Dominant Types
in British and American Literature

DOMINANT TYPES IN BRITISH & AMERICAN LITERATURE

Volume I. *Poetry and Drama*

WILLIAM H. DAVENPORT
University of Southern California

LOWRY C. WIMBERLY
University of Nebraska

HARRY SHAW
Humanities Editor, Harper & Brothers

New York

HARPER & BROTHERS PUBLISHERS

49-2373

CONTENTS

Preface xi

VOLUME I.

PART I. NARRATIVE AND LYRIC POETRY

* An asterisk after a poet's name signifies that he
is also represented in Lyric Poetry.

CONTENTS

CONTENTS

CONTENTS

PART II. THE DRAMA

PREFACE

Although practice differs widely in various sections of the United States, most colleges offer an introductory course in literature, often at the sophomore level. Such a course is usually a survey of English literature or a study of English and American literature by types. The former stresses historical development, background detail, and authors' lives, bringing the student from *Beowulf* to Thomas Hardy or thereabouts in measured stages; it usually serves to prepare the student for major work in English literature in the upper division, and ordinarily limits itself to poetry, a bit of drama, and the essay, with emphasis on poetry.

The latter course, "types," gives samples of the various broad divisions of literature—poetry, drama, essay, biography, and fiction—and often includes history, treatise, letter, and other subtypes. It usually serves to afford the general student experience in studying form and content, learning analysis and evaluation, achieving reading comprehension and enjoyment. The present text is designed for use in just such a course, although, because selections are arranged chronologically in each division, and because the introductory essays and the headnotes give a cumulative effect of developments and movements, it is readily adaptable to some survey or hybrid courses as well.

It is the feeling of the editors that an introductory course for the general student should be based on a different principle from that of a course for future majors; the course for the general student is a place to woo the uninitiated into the company of believers, a meeting-ground for a sort of secular evangelism. The ideal study materials, then, must be sound enough, but also, relatively speaking, appealing in their own right. Some "classic" material must be left out or de-emphasized because presumably the student may not be ready for

it; and there can be little good in forced feeding if only regurgitation is to result.

Thus poetry has been divided into only two broad types (see also I, 5) to minimize confusion and because editors and instructors alike do not always agree on which types and subtypes are most important. (Instructors will find, however, that the ballad, epic, sonnet, ode, epitaph, et cetera, can easily be located in the Table of Contents and rearranged for intensive study. A suggested listing is provided on I, pp. 633–639.) In classic poetry, the editors feel that there is adequate representation of major and minor figures; in modern poetry, with so many names of merit to select from, choices are more or less arbitrary (Aiken, Williams, MacLeish, Fearing, Patchen, Schwartz, and others could be represented here every bit as well as those who are). But space and permission costs call for some limit, and no anthology is, of course, wholly satisfactory. The editors realize that if a student could buy, or a library could furnish, sufficient copies of every important poet, an ideal situation would obtain.

The nine plays presented range from an early English comedy of the fourteenth century (*The Second Shepherds' Play*) to a recent American drama notable for its expressionism and satire (*The Adding Machine*). No nine plays can fully represent the growth and development of drama in England and America, but these have been selected to suggest those dramatic techniques and types of conflict which have positive reading appeal. Each of the nine represents a stage in the evolution of drama, and each is teachable, understandable, and readable.

In selecting essays the editors were governed by the following aims: to represent the work of both British and American writers; to illustrate the essay as a genre appearing in the several periods of British and American litera-ture; and to give examples of formal and in-formal essays, as well as of various subtypes found within those broad divisions, such as the critical essay, the satirical essay, and the hu-morous essay. In making their selections the editors had due regard, too, for essays which are both readable and teachable. They tried, moreover, to give a representation of the essay large enough to serve the varying purposes of teachers and to appeal to the diverse tastes of students.

Perhaps because of its historical and reflec-tive content, biography has not until recent years been popular among readers of college age. However, either because today's students are more mature or because biographical se-lections have been more judiciously made, the type has increased in popularity. The editors have attempted to choose, from the mass of English and American biography and auto-biography available, nineteen selections which entertainingly reveal human nature and pro-foundly affect our thinking about people.

The fiction included is not intended to rep-resent the "best" stories which have been writ-ten in England and America during the last century. Any attempt at such selection seems to the editors both silly and presumptuous. But the sixteen short stories and three long ones re-printed are as representative as possible of the widely varying forms and moods of the type. Each story is interesting, understandable, and, according to its kind, admirable or distinctive, or both. Their excellence should demonstrate the vitality of the genre and reveal sound rea-sons for its widespread popularity.

Selections are restricted to British and American authors because of tradition in that regard, because translations nearly always of-fer problems, and because, simply, there is ample material in British and American litera-ture. Any beginning student has a long way to go in his own tongue before he need adven-ture abroad; and there is no reason why im-portant foreign influences cannot be brought into class discussion by the instructor. Types and subtypes such as history, the letter, the treatise, and so on are omitted because they are relatively unimportant initially. There is no novel in this anthology, but the long stories by Henry James, Joseph Conrad, and Willa

Cather approach the novelette in length. Fur-thermore, in every anthology the instructor must be allowed to choose in two ways: from the material included and from the material excluded. The novel more than any other type belongs in the latter category, if only for the reason that there is ample freedom of choice in every other field properly representable.

Readers will note that the proportion of British to American authors (not necessarily in every section) is roughly fifty-fifty, and of old to new, about the same; that is, this collection presents relatively more American and more modern selections than any other comparable text. The introductory missionary work of proving that literature, good literature, can be understood and enjoyed should carry on after the course is completed; the non-major, after graduation, is likely to go on reading modern material (if he reads at all), and should there-fore have some grounding in it. And surely no one need apologize for including a great deal of American material, especially modern—not merely from a patriotic point of view, but on sheer merit alone.

Generally speaking, the editors have at-tempted to reprint whole samples or com-pletely independent parts of long works. Se-lections are intended to be "typical" of their authors and of their genres at the same time. Traditionalists may object to cutting Milton and Spenser to a few hundred lines each; the editors feel, frankly, that the purpose of the "types" and kindred courses is to place first emphasis on form and comprehension without slavish regard for the issue of major over minor writers. Special courses can do justice to the giants, whose work is difficult to anthologize at best. In some instances, especially modern choices, selections have been regulated by publishers' refusals to release material for re-print; some authors refuse reprint permission on any grounds.

Finally, there should be a word on notation principles and headnotes. Footnotes have been kept to a minimum, although the editors have not been unmindful of the fact that a reason-able amount of notation is welcomed by the teacher. Too much encyclopedic information tends, however, to obscure the personality of the selection itself and turn a course into a study *about* literature rather than *of* literature.

Terms so obscure as not to be found in the *American College Dictionary* have been explained; other terms ordinarily have been left to the student, part of whose regular chores should include looking up words. The headnotes, though brief, provide a running account of the development of each type and sufficient biographical or psychological details to explain the inclusion of each entry.

In addition to acknowledging permission for the use of copyrighted material (see text footnotes), the editors wish to thank the following publishers for their courtesy in making available certain texts or versions of material in print under their respective banners: Appleton-Century-Crofts; Ginn and Company; Harper & Brothers; Houghton Mifflin Company; Little, Brown & Company; Longmans, Green & Company; The Macmillan Company; W. W. Norton and Company; Random House; Charles Scribner's Sons; The Viking Press; Henry Holt and Company.

The editors also wish to thank the following for assistance of various kinds: Isobel Davenport and Kathryn Shriner; Frederick L. Christensen and Clarence Allen Forbes of the University of Nebraska; Miss Elizabeth Waggener, formerly of the University of Michigan; and Professor E. B. Knowles, Jr., of Pratt Institute.

For advice on general policy and plan the editors acknowledge indebtedness to friends, colleagues, and correspondents, including Professor John C. Gerber of the University of Iowa, Professor Thomas F. Dunn of Drake University, Professor Robert M. Estrich of Ohio State University, Professor Robert C. Pooley of the University of Wisconsin, Professor Edwin R. Steinberg of the Carnegie Institute of Technology, and Professor Lionel Stevenson of the University of Southern California.

W.H.D.
L.C.W.
H.S.

/

Terms so obscure as not to be found in the American College Dictionary have been explained; other terms ordinarily have been left to the student, part of whose regular chores should include looking up words. The head-notes, though brief, provide a running account of the development of each type and sufficient biographical or psychological details to explain the inclusion of each entry.

In addition to acknowledging permission for the use of copyrighted material (see text foot-notes), the editors wish to thank the following publishers for their courtesy in making available certain texts or sections of material in print under their respective banners: Apple-ton-Century-Crofts, Inc., and Company; Harper & Brothers, Houghton Mifflin Company, Little, Brown & Company, Longmans, Green & Company, The Macmillan Company, W. W. Norton and Company, Random House, Charles Scribner's Sons, The Viking Press, Henry Holt and Company.

The editors also wish to thank the following for assistance of various kinds: Isobel Daven-port and Kathryn Skinner; Professor L. Christiansen and Clarence Allen Forbes of the University of Nebraska; Miss Elizabeth Wag-ner, formerly of the University of Michigan; and Professor E. R. Knowles, Jr., of Pratt Institute.

For advice on general policy and plan the editors acknowledge indebtedness to friends, colleagues, and correspondents, including Pro-fessor John C. Gerber of the University of Iowa, Professor Thomas F. Dunn of Drake University, Professor Robert M. Estrich of Ohio State University, Professor Robert C. Pooley of the University of Wisconsin, Professor Edwin R. Steinberg of the Carnegie Institute of Tech-nology, and Professor David Stevenson of the University of Southern California.

W.H.D.
J.C.W.
H.S.

VOLUME I

PART I
NARRATIVE AND LYRIC POETRY

AN INTRODUCTORY NOTE
FOR THE STUDENT
OF POETRY

It is strange indeed that poetry should need any apology or explanation in a land as great as ours; it has been accepted and sought after in many other lands for centuries. It may be that as a nation we are just now leaving the pioneer stage, just beginning to develop a true culture and real interest in the arts.

Whatever the reason, poetry is not widely read; poetry magazines have small circulation, and in the schools, particularly, poetry encounters stubborn resistance almost everywhere. To be sure, in the past the poet was not always universally appreciated. From Plato to A. E. Housman, men have felt the need from time to time to redefine and defend the poet's position. But the poet has always survived, and the greatest works have stood the test of time. Writing styles have come and gone, some leaving their imprint on the present. Literary convention and revolt have swung in cycles with some fixed principles surviving and with some fringe changes as in morals, fashions, and means of making war—for always man has looked to his most inspired voices for emotional stimulation, teaching, or simple delight during the lulls in the storms of his development. In virtually all civilizations poetry has come first, before literary prose. Its roots are in the oldest and most obvious phenomena of existence—in the crash of surf, the rhythms of running streams, the hammer of the human pulse beat—and from simple cadences of religion and war the steady technical development has slowly come, like anything in evolution, with painful episodes, blank walls here, death there, mutation everywhere, but with

something elemental and universal preserved to the present day.

Poetry, then, is established; it has a long and honorable tradition in many languages, styles, and schools of thought. In America we are just beginning to take our rightful place in that tradition in terms of producing first-rate poets and first-rate audiences.

WHAT POETRY IS, AND DOES

"All right," you reply in student language, "but what is poetry, this term you bandy about so glibly, and what is its purpose? Seems as if everybody has a different slant on it." Well, in a way everybody almost must have a "different slant" on it. The poetic experience is something that exists in a shared way between writer and reader. Even if communication were perfect from a semantic point of view—which it rarely seems to be—the quality of the poetic experience would vary according to such factors as the relative age, training, and intelligence of both people concerned. But if the poet has something to say and if the reader or listener has something to work with in intelligence or interest, enough ought to come through to provide emotional release, teaching, or thought —or some combination. The experience, as Robinson has said, is indefinable but unmistakable.

To be sure, people have tried and still try to pin down the word "poetry." One man may concentrate on the music of verse; another on its moral force (not too long ago poetry was universally "taught" in secondary schools as a vehicle for moral principles); a third on sheer emotional impact, and so on. Or some critic will "bring out" poetry by contrasting it with prose: impression of fact *vs.* fact, intensity *vs.* low pitch, quality of experience *vs.* quantity, spiritual appeal *vs.* informative. To the ignorant, poetry is the product of the garret or the boudoir, or at best "high-falutin." Perhaps the truth is that poetry is indefinable in spite of Webster's stress on appropriate language, high thought, imagination, emotion, and rhythm. Certainly, while both Wordsworth and Sandburg are poets, the former's definition of poetry as the "spontaneous overflow of powerful feelings" is a different way of saying it from the latter's "synthesis of hyacinths and biscuits." And there are those who believe that poetry is a matter of inspiration as against those who feel that the major ingredient is perspiration. Even a casual reader can make out that one author's excitement leads to elevation and another's to sheer sensuality. And anyone who bothers to compare the set jingle of sentimental platitudes to be found in daily syndicated columns of "poetry" with the real simplicity, breathless simplicity, of Emily Dickinson's work may realize with a start that a poem is not merely a matter of stanza, type arrangement, or "what looks like a poem"—the poetic can be found in prose or in the motion involved in a well-executed end run, for that matter.

The definition of poetry varies with the age, with custom, with moral codes, with poets themselves. We have cults of aesthetes and cults of truth-seekers, for example. But the over-all traditional impression shows enough agreement on basic matters among writers and critics so that a qualified reader, with practice, can begin to work out his own definition, if he must define every worth-while experience. For one, hearing poetry read, like hearing a rich passage from Brahms, produces buzzing along the spine, kinesthetic sensations, wetness in the eyes, and eventually a sense of inward release. For some moderns the prime appeal is intellectual, and the poetic experience becomes a blending of mental recognitions of symbols (with or without the help of rhyme). For some, a poem's first value lies in its lofty presentation of a moral, religious, or philosophical theme. Note, then, that while we define by what it does, rather than saying what it is,

poetry is not trivial; it lives on a respectable level, it enriches one's life in some way or ways.

Forget about technicalities for the moment. Poetry somehow should entertain you in the best sense of that word. The more you grow, the more poetry will offer you. (Fortunately there is enough available so that you need never be bored, once you become a convert.) Thus, whether you think of poetry as frozen experience, sculpture on paper, a lofty expression of the best things in life, pure magic, or none of these, it really matters little. Poetry is rich enough to share something with almost any honest seeker. In Milton's day the reader might have sought an impassioned interpretation of the Scriptures; in Shakespeare's day he might have turned for escape to the Forest of Arden; in 1918 he might have felt that a picture of a steel mill best fitted his mood of the moment. No definition, then, can suffice here.

Poetry remains unmistakable and definable only in terms of reactions, a relative process. Relatively speaking, the trained student who catches an allusion by T. S. Eliot, the worldly-wise student who recognizes the emotional quality of a Millay sonnet, and the uninitiated freshman tackle who, parked on a sea cliff with his lady, becomes articulate enough to exclaim, "Gee, ain't that moonlight swell?"—all three belong somewhere in Poetry's train. There is no room for snobbery. The athlete may be ignorant and ungrammatical and slightly profane, but he is in the mood of poetry—he needs no definition for what he feels. With work, interest, guidance, he—and you—can find poetry actually, historically, sociologically a thrilling record of intense moments in the lives of human beings, dead and alive. For there is poetry in almost all of us, except for a few people who will live inevitably in a vegetable state. To repeat, then, it is strange that with poetry in and around us any defense should be necessary.

With the best intentions you will soon find that poetry can be hard work. If you are lucky, your first selections should not be too profound or dull, however "correct." And you must practice, just as you must sweat away on your tennis backhand or remember to keep your head down in golf—and perhaps without immediate signs of improvement. If you do not want to work to achieve eventual dividends, if you have no faith in your helpers, you may as well quit—and consider whether or not you are qualified to pursue higher education for legitimate reasons. Begin if you can with light verse or with the ballads, those charming tales of homicide and mayhem, and work up through longer narrative verse to the simplest lyrics. Sooner or later you will reach a limit. So do all of us. And whether you stop at simple lyrics or fight through to the metaphysicals or the modern obscurantists is again only a relative matter. Your life will be a bit richer for the effort.

COMPLICATIONS AND TABOOS

Somewhere in the early process you will recognize that poetry comes in many forms. Complications again! And what with human fads and fancies, forms change from time to time. More complications! Even "authorities" disagree on the labels for the basic types of poetry, let alone the subtypes. (This text is arranged around the two broad types, narrative and lyric, to simplify matters for the student. The subtypes—sonnet, ode, etc.—can be pointed out by the instructor.) At any rate, you will soon learn to distinguish one poem from another, to compare and contrast; this is the beginning of critical reading and of real enjoyment. And whether you learn to think of poetry as divisible into types according to purpose, mood, or meter-and-rhyme schemes, according to subject matter, or according to subtypes is largely a matter of splitting hairs—you can come back to such questions later on. (Actually, editors show a wide variance in approach to this question: one modern text divides poetry into narrative-lyric-didactic; another, narrative-lyric-reflective; a third, narrative-lyric-epic-ballad; a fourth into seven types, mixing technical forms and moods indiscriminately; and a fifth into no fewer than seventeen types!) You will have to learn other things some day: rhyme schemes, French forms, scansion, meters, technical terms; you will have to get historical perspective more clearly than you can from the chronological arrangement of poets in this volume or from the headnotes which are necessarily limited in scope.

But these matters need not be crammed together all at once, or discouragement and defeat might well result. Basic courses in poetry must first face the problem of wooing students to a point at which they can forget prejudices and honestly confess to an understanding and enjoyment of the assigned reading; any other approach may lead to memorizing of facts and dates, to learning "about" poets, even to assuming an air of culture for social effect—but for those trapped in the morass of mere facts the whole legacy of poetry in English will be only a hollow thing, never made real, never truly shared. "Types" courses with a variety of poetic subforms easily arrangeable according to relative difficulty offer materials for the wooing process, a process made necessary by the all-too-common experience among instructors of finding a large segment of their English classes, excluding gifted students and poseurs, made up of students who come to lectures with a "show-me" attitude. What basis is there for such an attitude?

All too often the novice in poetry (you may be he, or know someone like him) has a head stuffed with false concepts resembling tribal taboos—that is, if he has bothered to investigate the subject at all. He may be a good potential reader, even a writer, but he can hardly avoid reflecting his early background. Suppose the only poetry he knows is the over-sentimental, wooden doggerel ground out in the daily papers—he is hardly ready for Shakespeare. Suppose he has been forced to recite an ode to a daffodil or lines to keep a young man from a tavern—what can Keats mean to him? How can we expect a young undergraduate to understand Milton or Shelley or any Browning except "Pippa Passes" if he has been taught to look for a moral, and little else? Among the many false approaches he has met is very likely an embarrassed attempt to memorize Hamlet's fine soliloquy before he was ready to appreciate it, let alone ready to face a teen-age audience. It is a familiar psychological pattern to find a person unable to understand a work of art which he apparently should; it is easy for him to run away from the work, then become afraid because he is running; and because fear induces shame, the easiest way out via rationalizing is to convince himself loudly that the original work was not worth knowing in the first place.

Growing up in some social group, students meet modern taboos regarding poetry, and in several forms: poetry is "long-hair" stuff; poets are effeminate; poetry is meaningless; poets live brief, immoral lives; it is impossible to like poetry (except for the works of Guest and Service) and be a normal, red-blooded American, and so on. It requires a careful presentation of statistics to show that poets don't have to wear berets, that many of them were respectable graybeards, and, contrariwise, that some businessmen (the American ideal of the normal) die in disgrace. Here again work is necessary from both instructor and student— a good sporting "try" on the part of the latter particularly. And if in your private case the good try fails, there is no reason to feel depressed. Some of us are not destined to enjoy poetry any more than some of us will ever understand calculus.

TAKING INVENTORY

Let us assume at this point that you have temporarily, at least, suspended any prejudices you may have matriculated with, and that you are now facing a daily assignment in poetry. It may help your understanding to think a moment about certain barriers strewn on that meeting-ground; while bewilderment may ensue at first, ultimate clarification of the relationship between writer and reader will be worth a moment's thought. Certainly little is accomplished by an instructor's placing an epic before a student with the expressed or implied attitude that the poem is great and that any intelligent person should almost automatically appreciate the fact—after a bit of thought, of course.

First consider yourself in your capacity as reader, only one in a class made up of others like yourself in some respects and vastly different in others. Answer in your own heart for yourself and in silent comparison with your classmates the following questions, remembering that the poet and the instructor are facing an audience with various opinions, qualifications, and prejudices; it is at once an individual and a crowd problem.

(In facing this assignment, then:)

1. How intelligent am I, in terms of tests, I.Q., actions in the past, what people think of me?

2. How much thought have I given to the subject of taste—in dress, music, art, for example?

3. How much time and thought do I put on my assignments?

4. What are my basic prejudices? How did I get them? Can I jettison any?

5. What is my relationship with God and religion? Will my religious training condition my response to, say, passionate love poetry? Am I ready to face shock?

6. How many of what Richards calls "doctrinal adhesions" will my instructor and today's author have to compete with? If a poet's ideas and my family doctrine clash, can I keep an open mind?

7. What is my age in relation to others'? How experienced am I—in sport, travel, reading, earning a living, love, arts and crafts, tragedy, war? (The poet can't be blamed for being "dry" if you aren't ready to meet him.)

8. How well do I read *anything*? How fast? How do I rate on vocabulary tests? Do I bother to use exact adjectives in conversation, or is everything either "swell" or "lousy"?

9. How much technical training in poetry do I already have?

10. Have I already decided what I like and don't like in poetry? Am I like the musician who "loves" Tschaikowsky but can't "get" Bach?

11. Do I have an ear for music? Do people say I have imagination?

12. Am I emotionally mature? Can I separate literary and moral judgments? Can I distinguish between honest sentiment and sentimentality? (Remember that the Puritans, as Hillyer points out, fought emotion or possession by a mood—and produced very little poetry of first rank.)

13. Am I willing to work on poetry in return for future dividends?

Obviously all the foregoing questions cannot be answered in one sitting, and they should not be. Even a quick glance over the items that seem to fit you will give a reaction total good enough to go on for the moment.

COACHING AIDS

Now turn to the other side of the meeting-ground where stand the poet and the poem. Although it is possible to *enjoy* Shakespeare, say, without editorial help, it is not possible to *understand* him completely without some coaching; you have to be told that words like "wit" and "humour" meant something quite different to the Elizabethan from what you think they mean today. This need for coaching, discussion, breaking down of passages applies to all poetry in varying degrees; it should be apparent even to the student who objects that the classroom kills beauty. (This objection generally comes from poseurs and lazy people.) Occasionally a poem *is* mangled in class—so that dozens more may be correctly enjoyed. By and large, however, true beauty is much tougher than some young aesthetes pretend to think—it will rise again. And so now you begin to "study" the poet and his poem, using whatever equipment you possess in terms of the question list above. It becomes apparent almost at once that there is more to verse than symmetrical lines on a page, gushing about a heap o' living, or "dry" philosophy—or whatever was your private idea about the subject when you sat down. Some aspects immediately apparent include the following.

1. Poetry comes in various shapes and forms, types and subtypes. Although the matter is generally more important than the form, it is obvious that some day you will have to pick up information on ballads, epics, odes, sonnets, and so on.

2. Poetry has pronounced rhythms, generally resolvable into metrical patterns. It often has rhyme, and rhymes come in various patterns too. It often is musical and it relies heavily for effect on figurative language and allusion. Again, you may encounter "free verse," which upsets most of the foregoing. More to learn about!

3. Poetry has organization, purpose, style. Ideas and presentation vary from period to period. The Romantic of 1820 eschewed the neo-classic diction of Collins's day, for example. You will note eventually that both the romantic and the classic have something to offer, although you may develop a preference.

4. Poetry is a language phenomenon—a way of saying things. Whether to teach, preach, or simply thrill, to paint, inform, or spellbind, this is not the language of over-the-counter existence, although many of the words are the same.

A new blend of sound and sense is here, rich in connotation, imagery, impression, music—and offering new problems in semantics.

5. Poetry runs a wide gamut of subject matter and experience, familiar and unfamiliar. One age may sing of sea battle, another of a lady's eyes. Or in the same age one man may ponder the skylark while another weaves nightmarish dream-fantasies. Your modern poet may use conventional topics, new topics, or no topics at all, remaining content with patterns of sound and rhythm. In any period the gamut may be marked at one end by bright nonsense or folk song and at the other by metaphysics.

6. Poetry, like music and other arts, has an evocative factor which varies with the experience and personality of the audience. A passage may jog your memory suddenly and help you re-enjoy a lost moment. It may startle you into action or a new belief. Poetry may help you escape reality for a moment's peace. It may offer you new illusions to replace the old. But it will not sledge-hammer a skeptic into belief. The character in *Point Counter Point* who criticized Shelley for saying to the skylark, "Bird thou never wert" was incapable of, or scornful of, appreciating symbolism. For him most lyric poetry would always be alien territory. You must meet the poet halfway, then suspend disbelief for a time, "play along" sportingly. This is not to say that you should prostrate yourself as an ignoramus before genius; there is too much idolatry, devoid of thoughtful analysis, to be found in surprising surroundings—among self-styled "literary" clubs particularly. If after reading and thinking you honestly feel that your original poor impression of a poet, a poem, or poetry itself remains, maintain it stoutly; you will at least know by then why you feel the way you do—that knowledge itself is a step ahead.

SUGGESTIONS FOR STUDY

At this stage you should be aware that poetry has an honorable tradition, changing styles, various definitions, strange meanings in the public mind, barriers across communication lines—and that a poem itself is several things in one. Ahead of you is a parade of assignments, discussions, papers. In a short time you should find this introduction superficial. But what until then? In the first few days of confusion, how can the task be met? There is no easy road to the understanding of poetry; whole volumes (see the bibliography, I, 394) have been written on the subject. If, however, you have little idea of how to get started, the following check list may make reading have some significance:

1. Read the poem(s) through once quickly to get the general idea; reread several times carefully, slowly. Try reading key passages aloud.

2. Answer three questions clearly: what does the poem say; how is it said; was it worth saying or reading?

3. Does the poem have any physical effect on you? (Emily Dickinson said that if reading a book made her feel as if the top of her head were taken off, she was in the presence of poetry.)

4. How much idea content does the poem have? Is it "philosophical"? Does it preach? Is the thought commendable as thought but too heavy to allow the poem to move or soar?

5. What is the tone or mood of the poem as a whole?

6. Has the poem a claim to originality? How? Where? Does it present old notions in a fresh manner?

7. Study the vocabulary of the poem. How much "poetic" diction ('tis, lo!) is employed? How much language of ordinary men in extraordinary patterns? Point out what seem to you good or bad images. If you wrote the poem out in a prose statement, what would be gained, what lost—and what changes would occur?

8. Within the limits of your previous training, what technical features are recognizable for comment (rhyme, stanza form, figures of speech, etc.)?

9. What passages, if any, are obscure? Whose fault is it?

10. Check the poem for any evidence of sentimentalizing, use of stock phrases, "folksiness"—anything that will make it cheap or hackneyed material.

11. Check key allusions in a desk reference book. Does the poet seem to "show off" his knowledge, or are you not quite ready to meet him on even terms?

12. Does the poem appear labored or seemingly turned out with deftness and ease?

In your quest to add meaning to reading (and hence increase knowledge and pleasure), discuss specific assignments with good, average, and poor students alike—you can learn something from all of them. To sharpen your wits, argue points like these:

1. Must a poem have meaning?

2. Should a poem be criticized from the point of view of its day, our day, or both?

3. What effect, if any, has the machine age had on the poet's approach to life?

4. What effect did the Puritans have on early American poetry—and today's?

5. Why don't we have one or two "great" poets today? Is modern life too complex for poetry? Are readers to blame? (Remember Whitman's remark that great poets require great audiences.)

6. Is poetry succumbing before advances in the novel, short story, biography?

A FINAL WORD

Recall that your instructor has experience in reading, teaching, and absorbing student ideas; in other words, while pursuing the muse, you have some things to avoid, as well as cleave to or wrestle with. Some pointers:

1. When asked for a paraphrase of a poem, be sure you have it read through and thought about; don't make the common—and fatal—error of beginning your statement with what the poet says, then branching out into what *you* would have written on the assumption that you two are of one mind. Avoid composing, "reading-in."

2. When asked for an opinion, you will be better off to plead ignorance than to blurt out something you half-overheard or something you have memorized from notes without understanding them. Avoid parroting.

3. Watch out for insincerity, half-baked moralizing, making "impressions," sudden conversions, and the like. Although most of us are subject to flattery, the student who suddenly says, "Oh, professor, I never liked poetry, but you make Keats so alive!" *may* be simply naïve but is more likely to be angling for an A grade —and your instructor will be definitely not impressed. Avoid saying what you disbelieve.

4. Don't expect miracles, daily entertainment, or easy rewards. Some of the material which follows is dull but historically or soci-

ologically significant. Some of it you will like a few years from now. It is to be hoped that you will like enough to wish to investigate further on your own. Some of the selections are "good" for you. Some will puzzle you. Some will prove again that growth is sometimes painful. Some you will learn to repeat. But the wisdom and beauty of the ages will not come to you in a rush, as so many things do in youth. You are being asked to indulge in an act of faith based on experience, to believe that a life without poetry in it somewhere is a waste land indeed. But avoid expecting a short, swift trip to the promised land of plenty.

NARRATIVE POETRY

ANGLO-SAXON PERIOD

BEOWULF *

TRANSLATED BY J. DUNCAN SPAETH

Beowulf, *the oldest epic in English, is about Scandinavians, not Englishmen. Probably written in the eighth century, it has come down to us in a manuscript dating about* A.D. *1000. A mixture of pagan and Christian details and colorings, a hybrid of a little fact and a great deal of fiction, the poem has interested scholars and lay readers for a long time. Comparisons with other old tales will immediately suggest themselves. The story has a familiar three-part construction. (Following our selection, which is Part One of the original given here in modern English, there is a fight between Beowulf and the mother of Grendel, and a final episode fifty years later in which Beowulf, as King of the Geats, subdues a fire-dragon but loses his life.)* Beowulf *is rich in local color, contrast between pagan and Christian values, and old-fashioned blood-and-thunder. Note the use of "kennings" ("whale-road" for ocean, etc.), alliteration, and the four-foot line with pause after the second foot.*

THE MYTH OF THE SHEAF-CHILD

List to an old-time lay of the Spear-Danes,
Full of the prowess of famous kings,
Deeds of renown that were done by the heroes;
Scyld the Sheaf-Child[1] from scourging foemen,

From raiders a-many their mead-halls wrested.
He lived to be feared, though first as a waif,
Puny and frail he was found on the shore.
He grew to be great, and was girt with power
5 Till the border-tribes all obeyed his rule,
And sea-folk hardy that sit by the whale-path
Gave him tribute, a good king was he.
Many years after, an heir was born to him,
A goodly youth, whom God had sent
10 To stay and support his people in need.
(Long time leaderless living in woe,
The sorrow they suffered He saw full well.)
The Lord of Glory did lend him honor,
Beowulf's[2] fame afar was borne,
15 Son of old Scyld in the Scandian lands.
A youthful heir must be open-handed,
Furnish the friends of his father with plenty,
That thus in his age, in the hour of battle,
Willing comrades may crowd around him
20 Eager and true. In every tribe
Honorable deeds shall adorn an earl.
The aged Scyld, when his hour had come,
Famous and praised, departed to God.
His faithful comrades carried him down
25 To the brink of the sea, as himself had bidden,
The Scyldings' friend, before he fell silent,
Their lord beloved who long had ruled them.
Out in the bay a boat was waiting
Coated with ice, 'twas the king's own barge.
30 They lifted aboard their bracelet-bestower,
And down on the deck their dear lord laid,
Hard by the mast. Heaped-up treasure
Gathered from far they gave him along.
Never was ship more nobly laden

---

* The modern version by J. Duncan Spaeth is here reprinted by permission of the Princeton University Press.

[1] mythical ancestor of Danish house.

[2] another Beowulf, not our hero.

With wondrous weapons and warlike gear.
Swords and corselets covered his breast,
Floating riches to ride afar with him
Out o'er the waves at the will of the sea.
No less they dowered their lord with treasure, 5
Things of price, than those who at first
Had launched him forth as a little child
Alone on the deep to drift o'er the billows.
They gave him to boot a gilded banner,
High o'er his head they hung it aloft. 10
Then set him adrift, let the surges bear him.
Sad were their hearts, their spirits mournful;
Man hath not heard, no mortal can say
Who found that barge's floating burden.

1. THE LINE OF THE DANISH KINGS AND THE BUILDING OF HEOROT

Now Beowulf was king in the burgs of the
    Scyldings,
Famed among folk. (His father had left
The land of the living.) From his loins was
    sprung 20
Healfdene the royal, who ruled to old age,
Gray and battlegrim, the bold-hearted Scyld-
    ings.
Children four to this chief of the people
Woke unto life, one after another;
Heorogar and Hrothgar, and Halga the brave,
And winsome Sigeneow, a Scylfing she
    wedded;
Saewela's queen they say she became.
To Hrothgar was given such glory in battle,
Such fame he won, that his faithful band
Of youthful warriors waxed amain.
So great had grown his guard of kinsmen,
That it came in his mind to call on his people
To build a mead-hall, mightier far
Than any e'er seen by the sons of men,
Wherein to bestow upon old and young,
Gifts and rewards, as God vouchsafed them, 40
Save folk-share lands and freemen's lives.
Far and wide the work was published;
Many a tribe, the mid-earth round,
Helped to fashion the folk-stead fair.
With speed they built it, and soon 'twas 45
    finished,
Greatest of halls. Heorot[3] he named it,
Whose word was law o'er lands afar;
Nor failed in his promise, but freely dealt
Gifts at the feast. The fair hall towered 50

Wide-gabled and high, awaiting its doom,
The sweep of fire; not far was the time
That ancient feuds should open afresh,
And sword-hate sunder sons from fathers.

In the darkness dwelt a demon-sprite
Whose heart was filled with fury and hate,
When he heard each night the noise of revel
Loud in the hall, laughter and song.
To the sound of the harp the singer chanted 10
Lays he had learned, of long ago;
How the Almighty had made the earth,
Wonder-bright lands, washed by the ocean;
How he set, triumphant, sun and moon
To lighten all men that live on the earth. 15
He brightened the land with leaves and
    branches;
Life he created for every being,
Each in its kind, that moves upon earth.
So, happy in hall, the heroes lived, 20
Wanting naught, till one began
To work them woe, a wicked fiend.
The demon grim was Grendel called,
March-stalker huge, the moors he roamed. 25
The joyless creature had kept long time
The lonely fen, the lairs of monsters,
Cast out from men, an exile accurst.
On offspring of Cain, the killing of Abel
Was justly avenged by the Judge Eternal. 30
Nought gained by the feud the faithless mur-
    derer;
He was banished unblest from abode of men.
And hence arose the host of miscreants,
Monsters and elves and eldritch sprites,
Warlocks and giants, that warred against God; 35
Jotuns and goblins; He gave them their due.

2. THE RAVAGING OF HEOROT HALL BY THE MONSTER GRENDEL

When night had fallen, the fiend crept near 40
To the lofty hall, to learn how the Danes
In Heorot fared, when tho feasting was done.
The æthelings[4] all within he saw
Asleep after revel, not recking of danger,
And free from care. The fiend accurst, 45
Grim and greedy, his grip made ready;
Snatched in their sleep, with savage fury,
Thirty warriors; away he sprang
Proud of his prey, to repair to his home,
His blood-dripping booty to bring to his lair. 50

---

[3] hart, stag.

[4] princes.

At early dawn, when day-break came,
The vengeance of Grendel was revealed to all;
Their wails after wassail were widely heard,
Their morning-woe. The mighty ruler,
The ætheling brave, sat bowed with grief. 5
The fate of his followers filled him with sorrow,
When they traced the tracks of the treacherous foe,
Fiend accurst. Too fierce was that onset,
Too loathsome and long, nor left them respite. 10
The very next night, anew he began
To maim and to murder, nor was minded to slacken
His fury of hate, too hardened in crime.
'Twas easy to find then earls who preferred 15
A room elsewhere, for rest at night,
A bed in the bowers, when they brought this news
Of the hall-foe's hate; and henceforth all
Who escaped the demon, kept distance safe. 20

So Grendel wrongfully ruled the hall,
One against all till empty stood
That lordly mansion, and long remained so.
For the space of twelve winters the Scyldings' 25
  Friend⁵
Bore in his breast the brunt of this sorrow,
Measureless woe. In mournful lays
The tale became known; 'twas told abroad
In gleemen's songs, how Grendel had warred 30
Long against Hrothgar, and wreaked his hate
With murderous fury through many a year,
Refusing to end the feud perpetual,
Or decently deal with the Danes in parley,
Take their tribute for treaty of peace; 35
Nor could their leaders look to receive
Pay from his hands for the harm that he wrought.
The fell destroyer kept feeding his rage
On young and old. So all night long 40
He prowled o'er the fen and surprised his victims,
Death-shadow dark. (The dusky realms
Where the hell-runes haunt are hidden from men.) 45
So the exiled roamer his raids continued;
Wrong upon wrong in his wrath he heaped.
In midnights dark he dwelt alone
'Mongst Heorot's trophies and treasures rich.
Great was the grief of the gold-friend of Scyld- 50
  ings,

⁵ Hrothgar.

Vexed was his mood that he might not visit
His goodly throne, his gift-seat proud,
Deprived of joy by the judgment of God.
Many the wise men that met to discover
Ways of escape from the scourge of affliction.
Often they came for counsel together;
Often at heathen altars they made
Sacrifice-offerings, beseeching their idols
To send them deliverance from assault of the foe.
Such was their practice, they prayed to the Devil;
The hope of the heathen on hell was fixed,
The mood of their mind. Their Maker they knew not,
The righteous Judge and Ruler on high.
The Wielder of Glory they worshipped not,
The Warden of Heaven. Woe be to him
Whose soul is doomed through spite and envy,
In utter despair and agony hopeless
Forever to burn. But blessed is he
Who, after this life, the Lord shall seek,
Eager for peace in the arms of the Father.

3. THE VOYAGE OF BEOWULF TO THE HALL OF HROTHGAR

Thus boiled with care the breast of Hrothgar;
Ceaselessly sorrowed the son of Healfdene,
None of his chieftains might change his lot.
Too fell was the foe that afflicted the people
With wrongs unnumbered, and nightly horrors.
Then heard in his home king Hygelac's thane,⁶
The dauntless Jute,⁷ of the doings of Grendel.
In strength he outstripped the strongest of men
That dwell in the earth in the days of this life.
Gallant and bold, he gave command
To get him a boat, a good wave-skimmer.
O'er the swan-road, he said, he would seek the king
Noble and famous, who needed men.
Though dear to his kin, they discouraged him not;
The prudent in counsel praised the adventure,
Whetted his valor, awaiting good omens.

So Beowulf chose from the band of the Jutes
Heroes brave, the best he could find;
He with fourteen followers hardy,
Went to embark; he was wise in seamanship,

⁶ Beowulf.
⁷ here translated from original *Geat;* some think the Geats were Swedes.

Showed them the landmarks, leading the way.
Soon they descried their craft in the water,
At the foot of the cliff. Then climbed aboard
The chosen troop; the tide was churning
Sea against sand; they stowed away   5
In the hold of the ship their shining armor,
War-gear and weapons; the warriors launched
Their well-braced boat on her welcome voyage.

Swift o'er the waves with a wind that favored,   10
Foam on her breast, like a bird she flew;
A day and a night they drove to seaward,
Cut the waves with the curving prow,
Till the seamen that sailed her sighted the land,
Shining cliffs and coast-wise hills,   15
Headlands bold. The harbor opened,
Their cruise was ended. Then quickly the
     sailors,
The crew of Weder-folk, clambered ashore,
Moored their craft with clank of chainmail,   20
And goodly war-gear. God they thanked
That their way was smooth o'er the surging
     waves.

High on the shore, the Scylding coast-guard   25
Saw from the cliff where he kept his watch,
Glittering shields o'er the gang-plank carried,
Polished weapons: it puzzled him sore,
He wondered in mind who the men might be.
Down to the strand on his steed came riding   30
Hrothgar's thane, with threatening arm
Shook his war-spear and shouted this chal-
     lenge:
"Who are ye, men, all mailed and harnessed,
That brought yon ship o'er the broad seaways,   35
And hither have come across the water,
To land on our shores. Long have I stood
As coast-guard here, and kept my sea-watch,
Lest harrying foe with hostile fleet
Should dare to damage our Danish land.   40
Armed men never from overseas came
More openly hither. But how do ye know
That law of the land doth give ye leave
To come thus near. I never have seen
Statelier earl upon earth than him,—   45
Yon hero in harness. No house-carl he,
In lordly array, if looks speak true,
And noble bearing. But now I must learn
Your names and country, ere nearer ye come,
Underhand spies, for aught I know,   50
In Danish land. Now listen ye strangers,
In from the sea, to my open challenge:

Heed ye my words and haste me to know
What your errand and whence ye have come."

4. BEOWULF'S WORDS WITH THE COAST-GUARD

Him the hero hailed with an answer,
The war-troop's leader, his word-hoard un-
     locked:
"In truth we belong to the tribe of the Jutes;
We are Hygelac's own hearth-companions.
Far among folk my father was known,
A noble chieftain, his name was Ecgtheow.
Honored by all, he ended his days
Full of winters and famed in the land.
Wise men everywhere well remember him.
Hither we fare with friendly purpose
To seek thy lord, the son of Healfdene,
The land-protector. Instruct us kindly.
Bound on adventure we visit thy lord,
The prince of the Danes. Our purpose is open;
Nought keep we secret; thou surely wilt know
If the tale we were told is true or not:
That among the Scyldings a monster strange,
A nameless demon, when nights are dark,
With cruel cunning, for cause unknown,
Works havoc and slaughter. I have in mind
A way to help your wise king Hrothgar,
Your ruler to rid of the ravening foe,
If ever his tide of troubles shall turn,
The billows of care that boil in his breast
Shall cool and subside, and his sorrow be cured;
Else, failing my purpose, forever hereafter
He shall suffer distress, while stands on its hill,
Mounting on high, his matchless hall."
Straight answered the coast-guard, astride his
     horse,
The warrior brave: "Twixt words and deeds
A keen-witted thane, if he thinks aright,
Must well distinguish and weigh the difference.
Your words I believe, that you wish no evil
To the Scylding lord. I will let you bring
Your shields ashore and show you the way.
My comrades here shall keep the watch,
From meddling foe defend your craft,
Your fresh-tarred boat, fast by the beach,
And faithfully guard her till again she bear
With curving bow, o'er the bounding main,
Her master well-loved to the Wedermark.
Fortune oft favors the fighter who yields not;
Hero unflinching comes unhurt from the fray."
Landward they hastened, leaving behind them
Fast at her moorings the full-bosomed boat,

The ship at anchor. Shone the boar-heads,
Gleaming with gold, o'er the guards of their
    helmets;
Bright and fire-forged the beast kept watch.
Forward they pressed, proud and adventurous,
Fit for the fight, till afar they descried   5
The high-peaked radiant roof of the hall.
Of houses far-praised, 'neath heaven by the
    people
That inhabit the earth, this house was most 10
    famous,
The seat of King Hrothgar; its splendor
    gleamed bright
O'er many a land. Their leader well-armed
Showed them the shining shield-burg of heroes, 15
And set them right on the road to their goal.
Then, wheeling his steed, he wished them fare-
    well:
"'Tis time that I leave you; the Lord of
    Heaven, 20
The Father Almighty in mercy keep you
Safe on your journey; seaward I turn
Watch to keep and ward against foe."

5. BEOWULF'S ARRIVAL AT THE HALL AND THE MANNER OF HIS RECEPTION

The street was stone-paved; straight it led
To the goal of their journey. Glistened their
    byrnies[8]
Stout and strong-linked; sang the rings 30
Of their iron mail as they marched along,
In armor and helmet right up to the hall.
Sea-voyage-sated, they set their shields,
Their linden-woods broad, along the wall.
As they bent to the bench, their byrnies clat- 35
    tered.
They stacked their spears that stood in a row,
Ashwood tipped with iron above;
Well-equipped was the warlike band.
A stately Dane the strangers addressed, 40
Asked who they were and whence they had
    come:
"Whence do ye bear your burnished shields,
Your visored helmets and harness gray
Your heap of spear-shafts? A servant of Hroth- 45
    gar's,
His herald, am I. Hardier strangers,
Nobler in mien, have I never seen.
'Tis clear you come to the court of Hrothgar,
Not outlaws and beggars, but bent on adven- 50
    ture."

[8] coats of mail.

To him gave answer the hero brave,
The lord of the Weders these words returned,
Bold 'neath his helmet: "We are Hygelac's
    men,
His board-companions. I am Beowulf called.
Ready am I the ruler to answer,
To say to thy lord, the son of Healfdene,
Why we have come his court to seek,
If he will graciously grant us a hearing."
Wulfgar replied: (he was prince of the Wen- 10
    dles,
His noble renown was known to many,
His courage in war, and wisdom in counsel)
"I will carry thy quest to the king of the Danes,
And ask him whether he wishes to grant 15
The boon thou dost ask of the breaker-of-rings,
To speak to himself concerning thy journey;
And straight will I bring thee the answer he
    sends."
Swiftly he hied him where Hrothgar sat, 20
White-haired and old, his earls around him.
Stately he strode, till he stood in the presence
Of the king of the Danes,—in courtly ways
Was Wulfgar skilled; he spoke to his lord:
"Hither have fared from a far country, 25
A band of Jutes o'er the bounding sea.
Their leader and chief by his chosen comrades
Is Beowulf called; this boon they ask:
That they may find with thee, my lord,
Favor of speech; refuse them not, 30
But grant them, Hrothgar, gracious hearing
In armor clad, they claim respect
Of choicest earls; but chiefly their lord
Who lately hither hath led his comrades."

6. HROTHGAR'S WELCOME TO BEOWULF

Hrothgar spoke, the Scyldings' protector:
"Beowulf I knew in his boyhood days;
His aged father was Ecgtheow named.
To him, to take home, did Hrethel give 40
His only daughter. Their dauntless son
Now comes to my court in quest of a friend.
My sea-faring men whom I sent afar
To the land of the Jutes, with generous gifts,
In token of friendship, have told me this, 45
That the power of his grip was so great it
    equalled
The strength of thirty stout-armed thanes.
Him bold in battle, the blessed God
Hath sent in his mercy, to save our people 50
—So I hope in my heart—from the horror of
    Grendel.

I shall offer him gold for his gallant spirit.
Go now in haste, and greet the strangers;
Bid to the hall the whole of the company;
Welcome with words the warrior band,
To the home of the Danes." To the hall door
    went   5
Wulfgar the courtly, and called them in:
"My master commands me this message to give
    you,
The lord of the Danes your lineage knows;   10
Bids me to welcome you, brave-hearted war-
    riors,
Bound on adventure o'er the billowy main.
Ye may rise now and enter, arrayed in your
    armor,   15
Covered with helmets, the king to greet.
But leave your shields, and your shafts of
    slaughter,
Here by the wall to await the issue."
Then rose the leader, around him his com-   20
    rades,
Sturdy war-band; some waited without,
Bid by the bold one their battle-gear to guard.
Together they hastened where the herald led
    them,   25
Under Heorot's roof. The hero went first,
Strode under helmet, till he stood by the hearth.
Beowulf spoke, his byrnie glistened,
His corslet chain-linked by cunning of smith-
    craft: 30
"Hail, king Hrothgar! Hygelac's thane
And kinsman am I. Known is the record
Of deeds of renown I have done in my youth.
Far in my home, I heard of this Grendel;
Sea-farers tell the tale of the hall: 35
How bare of warriors, this best of buildings
Deserted stands, when the sun goes down
And twilight deepens to dark in the sky.
By comrades encouraged, I come on this jour-
    ney.   40
The best of them bade me, the bravest and
    wisest,
To go to thy succor, O good king Hrothgar;
For well they approved my prowess in battle,
They saw me themselves come safe from the   45
    conflict
When five of my foes I defeated and bound,
Beating in battle the brood of the monsters.
At night on the sea with nicors I wrestled,
Avenging the Weders, survived the sea-peril,   50
And crushed in my grip the grim sea-monsters

That harried my neighbors. Now I am come
To cope with Grendel in combat single,
And match my might against the monster,
    alone.
I pray thee therefore, prince of the Scyldings,   5
Not to refuse the favor I ask,
Having come so far, O friend of the Shield-
    Danes,
That I alone with my loyal comrades,
My hardy companions, may Heorot purge.   10
Moreover they say that the slaughterous fiend
In wanton mood all weapons despises.
Hence,—as I hope that Hygelac may,
My lord and king, be kind to me,—
Sword and buckler I scorn to bear,   15
Gold-adorned shield, as I go to the conflict.
With my grip will I grapple the gruesome
    fiend,
Foe against foe, to fight for our life.
And he that shall fall his faith must put   20
In the judgment of God. If Grendel wins,
He is minded to make his meal in the hall
Untroubled by fear, on the folk of the Jutes,
As often before he fed on the Danes.
No need for thee then to think of my burial.   25
If I lose my life, the lonely prowler
My blood-stained body will bear to his den,
Swallow me greedily, and splash with my gore
His lair in the marsh; no longer wilt then
Have need to find me food and sustenance.   30
To Hygelac send, if I sink in the battle,
This best of corslets that covers my breast,
Heirloom of Hrethel, rarest of byrnies,
The work of Weland.[9] So Wyrd[10] will be
    done."   35

7. THE FEASTING IN HEOROT AND THE CUSTOMS OF THE HALL

Hrothgar spoke, the Scyldings' defender:
"Thou has come, dear Beowulf, to bring us
    help,
For the sake of friendship to fight our bat-
    tles. . . .
*(Hrothgar recounts the exploits of Beowulf's
father.)*
Sad is my spirit and sore it grieves me
To tell to any the trouble and shame
That Grendel hath brought me with bitter
    hate,

_____
[9] legendary smith (Norse and Germanic).
[10] fate, destiny.

The havoc he wrought in my ranks in the hall.
My war-band dwindles, driven by Wyrd
Into Grendel's grasp; but God may easily
End this monster's mad career.
Full often they boasted, my beer-bold warriors, 5
Brave o'er their ale-cups, the best of my fight-
ers,
They'd meet in the mead-hall the mighty
Grendel,
End his orgies with edge of the sword.
But always the mead-hall, the morning after,
The splendid building, was blood-bespattered;
Daylight dawned on the drippings of swords;
Soiled with slaughter were sills and benches,
My liege-men perished, and left me poor. 15
Sit down to the board; unbend thy thoughts;
Speak to my men as thy mood shall prompt."
For the band of the Jutes a bench was cleared;
Room in the mead-hall was made for them all.
Then strode to their seats the strong-hearted 20
heroes.
The warriors' wants a waiting-thane served;
Held in his hand the highly-wrought ale-cup,
Poured sparkling mead, while the minstrel
sang
Gaily in Heorot. There was gladness of heroes, 25
A joyous company of Jutes and of Danes.

8. UNFERTH TAUNTS BEOWULF

Then up spoke Unferth, Ecglaf's son, 30
Who sat at the feet of the Scylding ruler;
He vented his jealousy. The journey of Beo-
wulf,
His sea-adventure, sorely displeased him.
It filled him with envy that any other 35
Should win among men more war-like glory,
More fame under heaven than he himself:
"Art thou the Beowulf that battled with Brecca,
Far out at sea, when ye swam together,
What time you two made trial of the billows, 40
Risking your lives in reckless folly,
On the open sea? None might dissuade you,
Friend nor foe, from the fool-hardy venture,
When straight from the shore you struck for
the open, 45
Breasted the waves and beat with your arms
The mounting billows, measured the seapaths
With lusty strokes. Stirred was the ocean
By wintry storms. Seven days and nights
Your sea-strife lasted; at length he beat you, 50
His strength was the better; at break of day

He made the beach where the Battle-Reamas
Dwell by the shore; and straightway returned
To his people beloved in the land of the Brond-
ings,
Where liegemen and towns and treasure were
his.
In sooth I say, the son of Beanstan
His boast against thee made good to the full.
But now I ween a worse fate awaits thee,
Though thy mettle be proved in many a battle
And grim encounter, if the coming of Grendel
Thou darest abide, in the dead of the night."
Beowulf spoke, the son of Ecgtheow:
"What a deal of stuff thou hast talked about
Brecca,
Garrulous with drink, my good friend Unferth.
Thou has lauded his deeds. Now listen to me!
More sea-strength had I, more ocean-endur-
ance,
Than any man else, the wide earth round.
'Tis true we planned in the pride of our youth
This ocean-adventure, and vowed we would
risk
Our lives in the deep, each daring the other.
We were both of us boys, but our boast we
fulfilled.
Our naked swords as we swam from the land,
We held in our grasp, to guard against whales.
Not a stroke could he gain on me, strive as
he would,
Make swifter speed through the swelling
waves,
Nor could I in swimming o'ercome him at sea.
Side by side in the surge we labored
Five nights long. At last we were parted
By furious seas and a freezing gale.
Night fell black; the norther wild
Rushed on us ruthless and roughened the sea.
Now was aroused the wrath of the monsters,
But my war-proof ring-mail, woven and hand-
locked,
Served me well 'gainst the sea-beasts' fury;
The close-linked battle-net covered my breast.
I was dragged to the bottom by a blood-thirsty
monster,
Firm in his clutch the furious sea-beast
Helpless held me. But my hand came free,
And my foe I pierced with point of my sword.
With my battle-blade good 'twas given me to
kill
The dragon of the deep, by dint of my blow."

[17]

9. BEOWULF COMPLETES THE STORY OF HIS SWIMMING ADVENTURE WITH BRECCA; HROTHGAR'S DEPARTURE FROM THE HALL

"Thus sore beset me sea-beasts thronging,
Murderous man-eaters. I met their charges,
Gave them their due with my goodly blade.
They failed of their fill, the feast they expected
In circle sitting on the sea-floor together
With me for their meal. I marred their pleasure.
When morning came, they were cast ashore 10
By the wash of the waves; their wounds proved fatal,
Bloated and dead on the beach they lay.
No more would they cross the course of the ships,
In the chop of the channel charge the sailors.
Day broke in the east, bright beacon of God;
The sea fell smooth. I saw old headlands, 20
Windy walls; for Wyrd oft saveth
A man not doomed, if he dauntless prove.
My luck did not fail me, my long sword finished
Nine of the nicors.[11] Ne'er have I heard 25
Of fiercer battle fought in the night,
Of hero more harried by horrors at sea.
Yet I saved my life from the sea-beasts' clutch.
Worn with the struggle, I was washed ashore
In the realm of the Finns by the run of the 30
tide,
The heave of the flood. I have failed to hear
Of like adventure laid to thee,
Battle so bitter. Brecca did never,—
Neither of you was known to achieve 35
Deed so valiant, adventure so daring,
Sword-play so nimble; not that I boast of it,
But mark me Unferth, you murdered your
brothers,
Your closest of kin. The curse of hell 40
For this you will suffer, though sharp be your
wit.
In sooth I say to you, son of Ecglaf,
Never had Grendel such grim deeds wrought,
Such havoc in Heorot, so harried your king 45
With bestial fury, if your boasted courage
In deeds as well as in words you had proved.
But now he has found he need not fear
Vengeance fierce from the Victory-Scyldings,
Ruthless attack in return for his raids. 50

He takes his toll of your tribe as he pleases,
Sparing none of your spearmen proud.
He ravens and rages and recks not the Dane
folk,
Safe from their sword-play. But soon I will
teach him
How the Jute-folk fight. Then freely may go
To the mead-hall who likes, when the light of
morning,
The next day's dawn, the dark shall dispel,
And the heaven-bright sun from the south
shall shine."

Glad in his heart was the giver of rings,
Hoped to have help, the hoar-headed king;
The Shield-Danes' shepherd was sure of relief,
When he found in Beowulf so firm a resolve.
There was laughter of heroes. Loud was their
revelry,
Words were winsome, as Wealhtheow rose,
Queen of Hrothgar, heedful of courtesy,
Gold-adorned greeted the guests in the hall.
First to her lord, the land-defender,
The high-born lady handed the cup;
Bade him be gleeful and gay at the board,
And good to his people. Gladly he took it,
Quaffed from the beaker, the battle-famed
king.
Then leaving her lord, the lady of the Helmings
Passed among her people in each part of the
hall,
Offered the ale-cup to old and young,
Till she came to the bench where Beowulf sat.
The jewel-laden queen in courteous manner
Beowulf greeted; to God gave thanks,
Wise in her words, that her wish was granted,
That at last in her trouble a trusted hero
Had come for comfort. The cup received
From Wealhtheow's hand the hardy warrior,
And made this reply, his mind on the battle;
Beowulf spoke, the son of Ecgtheow:
"I made up my mind when my mates and I
Embarked in our boat, outbound on the sea,
That fully I'd work the will of thy people,
Or fall in the fight, in the clutch of the fiend.
I surely shall do a deed of glory,
Worthy an earl, or end my days,
My morning of life, in the mead-hall here."
His words pleased well the wife of Hrothgar,
The Jutish lord's boast. The jewelled queen
Went to sit by the side of her lord.

---

[11] monsters of the deep.

Renewed was the sound of noisy revel,
Wassail of warriors. Brave words were spoken.
Mirth in the mead-hall mounted high,
Till Healfdene's son the sign did give
That he wished to retire. Full well he knew   5
The fiend would find a fight awaiting him,
When the light of the sun had left the hall,
And creeping night should close upon them,
And shadowy shapes come striding on
Dim through the dark. The Danes arose.   10
Hrothgar again gave greeting to Beowulf,
Wished him farewell; the wine-hall lofty
He left in his charge. These last words spoke
    he:
"Never before have I fully entrusted
To mortal man this mighty hall,   15
Since arm and shield I was able to lift.
To thee alone I leave it now,
To have and to hold it. Thy hardihood prove!
Be mindful of glory; keep watch for the foe!
No reward shalt thou lack if thou live through
    this fight."

10. BEOWULF'S WATCH IN HEOROT

Then Hrothgar went with his warrior-band,
The Arm-of-the-Scyldings, out of the hall.
Would the war-lord Wealhtheow seek,
The queen for his bed-mate. The best of kings
Had placed in the hall, so heroes report,
A watch against Grendel, to guard his house,
Deliverance bring to the land of the Danes.
But the lord of the Jutes joyfully trusted
In the might of his arm and the mercy of
    God.
Off he stripped his iron byrnie,
Helmet from head, and handed his sword,
Choicest of blades, to his body-thane,
And bade him keep the battle armor.
Then made his boast once more the warrior,
Beowulf the bold, ere his bed he sought,   40
Summoned his spirit; "Not second to Grendel
In combat I count me and courage of war.
But not with the sword will I slay this foeman,
Though light were the task to take his life.
Nothing at all does he know of such fighting,   45
Of hewing of shields, though shrewd be his
    malice
Ill deeds to contrive. We two in the night
Shall do without swords, if he dare to meet me
In hand to hand battle. May the holy Lord
To one or the other award the victory,   50
As it seems to Him right, Ruler all-wise."

Then he sought his bed. The bolster received
The head of the hero. In the hall about him,
Stretched in sleep, his sailormen lay.
Not one of them thought he would ever re-
    turn
Home to his country, nor hoped to see
His people again, and the place of his birth.
They had heard of too many men of the Danes
O'ertaken suddenly, slain without warning,
In the royal hall. But the Ruler on High   10
Through the woof of fate to the Wederfolk
    gave
Friendship and help, their foes to o'ercome,
By a single man's strength to slay the destroyer.
Thus all may learn that the Lord Almighty   15
Wields for aye the Wyrds of men.

    .   .   .   .   .   .

11. BEOWULF'S FIGHT WITH GRENDEL

Now Grendel came, from his crags of mist   20
Across the moor; he was curst of God.
The murderous prowler meant to surprise
In the high-built hall his human prey.
He stalked neath the clouds, till steep before
    him   25
The house of revelry rose in his path,
The gold-hall of heroes, the gaily adorned.
Hrothgar's home he had hunted full often,
But never before had he found to receive him
So hardy a hero, such hall-guards there.   30
Close to the building crept the slayer,
Doomed to misery. The door gave way,
Though fastened with bolts, when his fist fell
    on it.
Maddened he broke through the breach he   35
    had made;
Swoln with anger and eager to slay,
The ravening fiend o'er the bright-paved floor
Furious ran, while flashed from his eyes
An ugly glare like embers aglow.   40
He saw in the hall, all huddled together,
The heroes asleep. Then laughed in his heart
The hideous fiend; he hoped ere dawn
To sunder body from soul of each;
He looked to appease his lust of blood,   45
Glut his maw with the men he would slay.
But Wyrd had otherwise willed his doom;
Never again should he get a victim
After that night. Narrowly watched
Hygelac's thane how the horrible slayer   50
Forward should charge in fierce attack.
Nor was the monster minded to wait:

[19]

Sudden he sprang on a sleeping thane,
Ere he could stir, he slit him open;
Bit through the bone-joints, gulped the blood,
Greedily bolted the body piecemeal.
Soon he had swallowed the slain man wholly,
Hands and feet. Then forward he hastened,
Sprang at the hero, and seized him at rest;
Fiercely clutched him with fiendish claw.
But quickly Beowulf caught his forearm,
And threw himself on it with all his weight.
Straight discovered that crafty plotter,
That never in all midearth had he met
In any man a mightier grip.
Gone was his courage, and craven fear
Sat in his heart, yet helped him no sooner.
Fain would he hide in his hole in the fenland,
His devil's den. A different welcome
From former days he found that night!
Now Hygelac's thane, the hardy, remembered
His evening's boast, and bounding up,
Grendel he clenched, and cracked his fingers;
The monster tried flight, but the man pursued;
The ravager hoped to wrench himself free,
And gain the fen, for he felt his fingers
Helpless and limp in the hold of his foe.
'Twas a sorry visit the man-devourer
Made to the Hall of the Hart that night.
Dread was the din, the Danes were frighted
By the uproar wild of the ale-spilling fray.
The hardiest blenched as the hall-foes wrestled
In terrible rage. The rafters groaned;
'Twas wonder great that the wine-hall stood,
Firm 'gainst the fighters' furious onslaught,
Nor fell to the ground, that glorious building.
With bands of iron 'twas braced and stiffened
Within and without. But off from the sill
Many a mead-bench mounted with gold
Was wrung where they wrestled in wrath to-
    gether.
The Scylding nobles never imagined
That open attack, or treacherous cunning,
Could wreck or ruin their royal hall,
The lofty and antlered, unless the flames
Should some day swallow it up in smoke.
The din was renewed, the noise redoubled;
Each man of the Danes was mute with dread,
That heard from the wall the horrible wail,
The gruesome song of the godless foe,
His howl of defeat, as the fiend of hell
Bemoaned his hurt. The man held fast;
Greatest he was in grip of strength,
Of all that dwelt upon earth that day.

12. THE DEFEAT OF GRENDEL

Loath in his heart was the hero-deliverer
To let escape his slaughterous guest.
Of little use that life he deemed
To human kind. The comrades of Beowulf
Unsheathed their weapons to ward their leader,
Eagerly brandished their ancient blades,
The life of their peerless lord to defend.
Little they deemed, those dauntless warriors,
As they leaped to the fray, those lusty fighters,
Laying on boldly to left and to right,
Eager to slay, that no sword upon earth,
No keenest weapon, could wound that mon-
    ster:
Point would not pierce, he was proof against
    iron;
'Gainst victory-blades the devourer was
    charmed.
But a woful end awaited the wretch,
That very day he was doomed to depart,
And fare afar to the fiends' domain.

Now Grendel found, who in former days
So many a warrior had wantonly slain,
In brutish lust, abandoned of God,
That the frame of his body was breaking at
    last.
Keen of courage, the kinsman of Hygelac
Held him grimly gripped in his hands.
Loath was each to the other alive.
The grisly monster got his death-wound:
A huge split opened under his shoulder;
Crunched the socket, cracked the sinews,
Glory great was given to Beowulf.
But Grendel escaped with his gaping wound,
O'er the dreary moor his dark den sought,
Crawled to his lair. 'Twas clear to him then,
The count of his hours to end had come,
Done were his days. The Danes were glad,
The hard fight was over, they had their de-
    sire.
Cleared was the hall, 'twas cleansed by the
    hero
With keen heart and courage, who came from
    afar.
The lord of the Jutes rejoiced in his work,
The deed of renown he had done that night.
His boast to the Danes he bravely fulfilled;
From lingering woe delivered them all;
From heavy sorrow they suffered in heart;
From dire distress they endured so long;

From toil and from trouble. This token they
    saw:
The hero had laid the hand of Grendel
Both arm and claws, the whole forequarter
With clutches huge, 'neath the high-peaked
    roof.

13. THE CELEBRATION OF THE VICTORY AND
THE SONG OF THE GLEEMAN

When morning arrived, so runs the report,
Around the gift-hall gathered the warriors;
The folk-leaders fared from far and near,
The wide ways o'er, the wonder to view,
The wild beast's foot-prints. Not one of them
    felt
Regret that the creature had come to grief,
When they traced his retreat by the tracks on
    the moor;
Marked where he wearily made his way,
Harried and beaten, to the haunt of the nicors,
Slunk to the water, to save his life.
There they beheld the heaving surges,
Billows abrim with bloody froth,
Dyed with gore, where the gruesome fiend,
Stricken and doomed, in the struggle of death
Gave up his ghost in the gloom of the mere,
His heathen soul for hell to receive it.
Then from the mere the thanes turned back,
Men and youths from the merry hunt,
Home they rode on their horses gray,
Proudly sitting their prancing steeds.
Beowulf's prowess was praised by all.
They all agreed that go where you will,
'Twixt sea and sea, at the south or the north,
None better than he, no braver hero,
None worthier honor could ever be found,
(They meant no slight to their master and lord,
The good king Hrothgar their ruler kind.)

Now and again the noble chiefs
Gave rein to their steeds, and spurred them to
    race,
Galloped their grays where the ground was
    smooth.
Now and again a gallant thane,
Whose mind was stored with many a lay,
With songs of battle and sagas old,
Bound new words in well-knit bars,
Told in verse the valor of Beowulf,
Matched his lines and moulded his lay.

*Here is introduced an episode of the Nibelungen
Legend. The gleeman tells how Sigmund the Vol-*

*sung, with his son and nephew Fitela, ranged the
forests and slew wild beasts. Later, when Fitela was
no longer with him, Sigmund killed a dragon and
won a great treasure.*

5 When the lay was ended, they urged once
    more
Their racers fleet to fly o'er the plain.
As the morning sped, and the sun climbed
    higher,
10 Many went in, the marvellous sight
More closely to scan. The king himself,
With a troop of trusty retainers about him,
Strode from his bower; the bestower-of-rings
Came, and with him the queen, in state,
15 The meadow-path trod, by her maidens at-
    tended.

14. HROTHGAR'S PRAISE OF BEOWULF, AND BEO-
WULF'S REPLY

20 Hrothgar spoke when he reached the hall,
Stood on the step, and stared at the roof
Adorned with gold, and Grendel's hand:
"Prompt be my heart to praise the Almighty
For the sight I behold. Much harm have I suf-
    fered,
25 And grief from Grendel, but God still works
Wonder on wonder, the Warden of Glory.
But a little while since, I scarcely dared,
As long as I lived to look for escape
30 From my burden of sorrow, when blood-
    stained stood,
And dripping with slaughter, this stately hall.
Wide-spread woe my warriors scattered;
They never hoped this house to rid,
35 While life should last, this land-mark of people,
Of demons and devils. 'Tis done by the hero.
By the might of the Lord this man has finished
The feat that all of us failed to achieve
By wit or by war. And well may she say,
40 —Whoever she be,—that bore this son,
That the Ancient of Days dealt with her
    graciously,
And blest her in child-birth. Now Beowulf,
    hear!
45 I shall henceforth hold thee, hero beloved,
As child of my own, and cherish thee fondly
In kinship new. Thou shalt never lack
Meed of reward that is mine to give.
For deeds less mighty have I many times
50   granted
Fullest reward to warriors feebler,
In battle less brave. Thy boldness and valor

Afar shall be known; thy fame shall live
To be great among men. Now God the Almighty
With honor reward thee, as ever he doth."

Beowulf spoke, the son of Ecgtheow,
"Gladly we fought this good fight through,
Fearlessly faced the foe inhuman,
Grappled him gruesome; it grieves me sore
That the man-beast himself you may not see, 10
Dead in the hall, fordone in the fray.
I meant to master the monster quickly,
To his death-bed pin him by power of my grip,
Hold him hard till my hand could strangle him,
Bringing him low, but he broke away. 15
In vain I tried to prevent his escape.
The Lord was unwilling; I lost my hold
On the man-destroyer; too strong was the monster,
Too swift on his feet. But to save his life 20
He left behind him the whole of his fore-paw,
Arm and shoulder. 'Twas a useless shift.
Profiting nothing. He ne'er will prolong
His life by the loss, the loathly slayer,
Sunk in sin; but sorrow holds him, 25
Caught in the grasp of its grip relentless,
In woful bonds to await in anguish,
Guilty wretch, the rest of his doom,
As the Lord Almighty shall mete it to him."

More silent seemed the son of Ecglaf,[12] 30
Less boastful in bragging of brave deeds done,
When all of them, looking aloft, beheld
The hand on high, where it hung 'neath the roof,
The claw of the fiend; each finger was armed 35
With a steel-like spur instead of a nail,
The heathen's handspikes, the horrible paw
Of the evil fiend. They all declared
No iron blade could e'er have bit 40
On the monstrous bulk of the man-beast's hide,
Or hewn away that woful talon.

15. THE FEASTING AND GIVING OF TREASURE IN THE HALL

Now orders were given the guest-hall to
cleanse,
And furnish it fresh. Forth went hurrying
Men and maids. To the mead-hall they went
And busily worked. Woven tapestries, 50
Glinting with gold, hung gay on the walls,

[12] Unferth.

Marvellous wonders for men to look upon.
Ruin and wreck had been wrought in the
building,
Though braced within by iron bands,
5 The hinges were wrenched, the roof alone
stood
Undamaged and sound, when the sin-spotted
wretch,
The demon destroyer, in despair of his life,
10 Turned and made off,—not easy it is
To escape from death, essay it who will.
(So each of us all to his end must come,
Forced by fate to his final abode
Where his body, stretched on the bier of death,
15 Shall rest after revel.) Now right was the hour
For Healfdene's heir to enter the hall;
The king himself would come to the feast.
I never have heard of nobler bearing
'Mongst ranks of liegemen surrounding their
20 lord
As they took their seats, the trusty comrades,
And fell to feasting. Freely quaffed
Many a mead-cup the mighty kinsmen,
Hrothgar and Hrothulf, the high wall within.
25 Heorot was filled with a friendly host.
(Far was the day when the Scylding host
Should treachery plot, betraying each other.)
Then Healfdene's son bestowed on Beowulf
A gold-adorned banner for battle-reward,
30 A rich-broidered standard, breast-plate and
helmet.
The swordsmen assembled saw the treasures
Borne before the hero. Beowulf drank
The health of Hrothgar, nor had reason to feel
35 Ashamed before shieldmen to show his reward.
Never were offered by earls that I heard of,
In token of friendship four such treasures,
Never was equalled such ale-bench bounty.
Round the ridge of the helmet a rim of iron,
40 Wound with wire, warded the head,
That the offspring of files, with fearful stroke,
The hard-tempered sword-blade, might harm
it not,
When fierce in the battle the foemen should
45 join.
At a sign from the king, eight stallions proud,
Bitted and bridled, were brought into hall.
On the back of one was a wondrous saddle,
Bravely wrought and bordered with jewels,
50 The battle-seat bold of the best of kings,
When Hrothgar himself would ride to the
sword-play.

(Nor flinched from the foe the famous war-
    rior
In the front of the fight where fell the slain.)
To the hero delivered the lord of the Scyldings,
The heir of Ing, both armor and horses,   5
Gave them to Beowulf, and bade him enjoy
    them.
Thus royally, the ruler famous,
The heroes' hoard-guard, heaped his bounty;
Repaid the struggle with steeds and trophies, 10
Praised by all singers who speak the truth.

16. THE KING'S GIFTS TO BEOWULF'S MEN, AND
        THE GLEEMAN'S LAY OF FINN

The Lord of the earls then added gifts,   15
At the mead-bench remembered the men, each
    one,
That Beowulf brought o'er the briny deep,
With ancient heirlooms and offered to pay
In gold for the man that Grendel had slain,   20
As more of them surely the monster had
    killed
Had not holy God and the hero's courage
Averted their doom. (So daily o'errules
The Father Almighty the fortunes of men.   25
Therefore is insight ever the best,
And prudence of mind; for much shall suffer
Of lief and of loath who long endures
The days of his life in labor and toil.)
Now music and song were mingled together,   30
In the presence of Hrothgar, ruler in war.
Harp was struck and hero-lays told.
Along the mead-bench the minstrel spread
Cheer in hall, when he chanted the lay
Of the sudden assault on the sons of Finn.   35

*The episode which follows alludes obscurely to
details of a feud between Frisians and Danes. The
Finnsburg fragment contains a portion of the same
story; and one of the heroes, Hnaef, is also mentioned in* Widsith.

17. THE LAY OF FINN ENDED. THE SPEECH OF
        THE QUEEN

                    The lay was ended,
The gleeman's song. Sound of revelry   45
Rose again. Gladness brightened
Along bench and board. Beer-thanes poured
From flagons old the flowing wine.
Wealhtheow the queen walked in state,
Under her crown, where uncle and nephew   50
Together sat,—they still were friends.
There too sat Unferth, trusted counsellor,

At Hrothgar's feet; though faith he had broken
With his kinsmen in battle, his courage was
    proved.
Then the queen of the Scyldings spoke these
    words:
"Quaff of this cup my king and my lord,
Gold-friend of men. To thy guests be kind,
To the men of the Jutes be generous with gifts.
Far and near thou now hast peace.
I have heard thou dost wish the hero for son, 10
To hold as thy own, now Heorot is cleansed,
The jewel-bright hall. Enjoy while thou
    mayest,
Allotment of wealth, and leave to thy heirs
Kingdom and rule when arrives the hour   15
That hence thou shalt pass to thy place ap-
    pointed.
Well I know that my nephew Hrothulf
Will cherish in honor our children dear,
If thou leavest before him this life upon earth; 20
He will surely requite the kindness we showed
    him,
Faithfully tend our two young sons,
When to mind he recalls our care and affection,
How we helped him and housed him when *he*   25
    was a child."
She turned to the bench where her two boys
    sat,
Hrethric and Hrothmund, and the rest of the
    youth,
A riotous band, and right in their midst,   30
Between the two brothers, Beowulf sat.

18. THE QUEEN'S GIFTS TO BEOWULF

With courteous bow the cup she offered,   35
Greeted him graciously and gave him to boot
Two armlets rare of twisted gold,
A robe and rings, and the rarest collar;
A better was never known among men,
Since Hama brought to his bright-built hall   40
The jewelled necklace, the gem of the Bris-
    ings.[13]

*Lines 1200–1214 interrupt the narrative to tell of
the subsequent history of Wealhtheow's gift; how
Beowulf gave it to Hygelac, who wore it on his
famous raid against the Frisians, in which he was
slain by the Franks.*

Before the warriors Wealhtheow spoke:
"Accept, dear Beowulf, this bright-gemmed   50
    collar;

[13] originally owned by the goddess Freya.

Make happy use of this heirloom jewelled,
This ring and robe and royal treasure;
Be brave and bold. My boys instruct
In gentle manners; mine be the praise.
Thou hast done such a deed that in days to
    come
Men will proclaim thy might and valor
To the ends of the earth, where the ocean-
    wave
Washes the windy walls of the land.
I wish thee joy of thy jewelled treasure,
Long be thy life; enlarge thy prosperity,
Show thee a friend to my sons in deed.
Here each earl to the other is faithful,
True to his liege-lord, loyal and kind.
My warriors obey me, willing and prompt.
The Danes, carousing, do as I bid."
She went to her seat, the wine flowed free;
'Twas a glorious feast. The fate that impended,
None of them knew, though near to them all.

When darkness came, the king of the Danes
Went to his rest in the royal bower;
But a throng of his kinsmen kept the hall
As they used to do in the days of old.
They cleared the boards and covered the floor
With beds and bolsters. One beer-thane there
Lay down to sleep with his doom upon him.
They placed by their heads their polished
    shields,
Their battle-boards bright, on the bench
    nearby.
Above each earl, within easy reach,
Was his helmet high and his harness of mail
And the spear-shaft keen. 'Twas their custom
    so,
That always at rest they were ready for war
At home or abroad, where'er they might be,
At what hour soever for aid might call
Their lord and king; they were comrades true.

END OF THE FIRST ADVENTURE

THE BATTLE OF MALDON *

TRANSLATED BY
J. DUNCAN SPAETH

The Battle of Maldon, *along with* The Battle
of Brunanburh, *is a good example of Old Eng-*

* The modern version by J. Duncan Spaeth is
here reprinted by permission of the Princeton University Press.

lish battle poetry. Although the unknown author gives vent to lyrical emotion, the bulk of
the poem is a dramatic narrative. It sounds like
an eyewitness report. And, of course, it has the
concreteness of truth, for in 991 this battle took
place between Byrhtnoth, alderman of Essex,
and the invading Vikings. The account tells of
heroic and sporting defeat. Note the scorn for
the faint-hearted, the praise of loyalty. Note
also that literature sadly records, a thousand
years ago as it does today, the fundamental
stupidities and gallantries of human combat.

The beginning of the poem is lost. The first
sixteen lines of the remaining portion describe
how Byrhtnoth's men, arrived at the battle
field, dismount and turn their horses loose, how
one of them sends his hawk flying to the wood,
and how the East-Saxon alderman proceeds to
marshal his band on the banks of the stream.
The poem continues as follows:

Byrhtnoth encouraged his comrades heartily;
Rode through the ranks and roused their
    spirits;
Marshalled his men to meet the onset;
Showed them how they should hold their
    shields
Firm in their grip, and fearless stand.
When he had briskly whetted their courage,
He leaped from his steed and stood with his
    people,
His hearth-band beloved and household thanes.

Then strode to the strand a stalwart North-
    man,
The viking herald. They heard him shout,
Send o'er the tide the taunt of the pirates;
Hailing the earl, he hurled this challenge:
"Bold sea-rovers bade me tell thee
Straightway thou must send them tribute,
Rings for ransom, royal treasure;
Better with gifts ye buy us off,
Ere we deal hard blows and death in battle.
Why spill we blood when the bargain is easy?
Give us the pay and we grant ye peace.
If thou dost agree, who are greatest here,
To ransom thy folk with the fee we demand,
And give to the seamen the gold they ask,
Pay with tribute for treaty of peace,
We load the booty aboard our ships,
Haul to sea and hold the truce."

Byrhtnoth spake, he brandished his spear,
Lifted his shield and shouted aloud,
Grim was his wrath as he gave them his an-
    swer:
"Hearest thou, pirate, my people's reply?   5
Ancient swords they will send for ransom;
Poison-tipped points they will pay for tribute;
Treasure that scarce will serve you in battle.
Go back, pirate, give them my answer;
Bring them this word of bitter defiance;   10
Tell them here standeth, stern and intrepid,
The earl with his folk, to defend his country,
Æthelred's realm, the rights of my lord,
His house and his home; the heathen shall fall,
Pirates and robbers. My people were shamed,   15
If ye loaded our booty aboard your ships,
And floated them off unfought for, to sea,
Having sailed so far, to set foot on our soil.
Not all so easily earn ye our gold!
Sword-blades and spear-points we sell you   20
    first;
Battle-play grim, ere ye get our tribute!"
Forward he told his troop to come,
To step under shield and stand by the shore.
The breadth of the stream kept the bands   25
    asunder;
Strong came flowing the flood after ebb,
Filled the channel, and foamed between them.
Impatient stood by Panta stream,
East-Saxon host and horde of the pirates,   30
Longing to lock their lances in battle.
Neither could harass or harm the other,
Save that some fell by the flight of arrows.

Down went the tide, the Danes were ready;   35
Burned for battle the band of the Vikings;
On the bridge stood Wulfstan, and barred their
    way.
Byrhtnoth sent him, a seasoned warrior,
Ceola's son, with his kinsmen to hold it.
The first of the Vikings who ventured to set   40
Foot on the bridge, he felled with his spear.
Two sturdy warriors stood with Wulfstan,
Maccus and Ælfhere, mighty pair,
Kept the approach where the crossing was   45
    shallow;
Defended the bridge, and fought with the
    boldest,
As long as their hands could lift a sword.
When the strangers discovered and clearly saw   50
What bitter fighters the bridgewards proved,
They tried a trick, the treacherous robbers,

Begged they might cross, and bring their crews
Over the shallows, and up to the shore.
The earl was ready, in reckless daring,
To let them land too great a number.
Byrhthelm's son, while the seamen listened,   5
Called across, o'er the cold water:
"Come ye seamen, come and fight us!
We give you ground, but God alone knows
Who to-day shall hold the field."

Strode the battle-wolves bold through the
    water;
West over Panta waded the pirates:
Carried their shields o'er the shining waves;
Safely their lindenwoods landed the sailors.
Byrhtnoth awaited them, braced for the on-
    slaught,
Haughty and bold at the head of his band.
Bade them build the bristling war-hedge,
Shield against shield, to shatter the enemy.   20
Near was the battle, now for the glory,
Now for the death of the doomed in the field.
Swelled the war-cry, circled the ravens,
Screamed the eagle, eager for prey;
Sped from the hand the hard-forged spear-
    head,
Showers of darts, sharp from the grindstone.
Bows were busy, bolt stuck in buckler;
Bitter the battle-rush, brave men fell,
Heroes on either hand, hurt in the fray.   30
Wounded was Wulfmær, went to his battle-
    rest;
Cruelly mangled, kinsman of Byrhtnoth,
Son of his sister, slain on the field.

Pay of vengeance they paid the Vikings;
I heard of the deed of the doughty Edward:
He struck with his sword a stroke that was
    mighty,
Down fell the doomed man, dead at his feet.
For this the thane got the thanks of his leader,
Praise that was due for his prowess in fight.
Grimly they held their ground in the battle,
Strove with each other the stout-hearted he-
    roes,
Strove with each other, eager to strike
First with their darts the foe that was doomed.
Warriors thronged, the wounded lay thick.
Stalwart and steady they stood about Byrht-
    noth.
Bravely he heartened them, bade them to win
Glory in battle by beating the Danes.

Raising his shield, he rushed at the enemy;
Covered by buckler, he came at a Viking;
Charged him furious, earl against churl,
Each for the other had evil in store.
The sailorman sent from the south a javelin, 5
Sorely wounding the war-band's leader;
He shoved with his shield, the shaft snapped short;
The spear was splintered and sprang against him;
Wroth was Byrhtnoth, reached for his weapon: 10
Gored the Viking that gave him the wound.
Straight went the lance, strong was the leader;
Sheer through the throat of the pirate he thrust it.
His dart meant death, so deadly his aim.
Swiftly he sent him a second javelin,
That crashed through the corslet and cleft his bosom,
Wounded him sore through his woven mail; 20
The poisonous spear-head stood in his heart.
Blithe was the leader, laughed in his breast,
Thanked his Lord for that day's work.

Now one of the pirates poised his weapon;
Sped from his hand a spear that wounded 25
Through and through the thane of Æthelred.[1]
There stood at his side a stripling youth;
Brave was the boy; he bent o'er his lord,
Drew from his body the blood-dripping dart. 30
'Twas Wulfmær the youthful, Wulfstan's son;
Back he hurled the hard-forged spear.
In went the point, to earth fell the pirate
Who gave his master the mortal hurt.
A crafty seaman crept toward the earl, 35
Eager to rob him of armor and rings,
Bracelets and gear and graven sword.
Then Byrhtnoth drew his blade from the sheath,
Broad and blood-stained struck at the breast- 40
plate.
But one of the seamen stopped the warrior,
Beat down the arm of the earl with his lance.
Fell to the ground the gray-hilted sword;
No more he might grasp his goodly blade, 45
Wield his weapon; yet words he could utter;
The hoar-headed warrior heartened his men;
Bade them forward to fare and be brave.
When the stricken leader no longer could stand, 50

He looked to heaven and lifted his voice:
"I render Thee thanks, O Ruler of men,
For the joys Thou hast given, that gladdened my life.
Merciful Maker, now most I need, 5
Thy goodness to grant me a gracious end,
That my soul may swiftly speed to Thee.
Come to Thy keeping, O King of angels,
Depart in peace. I pray Thee Lord
That the fiends of hell may not harm my 10
spirit."
The heathen pirates then hewed him to pieces,
And both the brave men that by him stood;
Ælfnoth and Wulfmær, wounded to death, 15
Gave their lives for their lord in the fight.

Then quitted the field the cowards and faint-
hearts;
The son of Odda started the flight.
Godric abandoned his good lord in battle, 20
Who many a steed had bestowed on his thane.
Leaped on the horse that belonged to his leader,
Not *his* were the trappings, *he* had no right to 25
them.
Both of his brothers basely fled with him,
Godwin and Godwy, forgetful of honor,
Turned from the fight, and fled to the woods,
Seeking the cover, and saving their lives.
Those were with them, who would have re- 30
mained,
Had they remembered how many favors
Their lord had done them in days of old.
Offa foretold it, what time he arose
To speak where they met to muster their forces. 35
Many, he said, were mighty in words
Whose courage would fail when it came to fighting.
There lay on the field the lord of the people,
Æthelred's earl; all of them saw him, 40
His hearth-companions beheld him dead.
Forward went fighting the fearless warriors,
Their courage was kindled, no cowards were they;
Their will was fixed on one or the other: 45
To lose their life, or avenge their leader.
Ælfwiné spoke to them, son of Ælfric,
Youthful in years, but unyielding in battle;
Roused their courage, and called them to honor: 50
"Remember the time when we talked in the mead-hall,

---

[1] Byrhtnoth.

When bold on our benches we boasted our
    valor,
Deeds of daring we'd do in the battle!
Now we may prove whose prowess is true.
My birth and my breeding I boldly proclaim:
5 I am sprung from a mighty Mercian line.
Aldhelm the alderman, honored and prosper-
    ous,
He was my grandsire, great was his fame:
My people who know me shall never reproach 10
    me,
Say I was ready to run from the battle,
Back to my home, and abandon my leader,
Slain on the field. My sorrow is double,
Both kinsman and lord I've lost in the fight." 15
Forward he threw himself, thirsting for ven-
    geance;
Sent his javelin straight at a pirate.
Fell with a crash his foe to the earth,
His life-days ended. Then onward he strode, 20
Urging his comrades to keep in the thick of it.
Up spake Offa, with ashen spear lifted:
"Well has thou counselled us, well hast en-
    couraged;
Noble Ælfwiné, needs must we follow thee. 25
Now that our leader lies low on the field,
Needs must we steadfastly stand by each other,
Close in the conflict keeping together,
As long as our hands can hold a weapon,
Good blade wield. Godric the coward, 30
Son of Odda, deceived us all.
Too many believed 'twas our lord himself,
When they saw him astride the war-steed
    proud.
His run-away ride our ranks hath broken, 35
Shattered the shield-wall. Shame on the das-
    tard,
Who caused his comrades like cowards to fly!"
Up spake Leofsunu, lifted his linden-wood,
Answered his comrades from under his shield: 40
"Here I stand, and here shall I stay!
Not a foot will I flinch, but forward I'll go!
Vengeance I've vowed for my valiant leader.
Now that my friend is fallen in battle,
My people shall never reproach me, in Stour- 45
    mere;
Call me deserter, and say I returned,
Leaderless, lordless, alone from the fight.
Better is battle-death; boldly I welcome
The edge and the iron." Full angry he charged, 50
Daring all danger, disdaining to fly.
Up spake Dunheré, old and faithful,

Shook his lance and shouted aloud,
Bade them avenge the valiant Byrhtnoth:
"Wreak on the Danes the death of our lord!
Unfit is for vengeance who values his life."
5 Fell on the foe the faithful body-guard,
Battle-wroth spearmen, beseeching God
That they might avenge the thane of Æthel-
    red,
Pay the heathen with havoc and slaughter.
10 The son of Ecglaf, Æscferth by name,
Sprung from a hardy North-humbrian race,
—He was their hostage,—helped them man-
    fully.
Never he faltered or flinched in the war-play;
15 Lances a plenty he launched at the pirates,
Shot them on shield, or sheer through the
    breast-plate:
Rarely he missed them, many he wounded,
While he could wield his weapon in battle.
20 Still Edward the long held out at the front;
Brave and defiant, he boasted aloud
That he would not yield a hair's breadth of
    ground,
Nor turn his back where his better lay dead.
25 He broke through the shield-wall, breasted the
    foe,
Worthily paid the pirate warriors
For the life of his lord ere he laid him down.
Near him Æthelric, noble comrade,
30 Brother of Sibryht, brave and untiring,
Mightily fought, and many another;
Hacked the hollow shields, holding their own.
Bucklers were broken, the breast-plate sang
Its gruesome song. The sword of Offa
35 Went home to the hilt in the heart of a Viking.
But Offa himself soon had to pay for it,
The kinsman of Gadd succumbed in the fight.
Yet ere he fell, he fulfilled his pledge,
The promise he gave to his gracious lord,
40 That both should ride to their burg together,
Home to their friends, or fall in the battle,
Killed in conflict and covered with wounds;
He lay by his lord, a loyal thane.
Mid clash of shields the shipmen came on,
45 Maddened by battle. Full many a lance
Home was thrust to the heart of the doomed.
Then sallied forth Wistan, Wigelin's son;
Three of the pirates he pierced in the throng,
Ere he fell, by his friends, on the field of
    slaughter.
Bitter the battle-rush, bravely struggled
Heroes in armor, while all around them

The wounded dropped and the dead lay thick.
Oswold and Eadwold all the while
Their kinsmen and comrades encouraged
  bravely,
Both of the brothers bade their friends
Never to weaken or weary in battle,
But keep up their sword-play, keen to the end.
Up spake Byrhtwold, brandished his ash-
  spear,
—He was a tried and true old hero,—
Lifted his shield and loudly called to them:

"Heart must be keener, courage the hardier,
Bolder our mood as our band diminisheth.
Here lies in his blood our leader and comrade,
The brave on the beach. Bitter shall rue it
Who turns his back on the battle-field now.   5
Here I stay; I am stricken and old;
My life is done; I shall lay me down
Close by my lord and comrade dear."

10 *Six more lines and the MS. breaks off. There cannot have been much left. The battle is over.*

MIDDLE ENGLISH PERIOD

SIR GAWAIN AND THE GREEN KNIGHT*

Gawain *belongs in the same manuscript with*
The Pearl *and two other poems—perhaps all
by one poet. It extols the virtues of knighthood in presenting a Gawain rather different
from his counterpart in other familiar Arthurian
material. Whoever wrote this Middle English
poem, which appears here in part in a modern
translation, was no primitive writer; he has a
sense of scene, technical knowledge of hunting,
a good sense of humor, organizing ability, and
facility in verse, combining in the last the old
English four-stress line with French a, b, a, b, a
short lines at the end of verse-paragraphs.*

  *This romance begins with a challenge by the
mysterious Green Knight, who taunts Arthur's
men with the proposal that he will let one of
them chop his head off if in return his opponent
will appear a year later to receive a similar
blow. Gawain finally accepts, delivers the
stroke, and is surprised to see the Green Knight
pick up his head and ride away. Eventually
Gawain sets out to keep his word, meets with
difficulties on the way, but finally arrives near
his goal. He is given knightly hospitality by
Sir Bercilak, who proposes entertainment and*

a *bargain: Gawain, staying home with the lady
of the castle, will exchange trophies of each
day's activities (for three days) with his host,
who will successively hunt the deer, boar, and
fox. Gawain agrees. Our selection—roughly
one-third of the whole work—takes up the story
at this point and delightfully unwinds the plot.*

PART III

Betimes rose the folk ere the first of the day;
The guests that were going then summoned
  their grooms,
Who hastily sprang up to saddle their horses,
Packed their bags and prepared all their gear.   5
The nobles made ready, to ride all arrayed;
And quickly they leaped and caught up their
  bridles,
And started, each wight on the way that well
  pleased him,   10
The land's beloved lord not last was equipped
For riding, with many a man too. A morsel
He hurriedly ate when mass he had heard,
And promptly with horn to the hunting field
  hastened.   15
And ere any daylight had dawned upon earth,
Both he and his knights were high on their
  horses.

* Sir Gawain and the Green Knight, *the modern
version by Theodore Banks, is here reprinted by
permission of F. S. Crofts & Co., publishers.*

[28]

The dog-grooms, accomplished, the hounds then coupled,
The door of the kennel unclosed, called them out,
On the bugle mightily blew three single notes;
Whereupon bayed with a wild noise the brachets,[1]
And some they turned back that went straying, and punished.
The hunters, I heard, were a hundred. To station
        They go,
  The keepers of the hounds,
  And off the leashes throw.
  With noise the wood resounds
  From the good blasts they blow.

At the first sound of questing, the wild creatures quaked;
The deer fled, foolish from fright, in the dale,
To the high ground hastened, but quickly were halted
By beaters, loud shouting, stationed about
In a circle. The harts were let pass with their high heads,
And also the bucks, broad-antlered and bold;
For the generous lord by law had forbidden
All men with the male deer to meddle in close season.
The hinds were hemmed in with hey! and ware!
The does to the deep valleys driven with great din.
You might see as they loosed them the shafts swiftly soar—
At each turn of the forest their feathers went flying—
That deep into brown hides bit with their broad heads;
Lo! they brayed on the hill-sides, bled there, and died,
And hounds, fleet-footed, followed them head-long.
And hunters after them hastened with horns
So loud in their sharp burst of sound as to sunder
The cliffs. What creatures escaped from the shooters,
Hunted and harried from heights to the waters,
Were pulled down and rent at the places there ready;

_____
[1] female hounds.

Such skill the men showed at these low-lying stations,
So great were the greyhounds that quickly they got them
And dragged them down, fast as the folk there might look
        At the sight.
  Carried with bliss away,
  The lord did oft alight,
  Oft gallop; so that day
  He passed till the dark night.

Thus frolicked the lord on the fringe of the forest,
And Gawain the good in his gay bed reposed,
Lying snugly, till sunlight shone on the walls,
'Neath a coverlet bright with curtains about it.
As softly he slumbered, a slight sound he heard
At his door, made with caution, and quickly it opened.
The hero heaved up his head from the clothes;
By a corner he caught up the curtain a little,
And glanced out with heed to behold what had happened.
The lady it was, most lovely to look at,
Who shut the door after her stealthily, slyly,
And turned toward the bed. Then the brave man, embarrassed,
Lay down again subtly to seem as if sleeping;
And stilly she stepped, and stole to his bed,
There cast up the curtain, and creeping within it,
Seated herself on the bedside right softly,
And waited a long while to watch when he woke.
And the lord too, lurking, lay there a long while,
Wondering at heart what might come of this happening,
Or what it might mean—a marvel he thought it.
Yet he said to himself, " 'T would be surely more seemly
By speaking at once to see what she wishes."
Then roused he from sleep, and stretching turned toward her,
His eyelids unlocked, made believe that he wondered,
And signed himself so by his prayers to be safer
        From fall.
  Right sweet in chin and cheek,
  Both white and red withal,
  Full fairly she did speak
  With laughing lips and small.

"Good morrow, Sir Gawain," that gay lady
    said,
"You're a sleeper unwary, since so one may
    steal in.
In a trice you are ta'en! If we make not a truce, 5
In your bed, be you certain of this, I shall bind
    you."
All laughing, the lady delivered those jests.
"Good morrow, fair lady," said Gawain the
    merry,   10
"You may do what you will, and well it doth
    please me,
For quickly I yield me, crying for mercy;
This method to me seems the best—for I must!"
So the lord in turn jested with laughter right 15
    joyous.
"But if, lovely lady, you would, give me leave,
Your prisoner release and pray him to rise,
And I'd come from this bed and clothe myself
    better;   20
So could I converse with you then with more
    comfort."
"Indeed no, fair sir," that sweet lady said,
"You'll not move from your bed; I shall manage
    you better;   25
For here—and on that side too—I shall hold
    you,
And next I shall talk with the knight I have
    taken.
For well do I know that your name is Sir 30
    Gawain,
By everyone honored wherever you ride;
Most highly acclaimed is your courtly behav-
    ior
With lords and ladies and all who are living. 35
And now you're here, truly, and none but we
    two;
My lord and his followers far off have fared;
Other men remain in their beds, and my
    maidens;   40
The door is closed, and secured with a strong
    hasp;
Since who delights all I have in my house,
My time, as long as it lasts, I with talking
             Shall fill.   45
    My body's gladly yours;
    Upon me work your will.
    Your servant I, perforce,
    And now, and shall be still."
                    50
"In faith," quoth Sir Gawain, "a favor I
    think it,

Although I am now not the knight you speak
    of;
To reach to such fame as here you set forth,
I am one, as I well know myself, most un-
    worthy.
By God, should you think it were good, I'd be
    glad
If I could or in word or action accomplish
Your ladyship's pleasure—a pure joy 't would
    prove."
"In good faith, Sir Gawain," the gay lady said,
"Ill-bred I should be if I blamed or belittled
The worth and prowess that please all others.
There are ladies enough who'd be now more
    delighted
To have you in thraldom, as here, sir, I have
    you
To trifle gaily in talk most engaging,
To give themselves comfort and quiet their
    cares
Than have much of the gold and the goods they
    command.
But to Him I give praise that ruleth the heaven
That wholly I have in my hand what all wish."
                So she
    Gave him good cheer that day,
    She who was fair to see.
    To what she chanced to say
    With pure speech answered he.

    Quoth the merry man, "Madam, Mary re-
    ward you,
For noble, in faith, I've found you, and gen-
    erous.
People by others pattern their actions,
But more than I merit to me they give praise;
'T is your courteous self who can show naught
    but kindness."
"By Mary," said she, "to me it seems other!
Were I worth all the host of women now living,
And had I the wealth of the world in my hands,
Should I chaffer and choose to get me a
    champion,
Sir, from the signs I've seen in you here
Of courtesy, merry demeanor, and beauty,
From what I have heard, and hold to be true,
Before you no lord now alive would be chosen."
"A better choice, madam, you truly have made;
Yet I'm proud of the value you put now upon
    me.
Your servant as seemly, I hold you my sover-
    eign,

Become your knight, and Christ give you quit-
   tance."
Thus of much they talked till mid-morning was
   past.
The lady behaved as if greatly she loved him,   5
But Gawain, on guard, right gracefully acted.
"Though I were the most lovely of ladies," she
   thought,
"The less would he take with him love." He
   was seeking   10
               With speed,
   Grief that must be: the stroke
   That him should stun indeed.
   She then of leaving spoke,
   And promptly he agreed.

  Then she gave him good-day, and glanced
   at him, laughing,
And startled him, speaking sharp words as she
   stood:
"He who blesses all words reward this re-
   ception!
I doubt if indeed I may dub you Gawain."
"Wherefore?" he queried, quickly enquiring,
Afraid that he'd failed in his fashion of speech.   25
But the fair lady blesses him, speaking as fol-
   lows:
"One as good as is Gawain the gracious con-
   sidered,
(And courtly behavior's found wholly in him)   30
Not lightly so long could remain with a lady
Without, in courtesy, craving a kiss
At some slight subtle hint at the end of a story."
"Let it be as you like, lovely lady," said Gawain;
"As a knight is so bound, I'll kiss at your bid-   35
   ding,
And lest he displease you, so plead no longer."
Then closer she comes, and catches the knight
In her arms, and salutes him, leaning down
   affably.   40
Kindly each other to Christ they commend.
She goes forth at the door without further ado,
And he quickly makes ready to rise, and
   hastens,
Calls to his chamberlain, chooses his clothes,   45
And merrily marches, when ready, to mass.
Then he fared to his meat, and fitly he feasted,
Made merry all day with amusements till moon-
   rise.
          None knew   50
   A knight to better fare
   With dames so worthy, two:

One old, one younger. There
Much mirth did then ensue.

  Still was absent the lord of that land on his
   pleasure,
To hunt barren hinds in wood and in heath.
By the set of the sun he had slain such a num-
   ber
Of does and different deer that 't was wondrous.
Eagerly flocked in the folk at the finish,
And quickly made of the killed deer a quarry;
To this went the nobles with numerous men;
The game whose flesh was the fattest they
   gathered;
With care, as the case required, cut them open.
And some the deer searched at the spot of as-
   say,
And two fingers of fat they found in the poorest.
They slit at the base of the throat, seized the
   stomach,
Scraped it away with a sharp knife and sewed
   it;
Next slit the four limbs and stripped off the
   hide;
Then opened the belly and took out the bowels
And flesh of the knot, quickly flinging them
   out.
They laid hold of the throat, made haste to
   divide, then,
The windpipe and gullet, and tossed out the
   guts;
With their sharp knives carved out the shoul-
   ders and carried them
Held through a small hole to have the sides
   perfect.
The breast they sliced, and split it in two;
And then they began once again at the throat,
And quickly as far as its fork they cut it;
Pulled out the pluck, and promptly thereafter
Beside the ribs swiftly severed the fillets,
Cleared them off readily right by the backbone,
Straight down to the haunch, all hanging to-
   gether.
They heaved it up whole, and hewed it off
   there,
And the rest by the name of the numbles—and
   rightly—
           They knew.
   Then where divide the thighs,
   The folds behind they hew,
   Hasten to cut the prize
   Along the spine in two.

And next both the head and the neck off
they hewed;
The sides from the backbone swiftly they sun-
dered;
The fee of the ravens they flung in the 5
branches,
They ran through each thick side a hole by the
ribs,
And hung up both by the hocks of the
haunches, 10
Each fellow to have the fee that was fitting.
On the fair beast's hide, they fed their hounds
With the liver and lights[2] and the paunch's
lining,
Among which bread steeped in blood was 15
mingled.
They blew boldly the blast for the prize; the
hounds barked.
Then the venison took they and turned toward
home, 20
And stoutly many a shrill note they sounded.
Ere close of the daylight, the company came
To the comely castle where Gawain in comfort
Sojourned.
    And when he met the knight 25
    As thither he returned,
    Joy had they and delight,
    Where the fire brightly burned.

In the hall the lord bade all his household to 30
gather,
And both the dames to come down with their
damsels.
In the room there before all the folk he ordered
His followers, truly, to fetch him his venison. 35
Gawain he called with courteous gaiety,
Asked him to notice the number of nimble
beasts,
Showed him the fairness of flesh on the ribs.
"Are you pleased with this play? Have I won 40
your praise?
Have I thoroughly earned your thanks through
my cunning?"
"In faith," said Sir Gawain, "this game is the
fairest 45
I've seen in the season of winter these seven
years."
"The whole of it, Gawain, I give you," the host
said;
"Because of our compact, as yours you may 50
claim it."

_____
[2] lungs.

"That is true," the knight said, "and I tell you
the same:
That this I have worthily won within doors,
And surely to you with as good will I yield it."
With both of his arms his fair neck he em- 5
braced,
And the hero as courteously kissed as he could.
"I give you my gains. I got nothing further;
I freely would grant it, although it were
greater." 10
"It is good," said the good man; "I give you
my thanks.
Yet things so may be that you'd think it better
To tell where you won this same wealth by 15
your wit."
"'T was no part of our pact," said he; "press
me no more;
For trust entirely in this, that you've taken
        Your due."
    With laughing merriment
    And knightly speech and true
    To supper soon they went
    With store of dainties new.

In a chamber they sat, by the side of the
chimney,
Where men right frequently fetched them
mulled wine.
In their jesting, again they agreed on the mor-
row
To keep the same compact they came to be-
fore:
That whatever should chance, they'd exchange
at evening,
When greeting again, the new things they had
gotten.
Before all the court they agreed to the cove-
nant;
Then was the beverage brought forth in jest.
At last they politely took leave of each other,
And quickly each hero made haste to his couch.
When the cock but three times had crowed
and cackled,
The lord and his men had leaped from their
beds.
So that duly their meal was dealt with, and
mass,
And ere daylight they'd fared toward the forest,
on hunting
        Intent.
    The huntsmen with loud horns
    Through level fields soon went,

Uncoupling 'mid the thorns
The hounds swift on the scent.

Soon they cry for a search by the side of a
swamp.   5
The huntsmen encourage the hounds that first
catch there
The scent, and sharp words they shout at them
loudly;
And thither the hounds that heard them has- 10
tened,
And fast to the trail fell, forty at once.
Then such clamor and din from the dogs that
had come there
Arose that the rocks all around them rang.   15
With horn and with mouth the hunters heart-
ened them;
They gathered together then, all in a group,
'Twixt a pool in that copse and a crag most
forbidding.   20
At a stone-heap, beside the swamp, by a cliff,
Where the rough rock had fallen in rugged
confusion,
They fared to the finding, the folk coming
after.   25
Around both the crag and the rubble-heap
searched
The hunters, sure that within them was hidden
The beast whose presence was bayed by the
bloodhounds.   30
Then they beat on the bushes, and bade him
rise up,
And wildly he made for the men in his way,
Rushing suddenly forth, of swine the most
splendid.   35
Apart from the herd he'd grown hoary with
age,
For fierce was the beast, the biggest of boars.
Then many men grieved, full grim when he
grunted,   40
For three at his first thrust he threw to the
earth,
And then hurtled forth swiftly no harm doing
further.
They shrilly cried hi! and shouted hey! hey! 45
Put bugles to mouth, loudly blew the recall.
The men and dogs merry in voice were and
many;
With outcry they all hurry after this boar
    To slay.   50
He maims the pack when, fell,
He oftens stands at bay.

Loudly they howl and yell,
Sore wounded in the fray.

Then to shoot at him came up the company
quickly.   5
Arrows that hit him right often they aimed,
But their sharp points failed that fell on his
shoulders'
Tough skin, and the barbs would not bite in
his flesh;   10
But the smooth-shaven shafts were shivered in
pieces,
The heads wherever they hit him rebounding.
But when hurt by the strength of the strokes
they struck,   15
Then mad for the fray he falls on the men,
And deeply he wounds them as forward he
dashes.
Then many were frightened, and drew back in
fear;   20
But the lord galloped off on a light horse after
him,
Blew like a huntsman right bold the recall
On his bugle, and rode through the thick of
the bushes,   25
Pursuing this swine till the sun shone clearly.
Thus the day they passed in doing these deeds,
While bides our gracious knight Gawain in bed,
With bed-clothes in color right rich, at the
castle   30
                Behind.
The dame did not forget
To give him greetings kind.
She soon upon him set,
To make him change his mind.   35

Approaching the curtain, she peeps at the
prince,
And at once Sir Gawain welcomes her worthily.
Promptly the lady makes her reply.   40
By his side she seats herself softly, heartily
Laughs, and with lovely look these words de-
livers:
"If you, sir, are Gawain, greatly I wonder
That one so given at all times to goodness   45
Should be not well versed in social conven-
tions,
Or, made once to know, should dismiss them
from mind.
You have promptly forgotten what I in the   50
plainest
Of talk that I knew of yesterday taught you."

"What is that?" said the knight. "For truly I
    know not;
If it be as you say, I am surely to blame."
"Yet I taught you," quoth the fair lady, "of
    kissing;   5
When clearly he's favored, quickly to claim one
Becomes each knight who practices courtesy."
"Cease, dear lady, such speech," said the strong
    man;
"I dare not for fear of refusal do that.   10
'T would be wrong to proffer and then be re-
    pulsed."
"In faith, you may not be refused," said the
    fair one;
"Sir, if you pleased, you have strength to com- 15
    pel it,
Should one be so rude as to wish to deny you."
"By God, yes," said Gawain, "good is your
    speech;
But unlucky is force in the land I live in,   20
And every gift that with good will's not given.
Your word I await to embrace when you wish;
You may start when you please, and stop at
    your pleasure."
                With grace,   25
    The lady, bending low,
    Most sweetly kissed his face.
    Of joy in love and woe
    They talked for a long space.
                            30

    "I should like," said the lady, "from you, sir,
    to learn,
If I roused not your anger by asking, the reason
Why you, who are now so young and valiant,
So known far and wide as knightly and cour- 35
    teous
(And principally, picked from all knighthood,
    is praised
The sport of true love and the science of arms;
For to tell of these true knights' toil, it is surely 40
The title inscribed and the text of their deeds,
How men their lives for their real love ad-
    ventured,
Endured for their passion doleful days,
Then themselves with valor avenged, and their 45
    sorrow
Cast off, and brought bliss into bowers by their
    virtues),
Why you, thought the noblest knight of your
    time,   50
Whose renown and honor are everywhere
    noted,

Have so let me sit on two separate occasions
Beside you, and hear proceed from your head
Not one word relating to love, less or more.
You so goodly in vowing your service and
    gracious
Ought gladly to give to a young thing your
    guidance,
And show me some sign of the sleights of true
    love.
What! know you nothing, and have all renown?
Or else do you deem me too dull, for your
    talking
                Unfit?
    For shame! Alone I come;
    To learn some sport I sit;
    My lord is far from home;
    Now, teach me by your wit."

    "In good faith," said Gawain, "God you re-
    ward;
For great is the happiness, huge the gladness
That one so worthy should want to come hither,
And pains for so poor a man take, as in play
With your knight with looks of regard; it de-
    lights me.
But to take up the task of telling of true love,
To touch on those themes, and on tales of arms
To you who've more skill in that art, I am
    certain,
By half than a hundred men have such as I,
Or ever shall have while here upon earth,
By my faith, 't would be, madam, a manifold
    folly.
Your bidding I'll do, as in duty bound,
To the height of my power, and will hold my-
    self ever
Your ladyship's servant, so save me the Lord."
Thus the fair lady tempted and tested him
    often
To make the man sin—what'er more she'd in
    mind;
But so fair his defense was, no fault was ap-
    parent,
Nor evil on either side; each knew but joy
               On that day.
    At last she kissed him lightly,
    After long mirth and play,
    And took her leave politely,
    And went upon her way.

    The man bestirs himself, springs up for
    mass.

Then made ready and splendidly served was
    their dinner;
In sport with the ladies he spent all the day.
But the lord through fields oft dashed as he
    followed
The savage swine, that sped o'er the slopes, 5
And in two bit the backs of the best of his
    hounds
Where he stood at bay; till 't was broken by
    bowmen, 10
Who made him, despite himself, move to the
    open,
The shafts flew so thick when the throng had
    assembled.
Yet sometimes he forced the stoutest to flinch, 15
Till at last too weary he was to run longer,
But came with such haste as he could to a hole
In a mound, by a rock whence the rivulet runs
    out.
He started to scrape the soil, backed by the 20
    slope,
While froth from his mouth's ugly corners came
    foaming.
White were the tushes[3] he whetted. The bold
    men 25
Who stood round grew tired of trying from far
To annoy him, but dared not for danger draw
    nearer.
               Before,
     So many he did pierce 30
     That all were loth a boar
     So frenzied and so fierce
     Should tear with tusks once more,

 Till the hero himself came, spurring his 35
    horse,
Saw him standing at bay, the hunters beside
    him.
He leaped down right lordly, leaving his
    courser, 40
Unsheathed a bright sword and strode forth
    stoutly,
Made haste through the ford where that fierce
    one was waiting.
Aware of the hero with weapon in hand, 45
So savagely, bristling his back up, he snorted
All feared for the wight lest the worst befall
    him.
Then rushed out the boar directly upon him,
And man was mingled with beast in the midst 50

Of the wildest water. The boar had the worse,
For the man aimed a blow at the beast as he
    met him,
And surely with sharp blade struck o'er his
    breast bone,
That smote to the hilt, and his heart cleft
    asunder.
He squealing gave way, and swift through the
    water
               Went back.
     By a hundred hounds he's caught,
     Who fiercely him attack;
     To open ground he's brought,
     And killed there by the pack.

   The blast for the beast's death was blown on
    sharp horns,
And the lords there loudly and clearly hallooed.
At the beast bayed the brachets, as bid by their
    masters,
The chief, in that hard, long chase, of the
    hunters.
Then one who was wise in woodcraft began
To slice up this swine in the seemliest manner.
First he hews off his head, and sets it on high;
Then along the back roughly rends him apart.
He hales out the bowels, and broils them on hot
    coals,
With these mixed with bread, rewarding his
    brachets.
Then slices the flesh in fine, broad slabs,
And pulls out the edible entrails properly.
Whole, though, he gathers the halves together,
And proudly upon a stout pole he places them.
Homeward they now with this very swine
    hasten,
Bearing in front of the hero the boar's head,
Since him at the ford by the force of his strong
    hand
               He slew.
     It seemed long till he met
     In hall Sir Gawain, who
     Hastened, when called, to get
     The payment that was due.

   The lord called out loudly, merrily laughed
When Gawain he saw, and gladsomely spoke.
The good ladies were sent for, the household
    assembled;
He shows them the slices of flesh, and the story
He tells of his largeness and length, and how
    fierce

---

[3] tusks.

Was the war in the woods where the wild swine
  had fled.
Sir Gawain commended his deeds right gra-
  ciously,
Praised them as giving proof of great prowess. 5
Such brawn on a beast, the bold man declared,
And such sides on a swine he had ne'er before
  seen.
Then they handled the huge head; the cour-
  teous hero 10
Praised it, horror-struck, honoring his host.
Quoth the goodman, "Now, Gawain, yours is
  this game
By our covenant, fast and firm, you know truly."
"It is so," said the knight; "and as certain and 15
  sure
All I get I'll give you again as I pledged you."
He about the neck caught, with courtesy kissed
  him,
And soon a second time served him the same 20
  way.
Said Gawain, "We've fairly fulfilled the agree-
  ment
This evening we entered on, each to the other
               Most true."
  "I, by Saint Giles, have met 25
    None," said the lord, "like you.
    Riches you soon will get,
    If you such business do." 30

    And then the tables they raised upon trestles,
And laid on them cloths; the light leaped up
  clearly
Along by the walls, where the waxen torches
Were set by the henchmen who served in the 35
  hall.
A great sound of sport and merriment sprang
  up
Close by the fire, and on frequent occasions
At supper and afterward, many a splendid 40
  song,
Conduits[4] of Christmas, new carols, all kinds
Of mannerly mirth that a man may tell of.
Our seemly knight ever sat at the side
Of the lady, who made so agreeable her man- 45
  ner,
With sly, secret glances to glad him, so stalwart,
That greatly astonished was Gawain, and wroth
With himself; he in courtesy could not refuse
  her, 50

But acted becomingly, courtly, whatever
The end, good or bad, of his action might be.
          When quite
    Done was their play at last,
    The host called to the knight,
    And to his room they passed
    To where the fire burned bright.

    The men there make merry and drink, and
  once more 10
The same pact for New Year's Eve is proposed;
But the knight craved permission to mount on
  the morrow:
The appointment approached where he had to
  appear.
But the lord him persuaded to stay and linger,
And said, "On my word as a knight I assure
  you
You'll get to the Green Chapel, Gawain, on
  New Year's,
And far before prime,[5] to finish your business.
Remain in your room then, and take your rest.
I shall hunt in the wood and exchange with
  you winnings,
As bound by our bargain, when back I return, 25
For twice I've found you were faithful when
  tried:
In the morning 'best be the third time,' re-
  member.
Let's be mindful of mirth while we may, and 30
  make merry,
For care when one wants it is quickly en-
  countered."
At once this was granted, and Gawain is
  stayed; 35
Drink blithely was brought him; to bed they
  were lighted.
          The guest
    In quiet and comfort spent
    The night, and took his rest.
    On his affairs intent,
    The host was early dressed.

After mass a morsel he took with his men.
The morning was merry; his mount he de- 45
  manded.
The knights who'd ride in his train were in
  readiness,
Dressed and horsed at the door of the hall.

---

[4] songs, tunes.

[5] the first of the canonical hours, or the first hour
of the day.

Wondrous fair were the fields, for the frost was
   clinging;
Bright red in the cloud-rack rises the sun,
And full clear sails close past the clouds in the
   sky.
The hunters unleashed all the hounds by a
   woodside:
The rocks with the blast of their bugles were
   ringing.
Some dogs there fall on the scent where the 10
   fox is,
And trail oft a traitoress using her tricks.
A hound gives tongue at it; huntsmen call to
   him;
Hastens the pack to the hound sniffing hard, 15
And right on his track run off in a rabble,
He scampering before them. They started the
   fox soon;
When finally they saw him, they followed fast,
Denouncing him clearly with clamorous an- 20
   ger.
Through many a dense grove he dodges and
   twists,
Doubling back and harkening at hedges right
   often; 25
At last by a little ditch leaps o'er a thorn-hedge,
Steals out stealthily, skirting a thicket
In thought from the wood to escape by his
   wiles
From the hounds; then, unknowing, drew near 30
   to a hunting-stand.
There hurled themselves, three at once, on him
   strong hounds,
           All gray.
    With quick swerve he doth start 35
    Afresh without dismay.
    With great grief in his heart
    To the wood he goes away.

  Huge was the joy then to hark to the hounds. 40
When the pack all met him, mingled together,
Such curses they heaped on his head at the
   sight
That the clustering cliffs seemed to clatter down
   round them 45
In heaps. The men, when they met him, hailed
   him,
And loudly with chiding speeches hallooed him;
Threats were oft thrown at him, thief he was
   called;
At his tail were the greyhounds, that tarry he 50
   might not.

They rushed at him oft when he raced for the
   open,
And ran to the wood again, reynard the wily.
Thus he led them, all muddied, the lord and
   his men, 5
In this manner along through the hills until
   midday.
At home, the noble knight wholesomely slept
In the cold of the morn within comely curtains.
But the lady, for love, did not let herself sleep, 10
Or fail in the purpose fixed in her heart;
But quickly she roused herself, came there
   quickly,
Arrayed in a gay robe that reached to the
   ground, 15
The skins of the splendid fur skillfully trimmed
   close.
On her head no colors save jewels, well-cut,
That were twined in her hair-fret in clusters of
   twenty. 20
Her fair face was completely exposed, and her
   throat;
In front her breast too was bare, and her back.
She comes through the chamber-door, closes it
   after her, 25
Swings wide a window, speaks to the wight,
And rallies him soon in speech full of sport
           And good cheer.
    "Ah! man, how can you sleep?
    The morning is so clear."
    He was in sorrow deep,
    Yet her he then did hear.

  In a dream muttered Gawain, deep in its
   gloom,
Like a man by a throng of sad thoughts sorely
   moved
Of how fate was to deal out his destiny to him
That morn, when he met the man at the Green
   Chapel,
Bound to abide his blow, unresisting,
But as soon as that comely one came to his
   senses,
Started from slumber and speedily answered, 45
The lovely lady came near, sweetly laughing,
Bent down o'er his fair face and daintily kissed
   him.
And well, in a worthy manner, he welcomed
   her.
50 Seeing her glorious, gayly attired,
Without fault in her features, most fine in her
   color,

Deep joy came welling up, warming his heart.
With sweet, gentle smiling they straightway
 grew merry;
So passed naught between them but pleasure,
 joy,
     And delight.
  Goodly was their debate,
  Nor was their gladness slight.
  Their peril had been great
  Had Mary quit her knight. 10

For that noble princess pressed him so
 closely,
Brought him so near the last bound, that her
 love
He was forced to accept, or, offending, refuse
 her:
Concerned for his courtesy not to prove cai-
 tiff,
And more for his ruin if wrong he committed, 20
Betraying the hero, the head of that house.
"God forbid," said the knight; "that never shall
 be";
And lovingly laughing a little, he parried
The words of fondness that fell from her mouth. 25
She said to him, "Sir, you are surely to blame
If you love not the lady beside whom you're
 lying,
Of all the world's women most wounded in
 heart,
Unless you've one dearer, a lover you like more,
Your faith to her plighted, so firmly made fast
You desire not to loosen it—so I believe.
Now tell me truly I pray you; the truth.
By all of the loves that in life are, conceal not 35
   Through guile."
  The knight said, "By Saint John,"
  And pleasantly to smile
  Began, "In faith I've none,
  Nor will have for a while." 40

"Such words," said the lady, "the worst are
 of all;
But in sooth I am answered, and sad it seems
 to me. 45
Kiss me now kindly, and quickly I'll go;
I on earth may but mourn, as a much loving
 mortal."
Sighing she stoops down, and kisses him
 seemly;
Then starting away from him, says as she 50
 stands,

"Now, my dear, at parting, do me this pleasure:
Give me some gift, thy glove if it might be,
To bring you to mind, sir, my mourning to
 lessen."
"On my word," quoth the hero, "I would that
 I had here,
For thy sake, the thing that I think the dearest
I own, for in sooth you've deserved very often
A greater reward than one I could give.
But a pledge of love would profit but little;
'T would help not your honor to have at this
 time
For a keepsake a glove, as a gift of Gawain.
I've come on a mission to countries most
 strange;
I've no servants with splendid things filling
 their sacks:
That displeases me, lady, for love's sake, at
 present;
Yet each man without murmur must do what
 he may
     Nor repine."
  "Nay, lord of honors high,
  Though I have naught of thine,"
  Quoth the lovely lady, "I
  Shall give you gift of mine."

She offered a rich ring, wrought in red gold,
With a blazing stone that stood out above it,
And shot forth brilliant rays bright as the sun;
Wit you well that wealth right huge it was
 worth.
But promptly the hero replied, refusing it,
"Madam, I care not for gifts now to keep;
I have none to tender and naught will I take."
Thus he ever declined her offer right earnest,
And swore on his word that he would not ac-
 cept it;
And, sad he declined, she thereupon said,
"If my ring you refuse, since it seems too rich,
If you would not so highly to me be beholden,
My girdle, that profits you less, I'll give you."
She swiftly removed the belt circling her sides,
Round her tunic knotted, beneath her bright
 mantle;
'T was fashioned of green silk, and fair made
 with gold,
With gold, too, the borders embellished and
 beautiful.
To Gawain she gave it, and gaily besought him
To take it, although he thought it but trifling.
He swore by no manner of means he'd accept

Either gold or treasure ere God gave him grace
To attain the adventure he'd there undertaken.
"And, therefore, I pray, let it prove not dis-
pleasing,
But give up your suit, for to grant it I'll never 5
    Agree.
  I'm deeply in your debt
  For your kind ways to me.
  In hot and cold I yet
  Will your true servant be."   10

 "Refuse ye this silk," the lady then said,
"As slight in itself? Truly it seems so.
Lo! it is little, and less is its worth;
But one knowing the nature knit up within it, 15
Would give it a value more great, peradventure;
For no man girt with this girdle of green,
And bearing it fairly made fast about him,
Might ever be cut down by any on earth,
For his life in no way in the world could be 20
 taken."
Then mused the man, and it came to his mind
In the peril appointed him precious 't would
 prove
When he'd found the chapel, to face there his 25
 fortune.
The device, might he slaying evade, would be
 splendid.
Her suit then he suffered, and let her speak;
And the belt she offered him, earnestly urging 30
 it
(And Gawain consented), and gave it with
 good will,
And prayed him for her sake ne'er to display it,
But, true, from her husband to hide it. The 35
 hero
Agreed that no one should know of it ever.
    Then he
  Thanked her with all his might
  Of heart and thought; and she 40
  By then to this stout knight
  Had given kisses three.

 Then the lady departs, there leaving the
 lord,
For more pleasure she could not procure from 45
 that prince.
When she's gone, then quickly Sir Gawain
 clothes himself,
Rises and dresses in noble array,   50
Lays by the love-lace the lady had left him,
Faithfully hides it where later he'd find it.

At once then went on his way to the chapel,
Approached in private a priest, and prayed him
To make his life purer, more plainly him teach
How his soul, when he had to go hence, should
 be saved.
He declared his faults, confessing them fully,
The more and the less, and mercy besought,
And then of the priest implored absolution.
He surely absolved him, and made him as spot-
 less,
Indeed, as if doomsday were due on the mor-
 row.
Then among the fair ladies he made more
 merry
With lovely caroles, all kinds of delights,
That day than before, until darkness fell.
    All there
  Were treated courteously,
  "And never," they declare,
  "Has Gawain shown such glee
  Since hither he did fare."

 In that nook where his lot may be love let
 him linger!
The lord's in the meadow still, leading his
 men.
He has slain this fox that he followed so long;
As he vaulted a hedge to get view of the
 villain,
Hearing the hounds that hastened hard after
 him,
Reynard from out a rough thicket came run-
 ning,
And right at his heels in a rush all the rabble.
He, seeing that wild thing, wary, awaits him,
Unsheaths his bright brand and strikes at the
 beast.
And he swerved from its sharpness and back
 would have started;
A hound, ere he could, came hurrying up to
 him;
All of them fell on him fast by the horse's feet,
Worried that sly one with wrathful sound.
And quickly the lord alights, and catches him,
Takes him in haste from the teeth of the
 hounds,
And over his head holds him high, loudly
 shouting,
Where brachets, many and fierce, at him
 barked.
Thither huntsmen made haste with many a
 horn,

The recall, till they saw him, sounding right
    clearly.
As soon as his splendid troop had assembled,
All bearing a bugle blew them together,
The others having no horns all hallooed.
'T was the merriest baying that man ever
    heard
That was raised for the soul of reynard with
    sounding
                    Din.
        They fondle each dog's head
        Who his reward did win.
        Then take they reynard dead
        And strip him of his skin.

And now, since near was the night, they
    turned homeward,
Strongly and sturdily sounding their horns.
At last at his loved home the lord alighted,
A fire on the hearth found, the hero beside it,
Sir Gawain the good, who glad was withal,
For he had 'mong the ladies in love much de-
    light.
A blue robe that fell to the floor he was wear-
    ing;
His surcoat, that softly was furred, well be-
    seemed him;
A hood of the same hue hung on his shoulders,
And both were bordered with white all about.
He, mid-most, met the good man in the hall,
And greeted him gladly, graciously saying:
"Now shall I first fulfill our agreement
We struck to good purpose, when drink was
    not spared."
Then Gawain embraced him, gave him three
    kisses,
The sweetest and soundest a man could bestow.
"By Christ, you'd great happiness," quoth then
    the host,
"I'm getting these wares, if good were your
    bargains."
"Take no care for the cost," the other said
    quickly,
"Since plainly the debt that is due I have
    paid."
Said the other, "By Mary, mine's of less worth.
The whole of the day I have hunted, and got-
    ten
The skin of this fox—the fiend take its foul-
    ness!—
Right poor to pay for things of such price

As you've pressed on me here so heartily,
    kisses
            So good."
        "Say no more," Gawain saith;
        "I thank you, by the rood!"[6]
        How the fox met his death
        He told him as they stood.

With mirth and minstrelsy, meat at their
    pleasure
They made as merry as any men might
(With ladies' laughter, and launching of jests
Right glad were they both, the good man and
    Gawain)
Unless they had doted or else had been
    drunken.
Both the man and the company make many
    jokes,
Till the time is come when the two must be
    parted,
When finally the knights are forced to go bed-
    ward.
And first of the lord his respectful leave
This goodly man took, and graciously thanked
    him:
"May God you reward for the welcome you
    gave me
This high feast, the splendid sojourn I've had
    here.
I give you myself, if you'd like it, to serve you.
I must, as you know, on the morrow move on;
Give me someone to show me the path, as you
    said,
To the Green Chapel, there, as God will allow
    me,
On New Year the fate that is fixed to perform."
"With a good will, indeed," said the good man;
    "whatever
I promised to do I deem myself ready."
He a servant assigns on his way to set him,
To take him by hills that no trouble he'd have,
And through grove and wood by the way most
    direct
                Might repair.
        The lord he thanked again
        For the honor done him there.
        The knight his farewell then
        Took of those ladies fair.

    To them with sorrow and kissing he spoke,
    [6] the Cross.

[40]

And besought them his thanks most sincere to accept;
And they, replying, promptly returned them,
With sighings full sore to the Savior commended him.
Then he with courtesy quitted the company,
Giving each man that he met his thanks
For kindness, for trouble he'd taken, for care
Whereby each had sought to serve him right eagerly.
Pained was each person to part with him then,
As if long they in honor had lived with that noble.
With people and lights he was led to his chamber,
To bed gaily brought there to be at his rest;
Yet I dare not say whether soundly he slept,
For much, if he would, on the morn to remember

          Had he.
    Let him lie stilly there
    Near what he sought to see.
    What happened I'll declare,
    If you will silent be.

PART IV

The New Year draws near, and the night-time now passes;
The day, as the Lord bids, drives on to darkness.
Outside, there sprang up wild storms in the world;
The clouds cast keenly the cold to the earth
With enough of the north sting to trouble the naked;
Down shivered the snow, nipping sharply the wild beasts;
The wind from the heights, shrilly howling, came rushing,
And heaped up each dale full of drifts right huge.
Full well the man listened who lay in his bed.
Though he shut tight his lids, he slept but a little;
He knew by each cock that crowed 't was the tryst time,
And swiftly ere dawn of the day he arose,
For there shone then the light of a lamp in his room;
To his chamberlain called, who answered him quickly,

5 And bade him his saddle to bring and his mail-shirt.
The other man roused up and fetched him his raiment,
5 Arrayed then that knight in a fashion right noble.
First he clad him in clothes to ward off the cold,
Then his other equipment, carefully kept:
10 His pieces of plate armor, polished right cleanly,
The rings of his rich mail burnished from rust.
All was fresh as at first; he was fain to give thanks
15   To the men.
    He had on every piece
    Full brightly burnished then.
    He, gayest from here to Greece,
20   Ordered his steed again.

He garbed himself there in the loveliest garments
(His coat had its blazon of beautiful needlework
25 Stitched upon velvet for show, its rich stones
Set about it and studded, its seams all embroidered,
Its lovely fur in the fairest of linings),
Yet he left not the lace, the gift of the lady:
30 That, Gawain did not, for his own sake, forget.
When the brand on his rounded thighs he had belted,
He twisted the love-token two times about him.
That lord round his waist with delight quickly wound
35 The girdle of green silk, that seemed very gay
Upon royal red cloth that was rich to behold.
But Gawain the girdle wore not for its great price,
Or pride in its pendants although they were polished,
Though glittering gold there gleamed on the ends,
But himself to save when he needs must suffer
45 The death, nor could stroke then of sword or of knife
          Him defend.
    Then was the bold man dressed;
    Quickly his way did wend;
    To all the court expressed
    His great thanks without end.

Then was Gringolet ready that great was
   and huge,
Who had safely, as seemed to him pleasant,
   been stabled;
That proud horse pranced, in the pink of con- 5
   dition.
The lord then comes to him, looks at his coat,
And soberly says, and swears on his word,
"In this castle's a company mindful of courtesy,
Led by this hero. Delight may they have;
And may love the dear lady betide all her
   lifetime.
If they for charity cherish a guest,
And give so great welcome, may God reward
   them, 15
Who rules the heaven on high, and the rest of
   you.
Might I for long live my life on the earth,
Some repayment with pleasure I'd make, if
   't were possible." 20
He steps in the stirrup, strides into the saddle,
Receives on his shoulder the shield his man
   brings him,
And spurs into Gringolet strikes with his gilt
   heels;
Who leaps on the stones and lingers no longer
          To prance.
    The knight on his horse sits,
    Who bears his spear and lance,
    The house to Christ commits,
    And wishes it good chance.

Then down the drawbridge they dropped,
   the broad gates
Unbarred, and on both sides bore them wide 35
   open.
He blessed them quickly, and crossed o'er the
   planks there
(He praises the porter, who knelt by the
   prince 40
Begging God to save Gawain, and gave him
   good-day),
And went on his way with but one man at-
   tended
To show him the turns to that sorrowful spot 45
Where he must to that onerous onset submit.
By hillsides where branches were bare they
   both journeyed;
They climbed over cliffs where the cold was
   clinging. 50
The clouds hung aloft, but 't was lowering be-
   neath them.

On the moor dripped the mist, on the mountains melted;
Each hill had a hat, a mist-cloak right huge.
The brooks foamed and bubbled on hillsides
   about them,
And brightly broke on their banks as they
   rushed down.
Full wandering the way was they went
   through the wood,
Until soon it was time for the sun to be springing.
        Then they
    Were on a hill full high;
    White snow beside them lay.
    The servant who rode nigh
    Then bade his master stay.

"I have led you hither, my lord, at this time,
And not far are you now from that famous
   place 20
You have sought for, and asked so especially
   after.
Yet, sir, to you surely I'll say, since I know you,
A man in this world whom I love right well,
If you'd follow my judgment, the better you'd 25
   fare.
You make haste to a place that is held full of
   peril;
One dwells, the worst in the world, in that
   waste, 30
For he's strong and stern, and takes pleasure
   in striking.
No man on the earth can equal his might;
He is bigger in body than four of the best men
In Arthur's own household, Hector or others. 35
And thus he brings it about at the chapel:
That place no one passes so proud in his arms
That he smites him not dead with a stroke of
   his hand.
He's a man most immoderate, showing no 40
   mercy;
Be it chaplain or churl that rides by the chapel,
Monk or priest, any manner of man,
Him to slay seems as sweet as to still live him-
   self.
So I say, as sure as you sit in your saddle
You're killed, should the knight so choose, if
   you come here;
That take as the truth, though you twenty
   lives had 50
          To spend.
    He's lived in this place long

In battles without end.
Against his strokes right strong
You cannot you defend.

"So let him alone, good Sir Gawain, and 5
    leave
By a different road, for God's sake, and ride
To some other country where Christ may re-
    ward you.
And homeward again I will hie me, and prom- 10
    ise
To swear by the Lord and all his good saints
(So help me the oaths on God's halidom[7]
    sworn)
That I'll guard well your secret, and give out 15
    no story
You hastened to flee any hero I've heard of."
"Thank you," said Gawain, and grudgingly
    added,
"Good fortune go with you for wishing me well. 20
And truly I think you'd not tell; yet though
    never
So surely you hid it, if hence I should hasten,
Fearful, to fly in the fashion you tell of,
A coward I'd prove, and could not be par- 25
    doned.
The chapel I'll find whatsoever befalls,
And talk with that wight the way that I want
    to,
Let weal or woe follow as fate may wish. 30
            Though the knave,
        Hard to subdue and fell,
        Should stand there with a stave,
        Yet still the Lord knows well
        His servants how to save." 35

Quoth the man, "By Mary, you've said now
    this much:
That you wish to bring down your own doom
    on your head.
Since you'd lose your life, I will stay you no 40
    longer.
Put your helm on your head, take your spear in
    your hand,
And ride down this road by the side of that 45
    rock
Till it brings you down to the dale's rugged
    bottom;
Then look at the glade on the left hand a little:
You'll see in the valley that self-same chapel, 50

----

[7] holiness.

And near it the great-limbed knight who is
    guarding it.
Gawain the noble, farewell now, in God's
    name!
I would not go with thee for all the world's
    wealth,
Nor in fellowship ride one more foot through
    the forest."
The man in the trees there then turns his
    bridle,
As hard as he can hits his horse with his heels,
And across the fields gallops, there leaving
    Sir Gawain
                Alone.
        "By God," the knight said, "now
        I'll neither weep nor groan.
        Unto God's will I bow,
        And make myself his own."

He strikes spurs into Gringolet, starts on the
    path;
By a bank at the side of a small wood he pushes
    in,
Rides down the rugged slope right to the dale.
Then about him he looks, and the land seems
    wild,
And nowhere he sees any sign of a shelter,
But slopes on each side of him, high and steep,
And rocks, gnarled and rough, and stones right
    rugged.
The clouds there seemed to him scraped by
    the crags.
Then he halted and held back his horse at that
    time,
And spied on all sides in search of the chapel;
Such nowhere he saw, but soon, what seemed
    strange,
In the midst of a glade a mound, as it might
    be,
A smooth, swelling knoll by the side of the
    water,
The falls of a rivulet running close by;
In its banks the brook bubbled as though it
    were boiling.
The knight urged on Gringolet, came to the
    glade,
There leaped down lightly and tied to the
    limb
Of a tree, right rugged, the reins of his noble
    steed,
Went to the mound, and walked all about it,
Debating what manner of thing it might be;

On the end and on each side an opening; everywhere
Over it grass was growing in patches,
All hollow inside, it seemed an old cave
Or a crag's old cleft: which, he could not de- 5
cide.
        Said the knight,
   "Is this the chapel here?
   Alas, dear Lord! here might
   The fiend, when midnight's near, 10
   His matin prayers recite.

"Of a truth," said Gawain, "the glade here
is gloomy;
The Green Chapel's ugly, with herbs over- 15
grown.
It greatly becomes here that hero, green-clad,
To perform in the devil's own fashion his wor-
ship.
I feel in my five senses this is the fiend 20
Who has made me come to this meeting to
kill me.
Destruction fall on this church of ill-fortune!
The cursedest chapel that ever I came to!"
With helm on his head and lance in his hand 25
He went right to the rock of that rugged
abode.
From the high hill he heard, from a hard rock
over
The stream, on the hillside, a sound wondrous 30
loud.
Lo! it clattered on cliffs fit to cleave them, as
though
A scythe on a grindstone someone were grind-
ing. 35
It whirred, lo! and whizzed like a water-mill's
wheel;
Lo! it ground and it grated, grievous to hear.
"By God, this thing, as I think," then said
Gawain, 40
"Is done now for me, since my due turn to
meet it
          Is near.
   God's will be done! 'Ah woe!'
   No whit doth aid me here. 45
   Though I my life forego
   No sound shall make me fear."

And then the man there commenced to call
loudly,
"Who here is the master, with me to hold 50
tryst?

For Gawain the good now is going right near.
He who craves aught of me let him come hither
quickly;
'T is now or never; he needs to make haste."
Said somebody, "Stop," from the slope up
above him,
"And promptly you'll get what I promised to
give you."
Yet he kept up the whirring noise quickly a
while,
Turned to finish his sharpening before he'd
descend.
Then he came by a crag, from a cavern emerg-
ing,
Whirled out of a den with a dreadful weapon,
A new Danish ax to answer the blow with;
Its blade right heavy, curved back to the
handle,
Sharp filed with the filing tool, four feet in
length,
'T was no less, by the reach of that lace gleam-
ing brightly.
The fellow in green was garbed as at first,
Both his face and his legs, his locks and his
beard,
Save that fast o'er the earth on his feet he went
fairly,
The shaft on the stone set, and stalked on be-
side it.
On reaching the water, he would not wade
it;
On his ax he hopped over, and hastily strode,
Very fierce, through the broad field filled all
about him
          With snow.
   Sir Gawain met the man,
   And bowed by no means low,
   Who said, "Good sir, men can
   Trust you to tryst to go."

Said the green man, "Gawain, may God you
guard!
You are welcome indeed, sir knight, at my
dwelling.
Your travel you've timed as a true man should,
And you know the compact we came to be-
tween us;
A twelvemonth ago you took what chance
gave,
And I promptly at New Year was pledged to
repay you.
In truth, we are down in this dale all alone;

Though we fight as we please, here there's no
    one to part us.
Put your helm from your head, and have here
    your payment;
Debate no further than I did before,   5
When you slashed off my head with a single
    stroke."
"Nay," quoth Gawain, "by God who gave me
    my spirit,
I'll harbor no grudge whatever harm happens. 10
Exceed not one stroke and still I shall stand;
You may do as you please, I'll in no way op-
    pose
            The blow."
    He left the flesh all bare,
    Bending his neck down low   15
    As if he feared naught there,
    For fear he would not show.

  Then the man in green raiment quickly 20
    made ready,
Uplifted his grim tool Sir Gawain to smite;
With the whole of his strength he heaved it on
    high,
As threateningly swung it as though he would 25
    slay him.
Had it fallen again with the force he intended
That lord, ever-brave, from the blow had been
    lifeless.
But Gawain a side glance gave at the weapon 30
As down it came gliding to do him to death;
With his shoulders shrank from the sharp iron
    a little.
The other with sudden jerk stayed the bright
    ax,   35
And reproved then that prince with proud
    words in plenty:
"Not Gawain thou art who so good is con-
    sidered,
Ne'er daunted by host in hill or in dale;   40
Now in fear, ere thou feelest a hurt, thou art
    flinching;
Such cowardice never I knew of that knight.
When you swung at me, sir, I fled not nor
    started;   45
No cavil I offered in King Arthur's castle.
My head at my feet fell, yet never I flinched,
And thy heart is afraid ere a hurt thou feelest,
And therefore thy better I'm bound to be
    thought   50
          On that score."
    "I shrank once," Gawain said,

    "And I will shrink no more;
    Yet cannot I my head,
    If it fall down, restore.

  "But make ready, sir, quickly, and come to
    the point;
My destiny deal me, and do it forthwith;
For a stroke I will suffer, and start no further
Till hit with thy weapon; have here my pledged
    word."
Quoth the other, heaving it high, "Have at
    thee!"
As fierce in his manner as if he were mad,
He mightily swung but struck not the man.
Withheld on a sudden his hand ere it hurt him.
And firmly he waited and flinched in no mem-
    ber,
But stood there as still as a stone or a stump
In rocky ground held by a hundred roots.
Then the Green Knight again began to speak
    gaily:
"It behooves me to hit, now that whole is thy
    heart.
Thy high hood that Arthur once gave you now
    hold back,
Take care that your neck at this cut may re-
    cover."
And Gawain full fiercely said in a fury,
"Come! lay on, thou dread man; too long thou
    art threatening.
I think that afraid of your own self you feel."
"In sooth," said the other, "thy speech is so
    savage
No more will I hinder thy mission nor have it
          Delayed."
    With puckered lips and brow
    He stands with ready blade,
    Not strange 't is hateful now
    To him past hope of aid.

  He lifts his ax lightly, and lets it down deftly,
The blade's edge next to the naked neck.
Though he mightily hammered he hurt him no
    more
Than to give him a slight nick that severed the
    skin there.
Through fair skin the keen ax so cut to the flesh
That shining blood shot to the earth o'er his
    shoulders.
As soon as he saw his blood gleam on the snow
He sprang forth in one leap, for more than a
    spear length;

His helm fiercely caught up and clapped on his
head;
With his shoulders his fair shield shot round in
front of him,
Pulled out his bright sword, and said in a   5
passion
(And since he was mortal man born of his
mother
The hero was never so happy by half),
"Cease thy violence, man; no more to me offer,   10
For here I've received, unresisting, a stroke.
If a second thou strikest I soon will requite
thee,
And swiftly and fiercely, be certain of that,
        Will repay.   15
    One stroke on me might fall
    By bargain struck that way,
    Arranged in Arthur's hall;
    Therefore, sir knight, now stay!"

    The man turned away, on his weapon   20
rested,
The shaft on the ground set, leaned on the
sharp edge,
And gazed at Sir Gawain there in the glade;
Saw that bold man, unblenching, standing right   25
bravely,
Full-harnessed and gallant; at heart he was
glad.
Then gaily the Green Knight spoke in a great   30
voice,
And said to the man in speech that resounded,
"Now be not so savage, bold sir, for towards
you
None here has acted unhandsomely, save   35
In accord with the compact arranged in the
King's court.
I promised the stroke you've received, so hold
you
Well payed. I free you from all duties further. 40
If brisk I had been, peradventure a buffet
I'd harshly have dealt that harm would have
done you.
In mirth, with a feint I menaced you first,
With no direful wound rent you; right was   45
my deed,
By the bargain that bound us both on the first
night,
When, faithful and true, you fulfilled our agree-
ment,   50
And gave me your gain as a good man ought
to.

The second I struck at you, sir, for the morning
You kissed my fair wife and the kisses accorded
me.
Two mere feints for both times I made at you,
man,
        Without woe.
    True men restore by right,
    One fears no danger so;
    You failed the third time, knight,
    And therefore took that blow.

    "'Tis my garment you're wearing, that
woven girdle,
Bestowed by my wife, as in truth I know well.
I know also your kisses and all of your acts
And my wife's advances; myself, I devised   15
them.
I sent her to try you, and truly you seem
The most faultless of men that e'er fared on
his feet.
As a pearl compared to white peas is more   20
precious,
So next to the other gay knights is Sir Gawain.
But a little you lacked and loyalty wanted,
Yet truly 't was not for intrigue or for wooing,
But love of your life; the less do I blame you." 25
Sir Gawain stood in a study a great while,
So sunk in disgrace that in spirit he groaned;
To his face all the blood in his body was flow-
ing;
For shame, as the other was talking, he shrank. 30
And these were the first words that fell from
his lips:
"Be cowardice cursed, and coveting! In you
Are vice and villainy, virtue destroying."
The lace he then seized, and loosened the   35
strands,
And fiercely the girdle flung at the Green
Knight.
"Lo! there is faith-breaking! evil befall it.
To coveting came I, for cowardice caused me   40
From fear of your stroke to forsake in myself
What belongs to a knight: munificence, loyalty.
I'm faulty and false, who've been ever afraid
Of untruth and treachery; sorrow betide both
        And care!
    Here I confess my sin;
    All faulty did I fare.
    Your good will let me win,
    And then I will beware."   50

    Then the Green Knight laughed, and right
graciously said,

"I am sure that the harm is healed that I suf-
fered.
So clean you're confessed, so cleared of your
faults,
Having had the point of my weapon's plain   5
penance,
I hold you now purged of offense, and as per-
fectly
Spotless as though you'd ne'er sinned in your
life.   10
And I give to you, sir, the golden-hemmed
girdle,
As green as my gown. Sir Gawain, when go-
ing
Forth on your way among famous princes,   15
Think still of our strife and this token right
splendid,
'Mid chivalrous knights, of the chapel's ad-
venture.
This New Year you'll come to my castle again, 20
And the rest of this feast in revel most pleasant
Will go."
        Then pressed him hard the lord:
        "My wife and you, I know
        We surely will accord,   25
        Who was your bitter foe."

"No indeed," quoth the hero, his helm seized
and doffed it
Graciously, thanking the Green Knight; "I've   30
stayed
Long enough. May good fortune befall you;
may He
Who all fame doth confer give it fully to you,
sir.   35
To your lady, gracious and lovely, commend
me,
To her and that other, my honored ladies,
That so with their sleights deceived their
knight subtly.   40
But no marvel it is for a fool to act madly,
Through woman's wiles to be brought to woe.
So for certain was Adam deceived by some
woman,
By several Solomon, Samson besides;   45
Delilah dealt him his doom; and David
Was duped by Bath-sheba, enduring much sor-
row.
Since these were grieved by their guile, 't
would be great gain   50
To love them yet never believe them, if
knights could.

For formerly these were most noble and
fortunate,
More than all others who lived on the earth;
        And these few
        By women's wiles were caught
        With whom they had to do.
        Though I'm beguiled, I ought
        To be excused now too.

"But your girdle," said Gawain, "may God   10
you reward!
With a good will I'll use it, yet not for the
gold,
The sash or the silk, or the sweeping pendants,
Or fame, or its workmanship wondrous, or cost, 15
But in sign of my sin I shall see it oft.
When in glory I move, with remorse I'll re-
member
The frailty and fault of the stubborn flesh,
How soon 't is infected with stains of defile- 20
ment;
And thus when I'm proud of my prowess in
arms,
The sight of this sash shall humble my spirit.
But one thing I pray, if it prove not displeasing; 25
Because you are lord of the land where I
stayed
In your house with great worship (may He
now reward you
Who sitteth on high and upholdeth the heav-   30
ens),
What name do you bear? No more would I
know."
And then "That truly I'll tell," said the other;
"Bercilak de Hautdesert here am I called.   35
Through her might who lives with me, Morgan
le Fay,
Well-versed in the crafts and cunning of magic
(Many of Merlin's arts she has mastered,
For long since she dealt in the dalliance of love 40
With him whom your heroes at home know,
that sage
        Without blame.
        'Morgan the goddess,' so
        She's rightly known by name.
        No one so proud doth go
        That him she cannot tame).

"I was set in this way to your splendid hall
To make trial of your pride, and to see if the 50
people's
Tales were true of the Table's great glory.

This wonder she sent to unsettle your wits,
And to daunt so the Queen as to cause her to die
From fear at the sight of that phantom speaker
Holding his head in his hand at the high table. 5
Lives she at home there, that ancient lady;
She's even thine aunt, King Arthur's half-sister,
Tyntagel's duchess's daughter, whom Uther
Made later the mother of mighty Lord Arthur. 10
I beg thee, sir, therefore, come back to thine aunt;
In my castle make merry. My company love thee,
And I, sir, wish thee as well, on my word, 15
As any on earth for thy high sense of honor."
He said to him, nay, this he'd never consent to.
The men kiss, embrace, and each other commend 20
To the Prince of Paradise; there they part
            In the cold.
    Gawain on his fair horse
    To Arthur hastens bold;
    The bright Green Knight his course 25
    Doth at his pleasure hold.

    Through the wood now goes Sir Gawain by wild ways
On Gringolet, given by God's grace his life. 30
Oft in houses, and oft in the open he lodged,
Met many adventures, won many a victory:
These I intend not to tell in this tale.
Now whole was the hurt he had in his neck,
And about it the glimmering belt he was bear- 35
ing,
Bound to his side like a baldric obliquely,
Tied under his left arm, that lace, with a knot
As a sign that with stain of sin he'd been found.
And thus to the court he comes all securely. 40
Delight in that dwelling arose when its lord knew
That Gawain had come; a good thing he thought it.
The King kissed the lord, and the Queen did 45
likewise,
And next many knights drew near him to greet him
And ask how he'd fared; and he wondrously answered, 50
Confessed all the hardships that him had befallen,

The happenings at chapel, the hero's behavior,
The lady's love, and lastly the lace.
He showed them the nick in his neck all naked
The blow that the Green Knight gave for deceit
            Him to blame.
    In torment this he owned;
    Blood in his face did flame;
    With wrath and grief he groaned,
    When showing it with shame.

    Laying hold of the lace, quoth the hero,
        "Lo! lord!
    The band of this fault I bear on my neck;
And this is the scathe and damage I've suf- 15
fered,
For cowardice caught there, and coveting also,
The badge of untruth in which I was taken.
And this for as long as I live I must wear,
For his fault none may hide without meeting 20
misfortune,
For once it is fixed, it can ne'er be unfastened."
To the knight then the King gave comfort; the court too
Laughed greatly, and made this gracious agree- 25
ment:
That ladies and lords to the Table belonging,
All of the brotherhood, baldrics should bear
Obliquely about them, bands of bright green,
Thus following suit for the sake of the hero. 30
For the Round Table's glory was granted that lace,
And he held himself honored who had it there-
after,
As told in the book, the best of romances. 35
In the days of King Arthur this deed was done
Whereof witness is borne by Brutus's book.
Since Brutus, that bold man, first came here to Britain,
When ceased, indeed, had the siege and as- 40
sault
            At Troy's wall,
    Full many feats ere now
    Like this one did befall. 45
    May He with thorn-crowned brow
    To His bliss bring us all. Amen.

HONY SOYT QUI MAL PENCE[8]

50 ───────

[8] the motto of the Order of the Garter (Evil to him who evil thinks).

GEOFFREY CHAUCER*

Chaucer (1340?–1400) is the first great individual name on record in English literature; in spite of language difficulty (and surprisingly little labor here will be quickly rewarded) this versatile voice can reach across the centuries to amuse and edify modern readers of catholic taste. Chaucer was variously a page, a military man, a diplomat, an M.P., a scholar, a man of the world. In various periods of French, Italian, and English influence he wrote dream visions, a psychological novel in verse (Troilus and Criseyde), frame-tales, allegories, complaints, etc. He exhibits a reading background, a knowledge of human nature, a delightful sense of humor. Whether he writes a traveling salesman's story, a fable, a sermon, or a fantasy, Chaucer always has the right touch. He has that rare quality, universality.

THE PROLOGUE

Here bygynneth the Book of the Tales of Caunterbury

Whan that Aprille with his shoures soote[1]
The droghte of March hath perced to the roote,
And bathed every veyne in swich[2] licour
Of which vertu engendred is the flour;
Whan Zephirus eek[3] with his sweete breeth
Inspired hath in every holt and heeth
The tendre croppes, and the yonge sonne
Hath in the Ram his halve cours yronne,[4]
And smale foweles maken melodye,
That slepen al the nyght with open ye
(So priketh hem nature in hir corages);[5]
Thanne longen folk to goon on pilgrimages,
And palmeres for to seken straunge strondes,
To ferne halwes,[6] kowthe[7] in sondry londes;
And specially from every shires ende
Of Engelond to Caunterbury they wende,
The hooly blisful martir[8] for to seke,
That hem hath holpen whan that they were seeke.
Bifil that in that seson on a day,

In Southwerk at the Tabard[9] as I lay
Redy to wenden on my pilgrymage
To Caunterbury with ful devout corage,
At nyght was come into that hostelrye
5 Wel nyne and twenty in a compaignye,
Of sondry folk, by aventure yfalle
In felaweshipe, and pilgrimes were they alle,
That toward Caunterbury wolden ryde.
The chambres and the stables weren wyde,
10 And wel we weren esed[10] atte beste.
And shortly, whan the sonne was to reste,
So hadde I spoken with hem everichon
That I was of hir felaweshipe anon,
And made forward erly for to ryse,
15 To take oure wey ther as I yow devyse.
    But nathelees, whil I have tyme and space,
Er that I ferther in this tale pace,
Me thynketh it acordaunt to resoun
To telle yow al the condicioun
20 Of ech of hem, so as it semed me,
And whiche they weren, and of what degree,
And eek in what array that they were inne;
And at a knyght than wol I first bigynne.
    A KNYGHT ther was, and that a worthy man,
25 That fro the tyme that he first bigan
To riden out, he loved chivalrie,
Trouthe and honour, fredom and curteisie.
Ful worthy was he in his lordes werre,
And therto hadde he riden, no man ferre,[11]
30 As wel in cristendom as in hethenesse,
And evere honoured for his worthynesse.
At Alisaundre he was whan it was wonne.
Ful ofte tyme he hadde the bord bigonne
Aboven alle nacions in Pruce;[12]
35 In Lettow[13] hadde he reysed[14] and in Ruce,[15]
No Cristen man so ofte of his degree.
In Gernade[16] at the seege eek hadde he be
Of Algezir,[17] and riden in Belmarye.[18]
At Lyeys[19] was he and at Satalye,[20]
40 Whan they were wonne; and in the Grete See[21]
At many a noble armee hadde he be.
At mortal batailles hadde he been fiftene,
And foughten for oure feith at Tramyssene[22]
45

---

[1] sweet. [2] such.
[3] also. [4] run.
[5] dispositions. [6] shrines.
[7] known. [8] Thomas à Becket.
[9] name of inn in Southwark; a tabard is a short cloak.
[10] taken care of. [11] farther.
[12] Prussia. [13] Lithuania.
[14] campaigned. [15] Russia.
[16] Granada. [17] Algeciras.
[18] in Morocco. [19] in Armenia.
[20] in Asia Minor. [21] Mediterranean.
[22] in North Africa.

In lystes thries, and ay slayn his foo.
This ilke[23] worthy knyght hadde been also
Somtyme with the lord of Palatye[24]
Agayn another hethen in Turkye.
And everemoore he hadde a sovereyn prys;[25]   5
And though that he were worthy, he was wys,
And of his port as meeke as is a mayde.
He nevere yet no vileynye ne sayde
In al his lyf unto no maner wight.
He was a verray, parfit gentil knyght.   10
But, for to tellen yow of his array,
His hors were goode, but he was nat gay.
Of fustian[26] he wered a gypon[27]
Al bismotered[28] with his habergeon,[29]
For he was late ycome from his viage,   15
And wente for to doon his pilgrymage.
    With hym ther was his sone, a yong SQUIER,
A lovyere and a lusty bacheler,[30]
With lokkes crulle[31] as they were leyd in presse.
Of twenty yeer of age he was, I gesse.   20
Of his stature he was of evene lengthe,
And wonderly delyvere,[32] and of greet
    strengthe.
And he hadde been somtyme in chyvachie[33]
In Flaundres, in Artoys, and Pycardie,
And born hym weel, as of so litel space,   25
In hope to stonden in his lady grace.
Embrouded was he, as it were a meede
Al ful of fresshe floures, whyte and reede.
Syngynge he was, or floytynge,[34] al the day;
He was as fressh as is the month of May.   30
Short was his gowne, with sleves longe and
    wyde.
Wel koude he sitte on hors and faire ryde.
He koude songes make and wel endite,
Juste[35] and eek daunce, and weel purtreye and
    write,   35
So hoote he lovede that by nyghtertale[36]
He sleep namoore than dooth a nyghtyngale.
Curteis he was, lowely, and servysable,
And carf biforn his fader at the table.   40
    A YEMAN hadde he and servantz namo
At that tyme, for hym liste ride so;
And he was clad in cote and hood of grene.
A sheef of pecok arwes, bright and kene,   45

Under his belt he bar ful thriftily,
(Wel koude he dresse his takel yemanly:
His arwes drouped noght with fetheres lowe)
And in his hand he baar a myghty bowe.
A not heed[37] hadde he, with a broun visage.   5
Of wodecraft wel koude he al the usage.
Upon his arm he baar a gay bracer,
And by his syde a swerd and a bokeler,
And on that oother syde a gay daggere
Harneised wel and sharp as point of spere;   10
A Cristopher on his brest of silver sheene.
An horn he bar, the bawdryk was of grene;
A forster was he, soothly, as I gesse.
    Ther was also a Nonne, a PRIORESSE,
That of hir smylyng was ful symple and coy;   15
Hire gretteste ooth was but by Seinte Loy;
And she was cleped madame Eglentyne.
Ful weel she soong the service dyvyne,
Entuned in hir nose ful semely,
And Frenssh she spak ful faire and fetisly,[38]   20
After the scole of Stratford atte Bowe,
For Frenssh of Parys was to hire unknowe.
At mete wel ytaught was she with alle:
She leet no morsel from hir lippes falle,
Ne wette hir fyngres in hir sauce depe;   25
Wel koude she carie a morsel and wel kepe
That no drope ne fille upon hire brest.
In curteisie was set ful muchel hir lest.[39]
Hir over-lippe wyped she so clene
That in hir coppe ther was no ferthyng[40] sene   30
Of grece, whan she dronken hadde hir
    draughte.
Ful semely after hir mete she raughte.[41]
And sikerly she was of greet desport,
And ful plesaunt, and amyable of port,   35
And peyned hire to countrefete cheere
Of court, and to been estatlich of manere,
And to ben holden digne[42] of reverence.
But, for to speken of hire conscience,
She was so charitable and so pitous   40
She wolde wepe, if that she saugh a mous
Kaught in a trappe, if it were deed or bleede.
Of smale houndes hadde she that she fedde
With rosted flessh, or milk and wastel-breed.[43]
But soore wepte she if oon of hem were deed,   45
Or if men smoot it with a yerde[44] smerte;
And al was conscience and tendre herte.

---

[23] same.   [24] in Asia Minor.
[25] praise.   [26] coarse cloth.
[27] tunic.   [28] stained.
[29] coat of mail.   [30] aspirant to knighthood.
[31] curly.   [32] lively.
[33] expeditions.   [34] fluting, whistling.
[35] joust.   [36] night-time.

---

[37] close-cropped head.   [38] elegantly.
[39] desire.   [40] trace.
[41] reached.   [42] worthy.
[43] fine white bread.   [44] stick.

Ful semyly hir wympul pynched[45] was;
Hir nose tretys,[46] hir eyen greye as glas,
Hir mouth ful smal, and therto softe and reed;
But sikerly she hadde a fair forheed;
It was almoost a spanne brood, I trowe;
For, hardily, she was nat undergrowe.
Ful fetys[47] was hir cloke, as I was war.
Of smal coral aboute hire arm she bar
A peire of bedes, gauded al with grene,
And theron heng a brooch of gold ful sheene, 10
On which ther was first write a crowned A,
And after *Amor vincit omnia.*[48]
    Another NONNE with hire hadde she,
That was hir chapeleyne, and preestes thre.

    A MONK ther was, a fair for the maistrie, 15
An outridere, that lovede venerie,
A manly man, to been an abbot able.
Ful many a deyntee hors hadde he in stable,
And whan he rood, men myghte his brydel
    heere
Gynglen in a whistlynge wynd als cleere 20
And eek as loude as dooth the chapel belle.
Ther as this lord was kepere of the celle,
The reule of seint Maure or of seint Beneit,
By cause that it was old and somdel streit[49] 25
This ilke Monk leet olde thynges pace,
And heeld after the newe world the space.
He yaf nat of that text a pulled hen,
That seith that hunters ben nat hooly men,
Ne that a monk, whan he is recchelees,[50] 30
Is likned til a fissh that is waterlees,—
This is to seyn, a monk out of his cloystre.
But thilke text heeld he nat worth an oystre;
And I seyde his opinion was good.
What sholde he studie and make hymselven 35
    wood,[51]
Upon a book in cloystre alwey to poure,
Or swynken[52] with his handes, and laboure,
As Austyn bit?[53] How shal the world be served? 40
Lat Austyn have his swynk to hym reserved!
Therfore he was a prikasour[54] aright:
Grehoundes he hadde as swift as fowel in
    flight;
Of prikyng[55] and of huntyng for the hare
Was al his lust, for no cost wolde he spare. 45
I seigh his sleves purfiled[56] at the hond

With grys,[57] and that the fyneste of a lond;
And, for to festne his hood under his chyn,
He hadde of gold ywroght a ful curious pyn;
A love-knotte in the gretter ende ther was.
His heed was balled, that shoon as any glas, 5
And eek his face, as he hadde been enoynt.
He was a lord ful fat and in good poynt;
His eyen stepe,[58] and rollynge in his heed,
That stemed as a forneys of a leed;[59]
His bootes souple, his hors in greet estaat. 10
Now certeinly he was a fair prelaat;
He was nat pale as a forpyned[60] goost.
A fat swan loved he best of any roost.
His palfrey was as broun as is a berye.

    A FRERE ther was, a wantowne and a merye, 15
A lymytour,[61] a ful solempne man.
In alle the ordres foure is noon that kan
So muchel of daliaunce and fair langage.
He hadde maad ful many a mariage
Of yonge wommen at his owene cost. 20
Unto his ordre he was a noble post.
Ful wel biloved and famulier was he
With frankeleyns over al in his contree,
And eek with worthy wommen of the toun;
For he hadde power of confessioun, 25
As seyde hymself, moore than a curat,
For of his ordre he was licenciat.
Ful swetely herde he confessioun,
And plesaunt was his absolucioun:
He was an esy man to yeve[62] penaunce, 30
Ther as he wiste to have a good pitaunce.
For unto a povre ordre for to yive
Is signe that a man is wel yshryve;
For if he yaf, he dorste make avaunt,[63]
He wiste that a man was repentaunt; 35
For many a man so hard is of his herte,
He may nat wepe, althogh hym soore smerte.
Therfore in stede of wepynge and preyeres
Men moote yeve silver to the povre freres.
His typet was ay farsed[64] ful of knyves 40
And pynnes, for to yeven faire wyves.
And certeinly he hadde a murye note:
Wel koude he synge and pleyen on a rote;[65]
Of yeddynges[66] he baar outrely the pris.
His nekke whit was as the flour-de-lys; 45
Therto he strong was as a champioun.

---

[45] pleated.   [46] well-formed.
[47] neat.   [48] Love conquers all.
[49] strict.   [50] reckless.
[51] crazy.   [52] work.
[53] Augustine bids.   [54] keen rider.
[55] riding.   [56] trimmed.

[57] gray fur.   [58] prominent.
[59] cauldron.   [60] tormented.
[61] a friar licensed to beg in a certain district.
[62] or *yive* (past, *yaf*), give.
[63] boast.   [64] stuffed.
[65] stringed instrument.   [66] songs.

He knew the tavernes wel in every toun
And everich hostiler and tappestere
Bet than a lazar or a beggestere;
For unto swich a worthy man as he
Acorded nat, as by his facultee,
To have with sike lazars aqueyntaunce.
It is nat honest, it may nat avaunce,
For to deelen with no swich poraille,[67]
But al with riche and selleres of vitaille.
And over al, ther as profit sholde arise,   10
Curteis he was and lowely of servyse.
Ther nas no man nowher so vertuous.
He was the beste beggere in his hous;
For thogh a wydwe hadde noght a sho,
So plesaunt was his *"In principio,"*
Yet wolde he have a ferthyng, er he wente.
His purchas was well bettre than his rente.
And rage he koude, as it were right a whelp.
In love-dayes[68] ther koude he muchel help,
For ther he was nat lyk a cloysterer   20
With a thredbare cope, as is a povre scoler,
But he was lyk a maister or a pope.
Of double worstede was his semycope,[69]
That rounded as a belle out of the presse.
Somwhat he lipsed, for his wantownesse,
To make his Englissh sweete upon his tonge;
And in his harpyng, whan that he hadde songe,
His eyen twynkled in his heed aryght,
As doon the sterres in the frosty nyght.
This worthy lymytour was cleped Huberd.   30

A MARCHANT was ther with a forked berd,
In mottelee,[70] and hye on horse he sat;
Upon his heed a Flaundryssh bever hat,
His bootes clasped faire and fetisly.
His resons he spak ful solempnely,
Sownynge alwey th' encrees of his wynnyng.
He wolde the see were kept for any thyng
Bitwixe Middelburgh and Orewelle.[71]
Wel koude he in eschaunge sheeldes[72] selle.
This worthy man ful wel his wit bisette: 40
Ther wiste no wight that he was in dette,
So estatly was he of his governaunce
With his bargaynes and with his chevys-
   saunce.[73]
For sothe he was a worthy man with alle,
But, sooth to seyn, I noot how men hym calle.
A CLERK ther was of Oxenford also,

That unto logyk hadde longe ygo.
As leene was his hors as is a rake,
And he nas nat right fat, I undertake,
But looked holwe, and therto sobrely.
Ful thredbare was his overeste courtepy;[74]   5
For he hadde geten hym yet no benefice,
Ne was so worldly for to have office.
For hym was levere have at his beddes heed
Twenty bookes, clad in blak or reed,
Of Aristotle and his philosophie,   10
Than robes riche, or fithele,[75] or gay sautrie.[76]
But al be that he was a philosophre,
Yet hadde he but litel gold in cofre;
But al that he myghte of his freendes hente,[77]
On bookes and on lernynge he it spente,   15
And bisily gan for the soules preye
Of hem that yaf hym wherwith to scoleye.[78]
Of studie took he moost cure and moost heede.
Noght o word spak he moore than was neede,
And that was seyd in forme and reverence,   20
And short and quyk and ful of hy sentence;
Sownynge in moral vertu was his speche,
And gladly wolde he lerne and gladly teche.

A SERGEANT OF THE LAWE, war and wys,
That often hadde been at the Parvys,[79]   25
Ther was also, ful riche of excellence.
Discreet he was and of greet reverence—
He semed swich, his wordes weren so wise.
Justice he was full often in assise,
By patente and by pleyn commissioun.   30
For his science and for his heigh renoun,
Of fees and robes hadde he many oon.
So greet a purchasour was nowher noon:
Al was fee symple to hym in effect;
His purchasyng myghte nat been infect.[80]   35
Nowher so bisy a man as he ther nas,
And yet he semed bisier than he was.
In termes hadde he caas and doomes[81] alle
That from the tyme of kyng William were falle.
Therto he koude endite, and make a thyng,   40
Ther koude no wight pynche at his writyng;
And every statut koude he pleyn by rote.
He rood but hoomly in a medlee cote,
Girt with a ceint[82] of silk, with barress male;
Of his array telle I no lenger tale.   45
A FRANKELEYN[83] was in his compaignye.

---

[67] poor people.
[68] days set for arbitrating minor disputes.
[69] short cape.   [70] parti-colored cloth.
[71] Middelburgh in Holland, Orwell in England.
[72] French coins.   [73] dealings.
[74] short coat.   [75] fiddle.
[76] psaltery.   [77] get.
[78] go to school.
[79] porch of St. Paul's, used for lawyers' consultations.
[80] invalid.   [81] decisions.
[82] girdle.   [83] rich landowner.

Whit was his berd as is the dayesye;
Of his complexioun[84] he was sangwyn.
Wel loved he by the morwe a sop in wyn;
To lyven in delit was evere his wone,[85]
For he was Epicurus owene sone,
That heeld opinioun that pleyn delit
Was verraily felicitee parfit.
An housholdere, and that a greet, was he;
Seint Julian[86] he was in his contree.
His breed, his ale, was alweys after oon;[87]
A bettre envyned man was nowher noon.
Withoute bake mete was nevere his hous
Of fissh and flessh, and that so plentevous,
It snewed in his hous of mete and drynke,
Of alle deyntees that men koude thynke.
After the sondry sesons of the yeer,
So chaunged he his mete and his soper.
Ful many a fat partrich hadde he in muwe,[88]
And many a breem and many a luce in stuwe.[89]
Wo was his cook but if his sauce were
Poynaunt and sharp, and redy al his geere.
His table dormant in his halle alway
Stood redy covered al the longe day.
At sessiouns ther was he lord and sire;
Ful ofte tyme he was knyght of the shire.
An anlaas[90] and a gipser[91] al of silk
Heeng at his girdel, whit as morne milk.
A shirreve hadde he been, and a countour.
Was nowher swich a worthy vavasour.[92]
    An HABERDASSHERE and a CARPENTER,
A WEBBE,[93] a DYERE, and a TAPYCER,[94]—
And they were clothed alle in o lyveree
Of a solempne and a greet fraternitee.
Ful fressh and newe hir geere apiked[95] was;
Hir knyves were chaped[96] noght with bras
But al with silver; wroght ful clene and weel
Hire girdles and hir pouches everydeel.
Wel semed ech of hem a fair burgeys
To sitten in a yeldehalle on a deys.[97]
Everich, for the wisdom that he kan,
Was shaply for to been an alderman.
For catel[98] hadde they ynogh and rente,
And eek hir wyves wolde it wel assente;

And elles certeyn were they to blame.
It is ful fair to been ycleped "madame,"
And goon to vigilies al bifore,
And have a mantel roialliche ybore.
5 A COOK they hadde with hem for the nones
To boille the chiknes with the marybones,
And poudre-marchant[99] tart and galyngale.[100]
Wel koude he knowe a draughte of Londoun ale.
10 He koude rooste, and sethe, and broille, and frye,
Maken mortreux,[101] and wel bake a pye.
But greet harm was it, as it thoughte me,
That on his shyne a mormal[102] hadde he.
15 For blankmanger,[103] that made he with the beste.
    A SHIPMAN was ther, wonynge fer by weste;
For aught I woot, he was of Dertemouthe.
He rood upon a rouncy,[104] as he kouthe,
20 In a gowne of faldyng[105] to the knee.
A daggere hangynge on a laas hadde he
Aboute his nekke, under his arm adoun.
The hoote somer hadde maad his hewe al broun;
25 And certeinly he was a good felawe.
Ful many a draughte of wyn had he ydrawe
Fro Burdeux-ward, whil that the chapman sleep.
Of nyce conscience took he no keep.
30 If that he faught, and hadde the hyer hond,
By water he sente hem hoom to every lond.
But of his craft to rekene wel his tydes,
His stremes, and his daungers hym bisides,
His herberwe,[106] and his moone, his lode-
35 menage,[107]
Ther nas noon swich from Hulle to Cartage.[108]
Hardy he was and wys to undertake;
With many a tempest hadde his berd been shake.
40 He knew alle the havenes, as they were,
Fro Gootlond to the cape of Fynystere,
And every cryke in Britaigne and in Spayne.
His barge ycleped was the Maudelayne.
    With us ther was a DOCTOUR OF PHISIK;
45 In al this world ne was ther noon hym lik,
To speke of phisik and of surgerye,

---

[84] temperament.   [85] custom.
[86] patron saint of hospitality.
[87] uniformly good.   [88] coop.
[89] fish pond.   [90] dagger.
[91] purse.
[92] substantial landholder, below rank of baron.
[93] weaver.   [94] upholsterer.
[95] trimmed.   [96] mounted.
[97] in a guildhall on a dais.
[98] property.

---

[99] flavoring powder.   [100] spice.
[101] thick soup.   [102] sore.
[103] creamed meat with eggs, etc.
[104] nag.   [105] coarse cloth.
[106] harbor.   [107] steersmanship.
[108] Cartagena.

For he was grounded in astronomye.
He kepte his pacient a ful greet deel
In houres by his magyk natureel.
Wel koude he fortunen the ascendent
Of his ymages for his pacient.   5
He knew the cause of everich maladye,
Were it of hoot, or coold, or moyste, or drye,
And where they engendred, and of what
    humour.
He was a verray, parfit praktisour:
The cause yknowe, and of his harm the roote,   10
Anon he yaf the sike man his boote.[109]
Ful redy hadde he his apothecaries
To sende hym drogges and his letuaries,[110]
For ech of hem made oother for to wynne—
Hir frendshipe nas nat newe to bigynne.   15
Wel knew he the olde Esculapius,
And Deyscorides, and eek Rufus,
Olde Ypocras, Haly, and Galyen,
Serapion, Razis, and Avycen,
Averrois, Damascien, and Constantyn,   20
Bernard, and Gatesden, and Gilbertyn.
Of his diete mesurable was he,
For it was of no superfluitee,
But of greet norissyng and digestible.
His studie was but litel on the Bible.   25
In sangwyn and in pers[111] he clad was al,
Lyned with taffata and with sendal;[112]
And yet he was but esy of dispence;
He kepte that he wan in pestilence.
For gold in phisik is a cordial,   30
Therefore he lovede gold in special.

    A good WIF was ther OF biside BATHE,
But she was somdel[113] deef, and that was
    scathe.[114]
Of clooth-makyng she hadde swich an haunt,[115] 35
She passed hem of Ypres and of Gaunt.
In al the parisshe wif ne was ther noon
That to the offrynge bifore hire sholde goon;
And if ther dide, certeyn so wrooth was she,   40
That she was out of alle charitee.
Hir coverchiefs ful fyne weren of ground;[116]
I dorste swere they weyeden ten pound
That on a Sonday weren upon hir heed.
Hir hosen weren of fyn scarlet reed,   45
Ful streite yteyd, and shoes ful moyste and
    newe.
Boold was hir face, and fair, and reed of hewe.

She was a worthy womman al hir lyve:
Housbondes at chirche dore she hadde fyve,
Withouten oother compaignye in youthe,—
But therof nedeth nat to speke as nowthe.
And thries hadde she been at Jerusalem;   5
She hadde passed many a straunge strem;
At Rome she hadde been, and at Boloigne,
In Galice at Seint Jame, and at Cologne.
She koude muchel of wandrynge by the weye.
Gat-tothed was she, soothly for to seye.   10
Upon an amblere esily she sat,
Ywympled[117] wel, and on hir heed an hat
As brood as is a bokeler or a targe;
A foot-mantel aboute hir hipes large,
And on hir feet a paire of spores sharpe.   15
In felaweshipe wel koude she laughe and
    carpe.[118]
Of remedies of love she knew per chaunce,
For she koude of that art the olde daunce.

    A good man was ther of religioun,   20
And was a povre PERSOUN OF A TOUN,
But riche he was of hooly thoght and werk.
He was also a lerned man, a clerk,
That Cristes gospel trewely wolde preche;
His parisshens devoutly wolde he teche.   25
Benygne he was, and wonder diligent,
And in adversitee ful pacient,
And swich he was ypreved ofte sithes.
Ful looth were hym to cursen[119] for his tithes,
But rather wolde he yeven, out of doute,   30
Unto his povre parisshens aboute
Of his offryng and eek of his substaunce.
He koude in litel thyng have suffisaunce.
Wyd was his parisshe, and houses fer asonder,
But he ne lefte nat, for reyn ne thonder,   35
In siknesse nor in meschief to visite
The ferreste in his parisshe, muche and lite,
Upon his feet, and in his hand a staf.
This noble ensample to his sheep he yaf,
That first he wroghte, and afterward he   40
    taughte.
Out of the gospel he tho wordes caughte,
And this figure he added eek therto,
That if gold ruste, what shal iren do?
For if a preest be foul, on whom we truste,   45
No wonder is a lewed[120] man to ruste;
And shame it is, if a prest take keep,
A shiten shepherde and a clene sheep.
Wel oghte a preest ensample for to yive,

---

[109] remedy.   [110] syrups.
[111] light blue.   [112] light silk.
[113] somewhat.   [114] pity.
[115] skill.   [116] texture.

[117] with pleated head-covering.
[118] talk.   [119] excommunicate.
[120] ignorant.

By his clennesse, how that his sheep sholde
   lyve.
He sette nat his benefice to hyre
And leet his sheep encombred in the myre
And ran to Londoun unto Seinte Poules   5
To seken hym a chaunterie for soules,
Or with a bretherhed to been withholde;
But dwelte at hoom, and kepte wel his folde,
So that the wolf ne made it nat myscarie;
He was a shepherde and noght a mercenarie. 10
And though he hooly were and vertuous,
He was to synful men nat despitous,
Ne of his speche daungerous ne digne,[121]
But in his techyng discreet and benygne.
To drawen folk to hevene by fairnesse,   15
By good ensample, this was his bisynesse.
But it were any persone obstinat,
What so he were, of heigh or lough estat,
Hym wolde he snybben sharply for the nonys.
A bettre preest I trowe that nowher noon ys. 20
He waited after no pompe and reverence,
Ne maked him a spiced conscience,
But Cristes loore and his apostles twelve
He taughte, but first he folwed it hymselve.
   With hym ther was a PLOWMAN, was his 25
   brother,
That hadde ylad of dong ful many a fother;[122]
A trewe swynkere[123] and a good was he,
Lyvynge in pees and parfit charitee.
God loved he best with al his hoole herte 30
At alle tymes, thogh him gamed[124] or smerte,
And thanne his neighebor right as hymselve.
He wolde thresshe, and therto dyke and delve,
For Cristes sake, for every povre wight,
Withouten hire, if it lay in his myght.   35
His tithes payde he ful faire and wel,
Bothe of his propre swynk and his catel.
In a tabard he rood upon a mere.
   Ther was also a REVE,[125] and a MILLERE,
A SOMNOUR,[126] and a PARDONER,[127] also, 40
A MAUNCIPLE,[128] and myself—ther were
   namo.
The MILLERE was a stout carl for the nones;
Ful byg he was of brawn, and eek of bones.
That proved wel, for over al ther he cam, 45

At wrastlynge he wolde have alwey the ram.
He was short-sholdred, brood, a thikke
   knarre;[129]
Ther was no dore that he nolde heve of
   harre,[130]
Or breke it at a rennyng with his heed.
His berd as any sowe or fox was reed,
And therto brood, as though it were a spade.
Upon the cop[131] right of his nose he hade
A werte, and theron stood a toft of herys,
Reed as the brustles of a sowes erys;
His nosethirles blake were and wyde.
A swerd and bokeler bar he by his syde.
His mouth as greet was as a greet forneys.
He was a janglere and a goliardeys,[132]
And that was moost of synne and harlotries.
Wel koude he stelen corn and tollen[133] thries;
And yet he hadde a thombe of gold, pardee.
A whit cote and a blew hood wered he.
A baggepipe wel koude he blowe and sowne,
And therwithal he broghte us out of towne.
   A gentil MAUNCIPLE was ther of a temple,
Of which achatours[134] myghte take exemple
For to be wise in byynge of vitaille;
For wheither that he payde or took by taille,[135]
Algate he wayted so in his achaat
That he was ay biforn and in good staat.
Now is nat that of God a ful fair grace
That swich a lewed mannes wit shal pace
The wisdom of an heep of lerned men?
Of maistres hadde he mo than thries ten,
That weren of lawe expert and curious,
Of which ther were a duszeyne in that hous
Worthy to been stywardes of rente and lond
Of any lord that is in Engelond,
To make hym lyve by his propre good
In honour dettelees (but if he were wood),[136]
Or lyve as scarsly as hym list desire;
And able for to helpen al a shire
In any caas that myghte falle or happe;
And yet this Manciple sette hir aller cappe.[137]
   The REVE was a sclendre colerik man.
His berd was shave as ny as ever he kan;
His heer was by his erys ful round yshorn;
His top was dokked lyk a preest biforn.
Ful longe were his legges and ful lene,
Ylyk a staf, ther was no calf ysene.

---

[121] haughty.   [122] load.   [123] worker.
[124] whether it pleased him (or irritated him).
[125] steward of estate.
[126] officer responsible for appearance of offenders
at ecclesiastical courts.
[127] one licensed to sell indulgences.
[128] steward of a college.

[129] knotty-muscled fellow.   [130] hinge.
[131] tip.   [132] joker.
[133] take toll.   [134] buyers.
[135] on account.   [136] crazy.
[137] made fools of them all.

Wel koude he kepe a gerner and a bynne;
Ther was noon auditour koude on him wynne.
Wel wiste he by the droghte and by the reyn
The yeldynge of his seed and of his greyn.
His lordes sheep, his neet, his dayerye, 5
His swyn, his hors, his stoor, and his pultrye
Was hoolly in this Reves governyng,
And by his covenant yaf the rekenyng,
Syn that his lord was twenty yeer of age.
Ther koude no man brynge hym in arrerage. 10
Ther nas baillif, ne hierde, nor oother hyne,
That he ne knew his sleighte and his covyne;[138]
They were adrad of hym as of the deeth.
His wonyng was ful faire upon an heeth;
With grene trees yshadwed was his place. 15
He koude bettre than his lord purchace.
Ful riche he was astored pryvely:
His lord wel koude he plesen subtilly,
To yeve and lene hym of his owene good,
And have a thank, and yet a cote and hood. 20
In youthe he hadde lerned a good myster;[139]
He was a wel good wrighte, a carpenter.
This Reve sat upon a ful good stot,
That was al pomely[140] grey and highte Scot.
A long surcote of pers upon he hade, 25
And by his syde he baar a rusty blade.
Of Northfolk was this Reve of which I telle,
Biside a toun men clepen Baldeswelle.
Tukked he was as is a frere aboute,
And evere he rood the hyndreste of oure route. 30

A Somonour was ther with us in that place,
That hadde a fyr-reed cherubynnes face,
For saucefleem[141] he was, with eyen narwe.
As hoot he was and lecherous as a sparwe,
With scalled[142] browes blake and piled[143] berd. 35
Of his visage children were aferd.
Ther nas quyk-silver, lytarge, ne brymstoon,
Boras, ceruce, ne oille of tartre noon;
Ne oynement that wolde clense and byte,
That hym myghte helpen of his whelkes[144] 40
  white,
Nor of the knobbes sittynge on his chekes.
Wel loved he garleek, oynons, and eek lekes,
And for to drynken strong wyn, reed as blood;
Thanne wolde he speke and crie as he were 45
  wood.
And whan that he wel dronken hadde the wyn,
Thanne wolde he speke no word but Latyn.

A fewe termes hadde he, two or thre,
That he had lerned out of som decree—
No wonder is, he herde it al the day;
And eek ye knowen wel how that a jay
Kan clepen "Watte"[145] as wel as kan the pope.
But whoso koude in oother thyng hym grope,
Thanne hadde he spent al his philosophie;
Ay *"Questio quid iuris"*[146] wolde he crie.
He was a gentil harlot[147] and a kynde;
A bettre felawe sholde men noght fynde.
He wolde suffre for a quart of wyn
A good felawe to have his concubyn
A twelf month, and excuse hym atte fulle;
Ful prively a fynch eek koude he pulle.
And if he foond owher a good felawe,
He wolde techen him to have noon awe
In swich caas of the ercedekenes curs,
But if a mannes soule were in his purs;
For in his purs he sholde ypunysshed be.
"Purs is the ercedekenes helle," seyde he.
But wel I woot he lyed right in dede;
Of cursyng oghte ech gilty man him drede,
For curs wol slee right as assoillyng[148] savith,
And also war hym of a *Significavit*.[149]
In daunger[150] hadde he at his owene gise 25
The yonge girles[151] of the diocise,
And knew hir conseil, and was al hir reed.[152]
A gerland hadde he set upon his heed
As greet as it were for an ale-stake.
A bokeleer hadde he maad hym of a cake. 30

With hym ther rood a gentil Pardoner
Of Rouncivale, his freend and his compeer,
That streight was comen fro the court of Rome.
Ful loude he soong "Com hider, love, to me!"
This Somonour bar to hym a stif burdoun;
Was nevere trompe of half so greet a soun.
This Pardoner hadde heer as yelow as wex,
But smothe it heeng as dooth a strike of flex;
By ounces henge his lokkes that he hadde,
And therwith he his shuldres overspradde;
But thynne it lay, by colpons[153] oon and oon.
But hood, for jolitee, wered he noon,
For it was trussed up in his walet.
Hym thoughte he rood al of the newe jet;[154]
Dischevele, save his cappe, he rood al bare.
Swiche glarynge eyen hadde he as an hare.

[145] Walt (of a jay, as Polly for a modern parrot).
[146] The question is, what part of the law applies.
[147] rogue.   [148] absolution.
[149] writ of excommunication.   [150] control.
[151] people of both sexes.   [152] adviser.
[153] shreds.   [154] fashion.

[138] deceitfulness.   [139] trade.
[140] dappled.   [141] pimpled.
[142] scabby.   [143] thin.
[144] pimples.

A vernycle hadde he sowed upon his cappe.
His walet lay biforn hym in his lappe,
Bretful of pardoun, comen from Rome al hoot.
A voys he hadde as smal as hath a goot.
No berd hadde he, ne nevere sholde have;
As smothe it was as it were late shave.
I trowe he were a geldyng or a mare.
But of his craft, fro Berwyk into Ware,
Ne was ther swich another pardoner.
For in his male[155] he hadde a pilwe-beer,[156]
Which that he seyde was Oure Lady veyl:
He seyde he hadde a gobet of the seyl
That Seint Peter hadde, whan that he wente
Upon the see, til Jhesu Crist hym hente.
He hadde a croys of latoun[157] ful of stones,
And in a glas he hadde pigges bones.
But with thise relikes, whan that he fond
A povre person dwellynge upon lond,
Upon a day he gat hym moore moneye
Than that the person gat in monthes tweye;
And thus, with feyned flaterye and japes,
He made the person and the peple his apes.
But trewely to tellen atte laste,
He was in chirche a noble ecclesiaste.
Wel koude he rede a lessoun or a storie,
But alderbest he song an offertorie;
For wel he wiste, whan that song was songe,
He moste preche and wel affile his tonge
To wynne silver, as he ful wel koude;
Therefore he song the murierly and loude.
   Now have I toold you shortly, in a clause,
Th' estaat, th' array, the nombre, and eek the
    cause
Why that assembled was this compaignye
In Southwerk at this gentil hostelrye
That highte the Tabard, faste by the Belle.
But now is tyme to yow for to telle
How that we baren us that ilke nyght,
Whan we were in that hostelrie alyght,
And after wol I telle of our viage
And al the remenaunt of oure pilgrimage.
But first I pray yow, of youre curteisye,
That ye n'arette it nat my vileynye,
Thogh that I pleynly speke in this mateere,
To telle yow hir wordes and hir cheere,
Ne thogh I speke hir wordes proprely.
For this ye knowen al so wel as I,
Whoso shal telle a tale after a man,
He moot reherce as ny as evere he kan
Everich a word, if it be in his charge,

Al speke he never so rudeliche and large,
Or ellis he moot telle his tale untrewe,
Or feyne thyng, or fynde wordes newe.
5   He may nat spare, althogh he were his
    brother;
He moot as wel seye o word as another.
Crist spak hymself ful brode in hooly writ,
And wel ye woot no vileynye is it.
Eek Plato seith, whoso that kan hym rede,
10   The wordes moote be cosyn to the dede.
Also I prey yow to foryeve it me,
Al have I nat set folk in hir degree
Heere in this tale, as that they sholde stonde.
My wit is short, ye may wel understonde.
15   Greet chiere made oure Hoost us everichon,
And to the soper sette he us anon.
He served us with vitaille at the beste;
Strong was the wyn, and wel to drynke us
    leste.
20 A semely man Oure Hooste was withalle
For to han been a marchal in an halle.
A large man he was with eyen stepe—
A fairer burgeys is ther noon in Chepe[158]—
Boold of his speche, and wys, and wel ytaught,
25 And of manhod hym lakkede right naught.
Eek therto he was right a myrie man,
And after soper pleyen he bigan,
And spak of myrthe amonges othere thynges,
Whan that we hadde maad our rekenynges,
30 And seyde thus: "Now, lordynges, trewely,
Ye been to me right welcome, hertely;
For by my trouthe, if that I shal nat lye,
I saugh nat this yeer so myrie a compaignye
Atones in this herberwe as is now.
35 Fayn wolde I doon yow myrthe, wiste I how.
And of a myrthe I am right now bythoght,
To doon yow ese, and it shal coste noght.
    Ye goon to Caunterbury—God yow speede,
The blisful martir quite yow youre meede![159]
40 And wel I woot, as ye goon by the weye,
Ye shapen yow to talen[160] and to pleye;
For trewely, confort ne myrthe is noon
To ride by the weye doumb as a stoon;
And therfore wol I maken yow disport,
45 As I seyde erst, and doon yow som confort
And if yow liketh alle by oon assent
For to stonden at my juggement,
And for to werken as I shal yow seye,
To-morwe, whan ye riden by the weye,
50 ————

---

[155] bag.   [156] pillow case.   [157] alloy.
[158] Cheapside (London).   [159] reward.
[160] tell tales.

Now, by my fader soule that is deed,
But ye be myrie, I wol yeve yow myn heed!
Hoold up youre hondes, withouten moore
  speche."
    Oure conseil was nat longe for to seche.
Us thoughte it was noght worth to make it
  wys,[161]
And graunted hym withouten moore avys,
And bad him seye his voirdit as hym leste.
"Lordynges," quod he, "now herkneth for the 10
  beste;
But taak it nought, I prey yow, in desdeyn.
This is the poynt, to speken short and pleyn,
That ech of yow, to shorte with oure weye,
In this viage shal telle tales tweye 15
To Caunterbury-ward, I mene it so,
And homward he shal tellen othere two,
Of aventures that whilom han bifalle.
And which of yow that bereth hym best of alle,
That is to seyn, that telleth in this caas 20
Tales of best sentence and moost solaas,
Shal have a soper at oure aller cost
Heere in this place, sittynge by this post;
Whan that we come agayn fro Caunterbury.
And for to make yow the moore mury, 25
I wol myselven goodly with yow ryde,
Right at myn owene cost, and be youre gyde;
And whoso wole my juggement withseye
Shal paye al that we spenden by the weye.
And if ye vouche sauf that it be so, 30
Tel me anon, withouten wordes mo,
And I wol erly shape me therfore."
    This thyng was graunted, and oure othes
  swore
With ful glad herte, and preyden hym also 35
That he wolde vouche sauf for to do so,
And that he wolde been oure governour,
And of our tales juge and reportour,
And sette a soper at a certeyn pris,
And we wol reuled been at his devys 40
In heigh and lough; and thus by oon assent
We been acorded to his juggement.
And therupon the wyn was fet anon;
We dronken, and to reste wente echon,
Withouten any lenger taryynge. 45
    Amorwe, whan that day bigan to sprynge,
Up roos oure Hoost, and was oure aller cok,
And gadrede us togidre alle in a flok,
And forth we riden a litel moore than paas
Unto the wateryng of Seint Thomas; 50

And there oure Hoost bigan his hors areste
And seyde, "Lordynges, herkneth, if yow leste.
Ye woot youre foreward,[162] and I it yow re-
  corde.
If even-song and morwe-song accorde,
Lat se now who shal telle the firste tale.
As evere mote I drynke wyn or ale,
Whoso be rebel to my juggement
Shal paye for al that by the wey is spent.
Now draweth cut, er that we ferrer twynne;[163]
He which that hath the shorteste shal bigynne.
Sire Knyght," quod he, "my mayster and my
  lord,
Now draweth cut, for that is myn accord.
Cometh neer," quod he, "my lady Prioresse.
And ye, sire Clerk, lat be youre shamefastnesse,
Ne studieth noght; ley hond to, every man!"
Anon to drawen every wight bigan,
And shortly for to tellen as it was,
Were it by aventure, or sort, or cas,
The sothe is this, the cut fil to the Knyght,
Of which ful blithe and glad was every wyght,
And telle he moste his tale, as was resoun,
By foreward and by composicioun,
As ye han herd; what nedeth wordes mo?
And whan this goode man saugh that it was so,
As he that wys was and obedient
To kepe his foreward by his free assent,
He seyde, "Syn I shal bigynne the game,
What, welcome be the cut, a Goddes name!
Now lat us ryde, and herkneth what I seye."
And with that word we ryden forth oure weye,
And he bigan with right a myrie cheere
His tale anon, and seyde in this manere.

THE PARDONER'S TALE

The Pardoner's Prologue

HEERE FOLWETH THE PROLOGE OF THE
PARDONERS TALE.

Radix malorum est Cupiditas.
Ad Thimotheum, 6º.

"Lordynges," quod he, "in chirches whan
  I preche,
I peyne me to han an hauteyn speche,
And rynge it out as round as gooth a belle,
For I kan al by rote that I telle.
My theme is alwey oon, and evere was—

---

[161] deliberate.

[162] agreement.

[163] depart.

Radix malorum est Cupiditas.[164]
First I pronounce whennes that I come,
And thanne my bulles shewe I, alle and some.
Oure lige lordes seel on my patente,
That shewe I first, my body to warente,
That no man be so boold, ne preest ne clerk,
Me to destourbe of Cristes hooly werk.
And after that thanne telle I forth my tales;
Bulles of popes and of cardynales,
Of patriarkes and bishops I shewe,
And in Latyn I speke a wordes fewe,
To saffron with my predicacioun,
And for to stire hem to devocioun.
Thanne shewe I forth my longe cristal stones,
Ycrammed ful of cloutes and of bones,—
Relikes been they, as wenen they echoon.
Thanne have I in latoun a sholder-boon
Which that was of an hooly Jewes sheep.
'Goode men,' I seye, 'taak of my wordes keep;
If that this boon be wasshe in any welle,
If cow, or calf, or sheep, or oxe swelle
That any worm hath ete, or worm ystonge,
Taak water of that welle and wassh his tonge,
And it is hool anon; and forthermoore,
Of pokkes and of scabbe, and every soore
Shal every sheep be hool that of this welle
Drynketh a draughte. Taak kep eek what I
    telle:
If that the good-man that the beestes oweth
Wol every wyke, er that the cok hym croweth,
Fastynge, drynken of this welle a draughte,
As thilke hooly Jew oure eldres taughte,
His beestes and his stoor shal multiplie.
And, sires, also it heeleth jalousie;
For though a man be falle in jalous rage,
Lat maken with this water his potage,
And nevere shal he moore his wyf mystriste,
Though he the soothe of hir defaute wiste,
Al had she taken prestes two or thre.
Heere is a miteyn eek, that ye may se.
He that his hand wol putte in this mitayn,
He shal have multipliyng of his grayn,
Whan he hath sowen, be it whete or otes,
So that he offre pens, or elles grotes.
Goode men and wommen, o thyng warne I
    yow:
If any wight be in this chirche now
That hath doon synne horrible, that he
Dar nat, for shame, of it yshryven be,[165]

Or any womman, be she yong or old,
That hath ymaad hir housbonde cokewold,[166]
Swich folk shal have no power ne no grace
To offren to my relikes in this place.
And whoso fyndeth hym out of swich blame,
He wol come up and offre in Goddes name,
And I assoille him by the auctoritee
Which that by bulle ygraunted was to me.'
    By this gaude[167] have I wonne, yeer by yeer,
An hundred mark sith I was pardoner.
I stonde lyk a clerk in my pulpet,
And whan the lewed peple is doun yset,
I preche so as ye han herd bifoore,
And telle an hundred false japes moore.
Thanne peyne I me to strecche forth the nekke,
And est and west upon the peple I bekke,
As dooth a dowve sittynge on a berne.
Myne handes and my tonge goon so yerne[168]
That it is joye to se my bisynesse.
Of avarice and of swich cursednesse
Is al my prechyng, for to make hem free
To yeven hir pens, and namely unto me.
For myn entente is nat but for to wynne,
And nothyng for correccioun of synne.
I rekke nevere, whan that they been beryed,
Though that hir soules goon a-blakeberyed!
For certes, many a predicacioun
Comth ofte tyme of yvel entencioun;
Som for plesance of folk and flaterye,
To been avaunced by ypocrisye,
And som for veyne glorie, and som for hate.
For whan I dar noon oother weyes debate,
Thanne wol I stynge hym with my tonge
    smerte
In prechyng, so that he shal nat asterte[169]
To been defamed falsly, if that he
Hath trespased to my bretheren or to me.
For though I telle noght his propre name,
Men shal wel knowe that it is the same,
By signes, and by othere circumstances.
Thus quyte I folk that doon us displesances;
Thus spitte I out my venym under hewe
Of hoolynesse, to semen hooly and trewe.
    But shortly myn entente I wol devyse:
I preche of no thyng but for coveityse.
Therfore my theme is yet, and evere was,
Radix malorum est Cupiditas.
Thus kan I preche agayn that same vice
Which that I use, and that is avarice.

[164] The root of evils is love of money.
[165] confessed and absolved.
[166] cuckold.
[168] briskly.
[167] trick.
[169] escape.

But though myself be gilty in that synne,
Yet kan I maken oother folk to twynne
From avarice, and soore to repente.
But that is nat my principal entente;
I preche nothyng but for coveitise. 5
Of this mateere it oghte ynogh suffise.
    Thanne telle I hem ensamples many oon
Of olde stories longe tyme agoon.
For lewed peple loven tales olde;
Swiche thynges kan they wel reporte and 10
    holde.
What, trowe ye, that whiles I may preche,
And wynne gold and silver for I teche,
That I wol lyve in poverte wilfully?
Nay, nay, I thoghte it nevere, trewely! 15
For I wol preche and begge in sondry landes;
I wol nat do no labour with myne handes,
Ne make baskettes, and lyve therby,
By cause I wol nat beggen ydelly.
I wol noon of the apostles countrefete; 20
I wol have moneie, wolle, chese, and whete,
Al were it yeven of the povereste page,
Or of the povereste wydwe in a village,
Al sholde hir children sterve for famyne.
Nay, I wol drynke licour of the vyne, 25
And have a joly wenche in every toun.
But herkneth, lordynges, in conclusioun:
Youre likyng is that I shal telle a tale.
Now have I dronke a draughte of corny ale,
By God, I hope I shal yow telle a thyng 30
That shal by reson been at youre likyng.
For though myself be a full vicious man,
A moral tale yet I yow telle kan,
Which I am wont to preche for to wynne.
Now hoold youre pees! my tale I wol bigynne." 35

The Pardoner's Tale

HEERE BIGYNNETH THE PARDONERS TALE.

In Flaundres whilom was a compaignye 40
Of yonge folk that haunteden[170] folye,
As riot, hasard, stywes,[171] and tavernes,
Where as with harpes, lutes, and gyternes,
They daunce and pleyen at dees bothe day and
    nyght,
And eten also and drynken over hir myght, 40
Thurgh which they doon the devel sacrifise
Withinne that develes temple, in cursed wise,
By superfluytee abhomynable.
Hir othes been so grete and so dampnable 50

That it is grisly for to heere hem swere.
Oure blissed Lordes body they totere,[172]
Hem thoughte that Jewes rente hym noght
    ynough;
And ech of hem at otheres synne lough.
And right anon thanne comen tombesteres[173]
Fetys and smale, and yonge frutesteres,[174]
Syngeres with harpes, baudes, wafereres,
Whiche been the verray develes officeres
To kyndle and blowe the fyr of lecherye,
That is annexed unto glotonye.
The hooly writ take I to my witnesse
That luxurie is in wyn and dronkenesse.
    Lo, how that dronken Looth, unkyndely,[175]
Lay by his doghtres two, unwityngly;
So dronke he was, he nyste what he wroghte.
    Herodes, whoso wel the stories soghte,
Whan he of wyn was repleet at his feeste,
Right at his owene table he yaf his heeste[176]
To sleen the Baptist John, ful giltelees.
    Senec seith a good word doutelees;
He seith he kan no difference fynde
Bitwix a man that is out of his mynde
And a man which that is dronkelewe,
But that woodnesse, yfallen in a shrewe,[177]
Persevereth lenger than dooth dronkenesse.
    O glotonye, ful of cursednesse!
O cause first of oure confusioun!
O original of oure dampnacioun,
Til Crist hadde boght us with his blood agayn!
Lo, how deere, shortly for to sayn,
Aboght was thilke cursed vileynye!
Corrupt was al this world for glotonye.
    Adam oure fader, and his wyf also,
Fro Paradys to labour and to wo
Were dryven for that vice, it is no drede.
For whil that Adam fasted, as I rede,
He was in Paradys; and whan that he
Eet of the fruyt deffended[178] on the tree,
Anon he was out cast to wo and peyne.
O glotonye, on thee wel oghte us pleyne!
O, wiste a man how manye maladyes
Folwen of excesse and of glotonyes,
He wolde been the moore mesurable
Of his diete, sittynge at his table.
Allas! the shorte throte, the tendre mouth,
Maketh that est and west and north and south,
In erthe, in eir, in water, men to swynke

---

[170] practiced.   [171] brothels.

[172] tore in pieces.   [173] female tumblers.
[174] female fruit-sellers.   [175] unnaturally.
[176] command.   [177] scoundrel.
[178] forbidden.

To gete a glotoun deyntee mete and drynke!
Of this matiere, o Paul, wel kanstow trete:
"Mete unto wombe, and wombe eek unto
    mete,
Shal God destroyen bothe," as Paulus seith.
Allas! a foul thyng is it, by me feith,
To seye this word, and fouler is the dede,
Whan man so drynketh of the white and rede
That of his throte he maketh his pryvee,
Thurgh thilke cursed superfluitee.
    The apostel wepyng seith ful pitously,
"Ther walken manye of whiche yow toold
    have I—
I seye it now wepyng, with pitous voys—
That they been enemys of Cristes croys,
Of whiche the ende is deeth, wombe is hir
    god!"
O wombe! O bely! O stynkyng cod,[179]
Fulfilled of donge and of corrupcioun!
At either ende of thee foul is the soun.
How greet labour and cost is thee to fynde!
Thise cookes, how they stampe, and streyne,
    and grynde,
And turnen substaunce into accident,
To fulfille al thy likerous talent!
Out of the harde bones knokke they
The mary, for they caste noght awey
That may go thurgh the golet softe and swoote.
Of spicerie of leef, and bark, and roote
Shal been his sauce ymaked by delit,
To make hym yet a newer appetit.
But, certes, he that haunteth swiche delices
Is deed, whil that he lyveth in tho vices.
    A lecherous thyng is wyn, and dronkenesse
Is ful of stryvyng and of wrecchednesse.
O dronke man, disfigured is thy face,
Sour is thy breeth, foul artow to embrace,
And thurgh thy dronke nose semeth the soun
As though thou seydest ay "Sampsoun, Samp-
    soun!"
And yet, God woot, Sampsoun drank nevere no
    wyn.
Thou fallest as it were a styked swyn;
Thy tonge is lost, and al thyn honeste cure;
For dronkenesse is verray sepulture
Of mannes wit and his discrecioun.
In whom that drynke hath dominacioun
He kan no conseil kepe, it is no drede.[180]
Now kepe yow fro the white and fro the rede,
And namely fro the white wyn of Lepe,[181]

That is to selle in Fysshstrete or in Chepe.
This wyn of Spaigne crepeth subtilly
In othere wynes, growynge faste by,
Of which ther ryseth swich fumositee.
5 That whan a man hath dronken draughtes thre,
And weneth that he be at hoom in Chepe,
He is in Spaigne, right at the toune of Lepe,—
Nat at the Rochele, ne at Burdeux toun;
And thanne wol he seye "Sampsoun, Samp-
10   soun!"
    But herkneth, lordynges, o word, I yow
        preye,
That alle the sovereyn actes, dar I seye,
Of victories in the Olde Testament,
15 Thurgh verray God, that is omnipotent,
Were doon in abstinence and in preyere.
Looketh the Bible, and ther ye may it leere.
    Looke, Attilla, the grete conquerour,
Deyde in his sleep, with shame and dishonour,
20 Bledynge ay at his nose in dronkenesse.
A capitayn sholde lyve in sobrenesse.
And over al this, avyseth yow right wel
What was comaunded unto Lamuel—
Nat Samuel, but Lamuel, seye I—
25 Redeth the Bible, and fynde it expresly
Of wyn-yevyng to hem that han justise.
Namoore of this, for it may wel suffise.
    And now that I have spoken of glotonye,
Now wol I yow deffenden hasardrye.[182]
30 Hasard is verray mooder of lesynges,[183]
And of deceite, and cursed forswerynges,
Blaspheme of Crist, manslaughtre, and wast
    also
Of catel and of tyme; and forthermo,
35 It is repreeve and contrarie of honour
For to ben holde a commune hasardour.
And ever the hyer he is of estaat,
The moore is he yholden desolaat.
If that a prynce useth hasardrye,
40 In alle governaunce and policye
He is, as by commune opinioun,
Yholde the lasse in reputacioun.
    Stilboun, that was a wys embassadour,
Was sent to Corynthe, in ful greet honour,
45 Fro Lacidomye, to make hire alliaunce.
And whan he cam, hym happede, par chaunce,
That alle the gretteste that were of that lond,
Pleyynge atte hasard he hem fond.
For which, as soone as it myghte be,
50 He stal hym hoom agayn to his contree,

---

[179] bag.   [180] doubt.   [181] in Spain.   [182] gaming.   [183] lies.

And seyde, "Ther wol I nat lese my name,
Ne I wol nat take on me so greet defame,
Yow for to allie unto none hasardours.
Sendeth othere wise embassadours;
For, by my trouthe, me were levere dye   5
Than I yow sholde to hasardours allye.
For ye, that been so glorious in honours,
Shul nat allyen yow with hasardours
As by my wyl, ne as by my tretee."
This wise philosophre, thus seyde hee.   10
    Looke eek that to the kyng Demetrius
The kyng of Parthes, as the book seith us,
Sente him a paire of dees of gold in scorn,
For he hadde used hasard ther-biforn;
For which he heeld his glorie or his renoun   15
At no value or reputacioun.
Lordes may fynden oother maner pley
Honest ynough to dryve the day awey.
    Now wol I speke of othes false and grete
A word or two, as olde bookes trete.   20
Gret sweryng is a thyng abhominable,
And fals sweryng is yet moore reprevable.
The heighe God forbad sweryng at al,
Witnesse on Mathew; but in special
Of sweryng seith the hooly Jeremye,   25
"Thou shalt swere sooth thyne othes, and nat
        lye,
And swere in doom, and eek in rightwisnesse";
But ydel sweryng is a cursednesse.
Bihoold and se that in the first table
Of heighe Goddes heestes honurable,   30
Hou that the seconde heeste of hym is this:
"Take nat my name in ydel or amys."
Lo, rather he forbedeth swich sweryng
Than homycide or many a cursed thyng;
I seye that, as by ordre, thus it stondeth;   35
This knoweth, that his heestes understondeth,
How that the seconde heeste of God is that.
And forther over, I wol thee telle al plat,[184]
That vengeance shal nat parten from his hous   40
That of his othes is to outrageous.
"By Goddes precious herte," and "By his
        nayles,"
And "By the blood of Crist that is in Hayles,[185]
Sevene is my chaunce, and thyn is cynk[186] and 45
        treye!"
"By Goddes armes, if thou falsly pleye,
This daggere shal thurghout thyn herte go!"

---

[184] flat.
[185] abbey in Gloucestershire having as a relic a
vial of Christ's blood.
[186] five.

This fruyt cometh of the bicched bones two,
Forsweryng, ire, falsnesse, homycide.
Now, for the love of Crist, that for us dyde,
Lete youre othes, bothe gret and smale.
But, sires, now wol I telle forth my tale.   5
    Thise riotoures thre of whiche I telle,
Longe erst er prime rong of any belle,
Were set hem in a taverne for to drynke,
And as they sat, they herde a belle clynke
Biforn a cors, was caried to his grave.   10
That oon of hem gan callen to his knave:
"Go bet,"[187] quod he, "and axe redily
What cors is this that passeth heer forby;
And looke that thou reporte his name weel."
    "Sire," quod this boy, "it nedeth never-a-   15
        deel;
It was me toold er ye cam heer two houres.
He was, pardee, an old felawe of youres;
And sodeynly he was yslayn to-nyght,[188]
Fordronke, as he sat on his bench upright.   20
Ther cam a privee theef, men clepeth Deeth,
That in this contree al the peple sleeth,
And with his spere he smoot his herte atwo,
And wente his wey withouten wordes mo.
He hath a thousand slayn this pestilence.   25
And, maister, er ye come in his presence,
Me thynketh that it were necessarie
For to be war of swich an adversarie.
Beth redy for to meete hym everemoore;
Thus taughte me my dame; I sey namoore."   30
"By seinte Marie!" seyde this taverner
"The child seith sooth, for he hath slayn this
        yeer,
Henne over a mile, withinne a greet village,
Bothe man and womman, child, and hyne,[189]   35
        and page;
I trowe his habitacioun be there.
To been avysed greet wysdom it were,
Er that he dide a man a dishonour."
    "Ye, Goddes armes!" quod this riotour,
"Is it swich peril with hym for to meete?   40
I shal hym seke by wey and eek by strete,
I make avow to Goddes digne bones!
Herkneth, felawes, we thre been al ones;
Lat ech of us holde up his hand til oother,   45
And ech of us bicomen otheres brother,
And we wol sleen this false traytour Deeth.
He shal be slayn, he that so manye sleeth,
By Goddes dignitee, er it be nyght!"
    Togidres han thise thre hir trouthes plight 50

---

[187] hurry.   [188] last night.   [189] laborer.

To lyve and dyen ech of hem for oother,
As though he were his owene ybore brother.
And up they stirte, al dronken in this rage,
And forth they goon towardes that village
Of which the taverner hadde spoke biforn.
And many a grisly ooth thanne han they
    sworn,
And Cristes blessed body al torente—
Deeth shal be deed, if that they may hym
    hente!
    Whan they han goon nat fully half a mile,
Right as they wolde han troden over a stile,
An oold man and a povre with hem mette.
This olde man ful mekely hem grette,
And seyde thus, "Now, lordes, God yow
    see!"[190]
    The proudeste of thise riotoures three
Answerde agayn, "What, carl,[191] with sory
    grace!
Why artow al forwrapped save thy face?
Why lyvestow so longe in so greet age?"
    This olde man gan looke in his visage,
And seyde thus, "For I ne kan nat fynde
A man, though that I walked into Ynde,
Neither in citee ne in no village,
That wolde chaunge his youthe for myn age;
And therfore moot I han myn age stille,
As longe tyme as it is Goddes wille.
Ne Deeth, allas! ne wol nat han my lyf.
Thus walke I, lyk a resteleees kaityf,[192]
And on the ground, which is my moodres gate,
I knokke with my staf, bothe erly and late,
And seye 'Leeve mooder, leet me in!
Lo how I vanysshe, flessh, and blood, and
    skyn!
Allas! whan shul my bones been at reste?
Mooder, with yow wolde I chaunge my cheste
That in my chambre longe tyme hath be,
Ye, for an heyre clowt to wrappe in me!'
But yet to me she wol nat do that grace,
For which ful pale and welked is my face.
    But, sires, to yow it is no curteisye
To speken to an old man vileynye,
But he trespasse in word, or elles in dede.
In Hooly Writ ye may yourself wel rede:
'Agayns[193] an oold man, hoor upon his heed,
Ye sholde arise;' wherfore I yeve yow reed,
Ne dooth unto an oold man noon harm now,
Namoore than that ye wolde men did to yow

In age, if that ye so longe abyde.
And God be with yow, where ye go or ryde!
I moot go thider as I have to go."
    "Nay, olde cherl, by God, thou shalt nat so,"
5 Seyde this oother hasardour anon;
"Thou partest nat so lightly, by Seint John!
Thou spak right now of thilke traytour Deeth,
That in this contree alle oure freendes sleeth.
Have heer my trouthe, as thou art his espye,
10 Telle where he is, or thou shalt it abye,[194]
By God, and by the hooly sacrement!
For soothly thou art oon of his assent
To sleen us yonge folk, thou false theef!"
    "Now, sires," quod he, "if that ye be so leef
15 To fynde Deeth, turne up this croked wey,
For in that grove I lafte hym, by my fey,
Under a tree, and there he wole abyde;
Noght for youre boost he wole him no thyng
    hyde.
20 Se ye that ook? Right there ye shal hym fynde.
God save yow, that boghte agayn mankynde,
And yow amende!" Thus seyde this olde man;
And everich of thise riotoures ran
Til he cam to that tree, and ther they founde
25 Of floryns fyne of gold ycoyned rounde
Wel ny an eighte busshels, as hem thoughte.
No lenger thanne after Deeth they soughte,
But ech of hem so glad was of that sighte,
For that the floryns been so faire and brighte,
30 That doun they sette hem by this precious
    hoord.
The worste of hem, he spak the firste word.
    "Bretheren," quod he, "taak kep what that I
    seye;
35 My wit is greet, though that I bourde[195] and
    pleye.
This tresor hath Fortune unto us yiven,
In myrthe and joliftee oure lyf to lyven,
And lightly as it comth, so wol we spende.
40 Ey! Goddes precious dignitee! who wende
To-day that we sholde han so fair a grace?
But myghte this gold be caried fro this place
Hoom to myn hous, or elles unto youres—
For wel ye woot that al this gold is oures—
45 Thanne were we in heigh felicitee.
But trewely, by daye it may nat bee.
Men wolde seyn that we were theves stronge,
And for oure owene tresor doon us honge.
This tresor moste ycaried be by nyghte
50 As wisely and as slyly as it myghte.

---

[190] protect.   [191] churl.
[192] wretch.   [193] Before.   [194] pay for.   [195] jest.

Wherfore I rede that cut among us alle
Be drawe, and lat se wher the cut wol falle;
And he that hath the cut with herte blithe
Shal renne to the town, and that ful swithe,[196]
And brynge us breed and wyn ful prively. 5
And two of us shul kepen subtilly
This tresor wel; and if he wol nat tarie,
Whan it is nyght, we wol this tresor carie,
By oon assent, where as us thynketh best."
That oon of hem the cut broghte in his fest, 10
And bad hem drawe, and looke where it wol
    falle;
And it fil on the yongeste of hem alle,
And forth toward the toun he wente anon.
And also soone as that he was gon, 15
That oon of hem spak thus unto that oother:
"Thow knowest wel thou art my sworen
    brother;
Thy profit wol I telle thee anon.
Thou woost wel that oure felawe is agon, 20
And heere is gold, and that ful greet plentee,
That shal departed been among us thre.
But nathelees, if I kan shape it so
That it departed were among us two,
Hadde I nat doon a freendes torn to thee?" 25
    That oother answerde, "I noot hou that may
    be.
He woot wel that the gold is with us tweye;
What shal we doon? What shal we to hym
    seye?" 30
    "Shal it be conseil?" seyed the firste shrewe,
"And I shal tellen in a wordes fewe
What we shal doon, and brynge it wel aboute."
    "I graunte," quod that oother, "out of doute,
That, by my trouthe, I wol thee nat biwreye." 35
    "Now," quod the firste, "thou woost wel we
    be tweye,
And two of us shul strenger be than oon.
Looke whan that he is set, that right anoon
Arys as though thou woldest with hym pleye, 40
And I shal ryve hym thurgh the sydes tweye
Whil that thou strogelest with hym as in game,
And with thy daggere looke thou do the same;
And thanne shal al this gold departed be,
My deere freend, bitwixen me and thee. 45
Thanne may we bothe oure lustes all fulfille,
And pleye at dees right at oure owene wille."
And thus acorded been thise shrewes tweye
To sleen the thridde, as ye han herd me seye.
    This yongeste, which that wente to the toun, 50

Ful ofte in herte he rolleth up and doun
The beautee of thise floryns newe and brighte.
"O Lord!" quod he, "if so were that I myghte
Have al this tresor to myself allone,
Ther is no man that lyveth under the trone 5
Of God that sholde lyve so murye as I!"
And atte laste the feend, oure enemy,
Putte in his thought that he sholde poyson
    beye,
With which he myghte sleen his felawes tweye; 10
For-why the feend foond hym in swich lyvynge
That he hadde leve him to sorwe brynge.
For this was outrely his fulle entente,
To sleen hem bothe, and nevere to repente.
And forth he gooth, no lenger wolde he tarie, 15
Into the toun, unto a pothecarie,
And preyde hym that he hym wolde selle
Som poyson, that he myghte his rattes quelle;
And eek ther was a polcat in his hawe,[197]
That, as he seyde, his capouns hadde yslawe, 20
And fayn he wolde wreke hym, if he myghte,
On vermyn that destroyed hym by nyghte.
    The pothecarie answerde, "And thou shalt
    have
A thyng that, also God my soule save, 25
In al this world ther is no creature,
That eten or dronken hath of this confiture
Noght but the montance[198] of a corn of whete,
That he ne shal his lif anon forlete;
Ye, sterve[199] he shal, and that in lasse while 30
Than thou wolt goon a paas nat but a mile,
This poysoun is so strong and violent."
    This cursed man hath in his hond yhent
This poysoun in a box, and sith he ran
Into the nexte strete unto a man, 35
And borwed hym large botelles thre;
And in the two his poyson poured he;
The thridde he kepte clene for his drynke.
For al the nyght he shoop hym for to swynke
In cariynge of the gold out of that place. 40
And whan this riotour, with sory grace,
Hadde filled with wyn his grete botels thre,
To his felawes agayn repaireth he.
    What nedeth it to sermone of it moore?
For right as they hadde cast his deeth bifoore, 45
Right so they han hym slayn, and that anon.
And whan that this was doon, thus spak that
    oon:
"Now lat us sitte and drynke, and make us
    merie, 50

---

[196] quickly.　　　　　　　　　　[197] yard.　　　[198] amount.　　　[199] die.

And afterward we wol his body berie."
And with that word it happed hym, par cas,
To take the botel ther the poyson was,
And drank, and yaf his felawe drynke also,
For which anon they storven[200] bothe two.

But certes, I suppose that Avycen
Wroot nevere in no canon, ne in no fen,
Mo wonder signes of empoisonyng
Than hadde thise wrecches two, er hir endyng.
Thus ended been thise homycides two,
And eek the false empoysonere also.

O cursed synne of alle cursednesse!
O traytours homycide, O wikkednesse!
O glotonye, luxurie, and hasardrye!
Thou blasphemour of Crist with vileynye
And othes grete, of usage and of pride!
Allas! mankynde, how may it bitide
That to thy creatour, which that the wroghte,
And with his precious herte-blood thee boghte,
Thou art so fals and so unkynde, allas?

Now, goode men, God foryeve yow youre
   trespas,
And ware yow fro the synne of avarice!
Myn hooly pardoun may yow alle warice,[201]
So that he offre nobles or sterlynges,
Or elles silver broches, spoones, rynges.
Boweth youre heed under this hooly bulle!
Cometh up, ye wyves, offreth of youre wolle!
Youre names I entre heer in my rolle anon;
Into the blisse of hevene shul ye go.
I yow assoille, by myn heigh power,
Yow that wol offre, as clene and eek as cleer
As ye were born.—And lo, sires, thus I preche.
And Jhesu Crist, that is oure soules leche,
So graunte yow his pardoun to receyve,
For that is best; I wol yow nat deceyve.

But, Sires, o word forgat I in my tale:
I have relikes and pardoun in my male,
As faire as any man in Engelond,
Whiche were me yeven by the popes hond.
If any of yow wole, of devocion,
Offren, and han myn absolucion,
Com forth anon, and kneleth heere adoun,
And mekely receyveth my pardoun;
Or elles taketh pardoun as ye wende,
Al newe and fressh at every miles ende,
So that ye offren, alwey newe and newe,
Nobles or pens, whiche that be goode and
   trewe.
It is an honour to everich that is heer

5

10

15

20

25

30

35

40

45

50

That ye mowe have a suffisant pardoneer
T'assoille yow, in contree as ye ryde,
For aventures whiche that may bityde.
Paraventure ther may fallen oon or two
Doun of his hors, and breke his nekke atwo.
Looke which a seuretee is it to yow alle
That I am in youre felaweshipe yfalle,
That may assoille yow, bothe moore and lasse,
Whan that the soule shal fro the body passe.
I rede that oure Hoost heere shal bigynne,
For he is moost envoluped in synne.
Com forth, sire Hoost, and offre first anon,
And thou shalt kisse the relikes everychon,
Ye, for a grote! Unbokele anon thy purs.
"Nay, nay!" quod he, "thanne have I Cristes
   curs!
Lat be," quod he, "it shal nat be, so theech![202]
Thou woldest make me kisse thyn olde breech,
And swere it were a relyk of a seint,"

.   .   .   .

This Pardoner answerde nat a word;
So wrooth he was, no word ne wolde he seye.
"Now," quod oure Hoost, "I wol no lenger
   pleye
With thee, ne with noon oother angry man."
But right anon the worthy Knyght bigan,
Whan that he saugh that al the peple lough,
"Namoore of this, for it is right ynough!
Sire Pardoner, be glad and myrie of cheere;
And ye, sire Hoost, that been to me so deere,
I prey yow that ye kisse the Pardoner.
And Pardoner, I prey thee, drawe thee neer,
And, as we diden, lat us laughe and pleye."
Anon they kiste, and ryden forth hir weye.

HEERE IS ENDED THE PARDONERS TALE.

THE POPULAR BALLADS*

In most anthologies the ballads are listed for convenience under the fifteenth century; actually they go back several centuries before that, and we still have them with us. They stem from the people, who passed them down by word of mouth (the first extensive printed collection by Bishop Percy did not appear until 1765). Authorship is unknown. A compromise between

[200] died.   [201] cure.

[202] so may I prosper!
* The text of the ballads printed here in general follows that of F. J. Child, by permission of Houghton Mifflin Company.

two current theories of composition would suggest that capable individuals wrote the originals and that the people in communal songfests improvised changes and additions in the manner of modern campers about the fire.

Besides the popular ballad, which is still to be found in primitive form in mountain recesses of America, there was the broadside, a sixteenth-century song written by identified second-raters who seized the occasion of a murder, fire, or political event to scratch off verses to be sold on the street and sung to a familiar tune. The name comes from the fact that the ballad was printed on the full printer's sheet, generally with a crude woodcut illustration. Tin-Pan Alley still turns out what amounts to broadsides about the burning of the "Hindenburg" or the death of Floyd Collins in a Kentucky cave.

With the Romantic Movement a third major type of ballad—the literary—was developed. It is the work of competent artists who imitated the popular form. It has the virtues of literacy and art, but generally lacks the earthiness and pungent primitiveness of the original. In addition, there are many subtypes of ballad, both popular and literary, dealing with domestic crime, outlaws, the supernatural, history, and so on. Humorous ballads are relatively rare.

The common ballad stanza has four lines, of which the second and fourth rhyme. There are four stresses in the first and third lines, three in the others. However, especially in literary ballads, much variation in stanza length and rhyme occurs.

Though the ballad is relatively primitive, it has its own conventions. Some of these include the prominence of odd numbers; the use of incremental repetition; the refrain; sudden transitions; upper-class background; question-and-answer routines; brevity; stock epithets; and a number of small, but important, symbolic details—for example, a rose and a brier will grow from the graves of a couple who died for love, a sprig of birch in the hat will indicate a return from Paradise, and so on.

Since the ballads are meant to be sung, they do not always read well to a beginner's taste. The ideal remedy is to take advantage of the many recordings available in all good music libraries. Better yet, let everyone join in on the refrains, and the whole charm of the ballads will begin to assert itself. And if the old ballads seem too far removed, there are modern versions of them, and brand-new modern ballads —of the cowboys, for example. There is no better place to begin the study of literature.

LORD RANDAL

"O where hae ye been, Lord Randal, my son?
O where hae ye been, my handsome young
    man?"
"I hae been to the wild wood; mother, make
5   my bed soon,
For I'm weary wi hunting, and fain wald lie
    down."

"Where gat ye your dinner, Lord Randal, my
10 son?
Where gat ye your dinner, my handsome
    young man?"
"I dined wi my true-love; mother, make my
    bed soon,
15 For I'm weary wi hunting, and fain wald lie
    down."

"What gat ye to your dinner, Lord Randal,
    my son?
20 What gat ye to your dinner, my handsome
    young man?"
"I gat eels boiled in broo; mother, make my
    bed soon,
For I'm weary wi hunting, and fain wald lie
25 down."

"What became of your bloodhounds, Lord
    Randal, my son?
What became of your bloodhounds, my hand-
30 some young man?"
"O they swelld and they died; mother, make
    my bed soon,
For I'm weary wi hunting, and fain wald lie
    down."

35 "O I fear ye are poisond, Lord Randal, my
    son!
O I fear ye are poisond, my handsome young
    man!"
40 "O yes! I am poisond; mother, make my bed
    soon,
For I'm sick at the heart, and I fain wald lie
    down."

EDWARD

1. "Why dois your brand sae drap wi bluid,
    Edward, Edward,
Why dois your brand sae drap wi bluid,
    And why sae sad gang yee O?"
"O I hae killed my hauke sae guid,
    Mither, mither,
O I hae killed my hauke sae guid,
    And I had nae mair bot hee O."

2. "Your haukis bluid was nevir sae reid,
    Edward, Edward,
Your haukis bluid was nevir sae reid,
    My deir son I tell thee O."
"O I hae killed my reid-roan steid,
    Mither, mither,
O I hae killed my reid-roan steid,
    That erst was sae fair and frie O."

3. "Your steid was auld, and ye hae gat mair,
    Edward, Edward,
Your steid was auld, and ye hae gat mair,
    Sum other dule ye drie[1] O."
"O I hae killed my fadir deir,
    Mither, mither,
O I hae killed my fadir deir,
    Alas, and wae is mee O!"

4. "And whatten penance wul ye drie for that,
    Edward, Edward,
And whatten penance wul ye drie for that?
    My deir son, now tell me O."
"Ile set my feit in yonder boat,
    Mither, mither,
Ile set my feit in yonder boat,
    And Ile fare ovir the sea O."

5. "And what wul ye doe wi your towirs and
        your ha,
    Edward, Edward?
And what wul ye doe wi your towirs and your
        ha,
    That were sae fair to see O?"
"Ile let thame stand tul they doun fa,
    Mither, mither,
Ile let thame stand tul they doun fa,
    For here nevir mair maun I bee O."

6. "And what wul ye leive to your bairns and

your wife,
        Edward, Edward?
And what wul ye leive to your bairns and
        your wife,
    Whan ye gang ovir the sea O?"
"The warldis room, late them beg thrae life,
        Mither, mither,
The warldis room, late them beg thrae life,
    For thame nevir mair wul I see O."

7. "And what wul ye leive to your ain mither
        deir,
        Edward, Edward?
And what wul ye leive to your ain mither
        deir?
    My deir son, now tell me O."
"The curse of hell frae me sall ye beir,
        Mither, mither,
The curse of hell frae me sall ye beir,
    Sic counseils ye gave to me O."

THE TWA CORBIES

1. As I was walking all alane,
I herd twa corbies making a mane;[1]
The tane unto the t' other say,
"Where sall we gang and dine to-day?"

2. "In behint yon auld fail[2] dyke,
I wot there lies a new slain knight;
And naebody kens that he lies there,
But his hawk, his hound, and lady fair.

3. "His hound is to the hunting gane,
His hawk to fetch the wild-fowl hame,
His lady's ta'en another mate,
So we may mak our dinner sweet.

4. "Ye'll sit on his white hause-bane,[3]
And I'll pike out his bonny blue een;
Wi ae lock o his gowden hair
We'll theek[4] our nest when it grows bare.

5. "Mony a one for him makes mane,
But nane sall ken where he is gane;
Oer his white banes when they are bare,
The wind sall blaw for evermair."

___

[1] two ravens (crows) complaining (talking).
[2] turf.
[3] neck-bone.
[4] thatch.

___

[1] Some other grief ye suffer.

THE WIFE OF USHER'S WELL

1. There lived a wife at Usher's Well,
    And a wealthy wife was she;
She had three stout and stalwart sons,   5
    And sent them oer the sea.

2. They hadna been a week from her,
    A week but barely ane,
Whan word came to the carline wife[1]   10
    That her three sons were gane.

3. They hadna been a week from her,
    A week but barely three,
Whan word came to the carlin wife   15
    That her sons she'd never see.

4. "I wish the wind may never cease,
    Nor fashes[2] in the flood,
Till my three sons come hame to me,   20
    In earthly flesh and blood."

5. It fell about the Martinmass,[3]
    When nights are lang and mirk,
The carlin wife's three sons came hame,   25
    And their hats were o the birk.[4]

6. It neither grew in syke[5] nor ditch,
    Nor yet in ony sheugh;[6]
But at the gates o Paradise,
    That birk grew fair enough.

7. "Blow up the fire, my maidens,
    Bring water from the well;
For a' my house shall feast this night,
    Since my three sons are well."

8. And she has made to them a bed,
    She's made it large and wide,
And she's taen her mantle her about,
    Sat down at the bed-side.

9. Up then crew the red, red cock,   45
    And up and crew the gray,
The eldest to the youngest said,
    "'Tis time we were away."

10. The cock he hadna crawd but once,
    And clappd his wings at a',
When the youngest to the eldest said,
    "Brother, we must awa.

11. "The cock doth craw, the day doth daw,
    The channerin[7] worm doth chide;
Gin we be mist out o our place,
    A sair pain we maun bide.

12. "Fare ye weel, my mother dear!
    Fareweel to barn and byre![8]
And fare ye weel, the bonny lass
    That kindles my mother's fire!"

BONNY BARBARA ALLAN

It was in and about the Martinmas time,
    When the green leaves were a falling,
That Sir John Graeme, in the West Country,
    Fell in love with Barbara Allan.

He sent his men down through the town
    To the place where she was dwelling:
"O haste and come to my master dear,
    Gin[1] ye be Barbara Allan."

O hooly,[2] hooly rose she up,   30
    To the place where he was lying,
And when she drew the curtain by,
    "Young man, I think you're dying."

"O it's I'm sick, and very, very sick,   35
    And it's a' for Barbara Allan";
"O the better for me ye's never be,
    Tho your heart's blood were a spilling.

"O dinna ye mind, young man," said she,
    "When ye was in the tavern a drinking,   40
That ye made the healths gae round and round,
    And slighted Barbara Allan?"

He turned his face unto the wall,
    And death was with him dealing;   45
"Adieu, adieu, my dear friends all,
    And be kind to Barbara Allan."

And slowly, slowly raise she up,
    And slowly, slowly left him,   50

---

[1] old woman.   [2] disturbances.
[3] November 11.   [4] birch.
[5] trench.   [6] furrow.

[7] fretting.   [8] cow-shed.
[1] If.   [2] slowly.

And sighing said she coud not stay,
　　Since death of life had reft him.

She had not gane a mile but twa,
　　When she heard the dead-bell ringing,
And every jow[3] that the dead-bell geid,
　　It cry'd, Woe to Barbara Allan!

"O mother, mother, make my bed!
　　O make it saft and narrow!
Since my love died for me today,
　　I'll die for him tomorrow."

CHEVY CHASE

1. God prosper long our noble king,
　　our liffes and saftyes all!
A woefull hunting once there did
　　in Chevy Chase befall.

2. To drive the deere with hound and horne
　　Erle Pearcy took the way:
The child may rue that is unborne
　　the hunting of that day!

3. The stout Erle of Northumberland
　　a vow to God did make
His pleasure in the Scottish woods
　　three sommers days to take,

4. The cheefest harts in Chevy C[h]ase
　　to kill and beare away:
These tydings to Erle Douglas came
　　in Scotland, where he lay.

5. Who sent Erle Pearcy present word
　　he would prevent his sport:
The English erle, not fearing that,
　　did to the woods resort,

6. With fifteen hundred bowmen bold,
　　All chosen men of might,
Who knew ffull well in time of neede
　　to ayme their shafts arright.

7. The gallant greyhound swiftly ran
　　to chase the fallow deere;
On Munday they began to hunt,
　　ere daylight did appeare.

---

[3] stroke.

8. And long before high noone they had
　　a hundred fat buckes slaine;
Then having dined, the drovyers went
　　to rouze the deare againe.

9. The bowmen mustered on the hills,
　　well able to endure;
Theire backsids all with speciall care
　　that day were guarded sure.

10. The hounds ran swiftly through the woods
　　the nimble deere to take,
That with their cryes the hills and dales
　　an eccho shrill did make.

11. Lord Pearcy to the querry went
　　to view the tender deere;
Quoth he, "Erle Douglas promised once
　　this day to meete me heere;

12. "But if I thought he wold not come,
　　noe longer wold I stay."
With that a brave younge gentlman
　　thus to the erle did say:

13. "Loe, yonder doth Erle Douglas come,
　　hys men in armour bright;
Full twenty hundred Scottish speres
　　all marching in our sight.

14. "All men of pleasant Tivydale,
　　fast by the river Tweede:"
"O ceaze your sportts!" Erle Pearcy said,
　　"and take your bowes with speede.

15. "And now with me, my countrymen,
　　your courage forth advance!
For there was never champion yett,
　　in Scottland nor in Ffrance,

16. "That ever did on horsbacke come,
　　[but], and if my hap it were,
I durst encounter man for man,
　　with him to break a spere."

17. Erle Douglas on his milke-white steede,
　　most like a baron bold,
Rode formost of his company,
　　whose armor shone like gold.

18. "Shew me," sayd hee, "whose men you bee
　　that hunt soe boldly heere,

That without my consent doe chase
    and kill my fallow deere."

19. The first man that did answer make
    was noble Pearcy hee,   5
Who sayd, "Wee list not to declare
    nor shew whose men wee bee;

20. "Yett wee will spend our deerest blood
    thy cheefest harts to slay."   10
Then Douglas swore a solempne oathe,
    and thus in rage did say:

21. "Ere thus I will outbraved bee,
    one of us tow shall dye;   15
I know thee well, an erle thou art;
    Lord Pearcy, soe am I.

22. "But trust me, Pearcye, pittye it were,
    and great offence, to kill   20
Then any of these our guiltlesse men,
    for they have done none ill.

23. "Let thou and I the battell trye,
    and set our men aside:"   25
"Accurst bee [he!]" Erle Pearcye sayd,
    "by whome it is denyed."

24. Then stept a gallant squire forth—
    Witherington was his name—   30
Who said, "I wold not have it told
    To Henery our king, for shame,

25. "That ere my captaine fought on foote,
    and I stand looking on.   35
You bee two Erles," quoth Witherington,
    "and I a squier alone;

26. "I'le doe the best that doe I may,
    while I have power to stand;   40
While I have power to weeld my sword,
    I'le fight with hart and hand."

27. Our English archers bent thier bowes;
    their harts were good and trew;   45
Att the first flight of arrowes sent,
    full foure score Scotts the slew.

28. To drive the deere with hound and horne,
    Douglas bade on the bent;   50
Two captaines moved with mickle might,
    their speres to shivers went.

29. They closed full fast on everye side,
    noe slacknes there was found,
But many a gallant gentleman
    lay gasping on the ground.

30. O Christ! it was great greeve to see
    how eche man chose his spere,
And how the blood out of their brests
    did gush like water cleare.

31. At last these two stout erles did meet,
    like captaines of great might;
Like lyons woode[1] they layd on lude;
    the made a cruell fight.

32. The fought untill they both did sweat,
    with swords of tempered steele,
Till blood downe their cheekes like raine
    the trickling downe did feele.

33. "O yeeld thee, Pearcye!" Douglas sayd,
    "And in faith I will thee bringe
Where thou shall high advanced bee
    by James our Scottish king.

34. "Thy ransome I will freely give,
    and this report of thee,
Thou art the most couragious knight
    [that ever I did see.]"

35. "Noe, Douglas!" quoth Erle Percy then,
    "thy profer I doe scorne;
I will not yeelde to any Scott
    that ever yett was borne!"

36. With that there came an arrow keene,
    out of an English bow,
Which stroke Erle Douglas on the brest
    a deepe and deadlye blow.

37. Who never sayd more words than these;
    "Fight on, my merry men all!
For why, my life is att [an] end,
    lord Pearcy sees my fall."

38. Then leaving liffe, Erle Pearcy tooke
    the dead man by the hand;
Who said, "Erle Dowglas, for thy life,
    wold I had lost my land!

---

[1] mad, wild.

39. "O Christ! my verry hart doth bleed
    for sorrow for thy sake,
For sure, a more redoubted knight
    mischance cold never take."

40. A knight amongst the Scotts there was
    which saw Erle Douglas dye,
Who streight in hart did vow revenge
    upon the Lord Pearcye.

41. Sir Hugh Mountgomerye was he called,
    who, with a spere full bright,
Well mounted on a gallant steed,
    ran feircly through the fight,

42. And past the English archers all,
    without all dread or feare,
And through Erle Percyes body then
    he thrust his hatfull spere.

43. With such a vehement force and might
    his body he did gore,
The staff ran through the other side
    a large cloth-yard and more.

44. Thus did both those nobles dye,
    whose courage none cold staine;
An English archer then perceived
    the noble erle was slaine.

45. He had [a] good bow in his hand,
    made of a trusty tree;
An arrow of a cloth-yard long
    to the hard head haled hee.

46. Against Sir Hugh Mountgomerye
    his shaft full right he sett;
The grey-goose-winge that was there-on
    in his harts bloode was wett.

47. This fight from breake of day did last
    till setting of the sun,
For when the rung the evening-bell
    the battele scarse was done.

48. With stout Erle Percy there was slaine
    Sir John of Egerton,
Sir Robert Harcliffe and Sir William,
    Sir James, that bold barron.

49. And with Sir George and Sir James,
    both knights of good account,

Good Sir Raphe Rebbye there was slaine,
    whose prowesse did surmount.

50. For Witherington needs must I wayle
    as one in dolefull dumpes,
For when his leggs were smitten of,
    he fought upon his stumpes.

51. And with Erle Dowglas there was slaine
    Sir Hugh Mountgomerye,
And Sir Charles Morrell, that from feelde
    one foote wold never flee;

52. Sir Roger Hever of Harcliffe tow,
    his sisters sonne was hee;
Sir David Lambwell, well esteemed,
    but saved he cold not bee.

53. And the Lord Maxwell, in like case,
    with Douglas he did dye;
Of twenty hundred Scottish speeres,
    scarce fifty-five did flye.

54. Of fifteen hundred Englishmen
    went home but fifty-three;
The rest in Chevy Chase were slaine,
    under the greenwoode tree.

55. Next day did many widdowes come
    their husbands to bewayle;
They washt their wounds in brinish teares,
    but all wold not prevayle.

56. Theyr bodyes, bathed in purple blood,
    the bore with them away;
They kist them dead a thousand times
    ere the were cladd in clay.

57. The newes was brought to Eddenborrow,
    where Scottlands king did rayne,
That brave Erle Douglas soddainlye
    was with an arrow slaine.

58. "O heavy newes!" King James can say;
    "Scottland may wittenesse bee
I have not any captaine more
    of such account as hee."

59. Like tydings to King Henery came,
    within as short a space,
That Pearcy of Northumberland
    was slaine in Chevy Chase.

60. "Now God be with him!" said our king,
    "sith it will noe better bee;
I trust I have within my realme
    five hundred as good as hee.

61. "Yett shall not Scotts nor Scottland say
    but I will vengeance take,
And be revenged on them all
    for brave Erle Percyes sake."

62. This vow the king did well performe
    after on Humble-downe;
In one day fifty knights were slayne,
    with lords of great renowne.

63. And of the rest, of small account,
    did many hundreds dye:
Thus endeth the hunting in Chevy Chase,
    made by the Erle Pearcye.

64. God save our king, and blesse this land
    with plentye, joy, and peace,
And grant hencforth that foule debate
    twixt noble men may ceaze!

TAM LIN

1. O I forbid you, maidens a',
    That wear gowd on your hair,
To come or gae by Carterhaugh,
    For young Tam Lin is there.

2. There's nane that gaes by Carterhaugh
    But they leave him a wad,[1]
Either their rings, or green mantles,
    Or else their maidenhead.

3. Janet has kilted her green kirtle
    A little aboon[2] her knee,
And she has broded her yellow hair
    A little aboon her bree,[3]
And she's awa to Carterhaugh,
    As fast as she can hie.

4. When she came to Carterhaugh
    Tam Lin was at the well,
And there she fand his steed standing,
    But away was himsel.

5. She had na pu'd a double rose,
    A rose but only twa,

Till up then started young Tam Lin,
    Says, "Lady, thou's pu nae mae.[4]

6. "Why pu's thou the rose, Janet,
    And why breaks thou the wand?
Or why comes thou to Carterhaugh
    Withoutten my command?

7. "Carterhaugh, it is my ain,
    My daddie gave it me;
I'll come and gang by Carterhaugh,
    And ask nae leave at thee."

   .   .   .   .

8. Janet has kilted her green kirtle
    A little aboon her knee,
And she has snooded her yellow hair
    A little aboon her bree,
And she is to her father's ha,
    As fast as she can hie.

9. Four and twenty ladies fair
    Were playing at the ba,
And out then cam the fair Janet,
    Ance the flower amang them a'.

10. Four and twenty ladies fair
    Were playing at the chess,
And out then cam the fair Janet,
    As green as onie glass.

11. Out then spak an auld grey knight,
    Lay oer the castle wa,
And says, "Alas, fair Janet, for thee
    But we'll be blamed a'.

12. "Haud your tongue, ye auld fac'd knight,
    Some ill death may ye die!
Father my bairn on whom I will,
    I'll father nane on thee."

13. Out then spak her father dear,
    And he spak meek and mild;
"And ever alas, sweet Janet," he says,
    "I think thou gaes wi child."

14. "If that I gae wi child, father,
    Mysel maun bear the blame;
There's neer a laird about your ha
    Shall get the bairn's name.

---

[1] token.   [2] above.   [3] brow.   [4] thou shalt pull no more.

15. "If my love were an earthly knight,
    As he's an elfin grey,
I wad na gie my ain true-love
    For nae lord that ye hae.

16. "The steed that my true-love rides on
    Is lighter than the wind;
Wi siller[5] he is shod before,
    Wi burning gowd[6] behind."

17. Janet has kilted her green kirtle
    A little aboon her knee,
And she has snooded her yellow hair
    A little aboon her bree,
And she's awa to Carterhaugh,
    As fast as she can hie.

18. When she cam to Carterhaugh,
    Tam Lin was at the well,
And there she fand his steed standing,
    But away was himsel.

19. She had na pu'd a double rose,
    A rose but only twa,
Till up then started young Tam Lin,
    Says, "Lady thou pu's nae mae.

20. "Why pu's thou the rose, Janet,
    Amang the groves sae green,
And a' to kill the bonie babe
    That we gat us between?"

21. "O tell me, tell me, Tam Lin," she says,
    "For's sake that died on tree,
If eer ye was in holy chapel,
    Or christendom[7] did see?"

22. "Roxbrugh he was my grandfather,
    Took me with him to bide,
And ance it fell upon a day
    That wae did me betide.

23. "And ance it fell upon a day,
    A cauld day and a snell,[8]
When we were frae the hunting come,
    That frae my horse I fell;
The Queen o Fairies she caught me,
    In yon green hill to dwell.

24. "And pleasant is the fairy land,
    But, an eerie tale to tell,

Ay at the end of seven years
    We pay a tiend[9] to hell;
I am sae fair and fu o flesh,
    I'm feard it be mysel.

25. "But the night is Halloween, lady,
    The morn is Hallowday;
Then win me, win me, an ye will,
    For weel I wat ye may.

26. "Just at the mirk and midnight hour
    The fairy folk will ride,
And they that wad their true-love win,
    At Miles Cross they maun bide."

27. "But how shall I thee ken, Tam Lin,
    Or how my true-love know,
Amang sae mony unco[10] knights
    The like I never saw?"

28. "O first let pass the black, lady,
    And syne let pass the brown,
But quickly run to the milk-white steed,
    Pu ye his rider down.

29. "For I'll ride on the milk-white steed,
    And ay nearest the town;
Because I was an earthly knight
    They gie me that renown.

30. "My right hand will be glovd, lady,
    My left hand will be bare,
Cockt up shall my bonnet be,
    And kaimd down shall my hair,
And thae's the takens I gie thee,
    Nae doubt I will be there.

31. "They'll turn me in your arms, lady,
    Into an esk[11] and adder;
But hold me fast, and fear me not,
    I am your bairn's father.

32. "They'll turn me to a bear sae grim,
    And then a lion bold;
But hold me fast, and fear me not,
    As ye shall love your child.

33. "Again they'll turn me in your arms
    To a red het gaud[12] of airn;

_____

[5] silver. [6] gold. [7] christening. [8] bitter.

[9] tithe. [10] unfamiliar.
[11] lizard. [12] bar.

[73]

But hold me fast, and fear me not,
    I'll do to you nae harm.

34. "And last they'll turn me in your arms
    Into the burning gleed;[13]
Then throw me into well water,
    O throw me in wi speed.

35. "And then I'll be your ain true-love,
    I'll turn a naked knight;
Then cover me wi your green mantle,
    And cover me out o sight."

36. Gloomy, gloomy was the night,
    And eerie was the way,
As fair Jenny in her green mantle
    To Miles Cross she did gae.

37. About the middle o the night
    She heard the bridles ring;
This lady was as glad at that
    As any earthly thing.

38. First she let the black pass by,
    And syne she let the brown;
But quickly she ran to the milk-white steed,
    And pu'd the rider down.

39. Sae weel she minded whae he did say,
    And young Tam Lin did win;
Syne coverd him wi her green mantle,
    As blythe 's a bird in spring.

40. Out then spak the Queen o Fairies,
    Out of a bush o broom:
"Them that has gotten young Tam Lin
    Has gotten a stately groom."

41. Out then spak the Queen o Fairies,
    And an angry woman was she:
"Shame betide her ill-far'd face,
    And an ill death may she die,
For she's taen awa the boniest knight
    In a' my companie.

42. "But had I kend, Tam Lin," she says,
    "What now this night I see,
I wad hae taen out thy twa grey een,
    And put in twa een o tree."

----

[13] coal.

ROBIN HOOD AND ALLIN-A-DALE

Come listen to me, you gallants so free,
    All you that loves mirth for to hear,
5 And I will you tell of a bold outlaw,
    That lived in Nottinghamshire.
                (Twice.)

As Robin Hood in the forrest stood,
    All under the green-wood tree,
10 There he was ware of a brave young man,
    As fine as fine might be.

The youngster was cloathed in scarlet red,
    In scarlet fine and gay,
15 And he did frisk it over the plain,
    And chanted a roundelay.

As Robin Hood next morning stood,
    Amongst the leaves so gay,
20 There did he espy the same young man
    Come drooping along the way.

The scarlet he wore the day before,
    It was clean cast away;
25 And every step he fetcht a sigh,
    "Alack and a well a day!"

Then stepped forth brave Little John,
    And Nick the miller's son,
30 Which made the young man bend his bow,
    When as he see them come.

"Stand off, stand off," the young man said,
    "What is your will with me?"
35 "You must come before our master straight,
    Under yon greenwood tree."

And when he came bold Robin before,
    Robin asked him courteously,
40 "O hast thou any money to spare
    For my merry men and me?"

"I have no money," the young man said,
    "But five shillings and a ring;
45 And that I have kept this seven long years,
    To have it at my wedding.

"Yesterday I should have married a maid,
    But now she is from me tane,
50 And chosen to be an old knight's delight,
    Whereby my poor heart is slain."

"What is thy name?" then said Robin Hood,
  "Come tell me, without any fail."
"By the faith of my body," then said the young
    man,
  "My name it is Allin-a-Dale."   5

"What wilt thou give me," said Robin Hood,
  "In ready gold or fee,
To help thee to thy true-love again,
  And deliver her unto thee?"   10

"I have no money," then quoth the young man,
  "No ready gold nor fee.
But I will swear upon a book
  Thy true servant for to be."   15

"How many miles is it to thy true-love?
  Come tell me without any guile."
"By the faith of my body," then said the young
    man,
  "It is but five little mile."   20

Then Robin he hasted over the plain,
  He did neither stint nor lin,
Until he came unto the church   25
  Where Allin should keep his wedding.

"What dost thou do here?" the bishop he said,
  "I prethee now tell to me."
"I am a bold harper," quoth Robin Hood,   30
  "And the best in the north countrey."

"O welcome, O welcome," the bishop he said,
  "That music best pleaseth me."
"You shall have no music," quoth Robin Hood,   35
  "Till the bride and the bridegroom I see."

With that came in a wealthy knight,
  Which was both grave and old,
And after him a finikin lass,   40
  Did shine like glistering gold.

"This is no fit match," quoth bold Robin Hood,
  "That you do seem to make here;
For since we are come into the church,   45
  The bride she shall choose her own dear."

Then Robin Hood put his horn to his mouth,
  And blew blasts two or three;
When four and twenty bowmen bold   50
  Came leaping over the lea.

And when they came into the churchyard,
  Marching all on a row,
The first man was Allin-a-Dale,
  To give bold Robin his bow.

"This is thy true-love," Robin he said,
  "Young Allin, as I hear say;
And you shall be married at this same time,
  Before we depart away."

"That shall not be," the bishop he said,
  "For thy word shall not stand;
They shall be three times askt in the church,
  As the law is of our land."

Robin Hood pulld off the bishop's coat,
  And put it upon Little John;
"By the faith of my body," then Robin said,
  "This cloath doth make thee a man."

When Little John went into the quire,
  The people began for to laugh;
He askt them seven times in the church,
  Lest three times should not be enough.

"Who gives me this maid?" then said Little
    John;
  Quoth Robin, "That do I,
And he that doth take her from Allin-a-Dale
  Full dearly he shall her buy."

And thus having ended this merry wedding,
  The bride lookt as fresh as a queen,
And so they returned to the merry greenwood,
  Amongst the leaves so green.

GET UP AND BAR THE DOOR

It fell about the Martinmas time,
  And a gay time it was then,
When our goodwife got puddings to make,
  And she's boild them in the pan.

The wind sae cauld blew south and north,
  And blew into the floor;
Quoth our goodman to our goodwife,
  "Gae out and bar the door."

"My hand is in my hussyfskap,
  Goodman, as ye may see;

An it shoud nae be barrd this hundred year,
  It's no be barrd for me."

They made a paction tween them twa,
  They made it firm and sure,   5
That the first word whaeer shoud speak,
  Shoud rise and bar the door.

Then by there came two gentlemen,
  At twelve o'clock at night,   10
And they could neither see house nor hall,
  Nor coal nor candlelight.

"Now whether is this a rich man's house,
  Or whether is it a poor?"   15
But neer a word wad ane o' them speak,
  For barring of the door.

And first they ate the white puddings,
  And then they ate the black;   20
Tho muckle thought the goodwife to hersel,
  Yet neer a word she spake.

Then said the one unto the other,
  "Here, man, tak ye my knife;
Do ye tak aff the auld man's beard,
  And I'll kiss the goodwife."

"But there's nae water in the house,
  And what shall we do than?"
"What ails ye at the pudding-broo,
  That boils into the pan?"

O up then started our goodman,
  An angry man was he:
"Will ye kiss my wife before my een,
  And scad me wi pudding-bree?"

Then up and started our goodwife,
  Gied three skips on the floor:
"Goodman, you've spoken the foremost
      word;
  Get up and bar the door."

THE RENAISSANCE

BROADSIDE BALLADS[1]

THE KING'S HUNT IS UP

The hunt is up, the hunt is up,
And it is well nigh day;
And Harry our king is gone hunting,   5
To bring his deer to bay.

The east is bright with morning light,
And darkness it is fled;
And the merry horn wakes up the morn   10
To leave his idle bed.

Behold the skies with golden dyes
Are glowing all around;
The grass is green, and so are the treen,   15
All laughing with the sound.

The horses snort to be at the sport,
The dogs are running free;
The woods rejoice at the merry noise
Of hey tantara tee ree!

The sun is glad to see us clad
All in our lusty green,
And smiles in the sky as he riseth high
To see and to be seen.

Awake all men, I say again,
Be merry as you may;
For Harry our king is gone hunting
To bring his deer to bay.
              [Gray of Reading]

[1] See introduction to the ballad, I, 65.

THE VALOROUS ACTS PERFORMED
AT GAUNT[1] BY THE BRAVE BONNY
LASS, MARY AMBREE, WHO IN
REVENGE OF HER LOVER'S DEATH,
DID PLAY HER PART 5
MOST GALLANTLY

When Captain Courageous, whom death
    could not daunt,
Had roundly besieged the city of Gaunt, 10
And manly they marched by two and by three,
And foremost in battle was Mary Ambree.

Thus being enforced to fight with her foes,
On each side most fiercely they seemed to 15
    close;
Each one sought for honor in every degree,
But none so much won it as Mary Ambree.

When brave Sergeant Major was slain in the 20
    fight,
Who was her own true love, her joy and de-
    light,
She swore unrevenged his blood should not be;
Was not this a brave bonny lass, Mary Ambree? 25

She clothed herself from the top to the toe
With buff of the bravest and seemly to show;
A fair shirt of mail over that striped she;
Was not this a brave bonny lass, Mary Ambree? 30

A helmet of proof she put on her head,
A strong armed sword she girt on her side,
A fair goodly gauntlet on her hand wore she;
Was not this a brave bonny lass, Mary Ambree? 35

Then took she her sword and her target in
    hand,
And called all those that would be of her
    band,—
To wait on her person there came thousands 40
    three;
Was not this a brave bonny lass, Mary Ambree?

Before you shall perish, the worst of you all, 45
Or come to any danger of enemy's thrall,
This hand and this life of mine shall set you
    free;
Was not this a brave bonny lass, Mary Ambree?

The drums and the trumpets did sound out
    alarm,
And many a hundred did lose leg and arm,
And many a thousand she brought on their
    knee;
Was not this a brave bonny lass, Mary Ambree?

The sky then she filled with smoke of her
    shot,
And her enemies' bodies with bullets so hot,
For one of her own men, a score killed she;
Was not this a brave bonny lass, Mary Ambree?

And then her false gunner did spoil her intent,
Her powder and bullets away he had spent,
And then with her weapon she slashed them in
    three;
Was not this a brave bonny lass, Mary Ambree?

Then took she her castle where she did abide,
Her enemies besieged her on every side;
To beat down her castle walls they did agree,
And all for to overcome Mary Ambree.

Then took she her sword and her target in
    hand,
And on her castle walls stoutly did stand,
So daring the captains to match any three;
Oh, what a brave captain was Mary Ambree!

At her then they smiled, not thinking in heart
That she could have performed so valorous a
    part;
The one said to the other, we shortly shall see
This gallant brave captain before us to flee.

Why, what do you think or take me to be?
Unto these brave soldiers so valiant spoke she.
A knight, sir, of England, and captain, quoth
    they,
Whom shortly we mean to take prisoner away.

No captain of England behold in your sight,
Two breasts in my bosom, and therefore no
    knight;
No knight, sir, of England, nor captain, quoth
    she,
But even a poor bonny lass, Mary Ambree.

But art thou a woman as thou dost declare, 50
That hath made us thus spend our armor in
    war?

---

[1] Ghent.

[77]

The like in our lives we never did see,
And therefore we'll honor brave Mary Ambree.

The Prince of great Parma heard of her re-
    nown,
Who long had advanced for England's fair
    crown;   5
In token he sent a glove and a ring,
And said she should be his bride at his wed-
    ding.

Why, what do you think or take me to be?
Though he be a prince of great dignity,
It shall never be said in England so free
That a stranger did marry with Mary Ambree. 15

Then unto fair England she back did return,
Still holding the foes of brave England in
    scorn;
In valor no man was ever like she;
Was not this a brave bonny lass, Mary Ambree? 20

In this woman's praises I'll here end my song,
Whose heart was approved in valor most
    strong;   25
Let all sorts of people, whatever they be,
Sing forth the brave valors of Mary Ambree.

A SONNET UPON THE PITIFUL
BURNING OF THE GLOBE   30
PLAYHOUSE IN LONDON

Now sit thee down, Melpomene,[1]
Wrapped in a sea-coal robe,
And tell the doleful tragedy
That late was played at Globe;
For no man that can sing and say
Was scared on St. Peter's Day.
Oh sorrow, pitiful sorrow, and yet all this is
    true.

All you that please to understand,
Come listen to my story,
To see Death with his raking brand
'Mongst such an auditory;
Regarding neither Cardinal's might,   40
Nor yet the rugged face of Henry the eight.
    —Oh sorrow, &c.

This fearful fire began above,
A wonder strange and true,   50

And to the stage-house did remove,
As round as tailor's clew;
And burnt down both beam and snag,
And did not spare the silken flag.—Oh sor-
    row, &c.

Out run the knights, out run the lords,
And there was great ado;
Some lost their hats and some their swords,
Then out run Burbage too;   10
The reprobates, though drunk on Monday,
Prayed for the fool and Henry Condye.[2]—Oh
    sorrow, &c.

The periwigs and drum-heads fry,
Like to a butter firkin;
A woeful burning did betide
To many a good buff jerkin.
Then with swollen eyes, like drunken Flem-
    ings,   20
Distressèd stood old stuttering Hemings.—Oh
    sorrow, &c.

No shower his rain did there down force,
In all that sunshine weather,   25
To save that great renownèd house,
Nor thou, O ale-house, neither.
Had it begun below, *sans doute*,
Their wives for fear . . . —Oh sorrow, &c.

Be warned, you stage strutters all,
Lest you again be catched,
And such a burning do befall
As to them whose house was thatched;
Forbear your whoring, breeding biles,   35
And lay up that expense for tiles.—Oh sorrow,
    &c.

Go draw you a petition,
And do you not abhor it,   40
And get, with low submission,
A license to beg for it
In churches, *sans* churchwardens' checks,
In Surrey and in Middlesex.
Oh sorrow, pitiful sorrow, and yet all this is 45
    true.

EDMUND SPENSER

*Spenser (1552–1599) is the first great figure in
English poetry after Chaucer. Known as a*

---

[1] muse of tragedy.

[2] Condell.

poet's poet because of his technical versatility and originality, he is a difficult author for a beginner to follow, partly because his outstanding work, The Faerie Queene, *is remote historically and clouded with triple allegory; nevertheless his narrative and descriptive skill can be appreciated in even a brief selection. A Cambridge man, Spenser held various secretaryships, was a friend of the scholar Gabriel Harvey, lived for a time in Ireland, hoped for high position. He never quite realized his ambition although he was granted a modest pension. His important titles include* The Shepheardes (Shepherd's) Calendar *in the classic pastoral tradition—a work which gave impetus to English lyric poetry; two marriage poems,* Epithalamion *and* Prothalamion; *and the* Amoretti, *a sonnet sequence based on his love for Elizabeth Boyle, whom he married.*

The Faerie Queene, *originally planned to include twelve books, is made up of six and part of a seventh. Each book has a hero, who represents a virtue, and who is assigned by Gloriana, the Faerie Queene, to aid someone in distress. The hero and unifying force of the whole work is Prince Arthur, who plays prominent rescue roles in Books I and II. The poem contains a general moral allegory, a religious allegory (Protestantism vs. Catholicism and non-Christian elements), and a political allegory involving people and issues of the day. Thus any one character may represent virtue and Protestantism and Queen Elizabeth; another evil, Catholicism, and Mary, Queen of Scots; many intended identities are not clear today, and scholars disagree over the minor characters. As a matter of fact, a beginning student can read the poem simply as an adventure story, old style, and forget the allegory. Spenser tells us that the poem was "to fashion a gentleman . . . in vertuous and gentle discipline"; it is also an extravagant compliment to Elizabeth.*

Our selection, given chiefly to show a sample of Elizabethan narrative verse, includes only one canto of Book I. The remaining cantos tell of the separation of Una and the Red Cross Knight, their independent adventures with knights, wizards, lions, forest folk, and the like; the plotting of Archimago and Duessa, with the final discomfiture of the latter; the reunion of the principals, the restoration of the Knight's

spirit after a fatal slip, and the glorious conquest of the dragon. Though purposely brief, this selection will serve to show the student Spenser's deliberately archaic language, his descriptive ability, his stanza form and organization. If he cares to go on, the bibliography (I, 394) will help him on his way.

THE FIRST BOOK OF THE FAERIE QUEENE

Contayning the Legend of the Knight of the Red Crosse, or of Holinesse

1

Lo! I, the man whose Muse whylome did maske,
As time her taught, in lowly Shephards weeds,[1]
Am now enforst, a farre unfitter taske,
For trumpets sterne to chaunge mine Oaten reeds, 5
And sing of Knights and Ladies gentle deeds;
Whose praises having slept in silence long,
Me, all too meane, the sacred Muse areeds[2]
To blazon broade emongst her learned throng:
Fierce warres and faithful loves shall moralize my song.

2

Helpe then, O holy virgin! chiefe of nyne,[3] 15
Thy weaker Novice to performe thy will;
Lay forth out of thine everlasting scryne[4]
The antique rolles, which there lye hidden still,
Of Faerie knights, and fayrest Tanaquill,[5]
Whom that most noble Briton Prince[6] so long 20
Sought through the world, and suffered so much ill,
That I must rue his undeserved wrong:
O, helpe thou my weake wit, and sharpen my dull tong!

3

And thou, most dreaded impe of highest Jove,
Faire Venus sonne, that with thy cruell dart 30
At that good knight so cunningly didst rove,
That glorious fire it kindled in his hart;
Lay now thy deadly Heben[7] bowe apart,
And with thy mother mylde come to mine ayde;

---

[1] ref. to *Shepherd's Calendar.*   [2] designates.
[3] Clio, one of the nine muses.   [4] desk.
[5] ref. to Elizabeth.   [6] Arthur.   [7] ebony.

Come, both; and with you bring triumphant
    Mart,[8]
In loves and gentle jollities arraid,
After his murdrous spoyles and bloudie rage
    allayd.

4

And with them eke, O Goddesse[9] heavenly
    bright!
Mirrour of grace and Majestie divine,
Great Ladie of the greatest Isle, whose light
Like Phœbus lampe throughout the world doth
    shine,
Shed thy faire beames into my feeble eyne,
And raise my thoughts, too humble and too
    vile,
To thinke of that true glorious type of thine,
The argument of mine afflicted stile:
The which to heare vouchsafe, O dearest
    dread, a-while!

CANTO I

The Patrone of true Holinesse
Foule Errour doth defeate:
Hypocrisie, him to entrappe,
Doth to his home entreate.

1

A gentle Knight was pricking[10] on the
    plaine,
Ycladd in mightie armes and silver shielde,
Wherein old dints of deepe woundes did re-
    maine,
The cruell markes of many a bloody fielde;
Yet armes till that time did he never wield.
His angry steede did chide his foming bitt,
As much disdayning to the curbe to yield:
Full jolly knight he seemd, and faire did sitt,
As one for knightly giusts and fierce encounters
    fitt.

2

And on his brest a bloodie Crosse he bore,
The deare remembrance of his dying Lord,
For whose sweete sake that glorious badge he
    wore,
And dead, as living, ever him ador'd:
Upon his shield the like was also scor'd,
For soveraine hope which in his helpe he had.
Right faithfull true he was in deede and word,
But of his cheere did seeme too solemne sad;

Yet nothing did he dread, but ever was ydrad.[11]

3

Upon a great adventure he was bond,
That greatest Gloriana[12] to him gave,
(That greatest Glorious Queene of Faery lond)
To winne him worshippe, and her grace to
    have,
Which of all earthly things he most did crave:
And ever as he rode his hart did earne[13]
To prove his puissance in battell brave
Upon his foe, and his new force to learne,
Upon his foe, a Dragon horrible and stearne.

4

A lovely Ladie rode him faire beside,
Upon a lowly Asse more white then snow,
Yet she much whiter; but the same did hide
Under a vele, that wimpled was full low;
And over all a blacke stole shee did throw:
As one that inly mournd, so was she sad,
And heavie sate upon her palfrey slow;
Seemed in heart some hidden care she had,
And by her, in a line, a milkewhite lambe she
    lad.

5

So pure and innocent, as that same lambe,
She was in life and every vertuous lore;
And by descent from Royall lynage came
Of ancient Kinges and Queenes, that had of
    yore
Their scepters stretcht from East to Westerne
    shore,
And all the world in their subjection held;
Till that infernall feend with foule uprore
Forewasted all their land, and them expeld;
Whom to avenge she had this Knight from far
    compeld.

6

Behind her farre away a Dwarfe did lag,
That lasie seemd, in being ever last,
Or wearied with bearing of her bag
Of needments at his backe. Thus as they past,
The day with cloudes was suddeine overcast,
And angry Jove an hideous storme of raine
Did poure into his Lemans lap[14] so fast
That everie wight to shrowd it did constrain;

---

[8] Mars.   [9] Elizabeth.   [10] spurring.

[11] feared.   [12] Elizabeth.   [13] yearn.
[14] lover's lap; here, the earth.

And this faire couple eke to shroud themselves
were fain.

7

Enforst to seeke some covert high at hand,
A shadie grove not farr away they spide,
That promist ayde the tempest to withstand;
Whose loftie trees, yclad with sommers pride,
Did spred so broad, that heavens light did
hide,
Not perceable with power of any starr:
And all within were pathes and alleies wide,
With footing worne, and leading inward farr.
Faire harbour that them seems, so in they
entred ar.

8

And foorth they passe, with pleasure for-
ward led,
Joying to heare the birdes sweete harmony,
Which, therein shrouded from the tempest
dred,
Seemd in their song to scorne the cruell sky.
Much can they praise the trees so straight
and hy,
The sayling Pine; the Cedar proud and tall;
The vine-propp Elme; the Poplar never dry;
The builder Oake, sole king of forrests all;
The Aspine good for staves; the Cypresse fu-
nerall;

9

The Laurell, meed of mightie Conquerours
And Poets sage; the Firre that weepeth still:
The Willow, worne of forlorne Paramours;
The Eugh, obedient to the benders will;
The Birch for shaftes; the Sallow for the mill;
The Mirrhe sweete-bleeding in the bitter
wound;
The warlike Beech; the Ash for nothing ill;
The fruitfull Olive; and the Platane round;
The carver Holme; the Maple seeldom in-
ward sound.

10

Led with delight, they thus beguile the way,
Untill the blustring storme is overblowne;
When, weening to returne whence they did
stray,
They cannot finde that path, which first was
showne,
But wander too and fro in waies unknowne,

Furthest from end then, when they neerest
weene,
That makes them doubt their wits be not their
owne:
So many pathes, so many turnings seene,
That which of them to take in diverse doubt
they been.

11

At last resolving forward still to fare,
Till that some end they finde, or in or out,
That path they take that beaten seemd most
bare,
And like to lead the labyrinth about;
Which when by tract they hunted had through-
out,
At length it brought them to a hollowe cave
Amid the thickest woods. The Champion stout
Eftsoones dismounted from his courser brave,
And to the Dwarfe a while his needlesse spere
he gave.

12

"Be well aware," quoth then that Ladie
milde,
"Least suddaine mischiefe ye too rash provoke:
The danger hid, the place unknowne and
wilde,
Breedes dreadfull doubts. Oft fire is without
smoke,
And perill without show: therefore your stroke,
Sir Knight, with-hold, till further tryall made."
"Ah Ladie," (sayd he) "shame were to re-
voke
The forward footing for an hidden shade:
Vertue gives her selfe light through darknesse
for to wade."

13

"Yea but" (quoth she) "the perill of this
place
I better wot then you: though nowe too late
To wish you backe returne with foule dis-
grace,
Yet wisedome warnes, whilst foot is in the
gate,
To stay the steppe, ere forced to retrate.
This is the wandring wood, this *Errours* den,
A monster vile, whom God and man does hate:
Therefore I read[15] beware." "Fly, fly!" (quoth
then

---

[15] advise.

The fearfull Dwarfe) "this is no place for
living men."

14

But, full of fire and greedy hardiment,
The youthfull Knight could not for ought be
staide;
But forth unto the darksom hole he went,
And looked in: his glistring armoor made
A litle glooming light, much like a shade;
By which he saw the ugly monster plaine,
Halfe like a serpent horribly displaide,
But th'other halfe did womans shape retaine,
Most lothsom, filthie, foule, and full of vile
disdaine.

15

And, as she lay upon the durtie ground,
Her huge long taile her den all overspred,
Yet was in knots and many boughtes[16] up-
wound,
Pointed with mortall sting. Of her there bred
A thousand yong ones, which she dayly fed,
Sucking upon her poisnous dugs; each one
Of sundrie shapes, yet all ill-favored:
Soone as that uncouth light upon them shone,
Into her mouth they crept, and suddain all
were gone.

16

Their dam upstart out of her den effraide,
And rushed forth, hurling her hideous taile
About her cursed head; whose folds displaid
Were stretcht now forth at length without en-
traile.[17]
She lookt about, and seeing one in mayle,
Armed to point, sought backe to turne againe;
For light she hated as the deadly bale,
Ay wont in desert darknes to remaine,
Where plain none might see her, nor she see
any plaine.

17

Which when the valiant Elfe[18] perceiv'd, he
lept
As Lyon fierce upon the flying pray,
And with his trenchand blade her boldly kept
From turning backe, and forced her to stay:
Therewith enrag'd she loudly gan to bray,

And turning fierce her speckled taile advaunst,
Threatning her angrie sting, him to dismay;
Who, nought aghast, his mightie hand en-
haunst:[19]
5 The stroke down from her head unto her
shoulder glaunst.

18

Much daunted with that dint her sence was
dazd;
Yet kindling rage her selfe she gathered round,
And all attonce her beastly bodie raizd
With doubled forces high above the ground:
Tho, wrapping up her wrethed sterne arownd,
15 Lept fierce upon his shield, and her huge traine
All suddenly about his body wound,
That hand or foot to stirr he strove in vaine.
God helpe the man so wrapt in Errours end-
lesse traine!

19

His Lady, sad to see his sore constraint,
Cride out, "Now, now, Sir knight, shew what
ye bee:
25 Add faith unto your force, and be not faint;
Strangle her, els she sure will strangle thee."
That when he heard, in great perplexitie,
His gall did grate for griefe and high disdaine;
And, knitting all his force, got one hand free,
30 Wherewith he grypt her gorge with so great
paine,
That soone to loose her wicked bands did her
constraine.

20

Therewith she spewd out of her filthie maw
A floud of poyson horrible and blacke,
Full of great lumps of flesh and gobbets raw,
Which stunck so vildly, that it forst him slacke
40 His grasping hold, and from her turne him
backe.
Her vomit full of bookes and papers was,
With loathly frogs and toades, which eyes did
lacke,
45 And creeping sought way in the weedy gras:
Her filthie parbreake[20] all the place defiled has.

21

As when old father Nilus gins to swell
50 With timely pride above the Aegyptian vale

---

[16] coils.   [17] coiling.
[18] Red Cross Knight (of elfin birth).

[19] raised.   [20] vomit.

His fattie waves doe fertile slime outwell,
And overflow each plaine and lowly dale:
But, when his later spring gins to avale,[21]
Huge heapes of mudd he leaves, wherein there
    breed
Ten thousand kindes of creatures, partly male
And partly femall, of his fruitful seed;
Such ugly monstrous shapes elswher may no
    man reed.

22

The same so sore annoyed has the knight,
That, welnigh choked with the deadly stinke,
His forces faile, ne can no lenger fight
Whose corage when the feend perceivd to
    shrinke,
She poured forth out of her hellish sinke
Her fruitfull cursed spawne of serpents small,
Deformed monsters, fowle, and blacke as inke,
Which swarming all about his legs did crall,
And him encombred sore, but could not hurt
    at all.

23

As gentle shepheard in sweete eventide,
When ruddy Phebus gins to welke[22] in west,
High on an hill, his flocke to vewen wide,
Markes which doe byte their hasty supper best;
A cloud of cumbrous gnattes doe him molest,
All striving to infixe their feeble stinges,
That from their noyance he no where can rest;
But with his clownish hands their tender wings
He brusheth oft, and oft doth mar their mur-
    murings.

24

Thus ill bestedd, and fearefull more of
    shame
Then of the certeine perill he stood in
Halfe furious unto his foe he came,
Resolvd in minde all suddenly to win,
Or soone to lose, before he once would lin;[23]
And stroke at her with more than manly force,
That from her body, full of filthie sin,
He raft her hatefull heade without remorse:
A streame of cole-black blood forth gushed
    from her corse.

25

Her scattered brood, soone as their Parent
    deare

They saw so rudely falling to the ground,
Groning full deadly, all with troublous feare
Gathred themselves about her body round,
Weening their wonted entrance to have found
5 At her wide mouth; but being there with-
    stood,
They flocked all about her bleeding wound,
And sucked up their dying mothers bloud,
Making her death their life, and eke her hurt
10   their good.

26

That detestable sight him much amazde,
To see th' unkindly Impes, of heaven ac-
    curst,
Devoure·their dam; on whom while so he gazd,
Having all satisfide their bloudy thurst,
Their bellies swolne he saw with fulnesse
    burst,
And bowels gushing forth: well worthy end
Of such as drunke her life the which them
    nurst!
Now needeth him no lenger labour spend,
His foes have slaine themselves, with whom he
    should contend.

27

His Lady, seeing all that chaunst from farre,
Approcht in hast to greet his victorie;
And saide, "Faire knight, borne under happie
    starre,
Who see your vanquisht foes before you lye,
Well worthie be you of that Armory,
Wherein ye have great glory wonne this day,
And proov'd your strength on a strong enimie,
Your first adventure: many such I pray,
And henceforth ever wish that like succeed it
    may!"

28

Then mounted he upon his Steede againe,
And with the Lady backward sought to wend.
That path he kept which beaten was most
    plaine,
Ne ever would to any byway bend,
But still did follow one unto the end,
The which at last out of the wood them
    brought.
So forward on his way (with God to frend)
He passed forth, and new adventure sought:
Long way he traveiled before he heard of
    ought.

---

[21] subside.   [22] wane.   [23] cease.

29

At length they chaunst to meet upon the
way
An aged Sire, in long blacke weedes yclad, 5
His feete all bare, his beard all hoarie gray,
And by his belt his booke he hanging had:
Sober he seemde, and very sagely sad,
And to the ground his eyes were lowly bent,
Simple in shew, and voide of malice bad; 10
And all the way he prayed as he went,
And often knockt his brest, as one that did
repent.

30

He faire the knight saluted, louting[24] low,
Who faire him quited, as that courteous was;
And after asked him, if he did know
Of straunge adventures, which abroad did pas,
"Ah! my dear sonne," (quoth he) "how should, 20
alas!
Silly old man, that lives in hidden cell,
Bidding his beades all day for his trespas,
Tydings of warre and worldly trouble tell?
With holy father sits not with such things to 25
mell.[25]

31

"But if of daunger, which hereby doth
dwell,
And homebredd evil ye desire to heare,
Of a straunge man I can you tidings tell,
That wasteth all this countrie, farre and neare."
"Of such," (saide he,) "I chiefly doe inquere,
And shall thee well rewarde to shew the place, 35
In which that wicked wight his dayes doth
weare;
For to all knighthood it is foule disgrace,
That such a cursed creature lives so long a
space." 40

32

"Far hence" (quoth he) "in wastfull wilder-
nesse
His dwelling is, by which no living wight 45
May ever passe, but thorough great distresse."
"Now," (saide the Ladie,) "draweth toward
night,
And well I wote, that of your later fight
Ye all forwearied be; for what so strong, 50

But, wanting rest, will also want of might?
The Sunne, that measures heaven all day long,
At night doth baite his steedes the Ocean
waves emong.

33

"Then with the Sunne take, Sir, your timely
rest,
And with new day new worke at once begin:
Untroubled night, they say, gives counsell
best."
"Right well, Sir knight, ye have advised bin,"
Quoth then that aged man: "the way to win
Is wisely to advise; now day is spent:
Therefore with me ye may take up your In
For this same night." The knight was well
content;
So with that godly father to his home they
went.

34

A litle lowly Hermitage it was,
Downe in a dale, hard by a forests side,
Far from resort of people that did pas
In traveill to and froe: a litle wyde[26]
There was an holy chappell edifyde,[27]
Wherein the Hermite dewly wont to say
His holy thinges each morne and eventyde:
Thereby a christall streame did gently play,
Which from a sacred fountaine welled forth
alway.

35

Arrived there, the litle house they fill,
Ne looke for entertainment where none was;
Rest is their feast, and all thinges at their will:
The noblest mind the best contentment has.
With faire discourse the evening so they pas;
For that olde man of pleasing wordes had
store,
And well could file his tongue as smooth as
glas;
He told of Saintes and Popes, and evermore
He strowd an *Ave-Mary* after and before.

36

The drouping night thus creepeth on them
fast;
And the sad humor[28] loading their eyeliddes,
As messenger of Morpheus on them cast

---

[24] bending. [25] meddle. [26] way off. [27] built. [28] dampness.

Sweet slombring deaw, the which to sleep
    them biddes.
Unto their lodgings then his guestes he riddes:
Where when all drownd in deadly sleepe he
    findes,
He to his studie goes; and there amiddes
His magick bookes, and artes of sundrie kindes,
He seekes out mighty charmes to trouble sleepy
    minds.

37

Then choosing out few words most horrible,
(Let none them read) thereof did verses frame;
With which, and other spelles like terrible,
He bad awake blacke Plutoes griesly Dame;[29] 15
And cursed heven; and spake reprochful shame
Of highest God, the Lord of life and light:
A bold bad man, that dar'd to call by name
Great Gorgon, prince of darknes and dead
    night:
At which Cocytus[30] quakes, and Styx[30] is put to
    flight.

38

And forth he cald out of deepe darknes 25
    dredd
Legions of Sprights, the which, like litle flyes
Fluttering about his ever-damned hedd,
Awaite whereto their service he applyes,
To aide his friendes, or fray his enimies. 30
Of those he chose out two, the falsest twoo,
And fittest for to forge true-seeming lyes:
The one of them he gave a message too,
The other by him selfe staide, other worke to
    doo.

39

He, making speedy way through spersed
    ayre,
And through the world of waters wide and 40
    deepe,
To Morpheus house doth hastily repaire.
Amid the bowels of the earth full steepe,
And low, where dawning day doth never
    peepe, 45
His dwelling is; there Tethys[31] his wet bed
Doth ever wash, and Cynthia[32] still doth steepe
In silver deaw his ever-drouping hed,
Whiles sad Night over him her mantle black
    doth spred. 50

40

Whose double gates he findeth locked fast,
The one faire fram'd of burnisht Yvory,
The other all with silver overcast; 5
And wakeful dogges before them farre doe lye,
Watching to banish Care their enimy,
Who oft is wont to trouble gentle Sleepe.
By them the Sprite doth passe in quietly,
And unto Morpheus comes, whom drowned 10
    deepe
In drowsie fit he findes: of nothing he takes
    keepe.[33]

41

And more to lulle him in his slumber soft,
A trickling streame from high rock tumbling
    downe,
And ever-drizling raine upon the loft,
Mixt with a murmuring winde, much like the 20
    sowne
Of swarming Bees, did cast him in a swowne.
No other noyse, nor peoples troublous cryes,
As still are wont t'annoy the walled towne,
Might there be heard; but carelesse Quiet lyes 25
Wrapt in eternall silence farre from enimyes.

42

The Messenger approching to him spake;
But his waste wordes retournd to him in vaine:
So sound he slept, that nought mought him
    awake.
Then rudely he him thrust, and pusht with
    paine,
Whereat he gan to stretch; but he againe 35
Shooke him so hard, that forced him to speake.
As one then in a dreame, whose dryer braine
Is tost with troubled sights and fancies weake,
He mumbled soft, but would not all his silence
    breake.

43

The Sprite then gan more boldly him to
    wake,
And threatned unto him the dreaded name 45
Of Hecate:[34] whereat he gan to quake,
And, lifting up his lompish head, with blame
Halfe angrie asked him, for what he came.
"Hether" (quoth he,) "me Archimago sent,
He that the stubborne Sprites can wisely tame, 50
He bids thee to him send for his intent

---

[29] Proserpine.   [30] river in Hell.
[31] the ocean.   [32] the moon.   [33] care.   [34] goddess of magic.

A fit false dreame, that can delude the sleepers
sent."

44

The God obayde; and, calling forth straight
way
A diverse Dreame out of his prison darke,
Delivered it to him, and downe did lay
His heavie head, devoide of careful carke;[35]
Whose sences all were straight benumbd and
starke.
He, backe returning by the Yvorie dore,
Remounted up as light as chearefull Larke;
And on his litle winges the dreame he bore
In hast unto his Lord, where he him left afore.

45

Who all this while, with charmes and hidden
artes,
Had made a Lady of that other Spright,
And fram'd of liquid ayre her tender partes,
So lively and so like in all mens sight,
That weaker sence it could have ravisht
quight:
The maker selfe, for all his wondrous witt,
Was nigh beguiled with so goodly sight.
Her all in white he clad, and over it
Cast a black stole, most like to seeme for Una
fit.

46

Now, when that ydle dreame was to him
brought,
Unto that Elfin knight he bad him fly,
Where he slept soundly void of evil thought,
And with false shewes abuse his fantasy,
In sort as he him schooled privily:
And that new creature, borne without her
dew,[36]
Full of the makers guyle, with usage sly
He taught to imitate that Lady trew,
Whose semblance she did carrie under feigned
hew.

47

Thus well instructed, to their worke they
hast,
And comming where the knight in slomber lay,
The one upon his hardy head him plast,
And made him dreame of loves and lustfull
play,

That nigh his manly hart did melt away,
Bathed in wanton blis and wicked ioy:
Then seemed him his Lady by him lay,
And to him playnd, how that false winged boy
Her chast hart had subdewd, to learne Dame
pleasures toy.

48

And she her selfe of beautie soveraigne
Queene,
Faire Venus seemde unto his bed to bring
Her, whom he waking evermore did weene
To be the chastest flowre, that ay did spring
On earthly braunch, the daughter of a king,
Now a loose Leman to vile service bound:
And eke the Graces seemed all to sing,
Hymen iô Hymen, dauncing all around,
Whilst freshest Flora her with Yuie girlond
crownd.

49

In this great passion of unwonted lust,
Or wonted feare of doing ought amis,
He started up, as seeming to mistrust
Some secret ill, or hidden foe of his:
Lo there before his face his Lady is,
Under blake stole hyding her bayted hooke,
And as halfe blushing offred him to kis,
With gentle blandishment and lovely looke,
Most like that virgin true, which for her knight
him took.

50

All cleane dismayd to see so uncouth sight,
And halfe enraged at her shamelesse guise,
He thought have slaine her in his fierce de-
spight:
But hasty heat tempring with sufferance wise,
He stayde his hand, and gan himselfe advise
To prove his sense, and tempt her faigned
truth.
Wringing her hands in wemens pitteous wise,
Tho[37] can she weepe, to stirre up gentle ruth,[38]
Both for her noble bloud, and for her tender
youth.

51

And said, "Ah Sir, my liege Lord and my
love,
Shall I accuse the hidden cruell fate,
And mightie causes wrought in heaven above,

---

[35] worry.   [36] unnaturally.   [37] Then.   [38] pity.

Or the blind God, that doth me thus amate,[39]
For hoped love to winne me certaine hate?
Yet thus perforce he bids me do, or die.
Die is my dew: yet rew my wretched state
You, whom my hard avenging destinie
Hath made iudge of my life or death indif-
ferently.

52

"Your owne deare sake forst me at first to 10
leave
My Fathers kingdome." There she stopt with
teares;
Her swollen hart her speach seemd to bereave,
And then againe begun, "My weaker yeares 15
Captiv'd to fortune and frayle worldly feares,
Fly to your faith for succour and sure ayde:
Let me not dye in langour and long teares."
"Why Dame" (quoth he) "what hath ye thus
dismayd? 20
What frayes ye, that were wont to comfort me
affrayd?"

53

"Love of your selfe," she said, "and deare 25
constraint
Lets me not sleepe, but wast the wearie night
In secret anguish and unpittied plaint,
Whiles you in carelesse sleepe are drowned
quight."
Her doubtfull words made that redouted 30
knight
Suspect her truth: yet since no'untruth he
knew,

[39] dismay.

Her fawning love with foule disdainefull
spight
He would not shend,[40] but said, "Deare dame
I rew,
5 That for my sake unknowne such griefe unto
you grew.

54

"Assure your selfe, it fell not all to ground;
For all so deare as life is to my hart,
I deeme your love, and hold me to you bound;
Ne let vaine feares procure your needlesse
smart,
Where cause is none, but to your rest depart."
Not all content, yet seemd she to appease
Her mournefull plaintes, beguiled of her art,
And fed with words, that could not chuse but
please,
So slyding softly forth, she turnd as to her ease.

55

Long after lay he musing at her mood,
Much grieu'd to thinke that gentle Dame so
light,
For whose defence he was to shed his blood.
At last dull wearinesse of former fight
Having yrockt a sleepe his irkesome spright,
That troublous dreame gan freshly tosse his
braine
30 With bowres, and beds, and Ladies deare de-
light:
But when he saw his labour all was vaine,
With that misformed spright he backe returnd
againe.

[40] reproach.

SEVENTEENTH CENTURY

JOHN MILTON

*As with Chaucer, Spenser, and Shakespeare, it
is well-nigh ridiculous to confine the life of
Milton (1608–1674) to a few lines of editorial
comment. Nevertheless, if the reader happens
to be ignorant of the bare facts of the poet's*
*career, he may be interested to know that a
long, careful preparation for achievement was
the procedure in Milton's case: early reading,
language training, schooling at St. Paul's and
Cambridge, the Grand Tour. Milton was al-*

lowed to rusticate, to grow and develop without too many cares, except for those met while tutoring his nephews. Even so, trouble soon began to dog him: his friend Diodati died, and his wife Mary Powell left him. From 1642 on, life was a battle, and Milton fought like a Titan to the end. In prose he attacked episcopacy, advocated divorce, battled royalism, and defended free press (II, 21); he literally wrote himself blind under Cromwell in his defenses of England against foreign pamphleteers. In poetry, after preliminary exercises in the elegy, masque, and sonnet, along with a few occasional poems, Milton wrote the great epic, Paradise Lost, and followed it with Paradise Regained and the dramatic Samson Agonistes, a moving version of the old Biblical tale with unmistakable autobiographical passages drawn in.

Domestically the poet had fared badly: Mary, finally reconciled, had died after bearing three children; Katharine Woodcock, with whom he was happy, died with her baby just over a year after their marriage; a third wife, Elizabeth Minshull, was left as companion to an old man, alone, "blind among enemies." (Politically Milton was in hiding after the Restoration, tired and disillusioned; but the three works mentioned above were the products of his last years, nevertheless.)

Milton has undergone some unfavorable criticism in our day, whereas he was almost unanimously hailed as a literary giant a generation or two ago. Most of the argument settles around his language, the unattractive traits of his personality, his remote theological subject matter, and the like. But Milton is great enough —correct though some criticism may be—to offer much to the modern student. In his impact upon poets who came after him he has shown his stature; the ideas in his prose are still liberal in the twentieth century. Other poets may have more humor, warmth, human appeal; Milton, right or wrong, had nobility of purpose, great strength, and a deep, sincere interest in man's conduct, his struggle with evil, his attempts to reason, his war with himself. In the great sweep of his canvas, much that is ponderous or dated in Milton should be forgiven—in a sense, Paradise Lost is a period piece—in favor of much that is strong, solid, worthy of study in this age of indecision, of

groping toward strength and solidity.

PARADISE LOST

BOOK I

The Argument

This First Book proposes, first in brief, the whole subject—Man's disobedience, and the loss thereupon of Paradise, wherein he was placed: then touches the prime cause of his fall—the Serpent, or rather Satan in the Serpent; who, revolting from God, and drawing to his side many legions of Angels, was, by the command of God, driven out of Heaven, with all his crew, into the great Deep. Which action passed over, the Poem hastes into the midst of things; presenting Satan, with his Angels, now fallen into Hell—described here not in the Centre (for heaven and earth may be supposed as yet not made, certainly not yet accursed), but in a place of utter darkness, fitliest called Chaos. Here Satan, with his Angels lying on the burning lake, thunderstruck and astonished, after a certain space recovers, as from confusion; calls up him who, next in order and dignity, lay by him: they confer of their miserable fall. Satan awakens all his legions, who lay till then in the same manner confounded. They rise: their numbers; array of battle; their chief leaders named, according to the idols known afterwards in Canaan and the countries adjoining. To these Satan directs his speech; comforts them with hope yet of regaining Heaven; but tells them, lastly, of a new world and new kind of creature to be created, according to an ancient prophecy, or report, in Heaven —for that Angels were long before this visible creation was the opinion of many ancient Fathers. To find out the truth of this prophecy, and what to determine thereon, he refers to a full council. What his associates thence attempt. Pandemonium, the palace of Satan, rises, suddenly built out of the Deep: the infernal Peers there sit in council.

Of Man's first disobedience, and the fruit
Of that forbidden tree whose mortal taste
Brought death into the World, and all our woe,
With loss of Eden, till one greater Man

Restore us, and regain the blissful Seat,
Sing, Heavenly Muse, that, on the secret top
Of Oreb, or of Sinai, didst inspire
That Shepherd[1] who first taught the chosen
    seed 5
In the beginning how the heavens and earth
Rose out of Chaos: or, if Sion hill
Delight thee more, and Siloa's brook that
    flowed
Fast by the oracle of God, I thence 10
Invoke thy aid to my adventrous song,
That with no middle flight intends to soar
Above the Aonian mount, while it pursues
Things unattempted yet in prose or rhyme.
And chiefly Thou, O Spirit, that dost prefer 15
Before all temples the upright heart and pure,
Instruct me, for Thou know'st; Thou from the
    first
Wast present, and, with mighty wings out-
    spread, 20
Dove-like sat'st brooding on the vast Abyss,
And mad'st it pregnant: what in me is dark
Illumine, what is low raise and support;
That, to the highth of this great argument,
I may assert Eternal Providence, 25
And justify the ways of God to men.
    Say first—for Heaven hides nothing from
    thy view,
Nor the deep tract of Hell—say first what
    cause 30
Moved our grand Parents, in that happy state,
Favored of Heaven so highly, to fall off
From their Creator, and transgress his will
For one restraint, lords of the World besides.
Who first seduced them to that foul revolt? 35
    The infernal Serpent; he it was whose guile,
Stirred up with envy and revenge, deceived
The mother of mankind, what time his pride
Had cast him out from Heaven, with all his
    host
Of rebel Angels, by whose aid, aspiring
To set himself in glory above his peers,
He trusted to have equalled the Most High,
If he opposed, and, with ambitious aim
Against the throne and monarchy of God,
Raised impious war in Heaven and battle
    proud,
With vain attempt. Him the Almighty Power
Hurled headlong flaming from the ethereal sky,
With hideous ruin and combustion, down 50

To bottomless perdition, there to dwell
In adamantine chains and penal fire,
Who durst defy the Omnipotent to arms.
    Nine times the space that measures day and
    night
To mortal men, he, with his horrid crew,
Lay vanquished, rolling in the fiery gulf,
Confounded, though immortal. But his doom
Reserved him to more wrath; for now the
    thought
Both of lost happiness and lasting pain
Torments him: round he throws his baleful
    eyes,
That witnessed huge affliction and dismay,
Mixed with obdúrate pride and steadfast hate.
At once, as far as Angels ken, he views
The dismal situation waste and wild.
A dungeon horrible, on all sides round,
As one great furnace flamed; yet from those
    flames
No light; but rather darkness visible
Served only to discover sights of woe,
Regions of sorrow, doleful shades, where peace
And rest can never dwell, hope never comes
That comes to all, but torture without end
Still urges, and a fiery deluge, fed
With ever-burning sulphur unconsumed.
Such place Eternal Justice had prepared
For those rebellious; here their prison ordained
In utter darkness, and their portion set,
As far removed from God and the light of
    Heaven
As from the centre thrice to the utmost pole.
Oh how unlike the place from whence they
    fell!
There the companions of his fall, o'erwhelmed
With floods and whirlwinds of tempestuous
    fire,
He soon discerns; and, weltering by his side,
One next himself in power, and next in crime,
Long after known in Palestine, and named
Beëlzebub. To whom the Arch-Enemy,
And thence in Heaven called Satan, with bold
    words
Breaking the horrid silence, thus began:—
    "If thou beest he—but Oh how fallen! how
    changed
From him!—who, in the happy realms of light,
Clothed with transcendent brightness, didst
    outshine
Myriads, though bright—if he whom mutual
    league,

[1] Moses.

[89]

United thoughts and counsels, equal hope
And hazard in the glorious enterprise,
Joined with me once, now misery hath joined
In equal ruin; into what pit thou seest
From what highth fallen: so much the stronger 5
    proved
He with his thunder: and till then who knew
The force of those dire arms? Yet not for those,
Nor what the potent Victor in his rage
Can else inflict, do I repent, or change,
Though changed in outward lustre, that fixed 10
    mind,
And high disdain from sense of injured merit,
That with the Mightiest raised me to contend,
And to the fierce contention brought along 15
Innumerable force of Spirits armed,
That durst dislike his reign, and, me prefer-
    ring,
His utmost power with adverse power op-
    posed
In dubious battle on the plains of Heaven, 20
And shook his throne. What though the field
    be lost?
All is not lost—the unconquerable will,
And study of revenge, immortal hate, 25
And courage never to submit or yield:
And what is else not to be overcome?
That glory never shall his wrath or might
Extort from me. To bow and sue for grace
With suppliant knee, and deify his power 30
Who, from the terror of this arm, so late
Doubted his empire—that were low indeed;
That were an ignominy and shame beneath
This downfall; since, by fate, the strength of 35
    Gods,
And this empyreal substance, cannot fail;
Since, through experience of this great event,
In arms not worse, in foresight much advanced,
We may with more successful hope resolve
To wage by force or guile eternal war, 40
Irreconcilable to our grand Foe,
Who now triumphs, and in the excess of joy
Sole reigning holds the tyranny of Heaven."
    So spake the apostate Angel, though in pain, 45
Vaunting aloud, but racked with deep de-
    spair;
And him thus answered soon his bold Com-
    peer:—
    "O Prince, O Chief of many thronèd Powers 50
That led the embattled Seraphim to war
Under thy conduct, and, in dreadful deeds
Fearless, endangered Heaven's perpetual King,

And put to proof his high supremacy,
Whether upheld by strength, or chance, or
    fate!
Too well I see and rue the dire event
That, with sad overthrow and foul defeat, 5
Hath lost us Heaven, and all this mighty host
In horrible destruction laid thus low,
As far as Gods and Heavenly Essences
Can perish: for the mind and spirit remains
Invincible, and vigor soon returns, 10
Though all our glory extinct, and happy state
Here swallowed up in endless misery.
But what if He our Conqueror (whom I now
Of force believe almighty, since no less
Than such could have o'erpowered such force 15
    as ours)
Have left us this our spirit and strength entire,
Strongly to suffer and support our pains,
That we may so suffice his vengeful ire,
Or do him mightier service as his thralls 20
By right of war, whate'er his business be,
Here in the heart of Hell to work in fire,
Or do his errands in the gloomy Deep?
What can it then avail though yet we feel
Strength undiminished, or eternal being 25
To undergo eternal punishment?"
    Whereto with speedy words the Arch-Fiend
    replied:—
"Fallen Cherub, to be weak is miserable,
Doing or suffering: but of this be sure— 30
To do aught good never will be our task,
But ever to do ill our sole delight,
As being the contrary to His high will
Whom we resist. If then his providence
Out of our evil seek to bring forth good, 35
Our labor must be to pervert that end,
And out of good still to find means of evil;
Which ofttimes may succeed so as perhaps
Shall grieve him, if I fail not, and disturb
His inmost counsels from their destined aim. 40
But see! the angry Victor hath recalled
His ministers of vengeance and pursuit
Back to the gates of Heaven: the sulphurous
    hail,
Shot after us in storm, o'erblown hath laid 45
The fiery surge that from the precipice
Of Heaven received us falling; and the thun-
    der,
Winged with red lightning and impetuous rage,
Perhaps hath spent his shafts, and ceases now 50
To bellow through the vast and boundless
    Deep.

Let us not slip the occasion, whether scorn
Or satiate fury yield it from our Foe.
Seest thou yon dreary plain, forlorn and wild,
The seat of desolation, void of light,
Save what the glimmering of these livid flames 5
Casts pale and dreadful? Thither let us tend
From off the tossing of these fiery waves;
There rest, if any rest can harbor there;
And, re-assembling our afflicted powers,
Consult how we may henceforth most offend 10
Our Enemy, our own loss how repair,
How overcome this dire calamity,
What reinforcement we may gain from hope,
If not what resolution from despair."

    Thus Satan, talking to his nearest Mate, 15
With head uplift above the wave, and eyes
That sparkling blazed; his other parts besides
Prone on the flood, extended long and large,
Lay floating many a rood, in bulk as huge
As whom the fables name of monstrous size, 20
Titanian or Earth-born, that warred on Jove,
Briareos or Typhon,[2] whom the den
By ancient Tarsus held, or that sea-beast
Leviathan, which God of all his works
Created hugest that swim the ocean-stream. 25
Him, haply slumbering on the Norway foam,
The pilot of some small night-foundered skiff,
Deeming some island, oft, as seamen tell,
With fixèd anchor in his scaly rind,
Moors by his side under the lee, while night 30
Invests the sea, and wishèd morn delays.
So stretched out huge in length the Arch-Fiend
    lay,
Chained on the burning lake; nor ever thence
Had risen, or heaved his head, but that the 35
    will
And high permission of all-ruling Heaven
Left him at large to his own dark designs,
That with reiterated crimes he might
Heap on himself damnation, while he sought 40
Evil to others, and enraged might see
How all his malice served but to bring forth
Infinite goodness, grace, and mercy, shewn
On Man by him seduced, but on himself
Treble confusion, wrath, and vengeance 45
    poured.

    Forthwith upright he rears from off the pool
His mighty stature; on each hand the flames
Driven backward slope their pointing spires,
    and, rolled 50
In billows, leave i' the midst a horrid vale.

[2] Briareos, a Titan; Typhon, a giant.

Then with expanded wings he steers his flight
Aloft, incumbent on the dusky air,
That felt unusual weight; till on dry land
He lights—if it were land that ever burned
With solid, as the lake with liquid fire, 5
And such appeared in hue as when the force
Of subterranean wind transports a hill
Torn from Pelorus, or the shattered side
Of thundering Ætna, whose combustible
And fuelled entrails, thence conceiving fire, 10
Sublimed with mineral fury, aid the winds,
And leave a singèd bottom all involved
With stench and smoke. Such resting found
    the sole
Of unblest feet. Him followed his next Mate;
Both glorying to have scaped the Stygian flood
As gods, and by their own recovered strength,
Not by the sufferance of supernal power.

    "Is this the region, this the soil, the clime,"
Said then the lost Archangel, "this the seat 20
That we must change for Heaven?—this
    mournful gloom
For that celestial light? Be it so, since He
Who now is sovran can dispose and bid
What shall be right: farthest from Him is best, 25
Whom reason hath equalled, force hath made
    supreme
Above his equals. Farewell, happy fields,
Where joy for ever dwells! Hail, horrors!
    hail,
Infernal World! and thou, profoundest Hell,
Receive thy new possessor—one who brings
A mind not to be changed by place or time.
The mind is its own place, and in itself
Can make a Heaven of Hell, a Hell of Heaven. 35
What matter where, if I be still the same,
And what I should be, all but less than he
Whom thunder hath made greater? Here at
    least
We shall be free; the Almighty hath not built 40
Here for his envy, will not drive us hence:
Here we may reign secure; and, in my choice,
To reign is worth ambition, though in Hell:
Better to reign in Hell than serve in Heaven.
But wherefore let we then our faithful friends, 45
The associates and co-partners of our loss,
Lie thus astonished on the oblivious pool,
And call them not to share with us their part
In this unhappy mansion, or once more
With rallied arms to try what may be yet 50
Regained in Heaven, or what more lost in
    Hell?"

So Satan spake; and him Beëlzebub
Thus answered:—"Leader of those armies
   bright,
Which, but the Omnipotent, none could have
   foiled!
If once they hear that voice, their liveliest
   pledge
Of hope in fears and dangers—heard so oft
In worst extremes, and on the perilous edge
Of battle, when it raged, in all assaults
Their surest signal—they will soon resume
New courage and revive, though now they lie
Grovelling and prostrate on yon lake of fire,
As we erewhile, astounded and amazed;
No wonder, fallen such a pernicious highth!"
   He scarce had ceased when the superior
      Fiend
Was moving toward the shore; his ponderous
   shield,
Ethereal temper, massy, large, and round,
Behind him cast. The broad circumference
Hung on his shoulders like the moon, whose
   orb
Through optic glass the Tuscan artist[3] views
At evening, from the top of Fesolè,
Or in Valdarno, to descry new lands,
Rivers, or mountains, in her spotty globe.
His spear—to equal which the tallest pine
Hewn on Norwegian hills, to be the mast
Of some great Ammiral,[4] were but a wand—
He walked with, to support uneasy steps
Over the burning marle, not like those steps
On Heaven's azure; and the torrid clime
Smote on him sore besides, vaulted with fire.
Nathless[5] he so endured, till on the beach
Of that inflamèd sea he stood, and called
His legions—Angel Forms, who lay entranced
Thick as autumnal leaves that strow the brooks
In Vallombrosa, where the Etrurian shades
High over-arched embower; or scattered sedge
Afloat, when with fierce winds Orion armed
Hath vexed the Red-Sea coast, whose waves
   o'erthrew
Busiris and his Memphian chivalry,
While with perfidious hatred they pursued
The sojourners of Goshen, who beheld
From the safe shore their floating carcases
And broken chariot-wheels. So thick bestrown,
Abject and lost, lay these, covering the flood,

Under amazement of their hideous change.
He called so loud that all the hollow deep
Of Hell resounded:—"Princes, Potentates,
Warriors, the Flower of Heaven—once yours;
   now lost,
If such astonishment as this can seize
Eternal Spirits! Or have ye chosen this place
After the toil of battle to repose
Your wearied virtue, for the ease you find
To slumber here, as in the vales of Heaven?
Or in this abject posture have ye sworn
To adore the Conqueror, who now beholds
Cherub and Seraph rolling in the flood
With scattered arms and ensigns, till anon
His swift pursuers from Heaven-gates discern
The advantage, and, descending, tread us
   down
Thus drooping, or with linkèd thunderbolts
Transfix us to the bottom of this gulf?—
Awake, arise, or be for ever fallen!"
   They heard, and were abashed, and up they
      sprung
Upon the wing, as when men wont to watch,
On duty sleeping found by whom they dread,
Rouse and bestir themselves ere well awake.
Nor did they not perceive the evil plight
In which they were, or the fierce pains not
   feel;
Yet to their General's voice they soon obeyed
Innumerable. As when the potent rod
Of Amram's son, in Egypt's evil day,
Waved round the coast, up-called a pitchy
   cloud
Of locusts, warping on the eastern wind,
That o'er the realm of impious Pharaoh hung
Like Night, and darkened all the land of Nile;
So numberless were those bad Angels seen
Hovering on wing under the cope of Hell,
'Twixt upper, nether, and surrounding fires;
Till, as a signal given, the uplifted spear
Of their great Sultan waving to direct
Their course, in even balance down they light
On the firm brimstone, and fill all the plain:
A multitude like which the populous North
Poured never from her frozen loins to pass
Rhene or the Danaw,[6] when her barbarous
   sons
Came like a deluge on the South, and spread
Beneath Gibraltar to the Libyan sands.
Forthwith, from every squadron and each
   band,

---

[3] Galileo.
[4] the admiral, here the flagship.
[5] Nevertheless.

[6] Rhine or Danube.

The heads and leaders thither haste where
    stood
Their great Commander—godlike Shapes, and
    Forms
Excelling human; princely Dignities; 5
And Powers that erst in Heaven sat on thrones,
Though of their names in Heavenly records
    now
Be no memorial, blotted out and rased
By their rebellion from the Books of Life. 10
Nor had they yet among the sons of Eve
Got them new names, till, wandering o'er the
    earth,
Through God's high sufferance for the trial
    of man,
By falsities and lies the greatest part 15
Of mankind they corrupted to forsake
God their Creator, and the invisible
Glory of Him that made them to transform
Oft to the image of a brute, adorned 20
With gay religions full of pomp and gold,
And devils to adore for deities:
Then were they known to men by various
    names,
And various idols through the heathen 25
    world.[7] . . .

BOOK II

The Argument

   *The consultation begun, Satan debates
whether another battle be to be hazarded for
the recovery of Heaven: some advise it, others
dissuade. A third proposal is preferred, mentioned before by Satan—to search the truth of
that prophecy or tradition in Heaven concerning another world, and another kind of creature, equal, or not much inferior, to themselves,
about this time to be created. Their doubt who
shall be sent on this difficult search: Satan,
their chief, undertakes alone the voyage; is
honored and applauded. The council thus
ended, the rest betake them several ways and
to several employments, as their inclinations
lead them, to entertain the time till Satan return. He passes on his journey to Hell-gates;
finds them shut, and who sat there to guard
them; by whom at length they are opened, and
discover to him the great gulf between Hell*

and Heaven. *With what difficulty he passes
through, directed by Chaos, the Power of that
place, to the sight of this new World which he
sought.*

High on a throne of royal state, which far
Outshone the wealth of Ormus[1] and of Ind,
Or where the gorgeous East with richest hand
Showers on her kings barbaric pearl and gold,
Satan exalted sat, by merit raised 10
To that bad eminence; and, from despair
Thus high uplifted beyond hope, aspires
Beyond thus high, insatiate to pursue
Vain war with Heaven; and, by success un-
    taught, 15
His proud imaginations thus displayed:—
   "Powers and Dominions, Deities of Hea-
    ven!—
For, since no deep within her gulf can hold
Immortal vigor, though oppressed and fallen, 20
I give not Heaven for lost: from this descent
Celestial Virtues rising will appear
More glorious and more dread than from no
    fall,
And trust themselves to fear no second fate!— 25
Me though just right, and the fixed laws of
    Heaven,
Did first create your leader—next, free choice,
With what besides in council or in fight
Hath been achieved of merit—yet this loss, 30
Thus far at least recovered, hath much more
Established in a safe, unenvied throne,
Yielded with full consent. The happier state
In Heaven, which follows dignity, might draw
Envy from each inferior; but who here 35
Will envy whom the highest place exposes
Foremost to stand against the Thunderer's aim
Your bulwark, and condemns to greatest share
Of endless pain? Where there is, then, no good
For which to strive, no strife can grow up there 40
From faction: for none sure will claim in Hell
Precedence; none whose portion is so small
Of present pain that with ambitious mind
Will covet more! With this advantage, then,
To union, and firm faith, and firm accord, 45
More than can be in Heaven, we now return
To claim our just inheritance of old,
Surer to prosper than prosperity
Could have assured us; and by what best way,
Whether of open war or covert guile, 50

---

[7] For plot of remainder of Book 1, see "The
Argument," I, 88.

[1] in the Persian Gulf.

We now debate. Who can advise may speak."
   He ceased; and next him Moloch, sceptred
     king,
Stood up—the strongest and the fiercest Spirit
That fought in Heaven, now fiercer by despair. 5
His trust was with the Eternal to be deemed
Equal in strength, and rather than be less
Cared not to be at all; with that care lost
Went all his fear: of God, or Hell, or worse,
He recked not, and these words thereafter 10
     spake:—
   "My sentence is for open war. Of wiles,
More unexpert, I boast not: them let those
Contrive who need, or when they need; not
     now.
For, while they sit contriving, shall the rest— 15
Millions that stand in arms, and longing wait
The signal to ascend—sit lingering here,
Heaven's fugitives, and for their dwelling-place
Accept this dark opprobrious den of shame, 20
The prison of His tyranny who reigns
By our delay? No! let us rather choose,
Armed with Hell-flames and fury, all at once
O'er Heaven's high towers to force resistless
     way,
Turning our tortures into horrid[2] arms 25
Against the Torturer; when, to meet the noise
Of his almighty engine, he shall hear
Infernal thunder, and, for lightning, see
Black fire and horror shot with equal rage 30
Among his Angels, and his throne itself
Mixed with Tartarean sulphur and strange fire,
His own invented torments. But perhaps
The way seems difficult, and steep to scale
With upright wing against a higher foe! 35
Let such bethink them, if the sleepy drench
Of that forgeful lake benumb not still,
That in our proper motion we ascend
Up to our native seat; descent and fall
To us is adverse. Who but felt of late, 40
When the fierce foe hung on our broken rear
Insulting, and pursued us through the Deep,
With what compulsion and laborious flight
We sunk thus low? The ascent is easy, then;
The event is feared! Should we again provoke 45
Our stronger, some worse way his wrath may
     find
To our destruction, if there be in Hell
Fear to be worse destroyed! What can be
     worse 50

Than to dwell here, driven out from bliss, con-
     demned
In this abhorrèd deep to utter woe;
Where pain of unextinguishable fire
Must exercise us without hope of end 5
The vassals of his anger, when the scourge
Inexorably, and the torturing hour,
Calls us to penance? More destroyed than thus,
We should be quite abolished, and expire.
What fear we then? what doubt we to incense 10
His utmost ire? which, to the highth enraged,
Will either quite consume us, and reduce
To nothing this essential—happier far
Than miserable to have eternal being!—
Or, if our substance be indeed divine, 15
And cannot cease to be, we are at worst
On this side nothing; and by proof we feel
Our power sufficient to disturb his Heaven,
And with perpetual inroads to alarm,
Though inaccessible, his fatal Throne: 20
Which, if not victory, is yet revenge."
   He ended frowning, and his look denounced[3]
Desperate revenge, and battle dangerous
To less than gods. On the other side up rose
Belial, in act more graceful and humane. 25
A fairer person lost not heaven; he seemed
For dignity composed, and high exploit.
But all was false and hollow; though his tongue
Dropt manna, and could make the worse ap-
     pear 30
The better reason, to perplex and dash
Maturest counsels: for his thoughts were
     low—
To vice industrious, but to nobler deeds
Timorous and slothful. Yet he pleased the ear, 35
And with persuasive accent thus began:—
   "I should be much for open war, O Peers,
As not behind in hate, if what was urged
Main reason to persuade immediate war
Did not dissuade me most, and seem to cast 40
Ominous conjecture on the whole success;
When he who most excels in fact of arms,
In what he counsels and in what excels
Mistrustful, grounds his courage on despair
And utter dissolution, as the scope 45
Of all his aim, after some dire revenge.
First, what revenge? The towers of Heaven
     are filled
With armèd watch, that render all access
Impregnable: oft on the bordering Deep 50

---

[2] bristling.   [3] threatened.

Encamp their legions, or with obscure wing
Scout far and wide into the realm of Night,
Scorning surprise. Or, could we break our way
By force, and at our heels all Hell should rise
With blackest insurrection to confound
Heaven's purest light, yet our great Enemy,
All incorruptible, would on his throne
Sit unpolluted, and the ethereal mould,
Incapable of stain, would soon expel
Her mischief, and purge off the baser fire, 10
Victorious. Thus repulsed, our final hope
Is flat despair: we must exasperate
The Almighty Victor to spend all his rage;
And that must end us; that must be our cure—
To be no more. Sad cure! for who would lose, 15
Though full of pain, this intellectual being,
Those thoughts that wander through eternity,
To perish rather, swallowed up and lost
In the wide womb of uncreated Night,
Devoid of sense and motion? And who knows, 20
Let this be good, whether our angry Foe
Can give it, or will ever? How he can
Is doubtful; that he never will is sure.
Will He, so wise, let loose at once his ire,
Belike through impotence or unaware, 25
To give his enemies their wish, and end
Them in his anger whom his anger saves
To punish endless? 'Wherefore cease we, then?'
Say they who counsel war; 'we are decreed,
Reserved, and destined to eternal woe; 30
Whatever doing, what can we suffer more,
What can we suffer worse?' Is this, then,
      worst—
Thus sitting, thus consulting, thus in arms?
What when we fled amain, pursued and strook 35
With Heaven's afflicting thunder, and besought
The Deep to shelter us? This Hell then seemed
A refuge from those wounds. Or when we lay
Chained on the burning lake? That sure was
      worse.
What if the breath that kindled those grim
      fires, 40
Awaked, should blow them into sevenfold
      rage,
And plunge us in the flames; or from above
Should intermitted vengeance arm again
His red right hand to plague us? What if all
Her stores were opened, and this firmament
Of Hell should spout her cataracts of fire,
Impendent horrors, threatening hideous fall 50
One day upon our heads; while we perhaps,
Designing or exhorting glorious war,

Caught in a fiery tempest, shall be hurled,
Each on his rock transfixed, the sport and prey
Of racking whirlwinds, or for ever sunk
Under yon boiling ocean, wrapt in chains,
There to converse with everlasting groans, 5
Unrespited, unpitied, unreprieved,
Ages of hopeless end? This would be worse.
War, therefore, open or concealed, alike
My voice dissuades; for what can force or
      guile 10
With Him, or who deceive His mind, whose
      eye
Views all things at one view? He from Heaven's
      highth
All these our motions vain sees and derides, 15
Not more almighty to resist our might
Than wise to frustrate all our plots and wiles.
Shall we, then, live thus vile—the race of
      Heaven
Thus trampled, thus expelled, to suffer here 20
Chains and these torments? Better these than
      worse,
By my advice; since fate inevitable
Subdues us, and omnipotent decree,
The Victor's will. To suffer, as to do, 25
Our strength is equal; nor the law unjust
That so ordains. This was at first resolved,
If we were wise, against so great a foe
Contending, and so doubtful what might fall.
I laugh when those who at the spear are bold 30
And venturous, if that fail them, shrink, and
      fear
What yet they know must follow—to endure
Exile, or ignominy, or bonds, or pain,
The sentence of their conqueror. This is now 35
Our doom; which if we can sustain and bear,
Our Supreme Foe in time may much remit
His anger, and perhaps, thus far removed,
Not mind us not offending, satisfied
With what is punished; whence these raging 40
      fires
Will slacken, if his breath stir not their flames.
Our purer essence then will overcome
Their noxious vapor; or, inured, not feel;
Or, changed at length, and to the place con- 45
      formed
In temper and in nature, will receive
Familiar the fierce heat; and, void of pain,
This horror will grow mild, this darkness light;
Besides what hope the never-ending flight 50
Of future days may bring, what chance, what
      change

Worth waiting—since our present lot appears
For happy though but ill, for ill not worst,
If we procure not to ourselves more woe."

Thus Belial, with words clothed in reason's
garb,
Counselled ignoble ease and peaceful sloth,
Not peace; and after him thus Mammon
spake:—
"Either to disenthrone the King of Heaven
We war, if war be best, or to regain   10
Our own right lost. Him to unthrone we then
May hope, when everlasting Fate shall yield
To fickle Chance, and Chaos judge the strife.
The former, vain to hope, argues as vain
The latter; for what place can be for us   15
Within Heaven's bound, unless Heaven's Lord
Supreme
We overpower? Suppose he should relent,
And publish grace to all, on promise made
Of new subjection; with what eyes could we   20
Stand in his presence humble, and receive
Strict laws imposed, to celebrate his throne
With warbled hymns, and to his Godhead
sing
Forced Halleluiahs, while he lordly sits   25
Our envied sovran, and his altar breathes
Ambrosial odors and ambrosial flowers,
Our servile offerings? This must be our task
In Heaven, this our delight. How wearisome
Eternity so spent in worship paid   30
To whom we hate! Let us not then pursue,
By force impossible, by leave obtained
Unacceptáble, though in Heaven, our state
Of splendid vassalage; but rather seek
Our own good from ourselves, and from our   35
own
Live to ourselves, though in this vast recess,
Free and to none accountable, preferring
Hard liberty before the easy yoke
Of servile pomp. Our greatness will appear   40
Then most conspicuous when great things of
small,
Useful of hurtful, prosperous of adverse,
We can create, and in what place soe'er
Thrive under evil, and work ease out of pain 45
Through labor and endurance. This deep
world
Of darkness do we dread? How oft amidst
Thick clouds and dark doth Heaven's all-ruling
Sire   50
Choose to reside, his glory unobscured,
And with the majesty of darkness round

Covers his throne, from whence deep thunders
roar,
Mustering their rage, and Heaven resembles
Hell!
As He our darkness, cannot we His light   5
Imitate when we please? This desert soil
Wants not her hidden lustre, gems and gold;
Nor want we skill or art from whence to raise
Magnificence; and what can Heaven shew
more?   10
Our torments also may, in length of time,
Become our elements, these piercing fires
As soft as now severe, our temper changed
Into their temper; which must needs remove
The sensible[4] of pain. All things invite   15
To peaceful counsels, and the settled state
Of order, how in safety best we may
Compose our present evils, with regard
Of what we are and where, dismissing quite
All thoughts of war. Ye have what I advise." 20
He scarce had finished, when such murmur
filled
The assembly as when hollow rocks retain
The sound of blustering winds, which all night
long   25
Had roused the sea, now with hoarse cadence
lull
Seafaring men o'erwatched, whose bark by
chance,
Or pinnace, anchors in a craggy bay   30
After the tempest. Such applause was heard
As Mammon ended, and his sentence pleased,
Advising peace: for such another field
They dreaded worse than Hell; so much the
fear   35
Of thunder and the sword of Michaël
Wrought still within them; and no less desire
To found this nether empire, which might rise
By policy and long process of time,
In emulation opposite to Heaven.   40
Which when Beëlzebub perceived—than
whom,
Satan except, none higher sat—with grave
Aspect he rose, and in his rising seemed
A pillar of state. Deep on his front engraven 45
Deliberation sat, and public care;
And princely counsel in his face yet shone,
Majestic, though in ruin. Sage he stood,
With Atlantean shoulders, fit to bear
The weight of mightiest monarchies; his look 50
Drew audience and attention still as night

[4] susceptibility.

[96]

Or summer's noontide air, while thus he
　　spake:—
　"Thrones and Imperial Powers, Offspring
　　of Heaven,
Ethereal Virtues! or these titles now　　　　　5
Must we renounce, and, changing style, be
　　called
Princes of Hell? for so the popular vote
Inclines—here to continue, and build up here
A growing empire; doubtless! while we dream, 10
And know not that the King of Heaven hath
　　doomed
This place our dungeon—not our safe retreat
Beyond his potent arm, to live exempt
From Heaven's high jurisdiction, in new league 15
Banded against his throne, but to remain
In strictest bondage, though thus far removed,
Under the inevitable curb, reserved
His captive multitude. For He, be sure,
In highth or depth, still first and last will reign 20
Sole king, and of his kingdom lose no part
By our revolt, but over Hell extend
His empire, and with iron sceptre rule
Us here, as with his golden those in Heaven.
What sit we then projecting peace and war? 25
War hath determined us and foiled with loss
Irreparable; terms of peace yet none
Vouchsafed or sought; for what peace will be
　　given
To us enslaved, but custody severe,　　　　30
And stripes and arbitrary punishment
Inflicted? and what peace can we return,
But, to our power, hostility and hate,
Untamed reluctance, and revenge, though slow,
Yet ever plotting how the Conqueror least 35
May reap his conquest, and may least rejoice
In doing what we most in suffering feel?
Nor will occasion want, nor shall we need
With dangerous expedition to invade
Heaven, whose high walls fear no assault or 40
　　siege,
Or ambush from the Deep. What if we find
Some easier enterprise? There is a place
(If ancient and prophetic fame in Heaven
Err not)—another World, the happy seat 45
Of some new race, called Man, about this time
To be created like to us, though less
In power and excellence, but favored more
Of Him who rules above; so was His will
Pronounced among the gods, and by an oath 50
That shook Heaven's whole circumference con-
　　firmed.

Thither let us bend all our thoughts, to learn
What creatures there inhabit, of what mould
Or substance, how endued, and what their
　　power
And where their weakness: how attempted
　　best,
By force or subtlety. Though Heaven be shut,
And Heaven's high Arbitrator sit secure
In his own strength, this place may lie ex-
　　posed,
The utmost border of his kingdom, left
To their defence who hold it: here, perhaps,
Some advantageous act may be achieved
By sudden onset—either with Hell-fire
To waste his whole creation, or possess
All as our own, and drive, as we are driven,
The puny habitants; or, if not drive,
Seduce them to our party, that their God
May prove their foe, and with repenting hand
Abolish his own works. This would surpass
Common revenge, and interrupt His joy
In our confusion, and our joy upraise
In His disturbance; when his darling sons,
Hurled headlong to partake with us, shall
　　curse
Their frail original, and faded bliss—
Faded so soon! Advise if this be worth
Attempting, or to sit in darkness here
Hatching vain empires." Thus Beëlzebub
Pleaded his devilish counsel—first devised
By Satan, and in part proposed: for whence,
But from the author of all ill, could spring
So deep a malice, to confound the race
Of mankind in one root, and Earth with Hell
To mingle and involve, done all to spite
The great Creator? But their spite still serves
His glory to augment. The bold design
Pleased highly those Infernal States, and joy
Sparkled in all their eyes: with full assent
They vote: whereat his speech he thus re-
　　news:—
"Well have ye judged, well ended long debate,
Synod of Gods, and, like to what ye are,
Great things resolved, which from the lowest
　　deep
Will once more lift us up, in spite of fate,
Nearer our ancient Seat—perhaps in view
Of those bright confines, whence, with neigh-
　　boring arms,
And opportune excursion, we may chance
Re-enter Heaven; or else in some mild zone
Dwell, not unvisited of Heaven's fair light,

Secure, and at the brightening orient beam
Purge off this gloom: the soft delicious air,
To heal the scar of these corrosive fires,
Shall breathe her balm. But, first, whom shall
    we send 5
In search of this new World? whom shall we
    find
Sufficient? who shall tempt with wandering
    feet
The dark, unbottomed, infinite Abyss, 10
And through the palpable obscure find out
His uncouth way, or spread his aerie flight,
Upborne with indefatigable wings
Over the vast Abrupt, ere he arrive
The happy Isle? What strength, what art can 15
    then
Suffice, or what evasion bear him safe
Through the strict senteries and stations thick
Of Angels watching round? Here he had need
All circumspection: and we now no less 20
Choice in our suffrage; for on whom we send
The weight of all, and our last hope, relies."
    This said, he sat; and expectation held
His look suspense, awaiting who appeared
To second, or oppose, or undertake 25
The perilous attempt. But all sat mute,
Pondering the danger with deep thoughts; and
    each
In other's countenance read his own dismay,
Astonished. None among the choice and prime 30
Of those Heaven-warring champions could be
    found
So hardy as to proffer or accept,
Alone, the dreadful voyage; till, at last,
Satan, whom now transcendent glory raised 35
Above his fellows, with monarchal pride
Conscious of highest worth, unmoved thus
    spake:—
    "O Progeny of Heaven! Empyreal Thrones!
With reason hath deep silence and demur 40
Seized us, though undismayed. Long is the
    way
And hard, that out of Hell leads up to Light.
Our prison strong, this huge convex of fire,
Outrageous to devour, immures us round 45
Ninefold; and gates of burning adamant,
Barred over us, prohibit all egress.
These passed, if any pass, the void profound
Of unessential Night receives him next,
Wide-gaping, and with utter loss of being 50
Threatens him, plunged in that abortive gulf.
If thence he scape, into whatever world,

Or unknown region, what remains him less
Than unknown dangers, and as hard escape?
But I should ill become this throne, O Peers,
And this imperial sovranty, adorned
With splendor, armed with power, if aught
    proposed
And judged of public moment in the shape
Of difficulty or danger, could deter
Me from attempting. Wherefore do I assume
These royalties, and not refuse to reign,
Refusing to accept as great a share
Of hazard as of honor, due alike
To him who reigns, and so much to him due
Of hazard more as he above the rest
High honored sits? Go, therefore, mighty
    Powers,
Terror of Heaven, though fallen; intend at
    home,
While here shall be our home, what best may
    ease
The present misery, and render Hell
More tolerable; if there be cure or charm
To respite, or deceive, or slack the pain
Of this ill mansion: intermit no watch
Against a wakeful Foe, while I abroad
Through all the coasts of dark destruction seek
Deliverance for us all. This enterprise
None shall partake with me." Thus saying, rose
The Monarch, and prevented all reply;
Prudent lest, from his resolution raised,
Others among the chief might offer now,
Certain to be refused, what erst they feared,
And, so refused, might in opinion stand
His rivals, winning cheap the high repute
Which he through hazard huge must earn. But
    they
Dreaded not more the adventure than his
    voice
Forbidding; and at once with him they rose.
Their rising all at once was as the sound
Of thunder heard remote. Towards him they
    bend
With awful reverence prone, and as a God
Extol him equal to the Highest in Heaven.
Nor failed they to express how much they
    praised
That for the general safety he despised
His own: for neither do the Spirits damned
Lose all their virtue; lest bad men should
    boast
Their specious deeds on earth, which glory
    excites,

Or close ambition varnished o'er with zeal.
  Thus they their doubtful consultations dark
Ended, rejoicing in their matchless Chief:
As, when from mountain-tops the dusky clouds
Ascending, while the North-wind sleeps, o'er-   5
    spread
Heaven's cheerful face, the louring element
Scowls o'er the darkened landscape snow or
    shower,
If chance the radiant sun, with farewell sweet, 10
Extend his evening beam, the fields revive,
The birds their notes renew, and bleating herds
Attest their joy, that hill and valley rings.
O shame to men! Devil with devil damned
Firm concord holds; men only disagree   15
Of creatures rational, though under hope
Of heavenly grace, and, God proclaiming
    peace,
Yet live in hatred, enmity, and strife
Among themselves, and levy cruel wars   20
Wasting the earth, each other to destroy:
As if (which might induce us to accord)
Man had not hellish foes enow besides,
That day and night for his destruction wait!
  The Stygian council thus dissolved; and 25
    forth
In order came the grand Infernal Peers:
Midst came their mighty Paramount,[5] and
    seemed
Alone the Antagonist of Heaven, nor less   30
Than Hell's dread Emperor, with pomp su-
    preme,
And god-like imitated state: him round
A globe of fiery Seraphim inclosed
With bright emblazonry, and horrent[6] arms.   35
Then of their session ended they bid cry
With trumpet's regal sound the great result:
Toward the four winds four speedy Cherubim
Put to their mouths the sounding alchymy,
By harald's voice explained; the hollow Abyss 40
Heard far and wide, and all the host of Hell
With deafening shout returned them loud ac-
    claim.
Thence more at ease their minds, and some-
    what raised   45
By false presumptuous hope, the rangèd
    Powers
Disband; and, wandering, each his several way
Pursues, as inclination or sad choice
Leads him perplexed, where he may likeliest 50
    find

Truce to his restless thoughts, and entertain
The irksome hours, till his great Chief return.
Part on the plain, or in the air sublime,
Upon the wing or in swift race contend,
As at the Olympian games or Pythian fields;
Part curb their fiery steeds, or shun the goal
With rapid wheels, or fronted brigads form:
As when, to warn proud cities, war appears
Waged in the troubled sky, and armies rush
To battle in the clouds; before each van
Prick forth the aerie knights, and couch their
    spears,
Till thickest legions close; with feats of arms
From either end of heaven the welkin burns.
Others, with vast Typhœan[7] rage, more fell,
Rend up both rocks and hills, and ride the air
In whirlwind; Hell scarce holds the wild up-
    roar:—
As when Alcides, from Œchalia crowned
With conquest, felt the envenomed robe, and
    tore
Through pain up by the roots Thessalian pines,
And Lichas from the top of Œta. threw
Into the Euboic sea. Others, more mild,
Retreated in a silent valley, sing
With notes angelical to many a harp
Their own heroic deeds, and hapless fall
By doom of battle, and complain that Fate
Free Virtue should enthrall to Force or Chance.
Their song was partial;[8] but the harmony
(What could it less when Spirits immortal
    sing?)
Suspended Hell, and took with ravishment
The thronging audience. In discourse more
    sweet
(For Eloquence the Soul, Song charms the
    Sense)
Others apart sat on a hill retired,
In thoughts more elevate, and reasoned high
Of Providence, Foreknowledge, Will, and
    Fate—
Fixed fate, free will, foreknowledge absolute—
And found no end, in wandering mazes lost.
Of good and evil much they argued then,
Of happiness and final misery,
Passion and apathy, and glory and shame:
Vain wisdom all, and false philosophy!—
Yet, with a pleasing sorcery, could charm
Pain for a while or anguish, and excite

---

[5] leader.   [6] bristling.

[7] monstrous (after Typhon, a legendary monster).
[8] in parts.

Fallacious hope, or arm the obdurèd[9] breast
With stubborn patience as with triple steel.
Another part, in squadrons and gross bands,
On bold adventure to discover wide
That dismal world, if any clime perhaps   5
Might yield them easier habitation, bend
Four ways their flying march, along the banks
Of four infernal rivers, that disgorge
Into the burning lake their baleful streams—
Abhorrèd Styx, the flood of deadly hate;   10
Sad Acheron of sorrow, black and deep;
Cocytus, named of lamentation loud
Heard on the rueful stream; fierce Phlegeton,
Whose waves of torrent fire inflame with rage.
Far off from these, a slow and silent stream,   15
Lethe, the river of oblivion, rolls
Her watery labyrinth, whereof who drinks
Forthwith his former state and being forgets—
Forgets both joy and grief, pleasure and pain.
Beyond this flood a frozen continent   20
Lies dark and wild, beat with perpetual storms
Of whirlwind and dire hail, which on firm land
Thaws not, but gathers heap, and ruin seems
Of ancient pile; all else deep snow and ice,
A gulf profound as that Serbonian bog   25
Betwixt Damiata and Mount Casius old,
Where armies whole have sunk: the parching
   air
Burns frore, and cold performs the effect of
   fire.
Thither, by harpy-footed Furies haled,   30
At certain revolutions all the damned
Are brought; and feel by turns the bitter
   change
Of fierce extremes, extremes by change more 35
   fierce,
From beds of raging fire to starve in ice
Their soft ethereal warmth, and there to pine
Immovable, infixed, and frozen round
Periods of time,—thence hurried back to fire. 40
They ferry over this Lethean sound
Both to and fro, their sorrow to augment,
And wish and struggle, as they pass, to reach
The tempting stream, with one small drop to
   lose   45
In sweet forgetfulness all pain and woe,
All in one moment, and so near the brink;
But Fate withstands, and, to oppose the at-
   tempt,
Medusa with Gorgonian terror guards   50

The ford, and of itself the water flies
All taste of living wight, as once it fled
The lip of Tantalus. Thus roving on
In confused march forlorn, the adventrous
   bands,
With shuddering horror pale, and eyes aghast,
Viewed first their lamentable lot, and found
No rest. Through many a dark and dreary vale
They passed, and many a region dolorous,
O'er many a frozen, many a fiery Alp,
Rocks, caves, lakes, fens, bogs, dens, and
   shades of death—
A universe of death, which God by curse
Created evil, for evil only good;
Where all life dies, death lives, and Nature
   breeds,
Perverse, all monstrous, all prodigious things,
Abominable, inutterable, and worse
Than fables yet have feigned or fear con-
   ceived,
Gorgons, and Hydras, and Chimæras dire.
   Meanwhile the Adversary of God and Man,
Satan, with thoughts inflamed of highest de-
   sign,
Puts on swift wings, and toward the gates of
   Hell
Explores his solitary flight: sometimes
He scours the right hand coast, sometimes the
   left;
Now shaves with level wing the Deep, then
   soars
Up to the fiery concave towering high.
As when far off at sea a fleet descried
Hangs in the clouds, by equinoctial winds
Close sailing from Bengala, or the isles
Of Ternate and Tidore, whence merchants
   bring
Their spicy drugs; they on the trading flood,
Through the wide Ethiopian to the Cape,
Ply stemming nightly toward the pole: so
   seemed
Far off the flying Fiend. At last appear
Hell-bounds, high reaching to the horrid roof,
And thrice threefold the gates; three folds
   were brass,
Three iron, three of adamantine rock,
Impenetrable, impaled with circling fire,
Yet unconsumed.[10]

---

[9] hardened.

---

[10] For the plot of the remainder of Book II, see
"The Argument," I, 93. In the ten books that follow, much theological discussion ensues between

EIGHTEENTH CENTURY

ALEXANDER POPE

Ill and crippled, deprived of university training because of his Catholic faith, Pope (1688–1744) managed to become a literary leader in the Age of Reason. He won recognition in his twenties for his Pastorals, the Essay on Criticism, The Rape of the Lock (which follows), and other poems. His translations of Homer were very profitable. The complete list of his works is too long to give here, but mention must be made of the Epistle to Dr. Arbuthnot, The Dunciad, An Essay on Man, the editing of Shakespeare, and the satires. A spiteful little man, Pope attacked Theobald, his old friend. Lady Mary Wortley Montagu, and Colley Cibber, among others. He was an outstanding member of the Scriblerus Club, which included Swift and Gay. There is intellect but little emotion in Pope's poetry. His mastery of the heroic couplet makes him of interest to poets and critics. He had succinctness and a definite bite to his lines, but he leaves the modern reader wondering just how much poetry there was in his poems. His impact on his own age, however, made him quite definitely a major figure in the history of English literature.

If this poetry section were divided into three, rather than two, main "types," the third would probably be didactic; the selection given in the Lyric Poetry section (I, 242), from Essay on Man, is a good example of didactic poetry. The first epistle, "Of the Nature and State of Man, with Respect to the Universe," is there reprinted in full.

God and Christ; Raphael instructs Adam about the war in Heaven that led up to the expulsion (where Milton begins), about the Creation and operation of the Universe; Satan at last corrupts Adam and Eve (Bk. IX); finally, after a history of the world up to the Crucifixion and Redemption, told them by Michael, Adam and Eve are expelled from the Garden.

THE RAPE OF THE LOCK

AN HEROI-COMICAL POEM

The first canto of this poem, which is based on an actual event, announces the theme, and introduces Belinda. The fourth and fifth cantos, which normally follow the selection here given, describe her anger at the theft and the search for the Lock, which has risen to the heavens, where it becomes a new star.

CANTO II

Not with more glories, in th' ethereal plain
The sun first rises o'er the purpled main,
Than, issuing forth, the rival of his beams
Launched on the bosom of the silver Thames.
5 Fair nymphs, and well-dressed youths around
   her shone,
But every eye was fixed on her alone.
On her white breast a sparkling cross she wore,
Which Jews might kiss, and infidels adore.
10 Her lively looks a sprightly mind disclose,
Quick as her eyes, and as unfixed as those:
Favors to none, to all she smiles extends;
Oft she rejects, but never once offends.
Bright as the sun, her eyes the gazers strike,
15 And, like the sun, they shine on all alike.
Yet graceful ease, and sweetness void of pride,
Might hide her faults, if belles had faults to
   hide;
If to her share some female errors fall,
20 Look on her face, and you'll forget 'em all.
   This nymph, to the destruction of mankind,
Nourished two locks, which graceful hung be-
   hind
In equal curls, and well conspired to deck
25 With shining ringlets the smooth ivory neck.
Love in these labyrinths his slaves detains,

And mighty hearts are held in slender chains.
With hairy springes we the birds betray,
Slight lines of hair surprise the finny prey,
Fair tresses man's imperial race ensnare,
And beauty draws us with a single hair.
   Th' adventurous Baron the bright locks admired;
He saw, he wished, and to the prize aspired.
Resolved to win, he meditates the way,
By force to ravish, or by fraud betray;
For when success a lover's toil attends,
Few ask if fraud or force attained his ends.
   For this, ere Phœbus rose, he had implored
Propitious Heaven, and every Power adored,
But chiefly Love—to Love an altar built
Of twelve vast French romances, neatly gilt.
There lay three garters, half a pair of gloves,
And all the trophies of his former loves;
With tender billet-doux he lights the pyre,
And breathes three amorous sighs to raise the fire.
Then prostrate falls, and begs with ardent eyes
Soon to obtain, and long possess the prize:
The Powers gave ear, and granted half his prayer,
The rest the winds dispersed in empty air.
   But now secure the painted vessel glides,
The sunbeams trembling on the floating tides;
While melting music steals upon the sky,
And softened sounds along the waters die:
Smooth flow the waves, the zephyrs gently play,
Belinda smiled, and all the world was gay.
All but the Sylph—with careful thoughts opprest
Th' impending woe sat heavy on his breast.
He summons straight his denizens of air;
The lucid squadrons round the sails repair:
Soft o'er the shrouds aërial whispers breathe
That seemed but zephyrs to the train beneath.
Some to the sun their insect-wings unfold,
Waft on the breeze, or sink in clouds of gold;
Transparent forms too fine for mortal sight,
Their fluid bodies half dissolved in light,
Loose to the wind their airy garments flew,
Thin glittering textures of the filmy dew,
Dipt in the richest tincture of the skies,
Where light disports in ever-mingling dyes,
While every beam new transient colors flings,
Colors that change whene'er they wave their wings.
Amid the circle, on the gilded mast,

Superior by the head was Ariel placed;
His purple pinions opening to the sun,
He raised his azure wand, and thus begun:
   "Ye Sylphs and Sylphids, to your chief give ear.
Fays, Fairies, Genii, Elves, and Dæmons, hear!
Ye know the spheres and various tasks assigned
By laws eternal to th' aërial kind.
Some in the fields of purest ether play,
And bask and whiten in the blaze of day:
Some guide the course of wandering orbs on high,
Or roll the planets thro' the boundless sky:
Some, less refined, beneath the moon's pale light
Pursue the stars that shoot athwart the night,
Or suck the mists in grosser air below,
Or dip their pinions in the painted bow,
Or brew fierce tempests on the wintry main,
Or o'er the glebe distil the kindly rain.
Others, on earth, o'er human race preside,
Watch all their ways, and all their actions guide:
Of these the chief the care of nations own,
And guard with arms divine the British Throne.
   "Our humbler province is to tend the Fair,
Not a less pleasing, tho' less glorious care;
To save the Powder from too rude a gale;
Nor let th' imprisoned Essences exhale;
To draw fresh colors from the vernal flowers;
To steal from rainbows ere they drop in showers
A brighter Wash; to curl their waving hairs,
Assist their blushes and inspire their airs;
Nay oft, in dreams invention we bestow,
To change a Flounce, or add a Furbelow.
   "This day black omens threat the brightest Fair,
That e'er deserved a watchful spirit's care;
Some dire disaster, or by force or slight;
But what, or where, the Fates have wrapt in night.
Whether the nymph shall break Diana's law,[1]
Or some frail China jar receive a flaw;
Or stain her honor, or her new brocade,
Forget her prayers, or miss a masquerade,
Or lose her heart, or necklace, at a ball;
Or whether Heaven has doomed that Shock must fall.
Haste, then, ye Spirits! to your charge repair:

_____
[1] chastity.

The fluttering fan be Zephyretta's care;
The drops to thee, Brillante, we consign;
And, Momentilla, let the watch be thine;
Do thou, Crispissa, tend her favorite Lock;
Ariel himself shall be the guard of Shock. 5
    "To fifty chosen sylphs, of special note,
We trust th' important charge, the petticoat,
Oft have we known that seven-fold fence to fail,
Tho' stiff with hoops, and armed with ribs of 10 whale.
Form a strong line about the silver bound,
And guard the wide circumference around.
    "Whatever spirit, careless of his charge,
His post neglects, or leaves the Fair at large, 15
Shall feel sharp vengeance soon o'ertake his sins:
Be stopped·in vials, or transfixed with pins,
Or plunged in lakes of bitter washes lie,
Or wedged whole ages in a bodkin's eye; 20
Gums and pomatums shall his flight restrain,
While clogged he beats his silken wings in vain,
Or alum styptics with contracting power
Shrink his thin essence like a rivelled flower: 25
Or, as Ixion² fixed, the wretch shall feel
The giddy motion of the whirling mill,
In fumes of burning chocolate shall glow,
And tremble at the sea that froths below!"
    He spoke; the spirits from the sails descend; 30
Some, orb in orb, around the nymph extend;
Some thread the mazy ringlets of her hair;
Some hang upon the pendants of her ear;
With beating hearts the dire event they wait,
Anxious, and trembling for the birth of Fate. 35

CANTO III

Close by those meads, for ever crowned with flowers,
Where Thames with pride surveys his rising 40 towers
There stands a structure of majestic frame,
Which from the neighboring Hampton takes its name.³
Here Britain's statesmen oft the fall foredoom 45
Of foreign tyrants, and of nymphs at home;
Here, thou, great ANNA!⁴ whom three realms obey,

Dost sometimes counsel take—and sometimes tea.
    Hither the Heroes and the Nymphs resort,
To taste awhile the pleasures of a court;
In various talk th' instructive hours they past,
Who gave the ball, or paid the visit last;
One speaks the glory of the British Queen,
And one describes a charming Indian screen;
A third interprets motions, looks, and eyes;
At every word a reputation dies.
Snuff, or the fan, supply each pause of chat,
With singing, laughing, ogling, *and all that.*
    Meanwhile, declining from the noon of day,
The sun obliquely shoots his burning ray;
The hungry judges soon the sentence sign,
And wretches hang that jurymen may dine;
The merchant from th' Exchange returns in peace,
And the long labors of the toilet cease.
Belinda now, whom thirst of fame invites,
Burns to encounter two adventurous knights,
At Ombre singly to decide their doom,
And swells her breast with conquests yet to come.
Straight the three bands prepare in arms to join,
Each band the number of the sacred Nine.
Soon as she spreads her hand, th' aërial guard
Descend, and sit on each important card:
First Ariel perched upon a Matadore,⁵
Then each according to the rank they bore;
For Sylphs, yet mindful of their ancient race,
Are, as when women, wondrous fond of place.
    Behold four Kings in majesty revered,
With hoary whiskers and a forky beard;
And four fair Queens, whose hands sustain a flower,
Th' expressive emblem of their softer power;
Four Knaves, in garbs succinct, a trusty-band,
Caps on their heads, and halberts in their hand;
And party-colored troops, a shining train,
Draw forth to combat on the velvet plain.
    The skilful nymph reviews her force with care;
"Let Spades be trumps!" she said, and trumps they were.
    Now move to war her sable Matadores,
In show like leaders of the swarthy Moors.

---

² punished for making love to Juno; he was pinned to a turning wheel in Hades.
³ Hampton Court, a palace near London.
⁴ Queen Anne (reigned 1702–1714).

⁵ In ombre, a card game, a matadore was one of three high cards: Spadillio, Manillio, Basto—all named a few lines later.

Spadillio first, unconquerable lord!
Led off two captive trumps, and swept the
    board.
As many more Manillio forced to yield,
And marched a victor from the verdant field.
Him Basto followed, but his fate more hard
Gained but one trump and one plebeian card.
With his broad sabre next, a chief in years,
The hoary Majesty of Spades appears,
Puts forth one manly leg, to sight revealed;   10
The rest his many colored robe concealed.
The rebel Knave, who dares his prince engage,
Proves the just victim of his royal rage.
Even mighty Pam,[6] that kings and queens
    o'erthrew,   15
And mowed down armies in the fights of Loo,
Sad chance of war! now destitute of aid,
Falls undistinguished by the victor Spade.
    Thus far both armies to Belinda yield;
Now to the Baron Fate inclines the field.   20
His warlike amazon her host invades,
Th' imperial consort of the crown of Spades.
The Club's black tyrant first her victim died,
Spite of his haughty mien and barbarous pride:
What boots the regal circle on his head,   25
His giant limbs, in state unwieldy spread;
That long behind he trails his pompous robe,
And of all monarchs only grasps the globe?
    The Baron now his Diamonds pours apace;
Th' embroidered King who shows but half his   30
    face,
And his refulgent Queen, with powers com-
    bined,
Of broken troops an easy conquest find.
Clubs, Diamonds, Hearts, in wild disorder   35
    seen,
With throngs promiscuous strew the level
    green.
Thus when dispersed a routed army runs,
Of Asia's troops, and Afric's sable sons,   40
With like confusion different nations fly,
Of various habit, and of various dye;
The pierced battalions disunited fall
In heaps on heaps; one fate o'erwhelms them
    all.   45
    The Knave of Diamonds tries his wily arts,
And wins (oh shameful chance!) the Queen of
    Hearts.
At this, the blood the virgin's cheek forsook,
A livid paleness spreads o'er all her look;   50

She sees, and trembles at th' approaching ill,
Just in the jaws of ruin, and Codille.[7]
And now (as oft in some distempered state)
On one nice trick depends the general fate!
An Ace of Hearts steps forth: the King unseen
Lurked in her hand, and mourned his captive
    Queen.
He springs to vengeance with an eager pace,
And falls like thunder on the prostrate Ace.
The nymph, exulting, fills with shouts the sky;
The walls, the woods, and long canals reply.
    Oh thoughtless mortals! ever blind to fate,
Too soon dejected, and too soon elate.
Sudden these honors shall be snatched away,
And cursed for ever this victorious day.
    For lo! the board with cups and spoons is
    crowned,
The berries[8] crackle, and the mill turns round;
On shining altars of japan they raise
The silver lamp; the fiery spirits blaze:
From silver spouts the grateful liquors glide,
While China's earth receives the smoking tide.
At once they gratify their scent and taste,
And frequent cups prolong the rich repast.
Straight hover round the Fair her airy band;
Some, as she sipped, the fuming liquor fanned,
Some o'er her lap their careful plumes dis-
    played,
Trembling, and conscious of the rich brocade.
Coffee (which makes the politician wise,
And see thro' all things with his half-shut eyes)
Sent up in vapors to the Baron's brain
New stratagems, the radiant Lock to gain.
Ah, cease, rash youth! desist ere 'tis too late,
Fear the just Gods, and think of Scylla's fate!
Changed to a bird, and sent to flit in air,
She dearly pays for Nisus' injured hair!
    But when to mischief mortals bend their
    will,
How soon they find fit instruments of ill!
Just then, Clarissa drew with tempting grace
A two-edged weapon from her shining case:
So ladies in romance assist their knight,
Present the spear, and arm him for the fight.
He takes the gift with reverence, and extends
The little engine on his fingers' ends;
This just behind Belinda's neck he spread,
As o'er the fragrant steams she bends her
    head.
Swift to the Lock a thousand sprites repair;

---

[6] highest card in game of Loo.   [7] Codille equals "being set."   [8] coffee-beans.

A thousand wings, by turns, blow back the hair;
And thrice they twitched the diamond in her ear;
Thrice she looked back, and thrice the foe drew near.
Just in that instant, anxious Ariel sought
The close recesses of the virgin's thought.
As on the nosegay in her breast reclined,
He watched th' ideas rising in her mind, 10
Sudden he viewed, in spite of all her art,
An earthly Lover lurking at her heart.
Amazed, confused, he found his power expired,
Resigned to fate, and with a sigh retired. 15
 The Peer now spreads the glittering forfex wide,
To inclose the Lock; now joins it, to divide.
Even then, before the fatal engine closed,
A wretched Sylph too fondly interposed;
Fate urged the shears, and cut the Sylph in 20 twain
(But airy substance soon unites again).
The meeting points the sacred hair dissever
From the fair head, for ever, and for ever! 25
 Then flashed the living lightning from her eyes,
And screams of horror rend th' affrighted skies.
Not louder shrieks to pitying Heaven are cast,
When husbands, or when lapdogs breathe their 30 last;
Or when rich China vessels, fallen from high,
In glittering dust and painted fragments lie!
"Let wreaths of triumph now my temples twine," 35
The Victor cried, "the glorious prize is mine!
While fish in streams, or birds delight in air,
Or in a coach and six the British Fair,
As long as Atalantis[9] shall be read,
Or the small pillow grace a lady's bed, 40
While visits shall be paid on solemn days,
When numerous wax-lights in bright order blaze:
While nymphs take treats, or assignations give,
So long my honor, name, and praise shall live! 45
What Time would spare, from Steel receives its date,
And monuments, like men, submit to Fate!
Steel could the labor of the Gods destroy,

And strike to dust th' imperial towers of Troy;
Steel could the works of mortal pride confound
And hew triumphal arches to the ground. 5
What wonder, then, fair Nymph! thy hairs should feel
The conquering force of unresisted steel?"

ROBERT BURNS

Burns (1759–1796) was an obscure farmer who barely made a living and who drew no publicity—except when he was read out in church for affairs with women—until some of his verses reached the right people. Then the poet was lionized by city society, but he was not quite comfortable in such circles. An excise job kept him busy for a while, but he never really found a position which he fitted. Death came early, possibly because of hearty living, though more probably from hard labor in his youth. Burns is remembered as a great lover, of course, and as a nonconformist whose humanism was anathema to the strict Scots clergy. He was more than these, however; there is a strong nationalistic spirit in his poetry which kindles the spirit in any Scot today; there is pleasant sentiment in The Cotter; *there are wildness and romantic high color in* Tam, *keen satire in* Holy Fair, *homely philosophy scattered broadcast through his lines. Apart from the classroom, however, Burns is loved for his songs, his sad-sweet refrains that reach deep down to fundamental things (like the works of Stephen Foster in America), things people know all over the world. (For the lyrics, see I, 263.)*

TAM O'SHANTER

A TALE

When chapman billies[1] leave the street,
And drouthy[2] neebors neebors meet;
As market-days are wearing late,
An' folk begin to tak the gate;[3]
While we sit bousing at the nappy,[4]
An' getting fou and unco happy,
We think na on the lang Scots miles,

---

[9] *The New Atalantis,* by Mrs. Manley, was a contemporary best seller, largely gossip.

[1] peddler fellows.   [2] thirsty.
[3] go home.   [4] ale.

The mosses, waters, slaps,[5] and styles,
That lie between us and our hame,
Whare sits our sulky, sullen dame,
Gathering her brows like gathering storm,
Nursing her wrath to keep it warm.   5

This truth fand honest Tam o'Shanter,
As he frae Ayr ae night did canter:
(Auld Ayr, wham ne'er a town surpasses,
For honest men and bonie lasses).   10

O Tam, had'st thou but been sae wise,
As taen thy ain wife Kate's advice!
She tauld thee weel thou was a skellum,[6]
A blethering, blustering, drunken blellum;[7] 15
That frae November till October,
Ae market-day thou was nae sober;
That ilka melder[8] wi' the miller,
Thou sat as lang as thou had siller;
That ev'ry naig was ca'd a shoe on,   20
The smith and thee gat roaring fou on;
That at the Lord's house, even on Sunday,
Thou drank wi' Kirkton Jean till Monday.
She prophesied, that, late or soon,
Thou would be found deep drowned in   25
        Doon,
Or catched wi' warlocks[9] in the mirk
By Alloway's auld, haunted kirk.

Ah! gentle dames, it gars me greet,[10]   30
To think how monie counsels sweet,
How monie lengthened, sage advices
The husband frae the wife despises!

But to our tale: Ae market-night,   35
Tam had got planted unco right,
Fast by an ingle, bleezing finely,
Wi' reaming swats,[11] that drank divinely;
And at his elbow, Souter[12] Johnie,
His ancient, trusty, droughty cronie: 40
Tam lo'ed him like a very brither;
They had been fou for weeks thegither.
The night drave on wi' sangs and clatter;
And ay the ale was growing better:
The landlady and Tam grew gracious   45
Wi' secret favors, sweet and precious:
The Souter tauld his queerest stories;
The landlord's laugh was ready chorus:

The storm without might rair and rustle,
Tam did na mind the storm a whistle.

Care, mad to see a man sae happy,
E'en drowned himsel amang the nappy.
As bees flee hame wi' lades o' treasure,
The minutes winged their way wi' pleasure:
Kings may be blest but Tam was glorious,
O'er a' the ills o' life victorious!

But pleasures are like poppies spread:
You seize the flow'r, its bloom is shed;
Or like the snow falls in the river,
A moment white—then melts for ever;
Or like the borealis race,
That flit ere you can point their place;
Or like the rainbow's lovely form
Evanishing amid the storm.
Nae man can tether time or tide;
The hour approaches Tam maun ride:
That hour, o' night's black arch the keystane,
That dreary hour Tam mounts his beast in;
And sic a night he taks the road in,
As ne'er poor sinner was abroad in.

The wind blew as 't wad blawn its last;
The rattling showers rose on the blast;
The speedy gleams the darkness swallowed;
Loud, deep, and lang the thunder bellowed:
That night, a child might understand,
The Deil had business on his hand.

Weel mounted on his gray mare Meg,
A better never lifted leg,
Tam skelpit[13] on thro' dub[14] and mire,
Despising wind, and rain, and fire;
Whiles holding fast his guid blue bonnet,
Whiles crooning o'er some auld Scots sonnet,
Whiles glow'ring round wi' prudent cares,
Lest bogles[15] catch him unawares:
Kirk-Alloway was drawing nigh,
Whare ghaists and houlets nightly cry.

By this time he was cross the ford,
Whare in the snaw the chapman smoor'd;[16]
And past the birks and meikle stane,
Whare drunken Charlie brak's neck-bane;
And thro' the whin,[17] and by the cairn,
Whare hunters fand the murdered bairn;

---

[5] gates.   [6] good-for-nothing.
[7] babbler.   [8] every grinding.
[9] wizards.   [10] it makes me weep.
[11] creamy ale.   [12] Cobbler.

[13] hurried.   [14] puddle.
[15] hobgoblins.   [16] smothered.
[17] furze.

And near the thorn, aboon the well,
Whare Mungo's mither hanged hersel.
Before him Doon pours all his floods;
The doubling storm roars thro' the woods;
The lightnings flash from pole to pole; 5
Near and more near the thunders roll:
When, glimmering thro' the groaning trees,
Kirk-Alloway seemed in a bleeze,
Thro' ilka bore the beams were glancing,
And loud resounded mirth and dancing. 10

Inspiring bold John Barleycorn,
What dangers thou canst make us scorn!
Wi'tippenny,[18] we fear nae evil;
Wi' usquabae,[19] we'll face the Devil! 15
The swats sae reamed in Tammie's noddle,
Fair play, he cared na deils a boddle.[20]
But Maggie stood, right sair astonished,
Till, by the heel and hand admonished,
She ventured forward on the light; 20
And, vow! Tam saw an unco sight!

Warlocks and witches in a dance:
Nae cotillion, brent new frae France,
But hornpipes, jigs, strathspeys, and reels, 25
Put life and mettle in their heels.
A winnock-bunker[21] in the east,
There sat Auld Nick, in shape o' beast;
A tousie tyke,[22] black, grim, and large,
To gie them music was his charge: 30
He screwed the pipes, and gart them skirl,
Till roof and rafters a' did dirl.[23]
Coffins stood round, like open presses,
That shawed the dead in their last dresses;
And, by some devilish cantraip[24] sleight, 35
Each in its cauld hand held a light:
By which heroic Tam was able
To note upon the haly table,
A murderer's banes, in gibbet-airns;
Twa span-lang, wee, unchristened bairns; 40
A thief new-cutted frae a rape[25]—
Wi' his last gasp his gab did gape;
Five tomahawks wi' bluid red-rusted;
Five scymitars wi' murder crusted;
A garter which a babe had strangled; 45
A knife a father's throat had mangled—
Whom his ain son o' life bereft—

The grey-hairs yet stack to the heft;
Wi' mair of horrible and awefu',
Which even to name wad be unlawfu'.

As Tammie glowered, amazed, and curious,
The mirth and fun grew fast and furious;
The piper loud and louder blew,
The dancers quick and quicker flew,
They reeled, they set, they crossed, they cleekit,[26]
Till ilka carlin swat and reekit,[27]
And coost her duddies to the wark,[28]
And linket at it in her sark![29]

Now Tam, O Tam! had thae been queans,[30]
A' plump and strapping in their teens!
Their sarks, instead o' creeshie flannen,[31]
Been snaw-white seventeen hunder linen!—
Thir breeks o' mine, my only pair,
That ance were plush, o' guid blue hair,
I wad hae gi'en them off my hurdies[32]
For ae blink o' the bonie burdies!

But withered beldams, auld and droll,
Rigwoodie[33] hags wad spean[34] a foal,
Louping and flinging on a crummock,[35]
I wonder did na turn thy stomach!

But Tam kend what was what fu' brawlie:
There was ae winsome wench and wawlie,[36]
That night enlisted in the core,
Lang after kend on Carrick shore
(For monie a beast to dead she shot,
An' perished monie a bonie boat,
And shook baith meikle corn and bear,[37]
And kept the country-side in fear).
Her cutty sark,[38] o' Paisley harn,[39]
That while a lassie she had worn,
In longitude tho' sorely scanty,
It was her best, and she was vauntie.
Ah! little kend thy reverend grannie,

[18] two-penny ale.   [19] whisky.
[20] he didn't care a farthing for devils.
[21] window seat.   [22] shaggy cur.
[23] ring.   [24] magic.
[25] rope.

[26] clutched.
[27] every hag sweated and steamed.
[28] threw off her clothes for the work.
[29] went at it in her shirt.
[30] wenches.   [31] greasy flannel.
[32] bottom.   [33] withered.
[34] wean (from disgust).   [35] crooked staff.
[36] well-built.   [37] barley.
[38] shirt, smock, chemise.   [39] coarse cloth.

That sark she coft[40] for her wee Nannie,
Wi' twa pund Scots ('twas a' her riches),
Wad ever graced a dance of witches!

But here my Muse her wing maun cour,[41]   5
Sic flights are far beyond her power:
To sing how Nannie lap and flang
(A souple jad she was and strang),
And how Tam stood like ane bewitched,
And thought his very een enriched;   10
Even Satan glowered, and fidged fu' fain,[42]
And hotched[43] and blew wi' might and main;
Till first ae caper, syne anither,
Tam tint[44] his reason a' thegither,
And roars out: "Weel done, Cutty-sark!"   15
And in an instant all was dark;
And scarcely had he Maggie rallied,
When out the hellish legion sallied.

As bees bizz out wi' angry fyke,[45]   20
When plundering herds assail their byke;[46]
As open pussie's[47] mortal foes,
When, pop! she starts before their nose;
As eager runs the market-crowd,
When "Catch the thief!" resounds aloud: 25

So Maggie runs, the witches follow,
Wi' monie an eldritch[48] skriech and hollo.

Ah, Tam! ah, Tam! thou'll get thy fairin![49]
In hell they'll roast thee like a herrin!
In vain thy Kate awaits thy comin!
Kate soon will be a woefu' woman!
Now, do thy speedy utmost, Meg,
And win the key-stane of the brig;
There, at them thou thy tail may toss,
A running stream they dare na cross!
But ere the key-stane she could make,
The fient[50] a tail she had to shake;
For Nannie, far before the rest,
Hard upon noble Maggie prest,
And flew at Tam wi' furious ettle;[51]
But little wist she Maggie's mettle!
Ae spring brought off her master hale,
But left behind her ain grey tail:
The carlin claught her by the rump,
And left poor Maggie scarce a stump.

Now, wha this tale o' truth shall read,
Ilk man, and mother's son, take heed:
Whene'er to drink you are inclined,
Or cutty sarks run in your mind,
Think! ye may buy the joys o'er dear:
Remember Tam o'Shanter's mare.

---

40 bought.   41 lower.
42 fidgeted with pleasure.
43 jerked.   44 lost.
45 fuss.   46 hive.
47 a hare's.

---

48 unearthly.   49 reward.
50 devil.   51 intent.

NINETEENTH CENTURY

WILLIAM WORDSWORTH

The young Wordsworth touring Europe after college was a typical romantic liberal. Guided by his friend Beaupuy, he grew to pity the French common people and hoped for great things from the Revolution, only to be disillusioned by its aftermath; he had an affair with Annette Vallon, who reared his child, and to whom he never made full amends. (Several early lyrics seem to indicate a guilt complex in their persistent pity for woebegone, deserted females.) The rest of his long life (1770–1850) was, however, calm, conservative, even dull. With his sister Dorothy, wife Mary, and friend Coleridge, Wordsworth lived a well-ordered existence. He was a Nature romantic, a pantheist who packed thought and feeling into his lines. His Lyrical Ballads, in part a working-out of his own theories of simple language and powerful feeling, mark the official beginning of the Romantic Movement. With security and a laureateship, however, Wordsworth tended toward ultraconservatism and cold intellectualism. He criticized the later Romantics, whom he outlived. The best of his pieces are among the best in the language; but from Matthew Arnold's time to the present, the number of surviving reprinted poems has steadily dropped, even with friendly editors. Changing tastes account for some of the excisions. The lack of warmth in the poet himself keeps him away from many young readers. But few will argue against the poetic worth of the best sonnets, two or three odes, parts of the Prelude, Michael, *and a half-dozen imperishable lyrics. As a trailblazer in the Romantic Movement, Wordsworth deserves lasting credit for his attacks on neo-classic diction, which had all but wrecked the English language for poetic purposes. (For his lyrics, see I, 269.)*

MICHAEL

A PASTORAL POEM

If from the public way you turn your steps
Up the tumultuous brook of Greenhead Ghyll,[1]
You will suppose that with an upright path
Your feet must struggle; in such bold ascent
The pastoral mountains front you, face to face.
But, courage! for around that boisterous brook
The mountains have all opened out themselves, 30
And made a hidden valley of their own.
No habitation can be seen; but they
Who journey thither find themselves alone
With a few sheep, with rocks and stones, and
    kites
That overhead are sailing in the sky.
It is in truth an utter solitude;
Nor should I have made mention of this Dell
But for one object which you might pass by,
Might see and notice not. Beside the brook 40
Appears a straggling heap of unhewn stones!
And to that simple object appertains
A story—unenriched with strange events,
Yet not unfit, I deem, for the fireside,
Or for the summer shade. It was the first 45
Of those domestic tales that spake to me
Of shepherds, dwellers in the valleys, men
Whom I already loved; not verily
For their own sakes, but for the fields and hills
Where was their occupation and abode. 50

---

[1] ravine.

And hence this Tale, while I was yet a Boy
Careless of books, yet having felt the power
Of Nature, by the gentle agency
Of natural objects, led me on to feel
For passions that were not my own, and think 5
(At random and imperfectly indeed)
On man, the heart of man, and human life.
Therefore, although it be a history
Homely and rude, I will relate the same
For the delight of a few natural hearts; 10
And, with yet fonder feeling, for the sake
Of youthful Poets, who among these hills
Will be my second self when I am gone.

    Upon the forest-side in Grasmere Vale 15
There dwelt a Shepherd, Michael was his
    name;
An old man, stout of heart, and strong of limb.
His bodily frame had been from youth to age
Of an unusual strength: his mind was keen, 20
Intense, and frugal, apt for all affairs,
And in his shepherd's calling he was prompt
And watchful more than ordinary men.
Hence had he learned the meaning of all
    winds,
Of blasts of every tone; and, oftentimes,
When others heeded not, he heard the South
Make subterraneous music, like the noise
Of bagpipers on distant Highland hills.
The Shepherd, at such warning, of his flock
Bethought him, and he to himself would say,
"The winds are now devising work for me!"
And, truly, at all times, the storm, that drives
The traveller to a shelter, summoned him
Up to the mountains: he had been alone 35
Amid the heart of many thousand mists,
That came to him, and left him, on the heights.
So lived he till his eightieth year was past;
And grossly that man errs, who should suppose
That the green valleys, and the streams and 40
    rocks,
Were things indifferent to the Shepherd's
    thoughts.
Fields, where with cheerful spirits he had
    breathed
The common air; hills, which with vigorous
    step
He had so often climbed; which had impressed
So many incidents upon his mind
Of hardship, skill or courage, joy or fear; 50
Which, like a book, preserved the memory
Of the dumb animals, whom he had saved,

Had fed or sheltered, linking to such acts
The certainty of honorable gain;
Those fields, those hills—what could they less?
  —had laid
Strong hold on his affections, were to him   5
A pleasurable feeling of blind love,
The pleasure which there is in life itself.
  His days had not been passed in singleness.
His Helpmate was a comely matron, old,
Though younger than himself full twenty   10
  years.
She was a woman of a stirring life,
Whose heart was in her house: two wheels she
  had
Of antique form; this large, for spinning wool; 15
That small, for flax; and if one wheel had rest,
It was because the other was at work.
The Pair had but one inmate in their house,
An only Child, who had been born to them
When Michael, telling o'er his years, began   20
To deem that he was old,—in shepherd's
  phrase,
With one foot in the grave. This only Son,
With two brave sheep-dogs tried in many a
  storm,
The one of an inestimable worth,   25
Made all their household. I may truly say,
That they were as a proverb in the vale
For endless industry. When day was gone,
And from their occupations out of doors   30
The Son and Father were come home, even
  then,
Their labor did not cease; unless when all
Turned to the cleanly supper-board, and there,
Each with a mess of pottage and skimmed   35
  milk,
Sat round the basket piled with oaten cakes,
And their plain home-made cheese. Yet when
  the meal
Was ended, Luke (for so the Son was named)   40
And his old Father both betook themselves
To such convenient work as might employ
Their hands by the fireside; perhaps to card
Wool for the Housewife's spindle, or repair
Some injury done to sickle, flail, or scythe,   45
Or other implement of house or field.
  Down from the ceiling, by the chimney's
    edge,
That in our ancient uncouth country style
With huge and black projection overbrowed   50
Large space beneath, as duly as the light
Of day grew dim, the Housewife hung a lamp;

An aged utensil, which had performed
Service beyond all others of its kind.
Early at evening did it burn—and late,
Surviving comrade of uncounted hours,
Which, going by from year to year, had found,
And left, the couple neither gay perhaps
Nor cheerful, yet with objects and with hopes,
Living a life of eager industry.
And now, when Luke had reached his eight-
  eenth year,
There by the light of this old lamp they sate,
Father and Son, while far into the night
The Housewife plied her own peculiar work,
Making the cottage through the silent hours
Murmur as with the sound of summer flies.
This light was famous in its neighborhood,
And was a public symbol of the life
That thrifty Pair had lived. For, as it chanced,
Their cottage on a plot of rising ground
Stood single, with large prospect, north and
  south,
High into Easedale, up to Dunmail-Raise,
And westward to the village near the lake;
And from this constant light, so regular
And so far seen, the House itself, by all
Who dwelt within the limits of the vale,
Both old and young, was named THE EVENING
  STAR.
  Thus living on through such a length of
    years,
The Shepherd, if he loved himself, must needs
Have loved his Helpmate; but to Michael's
  heart
This son of his old age was yet more dear—
Less from instinctive tenderness, the same
Fond spirit that blindly works in the blood of
  all—
Than that a child, more than all other gifts
That earth can offer to declining man,
Brings hope with it, and forward-looking
  thoughts,
And stirrings of inquietude, when they
By tendency of nature needs must fail.
Exceeding was the love he bare to him,
His heart and his heart's joy! For often-times
Old Michael, while he was a babe in arms,
Had done him female service, not alone
For pastime and delight, as is the use
Of fathers, but with patient mind enforced
To acts of tenderness; and he had rocked
His cradle, as with a woman's gentle hand.
  And, in a later time, ere yet the Boy

Had put on boy's attire, did Michael love,
Albeit of a stern unbending mind,
To have the Young-one in his sight, when he
Wrought in the field, or on his shepherd's stool
Sat with a fettered sheep before him stretched   5
Under the large old oak, that near his door
Stood single, and, from matchless depth of
    shade,
Chosen for the Shearer's covert from the sun,
Thence in our rustic dialect was called   10
The CLIPPING TREE,[2] a name which yet it
    bears.
There, while they two were sitting in the
    shade,
With others round them, earnest all and blithe, 15
Would Michael exercise his heart with looks
Of fond correction and reproof bestowed
Upon the Child, if he disturbed the sheep
By catching at their legs, or with his shouts
Scared them, while they lay still beneath the   20
    shears.
    And when by Heaven's good grace the boy
        grew up
A healthy Lad, and carried in his cheek
Two steady roses that were five years old,   25
Then Michael from a winter coppice cut
With his own hand a sapling, which he hooped
With iron, making it throughout in all
Due requisites a perfect shepherd's staff,
And gave it to the Boy; wherewith equipt   30
He as a watchman oftentimes was placed
At gate or gap, to stem or turn the flock;
And, to his office prematurely called,
There stood the urchin, as you will divine,
Something between a hindrance and a help;   35
And for this cause not always, I believe,
Receiving from his Father hire or praise;
Though nought was left undone which staff,
    or voice,
Or looks, or threatening gestures, could per- 40
    form.
    But soon as Luke, full ten years old, could
        stand
Against the mountain blasts; and to the heights,
Not fearing toil, nor length of weary ways,   45
He with his Father daily went, and they
Were as companions, why should I relate
That objects which the Shepherd loved before
Were dearer now? that from the Boy there
    came   50

---

[2] Wordsworth notes that in the north "clipping"
is used for "shearing."

Feelings and emanations—things which were
Light to the sun and music to the wind;
And that the old Man's heart seemed born
    again?
    Thus in his Father's sight the Boy grew up:
And now, when he had reached his eighteenth
    year,
He was his comfort and his daily hope.
    While in this sort the simple household lived
From day to day, to Michael's ear there came
Distressful tidings. Long before the time
Of which I speak, the Shepherd had been
    bound
In surety for his brother's son, a man
Of an industrious life, and ample means;
But unforeseen misfortunes suddenly
Had prest upon him; and old Michael now
Was summoned to discharge the forfeiture,
A grievous penalty, but little less
Than half his substance. This unlooked-for
    claim,
At the first hearing, for a moment took
More hope out of his life than he supposed
That any old man ever could have lost.
As soon as he had armed himself with strength
To look his trouble in the face, it seemed
The Shepherd's sole resource to sell at once
A portion of his patrimonial fields.
Such was his first resolve; he thought again,
And his heart failed him. "Isabel," said he,
Two evenings after he had heard the news,
"I have been toiling more than seventy years,
And in the open sunshine of God's love
Have we all lived; yet if these fields of ours
Should pass into a stranger's hand, I think
That I could not lie quiet in my grave.
Our lot is a hard lot; the sun himself
Has scarcely been more diligent than I;
And I have lived to be a fool at last
To my own family. An evil man
That was, and made an evil choice, if he
Were false to us; and if he were not false,
There are ten thousand to whom loss like this
Had been no sorrow. I forgive him;—but
'Twere better to be dumb than to talk thus.
    "When I began, my purpose was to speak
Of remedies and of a cheerful hope.
Our Luke shall leave us, Isabel; the land
Shall not go from us, and it shall be free;
He shall possess it, free as is the wind
That passes over it. We have, thou know'st,
Another kinsman,—he will be our friend

In this distress. He is a prosperous man,
Thriving in trade,—and Luke to him shall go,
And with his kinsman's help and his own
    thrift
He quickly will repair this loss, and then
He may return to us. If here he stay,
What can be done? Where every one is poor,
What can be gained?"
        At this the old Man paused,
And Isabel sat silent, for her mind
Was busy, looking back into past times.
There's Richard Bateman, thought she to her-
    self,
He was a parish-boy;—at the church-door
They made a gathering for him, shillings,
    pence
And halfpennies, wherewith the neighbors
    bought
A basket, which they filled with pedlar's wares;
And, with this basket on his arm, the lad
Went up to London, found a master there,
Who, out of many, chose the trusty boy
To go and overlook his merchandise
Beyond the seas; where he grew wondrous
    rich,
And left estates and monies to the poor,
And, at his birth-place, built a chapel, floored
With marble which he sent from foreign lands.
These thoughts, and many others of like sort,
Passed quickly through the mind of Isabel,
And her face brightened. The old Man was
    glad,
And thus resumed:—"Well, Isabel! this scheme
These two days, has been meat and drink to
    me.
Far more than we have lost is left us yet.
—We have enough;—I wish indeed that I
Were younger;—but this hope is a good hope.
—Make ready Luke's best garments, of the
    best
Buy for him more, and let us send him forth
To-morrow, or the next day, or to-night:
—If he *could* go, the Boy should go to-night."
    Here Michael ceased, and to the fields went
    forth
With a light heart. The Housewife for five
    days
Was restless morn and night, and all day long
Wrought on with her best fingers to prepare
Things needful for the journey of her son.
But Isabel was glad when Sunday came
To stop her in her work: for, when she lay

By Michael's side, she through the last two
    nights
Heard him, how he was troubled in his sleep:
And when they rose at morning she could see
5 That all his hopes were gone. That day at noon
She said to Luke, while they two by them-
    selves
Were sitting at the door, "Thou must not go:
We have no other Child but thee to lose,
10 None to remember;—do not go away,
For if thou leave thy Father he will die."
The Youth made answer with a jocund voice;
And Isabel, when she had told her fears,
Recovered heart. That evening her best fare
15 Did she bring forth, and all together sat
Like happy people round a Christmas fire.
    With daylight Isabel resumed her work;
And all the ensuing week the house appeared
As cheerful as a grove in Spring: at length
20 The expected letter from their kinsman came,
With kind assurances that he would do
His utmost for the welfare of the Boy;
To which, requests were added, that forthwith
He might be sent to him. Ten times or more
25 The letter was read over; Isabel
Went forth to show it to the neighbors round;
Nor was there at that time on English land
A prouder heart than Luke's. When Isabel
Had to her house returned, the old Man said,
30 "He shall depart to-morrow." To this word
The Housewife answered, talking much of
    things
Which, if at such short notice he should go,
Would surely be forgotten. But at length
35 She gave consent, and Michael was at ease.
    Near the tumultuous brook of Greenhead
    Ghyll,
In that deep valley, Michael had designed
To build a Sheepfold; and, before he heard
40 The tidings of his melancholy loss,
For this same purpose he had gathered up
A heap of stones, which by the streamlet's
    edge
Lay thrown together, ready for the work.
45 With Luke that evening thitherward he
    walked:
And soon as they had reached the place he
    stopped,
And thus the old Man spake to him:—"My
50 Son,
To-morrow thou wilt leave me: with full heart
I look upon thee, for thou art the same

That wert a promise to me ere thy birth,
And all thy life has been my daily joy.
I will relate to thee some little part
Of our two histories; 'twill do thee good
When thou art from me, even if I should 5
  touch
On things thou canst not know of.——After
  thou
First cam'st into the world—as oft befalls
To new-born infants—thou didst sleep away 10
Two days, and blessings from thy Father's
  tongue
Then fell upon thee. Day by day passed on,
And still I loved thee with increasing love.
Never to living ear came sweeter sounds 15
Than when I heard thee by our own fireside
First uttering, without words, a natural tune;
While thou, a feeding babe, didst in thy joy
Sing at thy Mother's breast. Month followed
  month,
And in the open fields my life was passed
And on the mountains; else I think that thou
Hadst been brought up upon thy Father's
  knees.
But we were playmates, Luke: among these 25
  hills,
As well thou knowest, in us the old and young
Have played together, nor with me didst thou
Lack any pleasure which a boy can know."
Luke had a manly heart; but at these words 30
He sobbed aloud. The old Man grasped his
  hand,
And said, "Nay, do not take it so—I see
That these are things of which I need not
  speak.
—Even to the utmost I have been to thee 35
A kind and a good Father: and herein
I but repay a gift which I myself
Received at others' hands; for, though now
  old 40
Beyond the common life of man, I still
Remember them who loved me in my youth.
Both of them sleep together: here they lived,
As all their Forefathers had done; and when
At length their time was come, they were not 45
  loth
To give their bodies to the family mold.
I wished that thou should'st live the life they
  lived:
But, 'tis a long time to look back, my Son, 50
And see so little gain from threescore years.
These fields were burthened when they came

to me;
Till I was forty years of age, not more
Than half of my inheritance was mine.
I toiled and toiled; God blessed me in my
  work,
And till these three weeks past the land was
  free.
—It looks as if it never could endure
Another Master. Heaven forgive me, Luke,
If I judge ill for thee, but it seems good
That thou should'st go."
                    At this the old Man paused;
Then, pointing to the stones near which they
  stood,
Thus, after a short silence, he resumed: 15
"This was a work for us; and now, my Son,
It is a work for me. But, lay one stone,—
Here, lay it for me, Luke, with thine own
  hands.
Nay, Boy, be of good hope;—we both may live 20
To see a better day. At eighty-four
I still am strong and hale;—do thou thy part;
I will do mine.—I will begin again
With many tasks that were resigned to thee:
Up to the heights, and in among the storms,
Will I without thee go again, and do
All works which I was wont to do alone,
Before I knew thy face.—Heaven bless thee,
  Boy!
Thy heart these two weeks has been beating
  fast
With many hopes; it should be so;—yes—
  yes—
I knew that thou could'st never have a wish
To leave me, Luke: thou hast been bound to 35
  me
Only by links of love: when thou art gone,
What will be left to us!—But, I forget
My purposes. Lay now the corner-stone,
As I requested; and hereafter, Luke, 40
When thou art gone away, should evil men
Be thy companions, think of me, my Son,
And of this moment; hither turn thy thoughts,
And God will strengthen thee: amid all fear
And all temptation, Luke, I pray that thou 45
May'st bear in mind the life thy Fathers
  lived,
Who, being innocent, did for that cause
Bestir them in good deeds. Now, fare thee
  well; 50
When thou return'st, thou in this place wilt
  see

A work which is not here: a covenant
'Twill be between us; but, whatever fate
Befall thee, I shall love thee to the last,
And bear thy memory with me to the grave."
    The Shepherd ended here; and Luke stooped 5
        down,
And, as his Father had requested, laid
The first stone of the Sheepfold. At the sight
The old Man's grief broke from him; to his
        heart 10
He pressed his Son, he kissèd him and wept;
And to the house together they returned.
—Hushed was that House in peace, or seem-
        ing peace,
Ere the night fell:—with morrow's dawn the 15
        Boy
Began his journey, and when he had reached
The public way, he put on a bold face;
And all the neighbors, as he passed their doors,
Came forth with wishes and with farewell 20
        prayers,
That followed him till he was out of sight.
    A good report did from their Kinsman come,
Of Luke and his well-doing: and the Boy
Wrote loving letters, full of wondrous news, 25
Which, as the Housewife phrased it, were
        throughout
"The prettiest letters that were ever seen."
Both parents read them with rejoicing hearts.
So, many months passed on: and once again 30
The Shepherd went about his daily work
With confident and cheerful thoughts; and
        now
Sometimes when he could find a leisure hour
He to that valley took his way, and there 35
Wrought at the Sheepfold. Meantime Luke be-
        gan
To slacken in his duty; and, at length,
He in the dissolute city gave himself
To evil courses: ignominy and shame 40
Fell on him, so that he was driven at last
To seek a hiding-place beyond the seas.
    There is a comfort in the strength of love;
'Twill make a thing endurable, which else
Would overset the brain, or break the heart: 45
I have conversed with more than one who well
Remember the old Man, and what he was
Years after he had heard this heavy news.
His bodily frame had been from youth to age
Of an unusual strength. Among the rocks 50
He went, and still looked up to sun and cloud,
And listened to the wind; and, as before,

Performed all kinds of labor for his sheep,
And for the land, his small inheritance.
And to that hollow dell from time to time
Did he repair, to build the Fold of which
His flock had need. 'Tis not forgotten yet
The pity which was then in every heart
For the old Man—and 'tis believed by all
That many and many a day he thither went,
And never lifted up a single stone.
    There, by the Sheepfold, sometimes was he
        seen
Sitting alone, or with his faithful Dog,
Then old, beside him, lying at his feet.
The length of full seven years, from time to
        time,
He at the building of this Sheepfold wrought,
And left the work unfinished when he died.
Three years, or little more, did Isabel
Survive her Husband: at her death the estate
Was sold and went into a stranger's hand.
The Cottage which was named the EVENING
        STAR
Is gone;—the ploughshare has been through
        the ground
On which it stood; great changes have been
        wrought
In all the neighborhood:—yet the oak is left
That grew beside their door; and the remains
Of the unfinished Sheepfold may be seen
Beside the boisterous brook of Greenhead
        Ghyll.

SAMUEL TAYLOR COLERIDGE

*The career of Coleridge (1772–1834) is one of
tragic incompleteness, of isolated flashes of
brilliance against a backdrop of frustration. He
never quite realized his universally acknowledged potentialities. He left Cambridge, had a
comic-opera experience in the Army. He wrote,
he lectured, he traveled, he preached. As a
Romantic he naturally hoped for a change in
the world after the French Revolution; with
Southey, Coleridge conceived the idea of a
pantisocracy in America. Both ideals were un-
realized. One reason for his failure to finish
many pieces of poetry was, of course, his ad-
diction to narcotics, but this detail can be
easily exaggerated in importance. Equipped
with a magnificent memory and unusual conversational ability, Coleridge had moments*

when he was king. In The Ancient Mariner *and two fragments,* Kubla Khan *and* Christabel, *he shows to fine advantage his particular type of romanticism, marked by the welding of strangeness and beauty, of music and madness. And while scholars still argue the fine points, it seems safe to say that the future will know Coleridge the poet for only one or two pieces which show clear marks of genius. By then, however, others with more works in print may be completely forgotten; already Scott and Southey, for example, have begun to slip into the shadows.*

THE RIME OF THE ANCIENT MARINER

IN SEVEN PARTS

Argument

How a Ship having passed the Line was driven by storms to the cold Country towards the South Pole; and how from thence she made her course to the tropical Latitude of the Great Pacific Ocean; and of the strange things that befell: and in what manner the Ancyent Marinere came back to his own Country.

PART I

It is an ancient Mariner,
And he stoppeth one of three.
"By thy long gray beard and glittering eye,
Now wherefore stopp'st thou me?

An ancient Mariner meeteth three Gallants bidden to a wedding-feast, and detaineth one.

"The Bridegroom's doors are opened wide,
And I am next of kin,
The guests are met, the feast is set:
May'st hear the merry din."

He holds him with his skinny hand;
"There was a ship," quoth he.
"Hold off! unhand me, gray-beard loon!"
Eftsoons[1] his hand dropt he.

He holds him with his glittering eye—
The Wedding-Guest stood still,
And listens like a three years' child.
The Mariner hath his will.

---

[1] at once.

The Wedding-Guest sat on a stone:
He cannot choose but hear;
And thus spake on that ancient man,
5   The bright-eyed Mariner.

The Wedding-Guest is spellbound by the eye of the old seafaring man and constrained to hear his tale.

"The ship was cheered, the harbor cleared,
Merrily did we drop
10 Below the kirk, below the hill,
Below the light-house top.

"The sun came up upon the left,
Out of the sea came he!
15 And he shone bright, and on the right
Went down into the sea.

The Mariner tells how the ship sailed southward with a good wind and fair weather, till it reached the Line.

"Higher and higher every day,
20 Till over the mast at noon—"
The Wedding-Guest here beat his breast,
For he heard the loud bassoon.

The bride hath paced into the hall,
Red as a rose is she;
Nodding their heads before her goes
The merry minstrelsy.

The Wedding-Guest heareth the bridal music; but the Mariner continueth his tale.

30 The Wedding-Guest he beat his breast,
Yet he cannot choose but hear;
And thus spake on that ancient man,
The bright-eyed Mariner.

35 "And now the Storm-blast came, and he
Was tyrannous and strong:
He struck with his o'ertaking wings,
And chased us south along.

The ship driven by a storm toward the south pole.

40

"With sloping masts and dipping prow,
As who pursued with yell and blow
Still treads the shadow of his foe,
And forward bends his head,
45 The ship drove fast, loud roared the blast,
And southward aye we fled.

"And now there came both mist and snow,
And it grew wondrous cold:
50 And ice, mast-high, came floating by,
As green as emerald.

"And through the drifts the snowy clifts
Did send a dismal sheen:
Nor shapes of men nor beasts we ken—
The ice was all between.

The land of ice, and of fearful sounds where no living thing was to be seen.

"The ice was here, the ice was there,
The ice was all around:
It cracked and growled, and roared and howled, 10
Like noises in a swound!

"At length did cross an Albatross,
Thorough the fog it came;
As if it had been a Christian soul, 15
We hailed it in God's name.

Till a great sea-bird, called the Albatross, came through the snow-fog, and was received with great joy and hospitality.

"It ate the food it ne'er had eat,
And round and round it flew. 20
The ice did split with a thunder-fit;
The helmsman steered us through!

"And a good south wind sprung up behind;
The Albatross did follow, 25
And every day, for food or play,
Came to the mariners' hollo!

And lo! the Albatross proveth a bird of good omen, and followeth the ship as it returned northward through fog and floating ice.

"In mist or cloud, on mast or shroud,
It perched for vespers nine; 30
Whiles all the night, through fog-smoke white,
Glimmered the white moon-shine."

"God save thee, ancient Mariner!
From the fields, that plague thee thus!— 35
Why look'st thou so?"—"With my crossbow
I shot the Albatross! 40

The ancient Mariner inhospitably killeth the pious bird of good omen.

PART II

"The Sun now rose upon the right:
Out of the sea came he,
Still hid in mist, and on the left
Went down into the sea.

"And the good south wind still blew behind,
But no sweet bird did follow,
Nor any day for food or play 50
Came to the mariners' hollo!

"And I had done a hellish thing,
And it would work 'em woe:
For all averred, I had killed the bird
That made the breeze to blow. 5
Ah wretch! said they, the bird to slay,
That made the breeze to blow!

His shipmates cry out against the ancient Mariner, for killing the bird of good luck.

"Nor dim nor red, like God's own head,
The glorious Sun uprist:
Then all averred, I had killed the bird
That brought the fog and mist.
'Twas right, said they, such birds to slay, 15
That bring the fog and mist.

But when the fog cleared off they justify the same, and thus make themselves accomplices in the crime.

"The fair breeze blew, the white foam flew,
The furrow followed free;
We were the first that ever burst 20
Into that silent sea.

The fair breeze continues; the ship enters the Pacific Ocean, and sails northward, even till it reaches the Line.

"Down dropt the breeze, the sails dropt down,
'Twas sad as sad could be; 25
And we did speak only to break
The silence of the sea!

The ship hath been suddenly becalmed.

"All in a hot and copper sky,
The bloody Sun, at noon, 30
Right up above the mast did stand,
No bigger than the Moon.

"Day after day, day after day,
We stuck, nor breath nor motion; 35
As idle as a painted ship
Upon a painted ocean.

"Water, water, everywhere,
And all the boards did shrink; 40
Water, water, everywhere,
Nor any drop to drink.

And the Albatross begins to be avenged.

"The very deep did rot: O Christ!
That ever this should be! 45
Yea, slimy things did crawl with legs
Upon the slimy sea.

"About, about, in reel and rout
The death-fires danced at night; 50
The water, like a witch's oils,
Burnt green, and blue and white.

A Spirit had followed them; one of the invisible inhabitants of this planet, neither departed souls nor angels; concerning whom the learned

"And some in dreams assured were
Of the Spirit that plagued us so;
Nine fathom deep he had followed us
From the land of mist and snow.

Jew, Josephus, and the Platonic Constantinopolitan, Michael Psellus, may be consulted. They are very numerous, and there is no climate or element without one or more.

"And every tongue, through utter drought,
Was withered at the root;
We could not speak, no more than if
We had been choked with soot.

The shipmates, in their sore distress, would fain throw the whole guilt on the ancient Mariner: in sign whereof they hang the dead sea-bird round his neck.

"Ah! well-a-day! what evil looks
Had I from old and young!
Instead of the cross, the Albatross
About my neck was hung.   15

PART III

"There passed a weary time. Each throat
Was parched, and glazed each eye.
A weary time! a weary time!
How glazed each weary eye,
When looking westward, I beheld   25
A something in the sky.

The ancient Mariner beholdeth a sign in the element afar off.

"At first it seemed a little speck,
And then it seemed a mist;
It moved and moved, and took at last   30
A certain shape, I wist.

"A speck, a mist, a shape, I wist!
And still it neared and neared:
As if it dodged a water-sprite,
It plunged and tacked and veered.   35

"With throats unslaked, with black lips baked,
We could nor laugh nor wail;
Through utter drought all dumb we stood!   40
I bit my arm, I sucked the blood,
And cried, A sail! a sail!

At its nearer approach, it seemeth him to be a ship; and at a dear ransom he freeth his speech from the bonds of thirst.

"With throats unslaked, with black lips baked,   45
Agape they heard me call:
Gramercy! they for joy did grin,
And all at once their breath drew in,   50
As they were drinking all.

A flash of joy;

"See! see! (I cried) she tacks no more!
Hither to work us weal,—
Without a breeze, without a tide,
She steadies with upright keel!   5

And horror follows. For can it be a ship that comes onward without wind or tide?

"The western wave was all aflame,
The day was well nigh done!
Almost upon the western wave
Rested the broad bright Sun;
When that strange shape drove suddenly
Betwixt us and the Sun.

"And straight the Sun was flecked with bars,
(Heaven's Mother send us grace!)
As if through a dungeon-grate he peered
With broad and burning face.

It seemeth him but the skeleton of a ship.

"Alas! (thought I, and my heart beat loud)   20
How fast she nears and nears!
Are those her sails that glance in the Sun,
Like restless gossameres?

"Are those her ribs through which the Sun   25
Did peer, as through a grate?
And is that Woman all her crew?
Is that a Death? and are there two?   30
Is Death that woman's mate?

And its ribs are seen as bars on the face of the setting Sun.

The Spectre-Woman and her Deathmate, and no other on board the skeleton-ship.

"Her lips were red, her looks were free,
Her locks were yellow as gold:
Her skin was as white as leprosy,   35
The Night-mare Life-in-Death was she,
Who thicks man's blood with cold.

Like vessel, like crew!

"The naked hulk alongside came,
And the twain were casting dice;   40
'The game is done! I've won! I've won!'
Quoth she, and whistles thrice.

Death and Life-in-Death have diced for the ship's crew, and she (the latter) winneth the ancient Mariner.

"The Sun's rim dips; the stars rush out: 45
At one stride comes the dark;
With far-heard whisper, o'er the sea,
Off shot the spectre-bark.

No twilight within the courts of the Sun.

"We listened and looked sideways up!   50

At the rising of the Moon.

Fear at my heart, as at a cup,
My life-blood seemed to sip!
The stars were dim, and thick the night,
The steersman's face by his lamp gleamed
    white;
From the sails the dew did drip—
Till clomb above the eastern bar
The horned Moon, with one bright star
Within the nether tip.

"One after one, by the star-   *One after another,*
    dogged Moon,
Too quick for groan or sigh,
Each turned his face with a ghastly pang,
And cursed me with his eye.

"Four times fifty living men,   *His shipmates*
(And I heard nor sigh nor groan)   *drop down dead.*
With heavy thump, a lifeless lump,
They dropped down one by one.

"The souls did from their bodies   *But Life-in-Death*
    fly,—   *begins her work on*
They fled to bliss or woe!   *the ancient Mari-*
And every soul, it passed me by   *ner.*
Like the whizz of my cross-bow!"

PART IV

"I fear thee, ancient Mariner!   *The Wedding-*
I fear thy skinny hand!   *Guest feareth that*
And thou art long, and lank, and   *a Spirit is talking*
    brown,   *to him;*
As is the ribbed sea-sand.

"I fear thee and thy glittering eye,
And thy skinny hand, so brown."—
"Fear not, fear not, thou Wed-   *But the ancient*
    ding-Guest!   *Mariner assureth*
This body dropt not down.   *him of his bodily*
    life, and proceed-
    eth to relate his
    horrible penance.

"Alone, alone, all, all alone,
Alone on a wide, wide sea!
And never a saint took pity on
My soul in agony.

"The many men, so beautiful!   *He despiseth the*
And they all dead did lie: *creatures of the*
And a thousand thousand slimy things   *calm.*
Lived on; and so did I.

"I looked upon the rotting sea,   *And envieth that*
And drew my eyes away;   *they should live,*
    and so many lie
    dead.

I looked upon the rotting deck,
And there the dead men lay.

"I looked to heaven, and tried to pray;
But or ever a prayer had gusht,
A wicked whisper came, and made
My heart as dry as dust.

"I closed my lids, and kept them close,
And the balls like pulses beat;
For the sky and the sea, and the sea and the sky
Lay like a load on my weary eye,
And the dead were at my feet.

"The cold sweat melted from   *But the curse*
    their limbs,   *liveth for him in*
Nor rot nor reek did they: *the eye of the dead*
The look with which they looked on me   *men.*
Had never passed away.

"An orphan's curse would drag to hell
A spirit from on high;   *In his loneliness*
But oh! more horrible than that   *and fixedness he*
Is a curse in a dead man's eye!   *yearneth towards*
    the journeying
Seven days, seven nights, I saw   *Moon, and the*
    that curse,   *stars that still*
And yet I could not die.   *sojourn, yet still*
    move onward; and
    everywhere the
    blue sky belongs
    to them, and is
    their appointed
"The moving Moon went up the   *rest, and their*
    sky,   *native country*
And nowhere did abide: *and their own*
Softly she was going up,   *natural homes,*
And a star or two beside—   *which they enter*
    unannounced, as
    lords that are
    certainly ex-
"Her beams bemocked the sultry main,   *pected, and yet*
Like April hoar-frost spread;   *there is a silent*
But where the ship's huge shadow lay,   *joy at their ar-*
The charmèd water burnt alway   *rival.*
A still and awful red.

"Beyond the shadow of the ship,   *By the light of the*
I watched the water-snakes: *Moon he be-*
They moved in tracks of shining   *holdeth God's*
    white,   *creatures of the*
And when they reared, the elfish light   *great calm.*
Fell off in hoary flakes.

"Within the shadow of the ship
I watched their rich attire:
Blue, glossy green, and velvet black,
They coiled and swam; and every track
Was a flash of golden fire.

"O happy living things! no tongue
Their beauty might declare:
A spring of love gushed from my heart,
And I blessed them unaware;
Sure my kind saint took pity on
    me,
And I blessed them unaware;

Their beauty and their happiness.

He blesseth them in his heart.

The spell begins to break.

10 "The selfsame moment I could pray;
And from my neck so free
The Albatross fell off, and sank
Like lead into the sea.

PART V

"Oh sleep! it is a gentle thing,
Beloved from pole to pole!
To Mary Queen the praise be given!
She sent the gentle sleep from Heaven,
That slid into my soul.

"The silly² buckets on the deck,
That had so long remained,
I dreamt that they were filled
    with dew;
And when I awoke, it rained.

By grace of the holy Mother, the ancient Mariner is refreshed with rain.

"My lips were wet, my throat was cold,
My garments all were dank;
Sure I had drunken in my dreams,
And still my body drank.

"I moved, and could not feel my limbs:
I was so light—almost
I thought that I had died in sleep,
And was a blessed ghost.

"And soon I heard a roaring
    wind:
It did not come anear;
But with its sound it shook the
    sails,
That were so thin and sere.

He heareth sounds and seeth strange sights and commotions in the sky and the elements.

"The upper air burst into life!
And a hundred fire-flags sheen,
To and fro they were hurried about!
And to and fro, and in and out,
The wan stars danced between.

"And the coming wind did roar more loud,
And the sails did sigh like sedge;

² empty.

And the rain poured down from one black
    cloud;
The Moon was at its edge.

5 "The thick black cloud was cleft, and still
The Moon was at its side:
Like waters shot from some high crag,
The lightning fell with never a jag,
A river steep and wide.

10 "The loud wind never reached
    the ship,
Yet now the ship moved on!
Beneath the lightning and the Moon
15 The dead men gave a groan.

The bodies of the ship's crew are inspired, and the ship moves on;

"They groaned, they stirred, they all up-
    rose,
Nor spake, nor moved their eyes;
20 It had been strange, even in a dream,
To have seen those dead men rise.

"The helmsman steered, the ship moved on;
Yet never a breeze up blew;
25 The mariners all 'gan work the ropes,
Where they were wont to do;
They raised their limbs like lifeless tools—
We were a ghastly crew.

30 "The body of my brother's son
Stood by me, knee to knee:
The body and I pulled at one rope,
But he said nought to me."

35 "I fear thee, ancient Mariner!"
"Be calm, thou Wedding-Guest!
'Twas not those souls that fled
    in pain,
Which to their corses came again,
40 But a troop of spirits blest:

But not by the souls of the men, nor by demons of earth or middle air, but by a blessed troop of angelic spirits, sent down by the invocation of the guardian saint.

"For when it dawned—they dropped their
    arms,
And clustered round the mast;
45 Sweet sounds rose slowly through their
    mouths,
And from their bodies passed.

"Around, around, flew each sweet sound,
50 Then darted to the Sun;
Slowly the sounds came back again,
Now mixed, now one by one.

"Sometimes a-dropping from the sky
I heard the skylark sing;
Sometimes all little birds that are,
How they seemed to fill the sea and air
With their sweet jargoning!   5

"And now 'twas like all instruments,
Now like a lonely flute;
And now it is an angel's song,
That makes the heavens be mute.

"It ceased; yet still the sails made on   10
A pleasant noise till noon,
A noise like of a hidden brook
In the leafy month of June,
That to the sleeping woods all night
Singeth a quiet tune.   15

"Till noon we quietly sailed on,
Yet never a breeze did breathe:
Slowly and smoothly went the ship,   20
Moved onward from beneath.

"Under the keel nine fathom
   deep,   *The lonesome Spirit from the south-pole carries on the ship as far as the Line, in obedience to the angelic troop, but still requireth vengeance.*
From the land of mist and snow,   25
The Spirit slid: and it was he
That made the ship to go.
The sails at noon left off their tune,
And the ship stood still also.   30

"The Sun, right up above the mast,
Had fixed her to the ocean:
But in a minute she 'gan stir,
With a short uneasy motion—   35
Backwards and forwards half her length
With a short uneasy motion.

"Then like a pawing horse let go,
She made a sudden bound: 40
It flung the blood into my head,
And I fell down in a swound.

"How long in that same fit I lay,   *The Polar Spirit's fellow demons, the invisible inhabitants of the element, take part in his wrong; and two of them relate, one to the other, that penance long and heavy for the ancient Mariner hath been accorded to the Polar Spirit, who returneth southward.*
I have not to declare;   45
But ere my living life returned,
I heard, and in my soul discerned,
Two voices in the air.

" 'Is it he?' quoth one, 'Is this the
   man?   50
By him who died on cross,

With his cruel bow he laid full low
The harmless Albatross.

" 'The Spirit who bideth by himself
In the land of mist and snow,   5
He loved the bird that loved the man
Who shot him with his bow.'

"The other was a softer voice,
As soft as honey-dew: 10
Quoth he, 'The man hath penance done,
And penance more will do.' "

PART VI

First Voice

" 'But tell me, tell me! speak again,
Thy soft response renewing—
What makes that ship drive on so fast?   20
What is the ocean doing?'

Second Voice

" 'Still as a slave before his lord,
The ocean hath no blast;   25
His great bright eye most silently
Up to the Moon is cast—

" 'If he may know which way to go;
For she guides him smooth or grim.   30
See, brother, see! how graciously
She looketh down on him.'

First Voice

" 'But why drives on that ship   *The Mariner hath been cast into a trance; for the angelic power causeth the vessel to drive northward faster than human life could endure.*
   so fast,   35
Without or wave or wind?'

Second Voice

" 'The air is cut away before,   40
And closes from behind.'

" 'Fly, brother, fly! more high, more high!
Or we shall be belated:
For slow and slow that ship will go,   45
When the Mariner's trance is abated.'

"I woke, and we were sailing on   *The supernatural motion is retarded; the Mariner awakes, and his penance begins anew.*
As in a gentle weather:
'Twas night, calm night, the   50
   moon was high;
The dead men stood together.

"All stood together on the deck,
For a charnel-dungeon fitter:
All fixed on me their stony eyes,
That in the Moon did glitter.

"The pang, the curse, with which they died,
Had never passed away:
I could not draw my eyes from theirs,
Nor turn them up to pray.

"And now this spell was snapt: *The curse is finally expiated.*
    once more
I viewed the ocean green,
And looked far forth, yet little saw
Of what had else been seen—

"Like one, that on a lonesome road
Doth walk in fear and dread,
And having once turned round, walks on,
And turns no more his head;
Because he knows, a frightful fiend
Doth close behind him tread.

"But soon there breathed a wind on me,
Nor sound nor motion made:
Its path was not upon the sea,
In ripple or in shade.

"It raised my hair, it fanned my cheek
Like a meadow-gale of spring—
It mingled strangely with my fears,
Yet it felt like a welcoming.

"Swiftly, swiftly flew the ship,
Yet she sailed softly too:
Sweetly, sweetly blew the breeze—
On me alone it blew.

"Oh! dream of joy! is this indeed *And the ancient Mariner beholdeth his native country.*
The light-house top I see?
Is this the hill? is this the kirk?
Is this mine own countree?

"We drifted o'er the harbor-bar,
And I with sobs did pray—
O let me be awake, my God!
Or let me sleep alway.

"The harbor-bay was clear as glass,
So smoothly it was strewn!
And on the bay the moonlight lay,
And the shadow of the Moon.

"The rock shone bright, the kirk no less,
That stands above the rock:
The moonlight steeped in silentness
The steady weathercock.

5

"And the bay was white with silent light
Till, rising from the same,
Full many shapes, that shadows *The angelic spirits leave the dead bodies,*
    were,
10 In crimson colors came.

"A little distance from the prow
Those crimson shadows were:
I turned my eyes upon the deck—
15 Oh, Christ! what saw I there!

"Each corse lay flat, lifeless and flat,
And, by the holy rood!
A man all light, a seraph-man, *And appear in their own forms of light.*
20 On every corse there stood.

"This seraph-band, each waved his hand:
It was a heavenly sight!
They stood as signals to the land,
25 Each one a lovely light;

"This seraph-band, each waved his hand,
No voice did they impart—
No voice; but oh! the silence sank
30 Like music on my heart.

"But soon I heard the dash of oars,
I heard the Pilot's cheer;
My head was turned perforce away,
35 And I saw a boat appear.

"The Pilot and the Pilot's boy,
I heard them coming fast:
Dear Lord in Heaven! it was a joy
40 The dead men could not blast.

"I saw a third—I heard his voice:
It is the Hermit good!
He singeth loud his godly hymns
45 That he makes in the wood.
He'll shrieve my soul, he'll wash away
The Albatross's blood.

PART VII

50 "This Hermit good lives in that *The Hermit of the wood,*
    wood
Which slopes down to the sea.

How loudly his sweet voice he rears!
He loves to talk with marineres
That come from a far countree.

"He kneels at morn, and noon, and eve— 5
He hath a cushion plump:
It is the moss that wholly hides
The rotted old oak-stump.

"The skiff-boat neared: I heard them talk, 10
'Why, this is strange, I trow!
Where are those lights so many and fair,
That signal made but now?'

"'Strange, by my faith!' the Her-   *Approacheth the* 15
mit said—   *ship with wonder.*
'And they answered not our cheer!
The planks looked warped! and see those
    sails,
How thin they are and sere!
I never saw aught like to them,
Unless perchance it were

"'Brown skeletons of leaves that lag
My forest-brook along;
When the ivy-tod is heavy with snow, 25
And the owlet whoops to the wolf below,
That eats the she-wolf's young.'

"'Dear Lord! it hath a fiendish look— 30
(The Pilot made reply)
I am a-feared'—'Push on, push on!'
Said the Hermit cheerily.

"The boat came closer to the ship, 35
But I nor spake nor stirred;
The boat came close beneath the ship,
And straight a sound was heard.

"Under the water it rumbled on,   *The ship suddenly* 40
Still louder and more dread: *sinketh.*
It reached the ship, it split the bay;
The ship went down like lead.

"Stunned by that loud and dread-   *The ancient Mari-* 45
    ful sound,   *ner is saved in the*
Which sky and ocean smote,   *Pilot's boat.*
Like one that hath been seven days drowned
My body lay afloat;
But swift as dreams, myself I found 50
Within the Pilot's boat.

"Upon the whirl, where sank the ship,
The boat spun round and round;
And all was still, save that the hill
Was telling of the sound.

"I moved my lips—the Pilot shrieked
And fell down in a fit;
The holy Hermit raised his eyes,
And prayed where he did sit.

"I took the oars: the Pilot's boy,
Who now doth crazy go,
Laughed loud and long, and all the while
His eyes went to and fro.
'Ha! ha!' quoth he, 'full plain I see,
The Devil knows how to row.'

"And now, all in my own countree,
I stood on the firm land!
The Hermit stepped forth from the boat, 20
And scarcely he could stand.

"'O shrieve me, shrieve me, holy   *The ancient Mari-*
    man!'   *ner earnestly en-*
The Hermit crossed his brow. 25   *treateth the Her-*
'Say quick,' quoth he, 'I bid thee   *mit to shrieve*
    say—   *him; and the*
What manner of man art thou?'   *penance of life*
   falls on him.

"Forthwith this frame of mine was wrenched 30
With a woful agony,
Which forced me to begin my tale;
And then it left me free.

"Since then, at an uncertain hour,   *And ever and anon*
That agony returns; 35   *throughout his*
And till my ghastly tale is told,   *future life an*
This heart within me burns.   *agony constrain-*
   eth him to travel
   from land to land.

"I pass, like night, from land to land;
I have strange power of speech; 40
That moment that his face I see,
I know the man that must hear me:
To him my tale I teach.

"What loud uproar bursts from that door!
The wedding-guests are there: 45
But in the garden-bower the bride
And bride-maids singing are:
And hark the little vesper bell, 50
Which biddeth me to prayer!

"O Wedding-Guest! this soul hath been
Alone on a wide, wide sea:
So lonely 'twas, that God himself
Scarce seemèd there to be.

"Oh sweeter than the marriage-feast,
'Tis sweeter far to me,
To walk together to the kirk
With a goodly company!—

"To walk together to the kirk,
And all together pray,
While each to his great Father bends,
Old men, and babes, and loving friends,
And youths and maidens gay!

"Farewell, farewell! but this I
    tell
To thee, thou Wedding-Guest!
He prayeth well, who loveth well
Both man and bird and beast.

And to teach by his own example love and reverence to all things that God made and loveth.

"He prayeth best, who loveth best
All things both great and small;
For the dear God who loveth us,
He made and loveth all."

The Mariner, whose eye is bright,
Whose beard with age is hoar,
Is gone: and now the Wedding-Guest
Turned from the bridegroom's door.

He went like one that hath been stunned,
And is of sense forlorn:
A sadder and a wiser man,
He rose the morrow morn.

GEORGE GORDON, LORD BYRON

Space does not permit presentation of the classic arguments for and against Byron (1788–1824). As often happens, judgment of his case is difficult for some, because some cannot separate moral from literary values. With a grandfather whose ships perennially ran into storms, a father called "Mad Jack," and a mother who cursed him as a "lame brat," Byron was hardly destined for a dull life. His affairs with women were not entirely his fault; women rarely complained and often invited. But public opinion

forced him into exile, where he could continue to write and to live unconventionally. One is impressed with his vigor: his athletic attempts to compensate for a bad foot by becoming a

5 *fine swimmer; his headlong tilt with Southey over literature, politics, and morals; his boisterous escapades on the Continent (see his inimitable letters); his speed in writing. Byron was a success in his day, where Shelley was*

10 *almost unknown. Byron made money and spent it. He is the Romantic to the French, and, as a matter of fact, does show the best and worst of romanticism in his humanitarian interest in the Greek cause as against the maudlin self-*

15 *pity of the Oriental tales. We must remember, too, that Byron was a living paradox: the poets he praised most consistently were classic poets. There is little profound thought in Byron— but there are some deceivingly clever half-*

20 *truths. There is much that is gallant—and much that is not a little shameful, as in the treatment of his half-sister and his wife. As a poet, he wrote few lyrics in an age of lyricism. His plays and tales are dated or plainly inferior. Looked*

25 *at purely as a poet, Byron survives as an extremely able versifier and satirist; his original ability is seen in the twists and turns of* Don Juan, Beppo, *and* Vision of Judgment. *No one before or since has turned the English language*

30 *so cleverly in the tricksy* ottava rima *form; lyrics, satire, digressions, sermons, autobiography, forced rhymes, playfulness—in* Don Juan *especially—show Byron as master of the Italianate medley-poem.*

35

DON JUAN

The poem opens with a slashing "Dedication"
to Southey; the first canto gives details of
Juan's intrigue with Donna Julia; the second
40 *describes his "cooling-off" voyage, shipwreck,*
and casting away on a Greek island, where he
meets and woos Haidée.

45 CANTO THE THIRD

1

Hail, Muse! *et cetera.*—We left Juan sleeping,
    Pillowed upon a fair and happy breast,
50 And watched by eyes that never yet knew
    weeping,

And loved by a young heart, too deeply
    blest
To feel the poison through her spirit
    creeping,
Or know who rested there, a foe to rest,
Had soiled the current of her sinless years,
And turned her pure heart's purest blood to
    tears.

2

Oh, Love! what is it in this world of ours
    Which makes it fatal to be loved? Ah, why
With cypress branches hast thou wreathed
    thy bowers,
    And made thy best interpreter a sigh?
As those who dote on odors pluck the flowers,
    And place them on their breast—but place
    to die—
Thus the frail beings we would fondly cherish
Are laid within our bosoms but to perish.

3

In her first passion Woman loves her lover,
    In all the others all she loves is love,
Which grows a habit she can ne'er get over,
    And fits her loosely—like an easy glove,
As you may find, whene'er you like to prove
    her:
    One man alone at first her heart can move;
She then prefers him in the plural number,
Not finding that the additions much encumber.

4

I know not if the fault be men's or theirs;
    But one thing's pretty sure; a woman
    planted
(Unless at once she plunge for life in prayers)
    After a decent time must be gallanted;
Although, no doubt, her first of love affairs
    Is that to which her heart is wholly granted;
Yet there are some, they say, who have had
    none,
But those who have ne'er end with only *one.*

5

'Tis melancholy, and a fearful sign
    Of human frailty, folly, also crime,
That love and marriage rarely can combine,
    Although they both are born in the same
    clime;
Marriage from love, like vinegar from wine—
    A sad, sour, sober beverage—by time,

Is sharpened from its high celestial flavor
Down to a very homely household savor.

6

5   There's something of antipathy, as 'twere,
        Between their present and their future state;
    A kind of flattery that's hardly fair
        Is used until the truth arrives too late—
    Yet what can people do, except despair?
10   The same things change their names at
        such a rate;
    For instance—passion in a lover's glorious,
    But in a husband is pronounced uxorious.

7

    Men grow ashamed of being so very fond;
        They sometimes also get a little tired
    (But that, of course, is rare), and then
        despond:
20   The same things cannot always be admired,
    Yet 'tis "so nominated in the bond,"
        That both are tied till one shall have ex-
        pired.
    Sad thought! to lose the spouse that was
        adorning
    Our days, and put one's servants into
        mourning.

8

30 There's doubtless something in domestic
        doings
        Which forms, in fact, true love's antithesis;
    Romances paint at full length people's
        wooings,
35   But only give a bust of marriages;
    For no one cares for matrimonial cooings,
        There's nothing wrong in a connubial kiss:
    Think you, if Laura had been Petrarch's
        wife,
40 He would have written sonnets all his life?

9

    All tragedies are finished by a death,
        All comedies are ended by a marriage;
45 The future states of both are left to faith,
        For authors fear description might disparage
    The worlds to come of both, or fall beneath,
        And then both worlds would punish their
        miscarriage;
50 So leaving each their priest and prayerbook
        ready,
    They say no more of Death or of the Lady.

10

The only two that in my recollection
    Have sung of heaven and hell, or marriage,
    are
Dante and Milton, and of both the affection
    Was hapless in their nuptials, for some bar
Of fault or temper ruined the connection
    (Such things, in fact, it don't ask much to
    mar);
But Dante's Beatrice and Milton's Eve
Were not drawn from their spouses, you
    conceive.

11

Some persons say that Dante meant theology
    By Beatrice, and not a mistress—I,
Although my opinion may require apology,
    Deem this a commentator's phantasy,
Unless indeed it was from his own
    knowledge he
    Decided thus, and showed good reason
    why;
I think that Dante's more abstruse ecstatics
Meant to personify the mathematics.

12

Haidée and Juan were not married, but
    The fault was theirs, not mine: it is not fair,
Chaste reader, then, in any way to put
    The blame on me, unless you wish they
    were;
Then if you'd have them wedded, please to
    shut
    The book which treats of this erroneous
    pair,
Before the consequences grow too awful;
'Tis dangerous to read of loves unlawful.

13

Yet they were happy,—happy in the illicit
    Indulgence of their innocent desires;
But more imprudent grown with every visit,
    Haidée forgot the island was her sire's:
When we have what we like, 'tis hard to
    miss it,
    At least in the beginning, ere one tires;
Thus she came often, not a moment losing,
Whilst her piratical papa was cruising.

14

Let not his mode of raising cash seem strange,

Although he fleeced the flags of every
    nation,
For into a prime minister but change
    His title, and 'tis nothing but taxation;
But he, more modest, took an humbler range
    Of life, and in an honester vocation
Pursued o'er the high seas his watery journey,
And merely practiced as a sea-attorney.

15

The good old gentleman had been detain'd
    By winds and waves, and some important
    captures;
And, in the hope of more, at sea remain'd,
    Although a squall or two had damp'd his
    raptures,
By swamping one of the prizes; he had chain'd
    His prisoners, dividing them like chapters
In number'd lots; they all had cuffs and
    collars,
And averaged each from ten to a hundred
    dollars.

16

Some he disposed of off Cape Matapan
    Among his friends the Mainots; some he
    sold
To his Tunis correspondents, save one man
    Toss'd overboard unsaleable (being old):
The rest—save here and there some richer
    one,
    Reserved for future ransom—in the hold,
Were link'd alike, as for the common people
    he
Had a large order from the Dey of Tripoli.

17

The merchandise was served in the same way,
    Pieced out for different marts in the Levant,
Except some certain portions of the prey,
    Light classic articles of female want,
French stuffs, lace, tweezers, toothpicks, tea-
    pot, tray,
    Guitars and castanets from Alicant,
All which selected from the spoil he gathers,
Robb'd for his daughter by the best of fathers.

18

A monkey, a Dutch mastiff, a mackaw,
    Two parrots, with a Persian cat and kittens,
He chose from several animals he saw—
    A terrier, too, which once had been a

Briton's,
Who dying on the coast of Ithaca,
  The peasants gave the poor dumb thing a
    pittance.
These to secure in this strong blowing weather, 5
He caged in one huge hamper all together.

19

Then, having settled his marine affairs,
  Despatching single cruisers here and there, 10
His vessel having need of some repairs,
  He shaped his course to where his daughter
    fair
Continued still her hospitable cares;
  But that part of the coast being shoal and 15
    bare,
And rough with reefs which ran out many a
    mile,
His port lay on the other side o' the isle.

20

And there he went ashore without delay,
  Having no custom-house nor quarantine
To ask him awkward questions on the way,
  About the time and place where he had 25
    been: ,
He left his ship to be hove down next day,
  With orders to the people to careen;
So that all hands were busy beyond measure,
In getting out goods, ballast, guns, and 30
    treasure.

21

Arriving at the summit of a hill
  Which overlooked the white walls of his 35
    home,
He stopped.—What singular emotions fill
  Their bosoms who have been induced to
    roam!
With fluttering doubts if all be well or ill— 40
  With love for many, and with fears for
    some;
All feelings which o'erleap the years long lost,
And bring our hearts back to their starting-
    post. 45

22

The approach of home to husbands and to
  sires,
  After long traveling by land or water, 50
Most naturally some small doubt inspires—
  A female family's a serious matter

(None trusts the sex more, or so much
    admires—
  But they hate flattery, so I never flatter);
Wives in their husbands' absences grow
    subtler,
And daughters sometimes run off with the
    butler.

23

An honest gentleman at his return
  May not have the good fortune of Ulysses;
Not all lone matrons for their husbands
    mourn,
  Or show the same dislike to suitors' kisses;
The odds are that he finds a handsome urn
  To his memory—and two or three young
    misses
Born to some friend, who holds his wife and
    riches,—
And that *his* Argus[1]—bites him by the
    breeches.

24

If single, probably his plighted fair
  Has in his absence wedded some rich miser;
But all the better, for the happy pair
  May quarrel, and the lady growing wiser,
He may resume his amatory care
  As *cavalier servente*,[2] or despise her;
And that his sorrow may not be a dumb one,
Writes odes on the Inconstancy of Woman.

25

And oh! ye gentlemen who have already
  Some chaste *liaison* of the kind—I mean
An honest friendship with a married lady—
  The only thing of this sort ever seen
To last—of all connections the most steady,
  And the true Hymen (the first's but a
    screen)—
Yet, for all that, keep not too long away,
I've known the absent wronged four times a
    day.

26

Lambro, our sea-solicitor, who had
  Much less experience of dry land than ocean,
On seeing his own chimney-smoke, felt glad;

---

[1] Ulysses' dog, who recognized him after many
years.
[2] escort for married lady.

But not knowing metaphysics, had no notion
Of the true reason of his not being sad,
  Or that of any other strong emotion;
He loved his child, and would have wept the
    loss of her, 5
But knew the cause no more than a philosopher.

27

He saw his white walls shining in the sun,
  His garden trees all shadowy and green;
He heard his rivulet's light bubbling run, 10
  The distant dog-bark; and perceived be-
    tween
The umbrage of the wood, so cool and dun,
  The moving figures, and the sparkling sheen 15
Of arms (in the East all arm)—and various
    dyes
Of colored garbs, as bright as butterflies.

28

And as the spot where they appear he nears, 20
  Surprised at these unwonted signs of idling,
He hears—alas! no music of the spheres,
  But an unhallowed, earthly sound of
    fiddling!
A melody which made him doubt his ears, 25
  The cause being past his guessing or un-
    riddling;
A pipe, too, and a drum, and shortly after,
A most unoriental roar of laughter. 30

29

And still more nearly to the place advancing,
  Descending rather quickly the declivity,
Through the waved branches, o'er the green- 35
    sward glancing,
  'Midst other indications of festivity,
Seeing a troop of his domestics dancing
  Like dervises, who turn as on a pivot, he
Perceived it was the Pyrrhic dance so martial, 40
To which the Levantines are very partial.

30

And further on a group of Grecian girls,
  The first and tallest her white kerchief 45
    waving,
Were strung together like a row of pearls,
  Link'd hand in hand, and dancing: each too
    having
Down her white neck long floating auburn 50
    curls—
  (The least of which would set ten poets

  raving);
Their leader sang—and bounded to her song,
With choral step and voice, the virgin throng.

31

And here, assembled cross-legg'd round their
    trays,
  Small social parties just begun to dine;
Pilaus and meats of all sorts met the gaze,
  And flasks of Samian and of Chian wine,
And sherbet cooling in the porous vase;
  Above them their dessert grew on its vine,
The orange and pomegranate nodding o'er
Dropp'd in their laps, scarce pluck'd, their mel-
    low store.

32

A band of children, round a snow-white ram,
  There wreathe his venerable horns with
    flowers;
While peaceful as if still an unwean'd lamb,
  The patriarch of the flock all gently cowers
His sober head, majestically tame,
  Or eats from out the palm, or playful lowers
His brow, as if in act to butt, and then
Yielding to their small hands, draws back
    again.

33

Their classical profiles, and glittering dresses,
  Their large black eyes, and soft seraphic
    cheeks,
Crimson as cleft pomegranates, their long
    tresses,
  The gesture which enchants, the eye that
    speaks,
The innocence which happy childhood blesses,
  Made quite a picture of these little Greeks;
So that the philosophical beholder
Sigh'd for their sakes—that they should e'er
    grow older.

34

Afar, a dwarf buffoon stood telling tales
  To a sedate gray circle of old smokers,
Of secret treasures found in hidden vales,
  Of wonderful replies from Arab jokers,
Of charms to make good gold and cure bad
    ails,
  Of rocks bewitched that open to the
    knockers,
Of magic ladies who, by one sole act,

Transformed their lords to beasts (but that's a
    fact).

35

Here was no lack of innocent diversion
  For the imagination or the senses,
Song, dance, wine, music, stories from the
    Persian,
  All pretty pastimes in which no offense is;
But Lambro saw all these things with aversion, 10
  Perceiving in his absence such expenses,
Dreading that climax of all human ills,
The inflammation of his weekly bills.

36

Ah! what is man? what perils still environ
  The happiest mortals even after dinner!
A day of gold from out an age of iron
  Is all that Life allows the luckiest sinner;
Pleasure (whene'er she sings, at least) 's a
    siren, 20
  That lures, to flay alive, the young beginner;
Lambro's reception at his people's banquet
Was such as fire accords to a wet blanket.

37

He—being a man who seldom used a word
  Too much, and wishing gladly to surprise
(In general he surprised men with the sword)
  His daughter—had not sent before to
    advise 30
Of his arrival, so that no one stirred;
  And long he paused to re-assure his eyes,
In fact much more astonished than delighted,
To find so much good company invited. 35

38

He did not know (alas! how men will lie)
  That a report (especially the Greeks)
Avouched his death (such people never die), 40
  And put his house in mourning several
    weeks,—
But now their eyes and also lips were dry;
  The bloom, too, had returned to Haidée's
    cheeks. 45
Her tears, too, being returned into their fount,
She now kept house upon her own account.

39

Hence all this rice, meat, dancing, wine, and 50
  fiddling,
Which turned the isle into a place of
    pleasure;
The servants all were getting drunk or idling,
  A life which made them happy beyond
    measure.
5 Her father's hospitality seemed middling,
  Compared with what Haidée did with his
    treasure;
'Twas wonderful how things went on
    improving,
While she had not one hour to spare from
    loving.

40

Perhaps you think, in stumbling on this feast,
15 He flew into a passion, and in fact
There was no mighty reason to be pleased;
  Perhaps you prophesy some sudden act,
The whip, the rack, or dungeon at the least,
  To teach his people to be more exact,
20 And that, proceeding at a very high rate,
He showed the royal penchants of a pirate.

41

You're wrong.—He was the mildest manner'd
25 man
  That ever scuttled ship or cut a throat,
With such true breeding of a gentleman,
  You never could divine his real thought,
No courtier could, and scarcely woman can
  Gird more deceit within a petticoat;
Pity he loved adventurous life's variety,
He was so great a loss to good society.

42

Advancing to the nearest dinner tray,
  Tapping the shoulder of the nighest guest,
With a peculiar smile, which, by the way,
  Boded no good, whatever it expressed,
He asked the meaning of this holiday;
  The vinous Greek to whom he had
    addressed
His question, much too merry to divine
The questioner, filled up a glass of wine,

43

And without turning his facetious head,
  Over his shoulder, with a Bacchant air,
Presented the o'erflowing cup, and said,
  "Talking's dry work, I have no time to
    spare."
A second hiccuped, "Our old master's dead,
  You'd better ask our mistress who's his

heir."
"Our mistress!" quoth a third: "Our mistress!
—pooh!—
You mean our master—not the old, but new."

44

These rascals, being new comers, knew not
whom
They thus addressed—and Lambro's vis-
age fell—
And o'er his eye a momentary gloom
Passed, but he strove quite courteously to
quell
The expression, and endeavoring to resume
His smile, requested one of them to tell
The name and quality of his new patron,
Who seemed to have turned Haidée into a
matron.

45

"I know not," quoth the fellow, "who or what
He is, nor whence he came—and little care;
But this I know, that this roast capon's fat,
And that good wine ne'er washed down bet-
ter fare;
And if you are not satisfied with that,
Direct your questions to my neighbor there;
He'll answer all for better or worse,
For none likes more to hear himself converse."

46

I said that Lambro was a man of patience,
And certainly he showed the best of
breeding,
Which scarce France, the paragon of nations, 35
E'er saw her most polite of sons exceeding;
He bore these sneers against his near relations,
His own anxiety, his heart, too, bleeding,
The insults, too, of every servile glutton,
Who all the time was eating up his mutton. 40

47

Now in a person used to much command—
To bid men come, and go, and come again—
To see his orders done, too, out of hand—
Whether the word was death, or but the
chain—
It may seem strange to find his manners bland; 45
Yet such things are, which I cannot explain,
Though doubtless he who can command
himself
Is good to govern—almost as a Guelf.

48

Not that he was not sometimes rash or so,
But never in his real and serious mood;
5 Then calm, concentrated, and still, and slow,
He lay coil'd like the boa in the wood;
With him it never was a word and blow,
His angry word once o'er, he shed no blood,
But in his silence there was much to rue,
10 And his *one* blow left little work for *two*.

49

He ask'd no further questions, and proceeded
On to the house, but by a private way,
15 So that the few who met him hardly heeded,
So little they expected him that day;
If love paternal in his bosom pleaded
For Haidée's sake, is more than I can say,
But certainly to one deem'd dead returning,
20 This revel seem'd a curious mode of mourn-
ing.

50

If all the dead could now return to life,
(Which God forbid!) or some, or a great
25 many,
For instance, if a husband or his wife
(Nuptial examples are as good as any),
No doubt whate'er might be their former
30 strife,
The present weather would be much more
rainy—
Tears shed into the grave of the connexion
Would share most probably its resurrection.

51

He enter'd in the house no more his home,
A thing to human feelings the most trying,
And harder for the heart to overcome,
40 Perhaps, than even the mental pangs of
dying;
To find our hearthstone turn'd into a tomb,
And round its once warm precincts palely
lying
45 The ashes of our hopes, is a deep grief,
Beyond a single gentleman's belief.

52

He enter'd in the house—his home no more,
50 For without hearts there is no home;—and
felt
The solitude of passing his own door

Without a welcome: *there* he long had
    dwelt,
There his few peaceful days Time had swept
    o'er,
    There his warm bosom and keen eye would
    melt
Over the innocence of that sweet child,
His only shrine of feelings undefiled.

53

He was a man of a strange temperament,
    Of mild demeanour though of savage mood,
Moderate in all his habits, and content
    With temperance in pleasure, as in food,
Quick to perceive, and strong to bear, and
    meant
    For something better, if not wholly good;
His country's wrongs and his despair to save
    her
Had stung him from a slave to an enslaver.

54

The love of power, and rapid gain of gold,
    The hardness by long habitude produced,
The dangerous life in which he had grown old,
    The mercy he had granted oft abused,
The sights he was accustom'd to behold,
    The wild seas, and wild men with whom he
    cruised,
Had cost his enemies a long repentance,
And made him a good friend, but bad ac-
    quaintance.

55

But something of the spirit of old Greece
    Flash'd o'er his soul a few heroic rays,
Such as lit onward to the Golden Fleece
    His predecessors in the Colchian days;
'T is true he had no ardent love for peace—
    Alas! his country show'd no path to praise:
Hate to the world and war with every nation
He waged, in vengeance of her degradation.

56

Still o'er his mind the influence of the clime
    Shed its Ionian elegance, which showed
Its power unconsciously full many a time,—
    A taste seen in the choice of his abode,
A love of music and of scenes sublime,
    A pleasure in the gentle stream that flowed
Past him in crystal, and a joy in flowers,
Bedewed his spirit in his calmer hours.

57

But whatsoe'er he had of love reposed
    On that belovéd daughter; she had been
The only thing which kept his heart unclosed
    Amidst the savage deeds he had done and
    seen,
A lonely pure affection unopposed:
    There wanted but the loss of this to wean
His feelings from all milk of human
    kindness,
And turn him like the Cyclops mad with
    blindness.

58

The cubless tigress in her jungle raging
    Is dreadful to the shepherd and the flock;
The ocean when its yeasty war is waging
    Is awful to the vessel near the rock;
But violent things will sooner bear assuaging,
    Their fury being spent by its own shock,
Than the stern, single, deep, and wordless ire
Of a strong human heart, and in a sire.

59

It is a hard although a common case
    To find our children running restive—they
In whom our brightest days we would retrace,
    Our little selves re-formed in finer clay,
Just as old age is creeping on apace,
    And clouds come o'er the sunset of our day,
They kindly leave us, though not quite alone,
But in good company—the gout or stone.

60

Yet a fine family is a fine thing
    (Provided they don't come in after dinner);
'Tis beautiful to see a matron bring
    Her children up (if nursing them don't
    thin her);
Like cherubs round an altar-piece they cling
    To the fire-side (a sight to touch a sinner).
A lady with her daughters or her nieces
Shine like a guinea and seven-shilling pieces.

61

Old Lambro passed unseen a private gate,
    And stood within his hall at eventide;
Meantime the lady and her lover sate
    At wassail in their beauty and their pride:
An ivory inlaid table spread with state
    Before them, and fair slaves on every side;

Gems, gold, and silver, formed the service
mostly,
Mother of pearl and coral the less costly.

62

The dinner made about a hundred dishes;
  Lamb and pistachio nuts—in short, all
  meats,
And saffron soups, and sweetbreads; and the
  fishes
  Were of the finest that e'er flounced in nets,
Drest to a Sybarite's most pampered
  wishes;
  The beverage was various sherbets
Of raisin, orange, and pomegranate juice,
Squeezed through the rind, which makes it
  best for use.

63

These were ranged round, each in its crystal
  ewer,
  And fruits, and date-bread loaves closed the
  repast,
And Mocha's berry, from Arabia pure,
  In small fine China cups, came in at last;
Gold cups of filigree, made to secure
  The hand from burning, underneath them
  placed;
Cloves, cinnamon, and saffron too were boiled
Up with the coffee, which (I think) they
  spoiled.

64

The hangings of the room were tapestry,
  made
  Of velvet panels, each of different hue,
And thick with damask flowers of silk inlaid;
  And round them ran a yellow border too;
The upper border, richly wrought, displayed,
  Embroidered delicately o'er with blue,
Soft Persian sentences, in lilac letters,
From poets, or the moralists their betters.

65

These Oriental writings on the wall,
  Quite common in those countries, are a kind
Of monitors adapted to recall,
  Like skulls at Memphian banquets, to the
  mind,
The words which shook Belshazzar in his hall,
  And took his kingdom from him: you will
  find,

Though sages may pour out their wisdom's
  treasure,
There is no sterner moralist than Pleasure.

66

A beauty at the season's close grown hectic,
  A genius who has drunk himself to death,
A rake turned Methodistic, or Eclectic
  (For that's the name they like to pray be-
  neath)—
But most, an alderman struck apoplectic,
  Are things that really take away the
  breath,—
And show that late hours, wine, and love are
  able
To do not much less damage than the table.

67

Haidée and Juan carpeted their feet
  On crimson satin, bordered with pale blue;
Their sofa occupied three parts complete
  Of the apartment—and appeared quite
  new;
The velvet cushions (for a throne more meet)
  Were scarlet, from whose glowing center
  grew
A sun embossed in gold, whose rays of tissue,
Meridian-like, were seen all light to issue.

68

Crystal and marble, plate and porcelain,
  Had done their work of splendour; Indian
  mats
And Persian carpets, which the heart bled to
  stain,
  Over the floors were spread; gazelles and
  cats,
And dwarfs and blacks, and such like things
  that gain
  Their bread as ministers and favourites—
  (that's
To say, by degradation)—mingled there
As plentiful as in a court or fair.

69

There was no want of lofty mirrors, and
  The tables, most of ebony inlaid
With mother of pearl or ivory, stood at hand,
  Or were of tortoise-shell or rare woods
  made,
Fretted with gold or silver:—by command,
  The greater part of these were ready spread

With viands and sherbets in ice—and wine—
Kept for all comers at all hours to dine.

70

Of all the dresses I select Haidée's:
  She wore two jelicks—one was of pale
    yellow;
Of azure, pink, and white was her chemise—
  'Neath which her breast heaved like a little
    billow,
With buttons form'd of pearls as large as peas,
  All gold and crimson shone her jelick's
    fellow,
And the striped white gauze baracan that
    bound her,
Like fleecy clouds about the moon, flow'd
    round her.

71

One large gold bracelet clasp'd each lovely
    arm,
  Lockless—so pliable from the pure gold
That the hand stretch'd and shut it without
    harm,
  The limb which it adorn'd its only mould;
So beautiful—its very shape would charm,
  And clinging as if loath to lose its hold,
The purest ore enclosed the whitest skin
That e'er by precious metal was held in.

72

Around, as princess of her father's land,
  A like gold bar above her instep roll'd
Announced her rank; twelve rings were on her
    hand;
  Her hair was starr'd with gems; her veil's
    fine fold
Below her breast was fasten'd with a band
  Of lavish pearls, whose worth could scarce
    be told;
Her orange silk full Turkish trousers furl'd
About the prettiest ankle in the world.

73

Her hair's long auburn waves down to her
    heel
  Flow'd like an Alpine torrent which the sun
Dyes with his morning light,—and would con-
    ceal
  Her person if allow'd at large to run,
And still they seem'd resentfully to feel
  The silken fillet's curb, and sought to shun

Their bonds whene'er some Zephyr caught
    began
To offer his young pinion as her fan.

74

Round her she made an atmosphere of life,
  The very air seem'd lighter from her eyes,
They were so soft and beautiful, and rife
  With all we can imagine of the skies,
And pure as Psyche ere she grew a wife—
  Too pure even for the purest human ties;
Her overpowering presence made you feel
It would not be idolatry to kneel.

75

Her eyelashes, though dark as night, were
    tinged
  (It is the country's custom), but in vain;
For those large black eyes were so blackly
    fringed,
  The glossy rebels mock'd the jetty stain,
And in their native beauty stood avenged:
  Her nails were touch'd with henna; but
    again
The power of art was turn'd to nothing, for
They could not look more rosy than before.

76

The henna should be deeply dyed to make
  The skin relieved appear more fairly fair;
She had no need of this, day ne'er will break
  On mountain tops more heavenly white
    than her:
The eye might doubt if it were well awake,
  She was so like a vision; I might err,
But Shakespeare also says, 'tis very silly
"To gild refinéd gold, or paint the lily."[3]

77

Juan had on a shawl of black and gold,
  But a white baracan, and so transparent
The sparkling gems beneath you might be-
    hold,
  Like small stars through the milky way
    apparent;
His turban, furled in many a graceful fold,
  An emerald aigrette, with Haidée's hair in 't,
Surmounted, as its clasp, a glowing crescent,
Whose rays shone ever trembling, but
  incessant.

[3] *King John*, IV, 2, 11.

78

And now they were diverted by their suite,
  Dwarfs, dancing girls, black eunuchs, and
    a poet,
Which made their new establishment
  complete;
  The last was of great fame, and liked to
    show it;
His verses rarely wanted their due feet;   10
  And for his theme—he seldom sung below
    it,
He being paid to satirize or flatter,
As the Psalm says, "inditing a good matter."[4]

79

He praised the present, and abused the past,
  Reversing the good custom of old days,
An Eastern anti-jacobin at last
  He turned, preferring pudding to *no*   20
    praise—
For some few years his lot had been o'ercast
  By his seeming independent in his lays,
But now he sung the Sultan and the Pasha—
With truth like Southey, and with verse like 25
  Crashaw.

80

He was a man who had seen many changes,
  And always changed as true as any needle; 30
His polar star being one which rather ranges,
  And not the fixed—he knew the way to
    wheedle:
So vile he 'scaped the doom which oft
  avenges;   35
  And being fluent (save indeed when fee'd
    ill),
He lied with such a fervor of intention—
There was no doubt he earned his laureate
  pension.

81

But *he* had genius,—when a turncoat has it,
  The *Vates irritabilis*[5] takes care
That without notice few full moons shall pass 45
  it;
  Even good men like to make the public
    stare:—
But to my subject—let me see—what was it?—
  Oh!—the third canto—and the pretty pair— 50

Their loves, and feasts, and house, and dress,
  and mode
Of living in their insular abode.

82

Their poet, a sad trimmer, but, no less
  In company a very pleasant fellow,
Had been the favorite of full many a mess
  Of men, and made them speeches when
    half mellow;
And though his meaning they could rarely
  guess,
  Yet still they deigned to hiccup or to bellow
The glorious meed of popular applause,
Of which the first ne'er knows the second
  cause.

83

But now being lifted into high society,
  And having picked up several odds and ends
Of free thoughts in his travels for variety,
  He deemed, being in a lone isle, among
    friends,
That, without any danger of a riot, he
  Might for long lying make himself amends;
And, singing as he sung in his warm youth,
Agree to a short armistice with truth.

84

He had travelled 'mongst the Arabs, Turks,
  and Franks,
  And knew the self-loves of the different na-
    tions;
And having lived with people of all ranks,
  Had something ready upon most occasions—
Which got him a few presents and some
  thanks.
He varied with some skill his adulations;
To "do at Rome as Romans do," a piece
Of conduct was which *he* observed in Greece.

85

Thus, usually, when *he*[6] was asked to sing,
  He gave the different nations something
    national;
'Twas all the same to him—"God save the
  king,"
  Or *"Ça ira,"*[7] according to the fashion all:
His muse made increment of any thing,

---

[4] Psalm 45:1.   [5] irritable poet.

[6] Southey.
[7] French Revolutionary song.

From the high lyric down to the low ra-
   tional:
If Pindar[8] sang horse-races, what should hinder
Himself from being as pliable as Pindar?

86

In France, for instance, he would write a
   chanson;
   In England a six canto quarto tale;
In Spain, he'd make a ballad or romance on
   The last war—much the same in Portugal;
In Germany, the Pegasus he'd prance on
   Would be old Goethe's (see what says De
   Staël);[9]
In Italy he'd ape the "Trecentisti;"[10]
In Greece, he'd sing some sort of hymn like
   this t' ye:

1

The Isles of Greece, the Isles of Greece!
   Where burning Sappho loved and sung,
Where grew the arts of war and peace,
   Where Delos[11] rose, and Phœbus sprung!
Eternal summer gilds them yet,
But all, except their sun, is set.

2

The Scian[12] and the Teian[13] muse,
   The hero's harp, the lover's lute,
Have found the fame your shores refuse;
   Their place of birth alone is mute
To sounds which echo further west
Than your sires' "Islands of the Blest."

3

The mountains look on Marathon—
   And Marathon looks on the sea;
And musing there an hour alone,
   I dreamed that Greece might still be free;
For standing on the Persians' grave,
I could not deem myself a slave.

4

A king[14] sate on the rocky brow
   Which looks o'er sea-born Salamis;
And ships, by thousands, lay below,
   And men in nations;—all were his!
He counted them at break of day—
And when the sun set where were they?

5

And where are they? and where art thou,
   My country? On thy voiceless shore
The heroic lay is tuneless now—
   The heroic bosom beats no more!
And must thy lyre, so long divine,
Degenerate into hands like mine?

6

'Tis something, in the dearth of fame,
   Though linked among a fettered race,
To feel at least a patriot's shame,
   Even as I sing, suffuse my face;
For what is left the poet here?
For Greeks a blush—for Greece a tear.

7

Must *we* but weep o'er days more blest?
   Must *we* but blush?—Our fathers bled.
Earth! render back from out thy breast
   A remnant of our Spartan dead!
Of the three hundred grant but three,
To make a new Thermopylæ![15]

8

What, silent still? and silent all?
   Ah! no;—the voices of the dead
Sound like a distant torrent's fall,
   And answer, "Let one living head,
But one arise,—we come, we come!"
'Tis but the living who are dumb.

9

In vain—in vain: strike other chords;
   Fill high the cup with Samian[16] wine!
Leave battles to the Turkish hordes,
   And shed the blood of Scio's vine!
Hark! rising to the ignoble call—
How answers each bold Bacchanal!

10

You have the Pyrrhic dance as yet,
   Where is the Pyrrhic phalanx gone?
Of two such lessons, why forget
   The nobler and the manlier one?
You have the letters Cadmus[17] gave—
Think ye he meant them for a slave?

11

Fill high the bowl with Samian wine!
   We will not think of themes like these!

---

[8] Greek odic poet.   [9] French author.
[10] fourteenth-century Italian artists.
[11] Island, birthplace of Phœbus Apollo.
[12] Homer.   [13] Anacreon.   [14] Xerxes.

[15] scene of heroic defeat of Spartans by Xerxes.
[16] from island Samos.
[17] supposed inventor of alphabet.

It made Anacreon's song divine:
    He served—but served Polycrates—
A tyrant; but our masters then
Were still, at least, our countrymen.

12

The tyrant of the Chersonese[18]
    Was freedom's best and bravest friend;
That tyrant was Miltiades!
    Oh! that the present hour would lend
Another despot of the kind!
Such chains as his were sure to bind.

13

Fill high the bowl with Samian wine!
    On Suli's rock, and Parga's shore,[19]
Exists the remnant of a line
    Such as the Doric mothers bore;
And there, perhaps, some seed is sown,
The Heracleidan blood[20] might own.

14

Trust not for freedom to the Franks—
    They have a king who buys and sells:
In native swords, and native ranks,
    The only hope of courage dwells;
But Turkish force, and Latin fraud,
Would break your shield, however broad.

15

Fill high the bowl with Samian wine!
    Our virgins dance beneath the shade—
I see their glorious black eyes shine;
    But gazing on each glowing maid,
My own the burning tear-drop laves,
To think such breasts must suckle slaves.

16

Place me on Sunium's[21] marbled steep,
    Where nothing, save the waves and I,
May hear our mutual murmurs sweep;
    There, swan-like, let me sing and die:
A land of slaves shall ne'er be mine—
Dash down yon cup of Samian wine!

87

Thus sung, or would, or could, or should have
        sung,
    The modern Greek, in tolerable verse;
If not like Orpheus quite, when Greece was
        young,
    Yet in these times he might have done
        much worse:
His strain displayed some feeling—right or
        wrong;

And feeling, in a poet, is the source
    Of others' feeling; but they are such liars,
And take all colors—like the hands of dyers.

88

But words are things, and a small drop of ink,
    Falling like dew, upon a thought, produces
That which makes thousands, perhaps millions,
        think;
    'Tis strange, the shortest letter which man
        uses
Instead of speech, may form a lasting link
    Of ages; to what straits old Time reduces
Frail man, when paper—even a rag like this,
Survives himself, his tomb, and all that's his.

89

And when his bones are dust, his grave a
        blank,
    His station, generation, even his nation,
Become a thing, or nothing, save to rank
    In chronological commemoration,
Some dull MS. Oblivion long has sank,
    Or graven stone found in a barrack's station
In digging the foundation of a closet,
May turn his name up, as a rare deposit.

90

And Glory long has made the sages smile;
    'Tis something, nothing, words, illusion,
        wind—
Depending more upon the historian's style
    Than on the name a person leaves behind:
Troy owes to Homer what whist owes to
        Hoyle:
    The present century was growing blind
To the great Marlborough's skill in giving
        knocks,
Until his late Life by Archdeacon Coxe.

91

Milton's the Prince of Poets—so we say;
    A little heavy, but no less divine:
An independent being in his day—
    Learned, pious, temperate in love and wine;
But, his life falling into Johnson's way,
    We're told this great High Priest of all the
        Nine
Was whipt at college—a harsh sire—odd
        spouse,
For the first Mrs. Milton left his house.

[18] Gallipoli.   [20] blood of Hercules.
[19] in Albania.   [21] in Greece.

92

All these are, *certes,* entertaining facts,
  Like Shakespeare's stealing deer, Lord
    Bacon's bribes;
Like Titus' youth, and Caesar's earliest acts;
  Like Burns (whom Doctor Currie well de-
    scribes);
Like Cromwell's pranks;—but although Truth
    exacts
  These amiable descriptions from the scribes,
As most essential to their hero's story,
They do not much contribute to his glory.

93

All are not moralists, like Southey, when
  He prated to the world of "Pantisocracy;"
Or Wordsworth unexcised, unhired, who then
  Seasoned his pedlar poems with Democ-
    racy;
Or Coleridge, long before his flighty pen
  Let to the *Morning Post* its aristocracy;
When he and Southey, following the same
    path,
Espoused two partners (milliners of Bath).

94

Such names at present cut a convict figure,
  The very Botany Bay[22] in moral geography;
Their loyal treason, renegado rigor,
  Are good manure for their more bare biog-
    raphy.
Wordsworth's last quarto, by the way, is bigger
  Than any since the birthday of typography;
A drowsy frowsy poem, called the "*Excur-
    sion,*"
Writ in a manner which is my aversion.

95

He there builds up a formidable dyke
  Between his own and others' intellect;
But Wordsworth's poem, and his followers,
    like
  Joanna Southcote's[23] Shiloh, and her sect,
Are things which in this century don't strike
  The public mind,—so few are the elect;
And the new births of both their stale vir-
    ginities
Have proved but dropsies, taken for divinities.

[22] English convict colony in Australia.
[23] a crank who said she was to bear a new Mes-
siah.

96

But let me to my story: I must own,
  If I have any fault, it is digression—
5 Leaving my people to proceed alone,
  While I soliloquize beyond expression;
But these are my addresses from the throne,
  Which put off business to the ensuing
    session:
10 Forgetting each omission is a loss to
  The world, not quite so great as Ariosto.[24]

97

I know that what our neighbors call "*lon-
15   gueurs*"[25]
  (We've not so good a *word,* but have the
    thing,
In that complete perfection which insures
  An epic from Bob Southey every spring),
20 Form not the true temptation which allures
  The reader; but 'twould not be hard to bring
Some fine examples of the *epopée,*[26]
To prove its grand ingredient is *ennui.*

98

We learn from Horace, "Homer sometimes
    sleeps;"
  We feel without him,—Wordsworth some-
    times wakes,—
To show with what complacency he creeps,
30   With his dear "*Waggoners,*" around his
    lakes.
He wishes for "a boat" to sail the deeps—
  Of Ocean?—No, of air; and then he makes
35 Another outcry for "a little boat,"
And drivels seas to set it well afloat.

99

If he must fain sweep o'er the ethereal plain,
  And Pegasus runs restive in his "Waggon,"
Could he not beg the loan of Charles's Wain?[27]
  Or pray Medea for a single dragon?
Or if, too classic for his vulgar brain,
  He feared his neck to venture such a nag
    on,
And he must needs mount nearer to the moon,
Could not the blockhead ask for a balloon?

[24] author of *Orlando Furioso.*
[25] boredom.
[26] epic.
[27] Charles's Wagon, the constellation known as
the "Dipper."

100

"Pedlars," and "Boats," and "Waggons!"
    Oh! ye shades
Of Pope and Dryden, are we come to this?
That trash of such sort not alone evades
    Contempt, but from the bathos' vast abyss
Floats scumlike uppermost, and these Jack
    Cades
    Of sense and song above your graves may
    hiss—
The "little boatman" and his "Peter Bell"
Can sneer at him who drew "Achitophel"![28]

101

T' our tale.—The feast was over, the slaves
    gone,
    The dwarfs and dancing girls had all re-
    tired;
The Arab lore and Poet's song were done,
    And every sound of revelry expired;
The lady and her lover, left alone,
    The rosy flood of Twilight's sky admired;—
Ave Maria! o'er the earth and sea,
That heavenliest hour of Heaven is worthi-
    est thee!

102

Ave Maria! blessèd be the hour!
    The time, the clime, the spot, where I so oft
Have felt that moment in its fullest power
    Sink o'er the earth so beautiful and soft,
While swung the deep bell in the distant
    tower,
    Or the faint dying day-hymn stole aloft,
And not a breath crept through the rosy air,
And yet the forest leaves seemed stirred with
    prayer.

103

Ave Maria! 'tis the hour of prayer!
Ave Maria! 'tis the hour of Love!
Ave Maria! may our spirits dare
    Look up to thine and to thy Son's above!
Ave Maria! oh that face so fair!
    Those downcast eyes beneath the Almighty
    Dove—
What though 'tis but a pictured image?—
    strike—
That painting is no idol,—'tis too like.

104

Some kinder casuists are pleased to say,
    In nameless print—that I have no devotion;
But set those persons down with me to pray,
    And you shall see who has the properest
    notion
Of getting into Heaven the shortest way;
    My altars are the mountains and the Ocean,
Earth, air, stars,—all that springs from the
    great Whole,
Who hath produced, and will receive the Soul.

105

Sweet Hour of Twilight!—in the solitude
    Of the pine forest, and the silent shore
Which bounds Ravenna's immemorial wood,
    Rooted where once the Adrian wave flowed
    o'er,
To where the last Caesarean fortress stood,
    Evergreen forest! which Boccaccio's lore
And Dryden's lay made haunted ground to
    me,
How have I loved the twilight hour and thee!

106

The shrill cicalas, people of the pine,
    Making their summer lives one ceaseless
    song,
Were the sole echoes, save my steed's and
    mine,
    And Vesper bell's that rose the boughs
    along;
The spectre huntsman[29] of Onesti's line,
    His hell-dogs, and their chase, and the fair
    throng
Which learned from this example not to fly
From a true lover,—shadowed my mind's eye.

107

Oh, Hesperus! thou bringest all good things—
    Home to the weary, to the hungry cheer,
To the young bird the parent's brooding
    wings,
    The welcome stall to the o'erlabored steer;
Whate'er of peace about our hearthstone
    clings,
    Whate'er our household gods protect of
    dear,
Are gathered round us by thy look of rest;

---

[28] Dryden's *Absalom and Achitophel.*

[29] reference to story by Boccaccio.

Thou bring'st the child, too, to the mother's
  breast.

108

Soft Hour! which wakes the wish and melts 5
    the heart
  Of those who sail the seas, on the first day
When they from their sweet friends are torn
  apart;
  Or fills with love the pilgrim on his way 10
As the far bell of Vesper makes him start,
  Seeming to weep the dying day's decay;
Is this a fancy which our reason scorns?
Ah! surely Nothing dies but Something
    mourns! 15

109

When Nero perished by the justest doom
  Which ever the Destroyer yet destroyed,
Amidst the roar of liberated Rome,
  Of nations freed, and the world overjoyed, 20
Some hands unseen strewed flowers upon his
    tomb:
  Perhaps the weakness of a heart not void
Of feeling for some kindness done, when 25
    Power
Had left the wretch an uncorrupted hour.

110

But I'm digressing; what on earth has Nero, 30
  Or any such like sovereign buffoons,
To do with the transactions of my hero,
  More than such madmen's fellow man—
    the moon's?
Sure my invention must be down at zero, 35
  And I grown one of many "wooden spoons"
Of verse (the name with which we Cantabs[30]
    please
To dub the last of honors in degrees).

111

I feel this tediousness will never do—
  'Tis being *too* epic, and I must cut down
(In copying) this long canto into two;
  They'll never find it out, unless I own 45
The fact, excepting some experienced few;
  And then as an improvement 'twill be
    shown:
I'll prove that such the opinion of the critic is
From Aristotle *passim*.—See Ποιητ ικης.[31]

---

[30] Cambridge students.   [31] *The Poetics.*

The following cantos—the poem is sixteen cantos
in length—narrate the return of Haidée's father,
Lambro the pirate, who captures Juan and sells him
as a slave in Constantinople; the death of Haidée;
Juan's slavery under a sultana, from whom he
escapes, only to become involved in a Russian military campaign; his arrival at the court of Catharine
the Great; his appointment as ambassador to England; and finally, in the closing stages, his observations on English social life.

JOHN KEATS

*Where Shelley and Byron were literally of the
aristocracy, Keats (1795–1821) was of the people, respectable and successful innkeepers and
ostlers. From such origins came the poet who
lived fewer years than any other major figure
in English literature; whose death was, in its
prematurity, its frustration of high genius, perhaps the greatest tragedy in English letters.
The influences on his life are relatively clear:
school at Enfield, and the all-important friendship with Charles Cowden Clarke, who introduced Keats to Spenser and a love of poetry;
the death of his parents, leading to the guardi-
anship of the Abbeys and the subsequent study
of the surgeon's art, and a turning away to
literature; Leigh Hunt's circle with its entree
to a new world; Fanny Brawne, the one true
love whom he never could possess; and the
gnawing evil within him, tuberculosis. The first
poems were harshly criticized, but it is sheer
romance to say that Keats's death was hastened
by the reviews: Keats was a fighter. The rush
to Italy and possible salvation came too late—
but not before another volume had been well
received, not before the poet had turned out
in a few months a dozen or more masterpieces.
He had nursed his brother Tom and watched
him die. George, another brother, was in America. Pride and lack of money had presumably
kept Keats from marrying Fanny. The short
tragic life was over.
  In his sonnets and odes, in* Endymion *and*
Hyperion, *and in the longer narratives (particularly in* The Eve of St. Agnes) *John
Keats reached into another direction, a bit
apart from Byron's and Shelley's but, like
theirs, fundamentally "romantic." He was the
Romantic of rich color and imagery, of sensuous language and impression, of thoughtful*

pursuit of the truth beyond the object. In many ways he was the most well rounded of the whole group: bright, but not erratic; stable, but not dull; sensuous, but not sensual.

LA BELLE DAME SANS MERCI

"Ah, what can ail thee, Knight-at-arms,
    Alone and palely loitering?
The sedge has withered from the lake,
    And no birds sing. 10

"Ah, what can ail thee, Knight-at-arms,
    So haggard and so woe-begone?
The squirrel's granary is full,
    And the harvest's done. 15

"I see a lily on thy brow
    With anguish moist and fever-dew, 20
And on thy cheeks a fading rose
    Fast withereth too."

"I met a lady in the meads,
    Full beautiful—a faery's child; 25
Her hair was long, her foot was light,
    And her eyes were wild.

"I made a garland for her head,
    And bracelets too, and fragrant zone; 30
She looked at me as she did love,
    And made sweet moan.

"I set her on my pacing steed,
    And nothing else saw all day long; 35
For sidelong would she bend, and sing
    A faery's song.

"She found me roots of relish sweet,
    And honey wild and manna-dew; 40
And sure in language strange she said,
    'I love thee true.'

"She took me to her elfin grot,
    And there she gazed and sighed full sore, 45
And there I shut her wild, wild eyes—
    With kisses four.

"And there she lullèd me asleep,
    And there I dreamed—ah! woe betide!— 50
The latest dream I ever dreamed
    On the cold hill's side.

"I saw pale kings, and princes too,
    Pale warriors, death-pale were they all:
They cried—'La belle Dame sans Merci
    Hath thee in thrall!'

"I saw their starved lips in the gloam
    With horrid warning gapèd wide,
And I awoke, and found me here
    On the cold hill side.

"And this is why I sojourn here
    Alone and palely loitering,
Though the sedge is withered from the lake,
    And no birds sing."

THE EVE OF ST. AGNES

1

St. Agnes' Eve[1]—Ah, bitter chill it was!
The owl, for all his feathers, was a-cold;
The hare limped trembling through the frozen grass,
And silent was the flock in woolly fold:
Numb were the Beadsman's fingers, while he told
His rosary, and while his frosted breath,
Like pious incense from a censer old,
Seemed taking flight for heaven, without a death,
Past the sweet Virgin's picture, while his prayer he saith.

2

His prayer he saith, this patient, holy man;
Then takes his lamp, and riseth from his knees,
And back returneth, meagre, barefoot, wan,
Along the chapel aisle by slow degrees:
The sculptured dead, on each side, seem to freeze,
Emprisoned in black, purgatorial rails:
Knights, ladies, praying in dumb orat'ries,[2]
He passeth by; and his weak spirit fails
To think how they may ache in icy hoods and mails.

3

Northward he turneth through a little door,

[1] January 20. Legend ran that a girl would dream of her future husband on the Eve.
[2] small chapels with sculptured (dumb) figures.

And scarce three steps, ere Music's golden
tongue
Flattered to tears this aged man and poor;
But no—already had his death-bell rung:
The joys of all his life were said and sung: 5
His was harsh penance on St. Agnes' Eve:
Another way he went, and soon among
Rough ashes sat he for his soul's reprieve,
And all night kept awake, for sinners' sake to
grieve.   10

4

That ancient Beadsman heard the prelude
soft;
And so it chanced, for many a door was   15
wide,
From hurry to and fro. Soon, up aloft,
The silver, snarling trumpets 'gan to chide:
The level chambers, ready with their pride,
Were glowing to receive a thousand guests: 20
The carved angels, ever eager-eyed,
Stared, where upon their heads the cornice
rests,
With hair blown back, and wings put cross-
wise on their breasts.   25

5

At length burst in the argent revelry,
With plume, tiara, and all rich array,
Numerous as shadows haunting faerily   30
The brain, new-stuffed, in youth, with tri-
umphs gay
Of old romance. These let us wish away,
And turn, sole-thoughted, to one Lady there,
Whose heart had brooded, all that wintry   35
day,
On love, and winged St. Agnes' saintly care,
As she had heard old dames full many times
declare.

6   40

They told her how, upon St. Agnes' Eve,
Young virgins might have visions of de-
light,
And soft adorings from their loves receive   45
Upon the honeyed middle of the night,
If ceremonies due they did aright;
As, supperless to bed they must retire,
And couch supine their beauties, lily white;
Nor look behind, nor sideways, but require   50
Of Heaven with upward eyes for all that they
desire.

7

Full of this whim was thoughtful Madeline:
The music, yearning like a God in pain,
She scarcely heard: her maiden eyes divine,
Fixed on the floor, saw many a sweeping
train
Pass by—she heeded not at all: in vain
Came many a tiptoe, amorous cavalier,
And back retired; not cooled by high dis-
dain,
But she saw not: her heart was otherwhere;
She sighed for Agnes' dreams, the sweetest of
the year.

8

She danced along with vague, regardless
eyes,
Anxious her lips, her breathing quick and
short:
The hallowed hour was near at hand: she
sighs
Amid the timbrels, and the thronged resort
Of whisperers in anger, or in sport;
'Mid looks of love, defiance, hate, and scorn,
Hoodwinked with faery fancy; all amort,[3]
Save to St. Agnes and her lambs,[4] unshorn,
And all the bliss to be before to-morrow morn.

9

So, purposing each moment to retire,
She lingered still. Meantime, across the
moors,
Had come young Porphyro, with heart on
fire
For Madeline. Beside the portal doors,
Buttressed from moonlight, stands he, and
implores
All saints to give him sight of Madeline,
But for one moment in the tedious hours,
That he might gaze and worship all unseen;
Perchance speak, kneel, touch, kiss—in sooth
such things have been.

10

He ventures in: let no buzzed whisper tell:
All eyes be muffled, or a hundred swords

_____

[3] dead.
[4] On the anniversary of St. Agnes' martyrdom
two lambs, later shorn, were prominent in the
service; nuns wove the wool into cloth.

Will storm his heart, Love's fev'rous citadel:
For him, those chambers held barbarian
  hordes,
Hyena foemen, and hot-blooded lords,
Whose very dogs would execrations howl
Against his lineage: not one breast affords
Him any mercy, in that mansion foul,
Save one old beldame, weak in body and in
  soul.

11

Ah, happy chance! the aged creature came,
Shuffling along with ivory-headed wand,
To where he stood, hid from the torch's
  flame,
Behind a broad hall-pillar, far beyond
The sound of merriment and chorus bland:
He startled her; but soon she knew his face,
And grasped his fingers in her palsied hand,
Saying, "Mercy, Porphyro! hie thee from
  this place;
They are all here to-night, the whole blood-
  thirsty race!

12

"Get hence! get hence! there's dwarfish
  Hildebrand;
He had a fever late, and in the fit
He cursed thee and thine, both house and
  land:
Then there's that old Lord Maurice, not a
  whit
More tame for his gray hairs—Alas me! flit!
Flit like a ghost away."—"Ah, Gossip[5] dear,
We're safe enough; here in this armchair sit,
And tell me how"—"Good Saints! not here,
  not here;
Follow me, child, or else these stones will be
  thy bier."

13

He followed through a lowly arched way,
Brushing the cobwebs with his lofty plume;
And as she muttered "Well-a—well-a-day!"
He found him in a little moonlight room,
Pale, latticed, chill, and silent as a tomb.
"Now tell me where is Madeline," said he,
"O tell me, Angela, by the holy loom
Which none but secret sisterhood may see,
When they St. Agnes' wool are weaving,
  piously."

[5] here means "good old friend."

14

"St. Agnes! Ah! it is St. Agnes' Eve—
Yet men will murder upon holy days:
Thou must hold water in a witch's sieve,
And be liege-lord of all the Elves and Fays,
To venture so: it fills me with amaze
To see thee, Porphyro!—St. Agnes' Eve!
God's help! my lady fair the conjuror plays
This very night: good angels her deceive!
But let me laugh awhile, I've mickle[6] time to
  grieve."

15

Feebly she laugheth in the languid moon,
While Porphyro upon her face doth look,
Like puzzled urchin on an aged crone
Who keepeth closed a wond'rous riddle-
  book,
As spectacled she sits in chimney nook.
But soon his eyes grew brilliant, when she
  told
His lady's purpose; and he scarce could
  brook
Tears, at the thought of those enchantments
  cold,
And Madeline asleep in lap of legends old.

16

Sudden a thought came like a full-blown
  rose,
Flushing his brow, and in his pained heart
Made purple riot: then doth he propose
A stratagem, that makes the beldame start:
"A cruel man and impious thou art:
Sweet lady, let her pray, and sleep, and
  dream
Alone with her good angels, far apart
From wicked men like thee. Go, go! I deem
Thou canst not surely be the same that thou
  didst seem."

17

"I will not harm her, by all saints I swear,"
Quoth Porphyro: "O may I ne'er find grace
When my weak voice shall whisper its last
  prayer,
If one of her soft ringlets I displace,
Or look with ruffian passion in her face:
Good Angela, believe me by these tears;
Or I will, even in a moment's space,

[6] much.

Awake, with horrid shout, my foemen's ears,
And beard them, though they be more fanged
    than wolves and bears."

18

"Ah! why wilt thou affright a feeble soul?   5
A poor, weak, palsy-stricken, churchyard
    thing,
Whose passing-bell may ere the midnight
    toll;
Whose prayers for thee, each morn and
    evening,
Were never missed." Thus plaining, doth
    she bring
A gentler speech from burning Porphyro;   15
So woful, and of such deep sorrowing,
That Angela gives promise she will do
Whatever he shall wish, betide her weal or
    woe.

19

Which was, to lead him, in close secrecy,
Even to Madeline's chamber, and there hide
Him in a closet, of such privacy
That he might see her beauty unespied,   25
And win perhaps that night a peerless bride,
While legioned faeries paced the coverlet,
And pale enchantment held her sleepy-eyed.
Never on such a night have lovers met,
Since Merlin paid his Demon[7] all the mon-   30
    strous debt.

20

"It shall be as thou wishest," said the Dame:
"All cates[8] and dainties shall be stored there   35
Quickly on this feast-night: by the tambor
    frame[9]
Her own lute thou wilt see: no time to spare,
For I am slow and feeble, and scarce dare
On such a catering trust my dizzy head.   40
Wait here, my child, with patience; kneel
    in prayer
The while: Ah! thou must needs the lady
    wed,
Or may I never leave my grave among the   45
    dead."

21

So saying, she hobbled off with busy fear.

----

[7] his legendary father.
[8] delicacies.   [9] embroidery frame.

The lover's endless minutes slowly passed;
The Dame returned, and whispered in his
    ear
To follow her; with aged eyes aghast
From fright of dim espial. Safe at last,
Through many a dusky gallery, they gain
The maiden's chamber, silken, hushed and
    chaste;
Where Porphyro took covert, pleased amain.
His poor guide hurried back with agues in her   10
    brain.

22

Her faltering hand upon the balustrade,
Old Angela was feeling for the stair,
When Madeline, St. Agnes' charmed maid,
Rose, like a missioned spirit, unaware:
With silver taper's light, and pious care,
She turned, and down the aged gossip led
To a safe level matting. Now prepare,   20
Young Porphyro, for gazing on that bed;
She comes, she comes again, like ring-dove
    frayed and fled.

23

Out went the taper as she hurried in;
Its little smoke, in pallid moonshine, died:
She closed the door, she panted, all akin
To spirits of the air, and visions wide:
No uttered syllable, or, woe betide!
But to her heart, her heart was voluble,
Paining with eloquence her balmy side;
As though a tongueless nightingale should
    swell
Her throat in vain, and die, heart-stifled in her   35
    dell.

24

A casement high and triple-arched there was,
All garlanded with carven imag'ries
Of fruits, and flowers, and bunches of knot-
    grass,
And diamonded with panes of quaint de-
    vice,
Innumerable of stains and splendid dyes,
As are the tiger-moth's deep-damasked
    wings;
And in the mist, 'mong thousand herald-
    ries,
And twilight saints, and dim emblazonings,   50
A shielded scutcheon blushed with blood of
    queens and kings.

25

Full on this casement shone the wintry
    moon,
And threw warm gules[10] on Madeline's fair
    breast,
As down she knelt for heaven's grace and
    boon;
Rose-bloom fell on her hands, together prest,
And on her silver cross soft amethyst,
And on her hair a glory, like a saint:
She seem'd a splendid angel, newly drest,
Save wings, for heaven:—Porphyro grew
    faint:
She knelt, so pure a thing, so free from mortal
    taint.

26

Anon his heart revives: her vespers done,
Of all its wreathed pearls her hair she frees;
Unclasps her warmed jewels one by one;
Loosens her fragrant bodice; by degrees
Her rich attire creeps rustling to her knees:
Half-hidden, like a mermaid in sea-weed,
Pensive awhile she dreams awake, and sees,
In fancy, fair St. Agnes in her bed,
But dares not look behind, or all the charm
    is fled.

27

Soon, trembling in her soft and chilly nest,
In sort of wakeful swoon, perplexed she lay,
Until the poppied warmth of sleep oppressed
Her soothed limbs, and soul fatigued away;
Flown, like a thought, until the morrow-
    day;
Blissfully havened both from joy and pain;
Clasped like a missal where swart Paynims
    pray;[11]
Blinded alike from sunshine and from rain,
As though a rose should shut, and be a bud
    again.

28

Stol'n to this paradise, and so entranced,
Porphyro gazed upon her empty dress,
And listened to her breathing, if it chanced
To wake into a slumberous tenderness;

Which when he heard, that minute did he
    bless,
And breathed himself: then from the closet
    crept,
Noiseless as fear in a wide wilderness,
And over the hushed carpet, silent, stept,
And 'tween the curtains peeped, where lo!—
    how fast she slept.

29

Then by the bed-side, where the faded moon
Made a dim, silver twilight, soft he set
A table, and, half anguished, threw thereon
A cloth of woven crimson, gold, and jet:—
O for some drowsy Morphean amulet!
The boisterous, midnight, festive clarion,
The kettle-drum, and far-heard clarionet,
Affray his ears, though but in dying tone:—
The hall-door shuts again, and all the noise is
    gone.

30

And still she slept an azure-lidded sleep,
In blanched linen, smooth, and lavendered,
While he from forth the closet brought a
    heap
Of candied apple, quince, and plum, and
    gourd;
With jellies soother[12] than the creamy curd,
And lucent syrops, tinct with cinnamon;
Manna and dates, in argosy transferred
From Fez; and spiced dainties, every one,
From silken Samarcand to cedared Lebanon.

31

These delicates he heaped with glowing
    hand
On golden dishes and in baskets bright
Of wreathed silver: sumptuous they stand
In the retired quiet of the night,
Filling the chilly room with perfume light.—
"And now, my love, my seraph fair, awake!
Thou art my heaven, and I thine eremite:[13]
Open thine eyes, for meek St. Agnes' sake,
Or I shall drowse beside thee, so my soul doth
    ache."

32

Thus whispering, his warm, unnerved arm
Sank in her pillow. Shaded was her dream

---

[10] red (heraldry).
[11] shut like a prayer book (safe and secret) in
the company of non-believers.

[12] smoother.   [13] hermit (figuratively)

By the dusk curtains:—'twas a midnight
  charm
Impossible to melt as iced stream:
The lustrous salvers in the moonlight gleam;
Broad golden fringe upon the carpet lies: 5
It seemed he never, never could redeem
From such a steadfast spell his lady's eyes;
So mused awhile, entoiled in woofed phan-
  tasies.

33

Awakening up, he took her hollow lute,— 10
Tumultuous,—and, in chords that tender-
  est be,
He played an ancient ditty, long since mute, 15
In Provence called "La belle dame sans
  mercy:"
Close to her ear touching the melody;—
Wherewith disturbed, she uttered a soft
  moan: 20
He ceased—she panted quick—and sud-
  denly
Her blue affrayed eyes wide open shone:
Upon his knees he sank, pale as smooth-
  sculptured stone. 25

34

Her eyes were open, but she still beheld,
Now wide awake, the vision of her sleep:
There was a painful change, that nigh ex- 30
  pelled
The blisses of her dream so pure and deep
At which fair Madeline began to weep,
And moan forth witless words with many
  a sigh;
While still her gaze on Porphyro would 35
  keep;
Who knelt, with joined hands and piteous
  eye,
Fearing to move or speak, she looked so 40
  dreamingly.

35

"Ah, Porphyro!" said she, "but even now
Thy voice was at sweet tremble in mine ear, 45
Made tuneable with every sweetest vow;
And those sad eyes were spiritual and clear:
How changed thou art! how pallid, chill,
  and drear!
Give me that voice again, my Porphyro, 50
Those looks immortal, those complainings
  dear!

Oh leave me not in this eternal woe,
For if thou diest, my Love, I know not where
  to go."

36

Beyond a mortal man impassioned far
At these voluptuous accents, he arose,
Ethereal, flushed, and like a throbbing star
Seen mid the sapphire heaven's deep repose;
Into her dream he melted, as the rose 10
Blendeth its odor with the violet,—
Solution sweet: meantime the frost-wind
  blows
Like Love's alarum pattering the sharp sleet
Against the window-panes; St. Agnes' moon
  hath set.

37

'Tis dark: quick pattereth the flaw-blown[14]
  sleet:
"This is no dream, my bride, my Madeline!"
'Tis dark: the iced gusts still rave and beat:
"No dream, alas! alas! and woe is mine!
Porphyro will leave me here to fade and 25
  pine.—
Cruel! what traitor could thee hither bring?
I curse not, for my heart is lost in thine,
Though thou forsakest a deceived thing;—
A dove forlorn and lost with sick unpruned
  wing."

38

"My Madeline! sweet dreamer! lovely bride!
Say, may I be for aye thy vassal blest?
Thy beauty's shield, heart-shaped and ver-
  meil dyed?
Ah, silver shrine, here will I take my rest
After so many hours of toil and quest,
A famished pilgrim,—saved by miracle.
Though I have found, I will not rob thy
  nest
Saving of thy sweet self; if thou think'st well
To trust, fair Madeline, to no rude infidel.

39

"Hark! 'tis an elfin storm from faery land,
Of haggard seeming, but a boon indeed:
Arise—arise! the morning is at hand:—
The bloated wassailers will never heed:—
Let us away, my love, with happy speed;

[14] wind-blown.

There are no ears to hear, or eyes to see,—
Drowned all in Rhenish and the sleepy
    mead:
Awake! arise! my love, and fearless be,
For o'er the southern moors I have a home 5
    for thee."

40

She hurried at his words, beset with fears,
For there were sleeping dragons all around, 10
At glaring watch, perhaps, with ready
    spears—
Down the wide stairs a darkling way they
    found.—
In all the house was heard no human sound. 15
A chain-drooped lamp was flickering by
    each door;
The arras, rich with horseman, hawk, and
    hound,
Fluttered in the besieging wind's uproar; 20
And the long carpets rose along the gusty
    floor.

41

They glide, like phantoms, into the wide 25
    hall;
Like phantoms to the iron porch they glide,
Where lay the Porter, in uneasy sprawl,
With a huge empty flagon by his side:
The wakeful bloodhound rose, and shook 30
    his hide,
But his sagacious eye an inmate owns:
By one, and one, the bolts full easy slide:—
The chains lie silent on the footworn
    stones;—
The key turns, and the door upon its hinges
    groans.

42

And they are gone: ay, ages long ago 40
These lovers fled away into the storm.
That night the Baron dreamt of many a
    woe,
And all his warrior-guests, with shade and
    form
Of witch, and demon, and large coffin-worm,
Were long be-nightmared. Angela the old
Died palsy-twitched, with meagre face de-
    form;
The Beadsman, after thousand aves told, 50
For aye unsought-for slept among his ashes
    cold.

HENRY WADSWORTH LONGFELLOW

Evangeline, Hiawatha, and The Courtship of Miles Standish *are among America's most beloved poems, and Longfellow (1807–1882), their author, is to many the greatest name in traditional American literature. Like Bryant, however, he always seems "safe" but hardly moving; one plows through too much sweetness and looks almost in vain for flashes of wit or deep perception. Longfellow was educated at Bowdoin, became a professor there after travel abroad, and eventually taught at Harvard for almost twenty years. The death of his second wife (in a fire) stopped his writing for a time. The poet otherwise had little to worry about; through inheritance and large sales his income grew steadily. Although popular in his day and revered in the classroom down to the present, Longfellow does not impress people so much as he did; one regrets his avoidance of most real issues; his second-hand Germanic romanticism doesn't quite jell; with much good material to work with, he seldom goes below the surface. The future may judge him for the unfamiliar sonnets in this volume or for his sound service in helping America establish her reputation abroad—and forget the harmless tales which the public took to its bosom. (See also I, 292.)**

THE WRECK OF THE HESPERUS[1]

It was the schooner Hesperus, 35
    That sailed the wintry sea;
And the skipper had taken his little daughtèr,
    To bear him company.

Blue were her eyes as the fairy-flax, 40
    Her cheeks like the dawn of day,
And her bosom white as the hawthorn buds,
    That ope in the month of May.

The skipper he stood beside the helm, 45
    His pipe was in his mouth,

---

* The selections from Longfellow's poetry are reprinted through kind permission of the publisher, Houghton Mifflin Company.
[1] Based upon details of an actual wreck of a ship by this name.

And he watched how the veering flaw did blow
  The smoke now West, now South.

Then up and spake an old Sailòr,
  Had sailed to the Spanish Main,
'I pray thee, put into yonder port,
  For I fear a hurricane.   5

'Last night, the moon had a golden ring,
  And to-night no moon we see!'   10
The skipper, he blew a whiff from his pipe,
  And a scornful laugh laughed he.

Colder and louder blew the wind,
  A gale from the Northeast,   15
The snow fell hissing in the brine,
  And the billows frothed like yeast.

Down came the storm, and smote amain
  The vessel in its strength;   20
She shuddered and paused, like a frighted
    steed,
  Then leaped her cable's length.

'Come hither! come hither! my little daughtèr, 25
  And do not tremble so;
For I can weather the roughest gale
  That ever wind did blow.'

He wrapped her warm in his seaman's coat   30
  Against the stinging blast;
He cut a rope from a broken spar,
  And bound her to the mast.

'O father! I hear the church-bells ring,   35
  Oh say, what may it be?'
' 'T is a fog-bell on a rock-bound coast!'—
  And he steered for the open sea.

'O father! I hear the sound of guns,   40
  Oh say, what may it be?'
'Some ship in distress, that cannot live
  In such an angry sea!'

'O father! I see a gleaming light,   45
  Oh say, what may it be?'
But the father answered never a word,
  A frozen corpse was he.

Lashed to the helm, all stiff and stark,   50
  With his face turned to the skies,

The lantern gleamed through the gleaming
    snow
  On his fixed and glassy eyes.

Then the maiden clasped her hands and prayed
  That savèd she might be;
And she thought of Christ, who stilled the
    wave,
  On the Lake of Galilee.

And fast through the midnight dark and drear,
  Through the whistling sleet and snow,
Like a sheeted ghost, the vessel swept
  Tow'rds the reef of Norman's Woe.[2]

And ever the fitful gusts between
  A sound came from the land;
It was the sound of the trampling surf
  On the rocks and the hard sea-sand.

The breakers were right beneath her bows,
  She drifted a dreary wreck,
And a whooping billow swept the crew
  Like icicles from her deck.

She struck where the white and fleecy waves
  Looked soft as carded wool,
But the cruel rocks, they gored her side
  Like the horns of an angry bull.

Her rattling shrouds, all sheathed in ice,
  With the masts went by the board;
Like a vessel of glass, she stove and sank,
  Ho! ho! the breakers roared!

At daybreak, on the bleak sea-beach,
  A fisherman stood aghast,
To see the form of a maiden fair,
  Lashed close to a drifting mast.

The salt sea was frozen on her breast,
  The salt tears in her eyes;
And he saw her hair, like the brown seaweed,
  On the billows fall and rise.

Such was the wreck of the Hesperus,
  In the midnight and the snow!
Christ save us all from a death like this,
  On the reef of Norman's Woe!

              —————
[2] near Gloucester.

THE SKELETON IN ARMOR

Speak! speak! thou fearful guest!
Who, with thy hollow breast
Still in rude armor drest,   5
 Comest to daunt me!
Wrapt not in Eastern balms,
But with thy fleshless palms
Stretched, as if asking alms,
 Why dost thou haunt me?   10

Then, from those cavernous eyes
Pale flashes seemed to rise,
As when the Northern skies
 Gleam in December;   15
And, like the water's flow
Under December's snow,
Came a dull voice of woe
 From the heart's chamber.
          20
"I was a Viking old!
My deeds, though manifold,
No Skald in song has told,
 No Saga taught thee!
Take heed, that in thy verse   25
Thou dost the tale rehearse,
Else dread a dead man's curse;
 For this I sought thee.

"Far in the Northern Land,   30
By the wild Baltic's strand,
I, with my childish hand,
 Tamed the gerfalcon;
And, with my skates fast-bound,
Skimmed the half-frozen Sound, 35
That the poor whimpering hound
 Trembled to walk on.

"Oft to his frozen lair
Tracked I the grisly bear,   40
While from my path the hare
 Fled like a shadow;
Oft through the forest dark
Followed the were-wolf's bark,
Until the soaring lark   45
 Sang from the meadow.

"But when I older grew,
Joining a corsair's crew,
O'er the dark sea I flew   50
 With the marauders.

Wild was the life we led;
Many the souls that sped,
Many the hearts that bled,
 By our stern orders.

"Many a wassail-bout
Wore the long Winter out;
Often our midnight shout
 Set the cocks crowing,
As we the Berserk's tale
Measured in cups of ale,
Draining the oaken pail,
 Filled to o'erflowing.

"Once as I told in glee
Tales of the stormy sea,
Soft eyes did gaze on me,
 Burning yet tender;
And as the white stars shine
On the dark Norway pine,
On that dark heart of mine
 Fell their soft splendor.

"I wooed the blue-eyed maid,
Yielding, yet half afraid,
And in the forest's shade
 Our vows were plighted.
Under its loosened vest
Fluttered her little breast,
Like birds within their nest
 By the hawk frighted.

"Bright in her father's hall
Shields gleamed upon the wall,
Loud sang the minstrels all,
 Chanting his glory;
When of old Hildebrand
I asked his daughter's hand,
Mute did the minstrels stand
 To hear my story.

"While the brown ale he quaffed,
Loud then the champion laughed,
And as the wind-gusts waft
 The sea-foam brightly,
So the loud laugh of scorn
Out of those lips unshorn,
From the deep drinking-horn
 Blew the foam lightly.

"She was a Prince's child,

I but a Viking wild,
And though she blushed and smiled,
  I was discarded!
Should not the dove so white
Follow the sea-mew's flight?   5
Why did they leave that night
  Her nest unguarded?

"Scarce had I put to sea,
Bearing the maid with me,   10
Fairest of all was she
  Among the Norsemen!
When on the white sea-strand,
Waving his armèd hand,
Saw we old Hildebrand,   15
  With twenty horsemen.

"Then launched they to the blast,
Bent like a reed each mast,
Yet we were gaining fast,   20
  When the wind failed us;
And with a sudden flaw
Came round the gusty Skaw,
So that our foe we saw
  Laugh as he hailed us.   25

"And as to catch the gale
Round veered the flapping sail,
'Death!' was the helmsman's hail,
  'Death without quarter!'   30
Midships with iron keel
Struck we her ribs of steel;
Down her black hulk did reel
  Through the black water!   35

"As with his wings aslant,
Sails the fierce cormorant,
Seeking some rocky haunt,
  With his prey laden,—
So toward the open main,   40
Beating to sea again,
Through the wild hurricane,
  Bore I the maiden.

"Three weeks we westward bore,   45
And when the storm was o'er,
Cloud-like we saw the shore
  Stretching to leeward;
There for my lady's bower
Built I the lofty tower,   50
Which, to this very hour,
  Stands looking seaward.

"There lived we many years;
Time dried the maiden's tears;
She had forgot her fears,
  She was a mother;
Death closed her mild blue eyes;
Under that tower she lies;
Ne'er shall the sun arise
  On such another!

"Still grew my bosom then,
Still as a stagnant fen!
Hateful to me were men,
  The sunlight hateful!
In the vast forest here,
Clad in my warlike gear,
Fell I upon my spear,
  Oh, death was grateful!

"Thus, seamed with many scars,
Bursting these prison bars
Up to its native stars
  My soul ascended!
There from the flowing bowl
Deep drinks the warrior's soul,
Skoal! to the Northland! *skoal!*"
  Thus the tale ended.

JOHN GREENLEAF WHITTIER

*Whittier (1807–1892) was not so fortunate in his New England background as were Emerson and Longfellow; he had little formal education. However, he was at home in books and was sustained by his Quaker training. He wrote for country journals and had editorial experience —a pattern as familiar for the early American group as the Cambridge-diplomatic mission-court pattern was for young English Cavaliers. Whittier served in the legislature and was connected with the early Liberty party. As a devoted abolitionist he often used his pen to serve the cause of emancipation. His poetry is of the idyllic New England country scene and, generally speaking, has the solid virtues of morality and sentiment peculiar to his contemporaries. There is little that approaches great art in Whittier's work, but it had strong local appeal in its day. (See also I, 295.)**

* The selection from Whittier's poetry is reprinted by kind permission of the publisher, Houghton Mifflin Company.

SKIPPER IRESON'S RIDE[1]

Of all the rides since the birth of time,
Told in story or sung in rhyme,—
On Apuleius's Golden Ass,
Or one-eyed Calender's horse of brass,
Witch astride of a human back,
Islam's prophet on Al-Borák,—
The strangest ride that ever was sped
Was Ireson's, out from Marblehead!
    Old Floyd Ireson, for his hard heart,
    Tarred and feathered and carried in a cart
    By the women of Marblehead!

Body of turkey, head of owl,
Wings a-droop like a rained-on fowl,
Feathered and ruffled in every part,
Skipper Ireson stood in the cart.
Scores of women, old and young,
Strong of muscle, and glib of tongue,
Pushed and pulled up the rocky lane,
Shouting and singing the shrill refrain:
    'Here's Flud Oirson, fur his horrd horrt,
    Torr'd an' futherr'd an' corr'd in a corrt
    By the women o' Morble'ead!'

Wrinkled scolds with hands on hips,
Girls in bloom of cheek and lips,
Wild-eyed, free-limbed, such as chase
Bacchus round some antique vase,
Brief of skirt, with ankles bare,
Loose of kerchief and loose of hair,
With conch-shells blowing and fish-horns'
    twang,
Over and over the Mænads sang:
    'Here's Flud Oirson, fur his horrd horrt,
    Torr'd an' futherr'd an' corr'd in a corrt
    By the women o' Morble'ead!'

Small pity for him!—He sailed away
From a leaking ship in Chaleur Bay,—
Sailed away from a sinking wreck,
With his own town's-people on her deck!
'Lay by! lay by!' they called to him.
Back he answered, 'Sink or swim!
Brag of your catch of fish again!'
And off he sailed through the fog and rain!
    Old Floyd Ireson, for his hard heart,
    Tarred and feathered and carried in a cart
    By the women of Marblehead!

Fathoms deep in dark Chaleur
That wreck shall lie forevermore.
Mother and sister, wife and maid,
Looked from the rocks of Marblehead
Over the moaning and rainy sea,—
Looked for the coming that might not be!
What did the winds and the sea-birds say
Of the cruel captain who sailed away?—
    Old Floyd Ireson, for his hard heart,
    Tarred and feathered and carried in a cart
    By the women of Marblehead!

Through the street, on either side,
Up flew windows, doors swung wide;
Sharp-tongued spinsters, old wives gray,
Treble lent the fish-horn's bray.
Sea-worn grandsires, cripple-bound,
Hulks of old sailors run aground,
Shook head, and fist, and hat, and cane,
And cracked with curses the hoarse refrain:
    'Here's Flud Oirson, fur his horrd horrt,
    Torr'd an' futherr'd an' corr'd in a corrt
    By the women o' Morble'ead!'

Sweetly along the Salem road
Bloom of orchard and lilac showed.
Little the wicked skipper knew
Of the fields so green and the sky so blue.
Riding there in his sorry trim,
Like an Indian idol glum and grim,
Scarcely he seemed the sound to hear
Of voices shouting, far and near:
    'Here's Flud Oirson, fur his horrd horrt,
    Torr'd an' futherr'd an' corr'd in a corrt
    By the women o' Morble'ead!'

'Hear me, neighbors!' at last he cried,—
'What to me is this noisy ride?
What is the shame that clothes the skin
To the nameless horror that lives within?
Waking or sleeping, I see a wreck,
And hear a cry from a reeling deck!
Hate me and curse me,—I only dread
The hand of God and the face of the dead!'
    Said old Floyd Ireson, for his hard heart,
    Tarred and feathered and carried in a cart
    By the women of Marblehead!

Then the wife of the skipper lost at sea

[1] Whittier based this ballad on a story he heard in school. He began it in 1828, published it in 1857. He later learned that Ireson was not guilty of abandoning ship.

Said, 'God has touched him! why should we!'
Said an old wife mourning her only son,
'Cut the rogue's tether and let him run!'
So with soft relentings and rude excuse,
Half scorn, half pity, they cut him loose, 5
And gave him a cloak to hide him in,
And left him alone with his shame and sin.
   Poor Floyd Ireson, for his hard heart,
   Tarred and feathered and carried in a cart
     By the women of Marblehead! 10

ALFRED, LORD TENNYSON

Tennyson (1809–1892) had early impetus to-
ward literature from guided reading in the 15
family books. After leaving Cambridge he rusti-
cated, as Milton had done, and wrote verses
which were not well received. He experienced
grief over the death of his friend Hallam (see
In Memoriam); he had financial difficulties; 20
he found himself holding the family to-
gether after his father, the rector, died.
Something came of this hard growth. The
Poems of 1842 and the later Princess set
him on the road; from then on he won every- 25
thing a poet might hope for—money, wife,
laureateship, peerage, critical and popular ac-
claim. Tennyson is an artist, a painter of pretty
Arthurian pictures, a stanch moralist in a moral
age, a musician with an ear for melody and 30
hypnotic sound-effects. He dodges many of
the deeper questions in a time crowded with
questions, avoids unpleasant realities, remains
(like Spenser) strangely virginal. And yet his
best lyrics and Greek or Arthurian idylls con- 35
tinue to be effective, probably because their
author is such a sweet singer. If ever a major
poet fitted his period, that man was Tennyson.
(For lyric verse see I, 297.)**

40

THE LADY OF SHALOTT

PART I

On either side the river lie
Long fields of barley and of rye,
That clothe the wold and meet the sky; 45
And thro' the field the road runs by
     To many-towered Camelot;[1]

---

* The following selections are from Tennyson's
Poetical Works. By permission of The Macmillan 50
Company, publishers.
[1] King Arthur's city in Cornwall.

And up and down the people go,
Gazing where the lilies blow
Round an island there below,
     The island of Shalott.

Willows whiten, aspens quiver,
Little breezes dusk and shiver
Thro' the wave that runs for ever
By the island in the river
     Flowing down to Camelot.
Four gray walls, and four gray towers,
Overlook a space of flowers,
And the silent isle imbowers
     The Lady of Shalott.

By the margin, willow-veiled,
Slide the heavy barges trailed
By slow horses; and unhailed
The shallop flitteth silken-sailed
     Skimming down to Camelot:
But who hath seen her wave her hand?
Or at the casement seen her stand?
Or is she known in all the land,
     The Lady of Shalott?

Only reapers, reaping early
In among the bearded barley,
Hear a song that echoes cheerly
From the river winding clearly,
     Down to towered Camelot;
And by the moon the reaper weary,
Piling sheaves in uplands airy,
Listening, whispers " 'Tis the fairy
     Lady of Shalott."

PART II

There she weaves by night and day
A magic web with colors gay.
She has heard a whisper say,
A curse is on her if she stay
     To look down to Camelot.
She knows not what the curse may be,
And so she weaveth steadily,
And little other care hath she,
     The Lady of Shalott.

And moving thro' a mirror clear
That hangs before her all the year,
Shadows of the world appear.
There she sees the highway near
     Winding down to Camelot;
There the river eddy whirls,

And there the surly village-churls,
And the red cloaks of market girls,
      Pass onward from Shalott.

Sometimes a troop of damsels glad,
An abbot on an ambling pad,
Sometimes a curly shepherd-lad,
Or long-haired page in crimson clad,
      Goes by to towered Camelot;
And sometimes thro' the mirror blue
The knights come riding two and two:
She hath no loyal knight and true,
      The Lady of Shalott.

But in her web she still delights
To weave the mirror's magic sights,
For often thro' the silent nights
A funeral, with plumes and lights
      And music, went to Camelot;
Or when the moon was overhead,
Came two young lovers lately wed:
"I am half-sick of shadows," said
      The Lady of Shalott.

PART III

A bow-shot from her bower-eaves,
He rode between the barley-sheaves,
The sun came dazzling thro' the leaves,
And flamed upon the brazen greaves
      Of bold Sir Lancelot.
A redcross knight for ever kneeled
To a lady in his shield,
That sparkled on the yellow field,
      Beside remote Shalott.

The gemmy bridle glittered free,
Like to some branch of stars we see
Hung in the golden Galaxy.
The bridle bells rang merrily
      As he rode down to Camelot;
And from his blazoned baldric slung
A mighty silver bugle hung,
And as he rode his armor rung,
      Beside remote Shalott.

All in the blue unclouded weather
Thick-jewelled shone the saddle-leather,
The helmet and the helmet-feather
Burned like one burning flame together,
      As he rode down to Camelot;
As often thro' the purple night,

Below the starry clusters bright,
Some bearded meteor, trailing light,
      Moves over still Shalott.

His broad clear brow in sunlight glowed;
On burnished hooves his war-horse trode;
From underneath his helmet flowed
His coal-black curls as on he rode,
      As he rode down to Camelot.
From the bank and from the river
He flashed into the crystal mirror,
"Tirra lirra," by the river
      Sang Sir Lancelot.

She left the web, she left the loom,
She made three paces thro' the room,
She saw the water-lily bloom,
She saw the helmet and the plume,
      She looked down to Camelot.
Out flew the web and floated wide;
The mirror cracked from side to side;
"The curse is come upon me," cried
      The Lady of Shalott.

PART IV

In the stormy east-wind straining,
The pale yellow woods were waning,
The broad stream in his banks complaining,
Heavily the low sky raining
      Over towered Camelot;
Down she came and found a boat
Beneath a willow left afloat,
And round about the prow she wrote
      The Lady of Shalott.

And down the river's dim expanse—
Like some bold seër in a trance,
Seeing all his own mischance—
With a glassy countenance
      Did she look to Camelot.
And at the closing of the day
She loosed the chain, and down she lay;
The broad stream bore her far away,
      The Lady of Shalott.

Lying, robed in snowy white
That loosely flew to left and right—
The leaves upon her falling light—
Thro' the noises of the night
      She floated down to Camelot;
And as the boat-head wound along

The willowy hills and fields among,
They heard her singing her last song,
    The Lady of Shalott.

Heard a carol, mournful, holy,
Chanted loudly, chanted lowly,
Till her blood was frozen slowly,
And her eyes were darkened wholly,
    Turned to towered Camelot;
For ere she reached upon the tide
The first house by the water-side,
Singing in her song she died,
    The Lady of Shalott.

Under tower and balcony,
By garden-wall and gallery,
A gleaming shape she floated by,
A corse between the houses high,
    Silent into Camelot.
Out upon the wharfs they came,
Knight and burgher, lord and dame,
And round the prow they read her name,
    The Lady of Shalott.

Who is this? and what is here?
And in the lighted palace near
Died the sound of royal cheer;
And they crossed themselves for fear,
    All the knights at Camelot:
But Lancelot mused a little space;
He said, "She has a lovely face;
God in his mercy lend her grace,
    The Lady of Shalott."

ULYSSES

It little profits that an idle king,
By this still hearth, among these barren crags,
Matched with an aged wife, I mete and dole
Unequal laws unto a savage race,
That hoard, and sleep, and feed, and know not me.
I cannot rest from travel. I will drink
Life to the lees. All times I have enjoyed
Greatly, have suffered greatly, both with those
That loved me, and alone; on shore, and when
Through scudding drifts the rainy Hyades[1]
Vexed the dim sea. I am become a name;
For always roaming with a hungry heart

[1] group of stars in constellation Taurus.

5 Much have I seen and known; cities of men,
And manners, climates, councils, governments,
Myself not least, but honored of them all;
And drunk delight of battle with my peers,
Far on the ringing plains of windy Troy.
I am a part of all that I have met.
Yet all experience is an arch wherethrough
Gleams that untraveled world, whose margin fades
10 Forever and forever when I move.
How dull it is to pause, to make an end,
To rust unburnished, not to shine in use!
As though to breathe were life. Life piled on life
15 Were all too little, and of one to me
Little remains. But every hour is saved
From that eternal silence, something more,
A bringer of new things; and vile it were
For some three suns to store and hoard myself,
20 And this gray spirit yearning in desire
To follow knowledge like a sinking star,
Beyond the utmost bound of human thought.
This is my son, mine own Telemachus,
To whom I leave the scepter and the isle—
25 Well-loved of me, discerning to fulfill
This labor, by slow prudence to make mild
A rugged people, and through soft degrees
Subdue them to the useful and the good.
Most blameless is he, centered in the sphere
30 Of common duties, decent not to fail
In offices of tenderness, and pay
Meet adoration to my household gods,
When I am gone. He works his work, I mine.
There lies the port; the vessel puffs her sail;
35 There gloom the dark broad seas. My mariners,
Souls that have toiled, and wrought, and thought with me—
That ever with a frolic welcome took
The thunder and the sunshine, and opposed
40 Free hearts, free foreheads—you and I are old;
Old age hath yet his honor and his toil;
Death closes all. But something ere the end,
Some work of noble note, may yet be done,
45 Not unbecoming men that strove with gods.
The lights begin to twinkle from the rocks;
The long day wanes; the slow moon climbs; the deep
Moans round with many voices. Come, my
50   friends,
'Tis not too late to seek a newer world.
Push off, and sitting well in order smite

The sounding furrows; for my purpose holds
To sail beyond the sunset, and the baths
Of all the western stars, until I die.
It may be that the gulfs will wash us down
It may be we shall touch the Happy Isles,[2]
And see the great Achilles,[3] whom we knew.
Though much is taken, much abides; and
    though
We are not now that strength which in old
    days
Moved earth and heaven, that which we are,
    we are;
One equal temper of heroic hearts,
Made weak by time and fate, but strong in
    will
To strive, to seek, to find, and not to yield.

MORTE D'ARTHUR

So all day long the noise of battle rolled
Among the mountains by the winter sea,
Until King Arthur's table, man by man,
Had fallen in Lyonness about their lord,
King Arthur; then, because his wound was
    deep,
The bold Sir Bedivere uplifted him,
Sir Bedivere, the last of all his knights,
And bore him to a chapel nigh the field,
A broken chancel with a broken cross,
That stood on a dark strait of barren land.
On one side lay the Ocean and on one
Lay a great water, and the moon was full.
    Then spake King Arthur to Sir Bedivere:
"The sequel of to-day unsolders all
The goodliest fellowship of famous knights
Whereof this world holds record. Such a sleep
They sleep—the men I loved. I think that we
Shall never more, at any future time,
Delight our souls with talk of knightly deeds,
Walking about the gardens and the halls
Of Camelot, as in the days that were.
I perish by this people which I made,—
Tho' Merlin sware that I should come again
To rule once more—but let what will be, be,
I am so deeply smitten thro' the helm
That without help I cannot last till morn.
Thou therefore take my brand Excalibur,

Which was my pride; for thou rememberest
    how
In those old days, one summer noon, an arm
Rose up from out the bosom of the lake,
Clothed in white samite, mystic, wonderful,
Holding the sword—and how I rowed across
And took it, and have worn it, like a king;
And, wheresoever I am sung or told
In aftertime, this also shall be known.
But now delay not; take Excalibur,
And fling him far into the middle mere;
Watch what thou seest, and lightly bring me
    word."
    To him replied the bold Sir Bedivere:
"It is not meet, Sir King, to leave thee thus,
Aidless, alone, and smitten thro' the helm.
A little thing may harm a wounded man.
Yet I thy hest[1] will all perform at full,
Watch what I see, and lightly bring thee
    word."
    So saying, from the ruined shrine he stept
And in the moon athwart the place of tombs,
Where lay the mighty bones of ancient men,
Old knights, and over them the sea-wind sang
Shrill, chill, with flakes of foam. He, stepping
    down
By zigzag paths, and juts of pointed rock,
Came on the shining levels of the lake.
    There drew he forth the brand Excalibur,
And o'er him, drawing it, the winter moon,
Brightening the skirts of a long cloud, ran
    forth
And sparkled keen with frost against the hilt;
For all the haft twinkled with diamond sparks,
Myriads of topaz-lights, and jacinth-work
Of subtlest jewellery. He gazed so long
That both his eyes were dazzled, as he stood,
This way and that dividing the swift mind,
In act to throw; but at the last it seemed
Better to leave Excalibur concealed
There in the many-knotted waterflags,
That whistled stiff and dry about the marge.
So strode he back slow to the wounded king.
    Then spake King Arthur to Sir Bedivere:
"Hast thou performed my mission which I
    gave?
What is it thou hast seen? or what hast heard?"
    And answer made the bold Sir Bedivere:
"I heard the ripple washing in the reeds,
And the wild water lapping on the crag."

[2] Isles of the Blest, where god-favored elite went
after death.
[3] greatest warrior of the Greeks, slayer of Hector.

[1] bidding.

To whom replied King Arthur, faint and
    pale:
"Thou hast betrayed thy nature and thy name,
Not rendering true answer, as beseemed
Thy fealty, nor like a noble knight;
For surer sign had followed, either hand, 5
Or voice, or else a motion of the mere.
This is a shameful thing for men to lie.
Yet now, I charge thee, quickly go again
As thou art lief[2] and dear, and do the thing 10
I bade thee, watch, and lightly bring me
    word."
    Then went Sir Bedivere the second time
Across the ridge, and paced beside the mere,
Counting the dewy pebbles, fixed in thought; 15
But when he saw the wonder of the hilt,
How curiously and strangely chased, he smote
His palms together, and he cried aloud:
    "And if indeed I cast the brand away,
Surely a precious thing, one worthy note, 20
Should thus be lost forever from the earth,
Which might have pleased the eyes of many
    men.
What good should follow this, if this were
    done? 25
What harm, undone? deep harm to disobey,
Seeing obedience is the bond of rule.
Were it well to obey then, if a king demand
An act unprofitable, against himself?
The King is sick, and knows not what he does. 30
What record, or what relic of my lord
Should be to aftertime, but empty breath
And rumors of a doubt? but were this kept,
Stored in some treasure-house of mighty kings,
Some one might show it at a joust of arms, 35
Saying, 'King Arthur's sword, Excalibur,
Wrought by the lonely maiden of the lake;
Nine years she wrought it, sitting in the deeps
Upon the hidden bases of the hills.'
So might some old man speak in the aftertime 40
To all the people, winning reverence;
But now much honor and much fame were
    lost."
    So spake he, clouded with his own conceit,[3]
And hid Excalibur the second time, 45
And so strode back slow to the wounded King.
    Then spoke King Arthur, breathing heavily:
"What is it thou hast seen? or what hast
    heard?"
    And answer made the bold Sir Bedivere: 50

"I heard the water lapping on the crag,
And the long ripple washing in the reeds."
    To whom replied King Arthur, much in
    wrath:
"Ah, miserable and unkind, untrue,
Unknightly, traitor-hearted! Woe is me!
Authority forgets a dying king,
Laid widowed of the power in his eye
That bowed the will. I see thee what thou art,
For thou, the latest-left of all my knights,
In whom should meet the offices of all,
Thou wouldst betray me for the precious hilt;
Either from lust of gold, or like a girl
Valuing the giddy pleasure of the eyes.
Yet, for a man may fail in duty twice,
And the third time may prosper, get thee
    hence;
But, if thou spare to fling Excalibur,
I will arise and slay thee with my hands."
    Then quickly rose Sir Bedivere, and ran,
And, leaping down the ridges lightly, plunged
Among the bulrush-beds, and clutched the
    sword,
And strongly wheeled and threw it. The great
    brand
Made lightnings in the splendor of the moon,
And flashing round and round, and whirled in
    an arch,
Shot like a streamer of the northern morn,
Seen where the moving isles[4] of winter shock
By night, with noises of the northern sea.
So flashed and fell the brand Excalibur;
But ere he dipt the surface, rose an arm
Clothed in white samite, mystic, wonderful,
And caught him by the hilt, and brandished
    him
Three times, and drew him under in the mere.
And lightly went the other to the King.
    Then spoke King Arthur, drawing thicker
    breath:
"Now see I by thine eyes that this is done.
Speak out; what is it thou hast heard, or seen?"
    And answer made the bold Sir Bedivere:
"Sir King, I closed mine eyelids, lest the gems
Should blind my purpose, for I never saw,
Nor shall see, here or elsewhere, till I die,
Not tho' I live three lives of mortal men,
So great a miracle as yonder hilt.
Then with both hands I flung him, wheeling
    him;

---

[2] beloved.   [3] notion.   [4] icebergs.

But when I looked again, behold an arm,
Clothed in white samite, mystic, wonderful,
That caught him by the hilt, and brandished him
Three times, and drew him under in the mere."
    And answer made King Arthur, breathing hard:
"My end draws nigh; 'tis time that I were gone.
Make broad thy shoulders to receive my weight, 10
And bear me to the margin; yet I fear
My wound hath taken cold, and I shall die."
    So saying, from the pavement he half rose,
Slowly, with pain, reclining on his arm, 15
And looking wistfully with wide blue eyes
As in a picture. Him Sir Bedivere
Remorsefully regarded thro' his tears,
And would have spoken, but he found not words, 20
Then took with care, and kneeling on one knee,
O'er both his shoulders drew the languid hands,
And rising bore him thro' the place of tombs. 25
    But, as he walked, King Arthur panted hard,
Like one that feels a nightmare on his bed
When all the house is mute. So sighed the King,
Muttering and murmuring at his ear, "Quick, 30
quick!
I fear it is too late, and I shall die."
But the other swiftly strode from ridge to ridge,
Clothed with his breath, and looking, as he 35
walked,
Larger than human on the frozen hills.
He heard the deep behind him, and a cry
Before. His own thought drove him like a goad.
Dry clashed his harness in the icy caves 40
And barren chasms, and all to left and right
The bare black cliff clanged round him, as he based
His feet on juts of slippery crag that rang 45
Sharp-smitten with the dint of armed heels—
And on a sudden, lo! the level lake,
And the long glories of the winter moon.
    Then saw they how there hove a dusky barge,
Dark as a funeral scarf from stem to stern,
Beneath them; and descending they were ware

That all the decks were dense with stately forms
Black-stoled, black-hooded, like a dream—by these
Three Queens with crowns of gold—and from 5
them rose
A cry that shivered to the tingling stars,
And, as it were one voice, an agony
Of lamentation, like a wind, that shrills
All night in a waste land, where no one comes, 10
Or hath come, since the making of the world.
    Then murmured Arthur, "Place me in the barge,"
And to the barge they came. There those three 15
queens
Put forth their hands, and took the king, and wept.
But she, that rose the tallest of them all
And fairest, laid his head upon her lap,
And loosed the shattered casque, and chafed 20
his hands,
And called him by his name, complaining loud,
And dropping bitter tears against his brow
Striped with dark blood; for all his face was white
And colorless, and like the withered moon
Smote by the fresh beam of the springing east;
And all his greaves and cuisses dashed with drops
Of onset; and the light and lustrous curls— 30
That made his forehead like a rising sun
High from the dais-throne—were parched with dust;
Or, clotted into points and hanging loose,
Mixed with the knightly growth that fringed 35
his lips.
So like a shattered column lay the king;
Not like that Arthur who, with lance in rest,
From spur to plume a star of tournament,
Shot thro' the lists at Camelot, and charged 40
Before the eyes of ladies and of kings.
    Then loudly cried the bold Sir Bedivere:
"Ah! my Lord Arthur, whither shall I go?
Where shall I hide my forehead and my eyes?
For now I see the true old times are dead, 45
When every morning brought a noble chance,
And every chance brought out a noble knight.
Such times have been not since the light that led
The holy Elders[5] with the gift of myrrh. 50

————

[5] the Magi.

[155]

But now the whole ROUND TABLE is dissolved
Which was an image of the mighty world;
And I, the last, go forth companionless,
And the days darken round me, and the years,
Among new men, strange faces, other minds." 5
    And slowly answered Arthur from the barge:
"The old order changeth, yielding place to
    new,
And God fulfils himself in many ways,
Lest one good custom should corrupt the 10
    world.
Comfort thyself: what comfort is in me?
I have lived my life, and that which I have
    done
May He within himself make pure! but thou, 15
If thou shouldst never see my face again,
Pray for my soul. More things are wrought by
    prayer
Than this world dreams of. Wherefore, let thy
    voice 20
Rise like a fountain for me night and day.
For what are men better than sheep or goats
That nourish a blind life within the brain,
If, knowing God, they lift not hands of prayer
Both for themselves and those who call them 25
    friend?
For so the whole round earth is every way
Bound by gold chains about the feet of
    God.
But now farewell. I am going a long way 30
With these thou seest—if indeed I go—
(For all my mind is clouded with a doubt)
To the island-valley of Avilion;
Where falls not hail, or rain, or any snow,
Nor ever wind blows loudly; but it lies 35
Deep-meadowed, happy, fair with orchard
    lawns
And bowery hollows crowned with summer
    sea,
Where I will heal me of my grievous wound." 40
    So said he, and the barge with oar and
    sail
Moved from the brink, like some full-breasted
    swan
That, fluting a wild carol ere her death, 45
Ruffles her pure cold plume, and takes the
    flood
With swarthy webs. Long stood Sir Bedivere
Revolving many memories, till the hull
Looked one black dot against the verge of 50
    dawn,
And on the mere the wailing died away.

THE REVENGE

A BALLAD OF THE FLEET[1]

1

At Flores in the Azores Sir Richard Grenville
    lay,
And a pinnace, like a fluttered bird, came
    flying from far away:
"Spanish ships of war at sea! we have sighted
    fifty-three!"
Then sware Lord Thomas Howard: " 'Fore
    God I am no coward;
But I cannot meet them here, for my ships
    are out of gear,
And the half my men are sick. I must fly, but
    follow quick.
We are six ships of the line; can we fight with
    fifty-three?"

2

Then spake Sir Richard Grenville: "I know
    you are no coward;
You fly them for a moment to fight with them
    again.
But I've ninety men and more that are lying
    sick ashore.
I should count myself the coward if I left
    them, my Lord Howard,
To these Inquisition dogs and the devildoms
    of Spain."

3

So Lord Howard passed away with five ships
    of war that day,
Till he melted like a cloud in the silent sum-
    mer heaven;
But Sir Richard bore in hand all his sick men
    from the land
Very carefully and slow,
Men of Bideford in Devon,
And we laid them on the ballast down below;
For we brought them all aboard,
And they blessed him in their pain, that they
    were not left to Spain,
To the thumb-screw and the stake, for the
    glory of the Lord.

4

He had only a hundred seamen to work the

[1] Based on Ralegh's account of the actual engagement in 1591.

ship and to fight,
And he sailed away from Flores till the Span-
iard came in sight,
With his huge sea-castles heaving upon the
weather bow.
"Shall we fight or shall we fly? 5
Good Sir Richard, tell us now,
For to fight is but to die!
There'll be little of us left by the time this
sun be set."
And Sir Richard said again: "We be all good 10
English men.
Let us bang these dogs of Seville, the children
of the devil,
For I never turned my back upon Don or 15
devil yet."

5

Sir Richard spoke and he laughed, and we
roared a hurrah, and so 20
The little *Revenge* ran on sheer into the heart
of the foe,
With her hundred fighters on deck, and her
ninety sick below;
For half of their fleet to the right and half to 25
the left were seen,
And the little *Revenge* ran on through the
long sea-lane between.

6

Thousands of their soldiers looked down from 30
their decks and laughed,
Thousands of their seamen made mock at the
mad little craft
Running on and on, till delayed 35
By their mountain-like *San Philip* that, of
fifteen hundred tons,
And up-shadowing high above us with her
yawning tiers of guns,
Took the breath from our sails, and we 40
stayed.

7

And while now the great *San Philip* hung
above us like a cloud 45
Whence the thunderbolt will fall
Long and loud,
Four galleons drew away
From the Spanish fleet that day,
And two upon the larboard and two upon the 50
starboard lay,
And the battle-thunder broke from them all.

8

But anon the great *San Philip*, she bethought
herself and went,
Having that within her womb that had left 5
her ill content;
And the rest they came aboard us, and they
fought us hand to hand,
For a dozen times they came with their pikes
and musketeers,
And a dozen times we shook 'em off as a dog
that shakes his ears
When he leaps from the water to the land.

9

And the sun went down, and the stars came
out far over the summer sea,
But never a moment ceased the fight of the
one and the fifty-three.
Ship after ship, the whole night long, their 20
high-built galleons came,
Ship after ship, the whole night long, with
her battle-thunder and flame;
Ship after ship, the whole night long, drew
back with her dead and her shame.
For some were sunk and many were shattered,
and so could fight us no more—
God of battles, was ever a battle like this in
the world before?

10

For he said, "Fight on! fight on!"
Though his vessel was all but a wreck;
And it chanced that, when half of the short
summer night was gone,
With a grisly wound to be dressed he had left
the deck,
But a bullet struck him that was dressing it
suddenly dead,
And himself he was wounded again in the side
and the head,
And he said, "Fight on! fight on!"

11

And the night went down, and the sun smiled
out far over the summer sea,
And the Spanish fleet with broken sides lay
round us all in a ring;
But they dared not touch us again, for they
feared that we still could sting,
So they watched what the end would be.
And we had not fought them in vain,

But in perilous plight were we,
Seeing forty of our poor hundred were slain,
And half of the rest of us maimed for life
In the crash of the cannonades and the des-
    perate strife;
And the sick men down in the hold were most
    of them stark and cold,
And the pikes were all broken or bent, and
    the powder was all of it spent;
And the masts and the rigging were lying 10
    over the side;
But Sir Richard cried in his English pride:
"We have fought such a fight for a day and a
    night
As may never be fought again!
We have won great glory, my men!
And a day less or more
At sea or ashore,
We die—does it matter when?
Sink me the ship, Master Gunner—sink her, 20
    split her in twain!
Fall into the hands of God, not into the hands
    of Spain!"

12

And the gunner said, "Ay, ay," but the seamen
    made reply:
"We have children, we have wives,
And the Lord hath spared our lives.
We will make the Spaniard promise, if we 30
    yield, to let us go;
We shall live to fight again and to strike
    another blow."
And the lion there lay dying, and they yielded
    to the foe. 35

13

And the stately Spanish men to their flagship
    bore him then,
Where they laid him by the mast, old Sir 40
    Richard caught at last,
And they praised him to his face with their
    courtly foreign grace;
But he rose upon their decks, and he
    cried: 45
"I have fought for Queen and Faith like a
    valiant man and true;
I have only done my duty as a man is bound
    to do.
With a joyful spirit I Sir Richard Grenville 50
    die!"
And he fell upon their decks, and he died.

14

And they stared at the dead that had been
    so valiant and true,
And had holden the power and glory of Spain
    so cheap
That he dared her with one little ship and his
    English few;
Was he devil or man? He was devil for aught
    they knew,
But they sank his body with honor down into
    the deep,
And they manned the *Revenge* with a swarth-
    ier alien crew,
And away she sailed with her loss and longed
    for her own;
When a wind from the lands they had ruined
    awoke from sleep,
And the water began to heave and the weather
    to moan,
And or ever that evening ended a great gale
    blew,
And a wave like the wave that is raised by an
    earthquake grew,
Till it smote on their hulls and their sails and
    their masts and their flags,
And the whole sea plunged and fell on the
    shot-shattered navy of Spain,
And the little *Revenge* herself went down by
    the island crags
To be lost evermore in the main.

ROBERT BROWNING

*Like his famous contemporary, Tennyson,
Browning (1812–1889) had a literary start
in life—in his father's library. Like Tennyson,
he knew the Romantics and early felt their influence. Travel and tutors gave him fundamen-
tals to build on. Eventually Browning produced
a great quantity of verse, much of it first-rank,
some of it obscure, some of it (the later work)
unexciting. His reputation is almost unassaila-
ble at the present time; students coming to
Browning after difficulties with earlier authors
relax with understanding and enjoyment as
they read the best lyrics, the half-dozen outstanding dramatic monologues,* The Ring and
the Book; *something in Browning seems
modern to them. His love for Elizabeth Barrett
has been exploited on the stage, but it takes*

*more than a literary love duet to excite under-
graduates. They generally like his Renaissance
backgrounds, or his stream-of-consciousness
technique in the monologues, or his philosophy
of work and noble risks, or his ability to spin a* 5
*yarn, or his psychological approach to truth—
or some combination of these. One answer for
Browning's popularity, then, is that he has so
many facets: he is poet, thinker, psychologist.
And, of course, his language is modern. Finally,* 10
*his living men and women are dramatically
real, whereas much earlier literature too often
is remote or merely pretty. (See also I, 304.)**

MY LAST DUCHESS

FERRARA

That's my last Duchess painted on the wall,
Looking as if she were alive. I call   20
That piece a wonder, now: Frà Pandolf's[1] hand
Worked busily a day, and there she stands.
Will't please you sit and look at her? I said
"Frà Pandolf" by design, for never read
Strangers like you that pictured countenance,   25
The depth and passion of its earnest glance,
But to myself they turned (since none puts by
The curtain I have drawn for you, but I)
And seemed as they would ask me, if they
    durst,
How such a glance came there; so, not the first   30
Are you to turn and ask thus. Sir, 'twas not
Her husband's presence only, called that spot
Of joy into the Duchess' cheek: perhaps
Frà Pandolf chanced to say, "Her mantle laps   35
Over my lady's wrist too much," or "Paint
Must never hope to reproduce the faint
Half-flush that dies along her throat:" such
    stuff
Was courtesy, she thought, and cause enough   40
For calling up that spot of joy. She had
A heart—how shall I say?—too soon made
    glad,
Too easily impressed: she liked whate'er
She looked on, and her looks went every-   45
    where.
Sir, 'twas all one! My favor at her breast,
The dropping of the daylight in the West,

---

* The selections which follow are from Browning's *Poetical Works*. By permission of The Mac-   50
millan Company, publishers.
[1] imaginary painter.

The bough of cherries some officious fool
Broke in the orchard for her, the white mule
She rode with round the terrace—all and each
Would draw from her alike the approving
    speech,
Or blush, at least. She thanked men,—good!
    but thanked
Somehow—I know not how—as if she ranked
My gift of a nine-hundred-years-old name
With anybody's gift. Who'd stoop to blame
This sort of trifling? Even had you skill
In speech—(which I have not)—to make your
    will
Quite clear to such an one, and say, "Just this
Or that in you disgusts me; here you miss,
Or there exceed the mark"—and if she let
Herself be lessoned so, nor plainly set
Her wits to yours, forsooth, and made excuse,
—E'en then would be some stooping; and I
    choose
Never to stoop. Oh sir, she smiled, no doubt,
Whene'er I passed her; but who passed with-
    out
Much the same smile? This grew; I gave com-
    mands;
Then all smiles stopped together. There she
    stands
As if alive. Will't please you rise? We'll meet
The company below, then. I repeat,
The Count your master's known munificence
Is ample warrant that no just pretence
Of mine for dowry will be disallowed;
Though his fair daughter's self, as I avowed
At starting, is my object. Nay, we'll go
Together down, sir. Notice Neptune, though,
Taming a sea-horse, thought a rarity,
Which Claus of Innsbruck[2] cast in bronze for
    me!

SOLILOQUY OF THE SPANISH
CLOISTER

Gr-r-r—there go, my heart's abhorrence!
    Water your damned flower-pots, do!
If hate killed men, Brother Lawrence,
    God's blood, would not mine kill you!
What? your myrtle-bush wants trimming?
    Oh, that rose has prior claims—
Needs its leaden vase filled brimming?
    Hell dry you up with its flames!

---

[2] imaginary sculptor.

At the meal we sit together:
  Salve tibi![1] I must hear
Wise talk of the kind of weather,
  Sort of season, time of year:
Not a plenteous cork-crop: scarcely   5
Dare we hope oak-galls, I doubt:
What's the Latin name for "parsley"?
  What's the Greek name for Swine's Snout?

Whew! We'll have our platter burnished,   10
  Laid with care on our own shelf!
With a fire-new spoon we're furnished,
  And a goblet for ourself,
Rinsed like something sacrificial
  Ere 'tis fit to touch our chaps—   15
Marked with L for our initial!
  (He-he! There his lily snaps!)

Saint, forsooth! While brown Dolores
  Squats outside the Convent bank   20
With Sanchicha, telling stories,
  Steeping tresses in the tank,
Blue-black, lustrous, thick like horsehairs,
  —Can't I see his dead eye glow,
Bright as 'twere a Barbary corsair's?   25
  (That is, if he'd let it show!)

When he finishes refection,
  Knife and fork he never lays
Cross-wise, to my recollection,
  As do I, in Jesu's praise.   30
I the Trinity illustrate,
  Drinking watered orange-pulp—
In three sips the Arian[2] frustrate;
  While he drains his at one gulp.

Oh, those melons! If he's able   35
  We're to have a feast! so nice!
One goes to the Abbot's table,
  All of us get each a slice.
How go on your flowers? None double?   40
  Not one fruit-sort can you spy?
Strange!—And I, too, at such trouble
  Keep them close-nipped on the sly!

There's a great text in Galatians,
  Once you trip on it, entails
Twenty-nine distinct damnations,   45

One sure, if another fails:
If I trip him just a-dying,
  Sure of heaven as sure can be,
Spin him round and send him flying
  Off to hell, a Manichee?[3]

Or, my scrofulous French novel
  On gray paper with blunt type!
Simply glance at it, you grovel
  Hand and foot in Belial's[4] gripe:
If I double down its pages
  At the woeful sixteenth print,
When he gathers his greengages,
  Ope a sieve and slip it in't?

Or, there's Satan!—one might venture
  Pledge one's soul to him, yet leave
Such a flaw in the indenture
  As he'd miss till, past retrieve,
Blasted lay that rose-acacia
  We're so proud of! *Hy, Zy, Hine . . .*
'St, there's Vespers! *Plena gratiâ,*
  Ave, Virgo![5] Gr-r-r—you swine!

THE BISHOP ORDERS HIS TOMB
AT SAINT PRAXED'S CHURCH

ROME, 15—

Vanity, saith the preacher, vanity!
Draw round my bed: is Anselm keeping back?   30
Nephews—sons mine . . . ah God, I know
  not! Well—
She, men would have to be your mother once,
Old Gandolf envied me, so fair she was!
What's done is done, and she is dead beside,   35
Dead long ago, and I am Bishop since,
And as she died so must we die ourselves,
And thence ye may perceive the world's a
  dream.
Life, how and what is it? As here I lie   40
In this state-chamber, dying by degrees,
Hours and long hours in the dead night, I ask
"Do I live, am I dead?" Peace, peace seems all.
Saint Praxed's ever was the church for peace;
And so, about this tomb of mine. I fought   45
With tooth and nail to save my niche, ye know:
—Old Gandolf cozened me, despite my care;

---

[1] Hail to thee.
[2] a follower of Arius (fourth century), who believed Christ not co-equal with God, and was deemed heretical by the Council of Nicea.

[3] Manichean, heretical follower of Manes (third century), who mixed Christian and Zoroastrian doctrines.
[4] a prominent devil.
[5] Hail, Virgin, full of grace.

Shrewd was that snatch from out the corner
  South
He graced his carrion with, God curse the
  same!
Yet still my niche is not so cramped but thence
One sees the pulpit o' the epistle-side,
And somewhat of the choir, those silent seats,
And up into the aery dome where live
The angels, and a sunbeam's sure to lurk:
And I shall fill my slab of basalt there,
And 'neath my tabernacle take my rest,
With those nine columns round me, two and
  two,
The odd one at my feet where Anselm stands:
Peach-blossom marble all, the rare, the ripe
As fresh-poured red wine of a mighty pulse.
—Old Gandolf with his paltry onion-stone,
Put me where I may look at him! True peach,
Rosy and flawless: how I earned the prize!
Draw close: that conflagration of my church
—What then? So much was saved if aught
  were missed!
My sons, ye would not be my death? Go dig
The white-grape vineyard where the oil-press
  stood,
Drop water gently till the surface sink,
And if ye find . . . Ah God, I know not,
  I! . . .
Bedded in store of rotten fig-leaves soft,
And corded up in a tight olive-frail,[1]
Some lump, ah God, of *lapis lazuli*,
Big as a Jew's head cut off at the nape,
Blue as a vein o'er the Madonna's breast . . .
Sons, all have I bequeathed you, villas, all,
That brave Frascati villa with its bath,
So, let the blue lump poise between my knees,
Like God the Father's globe on both his hands
Ye worship in the Jesu Church so gay,
For Gandolf shall not choose but see and burst!
Swift as a weaver's shuttle fleet our years:
Man goeth to the grave, and where is he?
Did I say basalt for my slab, sons? Black—
'Twas ever antique-black I meant! How else
Shall ye contrast my frieze to come beneath?
The bas-relief in bronze ye promised me,
Those Pans and Nymphs ye wot of, and per-
  chance
Some tripod, thyrsus, with a vase or so,
The Savior at his sermon on the mount,
Saint Praxed in a glory, and one Pan

5 Ready to twitch the Nymph's last garment off,
And Moses with the tables . . . but I know
Ye mark me not! What do they whisper thee,
Child of my bowels, Anselm? Ah, ye hope
To revel down my villas while I gasp
Bricked o'er with beggar's moldy travertine
Which Gandolf from his tomb-top chuckles at!
Nay, boys, ye love me—all of jasper, then!
'Tis jasper ye stand pledged to, lest I grieve
10 My bath must needs be left behind, alas!
One block, pure green as a pistachio-nut,
There's plenty jasper somewhere in the
  world—
And have I not Saint Praxed's ear to pray
15 Horses for ye, and brown Greek manuscripts,
And mistresses with great smooth marbly
  limbs?
—That's if ye carve my epitaph aright,
Choice Latin, picked phrase, Tully's[2] every
  word,
20 No gaudy ware like Gandolf's second line—
Tully, my masters? Ulpian[3] serves his need!
And then how I shall lie through centuries,
And hear the blessed mutter of the mass,
25 And see God made and eaten all day long,
And feel the steady candle-flame, and taste
Good strong thick stupefying incense-smoke!
For as I lie here, hours of the dead night,
Dying in state and by such slow degrees,
30 I fold my arms as if they clasped a crook,
And stretch my feet forth straight as stone
  can point,
And let the bedclothes, for a mortcloth, drop
Into great laps and folds of sculptor's-work:
35 And as yon tapers dwindle, and strange
  thoughts
Grow, with a certain humming in my ears,
About the life before I lived this life,
And this life too, popes, cardinals and priests,
40 Saint Praxed at his sermon on the mount,
Your tall pale mother with her talking eyes,
And new-found agate urns as fresh as day,
And marble's language, Latin pure, discreet,
—Aha, ELUCESCEBAT[4] quoth our friend?
45 No Tully, said I, Ulpian at the best!
Evil and brief hath been my pilgrimage.
All *lapis*, all, sons! Else I give the Pope
My villas! Will ye ever eat my heart?
Ever your eyes were as a lizard's quick,
50 They glitter like your mother's for my soul,

---

[1] basket for holding olives.   [2] Cicero.   [3] Roman jurist.   [4] he was famous.

Or ye would heighten my impoverished frieze,
Piece out its starved design, and fill my vase
With grapes, and add a visor and a Term,[5]
And to the tripod ye would tie a lynx
That in his struggle throws the thyrsus down,　5
To comfort me on my entablature
Whereon I am to lie till I must ask
"Do I live, am I dead?" There, leave me,
　　there!
For ye have stabbed me with ingratitude　　10
To death—ye wish it—God, ye wish it!
Stone—
Gritstone, a-crumble! Clammy squares which
　　sweat
As if the corpse they keep were oozing　15
　　through—
And no more *lapis* to delight the world!
Well, go! I bless ye. Fewer tapers there,
But in a row: and, going, turn your backs
—Ay, like departing altar-ministrants,　　20
And leave me in my church, the church for
　　peace,
That I may watch at leisure if he leers—
Old Gandolf—at me, from his onion-stone,
As still he envied me, so fair she was!　　25

THE STATUE AND THE BUST

There's a palace in Florence, the world knows　30
　　well,
And a statue watches it from the square,
And this story both do our townsmen tell.

Ages ago, a lady there,　　35
At the farthest window facing the East
Asked, "Who rides by with the royal air?"

The bridesmaids' prattle around her ceased;
She leaned forth, one on either hand;　　40
They saw how the blush of the bride in-
　　creased—

They felt by its beats her heart expand—
As one at each ear and both in a breath　45
Whispered, "The Great-Duke Ferdinand."

That selfsame instant, underneath,
The Duke rode past in his idle way,
Empty and fine like a swordless sheath.　　50

Gay he rode, with a friend as gay,
Till he threw his head back—"Who is she?"
—"A bride the Riccardi brings home today."

Hair in heaps lay heavily
Over a pale brow spirit-pure—
Carved like the heart of the coal-black tree,

Crisped like a war-steed's encolure[1]—
And vainly sought to dissemble her eyes
Of the blackest black our eyes endure,

And lo, a blade for a knight's emprise
Filled the fine empty sheath of a man,—
The Duke grew straightway brave and wise.

He looked at her, as a lover can;
She looked at him, as one who awakes:
The past was a sleep, and her life began.

Now, love so ordered for both their sakes,
A feast was held that selfsame night
In the pile which the mighty shadow makes.

(For Via Larga is three-parts light,
But the palace overshadows one,
Because of a crime, which may God requite!

To Florence and God the wrong was done,
Through the first republic's murder there
By Cosimo and his cursed son.)

The Duke (with the statue's face in the square)
Turned in the midst of his multitude
At the bright approach of the bridal pair.

Face to face the lovers stood
A single minute and no more,
While the bridegroom bent as a man sub-
　　dued—

Bowed till his bonnet brushed the floor—
For the Duke on the lady a kiss conferred,
As the courtly custom was of yore.

In a minute can lovers exchange a word?
If a word did pass, which I do not think,
Only one out of a thousand heard.

That was the bridegroom. At day's brink

---

[5] bust on pedestal.

[1] mane.

He and his bride were alone at last
In a bed chamber by a taper's blink.

Calmly he said that her lot was cast,
That the door she had passed was shut on her
Till the final catafalk repassed.

The world meanwhile, its noise and stir,
Through a certain window facing the East
She could watch like a convent's chronicler.

Since passing the door might lead to a feast,
And a feast might lead to so much beside,
He, of many evils, chose the least.

"Freely I choose too," said the bride—
"Your window and its world suffice,"
Replied the tongue, while the heart replied—

"If I spend the night with that devil twice,
May his window serve as my loop of hell
Whence a damned soul looks on paradise!

"I fly to the Duke who loves me well,
Sit by his side and laugh at sorrow
Ere I count another ave-bell.

" 'Tis only the coat of a page to borrow,
And tie my hair in a horse-boy's trim,
And I save my soul—but not to-morrow"—

(She checked herself and her eye grew dim)
"My father tarries to bless my state:
I must keep it one day more for him.

"Is one day more so long to wait?
Moreover the Duke rides past, I know;
We shall see each other, sure as fate."

She turned on her side and slept. Just so!
So we resolve on a thing and sleep:
So did the lady, ages ago.

That night the Duke said, "Dear or cheap
As the cost of this cup of bliss may prove
To body or soul, I will drain it deep."

And on the morrow, bold with love,
He beckoned the bridegroom (close on call,
As his duty bade, by the Duke's alcove)

And smiled " 'Twas a very funeral,

Your lady will think, this feast of ours,—
A shame to efface, whate'er befall!

"What if we break from the Arno bowers,
5 And try if Petraja, cool and green,
Cure last night's fault with this morning's
    flowers?"

The bridegroom, not a thought to be seen
10 On his steady brow and quiet mouth,
Said, "Too much favor for me so mean!

"But, alas! my lady leaves[2] the South;
Each wind that comes from the Apennine
15 Is a menace to her tender youth:

"Nor a way exists, the wise opine,
If she quits her palace twice this year,
To avert the flower of life's decline."

20
Quoth the Duke, "A sage and a kindly fear.
Moreover Petraja is cold this spring:
Be our feast to-night as usual here!"

25 And then to himself—"Which night shall bring
Thy bride to her lover's embraces, fool—
Or I am the fool, and thou art the king!

"Yet my passion must wait a night, nor cool—
30 For to-night the Envoy arrives from France
Whose heart I unlock with thyself, my tool.

"I need thee still and might miss perchance.
To-day is not wholly lost, beside,
35 With its hope of my lady's countenance:

"For I ride—what should I do but ride?
And passing her palace, if I list,
May glance at its window—well betide!"

40
So said, so done: nor the lady missed
One ray that broke from the ardent brow,
Nor a curl of the lips where the spirit kissed.

45 Be sure that each renewed the vow,
No morrow's sun should arise and set
And leave them then as it left them now.

But next day passed, and next day yet,
50 With still fresh cause to wait one day more
Ere each leaped over the parapet.

_____
[2] comes from.

And still, as love's brief morning wore,
With a gentle start, half smile, half sigh,
They found love not as it seemed before.

They thought it would work infallibly,
But not in despite of heaven and earth:
The rose would blow when the storm passed
    by.

Meantime they could profit in winter's dearth
By store of fruits that supplant the rose:
The world and its ways have a certain worth:

And to press a point while these oppose
Were simple policy; better wait:
We lose no friends and we gain no foes.

Meantime, worse fates than a lover's fate,
Who daily may ride and pass and look
Where his lady watches behind the grate!

And she—she watched the square like a book
Holding one picture and only one,
Which daily to find she undertook:

When the picture was reached the book was
    done,
And she turned from the picture at night to
    scheme
Of tearing it out for herself next sun.

So weeks grew months, years; gleam by gleam
The glory dropped from their youth and
    love,
And both perceived they had dreamed a
    dream;

Which hovered as dreams do, still above:
But who can take a dream for a truth?
Oh, hide our eyes from the next remove!

One day as the lady saw her youth
Depart, and the silver thread that streaked
Her hair, and, worn by the serpent's tooth,

The brow so puckered, the chin so peaked,—
And wondered who the woman was,
Hollow-eyed and haggard-cheeked,

Fronting her silent in the glass—
"Summon here," she suddenly said,
"Before the rest of my old self pass,

"Him, the Carver, a hand to aid,
Who fashions the clay no love will change,
And fixes a beauty never to fade.

"Let Robbia's[3] craft so apt and strange
Arrest the remains of young and fair,
And rivet them while the seasons range.

"Make me a face on the window there,
Waiting as ever, mute the while,
My love to pass below in the square!

"And let me think that it may beguile
Dreary days which the dead must spend
Down in their darkness under the aisle,

"To say, 'What matters it at the end?
I did no more while my heart was warm
Than does that image, my pale-faced friend.'

"Where is the use of lip's red charm,
The heaven of hair, the pride of the brow,
And the blood that blues the inside arm—

"Unless we turn, as the soul knows how,
The earthly gift to an end divine?
A lady of clay is as good, I trow."

But long ere Robbia's cornice, fine,
With flowers and fruits which leaves enlace,
Was set where now is the empty shrine—

(And, leaning out of a bright blue space,
As a ghost might lean from a chink of sky,
The passionate pale lady's face—

Eying ever, with earnest eye
And quick-turned neck at its breathless stretch,
Some one who ever is passing by—)

The Duke had sighed like the simplest wretch
In Florence, "Youth—my dream escapes!
Will its record stay?" And he bade them fetch

Some subtle molder of brazen shapes—
"Can the soul, the will, die out of a man
Ere his body find the grave that gapes?

"John of Douay[4] shall effect my plan,

[3] The Della Robbias were a family famous for terra cotta work.
[4] sculptor of Bologna.

Set me on horseback here aloft,
Alive, as the crafty sculptor can,

"In the very square I have crossed so oft:
That men may admire, when future suns
Shall touch the eyes to a purpose soft,

"While the mouth and the brow stay brave in
    bronze—
Admire and say, 'When he was alive
How he would take his pleasure once!'

"And it shall go hard but I contrive
To listen the while, and laugh in my tomb
At idleness which aspires to strive."

    .   .   .   .   .

So! While these wait the trump of doom,
How do their spirits pass, I wonder,
Nights and days in the narrow room?

Still, I suppose, they sit and ponder
What a gift life was, ages ago,
Six steps out of the chapel yonder.

Only they see not God, I know,
Nor all that chivalry of his,
The soldier-saints who, row on row,

Burn upward each to his point of bliss—
Since, the end of life being manifest,
He had burned his way through the world to
    this.

I hear you reproach, "But delay was best,
For their end was a crime."—Oh, a crime will
    do
As well, I reply, to serve for a test,

As a virtue golden through and through,
Sufficient to vindicate itself
And prove its worth at a moment's view!

Must a game be played for the sake of pelf?
Where a button goes, 'twere an epigram
To offer the stamp of the very Guelph.[5]

The true has no value beyond the sham:
As well the counter as coin, I submit,

When your table's a hat, and your prize, a
    dram.

Stake your counter as boldly every whit,
5 Venture as warily, use the same skill,
Do your best, whether winning or losing it,

If you choose to play!—is my principle.
Let a man contend to the uttermost
10 For his life's set prize, be it what it will!
The counter our lovers staked was lost
As surely as if it were lawful coin:
And the sin I impute to each frustrate ghost

15 Is—the unlit lamp and the ungirt loin,
Though the end in sight was a vice, I say.
You of the virtue (we issue join)
How strive you? *De te, fabula!*[6]

20

ANDREA DEL SARTO

CALLED "THE FAULTLESS PAINTER"

But do not let us quarrel any more,
25 No, my Lucrezia; bear with me for once:
Sit down and all shall happen as you wish.
You turn your face, but does it bring your
    heart?
I'll work then for your friend's friend, never
30   fear,
Treat his own subject after his own way,
Fix his own time, accept too his own price,
And shut the money into this small hand
When next it takes mine. Will it? tenderly?
35 Oh, I'll content him,—but to-morrow, Love!
I often am much wearier than you think,
This evening more than usual, and it seems
As if—forgive now—should you let me sit
Here by the window with your hand in mine
40 And look a half-hour forth on Fiesole,
Both of one mind, as married people use,
Quietly, quietly the evening through,
I might get up to-morrow to my work
Cheerful and fresh as ever. Let us try.
45 To-morrow, how you shall be glad for this!
Your soft hand is a woman of itself,
And mine the man's bared breast she curls in-
    side.
Don't count the time lost, neither; you must
50   serve

[5] to offer a real coin with the ruler's mark or face
on it.

[6] This tale concerns you.

For each of the five pictures we require:
It saves a model. So! keep looking so—
My serpentining beauty, rounds on rounds!
—How could you ever prick those perfect ears,
Even to put the pearl there! oh, so sweet—   5
My face, my moon, my everybody's moon,
Which everybody looks on and calls his,
And, I suppose, is looked on by in turn,
While she looks—no one's: very dear, no less.
You smile? why, there's my picture ready   10
      made,
There's what we painters call our harmony!
A common grayness silvers everything,—
All in a twilight, you and I alike
—You, at the point of your first pride in me   15
(That's gone you know),—but I, at every
      point;
My youth, my hope, my art, being all toned
      down
To yonder sober pleasant Fiesole.
There's the bell clinking from the chapel-top;   20
That length of convent-wall across the way
Holds the trees safer, huddled more inside;
The last monk leaves the garden; days de-
      crease,
And autumn grows, autumn in everything.   25
Eh? the whole seems to fall into a shape
As if I saw alike my work and self
And all that I was born to be and do,
A twilight-piece. Love, we are in God's hand.   30
How strange now looks the life he makes us
      lead;
So free we seem, so fettered fast we are!
I feel he laid the fetter: let it lie!
This chamber for example—turn your head—   35
All that's behind us! You don't understand
Nor care to understand about my art,
But you can hear at least when people speak:
And that cartoon, the second from the door
—It is the thing, Love! so such things should   40
      be—
Behold Madonna!—I am bold to say.
I can do with my pencil what I know,
What I see, what at bottom of my heart
I wish for, if I ever wish so deep—   45
Do easily, too—when I say, perfectly,
I do not boast, perhaps: yourself are judge,
Who listened to the Legate's talk last week,
And just as much they used to say in France.
At any rate 'tis easy, all of it!   50
No sketches first, no studies, that's long past:
I do what many dream of all their lives,

—Dream? strive to do, and agonize to do,
And fail in doing. I could count twenty such
On twice your fingers, and not leave this town,
Who strive—you don't know how the others
      strive
To paint a little thing like that you smeared
Carelessly passing with your robes afloat,—
Yet do much less, so much less, Someone says,
(I know his name, no matter)—so much less!
Well, less is more, Lucrezia: I am judged.
There burns a truer light of God in them,
In their vexed beating stuffed and stopped-up
      brain,
Heart, or whate'er else, than goes on to prompt
This low-pulsed forthright craftsman's hand
      of mine.
Their works drop groundward, but themselves,
      I know,
Reach many a time a heaven that's shut to me,
Enter and take their place there sure enough,   20
Though they come back and cannot tell the
      world.
My works are nearer heaven, but I sit here.
The sudden blood of these men! at a word—
Praise them, it boils, or blame them, it boils   25
      too.
I, painting from myself and to myself,
Know what I do, am unmoved by men's blame
Or their praise either. Somebody remarks
Morello's[1] outline there is wrongly traced,   30
His hue mistaken; what of that? or else,
Rightly traced and well ordered; what of that?
Speak as they please, what does the mountain
      care?
Ah, but a man's reach should exceed his grasp,   35
Or what's a heaven for? All is silver-gray
Placid and perfect with my art: the worse!
I know both what I want and what might gain,
And yet how profitless to know, to sigh
"Had I been two, another and myself,   40
Our head would have o'erlooked the world!"
      No doubt.
Yonder's a work now, of that famous youth
The Urbinate[2] who died five years ago.
('Tis copied, George Vasari[3] sent it me.)   45
Well, I can fancy how he did it all,
Pouring his soul, with kings and popes to see,
Reaching, that heaven might so replenish him,

[1] mountain in the Apennines.
[2] Raphael.
[3] author of a standard work, biographies of
painters and artisans, source for the poem.

Above and through his art—for it gives way;
That arm is wrongly put—and there again—
A fault to pardon in the drawing's lines,
Its body, so to speak: its soul is right,
He means right—that, a child may understand.
Still, what an arm! and I could alter it:
But all the play, the insight and the stretch—
Out of me, out of me! And wherefore out?
Had you enjoined them on me, given me soul,
We might have risen to Rafael, I and you!
Nay, Love, you did give all I asked, I think—
More than I merit, yes, by many times.
But had you—oh, with the same perfect brow,
And perfect eyes, and more than perfect
mouth,
And the low voice my soul hears, as a bird
The fowler's pipe, and follows to the snare—
Had you, with these the same, but brought a
mind!
Some women do so. Had the mouth there
urged
"God and the glory! never care for gain.
The present by the future, what is that?
Live for fame, side by side with Agnolo!⁴
Rafael is waiting: up to God, all three!"
I might have done it for you. So it seems:
Perhaps not. All is as God overrules.
Besides, incentives come from the soul's self;
The rest avail not. Why do I need you?
What wife had Rafael, or has Agnolo?
In this world, who can do a thing, will not;
And who would do it, cannot, I perceive:
Yet the will's somewhat—somewhat, too, the
power—
And thus we half-men struggle. At the end,
God, I conclude, compensates, punishes.
'Tis safer for me, if the award be strict,
That I am something underrated here,
Poor this long while, despised, to speak the
truth.
I dared not, do you know, leave home all day,
For fear of chancing on the Paris lords.
The best is when they pass and look aside;
But they speak sometimes; I must bear it
all.
Well may they speak! That Francis,⁵ that first
time,

⁴ Michelangelo.
⁵ Francis I of France. Andrea is supposed to have
left his employ with money to buy him pictures,
money which went for building a house for Lucrezia.

And that long festal year at Fontainebleau!
I surely then could sometimes leave the
ground,
Put on the glory, Rafael's daily wear,
5 In that humane great monarch's golden look,—
One finger in his beard or twisted curl
Over his mouth's good mark that made the
smile,
One arm about my shoulder, round my neck,
10 The jingle of his gold chain in my ear,
I painting proudly with his breath on me,
All his court round him, seeing with his eyes,
Such frank French eyes, and such a fire of
souls
15 Profuse, my hand kept plying by those
hearts,—
And, best of all, this, this, this face beyond,
This in the background, waiting on my work,
To crown the issue with a last reward!
20 A good time, was it not, my kingly days?
And had you not grown restless . . . but I
know—
'Tis done and past; 'twas right, my instinct
said;
25 Too live the life grew, golden and not gray,
And I'm the weak-eyed bat no sun should
tempt
Out of the grange whose four walls make his
world.
30 How could it end in any other way?
You called me, and I came home to your heart.
The triumph was—to reach and stay there;
since
I reached it ere the triumph, what is lost?
35 Let my hands frame your face in your hair's
gold,
You beautiful Lucrezia that are mine!
"Rafael did this, Andrea painted that;
The Roman's is the better when you pray,
40 But still the other's Virgin was his wife"—
Men will excuse me. I am glad to judge
Both pictures in your presence; clearer grows
My better fortune, I resolve to think.
For, do you know, Lucrezia, as God lives,
45 Said one day Agnolo, his very self,
To Rafael . . . I have known it all these
years . . .
(When the young man was flaming out his
thoughts
50 Upon a palace-wall for Rome to see,
Too lifted up in heart because of it)
"Friend, there's a certain sorry little scrub

Goes up and down our Florence, none cares
  how,
Who, were he set to plan and execute
As you are, pricked on by your popes and
  kings,
Would bring the sweat into that brow of 5
  yours!"
To Rafael's!—And indeed the arm is wrong.
I hardly dare . . . yet, only you to see,
Give the chalk here—quick, thus the line 10
  should go!
Ay, but the soul! he's Rafael! rub it out!
Still, all I care for, if he spoke the truth,
(What he? why, who but Michel Agnolo?
Do you forget already words like those?) 15
If really there was such a chance, so lost,—
Is, whether you're—not grateful—but more
  pleased.
Well, let me think so. And you smile indeed!
This hour has been an hour! Another smile? 20
If you would sit thus by me every night
I should work better, do you comprehend?
I mean that I should earn more, give you more.
See, it is settled dusk now; there's a star;
Morello's gone, the watch-lights show the wall, 25
The cue-owls speak the name we call them by.
Come from the window, love,—come in, at
  last,
Inside the melancholy little house
We built to be so gay with. God is just. 30
King Francis may forgive me: oft at nights
When I look up from painting, eyes tired out,
The walls become illumined, brick from brick
Distinct, instead of mortar, fierce bright gold,
That gold of his I did cement them with! 35
Let us but love each other. Must you go?
That Cousin[6] here again? he waits outside?
Must see you—you, and not with me? Those
  loans?
More gaming debts to pay? you smiled for 40
  that?
Well, let smiles buy me! have you more to
  spend?
While hand and eye and something of a heart
Are left me, work's my ware, and what's it 45
  worth?
I'll pay my fancy. Only let me sit
The gray remainder of the evening out,
Idle, you call it, and muse perfectly
How I could paint, were I but back in France, 50
One picture, just one more—the Virgin's face,

Not yours this time! I want you at my side
To hear them—that is, Michel Agnolo—
Judge all I do and tell you of its worth.
Will you? To-morrow, satisfy your friend.
I take the subjects for his corridor,
Finish the portrait out of hand—there, there,
And throw him in another thing or two
If he demurs; the whole should prove enough
To pay for this same Cousin's freak. Beside,
What's better and what's all I care about,
Get you the thirteen scudi[7] for the ruff!
Love, does that please you? Ah, but what does
  he,
The Cousin! what does he to please you more?

  I am grown peaceful as old age to-night.
I regret little, I would change still less.
Since there my past life lies, why alter it?
The very wrong to Francis!—it is true
I took his coin, was tempted and complied,
And built this house and sinned, and all is
  said.
My father and my mother died of want.
Well, had I riches of my own? you see
How one gets rich! Let each one bear his lot.
They were born poor, lived poor, and poor
  they died:
And I have labored somewhat in my time
And not been paid profusely. Some good son
Paint my two hundred pictures—let him try!
No doubt, there's something strikes a balance.
  Yes,
You loved me quite enough, it seems to-night.
This must suffice me here. What would one
  have?
In heaven, perhaps, new chances, one more
  chance—
Four great walls in the New Jerusalem,
Meted on each side by the angel's reed,
For Leonard,[8] Rafael, Agnolo and me
To cover—the three first without a wife,
While I have mine! So—still they overcome
Because there's still Lucrezia,—as I choose.

  Again the Cousin's whistle! Go, my Love.

DANTE GABRIEL ROSSETTI

*Rossetti (1828–1882) was a member of an il-
lustrious household which included his gifted
sister Christina and his well-known brother*

---

[6] here, lover.

[7] plural of *scudo*, a coin worth about a dollar.
[8] Leonardo da Vinci.

artist, William Michael. Interested in both painting and poetry, Rossetti belonged to the Pre-Raphaelite Brotherhood, which derived its name from its desire to use artistic techniques known before Raphael. Millais, Holman Hunt, Morris, and Swinburne were among the famous names in the group, which at one time was criticized for theme and treatment by stodgy Victorians who attached to it the label "Fleshly School"—but without making it stick. Rossetti and his friends actually were second-crop Romantics, with color and imagination in their work, interest in old forms, versatility in the sonnet and ballad, and marked antagonism toward the new machine age. Rossetti's life was "romantic" in another sense as well: after his wife's death he buried his work, had visions, dug it up; suffered from real and imaginary disorders; took to the bottle and the needle. In spite of all this, he left some memorable ballads, an important sonnet sequence, and a standard translation of Dante's Vita Nuova.

THE BLESSED DAMOZEL

The blessed damozel leaned out
    From the gold bar of Heaven;
Her eyes were deeper than the depth
    Of waters stilled at even;
She had three lilies in her hand,   30
    And the stars in her hair were seven.

Her robe, ungirt from clasp to hem,
    No wrought flowers did adorn,
But a white rose of Mary's gift,   35
    For service meetly worn;
Her hair that lay along her back
    Was yellow like ripe corn.

Her seemed she scarce had been a day   40
    One of God's choristers;
The wonder was not yet quite gone
    From that still look of hers;
Albeit, to them she left, her day
    Had counted as ten years.   45

(To one, it is ten years of years.
    —Yet now, and in this place,
Surely she leaned o'er me—her hair
    Fell all about my face. . . .   50
Nothing: the autumn fall of leaves.
    The whole year sets apace.)

It was the rampart of God's house
    That she was standing on;
By God built over the sheer depth
    The which is Space begun;
So high, that looking downward thence
    She scarce could see the sun.

It lies in Heaven, across the flood
    Of ether, as a bridge.
Beneath, the tides of day and night
    With flame and darkness ridge
The void, as low as where this earth
    Spins like a fretful midge.

Around her, lovers, newly met
    'Mid deathless love's acclaims,
Spoke evermore among themselves
    Their heart-remembered names;
And the souls mounting up to God
    Went by her like thin flames.

And still she bowed herself and stooped
    Out of the circling charm;
Until her bosom must have made
    The bar she leaned on warm,
And the lilies lay as if asleep
    Along her bended arm.

From the fixed place of Heaven she saw
    Time, like a pulse, shake fierce
Through all the worlds. Her gaze still strove
    Within the gulf to pierce
Its path; and now she spoke as when
    The stars sang in their spheres.

The sun was gone now; the curled moon
    Was like a little feather
Fluttering far down the gulf; and now
    She spoke through the still weather.
Her voice was like the voice the stars
    Had when they sang together.

(Ah sweet! Even now, in that bird's song,
    Strove not her accents there,
Fain to be hearkened? When those bells
    Possessed the mid-day air,
Strove not her steps to reach my side
    Down all the echoing stair?)

"I wish that he were come to me.
    For he will come," she said.
"Have I not prayed in Heaven?—on earth,

Lord, Lord, has he not prayed?
Are not two prayers a perfect strength?
  And shall I feel afraid?

"When round his head the aureole clings,
  And he is clothed in white,
I'll take his hand and go with him
  To the deep wells of light;
As unto a stream we will step down,
  And bathe there in God's sight.

"We two will stand beside that shrine,
  Occult, withheld, untrod,
Whose lamps are stirred continually
  With prayer sent up to God;
And see our old prayers, granted, melt
  Each like a little cloud.

"We two will lie i' the shadow of
  That living mystic tree
Within whose secret growth the Dove
  Is sometimes felt to be,
While every leaf that His plumes touch
  Saith His Name audibly.

"And I myself will teach to him,
  I myself, lying so,
The songs I sing here; which his voice
  Shall pause in, hushed and slow,
And find some knowledge at each pause,
  Or some new thing to know."

(Alas! We two, we two, thou say'st!
  Yea, one wast thou with me
That once of old. But shall God lift
  To endless unity
The soul whose likeness with thy soul
  Was but its love for thee?)

"We two," she said, "will seek the groves
  Where the lady Mary is,
With her five handmaidens, whose names
  Are five sweet symphonies,
Cecily, Gertrude, Magdalen,
  Margaret, and Rosalys.

"Circlewise sit they, with bound locks
  And foreheads garlanded;
Into the fine cloth, white like flame
  Weaving the golden thread,
To fashion the birth-robes for them
  Who are just born, being dead.

"He shall fear, haply, and be dumb:
  Then will I lay my cheek
To his, and tell about our love,
  Not once abashed or weak;
And the dear Mother will approve
  My pride, and let me speak.

"Herself shall bring us, hand in hand,
  To Him round Whom all souls
Kneel, the clear-ranged unnumbered heads
  Bowed with their aureoles;
And angels meeting us shall sing
  To their citherns and citoles.[1]

"There will I ask of Christ the Lord
  Thus much for him and me:—
Only to live as once on earth
  With Love,—only to be,
As then awhile, forever now
  Together, I and he."

She gazed and listened and then said,
  Less sad of speech than mild,—
"All this is when he comes." She ceased.
  The light thrilled towards her, filled
With angels in strong level flight.
  Her eyes prayed, and she smiled.

(I saw her smile.) But soon their path
  Was vague in distant spheres:
And then she cast her arms along
  The golden barriers,
And laid her face between her hands,
  And wept. (I heard her tears.)

SISTER HELEN

"Why did you melt your waxen man,[1]
    Sister Helen?
To-day is the third since you began."
"The time was long, yet the time ran,
    Little brother."
  (*O Mother, Mary Mother,*
Three days to-day, between Hell and Heaven!)

"But if you have done your work aright,
    Sister Helen,
You'll let me play, for you said I might."

---

[1] stringed instruments.
[1] This poem is based on the superstition that melting an image of a person will bring death to him.

"Be very still in your play to-night,
          Little brother."
     (*O Mother, Mary Mother,*
Third night, to-night, between Hell and
     Heaven!)

"You said it must melt ere vesper-bell,
          Sister Helen;
If now it be molten, all is well."
"Even so,—nay, peace! you cannot tell,   10
          Little brother."
     (*O Mother, Mary Mother,*
What is this, between Hell and Heaven?)

"Oh the waxen knave was plump to-day,   15
          Sister Helen;
How like dead folk he has dropped away!"
"Nay now, of the dead what can you say,
          Little brother?"
     (*O Mother, Mary Mother,*   20
What of the dead, between Hell and Heaven?)

"See, see, the sunken pile of wood,
          Sister Helen,
Shines through the thinned wax red as blood!"   25
"Nay now, when looked you yet on blood,
          Little brother?"
     (*O Mother, Mary Mother,*
How pale she is, between Hell and Heaven!)
                                                          30
"Now close your eyes, for they're sick and sore,
          Sister Helen,
And I'll play without the gallery door."
"Ay, let me rest,—I'll lie on the floor,
          Little brother."   35
     (*O Mother, Mary Mother,*
What rest to-night, between Hell and Heaven?)

"Here high up in the balcony,
          Sister Helen,
The moon flies face to face with me."   40
"Ay, look and say whatever you see,
          Little brother."
     (*O Mother, Mary Mother,*
What sight to-night, between Hell and   45
     Heaven?)

"Outside it's merry in the wind's wake,
          Sister Helen;
In the shaken trees the chill stars shake."   50
"Hush, heard you a horse-tread as you spake,
          Little brother?"

     (*O Mother, Mary Mother,*
What sound to-night, between Hell and
     Heaven?)

"I hear a horse-tread, and I see,   5
          Sister Helen,
Three horsemen that ride terribly."
"Little brother, whence come the three,
          Little brother?"
     (*O Mother, Mary Mother,*
Whence should they come, between Hell and
     Heaven?)

"They come by the hill-verge from Boyne Bar,
          Sister Helen,
And one draws nigh, but two are afar."
"Look, look, do you know them who they are,
          Little brother?"
     (*O Mother, Mary Mother,*
Who should they be, between Hell and   20
     Heaven?)

"Oh, it's Keith of Eastholm rides so fast,
          Sister Helen,
For I know the white mane on the blast."   25
"The hour has come, has come at last,
          Little brother!"
     (*O Mother, Mary Mother,*
Her hour at last, between Hell and Heaven!)

"He has made a sign and called 'Halloo!'
          Sister Helen,
And he says that he would speak with you."
"Oh tell him I fear the frozen dew,
          Little brother."
     (*O Mother, Mary Mother,*
Why laughs she thus, between Hell and
     Heaven!)

"The wind is loud, but I hear him cry,   40
          Sister Helen,
That Keith of Ewern's like to die."
"And he and thou, and thou and I,
          Little brother."
     (*O Mother, Mary Mother,*
And they and we, between Hell and Heaven!)

"Three days ago, on his marriage-morn,
          Sister Helen,
He sickened, and lies since then forlorn."   50
"For bridegroom's side is the bride a thorn,
          Little brother?"

(*O Mother, Mary Mother,*
Cold bridal cheer, between Hell and Heaven!)

"Three days and nights he has lain abed,
    Sister Helen,
And he prays in torment to be dead."
"The thing may chance, if he have prayed,
    Little brother!"
    (*O Mother, Mary Mother,*
If he have prayed, between Hell and Heaven!) 10

"But he has not ceased to cry to-day,
    Sister Helen,
That you should take your curse away."
"*My* prayer was heard,—he need but pray, 15
    Little brother!"
    (*O Mother, Mary Mother,*
Shall God not hear, between Hell and
Heaven?)

20

"But he says, till you take back your ban,
    Sister Helen,
His soul would pass, yet never can."
"Nay then, shall I slay a living man, 25
    Little brother?"
    (*O Mother, Mary Mother,*
A living soul, between Hell and Heaven!)

"But he calls forever on your name, 30
    Sister Helen,
And says that he melts before a flame."
"My heart for his pleasure fared the same,
    Little brother."
    (*O Mother, Mary Mother,* 35
Fire at the heart, between Hell and Heaven!)

"Here's Keith of Westholm riding fast,
    Sister Helen,
For I know the white plume on the blast." 40
"The hour, the sweet hour I forecast,
    Little brother!"
    (*O Mother, Mary Mother,*
Is the hour sweet, between Hell and Heaven?)

45

"He stops to speak, and he stills his horse,
    Sister Helen;
But his words are drowned in the wind's
    course."
"Nay hear, nay hear, you must hear perforce, 50
    Little brother!"
    (*O Mother, Mary Mother,*

What word now heard, between Hell and
Heaven?)

"Oh he says that Keith of Ewern's cry,
    Sister Helen, 5
Is ever to see you ere he die."
"In all that his soul sees, there am I,
    Little brother!"
    (*O Mother, Mary Mother,*
The soul's one sight, between Hell and
Heaven!)

"He sends a ring and a broken coin,
    Sister Helen,
And bids you mind the banks of Boyne."
"What else he broke will he ever join,
    Little brother?"
    (*O Mother, Mary Mother,*
No, never joined, between Hell and Heaven!)

"He yields you these and craves full fain,
    Sister Helen,
You pardon him in his mortal pain."
"What else he took will he give again,
    Little brother?"
    (*O Mother, Mary Mother,*
Not twice to give, between Hell and Heaven!)

"He calls your name in an agony,
    Sister Helen,
That even dead Love must weep to see."
"Hate, born of Love, is blind as he,
    Little brother!"
    (*O Mother, Mary Mother,*
Love turned to hate, between Hell and
Heaven!)

"Oh it's Keith of Keith now that rides fast,
    Sister Helen,
For I know the white hair on the blast."
"The short, short hour will soon be past,
    Little brother!"
    (*O Mother, Mary Mother,*
Will soon be past, between Hell and Heaven!)

"He looks at me and he tries to speak,
    Sister Helen,
But oh his voice is sad and weak!"
"What here should the mighty Baron seek,
    Little brother?"
    (*O Mother, Mary Mother,*
Is this the end, between Hell and Heaven?)

"Oh his son still cries, if you forgive,
  Sister Helen,
The body dies, but the soul shall live."
"Fire shall forgive me as I forgive,
  Little brother!"   5
  (*O Mother, Mary Mother,*
As she forgives, between Hell and Heaven!)

"Oh he prays you, as his heart would rive,
  Sister Helen,   10
To save his dear son's soul alive."
"Fire cannot slay it, it shall thrive,
  Little brother!"
  (*O Mother, Mary Mother,*
Alas, alas, between Hell and Heaven!) 15

"He cries to you, kneeling in the road,
  Sister Helen,
To go with him for the love of God!"
"The way is long to his son's abode,
  Little brother."   20
  (*O Mother, Mary Mother,*
The way is long, between Hell and Heaven!)

"A lady's here, by a dark steed brought, 25
  Sister Helen,
So darkly clad, I saw her not."
"See her now or never see aught,
  Little brother!"
  (*O Mother, Mary Mother,* 30
What more to see, between Hell and Heaven!)

"Her hood falls back, and the moon shines fair,
  Sister Helen,
On the Lady of Ewern's golden hair." 35
"Blest hour of my power and her despair,
  Little brother!"
  (*O Mother, Mary Mother,*
Hour blest and banned, between Hell and
  Heaven!)   40

"Pale, pale her cheeks, that in pride did glow,
  Sister Helen,
'Neath the bridal-wreath three days ago."
"One morn for pride and three days for woe, 45
  Little brother!"
  (*O Mother, Mary Mother,*
Three days, three nights, between Hell and
  Heaven!)

"Her clasped hands stretch from her bending 50
  head,

  Sister Helen;
With the loud wind's wail her sobs are wed."
"What wedding-strains hath her bridal-bed,
  Little brother?"
  (*O Mother, Mary Mother,*
What strain but death's, between Hell and
  Heaven?)

"She may not speak, she sinks in a swoon,
  Sister Helen,—
She lifts her lips and gasps on the moon."
"Oh! might I but hear her soul's blithe tune,
  Little brother!"
  (*O Mother, Mary Mother,*
Her woe's dumb cry, between Hell and
  Heaven!)

"They've caught her to Westholm's saddle-
  bow,
  Sister Helen,
And her moonlit hair gleams white in its flow."
"Let it turn whiter than winter snow,
  Little brother!"
  (*O Mother, Mary Mother,*
Woe-withered gold, between Hell and
  Heaven!)

"O Sister Helen, you heard the bell,
  Sister Helen;
More loud than the vesper-chime it fell."
"No vesper-chime, but a dying knell,
  Little brother!"
  (*O Mother, Mary Mother,*
His dying knell, between Hell and Heaven!)

"Alas! but I fear the heavy sound,
  Sister Helen;
Is it in the sky or in the ground?"
"Say, have they turned their horses round,
  Little brother?"
  (*O Mother, Mary Mother,*
What would she more, between Hell and
  Heaven?)

"They have raised the old man from his
  knee,
  Sister Helen,
And they ride in silence hastily."
"More fast the naked soul doth flee,
  Little brother!"
  (*O Mother, Mary Mother,*
The naked soul, between Hell and Heaven!)

"Flank to flank are the three steeds gone,
    Sister Helen,
But the lady's dark steed goes alone."
"And lonely her bridegroom's soul hath flown,
    Little brother."
    (*O Mother, Mary Mother,*
The lonely ghost, between Hell and Heaven!)

"Oh the wind is sad in the iron chill,
    Sister Helen,
And weary sad they look by the hill."
"But he and I are sadder still,
    Little brother!"
    (*O Mother, Mary Mother,*
Most sad of all, between Hell and Heaven!) 15

"See, see, the wax has dropped from its place,
    Sister Helen,
And the flames are winning up apace!"
"Yet here they burn but for a space,   20
    Little brother!"
    (*O Mother, Mary Mother,*
Here for a space, between Hell and Heaven!)

"Ah! what white thing at the door has crossed, 25
    Sister Helen,
Ah! what is this that sighs in the frost?"
"A soul that's lost as mine is lost,
    Little brother!"
    (*O Mother, Mary Mother,*   30
Lost, lost, all lost, between Hell and Heaven!)

WILLIAM MORRIS

Coming from a well-to-do family and helped on 35
by an Oxford education, Morris (1834–1896)
developed into the most versatile and vigorous
artisan of his generation. He lent his energies
to the pursuit of religion, art, and architecture.
He labored for the socialist cause. He wrote 40
poetry, produced furniture, ran his own print-
ing press. Morris had zest for life, a virile
personality, joy in work which led him to make
his own paper and ink when he needed it. His
vigor and adaptability, curiosity and humor, re- 45
mind one of the American artist, George Bel-
lows—they would have made a great pair. The
student should compare Morris's Arthurian
poetry with Tennyson's, as art and as evidence
*of differences in personality.** 50

* Morris's poems are reprinted by arrangement
with Longmans, Green & Company.

THE DEFENCE OF GUENEVERE

But, knowing now that they would have her
    speak,
5 She threw her wet hair backward from her
    brow,
Her hand close to her mouth touching her
    cheek,

As though she had had there a shameful blow, 10
And feeling it shameful to feel ought but
    shame
All through her heart, yet felt her cheek
    burned so,

She must a little touch it; like one lame 15
She walked away from Gauwaine, with her
    head
Still lifted up; and on her cheek of flame

The tears dried quick; she stopped at last and
    said:
"O knights and lords, it seems but little skill
To talk of well-known things past now and
    dead.

"God wot I ought to say, I have done ill,
And pray you all forgiveness heartily!
Because you must be right such great lords—
    still

"Listen, suppose your time were come to die,
And you were quite alone and very weak;
Yea, laid a dying while very mightily

"The wind was ruffling up the narrow streak 35
Of river through your broad lands running
    well:
Suppose a hush should come, then some one
    speak:

"'One of these cloths is heaven, and one is
    hell,
Now choose one cloth for ever, which they be,
I will not tell you, you must somehow tell 45

"'Of your own strength and mightiness; here,
    see!'
Yea, yea, my Lord, and you to ope your eyes,
At foot of your familiar bed to see 50

"A great God's angel standing, with such dyes,

Not known on earth, on his great wings, and
    hands,
Held out two ways, light from the inner skies

"Showing him well, and making his commands 5
Seem to be God's commands, moreover, too,
Holding within his hands the cloths on wands;

"And one of these strange choosing cloths
    was blue, 10
Wavy and long, and one cut short and red;
No man could tell the better of the two.

"After a shivering half-hour you said,
'God help! heaven's color, the blue;' and he 15
    said, 'hell.'
Perhaps you then would roll upon your bed,

"And cry to all good men that loved you
    well, 20
'Ah Christ! if only I had known, known,
    known;'
Launcelot went away, then I could tell,

"Like wisest man how all things would be, 25
    moan,
And roll and hurt myself, and long to die,
And yet fear much to die for what was sown.

"Nevertheless you, O Sir Gauwaine, lie, 30
Whatever may have happened through these
    years,
God knows I speak truth, saying that you lie."

Her voice was low at first, being full of tears, 35
But as it cleared, it grew full loud and shrill,
Growing a windy shriek in all men's ears,

A ringing in their startled brains, until
She said that Gauwaine lied, then her voice 40
    sunk,
And her great eyes began again to fill,

Though still she stood right up, and never
    shrunk,
But spoke on bravely, glorious lady fair! 45
Whatever tears her full lips may have drunk,

She stood, and seemed to think, and wrung
    her hair, 50
Spoke out at last with no more trace of shame,
With passionate twisting of her body there:

"It chanced upon a day that Launcelot came
To dwell at Arthur's court: at Christmastime
This happened; when the heralds sung his
    name,

"'Son of King Ban of Benwick,' seemed to
    chime
Along with all the bells that rang that day,
O'er the white roofs, with little change of
    rhyme.

"Christmas and whitened winter passed away,
And over me the April sunshine came,
Made very awful with black hail-clouds, yea

"And in the Summer I grew white with flame,
And bowed my head down—Autumn, and the
    sick
Sure knowledge things would never be the
    same,

"However often Spring might be most thick
Of blossoms and buds, smote on me, and I
    grew
Careless of most things, let the clock tick, tick,

"To my unhappy pulse, that beat right through
My eager body: while I laughed out loud,
And let my lips curl up at false or true,

"Seemed cold and shallow without any cloud.
Behold my judges, then the cloths were
    brought:
While I was dizzied thus, old thoughts would
    crowd,

"Belonging to the time ere I was bought
By Arthur's great name and his little love,
Must I give up for ever then, I thought,

"That which I deemed would ever round me
    move
Glorifying all things; for a little word,
Scarce ever meant at all, must I now prove

"Stone-cold for ever? Pray you, does the Lord
Will that all folks should be quite happy and
    good?
I love God now a little, if this cord

"Were broken, once for all what striving could
Make me love anything in earth or heaven.

So day by day it grew, as if one should

"Slip slowly down some path worn smooth and
      even,
Down to a cool sea on a summer day;   5
Yet still in slipping was there some small
      leaven

"Of stretched hands catching small stones by
      the way,   10
Until one surely reached the sea at last,
And felt strange new joy as the worn head lay

"Back, with the hair like sea-weed; yea all past
Sweat of the forehead, dryness of the lips,   15
Washed utterly out by the dear waves o'er-
      cast,

"In the lone sea, far off from any ships!
Do I not know now of a day in Spring?   20
No minute of that wild day ever slips

"From out my memory; I hear thrushes sing,
And wheresoever I may be, straightway
Thoughts of it all come up with most fresh   25
      sting;

"I was half mad with beauty on that day,
And went without my ladies all alone,
In a quiet garden walled round every way;   30

"I was right joyful of that wall of stone,
That shut the flowers and trees up with the
      sky,
And trebled all the beauty: to the bone,   35

"Yea right through to my heart, grown very
      shy
With weary thoughts, it pierced, and made
      me glad;   40
Exceedingly glad, and I knew verily,

"A little thing just then had made me mad;
I dared not think, as I was wont to do,
Sometimes, upon my beauty; if I had   45

"Held out my long hand up against the blue,
And, looking on the tenderly darkened fingers,
Thought that by rights one ought to see quite
      through,   50

"There, see you, where the soft still light yet

lingers,
Round by the edges; what should I have done,
If this had joined with yellow spotted singers,

"And startling green drawn upward by the
      sun?
But shouting, loosed out, see now! all my
      hair,
And trancedly stood watching the west wind
      run

"With faintest half-heard breathing sound—
      why there
I lose my head e'en now in doing this;
But shortly listen—In that garden fair

"Came Launcelot walking; this is true, the kiss
Wherewith we kissed in meeting that spring
      day,
I scarce dare talk of the remembered bliss,

"When both our mouths went wandering in
      one way,
And aching sorely, met among the leaves;
Our hands being left behind strained far away.

"Never within a yard of my bright sleeves
Had Launcelot come before—and now, so
      nigh!
After that day why is it Guenevere grieves?

"Nevertheless you, O Sir Gauwaine, lie,
Whatever happened on through all those years,
God knows I speak truth, saying that you lie.

"Being such a lady could I weep these tears
If this were true? A great queen such as I
Having sinned this way, straight her conscience
      sears;

"And afterwards she liveth hatefully,
Slaying and poisoning, certes never weeps,—
Gauwaine be friends now, speak me lovingly.

"Do I not see how God's dear pity creeps
All through your frame, and trembles in your
      mouth?
Remember in what grave your mother sleeps,

"Buried in some place far down in the south,
Men are forgetting as I speak to you;
By her head severed in that awful drouth

"Of pity that drew Agravaine's fell blow,
I pray your pity! let me not scream out
For ever after, when the shrill winds blow

"Through half your castle-locks! let me not   5
        shout
For ever after in the winter night
When you ride out alone! in battle rout

"Let not my rusting tears make your sword 10
        light!
Ah! God of mercy how he turns away!
So, ever must I dress me to the fight,

"So—let God's justice work! Gauwaine, I say, 15
See me hew down your proofs: yea all men
        know
Even as you said how Mellyagraunce one day,

"One bitter day in *la Fausse Garde*,[1] for so   20
All good knights held it after, saw—
Yea, sirs, by cursed unknightly outrage; though

"You, Gauwaine, held his word without a flaw,
This Mellyagraunce saw blood upon my bed— 25
Whose blood then pray you? is there any law

"To make a queen say why some spots of red
Lie on her coverlet? or will you say,
'Your hands are white, lady, as when you wed, 30

"'Where did you bleed?' and must I stammer
        out—'Nay,
I blush indeed, fair lord, only to rend
My sleeve up to my shoulder, where there lay 35

"'A knife-point last night:' so must I defend
The honor of the lady Guenevere?
Not so, fair lords, even if the world should end

"This very day, and you were judges here   40
Instead of God. Did you see Mellyagraunce
When Launcelot stood by him? what white
        fear

"Curdled his blood, and how his teeth did   45
        dance,
His side sink in? as my knight cried and said,
'Slayer of unarmed men, here is a chance!

"'Setter of traps, I pray you guard your head, 50

By God I am so glad to fight with you,
Stripper of ladies, that my hand feels lead

"'For driving weight; hurrah now! draw and
        do,
For all my wounds are moving in my breast,
And I am getting mad with waiting so.'

"He struck his hands together o'er the beast,
Who fell down flat, and grovelled at his feet,
And groaned at being slain so young—'at least.'

"My knight said, 'Rise you, sir, who are so
        fleet
At catching ladies, half-armed will I fight,
My left side all uncovered!' then I weet,

"Up sprang Sir Mellyagraunce with great de-
        light
Upon his knave's face; not until just then
Did I quite hate him, as I saw my knight

"Along the lists look to my stake and pen
With such a joyous smile, it made me sigh
From agony beneath my waist-chain, when

"The fight began, and to me they drew nigh;
Ever Sir Launcelot kept him on the right,
And traversed warily, and ever high

"And fast leapt caitiff's sword, until my knight
Sudden threw up his sword to his left hand,
Caught it, and swung it; that was all the fight.

"Except a spout of blood on the hot land;
For it was hottest summer; and I know
I wondered how the fire, while I should stand,

"And burn, against the heat, would quiver so,
Yards above my head; thus these matters went;
Which things were only warnings of the woe

"That fell on me. Yet Mellyagraunce was
        shent,[2]
For Mellyagraunce had fought against the
        Lord;
Therefore, my lords, take heed lest you be
        blent[3]

"With all this wickedness; say no rash word
Against me, being so beautiful; my eyes,

---

[1] "The false prison."   [2] disgraced.   [3] blinded.

[177]

Wept all away to grey, may bring some sword

"To drown you in your blood; see my breast
    rise,
Like waves of purple sea, as here I stand;
And how my arms are moved in wonderful
    wise,

"Yea also at my full heart's strong command,
See through my long throat how the words 10
    go up
In ripples to my mouth; how in my hand

"The shadow lies like wine within a cup
Of marvellously colored gold; yea now
This little wind is rising, look you up, 15

"And wonder how the light is falling so
Within my moving tresses: will you dare,
When you have looked a little on my brow, 20

"To say this thing is vile? or will you care
For any plausible lies of cunning woof,
When you can see my face with no lie there
                                          25

"For ever? am I not a gracious proof—
'But in your chamber Launcelot was found'—
Is there a good knight then would stand aloof,

"When a queen says with gentle queenly 30
    sound:
'O true as steel come now and talk with me,
I love to see your step upon the ground

"'Unwavering, also well I love to see 35
That gracious smile light up your face, and
    hear
Your wonderful words, that all mean verily

"'The thing they seem to mean: good friend, 40
    so dear
To me in everything, come here to-night,
Or else the hours will pass most dull and
    drear;
                                          45
"'If you come not, I fear this time I might
Get thinking over much of times gone by,
When I was young, and green hope was in
    sight;
                                          50
"'For no man cares now to know why I sigh;
And no man comes to sing me pleasant songs,

Nor any brings me the sweet flowers that lie

"'So thick in the gardens; therefore one so
    longs
To see you, Launcelot; that we may be
Like children once again, free from all wrongs

"'Just for one night.' Did he not come to me?
What thing could keep true Launcelot away
If I said 'come'? there was one less than three

"In my quiet room that night, and we were
    gay;
Till sudden I rose up, weak, pale, and sick,
Because a bawling broke our dream up, yea

"I looked at Launcelot's face and could not
    speak,
For he looked helpless too, for a little while;
Then I remembered how I tried to shriek,

"And could not, but fell down; from tile to
    tile
The stones they threw up rattled o'er my head,
And made me dizzier; till within a while

"My maids were all about me, and my head
On Launcelot's breast was being soothed away
From its white chattering, until Launcelot
    said—

"By God! I will not tell you more to-day,
Judge any way you will—what matters it?
You know quite well the story of that fray,

"How Launcelot stilled their bawling, the mad
    fit
That caught up Gauwaine—all, all, verily,
But just that which would save me; these
    things flit.

"Nevertheless you, O Sir Gauwaine, lie,
Whatever may have happened these long
    years,
God knows I speak truth, saying that you lie!

"All I have said is truth, by Christ's dear tears."
She would not speak another word, but stood
Turned sideways; listening, like a man who
    hears

His brother's trumpet sounding through the

wood
Of his foes' lances. She leaned eagerly,
And gave a slight spring sometimes, as she
   could

At last hear something really; joyfully
Her cheek grew crimson, as the headlong speed
Of the roan charger drew all men to see,
The knight who came was Launcelot at good
   need.

THE HAYSTACK IN THE FLOODS[1]

Had she come all the way for this,
To part at last without a kiss?
Yea, had she borne the dirt and rain
That her own eyes might see him slain
Beside the haystack in the floods?

Along the dripping leafless woods,
The stirrup touching either shoe,
She rode astride as troopers do;
With kirtle kilted to her knee,
To which the mud splashed wretchedly;
And the wet dripped from every tree
Upon her head and heavy hair,
And on her eyelids broad and fair;
The tears and rain ran down her face.
By fits and starts they rode apace,
And very often was his place
Far off from her; he had to ride
Ahead, to see what might betide
When the roads crossed; and sometimes, when
There rose a murmuring from his men,
Had to turn back with promises;
Ah me! she had but little ease;
And often for pure doubt and dread
She sobbed, made giddy in the head
By the swift riding; while, for cold,
Her slender fingers scarce could hold
The wet reins; yea, and scarcely, too,
She felt the foot within her shoe
Against the stirrup: all for this,
To part at last without a kiss
Besides the haystack in the floods.

For when they neared that old soaked hay,

---

[1] This poem gives the story of the events which befell Sir Robert de Marny, an English knight, and his sweetheart, after they met Godmar, a French knight who ambushed them. The time is shortly after the battle of Poictiers (1356).

They saw across the only way
That Judas, Godmar, and the three
Red running lions dismally
Grinned from his pennon, under which,
5 In one straight line along the ditch,
They counted thirty heads.

           So then,
While Robert turned round to his men,
10 She saw at once the wretched end,
And, stooping down, tried hard to rend
Her coif the wrong way from her head,
And hid her eyes; while Robert said:
"Nay, love, 'tis scarcely two to one,
15 At Poictiers where we made them run
So fast—why, sweet my love, good cheer,
The Gascon frontier is so near,
Nought after this."

20   But, "O," she said,
"My God! my God! I have to tread
The long way back without you; then
The court at Paris; those six men;
The gratings of the Chatelet;
25 The swift Seine on some rainy day
Like this, and people standing by,
And laughing, while my weak hands try
To recollect how strong men swim.
All this, or else a life with him,
30 For which I should be damned at last,
Would God that this next hour were past!"

He answered not, but cried his cry,
"St. George for Marny!" cheerily;
35 And laid his hand upon her rein.
Alas! no man of all his train
Gave back that cheery cry again;
And, while for rage his thumb beat fast
Upon his sword-hilts, some one cast
40 About his neck a kerchief long,
And bound him.

           Then they went along
To Godmar; who said: "Now, Jehane,
45 Your lover's life is on the wane
So fast, that, if this very hour
You yield not as my paramour,
He will not see the rain leave off—
Nay, keep your tongue from gibe and scoff,
50 Sir Robert, or I slay you now."

She laid her hand upon her brow,

Then gazed upon the palm, as though
She thought her forehead bled, and—"No."
She said, and turned her head away,
As there were nothing else to say,
And everything were settled: red   5
Grew Godmar's face from chin to head:
"Jehane, on yonder hill there stands
My castle, guarding well my lands:
What hinders me from taking you,
And doing that I list to do   10
To your fair wilful body, while
Your knight lies dead?"

                A wicked smile
Wrinkled her face, her lips grew thin,
A long way out she thrust her chin: 15
"You know that I should strangle you
While you were sleeping; or bite through
Your throat, by God's help—ah!" she said,
"Lord Jesus, pity your poor maid!
For in such wise they hem me in,   20
I cannot choose but sin and sin,
Whatever happens: yet I think
They could not make me eat or drink,
And so should I just reach my rest."
"Nay, if you do not my behest,   25
O Jehane! though I love you well,"
Said Godmar, "would I fail to tell
All that I know." "Foul lies," she said.
"Eh? lies my Jehane? by God's head,
At Paris folks would deem them true!   30
Do you know, Jehane, they cry for you,
'Jehane the brown! Jehane the brown!
Give us Jehane to burn or drown!'—
Eh—gag me Robert!—sweet my friend,
This were indeed a piteous end   35
For those long fingers, and long feet,
And long neck, and smooth shoulders sweet;
An end that few men would forget
That saw it—So, an hour yet:
Consider, Jehane, which to take   40
Of life or death!"

              So, scarce awake,
Dismounting, did she leave that place,   45
And totter some yards: with her face
Turned upward to the sky she lay,

Her head on a wet heap of hay,
And fell asleep: and while she slept,
And did not dream, the minutes crept
Round to the twelve again; but she,
Being waked at last, sighed quietly,
And strangely childlike came, and said:
"I will not." Straightway Godmar's head,
As though it hung on strong wires, turned
Most sharply round, and his face burned.

For Robert—both his eyes were dry,
He could not weep, but gloomily
He seemed to watch the rain; yea, too,
His lips were firm; he tried once more
To touch her lips; she reached out, sore   15
And vain desire so tortured them,
The poor grey lips, and now the hem
Of his sleeve brushed them.

               With a start   20
Up Godmar rose, thrust them apart;
From Robert's throat he loosed the bands
Of silk and mail; with empty hands
Held out, she stood and gazed, and saw,
The long bright blade without a flaw   25
Glide out from Godmar's sheath, his hand
In Robert's hair; she saw him bend
Back Robert's head; she saw him send
The thin steel down; the blow told well,
Right backward the knight Robert fell,   30
And moaned as dogs do, being half dead,
Unwitting, as I deem: so then
Godmar turned grinning to his men,
Who ran, some five or six, and beat   35
His head to pieces at their feet.

Then Godmar turned again and said:
"So Jehane, the first fitte[2] is read!
Take note, my lady, that your way
Lies backward to the Chatelet!"   40
She shook her head and gazed awhile
At her cold hands with a rueful smile,
As though this thing had made her mad.

This was the parting that they had   45
Beside the haystack in the floods.

[2] chapter.

TWENTIETH CENTURY

EDWIN ARLINGTON ROBINSON

*Reading the early lives of Masefield, Sand-
burg, Lindsay, and other moderns, the student
may realize for himself that the popular myth
making the poet an exalted person apart is
just that, a myth. Who would guess, for ex-* 5
*ample, that the author of one of the most
popular long poems of the twentieth century—
Tristram—had once been a subway inspector
and clerk? With the early encouragement of
Theodore Roosevelt, Robinson (1869–1935)* 10
*went on to become one of the most prolific of
the first rank of modern American poets. A
frequent winner of the Pulitzer Prize, he developed an original idiom, mastered the art of
the short characterization, and also turned out* 15
*many long allegories in a pessimistic, though
not hopeless, vein. Robinson veers toward the
intellectual, sometimes grows monotonous in
his phrases and rhythms, but is not obscure or
over-symbolistic. (See also I, 345.)* 20

RICHARD CORY*

Whenever Richard Cory went down town,
  We people on the pavement looked at him: 25
He was a gentleman from sole to crown,
  Clean favored, and imperially slim.

And he was always quietly arrayed,
  And he was always human when he talked; 30
But still he fluttered pulses when he said,
  "Good-morning," and he glittered when he
    walked.

And he was rich—yes, richer than a king— 35
  And admirably schooled in every grace:
In fine, we thought that he was everything
  To make us wish that we were in his place.

So on we worked, and waited for the light, 40
  And went without the meat, and cursed the

* From *Collected Poems* by Edwin Arlington
Robinson; by permission of Charles Scribner's Sons.

bread;
And Richard Cory, one calm summer night,
  Went home and put a bullet through his
    head.

MINIVER CHEEVY*

Miniver Cheevy, child of scorn,
  Grew lean while he assailed the seasons;
He wept that he was ever born,
  And he had reasons.

Miniver loved the days of old
  When swords were bright and steeds were
    prancing;
The vision of a warrior bold
  Would set him dancing.

Miniver sighed for what was not,
  And dreamed, and rested from his labors;
He dreamed of Thebes and Camelot,
  And Priam's neighbors.

Miniver mourned the ripe renown
  That made so many a name so fragrant;
He mourned Romance, now on the town,
  And Art, a vagrant.

Miniver loved the Medici,
  Albeit he had never seen one;
He would have sinned incessantly
  Could he have been one.

Miniver cursed the commonplace
  And eyed a khaki suit with loathing;
He missed the medieval grace
  Of iron clothing.

Miniver scorned the gold he sought,

* Reprinted from *The Town Down the River* by
Edwin Arlington Robinson; copyright 1910 by
Charles Scribner's Sons, 1938 by Ruth Niveson;
used by permission of the publishers.

But sore annoyed was he without it;
Miniver thought, and thought, and thought,
  And thought about it.

Miniver Cheevy, born too late,
  Scratched his head and kept on thinking;
Miniver coughed, and called it fate,
  And kept on drinking.

BEN JONSON ENTERTAINS A MAN FROM STRATFORD*

You are a friend then, as I make it out,
Of our man Shakespeare, who alone of us
Will put an ass's head in Fairyland
As he would add a shilling to more shillings,
All most harmonious—and out of his
Miraculous inviolable increase
Fills Ilion,[1] Rome, or any town you like
Of olden time with timeless Englishmen;
And I must wonder what you think of him—
All you down there where your small Avon
    flows
By Stratford, and where you're an Alderman.
Some, for a guess, would have him riding back
To be a farrier there, or say a dyer;
Or maybe one of your adept surveyors;
Or like enough the wizard of all tanners.
Not you—no fear of that; for I discern
In you a kindling of the flame that saves—
The nimble element, the true caloric;
I see it, and was told of it, moreover,
By our discriminate friend himself, no other.
Had you been one of the sad average,
As he would have it—meaning, as I take it,
The sinew and the solvent of our Island,
You'd not be buying beer for this Terpander's[2]
Approved and estimated friend Ben Jonson;
He'd never foist it as a part of his
Contingent entertainment of a townsman
While he goes off rehearsing, as he must,
If he shall ever be the Duke of Stratford.
And my words are no shadow on your town—
Far from it; for one town's like another
As all are unlike London. Oh, he knows it—

And there's the Stratford in him; he denies it,
And there's the Shakespeare in him. So, God
  help him!

5 I tell him he needs Greek; but neither God
Nor Greek will help him. Nothing will help
  that man.
You see the fates have given him so much,
He must have all or perish—or look out
10 Of London, where he sees too many lords.
They're part of half what ails him: I suppose
There's nothing fouler down among the
  demons
Than what it is he feels when he remembers
15 The dust and sweat and ointment of his calling
With his lords looking on and laughing at him.
King as he is, he can't be king de facto,
And that's as well, because he wouldn't like it;
He'd frame a lower rating of men then
20 Than he has now; and after that would come
An abdication or an apoplexy.
He can't be king, not even king of Stratford—
Though half the world, if not the whole of it,
May crown him with a crown that fits no king
25 Save Lord Apollo's homesick emissary:
Not there on Avon, or on any stream
Where Naiads and their white arms are no
  more
Shall he find home again. It's all too bad.
30 But there's a comfort, for he'll have that
    House—
The best you ever saw; and he'll be there
Anon, as you're an Alderman. Good God!
He makes me lie awake o' nights and laugh.

35

And you have known him from his origin,
You tell me; and a most uncommon urchin
He must have been to the few seeing ones—
A trifle terrifying, I dare say,
40 Discovering a world with his man's eyes,
Quite as another lad might see some finches,
If he looked hard and had an eye for Nature.
But this one had his eyes and their foretelling,
And he had you to fare with, and what else?
45 He must have had a father and a mother—
In fact I've heard him say so—and a dog,
As a boy should, I venture; and the dog,
Most likely, was the only man who knew him.
A dog, for all I know, is what he needs
50 As much as anything right here today,
To counsel him about his disillusions,
Old aches, and parturitions of what's coming—

A dog of orders, an emeritus,
To wag his tail at him when he comes home,
And then to put his paws up on his knees
And say, "For God's sake, what's it all about?"

I don't know whether he needs a dog or not—
Or what he needs. I tell him he needs Greek;
I'll talk of rules and Aristotle with him,
And if his tongue's at home he'll say to that,
"I have your word that Aristotle knows,
And you mine that I don't know Aristotle."
He's all at odds with all the unities,
And what's yet worse, it doesn't seem to matter;
He treads along through Time's old wilderness
As if the tramp of all the centuries
Had left no roads—and there are none, for
  him;
He doesn't see them, even with those eyes,—
And that's a pity, or I say it is.
Accordingly we have him as we have him—
Going his way, the way that he goes best,
A pleasant animal with no great noise
Or nonsense anywhere to set him off—
Save only divers and inclement devils
Have made of late his heart their dwelling
  place.
A flame half ready to fly out sometimes
At some annoyance may be fanned up in him,
But soon it falls, and when it falls goes out;
He knows how little room there is in there
For crude and futile animosities,
And how much for the joy of being whole,
And how much for long sorrow and old pain.
On our side there are some who may be given
To grow old wondering what he thinks of us
And some above us, who are, in his eyes,
Above himself,—and that's quite right and
  English.
Yet here we smile, or disappoint the gods
Who made it so: the gods have always eyes
To see men scratch; and they see one down
  here
Who itches, manor-bitten to the bone,
Albeit he knows himself—yes, yes, he knows—
The lord of more than England and of more
Than all the seas of England in all time
Shall ever wash. D'ye wonder that I laugh?
He sees me, and he doesn't seem to care;
And why the devil should he? I can't tell you.

I'll meet him out alone of a bright Sunday,
Trim, rather spruce, and quite the gentleman.

"What ho, my lord!" say I. He doesn't
  hear me;
Wherefore I have to pause and look at him.
He's not enormous, but one looks at him.
5 A little on the round if you insist,
For now, God save the mark, he's growing old;
He's five and forty, and to hear him talk
These days you'd call him eighty; then you'd
  add
10 More years to that. He's old enough to be
The father of a world, and so he is.
"Ben, you're a scholar, what's the time of day?"
Says he; and there shines out of him again
An aged light that has no age or station—
15 The mystery that's his—a mischievous
Half-mad serenity that laughs at fame
For being won so easy, and at friends
Who laugh at him for what he wants the
  most,
And for his dukedom down in Warwick-
20   shire;—
By which you see we're all a little jealous. . . .
Poor Greene![3] I fear the color of his name
Was even as that of his ascending soul;
25 And he was one where there are many
  others,—
Some scrivening to the end against their fate,
Their puppets all in ink and all to die there;
And some with hands that once would shade
30   an eye
That scanned Euripides and Æschylus[4]
Will reach by this time for a pot-house mop
To slush their first and last of royalties.
Poor devils! and they all play to his hand;
35 For so it was in Athens and old Rome.
But that's not here or there; I've wandered off.
Greene does it, or I'm careful. Where's that
  boy?

40 Yes, he'll go back to Stratford. And we'll miss
  him?
Dear sir, there'll be no London here without
  him.
We'll all be riding, one of these fine days,
45 Down there to see him—and his wife won't
  like us;
And then we'll think of what he never said
Of women—which, if taken all in all

50 [3] Robert Greene, contemporary of Shakespeare,
also a playwright, who attacked Shakespeare in
"Groatsworth of Wit."
[4] Greek tragic dramatists.

With what he did say, would buy many
    horses.
Though nowadays he's not so much for
    women:
"So few of them," he says, "are worth the 5
    guessing."
But there's a worm at work when he says
    that,
And while he says it one feels in the air
A deal of circumambient hocus-pocus. 10
They've had him dancing till his toes were
    tender,
And he can feel 'em now, come chilly rains.
There's no long cry for going into it,
However, and we don't know much about it. 15
But you in Stratford, like most here in London,
Have more now in the *Sonnets* than you paid
    for;
He's put one there with all her poison on,
To make a singing fiction of a shadow 20
That's in his life a fact, and always will be.
But she's no care of ours, though Time, I fear,
Will have a more reverberant ado
About her than about another one
Who seems to have decoyed him, married 25
    him,
And sent him scuttling on his way to London—
With much already learned, and more to
    learn,
And more to follow. Lord! how I see him now, 30
Pretending, maybe trying, to be like us.
Whatever he may have meant, we never had
    him;
He failed us, or escaped, or what you will—
And there was that about him (God knows 35
    what—
We'd flayed another had he tried it on us)
That made as many of us as had wits
More fond of all his easy distances
Than one another's noise and clap-your- 40
    shoulder.
But think you not, my friend, he'd never talk!
Talk? He was eldritch at it; and we listened—
Thereby acquiring much we knew before
About ourselves, and hitherto had held 45
Irrelevant, or not prime to the purpose.
And there were some, of course, and there be
    now,
Disordered and reduced amazedly
To resignation by the mystic seal 50
Of young finality the gods had laid
On everything that made him a young demon;

And one or two shot looks at him already
As he had been their executioner;
And once or twice he was, not knowing it—
Or knowing, being sorry for poor clay
And saying nothing . . . Yet, for all his
    engines,
You'll meet a thousand of an afternoon
Who strut and sun themselves and see
    around 'em
A world made out of more that has a reason
Than his, I swear, that he sees here today;
Though he may scarcely give a Fool an exit
But we mark how he sees in everything
A law that, given that we flout it once too
    often,
Brings fire and iron down on our naked heads.
To me it looks as if the power that made him,
For fear of giving all things to one creature,
Left out the first—faith, innocence, illusion,
Whatever 'tis that keeps us out o' Bedlam—
And thereby, for his too consuming vision,
Empowered him out of nature; though to see
    him,
You'd never guess what's going on inside him.
He'll break out some day like a keg of ale
With too much independent frenzy in it;
And all for cellaring what he knows won't
    keep,
And what he'd best forget—but that he can't.
You'll have it, and have more than I'm foretell-
    ing;
And there'll be such a roaring at the Globe
As never stunned the bleeding gladiators.
He'll have to change the color of its hair
A bit, for now he calls it Cleopatra.
Black hair woud never do for Cleopatra.
But you and I are not yet two old women,
And you're a man of office. What he does
Is more to you than how it is he does it—
And that's what the Lord God has never told
    him.
They worked together, and the Devil
    helps 'em;
They do it of a morning, or if not,
They do it of a night; in which event
He's peevish of a morning. He seems old;
He's not the proper stomach or the sleep—
And they're two sovran agents to conserve
    him
Against the fiery art that has no mercy
But what's in that prodigious grand new
    House.

I gather something happening in his boyhood
Fulfilled him with a boy's determination
To make all Stratford 'ware of him. Well,
    well,
I hope at last he'll have his joy of it,
And all his pigs and sheep and bellowing
    beeves,
And frogs and owls and unicorns, moreover,
Be less than hell to his attendant ears.
Oh, past a doubt we'll all go down to see him.

He may be wise. With London two days off,
Down there some wind of heaven may yet re-
    vive him,
But there's no quickening breath from
    anywhere
Shall make of him again the young poised faun
From Warwickshire, who'd made, it seems,
    already
A legend of himself before I came
To blink before the last of his first lightning.
Whatever there be, there'll be no more of that;
The coming on of his old monster Time
Has made him a still man; and he has dreams
Were fair to think on once, and all found
    hollow.
He knows how much of what men paint them-
    selves
Would blister in the light of what they are;
He sees how much of what was great now
    shares
An eminence transformed and ordinary;
He knows too much of what the world has
    hushed
In others, to be loud now for himself;
He knows now at what height low enemies
May reach his heart, and high friends let him
    fall;
But what not even such as he may know
Bedevils him the worst: his lark may sing
At heaven's gate how he will, and for as long
As joy may listen, but he sees no gate,
Save one whereat the spent clay waits a little
Before the churchyard has it, and the worm.

Not long ago, late in an afternoon,
I came on him unseen down Lambeth way,
And on my life I was afear'd of him:
He gloomed and mumbled like a soul from
    Tophet,
His hands behind him and his head bent
    solemn.

"What is it now," said I,—"another woman?"
That made him sorry for me, and he smiled.
"No, Ben," he mused; "it's Nothing. It's all
    Nothing.
5 We come, we go; and when we're done, we're
    done."
Spiders and flies—we're mostly one or
    t'other—
We come, we go; and when we're done, we're
    done;
"By God, you sing that song as if you knew it!"
Said I, by way of cheering him; "what ails ye?"
"I think I must have come down here to
    think,"
15 Says he to that, and pulls his little beard;
"Your fly will serve as well as anybody,
And what's his hour? He flies, and flies, and
    flies,
And in his fly's mind has a brave appearance;
20 And then your spider gets him in her net,
And eats him out, and hangs him up to dry.
That's Nature, the kind mother of us all.
And then your slattern housemaid swings her
    broom,
25 And where's your spider? And that's Nature,
    also.
It's Nature, and it's Nothing. It's all Nothing.
It's all a world where bugs and emperors
Go singularly back to the same dust,
30 Each in his time; and the old, ordered stars
That sang together, Ben, will sing the same
Old stave to-morrow."

                        When he talks like that,
35 There's nothing for a human man to do
But lead him to some grateful nook like this
Where we be now, and there to make him
    drink.
He'll drink, for love of me, and then be sick;
40 A sad sign always in a man of parts,
And always very ominous. The great
Should be as large in liquor as in love,—
And our great friend is not so large in either:
One disaffects him, and the other fails him;
45 Whatso he drinks that has an antic in it,
He's wondering what's to pay in his insides;
And while his eyes are on the Cyprian[5]
He's fribbling all the time with that damned
    House.
50 We laugh here at his thrift, but after all
    _____
        [5] here, a wench.

It may be thrift that saves him from the
    devil;
God gave it, anyhow,—and we'll suppose
He knew the compound of his handiwork.
To-day the clouds are with him, but anon
He'll out of 'em enough to shake the tree
Of life itself and bring down fruit
    unheard-of,—
And, throwing in the bruised and whole
    together,
Prepare a wine to make us drunk with
    wonder;
And if he live, there'll be a sunset spell
Thrown over him as over a glassed lake
That yesterday was all a black wild water.

God send he live to give us, if no more,
What now's a-rampage in him, and exhibit,
With a decent half-allegiance to the ages
An earnest of at least a casual eye
Turned once on what he owes to Gutenberg,
And to the fealty of more centuries
Than are as yet a picture in our vision.
"There's time enough,—I'll do it when I'm
    old,
And we're immortal men," he says to that;
And then he says to me, "Ben, what's
    'immortal'?
Think you by any force of ordination
It may be nothing of a sort more noisy
Than a small oblivion of component ashes
That of a dream-addicted world was once
A moving atomy much like your friend here?"
Nothing will help that man. To make him
    laugh,
I said then he was a mad mountebank,—
And by the Lord I nearer made him cry.
I could have eat an eft then, on my knees,
Tail, claws, and all of him; for I had stung
The king of men, who had no sting for me,
And I had hurt him in his memories;
And I say now, as I shall say again,
I love the man this side idolatry.
He'll do it when he's old, he says. I wonder.
He may not be so ancient as all that.
For such as he the thing that is to do
Will do itself—but there's a reckoning;
The sessions that are now too much his own,
The roiling inward of a still outside,
The churning out of all those blood-fed lines,
The nights of many schemes and little sleep,
The full brain hammered hot with too much

5

10

15

20

25

30

35

40

45

50

thinking,
The vexed heart over-worn with too much
    aching—
This weary jangling of conjoined affairs
Made out of elements that have no end,
And all confused at once, I understand,
Is not what makes a man to live forever.
O, no, not now! He'll not be going now:
There'll be time yet for God knows what
    explosions
Before he goes. He'll stay awhile. Just wait:
Just wait a year or two for Cleopatra,
For she's to be a balsam and a comfort;
And that's not all a jape of mine now, either.
For granted once the old way of Apollo
Sings in a man, he may then, if he's able,
Strike unafraid whatever strings he will
Upon the last and wildest of new lyres;
Nor out of his new magic, though it hymn
The shrieks of dungeoned hell, shall he create
A madness or a gloom to shut quite out
A cleaving daylight, and a last great calm
Triumphant over shipwreck and all storms.
He might have given Aristotle creeps,
But surely would have given him his *katharsis*.
He'll not be going yet. There's too much yet
Unsung within the man. But when he goes,
I'd stake ye coin o' the realm his only care
For a phantom world he sounded and found
    wanting
Will be a portion here, a portion there,
Of this or that thing or some other thing
That has a patent and intrinsical
Equivalence in those egregious shillings.
And yet he knows, God help him! Tell me,
    now,
If ever there was anything let loose
On earth by gods or devils heretofore
Like this mad, careful, proud, indifferent
    Shakespeare!
Where was it, if it ever was? By heaven,
'Twas never yet in Rhodes or Pergamon—
In Thebes or Nineveh, a thing like this!
No thing like this was ever out of England;
And that he knows. I wonder if he cares.
Perhaps he does. . . . O Lord, that House in
    Stratford!

ROBERT FROST

*Although he was born in San Francisco, Frost
(1875–   ) belongs to New England by res-*

idence and poetic citizenship. With the farm, the factory, journalism, and teaching in his background, he developed from the early volume, A Boy's Will, to a point at which he was accepted abroad and at home as one of the finest poetic voices in America. Long associated with various colleges as artist-in-residence (he is now Ticknor Fellow in Humanities at Dartmouth), Frost has won countless honors and prizes. He is the poet of the rural scene with no false sentiment or "philosophy" so dear to newspaper scribblers. He has wit, simplicity, and easy grace—few men have been so devoid of pose, so truly natural. Perhaps the most startling fact about Frost's literary fame is that it came relatively late in life. (See also I, 352.)

THE DEATH OF THE HIRED MAN*

Mary sat musing on the lamp-flame at the table
Waiting for Warren. When she heard his step,
She ran on tip-toe down the darkened passage
To meet him in the doorway with the news
And put him on his guard. "Silas is back."
She pushed him outward with her through the door
And shut it after her. "Be kind," she said.
She took the market things from Warren's arms
And set them on the porch, then drew him down
To sit beside her on the wooden steps.
"When was I ever anything but kind to him?
But I'll not have the fellow back," he said.
"I told him so last haying, didn't I?
'If he left then,' I said, 'that ended it.'
What good is he? Who else will harbour him
At his age for the little he can do?
What help he is there's no depending on.
Off he goes always when I need him most.
'He thinks he ought to earn a little pay,
Enough at least to buy tobacco with,
So he won't have to beg and be beholden.'
'All right,' I say, 'I can't afford to pay
Any fixed wages, though I wish I could.'
'Someone else can.' 'Then someone else will have to.'
I shouldn't mind his bettering himself
If that was what it was. You can be certain,

When he begins like that, there's someone at him
Trying to coax him off with pocket-money,—
In haying time, when any help is scarce.
In winter he comes back to us. I'm done."

"Sh! not so loud: he'll hear you," Mary said.

"I want him to: he'll have to soon or late."

"He's worn out. He's asleep beside the stove.
When I came up from Rowe's I found him here,
Huddled against the barn-door fast asleep,
A miserable sight, and frightening, too—
You needn't smile—I didn't recognise him—
I wasn't looking for him—and he's changed.
Wait till you see."

      "Where did you say he'd been?"

"He didn't say. I dragged him to the house,
And gave him tea and tried to make him smoke.
I tried to make him talk about his travels.
Nothing would do: he just kept nodding off."

"What did he say? Did he say anything?"

"But little."

            "Anything? Mary, confess
He said he'd come to ditch the meadow for me."

"Warren!"

        "But did he? I just want to know."

"Of course he did. What would you have him say?
Surely you wouldn't grudge the poor old man
Some humble way to save his self-respect.
He added, if you really care to know,
He meant to clear the upper pasture, too.
That sounds like something you have heard before?
Warren, I wish you could have heard the way
He jumbled everything. I stopped to look
Two or three times—he made me feel so queer—
To see if he was talking in his sleep.
He ran on Harold Wilson—you remember—

The boy you had in haying four years since.
He's finished school, and teaching in his col-
        lege.
Silas declares you'll have to get him back.
He says they two will make a team for work:
Between them they will lay this farm as
        smooth!
The way he mixed that in with other things.
He thinks young Wilson a likely lad, though
        daft
On education—you know how they fought
All through July under the blazing sun,
Silas up on the cart to build the load,
Harold along beside to pitch it on."

"Yes, I took care to keep well out of earshot."

"Well, those days trouble Silas like a dream.
You wouldn't think they would. How some
        things linger!
Harold's young college boy's assurance piqued
        him.
After so many years he still keeps finding
Good arguments he sees he might have used.
I sympathize. I know just how it feels
To think of the right thing to say too late.
Harold's associated in his mind with Latin.
He asked me what I thought of Harold's saying
He studied Latin like the violin
Because he liked it—that an argument!
He said he couldn't make the boy believe
He could find water with a hazel prong—
Which showed how much good school had
        ever done him.
He wanted to go over that. But most of all
He thinks if he could have another chance
To teach him how to build a load of hay—"

"I know, that's Silas' one accomplishment.
He bundles every forkful in its place,
And tags and numbers it for future reference,
So he can find and easily dislodge it
In the unloading. Silas does that well.
He takes it out in bunches like big birds' nests.
You never see him standing on the hay
He's trying to lift, straining to lift himself."

"He thinks if he could teach him that, he'd be
Some good perhaps to someone in the world.
He hates to see a boy the fool of books.
Poor Silas, so concerned for other folk,
And nothing to look backward to with pride,

5

10

15

20

25

30

35

40

45

50

And nothing to look forward to with hope,
So now and never any different."

Part of a moon was falling down the west,
Dragging the whole sky with it to the hills.
Its light poured softly in her lap. She saw
And spread her apron to it. She put out her
        hand
Among the harp-like morning-glory strings,
Taut with the dew from garden bed to eaves,
As if she played unheard the tenderness
That wrought on him beside her in the night.
"Warren," she said, "he has come home to die:
You needn't be afraid he'll leave you this time."

"Home," he mocked gently.

                "Yes, what else but home?
It all depends on what you mean by home.
Of course he's nothing to us, any more
Than was the hound that came a stranger to us
Out of the woods, worn out upon the trail."

"Home is the place where, when you have to
        go there,
They have to take you in."

                "I should have called it
Something you somehow haven't to deserve."

Warren leaned out and took a step or two,
Picked up a little stick, and brought it back
And broke it in his hand and tossed it by.
"Silas has better claim on us, you think,
Than on his brother? Thirteen little miles
As the road winds would bring him to his door.
Silas has walked that far no doubt today.
Why didn't he go there? His brother's rich,
A somebody—director in the bank."

"He never told us that."

                "We know it though."

"I think his brother ought to help, of course.
I'll see to that if there is need. He ought of right
To take him in, and might be willing to—
He may be better than appearances.
But have some pity on Silas. Do you think
If he'd had any pride in claiming kin
Or anything he looked for from his brother,
He'd keep so still about him all this time?"

"I wonder what's between them."

                     "I can tell you.
Silas is what he is—we wouldn't mind him—
But just the kind that kinsfolk can't abide.
He never did a thing so very bad.
He don't know why he isn't quite as good
As anyone. He won't be made ashamed
To please his brother, worthless though he is."

"I can't think Si ever hurt anyone."

"No, but he hurt my heart the way he lay
And rolled his old head on that sharp-edged
    chair-back.
He wouldn't let me put him on the lounge.
You must go in and see what you can do.
I made the bed up for him there tonight.
You'll be surprised at him—how much he's
    broken.
His working days are done; I'm sure of it."

"I'd not be in a hurry to say that."

"I haven't been. Go, look, see for yourself.
But, Warren, please remember how it is:
He's come to help you ditch the meadow.
He has a plan. You mustn't laugh at him.
He may not speak of it, and then he may.
I'll sit and see if that small sailing cloud
Will hit or miss the moon."

                    It hit the moon.
Then there were three there, making a dim
    row,
The moon, the little silver cloud, and she.

Warren returned—too soon, it seemed to her,
Slipped to her side, caught up her hand and
    waited.

"Warren?" she questioned.

               "Dead," was all he answered.

JOHN CROWE RANSOM

*Ransom (1888–   ) grew up in the American
South, studied at Vanderbilt and Oxford, and
became known as a writer, editor, and professor of English—generally all at once, as at
Kenyon, where he has taught and edited the*

Review. In his early days with the Fugitive
*group, Ransom, along with Warren and Tate,
was an outspoken sectionalist, believing in
shaping one's life according to the traditions of*
5 *one's region. There is something of the Waste
Land, of decay, of irony in his work; occasionally, allusions are difficult to fathom; but again,
there are pleasant satire, freedom with words—
a mixture of sweet and sour—which make for*
10 *rewarding experience. (See also I, 376.)*

CAPTAIN CARPENTER*

Captain Carpenter rose up in his prime
15 Put on his pistols and went riding out
But had got wellnigh nowhere at that time
Till he fell in with ladies in a rout.

It was a pretty lady and all her train
20 That played with him so sweetly but before
An hour she'd taken a sword with all her main
And twined him of his nose for evermore.

Captain Carpenter mounted up one day
25 And rode straightway into a stranger rogue
That looked unchristian but be that as may
The Captain did not wait upon prologue.

But drew upon him out of his great heart
30 The other swung against him with a club
And cracked his two legs at the shinny part
And let him roll and stick like any tub.

Captain Carpenter rode many a time
35 From male and female took he sundry harms
He met the wife of Satan crying "I'm
The she-wolf bids you shall bear no more
    arms."

40 Their strokes and counters whistled in the wind
I wish he had delivered half his blows
But where she should have made off like a
    hind
The bitch bit off his arms at the elbows.

45

And Captain Carpenter parted with his ears
To a black devil that used him in this wise
O Jesus ere his threescore and ten years
Another had plucked out his sweet blue eyes.

Captain Carpenter got up on his roan
And sallied from the gate in hell's despite
I heard him asking in the grimmest tone
If any enemy yet there was to fight?

"To any adversary it is fame
If he risk to be wounded by my tongue
Or burnt in two beneath my red heart's flame
Such are the perils he is cast among.

"But if he can he has a pretty choice
From an anatomy with little to lose
Whether he cut my tongue and take my voice
Or whether it be my round red heart he
    choose."

It was the neatest knave that ever was seen
Stepping in perfume from his lady's bower
Who at this word put in his merry mien
And fell on Captain Carpenter like a tower.

I would not knock old fellows in the dust
But there lay Captain Carpenter on his back
His weapons were the old heart in his bust
And a blade shook between rotten teeth alack.

The rogue in scarlet and grey soon knew his
    mind
He wished to get his trophy and depart
With gentle apology and touch refined
He pierced him and produced the Captain's
    heart.

God's mercy rest on Captain Carpenter now
I thought him Sirs an honest gentleman
Citizen husband soldier and scholar enow
Let jangling kites eat of him if they can.

But God's deep curses follow after those
That shore him of his goodly nose and ears
His legs and strong arms at the two elbows
And eyes that had not watered seventy years.

The curse of hell upon the sleek upstart
That got the Captain finally on his back
And took the red red vitals of his heart
And made the kites to whet their beaks clack
    clack.

STEPHEN VINCENT BENÉT

*Benét (1898–1943) was brought up at Army
posts and educated at Yale, where he broke
into publication early. A member of a writing
family, he turned out poems, novels, short
stories, and two librettos for operas. His* John
Brown's Body, *which used various verse forms
and prose, is a noble attempt to achieve the
panoramic sweep of an epic struggle; it won
the Pulitzer Prize as well as popular acclaim,
and was proof that narrative verse is definitely not dead. In short pieces Benét showed
lyric ability, a satirical touch, and ballad technique on various occasions, thus refusing to be
typed. His famous short story,* The Devil and
Daniel Webster, *appears on II, 514.*

THE BALLAD OF
WILLIAM SYCAMORE*

My father, he was a mountaineer,
His fist was a knotty hammer;
He was quick on his feet as a running deer,
And he spoke with a Yankee stammer.

My mother, she was merry and brave,
And so she came to her labor,
With a tall green fir for her doctor grave
And a stream for her comforting neighbor.

And some are wrapped in the linen fine,
And some like a godling's scion;
But I was cradled on twigs of pine
In the skin of a mountain lion.

And some remember a white, starched lap
And a ewer with silver handles;
But I remember a coonskin cap
And the smell of bayberry candles.

The cabin logs with the bark still rough,
And my mother who laughed at trifles,
And the tall, lank visitors, brown as snuff,
With their long, straight squirrel-rifles.

I can hear them dance, like a foggy song,
Through the deepest one of my slumbers,
The fiddle squeaking the boots along
And my father calling the numbers.

The quick feet shaking the puncheon-floor,
And the fiddle squeaking and squealing,

* From *Selected Works of Stephen Vincent
Benét*, published by Rinehart & Co., Inc. Copyright, 1922, by Stephen Vincent Benét.

Till the dried herbs rattled above the door
And the dust went up to the ceiling.

There are children lucky from dawn till dusk,
But never a child so lucky!
For I cut my teeth on "Money Musk"
In the Bloody Ground of Kentucky!

When I grew tall as the Indian corn,
My father had little to lend me,
But he gave me his great, old powder-horn
And his woodsman's skill to befriend me.

With a leather shirt to cover my back,
And a redskin nose to unravel
Each forest sign, I carried my pack
As far as a scout could travel.

Till I lost my boyhood and found my wife,
A girl like a Salem clipper!
A woman straight as a hunting-knife
With eyes as bright as the Dipper!

We cleared our camp where the buffalo feed,
Unheard-of streams were our flagons;
And I sowed my sons like apple-seed
On the trail of the Western wagons.

They were right, tight boys, never sulky or
slow,
A fruitful, a goodly muster.
The eldest died at the Alamo.
The youngest fell with Custer.

The letter that told it burned my hand.
Yet we smiled and said, "So be it!"
But I could not live when they fenced the
land,
For it broke my heart to see it.

I saddled a red, unbroken colt
And rode him into the day there;
And he threw me down like a thunderbolt
And rolled on me as I lay there.

The hunter's whistle hummed in my ear
As the city-men tried to move me,
And I died in my boots like a pioneer
With the whole wide sky above me.

Now I lie in the heart of the fat, black soil,
Like the seed of a prairie-thistle;

It has washed my bones with honey and oil
And picked them clean as a whistle.

And my youth returns, like the rains of Spring,
5 And my sons, like the wild-geese flying;
And I lie and hear the meadow-lark sing
And have much content in my dying.

Go play with the towns you have built of blocks
10 The towns where you would have bound me!
I sleep in my earth like a tired fox,
And my buffalo have found me.

15 *METROPOLITAN NIGHTMARE**

It rained quite a lot, that spring. You woke in
the morning
And saw the sky still clouded, the streets still
20 wet,
But nobody noticed so much, except the taxis
And the people who parade. You don't, in a
city.
The parks got very green. All the trees were
25 green
Far into July and August, heavy with leaf,
Heavy with leaf and the long roots boring and
spreading,
But nobody noticed that but the city gardeners
30 And they don't talk.

        Oh, on Sundays, perhaps, you'd notice:
Walking through certain blocks, by the shut,
proud houses
35 With the windows boarded, the people gone
away,
You'd suddenly see the queerest small shoots of
green
Poking through cracks and crevices in the stone
40 And a bird-sown flower, red on a balcony,
But then you made jokes about grass growing
in the streets
And politics and grass-roots—and there were
songs
45 And gags and a musical show called "Hot and
Wet."
It all made a good box for the papers. When
the flamingo
Flew into a meeting of the Board of Estimate,

50 * From *Selected Works of Stephen Vincent
Benét,* published by Rinehart & Co., Inc. Copyright, 1933, by Stephen Vincent Benét.

The new Mayor acted at once and called the
    photographers.
When the first green creeper crawled upon
    Brooklyn Bridge,
They thought it was ornamental. They let it   5
    stay.

There was the year the termites came to New
    York
And they don't do well in cold climates—but   10
    listen, Joe,
They're only ants and ants are nothing but in-
    sects.
It was funny and yet rather wistful, in a way
(As Heywood Broun pointed out in the *World-*   15
    Telegram)
To think of them looking for wood in a steel
    city.
It made you feel about life. It was too divine.
There were funny pictures by all the smart,   20
    funny artists
And Macy's ran a terribly clever ad:
"The Widow's Termite" or something.

                                        There was no   25
Disturbance. Even the Communists didn't pro-
    test
And say they were Morgan hirelings. It was too
    hot,
Too hot to protest, too hot to get excited,   30
An even, African heat, lush, fertile and steamy,
That soaked into bone and mind and never
    once broke.
The warm rain fell in fierce showers and ceased
    and fell.   35
Pretty soon you got used to its always being
    that way.

You got used to the changed rhythm, the al-
    tered beat,   40
To people walking slower, to the whole bright
Fierce pulse of the city slowing, to men in
    shorts,
To the new sun-helmets from Best's and the
    cops' white uniforms,   45
And the long noon-rest in the offices, every-
    where.
It wasn't a plan or anything. It just happened.
The fingers tapped the keys slower, the office-
    boys   50
Dozed on their benches, the bookkeeper
    yawned at his desk.

The A. T. & T. was the first to change the
    shifts
And establish an official siesta-room,
But they were always efficient. Mostly it just
Happened like sleep itself, like a tropic sleep,
Till even the Thirties were deserted at noon
Except for a few tourists and one damp cop.
They ran boats to see the big lilies on the
    North River
But it was only the tourists who really noticed
The flocks of rose-and-green parrots and par-
    rakeets
Nesting in the stone crannies of the Cathedral.
The rest of us had forgotten when they first
    came.
There wasn't any real change, it was just a
    heat spell,
A rain spell, a funny summer, a weather-man's
    joke,
In spite of the geraniums three feet high
In the tin-can gardens of Hester and Des-
    brosses.
New York was New York. It couldn't turn in-
    side out.
When they got the news from Woods Hole
    about the Gulf Stream,
The *Times* ran an adequate story.
But nobody reads those stories but science-
    cranks.

Until, one day, a somnolent city-editor
Gave a new cub the termite yarn to break his
    teeth on.
The cub was just down from Vermont, so he
    took the time.
He was serious about it. He went around.
He read all about termites in the Public Library
And it made him sore when they fired him.

                                        So, one evening,
Talking with an old watchman, beside the first
Raw girders of the new Planetopolis Build-
    ing
(Ten thousand brine-cooled offices, each with
    shower)
He saw a dark line creeping across the rubble
And turned a flashlight on it.

                            "Say, buddy," he said,
"You better look out for those ants. They eat
    wood, you know,
They'll have your shack down in no time."

The watchman spat.
"Oh, they've quit eating wood," he said, in a
    casual voice,
"I thought everybody knew that."

                    —and, reaching down,
He pried from the insect jaws the bright crumb
    of steel.

NIGHTMARE NUMBER THREE*

We had expected everything but revolt
And I kind of wonder myself when they
    started thinking—
But there's no dice in that now.

                    I've heard fellows say
They must have planned it for years and
    maybe they did.
Looking back, you can find little incidents here 20
    and there,
Like the concrete-mixer in Jersey eating the
    wop
Or the roto press that printed "Fiddle-dee-
    dee!"
In a three-color process all over Senator Sloop,
Just as he was making a speech. The thing
    about that
Was, how could it walk upstairs? But it was
    upstairs,
Clicking and mumbling in the Senate Chamber.
They had to knock out the wall to take it away
And the wrecking-crew said it grinned.

                    It was only the best 35
Machines, of course, the superhuman machines,
The ones we'd built to be better than flesh and
    bone,
But the cars were in it, of course . . .

                    and they hunted us
Like rabbits through the cramped streets on
    that Bloody Monday,
The Madison Avenue busses leading the
    charge.
The busses were pretty bad—but I'll not for-
    get
The smash of glass when the Duesenberg left
    the show-room

* From *Selected Works of Stephen Vincent
Benét*, published by Rinehart & Co., Inc. Copyright, 1935, by Stephen Vincent Benét.

And pinned three brokers to the Racquet Club
    steps
Or the long howl of the horns when they saw
    men run,
5 When they saw them looking for holes in the
    solid ground . . .

I guess they were tired of being ridden in
And stopped and started by pygmies for silly
10 ends,
Of wrapping cheap cigarettes and bad choco-
    late bars,
Collecting nickels and waving platinum hair
And letting six million people live in a town.
15 I guess it was that. I guess they got tired of us
And the whole smell of human hands.

                    But it was a shock
To climb sixteen flights of stairs to Art Zuck-
    ow's office
(Nobody took the elevators twice)
And find him strangled to death in a nest of
    telephones,
The octopus-tendrils waving over his head,
25 And a sort of quiet humming filling the
    air. . . .
Do they eat? . . . There was red . . . But I
    did not stop to look.
I don't know yet how I got to the roof in time
30 And it's lonely, here on the roof.

                    For a while, I thought
That window-cleaner would make it, and keep
    me company.
35 But they got him with his own hoist at the
    sixteenth floor
And dragged him in, with a squeal.
You see, they coöperate. Well, we taught them
    that
40 And it's fair enough, I suppose. You see, we
    built them.
We taught them to think for themselves.
It was bound to come. You can see that it was
    bound to come.
45 And it won't be so bad, in the country. I hate
    to think
Of the reapers, running wild in the Kansas
    fields,
And the transport planes like hawks on a
50 chickenyard,
But the horses might help. We might make a
    deal with the horses.

At least, you've more chance, out there.

               And they need us, too.
They're bound to realize that when they once
    calm down.
They'll need oil and spare parts and adjust-
    ments and tuning up.
Slaves? Well, in a way, you know, we were
    slaves before.
There won't be so much real difference—
    honest, there won't.
(I wish I hadn't looked into that beauty-parlor
And seen what was happening there.
But those are female machines and a bit high-
    strung.)
Oh, we'll settle down. We'll arrange it. We'll
    compromise.
It wouldn't make sense to wipe out the whole
    human race.
Why, I bet if I went to my old Plymouth now

(Of course you'd have to do it the tactful way)
And said, "Look here! Who got you the swell
    French horn?"
He wouldn't turn me over to those police cars;
5 At least I don't think he would.

               Oh, it's going to be jake.
There won't be so much real difference—
    honest, there won't—
10 And I'd go down in a minute and take my
    chance—
I'm a good American and I always liked
    them—
Except for one small detail that bothers me
15 And that's the food proposition. Because, you
    see,
The concrete-mixer may have made a mistake,
And it looks like just high spirits,
But, if it's got so they like the flavor . . .
20   well . .

LYRIC POETRY

SIXTEENTH CENTURY

─────────

SIR THOMAS WYATT

*Living in an age of political intrigue and high
adventure, Thomas Wyatt (1503–1542) knew
the confines of prison life on at least two occasions. Cambridge-trained, well-traveled, he cut
an attractive figure before Anne Boleyn but
had to retire before a more formidable adversary, Henry VIII. As a contributor to* Tottel's
Miscellany, *Wyatt was a pioneer in introducing
the Italian sonnet to England and in developing the possibilities of native song.*

THE LOVER COMPARETH HIS
STATE TO A SHIP IN PERILOUS
STORM TOSSED ON THE SEA

My galley charged with forgetfulness
Thorough sharp seas, in winter nights doth
    pass,
'Tween rock and rock; and eke my foe, alas,
That is my lord, steereth with cruelness,
And every hour, a thought in readiness,
As though that death were light in such a case.
An endless wind doth tear the sail apace
Of forced sighs, and trusty fearfulness.
A rain of tears, a cloud of dark disdain
Hath done the wearied cords great hinderance,
Wreathed with error, and with ignorance.
The stars be hid that led me to this pain;
  Drowned is reason that should be my com-
    fort,
  And I remain, despairing of the port.

A RENOUNCING OF LOVE

Farewell, Love, and all thy laws for ever!
Thy baited hooks shall tangle me no more:

Senec and Plato call me from thy lore
To perfect wealth my wit for to endeavor.
In blind error when I did persever,
Thy sharp repulse, that pricketh aye so sore,
5 Taught me in trifles that I set no store;
But 'scape forth thence, since liberty is lever.[1]
Therefore, farewell! go trouble younger hearts,
And in me claim no more authority.
With idle youth go use thy property,
10 And thereon spend thy many brittle darts;
  For hitherto though I have lost my time,
  Me list no longer rotten boughs to climb.

15 ### THE LOVER COMPLAINETH THE
UNKINDNESS OF HIS LOVE

  My lute, awake, perform the last
  Labor that thou and I shall waste,
  And end that I have now begun;
  And when this song is sung and past,
20   My lute, be still, for I have done.

  As to be heard where ear is none,
  As lead to grave[1] in marble stone,
  My song may pierce her heart as soon.
  Should we then sigh, or sing, or moan?
25   No, no, my lute, for I have done.

  The rocks do not so cruelly
  Repulse the waves continually,
  As she my suit and affection;
  So that I am past remedy,
  Whereby my lute and I have done.

35 ─────────
[1] more desirable.
[1] carve.

Proud of the spoil that thou hast got
Of simple hearts, through lovë's shot;
By whom unkind thou hast them won,
Think not he hath his bow forgot,
Although my lute and I have done.

Vengeance shall fall on thy disdain,
That makest but game on earnest pain;
Think not alone under the sun
Unquit to cause thy lovers plain,
Although my lute and I have done.

May chance thee lie withered and old,
In winter nights that are so cold,
Plaining in vain unto the moon;
Thy wishes then dare not be told.
Care then who list, for I have done.

And then may chance thee to repent
The time that thou hast lost and spent
To cause thy lovers sigh and swoon;
Then shalt thou know beauty but lent,
And wish and want as I have done.

Now cease, my lute, this is the last
Labor that thou and I shall waste,
And ended is that we begun.
Now is this song both sung and past,
My lute, be still, for I have done.

HENRY HOWARD, EARL OF SURREY

The name of Surrey (1517–1547) is almost invariably linked with that of Wyatt as a team, although actually he was much younger and was a follower of, occasionally an improver upon, the work of the older man. With a reputation as a prankster, and with a family background studded with royal names, Surrey, that "most foolish" boy, was executed for treason on manufactured evidence. He is significant for developing the sonnet pattern now known as "Shakespearean" and for introducing blank verse to non-dramatic English literature (in a translation of two books of the Aeneid*).*

DESCRIPTION OF SPRING, WHEREIN EACH THING RENEWS SAVE ONLY THE LOVER

The soote[1] season that bud and bloom forth 50
    brings

With green hath clad the hill and eke the vale,
The nightingale with feathers new she sings,
The turtle[2] to her make[3] hath told her tale.
Summer is come, for every spray now springs,
5 The hart hath hung his old head on the pale,
The buck in brake his winter coat he flings,
The fishes float with new repairëd scale,
The adder all her slough away she slings,
The swift swallow pursueth the flyës smale,
10 The busy bee her honey now she mings,[4]—
Winter is worn, that was the flowers' bale:
And thus I see, among these pleasant things
Each care decays—and yet my sorrow springs.

15

[LOVE, THAT DOTH REIGN]

Love, that doth reign and live within my
    thought,
20 And built his seat within my captive breast,
Clad in the arms wherein with me he fought,
Oft in my face he doth his banner rest.
But she that taught me love and suffer pain,
My doubtful hope and eke my hot desire
25 With shamefast look to shadow and refrain,
Her smiling grace converteth straight to ire.
And coward Love, then, to the heart apace
Taketh his flight, where he doth lurk and plain[1]
His purpose lost, and dare not show his face.
30 For my lord's guilt thus faultless bide I pain;
Yet from my lord shall not my foot remove.
Sweet is the death that taketh end by love.

35

THE MEANS TO ATTAIN HAPPY LIFE

Martial,[1] the things that do attain
    The happy life be these, I find;
    The riches left, not got with pain;
40   The fruitful ground, the quiet mind.

The equal friend, no grudge, no strife,
    No charge of rule nor governance;
Without disease, the healthful life;
45   The household of continuance.

The mean[2] diet, no delicate fare;

---

[1] sweet.

[2] turtle dove.   [3] mate.   [4] remembers.
[1] complain.
[1] Roman poet, first century. Surrey's verses translate one of Martial's epigrams.
[2] moderate.

True wisdom joined with simpleness;
  The night discharged of all care,
  Where wine the wit may not oppress.

The faithful wife, without debate;
  Such sleeps as may beguile the night;
Contented with thine own estate,
  Ne wish for death, ne fear his might.

SIR PHILIP SIDNEY

Sidney (1554–1586) is remembered as the perfect courtier—intelligent, accomplished, virile. Whether or not he actually gave his cup of water to a dying soldier on the field of Zutphen, the legend fits his reputation. His unrequited love for Penelope Devereux produced a memorable sonnet sequence, Astrophel and Stella. *In the field of fiction his* Arcadia, *a pastoral romance, is important in the development of the English novel. And in a third category, criticism, Sidney wrote the monumental* Apology for Poetry.

FROM *Astrophel and Stella*

31

With how sad steps, O Moon, thou climb'st the
  skies!
How silently, and with how wan a face!
What, may it be that even in heavenly place
That busy archer his sharp arrows tries?
Sure, if that long-with-love-acquainted eyes
Can judge of love, thou feel'st a lover's case.
I read it in thy looks; thy languished grace,
To me that feel the like, thy state descries.
Then, even of fellowship, O Moon, tell me,
Is constant love deemed there but want of wit?
Are beauties there as proud as here they be?
Do they above love to be loved, and yet
Those lovers scorn whom that love doth possess?
Do they call virtue there ungratefulness?

39

Come, Sleep! O Sleep, the certain knot of
  peace,
The baiting-place[1] of wit, the balm of woe,
The poor man's wealth, the prisoner's release,
The indifferent judge between the high and
  low;

---
[1] resting place.

With shield of proof shield me from out the
  press
Of those fierce darts Despair at me doth throw;
Oh make in me those civil wars to cease.
I will good tribute pay, if thou do so.
Take thou of me smooth pillows, sweetest bed,
A chamber deaf to noise and blind to light,
A rosy garland and a weary head;
And if these things, as being thine by right,
Move not thy heavy grace, thou shalt in me,
Livelier than elsewhere, Stella's image see.

41

Having this day my horse, my hand, my lance
  Guided so well that I obtained the prize,
  Both by the judgment of the English eyes
  And of some sent from that sweet enemy,
  France;
Horsemen my skill in horsemanship advance,
  Town-folks my strength; a daintier judge applies
  His praise to sleight which from good use
  doth rise;
  Some lucky wits impute it but to chance;
Others, because of both sides I do take
  My blood from them who did excel in this,
  Think nature me a man of arms did make.
How far they shot awry! The true cause is,
  Stella looked on, and from her heav'nly face
  Sent forth the beams which made so fair
  my race.

[LEAVE ME, O LOVE]

Leave me, O Love, which reachest but to dust;
And thou, my mind, aspire to higher things;
Grow rich in that which never taketh rust.
Whatever fades but fading pleasure brings.
Draw in thy beams, and humble all thy might
To that sweet yoke where lasting freedoms be,
Which breaks the clouds and opens forth the
  light
That doth both shine and give us sight to see.
Oh take fast hold; let that light be thy guide
In this small course which birth draws out to
  death,
And think how evil becometh him to slide
Who seeketh heaven, and comes of heavenly
  breath.
Then farewell, world; thy uttermost I see.
Eternal Love, maintain thy life in me.

CHRISTOPHER MARLOWE

The life of Marlowe (1564–1593) is filled with intrigue and mystery: he was granted a Cambridge degree after an unexplained political mission; he was involved in tavern scuffles; he was tried for atheism; and he was killed in a dispute over an inn bill. Like Keats, Marlowe showed genius and died prematurely; one speculates futilely on what might have happened if the fates had been more kind to both. Although Marlowe showed wit and intelligence in non-dramatic verse, his reputation is based primarily on four powerful dramatic studies of men ruled by passion: Tamburlaine, The Jew of Malta, Edward II, and Dr. Faustus. He was the first to handle English dramatic blank verse with professional ability, thus paving the way for Shakespeare.

THE PASSIONATE SHEPHERD TO HIS LOVE

Come live with me, and be my love;
And we will all the pleasures prove
That hills and valleys, dales and fields,
Woods, or steepy mountain yields.

And we will sit upon the rocks,
Seeing the shepherds feed their flocks
By shallow rivers, to whose falls
Melodious birds sing madrigals.

And I will make thee beds of roses,
And a thousand fragrant posies;
A cap of flowers, and a kirtle
Embroidered all with leaves of myrtle;

A gown made of the finest wool
Which from our pretty lambs we pull;
Fair-lined slippers for the cold,
With buckles of the purest gold;

A belt of straw and ivy-buds,
With coral clasps and amber studs;
And if these pleasures may thee move,
Come live with me, and be my love.

The shepherd-swains shall dance and sing
For thy delight each May morning;
If these delights thy mind may move,
Then live with me, and be my love.

SIR WALTER RALEIGH

Along with Sidney, Raleigh (1552–1618) was an outstanding courtier of the Elizabethan period. Like his contemporary, he combined ability in the field with grace in the salon and achievement in letters. After many a sea adventure Raleigh was executed for treason in a purely political move. We note, however, in our age of specialization, that this poet was a champion exponent of Renaissance versatility; even in the Tower he found ways and means to cultivate hothouse plants, distill liquors, and begin the writing of a history of the world. Some of Raleigh's verse is unique in its day; along with the usual sweet or conventional lines go such works as The Lie, with its "modern" skepticism and originality so marked as to win from one authority the label "new poetry."

A VISION UPON THIS CONCEIT OF THE FAIRY QUEEN

Methought I saw the grave where Laura lay,[1]
Within that temple where the vestal flame
Was wont to burn; and passing by that way
To see that buried dust of living fame,
Whose tomb fair Love and fairer Virtue kept,
All suddenly I saw the Fairy Queen;
At whose approach the soul of Petrarch wept,
And from thenceforth those graces were not seen,
For they this Queen attended; in whose stead
Oblivion laid him down on Laura's hearse.
Hereat the hardest stones were seen to bleed,
And groans of buried ghosts the heavens did pierce,
Where Homer's sprite did tremble all for grief,
And cursed th' access of that celestial thief.

THE NYMPH'S REPLY TO THE SHEPHERD[1]

If all the world and love were young,
And truth in every shepherd's tongue,
These pretty pleasures might me move,
To live with thee and be thy love.

---

[1] sonnet prefixed to *Faerie Queene;* Laura is Petrarch's lady.
[1] See column I, this page.

But time drives flocks from field to fold,
When rivers rage, and rocks grow cold;
And Philomel[2] becometh dumb;
The rest complains of cares to come.

The flowers do fade, and wanton fields
To wayward Winter reckoning yields;
A honey tongue, a heart of gall,
Is fancy's spring, but sorrow's fall.

Thy gowns, thy shoes, thy beds of roses,
Thy cap, thy kirtle, and thy posies,
Soon break, soon wither, soon forgotten,
In folly ripe, in reason rotten.

Thy belt of straw and ivy buds,
Thy coral clasps and amber studs,
All these in me no means can move,
To come to thee and be thy love.

But could youth last, and love still breed,
Had joys no date, nor age no need,
Then these delights my mind might move,
To live with thee and be thy love.

THE LIE

Go, Soul, the body's guest
  Upon a thankless arrant;[1]
Fear not to touch the best;
  The truth shall be thy warrant:
    Go, since I needs must die,
    And give the world the lie.

Say to the court, it glows
  And shines like rotten wood;
Say to the church, it shows
  What's good, and doth no good:
    If court and church reply,
    Then give them both the lie.

Tell potentates, they live
  Acting by others' action;
Not loved unless they give,
  Not strong but by a faction:
    If potentates reply,
    Give potentates the lie.

Tell men of high condition,
  That manage the estate,

Their purpose is ambition,
  Their practice only hate:
    And if they once reply,
    Then give them all the lie.

Tell them that brave it most,
  They beg for more by spending,
Who, in their greatest cost,
  Seek nothing but commending:
    And if they make reply,
    Then give them all the lie.

Tell zeal it wants devotion;
  Tell love it is but lust;
Tell time it is but motion;
  Tell flesh it is but dust:
    And wish them not reply,
    For thou must give the lie.

Tell age it daily wasteth;
  Tell honour how it alters;
Tell beauty how she blasteth;
  Tell favour how it falters:
    And as they shall reply,
    Give every one the lie.

Tell wit how much it wrangles
  In tickle[2] points of niceness;
Tell wisdom she entangles
  Herself in over-wiseness:
    And when they do reply,
    Straight give them both the lie.

Tell physic of her boldness;
  Tell skill it is pretension;
Tell charity of coldness;
  Tell law it is contention:
    And as they do reply,
    So give them still the lie.

Tell fortune of her blindness;
  Tell nature of decay;
Tell friendship of unkindness;
  Tell justice of delay:
    And if they will reply,
    Then give them all the lie.

Tell arts they have no soundness,
  But vary by esteeming;
Tell schools they want profoundness,
  And stand too much on seeming:

5

10

15

20

25

30

35

40

45

50

---

[2] nightingale.   [1] errand.   [2] delicate.

If arts and schools reply,
Give arts and schools the lie.

Tell faith it's fled the city;
Tell how the country erreth;
Tell manhood shakes off pity;
Tell virtue least preferreth:
    And if they do reply,
    Spare not to give the lie.

So when thou hast, as I
Commanded thee, done blabbing,—
Although to give the lie
Deserves no less than stabbing,—
    Stab at thee he that will,
    No stab the soul can kill.

MICHAEL DRAYTON

*Drayton (1563–1631) handled more verse
forms ably than any other sixteenth-century
poet: lyrics, fantasy, sonnets, odes, map poetry, pastorals, epistles, etc. Unlike most of his
contemporaries included in this volume, he
cannot show a record of university education,
missions abroad, and blue-blood ancestry.
Brought up by the Goodere family, he lived
largely on the bounty of influential friends.
Nevertheless, his reputation, based on* Nymphi-
dia, Poly-Olbion, England's Heroical Epistles,
*etc., is considerable. He was buried in West-
minster Abbey.*

[AS OTHER MEN, SO I]

As other men, so I myself do muse
Why in this sort I wrest invention so,
And why these giddy metaphors I use,
Leaving the path the greater part do go.
I will resolve you. I am lunatic,
And ever this in madmen you shall find,
What they last thought on when the brain
    grew sick
In most distraction keep that still in mind.
Thus talking idly in this bedlam fit,
Reason and I, you must conceive, are twain;
'Tis nine years, now, since first I lost my wit.
Bear with me, then, though troubled be my
    brain.
    With diet and correction men distraught
    (Not too far past) may to their wits be
    brought.

[SINCE THERE'S NO HELP]

Since there's no help, come, let us kiss and
    part.
5 Nay, I have done; you get no more of me.
And I am glad, yea, glad with all my heart
That thus so cleanly I myself can free.
Shake hands for ever; cancel all our vows;
And when we meet at any time again,
10 Be it not seen in either of our brows
That we one jot of former love retain.
Now at the last gasp of Love's latest breath,
When, his pulse failing, Passion speechless lies,
When Faith is kneeling by his bed of death,
15 And Innocence is closing up his eyes—
    Now, if thou wouldst, when all have given
        him over,
    From death to life thou might'st him yet re-
        cover.

ODE

TO THE VIRGINIAN VOYAGE

You brave heroic minds,
Worthy your country's name,
    That honor still pursue,
    Go, and subdue,
Whilst loitering hinds
Lurk here at home, with shame.

Britons, you stay too long.
Quickly aboard bestow you,
    And with a merry gale
    Swell your stretched sail,
With vows as strong
As the winds that blow you.

Your course securely steer,
West and by south forth keep,
    Rocks, lee-shores, nor shoals,
    When Eolus scowls,
You need not fear,
So absolute the deep.

And cheerfully at sea
Success you still entice,
    To get the pearl and gold,
    And ours to hold
Virginia,
Earth's only paradise.

Where Nature hath in store

Fowl, venison, and fish,
  And the fruitfull'st soil
  Without your toil
Three harvests more,
All greater than your wish.   5

And the ambitious vine
Crowns with his purple mass
  The cedar reaching high
  To kiss the sky;   10
The cypress, pine,
And useful sassafras.

To whom the golden age
Still Nature's laws doth give,
  No other cares that tend   15
  But them to defend
From Winter's rage,
That long there doth not live.

When as the luscious smell
Of that delicious land,   20
  Above the seas that flows,
  The clear wind throws,
Your hearts to swell
Approaching the dear strand,

In kenning of the shore   25
(Thanks to God first given)
  O you the happiest men,
  Be frolic then,
Let cannons roar,
Frighting the wide heaven.   30

And in regions far
Such heroes bring ye forth
  As those from whom we came,
  And plant our name   35
Under that star
Not known unto our north.   40

And as there plenty grows
Of laurel everywhere,
  Apollo's sacred tree,
  You may it see   45
A poet's brows
To crown, that may sing there.

Thy Voyages attend,
Industrious Hakluyt,[1]   50

¹ Elizabethan editor of *Principall Navigations,*
etc.

Whose reading shall inflame
  Men to seek fame,
And much commend
To after-times thy wit.

WILLIAM SHAKESPEARE

*Shakespeare (1564–1616) is known the world
over as the greatest dramatist of modern times,
if not of all time (see I, 419) for a sketch of his
life and work). It is easy to forget, perhaps,
that he also wrote miscellaneous verse, two
long, erotic, non-dramatic poems, songs (which
played functional roles in the plays), and 154
sonnets, some of which appear in the following pages. The best of the songs and sonnets
are among the best in the language.*

*The sonnets are addressed apparently to a
young man and, in later stages, to the famous
Dark Lady. They likewise seem to tell a story,
probably autobiographical, in two parts. They
are dedicated to a "Mr. W. H." whose identity,
like that of the people in the verse itself, is uncertain; most modern critics relate the dedication to the poet's patron, Southampton. In an
age of sonnets, Shakespeare, using for the most
part the sonnet form which bears his name (although he did not invent it), reached new
heights of expression and technical excellence.
The welding of sound and sense has seldom
been accomplished so successfully. The ama-
teur should note the simplicity of the vocabulary (most of it monosyllabic), the effective
openings, the use of the final "thrust" couplet,
the tight engineering of the whole—and, in
another direction, the dignity, drama, passion,
lyricism, and high intelligence that exist in
various proportions in the poetry itself.*

SONGS FROM THE PLAYS

FROM *The Two Gentlemen of Verona*

Who is Silvia? what is she,
  That all our swains commend her?
Holy, fair, and wise is she;
  The heaven such grace did lend her,
That she might admired be.

Is she kind as she is fair?
  For beauty lives with kindness:
Love doth to her eyes repair

To help him of his blindness,
And, being helped, inhabits there.

Then to Silvia let us sing,
  That Silvia is excelling;   5
She excels each mortal thing
  Upon the dull earth dwelling:
To her let us garlands bring.

FROM *The Merchant of Venice*   10

Tell me where is fancy bred,
Or in the heart, or in the head?
How begot, how nourishëd?
    Reply, reply.   15
It is engend'rëd in the eyes,
With gazing fed; and fancy dies
In the cradle where it lies.
Let us all ring fancy's knell;
I'll begin it—Ding, dong, bell.   20
    Ding, dong, bell.

FROM *Much Ado About Nothing*

Sigh no more, ladies, sigh no more;   25
  Men were deceivers ever;
One foot in sea, and one on shore,
  To one thing constant never.
Then sigh not so, but let them go,
  And be you blithe and bonny,   30
Converting all your sounds of woe
  Into "Hey nonny, nonny!"

Sing no more ditties, sing no moe
  Of dumps so dull and heavy;   35
The fraud of men was ever so,
  Since summer first was leavy.
Then sigh not so, but let them go,
  And be you blithe and bonny,
Converting all your sounds of woe   40
  Into "Hey nonny, nonny!"

FROM *As You Like It*

Blow, blow, thou winter wind!   45
Thou art not so unkind
  As man's ingratitude;
Thy tooth is not so keen,
Because thou art not seen,
  Although thy breath be rude.   50

Heigh ho! sing, heigh ho! unto the green holly;

Most friendship is feigning, most loving mere
    folly.
  Then, heigh ho, the holly!
  This life is most jolly.

Freeze, freeze, thou bitter sky!
That dost not bite so nigh
  As benefits forgot;
Though thou the waters warp,
Thy sting is not so sharp
  As friend remembered not.

Heigh ho! sing, heigh ho! etc.

FROM *Twelfth Night*

O mistress mine, where are you roaming?
O, stay and hear; your true love's coming,
  That can sing both high and low.
Trip no further, pretty sweeting,
Journeys end in lovers meeting,
  Every wise man's son doth know.

What is love? 'Tis not hereafter;
Present mirth hath present laughter;
  What's to come is still unsure.
In delay there lies no plenty;
Then come kiss me, sweet and twenty,
  Youth's a stuff will not endure.

FROM *Twelfth Night*

When that I was and a little tiny boy,
  With hey, ho, the wind and the rain,
A foolish thing was but a toy,
  For the rain it raineth every day.

But when I came to man's estate,
  With hey, ho, the wind and the rain,
'Gainst knaves and thieves men shut their
    gate,
  For the rain it raineth every day.

But when I came, alas! to wive,
  With hey, ho, the wind and the rain,
By swaggering could I never thrive,
  For the rain it raineth every day.

But when I came unto my beds,
  With hey, ho, the wind and the rain,
With toss-pots still had drunken heads,
  For the rain it raineth every day.

A great while ago the world begun,
    With hey, ho, the wind and the rain,
But that's all one, our play is done,
    And we'll strive to please you every
        day.

FROM *Measure for Measure*

Take, oh, take those lips away,
    That so sweetly were forsworn;
And those eyes, the break of day,
    Lights that do mislead the morn.
But my kisses bring again,
        Bring again;
Seals of love, but sealed in vain,
        Sealed in vain.

FROM *Cymbeline*

Hark, hark! The lark at heaven's gate sings,
    And Phoebus gins arise,
His steeds to water at those springs
    On chaliced flowers that lies;
And winking Mary-buds begin
    To ope their golden eyes.
With every thing that pretty is,
    My lady sweet, arise!
        Arise, arise!

SONNETS

15

When I consider every thing that grows
Holds in perfection but a little moment,
That this huge stage presenteth naught but
    shows
Whereon the stars in secret influence com-
    ment;
When I perceive that men as plants increase,
Cheered and checked even by the self-same
    sky,
Vaunt in their youthful sap, at height decrease,
And wear their brave state out of memory;
Then the conceit[1] of this inconstant stay
Sets you most rich in youth, before my sight,
Where wasteful Time debateth with Decay,
To change your day of youth to sullied night;
    And, all in war with Time for love of you,
    As he takes from you, I engraft[2] you new.

18

Shall I compare thee to a summer's day?
Thou art more lovely and more temperate:
5 Rough winds do shake the darling buds of
    May,
And summer's lease hath all too short a date:
Sometimes too hot the eye of heaven shines,
And often is his gold complexion dimmed;
10 And every fair from fair sometime declines,
By chance, or nature's changing course un-
    trimmed;
But thy eternal summer shall not fade,
Nor lose possession of that fair thou owest[3]
15 Nor shall Death brag thou wander'st in his
    shade,
When in eternal lines to time thou growest:
    So long as men can breathe or eyes can see,
    So long lives this, and this gives life to thee.
20

29

When, in disgrace with fortune and men's
    eyes,
I all alone beweep my outcast state,
25 And trouble deaf heaven with my bootless[4]
    cries,
And look upon myself and curse my fate,
Wishing me like to one more rich in hope,
Featured like him, like him with friends pos-
30   sessed,
Desiring this man's art and that man's scope,
With what I most enjoy contented least;
Yet in these thoughts myself almost despising,
Haply I think on thee,—and then my state,
35 Like to the lark at break of day arising
From sullen earth, sings hymns at heaven's
    gate;
    For thy sweet love remembered such wealth
      brings
    That then I scorn to change my state with
40   kings.

30

When to the sessions of sweet silent thought
I summon up remembrance of things past,
I sigh the lack of many a thing I sought,
And with old woes new wail my dear time's
    waste:
Then can I drown an eye, unused to flow,
50 For precious friends hid in death's dateless
    night,

---

[1] idea.   [2] keep alive.   [3] ownest.   [4] useless.

And weep afresh love's long since cancelled
woe,
And moan the expense of many a vanished
sight:
Then can I grieve at grievances foregone,
And heavily from woe to woe tell o'er
The sad account of fore-bemoaned moan,
Which I new pay as if not paid before.
  But if the while I think on thee, dear friend,
  All losses are restored and sorrows end.

55

Not marble, nor the gilded monuments
Of princes, shall outlive this powerful rime;
But you shall shine more bright in these con-
tents
Than unswept stone, besmeared with sluttish
time.
When wasteful war shall statues overturn,
And broils root out the work of masonry,
Nor Mars his sword nor war's quick fire shall
burn
The living record of your memory.
'Gainst death and all-oblivious enmity
Shall you pace forth; your praise shall still find
room
Even in the eyes of all posterity
That wear this world out to the ending doom.
  So, till the judgment that yourself arise,
  You live in this, and dwell in lovers' eyes.

71

No longer mourn for me when I am dead
Than you shall hear the surly sullen bell
Give warning to the world that I am fled
From this vile world, with vilest worms to
dwell:
Nay, if you read this line, remember not
The hand that writ it; for I love you so,
That I in your sweet thoughts would be for-
got,
If thinking on me then should make you woe.
O, if, I say, you look upon this verse,
When I perhaps compounded am with clay,
Do not so much as my poor name rehearse,
But let your love even with my life decay;
  Lest the wise world should look into your
  moan
  And mock you with me after I am gone.

90

Then hate me when thou wilt; if ever, now;

Now, while the world is bent my deeds to
cross,
Join with the spite of fortune, make me bow,
And do not drop in for an after-loss:
Ah, do not, when my heart hath 'scaped this
sorrow,
Come in the rearward of a conquered woe,
Give not a windy night a rainy morrow,
To linger out a purposed overthrow.
If thou wilt leave me, do not leave me last,
When other petty griefs have done their spite,
But in the onset come; so shall I taste
At first the very worst of fortune's might;
  And other strains of woe, which now seem
  woe,
  Compared with loss of thee will not seem so.

106

When in the chronicle of wasted time
I see descriptions of the fairest wights,[5]
And beauty making beautiful old rime
In praise of ladies dead and lovely knights,
Then, in the blazon of sweet beauty's best,
Of hand, of foot, of lip, of eye, of brow,
I see their antique pen would have expressed
Even such a beauty as you master now.
So all their praises are but prophecies
Of this our time, all you prefiguring;
And, for they looked but with divining eyes,
They had not skill enough your worth to sing:
  For we, which now behold these present
  days,
  Have eyes to wonder, but lack tongues to
  praise.

116

Let me not to the marriage of true minds
Admit impediments. Love is not love
Which alters when it alteration finds,
Or bends with the remover to remove:
O, no! it is an ever-fixed mark
That looks on tempests and is never shaken;
It is the star to every wandering bark,
Whose worth's unknown, although his height
be taken.
Love's not Time's fool, though rosy lips and
cheeks
Within his bending sickle's compass come;
Love alters not with his brief hours and weeks,
But bears it out even to the edge of doom.

---

[5] creatures.

If this be error and upon me proved,
I never writ, nor no man ever loved.

130

My mistress' eyes are nothing like the sun;
Coral is far more red than her lips' red;
If snow be white, why then her breasts are
    dun;
If hairs be wires, black wires grow on her head.
I have seen roses damasked, red and white,
But no such roses see I in her cheeks;
And in some perfumes is there more delight
Than in the breath that from my mistress reeks.
I love to hear her speak, yet well I know
That music hath a far more pleasing sound;
I grant I never saw a goddess go;
My mistress, when she walks, treads on the
    ground:
    And yet, by heaven, I think my love as rare
    As any she belied with false compare.

SONGS FROM THE PLAYS,
ANONYMOUS LYRICS,
LYRICS FROM SONGBOOKS
16th and early 17th century

*Elizabethan England has been called a "nest
of singing birds." The professionals and versatile amateurs who wrote sonnets and erotic
verse were not the only vocalists—the crafts-
men, the tavern crowd, and the after-supper
guests all sang. Three-man's songs, airs, madrigals all found their way into the songbooks.*

*Songs were an important part of sixteenth-
century drama. Most of them were sung by
one actor with a good voice. Those familiar
with the plays of Shakespeare, for example,
know how prominent these songs were, and
that they fitted the roles and were not "spe-
cialty numbers" at all. They could be used for
everything from reflecting stage moods to
clearing the scene itself. Many of the boy actors
were trained singers.*

*The songs as a group had considerable range
as to type and subject matter. Drinking songs,
tobacco songs, songs of the trades, lullabies,
moralizing airs, love songs, swan songs—they
ran the gamut of moods and attitudes. But
the main point is that people in this age of
rebirth sang. The Puritan had not yet become
politically powerful enough to focus the Englishman's mind once more on the hereafter.*

BACK AND SIDE, GO BARE,
GO BARE

FROM *Gammer Gurton's Needle*

Back and side, go bare, go bare,
    Both foot and hand go cold;
But, belly, God send thee good ale enough,
    Whether it be new or old.

I cannot eat but little meat,
    My stomach is not good;
But, sure, I think that I can drink
    With him that wears a hood.
Though I go bare, take ye no care,
    I am nothing a-cold;
I stuff my skin so full within
    Of jolly good ale and old.

    Back and side, go bare, go bare, etc.

I love no roast, but a nut-brown toast,
    And a crab[1] laid in the fire;
A little bread shall do me stead,
    Much bread I not desire.
No frost nor snow, no wind, I trow,
    Can hurt me if i[t] would,
I am so wrapt and throughly lapt
    Of jolly good ale and old.

    Back and side, go bare, go bare, etc.

And Tib, my wife, that as her life
    Loveth well good ale to seek,
Full oft drinks she till ye may see
    The tears run down her cheek;
Then doth she trowl to me the bowl,
    Even as malt-worm should,
And saith, "Sweetheart, I took my part
    Of this jolly good ale and old."

    Back and side, go bare, go bare, etc.

Now let them drink till they nod and wink,
    Even as good fellows should do;
They shall not miss to have the bliss
    Good ale doth bring men to.
And all poor souls that have scoured bowls,
    Or have them lustily trowled,
God save the lives of them and their wives,
    Whether they be young or old.

    Back and side, go bare, go bare, etc.

_____
[1] apple.

APELLES' SONG

FROM *Campaspe* (LYLY)

Cupid and my Campaspe played
At cards for kisses; Cupid paid.
He stakes his quiver, bow, and arrows,
His mother's doves and team of sparrows;
Loses them too. Then down he throws
The coral of his lip, the rose
Growing on's cheek (but none knows how);
With these, the crystal of his brow,
And then the dimple of his chin;
All these did my Campaspe win.
At last he set her both his eyes;
She won, and Cupid blind did rise.
O Love, has she done this to thee?
What shall, alas! become of me?

GOLDEN SLUMBERS KISS YOUR EYES

FROM *Patient Grissill* (DEKKER)

Golden slumbers kiss your eyes,
Smiles awake you when you rise;
Sleep, pretty wantons, do not cry,
And I will sing a lullaby,
Rock them, rock them, lullaby.

Care is heavy, therefore sleep you,
You are care, and care must keep you;
Sleep, pretty wantons, do not cry,
And I will sing a lullaby,
Rock them, rock them, lullaby.

DRINKING SONG

FROM *Bloody Brother* (J. FLETCHER)

Drink to-day, and drown all sorrow,
You shall perhaps not do it to-morrow.
But, while you have it, use your breath;
There is no drinking after death.

Wine works the heart up, wakes the wit;
There is no cure 'gainst age but it.
It helps the headache, cough, and tisic,
And is for all diseases physic.

Then let us swill, boys, for our health;
Who drinks well, loves the commonwealth.
And he that will to bed go sober,
Falls with the leaf still in October.

COLD'S THE WIND

FROM *Shoemaker's Holiday* (DEKKER)

Cold's the wind, and wet's the rain,
    Saint Hugh be our good speed;
Ill is the weather that bringeth no gain,
    Nor helps good hearts in need.

Trowl the bowl, the jolly nut-brown bowl,
    And here, kind mate, to thee;
Let's sing a dirge for Saint Hugh's soul,
    And down it merrily.

Down-a-down, hey, down-a-down,
    Hey derry derry down-a-down,
    Close with the tenor, boy;
Ho! well done, to me let come,
    Ring compass, gentle joy.

Troll the bowl, the nut-brown bowl,
    And here, kind, &c. (*As often as there be
    men to drink.*)
        (*At last, when all have drunk, this
        verse.*)

Cold's the wind, and wet's the rain,
    Saint Hugh be our good speed;
Ill is the weather that bringeth no gain,
    Nor helps good hearts in need.

CRABBÉD AGE AND YOUTH

FROM *The Passionate Pilgrim*, 1599

Crabbéd Age and Youth
Cannot live together:
Youth is full of pleasance,
Age is full of care;
Youth like summer morn,
Age like winter weather;
Youth like summer brave,
Age like winter bare.
Youth is full of sport,
Age's breath is short;
Youth is nimble, Age is lame;
Youth is hot and bold,
Age is weak and cold;
Youth is wild, and Age is tame.
Age, I do abhor thee;
Youth, I do adore thee.
O, my Love, my Love is young!
Age, I do defy thee:

5

10

15

20

25

30

35

40

45

50

O, sweet shepherd, hie thee!
For methinks thou stay'st too long.

MAIDS AND WIDOWS

If ever I marry, I'll marry a maid;
To marry a widow, I am sore afraid;
For maids they are simple, and never will
grutch,
But widows full oft, as they say, know too
much.

A maid is so sweet, and so gentle of kind,
That a maid is the wife I will choose to my
mind
A widow is froward, and never will yield;
Or if such there be, you will meet them but
seeld.

A maid ne'er complaineth, do what so you will;
But what you mean well, a widow takes ill.
A widow will make you a drudge and a slave,
And, cost ne'er so much, she will ever go brave.

A maid is so modest, she seemeth a rose
When it first beginneth the bud to unclose;
But a widow full-blown full often deceives,
And the next wind that bloweth shakes down
all her leaves.

The widows be lovely, I never gainsay,
But too well all their beauty they know to
display;
But a maid hath so great hidden beauty in
store,
She can spare to a widow, yet never be poor.

Then, if ever I marry, give me a fresh maid,
If to marry with any I be not afraid;
But to marry with any, it asketh much care;
And some bachelors hold they are best as they
are.

PHILLIDA FLOUTS ME

Oh! What a pain is love!
How shall I bear it?
She will inconstant prove,
I greatly fear it.
She so torments my mind
That my strength faileth;
And wavers with the wind,

As a ship that saileth.
Please her the best I may,
She looks another way,
Alack and wel-a-day!
Phillida flouts me.

At the fair yesterday,
She did pass by me;
She looked another way,
And would not spy me.
I wooed her for to dine,
But could not get her.
Will had her to the wine,
He might intreat her.
With Daniel she did dance,
On me she looked askance.
Oh, thrice unhappy chance!
Phillida flouts me.

Fair maid, be not so coy,
Do not disdain me.
I am my mother's joy;
Sweet, entertain me!
She'll give me, when she dies,
All that is fitting,
Her poultry and her bees
And her geese sitting,
A pair of mattress beds,
And a bag full of shreds.
And yet for all this goods
Phillida flouts me.

She hath a clout of mine
Wrought with good Coventry,
Which she keeps for a sign
Of my fidelity.
But i' faith, if she flinch,
She shall not wear it.
To Tib, my t'other wench,
I mean to bear it.
And yet it grieves my heart
So soon from her to part.
Death strikes me with his dart!
Phillida flouts me.

Thou shalt eat curds and cream,
All the year lasting;
And drink the crystal stream,
Pleasant in tasting;
Whig and whey whilst thou burst,
And bramble berries,
Pie-lid and pasty crust,

Pears, plums, and cherries.
Thy raiment shall be thin,
Made of a wether's skin—
Yet all's not worth a pin.
    Phillida flouts me.   5

Fair maiden, have a care,
  And in time take me.
I can have those as fair,
  If you forsake me.   10
For Doll, the dairymaid,
  Laughed on me lately,
And wanton Winifred
  Favors me greatly.
One throws milk on my clothes, 15
T'other plays with my nose;
What wanton signs are those!
    Phillida flouts me.

I cannot work and sleep
  All at a season;   20
Love wounds my heart so deep,
  Without all reason.
I gin to pine away
  With grief and sorrow,
Like to a fatted beast,   25
  Penned in a meadow.
I shall be dead, I fear,
Within this thousand year;
And all for very fear,   30
    Phillida flouts me.

[THOUGH AMARYLLIS DANCE]

FROM

WILLIAM BYRD's *Psalms, Sonnets, and Songs
of Sadness and Piety* (1588)

Though Amaryllis dance in green
  Like fairy queen;
  And sing full clear
Corinna can, with smiling, cheer.
Yet since their eyes make heart so sore,
Heigh ho, heigh ho, 'chill[1] love no more.   45

My sheep are lost for want of food,
  And I so wood,[2]
  That all the day
I sit and watch a herdmaid gay,   50

___
[1] I will.   [2] mad.

Who laughs to see me sigh so sore,
Heigh ho, heigh ho, 'chill love no more.

Her loving looks, her beauty bright
  Is such delight,
  That all in vain
I love to like and lose my gain,
For her that thanks me not therefor,
Heigh ho, heigh ho, 'chill love no more.

Ah wanton eyes, my friendly foes,
  And cause of woes,
  Your sweet desire
Breeds flames of ice and freeze in fire.
Ye scorn to see me weep so sore,
Heigh ho, heigh ho, 'chill love no more.

Love ye who list, I force him not,
  Sith, God it wot,
  The more I wail,
The less my sighs and tears prevail.
What shall I do but say therefore,
Heigh ho, heigh ho, 'chill love no more.

[ARISE, GET UP, MY DEAR LOVE]

FROM THOMAS MORLEY's *Canzonets*, 1593

Arise, get up, my dear love, rise, make haste,
  begone thee!
Lo, where the bride, fair Daphne bright, still
  stays on thee!
Hark! O hark! Yon merry wanton maidens
  squealing!
Spice cake, sops in wine, spice cakes, are
  a-dealing!
    Run then, run apace,
    Get a bride lace
And a gilt rosemary branch while yet there
  is catching,
And then hold fast for fear of old snatching.
    Alas, my love, why weep ye?
    O fear not that, dear love, the next
  day keep we.
List, hark yon minstrels! How fine they firk it!
And see how the maids jerk it!
    With Kate and Will,
    Tom and Jill,
    Hey ho brave,
    Now a skip,
    There a trip,

Finely set aloft,
On a fine wedding day,
All for fair Daphne's wedding day!

[TOBACCO, TOBACCO]

FROM TOBIAS HUME'S *Musical Humors.*
The first part of Airs, 1605

Tobacco, tobacco, sing sweetly for tobacco!
    Tobacco is like love, oh love it;
    For you see, I will prove it.
Love maketh lean the fat men's tumor,
    So doth tobacco.
Love still dries up the wanton humor,
    So doth tobacco.
Love makes men sail from shore to shore,
    So doth tobacco.
'Tis fond love often makes men poor,
    So doth tobacco.
Love makes men scorn all coward fears,
    So doth tobacco.
Love often sets men by the ears,
    So doth tobacco.
    Tobacco, tobacco,
Sing sweetly for tobacco.
Tobacco is like love, oh love it;
For you see I have proved it.

[THOUGH MY CARRIAGE]

FROM THOMAS WEELKES'S *Airs or Fantastic
Spirits,* 1608

Though my carriage be but careless,
    Though my looks be of the sternest,
Yet my passions are compareless;
    When I love, I love in earnest.

No, my wits are not so wild,
    But a gentle soul may yoke me;
Nor my heart so hard compiled,
    But it melts if love provoke me.

THOMAS CAMPION

*Campion (1567–1620) is unique in his day as
author of both words and music for his delightful songs. A former law student, he found
lyrics more to his liking, as various books of airs
can testify. He became involved in a battle*
*of treatises with Samuel Daniel over the ques-
tion of the relative merits of rhyme and quanti-
tative verse. Curiously enough, Campion, who
lost the battle, attacked the very rhyme which
he used so effectively. The controversy is all
but forgotten; the man is remembered for felicity and variety in the lyric form.*

WHEN TO HER LUTE
CORINNA SINGS

When to her lute Corinna sings,
Her voice revives the leaden strings,
And doth in highest notes appear,
As any challenged echo clear;
But when she doth of mourning speak,
E'en with her sighs the strings do break.

And as her lute doth live or die,
Led by her passion, so must I!
For when of pleasure she doth sing,
My thoughts enjoy a sudden spring;
But if she doth of sorrow speak,
Ev'n from my heart the strings do break.

FOLLOW YOUR SAINT

Follow your saint, follow with accents sweet;
Haste you, sad notes, fall at her flying feet.
There, wrapped in cloud of sorrow, pity move,
And tell the ravisher of my soul I perish for
    her love.
But if she scorns my never-ceasing pain,
Then burst with sighing in her sight and ne'er
    return again.

All that I sung still to her praise did tend,
Still she was first, still she my songs did end.
Yet she my love and music both doth fly,
The music that her echo is and beauty's
    sympathy.
Then let my notes pursue her scornful flight:
It shall suffice that they were breathed and
    died for her delight.

ROSE-CHEEKED LAURA

Rose-cheeked Laura, come,
Sing thou smoothly with thy beauty's
Silent music, either other
    Sweetly gracing.

Lovely forms do flow
From concent divinely framèd;
Heav'n is music, and thy beauty's
    Birth is heavenly.

These dull notes we sing
Discords need for helps to grace them;

Only beauty purely loving
    Knows no discord,

But still moves delight,
5 Like clear springs renewed by flowing,
Ever perfect, ever in them-
    Selves eternal.

SEVENTEENTH CENTURY

JOHN DONNE

Donne (1572–1631) has recently been redis-covered by writers and readers alike. (Among the many modern poets who owe something to Donne are Eliot, MacNeice, and Warren.) His life and work are both crowded with interest-ing details. With the traditional background of Oxford and the Inns of Court, he saw adven-ture at sea with Essex and adventure ashore with Anne More, whom he married in a stormy affair. Born a Catholic in an age of religious doubts, Donne "turned" and eventually be-came Dean of St. Paul's, though not without spiritual turmoil which his Holy Sonnets re-veal. The student will note that Donne is typi-cal of the turn away from the sweet song of the earlier Elizabethans when he tries for intel-lectual effects; that he, nevertheless, retains lyrical sweetness at times ("Sweetest love, I do not go"); that he shows high seriousness in his religious verse. His directness, violations of classic rules as to lines and rhythm, and un-conventional attitudes toward love are likely to interest many readers. More soberly, however, it should be noted that Donne had tremendous influence on the method and manner of the en-tire seventeenth-century metaphysical group.

Or who cleft the Devil's foot;
Teach me to hear mermaids singing,
Or to keep off envy's stinging,
    And find
5   What wind
Serves to advance an honest mind.

If thou be'st born to strange sights,
    Things invisible to see,
10 Ride ten thousand days and nights
    Till age snow white hairs on thee;
Thou, when thou return'st wilt tell me
All strange wonders that befell thee,
    And swear
15   No where
Lives a woman true and fair.

If thou find'st one let me know,
    Such a pilgrimage were sweet;
20 Yet do not, I would not go,
    Though at next door we might meet;
Though she were true when you met her,
And last till you write your letter,
    Yet she
    Will be
False, ere I come, to two or three.

SONG

Go and catch a falling star,
    Get with child a mandrake[1] root,
Tell me where all past years are,

THE CANONIZATION

30 For God's sake hold your tongue, and let me
    love;
    Or chide my palsy, or my gout;
    My five gray hairs, or ruined fortune flout;

---

[1] supposed to look like human body.

With wealth your state, your mind with arts
    improve;
    Take you a course, get you a place,
    Observe his Honor, or his Grace;
Or the king's real, or his stamped face
    Contemplate; what you will, approve,
    So you will let me love.

Alas! alas! who's injured by my love?
    What merchant's ships have my sighs
        drowned?
    Who says my tears have overflowed his
        ground?
When did my colds a forward spring remove?
    When did the heats which my veins fill
    Add one more to the plaguy bill?
Soldiers find wars, and lawyers find out still
    Litigious men, which quarrels move,
    Though she and I do love.

Call us what you will, we are made such by
    love;
    Call her one, me another fly;
    We're tapers too, and at our own cost die,
And we in us find th' eagle and the dove.
    The phœnix[1] riddle hath more wit
    By us; we two being one, are it;
So, to one neutral thing both sexes fit.
    We die and rise the same, and prove
    Mysterious by this love.

We can die by it, if not live by love,
    And if unfit for tomb or hearse,
    Our legend be, it will be fit for verse;
And if no piece of chronicle we prove,
    We'll build in sonnets pretty rooms;
    As well a well-wrought urn becomes
The greatest ashes, as half-acre tombs,
    And by these hymns all shall approve
    Us canonized for love;

And thus invoke us: "You, whom reverend
    love
    Made one another's hermitage;
    You, to whom love was peace, that now is
        rage;
Who did the whole world's soul contract, and
        drove
    Into the glasses of your eyes;

---

[1] mythical bird which renewed its life in fire every 500 years.

    So made such mirrors, and such spies,
That they did all to you epitomize,
    Countries, towns, courts, beg from above
    A pattern of your love."
5

SONG

    Sweetest love, I do not go
10   For weariness of thee,
Nor in hope the world can show
    A fitter love for me;
    But since that I
Must die at last, 'tis best
15 To use myself in jest,
    By feigned deaths to die.

Yesternight the sun went hence,
    And yet is here to-day;
20 He hath no desire nor sense,
    Nor half so short a way;
    Then fear not me,
But believe that I shall make
Speedier journeys, since I take
25   More wings and spurs than he.

O how feeble is man's power,
    That, if good fortune fall,
Cannot add another hour,
30   Nor a last hour recall;
    But come bad chance,
And we join to it our strength,
And we teach it art and length,
    Itself o'er us to advance.
35

When thou sigh'st, thou sigh'st not wind,
    But sigh'st my soul away;
When thou weep'st, unkindly kind,
    My life's blood doth decay:
40   It cannot be
That thou lovest me as thou say'st,
If in thine my life thou waste,
    That art the best of me.

45 Let not thy divining heart
    Forethink me any ill;
Destiny may take thy part
    And may thy fears fulfil.
    But think that we
50 Are but turned aside to sleep:
They who one another keep
    Alive, ne'er parted be.

LOVE'S DEITY

I long to talk with some old lover's ghost,
  Who died before the god of love was born.
I cannot think that he, who then loved most,
  Sunk so low as to love one which did scorn.
But since this god produced a destiny,
And that vice-nature, custom, lets it be,
  I must love her that loves not me.

Sure, they which made him god meant not so
    much,
  Nor he in his young godhead practiced it;
But when an even flame two hearts did touch,
  His office was indulgently to fit
Actives to passives. Correspondency
Only his subject was; it cannot be
  Love till I love her that loves me.

But every modern god will now extend
  His vast prerogative as far as Jove.
To rage, to lust, to write to, to commend,
  All is the purlieu of the god of love.
Oh, were we wakened by this tyranny
To ungod this child again, it could not be
  I should love her who loves not me.

Rebel and atheist too, why murmur I,
  As though I felt the worst that love
    could do?
Love might make me leave loving, or might try
  A deeper plague, to make her love me too;
Which, since she loves before, I am loth to see.
Falsehood is worse than hate; and that
    must be
  If she whom I love should love me.

[DEATH, BE NOT PROUD]

Death, be not proud, though some have called
  thee
Mighty and dreadful, for thou art not so;
For those whom thou think'st thou dost over-
  throw
Die not, poor Death, nor yet canst thou kill me.
From rest and sleep, which but thy pictures be,
Much pleasure; then from thee much more
  must flow,
And soonest our best men with thee do go,
Rest of their bones, and souls' delivery.
Thou art slave to fate, chance, kings, and des-
  perate men,

And dost with poison, war, and sickness dwell,
And poppy or charms can make us sleep as well
And better than thy stroke; why swell'st thou,
  then?
One short sleep past, we wake eternally,
And Death shall be no more; Death, thou shalt
  die.

A HYMN TO GOD THE FATHER

1

Wilt Thou forgive that sin where I begun,
  Which is my sin, though it were done be-
    fore?
Wilt Thou forgive those sins, through which I
    run,
  And do run still, though still I do deplore?
    When Thou hast done, Thou hast not
    done,
      For I have more.

2

Wilt Thou forgive that sin which I have won
  Others to sin? and made my sin their door?
Wilt Thou forgive that sin which I did shun
  A year or two, but wallowed in a score?
    When Thou hast done, Thou hast not
    done,
      For I have more.

3

I have a sin of fear, that when I have spun
  My last thread, I shall perish on the shore;
But swear by Thyself, that at my death Thy
  Son
  Shall shine as He shines now, and hereto-
    fore;
    And, having done that, Thou hast done,
      I fear no more.

BEN JONSON

*Jonson (1572–1637) rose from bricklayer to ar-
biter of a literary group known as the "Sons
of Ben"; they included the Cavalier poets represented in this volume. With little formal
education Jonson lived a life full of army adventure, brawls, duels, and jail sentences because of references in his Works. It was also
full of literary achievement. Jonson developed
the comedy of humors, produced able tragedy,*

and became the best writer of masques in his day. A classicist who followed Horace and Martial, and who criticized Donne for not keeping meter and accent straight, he was, after Shakespeare, the leading literary figure of the period. 5

ON MY FIRST SON

Farewell, thou child of my right hand, and joy; 10
My sin was too much hope of thee, loved boy:
Seven years thou wert lent to me, and I thee
    pay,
Exacted by thy fate, on the just day.
O could I lose all father now! for why 15
Will man lament the state he should envy—
To have so soon 'scaped world's and flesh's
    rage,
And, if no other misery, yet age? 20
Rest in soft peace, and asked, say, "Here doth
    lie
Ben Jonson his best piece of poetry;
For whose sake henceforth all his vows be
    such 25
As what he loves may never like too much."

AN EPITAPH ON S[ALATHIEL] P[AVY], A CHILD OF Q[UEEN] 30 EL[IZABETH'S] CHAPEL¹

Weep with me, all you that read
    This little story;
And know, for whom a tear you shed 35
    Death's self is sorry.
'Twas a child that so did thrive
    In grace and feature,
As heaven and nature seemed to strive
    Which owned the creature. 40
Years he numbered scarce thirteen
    When fates turned cruel,
Yet three filled zodiacs had he been
    The stage's jewel;
And did act, what now we moan, 45
    Old men so duly,
As, sooth, the Parcæ² thought him one.
    He played so truly.
So by error, to his fate 50

¹ Traditional title; S. may stand for Solomon.
² the Fates.

They all consented;
But viewing him since, alas too late,
    They have repented,
And have sought, to give new birth,
    In baths to steep him;
But being so much too good for earth,
    Heaven vows to keep him.

SONG

TO CELIA

Drink to me only with thine eyes,
    And I will pledge with mine;
Or leave a kiss but in the cup,
    And I'll not look for wine.
The thirst that from the soul doth rise
    Doth ask a drink divine;
But might I of Jove's nectar sup,
    I would not change for thine.

I sent thee late a rosy wreath,
    Not so much honoring thee
As giving it a hope, that there
    It could not withered be.
But thou thereon didst only breathe,
    And sent'st it back to me;
Since when it grows, and smells, I swear,
    Not of itself but thee.

TO THE MEMORY OF MY BELOVED, MASTER WILLIAM SHAKESPEARE

To draw no envy, Shakespeare, on thy name,
Am I thus ample to thy book and fame;
While I confess thy writings to be such
As neither man, nor muse, can praise too
    much. 40
'Tis true, and all men's suffrage. But these
    ways
Were not the paths I meant unto thy praise;
For seeliest ignorance on these may light,
Which, when it sounds at best, but echoes 45
    right;
Or blind affection, which doth ne'er advance
The truth, but gropes, and urgeth all by
    chance;
Or crafty malice might pretend this praise, 50
And think to ruin, where it seemed to raise.
These are, as some infamous bawd or whore

Should praise a matron. What could hurt her
    more?
But thou art proof against them, and, indeed,
Above the ill fortune of them, or the need.
I therefore will begin. Soul of the age!   5
The applause, delight, the wonder of our
    stage!
My Shakespeare, rise! I will not lodge thee by
Chaucer, or Spenser, or bid Beaumont lie
A little farther off, to make thee a room:
Thou art a monument without a tomb,
And art alive still while thy book doth live
And we have wits to read and praise to give.
That I not mix thee so, my brain excuses,
I mean with great, but disproportioned Muses;
For if I thought my judgment were of years,   15
I should commit thee surely with thy peers,
And tell how far thou didst our Lyly outshine,
Or sporting Kyd, or Marlowe's mighty line.
And though thou hadst small Latin and less   20
    Greek,
From thence to honor thee, I would not seek
For names; but call forth thundering Æschy-
    lus,
Euripides, and Sophocles to us;[1]
Pacuvius, Accius,[2] him of Cordova[3] dead,
To life again, to hear thy buskin tread,
And shake a stage; or, when thy socks were on,
Leave thee alone for the comparison
Of all that insolent Greece or haughty Rome   30
Sent forth, or since did from their ashes come.
Triumph, my Britain, thou hast one to show
To whom all scenes of Europe homage owe.
He was not of an age, but for all time!
And all the Muses still were in their prime,   35
When, like Apollo, he came forth to warm
Our ears, or like a Mercury to charm!
Nature herself was proud of his designs,
And joyed to wear the dressing of his lines!
Which were so richly spun, and woven so fit,   40
As, since, she will vouchsafe no other wit.
The merry Greek, tart Aristophanes,[4]
Neat Terence, witty Plautus,[5] now not please;
But antiquated and deserted lie,
As they were not of Nature's family.   45
Yet must I not give Nature all; thy art,
My gentle Shakespeare, must enjoy a part.

---

[1] three great Greek dramatists.
[2] minor Roman poets.
[3] Seneca, Roman playwright.
[4] Greek comic dramatist.
[5] Roman comic dramatists.

For though the poet's matter nature be,
His art doth give the fashion; and, that he
Who casts to write a living line, must sweat,
(Such as thine are) and strike the second
    heat
Upon the Muses' anvil; turn the same
(And himself with it) that he thinks to frame,
Or, for the laurel, he may gain a scorn;
For a good poet's made, as well as born.
And such wert thou! Look how the father's   10
    face
Lives in his issue, even so the race
Of Shakespeare's mind and manners brightly
    shines
In his well turned, and true filed lines;   15
In each of which he seems to shake a lance,
As brandished at the eyes of ignorance.
Sweet Swan of Avon! what a sight it were
To see thee in our water yet appear,
And make those flights upon the banks of   20
    Thames,
That so did take Eliza, and our James!
But stay, I see thee in the hemisphere
Advanced, and made a constellation there!
Shine forth, thou star of poets, and with rage   25
Or influence, chide or cheer the drooping
    stage,
Which, since thy flight from hence, hath
    mourned like night,
And despairs day, but for thy volume's light.   30

SONG, TO CELIA

Come, my Celia, let us prove
While we may the sports of love;
Time will not be ours forever,
He at length our good will sever.
Spend not then his gifts in vain;
Suns that set may rise again,
But if once we lose this light,
'Tis with us perpetual night.
Why should we defer our joys?
Fame and rumor are but toys.
Cannot we delude the eyes
Of a few poor household spies?
Or his easier ears beguile,
So removèd by our wile?
'Tis no sin love's fruit to steal;
But the sweet theft to reveal,
To be taken, to be seen,
These have crimes accounted been.

SIMPLEX MUNDITIIS

Still to be neat, still to be drest,
As you were going to a feast;
Still to be powdered, still perfumed: 5
Lady, it is to be presumed,
Though art's hid causes are not found,
All is not sweet, all is not sound.
Give me a look, give me a face
That makes simplicity a grace;   10
Robes loosely flowing, hair as free:
Such sweet neglect more taketh me
Than all th' adulteries of art;
They strike mine eyes, but not my heart.

ROBERT HERRICK

*Herrick (1591–1674) was the ablest disciple of
Ben Jonson, whom he praised in many short
pieces. Beginning life as a goldsmith's appren-
tice, he transferred his lightness of touch to
the lyric form in poetry, where he easily out-
distanced all contemporary competition. As a
churchman in Dean Prior, Herrick could well
observe the holiday customs and rural super-
stitions of Devonshire which he was to immortalize in verse. When country life palled, there
were always London and the conversations at
the Mermaid. To read Herrick is to enjoy life
at its best—rich, warm, simple, humorous, col-
orful, filled with pleasant music.*

TO DAFFODILS

Fair daffodils, we weep to see
  You haste away so soon:
As yet the early-rising sun
  Hast not attained his noon.
    Stay, stay,
  Until the hasting day
    Has run
  But to the evensong;
And, having prayed together, we
  Will go with you along.

We have short time to stay as you;
  We have as short a spring;
As quick a growth to meet decay,
  As you or anything.
    We die,
  As your hours do, and dry

Away
Like to the summer's rain;
Or as the pearls of morning's dew,
  Ne'er to be found again.

CORINNA'S GOING A-MAYING

Get up, get up for shame, the blooming morn
Upon her wings presents the god unshorn.   10
    See how Aurora throws her fair
    Fresh-quilted colors through the air:
    Get up, sweet slug-a-bed, and see
    The dew bespangling herb and tree.
Each flower has wept and bowed toward the   15
    east
Above an hour since; yet you not dressed;
    Nay! not so much as out of bed?
    When all the birds have matins said
And sung their thankful hymns, 'tis sin,   20
    Nay, profanation, to keep in,
Whenas a thousand virgins on this day
Spring, sooner than the lark, to fetch in May.

Rise, and put on your foliage, and be seen   25
To come forth, like the spring-time, fresh and
    green,
    And sweet as Flora. Take no care
    For jewels for your gown or hair:
    Fear not; the leaves will strew   30
    Gems in abundance upon you:
Besides, the childhood of the day has kept,
Against you come, some orient pearls unwept;
    Come and receive them while the light
    Hangs on the dew-locks of the night: 35
    And Titan on the eastern hill
    Retires himself, or else stands still
Till you come forth. Wash, dress, be brief in
    praying:
Few beads are best, when once we go a-May-   40
    ing.

Come, my Corinna, come; and, coming mark
How each field turns a street, each street a
    park   45
    Made green and trimmed with trees; see
    how
    Devotion gives each house a bough
    Or branch: each porch, each door, ere this,
    An ark, a tabernacle is,   50
Made up of white-thorn, neatly interwove;
As if here were those cooler shades of love.

Can such delights be in the street
And open fields and we not see't?
Come, we'll abroad; and let's obey
The proclamation made for May:
And sin no more, as we have done, by staying;　5
But, my Corinna, come, let's go a-Maying.

There's not a budding boy or girl this day
But is got up, and gone to bring in May.
　A deal of youth, ere this, is come　10
　Back, and with white-thorn laden home.
　Some have despatched their cakes and
　　cream
　Before that we have left to dream;
And some have wept, and wooed, and plighted　15
　　troth,
And chose their priest, ere we can cast off
　　sloth:
　Many a green-gown has been given;
　Many a kiss, both odd and even:　20
　Many a glance, too, has been sent
　From out the eye, love's firmament;
Many a jest told of the keys betraying
This night, and locks picked, yet we're not
　　a-Maying.　25

Come, let us go while we are in our prime;
And take the harmless folly of the time!
　We shall grow old apace, and die
　Before we know our liberty.　30
　Our life is short, and our days run
　As fast away as does the sun;
And, as a vapor or a drop of rain,
Once lost, can ne'er be found again:
　So when or you or I are made　35
　A fable, song, or fleeting shade,
　All love, all liking, all delight
　Lies drowned with us in endless night.
Then while time serves, and we are but de-
　　caying,　40
Come, my Corinna, come, let's go a-Maying.

DELIGHT IN DISORDER

A sweet disorder in the dress
Kindles in clothes a wantonness:
A lawn about the shoulders thrown
Into a fine distraction;
An erring lace, which here and there　50
Enthrals the crimson stomacher;
A cuff neglectful, and thereby

Ribbons to flow confusedly;
A winning wave, deserving note,
In the tempestuous petticoat;
A careless shoe-string, in whose tie
I see a wild civility;
Do more bewitch me, than when art
Is too precise in every part.

TO THE VIRGINS, TO MAKE MUCH OF TIME

Gather ye rosebuds while ye may,
　Old Time is still a-flying;
And this same flower that smiles to-day,
　To-morrow will be dying.

The glorious lamp of heaven, the sun,
　The higher he's a-getting,
The sooner will his race be run,
　And nearer he's to setting.

That age is best which is the first,
　When youth and blood are warmer;
But being spent, the worse, and worst
　Times, still succeed the former.

Then be not coy, but use your time,
　And while ye may, go marry;
For, having lost but once your prime,
　You may forever tarry.

THE HOCK CART; OR, HARVEST HOME

TO THE RIGHT HONORABLE MILDMAY,
EARL OF WESTMORELAND

Come, sons of summer, by whose toil,
We are the lords of wine and oil;
By whose tough labors and rough hands,
We rip up first, then reap our lands.
Crowned with the ears of corn, now come,
And to the pipe sing harvest home.
Come forth, my lord, and see the cart
Dressed up with all the country art.
See, here a malkin, there a sheet,
As spotless pure as it is sweet;
The horses, mares, and frisking fillies,
Clad all in linen white as lilies.
The harvest swains and wenches bound
For joy, to see the hock cart crowned.

About the cart, hear how the rout
Of rural younglings raise the shout,
Pressing before, some coming after,
Those with a shout, and these with laughter.
Some bless the cart, some kiss the sheaves,   5
Some prank them up with oaken leaves;
Some cross the fill-horse, some with great
Devotion stroke the home-borne wheat;
While other rustics, less attent
To prayers than to merriment,   10
Run after with their breeches rent.
Well, on, brave boys, to your lord's hearth,
Glitt'ring with fire, where, for your mirth,
Ye shall see first the large and chief
Foundation of your feast, fat beef;   15
With upper stories, mutton, veal,
And bacon, which makes full the meal,
With sev'ral dishes standing by,
As, here a custard, there a pie,
And here all-tempting frumenty.   20
And for to make the merry cheer,
If smirking wine be wanting here,
There's that which drowns all care, stout beer,
Which freely drink to your lord's health,
Then to the plough (the commonwealth),   25
Next to your flails, your fans, your vats;
Then to the maids with wheaten hats;
To the rough sickle, and the crook'd scythe,
Drink, frolic boys, till all be blithe.
Feed and grow fat; and as ye eat,   30
Be mindful that the lab'ring neat,
As you, may have their fill of meat.
And know, besides, ye must revoke
The patient ox unto the yoke,
And all go back unto the plough   35
And harrow, though they're hanged up now.
And, you must know, your lord's word's true,
Feed him ye must, whose food fills you.
And that this pleasure is like rain,
Not sent ye for to drown your pain,   40
But for to make it spring again.

A THANKSGIVING TO GOD
FOR HIS HOUSE

    45

Lord, thou hast given me a cell
    Wherein to dwell,
A little house, whose humble roof
    Is weather-proof;   50
Under the spars of which I lie
    Both soft and dry,

Where thou my chamber for to ward
    Hast set a guard
Of harmless thoughts, to watch and keep
    Me while I sleep.
Low is my porch, as is my fate,
    Both void of state;
And yet the threshold of my door
    Is worn by th' poor,
Who thither come and freely get
    Good words or meat;
Like as my parlor, so my hall
    And kitchen's small;
A little buttery, and therein
    A little bin
Which keeps my little loaf of bread
    Unchipped, unflead.
Some brittle sticks of thorn or briar
    Make me a fire,
Close by whose living coal I sit,
    And glow like it.
Lord, I confess, too, when I dine,
    The pulse is thine,
And all those other bits that be
    There placed by thee:
The worts, the purslain, and the mess
    Of water-cress,
Which of thy kindness thou hast sent;
    And my content
Makes those, and my beloved beet,
    To be more sweet.
'Tis thou that crown'st my glittering hearth
    With guiltless mirth;
And giv'st me wassail bowls to drink,
    Spiced to the brink.
Lord, 'tis thy plenty-dropping hand
    That soils my land,
And giv'st me for my bushel sown
    Twice ten for one.
Thou mak'st my teeming hen to lay
    Her egg each day;
Besides my healthful ewes to bear
    Me twins each year,
The while the conduits of my kine
    Run cream for wine.
All these, and better, thou dost send
    Me to this end:
That I should render, for my part,
    A thankful heart,
Which, fired with incense, I resign
    As wholly thine;
But the acceptance, that must be,
    My Christ, by thee.

HIS LITANY TO THE HOLY SPIRIT

In the hour of my distress,
When temptations me oppress,
And when I my sins confess,
    Sweet Spirit, comfort me!

When I lie within my bed,
Sick in heart and sick in head,
And with doubts discomforted,
    Sweet Spirit, comfort me!   10

When the house doth sigh and weep,
And the world is drowned in sleep,
Yet mine eyes the watch do keep,
    Sweet Spirit, comfort me!   15

When the artless doctor sees
No one hope, but of his fees,
And his skill runs on the lees,
    Sweet Spirit, comfort me!

When his potion and his pill,
His, or none, or little skill,
Meet for nothing but to kill,
    Sweet Spirit, comfort me!

When the passing-bell doth toll,
And the furies in a shoal
Come to fright a parting soul,
    Sweet Spirit, comfort me!

When the tapers now burn blue,
And the comforters are few,
And that number more than true,
    Sweet Spirit, comfort me!

When the priest his last hath prayed,
And I nod to what is said,
'Cause my speech is now decayed,
    Sweet Spirit, comfort me!

When, God knows, I'm tossed about,
Either with despair or doubt,
Yet, before the glass be out,
    Sweet Spirit, comfort me!

When the tempter me pursu'th
With the sins of all my youth,
And half damns me with untruth,
    Sweet Spirit, comfort me!

When the flames and hellish cries
Fright mine ears and fright mine eyes,
And all terrors me surprise,
    Sweet Spirit, comfort me!

When the Judgment is revealed,
And that opened which was sealed,
When to thee I have appealed,
    Sweet Spirit, comfort me!

GEORGE HERBERT

John Donne and George Herbert's mother were friends; thus it is not surprising to find the older poet influencing somewhat the verse of the younger. Herbert (1593–1633) was early consecrated to God's service; at Cambridge he showed a Miltonic seriousness which led him to the Oratorship and eventually the priesthood. While his brother, Lord Herbert of Cherbury, cut a brilliant figure in the circles of high society, George set out to write straightforward verses in praise of God. As a stylist he shows recognizable tags: a fondness for monosyllabic titles; experiments with stanza arrangements which appear as wings, pillars, etc.; a tendency to catalogue various alternatives, with God always the direct and conclusive answer; and an amazing ability to make up rhyme patterns, most of which he used only once.

THE PULLEY

When God at first made man,   35
Having a glass of blessings standing by,
  "Let us," said He, "pour on him all we can.
Let the world's riches, which dispersed lie,
  Contract into a span."   40

  So strength first made a way;
Then beauty flowed, then wisdom, honor, pleasure.
  When almost all was out, God made a stay,
Perceiving that, alone of all His treasure,   45
  Rest in the bottom lay.

  "For if I should," said He,
"Bestow this jewel also on my creature,
  He would adore my gifts instead of me   50
And rest in nature, not the God of nature;
  So both should losers be.

"Yet let him keep the rest,
But keep them with repining restlessness.
    Let him be rich and weary, that at least,
If goodness lead him not, yet weariness
    May toss him to my breast."

THE COLLAR

I struck the board and cried, No more!
            I will abroad.
What? Shall I ever sigh and pine?
My lines and life are free, free as the road,
    Loose as the wind, as large as store.
        Shall I be still in suit?
Have I no harvest but a thorn
To let me blood, and not restore
What I have lost with cordial fruit?
        Sure there was wine
Before my sighs did dry it; there was corn
    Before my tears did drown it.
    Is the year only lost to me?
        Have I no bays to crown it?
No flowers, no garlands gay? All blasted?
            All wasted?
Not so, my heart! But there is fruit,
        And thou hast hands.
    Recover all thy sigh-blown age
On double pleasures. Leave thy cold dispute
Of what is fit and not. Forsake thy cage,
        Thy rope of sands,
Which petty thoughts have made, and made
    to thee
    Good cable, to enforce and draw,
        And be thy law,
While thou didst wink and wouldst not see.

        Away! Take heed!
        I will abroad.
Call in thy death's head there. Tie up thy
    fears.
        He that forbears
        To suit and serve his need
        Deserves his load.
But as I raved and grew more fierce and wild
        At every word,
Me thoughts I heard one calling, Child!
        And I replied, My Lord.

THE QUIP

The merry world did on a day
    With his train-bands and mates agree

To meet together where I lay,
    And all in sport to jeer at me.

First Beauty crept into a rose;
5   Which when I plucked not, "Sir," said she,
"Tell me, I pray, whose hands are those?"
    But Thou shalt answer, Lord, for me.

Then Money came, and chinking still,
10 "What tune is this, poor man?" said he;
"I heard in music you had skill."
    But Thou shalt answer, Lord, for me.

Then came brave Glory puffing by
15 In silks that whistled, who but he?
He scarce allowed me half an eye.
    But Thou shalt answer, Lord, for me.

Then came quick Wit and Conversation,
20 And he would needs a comfort be,
And, to be short, make an oration.
    But Thou shalt answer, Lord, for me.

Yet when the hour of Thy design
25 To answer these fine things shall come,
Speak not at large; say I am Thine;
    And then they have their answer home.

LOVE

Love bade me welcome, yet my soul drew
        back,
    Guilty of dust and sin.
35 But quick-eyed Love, observing me grow slack
    From my first entrance in,
Drew nearer to me, sweetly questioning
    If I lacked anything.

40 A guest, I answered, worthy to be here.
    Love said, You shall be he.
I, the unkind, the ungrateful? ah, my dear,
    I cannot look on thee.
Love took my hand and smiling did reply,
45 Who made the eyes but I?

Truth, Lord, but I have marred them; let my
        shame
    Go where it doth deserve.
50 And know you not, says Love, who bore the
        blame?
    My dear, then I will serve.

You must sit down, says Love, and taste my
    meat.
So I did sit and eat.

VIRTUE
       5

Sweet day, so cool, so calm, so bright,
    The bridal of the earth and sky!
The dew shall weep thy fall to-night;
    For thou must die.   10

Sweet rose, whose hue, angry and brave,
    Bids the rash gazer wipe his eye,
Thy root is ever in its grave,
    And thou must die.   15

Sweet spring, full of sweet days and roses,
    A box where sweets compacted lie,
My music shows ye have your closes,
    And all must die.   20

Only a sweet and virtuous soul,
    Like seasoned timber, never gives;
But though the whole world turn to coal,
    Then chiefly lives.   25

THOMAS CAREW

*The early life of Carew (1595?–1639?) is
marked by failure in college and the law and* 30
*by half-performed offices as secretary to Eng-
lish ambassadors on the Continent. He later
led a gay life at court and became a great favorite. On the other hand, Carew was also a
friend of most of the famous men in literature* 35
*during the period (Donne, Jonson, Suckling,
Davenant); he turned out a few memorable
lyrics, some set to music by Henry Lawes; and
he distinguished himself among the Sons of
Ben for his care in composition—he polished* 40
*his lines more than the other Cavaliers did.
The result is that his best-known songs never
acquire the ease of Suckling (who criticized
Carew for his "trouble and pain"), but do present a technical perfection which the other was* 45
*incapable of, or which he scorned to work to-
ward.*

SONG
       50

Ask me no more where Jove bestows,
When June is past, the fading rose;

For in your beauty's orient deep
These flowers, as in their causes, sleep.

Ask me no more whither do stray
The golden atoms of the day;
For, in pure love, heaven did prepare
Those powders to enrich your hair.

Ask me no more whither doth haste
The nightingale when May is past;
For in your sweet dividing throat
She winters and keeps warm her note.

Ask me no more where those stars light
That downwards fall in dead of night;
For in your eyes they sit, and there
Fixed become as in their sphere.

Ask me no more if east or west
The Phœnix builds her spicy nest;
For unto you at last she flies,
And in your fragrant bosom dies.

MEDIOCRITY IN LOVE
REJECTED

Give me more love or more disdain:
    The torrid or the frozen zone
Bring equal ease unto my pain,
    The temperate affords me none;
Either extreme of love or hate
Is sweeter than a calm estate.

Give me a storm; if it be love,
    Like Danaë[1] in that golden shower,
I swim in pleasure; if it prove
    Disdain, that torrent will devour
My vulture-hopes; and he's possessed
Of heaven, that's but from hell released.
    Then crown my joys or cure my pain;
    Give me more love or more disdain.

DISDAIN RETURNED

He that loves a rosy cheek,
    Or a coral lip admires,
Or from star-like eyes doth seek
    Fuel to maintain his fires;
As old time makes these decay,
So his flames must waste away.

---

[1] Locked in a tower by her father, Danaë was
visited by Zeus in a shower of gold.

But a smooth and steadfast mind,
  Gentle thoughts and calm desires,
Hearts with equal love combined,
  Kindle never-dying fires.
Where these are not, I despise
Lovely cheeks, or lips, or eyes.

No tears, Celia, now shall win
  My resolved heart to return;
I have searched thy soul within,
  And find nought but pride and scorn;
I have learned thy arts, and now
Can disdain as much as thou.
  Some power, in my revenge, convey
  That love to her I cast away.

                        15

PERSUASIONS TO ENJOY

SONG

If the quick spirits in your eye
  Now languish, and anon must die;
If every sweet and every grace
Must fly from that forsaken face;
  Then, Celia, let us reap our joys
  Ere time such goodly fruit destroys.

Or, if that golden fleece must grow
Forever free from aged snow;
If those bright suns must know no shade,
Nor your fresh beauties ever fade;
Then, fear not, Celia, to bestow
What, still being gathered, still must grow.
  Thus, either Time his sickle brings
  In vain, or else in vain his wings.

EDMUND WALLER

After beginning his career with the familiar
university and law school pattern, Waller
(1606–1687) went on to become a Member of
Parliament under three kings. His political life
was stormy. Possessed of a fortune and good
connections, Waller played both sides: he was
friendly toward Cromwell and yet engineered
"Waller's Plot" to win London for the Royal-
ists—its discovery cost fellow plotters their
heads. But the leader survived by paying a
huge fine and accepting banishment to France.
His domestic life was likewise active, with
three ladies—Anne Bankes, Lady Dorothy Sid-

ney, and Mary Bracey—playing central roles
in a legal suit, an unrequited love affair, and
exile, respectively. A born diplomat, Waller
managed to write in praise of Cromwell after
exile and still convince Charles II after the
Restoration that he had been only shamming.
Waller, like Suckling, Lovelace, and so many
gentlemen-poets, is remembered for only two
or three first-rate poems. In these he is not ob-
scure; his lines are clean, and the lyric touch
is sure.

SONG

  Go, lovely rose!
Tell her that wastes her time and me
  That now she knows,
When I resemble her to thee,
How sweet and fair she seems to be.

  Tell her that's young,
And shuns to have her graces spied,
  That hadst thou sprung
In deserts, where no men abide,
Thou must have uncommended died.

  Small is the worth
Of beauty from the light retired;
  Bid her come forth,
Suffer herself to be desired,
And not blush so to be admired.

  Then die! that she
The common fate of all things rare
  May read in thee;
How small a part of time they share
That are so wondrous sweet and fair!

ON A GIRDLE

That which her slender waist confined,
Shall now my joyful temples bind;
No monarch but would give his crown,
His arms might do what this has done.

It was my heaven's extremest sphere,
The pale[1] which held that lovely deer;
My joy, my grief, my hope, my love
Did all within this circle move!

_____
[1] enclosure.

A narrow compass! and yet there
Dwelt all that's good and all that's fair;
Give me but what this ribbon bound,
Take all the rest the sun goes round!

JOHN MILTON*

L'ALLEGRO

Hence, loathèd Melancholy,
  Of Cerberus and blackest Midnight born,
In Stygian cave forlorn,
  'Mongst horrid shapes, and shrieks, and
    sights unholy,
Find out some uncouth cell,
  Where brooding Darkness spreads his jeal-
    ous wings,
And the night-raven sings;
  There under ebon shades, and low-browed 20
    rocks,
As ragged as thy locks,
  In dark Cimmerian desert[1] ever dwell.
But come, thou Goddess fair and free,
In heaven ycleped Euphrosyne,
  And by men, heart-easing Mirth,
Whom lovely Venus at a birth
With two sister Graces more
To ivy-crownèd Bacchus bore;
Or whether (as some sager sing)
The frolic Wind that breathes the spring,
Zephyr with Aurora playing,
As he met her once a-Maying,
There on beds of violets blue,
And fresh-blown roses washed in dew,
Filled her with thee, a daughter fair,
So buxom, blithe, and debonair.
  Haste thee, Nymph, and bring with thee
Jest and youthful Jollity,
Quips, and Cranks,[2] and wanton Wiles,
Nods, and Becks, and wreathèd Smiles
Such as hang on Hebe's cheek,
And love to live in dimple sleek;
Sport that wrinkled Care derides,
And Laughter holding both his sides.
Come, and trip it as ye go,
On the light fantastic toe;
And in thy right hand lead with thee

The mountain Nymph, sweet Liberty;
And, if I give thee honor due,
Mirth, admit me of thy crew,
To live with her, and live with thee,
  In unreproved pleasures free;
To hear the lark begin his flight,
And singing startle the dull night,
From his watch-tower in the skies,
Till the dappled Dawn doth rise;
Then to come, in spite of sorrow,
And at my window bid good-morrow,
Through the sweet-briar or the vine,
Or the twisted eglantine;
While the cock with lively din
  Scatters the rear of Darkness thin;
And to the stack, or the barn-door,
Stoutly struts his dames before:
Oft listening how the hounds and horn
Cheerly rouse the slumbering Morn,
From the side of some hoar hill,
Through the high wood echoing shrill:
Sometime walking, not unseen,
By hedgerow elms, on hillocks green,
Right against the eastern gate,
  Where the great Sun begins his state,
Robed in flames and amber light,
The clouds in thousand liveries dight;
While the ploughman, near at hand,
Whistles o'er the furrowed land,
And the milkmaid singeth blithe,
And the mower whets his scythe,
And every shepherd tells his tale
Under the hawthorn in the dale.
    Straight mine eye hath caught new
    pleasures,
Whilst the landscape round it measures:
Russet lawns, and fallows gray,
Where the nibbling flocks do stray;
Mountains on whose barren breast
The laboring clouds do often rest;
Meadows trim with daisies pied;
Shallow brooks, and rivers wide.
Towers and battlements it sees
Bosomed high in tufted trees,
  Where perhaps some Beauty lies,
The Cynosure of neighboring eyes.
Hard by, a cottage chimney smokes
From betwixt two aged oaks,
Where Corydon and Thyrsis met
  Are at their savory dinner set
Of herbs and other country messes,
Which the neat-handed Phillis dresses;

----

* For introductory sketch and selection from
Paradise Lost, see I, 87–100.
[1] allusion to Homeric geography.
[2] jests.

And then in haste her bower she leaves,
With Thestylis to bind the sheaves;
Or, if the earlier season lead,
To the tanned haycock in the mead.
   Sometimes with secure delight
The upland hamlets will invite,
When the merry bells ring round,
And the jocund rebecks[3] sound
To many a youth and many a maid
Dancing in the chequered shade;
And young and old come forth to play
On a sunshine holiday,
Till the livelong daylight fail:
Then to the spicy nut-brown ale,
With stories told of many a feat,
How fairy Mab the junkets eat:
She was pinched and pulled, she said;
And he, by Friar's lantern[4] led,
Tells how the drudging Goblin sweat
To earn his cream-bowl duly set,
When in one night, ere glimpse of morn,
His shadowy flail hath threshed the corn
That ten day-laborers could not end;
Then lies him down, the lubber[5] fiend,
And, stretched out all the chimney's length,
Basks at the fire his hairy strength,
And crop-full out of doors he flings,
Ere the first cock his matin rings.
Thus done the tales, to bed they creep,
By whispering winds soon lulled asleep.
Towered cities please us then,
And the busy hum of men,
Where throngs of Knights and Barons bold,
In weeds of peace, high triumphs hold,
With store of Ladies, whose bright eyes
Rain influence, and judge the prize
Of wit or arms, while both contend
To win her grace whom all commend.
There let Hymen oft appear
In saffron robe, with taper clear,
And pomp, and feast, and revelry,
With mask and antique pageantry;
Such sights as youthful Poets dream
On summer eves by haunted stream.
Then to the well-trod stage anon,
If Jonson's learned sock be on,
Or sweetest Shakespeare, Fancy's child,
Warble his native wood-notes wild.
And ever, against eating cares,
Lap me in soft Lydian airs,

Married to immortal verse,
Such as the meeting soul may pierce,
In notes with many a winding bout
Of linkèd sweetness long drawn out
5 With wanton heed and giddy cunning,
The melting voice through mazes running,
Untwisting all the chains that tie
The hidden soul of harmony;
That Orpheus' self may heave his head
10 From golden slumber on a bed
Of heaped Elysian flowers, and hear
Such strains as would have won the ear
Of Pluto to have quite set free
His half-regained Eurydice.
15 These delights if thou canst give,
Mirth, with thee I mean to live.

IL PENSEROSO

20
   Hence, vain deluding Joys,
     The brood of Folly without father bred!
How little you bested,[1]
     Or fill the fixèd mind with all your toys!
25 Dwell in some idle brain,
     And fancies fond with gaudy shapes possess,
As thick and numberless
     As the gay motes that people the sunbeams,
Or likest hovering dreams,
30   The fickle pensioners of Morpheus' train.
But, hail! thou Goddess sage and holy!
Hail, divinest Melancholy!
Whose saintly visage is too bright
To hit the sense of human sight,
35 And therefore to our weaker view
O'erlaid with black, staid Wisdom's hue;
Black, but such as in esteem
Prince Memnon's sister[2] might beseem,
Or that starred Ethiop Queen[3] that strove
40 To set her beauty's praise above
The Sea-Nymphs, and their powers offended.
Yet thou art higher far descended:
Thee bright-haired Vesta long of yore
To solitary Saturn bore;
45 His daughter she; in Saturn's reign
Such mixture was not held a stain.
Oft in glimmering bowers and glades
He met her, and in secret shades
Of woody Ida's[4] inmost grove,
50 ——————

---

[3] fiddles.   [4] will o' the wisp.   [5] clumsy.

[1] avail.   [2] Hemera (*Odyssey*).
[3] Cassiopeia.   [4] Mount Ida, in Crete.

Whilst yet there was no fear of Jove.
Come, pensive Nun, devout and pure,
Sober, steadfast, and demure,
All in a robe of darkest grain,
Flowing with majestic train,
And sable stole of cypress lawn
Over thy decent shoulders drawn.
Come; but keep thy wonted state,
With even step, and musing gait,
And looks commercing with the skies,
Thy rapt soul sitting in thine eyes:
There, held in holy passion still,
Forget thyself to marble, till
With a sad leaden downward cast
Thou fix them on the earth as fast.
And join with thee calm Peace and Quiet,
Spare Fast, that oft with gods doth diet,
And hears the Muses in a ring
Aye round about Jove's altar sing;
And add to these retirèd Leisure,
That in trim gardens takes his pleasure;
But, first and chiefest, with thee bring
Him that yon soars on golden wing,
Guiding the fiery-wheelèd throne,
The Cherub Contemplation;
And the mute Silence hist along,
'Less Philomel will deign a song,
In her sweetest saddest plight,
Smoothing the rugged brow of Night,
While Cynthia checks her dragon yoke
Gently o'er the accustomed oak.
Sweet bird, that shunn'st the noise of folly,
Most musical, most melancholy!
Thee, Chauntress, oft the woods among
I woo, to hear thy even-song;
And, missing thee, I walk unseen
On the dry smooth-shaven green,
To behold the wandering Moon,
Riding near her highest noon,
Like one that had been led astray
Through the heaven's wide pathless way,
And oft, as if her head she bowed,
Stooping through a fleecy cloud.
Oft, on a plat of rising ground,
I hear the far-off curfew sound,
Over some wide-watered shore,
Swinging slow with sullen roar;
Or, if the air will not permit,
Some still removèd place will fit,
Where glowing embers through the room
Teach light to counterfeit a gloom,
Far from all resort of mirth,

Save the cricket on the hearth,
Or the Bellman's drowsy charm
To bless the doors from nightly harm,
Or let my lamp, at midnight hour,
5 Be seen in some high lonely tower,
Where I may oft outwatch the Bear,[5]
With thrice-great Hermes,[6] or unsphere
The spirit of Plato, to unfold
What worlds or what vast regions hold
10 The immortal mind that hath forsook
Her mansion in this fleshly nook;
And of those demons that are found
In fire, air, flood, or underground,
Whose power hath a true consent
15 With planet or with element.
Sometime let gorgeous Tragedy
In sceptred pall come sweeping by,
Presenting Thebes, or Pelops' line,
Or the tale of Troy divine,
20 Or what (though rare) of later age
Ennobled hath the buskined stage.
But, O sad Virgin! that thy power
Might raise Musæus[7] from his bower;
Or bid the soul of Orpheus sing
25 Such notes as, warbled to the string,
Drew iron tears down Pluto's cheek,
And made Hell grant what Love did seek;
Or call up him[8] that left half-told
The story of Cambuscan bold,
30 Of Camball, and of Algarsife,
And who had Canace to wife,
That owned the virtuous ring and glass,
And of the wondrous horse of brass
On which the Tartar King did ride;
35 And if aught else great Bards beside
In sage and solemn tunes have sung,
Of tourneys, and of trophies hung,
Of forests, and enchantments drear,
Where more is meant than meets the ear.
40 Thus, Night, oft see me in thy pale career,
Till civil-suited Morn appear,
Not tricked and frounced, as she was wont
With the Attic boy[9] to hunt,
But kerchieft in a comely cloud,
45 While rocking winds are piping loud,
Or ushered with a shower still,

50

[5] the constellation.
[6] Hermes Trismegistus, mythical magician.
[7] mythical Greek poet.
[8] Chaucer; the following names are from *Squire's Tale*.
[9] Cephalus, loved by dawn goddess.

When the gust hath blown his fill,
Ending on the rustling leaves,
With minute-drops from off the eaves.
And, when the sun begins to fling
His flaring beams, me, Goddess, bring
To archèd walks of twilight groves,
And shadows brown, that Sylvan[10] loves,
Of pine, or monumental oak,
Where the rude axe with heavèd stroke
Was never heard the Nymphs to daunt,
Or fright them from their hallowed haunt.
There, in close covert, by some brook,
Where no profaner eye may look,
Hide me from Day's garish eye,
While the bee with honeyed thigh,
That at her flowery work doth sing,
And the waters murmuring,
With such consort as they keep,
Entice the dewy-feathered Sleep.
And let some strange mysterious dream
Wave at his wings, in airy stream
Of lively portraiture displayed,
Softly on my eyelids laid.
And as I wake, sweet music breathe
Above, about, or underneath,
Sent by some Spirit to mortals good,
Or the unseen Genius of the wood.
But let my due feet never fail
To walk the studious cloister's pale,
And love the high embowèd roof,
With antique pillars massy proof,
And storied windows richly dight,
Casting a dim religious light.
There let the pealing organ blow,
To the full voiced Quire below,
In service high and anthems clear,
As may with sweetness, through mine ear,
Dissolve me into ecstasies,
And bring all Heaven before mine eyes.
And may at last my weary age
Find out the peaceful hermitage,
The hairy gown and mossy cell,
Where I may sit and rightly spell
Of every star that Heaven doth shew,
And every herb that sips the dew;
Till old experience do attain
To something like prophetic strain.
These pleasures, Melancholy, give,
And I with thee will choose to live.

---

[10] Sylvanus, wood god.

ON HIS HAVING ARRIVED TO THE AGE OF TWENTY-THREE

How soon hath Time, the subtle thief of
5   youth,
    Stolen on his wing my three and twentieth
      year!
    My hasting days fly on with full career,
    But my late spring no bud or blossom
10   shew'th.
Perhaps my semblance might deceive the
    truth,
    That I to manhood am arrived so near,
    And inward ripeness doth much less appear,
15   That some more timely-happy spirits
      endu'th.
Yet be it less or more, or soon or slow,
    It shall be still in strictest measure even
    To that same lot, however mean or high,
20 Toward which Time leads me, and the will of
    Heaven.
    All is, if I have grace to use it so,
    As ever in my great Task-master's eye.

LYCIDAS[1]

25

Yet once more, O ye Laurels, and once more,
Ye Myrtles brown, with ivy never sere,
I come to pluck your berries harsh and crude,
30 And with forced fingers rude
Shatter your leaves before the mellowing
    year.
Bitter constraint and sad occasion dear
Compels me to disturb your season due;
35 For Lycidas is dead, dead ere his prime,
Young Lycidas, and hath not left his peer.
Who would not sing for Lycidas? he knew
Himself to sing, and build the lofty rhyme.
He must not float upon his watery bier
40 Unwept, and welter to the parching wind,
Without the meed of some melodious tear.
    Begin, then, Sisters of the sacred well[2]
That from beneath the seat of Jove doth
    spring;
45 Begin, and somewhat loudly sweep the string.
Hence with denial vain and coy excuse:
So may some gentle Muse
With lucky words favor *my* destined urn,
And as he passes turn,

---

[1] written in memory of Edward King, a college friend who was drowned at sea.
[2] the muses.

And bid fair peace be to my sable shroud!
  For we were nursed upon the self-same hill,
Fed the same flock, by fountain, shade, and
    rill;
Together both, ere the high lawns appeared
Under the opening eyelids of the Morn,   5
We drove a-field, and both together heard
What time the grey-fly winds her sultry horn,
Battening our flocks with the fresh dews of
    night,
Oft till the star that rose at evening bright
Toward heaven's descent had sloped his
    westering wheel.
Meanwhile the rural ditties were not mute;
Tempered to the oaten flute
Rough Satyrs danced, and Fauns with cloven   15
    heel
From the glad sound would not be absent
    long;
And old Damœtas loved to hear our song.
  But, oh! the heavy change, now thou art
    gone,   20
Now thou art gone and never must return!
Thee, Shepherd, thee the woods and desert
    caves,
With wild thyme and the gadding vine
    o'ergrown,
And all their echoes, mourn.
The willows, and the hazel copses green,
Shall now no more be seen   30
Fanning their joyous leaves to thy soft lays.
As killing as the canker to the rose,
Or taint-worm to the weanling herds that
    graze,
Or frost to flowers, that their gay wardrobe   35
    wear,
When first the white-thorn blows;
Such, Lycidas, thy loss to shepherd's ear.
  Where were ye, Nymphs, when the remorse-
    less deep   40
Closed o'er the head of your loved Lycidas?
For neither were ye playing on the steep
Where your old Bards, the famous Druids, lie,
Nor on the shaggy top of Mona high,
Nor yet where Deva spreads her wizard   45
    stream.
Ay me! I fondly dream
"Had ye been there," . . . for what could
    that have done?
What could the Muse[3] herself that Orpheus   50

    bore,
The Muse herself, for her enchanting son,
Whom universal nature did lament,
When, by the rout that made the hideous roar,
His gory visage down the stream was sent,
Down the swift Hebrus to the Lesbian shore?
  Alas! what boots it with uncessant care
To tend the homely slighted Shepherd's
    trade,
And strictly meditate the thankless Muse?
Were it not better done, as others use,
To sport with Amaryllis in the shade,
Or with the tangles of Neæra's hair?
Fame is the spur that the clear spirit doth
    raise
(That last infirmity of noble mind)
To scorn delights and live laborious days;
But the fair guerdon when we hope to find,
And think to burst out into sudden blaze,
Comes the blind Fury with the abhorrèd
    shears,
And slits the thin-spun life. "But not the
    praise,"
Phœbus replied, and touched my trembling
    ears:
"Fame is no plant that grows on mortal soil,
Nor in the glistering foil
Set off to the world, nor in broad rumor lies,
But lives and spreads aloft by those pure eyes
And perfect witness of all-judging Jove;
As he pronounces lastly on each deed,
Of so much fame in heaven expect thy
    meed."
  O fountain Arethuse,[4] and thou
    honored flood,
Smooth-sliding Mincius, crowned with vocal
    reeds,
That strain I heard was of a higher mood.
But now my oat proceeds,
And listens to the Herald of the Sea,[5]
That came in Neptune's plea.
He asked the waves, and asked the felon
    winds,
What hard mishap hath doomed this gentle
    swain?
And questioned every gust of rugged wings
That blows from off each beakèd promontory.
They knew not of his story;
And sage Hippotades[6] their answer brings,

---

[3] Calliope.

[4] in Sicily; symbolizes pastoral poetry.
[5] Triton.
[6] Aeolus, god of winds.

That not a blast was from his dungeon strayed:
The air was calm, and on the level brine
Sleek Panope[7] with all her sisters played.
It was that fatal and perfidious bark,
Built in the eclipse, and rigged with curses
    dark,
That sunk so low that sacred head of thine.
    Next, Camus,[8] reverend Sire, went footing
    slow,
His mantle hairy and his bonnet sedge,
Inwrought with figures dim, and on the edge
Like to that sanguine flower inscribed with
    woe.
"Ah! who hath reft," quoth he, "my dearest
    pledge?"
Last came, and last did go,
The Pilot of the Galilean Lake,[9]
Two massy keys he bore of metals twain
(The golden opes, the iron shuts amain).
He shook his mitred locks, and stern be-
    spake:—
"How well could I have spared for thee,
    young swain,
Enow of such as, for their bellies' sake,
Creep, and intrude, and climb into the fold!
Of other care they little reckoning make
Than how to scramble at the shearers' feast,
And shove away the worthy bidden guest.
Blind mouths! that scarce themselves know
    how to hold
A sheep-hook, or have learnt aught else the
    least
That to the faithful Herdman's art belongs!
What recks it them? What need they?
    They are sped;
And, when they list, their lean and flashy
    songs
Grate on their scrannel pipes of wretched
    straw;
The hungry sheep look up, and are not fed,
But, swoln with wind and the rank mist they
    draw,
Rot inwardly, and foul contagion spread;
Besides what the grim Wolf[10] with privy paw
Daily devours apace, and nothing said.
But that two-handed engine[11] at the door
Stands ready to smite once, and smite no
    more."

Return, Alpheus;[12] the dread voice is past
That shrunk thy streams; return, Sicilian
    Muse,
And call the vales, and bid them hither cast
5 Their bells and flowerets of a thousand hues.
Ye valleys low, where the mild whispers use
Of shades, and wanton winds, and gushing
    brooks,
On whose fresh lap the swart star sparely
10   looks,
Throw hither all your quaint enamelled eyes,
That on the green turf suck the honeyed
    showers,
And purple all the ground with vernal flowers.
15 Bring the rathe[13] primrose that forsaken dies,
The tufted crow-toe, and pale jessamine,
The white pink, and the pansy freaked with
    jet,
The glowing violet,
20 The musk-rose, and the well-attired woodbine,
With cowslips wan that hang the pensive
    head,
And every flower that sad embroidery wears;
Bid amaranthus all his beauty shed,
25 And daffadillies fill their cups with tears,
To strew the laureate hearse where Lycid lies.
For so, to interpose a little ease,
Let our frail thoughts dally with false
    surmise.
30 Ay me! whilst thee the shores and sounding
    seas
Wash far away, where'er thy bones are hurled;
Whether beyond the stormy Hebrides,
Where thou perhaps under the whelming tide
35 Visit'st the bottom of the monstrous world;
Or whether thou, to our moist vows denied,
Sleep'st by the fable of Bellerus[14] old,
Where the great Vision of the guarded mount[15]
Looks toward Namancos and Bayona's hold.[16]
40 Look homeward, Angel, now, and melt with
    ruth:
And, O ye dolphins, waft the hapless youth.
    Weep no more, woeful shepherds, weep no
    more,
45 For Lycidas, your sorrow, is not dead,
Sunk though he be beneath the watery floor.
So sinks the day-star in the ocean bed,

---

[12] pastoral figure; Milton is returning to pastoral mood.
[13] early.   [14] Land's End.
[15] St. Michael's Mount (Cornwall).
[16] in Spain.

---

[7] sea nymph.   [8] personification of river Cam.
[9] Saint Peter.   [10] Roman Catholic Church.
[11] obscure reference.

And yet anon repairs his drooping head,
And tricks his beams, and with new-spangled
 ore
Flames in the forehead of the morning sky:
So Lycidas sunk low, but mounted high,   5
Through the dear might of Him that walked
 the waves,
Where, other groves and other streams along,
With nectar pure his oozy locks he laves,
And hears the unexpressive nuptial song,
In the blest kingdoms meek of joy and love. 10
There entertain him all the Saints above,
In solemn troops, and sweet societies,
That sing, and singing in their glory move,
And wipe the tears for ever from his eyes.
Now, Lycidas, the Shepherds weep no more; 15
Henceforth thou art the Genius of the shore,
In thy large recompense, and shalt be good
To all that wander in that perilous flood.

Thus sang the uncouth[17] Swain to the oaks
 and rills,
While the still Morn went out with sandals
 grey:
He touched the tender stops of various quills, 25
With eager thought warbling his Doric lay:
And now the sun had stretched out all the
 hills,
And now was dropt into the western bay.
At last he rose, and twitched his mantle blue: 30
To-morrow to fresh woods, and pastures new.

ON HIS BLINDNESS

              35
When I consider how my light is spent
Ere half my days, in this dark world and wide,
And that one talent which is death to hide
Lodged with me useless, though my soul
 more bent   40
To serve therewith my Maker, and present
My true account, lest he returning chide;
"Doth God exact day-labor, light denied?"
I fondly ask. But Patience, to prevent
That murmur, soon replies, "God doth not 45
 need
Either man's work or his own gifts. Who best
Bear his mild yoke, they serve him best. His
 state
Is kingly: thousands at his bidding speed, 50

---

[17] rustic, unknown.

And post o'er land and ocean without rest;
They also serve who only stand and wait."

SIR JOHN SUCKLING

*Cambridge, Inns of Court, travel, military serv-
ice—these details in the life of Suckling (1609–
1642) merely fit the pattern for the moneyed
young man of the day, as we have seen. But
Suckling had his own individuality within the
pattern; he was the gay, insouciant sort that
could toss away thousands on bright (and im-
practical!) uniforms for a private troop of horse,
gamble away a fortune at dice and cards,
squander youth on the ladies, and eventually
(and typically) throw life itself away after the
last spin of the wheel. "Easy, natural Suckling,"
with his bad plays and good light verse, his
banter, his lampooning of the too-serious, was,
in spite of his own waste and tragedy, one of
those who seem designed by Fate, yesterday
or today, to make life pleasant for the rest of
us. He is the legendary Cavalier come to life,
one of the last to cry "Carpe diem" before the
gloom of Puritanism descended.*

THE CONSTANT LOVER

 Out upon it, I have loved
  Three whole days together!
 And am like to love three more,
  If it prove fair weather.

 Time shall moult away his wings,
  Ere he shall discover
 In the whole wide world again
  Such a constant lover.

 But the spite on't is, no praise
  Is due at all to me:
 Love with me had made no stays,
  Had it any been but she.

 Had it any been but she,
  And that very face,
 There had been at least ere this
  A dozen dozen in her place.

WHY SO PALE AND WAN?

 Why so pale and wan, fond lover?
  Prithee, why so pale?

Will, when looking well can't move her,
    Looking ill prevail?
    Prithee, why so pale?

Why so dull and mute, young sinner?
    Prithee, why so mute?
Will, when speaking well can't win her,
    Saying nothing do't?
    Prithee, why so mute?

Quit, quit for shame! This will not move
    This cannot take her.
If of herself she will not love,
    Nothing can make her:
    The devil take her!

SONG

I prithee send me back my heart,
    Since I cannot have thine;
For, if from yours you will not part,
    Why then shouldst thou have mine?

Yet now I think on it, let it lie;
    To find it were in vain,
For thou hast a thief in either eye
    Would steal it back again.

Why should two hearts in one breast lie
    And yet not lodge together?
O love, where is thy sympathy,
    If thus our breasts thou sever?

But love is such a mystery,
    I cannot find it out;
For when I think I'm best resolved,
    I then am in most doubt.

Then farewell care, and farewell woe,
    I will no longer pine;
For I'll believe I have her heart
    As much as she hath mine.

RICHARD CRASHAW

Crashaw (1612?–1649), like Donne, went through the pains of religious doubts, but came to an opposite decision. Brought up a Puritan, he eventually became a Catholic priest and, fascinated by the life of St. Theresa, wrote flaming verses, mystical verses, in her honor.

Although disillusioned by practices of certain members of Cardinal Palotta's retinue, Crashaw never recanted; his is the only significant Catholic poetic voice in seventeenth-century 5 *England. Influenced by Herbert (but more intense and less clear) and friendly with Cowley, Crashaw was capable of producing some of the best and some of the worst similes and metaphors in English. His life was cut short either* 10 *through heat prostration or (some say) through poisoning by churchmen who had resented his prying criticisms.*

15 *A HYMN TO THE NAME AND HONOR OF THE ADMIRABLE SAINT TERESA*

Foundress of the reformation of the Discalced[1] Carmelites, both men and women. A 20 *woman for angelical height of speculation, for masculine courage of performance, more than a woman, who yet a child outran maturity, and durst plot a martyrdom.*

25 Love, thou art absolute sole lord
Of life and death. To prove the word,
We'll now appeal to none of all
Those thy old soldiers, great and tall,
Ripe men of martyrdom, that could reach
30   down
With strong arms their triumphant crown,
Such as could with lusty breath
Speak loud into the face of death
Their great Lord's glorious name; to none
35 Of those whose spacious bosoms spread a
    throne
For love at large to fill; spare blood and
    sweat,
And see him take a private seat,
40 Making his mansion in the mild
And milky soul of a soft child.
    Scarce has she learned to lisp the name
Of martyr, yet she thinks it shame
Life should so long play with that breath
45 Which spent can buy so brave a death.
She never undertook to know
What death with love should have to do;
Nor has she e'er yet understood
Why to show love she should shed blood;
50 Yet though she cannot tell you why,

_____
[1] barefoot.

She can love and she can die.
Scarce has she blood enough to make
A guilty sword blush for her sake;
Yet has she a heart dares hope to prove
How much less strong is death than love.
Be love but there, let poor six years
Be posed with the maturest fears
Man trembles at, you straight shall find
Love knows no nonage, nor the mind.
'Tis love, not years or limbs that can
Make the martyr or the man.
Love touched her heart, and lo it beats
High, and burns with such brave heats,
Such thirsts to die, as dares drink up
A thousand cold deaths in one cup.
Good reason, for she breathes all fire;
Her weak breast heaves with strong desire
Of what she may with fruitless wishes
Seek for amongst her mother's kisses.
Since 'tis not to be had at home,
She'll travel to a martyrdom.
No home for hers confesses she
But where she may a martyr be.
She'll to the Moors, and trade with them
For this unvalued diadem.
She'll offer them her dearest breath,
With Christ's name in 't, in change for death.
She'll bargain with them, and will give
Them God, teach them how to live
In him; or if they this deny,
For him she'll teach them how to die.
So shall she leave amongst them sown
Her Lord's blood, or at least her own.
Farewell then, all the world, adieu!
Teresa is no more for you.
Farewell, all pleasures, sports, and joys,
Never till now esteemèd toys;
Farewell, whatever dear may be,
Mother's arms, or father's knee;
Farewell house and farewell home,
She's for the Moors and martyrdom!
Sweet, not so fast! lo, thy fair Spouse
Whom thou seek'st with so swift vows
Calls thee back, and bids thee come
To embrace a milder martyrdom.
Blest powers forbid thy tender life
Should bleed upon a barbarous knife,
Or some base hand have power to rase
Thy breast's chaste cabinet, and uncase
A soul kept there so sweet; O no,
Wise Heaven will never have it so:
Thou art Love's victim, and must die

A death more mystical and high.
Into Love's arms thou shalt let fall
A still-surviving funeral.
His is the dart must make the death
5 Whose stroke shall taste thy hallowed breath;
A dart thrice dipped in that rich flame
Which writes thy spouse's radiant name
Upon the roof of heaven, where aye
It shines, and with a sovereign ray
10 Beats bright upon the burning faces
Of souls, which in that name's sweet graces
Find everlasting smiles. So rare,
So spiritual, pure, and fair
Must be the immortal instrument
15 Upon whose choice point shall be sent
A life so loved; and that there be
Fit executioners for thee,
The fairest and first-born sons of fire,
Blest seraphim, shall leave their quire,
20 And turn Love's soldiers, upon thee
To exercise their archery.
O how oft shalt thou complain
Of a sweet and subtle pain;
Of intolerable joys;
25 Of a death in which who dies
Loves his death, and dies again,
And would forever so be slain,
And lives, and dies, and knows not why
To live, but that he thus may never leave to
30   die.
How kindly will thy gentle heart
Kiss the sweetly killing dart,
And close in his embraces keep
Those delicious wounds, that weep
35 Balsam to heal themselves with. Thus
When these thy deaths, so numerous,
Shall all at last die into one,
And melt thy soul's sweet mansion,
Like a soft lump of incense, hasted
40 By too hot a fire, and wasted
Into perfuming clouds, so fast
Shalt thou exhale to heaven at last
In a resolving sigh, and then,—
O what? Ask not the tongues of men.
45 Angels cannot tell; suffice
Thyself shall feel thine own full joys
And hold them fast forever there.
So soon as thou shalt first appear,
The moon of maiden stars, thy white
50 Mistress, attended by such bright
Souls as thy shining self, shall come,
And in her first ranks make thee room;

Where 'mongst her snowy family
Immortal welcomes wait for thee.
  O what delight, when revealed Life shall
    stand,
And teach thy lips heaven with His hand;
On which thou now may'st to thy wishes
Heap up thy consecrated kisses.
What joys shall seize thy soul when she,
Bending her blessed eyes on thee
(Those second smiles of heaven, shall dart 10
Her mild rays through thy melting heart!
  Angels, thy old friends, there shall greet
    thee,
Glad at their own home now to meet thee.
  All thy good works which went before
And waited for thee at the door
Shall own thee there, and all in one
Weave a constellation
Of crowns, with which the King, thy Spouse,
Shall build up thy triumphant brows.
  All thy old woes shall now smile on thee,
And thy pains sit bright upon thee;
All thy sorrows here shall shine,
All thy sufferings be divine;
Tears shall take comfort and turn gems,
And wrongs repent to diadems.
Even thy deaths shall live, and new
Dress the soul that erst they slew;
Thy wounds shall blush to such bright scars
As keep account of the Lamb's wars.
  Those rare works where thou shalt leave writ
Love's noble history, with wit
Taught thee by none but him, while here
They feed our souls, shall clothe thine there.
Each heavn'ly word by whose hid flame
Our hard hearts shall strike fire, the same
Shall flourish on thy brows, and be
Both fire to us and flame to thee,
Whose light shall live bright in thy face
By glory, in our hearts by grace.
  Thou shalt look round about and see
Thousands of crowned souls throng to be
Themselves thy crown; sons of thy vows,
The virgin-births with which thy sovereign
    spouse
Made fruitful thy fair soul, go now
And with them all about thee, bow
To him. Put on, he'll say, put on,
My rosy love, that thy rich zone
Sparkling with the sacred flames
Of thousand souls whose happy names
Heav'n keeps upon thy score. Thy bright

Life brought them first to kiss the light
That kindled them to stars. And so
Thou with the Lamb, thy Lord, shalt go,
And wheresoe'er he sets his white
5 Steps, walk with him those ways of light
Which who in death would live to see
Must learn in life to die like thee.

CHARITAS NIMIA; OR, THE DEAR BARGAIN

Lord, what is man? why should he cost Thee
So dear? what had his ruin lost Thee?
15 Lord, what is man, that Thou hast over-bought
So much a thing of naught?

Love is too kind, I see, and can
Make but a simple merchant-man.
20 'Twas for such sorry merchandise
Bold painters have put out his eyes.

Alas, sweet Lord! what were't to Thee
If there were no such worms as we?
25 Heav'n ne'er the less still Heav'n would be,
  Should mankind dwell
  In the deep hell.
What have his woes to do with Thee?

30   Let him go weep
  O'er his own wounds;
  Seraphims will not sleep,
Nor spheres let fall their faithful rounds.

35   Still would the youthful spirits sing,
And still Thy spacious palace ring;
Still would those beauteous ministers of light
  Burn all as bright,
And bow their flaming heads before Thee;
40 Still thrones and dominations would adore
  Thee.
Still would those ever-wakeful sons of fire
  Keep warm Thy praise
  Both nights and days,
45 And teach Thy loved name to their noble
  lyre.

Let froward dust then do its kind,
And give itself for sport to the proud wind.
50 Why should a piece of peevish clay plead
  shares
In the eternity of Thy old cares?

Why shouldst Thou bow Thy awful breast to
    see
What mine own madnesses have done with
    me?
Should not the king still keep his throne   5
Because some desperate fool's undone?
Or will the world's illustrious eyes
Weep for every worm that dies?

    Will the gallant sun   10
    E'er the less glorious run?
Will he hang down his golden head,
Or e'er the sooner seek his western bed,
    Because some foolish fly
    Grows wanton, and will die?   15

If I were lost in misery,
What was it to Thy heaven and Thee?
What was it to Thy precious blood
If my foul heart called for a flood?   20

What if my faithless soul and I
    Would needs fall in
    With guilt and sin;
What did the Lamb that he should die?   25
What did the Lamb that He should need,
When the wolf sins, Himself to bleed?

    If my base lust
Bargained with death and well-beseeming   30
    dust,
    Why should the white
    Lamb's bosom write
    The purple name
    Of my sin's shame?   35
Why should His unstained breast make good
My blushes with His own heart-blood?

O my Saviour, make me see
How dearly Thou hast paid for me;   40
That, lost again, my life may prove,
As then in death, so now in love.

A SONG   45

    Lord, when the sense of Thy sweet grace
    Sends up my soul to seek Thy face,
    Thy blessed eyes breed such desire
    I die in love's delicious fire.   50
      O love, I am thy sacrifice.
    Be still triumphant, blessed eyes;

Still shine on me, fair suns! that I
Still may behold, though still I die.

SECOND PART

Though still I die, I live again,
Still longing so to be still slain;
So gainful is such loss of breath,
I die even in desire of death.
    Still live in me this loving strife
Of living death and dying life;
For while Thou sweetly slayest me,
Dead to myself, I live in Thee.

RICHARD LOVELACE

*Lovelace (1618–1657) represents the ideal
Cavalier: brave, loyal, self-controlled. By comparison with the flamboyant Suckling and the
opportunist Carew he seems almost as dainty
as his name. Lovelace is the stanch royalist in
defeat, for twice he was imprisoned; and in
prison he wrote his best-known lyrics. We do
not know much about him. He apparently won
an Oxford M.A. simply because of "influence"
—he had been a student for only two years.
His life after prison is obscure. But like his fellows, he has left a slender legacy of verses;
unlike some of his contemporaries, he shows
that love poetry need not be flip or cynical or
sensual to be effective. Lovelace will shock no
one; he does not run deep; but for all his grace
and decency, he is never anything but virile.*

TO LUCASTA, ON GOING TO THE WARS

    Tell me not, sweet, I am unkind,
      That from the nunnery
    Of thy chaste breast and quiet mind
      To war and arms I fly.

    True, a new mistress now I chase,
      The first foe in the field;
    And with a stronger faith embrace
      A sword, a horse, a shield.

    Yet this inconstancy is such
      As thou too shalt adore:
    I could not love thee, dear, so much,
      Loved I not honor more.

TO ALTHEA, FROM PRISON

When Love with unconfinèd wings
  Hovers within my gates,
And my divine Althea brings
  To whisper at the grates;
When I lie tangled in her hair
  And fettered to her eye,
The gods that wanton in the air
  Know no such liberty.

When flowing cups run swiftly round
  With no allaying Thames,
Our careless heads with roses bound,
  Our hearts with loyal flames;
When thirsty grief in wine we steep,
  When healths and draughts go free,
Fishes that tipple in the deep
  Know no such liberty.

When, like committed[1] linnets, I
  With shriller throat will sing
The sweetness, mercy, majesty,
  And glories of my king;
When I shall voice aloud how good
  He is, how great should be,
Enlargèd winds, that curl the flood,
  Know no such liberty.

Stone walls do not a prison make,
  Nor iron bars a cage:
Minds innocent and quiet take
  That for an hermitage:
If I have freedom in my love,
  And in my soul am free,
Angels alone, that soar above,
  Enjoy such liberty.

GRATIANA DANCING AND SINGING

See! with what constant motion,
Even, and glorious, as the sun,
  Gratiana steers that noble frame.
Soft as her breast, sweet as her voice
That gave each winding law and poise,
  And swifter than the wings of fame,

She beat the happy pavement,
By such a star made firmament,

Which now no more the roof envies;
But swells up high with Atlas even,
Bearing the brighter, nobler heaven,
  And in her, all the deities.

Each step trod out a lover's thought,
And the ambitious hopes he brought
  Chained to her brave feet with such arts,
Such sweet command, and gentle awe,
As when she ceased, we sighing saw
  The floor lay paved with broken hearts.

So did she move; so did she sing
Like the harmonious spheres that bring
  Unto their rounds their music's aid;[1]
Which she performed such a way,
As all the enamoured world will say,
  "The Graces danced, and Apollo played."

ANDREW MARVELL

Somewhat obscured by the great shadow of Milton, under whom he worked at one time as assistant Latin secretary, Marvell (1621–1678) has recently experienced a sort of revival much like John Donne's. Recent scholarship makes much more of him than author of an unpuritanical poem of amatory opportunism, To His Coy Mistress, *clever as this is. Before and after Cambridge, Marvell got about a great deal, not always in genteel company. His knowledge of languages was amazing. As tutor to Mary Fairfax and, later, to a ward of John Oxenbridge, the poet found opportunities for composition (the gardens of Nun Appleton House inspiring him in the first instance and the talk about Bermuda from Oxenbridge setting him off in the second). For a long time Marvell was M.P. for Hull. His poetry runs the gamut from conventional persuasions to enjoy life, through simple lyrics or diplomatic occasional poetry, to the metaphysics of* The Garden, *where now and then a reader may think he is in the early nineteenth century.*

THE GARDEN

How vainly men themselves amaze
To win the palm, the oak, or bays,

---

[1] imprisoned.

[1] In the Ptolemaic system, the spheres were supposed to make music as they revolved.

And their incessant labors see
Crowned from some single herb, or tree,
Whose short and narrow-vergèd shade
Does prudently their toils upbraid;
While all flowers and all trees do close   5
To weave the garlands of repose!

   Fair Quiet, have I found thee here,
And Innocence, thy sister dear?
Mistaken long, I sought you then   10
In busy companies of men.
Your sacred plants, if here below,
Only among the plants will grow;
Society is all but rude
To this delicious solitude.   15

   No white nor red was ever seen
So amorous as this lovely green.
Fond lovers, cruel as their flame,
Cut in these trees their mistress' name: 20
Little, alas, they know or heed
How far these beauties hers exceed!
Fair trees, wheresoe'er your barks I wound,
No name shall but your own be found.

   When we have run our passion's heat,   25
Love hither makes his best retreat.
The gods, that mortal beauty chase,
Still in a tree did end their race:
Apollo hunted Daphne so,   30
Only that she might laurel grow;
And Pan did after Syrinx speed,
Not as a nymph, but for a reed.[1]

   What wondrous life is this I lead!   35
Ripe apples drop about my head;
The luscious clusters of the vine
Upon my mouth do crush their wine;
The nectarine and curious peach
Into my hands themselves do reach;   40
Stumbling on melons, as I pass,
Ensnared with flowers, I fall on grass.

   Meanwhile the mind from pleasure less
Withdraws into its happiness;   45
The mind, that ocean where each kind
Does straight its own resemblance find;
Yet it creates, transcending these,
Far other worlds and other seas,
                                                 50

Annihilating all that's made
To a green thought in a green shade.

   Here at the fountain's sliding foot,
Or at some fruit-tree's mossy root,
Casting the body's vest aside,
My soul into the boughs does glide:
There, like a bird, it sits and sings,
Then whets and combs its silver wings,
And, till prepared for longer flight,
Waves in its plumes the various light.

   Such was that happy garden-state,
While man there walked without a mate:
After a place so pure and sweet,
What other help could yet be meet!
But 'twas beyond a mortal's share
To wander solitary there:
Two paradises 'twere in one
To live in Paradise alone.

   How well the skilful gardener drew,
Of flowers and herbs, this dial new;
Where, from above, the milder sun
Does through a fragrant zodiac run;
And, as it works, the industrious bee
Computes its time as well as we!
How could such sweet and wholesome hours
Be reckoned but with herbs and flowers?

THE DEFINITION OF LOVE

My love is of a birth as rare
As 'tis, for object, strange and high;
It was begotten by Despair
Upon Impossibility.

Magnanimous Despair alone
Could show me so divine a thing,
Where feeble Hope could ne'er have flown,
But vainly flapped its tinsel wing.

And yet I quickly might arrive
Where my extended soul is fixed;
But Fate does iron wedges drive,
And always crowds itself betwixt.

For Fate with jealous eyes does see
Two perfect loves, nor lets them close;
Their union would her ruin be,
And her tyrannic power depose.

---

[1] Both mythological maidens were saved from pursuit by similar metamorphoses.

And therefore her decrees of steel
Us as the distant poles have placed
(Though Love's whole world on us doth
    wheel),
Not by themselves to be embraced;   5

Unless the giddy heaven fall,
And earth some new convulsion tear,
And, us to join, the world should all
Be cramped into a planisphere.[1]   10

As lines, so loves, oblique may well
Themselves in every angle greet;
But ours, so truly parallel,
Though infinite, can never meet.   15

Therefore the love which us doth bind,
But Fate so enviously debars,
Is the conjunction of the mind,
And opposition of the stars.   20

TO HIS COY MISTRESS

Had we but world enough, and time,
This coyness, Lady, were no crime.   25
We would sit down, and think which way
To walk, and pass our long love's day.
Thou by the Indian Ganges' side
Shouldst rubies find; I by the tide
Of Humber would complain. I would   30
Love you ten years before the Flood,
And you should, if you please, refuse
Till the conversion of the Jews.
My vegetable[1] love should grow
Vaster than empires and more slow;   35
An hundred years should go to praise
Thine eyes, and on thy forehead gaze;
Two hundred to adore each breast,
But thirty thousand to the rest;
An age at least to every part,   40
And the last age should show your heart.
For, Lady, you deserve this state,
Nor would I love at lower rate.
    But at my back I always hear
Time's wingèd chariot hurrying near;   45
And yonder all before us lie
Deserts of vast eternity.
Thy beauty shall no more be found,
Nor, in thy marble vault, shall sound

My echoing song; then worms shall try
That long-preserved virginity,
And your quaint honor turn to dust,
And into ashes all my lust:
The grave's a fine and private place,
But none, I think, do there embrace.
    Now therefore, while the youthful hue
Sits on thy skin like morning dew,
And while thy willing soul transpires
At every pore with instant fires,
Now let us sport us while we may,
And now, like amorous birds of prey,
Rather at once our time devour
Than languish in his slow-chapped power.
Let us roll all our strength and all
Our sweetness up into one ball,
And tear our pleasures with rough strife
Thorough the iron gates of life;
Thus, though we cannot make our sun
Stand still, yet we will make him run.

BERMUDAS

Where the remote Bermudas ride,
In the ocean's bosom unespied,
From a small boat that rowed along,
The listening winds received this song:[1]

"What should we do but sing His praise,
That led us through the watery maze
Unto an isle so long unknown,
And yet far kinder than our own?
Where He the huge sea-monsters wracks,
That lift the deep upon their backs;
He lands us on a grassy stage,
Safe from the storms, and prelate's rage.
He gave us this eternal spring
Which here enamels everything,
And sends the fowls to us in care,
On daily visits through the air;
He hangs in shades the orange bright,
Like golden lamps in a green night,
And does in the pomegranates close
Jewels more rich than Ormus[2] shows;
He makes the figs our mouths to meet,
And throws the melons at our feet;
But apples plants of such a price,
No tree could ever bear them twice;

---

[1] a flat map of the world.
[1] active.

[1] This song is sung by colonists granted religious freedom in Bermuda.
[2] See *Paradise Lost*, II, 2.

With cedars, chosen by His hand,
From Lebanon, He stores the land;
And makes the hollow seas, that roar,
Proclaim the ambergris on shore;
He cast (of which we rather boast)   5
The Gospel's pearl upon our coast,
And in these rocks for us did frame
A temple, where to sound His name.
Oh! let our voice His praise exalt,
Till it arrive at heaven's vault,   10
Which, thence (perhaps) rebounding, may
Echo beyond the Mexique Bay."

    Thus sung they in the English boat,
An holy and a cheerful note;   15
And all the way, to guide their chime,
With falling oars they kept the time.

HENRY VAUGHAN   20

Vaughan (1621–1695) left Oxford for the law only to have his studies interrupted by the wars, in which he may have served. He appears again in his native Wales, writing first secular and finally religious poetry, and practicing medicine. Taking the name of The Silurist, after the Latin for his area, Vaughan turned out four volumes of verse under the influence of Herbert, but more mystical. Politics and family troubles caused him concern which led to brooding which led to spiritual awakening; Vaughan reached God almost intuitively through Nature. Called the "mystic of light" because of his favorite imagery, he anticipates, in his personal relation with Nature and his interest in children, the work of Wordsworth and the Romantic school.

THE RETREAT   40

Happy those early days, when I
Shined in my angel infancy;
Before I understood this place
Appointed for my second race,
Or taught my soul to fancy aught   45
But a white, celestial thought;
When yet I had not walked above
A mile or two from my first Love,
And looking back, at that short space,   50
Could see a glimpse of His bright face;
When on some gilded cloud or flower

My gazing soul would dwell an hour,
And in those weaker glories spy
Some shadows of eternity;
Before I taught my tongue to wound
My conscience with a sinful sound,
Or had the black art to dispense
A several sin to every sense,
But felt through all this fleshly dress
Bright shoots of everlastingness.
    Oh, how I long to travel back,
And tread again that ancient track!
That I might once more reach that plain
Where first I left my glorious train,
From whence the enlightened spirit sees
That shady city of palm trees.
But, ah! my soul with too much stay
Is drunk, and staggers in the way.
Some men a forward motion love;
But I by backward steps would move,
And when this dust falls to the urn,
In that state I came, return.

CHILDHOOD

I cannot reach it; and my striving eye
Dazzles at it, as at eternity.

    Were now that chronicle alive,
Those white designs which children drive,
And the thoughts of each harmless hour,
With their content, too, in my power,
Quickly would I make my path even,
And by mere playing go to heaven.

    Why should men love
A wolf more than a lamb or dove?
Or choose hell-fire and brimstone streams
Before bright stars and God's own beams?
Who kisseth thorns will hurt his face,
But flowers do both refresh and grace,
And sweetly living—fie on men!—
Are, when dead, medicinal then;
If seeing much should make staid eyes,
And long experience should make wise,
Since all that age doth teach is ill,
Why should I not love childhood still?
Why, if I see a rock or shelf,
Shall I from thence cast down myself?
Or by complying with the world,
From the same precipice be hurled?
Those observations are but foul
Which make me wise to lose my soul.

And yet the practice worldlings call
Business, and weighty action all,
Checking the poor child for his play,
But gravely cast themselves away.

THE WORLD

I saw eternity the other night
Like a great ring of pure and endless light,   10
  All calm as it was bright;
And round beneath it, time, in hours, days,
    years,
  Driven by the spheres,
Like a vast shadow moved, in which the 15
    world
  And all her train were hurled.
The doting lover in his quaintest strain
  Did there complain;
Near him, his lute, his fancy, and his flights, 20
  Wit's sour delights,
With gloves and knots, the silly snares of pleas-
  ure,
  Yet his dear treasure,
All scattered lay, while he his eyes did pour 25
  Upon a flower.

The darksome statesman, hung with weights
  and woe,
Like a thick midnight fog, moved there so slow 30
  He did nor stay nor go;
Condemning thoughts, like mad eclipses,
  scowl
  Upon his soul,
And clouds of crying witnesses without 35
  Pursued him with one shout.
Yet digged the mole, and, lest his ways be
  found,
  Worked under ground,
Where he did clutch his prey. But one did see 40
  That policy:
Churches and altars fed him; perjuries
  Were gnats and flies;
It rained about him blood and tears; but he
  Drank them as free. 45

The fearful miser on a heap of rust
Sat pining all his life there, did scarce trust
  His own hands with the dust;
Yet would not place one piece above, but lives 50
  In fear of thieves.
Thousands there were as frantic as himself,

And hugged each one his pelf:
The downright epicure placed heaven in
  sense,
  And scorned pretense;
While others, slipped into a wide excess,
  Said little less;
The weaker sort, slight, trivial wares enslave,
  Who think them brave;
And poor, despised Truth sat counting by
  Their victory.

Yet some, who all this while did weep and
  sing,
And sing and weep, soared up into the ring;
  But most would use no wing.
"O fools!" said I, "thus to prefer dark night
  Before true light!
To live in grots and caves, and hate the day
  Because it shows the way,
The way which from this dead and dark abode
  Leads up to God,
A way where you might tread the sun and be
  More bright than he!"
But, as I did their madness so discuss,
  One whispered thus:
"This ring the bridegroom did for none pro-
  vide,
  But for his bride."

DEPARTED FRIENDS

They are all gone into the world of light!
  And I alone sit lingering here;
Their very memory is fair and bright, 35
  And my sad thoughts doth clear.

It glows and glitters in my cloudy breast,
  Like stars upon some gloomy grove,
Or those faint beams in which this hill is drest,
  After the sun's remove.

I see them walking in an air of glory,
  Whose light doth trample on my days;
My days, which are at best but dull and hoary, 45
  Mere glimmering and decays.

O holy hope! and high humility,
  High as the heavens above!
These are your walks, and you have showed 50
  them me,
  To kindle my cold love.

Dear, beauteous death! the jewel of the just,
  Shining nowhere, but in the dark,
What mysteries do lie beyond thy dust,
  Could man outlook that mark!

                                5

He that hath found some fledged bird's nest
    may know
  At first sight if the bird be flown;
But what fair well or grove he sings in now,
  That is to him unknown.   10

And yet, as angels in some brighter dreams
  Call to the soul, when man doth sleep,
So some strange thoughts transcend our
    wonted themes,   15
  And into glory peep.

If a star were confined into a tomb,
  The captive flames must needs burn there;
But when the hand that locked her up gives 20
    room,
  She'll shine through all the sphere.

O Father of eternal life, and all
  Created glories under Thee,
Resume Thy spirit from this world of thrall 25
  Into true liberty!

Either disperse these mists, which blot and fill
  My perspective still as they pass;
Or else remove me hence unto that hill, 30
  Where I shall need no glass.

PEACE

                           35

My soul, there is a country
    Far beyond the stars,
Where stands a winged sentry
    All skilful in the wars.
There, above noise and danger, 40
    Sweet Peace sits crowned with smiles,
And One born in a manger
    Commands the beauteous files.
He is thy gracious friend,
    And—O my soul, awake!— 45
Did in pure love descend
    To die here for thy sake.
If thou canst get but thither,
    There grows the flower of peace,
The rose that cannot wither, 50
    Thy fortress and thy ease.
Leave, then, thy foolish ranges;

For none can thee secure
  But One who never changes,
    Thy God, thy life, thy cure.

JOHN DRYDEN

The name of Dryden (1631–1700) is more significant than the size of the selection from his work may here indicate. He is a difficult subject for an anthologist: much of his fame depends on his criticism or his drama, neither of which belongs in this section of our text. Of his non-dramatic verse, much (especially the satires) is lost on the modern reader; most of it is too long to reprint conveniently. It is now established that Dryden (with a background of Cambridge and the inevitable secretaryships) excelled in four fields—satire, heroic drama, criticism, and lyric poetry—to which we may add a fifth, translation. Poet laureate and one of the great literary arbiters of English literature, Dryden is something of a paradox: he tried Protestantism and Catholicism and wrote poems favoring each; he tried rhyme and blank verse, assailing each on occasion. Whatever may have been his motives, however dull or cold his work may seem to a modern reader, there is, nevertheless, no one else of his versatility and energy in the annals of late seventeenth-century English literature.

A SONG FOR ST. CECILIA'S DAY, NOVEMBER 22, 1687

From harmony, from heavenly harmony
    This universal frame began;
    When Nature underneath a heap
      Of jarring atoms lay,
    And could not heave her head,
The tuneful voice was heard from high,
    "Arise, ye more than dead."

Then cold and hot and moist and dry 45
    In order to their stations leap,
    And Music's power obey.
From harmony, from heavenly harmony,
    This universal frame began:
    From harmony to harmony 50
Through all the compass of the notes it ran,
The diapason closing full in Man.

What passion cannot Music raise and quell!
  When Jubal[1] struck the chorded shell,
  His listening brethren stood around,
    And, wondering, on their faces fell
To worship that celestial sound: 5
Less than a god they thought there could not
    dwell
  Within the hollow of that shell,
  That spoke so sweetly, and so well.
What passion cannot Music raise and quell! 10

    The trumpet's loud clangor
      Excites us to arms
    With shrill notes of anger
      And mortal alarms.
    The double, double, double beat   15
      Of the thundering drum
    Cries, "Hark! the foes come;
  Charge, charge, 'tis too late to retreat!"

    The soft complaining flute
      In dying notes discovers   20
    The woes of hopeless lovers,
  Whose dirge is whispered by the war-
    bling lute.

    Sharp violins proclaim   25
Their jealous pangs and desperation,
Fury, frantic indignation,
Depth of pains and height of passion,   30
    For the fair, disdainful dame.

  But oh! what art can teach,
  What human voice can reach
    The sacred organ's praise?   35
  Notes inspiring holy love,
    Notes that wing their heavenly ways
  To mend the choirs above.

Orpheus could lead the savage race,   40
And trees unrooted left their place,
  Sequacious of the lyre;
But bright Cecilia raised the wonder higher;
When to her organ vocal breath was given,
An angel heard, and straight appeared,   45
  Mistaking earth for heaven.

GRAND CHORUS

  As from the power of sacred lays
    The spheres began to move,   50

[1] See Genesis 4:21.

  And sung that great Creator's praise
    To all the blessed above;
  So, when the last and dreadful hour
  This crumbling pageant shall devour,
  The trumpet shall be heard on high,
  The dead shall live, the living die,
  And Music shall untune the sky.

ALEXANDER'S FEAST; OR, THE POWER OF MUSIC

A SONG IN HONOR OF ST. CECILIA'S DAY, 1697

'Twas at the royal feast, for Persia won
  By Philip's warlike son:[1]
  Aloft in awful state
  The godlike hero sate
    On his imperial throne;
  His valiant peers were placed around;
Their brows with roses and with myrtles
    bound:
(So should desert in arms be crowned.)
The lovely Thais, by his side,
Sate like a blooming Eastern bride,
In flower of youth and beauty's pride.
    Happy, happy, happy pair!
      None but the brave,
      None but the brave,
    None but the brave deserves the fair.

CHORUS

    Happy, happy, happy pair!
      None but the brave,
      None but the brave,
    None but the brave deserves the fair.

  Timotheus,[2] placed on high
    Amid the tuneful quire,
    With flying fingers touched the lyre:
  The trembling notes ascend the sky,
    And heavenly joys inspire.
The song began from Jove,
Who left his blissful seats above,
(Such is the power of mighty love).
A dragon's fiery form belied the god:
Sublime on radiant spires he rode,
When he to fair Olympia[3] pressed;
And while he sought her snowy breast,

[1] Alexander.
[2] Alexander's favorite musician.
[3] Alexander's mother.

Then round her slender waist he curled,
And stamped an image of himself, a sovereign
   of the world.
The listening crowd admire the lofty sound,
"A present deity," they shout around;   5
"A present deity," the vaulted roofs re-
   bound:
    With ravished ears
    The monarch hears,
    Assumes the god,   10
    Affects to nod,
And seems to shake the spheres.

CHORUS

    With ravished ears
    The monarch hears,
    Assumes the god,
    Affects to nod,
And seems to shake the spheres.   20

The praise of Bacchus then the sweet musi-
   cian sung,
Of Bacchus ever fair, and ever young.
   The jolly god in triumph comes;   25
   Sound the trumpets, beat the drums;
    Flushed with a purple grace
    He shows his honest face:
Now give the hautboys breath; he comes, he
   comes.   30
   Bacchus, ever fair and young,
    Drinking joys did first ordain;
   Bacchus' blessings are a treasure,
   Drinking is the soldier's pleasure;
    Rich the treasure,   35
    Sweet the pleasure,
    Sweet is pleasure after pain.

CHORUS

   Bacchus' blessings are a treasure,
   Drinking is the soldier's pleasure;
    Rich the treasure,   40
    Sweet the pleasure,
    Sweet is pleasure after pain.   45

Soothed with the sound the king grew vain;
   Fought all his battles o'er again;
And thrice he routed all his foes, and thrice
   he slew the slain.   50
   The master saw the madness rise,
   His glowing cheeks, his ardent eyes;

And while he heaven and earth defied,
   Changed his hand, and checked his pride.
    He chose a mournful Muse,
    Soft pity to infuse;
   He sung Darius great and good,
    By too severe a fate,
   Fallen, fallen, fallen, fallen,
    Fallen from his high estate,
   And weltering in his blood;
   Deserted at his utmost need
   By those his former bounty fed;
   On the bare earth exposed he lies,
   With not a friend to close his eyes.

15 With downcast looks the joyless victor sate,
    Revolving in his altered soul
      The various turns of chance below;
    And, now and then, a sigh he stole,
      And tears began to flow.

CHORUS

    Revolving in his altered soul
      The various turns of chance below;
    And, now and then, a sigh he stole,
      And tears began to flow.

   The mighty master smiled to see
   That love was in the next degree;
   'Twas but a kindred sound to move,
   For pity melts the mind to love.
    Softly sweet, in Lydian measures,
    Soon he soothed his soul to pleasures.
   "War," he sung, "is toil and trouble;
   Honor but an empty bubble;
    Never ending, still beginning,
   Fighting still, and still destroying:
    If the world be worth thy winning,
   Think, O think it worth enjoying:
    Lovely Thais sits beside thee,
    Take the good the gods provide thee."

The many rend the skies with loud applause;
So Love was crowned, but Music won the
   cause.
   The prince, unable to conceal his pain,
    Gazed on the fair
    Who caused his care,
   And sighed and looked, sighed and looked,
   Sighed and looked, and sighed again;
50 At length, with love and wine at once op-
   pressed,
The vanquished victor sunk upon her breast.

[240]

CHORUS

The prince, unable to conceal his pain,
    Gazed on the fair
    Who caused his care,
And sighed and looked, sighed and looked,
Sighed and looked, and sighed again;
At length, with love and wine at once op-
    pressed,
The vanquished victor sunk upon her breast. 10

Now strike the golden lyre again;
A louder yet, and yet a louder strain.
Break his bands of sleep asunder,
And rouse him, like a rattling peal of 15
    thunder.
    Hark, hark, the horrid sound
      Has raised up his head;
      As awaked from the dead,
    And, amazed, he stares around. 20
"Revenge, revenge!" Timotheus cries;
    "See the Furies arise;
    See the snakes that they rear,
    How they hiss in their hair,
And the sparkles that flash from their 25
    eyes?
    Behold a ghastly band,
    Each a torch in his hand!
Those are Grecian ghosts, that in battle were
    slain, 30
      And unburied remain
      Inglorious on the plain:
    Give the vengeance due
    To the valiant crew.
Behold how they toss their torches on high, 35
    How they point to the Persian abodes,
And glittering temples of their hostile gods!"
The princes applaud with a furious joy;
And the king seized a flambeau with zeal to
    destroy; 40
    Thais led the way,

    To light him to his prey,
And, like another Helen, fired another Troy.

CHORUS

And the king seized a flambeau with zeal to
    destroy;
    Thais led the way,
    To light him to his prey,
And, like another Helen, fired another Troy.

    Thus long ago,
    Ere heaving bellows learned to blow,
      While organs yet were mute,
      Timotheus, to his breathing flute
      And sounding lyre,
Could swell the soul to rage, or kindle soft
    desire.
    At last divine Cecilia came,
    Inventress of the vocal frame;
The sweet enthusiast, from her sacred store,
    Enlarged the former narrow bounds,
    And added length to solemn sounds,
With Nature's mother wit, and arts unknown
    before.
    Let old Timotheus yield the prize,
      Or both divide the crown:
    He raised a mortal to the skies;
      She drew an angel down.

GRAND CHORUS

    At last divine Cecilia came,
    Inventress of the vocal frame;
The sweet enthusiast, from her sacred store
    Enlarged the former narrow bounds,
    And added length to solemn sounds,
With Nature's mother wit, and arts unknown
    before.
    Let old Timotheus yield the prize,
      Or both divide the crown:
    He raised a mortal to the skies;
      She drew an angel down.

EIGHTEENTH CENTURY

ALEXANDER POPE *

AN ESSAY ON MAN

EPISTLE I

OF THE NATURE AND STATE OF MAN, WITH RESPECT TO THE UNIVERSE

Argument

Of Man in the abstract. I. That we can judge only with regard to our own system, being ignorant of the relations of systems and things, verse 17, etc. II. That Man is not to be deemed imperfect, but a being suited to his place and rank in the creation, agreeable to the general order of things, and conformable to ends and relations to him unknown, verse 35, etc. III. That it is partly upon his ignorance of future events, and partly upon the hope of a future state, that all his happiness in the present depends, verse 77, etc. IV. The pride of aiming at more knowledge, and pretending to more perfection, the cause of Man's error and misery. The impiety of putting himself in the place of God, and judging of the fitness or unfitness, perfection or imperfection, justice or injustice, of his dispensations, verse 113, etc. V. The absurdity of conceiving himself the final cause of the creation, or expecting that perfection in the moral world which is not in the natural, verse 131, etc. VI. The unreasonableness of his complaints against Providence, while, on the one hand, he demands the perfections of the angels, and, on the other, the bodily qualifications of the brutes; though to possess any of the sensitive faculties in a higher degree would render him miserable, verse 173, etc. VII. That throughout the whole visible world a universal order and gradation in the sensual and mental faculties is observed, which causes a subordination of creature to creature, and of all creatures to man. The gradations of Sense, Instinct, Thought, Reflection, Reason: that Reason alone countervails all the other faculties, verse 207, etc. VIII. How much further this order and subordination of living creatures may extend above and below us; were any part of which broken, not that part only, but the whole connected creation must be destroyed, verse 213, etc. IX. The extravagance, madness, and pride of such a desire, verse 290, etc. X. The consequence of all, the absolute submission due to Providence, both as to our present and future state, verse 281, etc., to the end.

Awake, my St. John![1] leave all meaner things
To low ambition and the pride of Kings.
Let us, since life can little more supply
Than just to look about us and to die,
Expatiate free o'er all this scene of man;   5
A mighty maze! but not without a plan;
A wild, where weeds and flowers promiscuous
   shoot,
Or garden, tempting with forbidden fruit.
Together let us beat this ample field,
Try what the open, what the covert yield;   10
The latent tracts, the giddy heights, explore
Of all who blindly creep or sightless soar;
Eye Nature's walks, shoot folly as it flies,
And catch the manners living as they rise;   15
Laugh where we must, be candid where we
   can,
But vindicate the ways of God to man.
  I. Say first, of God above or Man below
What can we reason but from what we know?   20
Of man what see we but his station here,
From which to reason, or to which refer?
Thro' worlds unnumbered tho' the God be
   known,
'Tis ours to trace him only in our own.   25

* For introductory sketch see I, 101.

[1] Henry St. John, Lord Bolingbroke, friend of Pope, inspirer of much of the poet's philosophy.

He who thro' vast immensity can pierce,
See worlds on worlds compose one universe,
Observe how system into system runs,
What other planets circle other suns,
What varied being peoples every star,
May tell why Heaven has made us as we are:
But of this frame, the bearings and the ties,
The strong connections, nice dependencies,
Gradations just, has thy pervading soul
Looked thro'; or can a part contain the whole? 10
  Is the great chain that draws all to agree,
And drawn supports, upheld by God or thee?
  II. Presumptuous man! the reason wouldst
    thou find,
Why formed so weak, so little, and so blind? 15
First, if thou canst, the harder reason guess
Why formed no weaker, blinder, and no less!
Ask of thy mother earth why oaks are made
Taller or stronger than the weeds they shade!
Or ask of yonder argent fields above
Why Jove's satellites are less than Jove! 20
  Of systems possible, if 'tis confest
That wisdom infinite must form the best,
Where all must fall or not coherent be,
And all that rises rise in due degree;
Then in the scale of reasoning life 'tis plain 25
There must be, somewhere, such a rank as
    Man:
And all the question (wrangle e'er so long)
Is only this,—if God has placed him wrong? 30
  Respecting Man, whatever wrong we call,
May, must be right, as relative to all.
In human works, tho' labored on with pain,
A thousand movements scarce one purpose
    gain;
In God's, one single can its end produce,
Yet serve to second too some other use:
So man, who here seems principal alone,
Perhaps acts second to some sphere unknown,
Touches some wheel, or verges to some goal: 40
'Tis but a part we see, and not a whole.
  When the proud steed shall know why man
    restrains
His fiery course, or drives him o'er the plains;
When the dull ox, why now he breaks the clod, 45
Is now a victim, and now Egypt's God;
Then shall man's pride and dulness compre-
    hend
His actions', passions', being's, use and end;
Why doing, suffering, checked, impelled; and 50
    why
This hour a Slave, the next a Deity.

  Then say not man's imperfect, Heaven in
    fault;
Say rather man's as perfect as he ought;
His knowledge measured to his state and 5
    place,
His time a moment, and a point his space.
If to be perfect in a certain sphere,
What matter soon or late, or here or there?
The blest to-day is as completely so
As who began a thousand years ago. 10
  III. Heaven from all creatures hides the
    book of Fate,
All but the page prescribed, their present
    state;
From brutes what men, from men what spirits 15
    know;
Or who could suffer being here below?
The lamb thy riot dooms to bleed to-day,
Had he thy reason would he skip and play?
Pleased to the last he crops the flowery food, 20
And licks the hand just raised to shed his
    blood.
O blindness to the future! kindly given,
That each may fill the circle marked by
    Heaven; 25
Who sees with equal eye, as God of all,
A hero perish or a sparrow fall,
Atoms or systems into ruin hurled,
And now a bubble burst, and now a world.
  Hope humbly then; with trembling pinions 30
    soar;
Wait the great teacher Death, and God adore.
What future bliss He gives not thee to know,
But gives that hope to be thy blessing now.
Hope springs eternal in the human breast: 35
Man never is, but always to be, blest.
The soul, uneasy and confined from home,
Rests and expatiates in a life to come.
  Lo, the poor Indian! whose untutored mind
Sees God in clouds, or hears him in the wind;
His soul proud Science never taught to stray
Far as the solar walk or milky way;
Yet simple nature to his hope has given,
Behind the cloud-topt hill, an humbler 45
    Heaven,
Some safer world in depth of woods embraced,
Some happier island in the watery waste,
Where slaves once more their native land be-
    hold,
No fiends torment, no Christians thirst for 50
    gold.
To be, contents his natural desire;

He asks no Angel's wing, no Seraph's fire;
But thinks, admitted to that equal sky,
His faithful dog shall bear him company.
    IV. Go, wiser thou! and in thy scale of sense
Weigh thy opinion against Providence;
Call imperfection what thou fanciest such;
Say, here he gives too little, there too much;
Destroy all creatures for thy sport or gust,[2]
Yet cry, if man's unhappy, God's unjust;
If man alone engross not Heaven's high care,
Alone made perfect here, immortal there:
Snatch from his hand the balance and the rod,
Rejudge his justice, be the god of God.
In pride, in reasoning pride, our error lies;
All quit their sphere, and rush into the skies!
Pride still is aiming at the blessed abodes,
Men would be Angels, Angels would be Gods.
Aspiring to be Gods if Angels fell,
Aspiring to be Angels men rebel:
And who but wishes to invert the laws
Of order, sins against th' Eternal Cause.
    V. Ask for what end the heav'nly bodies shine,
Earth for whose use,—Pride answers, " 'Tis for mine:
For me kind Nature wakes her genial power,
Suckles each herb, and spreads out every flower;
Annual for me the grape, the rose, renew
The juice nectareous and the balmy dew;
For me the mine a thousand treasures brings;
For me health gushes from a thousand springs;
Seas roll to waft me, suns to light me rise;
My footstool earth, my canopy the skies."
    But errs not Nature from this gracious end,
From burning suns when livid deaths descend,
When earthquakes swallow, or when tempests sweep
Towns to one grave, whole nations to the deep?
"No," 'tis replied, "the first Almighty Cause
Acts not by partial but by general laws;
Th' exceptions few; some change since all began;
And what created perfect?"—Why then man? 45
If the great end be human happiness,
Then Nature deviates; and can man do less?
As much that end a constant course requires
Of showers and sunshine, as of man's desires;
As much eternal springs and cloudless skies, 50

As men for ever temperate, calm, and wise.
If plagues or earthquakes break not Heaven's design,
Why then a Borgia or a Catiline?
5 Who knows but He, whose hand the lightning forms,
Who heaves old ocean, and who wings the storms;
Pours fierce ambition in a Caesar's mind,
10 Or turns young Ammon[3] loose to scourge mankind?
From pride, from pride, our very reasoning springs;
Account for moral as for natural things:
15 Why charge we Heaven in those, in these acquit?
In both, to reason right is to submit.
    Better for us, perhaps, it might appear,
Were there all harmony, all virtue here;
20 That never air or ocean felt the wind,
That never passion discomposed the mind:
But all subsists by elemental strife;
And passions are the elements of life.
The general order, since the whole began,
25 Is kept in Nature, and is kept in Man.
    VI. What would this Man? Now upward will he soar,
And little less than Angel, would be more;
Now looking downwards, just as grieved appears
30 To want the strength of bulls, the fur of bears.
Made for his use all creatures if he call,
Say what their use, had he the powers of all?
Nature to these without profusion kind,
35 The proper organs, proper powers assigned;
Each seeming want compensated of course,
Here with degrees of swiftness, there of force;
All in exact proportion to the state;
Nothing to add, and nothing to abate;
40 Each beast, each insect, happy in its own:
Is Heaven unkind to man, and man alone?
Shall he alone, whom rational we call,
Be pleased with nothing if not blessed with all?
    The bliss of man (could pride that blessing find)
Is not to act or think beyond mankind;
No powers of body or of soul to share,
But what his nature and his state can bear.
50 Why has not man a microscopic eye?

---

[2] delight.

[3] Alexander the Great.

For this plain reason, man is not a fly.
Say, what the use, were finer optics given,
To inspect a mite, not comprehend the
  Heaven?
Or touch, if tremblingly alive all o'er,
To smart and agonize at every pore?
Or quick effluvia darting thro' the brain,
Die of a rose in aromatic pain?
If Nature thundered in his opening ears,
And stunned him with the music of the
  spheres,
How would he wish that Heaven had left him
  still
The whispering zephyr and the purling rill?
Who finds not Providence all good and wise,
Alike in what it gives and what denies?
  VII. Far as creation's ample range extends,
The scale of sensual, mental powers ascends.
Mark how it mounts to man's imperial race
From the green myriads in the peopled grass:
What modes of sight betwixt each wide ex-
  treme,
The mole's dim curtain and the lynx's beam:
Of smell, the headlong lioness between
And hound sagacious on the tainted green:
Of hearing, from the life that fills the flood
To that which warbles thro' the vernal wood.
The spider's touch, how exquisitely fine,
Feels at each thread, and lives along the line:
In the nice bee what sense so subtly true,
From poisonous herbs extracts the healing
  dew!
How instinct varies in the grovelling swine,
Compared, half-reasoning elephant, with
  thine!
'Twixt that and reason what a nice barrier!
For ever separate, yet for ever near!
Remembrance and reflection how allied!
What thin partitions Sense from Thought
  divide!
And middle natures how they long to join,
Yet never pass th' insuperable line!
Without this just gradation could they be
Subjected these to those, or all to thee!
The powers of all subdued by thee alone,
Is not thy Reason all these powers in one?
  VIII. See thro' this air, this ocean, and this
  earth
All matter quick, and bursting into birth:
Above, how high progressive life may go!
Around, how wide! how deep extend below!
Vast chain of being! which from God began;

Natures ethereal, human, angel, man,
Beast, bird, fish, insect, what no eye can see,
No glass can reach; from infinite to thee;
From thee to nothing.—On superior powers
5 Were we to press, inferior might on ours;
Or in the full creation leave a void,
Where, one step broken, the great scale's de-
  stroyed:
From Nature's chain whatever link you like,
10 Tenth, or ten thousandth, breaks the chain
  alike.
  And if each system in gradation roll,
Alike essential to th' amazing Whole,
The least confusion but in one, not all
15 That system only, but the Whole must fall.
Let earth unbalanced from her orbit fly,
Planets and stars run lawless thro' the sky;
Let ruling angels from their spheres be hurled,
Being on being wrecked, and world on world;
20 Heaven's whole foundations to their centre
  nod,
And Nature tremble to the throne of God!
All this dread order break—for whom? for
  thee?
25 Vile worm!—O madness! pride! impiety!
  IX. What if the foot, ordained the dust to
  tread,
Or hand to toil, aspired to be the head?
What if the head, the eye, or ear repined
30 To serve mere engines to the ruling mind?
Just as absurd for any part to claim
To be another in this general frame;
Just as absurd to mourn the tasks or pains
The great directing Mind of All ordains.
35   All are but parts of one stupendous Whole,
Whose body Nature is, and God the soul;
That changed thro' all, and yet in all the
  same,
Great in the earth as in th' ethereal frame,
40 Warms in the sun, refreshes in the breeze,
Glows in the stars, and blossoms in the trees;
Lives thro' all life, extends thro' all extent,
Spreads undivided, operates unspent;
Breathes in our soul, informs our mortal part,
45 As full, as perfect, in a hair as heart;
As full, as perfect, in vile man that mourns,
As the rapt Seraph that adores and burns.
To him no high, no low, no great, no small;
He fills, he bounds, connects, and equals all!
50   X. Cease, then, nor Order imperfection
  name;
Our proper bliss depends on what we blame.

Know thy own point: this kind, this due de-
 gree
Of blindness, weakness, Heaven bestows on
 thee.
Submit: in this or any other sphere,
Secure to be as blessed as thou canst bear; 5
Safe in the hand of one disposing Power,
Or in the natal or the mortal hour.
All Nature is but Art unknown to thee;
All Chance, Direction, which thou canst not 10
 see;
All Discord, Harmony not understood;
All partial Evil, universal Good:
And spite of Pride, in erring Reason's spite,
One truth is clear, *Whatever is, is right.* 15

JAMES THOMSON

Thomson (1700–1748) was born in Scotland; his father was a minister, and the young Thomson was destined likewise for the clergy when he entered the University of Edinburgh. In 1725, however, he boldly went to London to seek his fortune as a poet. The Seasons was an early success. By its very length and its sub- ject, Nature, it was an unusual work. In spite of the production of five undistinguished tragedies over the next few years, Thomson showed definite signs of being tired of work; he coasted along, living on royalties and pen- sions arranged by influential friends. The Cas- tle of Indolence, an imitation of Spenser, was, however, an unusual final work. By his interest in Nature and use of blank verse and Spen- serian stanza (thus turning away from the pre- scribed couplet) Thomson was a pioneer in the new poetry which was one day to blossom forth under the banner of the Romantic Move- ment.

WINTER
(lines 1–321)

FROM *The Seasons*

The subject proposed. Address to the Earl of Wilmington. First approach of Winter. Ac- cording to the natural course of the season, various storms described. Rain. Wind. Snow. The driving of the snows: a man perishing among them; whence reflections on the wants and miseries of human life. The wolves de- scending from the Alps and Apennines. A win-

ter evening described; as spent by philoso- phers; by the country people; in the city. Frost. A view of Winter within the polar circle. A thaw. The whole concluding with moral re- flections on a future state.

See, Winter comes, to rule the varied year,
Sullen and sad, with all his rising train—
Vapors, and clouds, and storms. Be these
 my theme,
These, that exalt the soul to solemn thought,
And heavenly musing. Welcome, kindred
 glooms!
Congenial horrors, hail! with frequent foot,
Pleased have I, in my cheerful morn of life, 15
When nursed by careless solitude I lived,
And sung of Nature with unceasing joy,
Pleased have I wandered through your rough
 domain;
Trod the pure virgin-snows, myself as pure; 20
Heard the winds roar, and the big torrent
 burst;
Or seen the deep-fermenting tempest brewed,
In the grim evening-sky. Thus passed the
 time, 25
Till through the lucid chambers of the south
Looked out the joyous Spring, looked out,
 and smiled.
  To thee, the patron of this first essay,
The Muse, O Wilmington! renews her song. 30
Since has she rounded the revolving year:
Skimmed the gay Spring; on eagle-pinions
 borne,
Attempted through the Summer-blaze to rise;
Then swept o'er Autumn with the shadowy 35
 gale;
And now among the Wintry clouds again,
Rolled in the doubling storm, she tries to soar;
To swell her note with all the rushing winds;
To suit her sounding cadence to the floods; 40
As is her theme, her numbers wildly great:
Thrice happy, could she fill thy judging ear
With bold description, and with manly
 thought.
Nor art thou skilled in awful schemes alone, 45
And how to make a mighty people thrive;
But equal goodness, sound integrity,
A firm, unshaken, uncorrupted soul
Amid a sliding age, and burning strong,
Not vainly blazing, for thy country's weal, 50
A steady spirit, regularly free—
These, each exalting each, the statesman's light

Into the patriot; these, the public hope
And eye to thee converting, bid the Muse
Record what envy dares not flattery call.
   Now when the cheerless empire of the sky
To Capricorn the Centaur-Archer yields,
And fierce Aquarius stains the inverted year;
Hung o'er the farthest verge of heaven, the sun
Scarce spreads o'er ether the dejected day.
Faint are his gleams, and ineffectual shoot
His struggling rays, in horizontal lines,
Through the thick air; as clothed in cloudy
    storm,
Weak, wan, and broad, he skirts the southern
    sky;
And, soon descending, to the long dark night,
Wide-shading all, the prostrate world resigns.
Nor is the night unwished; while vital heat,
Light, life, and joy the dubious day forsake.
Meantime, in sable cincture, shadows vast,
Deep tinged and damp, and congregated
    clouds,
And all the vapory turbulence of heaven,
Involve the face of things. Thus Winter falls,
A heavy gloom oppressive o'er the world,
Through Nature shedding influence malign,
And rouses up the seeds of dark disease.
The soul of man dies in him, loathing life,
And black with more than melancholy views.
The cattle droop; and o'er the furrowed land,
Fresh from the plough, the dun discolored
    flocks,
Untended spreading, crop the wholesome root.
Along the woods, along the moorish fens,
Sighs the sad genius of the coming storm;
And up among the loose disjointed cliffs,
And fractured mountains wild, the brawling
    brook,
And cave, presageful, send a hollow moan,
Resounding long in listening fancy's ear.
   Then comes the father of the tempest forth,
Wrapt in black glooms. First, joyless rains
    obscure
Drive through the mingling skies with vapor
    foul,
Dash on the mountain's brow, and shake the
    woods,
That grumbling wave below. The unsightly
    plain
Lies a brown deluge; as the low-bent clouds
Pour flood on flood, yet unexhausted still
Combine, and deepening into night, shut up
The day's fair face. The wanderers of heaven,

Each to his home, retire; save those that love
To take their pastime in the troubled air,
Or skimming flutter round the dimply pool.
The cattle from the untasted fields return,
5 And ask, with meaning low, their wonted
    stalls,
Or ruminate in the contiguous shade.
Thither the household feathery people crowd,
The crested cock, with all his female train,
10 Pensive, and dripping; while the cottage-hind
Hangs o'er th' enlivening blaze, and taleful
    there
Recounts his simple frolic: much he talks,
And much he laughs, nor recks the storm
15   that blows
Without, and rattles on his humble roof.
   Wide o'er the brim, with many a torrent
    swelled,
And the mixed ruin of its banks o'erspread,
20 At last the roused-up river pours along:
Resistless, roaring, dreadful, down it comes,
From the rude mountain and the mossy wild,
Tumbling through rocks abrupt, and sounding
    far;
25 Then o'er the sanded valley floating spreads,
Calm, sluggish, silent; till again, constrained
Between two meeting hills, it bursts away,
Where rocks and woods o'erhang the turbid
    stream;
30 There gathering triple force, rapid and deep,
It boils, and wheels, and foams, and thunders
    through.
   Nature! great parent! whose unceasing hand
Rolls round the seasons of the changeful year,
35 How mighty, how majestic, are thy works!
With what a pleasing dread they swell the
    soul,
That sees astonished! and astonished sings!
Ye too, ye winds! that now begin to blow
40 With boisterous sweep, I raise my voice to you.
Where are your stores, ye powerful beings!
    say,
Where your aerial magazines reserved,
To swell the brooding terrors of the storm?
45 In what far-distant region of the sky,
Hushed in deep silence, sleep ye when 'tis
    calm?
   When from the pallid sky the Sun descends,
With many a spot, that o'er his glaring orb
50 Uncertain wanders, stained; red fiery streaks
Begin to flush around. The reeling clouds
Stagger with dizzy poise, as doubting yet

Which master to obey; while, rising slow,
Blank in the leaden-colored east, the moon
Wears a wan circle round her blunted horns.
Seen through the turbid, fluctuating air,
The stars obtuse emit a shivering ray;
Or frequent seem to shoot athwart the gloom,
And long behind them trail the whitening
    blaze.
Snatched in short eddies, plays the withered
    leaf;
And on the flood the dancing feather floats.
With broadened nostrils to the sky upturned,
The conscious heifer snuffs the stormy gale.
E'en as the matron, at her nightly task,
With pensive labor draws the flaxen thread,
The wasted taper and the crackling flame
Foretell the blast. But chief the plumy race,
The tenants of the sky, its changes speak.
Retiring from the downs, where all day long
They picked their scanty fare, a blackening
    train
Of clamorous rooks thick-urge their weary
    flight,
And seek the closing shelter of the grove;
Assiduous, in his bower, the wailing owl
Plies his sad song. The cormorant on high
Wheels from the deep, and screams along the
    land.
Loud shrieks the soaring hern; and with wild
    wing
The circling sea-fowl cleave the flaky clouds.
Ocean, unequal pressed, with broken tide
And blind commotion heaves; while from the
    shore,
Eat into caverns by the restless wave,
And forest-rustling mountains, comes a voice
That, solemn sounding, bids the world
    prepare.
Then issues forth the storm with sudden
    burst,
And hurls the whole precipitated air
Down in a torrent. On the passive main
Descends the ethereal force, and with strong
    gust
Turns from its bottom the discolored deep.
Through the black night that sits immense
    around,
Lashed into foam, the fierce conflicting brine
Seems o'er a thousand raging waves to burn:
Meantime the mountain-billows, to the clouds
In dreadful tumult swelled, surge above surge,
Burst into chaos with tremendous roar,

And anchored navies from their stations drive,
Wild as the winds, across the howling waste
Of mighty waters: now the inflated wave
Straining they scale, and now impetuous shoot
Into the secret chambers of the deep,
The wintry Baltic thundering o'er their head.
Emerging thence again, before the breath
Of full-exerted heaven they wing their course,
And dart on distant coasts—if some sharp
    rock,
Or shoal insidious, break not their career,
And in loose fragments fling them floating
    round.
  Nor less at hand the loosened tempest
    reigns:
The mountain thunders; and its sturdy sons
Stoop to the bottom of the rocks they shed.
Lone on the midnight steep, and all aghast,
The dark wayfaring stranger breathless toils,
And, often falling, climbs against the blast.
Low waves the rooted forest, vexed, and sheds
What of its tarnished honors yet remain—
Dashed down, and scattered by the tearing
    wind's
Assiduous fury, its gigantic limbs.
Thus struggling through the dissipated grove,
The whirling tempest raves along the plain;
And, on the cottage thatched, or lordly roof,
Keen-fastening, shakes them to the solid base.
Sleep frighted flies; and round the rocking
    dome,
For entrance eager, howls the savage blast.
Then too, they say, through all the burthened
    air,
Long groans are heard, shrill sounds, and
    distant sighs,
That uttered by the demon of the night,
Warned the devoted[1] wretch of woe and
    death.
  Huge uproar lords it wide. The clouds
    commixed
With stars swift-gliding, sweep along the sky.
All Nature reels: till Nature's King, who oft
Amid tempestuous darkness dwells along,
And on the wings of the careering wind
Walks dreadfully serene, commands a calm:
Then straight air, sea, and earth, are hushed at
    once.
  As yet 'tis midnight deep. The weary
    clouds,
Slow-meeting, mingle into solid gloom.

---
[1] doomed.

Now, while the drowsy world lies lost in
   sleep,
Let me associate with the serious Night,
And Contemplation, her sedate compeer;
Let me shake off the intrusive cares of day,
And lay the meddling senses all aside.
   Where now, ye lying vanities of life!
Ye ever-tempting, ever-cheating train!
Where are you now? and what is your amount?
Vexation, disappointment, and remorse.
Sad, sickening thought! And yet, deluded
   man,
A scene of crude disjointed visions past,
And broken slumbers, rises still resolved,
With new-flushed hopes, to run the giddy
   round.
   Father of light and life! thou Good
      Supreme!
O teach me what is good! teach me Thyself!
Save me from folly, vanity, and vice,
From every low pursuit; and feed my soul
With knowledge, conscious peace, and virtue
   pure—
Sacred, substantial, never-fading bliss!
   The keener tempests come: and fuming dun
From all the livid east, or piercing north,
Thick clouds ascend: in whose capacious
   womb
A vapory deluge lies, to snow congealed.
Heavy they roll their fleecy world along;
And the sky saddens with the gathered storm.
Through the hushed air the whitening shower
   descends,
At first thin-wavering; till at last the flakes
Fall broad and wide and fast, dimming the
   day,
With a continual flow. The cherished fields
Put on their winter-robe of purest white.
'Tis brightness all; save where the new snow
   melts
Along the mazy current. Low the woods
Bow their hoar head; and, ere the languid sun
Faint from the west emits his evening ray,
Earth's universal face, deep-hid, and chill,
Is one wild dazzling waste, that buries wide
The works of man. Drooping, the laborer-ox
Stands covered o'er with snow, and then
   demands
The fruit of all his toil. The fowls of heaven,
Tamed by the cruel season, crowd around
The winnowing store, and claim the little
   boon

Which Providence assigns them. One alone,
The redbreast, sacred to the household gods,
Wisely regardful of the embroiling sky,
In joyless fields, and thorny thickets, leaves
5 His shivering mates, and pays to trusted man
His annual visit. Half afraid, he first
Against the window beats; then brisk alights
On the warm hearth; then, hopping o'er the
   floor,
10 Eyes all the smiling family askance,
And pecks, and starts, and wonders where
   he is—
Till, more familiar grown, the table-crumbs
Attract his slender feet. The foodless wilds
15 Pour forth their brown inhabitants. The hare,
Though timorous of heart, and hard beset
By death in various forms, dark snares, and
   dogs,
And more unpitying men, the garden seeks,
20 Urged on by fearless want. The bleating kind
Eye the bleak heaven, and next the glistening
   earth,
With looks of dumb despair; then, sad
   dispersed,
25 Dig for the withered herb through heaps of
   snow.
   Now, shepherds, to your helpless charge be
      kind:
Baffle the raging year, and fill their pens
30 With food at will; lodge them below the
   storm,
And watch them strict; for from the bellowing
   east,
In this dire season, oft the whirlwind's wing
35 Sweeps up the burden of whole wintry plains
In one wide waft, and o'er the hapless flocks,
Hid in the hollow of two neighboring hills,
The billowy tempest whelms; till, upward
   urged,
40 The valley to a shining mountain swells,
Tipped with a wreath high-curling in the sky.
   As thus the snows arise, and, foul and
      fierce,
All Winter drives along the darkened air,
45 In his own loose-revolving fields, the swain
Disastered stands: sees other hills ascend,
Of unknown joyless brow; and other scenes,
Of horrid prospect, shag the trackless plain:
Nor finds the river nor the forest, hid
50 Beneath the formless wild: but wanders on
From hill to dale, still more and more astray—
Impatient flouncing through the drifted heaps,

Stung with the thoughts of home; the thoughts
    of home
Rush on his nerves, and call their vigor forth
In many a vain attempt. How sinks his soul!
What black despair, what horror fills his heart, 5
When, for the dusky spot which fancy feigned
His tufted cottage rising through the snow,
He meets the roughness of the middle waste,
Far from the track and blest abode of man;
While round him night resistless closes fast, 10
And every tempest, howling o'er his head,
Renders the savage wilderness more wild.
Then throng the busy shapes into his mind,
Of covered pits, unfathomably deep,
A dire descent! beyond the power of frost; 15
Of faithless bogs; of precipices huge,
Smoothed up with snow; and, what is land,
    unknown,
What water, of the still unfrozen spring,
In the loose marsh or solitary lake,
Where the fresh fountain from the bottom
    boils.
These check his fearful steps; and down he
    sinks
Beneath the shelter of the shapeless drift, 25
Thinking o'er all the bitterness of death,
Mixed with the tender anguish nature shoots
Through the wrung bosom of the dying man—
His wife, his children, and his friends unseen.
In vain for him the officious wife prepares 30
The fire fair-blazing, and the vestment warm;
In vain his little children, peeping out
Into the mingling storm, demand their sire,
With tears of artless innocence. Alas!
Nor wife, nor children, more shall he behold; 35
Nor friends, nor sacred home. On every
    nerve
The deadly Winter seizes, shuts up sense,
And, o'er his inmost vitals creeping cold,
Lays him along the snows, a stiffened corse! 40
Stretched out and bleaching in the northern
    blast . . . .

THOMAS GRAY

*When Gray (1716–1771) wrote odes to spring
or adversity he wrote like a classicist. When he
penned his famous* Elegy *he managed to introduce a note of personal curiosity and melancholy which was not wholly in the classical 50
pattern. When he wrote* The Bard *he created
a romantic scene which Scott could not have*

*done better. Thus Gray, for all his slender
sheaf, is interesting to study in the classroom
from a technical point of view. For the modern
reader, most of the human charm of this old
Etonian and Cantabrigian, professor and anti-
quarian, lies in his letters or in the* Journal. *A
student perplexed by the rush of twentieth-
century living might learn something from this
quiet scholar who once refused the laureateship; here was one man who had worked out a
personal answer to the problem of intelligent
living.*

ELEGY

WRITTEN IN A COUNTRY CHURCHYARD

The curfew tolls the knell of parting day,
    The lowing herd wind slowly o'er the lea,
The ploughman homeward plods his weary 20
    way,
    And leaves the world to darkness and to me.

Now fades the glimmering landscape on the
    sight, 25
    And all the air a solemn stillness holds,
Save where the beetle wheels his droning
    flight,
    And drowsy tinklings lull the distant folds;

Save that from yonder ivy-mantled tower,
    The moping owl does to the moon complain
Of such, as wandering near her secret bower,
    Molest her ancient solitary reign.

Beneath those rugged elms, that yew-tree's
    shade,
    Where heaves the turf in many a moldering
    heap,
Each in his narrow cell for ever laid, 40
    The rude forefathers of the hamlet sleep.

The breezy call of incense-breathing Morn,
    The swallow twittering from the straw- 45
    built shed,
The cock's shrill clarion, or the echoing horn,
    No more shall rouse them from their lowly
    bed.

For them no more the blazing hearth shall 50
    burn,
    Or busy housewife ply her evening care:

No children run to lisp their sire's return,
  Or climb his knees the the envied kiss to
    share.

Oft did the harvest to their sickle yield, 5
  Their furrow oft the stubborn glebe has
    broke;
How jocund did they drive their team afield!
  How bowed the woods beneath their sturdy
    stroke!

Let not Ambition mock their useful toil,
  Their homely joys, and destiny obscure;
Nor Grandeur hear with a disdainful smile,
  The short and simple annals of the poor. 15

The boast of heraldry, the pomp of power,
  And all that beauty, all that wealth e'er
    gave,
Awaits alike th' inevitable hour: 20
  The paths of glory lead but to the grave.

Nor you, ye proud, impute to these the fault,
  If Memory o'er their tomb no trophies raise,
Where thro' the long-drawn aisle and fretted 25
    vault
  The pealing anthem swells the note of
    praise.

Can storied urn or animated bust 30
  Back to its mansion call the fleeting breath?
Can Honor's voice provoke the silent dust,
  Or Flattery soothe the dull cold ear of
    Death?
35
Perhaps in this neglected spot is laid
  Some heart once pregnant with celestial
    fire;
Hands, that the rod of empire might have
    swayed, 40
  Or waked to extasy the living lyre.

But Knowledge to their eyes her ample page
  Rich with the spoils of time did ne'er un-
    roll; 45
Chill Penury repressed their noble rage,
  And froze the genial current of the soul.

Full many a gem of purest ray serene,
  The dark unfathomed caves of ocean bear: 50
Full many a flower is born to blush unseen,
  And waste its sweetness on the desert air.

Some village-Hampden,[1] that with dauntless
    breast
  The little tyrant of his fields withstood;
Some mute inglorious Milton here may rest,
  Some Cromwell, guiltless of his country's
    blood.

Th' applause of listening senates to command,
  The threats of pain and ruin to despise,
To scatter plenty o'er a smiling land,
  And read their history in a nation's eyes,

Their lot forbad: not circumscribed alone
  Their growing virtues, but their crimes con-
    fined;
Forbad to wade through slaughter to a throne,
  And shut the gates of mercy on mankind;

The struggling pangs of conscious truth to
    hide,
  To quench the blushes of ingenuous shame,
Or heap the shrine of Luxury and Pride
  With incense kindled at the Muse's flame.

Far from the madding crowd's ignoble strife,
  Their sober wishes never learned to stray;
Along the cool sequestered vale of life
  They•kept the noiseless tenor of their way.

Yet even these bones from insult to protect
  Some frail memorial still erected nigh,
With uncouth rhymes and shapeless sculpture
    decked,
  Implores the passing tribute of a sigh.

Their name, their years, spelt by th' unlettered
    muse,
  The place of fame and elegy supply:
And many a holy text around she strews,
  That teach the rustic moralist to die.

For who, to dumb Forgetfulness a prey,
  This pleasing anxious being e'er resigned.
Left the warm precincts of the cheerful day,
  Nor cast one longing lingering look behind?

On some fond breast the parting soul relies,
  Some pious drops the closing eye requires;
Even from the tomb the voice of Nature cries,
  Even in our ashes live their wonted fires.

[1] John Hampden (1594–1643), patriot who opposed unjust taxes.

[251]

For thee, who, mindful of th' unhonored dead,
   Dost in these lines their artless tale relate;
If chance, by lonely contemplation led,
   Some kindred spirit shall inquire thy fate,— 5

Haply some hoary-headed swain may say,
   "Oft have we seen him at the peep of dawn
Brushing with hasty steps the dews away
   To meet the sun upon the upland lawn.

"There at the foot of yonder nodding beech 10
   That wreathes its old fantastic roots so high,
His listless length at noontide would he
      stretch,
   And pore upon the brook that babbles by. 15

"Hard by yon wood, now smiling as in scorn,
   Muttering his wayward fancies he would
      rove;
Now drooping, woeful wan, like one forlorn, 20
   Or crazed with care, or crossed in hopeless
      love.

"One morn I missed him on the customed hill,
   Along the heath and near his favorite tree; 25
Another came; nor yet beside the rill,
   Nor up the lawn, nor at the wood was he;

"The next, with dirges due in sad array
   Slow thro' the church-way path we saw him 30
      borne;—
Approach and read (for thou can'st read) the
      lay,
   Graved on the stone beneath yon aged
      thorn."

THE EPITAPH

Here rests his head upon the lap of Earth,
   A Youth, to Fortune and to Fame unknown:
Fair Science frowned not on his humble birth, 40
   And Melancholy marked him for her own.

Large was his bounty, and his soul sincere,
   Heaven did a recompence as largely send:
He gave to Misery all he had, a tear, 45
   He gained from Heaven ('twas all he
      wished) a friend.

No farther seek his merits to disclose,
   Or draw his frailties from their dread abode, 50
(There they alike in trembling hope repose,)
   The bosom of his Father and his God.

THE BARD

A PINDARIC ODE[1]

I. 1

"Ruin seize thee, ruthless King!
Confusion on thy banners wait,
Tho' fanned by conquest's crimson wing
They mock the air with idle state.
Helm, nor hauberk's twisted mail,
Nor e'en thy virtues, Tyrant, shall avail
To save thy secret soul from nightly fears,
From Cambria's[2] curse, from Cambria's tears!"
Such were the sounds that o'er the crested
   pride
   Of the first Edward scattered wild dismay,
As down the steep of Snowdon's shaggy side
He wound with toilsome march his long array.
Stout Glos'ter stood aghast in speechless
   trance:
To arms! cried Mortimer, and couched his
   quivering lance.

I. 2

On a rock, whose haughty brow
Frowns o'er old Conway's foaming flood,
Robed in the sable garb of woe,
With haggard eyes the Poet stood;
(Loose his beard, and hoary hair
Streamed, like a meteor, to the troubled air)
And with a master's hand, and prophet's fire,
Struck the deep sorrows of his lyre.
"Hark, how each giant-oak, and desert cave,
Sighs to the torrent's awful voice beneath!
O'er thee, oh King! their hundred arms they
   wave,
Revenge on thee in hoarser murmurs breathe;
Vocal no more, since Cambria's fatal day,
To high-born Hoel's harp, or soft Llewellyn's
   lay.

I. 3

"Cold is Cadwallo's tongue,
That hushed the stormy main:
Brave Urien sleeps upon his craggy bed;
Mountains, ye mourn in vain
Modred, whose magic song

---

[1] Gray based this ode on a tradition that Edward I, after conquering Wales, ordered all bards to be killed.
[2] Wales.

Made huge Plinlimmon[3] bow his cloud-topped
    head.
On dreary Arvon's shore they lie,
Smeared with gore, and ghastly pale:
Far, far aloof th' affrighted ravens sail;
The famished eagle screams, and passes by.
Dear lost companions of my tuneful art,
Dear, as the light that visits these sad eyes,
Dear, as the ruddy drops that warm my heart,
Ye died amidst your dying country's cries—   10
No more I weep. They do not sleep.
On yonder cliffs, a grisly band,
I see them sit, they linger yet,
Avengers of their native land:
With me in dreadful harmony they join,   15
And weave with bloody hands the tissue of
    thy line.

II. 1

"Weave the warp, and weave the woof,   20
The winding-sheet of Edward's race.
Give ample room, and verge enough
The characters of hell to trace.
Mark the year, and mark the night,
When Severn shall re-echo with affright
The shrieks of death, thro' Berkley's roof that
    ring,
Shrieks of an agonizing King![4]
She-wolf of France, with unrelenting fangs,[5]
That tear'st the bowels of thy mangled mate,   30
From thee be born, who o'er thy country
    hangs,
The scourge of Heaven. What terrors round
    him wait!
Amazement in his van, with Flight combined,   35
And Sorrow's faded form, and Solitude be-
    hind.

II. 2

"Mighty Victor, mighty Lord,
Low on his funeral couch he lies!
No pitying heart, no eye, afford
A tear to grace his obsequies.
Is the sable Warrior fled?[6]
Thy son is gone. He rests among the dead.
The swarm that in thy noon-tide beam were
    born?

Gone to salute the rising morn.
Fair laughs the morn, and soft the zephyr
    blows,
While proudly riding o'er the azure realm
In gallant trim the gilded vessel goes;   5
Youth on the prow, and Pleasure at the helm;
Regardless of the sweeping whirlwind's sway,
That, hushed in grim repose, expects his eve-
    ning prey.

II. 3

"Fill high the sparkling bowl,
The rich repast prepare,
Reft of a crown, he yet may share the feast:
Close by the regal chair   15
Fell Thirst and Famine scowl
A baleful smile upon their baffled guest.
Heard ye the din of battle bray,
Lance to lance, and horse to horse?
Long years of havoc urge their destined   20
    course,
And thro' the kindred squadrons mow their
    way.
Ye towers of Julius, London's lasting shame,
With many a foul and midnight murder fed,   25
Revere his consort's[7] faith, his father's[8] fame,
And spare the meek usurper's holy head.[9]
Above, below, the rose of snow,
Twined with her blushing foe, we spread:
The bristled boar in infant gore   30
Wallows beneath the thorny shade.
Now, brothers, bending o'er th' accursèd loom,
Stamp we our vengeance deep, and ratify his
    doom.

III. 1

"Edward, lo! to sudden fate
(Weave we the woof. The thread is spun.)
Half of thy heart we consecrate.
(The web is wove. The work is done.)"   40
"Stay, oh stay! nor thus forlorn
Leave me unblessed, unpitied, here to mourn:
In yon bright track, that fires the western skies,
They melt, they vanish from my eyes.
But oh! what solemn scenes on Snowdon's   45
    height
Descending slow their glittering skirts unroll?
Visions of glory, spare my aching sight,

---

[3] mountain in Wales.   [4] Edward II.
[5] Isabella, wife of Edward II, an adulteress and
plotter.
[6] the Black Prince.

[7] Margaret of Anjou.
[8] Henry V.
[9] Henry VI.

Ye unborn ages, crowd not on my soul!
No more our long-lost Arthur we bewail.
All hail, ye genuine Kings, Britannia's issue,
    hail.

III. 2

"Girt with many a Baron bold
Sublime their starry fronts they rear;
And gorgeous dames, and statesmen old
In bearded majesty, appear.
In the midst a form divine!
Her eye proclaims her of the Briton-line;
Her lion-port, her awe-commanding face.
Attempered sweet to virgin-grace.
What strings symphonious tremble in the air,
What strains of vocal transport round her play!
Hear from the grave, great Taliessin,[10] hear;
They breathe a soul to animate thy clay.
Bright Rapture calls, and soaring, as she sings,
Waves in the eye of Heaven her many-colored
    wings.

III. 3

"The verse adorn again
Fierce War, and faithful Love,
And Truth severe, by fairy fiction drest.[11]
In buskined measures move[12]
Pale Grief, and pleasing Pain,
With Horror, tyrant of the throbbing breast.
A voice as of the cherub-choir,[13]
Gales from blooming Eden bear;
And distant warblings lessen on my ear,
That lost in long futurity expire.
Fond impious Man, think'st thou yon sanguine
    cloud,
Raised by thy breath, has quenched the orb of
    day?
To-morrow he repairs the golden flood,
And warms the nations with redoubled ray.
Enough for me: with joy I see
The different doom our fates assign.
Be thine Despair, and sceptered Care,
To triumph, and to die, are mine."
He spoke, and headlong from the mountain's
    height
Deep in the roaring tide he plunged to endless
    night.

---

[10] famous sixth-century bard.
[11] Spenser.
[12] Shakespeare.
[13] Milton.

WILLIAM COLLINS

Collins (1721–1759) continues to appear in collections of poetry partly because a faithful, though small, group of adherents keeps his name alive; and partly because his small volume of work is so typical of the best and worst of eighteenth-century neo-classicism that it offers excellent material for comparative reading and discussion. Let the student compare an ode by Collins with one by Wordsworth or Keats, for example, to see how various authors treat a recognized form. We do not know much about this poet. He had a small output and a short life. He did hack work. He was mad at one time. He knew respectable poverty. And yet somehow he managed to chisel out a classical ode in professional manner, with knowledge, intelligence, and decorum. Now and then, without knowing it, he handled patriotic or supernatural themes with just a touch of the romanticism that lurked around the distant turn of the century.

ODE TO EVENING

If aught of oaten stop,[1] or pastoral song,
May hope, chaste Eve, to soothe thy modest
    ear,
    Like thy own solemn springs,
    Thy springs, and dying gales;

O nymph reserved, while now the bright-
    haired sun
Sits in yon western tent, whose cloudy skirts,
    With brede[2] ethereal wove,
    O'erhang his wavy bed:

Now air is hushed, save where the weak-eyed
    bat,
With short shrill shriek, flits by on leathern
    wing;
    Or where the beetle winds
    His small but sullen horn,

As oft he rises 'midst the twilight path,
Against the pilgrim borne in heedless hum:
    Now teach me, maid composed,
    To breathe some softened strain,

---

[1] anything played on a shepherd's pipe.
[2] embroidery.

Whose numbers, stealing through thy darken-
 ing vale,
May not unseemly with its stillness suit;
  As, musing slow, I hail
  Thy genial loved return!   5

For when thy folding-star arising shows
His paly circlet, at his warning lamp
  The fragrant Hours, and elves
  Who slept in flowers the day,   10

And many a nymph who wreathes her brows
 with sedge,
And sheds the freshening dew, and, lovelier
 still,   15
  The pensive Pleasures sweet,
  Prepare thy shadowy car.

Then lead, calm votaress, where some sheety
 lake   20
Cheers the lone heath, or some time-hallowed
 pile,
  Or upland fallows grey,
  Reflect its last cool gleam.

But when chill blustering winds, or driving 25
 rain,
Forbid my willing feet, be mine the hut,
  That from the mountain's side,
  Views wilds, and swelling floods, 30

And hamlets brown, and dim-discovered
 spires,
And hears their simple bell, and marks o'er all
  Thy dewy fingers draw
  The gradual dusky veil.   35

While Spring shall pour his showers, as oft he
 wont,
And bathe thy breathing tresses, meekest Eve!
  While Summer loves to sport 40
  Beneath thy lingering light;

While sallow Autumn fills thy lap with leaves;
Or Winter, yelling through the troublous air,
  Affrights thy shrinking train, 45
  And rudely rends thy robes;

So long, sure-found beneath the sylvan shed,
Shall Fancy, Friendship, Science, rose-lipped
 Health,   50
  Thy gentlest influence own,
  And hymn thy favorite name!

ODE

WRITTEN IN THE BEGINNING OF THE
YEAR 1746

How sleep the brave, who sink to rest,
By all their country's wishes blest!
When Spring, with dewy fingers cold,
Returns to deck their hallowed mold,
She there shall dress a sweeter sod
Than Fancy's feet have ever trod.

By fairy hands their knell is rung;
By forms unseen their dirge is sung;
There Honor comes, a pilgrim gray,
To bless the turf that wraps their clay;
And Freedom shall a while repair,
To dwell a weeping hermit there!

OLIVER GOLDSMITH

Boswell relates that Goldsmith (1728–1774) tried too hard to "shine," but the epitaph on his monument in Westminster Abbey says that he touched nothing which he did not adorn. He seems to have been a bundle of opposing traits; he died before he could integrate them on a grand scale. Goldsmith's early life was marked by failure at college in his native Ireland, vagabonding on the Continent (where he presumably picked up a medical degree), starving in London as a doctor, ruining himself at hack writing, and so on. Dr. Johnson befriended Goldsmith, who was a charter member of "The Club." His later successes included a novel, The Vicar of Wakefield, *a play,* She Stoops to Conquer, *and many sketches, essays (see II, 52), and poems. "The Deserted Village" (see below) may not be the best piece Goldsmith ever wrote, but it is a minor classic in the century, along with Gray's "Elegy" and Burns's "Cotter." The curious student who likes to study variations on a theme might look up George Crabbe's "The Village" for contrast.*

THE DESERTED VILLAGE

Sweet Auburn! loveliest village of the plain,
Where health and plenty cheered the laboring
 swain,
Where smiling spring its earliest visit paid, 50
And parting summer's lingering blooms de-
 layed:

Dear lovely bowers of innocence and ease,
Seats of my youth, when every sport could please;
How often have I loitered o'er thy green,
Where humble happiness endeared each 5 scene!
How often have I paused on every charm,
The sheltered cot, the cultivated farm,
The never failing brook, the busy mill,
The decent church that topt the neighboring 10 hill,
The hawthorn bush, with seats beneath the shade,
For talking age and whispering lovers made!
How often have I blest the coming day, 15
When toil remitting lent its turn to play,
And all the village train, from labor free,
Led up their sports beneath the spreading tree;
While many a pastime circled in the shade,
The young contending as the old surveyed; 20
And many a gambol frolicked o'er the ground,
And sleights of art and feats of strength went round.
And still, as each repeated pleasure tired, 25
Succeeding sports the mirthful band inspired;
The dancing pair that simply sought renown,
By holding out to tire each other down;
The swain, mistrustless of his smutted face,
While secret laughter tittered round the place; 30
The bashful virgin's sidelong looks of love,
The matron's glance that would those looks reprove.
These were thy charms, sweet village! sports like these,
With sweet succession taught even toil to 35 please;
These round thy bowers their cheerful influence shed,
These were thy charms—but all these charms 40 are fled.
  Sweet smiling village, loveliest of the lawn,
Thy sports are fled, and all thy charms withdrawn;
Amidst thy bowers the tyrant's hand is seen, 45
And desolation saddens all thy green:
One only master grasps the whole domain,
And half a tillage stints thy smiling plain;
No more thy glassy brook reflects the day,
But choked with sedges works its weedy way; 50
Along thy glades, a solitary guest,
The hollow-sounding bittern guards its nest;

Amidst thy desert walks the lapwing flies,
And tires their echoes with unvaried cries.
Sunk are thy bowers in shapeless ruin all,
And the long grass o'ertops the mouldering wall;
And, trembling, shrinking from the spoiler's hand,
Far, far away thy children leave the land.
  Ill fares the land, to hastening ills a prey,
Where wealth accumulates, and men decay;
Princes and lords may flourish, or may fade;
A breath can make them, as a breath has made:
But a bold peasantry, their country's pride,
When once destroyed, can never be supplied.
  A time there was, ere England's griefs began,
When every rood of ground maintained its man;
For him light labor spread her wholesome store,
Just gave what life required, but gave no more:
His best companions, innocence and health,
And his best riches, ignorance of wealth.
  But times are altered; trade's unfeeling train
Usurp the land, and dispossess the swain;
Along the lawn, where scattered hamlets rose,
Unwieldy wealth, and cumbrous pomp repose;
And every want to opulence allied,
And every pang that folly pays to pride.
Those gentle hours that plenty bade to bloom,
Those calm desires that asked but little room,
Those healthful sports that graced the peaceful scene,
Lived in each look, and brightened all the green;
These, far departing, seek a kinder shore,
And rural mirth and manners are no more.
  Sweet Auburn! parent of the blissful hour,
Thy glades forlorn confess the tyrant's power.
Here, as I take my solitary rounds,
Amidst thy tangling walks and ruined grounds,
And, many a year elapsed, return to view
Where once the cottage stood, the hawthorn grew,
Remembrance wakes with all her busy train,
Swells at my breast, and turns the past to pain.
  In all my wanderings round this world of care,

In all my griefs—and God has given my
    share—
I still had hopes, my latest hours to crown,
Amidst these humble bowers to lay me down;
To husband out life's taper at the close,
And keep the flame from wasting by repose: 5
I still had hopes, for pride attends us still,
Amidst the swains to show my book-learned
    skill,
Around my fire an evening group to draw, 10
And tell of all I felt, and all I saw;
And as a hare, whom hounds and horns pur-
    sue,
Pants to the place from whence at first she
    flew,
I still had hopes, my long vexations past, 15
Here to return—and die at home at last.
    O blest retirement, friend to life's decline,
Retreats from care, that never must be mine,
How happy he who crowns, in shades like 20
    these,
A youth of labor with an age of ease;
Who quits a world where strong temptations
    try,
And, since 'tis hard to combat, learns to fly! 25
For him no wretches, born to work and weep,
Explore the mine, or tempt the dangerous
    deep;
No surly porter stands, in guilty state,
To spurn imploring famine from the gate; 30
But on he moves to meet his latter end,
Angels around befriending Virtue's friend;
Sinks to the grave with unperceived decay,
While Resignation gently slopes the way;
And, all his prospects brightening to the last, 35
His Heaven commences ere the world be past.
    Sweet was the sound, when oft at evening's
    close
Up yonder hill the village murmur rose;
There, as I past with careless steps and slow, 40
The mingling notes came softened from be-
    low;
The swain responsive as the milkmaid sung,
The sober herd that lowed to meet their
    young; 45
The noisy geese that gabbled o'er the pool,
The playful children just let loose from school,
The watch-dog's voice that bayed the whisper-
    ing wind,
And the loud laugh that spoke the vacant 50
    mind;
These all in sweet confusion sought the shade,

And filled each pause the nightingale had
    made.
But now the sounds of population fail,
No cheerful murmurs fluctuate in the gale,
No busy steps the grass-grown footway tread,
But all the bloomy flush of life is fled;
All but yon widowed solitary thing,
That feebly bends beside the plashy spring;
She, wretched matron, forced, in age, for
    bread,
To strip the brook with mantling cresses
    spread,
To pick her wintry faggot from the thorn,
To seek her nightly shed, and weep till morn;
She only left of all the harmless train,
The sad historian of the pensive plain.
    Near yonder copse, where once the garden
    smiled,
And still where many a garden flower grows
    wild,
There, where a few torn shrubs the place dis-
    close,
The village preacher's modest mansion rose.
A man he was to all the country dear,
And passing rich with forty pounds a year;
Remote from towns he ran his godly race,
Nor e'er had changed, nor wished to change
    his place;
Unpractised he to fawn, or seek for power,
By doctrines fashioned to the varying hour;
For other aims his heart had learned to prize,
More skilled to raise the wretched than to
    rise.
His house was known to all the vagrant train,
He chid their wanderings, but relieved their
    pain;
The long remembered beggar was his guest,
Whose beard descending swept his aged
    breast;
The ruined spendthrift, now no longer proud,
Claimed kindred there, and had his claims al-
    lowed;
The broken soldier, kindly bade to stay,
Sat by his fire, and talked the night away;
Wept o'er his wounds, or, tales of sorrow done,
Shouldered his crutch, and shewed how fields
    were won.
Pleased with his guests, the good man learned
    to glow,
And quite forgot their vices in their woe;
Careless their merits or their faults to scan,
His pity gave ere charity began.

Thus to relieve the wretched was his pride,
And e'en his failings leaned to Virtue's side;
But in his duty prompt, at every call,
He watched and wept, he prayed and felt for
    all:
And, as a bird each fond endearment tries, 5
To tempt its new-fledged offspring to the skies,
He tried each art, reproved each dull delay,
Allured to brighter worlds, and led the way.
    Beside the bed where parting life was laid, 10
And sorrow, guilt, and pain, by turns dis-
    mayed,
The reverend champion stood. At his control
Despair and anguish fled the struggling soul;
Comfort came down the trembling wretch to 15
    raise,
And his last faltering accents whispered praise.
    At church, with meek and unaffected grace,
His looks adorned the venerable place;
Truth from his lips prevailed with double 20
    sway,
And fools, who came to scoff, remained to
    pray.
The service past, around the pious man,
With steady zeal, each honest rustic ran: 25
E'en children followed, with endearing wile,
And plucked his gown, to share the good man's
    smile.
His ready smile a parent's warmth exprest,
Their welfare pleased him, and their cares dis- 30
    trest;
To them his heart, his love, his griefs were
    given,
But all his serious thoughts had rest in heaven.
As some tall cliff, that lifts its awful form, 35
Swells from the vale, and midway leaves the
    storm,
Though round its breast the rolling clouds are
    spread,
Eternal sunshine settles on its head. 40
    Beside yon straggling fence that skirts the
    way
With blossomed furze, unprofitably gay,
There, in his noisy mansion, skilled to rule,
The village master taught his little school: 45
A man severe he was, and stern to view,
I knew him well, and every truant knew;
Well had the boding tremblers learned to trace
The day's disasters in his morning face;
Full well they laughed with counterfeited glee 50
At all his jokes, for many a joke had he;
Full well the busy whisper, circling round,

Conveyed the dismal tidings when he frowned;
Yet he was kind, or if severe in aught,
The love he bore to learning was in fault;
The village all declared how much he knew,
'Twas certain he could write, and cipher too;
Lands he could measure, terms and tides
    presage,
And even the story ran that he could gauge:
In arguing too, the parson owned his skill,
For even though vanquished, he could argue
    still;
While words of learned length and thundering
    sound
Amazed the gazing rustics ranged around;
And still they gazed, and still the wonder grew
That one small head could carry all he knew.
    But past is all his fame. The very spot,
Where many a time he triumphed, is forgot.
Near yonder thorn, that lifts its head on high,
Where once the sign-post caught the passing
    eye,
Low lies that house where nut-brown draughts
    inspired,
Where gray-beard mirth and smiling toil re-
    tired,
Where village statesmen talked with looks pro-
    found,
And news much older than their ale went
    round.
Imagination fondly stoops to trace
The parlor splendors of that festive place;
The whitewashed wall, the nicely sanded floor,
The varnished clock that clicked behind the
    door:
The chest contrived a double debt to pay,
A bed by night, a chest of drawers by day;
The pictures placed for ornament and use,
The twelve good rules, the royal game of
    goose;
The hearth, except when winter chilled the
    day,
With aspen boughs, and flowers, and fennel
    gay;
While broken teacups, wisely kept for show,
Ranged o'er the chimney, glistened in a row.
    Vain transitory splendors! could not all
Reprieve the tottering mansion from its fall?
Obscure it sinks, nor shall it more impart
An hour's importance to the poor man's heart;
Thither no more the peasant shall repair
To sweet oblivion of his daily care;
No more the farmer's news, the barber's tale,

No more the woodman's ballad shall prevail;
No more the smith his dusky brow shall clear,
Relax his ponderous strength, and lean to hear;
The host himself no longer shall be found
Careful to see the mantling bliss go round; 5
Nor the coy maid, half willing to be prest,
Shall kiss the cup to pass it to the rest.

Yes! let the rich deride, the proud disdain,
These simple blessings of the lowly train;
To me more dear, congenial to my heart, 10
One native charm, than all the gloss of art;
Spontaneous joys, where Nature has its play,
The soul adopts, and owns their first-born
sway;
Lightly they frolic o'er the vacant mind, 15
Unenvied, unmolested, unconfined.
But the long pomp, the midnight masquerade,
With all the freaks of wanton wealth arrayed,
In these, ere triflers half their wish obtain,
The toiling pleasure sickens into pain; 20
And, even while fashion's brightest arts decoy,
The heart distrusting asks, if this be joy?

Ye friends to truth, ye statesmen, who sur-
vey
The rich man's joys increase, the poor's decay, 25
'Tis yours to judge how wide the limits stand
Between a splendid and a happy land.
Proud swells the tide with loads of freighted
ore,
And shouting Folly hails them from her shore; 30
Hoards e'en beyond the miser's wish abound,
And rich men flock from all the world around.
Yet count our gains. This wealth is but a name,
That leaves our useful products still the same.
Not so the loss. The man of wealth and pride 35
Takes up a space that many poor supplied;
Space for his lake, his park's extended bounds,
Space for his horses, equipage, and hounds;
The robe that wraps his limbs in silken sloth
Has robbed the neighboring fields of half their 40
growth;
His seat, where solitary sports are seen,
Indignant spurns the cottage from the green,
Around the world each needful product flies,
For all the luxuries the world supplies; 45
While thus the land, adorned for pleasure all,
In barren splendor feebly waits the fall.

As some fair female, unadorned and plain,
Secure to please while youth confirms her
reign, 50
Slights every borrowed charm that dress supplies,

Nor shares with art the triumph of her eyes;
But when those charms are past, for charms
are frail,
When time advances, and when lovers fail,
She then shines forth, solicitous to bless,
In all the glaring impotence of dress:
Thus fares the land, by luxury betrayed,
In nature's simplest charms at first arrayed:
But verging to decline, its splendors rise,
Its vistas strike, its palaces surprise;
While, scourged by famine, from the smiling
land,
The mournful peasant leads his humble band;
And while he sinks, without one arm to save,
The country blooms—a garden and a grave. 15

Where then, ah! where shall poverty reside,
To 'scape the pressure of contiguous pride?
If to some common's fenceless limits strayed,
He drives his flock to pick the scanty blade,
Those fenceless fields the sons of wealth di- 20
vide,
And even the bare-worn common is denied.

If to the city sped—What waits him there?
To see profusion that he must not share;
To see ten thousand baneful arts combined 25
To pamper luxury, and thin mankind:
To see those joys the sons of pleasure know,
Extorted from his fellow-creatures' woe.
Here, while the courtier glitters in brocade,
There the pale artist plies the sickly trade; 30
Here, while the proud their long-drawn pomp
display,
There the black gibbet glooms beside the way;
The dome where Pleasure holds her midnight
reign,
Here, richly decked, admits the gorgeous train; 35
Tumultuous grandeur crowds the blazing
square,
The rattling chariots clash, the torches glare.
Sure scenes like these no troubles e'er annoy! 40
Sure these denote one universal joy!
Are these thy serious thoughts?—Ah, turn
thine eyes
Where the poor houseless shivering female
lies:
She once, perhaps, in village plenty blest,
Has wept at tales of innocence distrest;
Her modest looks the cottage might adorn,
Sweet as the primrose peeps beneath the
thorn; 50
Now lost to all; her friends, her virtue fled,
Near her betrayer's door she lays her head,

And, pinched with cold, and shrinking from
  the shower,
With heavy heart, deplores that luckless hour,
When idly first, ambitious of the town,
She left her wheel and robes of country brown. 5
  Do thine, sweet Auburn, thine, the loveliest
    train,
Do thy fair tribes participate her pain?
Even now, perhaps, by cold and hunger led,
At proud men's doors they ask a little bread! 10
  Ah, no. To distant climes, a dreary scene,
Where half the convex world intrudes be-
  tween,
Through torrid tracts with fainting steps they
  go, 15
Where wild Altama[1] murmurs to their woe.
Far different there from all that charmed be-
  fore,
The various terrors of that horrid shore;
Those blazing suns that dart a downward ray, 20
And fiercely shed intolerable day;
Those matted woods where birds forget to
  sing,
But silent bats in drowsy clusters cling;
Those poisonous fields with rank luxuriance 25
  crowned,
Where the dark scorpion gathers death
  around:
Where at each step the stranger fears to wake
The rattling terrors of the vengeful snake; 30
Where crouching tigers wait their hapless
  prey,
And savage men more murderous still than
  they:
While oft in whirls the mad tornado flies, 35
Mingling the ravaged landscape with the skies.
Far different these from every former scene,
The cooling brook, the grassy vested green,
The breezy covert of the warbling grove,
That only sheltered thefts of harmless love. 40
  Good Heaven! what sorrows gloomed that
    parting day,
That called them from their native walks
  away;
When the poor exiles, every pleasure past, 45
Hung round the bowers, and fondly looked
  their last,
And took a long farewell, and wished in vain
For seats like these beyond the western main;
And, shuddering still to face the distant deep, 50

[1] river in Georgia.

Returned and wept, and still returned to weep.
The good old sire the first prepared to go,
To new-found worlds, and wept for others'
  woe;
But for himself, in conscious virtue brave,
He only wished for worlds beyond the grave.
His lovely daughter, lovelier in her tears,
The fond companion of his helpless years,
Silent went next, neglectful of her charms,
And left a lover's for a father's arms.
With louder plaints the mother spoke her
  woes,
And blest the cot where every pleasure rose;
And kissed her thoughtless babes with many
  a tear,
And clasped them close, in sorrow doubly
  dear;
Whilst her fond husband strove to lend relief
In all the silent manliness of grief.
  O Luxury! thou curst by Heaven's decree,
How ill exchanged are things like these for
  thee!
How do thy potions, with insidious joy,
Diffuse their pleasures only to destroy!
Kingdoms by thee, to sickly greatness grown,
Boast of a florid vigor not their own:
At every draught more large and large they
  grow,
A bloated mass of rank unwieldy woe;
Till sapped their strength, and every part un-
  sound,
Down, down they sink, and spread a ruin
  round.
  Even now the devastation is begun,
And half the business of destruction done;
Even now, methinks, as pondering here I
  stand,
I see the rural Virtues leave the land.
Down where yon anchoring vessel spreads the
  sail,
That idly waiting flaps with every gale,
Downward they move, a melancholy band,
Pass from the shore, and darken all the strand.
Contented toil, and hospitable care,
And kind connubial tenderness are there;
And piety with wishes placed above,
And steady loyalty, and faithful love.
And thou, sweet Poetry, thou loveliest maid,
Still first to fly where sensual joys invade;
Unfit in these degenerate times of shame,
To catch the heart, or strike for honest fame;
Dear charming nymph, neglected and decried,

My shame in crowds, my solitary pride;
Thou source of all my bliss, and all my woe,
That found'st me poor at first, and keep'st me
    so;
Thou guide, by which the nobler arts excel,   5
Thou nurse of every virtue, fare thee well;
Farewell! and O! where'er thy voice be tried,
On Torno's cliffs,[2] or Pambamarca's[3] side,
Whether where equinoctial fervors glow,
Or winter wraps the polar world in snow,   10
Still let thy voice, prevailing over time,
Redress the rigors of the inclement clime;
Aid slighted truth with thy persuasive strain;
Teach erring man to spurn the rage of gain;
Teach him, that states of native strength   15
    possest,
Though very poor, may still be very blest;
That trade's proud empire hastes to swift de-
    cay,
As ocean sweeps the labored mole away;   20
While self-dependent power can time defy,
As rocks resist the billows and the sky.

WILLIAM BLAKE

*If Blake (1757–1827) had had larger circu-
lation (by commercial processes instead of random handing-around of hand-made books), he
might have been the first name in the Romantic Movement, for he wrote "romantically" fif- 30
teen years before Wordsworth's pronounce-
ments to the world. Blake, like Morris later,
was a craftsman, a virtuoso—he wrote, illustrated, engraved, colored. A mystic whose
longer pieces often defy explanation, at least 35
for most of us, Blake indicated his course
when, at the age of four, he "saw God through
a window." Nevertheless, in the shorter pieces,
the poet is anything but obscure; musically,
simply, but always with an other-worldly 40
touch, he sings the songs of innocence and experience, pitying poor chimney-sweepers, extending a hand to the Negro, limning the
beauties of external Nature, the creation of
God. This was a new touch in eighteenth-cen- 45
tury England—odes to evening or flat photographs of country scenes were pale things beside Blake's color and imagery; the "spontaneous overflow of powerful feeling" began right
here; the record, however, will say 1798 or 50*

[2] in Sweden.   [3] in Ecuador.

*1802, for convenience, because those dates ap-
peared on well-publicized volumes of the* Lyrical Ballads.

FROM *Songs of Innocence*

INTRODUCTION

Piping down the valleys wild,
    Piping songs of pleasant glee,
On a cloud I saw a child,
    And he laughing said to me:

"Pipe a song about a Lamb!"
    So I piped with merry cheer.
"Piper, pipe that song again;"
    So I piped: he wept to hear.

"Drop thy pipe, thy happy pipe;
    Sing thy songs of happy cheer!"
So I sang the same again,
    While he wept with joy to hear.

"Piper, sit thee down and write
    In a book, that all may read."
So he vanished from my sight,
    And I plucked a hollow reed,

And I made a rural pen,
    And I stained the water clear,
And I wrote my happy songs
    Every child may joy to hear.

THE LAMB

Little Lamb, who made thee?
    Dost thou know who made thee?
Gave thee life, and bid thee feed,
By the stream and o'er the mead;
Gave thee clothing of delight,
Softest clothing, woolly, bright;
Gave thee such a tender voice,
Making all the vales rejoice?
    Little Lamb, who made thee?
    Dost thou know who made thee?

    Little Lamb, I'll tell thee,
    Little Lamb, I'll tell thee:
He is callèd by thy name,
For He calls Himself a Lamb,
He is meek, and He is mild;
He became a little child.
I a child, and thou a lamb,

We are callèd by His name.
Little Lamb, God bless thee!
Little Lamb, God bless thee!

HOLY THURSDAY

'Twas on a Holy Thursday, their innocent faces
    clean,
The children walking two and two, in red and
    blue and green,
Grey-headed beadles walk'd before, with
    wands as white as snow,
Till into the high dome of Paul's they like
    Thames' waters flow.

O what a multitude they seem'd, these flowers
    of London town!
Seated in companies they sit with radiance all
    their own.
The hum of multitudes was there, but multi-
    tudes of lambs,
Thousands of little boys and girls raising their
    innocent hands.

Now like a mighty wind they raise to Heaven
    the voice of song,
Or like harmonious thunderings the seats of
    Heaven among.
Beneath them sit the agèd men, wise guardians
    of the poor;
Then cherish pity, lest you drive an angel from
    your door.

From *Songs of Experience*
THE CHIMNEY-SWEEPER

A little black thing among the snow,
Crying "weep! weep!" in notes of woe!
"Where are thy father and mother? Say!"—
"They are both gone up to church to pray.

"Because I was happy upon the heath,
And smiled among the winter's snow,
They clothed me in the clothes of death,
And taught me to sing the notes of woe.

"And because I am happy, and dance and sing,
They think they have done me no injury,
And are gone to praise God and His priest and
    king,
Who make up a heaven of our misery."

THE CLOD AND THE PEBBLE

"Love seeketh not itself to please,
    Nor for itself hath any care,
But for another gives its ease,
    And builds a Heaven in Hell's despair."

So sung a little Clod of Clay,
    Trodden with the cattle's feet,
But a Pebble of the brook
    Warbled out these metres meet:

"Love seeketh only Self to please,
    To bind another to Its delight,
Joys in another's loss of ease,
    And builds a Hell in Heaven's despite."

THE TIGER

Tiger! Tiger! burning bright
In the forests of the night,
What immortal hand or eye
Could frame thy fearful symmetry?

In what distant deeps or skies
Burnt the fire of thine eyes?
On what wings dare he aspire?
What the hand dare seize the fire?

And what shoulder, and what art,
Could twist the sinews of thy heart?
And when thy heart began to beat,
What dread hand and what dread feet?

What the hammer? what the chain?
In what furnace was thy brain?
What the anvil? what dread grasp
Dare its deadly terrors clasp?

When the stars threw down their spears,
And watered heaven with their tears,
Did He smile his work to see?
Did He who made the Lamb make thee?

Tiger! Tiger! burning bright
In the forests of the night,
What immortal hand or eye
Dare frame thy fearful symmetry?

LONDON

I wander through each chartered street,
Near where the chartered Thames does flow,

5

10

15

20

25

30

35

40

45

50

And mark in every face I meet
Marks of weakness, marks of woe.

In every cry of every man,
In every infant's cry of fear,   5
In every voice, in every ban,
The mind-forged manacles I hear:

How the chimney-sweeper's cry
Every blackening church appalls,   10
And the hapless soldier's sigh
Runs in blood down palace walls.

But most, through midnight streets I hear
How the youthful harlot's curse   15
Blasts the new-born infant's tear,
And blights with plagues the marriage hearse.

ROBERT BURNS*

MARY MORISON

1

O Mary, at thy window be!
    It is the wished, the trysted hour.
Those smiles and glances let me see,
    That make the miser's treasure poor.
    How blythely wad I bide the stoure,[1]
A weary slave frae sun to sun,
    Could I the rich reward secure—
The lovely Mary Morison!

2

Yestreen, when to the trembling string
    The dance gaed thro' the lighted ha',
To thee my fancy took its wing,
    I sat, but neither heard or saw:
Tho' this was fair, and that was braw.
And yon the toast of a' the town,
    I sighed and said amang them a':—
"Ye are na Mary Morison!"

3

O Mary, canst thou wreck his peace
    Wha for thy sake wad gladly die?
Or canst thou break that heart of his
    Whase only faut is loving thee?
    If love for love thou wilt na gie,
At least be pity to me shown:

---
* For introductory sketch see I, 105.
[1] endure the struggle.

A thought ungentle canna be
The thought o' Mary Morison.

THE COTTER'S SATURDAY NIGHT

INSCRIBED TO R. AIKEN, ESQ.

Let not Ambition mock their useful toil,
    Their homely joys, and destiny obscure;
Nor Grandeur hear, with a disdainful smile,   10
    The short and simple annals of the poor.
                                                    GRAY.

My loved, my honored, much respected friend!
    No mercenary bard his homage pays;   15
With honest pride, I scorn each selfish end,
    My dearest meed, a friend's esteem and
        praise:
To you I sing, in simple Scottish lays,
    The lowly train in life's sequestered scene;   20
    The native feelings strong, the guileless
        ways;
What Aiken in a cottage would have been;
Ah! tho' his worth unknown, far happier there
    I ween!   25

November chill blaws loud wi' angry sugh;
    The short'ning winter-day is near a close;
The miry beasts retreating frae the pleugh;
    The black'ning trains o' craws to their re-   30
        pose:
    The toil-worn Cotter frae his labor goes—
This night his weekly moil is at an end,
    Collects his spades, his mattocks, and his
        hoes,   35
Hoping the morn in ease and rest to spend,
    And weary, o'er the moor, his course does
        homeward bend.

At length his lonely cot appears in view,   40
    Beneath the shelter of an aged tree;
Th' expectant wee-things, toddlin, stacher[1]
        through
    To meet their dad, wi' flichterin'[2] noise and
        glee.   45
    His wee bit ingle,[3] blinkin bonilie,
His clean hearth-stane, his thrifty wifie's smile,
    The lisping infant, prattling on his knee,
Does a' his weary kiaugh[4] and care beguile,

---
[1] stagger.   [2] fluttering.
[3] fire.   [4] anxiety.

And makes him quite forget his labor and his
    toil.

Belyve,[5] the elder bairns come drapping in,
    At service out, amang the farmers roun'; 5
Some ca' the pleugh, some herd, some tentie[6]
    rin
    A cannie errand to a neebor town:
    Their eldest hope, their Jenny, woman
        grown, 10
In youthfu' bloom, love sparkling in her e'e,
    Comes hame: perhaps, to shew a braw new
        gown,
Or deposit her sair-won penny-fee,
To help her parents dear, if they in hardship 15
    be.

With joy unfeigned, brothers and sisters meet,
    And each for other's weelfare kindly spiers:[7]
The social hours, swift-winged, unnoticed 20
    fleet;
    Each tells the uncos[8] that he sees or hears.
    The parents partial eye their hopeful years;
Anticipation forward points the view;
    The mother, wi' her needle and her sheers, 25
Gars[9] auld claes look amaist as weel's the new;
The father mixes a' wi' admonition due.

Their master's and their mistress's command
    The younkers a' are warnèd to obey; 30
And mind their labors wi' an eydent[10] hand,
    And ne'er, tho' out o' sight, to jauk or play:
"And O! be sure to fear the Lord alway,
And mind your duty, duly, morn and night;
    Lest in temptation's path ye gang astray, 35
Implore His counsel and assisting might:
They never sought in vain that sought the
    Lord aright."

But hark! a rap comes gently to the door; 40
    Jenny, wha kens the meaning o' the same,
Tells how a neebor lad came o'er the moor,
    To do some errands, and convoy her hame.
The wily mother sees the conscious flame
Sparkle in Jenny's e'e, and flush her cheek; 45
    With heart-struck anxious care, enquires his
        name,
While Jenny hafflins is afraid to speak;

Weel-pleased the mother hears, it's nae wild,
    worthless rake.

With kindly welcome, Jenny brings him ben;[11]
    A strappin' youth, he takes the mother's eye;
Blythe Jenny sees the visit's no ill taen;
    The father cracks of horses, pleughs, and
        kye.
    The youngster's artless heart o'erflows wi'
        joy,
But blate and laithfu',[12] scarce can weel be-
    have;
    The mother, wi' a woman's wiles, can spy
What makes the youth sae bashfu' and sae
    grave;
Weel-pleased to think her bairn's respected
    like the lave.[13]

O happy love! where love like this is found;
    O heart-felt raptures! bliss beyond com-
        pare!
I've pacèd much this weary, mortal round,
    And sage experience bids me this declare:—
"If Heaven a draught of heavenly pleasure
    spare,
One cordial in this melancholy vale,
'Tis when a youthful, loving, modest pair,
In other's arms, breathe out the tender tale
Beneath the milk-white thorn that scents the
    ev'ning gale."

Is there, in human form, that bears a heart,
    A wretch! a villain! lost to love and truth!
That can, with studied, sly, ensnaring art,
    Betray sweet Jenny's unsuspecting youth?
    Curse on his perjured arts! dissembling,
        smooth!
Are honor, virtue, conscience, all exiled?
    Is there no pity, no relenting ruth,
Points to the parents fondling o'er their child?
Then paints the ruined maid, and their distrac-
    tion wild?

But now the supper crowns their simple board,
    The healsome parritch, chief o' Scotia's
        food;
The soupe their only hawkie[14] does afford,
    That 'yont the hallan[15] snugly chows her
        cood;

---

[5] soon.   [6] watchful.
[7] asks.   [8] unusual news.
[9] makes.   [10] diligent.
[11] inside.   [12] shy and bashful.
[13] the rest.   [14] cow.
[15] partition.

The dame brings forth, in complimental
  mood,
To grace the lad, her weel-hained kebbuck,[16]
  fell;[17]
And aft he's prest, and aft he ca's it guid;
The frugal wifie, garrulous, will tell,
How 'twas a towmond[18] auld, sin' lint was i'
  the bell.[19]

The chearfu' supper done, wi' serious face,
  They, round the ingle, form a circle wide;
The sire turns o'er, wi' patriarchal grace,
  The big ha'-Bible, ance his father's pride.
His bonnet rev'rently is laid aside,
His lyart haffets[20] wearing thin and bare;
  Those strains that once did sweet in Zion
    glide,
He wales[21] a portion with judicious care,
And "Let us worship God!" he says, with sol-
  emn air.

They chant their artless notes in simple guise,
  They tune their hearts, by far the noblest
    aim;
Perhaps *Dundee's* wild-warbling measures rise,
  Or plaintive *Martyrs*, worthy of the name;
  Or noble *Elgin* beets the heaven-ward
    flame,
The sweetest far of Scotia's holy lays:
  Compared with these, Italian trills are tame;
The tickled ears no heart-felt raptures raise;
Nae unison hae they, with our Creator's praise.

The priest-like father reads the sacred page,
  How Abram was the friend of God on high;
Or, Moses bade eternal warfare wage
  With Amalek's ungracious progeny;
  Or, how the royal Bard[22] did groaning lie
Beneath the stroke of Heaven's avenging ire;
  Or Job's pathetic plaint, and wailing cry;
  Or rapt Isaiah's wild, seraphic fire;
Or other holy Seers that tune the sacred lyre.

Perhaps the Christian volume is the theme:
  How guiltless blood for guilty man was
    shed;
How He, who bore in Heaven the second
  name,

Had not on earth whereon to lay His head;
  How His first followers and servants sped;
The precepts sage they wrote to many a land:
  How he, who lone in Patmos banishèd,[23]
Saw in the sun a mighty angel stand,
And heard great Bab'lon's doom pronounced
  by Heaven's command.

Then kneeling down to Heaven's Eternal King,
  The saint, the father, and the husband
    prays:
Hope "springs exulting on triumphant wing,"[24]
  That thus they all shall meet in future days,
  There, ever bask in uncreated rays,
No more to sigh or shed the bitter tear,
  Together hymning their Creator's praise,
In such society, yet still more dear;
While circling Time moves round in an eternal
  sphere.

Compared with this, how poor Religion's
  pride,
  In all the pomp of method, and of art;
When men display to congregations wide
  Devotion's ev'ry grace, except the heart,
  The Power, incensed, the pageant will de-
    sert,
The pompous strain, the sacerdotal stole;
  But haply, in some cottage far apart,
May hear, well-pleased, the language of the
  soul,
And in His Book of Life the inmates poor
  enroll.

Then homeward all take off their sev'ral way;
  The youngling cottagers retire to rest:
The parent-pair their secret homage pay,
  And proffer up to Heaven the warm request,
  That He who stills the raven's clam'rous
    nest,
And decks the lily fair in flow'ry pride,
  Would, in the way His wisdom sees the
    best,
For them and for their little ones provide;
But, chiefly, in their hearts with Grace Divine
  preside.

From scenes like these, old Scotia's grandeur
  springs,

---

[16] well-saved cheese.   [17] strong.
[18] twelve-month.   [19] flax was in blossom.
[20] gray temples.   [21] chooses.
[22] David.

---

[23] St. John.
[24] Pope's "Windsor Forest."

That makes her loved at home, revered
   abroad:
Princes and lords are but the breath of kings,
   "An honest man's the noblest work of
     God";[25]   5
   And certes, in fair Virtue's heavenly road,
The cottage leaves the palace far behind;
   What is a lordling's pomp? a cumbrous load,
Disguising oft the wretch of human kind,
Studied in arts of Hell, in wickedness refined! 10

O Scotia! my dear, my native soil!
   For whom my warmest wish to Heaven is
     sent!
Long may thy hardy sons of rustic toil   15
   Be blest with health, and peace, and sweet
     content!
   And O! may Heaven their simple lives pre-
     vent
From Luxury's contagion, weak and vile!   20
   Then, howe'er crowns and coronets be rent,
A virtuous populace may rise the while,
And stand a wall of fire around their much-
   loved Isle.

                  25
O Thou! who poured the patriotic tide,
   That streamed thro' Wallace's undaunted
     heart,
Who dared to, nobly, stem tyrannic pride,
   Or nobly die, the second glorious part: 30
(The patriot's God, peculiarly Thou art,
His friend, inspirer, guardian, and reward!)
   O never, never Scotia's realm desert;
But still the patriot, and the patriot-bard
In bright succession raise, her ornament and 35
   guard!

TO A MOUSE

ON TURNING HER UP IN HER NEST WITH THE   40
PLOUGH, NOVEMBER, 1785

Wee, sleekit,[1] cowrin, tim'rous beastie,
O, what a panic's in thy breastie!
Thou need na start awa sae hasty
     Wi' bickering brattle![2]   45
I wad be laith to rin an' chase thee,
     Wi' murdering pattle![3]

---

[25] Pope's *Essay on Man*.
[1] sleek.
[2] sudden scamper.
[3] stick.

I'm truly sorry man's dominion
Has broken Nature's social union,
An' justifies that ill opinion
     Which makes thee startle
At me, thy poor, earth-born companion
     An' fellow mortal!

I doubt na, whyles, but thou may thieve;
What then? poor beastie, thou maun live!
A daimen icker in a thrave[4]
     'S a sma' request;
I'll get a blessin wi' the lave,
     An' never miss 't!

Thy wee-bit housie, too, in ruin!
Its silly wa's the win's are strewin!
An' naething, now, to big a new ane,
     O' foggage green!
An' bleak December's win's ensuin,
     Baith snell[5] an' keen!

Thou saw the fields laid bare an' waste,
An' weary winter comin fast,
An' cozie here, beneath the blast,
     Thou thought to dwell,
Till crash! the cruel coulter past
     Out thro' thy cell.

That wee bit heap o' leaves an' stibble,
Hast cost thee monie a weary nibble!
Now thou's turned out, for a' thy trouble,
     But house or hald,[6]
To thole the winter's sleety dribble,
     An' cranreuch[7] cauld!

But Mousie, thou art no thy lane,
In proving foresight may be vain:
The best-laid schemes o' mice an' men
     Gang aft agley,[8]
An' lea'e us nought but grief an' pain,
     For promised joy!

Still thou art blest, compared wi' me!
The present only toucheth thee:
But och! I backward cast my e'e,
     On prospects drear!
An' forward, tho' I canna see,
     I guess an' fear!

---

[4] occasional ear in twenty-four sheaves.
[5] sharp.
[6] Without house or abode.
[7] hoar-frost.   [8] astray.

AULD LANG SYNE

CHORUS

For auld lang syne, my dear,
  For auld lang syne,
We'll tak a cup o' kindness yet
  For auld lang syne!¹

Should auld acquaintance be forgot,
  And never brought to mind?   10
Should auld acquaintance be forgot,
  And auld lang syne!

And surely ye'll be your pint-stowp,²
  And surely I'll be mine,   15
And we'll tak a cup o' kindness yet
  For auld lang syne!

We two hae run about the braes,³
  And pou'd the gowans⁴ fine,   20
But we've wandered monie a weary fit⁵
  Sin' auld lang syne.

We twa hae paidled in the burn⁶
  Frae morning sun till dine,   25
But seas between us braid hae roared
  Sin' auld lang syne.

And there's a hand, my trusty fiere,⁷
  And gie's a hand o' thine,   30
And we'll tak a right guid-willie waught⁸
  For auld lang syne!

CHORUS

For auld lang syne, my dear,   35
  For auld lang syne,
We'll tak a cup o' kindness yet
  For auld lang syne!

JOHN ANDERSON MY JO

John Anderson my jo,¹ John,
  When we were first acquent,
Your locks were like the raven,
  Your bonie brow was brent;²   45
But now your brow is beld, John,

Your locks are like the snaw,
But blessings on your frosty pow,³
  John Anderson my jo!

John Anderson my jo, John,   5
  We clamb the hill thegither,
And monie a cantie⁴ day, John,
  We've had wi' ane anither:
Now we maun totter down, John,
  And hand in hand we'll go,
And sleep thegither at the foot,
  John Anderson my jo!

A RED, RED ROSE

O, my luve is like a red, red rose,
  That's newly sprung in June.
O, my luve is like the melodie,
  That's sweetly played in tune.

As fair art thou, my bonie lass,
  So deep in luve am I,
And I will luve thee still, my dear,
  Till a' the seas gang dry.

Till a' the seas gang dry, my dear,
  And the rocks melt wi' the sun!
And I will luve thee still, my dear,
  While the sands o' life shall run.

And fare thee weel, my only luve,
  And fare thee weel a while!
And I will come again, my luve,
  Tho' it were ten thousand mile!

A MAN'S A MAN FOR A' THAT

Is there, for honest poverty,
  That hings his head, an' a' that?
The coward slave, we pass him by,   40
  We dare be poor for a' that!
For a' that, an' a' that,
  Our toils obscure, an' a' that;
The rank is but the guinea's stamp;
  The man's the gowd for a' that.

What though on hamely fare we dine,
  Wear hodden-gray, an' a' that;
Gie fools their silks, and knaves their wine,   50
  A man's a man for a' that.

---

¹ good old days.
² you'll pay for your pint.
³ hillsides.   ⁴ daisies.
⁵ foot.   ⁶ brook.
⁷ friend.   ⁸ swig.
¹ sweetheart.   ² smooth.

³ head.   ⁴ happy.

For a' that, an' a' that,
  Their tinsel show, an' a' that;
The honest man, though e'er sae poor,
  Is king o' men for a' that.

Ye see yon birkie, ca'd a lord,   5
  Wha struts, an' stares, an' a' that;
Though hundreds worship at his word,
  He's but a coof[1] for a' that.
      For a' that, an' a' that,   10
      His riband, star, an' a' that,
  The man o' independent mind,
      He looks and laughs at a' that.

A prince can mak a belted knight,   15
  A marquis, duke, an' a' that;
But an honest man's aboon[2] his might,
  Guid faith he mauna fa' that!
      For a' that, an' a' that,
      Their dignities, an' a' that,   20
  The pith o' sense, an' pride o' worth,
      Are higher rank than a' that.

Then let us pray that come it may,
  As come it will for a' that,
That sense and worth, o'er a' the earth,   25
  May bear the gree, an' a' that.
      For a' that, an' a' that,
      It's coming yet, for a' that,
  That man to man, the warld o'er,   30
      Shall brothers be for a' that.

ADDRESS TO THE UNCO GUID; OR, THE RIGIDLY RIGHTEOUS

35

My Son, these maxims make a rule,
  An' lump them ay thegither:
The Rigid Righteous is a fool,
  The Rigid Wise anither;
The cleanest corn that e'er was dight   40
  May hae some pyles o' caff in;
So ne'er a fellow-creature slight
  For random fits o' daffin.
          SOLOMON.—*Eccles.*, 7:16.

45

O ye who are sae guid yoursel,
  Sae pious and sae holy,
Ye've nought to do but mark and tell
  Your neebors' fauts and folly;
Whase life is like a weel-gaun mill,   50

Supplied wi' store o' water;
The heapet happer's[1] ebbing still,
  An' still the clap plays clatter!

Hear me, ye venerable core,[2]
  As counsel for poor mortals
That frequent pass douce[3] Wisdom's door
  For glaikit[4] Folly's portals;
I, for their thoughtless, careless sakes,
  Would here propone defences—
Their donsie tricks, their black mistakes,
  Their failings and mischances.

Ye see your state wi' theirs compared,
  And shudder at the niffer;[5]
But cast a moment's fair regard,
  What makes the mighty differ?
Discount what scant occasion gave,
  That purity ye pride in,
And (what's aft mair than a' the lave)
  Your better art o' hidin.

Think, when your castigated pulse
  Gies now and then a wallop,
What ragings must his veins convulse,
  That still eternal gallop!
Wi' wind and tide fair i' your tail,
  Right on ye scud your sea-way;
But in the teeth o' baith to sail,
  It makes an unco lee-way.

See Social-life and Glee sit down,
  All joyous and unthinking,
Till, quite transmogrify'd, they're grown
  Debauchery and Drinking:
O, would they stay to calculate
  Th' eternal consequences,
Or—your more dreadful hell to state—
  Damnation of expenses!

Ye high, exalted, virtuous dames,
  Tied up in godly laces,
Before ye gie poor Frailty names,
  Suppose a change o' cases;
A dear-lov'd lad, convenience snug,
  A treach'rous inclination—
But, let me whisper i' your lug,[6]
  Ye're aiblins[7] nae temptation.

---

[1] fool.   [2] above.

[1] heaped-up hopper.   [2] crew.
[3] grave.   [4] giddy.
[5] exchange.   [6] ear.
[7] perhaps.

Then gently scan your brother man,
　Still gentler sister woman;
Tho' they may gang a kennin[8] wrang,
　To step aside is human:
One point must still be greatly dark,　5
　The moving *Why* they do it;
And just as lamely can ye mark,
　How far perhaps they rue it.

Who made the heart, 't is He alone
　Decidedly can try us,
He knows each chord, its various tone,
　Each spring, its various bias:
Then at the balance, let's be mute,
　We never can adjust it;
What's *done* we partly can compute,
　But know not what's *resisted.*

[8] a little bit.

NINETEENTH CENTURY

WILLIAM WORDSWORTH*

LINES WRITTEN IN EARLY SPRING

I heard a thousand blended notes
While in a grove I sate reclined,　5
In that sweet mood when pleasant thoughts
Bring sad thoughts to the mind.

To her fair works did Nature link
The human soul that through me ran;
And much it grieved my heart to think
What Man has made of Man.

Through primrose tufts, in that sweet bower,
The periwinkle trailed its wreaths;
And 'tis my faith that every flower
Enjoys the air it breathes.

The birds around me hopped and played,
Their thoughts I cannot measure,—　20
But the least motion which they made,
It seemed a thrill of pleasure.

The budding twigs spread out their fan
To catch the breezy air;
And I must think, do all I can,
That there was pleasure there.

* For introductory sketch see I, 108.

If this belief from heaven be sent,
If such be Nature's holy plan,
Have I not reason to lament
What Man has made of Man?

LINES

COMPOSED A FEW MILES ABOVE TINTERN
ABBEY, ON REVISITING THE BANKS OF THE WYE
DURING A TOUR JULY 13, 1798

Five years have past; five summers, with the
　length
Of five long winters! and again I hear
These waters, rolling from their mountain-
　springs
With a soft inland murmur.—Once again
Do I behold these steep and lofty cliffs,
That on a wild, secluded scene impress
Thoughts of more deep seclusion; and connect
The landscape with the quiet of the sky.
The day is come when I again repose
Here, under this dark sycamore, and view
These plots of cottage-ground, these orchard-
　tufts,
Which at this season, with their unripe fruits,
Are clad in one green hue, and lose them-
　selves
'Mid groves and copses. Once again I see

These hedge-rows, hardly hedge-rows, little
    lines
Of sportive wood run wild: these pastoral
    farms,
Green to the very door; and wreaths of smoke
Sent up, in silence, from among the trees!
With some uncertain notice, as might seem
Of vagrant dwellers in the houseless woods,
Or of some Hermit's cave, where by his fire
The Hermit sits alone.
             These beauteous forms,
Through a long absence, have not been to me
As is a landscape to a blind man's eye:
But oft, in lonely rooms, and 'mid the din
Of towns and cities, I have owed to them,
In hours of weariness, sensations sweet,
Felt in the blood, and felt along the heart;
And passing even into my purer mind,
With tranquil restoration:—feelings too
Of unremembered pleasure: such, perhaps,
As have no slight or trivial influence
On that best portion of a good man's life,
His little, nameless, unremembered acts
Of kindness and of love. Nor less, I trust,
To them I may have owed another gift,
Of aspect more sublime; that blessed mood
In which the burden of the mystery,
In which the heavy and the weary weight
Of all this unintelligible world,
Is lightened:—that serene and blessed mood,
In which the affections gently lead us on,—
Until, the breath of this corporeal frame
And even the motion of our human blood
Almost suspended, we are laid asleep
In body, and become a living soul:
While with an eye made quiet by the power
Of harmony, and the deep power of joy,
We see into the life of things.
                If this
Be but a vain belief, yet, oh! how oft—
In darkness and amid the many shapes
Of joyless daylight; when the fretful stir
Unprofitable, and the fever of the world,
Have hung upon the beatings of my heart—
How oft, in spirit, have I turned to thee,
O sylvan Wye! thou wanderer thro' the woods,
How often has my spirit turned to thee!
    And now, with gleams of half-extinguished
        thought,
With many recognitions dim and faint,
And somewhat of a sad perplexity,
The picture of the mind revives again:

While here I stand, not only with the sense
Of present pleasure, but with pleasing
    thoughts
That in this moment there is life and food
5 For future years. And so I dare to hope,
Though changed, no doubt, from what I was
    when first
I came among these hills; when like a roe
I bounded o'er the mountains, by the sides
10 Of the deep rivers, and the lonely streams,
Wherever nature led: more like a man
Flying from something that he dreads, than
    one
Who sought the thing he loved. For nature
15   then
(The coarser pleasures of my boyish days,
And their glad animal movements all gone by)
To me was all in all.—I cannot paint
What then I was. The sounding cataract
20 Haunted me like a passion: the tall rock,
The mountain, and the deep and gloomy
    wood,
Their colors and their forms, were then to me
An appetite; a feeling and a love,
25 That had no need of a remoter charm,
By thought supplied, nor any interest
Unborrowed from the eye.—That time is past,
And all its aching joys are now no more,
And all its dizzy raptures. Not for this
30 Faint I, nor mourn nor murmur; other gifts
Have followed; for such loss, I would believe,
Abundant recompense. For I have learned
To look on nature, not as in the hour
Of thoughtless youth; but hearing oftentimes
35 The still, sad music of humanity,
Nor harsh nor grating, though of ample power
To chasten and subdue. And I have felt
A presence that disturbs me with the joy
Of elevated thoughts; a sense sublime
40 Of something far more deeply interfused,
Whose dwelling is the light of setting suns,
And the round ocean and the living air,
And the blue sky, and in the mind of man;
A motion and a spirit, that impels
45 All thinking things, all objects of all thought,
And rolls through all things. Therefore am I
    still
A lover of the meadows and the woods,
And mountains; and of all that we behold
50 From this green earth; of all the mighty world
Of eye, and ear,—both what they half create,
And what perceive; well pleased to recognize

In nature and the language of the sense,
The anchor of my purest thoughts, the nurse,
The guide, the guardian of my heart, and soul
Of all my moral being.
                  Nor perchance,
If I were not thus taught, should I the more   5
Suffer my genial spirits to decay:
For thou art with me here upon the banks
Of this fair river; thou my dearest Friend,
My dear, dear Friend,[1] and in thy voice I 10
   catch
The language of my former heart, and read
My former pleasures in the shooting lights
Of thy wild eyes. Oh! yet a little while
May I behold in thee what I was once,   15
My dear, dear Sister! and this prayer I make,
Knowing that Nature never did betray
The heart that loved her; 'tis her privilege,
Through all the years of this our life, to lead
From joy to joy: for she can so inform   20
The mind that is within us, so impress
With quietness and beauty, and so feed
With lofty thoughts, that neither evil tongues,
Rash judgments, nor the sneers of selfish men,
Nor greetings where no kindness is, nor all   25
The dreary intercourse of daily life,
Shall e'er prevail against us, or disturb
Our cheerful faith, that all which we behold
Is full of blessings. Therefore let the moon
Shine on thee in thy solitary walk;   30
And let the misty mountain-winds be free
To blow against thee: and, in after years,
When these wild ecstasies shall be matured
Into a sober pleasure; when thy mind
Shall be a mansion for all lovely forms,   35
Thy memory be as a dwelling-place
For all sweet sounds and harmonies; oh! then,
If solitude, or fear, or pain, or grief,
Should be thy portion, with what healing
   thoughts   40
Of tender joy wilt thou remember me,
And these my exhortations! Nor, perchance—
If I should be where I no more can hear
Thy voice, nor catch from thy wild eyes these
   gleams   45
Of past existence—wilt thou then forget
That on the banks of this delightful stream
We stood together; and that I, so long
A worshipper of Nature, hither came
Unwearied in that service: rather say   50

---

[1] his sister, Dorothy.

With warmer love—oh! with far deeper zeal
Of holier love. Nor wilt thou then forget,
That after many wanderings, many years
Of absence, these steep woods and lofty cliffs,
And this green pastoral landscape, were to me
More dear, both for themselves and for thy
   sake!

SHE DWELT AMONG THE
UNTRODDEN WAYS

She dwelt among the untrodden ways
   Beside the springs of Dove,
A maid whom there were none to praise
   And very few to love;

A violet by a mossy stone
   Half hidden from the eye!
Fair as a star, when only one
   Is shining in the sky.

She lived unknown, and few could know
   When Lucy ceased to be;
But she is in her grave, and, oh!
   The difference to me!

A SLUMBER DID MY SPIRIT
SEAL

A slumber did my spirit seal;
   I had no human fears—
She seemed a thing that could not feel
   The touch of earthly years.

No motion has she now, no force;
   She neither hears nor sees;
Rolled round in earth's diurnal course,
   With rocks, and stones, and trees.

MY HEART LEAPS UP

My heart leaps up when I behold
   A rainbow in the sky:
So was it when my life began,
So is it now I am a man,
So be it when I shall grow old,
   Or let me die!
The Child is father of the Man:
And I could wish my days to be
Bound each to each by natural piety.

COMPOSED UPON WESTMINSTER BRIDGE, SEPTEMBER 3, 1802

Earth has not anything to show more fair:
Dull would he be of soul who could pass by
A sight so touching in its majesty:
This City now doth like a garment wear
The beauty of the morning: silent, bare,
Ships, towers, domes, theatres, and temples lie
Open unto the fields, and to the sky,—
All bright and glittering in the smokeless air.
Never did sun more beautifully steep
In his first splendor valley, rock, or hill;
Ne'er saw I, never felt, a calm so deep!
The river glideth at his own sweet will:
Dear God! the very houses seem asleep;
And all that mighty heart is lying still!

LONDON, 1802

Milton! thou shouldst be living at this hour:
England hath need of thee: she is a fen
Of stagnant waters: altar, sword, and pen,
Fireside, the heroic wealth of hall and bower,
Have forfeited their ancient English dower
Of inward happiness. We are selfish men;
Oh! raise us up, return to us again;
And give us manners, virtue, freedom, power.
Thy soul was like a Star, and dwelt apart:
Thou hadst a voice whose sound was like the
      sea,
Pure as the naked heavens, majestic, free;
So didst thou travel on life's common way
In cheerful godliness; and yet thy heart
The lowliest duties on herself did lay.

I WANDERED LONELY AS A CLOUD

I wandered lonely as a cloud
That floats on high o'er vales and hills,
When all at once I saw a crowd,
A host of golden daffodils,
Beside the lake, beneath the trees,
Fluttering and dancing in the breeze.

Continuous as the stars that shine
And twinkle on the milky way,
They stretched in never-ending line
Along the margin of a bay;
Ten thousand saw I at a glance,
Tossing their heads in sprightly dance.

The waves beside them danced, but they
Outdid the sparkling waves in glee—
A poet could not but be gay
In such a jocund company.
I gazed—and gazed—but little thought
What wealth the show to me had brought.

For oft when on my couch I lie
In vacant or in pensive mood,
They flash upon that inward eye
Which is the bliss of solitude,
And then my heart with pleasure fills,
And dances with the daffodils.

ODE: INTIMATIONS OF IMMORTALITY FROM RECOLLECTIONS OF EARLY CHILDHOOD

There was a time when meadow, grove, and
      stream,
The earth, and every common sight
            To me did seem
            Apparelled in celestial light,
The glory and the freshness of a dream.
It is not now as it hath been of yore;—
            Turn wheresoe'er I may,
            By night or day,
The things which I have seen I now can see
      no more.
            The rainbow comes and goes,
            And lovely is the rose;
            The Moon doth with delight
Look round her when the heavens are
      bare;
            Waters on a starry night
            Are beautiful and fair;
      The sunshine is a glorious birth;
      But yet I know, where'er I go,
That there hath past away a glory from the
      earth.

Now, while the birds thus sing a joyous song,
      And while the young lambs bound
            As to the tabor's sound,
To me alone there came a thought of grief:
A timely utterance gave that thought relief,
            And I again am strong.
The cataracts blow their trumpets from the
      steep;—
No more shall grief of mine the season wrong:
I hear the echoes through the mountains
      throng,

The winds come to me from the fields of sleep,
    And all the earth is gay;
        Land and sea
    Give themselves up to jollity,
        And with the heart of May
    Doth every beast keep holiday;—
        Thou child of joy,
Shout round me, let me hear thy shouts, thou happy
        Shepherd-boy!

Ye blessèd Creatures, I have heard the call
    Ye to each other make; I see
The heavens laugh with you in your jubilee;
    My heart is at your festival,
    My head hath its coronal,
The fulness of your bliss, I feel—I feel it all.
      Oh evil day! if I were sullen
      While Earth herself is adorning
        This sweet May-morning;
      And the children are culling
        On every side
    In a thousand valleys far and wide,
    Fresh flowers; while the sun shines warm,
And the babe leaps up on his mother's arm:—
    I hear, I hear, with joy I hear!
    —But there's a tree, of many, one,
A single field which I have looked upon,
Both of them speak of something that is gone:
      The pansy at my feet
      Doth the same tale repeat:
Whither is fled the visionary gleam?
Where is it now, the glory and the dream?

Our birth is but a sleep and a forgetting;
The Soul that rises with us, our life's Star,
      Hath had elsewhere its setting,
        And cometh from afar;
      Not in entire forgetfulness,
      And not in utter nakedness,
But trailing clouds of glory do we come
        From God, who is our home:
Heaven lies about us in our infancy!
Shades of the prison-house begin to close
      Upon the growing Boy,
But he beholds the light, and whence it flows,
      He sees it in his joy;
The Youth, who daily farther from the east
    Must travel, still is Nature's priest,
      And by the vision splendid
      Is on his way attended;

At length the Man perceives it die away,
And fade into the light of common day.

Earth fills her lap with pleasures of her own;
5 Yearnings she hath in her own natural kind,
And, even with something of a mother's mind
        And no unworthy aim,
      The homely nurse doth all she can
To make her foster-child, her inmate, Man,
10   Forget the glories he hath known,
And that imperial palace whence he came.

Behold the Child among his new-born blisses,
15 A six years' darling of a pigmy size!
See, where 'mid work of his own hand he lies,
Fretted by sallies of his mother's kisses,
With light upon him from his father's eyes!
See, at his feet, some little plan or chart,
20 Some fragment from his dream of human life,
Shaped by himself with newly-learnèd art;
      A wedding or a festival,
      A mourning or a funeral;
        And this hath now his heart,
        And unto this he frames his song:
25   Then will he fit his tongue
To dialogues of business, love, or strife;
      But it will not be long
      Ere this be thrown aside,
      And with new joy and pride
The little actor cons another part;
Filling from time to time his "humorous stage"
With all the Persons, down to palsied Age,
35 That life brings with her in her equipage;
      As if his whole vocation
      Were endless imitation.

Thou, whose exterior semblance doth belie
40   Thy soul's immensity;
Thou best philosopher, who yet dost keep
Thy heritage, thou eye among the blind,
That, deaf and silent, read'st the eternal deep,
Haunted for ever by the eternal Mind,—
45   Mighty Prophet! Seer blest!
      On whom those truths do rest
Which we are toiling all our lives to find,
In darkness lost, the darkness of the grave;
Thou, over whom thy Immortality
50 Broods like the day, a master o'er a slave,
A Presence which is not to be put by;
Thou little child, yet glorious in the might

Of heaven-born freedom on thy being's
    height,
Why with such earnest pains dost thou pro-
    voke
The years to bring the inevitable yoke,
Thus blindly with thy blessedness at strife?
Full soon thy soul shall have her earthly
    freight,
And custom lie upon thee with a weight
Heavy as frost, and deep almost as life!

      O joy! that in our embers
      Is something that doth live,
      That Nature yet remembers
      What was so fugitive!
The thought of our past years in me doth
    breed
Perpetual benediction: not indeed
For that which is most worthy to be blest,
Delight and liberty, the simple creed
Of Childhood, whether busy or at rest,
With new-fledged hope still fluttering in his
    breast:—
      —Not for these I raise
      The song of thanks and praise;
      But for those obstinate questionings
      Of sense and outward things,
      Fallings from us, vanishings;
      Blank misgivings of a creature
Moving about in worlds not realized,
High instincts, before which our mortal nature
Did tremble like a guilty thing surprised:
      But for those first affections,
      Those shadowy recollections,
      Which, be they what they may,
Are yet the fountain-light of all our day,
Are yet a master-light of all our seeing;
      Uphold us, cherish, and have power to
      make
Our noisy years seem moments in the being
Of the eternal Silence: truths that wake,
      To perish never;
Which neither listlessness, nor mad endeavor,
      Nor man nor boy,
Nor all that is at enmity with joy,
Can utterly abolish or destroy!
      Hence, in a season of calm weather
      Though inland far we be,
Our souls have sight of that immortal sea
      Which brought us hither;
      Can in a moment travel thither—

And see the children sport upon the shore,
And hear the mighty waters rolling ever-
    more.

Then, sing ye birds, sing, sing a joyous song!
      And let the young lambs bound
      As to the tabor's sound!
We, in thought, will join your throng,
      Ye that pipe and ye that play,
      Ye that through your hearts to-day
      Feel the gladness of the May!
What though the radiance which was once
    so bright
Be now for ever taken from my sight,
      Though nothing can bring back the
      hour
Of splendor in the grass, of glory in the flower;
      We will grieve not, rather find
      Strength in what remains be-
      hind;
      In the primal sympathy
      Which having been must ever
      be;
      In the soothing thoughts that
      spring
      Out of human suffering;
      In the faith that looks through
      death,
In years that bring the philosophic mind.

And O, ye Fountains, Meadows, Hills, and
    Groves,
Forbode not any severing of our loves!
Yet in my heart of hearts I feel your might;
I only have relinquished one delight
To live beneath your more habitual sway:
I love the brooks which down their channels
    fret
Even more than when I tripped lightly as
    they;
The innocent brightness of a new-born day
      Is lovely yet;
The clouds that gather round the setting sun
Do take a sober coloring from an eye
That hath kept watch o'er man's mortality;
Another race hath been, and other palms are
    won.
Thanks to the human heart by which we live,
Thanks to its tenderness, its joys, and fears,
To me the meanest flower that blows can give
Thoughts that do often lie too deep for tears.

THE WORLD IS TOO MUCH WITH US

The world is too much with us; late and soon,
Getting and spending, we lay waste our   5
  powers:
Little we see in Nature that is ours;
We have given our hearts away, a sordid
  boon!
The Sea that bares her bosom to the moon;   10
The winds that will be howling at all hours
And are up-gathered now like sleeping flow-
  ers;
For this, for every thing, we are out of tune;
It moves us not.—Great God! I'd rather be   15
A Pagan suckled in a creed outworn;
So might I, standing on this pleasant lea,
Have glimpses that would make me less for-
  lorn;
Have sight of Proteus[1] rising from the sea;   20
Or hear old Triton blow his wreathèd horn.

GEORGE GORDON, LORD BYRON*   25

SHE WALKS IN BEAUTY

She walks in beauty, like the night
  Of cloudless climes and starry skies;   30
And all that's best of dark and bright
  Meet in her aspect and her eyes:
Thus mellowed to that tender light
  Which heaven to gaudy day denies.

  35

One shade the more, one ray the less,
  Had half impaired the nameless grace
Which waves in every raven tress,
  Or softly lightens o'er her face;
Where thoughts serenely sweet express   40
  How pure, how dear their dwelling-place.

And on that cheek, and o'er that brow,
  So soft, so calm, yet eloquent,
The smiles that win, the tints that glow,   45
  But tell of days in goodness spent,
A mind at peace with all below,
  A heart whose love is innocent!

---

[1] Proteus and Triton, sea gods.
* For introductory sketch see I, 123.

WHEN WE TWO PARTED

When we two parted
  In silence and tears,
Half broken-hearted
  To sever for years,
Pale grew thy cheek and cold,
  Colder thy kiss;
Truly that hour foretold
  Sorrow to this.

The dew of the morning
  Sunk chill on my brow—
It felt like the warning
  Of what I feel now.
Thy vows are all broken,
  And light is thy fame;
I hear thy name spoken,
  And share in its shame.

They name thee before me,
  A knell to mine ear;
A shudder comes o'er me—
  Why wert thou so dear?
They know not I knew thee,
  Who knew thee too well:—
Long, long shall I rue thee,
  Too deeply to tell.

In secret we met—
  In silence I grieve
That thy heart could forget,
  Thy spirit deceive.
If I should meet thee
  After long years,
How should I greet thee?—
  With silence and tears.

THE DESTRUCTION OF SENNACHERIB[1]

The Assyrian came down like the wolf on the
  fold,
And his cohorts were gleaming in purple and
  gold;
And the sheen of their spears was like stars
  on the sea,
When the blue wave rolls nightly on deep
  Galilee.

---

[1] See II Kings 19.

Like the leaves of the forest when Summer is
green,
That host with their banners at sunset were
seen:
Like the leaves of the forest when Autumn
hath blown, 5
That host on the morrow lay withered and
strown.

For the Angel of Death spread his wings on
the blast, 10
And breathed in the face of the foe as he
passed;
And the eyes of the sleepers waxed deadly
and chill,
And their hearts but once heaved, and forever
grew still! 15

And there lay the steed with his nostril all
wide, 20
But through it there rolled not the breath of
his pride;
And the foam of his gasping lay white on the
turf,
And cold as the spray of the rock-beating surf. 25

And there lay the rider distorted and pale,
With the dew on his brow, and the rust on his
mail:
And the tents were all silent—the banners 30
alone—
The lances unlifted—the trumpet unblown.

And the widows of Ashur are loud in their
wail, 35
And the idols are broke in the temple of Baal;
And the might of the Gentile, unsmote by the
sword,
Hath melted like snow in the glance of the
Lord! 40

STANZAS FOR MUSIC

There's not a joy the world can give like that 45
it takes away,
When the glow of early thought declines in
feeling's dull decay;
'Tis not on youth's smooth cheek the blush
alone, which fades so fast, 50
But the tender bloom of heart is gone, ere
youth itself be past.

Then the few whose spirits float above the
wreck of happiness
Are driven o'er the shoals of guilt or ocean of
excess:
The magnet of their course is gone, or only
points in vain
The shore to which their shivered sail shall
never stretch again.

Then the mortal coldness of the soul like death
itself comes down;
It cannot feel for others' woes, it dare not
dream its own;
That heavy chill has frozen o'er the fountain
of our tears,
And though the eye may sparkle still, 'tis
where the ice appears.

Though wit may flash from fluent lips, and
mirth distract the breast,
Through midnight hours that yield no more
their former hope of rest;
'Tis but as ivy-leaves around the ruined turret
wreath,
All green and wildly fresh without, but worn
and grey beneath.

Oh, could I feel as I have felt,—or be what I
have been,
Or weep as I could once have wept, o'er many
a vanished scene;
As springs, in deserts found, seem sweet, all
brackish though they be,
So, midst the withered waste of life, those
tears would flow to me.

PERCY BYSSHE SHELLEY

*Shelley (1792–1822) early acquired the nick-
name "Mad" when he distinguished himself at
school by blowing up trees, wearing strange
costumes, concocting chemical brews, and so
on. He was expelled from Oxford for writing
"The Necessity of Atheism," a treatise which
was less wicked than its title. After an elopement with Harriet Westbrook, Shelley, full of
Godwin and French materialism, conceived
the idea of saving the Irish from the English
by writing and lecturing on political reform
(years later he was to try a reform program on
the English themselves); as a reformer Shelley*

was socialistic in principle but conservative in method—he hated prelates, lawyers, tyrants, and in both poetry and prose attacked them. On returning to England Shelley had financial trouble, family trouble, wife trouble—Harriet eventually drowned herself after the poet had run off with Mary Godwin, who later became his second wife. Lawsuits, social ostracism, legal separation from his children sent Shelley into exile for the rest of his life. There were other episodes with women, strange experiences with imaginary assailants, repeated domestic illnesses and deaths—and yet the poetry, which had realized itself early in Queen Mab, *had gone on and on. Some of it is political. Some of it is obscure or dull, especially parts of* Rosalind and Helen *or* Revolt of Islam. *But when Shelley wrote in his most personal vein—as a lyricist singing with a bursting throat—he revealed a new voice, an incomparable soaring power. Apart from his sex life Shelley, like many other artists, led a life of kindness to friends, hard work, interest in the common man, and, in general, ironic as it may sound, of functional Christianity. An untimely sailing accident ended abruptly a poetic career still in the developing stage.*

HYMN TO INTELLECTUAL BEAUTY

1

The awful shadow of some unseen Power
  Floats though unseen among us, visiting
  This various world with as inconstant wing
As summer winds that creep from flower to
    flower;
Like moonbeams that behind some piny
    mountain shower,
    It visits with inconstant glance
    Each human heart and countenance;
Like hues and harmonies of evening,
    Like clouds in starlight widely spread,
    Like memory of music fled,
    Like aught that for its grace may be
Dear, and yet dearer for its mystery.

2

Spirit of BEAUTY, that dost consecrate
  With thine own hues all thou dost shine
    upon

Of human thought or form, where art thou
    gone?
Why dost thou pass away, and leave our state,
This dim vast vale of tears, vacant and deso-
    late?
    Ask why the sunlight not forever
    Weaves rainbows o'er yon mountain
      river;
Why aught should fail and fade that once is
    shown;
    Why fear and dream and death and birth
    Cast on the daylight of this earth
    Such gloom; why man has such a scope
For love and hate, despondency and hope.

3

No voice from some sublimer world hath ever
  To sage or poet these responses given;
  Therefore the names of Demon, Ghost, and
    Heaven,
Remain the records of their vain endeavor,
Frail spells, whose uttered charm might not
    avail to sever,
    From all we hear and all we see,
    Doubt, chance, and mutability.
Thy light alone, like mist o'er mountains
    driven,
    Or music by the night wind sent
    Through strings of some still instrument,
    Or moonlight on a midnight stream,
Gives grace and truth to life's unquiet dream.

4

Love, Hope, and Self-esteem, like clouds, de-
    part
  And come, for some uncertain moments lent.
  Man were immortal and omnipotent,
Didst thou, unknown and awful as thou art,
Keep with thy glorious train firm state within
    his heart.
    Thou messenger of sympathies
    That wax and wane in lovers' eyes!
Thou, that to human thought art nourishment,
    Like darkness to a dying flame,
    Depart not as thy shadow came,
    Depart not, lest the grave should be,
Like life and fear, a dark reality!

5

While yet a boy I sought for ghosts, and sped
  Through many a listening chamber, cave
    and ruin,

And starlight wood, with fearful steps pur-
   suing
Hopes of high talk with the departed dead;
I called on poisonous names with which our
   youth is fed.   5
   I was not heard—I saw them not—
   When, musing deeply on the lot
Of life, at that sweet time when winds are
   wooing
   All vital things that wake to bring   10
   News of birds and blossoming,—
   Sudden, thy shadow fell on me;
I shrieked, and clasped my hands in ecstasy!

6

I vowed that I would dedicate my powers
   To thee and thine—have I not kept the
      vow?
   With beating heart and streaming eyes,
      even now   20
I call the phantoms of a thousand hours
Each from his voiceless grave: they have in
   visioned bowers
   Of studious zeal or love's delight
   Outwatched with me the envious night— 25
They know that never joy illumed my brow
   Unlinked with hope that thou wouldst
      free
   This world from its dark slavery,
   That thou, O awful LOVELINESS,   30
Wouldst give whate'er these words cannot
   express.

The day becomes more solemn and serene   35
   When noon is past; there is a harmony
   In autumn, and a luster in its sky,
Which through the summer is not heard or
   seen,
As if it could not be, as if it had not been!   40
   Thus let thy power, which like the truth
   Of nature on my passive youth
Descended, to my onward life supply
   Its calm,—to one who worships thee,
   And every form containing thee,   45
   Whom, SPIRIT fair, thy spells did bind
To fear himself, and love all humankind.

OZYMANDIAS

I met a traveler from an antique land   50
Who said: "Two vast and trunkless legs of
   stone

Stand in the desert. Near them, on the sand,
Half sunk, a shattered visage lies, whose
   frown,
And wrinkled lip, and sneer of cold com-
   mand,
Tell that its sculptor well those passions read
Which yet survive, stamped on these lifeless
   things,
The hand that mocked them, and the heart
   that fed:
And on the pedestal these words appear:
'My name is Ozymandias, King of Kings:
Look on my works, ye Mighty, and despair!'
Nothing beside remains. Round the decay
Of that colossal wreck, boundless and bare
The lone and level sands stretch far away."

SONG TO THE MEN OF ENGLAND

Men of England, wherefore plow
For the lords who lay ye low?
Wherefore weave with toil and care
The rich robes your tyrants wear?

Wherefore feed, and clothe, and save,
From the cradle to the grave,
Those ungrateful drones who would
Drain your sweat—nay, drink your blood?

Wherefore, bees of England, forge
Many a weapon, chain, and scourge,
That these stingless drones may spoil
The forced produce of your toil?

Have ye leisure, comfort, calm,
Shelter, food, love's gentle balm?
Or what is it ye buy so dear
With your pain and with your fear?

The seed ye sow, another reaps;
The wealth ye find, another keeps;
The robes ye weave, another wears;
The arms ye forge, another bears.

Sow seed—but let no tyrant reap;
Find wealth—let no impostor heap;
Weave robes—let not the idle wear;
Forge arms—in your defense to bear.

Shrink to your cellars, holes, and cells;
In halls ye deck another dwells.

Why shake the chains ye wrought? Ye see
The steel ye tempered glance on ye.

With plow and spade, and hoe and loom,
Trace your grave, and build your tomb,
And weave your winding-sheet, till fair
England be your sepulcher.

ODE TO THE WEST WIND

1

O wild West Wind, thou breath of Autumn's
    being,
Thou, from whose unseen presence the leaves
    dead
Are driven, like ghosts from an enchanter
    fleeing,

Yellow, and black, and pale, and hectic red,
Pestilence-stricken multitudes! O thou
Who chariotest to their dark wintry bed

The wingèd seeds, where they lie cold and
    low,
Each like a corpse within its grave, until
Thine azure sister of the Spring shall blow

Her clarion o'er the dreaming earth, and fill
(Driving sweet buds like flocks to feed in air)
With living hues and odors plain and hill:

Wild Spirit, which art moving everywhere;
Destroyer and Preserver; hear, oh hear!

2

Thou on whose stream, 'mid the steep sky's
    commotion,
Loose clouds like earth's decaying leaves are
    shed,
Shook from the tangled boughs of heaven and
    ocean,

Angels of rain and lightning! there are spread
On the blue surface of thine airy surge,
Like the bright hair uplifted from the head

Of some fierce Mænad,[1] even from the dim
    verge
Of the horizon to the zenith's height,

The locks of the approaching storm. Thou
    dirge

Of the dying year, to which this closing night
Will be the dome of a vast sepulchre,
Vaulted with all thy congregated might

Of vapors, from whose solid atmosphere
Black rain, and fire, and hail, will burst: Oh
    hear!

3

Thou who didst waken from his summer-
    dreams
The blue Mediterranean, where he lay,
Lulled by the coil of his crystalline streams,

Beside a pumice isle in Baiae's[2] bay,
And saw in sleep old palaces and towers
Quivering within the wave's intenser day,

All overgrown with azure moss, and flowers
So sweet, the sense faints picturing them!
    Thou
For whose path the Atlantic's level powers

Cleave themselves into chasms, while far be-
    low
The sea-blooms and the oozy woods which
    wear
The sapless foliage of the ocean know

Thy voice, and suddenly grow gray with fear
And tremble and despoil themselves: Oh hear!

4

If I were a dead leaf thou mightest bear;
If I were a swift cloud to fly with thee;
A wave to pant beneath thy power, and share

The impulse of thy strength, only less free
Than Thou, O uncontrollable! If even
I were as in my boyhood, and could be

The comrade of thy wanderings over heaven,
As then, when to outstrip thy skyey speed
Scarce seemed a vision; I would ne'er have
    striven

As thus with thee in prayer in my sore need.

---

[1] bacchante.

[2] seaport near Naples.

Oh! lift me as a wave, a leaf, a cloud!
I fall upon the thorns of life! I bleed!

A heavy weight of hours has chained and
    bowed
One too like thee—tameless, and swift, and
    proud.

5

Make me thy lyre, ev'n as the forest is:
What if my leaves are falling like its own!
The tumult of thy mighty harmonies

Will take from both a deep, autumnal tone,
Sweet though in sadness. Be thou, Spirit fierce,
My spirit! be thou me, impetuous one!

Drive my dead thoughts over the universe,
Like withered leaves, to quicken a new birth!
And, by the incantation of this verse,

Scatter, as from an unextinguished hearth
Ashes and sparks, my words among mankind!
Be through my lips to unawakened earth

The trumpet of a prophecy! O wind,
If Winter comes, can Spring be far behind?

THE CLOUD

I bring fresh showers for the thirsting flowers,
    From the seas and the streams;
I bear light shade for the leaves when laid
    In their noonday dreams.
From my wings are shaken the dews that
    waken
    The sweet buds every one,
When rocked to rest on their mother's breast,
    As she dances about the sun.
I wield the flail of the lashing hail,
    And whiten the green plains under,
And then again I dissolve it in rain,
    And laugh as I pass in thunder.

I sift the snow on the mountains below,
    And their great pines groan aghast;
And all the night 'tis my pillow white,
    While I sleep in the arms of the blast.
Sublime on the towers of my skyey bowers,
    Lightning my pilot sits;
In a cavern under is fettered the thunder,
    It struggles and howls at fits;

Over earth and ocean, with gentle motion,
    This pilot is guiding me,
Lured by the love of the genii that move
    In the depths of the purple sea;
Over the rills, and the crags, and the hills,
    Over the lakes and the plains,
Wherever he dream, under mountain or stream,
    The Spirit he loves remains;
And I all the while bask in Heaven's blue
    smile,
    Whilst he is dissolving in rains.

The sanguine Sunrise, with his meteor eyes,
    And his burning plumes outspread,
Leaps on the back of my sailing rack,
    When the morning star shines dead;
As on the jag of a mountain crag,
    Which an earthquake rocks and swings,
An eagle alit one moment may sit
    In the light of its golden wings.
And when Sunset may breathe, from the lit sea
    beneath,
    Its ardors of rest and of love,
And the crimson pall of eve may fall
    From the depth of Heaven above,
With wings folded I rest, on mine airy nest,
    As still as a brooding dove.

That orbèd maiden with white fire laden,
    Whom mortals call the Moon,
Glides glimmering o'er my fleece-like floor,
    By the midnight breezes strewn;
And wherever the beat of her unseen feet,
    Which only the angels hear,
May have broken the woof of my tent's thin
    roof,
    The stars peep behind her and peer;
And I laugh to see them whirl and flee,
    Like a swarm of golden bees,
When I widen the rent in my wind-built tent,
    Till the calm rivers, lakes, and seas,
Like strips of the sky fallen through me on
    high,
    Are each paved with the moon and these.

I bind the Sun's throne with a burning zone,
    And the Moon's with a girdle of pearl;
The volcanoes are dim, and the stars reel and
    swim
    When the whirlwinds my banner unfurl.
From cape to cape, with a bridge-like shape,
    Over a torrent sea,

Sunbeam-proof, I hang like a roof,—
  The mountains its columns be.
The triumphal arch, through which I march,
  With hurricane, fire, and snow,
When the Powers of the air are chained to my   5
    chair,
  Is the million-colored bow;
The sphere-fire above its soft colors wove,
  While the moist Earth was laughing below.

I am the daughter of Earth and Water,
  And the nursling of the Sky;
I pass through the pores of the ocean and
    shores,
  I change, but I cannot die.   15
For after the rain when with never a stain
  The pavilion of Heaven is bare,
And the winds and sunbeams with their con-
    vex gleams
  Build up the blue dome of air,   20
I silently laugh at my own cenotaph,
  And out of the caverns of rain,
Like a child from the womb, like a ghost from
    the tomb,
  I arise and unbuild it again.   25

TO A SKYLARK

Hail to thee, blithe Spirit!   30
  Bird thou never wert,
That from Heaven, or near it,
  Pourest thy full heart
In profuse strains of unpremeditated art.

Higher still and higher
  From the earth thou springest
Like a cloud of fire;
  The blue deep thou wingest,
And singing still dost soar, and soaring ever 40
    singest.

In the golden lightning
  Of the sunken sun,
O'er which clouds are bright'ning,   45
  Thou dost float and run;
Like an unbodied joy whose race is just begun.

The pale purple even
  Melts around thy flight;   50
Like a star of Heaven,
  In the broad daylight

Thou art unseen,—but yet I hear thy shrill
  delight,

  Keen as are the arrows
    Of that silver sphere,
  Whose intense lamp narrows
    In the white dawn clear
Until we hardly see—we feel that it is there;

  All the earth and air
    With thy voice is loud,
  As, when night is bare,
    From one lonely cloud
The moon rains out her beams, and Heaven is
    overflowed.

  What thou art we know not;
    What is most like thee?
  From rainbow clouds there flow not
    Drops so bright to see
As from thy presence showers a rain of melody.

  Like a Poet hidden
    In the light of thought,
  Singing hymns unbidden,
    Till the world is wrought
To sympathy with hopes and fears it heeded
    not:

  Like a high-born maiden
    In a palace-tower,
  Soothing her love-laden
    Soul in secret hour
With music sweet as love,—which overflows
    her bower:

  Like a glowworm golden
    In a dell of dew,
  Scattering unbeholden
    Its aërial hue
Among the flowers and grass which screen it
    from the view:

  Like a rose embowered
    In its own green leaves,
  By warm winds deflowered,
    Till the scent it gives
Makes faint with too much sweet those heavy
    wingèd thieves.

  Sound of vernal showers
    On the twinkling grass,

Rain-awakened flowers,
    All that ever was
Joyous and clear and fresh, thy music doth
    surpass.

Teach us, Sprite or Bird,
    What sweet thoughts are thine;
I have never heard
    Praise of love or wine
That panted forth a flood of rapture so di- 10
    vine.

Chorus Hymeneal,
    Or triumphal chant,
Matched with thine, would be all   15
    But an empty vaunt,
A thing wherein we feel there is some hidden
    want.

What objects are the fountains   20
    Of thy happy strain?
What fields or waves or mountains?
    What shapes of sky or plain?
What love of thine own kind? what ignorance
    of pain?   25

With thy clear keen joyance
    Languor cannot be;
Shadow of annoyance
    Never came near thee;   30
Thou lovest—but ne'er knew love's sad satiety.

Waking or asleep,
    Thou of death must deem
Things more true and deep   35
    Than we mortals dream—
Or how could thy notes flow in such a crystal
    stream?

We look before and after,
    And pine for what is not;   40
Our sincerest laughter
    With some pain is fraught;
Our sweetest songs are those that tell of sad-
    dest thought.

Yet if we could scorn   45
    Hate, and pride, and fear;
If we were things born
    Not to shed a tear,   50
I know not how thy joy we ever should come
    near.

Better than all measures
    Of delightful sound,
Better than all treasures
    That in books are found,
5 Thy skill to poet were, thou scorner of the
    ground!

Teach me half the gladness
    That thy brain must know,
Such harmonious madness
    From my lips would flow
The world should listen then—as I am listen-
    ing now.

TO ——

Music, when soft voices die,
Vibrates in the memory—
Odors, when sweet violets sicken,
Live within the sense they quicken,

Rose leaves, when the rose is dead,
Are heaped for the beloved's bed;
And so thy thoughts, when thou art gone
Love itself shall slumber on.

JOHN KEATS*

SONNET

ON FIRST LOOKING INTO CHAPMAN'S HOMER

Much have I travelled in the realms of gold,
    And many goodly states and kingdoms seen;
    Round many western islands have I been
Which bards in fealty to Apollo hold.
Oft of one wide expanse had I been told
    That deep-browed Homer ruled as his de-
    mesne:
    Yet did I never breathe its pure serene
Till I heard Chapman[1] speak out loud and
    bold:
Then felt I like some watcher of the skies
    When a new planet swims into his ken;
Or like stout Cortez[2] when with eagle eyes
    He stared at the Pacific—and all his men
Looked at each other with a wild surmise—
    Silent, upon a peak in Darien.[3]

---

* For introductory sketch see I, 138.
[1] Elizabethan dramatist and translator, George
Chapman, "Englished" Homer.
[2] error for Balboa.   [3] on Isthmus of Panama.

WHEN I HAVE FEARS THAT I MAY CEASE TO BE

When I have fears that I may cease to be
  Before my pen has gleaned my teeming 5
    brain,
Before high-piled books, in charactery,
  Hold like rich garners the full-ripened grain;
When I behold, upon the night's starred face,
  Huge cloudy symbols of a high romance, 10
And think that I may never live to trace
  Their shadows, with the magic hand of
    chance;
And when I feel, fair creature of an hour,
  That I shall never look upon thee more, 15
Never have relish in the faery power
  Of unreflecting love;—then on the shore
Of the wide world I stand alone, and think
Till love and fame to nothingness do sink.
    20

ODE ON MELANCHOLY

No, no, go not to Lethe,[1] neither twist
  Wolf's-bane,[2] tight-rooted, for its poisonous
    wine;
Nor suffer thy pale forehead to be kissed
  By nightshade, ruby grape of Prosperpine;[3] 25
Make not your rosary of yew-berries,[4]
  Nor let the beetle,[5] nor the death-moth[6] be
    Your mournful Psyche,[7] nor the downy 30
    owl
A partner in your sorrow's mysteries;
  For shade to shade will come too drowsily,
    And drown the wakeful anguish of the
    soul. 35

But when the melancholy fit shall fall
  Sudden from heaven like a weeping cloud,
That fosters the droop-headed flowers all,
  And hides the green hill in an April shroud; 40
Then glut thy sorrow on a morning rose,
  Or on the rainbow of the salt sand-wave,
   Or on the wealth of globed peonies;
Or if thy mistress some rich anger shows,
  Emprison her soft hand, and let her rave, 45

[1] river of oblivion in Hades.
[2] poisonous plant; nightshade also poisonous.
[3] queen of the lower regions.
[4] Yew is symbol of grief.
[5] The ancients placed beetles in coffins.
[6] moth with skull markings.
[7] the soul.

And feed deep, deep upon her peerless
  eyes.

She dwells with Beauty—Beauty that must
  die;
  And Joy, whose hand is ever at his lips
Bidding adieu; and aching Pleasure nigh,
  Turning to poison while the bee-mouth sips:
Ay, in the very temple of Delight
  Veiled Melancholy has her sovran shrine,
    Though seen of none save him whose
    strenuous tongue
  Can burst Joy's grape against his palate fine;
His soul shall taste the sadness of her might,
  And be among her cloudy trophies hung.

ODE ON A GRECIAN URN

1

Thou still unravished bride of quietness,
  Thou foster-child of Silence and slow Time,
Sylvan historian, who canst thus express
  A flowery tale more sweetly than our rhyme:
What leaf-fringed legend haunts about thy
  shape
  Of deities or mortals, or of both,
    In Tempe or the dales of Arcady?[1]
What men or gods are these? What maidens
  loth?
What mad pursuit? What struggle to escape?
    What pipes and timbrels? What wild ec-
    stasy?

2

Heard melodies are sweet, but those unheard
  Are sweeter; therefore, ye soft pipes, play
    on;
Not to the sensual ear, but, more endeared,
  Pipe to the spirit ditties of no tone:
Fair youth, beneath the trees, thou canst not
  leave
  Thy song, nor ever can those trees be bare;
    Bold Lover, never, never canst thou kiss,
Though winning near the goal—yet, do not
  grieve;
  She cannot fade, though thou hast not thy
  bliss,
  For ever wilt thou love, and she be fair!

[1] regions in Greece suggesting pastoral background.

3

Ah, happy, happy boughs! that cannot shed
　Your leaves, nor ever bid the Spring adieu;
And, happy melodist, unwearied,
　For ever piping songs for ever new.
More happy love! more happy, happy love!
　For ever warm and still to be enjoyed,
　For ever panting, and for ever young;
All breathing human passion far above,
　That leaves a heart high-sorrowful and
　　cloyed,
　　A burning forehead, and a parching
　　tongue.

4

Who are these coming to the sacrifice?
　To what green altar, O mysterious priest,
Lead'st thou that heifer lowing at the skies,
　And all her silken flanks with garlands
　　drest?
What little town by river or sea shore,
　Or mountain-built with peaceful citadel,
　Is emptied of this folk, this pious morn?
And, little town, thy streets for evermore
　Will silent be; and not a soul to tell
　Why thou art desolate, can e'er return.

5

O Attic shape! Fair attitude! with brede
Of marble men and maidens overwrought,
With forest branches and the trodden weed;
　Thou, silent form! dost tease us out of
　　thought
As doth eternity: Cold Pastoral!
　When old age shall this generation waste,
　Thou shalt remain, in midst of other woe
Than ours, a friend to man, to whom thou
　say'st,
"Beauty is truth, truth beauty,"—that is all
　Ye know on earth, and all ye need to
　know.

ODE TO A NIGHTINGALE

1

My heart aches, and a drowsy numbness pains
　My sense, as though of hemlock[1] I had
　　drunk,
Or emptied some dull opiate to the drains

One minute past, and Lethe-wards had
　sunk:
'Tis not through envy of thy happy lot,
　But being too happy in thine happiness,—
　That thou, light-winged Dryad[2] of the
　　trees,
　　In some melodious plot
Of beechen green, and shadows numberless,
　Singest of summer in full-throated ease.

2

O for a draught of vintage! that hath been
　Cooled a long age in the deep-delved earth,
Tasting of Flora[3] and the country green,
　Dance, and Provençal[4] song, and sunburnt
　　mirth!
O for a beaker full of the warm South,
　Full of the true, the blushful Hippocrene,[5]
　With beaded bubbles winking at the
　　brim,
　　And purple-stained mouth;
That I might drink, and leave the world
　unseen,
And with thee fade away into the forest
　dim:

3

Fade far away, dissolve, and quite forget
　What thou among the leaves hast never
　known,
The weariness, the fever, and the fret
　Here, where men sit and hear each other
　　groan;
Where palsy shakes a few, sad, last gray hairs,
　Where youth grows pale, and spectre-thin,
　　and dies;
　　Where but to think is to be full of sorrow
　　And leaden-eyed despairs,
Where Beauty cannot keep her lustrous
　eyes,
　Or new Love pine at them beyond to-
　morrow.

4

Away! away! for I will fly to thee,
　Not charioted by Bacchus and his pards,[6]

---

[1] poison.

[2] tree nymph.　　　[3] goddess of flowers.
[4] Medieval home of troubadours was in Provence
(southern France).
[5] fountain sacred to muses.
[6] Bacchus, god of wine, was accompanied by
leopards (pards) and other beasts.

But on the viewless wings of Poesy,
  Though the dull brain perplexes and re-
    tards:
Already with thee! tender is the night,
  And haply the Queen-Moon is on her   5
    throne,
    Clustered around by all her starry Fays;
      But here there is no light,
  Save what from heaven is with the breezes
    blown   10
    Through verdurous glooms and winding
      mossy ways.

5

I cannot see what flowers are at my feet,   15
  Nor what soft incense hangs upon the
    boughs,
But, in embalmed darkness, guess each sweet
  Wherewith the seasonable month endows
The grass, the thicket, and the fruit-tree wild; 20
  White hawthorn, and the pastoral eglantine;
    Fast-fading violets covered up in leaves;
      And mid-May's eldest child,
  The coming musk-rose, full of dewy wine,
    The murmurous haunt of flies on summer   25
      eves.

6

Darkling I listen; and for many a time
  I have been half in love with easeful Death, 30
Called him soft names in many a mused rhyme,
  To take into the air my quiet breath;
Now more than ever seems it rich to die,
  To cease upon the midnight with no pain,
    While thou art pouring forth thy soul   35
      abroad
        In such an ecstasy!
  Still wouldst thou sing, and I have ears in
    vain—
    To thy high requiem become a sod.   40

7

Thou wast not born for death, immortal Bird!
  No hungry generations tread thee down;
The voice I hear this passing night was heard 45
  In ancient days by emperor and clown:
Perhaps the self-same song that found a path
  Through the sad heart of Ruth, when, sick
    for home,
    She stood in tears amid the alien corn;[7] 50

The same that oft-times hath
  Charmed magic casements, opening on the
    foam
    Of perilous seas, in faery lands forlorn.

8

Forlorn! the very word is like a bell
  To toll me back from thee to my sole self!
Adieu! the fancy cannot cheat so well
  As she is famed to do, deceiving elf.   10
Adieu! adieu! thy plaintive anthem fades
  Past the near meadows, over the still stream,
    Up the hill-side; and now 'tis buried deep
      In the next valley-glades:
  Was it a vision, or a waking dream?   15
    Fled is that music:—Do I wake or sleep?

WILLIAM CULLEN BRYANT

Bryant (1794–1878) was educated at Williams 20
College in his native Massachusetts and set out
to practice law. The publication of "Thanatop-
sis" led to the Poems of 1821, *and finally, in*
1825, Bryant decided to give up law. He was
later to become editor of the New York Eve- 25
ning Post *for several decades. His poems kept*
coming out meanwhile. Although at one time
Bryant was considered the best living Amer-
ican poet, his work is limited in its field of Na-
ture; his emotion is low-pitched; some poems 30
sound like second-rate Shelley or Wordsworth.
Nevertheless he has his followers among those
who value his fundamental decency, intelli-
gence, and didacticism, and who forgive his
*lack of depth or originality.** 35

THANATOPSIS[1]

To him who in the love of Nature holds
Communion with her visible forms, she speaks
A various language: for his gayer hours
She has a voice of gladness, and a smile
And eloquence of beauty; and she glides
Into his darker musings, with a mild
And healing sympathy that steals away
Their sharpness ere he is aware. When
  thoughts
Of the last bitter hour come like a blight

---

* The selections from Bryant's poetry are printed
with the permission of the publisher, Appleton-
Century-Crofts, Inc.
[1] View of death.

---

[7] See Book of Ruth in the Bible.

Over thy spirit, and sad images
Of the stern agony and shroud and pall
And breathless darkness and the narrow house
Make thee to shudder and grow sick at heart,
Go forth under the open sky and list   5
To Nature's teachings, while from all around—
Earth and her waters and the depths of air—
Comes a still voice:
                         Yet a few days, and thee
The all-beholding sun shall see no more
In all his course; nor yet in the cold ground,   10
Where thy pale form was laid with many tears,
Nor in the embrace of ocean, shall exist
Thy image. Earth, that nourished thee, shall
        claim   15
Thy growth, to be resolved to earth again,
And, lost each human trace, surrendering up
Thine individual being, shalt thou go
To mix for ever with the elements,
To be a brother to the insensible rock   20
And to the sluggish clod, which the rude swain
Turns with his share and treads upon; the oak
Shall send his roots abroad and pierce thy
        mould.

    Yet not to thine eternal resting-place   25
Shalt thou retire alone, nor couldst thou wish
Couch more magnificent. Thou shalt lie down
With patriarchs of the infant world, with
        kings,
The powerful of the earth, the wise, the good,
Fair forms, and hoary seers of ages past,
All in one mighty sepulchre. The hills
Rock-ribbed and ancient as the sun; the vales
Stretching in pensive quietness between;
The venerable woods, rivers that move
In majesty, and the complaining brooks
That make the meadows green; and, poured
        round all,
Old Ocean's gray and melancholy waste,—   40
Are but the solemn decorations all
Of the great tomb of man. The golden sun,
The planets, all the infinite host of heaven,
Are shining on the sad abodes of death,
Through the still lapse of ages. All that tread   45
The globe are but a handful to the tribes
That slumber in its bosom. Take the wings
Of morning, pierce the Barcan[2] wilderness,
Or lose thyself in the continuous woods
Where rolls the Oregon, and hears no sound   50

───────────
    [2] African.

Save his own dashings; yet the dead are there,
And millions in those solitudes, since first
The flight of years began, have laid them down
In their last sleep: the dead reign there alone.
So shalt thou rest; and what if thou withdraw   5
In silence from the living, and no friend
Take note of thy departure? All that breathe
Will share thy destiny. The gay will laugh
When thou art gone, the solemn brood of care
Plod on, and each one as before will chase   10
His favorite phantom; yet all these shall leave
Their mirth and their employments, and shall
        come
And make their bed with thee. As the long
        train   15
Of ages glide away, the sons of men—
The youth in life's green spring, and he who
        goes
In the full strength of years, matron and maid,
The speechless babe, and the gray-headed   20
        man—
Shall one by one be gathered to thy side
By those who in their turn shall follow them.

    So live that when thy summons comes to   25
        join
The innumerable caravan which moves
To that mysterious realm where each shall take
His chamber in the silent halls of death,
Thou go not, like the quarry-slave at night,   30
Scourged to his dungeon, but, sustained and
        soothed
By an unfaltering trust, approach thy grave
Like one who wraps the drapery of his couch
About him and lies down to pleasant dreams.   35

TO A WATERFOWL

    Whither, midst falling dew,
While glow the heavens with the last steps of   40
        day,
Far, through their rosy depths, dost thou pur-
        sue
    Thy solitary way?

    Vainly the fowler's eye
Might mark thy distant flight to do thee wrong,
As, darkly seen against the crimson sky,
    Thy figure floats along.

    Seek'st thou the plashy brink
Of weedy lake, or marge of river wide,

Or where the rocking billows rise and sink
  On the chafed ocean-side?

There is a Power whose care
Teaches thy way along that pathless coast— 5
The desert and illimitable air—
  Lone wandering, but not lost.

All day thy wings have fanned,
At that far height, the cold thin atmosphere, 10
Yet stoop not, weary, to the welcome land,
  Though the dark night is near.

And soon that toil shall end:
Soon shalt thou find a summer home, and rest, 15
And scream among thy fellows; reeds shall
    bend,
  Soon, o'er thy sheltered nest.

Thou'rt gone, the abyss of heaven
Hath swallowed up thy form; yet, on my heart 20
Deeply has sunk the lesson thou hast given,
  And shall not soon depart.

He who, from zone to zone, 25
Guides through the boundless sky thy certain
    flight,
In the long way that I must tread alone,
  Will lead my steps aright.

TO THE FRINGED GENTIAN

Thou blossom bright with autumn dew,
And colored with the heaven's own blue,
That openest when the quiet light
Succeeds the keen and frosty night,

Thou comest not when violets lean
O'er wandering brooks and springs unseen, 40
Or columbines, in purple dressed,
Nod o'er the ground-bird's hidden nest.

Thou waitest late and com'st alone,
When woods are bare and birds are flown, 45
And frosts and shortening days portend
The aged year is near his end.

Then doth thy sweet and quiet eye
Look through its fringes to the sky, 50
Blue—blue—as if that sky let fall
A flower from its cerulean wall.

I would that thus, when I shall see
The hour of death draw near to me,
Hope, blossoming within my heart,
May look to heaven as I depart.

EDGAR ALLAN POE

If poets must suffer or live Bohemian lives (as some lay opinion would have it), Poe (1809–1849) would qualify on both counts. He is the sole member of the early American group of "major" writers who was weak, poor, or abandoned, the only one to die young. Ironically, while the others had respectability, not one had the touch, the genius of this erratic individual.

Poe's life is a series of troubles and frustrations. Bereft of parents by death and desertion, he quarreled with his benefactor, John Allan. He was involved in family scandal. He got nowhere at the University of Virginia, was dismissed from West Point. He lost editorial jobs —though writing poems and stories for many reputable magazines—because he drank. His wife Virginia died of tuberculosis. A good bit of the time Poe was in poverty because of his habits. He could never quite achieve stability. After attempted suicide and following indecision over three ladies, Poe became engaged, but never reached his wedding: he was found in bad shape under strange circumstances near a Baltimore saloon. He died shortly afterward.

Separating moral criticism from literary criticism, few will dispute Poe's claim to a significant place in American letters, though all will not agree on details. English, American, and French writers have confessed his influence. In developing detective and horror stories and experimenting with mood poetry in place of conventional rhapsodies, Poe had both originality and power. (For further comment on Poe, see II, 430.)

ROMANCE

Romance, who loves to nod and sing,
With drowsy head and folded wing,
Among the green leaves as they shake
Far down within some shadowy lake,
To me a painted paroquet
Hath been—a most familiar bird—
Taught me my alphabet to say—

To lisp my very earliest word
While in the wild wood I did lie,
A child—with a most knowing eye.

Of late, eternal Condor years   5
So shake the very Heaven on high
With tumult as they thunder by,
I have no time for idle cares
Through gazing on the unquiet sky.
And when an hour with calmer wings   10
Its down upon my spirit flings—
That little time with lyre and rhyme
To while away—forbidden things!
My heart would feel to be a crime
Unless it trembled with the strings.   15

THE CITY IN THE SEA

Lo! Death has reared himself a throne
In a strange city lying alone   20
Far down within the dim West,
Where the good and the bad and the
        worst and the best
Have gone to their eternal rest.
There shrines and palaces and towers   25
(Time-eaten towers that tremble not!)
Resemble nothing that is ours.
Around, by lifting winds forgot,
Resignedly beneath the sky
The melancholy waters lie.   30

No rays from the holy heaven come down
On the long night-time of that town;
But light from out the lurid sea
Streams up the turrets silently—   35
Gleams up the pinnacles far and free—
Up domes—up spires—up kingly halls—
Up fanes—up Babylon-like walls—
Up shadowy long-forgotten bowers
Of sculptured ivy and stone flowers—   40
Up many and many a marvellous shrine
Whose wreathèd friezes intertwine
The viol, the violet, and the vine.
Resignedly beneath the sky
The melancholy waters lie.   45
So blend the turrets and shadows there
That all seem pendulous in air,
While from a proud tower in the town
Death looks gigantically down.
                                                 50
There open fanes and gaping graves
Yawn level with the luminous waves

But not the riches there that lie
In each idol's diamond eye—
Not the gayly-jewelled dead
Tempt the waters from their bed;
For no ripples curl, alas!
Along that wilderness of glass—
No swellings tell that winds may be
Upon some far-off happier sea—
No heavings hint that winds have been
On seas less hideously serene.

But lo, a stir is in the air!
The wave—there is a movement there!
As if the towers had thrust aside,
In slightly sinking, the dull tide—
As if their tops had feebly given
A void within the filmy Heaven.
The waves have now a redder glow—
The hours are breathing faint and low—
And when, amid no earthly moans,
Down, down that town shall settle hence,
Hell, rising from a thousand thrones,
Shall do it reverence.

THE CONQUEROR WORM

Lo! 't is a gala night
    Within the lonesome latter years!
An angel throng, bewinged, bedight
    In veils, and drowned in tears,
Sit in a theatre, to see
    A play of hopes and fears,
While the orchestra breathes fitfully
    The music of the spheres.

Mimes, in the form of God on high,
    Mutter and mumble low,
And hither and thither fly—
    Mere puppets they, who come and go
At bidding of vast formless things
    That shift the scenery to and fro,
Flapping from out their Condor wings
    Invisible Woe!

That motley drama—oh, be sure
    It shall not be forgot!
With its Phantom chased for evermore,
    By a crowd that seize it not,
Through a circle that ever returneth in
    To the self-same spot,
And much of Madness, and more of Sin,
    And Horror the soul of the plot.

But see, amid the mimic rout
  A crawling shape intrude!
A blood-red thing that writhes from out
  The scenic solitude!
It writhes!—it writhes!—with mortal
    pangs   5
  The mimes become its food,
And seraphs sob at vermin fangs
  In human gore imbued.

Out—out are the lights—out all!
  And, over each quivering form,
The curtain, a funeral pall,   10
  Comes down with the rush of a storm,
While the angels, all pallid and wan,   15
  Uprising, unveiling, affirm
That the play is the tragedy, 'Man,'
  And its hero the Conqueror Worm.

THE HAUNTED PALACE

In the greenest of our valleys
  By good angels tenanted,
Once a fair and stately palace—
  Radiant palace—reared its head.
In the monarch Thought's dominion—
  It stood there!
Never seraph spread a pinion
  Over fabric half so fair!

Banners yellow, glorious, golden,
  On its roof did float and flow,
(This—all this—was in the olden
  Time long ago)
And every gentle air that dallied
  In that sweet day
Along the ramparts plumed and pallid,
  A wingèd odor went away.

Wanderers in that happy valley,
  Through two luminous windows saw
Spirits moving musically
  To a lute's well-tunèd law,
Round about a throne where, sitting,
  (Porphyrogene!)
In state his glory well befitting,
  The ruler of the realm was seen.

And all with pearl and ruby glowing
  Was the fair palace door,
Through which came flowing, flowing,
    flowing

  And sparkling evermore,
A troop of Echoes, whose sweet duty
  Was but to sing,
In voices of surpassing beauty,
  The wit and wisdom of their king.

But evil things, in robes of sorrow,
  Assailed the monarch's high estate.
(Ah, let us mourn!—for never morrow
  Shall dawn upon him desolate!)
And round about his home the glory
  That blushed and bloomed,
Is but a dim-remembered story
  Of the old time entombed.

And travellers, now, within that valley,
  Through the red-litten windows see
Vast forms, that move fantastically
  To a discordant melody,
While, like a ghastly rapid river,   20
  Through the pale door
A hideous throng rush out forever
  And laugh—but smile no more.

25

ULALUME

The skies they were ashen and sober;
  The leaves they were crispèd and sere—
  The leaves they were withering and sere;
30 It was night in the lonesome October
  Of my most immemorial year;
It was hard by the dim lake of Auber,
  In the misty mid region of Weir—
It was down by the dank tarn of Auber,
35 In the ghoul-haunted woodland of Weir.

Here once, through an alley Titanic,
  Of cypress, I roamed with my Soul—
  Of cypress, with Psyche, my Soul.
40 These were days when my heart was volcanic
  As the scoriac rivers that roll—
  As the lavas that restlessly roll
Their sulphurous currents down Yaanek
  In the ultimate climes of the pole—
45 That groan as they roll down Mount Yaanek
  In the realms of the boreal pole.

Our talk had been serious and sober,
  But our thoughts they were palsied and
50   sere—
  Our memories were treacherous and sere—
For we knew not the month was October,

And we marked not the night of the year—
(Ah, night of all nights in the year!)
We noted not the dim lake of Auber—
(Though once we have journeyed down
here)—
Remembered not the dank tarn of Auber,
Nor the ghoul-haunted woodland of Weir.

And now, as the night was senescent
And star-dials pointed to morn—
As the star-dials hinted of morn—
At the end of our path a liquescent
And nebulous lustre was born,
Out of which a miraculous crescent
Arose with a duplicate horn—
Astarte's bediamonded crescent
Distinct with its duplicate horn.

And I said—"She is warmer than Dian:
She rolls through an ether of sighs—
She revels in a region of sighs:
She has seen that the tears are not dry on
These cheeks, where the worm never dies
And has come past the stars of the Lion
To point us the path to the skies—
To the Lethean peace of the skies—
Come up, in despite of the Lion,
To shine on us with her bright eyes—
Come up through the lair of the Lion,
With love in her luminous eyes."

But Psyche, uplifting her finger,
Said—"Sadly this star I mistrust—
Her pallor I strangely mistrust:—
Oh, hasten!—oh, let us not linger!
Oh, fly!—let us fly!—for we must."
In terror she spoke, letting sink her
Wings until they trailed in the dust—
In agony sobbed, letting sink her
Plumes till they trailed in the dust—
Till they sorrowfully trailed in the dust.

I replied—"This is nothing but dreaming:
Let us on by this tremulous light!
Let us bathe in the crystalline light!
Its Sibyllic splendor is beaming
With Hope and in Beauty to-night:—
See!—it flickers up the sky through the night!
Ah, we safely may trust to its gleaming,
And be sure it will lead us aright—
We safely may trust to a gleaming
That cannot but guide us aright,

Since it flickers up to Heaven through the
night."

5   Thus I pacified Psyche and kissed her,
And tempted her out of her gloom—
And conquered her scruples and gloom;
And we passed to the end of the vista,
But were stopped by the door of a tomb—
By the door of a legended tomb;
10   And I said—"What is written, sweet sister,
On the door of this legended tomb?"
She replied—"Ulalume—Ulalume—
'Tis the vault of thy lost Ulalume!"

15   Then my heart it grew ashen and sober
As the leaves that were crispèd and sere—
As the leaves that were withering and sere,
And I cried—"It was surely October
On *this* very night of last year
20   That I journeyed—I journeyed down here—
That I brought a dread burden down here—
On this night of all nights in the year,
Ah, what demon has tempted me here?
Well I know, now, this dim lake of Auber—
25   This misty mid region of Weir—
Well I know, now, this dank tarn of Auber,
This ghoul-haunted woodland of Weir."

RALPH WALDO EMERSON

*Another New Englander with solid back-
ground, Emerson (1803–1882) headed for
Harvard and what was to have been a career
in divine service. Unanswerable doubts, how-*
35 *ever, drove him from the church (it is disap-
pointing that, unlike Donne or Crashaw, he
produced no significant poetry from the turmoil). Emerson lived the quiet literary life—
writing, traveling, making friends with great*
40 *literary men (Carlyle), reading, lecturing, and
hovering among the Transcendentalists. In
reading his poems today, one is rarely lifted off
the ground or deeply stirred; but one never
misses for a moment the feeling of being in the*
45 *presence of a strong mind and sound thought.
Emerson had the self-reliance he wrote about.
He commanded respect in his day, and still
does—but not primarily as a creative poet.
(See also II, 88.)**

50   ———————
* The selections from Emerson's poetry are reprinted by kind permission of the publisher, Houghton Mifflin Company.

THE RHODORA:

ON BEING ASKED, WHENCE IS THE FLOWER?

In May, when sea-winds pierced our solitudes,
I found the fresh Rhodora in the woods,
Spreading its leafless blooms in a damp nook,
To please the desert and the sluggish brook.
The purple petals, fallen in the pool,
Made the black water with their beauty gay;
Here might the redbird come his plumes to 10
  cool,
And court the flower that cheapens his array.
Rhodora! if the sages ask thee why
This charm is wasted on the earth and sky,
Tell them, dear, that if eyes were made for 15
  seeing,
Then Beauty is its own excuse for being:
Why thou wert there, O rival of the rose!
I never thought to ask, I never knew:
But, in my simple ignorance, suppose
The self-same Power that brought me there
  brought you.

THE SNOW-STORM

Announced by all the trumpets of the sky,
Arrives the snow, and, driving o'er the fields,
Seems nowhere to alight: the whited air
Hides hills and woods, the river, and the
  heaven,
And veils the farm-house at the garden's end.
The sled and traveller stopped, the courier's
  feet
Delayed, all friends shut out, the housemates
  sit
Around the radiant fireplace, enclosed
In a tumultuous privacy of storm.

Come see the north wind's masonry.
Out of an unseen quarry evermore
Furnished with tile, the fierce artificer
Curves his white bastions with projected roof
Round every windward stake, or tree, or door.
Speeding, the myriad-handed, his wild work
So fanciful, so savage, nought cares he
For number or proportion. Mockingly,
On coop or kennel he hangs Parian wreaths;
A swan-like form invests the hidden thorn;
Fills up the farmer's lane from wall to wall,
Maugre[1] the farmer's sighs; and at the gate

_____
[1] in spite of.

A tapering turret overtops the work.
And when his hours are numbered, and the
  world
Is all his own, retiring, as he were not,
5 Leaves, when the sun appears, astonished Art
To mimic in slow structures, stone by stone,
Built in an age, the mad wind's nightwork,
The frolic architecture of the snow.

MUSKETAQUID

Because I was content with these poor fields,
Low, open meads, slender and sluggish
  streams,
And found a home in haunts which others
  scorned,
The partial wood-gods overpaid my love,
And granted me the freedom of their state,
20 And in their secret senate have prevailed
With the dear, dangerous lords that rule our
  life,
Made moon and planets parties to their bond,
And through my rock-like, solitary wont
25 Shot million rays of thought and tenderness.
For me, in showers, in sweeping showers, the
  Spring
Visits the valley;—break away the clouds,—
I bathe in the morn's soft and silvered air,
30 And loiter willing by yon loitering stream.
Sparrows far off, and nearer, April's bird,
Blue-coated,—flying before from tree to tree,
Courageous sing a delicate overture
To lead the tardy concert of the year.
35 Onward and nearer rides the sun of May;
And wide around, the marriage of the plants
Is sweetly solemnized. Then flows amain
The surge of summer's beauty; dell and crag,
Hollow and lake, hillside and pine arcade,
40 Are touched with genius. Yonder ragged cliff
Has thousand faces in a thousand hours.

Beneath low hills, in the broad interval
Through which at will our Indian rivulet
45 Winds mindful still of sannup and of squaw,
Whose pipe and arrow oft the plough un-
  buries,
Here in pine houses built of new-fallen trees,
Supplanters of the tribe, the farmers dwell.
50 Traveller, to thee, perchance, a tedious road,
Or, it may be, a picture; to these men,
The landscape is an armory of powers,

Which, one by one, they know to draw and
   use.
They harness beast, bird, insect, to their work;
They prove the virtues of each bed of rock,
And, like the chemist 'mid his loaded jars,   5
Draw from each stratum its adapted use
To drug their crops or weapon their arts
   withal.
They turn the frost upon their chemic heap,
They set the wind to winnow pulse and grain, 10
They thank the spring-flood for its fertile slime,
And, on cheap summit-levels of the snow,
Slide with the sledge to inaccessible woods
O'er meadows bottomless. So, year by year,
They fight the elements with elements 15
(That one would say, meadow and forest
   walked,
Transmuted in these men to rule their like),
And by the order in the field disclose
The order regnant in the yeoman's brain. 20

What these strong masters wrote at large in
   miles,
I followed in small copy in my acre;
For there's no rood has not a star above it; 25
The cordial quality of pear or plum
Ascends as gladly in a single tree
As in broad orchards resonant with bees;
And every atom poises for itself,
And for the whole. The gentle deities 30
Showed me the lore of colors and of sounds,
The innumerable tenements of beauty,
The miracle of generative force,
Far-reaching concords of astronomy
Felt in the plants and in the punctual birds; 35
Better, the linked purpose of the whole,
And, chiefest prize, found I true liberty
In the glad home plain-dealing Nature gave.
The polite found me impolite; the great
Would mortify me, but in vain; for still 40
I am a willow of the wilderness,
Loving the wind that bent me. All my hurts
My garden spade can heal. A woodland walk,
A quest of river-grapes, a mocking thrush,
A wild-rose, or rock-loving columbine, 45
Salve my worst wounds.
For thus the wood-gods murmured in my ear:
'Dost love our manners? Canst thou silent lie?
Canst thou, thy pride forgot, like Nature pass
Into the winter night's extinguished mood? 50
Canst thou shine now, then darkle,
And being latent, feel thyself no less?

As, when the all-worshipped moon attracts the
   eye,
The river, hill, stems, foliage are obscure,
Yet envies none, none are unenviable.'

DAYS

Daughters of Time, the hypocritic Days,
Muffled and dumb like barefoot dervishes,
And marching single in an endless file,
Bring diadems and fagots in their hands.
To each they offer gifts after his will,
Bread, kingdoms, stars, and sky that holds
   them all.
I, in my pleachèd garden, watched the pomp,
Forgot my morning wishes, hastily
Took a few herbs and apples, and the Day
Turned and departed silent. I, too late,
Under her solemn fillet saw the scorn.

BRAHMA

If the red slayer think he slays,
   Or if the slain think he is slain,
They know not well the subtle ways
   I keep, and pass, and turn again.

Far or forgot to me is near;
   Shadow and sunlight are the same;
The vanished gods to me appear;
   And one to me are shame and fame.

They reckon ill who leave me out;
   When me they fly, I am the wings;
I am the doubter and the doubt,
   And I the hymn the Brahmin sings.

The strong gods pine for my abode,
   And pine in vain the sacred Seven;
But thou, meek lover of the good!
   Find me, and turn thy back on heaven.

HENRY WADSWORTH
LONGFELLOW*

THE DAY IS DONE

The day is done, and the darkness
   Falls from the wings of Night,

* For introductory sketch see I, 145. Longfellow's
poems are reprinted by permission of the publisher,
Houghton Mifflin Company.

As a feather is wafted downward
  From an eagle in his flight.

I see the lights of the village
  Gleam through the rain and the mist,
And a feeling of sadness comes o'er me
  That my soul cannot resist:

A feeling of sadness and longing,
  That is not akin to pain,
And resembles sorrow only
  As the mist resembles the rain.

Come, read to me some poem,
  Some simple and heartfelt lay,
That shall soothe this restless feeling,
  And banish the thoughts of day.

Not from the grand old masters,
  Not from the bards sublime,
Whose distant footsteps echo
  Through the corridors of Time.

For, like strains of martial music,
  Their mighty thoughts suggest
Life's endless toil and endeavor;
  And to-night I long for rest.

Read from some humbler poet,
  Whose songs gushed from his heart,
As showers from the clouds of summer,
  Or tears from the eyelids start;

Who, through long days of labor,
  And nights devoid of ease,
Still heard in his soul the music
  Of wonderful melodies.

Such songs have power to quiet
  The restless pulse of care,
And come like the benediction
  That follows after prayer.

Then read from the treasured volume
  The poem of thy choice,
And lend to the rhyme of the poet
  The beauty of thy voice.

And the night shall be filled with music,
  And the cares that infest the day
Shall fold their tents, like the Arabs,
  And as silently steal away.

MY LOST YOUTH

Often I think of the beautiful town[1]
  That is seated by the sea;
5 Often in thought go up and down
  The pleasant streets of that dear old town,
    And my youth comes back to me.
      And a verse of a Lapland song
      Is haunting my memory still:
10   'A boy's will is the wind's will,
  And the thoughts of youth are long, long
      thoughts.'

I can see the shadowy lines of its trees,
15   And catch, in sudden gleams,
  The sheen of the far-surrounding seas,
  And islands that were the Hesperides
    Of all my boyish dreams.
      And the burden of that old song,
20   It murmurs and whispers still:
      'A boy's will is the wind's will,
  And the thoughts of youth are long, long
      thoughts.'

25 I remember the black wharves and the slips,
    And the sea-tides tossing free;
  And the Spanish sailors with bearded lips,
  And the beauty and mystery of the ships,
    And the magic of the sea.
30   And the voice of that wayward song
      Is singing and saying still:
      'A boy's will is the wind's will,
  And the thoughts of youth are long, long
      thoughts.'
35

  I remember the bulwarks by the shore,
    And the fort upon the hill;
  The sunrise gun, with its hollow roar,
  The drum-beat repeated o'er and o'er,
40   And the bugle wild and shrill.
      And the music of that old song
      Throbs in my memory still:
      'A boy's will is the wind's will,
  And the thoughts of youth are long, long
45   thoughts.'

  I remember the sea-fight far away,[2]
    How it thundered o'er the tide!
  And the dead captains, as they lay
50 In their graves, o'erlooking the tranquil bay

----
[1] Portland, Maine.
[2] *Enterprise* vs. *Boxer,* 1813.

Where they in battle died.
  And the sound of that mournful song
  Goes through me with a thrill:
  'A boy's will is the wind's will,
And the thoughts of youth are long, long   5
    thoughts.'

I can see the breezy dome of groves,
  The shadows of Deering's Woods;
And the friendships old and the early loves   10
Come back with a Sabbath sound, as of doves
  In quiet neighborhoods.
  And the verse of that sweet old song,
  It flutters and murmurs still:
  'A boy's will is the wind's will,   15
And the thoughts of youth are long, long
    thoughts.'

I remember the gleams and glooms that dart
  Across the school-boy's brain;
The song and the silence in the heart,   20
That in part are prophecies, and in part
  Are longings wild and vain.
  And the voice of that fitful song
  Sings on, and is never still: 25
  'A boy's will is the wind's will,
And the thoughts of youth are long, long
    thoughts.'

There are things of which I may not speak;   30
  There are dreams that cannot die;
There are thoughts that make the strong heart
    weak,
And bring a pallor into the cheek,
  And a mist before the eye.   35
  And the words of that fatal song
  Come over me like a chill:
  'A boy's will is the wind's will,
And the thoughts of youth are long, long
    thoughts.'   40

Strange to me now are the forms I meet
  When I visit the dear old town;
But the native air is pure and sweet,
And the trees that o'ershadow each well-   45
    known street,
  As they balance up and down,
  Are singing the beautiful song,
  Are sighing and whispering still:
  'A boy's will is the wind's will,   50
And the thoughts of youth are long, long
    thoughts.'

And Deering's Woods are fresh and fair,
  And with joy that is almost pain
My heart goes back to wander there,
And among the dreams of the days that were,
  I find my lost youth again.
  And the strange and beautiful song,
  The groves are repeating it still:
  'A boy's will is the wind's will,
And the thoughts of youth are long, long
    thoughts.'

DIVINA COMMEDIA[1]

1

Oft have I seen at some cathedral door   15
A laborer, pausing in the dust and heat,
Lay down his burden, and with reverent feet
Enter, and cross himself, and on the floor
Kneel to repeat his paternoster o'er;
Far off the noises of the world retreat;   20
The loud vociferations of the street
Become an undistinguishable roar.
So, as I enter here from day to day,
And leave my burden at this minster gate,
Kneeling in prayer, and not ashamed to pray,   25
The tumult of the time disconsolate
To inarticulate murmurs dies away,
While the eternal ages watch and wait.

2

How strange the sculptures that adorn these
    towers!
This crowd of statues, in whose folded sleeves
Birds build their nests; while canopied with
    leaves
Parvis and portal bloom like trellised bowers,
And the vast minster seems a cross of flowers!
But fiends and dragons on the gargoyled eaves
Watch the dead Christ between the living
    thieves,
And, underneath, the traitor Judas lowers!
Ah! from what agonies of heart and brain,
What exultations trampling on despair,
What tenderness, what tears, what hate of
    wrong,
What passionate outcry of a soul in pain,
Uprose this poem of the earth and air,
This mediæval miracle of song!

---

[1] Longfellow's translation of Dante's *Divine Comedy* is divided into three parts, each of which is preceded and followed by one sonnet from this sequence.

3

I enter, and I see thee in the gloom
Of the long aisles, O poet saturnine!
And strive to make my steps keep pace with 5
    thine.
The air is filled with some unknown perfume;
The congregation of the dead make room
For thee to pass; the votive tapers shine;
Like rooks that haunt Ravenna's groves of pine 10
The hovering echoes fly from tomb to tomb.
From the confessionals I hear arise
Rehearsals of forgotten tragedies,
And lamentations from the crypts below;
And then a voice celestial that begins 15
With the pathetic words, 'Although your sins
As scarlet be,' and ends with 'as the snow.'

4

With snow-white veil and garments as of 20
    flame,
She stands before thee, who so long ago
Filled thy young heart with passion and the
    woe
From which thy song and all its splendors 25
    came;
And while with stern rebuke she speaks thy
    name,
The ice about thy heart melts as the snow
On mountain heights, and in swift overflow 30
Comes gushing from thy lips in sobs of shame.
Thou makest full confession; and a gleam,
As of the dawn on some dark forest cast,
Seems on thy lifted forehead to increase;
Lethe and Eunoë—the remembered dream 35
And the forgotten sorrow—bring at last
That perfect pardon which is perfect peace.

5

I lift mine eyes, and all the windows blaze 40
With forms of Saints and holy men who died,
Here martyred and hereafter glorified;
And the great Rose upon its leaves displays
Christ's Triumph, and the angelic roundelays,
With splendor upon splendor multiplied; 45
And Beatrice again at Dante's side
No more rebukes, but smiles her words of
    praise.
And then the organ sounds, and unseen choirs
Sing the old Latin hymns of peace and love 50
And benedictions of the Holy Ghost;
And the melodious bells among the spires
O'er all the house-tops and through heaven
    above
Proclaim the elevation of the Host!

6

O star of morning and of liberty!
O bringer of the light, whose splendor shines
Above the darkness of the Apennines,
Forerunner of the day that is to be!
The voices of the city and the sea,
The voices of the mountains and the pines,
Repeat thy song, till the familiar lines
Are footpaths for the thought of Italy!
Thy flame is blown abroad from all the
    heights,
Through all the nations, and a sound is heard,
As of a mighty wind, and men devout,
Strangers of Rome, and the new proselytes,
In their own language hear the wondrous
    word,
And many are amazed and many doubt.

CHAUCER

An old man in a lodge within a park;
The chamber walls depicted all around
With portraitures of huntsman, hawk, and
    hound,
And the hurt deer. He listeneth to the lark,
Whose song comes with the sunshine through
    the dark
Of painted glass in leaden lattice bound;
He listeneth and he laugheth at the sound,
Then writeth in a book like any clerk.
He is the poet of the dawn, who wrote
The Canterbury Tales, and his old age
Made beautiful with song; and as I read
I hear the crowing cock, I hear the note
Of lark and linnet, and from every page
Rise odors of ploughed field or flowery mead.

JOHN GREENLEAF WHITTIER*

ASTRÆA

Jove means to settle
Astræa in her seat again,
And let down from his golden chain
An age of better metal.
             Ben Jonson.

---

* For introductory sketch see I, 148. Whittier's poems are reprinted by permission of the publisher, Houghton Mifflin Company.

O poet rare and old!
  Thy words are prophecies;
Forward the age of gold,
  The new Saturnian lies.

The universal prayer
  And hope are not in vain;
Rise, brothers! and prepare
  The way for Saturn's reign.

Perish shall all which takes
  From labor's board and can;
Perish shall all which makes
  A spaniel of the man!

Free from its bonds the mind,
  The body from the rod;
Broken all chains that bind
  The image of our God.

Just men no longer pine
  Behind their prison-bars;
Through the rent dungeon shine
  The free sun and the stars.

Earth own, at last, untrod
  By sect, or caste, or clan,
The fatherhood of God,
  The brotherhood of man!

Fraud fail, craft perish, forth
  The money-changers driven,
And God's will done on earth,
  As now in heaven!

THE RENDITION[1]

I heard the train's shrill whistle call,
  I saw an earnest look beseech,
  And rather by that look than speech
My neighbor told me all.

And, as I thought of Liberty
  Marched handcuffed down that sworded
    street,
  The solid earth beneath my feet
Reeled fluid as the sea.

---

[1] Written after learning that Anthony Burns, fugitive slave, was to be returned to Virginia by the Massachusetts authorities.

I felt a sense of bitter loss,—
  Shame, tearless grief, and stifling wrath,
  And loathing fear, as if my path
A serpent stretched across.

All love of home, all pride of place,
  All generous confidence and trust,
  Sank smothering in that deep disgust
And anguish of disgrace.

Down on my native hills of June,
  And home's green quiet, hiding all,
  Fell sudden darkness like the fall
Of midnight upon noon!

And Law, an unloosed maniac, strong,
  Blood-drunken, through the blackness trod,
  Hoarse-shouting in the ear of God
The blasphemy of wrong.

'O Mother, from thy memories proud,
  Thy old renown, dear Commonwealth,
  Lend this dead air a breeze of health,
And smite with stars this cloud.

'Mother of Freedom, wise and brave,
  Rise awful in thy strength,' I said;
  Ah me! I spake but to the dead;
I stood upon her grave!

THE ETERNAL GOODNESS

O Friends! with whom my feet have trod
  The quiet aisles of prayer,
Glad witness to your zeal for God
  And love of man I bear.

I trace your lines of argument;
  Your logic linked and strong
I weigh as one who dreads dissent,
  And fears a doubt as wrong.

But still my human hands are weak
  To hold your iron creeds:
Against the words ye bid me speak
  My heart within me pleads.

Who fathoms the Eternal Thought?
  Who talks of scheme and plan?
The Lord is God! He needeth not
  The poor device of man.

I walk with bare, hushed feet the ground
  Ye tread with boldness shod;
I dare not fix with mete and bound
  The love and power of God.

Ye praise his justice; even such
  His pitying love I deem:
Ye seek a king; I fain would touch
  The robe that hath no seam.

Ye see the curse which overbroods
  A world of pain and loss;
I hear our Lord's beatitudes
  And prayer upon the cross.

More than your schoolmen teach, within
  Myself, alas! I know:
Too dark ye cannot paint the sin,
  Too small the merit show.

I bow my forehead to the dust,
  I veil mine eyes for shame,
And urge, in trembling self-distrust,
  A prayer without a claim.

I see the wrong that round me lies,
  I feel the guilt within;
I hear, with groan and travail-cries,
  The world confess its sin.

Yet, in the maddening maze of things,
  And tossed by storm and flood,
To one fixed trust my spirit clings;
  I know that God is good!

Not mine to look where cherubim
  And seraphs may not see,
But nothing can be good in Him
  Which evil is in me.

The wrong that pains my soul below
  I dare not throne above,
I know not of his hate,—I know
  His goodness and his love.

I dimly guess from blessings known
  Of greater out of sight,
And, with the chastened Psalmist, own
  His judgments too are right.

I long for household voices gone,
  For vanished smiles I long,

But God hath led my dear ones on,
  And He can do no wrong.

I know not what the future hath
  Of marvel or surprise,
Assured alone that life and death
  His mercy underlies.

And if my heart and flesh are weak
  To bear an untried pain,
The bruisèd reed He will not break,
  But strengthen and sustain.

No offering of my own I have,
  Nor works my faith to prove;
I can but give the gifts He gave,
  And plead his love for love.

And so beside the Silent Sea
  I wait the muffled oar;
No harm from Him can come to me
  On ocean or on shore.

I know not where his islands lift
  Their fronded palms in air;
I only know I cannot drift
  Beyond his love and care.

O brothers! if my faith is vain,
  If hopes like these betray,
Pray for me that my feet may gain
  The sure and safer way.

And Thou, O Lord! by whom are seen
  Thy creatures as they be,
Forgive me if too close I lean
  My human heart on Thee!

ALFRED, LORD TENNYSON*

THE LOTOS-EATERS

"Courage!" he[1] said, and pointed toward the
  land,

---

* For introductory sketch see I, 150. The following selections are from Tennyson's *Poetical Works.* By permission of The Macmillan Company, publishers.

[1] Ulysses and his men visited the lotos-eaters on the long way home from Troy. See *Odyssey,* Bk. IX.

"This mounting wave will roll us shoreward
    soon."
In the afternoon they came unto a land,
In which it seemed always afternoon.
All round the coast the languid air did swoon,
Breathing like one that hath a weary dream.
Full-faced above the valley stood the moon;
And like a downward smoke, the slender
    stream
Along the cliff to fall and pause and fall did 10
    seem.

A land of streams! some, like a downward
    smoke,
Slow-dropping veils of thinnest lawn, did go; 15
And some thro' wavering lights and shadows
    broke,
Rolling a slumbrous sheet of foam below.
They saw the gleaming river seaward flow
From the inner land; far off, three mountain- 20
    tops,
Three silent pinnacles of aged snow,
Stood sunset-flushed; and, dewed with show-
    ery drops,
Up-clomb the shadowy pine above the woven 25
    copse.

The charmed sunset lingered low adown
In the red West; thro' mountain clefts the dale
Was seen far inland, and the yellow down 30
Bordered with palm, and many a winding vale
And meadow, set with slender galingale;
A land where all things always seemed the
    same!
And round about the keel with faces pale, 35
Dark faces pale against that rosy flame,
The mild-eyed melancholy Lotos-eaters came.

Branches they bore of that enchanted stem,
Laden with flower and fruit, whereof they 40
    gave
To each, but whoso did receive of them
And taste, to him the gushing of the wave
Far, far away did seem to mourn and rave
On alien shores; and if his fellow spake, 45
His voice was thin, as voices from the grave;
And deep-asleep he seemed, yet all awake,
And music in his ears his beating heart did
    make.

They sat them down upon the yellow sand,
Between the sun and moon upon the shore;

And sweet it was to dream of Fatherland,
Of child, and wife, and slave; but evermore
Most weary seemed the sea, weary the oar,
Weary the wandering fields of barren foam.
Then some one said, "We will return no 5
    more;"
And all at once they sang, "Our island home[2]
Is far beyond the wave; we will no longer
    roam."

CHORIC SONG

1

There is sweet music here that softer falls
Than petals from blown roses on the grass,
Or night-dews on still waters between walls
Of shadowy granite, in a gleaming pass;
Music that gentlier on the spirit lies,
Than tired eyelids upon tired eyes;
Music that brings sweet sleep down from the 20
    blissful skies.
Here are cool mosses deep,
And thro' the moss the ivies creep,
And in the stream the long-leaved flowers
    weep,
And from the craggy ledge the poppy hangs 25
    in sleep.

2

Why are we weighed upon with heaviness,
And utterly consumed with sharp distress,
While all things else have rest from weariness?
All things have rest: why should we toil alone,
We only toil, who are the first of things,
And make perpetual moan,
Still from one sorrow to another thrown;
Nor ever fold our wings,
And cease from wanderings,
Nor steep our brows in slumber's holy balm;
Nor harken what the inner spirit sings,
"There is no joy but calm!"—
Why should we only toil, the roof and crown
    of things?

3

Lo! in the middle of the wood,
The folded leaf is wooed from out the bud
With winds upon the branch, and there
Grows green and broad, and takes no care,
Sun-steeped at noon, and in the moon

_____
[2] Ithaca.

Nightly dew-fed; and turning yellow
Falls, and floats adown the air.
Lo! sweetened with the summer light,
The full-juiced apple, waxing over-mellow,
Drops in a silent autumn night.
All its allotted length of days
The flower ripens in its place,
Ripens and fades, and falls, and hath no toil,
Fast-rooted in the fruitful soil.

4

Hateful is the dark-blue sky,
Vaulted o'er the dark-blue sea.
Death is the end of life; ah, why
Should life all labor be?
Let us alone. Time driveth onward fast,
And in a little while our lips are dumb.
Let us alone. What is it that will last?
All things are taken from us, and become
Portions and parcels of the dreadful past.
Let us alone. What pleasure can we have
To war with evil? Is there any peace
In ever climbing up the climbing wave?
All things have rest, and ripen toward the
        grave
In silence—ripen, fall and cease:
Give us long rest or death, dark death, or
        dreamful ease.

5

How sweet it were, hearing the downward
        stream,
With half-shut eyes ever to seem
Falling asleep in a half-dream!
To dream and dream, like yonder amber light, 35
Which will not leave the myrrh-bush on the
        height;
To hear each other's whispered speech;
Eating the Lotos day by day,
To watch the crisping ripples on the beach,   40
And tender curving lines of creamy spray;
To lend our hearts and spirits wholly
To the influence of mild-minded melancholy;
To muse and brood and live again in memory,
With those old faces of our infancy   45
Heaped over with a mound of grass,
Two handfuls of white dust, shut in an urn of
        brass!

6

Dear is the memory of our wedded lives,
And dear the last embraces of our wives

And their warm tears; but all hath suffered
        change;
For surely now our household hearths are
        cold,
5 Our sons inherit us, our looks are strange,
And we should come like ghosts to trouble joy.
Or else the island princes[3] over-bold
Have eat our substance, and the minstrel sings
Before them of the ten-years' war in Troy,
10 And our great deeds, as half-forgotten things.
Is there confusion in the little isle?
Let what is broken so remain.
The Gods are hard to reconcile;
'Tis hard to settle order once again.
15 There *is* confusion worse than death,
Trouble on trouble, pain on pain,
Long labor unto aged breath,
Sore task to hearts worn out by many wars
And eyes grown dim with gazing on the pilot-
20   stars.

7

But, propt on beds of amaranth and moly,
How sweet (while warm airs lull us, blowing
25   lowly)
With half-dropt eyelids still,
Beneath a heaven dark and holy,
To watch the long bright river drawing
        slowly
30 His waters from the purple hill—
To hear the dewy echoes calling
From cave to cave thro' the thick-twined
        vine—
To watch the emerald-colored water falling
35 Thro' many a woven acanthus-wreath divine!
Only to hear and see the far-off sparkling
        brine,
Only to hear were sweet, stretched out be-
        neath the pine.

8

The Lotos blooms below the barren peak,
The Lotos blows by every winding creek;
All day the wind breathes low with mellower
        tone;
Thro' every hollow cave and alley lone
Round and round the spicy downs the yellow
        Lotos-dust is blown.
We have had enough of action, and of mo-
50   tion we,

[3] suitors for hand of Penelope, wife of Ulysses,
the latter believed lost at sea.

Rolled to starboard, rolled to larboard, when
   the surge was seething free,
Where the wallowing monster spouted his
   foam-fountains in the sea.
Let us swear an oath, and keep it with an 5
   equal mind,
In the hollow Lotos-land to live and lie reclined
On the hills like Gods together, careless of
   mankind.   10
For they lie beside their nectar, and the bolts
   are hurled
Far below them in the valleys, and the clouds
   are lightly curled
Round their golden houses, girdled with the 15
   gleaming world;
Where they smile in secret, looking over
   wasted lands,
Blight and famine, plague and earthquake,
   roaring deeps and fiery sands,   20
Clanging fights, and flaming towns, and sink-
   ing ships, and praying hands.
But they smile, they find a music centred in a
   doleful song
Steaming up, a lamentation and an ancient tale 25
   of wrong,
Like a tale of little meaning tho' the words
   are strong;
Chanted from an ill-used race of men that
   cleave the soil,   30
Sow the seed, and reap the harvest with enduring toil,
Storing yearly little dues of wheat, and wine
   and oil;
Till they perish and they suffer—some, 'tis 35
   whispered—down in hell
Suffer endless anguish, others in Elysian valleys[4] dwell,
Resting weary limbs at last on beds of aspho-
   del.   40
Surely, surely, slumber is more sweet than
   toil, the shore
Than labor in the deep mid-ocean, wind and
   wave and oar;
O, rest ye, brother mariners, we will not 45
   wander more.

BREAK, BREAK, BREAK

Break, break, break,
   On thy cold gray stones, O Sea!

[4] Greek paradise.

And I would that my tongue could utter
   The thoughts that arise in me.

O well for the fisherman's boy,
   That he shouts with his sister at play!
O well for the sailor lad,
   That he sings in his boat on the bay!

And the stately ships go on
   To their haven under the hill;
But O for the touch of a vanished hand,
   And the sound of a voice that is still!

SONGS FROM *The Princess*

1

The splendor falls on castle walls
   And snowy summits old in story;
The long light shakes across the lakes,
   And the wild cataract leaps in glory.
Blow, bugle, blow, set the wild echoes flying,
Blow, bugle; answer, echoes, dying, dying,
   dying.

O, hark, O, hear! how thin and clear,
   And thinner, clearer, farther going!
O, sweet and far from cliff and scar
   The horns of Elfland faintly blowing!
Blow, let us hear the purple glens replying,
Blow, bugle; answer, echoes, dying, dying,
   dying.

O love, they die in yon rich sky,
   They faint on hill or field or river;
Our echoes roll from soul to soul,
   And grow for ever and for ever.
Blow, bugle, blow, set the wild echoes flying,
And answer, echoes, answer, dying, dying,
   dying.

2

Tears, idle tears, I know not what they
   mean,
Tears from the depth of some divine despair
Rise in the heart, and gather to the eyes,
In looking on the happy autumn-fields,
And thinking of the days that are no more.

50   Fresh as the first beam glittering on a sail,
That brings our friends up from the under-
   world,

Sad as the last which reddens over one
That sinks with all we love below the verge;
So sad, so fresh, the days that are no more.

Ah, sad and strange as in dark summer 5
    dawns
The earliest pipe of half-awakened birds
To dying ears, when unto dying eyes
The casement slowly grows a glimmering
    square; 10
So sad, so strange, the days that are no more.

Dear as remembered kisses after death,
And sweet as those by hopeless fancy feigned
On lips that are for others; deep as love,
Deep as first love, and wild with all regret;
O Death in Life, the days that are no more.

3

Now sleeps the crimson petal, now the 20
    white;
Nor waves the cypress in the palace walk;
Nor winks the gold fin in the porphyry font.
The fire-fly wakens; waken thou with me.

Now droops the milkwhite peacock like a
    ghost,
And like a ghost she glimmers on to me.

Now lies the Earth all Danaë[1] to the stars, 30
And all thy heart lies open unto me.

Now slides the silent meteor on, and leaves
A shining furrow, as thy thoughts in me.

Now folds the lily all her sweetness up,
And slips into the bosom of the lake.
So fold thyself, my dearest, thou, and slip
Into my bosom and be lost in me.

4

Come down, O maid, from yonder moun-
    tain height:
What pleasure lives in height (the shepherd
    sang) 45
In height and cold, the splendor of the hills?
But cease to move so near the heavens, and
    cease
To glide a sunbeam by the blasted pine,
To sit a star upon the sparkling spire; 50

[1] Greek legendary maiden visited by Zeus in the form of a shower of gold.

And come, for Love is of the valley, come,
For Love is of the valley, come thou down
And find him; by the happy threshold, he,
Or hand in hand with Plenty in the maize,
Or red with spirted purple of the vats, 5
Or foxlike in the vine; nor cares to walk
With Death and Morning on the Silver Horns,[2]
Nor wilt thou snare him in the white ravine
Nor find him dropt upon the firths of ice,
That huddling slant in furrow-cloven falls 10
To roll the torrent out of dusky doors.
But follow; let the torrent dance thee down
To find him in the valley; let the wild
Lean-headed Eagles yelp alone, and leave
The monstrous ledges there to slope, and spill 15
Their thousand wreaths of dangling water-
    smoke,
That like a broken purpose waste in air.
So waste not thou, but come; for all the vales
Await thee; azure pillars of the hearth 20
Arise to thee; the children call, and I
Thy shepherd pipe, and sweet is every sound,
Sweeter thy voice, but every sound is sweet;
Myriads of rivulets hurrying thro' the lawn,
The moan of doves in immemorial elms, 25
And murmuring of innumerable bees.

FROM *In Memoriam* A. H. H.[1]

1

I held in truth, with him[2] who sings
    To one clear harp in divers tones,
    That men may rise on stepping-stones
Of their dead selves to higher things. 35

But who shall so forecast the years
    And find in loss a gain to match?
    Or reach a hand thro' time to catch
The far-off interest of tears? 40

Let Love clasp Grief lest both be drowned,
    Let darkness keep her raven gloss.
    Ah, sweeter to be drunk with loss,
To dance with Death, to beat the ground, 45

[2] mountain peaks.
[1] Arthur Henry Hallam was Tennyson's close friend at Cambridge. Engaged to Tennyson's sister Emily, he died suddenly in Vienna in 1833. The poet wrote *In Memoriam* in sections, the whole appearing seventeen years later.
[2] perhaps Goethe.

Than that the victor Hours should scorn
   The long result of love, and boast,
   "Behold the man that loved and lost,
But all he was is overworn."

9

Fair ship, that from the Italian shore
   Sailest the placid ocean-plains
   With my lost Arthur's loved remains,
Spread thy full wings, and waft him o'er.

So draw him home to those that mourn
   In vain; a favorable speed
   Ruffle thy mirrored mast, and lead
Through prosperous floods his holy urn.

All night no ruder air perplex
   Thy sliding keel, till Phosphor, bright
   As our pure love, through early light
Shall glimmer on the dewy decks.

Sphere all your lights around, above;
   Sleep, gentle heavens, before the prow;
   Sleep, gentle winds, as he sleeps now,
My friend, the brother of my love;

My Arthur, whom I shall not see
   Till all my widowed race be run;
   Dear as the mother to the son,
More than my brothers are to me.

11

Calm is the morn without a sound,
   Calm as to suit a calmer grief,
   And only through the faded leaf
The chestnut pattering to the ground:

Calm and deep peace on this high wold,
   And on these dews that drench the furze,
   And all the silvery gossamers
That twinkle into green and gold:

Calm and still light on yon great plain
   That sweeps with all its autumn bowers,
   And crowded farms and lessening towers,
To mingle with the bounding main:

Calm and deep peace in this wide air,
   These leaves that redden to the fall;
   And in my heart, if calm at all,
If any calm, a calm despair:

Calm on the seas, and silver sleep,
   And waves that sway themselves in rest,
   And dead calm in that noble breast
Which heaves but with the heaving deep.

27

I envy not in any moods
   The captive void of noble rage,
   The linnet born within the cage,
That never knew the summer woods;

I envy not the beast that takes
   His license in the field of time,
   Unfettered by the sense of crime,
To whom a conscience never wakes;

Nor, what may count itself as blest,
   The heart that never plighted troth
   But stagnates in the weeds of sloth;
Nor any want-begotten rest.

I hold it true, whate'er befall;
   I feel it, when I sorrow most;
   'Tis better to have loved and lost
Than never to have loved at all.

28

The time draws near the birth of Christ.
   The moon is hid, the night is still;
   The Christmas bells from hill to hill
Answer each other in the mist.

Four voices of four hamlets round,
   From far and near, on mead and moor,
   Swell out and fail, as if a door
Were shut between me and the sound;

Each voice four changes on the wind,
   That now dilate, and now decrease,
   Peace and goodwill, goodwill and peace,
Peace and goodwill, to all mankind.

This year I slept and woke with pain,
   I almost wished no more to wake,
   And that my hold on life would break
Before I heard those bells again;

But they my troubled spirit rule,
   For they controlled me when a boy;
   They bring me sorrow touched with joy,
The merry, merry bells of Yule.

54

O, yet we trust that somehow good
  Will be the final goal of ill,
  To pangs of nature, sins of will,
Defects of doubt, and taints of blood;

That nothing walks with aimless feet;
  That not one life shall be destroyed,
  Or cast as rubbish to the void,
When God hath made the pile complete;

That not a worm is cloven in vain;
  That not a moth with vain desire
  Is shriveled in a fruitless fire,
Or but subserves another's gain.

Behold, we know not anything;
  I can but trust that good shall fall
  At last—far off—at last, to all,
And every winter change to spring.

So runs my dream; but what am I?
  An infant crying in the night;
  An infant crying for the light,
And with no language but a cry.

55

The wish, that of the living whole
  No life may fail beyond the grave,
  Derives it not from what we have
The likest God within the soul?

Are God and Nature then at strife,
  That Nature lends such evil dreams?
  So careful of the type she seems,
So careless of the single life,

That I, considering everywhere
  Her secret meaning in her deeds,
  And finding that of fifty seeds
She often brings but one to bear,

I falter where I firmly trod,
  And falling with my weight of cares
  Upon the great world's altar-stairs
That slope thro' darkness up to God,

I stretch lame hands of faith, and grope,
  And gather dust and chaff, and call
  To what I feel is Lord of all,
And faintly trust the larger hope.

106

Ring out, wild bells, to the wild sky,
  The flying cloud, the frosty light:
5   The year is dying in the night;
Ring out, wild bells, and let him die.

Ring out the old, ring in the new,
  Ring, happy bells, across the snow:
10   The year is going, let him go;
Ring out the false, ring in the true.

Ring out the grief that saps the mind,
  For those that here we see no more;
15   Ring out the feud of rich and poor,
Ring in redress to all mankind.

Ring out a slowly dying cause,
  And ancient forms of party strife;
20   Ring in the nobler modes of life,
With sweeter manners, purer laws.

Ring out the want, the care, the sin,
  The faithless coldness of the times;
25   Ring out, ring out my mournful rhymes,
But ring the fuller minstrel in.

Ring out false pride in place and blood,
  The civic slander and the spite;
30   Ring in the love of truth and right,
Ring in the common love of good.

Ring out old shapes of foul disease;
  Ring out the narrowing lust of gold;
35   Ring out the thousand wars of old,
Ring in the thousand years of peace.

Ring in the valiant man and free,
  The larger heart, the kindlier hand;
40   Ring out the darkness of the land,
Ring in the Christ that is to be.

126

Love is and was my lord and king,
  And in his presence I attend
45   To hear the tidings of my friend,
Which every hour his couriers bring.

Love is and was my king and lord,
50   And will be, tho' as yet I keep
  Within his court on earth, and sleep
Encompassed by his faithful guard,

And hear at times a sentinel
  That moves about from place to place,
  And whispers to the worlds of space,
In the deep night, that all is well.

131

O living will that shalt endure
  When all that seems shall suffer shock,
  Rise in the spiritual rock,
Flow through our deeds and make them pure, 10

That we may lift from out of dust
  A voice as unto him that hears,
  A cry above the conquered years
To one that with us works, and trust, 15

With faith that comes of self-control,
  The truths that never can be proved
  Until we close with all we loved,
And all we flow from, soul in soul. 20

CROSSING THE BAR

Sunset and evening star,
  And one clear call for me!
And may there be no moaning of the bar, 25
  When I put out to sea,

But such a tide as moving seems asleep,
  Too full for sound and foam,
When that which drew from out the bound- 30
    less deep
  Turns again home.

Twilight and evening bell,
  And after that the dark! 35
And may there be no sadness of farewell,
  When I embark;

For though from out our bourne of Time and
    Place 40
  The flood may bear me far,
I hope to see my Pilot face to face
  When I have crost the bar.

ROBERT BROWNING* 45

THE LOST LEADER

Just for the handful of silver he left us,
  Just for a riband to stick in his coat— 50

---

* For introductory sketch see I, 158. The selec-

Found the one gift of which fortune bereft us,
  Lost all the others she lets us devote;
They, with the gold to give, doled him out
    silver,
  So much was theirs who so little allowed:
How all our copper had gone for his service!
  Rags—were they purple, his heart had been
    proud!
We that had loved him so, followed him, hon-
    ored him,
  Lived in his mild and magnificent eye,
Learned his great language, caught his clear
    accents,
  Made him our pattern to live and to die!
Shakespeare was of us, Milton was for us,
  Burns, Shelley, were with us,—they watch
    from their graves!
He alone breaks from the van and the free-
    men,—
  He alone sinks to the rear and the slaves!

We shall march prospering,—not through his
    presence;
  Songs may inspirit us,—not from his lyre;
Deeds will be done,—while he boasts his
    quiescence,
  Still bidding crouch whom the rest bade
    aspire:
Blot out his name, then, record one lost soul
    more,
  One task more declined, one more footpath
    untrod,
One more devils'-triumph and sorrow for
    angels,
  One wrong more to man, one more insult
    to God!
Life's night begins: let him never come back
    to us!
  There would be doubt, hesitation and pain,
Forced praise on our part—the glimmer of
    twilight,
  Never glad confident morning again!
Best fight on well, for we taught him—strike
    gallantly,
  Menace our heart ere we master his own;
Then let him receive the new knowledge and
    wait us,
  Pardoned in heaven, the first by the throne!

---

tions which follow are from Browning's *Poetical Works*. By permission of The Macmillan Company, publishers.

HOME-THOUGHTS FROM ABROAD

Oh, to be in England
Now that April's there,
And whoever wakes in England
Sees, some morning, unaware,
That the lowest boughs and the brush-wood sheaf
Round the elm-tree bole are in tiny leaf,
While the chaffinch sings on the orchard bough
In England—now!
And after April, when May follows,
And the whitethroat builds, and all the swallows!
Hark, where my blossomed pear-tree in the hedge
Leans to the field and scatters on the clover
Blossoms and dewdrops—at the bent spray's edge—
That's the wise thrush; he sings each song twice over,
Lest you should think he never could recapture
The first fine careless rapture!
And though the fields look rough with hoary dew,
All will be gay when noontide wakes anew
The buttercups, the little children's dower
—Far brighter than this gaudy melon-flower!

THE LAST RIDE TOGETHER

I said—Then, dearest, since 'tis so,
Since now at length my fate I know,
Since nothing all my love avails,
Since all, my life seemed meant for, fails,
  Since this was written and needs must be—
My whole heart rises up to bless
Your name in pride and thankfulness!
Take back the hope you gave,—I claim
Only a memory of the same,
—And this beside, if you will not blame,
  Your leave for one more last ride with me.

My mistress bent that brow of hers;
Those deep dark eyes where pride demurs
When pity would be softening through,
Fixed me a breathing-while or two
  With life or death in the balance: right!
5 The blood replenished me again;
My last thought was at least not vain:
I and my mistress, side by side
Shall be together, breathe and ride,
So, one day more am I deified.
  Who knows but the world may end tonight?

Hush! if you saw some western cloud
All billowy-bosomed, over-bowed
10 By many benedictions—sun's
And moon's and evening-star's at once—
  And so, you, looking and loving best,
Conscious grew, your passion drew
Cloud, sunset, moonrise, star-shine too,
15 Down on you, near and yet more near,
Till flesh must fade for heaven was here!—
Thus leant she and lingered—joy and fear!
  Thus lay she a moment on my breast.

20 Then we began to ride. My soul
Smoothed itself out, a long-cramped scroll
Freshening and fluttering in the wind.
Past hopes already lay behind.
  What need to strive with a life awry?
25 Had I said that, had I done this,
So might I gain, so might I miss.
Might she have loved me? just as well
She might have hated, who can tell!
Where had I been now if the worst befell?
30   And here we are riding, she and I.

Fail I alone, in words and deeds?
Why, all men strive, and who succeeds?
We rode; it seemed my spirit flew,
35 Saw other regions, cities new,
  As the world rushed by on either side.
I thought,—All labor, yet no less
Bear up beneath their unsuccess.
Look at the end of work, contrast
40 The petty done, the undone vast,
This present of theirs with the hopeful past!
  I hoped she would love me; here we ride.

What hand and brain went ever paired?
45 What heart alike conceived and dared?
What act proved all its thought had been?
What will but felt the fleshly screen?
  We ride and I see her bosom heave.
There's many a crown for who can reach.
50 Ten lines, a statesman's life in each!
The flag stuck on a heap of bones,
A soldier's doing! what atones?

They scratch his name on the Abbey stones,
   My riding is better, by their leave.

What does it all mean, poet? Well,
Your brains beat into rhythm, you tell
What we felt only; you expressed
You hold things beautiful the best,
   And place them in rhyme so, side by side.
'Tis something, nay 'tis much: but then,
Have you yourself what's best for men?
Are you—poor, sick, old ere your time—
Nearer one whit your own sublime
Than we who never have turned a rhyme?
   Sing, riding's a joy! For me, I ride.

And you, great sculptor—so, you gave
A score of years to Art, her slave,
And that's your Venus, whence we turn
To yonder girl that fords the burn!
   You acquiesce, and shall I repine?
What, man of music, you grown gray
With notes and nothing else to say,
Is this your sole praise from a friend,
"Greatly his opera's strains intend,
But in music we know how fashions end!"
   I gave my youth; but we ride, in fine.

Who knows what's fit for us? Had fate
Proposed bliss here should sublimate
My being—had I signed the bond—
Still one must lead some life beyond,
   Have a bliss to die with, dim-descried.
This foot once planted on the goal,
This glory-garland round my soul,
Could I descry such? Try and test!
I sink back shuddering from the quest.
Earth being so good, would heaven seem best?
   Now, heaven and she are beyond this ride.

And yet—she has not spoke so long!
What if heaven be that, fair and strong
At life's best, with our eyes upturned
Whither life's flower is first discerned,
   We, fixed so, ever should so abide?
What if we still ride on, we two,
With life forever old yet new,
Changed not in kind but in degree,
The instant made eternity,—
And heaven just proved that I and she
   Ride, ride together, forever ride?

UP AT A VILLA—DOWN IN THE CITY

AS DISTINGUISHED BY AN ITALIAN PERSON OF QUALITY

5 Had I but plenty of money, money enough
     and to spare,
The house for me, no doubt, were a house in
     the city-square;
10 Ah, such a life, such a life, as one leads at the
     window there!

Something to see, by Bacchus, something to
     hear, at least!
15 There, the whole day long, one's life is a per-
     fect feast;
While up at a villa one lives, I maintain it, no
     more than a beast.

20 Well now, look at our villa! stuck like the
     horn of a bull
Just on a mountain-edge as bare as the crea-
     ture's skull,
Save a mere shag of a bush with hardly a leaf
25   to pull!
—I scratch my own, sometimes, to see if the
     hair's turned wool.

But the city, oh the city—the square with the
30   houses! Why?
They are stone-faced, white as a curd, there's
     something to take the eye!
Houses in four straight lines, not a single front
     awry;
35 You watch who crosses and gossips, who
     saunters, who hurries by;
Green blinds, as a matter of course, to draw
     when the sun gets high;
And the shops with fanciful signs which are
40   painted properly.

What of a villa? Though winter be over in
     March by rights,
'Tis May perhaps ere the snow shall have
45   withered well off the heights:
You've the brown ploughed land before, where
     the oxen steam and wheeze,
And the hills over-smoked behind by the faint
     gray olive-trees.

50 Is it better in May, I ask you? You've summer
     all at once;

In a day he leaps complete with a few strong April suns.
'Mid the sharp short emerald wheat, scarce risen three fingers well,
The wild tulip, at end of its tube, blows out 5 its great red bell
Like a thin clear bubble of blood, for the children to pick and sell.

Is it ever hot in the square? There's a fountain 10 to spout and splash!
In the shade it sings and springs; in the shine such foambows flash
On the horses with curling fish-tails, that prance and paddle and pash 15
Round the lady atop in her conch—fifty gazers do not abash,
Though all that she wears is some weeds round her waist in a sort of sash. 20

All the year long at the villa, nothing to see though you linger,
Except yon cypress that points like death's lean lifted forefinger.
Some think fireflies pretty, when they mix i' 25 the corn and mingle,
Or thrid the stinking hemp till the stalks of it seem a-tingle.
Late August or early September, the stunning cicala is shrill, 30
And the bees keep their tiresome whine round the resinous firs on the hill.
Enough of the seasons,—I spare you the months of the fever and chill.

35
Ere you open your eyes in the city, the blessed church-bells begin:
No sooner the bells leave off than the diligence rattles in:
You get the pick of the news, and it costs you 40 never a pin.
By and by there's the travelling doctor gives pills, lets blood, draws teeth;
Or the Pulcinello-trumpet breaks up the market beneath.
At the post-office such a scene-picture—the 45 new play, piping hot!
And a notice how, only this morning, three liberal thieves were shot.
Above it, behold the Archbishop's most 50 fatherly of rebukes,
And beneath, with his crown and his lion,

some little new law of the Duke's!
Or a sonnet with flowery marge, to the Reverend Don So-and-so,
Who is Dante, Boccaccio, Petrarca, Saint Jerome, and Cicero,
"And moreover," (the sonnet goes rhyming,) "the skirts of Saint Paul has reached,
Having preached us those six Lent-lectures more unctuous than ever he preached."
Noon strikes,—here sweeps the procession! our Lady borne smiling and smart
With a pink gauze gown all spangles, and seven swords stuck in her heart!
Bang-whang-whang goes the drum, *tootle-te-tootle* the fife;
No keeping one's haunches still: it's the greatest pleasure in life.

But bless you, it's dear—it's dear! fowls, wine, at double the rate.
They have clapped a new tax upon salt, and what oil pays passing the gate
It's horror to think of. And so, the villa for me, not the city!
Beggars can scarcely be choosers: but still, ah, the pity, the pity!
Look, two and two go the priests, then the monks with cowls and sandals,
And the penitents dressed in white shirts, a-holding the yellow candles;
One, he carries a flag up straight, and another a cross with handles,
And the Duke's guard brings up the rear, for the better prevention of scandals:
Bang-whang-whang goes the drum, *tootle-te-tootle* the fife.
Oh, a day in the city-square, there is no such pleasure in life!

PROSPICE[1]

Fear death?—to feel the fog in my throat,
    The mist in my face,
When the snows begin, and the blasts denote
    I am nearing the place,
The power of the night, the press of the storm,
    The post of the foe;
Where he stands, the Arch Fear in a visible form,
    Yet the strong man must go:

_____
[1] Look forward.

For the journey is done and the summit attained,
    And the barriers fall,
Though a battle's to fight ere the guerdon be
gained,
    The reward of it all.

I was ever a fighter, so—one fight more,
    The best and the last!
I would hate that death bandaged my eyes,
and forbore,
    And bade me creep past.
No! let me taste the whole of it, fare like my
peers
    The heroes of old,
Bear the brunt, in a minute pay life's glad
arrears
    Of pain, darkness and cold.

For sudden the worst turns the best to the
brave,
    The black minute's at end,
And the elements' rage, the fiend-voices that
rave,
    Shall dwindle, shall blend,
Shall change, shall become first a peace out of
pain,
    Then a light, then thy breast,
O thou soul of my soul! I shall clasp thee
again,
    And with God be the rest!

WALT WHITMAN

*A product of the New York area, Whitman
(1819–1892) was at various times printer,
teacher, editor, Civil War nurse; he read
widely in both American and Continental
writers, traveled around a good portion of the
country, more or less a vagabond. There are
many disputed episodes in his life involving a
mysterious New Orleans girl, strange friendships, a possible mystic experience in 1855.
His* Leaves of Grass *is a monument in the history of American poetry; with the possible exception of Poe, it can be said that Whitman's
was the first original voice to reach beyond the
sea, to sing the arrival of America in the universal family of poetry. His passion combined
with a free verse form cleansed American verse
of its tendency to imitate the English and to
substitute moralizing for poetic truth. Thanks
to Whitman, the road was made easier for
Sandburg, Jeffers, and others.** *

FROM *Song of Myself*

1

I celebrate myself, and sing myself,
And what I assume you shall assume,
For every atom belonging to me as good be-
longs to you.

I loafe and invite my soul,
I learn and loafe at my ease observing a spear
of summer grass.

My tongue, every atom of my blood, form'd
from this soil, this air,
Born here of parents born here from parents
the same, and their parents the same,
I, now thirty-seven years old in perfect health
begin,
Hoping to cease not till death.
Creeds and schools in abeyance,
Retiring back a while sufficed at what they
are, but never forgotten,
I harbor for good or bad, I permit to speak at
every hazard,
Nature without check with original energy.

2

Houses and rooms are full of perfumes, the
shelves are crowded with perfumes,
I breathe the fragrance myself and know it
and like it,
The distillation would intoxicate me also, but
I shall not let it.

The atmosphere is not a perfume, it has no
taste of the distillation, it is odorless,
It is for my mouth forever, I am in love with
it,
I will go to the bank by the wood and become
undisguised and naked,
I am mad for it to be in contact with me.

The smoke of my own breath,
Echoes, ripples, buzz'd whispers, love-root,
silk-thread, crotch and vine,
My respiration and inspiration, the beating of

---

my heart, the passing of blood and air through my lungs,
The sniff of green leaves and dry leaves, and of the shore and dark-color'd sea-rocks, and of hay in the barn,
The sound of the belch'd words of my voice loos'd to the eddies of the wind,
A few light kisses, a few embraces, a reaching around of arms,
The play of shine and shade on the trees as the supple boughs wag,
The delight alone or in the rush of the streets, or along the fields and hill-sides,
The feeling of health, the full-moon trill, the song of me rising from bed and meeting the sun.
Have you reckon'd a thousand acres much? have you reckon'd the earth much?
Have you practic'd so long to learn to read?
Have you felt so proud to get at the meaning of poems?
Stop this day and night with me and you shall possess the origin of all poems,
You shall possess the good of the earth and sun, (there are millions of suns left,)
You shall no longer take things at second or third hand, nor look through the eyes of the dead, nor feed on the specters in books,
You shall not look through my eyes either, nor take things from me,
You shall listen to all sides and filter them from your self.

3

I have heard what the talkers were talking, the talk of the beginning and the end,
But I do not talk of the beginning or the end.

There was never any more inception than there is now,
Nor any more youth or age than there is now,
And will never be any more perfection than there is now,
Nor any more heaven or hell than there is now.

Urge and urge and urge,
Always the procreant urge of the world.
Out of the dimness opposite equals advance, always substance and increase, always sex,

Always a knit of identity, always distinction, always a breed of life.

To elaborate is no avail, learn'd and unlearn'd feel that it is so.

Sure as the most certain sure, plumb in the uprights, well center-tied, braced in the beams,
Stout as a horse, affectionate, haughty, electrical,
I and this mystery here we stand.
Clear and sweet is my soul, and clear and sweet is all that is not my soul.

Lack one lacks both, and the unseen is proved by the seen,
Till that becomes unseen and receives proof in its turn.

Showing the best and dividing it from the worst age vexes age,
Knowing the perfect fitness and equanimity of things, while they discuss I am silent, and go bathe and admire myself.

Welcome is every organ and attribute of me, and of any man hearty and clean,
Not an inch nor a particle of an inch is vile, and none shall be less familiar than the rest.

I am satisfied—I see, dance, laugh, sing;
As the hugging and loving bed-fellow sleeps at my side through the night, and withdraws at the peep of the day with stealthy tread,
Leaving me baskets cover'd with white towels swelling the house with their plenty,
Shall I postpone my acceptation and realization and scream at my eyes,
That they turn from gazing after and down the road,
And forthwith cipher and show to me a cent,
Exactly the value of one and exactly the value of two, and which is ahead?

4

Trippers and askers surround me,
People I meet, the effect upon me of my early life or the ward and city I live in, or the nation,

The latest dates, discoveries, inventions, soci-
    eties, authors old and new,
My dinner, dress, associates, looks, compli-
    ments, dues,
The real or fancied indifference of some man 5
    or woman I love,
The sickness of one of my folks or of myself, or
    ill-doing or loss or lack of money, or de-
    pressions of exaltations,
Battles, the horrors of fratricidal war, the fever 10
    of doubtful news, the fitful events;
These come to me days and nights and go from
    me again,
But they are not the Me myself.
Apart from the pulling and hauling stands what 15
    I am,
Stands amused, complacent, compassionating,
    idle, unitary,
Looks down, is erect, or bends an arm on an
    impalpable certain rest, 20
Looking with side-curved head curious what
    will come next,
Both in and out of the game and watching and
    wondering at it.

Backward I see in my own days where I 25
    sweated through fog with linguists and
    contenders,
I have no mockings or arguments, I witness
    and wait. 30

6

A child said *What is the grass?* fetching it to
    me with full hands, 35
How could I answer the child? I do not know
    what it is any more than he.

I guess it must be the flag of my disposition,
    out of hopeful green stuff woven. 40
Or I guess it is the handkerchief of the Lord,
A scented gift and remembrancer designedly
    dropt,
Bearing the owner's name someway in the cor-
    ners, that we may see and remark, and 45
    say *Whose?*

Or I guess the grass is itself a child, the pro-
    duced babe of the vegetation.

Or I guess it is a uniform hieroglyphic, 50
And it means, Sprouting alike in broad zones
    and narrow zones,
Growing among black folks as among white,
Kanuck, Tuckahoe, Congressman, Cuff, I give
    them the same, I receive them the same.

And now it seems to me the beautiful uncut
    hair of graves.

Tenderly will I use you curling grass,
It may be you transpire from the breasts of
    young men,
It may be if I had known them I would have
    loved them,
It may be you are from old people, or from off-
    spring taken soon out of their mothers'
    laps,
And here you are the mothers' laps.

This grass is very dark to be from the white
    heads of old mothers,
Darker than the colorless beards of old men,
Dark to come from under the faint red roofs of
    mouths.

O I perceive after all so many uttering tongues,
And I perceive they do not come from the roofs
    of mouths for nothing.

I wish I could translate the hints about the
    dead young men and women,
And the hints about old men and mothers, and
    the offspring taken soon out of their laps.

What do you think has become of the young
    and old men?
And what do you think has become of the
    women and children?

They are alive and well somewhere,
The smallest sprout shows there is really no
    death,
And if ever there was it led forward life, and
    does not wait at the end to arrest it,
And ceas'd the moment life appear'd.

All goes onward and outward, nothing col-
    lapses,
And to die is different from what any one sup-
    posed, and luckier.

7

Has anyone supposed it lucky to be born?

I hasten to inform him or her it is just as lucky
   to die, and I know it.

I pass death with the dying and birth with the
   new-wash'd babe, and am not contain'd 5
   between my hat and boots,
And peruse manifold objects, no two alike and
   every one good,
The earth good and the stars good, and their
   adjuncts all good. 10

I am not an earth nor an adjunct of an earth,
I am the mate and companion of people, all
   just as immortal and fathomless as myself,
(They do not know how immortal, but I 15
   know.)
Every kind for itself and its own, for me mine
   male and female,
For me those that have been boys and that
   love women, 20
For me the man that is proud and feels how it
   stings to be slighted,
For me the sweet-heart and the old maid, for
   me mothers and the mothers of mothers,
For me lips that have smiled, eyes that have 25
   shed tears,
For me children and the begetters of children.

Undrape! you are not guilty to me, nor stale
   nor discarded, 30
I see through the broadcloth and gingham
   whether or no,
And am around, tenacious, acquisitive, tireless,
   and cannot be shaken away. 35

8

The little one sleeps in its cradle,
I lift the gauze and look a long time, and
   silently brush away flies with my hand. 40

The youngster and the red-faced girl turn
   aside up the bushy hill,
I peeringly view them from the top.

The suicide sprawls on the bloody floor of the
   bedroom,
I witness the corpse with its dabbled hair, I
   note where the pistol has fallen.

The blab of the pave, tires of carts, sluff of 50
   boot-soles, talk of the promenaders,

The heavy omnibus, the driver with his inter-
   rogating thumb, the clank of the shod
   horses on the granite floor,
The snow-sleighs, clinking, shouted jokes, pelts
   of snow-balls,
The hurrahs for popular favorites, the fury of
   rous'd mobs,
The flap of the curtain'd litter, a sick man inside borne to the hospital,
The meeting of enemies, the sudden oath, the
   blows and fall,
The excited crowd, the policeman with his star
   quickly working his passage to the centre
   of the crowd,
The impassive stones that receive and return
   so many echoes,
What groans of over-fed or half-starv'd who
   fall sunstruck or in fits,
What exclamations of women taken suddenly
   who hurry home and give birth to babes,
What living and buried speech is always vibrating here, what howls restrain'd by decorum,
Arrests of criminals, slights, adulterous offers
   made, acceptances, rejections with convex lips,
I mind them or the show or resonance of them
   —I come and I depart.

9

The big doors of the country barn stand open
   and ready,
The dried grass of the harvest-time loads the
   slow-drawn wagon,
The clear light plays on the brown gray and
   green intertinged,
The armfuls are pack'd to the sagging mow.

I am there, I help, I came stretch'd atop of the
   load,
I felt its soft jolts, one leg reclined on the other,
I jump from the cross-beams and seize the
   clover and timothy,
And roll head over heels and tangle my hair
   full of wisps.

10

Alone far in the wilds and mountains I hunt,
Wandering amazed at my own lightness and
   glee,

In the late afternoon choosing a safe spot to
    pass the night,
Kindling a fire and broiling the fresh-kill'd
    game,
Falling asleep on the gather'd leaves with my   5
    dog and gun by my side.

The Yankee clipper is under her sky-sails, she
    cuts the sparkle and scud,
My eyes settle the land, I bend at her prow or   10
    shout joyously from the deck.

The boatmen and clam-diggers arose early and
    stopt for me,
I tuck'd my trowser-ends in my boots and went   15
    and had a good time;
You should have been with us that day round
    the chowder-kettle.

I saw the marriage of the trapper in the open   20
    air in the far west, the bride was a red
    girl,
Her father and his friends sat near cross-legged
    and dumbly smoking, they had moccasins
    to their feet and large thick blankets   25
    hanging from their shoulders,
On a bank lounged the trapper, he was drest
    mostly in skins, his luxuriant beard and
    curls protected his neck, he held his bride
    by the hand,   30
She had long eyelashes, her head was bare, her
    coarse straight locks descended upon her
    voluptuous limbs and reach'd to her feet.

The runaway slave came to my house and   35
    stopt outside,
I heard his motions crackling the twigs of the
    woodpile,
Through the swung half-door of the kitchen I
    saw him limpsy and weak,   40
And went where he sat on a log and led him
    in and assured him,
And brought water and fill'd a tub for his
    sweated body and bruis'd feet,
And gave him a room that enter'd from my   45
    own, and gave him some coarse clean
    clothes,
And remember perfectly well his revolving
    eyes and his awkwardness,
And remember putting plasters on the galls of   50
    his neck and ankles;
He staid with me a week before he was recu-

perated and pass'd north,
I had him sit next me at table, my fire-lock
    lean'd in the corner.

14

The wild gander leads his flock through the
    cool night,
Ya-honk he says, and sounds it down to me
    like an invitation,
The pert may suppose it meaningless, but I
    listening close,
Fine its purpose and place up there toward the
    wintry sky.

The sharp-hoof'd moose of the north, the cat
    on the the house-sill, the chickadee, the
    prairie-dog,
The litter of the grunting sow as they tug at
    her teats,
The brood of the turkey-hen and she with her
    half-spread wings,
I see in them and myself the same old law.

The press of my foot to the earth springs a
    hundred affections,
They scorn the best I can do to relate them.

I am enamour'd of growing out-doors,
Of men that live among cattle or taste of the
    ocean or woods,
Of the builders and steerers of ships and the
    wielders of axes and mauls, and the driv-
    ers of horses,
I can eat and sleep with them week in and
    week out.
What is commonest, cheapest, nearest, easiest,
    is Me,
Me going in for my chances, spending for vast
    returns,
Adorning myself to bestow myself on the first
    that will take me,
Not asking the sky to come down to my good
    will,
Scattering it freely forever.

15

The pure contralto sings in the organ loft,
The carpenter dresses his plank, the tongue of
    his foreplane whistles its wild ascending
    lisp,
The married and unmarried children ride
    home to their Thanksgiving dinner,

The pilot seizes the king-pin, he heaves down with a strong arm,

The mate stands braced in the whale-boat, lance and harpoon are ready,

The duck-shooter walks by silent and cautious stretches,

The deacons are ordain'd with cross'd hands at the altar,

The spinning-girl retreats and advances to the hum of the big wheel,

The farmer stops by the bars as he walks on a First-day loafe and looks at the oats and rye,

The lunatic is carried at last to the asylum a confirm'd case,

(He will never sleep any more as he did in the cot in his mother's bed-room;)

The jour printer with gray head and gaunt jaws works at his case,

He turns his quid of tobacco while his eyes blurr with the manuscript;

The malform'd limbs are tied to the surgeon's table,

What is removed drops horridly in a pail;

The quadroon girl is sold at the auction-stand, the drunkard nods by the bar-room stove,

The machinist rolls up his sleeves, the policeman travels his beat, the gate-keeper marks who pass,

The young fellow drives the express-wagon, (I love him, though I do not know him;)

The half-breed straps on his light boots to compete in the race,

The western turkey-shooting draws old and young, some lean on their rifles, some sit on logs,

Out from the crowd steps the marksman, takes his position, levels his piece;

The groups of newly-come immigrants cover the wharf or levee,

As the woolly-pates hoe in the sugar-field, the overseer views them from his saddle,

The bugle calls in the ball-room, the gentlemen run for their partners, the dancers bow to each other,

The youth lies awake in the cedar-roof'd garret and harks to the musical rain,

The Wolverine sets traps on the creek that helps fill the Huron,

The squaw wrapt in her yellow-hemm'd cloth is offering moccasins and bead-bags for sale,

The connoisseur peers along the exhibition-gallery with half-shut eyes bent sideways,

As the deck-hands make fast the steamboat the plank is thrown for the shore-going passengers,

The young sister holds out the skein while the elder sister winds it off in a ball, and stops now and then for the knots,

The one-year wife is recovering and happy having a week ago borne her first child,

The clean-hair'd Yankee girl works with her sewing-machine or in the factory or mill,

The paving-man leans on his two-handed rammer, the reporter's lead flies swiftly over the note-book, the sign-painter is lettering with blue and gold,

The canal boy trots on the tow-path, the book-keeper counts at his desk, the shoemaker waxes his thread,

The conductor beats time for the band and all the performers follow him,

The child is baptized, the convert is making his first professions,

The regatta is spread on the bay, the race is begun, (how the white sails sparkle!)

The drover watching his drove sings out to them that would stray,

The pedler sweats with his pack on his back, (the purchaser higgling about the odd cent;)

The bride unrumples her white dress, the minute-hand of the clock moves slowly,

The opium-eater reclines with rigid head and just-open'd lips,

The prostitute draggles her shawl, her bonnet bobs on her tipsy and pimpled neck,

The crowd laugh at her blackguard oaths, the men jeer and wink to each other,

(Miserable! I do not laugh at your oaths nor jeer you;)

The President holding a cabinet council is surrounded by the great Secretaries,

On the piazza walk three matrons stately and friendly with twined arms,

The crew of the fish-smack pack repeated layers of halibut in the hold,

The Missourian crosses the plains toting his wares and his cattle,

As the fare-collector goes through the train he gives notice by the jingling of loose change,

The floor-men are laying the floor, the tinners

are tinning the roof, the masons are calling for mortar,
In single file each shouldering his hod pass onward the laborers;
Seasons pursuing each other the indescribable 5
crowd is gather'd, it is the fourth of
Seventh-month, (what salutes of cannon
and small arms!)
Seasons pursuing each other the plougher
ploughs, the mower mows, and the win- 10
ter-grain falls in the ground;
Off on the lakes the pike-fisher watches and
waits by the hole in the frozen surface,
The stumps stand thick round the clearing, the
squatter strikes deep with his axe, 15
Flatboatmen make fast towards dusk near the
cotton-wood or pecan-trees,
Coon-seekers go through the regions of the
Red river or through those drain'd by the
Tennessee, or through those of the Ar- 20
kansas,
Torches shine in the dark that hangs on the
Chattahooche or Altamahaw,
Patriarchs sit at supper with sons and grand-
sons and great-grandsons around them, 25
In walls of adobie, in canvas tents, rest hunters
and trappers after their day's sport,
The city sleeps and the country sleeps,
The living sleep for their time, the dead sleep
for their time, 30
The old husband sleeps by his wife and the
young husband sleeps by his wife;
And these tend inward to me, and I tend out-
ward to them,
And such as it is to be of these more or less I 35
am,
And of these one and all I weave the song of
myself.

16

I am of old and young, of the foolish as much 40
as the wise,
Regardless of others, ever regardful of others,
Maternal as well as paternal, a child as well as
a man, 45
Stuff'd with the stuff that is coarse and stuff'd
with the stuff that is fine,
One of the Nation of many nations, the small-
est the same and the largest the same,
A Southerner soon as a Northerner, a planter 50
nonchalant and hospitable down by the
Oconee I live,

A Yankee bound my own way ready for trade,
my joints the limberest joints on earth and
the sternest joints on earth,
A Kentuckian walking the vale of the Elkhorn
in my deer-skin leggings, a Louisianian or
Georgian,
A boatman over lakes or bays or along coasts,
a Hoosier, Badger, Buckeye;
At home on Kanadian snow-shoes or up in the
bush, or with fishermen off Newfound-
land,
At home in the fleet of ice-boats, sailing with
the rest and tacking,
At home on the hills of Vermont or in the
woods of Maine, or the Texan ranch,
Comrade of Californians, comrade of free
North-Westerners, (loving their big proportions,)
Comrade of raftsmen and coalmen, comrade of
all who shake hands and welcome to drink
and meat,
A learner with the simplest, a teacher of the
thoughtfullest,
A novice beginning yet experient of myriads of
seasons,
Of every hue and caste am I, of every rank and
religion,
A farmer, mechanic, artist, gentleman, sailor,
quaker,
Prisoner, fancy-man, rowdy, lawyer, physician,
priest.

I resist any thing better than my own diver-
sity,
Breathe the air but leave plenty after me,
And am not stuck up, and am in my place.

(The moth and the fish-eggs are in their place,
The bright suns I see and the dark suns I cannot see are in their place,
The palpable is in its place and the impalpable
is in its place.)

18

With music strong I come, with my cornets
and my drums,
I play not marches for accepted victors only, I
play marches for conquer'd and slain persons.

Have you heard that it was good to gain the
day?

I also say it is good to fall, battles are lost in
the same spirit in which they are won.

I beat and pound for the dead,
I blow through my embouchures my loudest 5
and gayest for them.

Vivas to those who have fail'd!
And to those whose war-vessels sank in the
sea!
And to those themselves who sank in the sea! 10
And to all generals that lost engagements, and
all overcome heroes!
And the numberless unknown heroes equal to
the greatest heroes known!

19

This is the meal equally set, this the meat for
natural hunger,
It is for the wicked just the same as the right- 20
eous, I make appointments with all,
I will not have a single person slighted or left
away,
The kept-woman, sponger, thief, are hereby invited, 25
There shall be no difference between them and
the rest.

This is the press of a bashful hand, this the
float and odor of hair,
This the touch of my lips to yours, this the 30
murmur of yearning,
This the far-off depth and height reflecting my
own face,
This the thoughtful merge of myself, and the 35
outlet again.
Do you guess I have some intricate purpose?
Well I have, for the Fourth-month showers
have, and the mica on the side of the rock
has.

Do you take it I would astonish?
Does the daylight astonish? does the early red-
start twittering through the woods?
Do I astonish more than they?
This hour I tell things in confidence, 45
I might not tell everybody, but I will tell
you.

20

Who goes there? hankering, gross, mystical,
nude;

How is it I extract strength from the beef I
eat?

What is a man anyhow? what am I? what **are**
you?

All I mark as my own you shall offset it with
your own,
Else it were time lost listening to me.

I do not snivel that snivel the world over,
That months are vacuums and the ground but
wallow and filth.

15 Whimpering and truckling fold with powders
for invalids, conformity goes to the fourth-
remov'd,
I wear my hat as I please indoors or out.

20 Why should I pray? why should I venerate and
be ceremonious?

Having pried through the strata, analyzed to a
hair, counsel'd with doctors and calcu-
25 lated close,
I find no sweeter fat than sticks to my own
bones.

In all people I see myself, none more and not
30 one a barleycorn less,
And the good or bad I say of myself I say of
them.
I know I am solid and sound,
To me the converging objects of the universe
35 perpetually flow,
All are written to me, and I must get what the
writing means.

I know I am deathless,
40 I know this orbit of mine cannot be swept by a
carpenter's compass,
I know I shall not pass like a child's carlacue
cut with a burnt stick at night.

45 I know I am august,
I do not trouble my spirit to vindicate itself or
be understood,
I see that the elementary laws never apologize,
(I reckon I behave no prouder than the level I
50 plant my house by, after all.)

I exist as I am, that is enough,

If no other in the world be aware I sit content,
And if each and all be aware I sit content.

One world is aware and by far the largest to
   me, and that is myself,
And whether I come to my own today or in ten
   thousand or ten million years,
I can cheerfully take it now, or with equal
   cheerfulness I can wait.

My foothold is tenon'd and mortis'd in granite,
I laugh at what you call dissolution,
And I know the amplitude of time.

21

I am the poet of the Body and I am the poet of
   the Soul,
The pleasures of heaven are with me and the
   pains of hell are with me,

The first I graft and increase upon myself, the
   latter I translate into a new tongue.

I am the poet of the woman the same as the
   man,
And I say it is as great to be a woman as to be
   a man,
And I say there is nothing greater than the
   mother of men.

I chant the chant of dilation or pride,
We have had ducking and deprecating about
   enough,
I show that size is only development.

Have you outstript the rest? are you the President?
It is a trifle, they will more than arrive there
   every one, and still pass on.

I am he that walks with the tender and growing night,
I call to the earth and sea half-held by the
   night.

Press close bare-bosom'd night—press close
   magnetic nourishing night!
Night of south winds—night of the large few
   stars!
Still nodding night—mad naked summer night.

Smile O voluptuous cool-breath'd earth!

Earth of the slumbering and liquid trees!
Earth of departed sunset—earth of the mountains misty-topt!
5 Earth of the vitreous pour of the full moon
   just tinged with blue!
Earth of shine and dark mottling the tide of
   the river!
Earth of the limpid gray of clouds brighter and
   clearer for my sake!
10 Far-swooping elbow'd earth—rich apple-blos-
   som'd earth!
Smile, for your lover comes.

Prodigal, you have given me love—therefore
15   I to you give love!
O unspeakable passionate love.

22

You sea! I resign myself to you also—I guess
20   what you mean,
I behold from the beach your crooked inviting
   fingers,
I believe you refuse to go back without feeling
   of me,
25 We must have a turn together, I undress, hurry
   me out of sight of the land,
Cushion me soft, rock me in billowy drowse,
Dash me with amorous wet, I can repay you.

30 Sea of stretch'd ground-swells,
Sea breathing broad and convulsive breaths,
Sea of the brine of life and of unshovell'd yet
   always-ready graves,
Howler and scooper of storms, capricious and
35   dainty sea,
I am integral with you, I too am of one phase
   and of all phases.

Partaker of influx and efflux, I, extoller of hate
40   and conciliation,
Extoller of armies and those that sleep in each
   others' arms.

I am he attesting sympathy,
45 (Shall I make my list of things in the house
   and skip the house that supports them?)

I am not the poet of goodness only, I do not
   decline to be the poet of wickedness also.

50 What blurt is this about virtue and about vice?
Evil propels me and reform of evil propels me,

I stand indifferent,
My gait is no fault-finder's or rejecter's gait,
I moisten the roots of all that has grown.

Did you fear some scrofula out of the unflag- 5
ging pregnancy?
Did you guess the celestial laws are yet to be
work'd over and rectified?

I find one side a balance and the antipodal side 10
a balance,
Soft doctrine as steady help as stable doctrine,
Thoughts and deeds of the present our rouse
and early start.
This minute that comes to me over the past 15
decillions,
There is no better than it and now.

What behaved well in the past or behaves well
to-day is not such a wonder, 20
The wonder is always and always how there
can be a mean man or an infidel.

25

Dazzling and tremendous how quick the sun- 25
rise would kill me,
If I could not now and always send sun-rise
out of me.

We also ascend dazzling and tremendous as 30
the sun,
We found our own O my soul in the calm and
cool of the daybreak.

My voice goes after what my eyes cannot 35
reach,
With the twirl of my tongue I encompass
worlds and volumes of worlds.

Speech is the twin of my vision, it is unequal 40
to measure itself,
It provokes me forever, it says sarcastically,
*Walt you contain enough, why don't you let it
out then?*

45
Come now I will not be tantalized, you con-
ceive too much of articulation,
Do you not know O speech how the buds be-
neath you are folded?
Waiting in gloom, protected by frost, 50
The dirt receding before my prophetical
screams,

I underlying causes to balance them at last,
My knowledge my live parts, it keeping tally
with the meaning of all things,
Happiness, (which whoever hears me let him
or her set out in search of this day.)

My final merit I refuse you, I refuse putting
from me what I really am,
Encompass worlds, but never try to encompass
me,
I crowd your sleekest and best by simply looking toward you.

Writing and talking do not prove me,
I carry the plenum of proof and every thing
else in my face,
With the hush of my lips I wholly confound
the skeptic.

26

Now I will do nothing but listen,
To accrue what I hear into this song, to let
sounds contribute toward it.

I hear bravuras of birds, bustle of growing
wheat, gossip of flames, clack of sticks
cooking my meals,
I hear the sound I love, the sound of the human voice,
I hear all sounds running together, combined,
fused or following,
Sounds of the city and sounds out of the city,
sounds of the day and night,
Talkative young ones to those that like them,
the loud laugh of work-people at their
meals,
The angry base of disjointed friendship, the
faint tones of the sick,
The judge with hands tight to the desk, his
pallid lips pronouncing a death-sentence,
The heave'e'yo of stevedores unlading ships by
the wharves, the refrain of the anchor-
lifters,
The ring of alarm-bells, the cry of fire, the
whirr of swift-streaking engines and hose-
carts with premonitory tinkles and color'd
lights,
The steam-whistle, the solid roll of the train of
approaching cars,
The slow march play'd at the head of the as-
sociation marching two and two,

(**They** go to guard some corpse, the flag-tops
are draped with black muslin.)

I hear the violoncello, ('tis the young man's
heart's complaint,)
I hear the key'd cornet, it glides quickly in
through my ears,
It shakes mad-sweet pangs through my belly
and breast.
I hear the chorus, it is a grand opera, 10
Ah this indeed is music—this suits me.

A tenor large and fresh as the creation fills me,
The orbic flex of his mouth is pouring and filling me full.

I hear the train'd soprano (what work with
hers is this?)
The orchestra whirls me wider than Uranus
flies,
It wrenches such ardors from me I did not
know I possess'd them,
It sails me, I dab with bare feet, they are lick'd
by the indolent waves,
I am cut by bitter and angry hail, I lose my 25
breath,
Steep'd amid honey'd morphine, my windpipe
throttled in fakes of death,
At length let up again to feel the puzzle of
puzzles,
And that we call Being.

30

All truths wait in all things,
They neither hasten their own delivery nor re-
sist it,
They do not need the obstetric forceps of the
surgeon,
The insignificant is as big to me as any, 40
(What is less or more than a touch?)
Logic and sermons never convince,
The damp of the night drives deeper into my
soul.

(Only what proves itself to every man and 45
woman is so,
Only what nobody denies is so.)

A minute and a drop of me settle my brain, 50
I believe the soggy clods shall become lovers
and lamps,

And a compend of compends is the meat of a
man or woman,
And a summit and flower there is the feeling
they have for each other,
And they are to branch boundlessly out of that 5
lesson until it becomes omnific,
And until one and all shall delight us, and we
them.

31

I believe a leaf of grass is no less than the
journey-work of the stars,
And the pismire is equally perfect, and a grain
of sand, and the egg of the wren,
And the tree-toad is a chef-d'œuvre for the 15
highest,
And the running blackberry would adorn the
parlours of heaven,
And the narrowest hinge in my hand puts to
scorn all machinery, 20
And the cow crunching with depress'd head
surpasses any statue,
And a mouse is miracle enough to stagger sex-
tillions of infidels.

I find I incorporate gneiss, coal, long-threaded
moss, fruits, grains, esculent roots.
And am stucco'd with quadrupeds and birds
all over,
And have distanced what is behind me for 30
good reasons,
But call anything back again when I desire it.

In vain the speeding or shyness,
In vain the plutonic rocks send their old heat 35
against my approach,
In vain the mastodon retreats beneath its own
powder'd bones,
In vain objects stand leagues off and assume
manifold shapes, 40
In vain the ocean settling in hollows and the
great monsters lying low,
In vain the buzzard houses herself with the
sky,
In vain the snake slides through the creepers 45
and logs,
In vain the elk takes to the inner passes of the
woods,
In vain the razor-bill'd auk sails far north to
Labrador, 50
I follow quickly, I ascend to the nest in the
fissure of the cliff.

44

It is time to explain myself—let us stand up.

What is known I strip away,
I launch all men and women forward with
  me into the Unknown.
The clock indicates the moment—but what
  does eternity indicate?

We have thus far exhausted trillions of winters
  and summers,
There are trillions ahead, and trillions ahead of
  them.

Births have brought us richness and variety,
And other births will bring us richness and
  variety.

I do not call one greater and one smaller,
That which fills its period and place is equal to
  any.

Were mankind murderous or jealous upon you,
  my brother, my sister?
I am sorry for you, they are not murderous or
  jealous upon me,
All has been gentle with me, I keep no account
  with lamentation,
(What have I to do with lamentation?)

I am an acme of things accomplish'd, and I an
  encloser of things to be.

My feet strike an apex of the apices of the
  stairs,
On every step bunches of ages, and larger
  bunches between the steps,
All below duly travel'd, and still I mount and
  mount.

Rise after rise bow the phantoms behind me,
Afar down I see the huge first Nothing, I
  know I was even there,
I waited unseen and always, and slept through
  the lethargic mist,
And took my time, and took no hurt from the
  fetid carbon.

Long I was hugg'd close—long and long.

Immense have been the preparations for me,

Faithful and friendly the arms that have help'd
  me.

Cycles ferried my cradle, rowing and rowing
  like cheerful boatmen,

For room to me stars kept aside in their own
  rings,
They sent influences to look after what was to
  hold me.

Before I was born out of my mother generations guided me,
My embryo has never been torpid, nothing
  could overlay it.

For it the nebula cohered to an orb,
The long slow strata piled to rest it on,
Vast vegetables gave it sustenance,
Monstrous sauroids transported it in their
  mouths and deposited it with care.
All forces have been steadily employ'd to com-
  plete and delight me,
Now on this spot I stand with my robust soul.

46

I know I have the best of time and space, and
  was never measured and never will be
  measured.

I tramp a perpetual journey (come listen all!)
My signs are a rain-proof coat, good shoes, and
  a staff cut from the woods,
No friend of mine takes his ease in my chair,
I have no chair, no church, no philosophy,
I lead no man to a dinner-table, library, ex-
  change,
But each man and each woman of you I lead
  upon a knoll,
My left hand hooking you round the waist,
My right hand pointing to landscapes of conti-
  nents and the public road.

Not I, not any one else can travel that road
  for you,
You must travel it for yourself.

It is not far, it is within reach,
Perhaps you have been on it since you were
  born and did not know,
Perhaps it is everywhere on water and on land.

Shoulder your duds, dear son, and I will mine, and let us hasten forth,
Wonderful cities and free nations we shall fetch as we go.

If you tire, give me both burdens, and rest the chuff of your hand on my hip,
And in due time you shall repay the same service to me,
For after we start we never lie by again.

This day before dawn I ascend a hill and look'd at the crowded heaven,
And I said to my spirit, *When we become the enfolders of those orbs, and the pleasure and knowledge of everything in them, shall we be fill'd and satisfied then?*
And my spirit said, *No, we but level that lift to pass and continue beyond.*

You are also asking me questions and I hear you,
I answer that I cannot answer, you must find out for yourself.

Sit a while, dear son,
Here are biscuits to eat and here is milk to drink,
But as soon as you sleep and renew yourself in sweet clothes, I kiss you with a good-bye kiss and open the gate for your egress hence.

Long enough have you dream'd contemptible dreams,
Now I wash the gum from your eyes,
You must habit yourself to the dazzle of the light and of every moment of your life.
Long have you timidly waded holding a plank by the shore,
Now I will you to be a bold swimmer,
To jump off in the midst of the sea, rise again, nod to me, shout, and laughingly dash with your hair.

48

I have said that the soul is not more than the body,
And I have said that the body is not more than the soul,
And nothing, not God, is greater to one than one's self is,

And whoever walks a furlong without sympathy walks to his own funeral drest in his shroud,
And I or you pocketless of a dime may purchase the pick of the earth,
And to glance with an eye or show a bean in its pod confounds the learning of all times,
And there is no trade or employment but the young man following it may become a hero,
And there is no object so soft but it makes a hub for the wheel'd universe,
And I say to any man or woman, Let your soul stand cool and composed before a million universes.

And I say to mankind, Be not curious about God,
For I who am curious about each am not curious about God,
(No array of terms can say how much I am at peace about God and about death.)

I hear and behold God in every object, yet understand God not in the least,
Nor do I understand who there can be more wonderful than myself.

Why should I wish to see God better than this day?
I see something of God each hour of the twenty-four, and each moment then,
In the faces of men and women I see God, and in my own face in the glass,
I find letters from God dropt in the street, and every one is sign'd by God's name,
And I leave them where they are, for I know that wheresoe'er I go,
Others will punctually come for ever and ever.

49

And as to you Death, and you bitter hug of mortality, it is idle to try to alarm me.

To his work without flinching the accoucheur comes,
I see the elder-hand pressing receiving supporting,
I recline by the sills of the exquisite flexible doors,
And mark the outlet, and mark the relief and escape.

And as to you Corpse I think you are good
   manure, but that does not offend me,
I smell the white roses sweet-scented and
   growing,
I reach to the leafy lips, I reach to the polish'd 5
   breasts of melons.

And as to you Life I reckon you are the leav-
   ings of many deaths,
(No doubt I have died myself ten thousand 10
   times before.)

I hear you whispering there O stars of heaven,
O suns—O grass of graves—O perpetual trans-
   fers and promotions, 15
If you do not say any thing how can I say any
   thing?

Of the turbid pool that lies in the autumn forest, 20
Of the moon that descends the steeps of the
   soughing twilight,
Toss, sparkles of day and dusk—toss on the
   black stems that decay in the muck,
Toss to the moaning gibberish of the dry 25
   limbs.

I ascend from the moon, I ascend from the
   night,
I perceive that the ghastly glimmer is noon- 30
   day sunbeams reflected,
And debouch to the steady and central from
   the offspring great or small.

50
35
There is that in me—I do not know what it is
   —but I know it is in me.

Wrench'd and sweaty—calm and cool then my
   body becomes, 40
I sleep—I sleep long.

I do not know it—it is without name—it is a
   word unsaid,
It is not in any dictionary, utterance, symbol. 45

Something it swings on more than the earth I
   swing on,
To it the creation is the friend whose embrac-
   ing awakes me. 50

Perhaps I might tell more. Outlines! I plead for

my brothers and sisters.

Do you see O my brothers and sisters?
It is not chaos or death—it is form, union, plan
   —it is eternal life—it is Happiness.

51

The past and present wilt—I have fill'd them,
   emptied them,
And proceed to fill my next fold of the future.

Listener up there! what have you to confide to
   me?
Look in my face while I snuff the sidle of
   evening,
(Talk honestly, no one else hears you, and I
   stay only a minute longer.)

Do I contradict myself?
Very well then I contradict myself,
(I am large, I contain multitudes.)

I concentrate toward them that are nigh, I wait
   on the door-slab.

Who has done his day's work? who will soonest
   be through with his supper?
Who wishes to walk with me?

Will you speak before I am gone? will you
   prove already too late?

52

The spotted hawk swoops by and accuses me,
   he complains of my gab and my loitering.

I too am not a bit tamed, I too am untranslata-
   ble,
I sound my barbaric yawp over the roofs of the
   world.

The last scud of day holds back for me,
It flings my likeness after the rest and true as
   any on the shadow'd wilds,
It coaxes me to the vapor and the dusk.

I depart as air, I shake my white locks at the
   runaway sun,
I effuse my flesh in eddies, and drift it in lacy
   jags.

I bequeath myself to the dirt to grow from the
grass I love,
If you want me again look for me under your
boot-soles.

You will hardly know who I am or what I
mean,
But I shall be good health to you nevertheless,
And filter and fiber your blood.

Failing to fetch me at first keep encouraged,
Missing me one place search another,
I stop somewhere waiting for you.

GIVE ME THE SPLENDID SILENT SUN

1

Give me the splendid silent sun with all his
beams full-dazzling,
Give me juicy autumnal fruit ripe and red
from the orchard,
Give me a field where the unmowed grass
grows,
Give me an arbor, give me the trellised grape,
Give me fresh corn and wheat, give me serene-
moving animals teaching content,
Give me nights perfectly quiet as on high pla-
teaus west of the Mississippi, and I looking up at the stars,
Give me odorous at sunrise a garden of beautiful flowers where I can walk undisturbed,
Give me for marriage a sweet-breathed woman
of whom I should never tire,
Give me a perfect child, give me, away, aside
from the noise of the world, a rural, domestic life,
Give me to warble spontaneous songs recluse
by myself, for my own ears only,
Give me solitude, give me Nature, give me
again, O Nature, your primal sanities!

These demanding to have them (tired with
ceaseless excitement, and racked by the
war-strife,)
These to procure incessantly asking, rising in
cries from my heart,
While yet incessantly asking still I adhere to
my city,
Day upon day and year upon year, O city,
walking your streets,

Where you hold me enchained a certain time
refusing to give me up,
Yet giving to make me glutted, enriched of
soul, you give me forever faces;
(O I see what I sought to escape, confronting,
reversing my cries,
I see my own soul trampling down what it
asked for.)

2

Keep your splendid silent sun,
Keep your woods, O Nature, and the quiet
places by the woods,
Keep your fields of clover and timothy, and
your cornfields and orchards,
Keep the blossoming buckwheat fields where
the ninth-month bees hum;
Give me faces and streets—give me these
phantoms incessant and endless along the
trottoirs!
Give me interminable eyes—give me women—
give me comrades and lovers by the thousand!
Let me see new ones every day—let me hold
new ones by the hand every day!
Give me such shows—give me the streets of
Manhattan!
Give me Broadway, with the soldiers marching—give me the sound of the trumpets
and drums!
(The soldiers in companies or regiments—
some starting away, flushed and reckless,
Some, their time up, returning with thinned
ranks, young, yet very old, worn, marching, noticing nothing;)
Give me the shores and wharves heavy-fringed
with black ships!
O such for me! O an intense life, full to reple-
tion and varied!
The life of the theater, barroom, huge hotel,
for me!
The saloon of the steamer! the crowded excursion for me! the torchlight procession!
The dense brigade bound for the war, with
high-piled military wagons following;
People, endless, streaming, with strong voices,
passions, pageants,
Manhattan streets with their powerful throbs,
with beating drums as now,
The endless and noisy chorus, the rustle and
clank of muskets (even the sight of the
wounded,)

Manhattan crowds, with their turbulent musical chorus!
Manhattan faces and eyes forever for me.

WHEN I HEARD THE LEARN'D ASTRONOMER

When I heard the learn'd astronomer,
When the proofs, the figures, were ranged in columns before me,
When I was shown the charts and diagrams, to add, divide, and measure them,
When I sitting heard the astronomer where he lectured with much applause in the lecture-room,
How soon unaccountable I became tired and sick,
Till rising and gliding out I wander'd off by myself,
In the mystical moist night-air, and from time to time,
Look'd up in perfect silence at the stars.

WHEN LILACS LAST IN THE DOORYARD BLOOM'D

1

When lilacs last in the dooryard bloom'd,
And the great star early droop'd in the western sky in the night,
I mourn'd, and yet shall mourn with ever-returning spring.

Ever-returning spring, trinity sure to me you bring,
Lilac blooming perennial and drooping star in the west,
And thought of him I love.

2

O powerful western fallen star!
O shades of night—O moody, tearful night!
O great star disappear'd—O the black murk that hides the star!
O cruel hands that hold me powerless—O helpless soul of me!
O harsh surrounding cloud that will not free my soul.

3

In the dooryard fronting an old farm-house near the white-wash'd palings,

Stands the lilac-bush tall-growing with heart-shaped leaves of rich green,
With many a pointed blossom rising delicate, with the perfume strong I love,
With every leaf a miracle—and from this bush in the dooryard,
With delicate-color'd blossoms and heart-shaped leaves of rich green,
A sprig with its flower I break.

4

In the swamp in secluded recesses,
A shy and hidden bird is warbling a song.

Solitary the thrush,
The hermit withdrawn to himself, avoiding the settlements,
Sings by himself a song.

Song of the bleeding throat,
Death's outlet song of life, (for well dear brother I know,
If thou wast not granted to sing thou would'st surely die.)

5

Over the breast of the spring, the land, amid cities,
Amid lanes and through old woods, where lately the violets peep'd from the ground, spotting the gray debris,
Amid the grass in the fields each side of the lanes, passing the endless grass,
Passing the yellow-spear'd wheat, every grain from its shroud in the dark-brown fields uprisen,
Passing the apple-tree blows of white and pink in the orchards,
Carrying a corpse to where it shall rest in the grave,
Night and day journeys a coffin.

6

Coffin that passes through lanes and streets,
Through day and night with the great cloud darkening the land,
With the pomp of the inloop'd flags with the cities draped in black,
With the show of the States themselves as of crape-veil'd women standing,
With processions long and winding and the flambeaus of the night,

With the countless torches lit, with the silent
    sea of faces and the unbared heads,
With the waiting depot, the arriving coffin,
    and the somber faces,
With dirges through the night, with the thou- 5
    sand voices rising strong and solemn,
With all the mournful voices of the dirges
    pour'd around the coffin,
The dim-lit churches and the shuddering or-
    gans—where amid these you journey, 10
With the tolling tolling bells' perpetual clang,
Here, coffin that slowly passes,
I give you my sprig of lilac.

7

(Nor for you, for one alone, 15
Blossoms and branches green to coffins all I
    bring,
For fresh as the morning, thus would I chant a
    song for you O sane and sacred death. 20

All over bouquets of roses,
O death, I cover you over with roses and early
    lilies,
But mostly and now the lilac that blooms the 25
    first,
Copious I break, I break the sprigs from the
    bushes,
With loaded arms I come, pouring for you,
For you and the coffins all of you O death.) 30

8

O western orb sailing the heaven,
Now I know what you must have meant as a
    month since I walk'd, 35
As I walk'd in silence the transparent shadowy
    night,
As I saw you had something to tell as you bent
    to me night after night,
As you droop'd from the sky low down as if to 40
    my side, (while the other stars all look'd
    on,)
As we wander'd together the solemn night,
    (for something I know not what kept me
    from sleep,) 45
As the night advanced, and I saw on the rim
    of the west how full you were of woe,
As I stood on the rising ground in the breeze
    in the cool transparent night,
As I watch'd where you pass'd and was lost in 50
    the netherward black of the night,
As my soul in its trouble dissatisfied sank, as

where you sad orb,
Concluded, dropt in the night, and was gone.

9

Sing on there in the swamp, 5
O singer bashful and tender, I hear your notes,
    I hear your call,
I hear, I come presently, I understand you,
But a moment I linger, for the lustrous star has
    detain'd me, 10
The star my departing comrade holds and de-
    tains me.

10

O how shall I warble myself for the dead one
    there I loved?
And how shall I deck my song for the large
    sweet soul that has gone?
And what shall my perfume be for the grave of
    him I love?

Sea-winds blown from east and west,
Blown from the Eastern sea and blown from
    the Western sea, till there on the prairies
    meeting,
These and with these and the breath of my
    chant,
I'll perfume the grave of him I love.

11

O what shall I hang on the chamber walls?
And what shall the pictures be that I hang on
    the walls,
To adorn the burial-house of him I love?
Pictures of growing spring and farms and 35
    homes,
With the Fourth-month eve at sundown, and
    the gray smoke lucid and bright,
With floods of the yellow gold of the gorgeous,
    indolent, sinking sun, burning, expanding
    the air,
With the fresh sweet herbage under foot, and
    the pale green leaves of the trees prolific,
In the distance the flowing glaze, the breast
    of the river, with a wind-dapple here and
    there,
With ranging hills on the banks, with many a
    line against the sky, and shadows,
And the city at hand, with dwellings so dense,
    and stacks of chimneys,
And all the scenes of life and the workshops,
    and the workmen homeward returning.

12

Lo, body and soul—this land,
My own Manhattan with spires, and the spar-
kling and hurrying tides, and the ships,
The varied and ample land, the South and the
North in the light, Ohio's shores and flash-
ing Missouri,
And ever the far-spreading prairies cover'd
with grass and corn.

Lo, the most excellent sun so calm and
haughty,
The violet and purple morn with just-felt
breezes,
The gentle soft-born measureless light,
The miracle spreading bathing all, the fulfill'd
noon,
The coming eve delicious, the welcome night
and the stars,
Over my cities shining all, enveloping man and
land.

13

Sing on, sing on, you grey-brown bird,
Sing from the swamps, the recesses, pour your
chant from the bushes,
Limitless out of the dusk, out of the cedars
and pines.

Sing on, dearest brother, warble your reedy
song,
Loud human song, with voice of uttermost
woe.

O liquid and free and tender!
O wild and loose to my soul—O wondrous
singer!
You only I hear—yet the star holds me (but
will soon depart,)
Yet the lilac with mastering odour holds me.

14

Now while I sat in the day and look'd forth,
In the close of the day with its light and the
fields of spring, and the farmers preparing
their crops,
In the large unconscious scenery of my land
with its lakes and forests,
In the heavenly aerial beauty, (after the per-
turb'd winds and the storms,)

Under the arching heavens of the afternoon
swift passing, and the voices of children
and women,
The many-moving sea-tides, and I saw the
ships how they sail'd,
And the summer approaching with richness,
and the fields all busy with labor,
And the infinite separate houses, how they all
went on, each with its meals and minutia
of daily usages,
And the streets how their throbbings throbb'd,
and the cities pent—lo, then and there,
Falling upon them all and among them all, enveloping me with the rest,
Appear'd the cloud, appear'd the long black
trail,
And I knew death, its thought, and the sacred
knowledge of death.

Then with the knowledge of death as walking
one side of me,
And the thought of death close-walking the
other side of me,
And I in the middle as with companions, and
as holding the hands of companions,
I fled forth to the hiding receiving night that
talks not,
Down to the shores of the water, the path by
the swamp in the dimness,
To the solemn shadowy cedars and ghostly
pines so still.

And the singer so shy to the rest receiv'd me,
The gray-brown bird I know receiv'd us comrades three,
And he sang the carol of death, and a verse for
him I love.

From deep secluded recesses,
From the fragrant cedars and the ghostly pines
so still,
Came the carol of the bird.

And the charm of the carol rapt me,
As I held as if by their hands my comrades in
the night,
And the voice of my spirit tallied the song of
the bird.

Come lovely and soothing death,
Undulate round the world, serenely arriving,
arriving,

In the day, in the night, to all, to each,
Sooner or later delicate death.

Prais'd be the fathomless universe,
For life and joy, and for objects and knowledge 5
curious,
And for love, sweet love—but praise! praise!
praise!
For the sure-enwinding arms of cool-enfolding
death. 10

Dark mother always gliding near with soft
feet,
Have none chanted for thee a chant of fullest
welcome? 15
Then I chant it for thee, I glorify thee above
all,
I bring thee a song that when thou must in-
deed come, come unfalteringly.

Approach strong deliveress,
When it is so, when thou hast taken them, I
joyously sing the dead,
Lost in the loving floating ocean of thee,
Laved in the flood of thy bliss O death. 25

From me to thee glad serenades,
Dances for thee I propose saluting thee, adorn-
ments and feastings for thee,
And the sights of the open landscape and the 30
high-spread sky are fitting,
And life and the fields, and the huge and
thoughtful night.

The night in silence under many a star, 35
The ocean shore and the husky whispering
wave whose voice I know,
And the soul turning to thee O vast and well-
veil'd death,
And the body gratefully nestling close to thee. 40

Over the tree-tops I float thee a song,
Over the rising and sinking waves, over the
myriad fields and the prairies wide,
Over the dense-pack'd cities all and the teem- 45
ing wharves and ways,
I float this carol with joy, with joy to thee O
death.

15

To the tally of my soul, 50
Loud and strong kept up the gray-brown bird,

With pure deliberate notes spreading filling
the night.

Loud in the pines and cedars dim,
Clear in the freshness moist and swamp-per-
fume,
And I with my comrades there in the night.

While my sight that was bound in my eyes unclosed,
As to long panoramas of visions.

And I saw askant the armies,
I saw as in noiseless dreams hundreds of bat-
tle flags,
Borne through the smoke of the battles and
pierc'd with missiles I saw them,
And carried hither and yon through the smoke,
and torn and bloody,
And at last but a few shreds left on the staffs,
(and all in silence,)
And the staffs all splinter'd and broken.

I saw battle-corpses, myriads of them,
And the white skeletons of young men, I saw
them,
I saw the debris and debris of all the slain sol-
diers of the war,
But I saw they were not as was thought,
They themselves were fully at rest, they suf-
fer'd not,
The living remain'd and suffer'd, the mother
suffer'd,
And the wife and the child and the musing
comrade suffer'd,
And the armies that remain'd suffer'd.

16

Passing the visions, passing the night,
Passing, unloosing the hold of my comrades'
hands,
Passing the song of the hermit bird and the
tallying song of my soul,
Victorious song, death's outlet song, yet varying ever-altering song,
As low and wailing, yet clear the notes, rising
and falling, flooding the night,
Sadly sinking and fainting, as warning and
warning, and yet again bursting with joy,
Covering the earth and filling the spread of
the heaven,

As that powerful psalm in the night I heard
   from recesses,
Passing, I leave thee lilac with heart-shaped
   leaves,
I leave thee there in the door-yard, blooming,
   returning with spring.

I cease from my song for thee,
From my gaze on thee in the west, fronting
   the west, communing with thee,
O comrade lustrous with silver face in the
   night.

Yet each to keep and all, retrievements out of
   the night,
The song, the wondrous chant of the gray-
   brown bird,
And the tallying chant, the echo arous'd in my
   soul,
With the lustrous and drooping star with the
   countenance full of woe,
With the holders holding my hand nearing the
   call of the bird,
Comrades mine and I in the midst, and their
   memory ever to keep, for the dead I loved
   so well,
For the sweetest, wisest soul of all my days
   and lands—and this for his dear sake,
Lilac and star and bird twined with the chant
   of my soul,
There in the fragrant pines and the cedars
   dusk and dim.

MATTHEW ARNOLD

Dryden, Pope, Dr. Johnson were literary arbiters in their day; Arnold (1822–1888) was their Victorian equivalent. He seemed destined for some Olympian function. Son of the famous headmaster of Rugby, with an Oxford background (and friendship with Arthur Hugh Clough), with reading and traveling playing important roles in his growth, Arnold never got away from literature and art. He became inspector of schools, university professor, lecturer, poet, essayist, critic. He fancied himself a good combination of Tennyson and Browning. With classic attitude and serious mien Arnold attacked the Philistines around him for their narrowness and vulgarity. His Essays in Criticism *are still classics in their field. Whether friend or antagonist, Arnold is always a formidable figure: vigorous, intelligent, respectable without being stuffy.**

THE FORSAKEN MERMAN

Come, dear children, let us away;
Down and away below!
Now my brothers call from the bay, ·
10 Now the great winds shorewards blow,
Now the salt tides seawards flow,
Now the wild white horses play,
Champ and chafe and toss in the spray.
Children dear, let us away!
15 This way, this way!

Call her once before you go—
Call once yet!
In a voice that she will know:
20 "Margaret! Margaret!"
Children's voices should be dear
(Call once more) to a mother's ear;
Children's voices, wild with pain—
Surely she will come again!
25 Call her once and come away;
This way, this way!
"Mother dear, we cannot stay!
The wild white horses foam and fret."
Margaret! Margaret!
30

Come, dear children, come away down;
Call no more!
One last look at the white-walled town,
And the little grey church on the windy shore;
35 Then come down!
She will not come though you call all day;
Come away, come away!

Children dear, was it yesterday
40 We heard the sweet bells over the bay?
In the caverns where we lay,
Through the surf and through the swell,
The far-off sound of a silver bell?
Sand-strewn caverns, cool and deep,
45 Where the winds are all asleep;
Where the spent lights quiver and gleam,
Where the salt weed sways in the stream,
Where the sea-beasts, ranged all round,
Feed in the ooze of their pasture-ground;

* The selections which follow are from Arnold's *Poetical Works.* By permission of The Macmillan Company, publishers.

Where the sea-snakes coil and twine,
Dry their mail and bask in the brine;
Where great whales come sailing by,
Sail and sail, with unshut eye,
Round the world for ever and aye?
When did music come this way?
Children dear, was it yesterday?

Children dear, was it yesterday
(Call yet once) that she went away?
Once she sate with you and me,
On a red gold throne in the heart of the sea,
And the youngest sate on her knee.
She combed its bright hair, and she tended it
    well,
When down swung the sound of the far-off
    bell.
She sighed, she looked up through the clear
    green sea.
She said: "I must go, for my kinsfolk pray
In the little grey church on the shore to-day.
'Twill be Easter-time in the world—ah me!
And I lose my poor soul, Merman, here with
    thee."
I said: "Go up, dear heart, through the waves;
Say thy prayer, and come back to the kind sea-
    caves."
She smiled, she went up through the surf in
    the bay.
Children dear, was it yesterday?

Children dear, were we long alone?
"The sea grows stormy, the little ones moan.
Long prayers," I said, "in the world they say;
Come!" I said; and we rose through the surf
    in the bay.
We went up the beach, by the sandy down
Where the sea-stocks bloom, to the white-
    walled town;
Through the narrow paved streets, where all
    was still,
To the little grey church on the windy hill.
From the church came a murmur of folk at
    their prayers,
But we stood without in the cold blowing airs.
We climbed on the graves, on the stones worn
    with rains,
And we gazed up the aisle through the small
    leaded panes.
She sate by the pillar; we saw her clear:
"Margaret, hist! come quick, we are here!
Dear heart," I said, "we are long alone;

The sea grows stormy, the little ones moan."
But, ah, she gave me never a look,
For her eyes were sealed to the holy book!
Loud prays the priest; shut stands the door.
5 Come away, children, call no more!
Come away, come down, call no more!

Down, down, down!
Down to the depths of the sea!
10 She sits at her wheel in the humming town,
Singing most joyfully.
Hark, what she sings: "O joy, O joy,
For the humming street, and the child with its
    toy!
15 For the priest, and the bell, and the holy well;
For the wheel where I spun,
And the blessed light of the sun!"
And so she sings her fill,
Singing most joyfully,
20 Till the spindle falls from her hand,
And the whizzing wheel stands still.
She steals to the window, and looks at the
    sand,
And over the sand at the sea;
25 And her eyes are set in a stare;
And anon there breaks a sigh,
And anon there drops a tear,
From a sorrow-clouded eye,
And a heart sorrow-laden,
30 A long, long sigh;
For the cold strange eyes of a little Mermaiden
And the gleam of her golden hair.

Come away, away children;
35 Come children, come down!
The hoarse wind blows colder;
Lights shine in the town.
She will start from her slumber
When gusts shake the door;
40 She will hear the winds howling,
Will hear the waves roar.
We shall see, while above us
The waves roar and whirl,
A ceiling of amber,
45 A pavement of pearl.
Singing, "Here came a mortal,
But faithless was she!
And alone dwell for ever
The kings of the sea."

50 But, children, at midnight,
When soft the winds blow,

When clear falls the moonlight,
When spring-tides are low;
When sweet airs come seaward
From heaths starred with broom,
5 And high rocks throw mildly
On the blanched sands a gloom;
Up the still, glistening beaches,
Up the creeks we will hie,
Over banks of bright seaweed
The ebb-tide leaves dry.
We will gaze, from the sand-hills,
At the white, sleeping town;
At the church on the hill-side—
And then come back down.
Singing, "There dwells a loved one,
But cruel is she!
She left lonely for ever
The kings of the sea."

THE BURIED LIFE

Light flows our war of mocking words, and
    yet,
Behold, with tears my eyes are wet!
I feel a nameless sadness o'er me roll.
Yes, yes, we know that we can jest,
We know, we know that we can smile!
But there's a something in this breast,
To which thy light words bring no rest,
And thy gay smiles no anodyne.
Give me thy hand, and hush awhile,
And turn those limpid eyes on mine,
And let me read there, love, thy inmost soul.

Alas, is even love too weak
To unlock the heart, and let it speak?
Are even lovers powerless to reveal
To one another what indeed they feel?
I knew the mass of men concealed
Their thoughts, for fear that if revealed
They would by other men be met
With blank indifference, or with blame re-
    proved;
I knew they lived and moved
Tricked in disguises, alien to the rest
Of men, and alien to themselves—and yet
The same heart beats in every human breast!

But we, my love!—does a like spell benumb
Our hearts, our voices?—must we too be
    dumb?

Ah, well for us, if even we,
Even for a moment, can get free
Our heart, and have our lips unchained;
For that which seals them hath been deep-
5   ordained.

Fate, which foresaw
How frivolous a baby man would be—
By what distractions he would be possessed,
10 How he would pour himself in every strife,
And well-nigh change his own identity—
That it might keep from his capricious play
His genuine self, and force him to obey
Even in his own despite his being's law,
15 Bade through the deep recesses of our breast
The unregarded river of our life
Pursue with indiscernible flow its way;
And that we should not see
The buried stream, and seem to be
20 Eddying about in blind uncertainty,
Though driving on with it eternally.

But often, in the world's most crowded streets,
But often, in the din of strife,
25 There rises an unspeakable desire
After the knowledge of our buried life;
A thirst to spend our fire and restless force
In tracking out our true, original course;
A longing to inquire
30 Into the mystery of this heart that beats
So wild, so deep in us—to know
Whence our lives come, and where they go.
And many a man in his own breast then delves,
But deep enough, alas, none ever mines.
35 And we have been on many thousand lines,
And we have shown, on each, spirit and
    power;
But hardly have we, for one little hour,
Been on our own line, have we been our-
40   selves—
Hardly had skill to utter one of all
The nameless feelings that course through our
    breast,
But they course on for ever unexpressed.
45 And long we try in vain to speak and act
Our hidden self, and what we say and do
Is eloquent, is well—but 'tis not true!
And then we will no more be racked
With inward striving, and demand
50 Of all the thousand nothings of the hour
Their stupefying power;
Ah yes, and they benumb us at our call!

Yet still, from time to time, vague and for-
    lorn,
From the soul's subterranean depth upborne
As from an infinitely distant land,
Come airs, and floating echoes, and convey   5
A melancholy into all our day.
Only—but this is rare—
When a beloved hand is laid in ours,
When, jaded with the rush and glare
Of the interminable hours,   10
Our eyes can in another's eyes read clear,
When our world-deafened ear
Is by the tones of a loved voice caressed—
A bolt is shot back somewhere in our breast,
And a lost pulse of feeling stirs again.   15
The eye sinks inward, and the heart lies plain,
And what we mean, we say, and what we
    would, we know.
A man becomes aware of his life's flow,
And hears its winding murmur; and he sees   20
The meadows where it glides, the sun, the
    breeze.

And there arrives a lull in the hot race
Wherein he doth for ever chase
That flying and elusive shadow, rest.   25
An air of coolness plays upon his face,
And an unwonted calm pervades his breast.
And then he thinks he knows
The hills where his life rose,   30
And the sea where it goes.

DOVER BEACH

The sea is calm to-night,   35
The tide is full, the moon lies fair
Upon the straits; on the French coast the light
Gleams and is gone; the cliffs of England
    stand,   40
Glimmering and vast, out in the tranquil bay.
Come to the window, sweet is the night-
    air!
Only, from the long line of spray
Where the sea meets the moon-blanched sand,   45
Listen! you hear the grating roar
Of pebbles which the waves draw back, and
    fling,
At their return, up the high strand,
Begin, and cease; and then again begin,   50
With tremulous cadence slow; and bring
The eternal note of sadness in.

Sophocles, long ago,
Heard it on the Ægæan, and it brought
Into his mind the turbid ebb and flow
Of human misery; we
Find also in the sound a thought,   5
Hearing it by this distant northern sea.

The Sea of Faith
Was once, too, at the full, and round earth's
    shore   10
Lay like the folds of a bright girdle furled;
But now I only hear
Its melancholy, long, withdrawing roar,
Retreating, to the breath
Of the night-wind, down the vast edges drear   15
And naked shingles of the world.

Ah, love, let us be true
To one another! for the world, which seems
To lie before us like a land of dreams,   20
So various, so beautiful, so new,
Hath really neither joy, nor love, nor light,
Nor certitude, nor peace, nor help for pain;
And we are here as on a darkling plain,
Swept with confused alarms of struggle and   25
    flight,
Where ignorant armies clash by night.

RUGBY CHAPEL

NOVEMBER, 1857

Coldly, sadly descends
The autumn-evening. The field
Strewn with its dank yellow drifts
Of withered leaves, and the elms,
Fade into dimness apace,
Silent;—hardly a shout
From a few boys late at their play!
The lights come out in the street,
In the school-room windows;—but cold,
Solemn, unlighted, austere,
Through the gathering darkness, arise
The chapel-walls, in whose bound
Thou, my father! art laid.

There thou dost lie, in the gloom
Of the autumn evening. But ah!
That word, *gloom*, to my mind
Brings thee back, in the light
Of thy radiant vigor again;
In the gloom of November we passed

Days not dark at thy side;
Seasons impaired not the ray
Of thy buoyant cheerfulness clear.
Such thou wast! and I stand
In the autumn evening, and think   5
Of bygone autumns with thee.

Fifteen years have gone round
Since thou arosest to tread,
In the summer-morning, the road   10
Of death, at a call unforeseen,
Sudden. For fifteen years,
We who till then in thy shade
Rested as under the boughs
Of a mighty oak, have endured   15
Sunshine and rain as we might,
Bare, unshaded, alone,
Lacking the shelter of thee.

O strong soul, by what shore   20
Tarriest thou now? For that force,
Surely, has not been left vain!
Somewhere, surely, afar,
In the sounding labor-house vast
Of being, is practised that strength,   25
Zealous, beneficent, firm!
Yes, in some far-shining sphere,
Conscious or not of the past,
Still thou performest the word
Of the Spirit in whom thou dost live—   30
Prompt, unwearied, as here!
Still thou upraisest with zeal
The humble good from the ground,
Sternly repressest the bad!
Still, like a trumpet, doth rouse   35
Those who with half-open eyes
Tread the border-land dim
'Twixt vice and virtue; reviv'st,
Succorest!—this was thy work,
This was thy life upon earth.   40

What is the course of the life
Of mortal men on the earth?
Most men eddy about
Here and there—eat and drink,   45
Chatter and love and hate,
Gather and squander, are raised
Aloft, are hurled in the dust,
Striving blindly, achieving
Nothing; and then they die—   50
Perish;—and no one asks
Who or what they have been,

More than he asks what waves,
In the moonlit solitudes mild
Of the midmost Ocean, have swelled,
Foamed for a moment, and gone.

And there are some, whom a thirst
Ardent, unquenchable, fires,
Not with the crowd to be spent,
Not without aim to go round
In an eddy of purposeless dust,
Effort unmeaning and vain.
Ah yes! some of us strive
Not without action to die
Fruitless, but something to snatch
From dull oblivion, nor all
Glut the devouring grave!
We, we have chosen our path—
Path to a clear-purposed goal,
Path of advance!—but it leads
A long, steep journey, through sunk
Gorges, o'er the mountains in snow.
Cheerful, with friends, we set forth—
Then, on the height, comes the storm.
Thunder crashes from rock
To rock, the cataracts reply,
Lightnings dazzle our eyes.
Roaring torrents have breached
The track, the stream-bed descends
In the place where the wayfarer once
Planted his footstep—the spray
Boils o'er its borders! aloft
The unseen snow-beds dislodge
Their hanging ruin; alas,
Havoc is made in our train!
Friends, who set forth at our side,
Falter, are lost in the storm.
We, we only are left!
With frowning foreheads, with lips
Sternly compressed, we strain on,
On—and at nightfall at last
Come to the end of our way,
To the lonely inn 'mid the rocks;
Where the gaunt and taciturn host
Stands on the threshold, the wind
Shaking his thin white hairs—
Holds his lantern to scan
Our storm-beat figures, and asks:
Whom in our party we bring?
Whom we have left in the snow?

Sadly we answer: We bring
Only ourselves! we lost

Sight of the rest in the storm.
Hardly ourselves we fought through,
Stripped, without friends, as we are.
Friends, companions, and train,
The avalanche swept from our side.   5

But thou would'st not *alone*
Be saved, my father! *alone*
Conquer and come to thy goal,
Leaving the rest in the wild.   10
We were weary, and we
Fearful, and we in our march
Fain to drop down and to die.
Still thou turnedst, and still
Beckonedst the trembler, and still   15
Gavest the weary thy hand.
If, in the paths of the world,
Stones might have wounded thy feet,
Toil or dejection have tried
Thy spirit, of that we saw   20
Nothing—to us thou wast still
Cheerful, and helpful and firm!
Therefore to thee it was given
Many to save with thyself;
And, at the end of thy day,   25
O faithful shepherd! to come,
Bringing thy sheep in thy hand.

And through thee I believe
In the noble and great who are gone;   30
Pure souls honored and blest
By former ages, who else—
Such, so soulless, so poor,
Is the race of men whom I see—
Seemed but a dream of the heart,   35
Seemed but a cry of desire.
Yes! I believe that there lived
Others like thee in the past,
Not like the men of the crowd
Who all round me to-day   40
Bluster or cringe, and make life
Hideous, and arid, and vile;
But souls tempered with fire,
Fervent, heroic, and good,
Helpers and friends of mankind.   45

Servants of God!—or sons
Shall I not call you? because
Not as servants ye knew
Your Father's innermost mind,
His, who unwillingly sees   50

One of his little ones lost—
Yours is the praise, if mankind
Hath not as yet in its march
Fainted, and fallen, and died!

See! In the rocks of the world
Marches the host of mankind,
A feeble, wavering line.
Where are they tending?—A God
Marshalled them, gave them their goal.
Ah, but the way is so long!
Years they have been in the wild!
Sore thirst plagues them; the rocks,
Rising all round, overawe;
Factions divide them, their host
Threatens to break, to dissolve.
—Ah, keep, keep them combined!
Else, of the myriads who fill
That army, not one shall arrive;
Sole they shall stray; in the rocks
Stagger for ever in vain,
Die one by one in the waste.

Then, in such hour of need
Of your fainting, dispirited race,
Ye, like angels, appear,
Radiant with ardor divine!
Beacons of hope, ye appear!
Languor is not in your heart,
Weakness is not in your word,
Weariness not on your brow.
Ye alight in our van! at your voice,
Panic, despair, flee away.
Ye move through the ranks, recall
The stragglers, refresh the outworn,
Praise, re-inspire the brave!
Order, courage, return.
Eyes rekindling, and prayers,
Follow your steps as ye go.
Ye fill up the gaps in our files,
Strengthen the wavering line,
Stablish, continuing our march,
On, to the bound of the waste,
On, to the City of God.

GROWING OLD

What is it to grow old?
Is it to lose the glory of the form,
The luster of the eye?

Is it for beauty to forego her wreath?
—Yes, but not this alone.

Is it to feel our strength—
Not our bloom only, but our strength—decay? 5
Is it to feel each limb
Grow stiffer, every function less exact,
Each nerve more loosely strung?

Yes, this, and more; but not 10
Ah, 'tis not what in youth we dreamed 'twould
    be!
'Tis not to have our life
Mellowed and softened as with sunset-glow,
A golden day's decline. 15

'Tis not to see the world
As from a height, with rapt prophetic eyes,
And heart profoundly stirred;
And weep, and feel the fullness of the past, 20
The years that are no more.

It is to spend long days
And not once feel that we were ever young;
It is to add, immured 25
In the hot prison of the present, month
To month with weary pain.

It is to suffer this,
And feel but half, and feebly, what we feel. 30
Deep in our hidden heart
Festers the dull remembrance of a change,
But no emotion—none.

It is—last stage of all— 35
When we are frozen up within, and quite
The phantom of ourselves,
To hear the world applaud the hollow ghost
Which blamed the living man.
40

EMILY DICKINSON

*Emily Dickinson (1830–1886) was for a long
period an obscure lyricist in New England.* 45
*She was "discovered" late and is still being un-
covered, so to speak. By her own choice (perhaps because of an unhappy love affair) Miss
Dickinson remained in the seclusion of her
home, keeping most of her work secret. Her
epistolary friends were many, however. If she*
*had chosen to publish (only four of her hun-
dreds of pieces were circulated in her lifetime),
she might well have altered the course of
American poetry years before it became "modern"; as it is, Miss Dickinson's original voice
has influenced many. In images and rhymes,
wit and conciseness, economy and swiftness,
she was far ahead of her time. Today her reputation is high. Even a cursory reading of the
lyrics produces the indefinable yet undeniable
feeling that one is in the presence of a genius
with words.**

I TASTE A LIQUOR NEVER
BREWED

I taste a liquor never brewed,
From tankards scooped in pearl;
Not all the vats upon the Rhine
Yield such an alcohol!

Inebriate of air am I,
And debauchee of dew,
Reeling, through endless summer days,
From inns of molten blue.

When landlords turn the drunken bee
Out of the foxglove's door,
When butterflies renounce their drams,
I shall but drink the more!

Till seraphs swing their snowy hats,
And saints to windows run,
To see the little tippler
Leaning against the sun!

I NEVER SAW A MOOR

I never saw a moor,
I never saw the sea;
Yet know I how the heather looks,
And what a wave must be.

I never spoke with God,
Nor visited in heaven;
Yet certain am I of the spot
As if the chart were given.

* The following selections are reprinted from
The Poems of Emily Dickinson, edited by Martha
Dickinson Bianchi and Alfred Leete Hampson, by
permission of the publisher, Little, Brown & Company.

BRING ME THE SUNSET
IN A CUP

Bring me the sunset in a cup,
Reckon the morning's flagons up,
  And say how many dew;
Tell me how far the morning leaps,
Tell me what time the weaver sleeps
  Who spun the breadths of blue!

Write me how many notes there be
In the new robin's ecstasy
  Among astonished boughs;
How many trips the tortoise makes,
How many cups the bee partakes,—
  The debauchee of dews!

Also, who laid the rainbow's piers,
Also, who leads the docile spheres
  By withes of supple blue?
Whose fingers string the stalactite,
Who counts the wampum of the night,
  To see that none is due?

Who built this little Alban house
And shut the windows down so close
  My spirit cannot see?
Who'll let me out some gala day,
With implements to fly away,
  Passing pomposity?

SUCCESS IS COUNTED SWEETEST

Success is counted sweetest
By those who ne'er succeed.
To comprehend a nectar
Requires sorest need.

Not one of all the purple host
Who took the flag today
Can tell the definition,
So clear, of victory,

As he, defeated, dying,
On whose forbidden ear
The distant strains of triumph
Break, agonized and clear.

I DIED FOR BEAUTY

I died for beauty, but was scarce
Adjusted in the tomb,

When one who died for truth was lain
In an adjoining room.

He questioned softly why I failed?
"For beauty," I replied.
"And I for truth,—the two are one;
We brethren are," he said.

And so, as kinsmen met a night,
We talked between the rooms,
Until the moss had reached our lips
And covered up our names.

ELYSIUM IS AS FAR

Elysium is as far as to
The very nearest room,
If in that room a friend await
Felicity or doom.

What fortitude the soul contains,
That it can so endure
The accent of a coming foot,
The opening of a door!

SIDNEY LANIER

*Lanier (1842–1881) spent four years in the
Confederate Army, was captured, developed
tuberculosis. He was university-trained, dabbled in law, wrote, taught, and played the flute
professionally. His interest in music led to his
writing on the relation of music to verse, with
time (not accent) supposedly being the clue to
successful poetizing. He is generally thought of
as being among the chief American poets of
the traditional school, and considerable scholarly research is still being done in his works.** *

SONG OF THE CHATTAHOOCHEE

Out of the hills of Habersham,
  Down the valleys of Hall,
I hurry amain to reach the plain,
Run the rapid and leap the fall,

* The selections which follow are from *Poems*
by Sidney Lanier; reprinted by permission of the
publisher, Charles Scribner's Sons.

Split at the rock and together again,
Accept my bed, or narrow or wide,
And flee from folly on every side
With a lover's pain to attain the plain
    Far from the hills of Habersham,
    Far from the valleys of Hall.

    All down the hills of Habersham,
    All through the valleys of Hall,
The rushes cried *Abide, abide,*
The willful waterweeds held me thrall,
The laving laurel turned my tide,
The ferns and the fondling grass said *Stay,*
The dewberry dipped for to work delay,
And the little reeds sighed *Abide, abide,*
    Here in the hills of Habersham,
    Here in the valleys of Hall.

    High o'er the hills of Habersham,
    Veiling the valleys of Hall,
The hickory told me manifold
Fair tales of shade, the poplar tall
Wrought me her shadowy self to hold,
The chestnut, the oak, the walnut, the pine,
Overleaning, with flickering meaning and sign,
Said, *Pass not, so cold, these manifold*
    Deep shades of the hills of Habersham,
    These glades in the valleys of Hall.

    And oft in the hills of Habersham,
    And oft in the valleys of Hall,
The white quartz shone, and the smooth
    brook-stone
Did bar me of passage with friendly brawl,
And many a luminous jewel lone
—Crystals clear or a-cloud with mist,
Ruby, garnet and amethyst—
Made lures with the lights of streaming stone
    In the clefts of the hills of Habersham,
    In the beds of the valleys of Hall.

    But oh, not the hills of Habersham,
    And oh, not the valleys of Hall
Avail: I am fain for to water the plain.
Downward the voices of Duty call—
Downward, to toil and be mixed with the
    main,
The dry fields burn, and the mills are to turn,
And a myriad flowers mortally yearn,
And the lordly main from beyond the plain
    Calls o'er the hills of Habersham,
    Calls through the valleys of Hall.

THE MARSHES OF GLYNN

Glooms of the live-oaks, beautiful-braided and
    woven
5 With intricate shades of the vines that myriad-
    cloven
    Clamber the forks of the multiform
        boughs,—
        Emerald twilights,—
10   Virginal shy lights,
Wrought of the leaves to allure to the whisper
    of vows,
When lovers pace timidly down through the
    green colonnades
15 Of the dim sweet woods, of the dear dark
    woods,
    Of the heavenly woods and glades,
That run to the radiant marginal sand-beach
    within
20   The wide sea-marshes of Glynn;—

Beautiful glooms, soft dusks in the noon-day
    fire,—
Wildwood privacies, closets of lone desire,
25 Chamber from chamber parted with wavering
    arras of leaves,—
Cells for the passionate pleasure of prayer to
    the soul that grieves,
Pure with a sense of the passing of saints
    through the wood,
Cool for the dutiful weighing of ill with
    good;—

O braided dusks of the oak and woven shades
35   of the vine,
While the riotous noon-day sun of the June-
    day long did shine
Ye held me fast in your heart and I held you
    fast in mine;
40

But now when the noon is no more, and riot
    is rest,
And the sun is a-wait at the ponderous gate of
    the West,
45 And the slant yellow beam down the wood-
    aisle doth seem
Like a lane into heaven that leads from a
    dream,—

50 Ay, now, when my soul all day hath drunken
    the soul of the oak,
And my heart is at ease from men, and the

wearisome sound of the stroke
Of the scythe of time and the trowel of
    trade is low,
And belief overmasters doubt, and I know
    that I know,
And my spirit is grown to a lordly great
    compass within,
That the length and the breadth and the
    sweep of the Marshes of Glynn
Will work me no fear like the fear they have
    wrought me of yore
When length was fatigue, and when breadth
    was but bitterness sore,
And when terror and shrinking and dreary
    unnamable pain
Drew over me out of the merciless miles of the
    plain,—

Oh, now, unafraid, I am fain to face
    The vast sweet visage of space.
To the edge of the wood I am drawn, I am
    drawn,
Where the gray beach glimmering runs, as a
    belt of the dawn,
    For a mete and a mark
        To the forest-dark:—
            So:
Affable live-oak, leaning low,—
Thus—with your favor—soft, with a reverent
    hand
(Not lightly touching your person, Lord of the
    land!),
Bending your beauty aside, with a step I
    stand
On the firm-packed sand,
        Free
By a world of marsh that borders a world of
    sea.
    Sinuous southward and sinuous northward
        the shimmering band
Of the sand-beach fastens the fringe of the
    marsh to the folds of the land.
Inward and outward to northward and south-
    ward the beach-lines linger and curl
As a silver-wrought garment that clings to and
    follows the firm sweet limbs of a girl.
Vanishing, swerving, evermore curving again
    into sight,
Softly the sand-beach wavers away to a dim
    gray looping of light.
And what if behind me to westward the wall
    of the woods stands high?

The world lies east: how ample, the marsh and
    the sea and the sky!
A league and a league of marsh-grass, waist-
    high, broad in the blade,
Green, and all of a height, and unflecked with
    a light or a shade,
Stretch leisurely off, in a pleasant plain,
To the terminal blue of the main.

Oh, what is abroad in the marsh and the
    terminal sea?
    Somehow my soul seems suddenly free
From the weighing of fate and the sad discus-
    sion of sin,
By the length and the breadth and the sweep
    of the marshes of Glynn.

Ye marshes, how candid and simple and noth-
    ing-withholding and free
Ye publish yourselves to the sky and offer
    yourselves to the sea!
Tolerant plains, that suffer the sea and the
    rains and the sun,
Ye spread and span like the catholic man who
    hath mightily won
God out of knowledge and good out of infinite
    pain
And sight out of blindness and purity out of a
    stain.

As the marsh-hen secretly builds on the
    watery sod,
Behold I will build me a nest on the greatness
    of God:
I will fly in the greatness of God as the marsh-
    hen flies
In the freedom that fills all the space 'twixt
    the marsh and the skies:
By so many roots as the marsh-grass sends in
    the sod
I will heartily lay me a-hold on the greatness
    of God:
Oh, like to the greatness of God is the great-
    ness within
The range of the marshes, the liberal marshes
    of Glynn.

And the sea lends large, as the marsh: lo, out
    of his plenty the sea
Pours fast: full soon the time of the flood-tide
    must be:
Look how the grace of the sea doth go

About and about through the intricate chan-
    nels that flow
      Here and there,
        Everywhere,
Till his waters have flooded the uttermost
    creeks and the low-lying lanes,
And the marsh is meshed with a million veins,
That like as with rosy and silvery essences
    flow
    In the rose-and-silver evening glow.
      Farewell, my lord Sun!
The creeks overflow: a thousand rivulets run
'Twixt the roots of the sod; the blades of the
    marsh-grass stir;
Passeth a hurrying sound of wings that west-
    ward whirr;
Passeth, and all is still; and the currents cease
    to run;

And the sea and the marsh are one.

How still the plains of the waters be!
The tide is in his ecstasy.
5 The tide is at his highest height:
    And it is night.

And now from the Vast of the Lord will the
    waters of sleep
Roll in on the souls of men,
But who will reveal to our waking ken
The forms that swim and the shapes that creep
    Under the waters of sleep?
And I would I could know what swimmeth be-
    low when the tide comes in
On the length and the breadth of the marvel-
    lous marshes of Glynn.

TWENTIETH CENTURY

THOMAS HARDY

Before writing The Return of the Native *and*
The Mayor of Casterbridge *Hardy had written
some verse and had practiced architecture. His
novels are pessimistic, ironic, sometimes fa-
talistic. The gloom, however, is now and then
lightened with humor. (The novelist confesses
to having learned much from George Crabbe.)
Hardy's* Jude the Obscure *(1895) was too
realistic for public taste; the author turned in
disgust to verse again, also wrote a nineteen-
act drama,* The Dynasts, *but never returned to
the novel. Much of Hardy's poetry is like his
prose—the satires, for example, show up man's
greed and pettiness; but the verse cannot be
labeled with any single adjective, for it is possible in the lyrics to find all moods and lighting
effects, nearly all subtypes. With Hardy (1840–
1928) one literary era ends and another begins.
He remains a large, solid figure, honest and
sincere, unruffled by the new isms of our century. (See also II, 446.)*

HAP

If but some vengeful god would call to me
From up the sky, and laugh: "Thou suffering
    thing,
Know that thy sorrow is my ecstasy,
5 That thy love's loss is my hate's profiting!"

Then would I bear it, clench myself, and die,
Steeled by the sense of ire unmerited;
Half-eased in that a Powerfuller than I
10 Had willed and meted me the tears I shed.

But not so. How arrives it joy lies slain,

And why unblooms the best hope ever sown?
—Crass Casualty obstructs the sun and rain,
And dicing Time for gladness casts a moan. . . .
These purblind Doomsters had as readily
    strown   5
Blisses about my pilgrimage as pain.

AT THE DRAPER'S[1]

"I stood at the back of the shop, my dear,   10
But you did not perceive me.
Well, when they deliver what you were shown
I shall know nothing of it, believe me!"
And he coughed and coughed as she paled and
    said,   15
"Oh, I didn't see you come in there—
Why couldn't you speak?"—"Well, I didn't. I
    left
That you should not notice I'd been there.
                                                   20
"You were viewing some lovely things.
'Soon required for a widow of latest fashion';
And I knew 'twould upset you to meet the
    man
Who had to be cold and ashen,   25
And screwed in a box before they could dress
    you
'In the last new note in mourning,'
As they defined it. So, not to distress you,
I left you to your adorning."   30

THE DARKLING THRUSH

I leant upon a coppice gate
    When Frost was specter-gray,   35
And Winter's dregs made desolate
    The weakening eye of day.
The tangled bine-stems scored the sky
    Like strings of broken lyres,
And all mankind that haunted nigh   40
    Had sought their household fires.

The land's sharp features seemed to be
    The Century's corpse outleant,
His crypt the cloudy canopy,   45
    The wind his death-lament.
The ancient pulse of germ and birth
    Was shrunken hard and dry,
And every spirit upon earth
    Seemed fervorless as I.   50

---

[1] one of the *Satires of Circumstance*.

At once a voice arose among
    The bleak twigs overhead
In a full-hearted evensong
    Of joy illimited;
An aged thrush, frail, gaunt, and small,
    In blast-beruffled plume,
Had chosen thus to fling his soul
    Upon the growing gloom.

So little cause for carolings
    Of such ecstatic sound
Was written on terrestrial things
    Afar or nigh around,
That I could think there trembled through
    His happy good-night air
Some blessed Hope, whereof he knew
    And I was unaware.

THE MAN HE KILLED

"Had he and I but met
    By some old ancient inn,
We should have sat us down to wet
    Right many a nipperkin!

"But ranged as infantry,
    And staring face to face,
I shot at him as he at me,
    And killed him in his place.

"I shot him dead because—
    Because he was my foe,
Just so: my foe of course he was;
    That's clear enough; although

"He thought he'd 'list, perhaps,
    Off-hand like—just as I—
Was out of work—had sold his traps—
    No other reason why.

"Yes; quaint and curious war is!
    You shoot a fellow down
You'd treat if met where any bar is,
    Or help to half-a-crown."

AFTERWARDS

When the Present has latched its postern be-
    hind my tremulous stay,
And the May month flaps its glad green
    leaves like wings,
Delicate-filmed as new-spun silk, will the

neighbors say,
  "He was a man who used to notice such
    things"?

If it be in the dusk when, like an eyelid's 5
    soundless blink,
  The dewfall-hawk comes crossing the shades
    to alight
Upon the wind-warped upland thorn, a gazer
    may think,
  "To him this must have been a familiar
    sight." 10

If I pass during some nocturnal blackness,
    mothy and warm, 15
  When the hedgehog travels furtively over
    the lawn,
One may say, "He strove that such innocent
    creatures should come to no harm,
  But he could do little for them; and now he 20
    is gone."

If, when hearing that I have been stilled at
    last, they stand at the door,
  Watching the full-starred heavens that win- 25
    ter sees,
Will this thought rise on those who will meet
    my face no more,
  "He was one who had an eye for such
    mysteries"? 30

And will any say when my bell of quittance is
    heard in the gloom,
  And a crossing breeze cuts a pause in its
    outrollings, 35
Till they rise again, as they were a new bell's
    boom,
  "He hears it not now, but used to notice
    such things"?

40

A. E. HOUSMAN

*Housman (1859–1936), an Oxford man, even-
tually found himself teaching Latin at University College, London, and at Cambridge, 45
acquiring considerable reputation as a classical
scholar. One of his collections of verse, A
Shropshire Lad, became so popular that it was
possible for other versifiers to burlesque the
original with considerable success. Although
Housman's lyrics seem simple, almost blithe,
underneath they sing a sad message about life;*

*technically they are the work of a master who
believed in inspiration and who turned his
lines with apparent ease. The fact that they
seem easily done is a tribute to the poet's art;
by his own testimony, after phrases came to
him out of the air, only painful labor could
put them together and fill in the gaps.**

WITH RUE MY HEART IS LADEN

With rue my heart is laden
  For golden friends I had,
For many a rose-lipt maiden
  And many a lightfoot lad.

By brooks too broad for leaping
  The lightfoot boys are laid;
The rose-lipt girls are sleeping
  In fields where roses fade.

WHEN I WAS ONE-AND-TWENTY

When I was one-and-twenty
  I heard a wise man say,
"Give crowns and pounds and guineas
  But not your heart away;
Give pearls away and rubies
  But keep your fancy free."
But I was one-and-twenty,
  No use to talk to me.

When I was one-and-twenty
  I heard him say again,
"The heart out of the bosom
  Was never given in vain;
'Tis paid with sighs a-plenty
  And sold for endless rue."
And I am two-and-twenty,
  And oh, 'tis true, 'tis true.

TO AN ATHLETE DYING YOUNG

The time you won your town the race
We chaired you through the market-place;
Man and boy stood cheering by,
And home we brought you shoulder-high.

_____

* The poems which follow are reprinted from
A Shropshire Lad by A. E. Housman by permission

[339]

Today, the road all runners come,
Shoulder-high we bring you home,
And set you at your threshold down,
Townsman of a stiller town.

Smart lad, to slip betimes away
From fields where glory does not stay,
And early though the laurel grows
It withers quicker than the rose.

Eyes the shady night has shut
Cannot see the record cut,
And silence sounds no worse than cheers
After earth has stopped the ears:

Now you will not swell the rout
Of lads that wore their honors out,
Runners whom renown outran
And the name died before the man.

So set, before its echoes fade,
The fleet foot on the sill of shade,
And hold to the low lintel up
The still-defended challenge-cup.

And round that early-laureled head
Will flock to gaze the strengthless dead,
And find unwithered on its curls
The garland briefer than a girl's.

LOVELIEST OF TREES

Loveliest of trees, the cherry now
Is hung with bloom along the bough,
And stands about the woodland ride
Wearing white for Eastertide.

Now, of my threescore years and ten,
Twenty will not come again,
And take from seventy springs a score,
It only leaves me fifty more.

And since to look at things in bloom
Fifty springs are little room,
About the woodlands I will go
To see the cherry hung with snow.

OH, WHEN I WAS IN LOVE WITH YOU

Oh, when I was in love with you,
5   Then I was clean and brave,
And miles around the wonder grew
How well did I behave.

And now the fancy passes by,
10   And nothing will remain,
And miles around they'll say that I
Am quite myself again.

15 # WILLIAM BUTLER YEATS

*Born and bred in Ireland, Yeats (1865–1939)
went to London in 1888 and later traveled on
the Riviera. He was ever concerned with*
20 *Irish lore, much of which found its way into
his plays and poetry; as an editor he was vocal in yet a third field. Yeats was particularly
active in the great Celtic revival of drama. A
prolific writer, he eventually won the Nobel*
25 *Prize. His early poetry is filled with music,
with Irish magic and mysticism. The later
poetry is often tougher, a bit disillusioned, but
not decadent.** *

30 ## THE LAKE ISLE OF INNISFREE

I will arise and go now, and go to Innisfree,
And a small cabin build there, of clay and wat-
        tles made;
35 Nine bean rows will I have there, a hive for
        the honey bee,
And live alone in the bee-loud glade.

And I shall have some peace there, for peace
40   comes dropping slow,
Dropping from the veils of the morning to
        where the cricket sings;
There midnight's all a glimmer, and noon a
        purple glow,
45 And evening full of the linnet's wings.

I will arise and go now, for always night and
        day

I hear lake water lapping with low sounds by
the shore;
While I stand on the roadway, or on the pave-
ments gray,
I hear it in the deep heart's core.

WHEN YOU ARE OLD

When you are old and gray and full of sleep,
And nodding by the fire, take down this book,
And slowly read, and dream of the soft look
Your eyes had once, and of their shadows
deep;

How many loved your moments of glad grace,
And loved your beauty with love false or true;
But one man loved the pilgrim soul in you,
And loved the sorrows of your changing face.

And bending down beside the glowing bars
Murmur, a little sadly, how love fled
And paced upon the mountains overhead
And hid his face amid a crowd of stars.

THE INDIAN UPON GOD

I passed along the water's edge below the
humid trees,
My spirit rocked in evening light, the rushes
round my knees,
My spirit rocked in sleep and sighs; and saw
the moorfowl pace
All dripping on a grassy slope, and saw them
cease to chase
Each other round in circles, and heard the
eldest speak:
*Who holds the world between His bill and
made us strong or weak*
*Is an undying moorfowl, and He lives beyond
the sky.*
*The rains are from His dripping wings, the
moonbeams from His eye.*
I passed a little further on and heard a lotus
talk:
*Who made the world and ruleth it, He hang-
eth on a stalk,*
*For I am in His image made, and all this
tinkling tide*
*Is but a sliding drop of rain between His petals
wide.*
A little way within the gloom a roebuck raised
his eyes

Brimful of starlight, and he said: *The Stamper
of the Skies,*
*He is a gentle roebuck; for how else, I pray,
could He*
*Conceive a thing so sad and soft, a gentle
thing like me?*
I passed a little further on and heard a peacock say:
*Who made the grass and made the worms and
made my feathers gay,*
*He is a monstrous peacock, and He waveth all
the night*
*His languid tail above us, lit with myriad spots
of light.*

SAILING TO BYZANTIUM

1

That is no country for old men. The young
In one another's arms, birds in the trees,
—Those dying generations—at their song,
The salmon-falls, the mackerel-crowded seas,
Fish, flesh, or fowl, commend all summer long
Whatever is begotten, born, and dies.
Caught in that sensual music all neglect
Monuments of unaging intellect.

2

An aged man is but a paltry thing,
A tattered coat upon a stick, unless
Soul clap its hands and sing, and louder sing
For every tatter in its mortal dress,
Nor is there singing school but studying
Monuments of its own magnificence;
And therefore I have sailed the seas and come
To the holy city of Byzantium.

3

O sages standing in God's holy fire
As in the gold mosaic of a wall,
Come from the holy fire, perne[1] in a gyre,
And be the singing-masters of my soul.
Consume my heart away; sick with desire
And fastened to a dying animal
It knows not what it is; and gather me
Into the artifice of eternity.

4

Once out of nature I shall never take
My bodily form from any natural thing,

―――――――
[1] wheeling in a circle like a hawk or buzzard.

But such a form as Grecian goldsmiths make
Of hammered gold and gold enameling
To keep a drowsy Emperor awake;
Or set upon a golden bough to sing
To lords and ladies of Byzantium   5
Of what is past, or passing, or to come.

RUDYARD KIPLING

Kipling (1865–1936), born in India, schooled 10
in England, returned to his native land for a
career in journalism. He later spent some time
in Vermont with his American wife. Mean-
while, tales and verses had poured forth from a
ready pen. He wrote of the ordinary man, of 15
"real life," in a ballad style that was tre-
mendously popular. Something of a flag waver,
Kipling has been criticized by some writers for
an overabundance of patriotism. Nevertheless,
he won a Nobel Prize and, critics or no, be- 20
came the most widely known English poet of
his day. (For further details concerning Kipling
see II, 457.)

GUNGA DIN*

You may talk o' gin an' beer
When you're quartered safe out 'ere,
An' you're sent to penny-fights an' Aldershot
    it:
But if it comes to slaughter,
You will do your work on water,
An' you'll lick the bloomin' boots of 'im that's
    got it.
Now in Injia's sunny clime,
Where I used to spend my time
A-servin' of 'Er Majesty the Queen,
Of all them black-faced crew
The finest man I knew
Was our regimental Bhisti,[1] Gunga Din,   40
He was "Din! Din! Din!
You limping lump o' brick-dust, Gunga Din!
Hi! slippy hitherao!
Water! Get it! Panee lao![2]
You squidgy-nosed old idol, Gunga Din!"   45

---

* From *Departmental Ditties and Barrack-Room
Ballads,* by Rudyard Kipling, copyright, 1892,
1893, 1899, 1927, by Rudyard Kipling, reprinted
by permission of Mrs. George Bambridge, Doubleday & Company, Inc., and The Macmillan Company of Canada, Ltd.

[1] water carrier.   [2] bring water swiftly.

The uniform 'e wore
Was nothin' much before,
An' rather less than 'arf o' that be'ind;
For a twisty piece o' rag
An' a goatskin water-bag   5
Was all the field-equipment 'e could find.
When the sweatin' troop-train lay
In a sidin' through the day,
Where the 'eat would make your bloomin' eye-
    brows crawl,
We shouted "Harry By!"[3]
Till our throats were bricky-dry,
Then we wopped 'im cause 'e couldn't serve
    us all.
It was "Din! Din! Din!
You 'eathen, where the mischief 'ave you been?
You put some juldee[4] in it,
Or I'll marrow[5] you this minute
If you don't fill up my helmet, Gunga Din!"

'E would dot an' carry one
Till the longest day was done,
An' 'e didn't seem to know the use o' fear.
If we charged or broke or cut,
You could bet your bloomin' nut,   25
'E'd be waitin' fifty paces right flank rear.
With 'is mussick[6] on 'is back,
'E would skip with our attack,
An' watch us till the bugles made "Retire,"
An' for all 'is dirty 'ide   30
'E was white, clear white, inside,
When 'e went to tend the wounded under fire!
It was "Din! Din! Din!"
With the bullets kickin' dust-spots on the
    green.   35
When the cartridges ran out,
You could 'ear the front-files shout:
"Hi! ammunition mules an' Gunga Din!"

I sha'n't forget the night   40
When I dropped be'ind the fight
With a bullet where my belt-plate should a'
    been.
I was chokin' mad with thirst,
An' the man that spied me first   45
Was our good old grinnin', gruntin' Gunga
    Din.
'E lifted up my 'ead,
An' e' guv me 'arf a pint o' water—green:

---

[3] O Brother.   [4] snap.
[5] hit.   [6] water bag.

It was crawlin' and it stunk,
But of all the drinks I've drunk,
I'm gratefullest to one from Gunga Din.
It was "Din! Din! Din!
'Ere's a beggar with a bullet through 'is spleen; 5
'E's chawin' up the ground an' 'e's kickin' all
    around:
For Gawd's sake git the water, Gunga Din!"

'E carried me away
To where a dooli[7] lay, 10
An' a bullet come an' drilled the beggar clean.
'E put me safe inside,
An' just before 'e died:
"I 'ope you liked your drink," sez Gunga Din. 15
So I'll meet 'im later on
In the place where 'e is gone—
Where its always double drill and no can-
    teen;
'E'll be squattin' on the coals 20
Givin' drink to pore damned souls,
An I'll get a swig in Hell from Gunga Din.
Din! Din! Din!
You Lazarushian-leather Gunga Din!
Tho' I've belted you an' flayed you, 25
By the livin' God that made you,
You're a better man than I am, Gunga Din.

DANNY DEEVER*

"What are the bugles blowin' for?" said Files- 30
    on-Parade.
"To turn you out, to turn you out," the Color-
    Sergeant said.
"What makes you look so white, so white?" 35
    said Files-on-Parade.
"I'm dreadin' what I've got to watch," the
    Color-Sergeant said.
  For they're hangin' Danny Deever, you can 40
    'ear the Dead March play,
  The regiment's in 'ollow square—they're
    hangin' him today;
  They've taken of his buttons off an' cut his
    stripes away, 45

---

[7] stretcher.
* From *Departmental Ditties and Barrack-Room
Ballads,* by Rudyard Kipling, copyright, 1892, 1893,
1899, 1927, by Rudyard Kipling, reprinted by per- 50
mission of Mrs. George Bambridge, Doubleday
& Company, Inc., and The Macmillan Company of
Canada, Ltd.

  An' they're hangin' Danny Deever in the
    mornin'.

"What makes the rear-rank breathe so 'ard?"
    said Files-on-Parade.
"It's bitter cold, it's bitter cold," the Color-
    Sergeant said.
"What makes that front-rank man fall down?"
    says Files-on-Parade.
"A touch of sun, a touch of sun," the Color-
    Sergeant said.
  They are hangin' Danny Deever, they are
    marchin' of 'im round.
  They 'ave 'alted Danny Deever by 'is coffin
    on the ground:
  An 'e'll swing in 'arf a minute for a sneakin'
    shootin' hound—
  O they're hangin' Danny Deever in the
    mornin'!

" 'Is cot was right-'and cot to mine," said Files-
    on-Parade.
" 'E's sleepin' out an' far tonight," the Color-
    Sergeant said.
"I've drunk 'is beer a score o' times," said Files-
    on-Parade.
" 'E's drinkin' bitter beer alone," the Color-
    Sergeant said.
  They are hangin' Danny Deever, you must
    mark 'im to 'is place,
  For 'e shot a comrade sleepin'—you must
    look 'im in the face;
  Nine 'undred of 'is county an' the regiment's
    disgrace,
  While they're hangin' Danny Deever in the
    mornin'.

"What's that so black agin' the sun?" said
    Files-on-Parade.
"It's Danny fightin' 'ard for life," the Color-
    Sergeant said.
"What's that that whimpers over'ead?" said
    Files-on-Parade.
"It's Danny's soul that's passin' now," the
    Color-Sergeant said.
  For they're done with Danny Deever, you
    can 'ear the quickstep play,
  The regiment's in column, an' they're
    marchin' us away;
  Ho! the young recruits are shakin', an' they'll
    want their beer today,
  After hangin' Danny Deever in the mornin'.

RECESSIONAL*

God of our fathers, known of old,
    Lord of our far-flung battle-line,
Beneath whose awful hand we hold   5
    Dominion over palm and pine—
Lord God of Hosts, be with us yet,
Lest we forget—lest we forget!

The tumult and the shouting dies;   10
    The captains and the kings depart:
Still stands Thine ancient sacrifice,
    An humble and a contrite heart.
Lord God of Hosts, be with us yet,
Lest we forget—lest we forget!   15

Far-called, our navies melt away;
    On dune and headland sinks the fire:
Lo, all our pomp of yesterday
    Is one with Nineveh and Tyre![1]   20
Judge of the Nations, spare us yet,
Lest we forget—lest we forget!

If, drunk with sight of power, we loose
    Wild tongues that have not Thee in awe, 25
Such boastings as the Gentiles use,
    Or lesser breeds without the Law—
Lord God of Hosts, be with us yet,
Lest we forget—lest we forget!

      30
For heathen heart that puts her trust
    In reeking tube and iron shard,
All valiant dust that builds on dust,
    And, guarding, calls not Thee to guard,
For frantic boast and foolish word—   35
Thy Mercy on Thy People, Lord!

FOR TO ADMIRE**

The Injian Ocean sets an' smiles
    So sof', so bright, so bloomin' blue;   40

There aren't a wave for miles an' miles
Excep' the jiggle from the screw.
The ship is swep', the day is done,
    The bugle's gone for smoke and play;
An' black agin' the settin' sun
    The Lascar sings, *"Hum deckty hai!"*

    For to admire an' for to see,
      For to be'old this world so wide—
    It never done no good to me,
      But I can't drop it if I tried!

I see the sergeants pitchin' quoits,
    I 'ear the women laugh an' talk,
I spy upon the quarter-deck
    The orficers an' lydies walk.
I thinks about the things that was,
    An' leans an' looks acrost the sea,
Till spite of all the crowded ship
    There's no one lef' alive but me.

The things that was which I 'ave seen,
    In barrick, camp, an' action too,
I tells them over by myself,
    An' sometimes wonders if they're true;
For they was odd—most awful odd—
    But all the same now they are o'er,
There must be 'eaps o' plenty such,
    An' if I wait I'll see some more.

Oh, I 'ave come upon the books,
    An' frequent broke a barrick rule,
An' stood beside an' watched myself
    Be'avin' like a bloomin' fool.
I paid my price for findin' out,
    Nor never grutched the price I paid,
But sat in Clink without my boots,
    Admirin' 'ow the world was made.

Be'old a crowd upon the beam,
    An' 'umped above the sea appears
Old Aden, like a barrick-stove
    That no one's lit for years an' years!
I passed by that when I began,
    An' I go 'ome the road I came,
A time-expired soldier-man
    With six years' service to 'is name.

My girl she said, "Oh, stay with me!"
    My mother 'eld me to 'er breast.
They've never written none, an' so
    They must 'ave gone with all the rest—

With all the rest which I 'ave seen
  An' found an' known an' met along.
I cannot say the things I feel,
  And so I sing my evenin' song:

    For to admire an' for to see,
      For to be'old this world so wide—
    It never done no good to me,
      But I can't drop it if I tried!

EDWIN ARLINGTON ROBINSON*

THE MAN AGAINST THE SKY

Between me and the sunset, like a dome
Against the glory of a world on fire,
Now burned a sudden hill,
Bleak, round and high, by flame-lit height
  made higher,
With nothing on it for the flame to kill
Save one who moved and was alone up there
To loom before the chaos and the glare
As if he were the last god going home
Unto his last desire.
Dark, marvellous, and inscrutable he moved on
Till down the fiery distance he was gone,
Like one of those eternal, remote things
That range across a man's imaginings
When a sure music fills him and he knows
What he may say thereafter to few men—
The touch of ages having wrought
An echo and a glimpse of what he thought
A phantom or a legend until then;
For whether lighted over ways that save,
Or lured from all repose,
If he go on too far to find a grave,
Mostly alone he goes.

Even he, who stood where I had found him,
On high with fire all around him,
Who moved along the molten west,
And over the round hill's crest
That seemed half ready with him to go down,
Flame-bitten and flame-cleft
As if there were to be no last thing left
Of a nameless unimaginable town—
Even he who climbed and vanished may have
  taken

Down to the perils of a depth not known,
From death defended, though by men for-
  saken,
The bread that every man must eat alone;
5 He may have walked while others hardly dared
Look on to see him stand where many fell;
And upward out of that as out of hell,
He may have sung and striven
To mount where more of him shall yet be
10 given,
Bereft of all retreat,
To sevenfold heat—
As on a day when three in Dura[1] shared
The furnace, and were spared
15 For glory by that king of Babylon
Who made himself so great that God, who
  heard,
Covered him with long feathers, like a bird.

20 Again, he may have gone down easily,
By comfortable altitudes, and found,
As always, underneath him solid ground
Whereon to be sufficient and to stand
Possessed already of the promised land,
25 Far stretched and fair to see:
A good sight, verily,
And one to make the eyes of her who bore him
Shine glad with hidden tears.
Why question of his ease of who before him,
30 In one place or another where they left
Their names as far behind them as their bones,
And yet by dint of slaughter, toil and theft,
And shrewdly sharpened stones,
Carved hard the way for his ascendency
35 Through deserts of lost years?
Why trouble him now who sees and hears
No more than what his innocence requires,
And therefore to no other height aspires
Than one at which he neither quails nor tires?
40 He may do more by seeing what he sees
Than others eager for iniquities;
He may, by seeing all things for the best,
Incite futurity to do the rest.

45 Or with an even likelihood,
He may have met with atrabilious eyes
The fires of time on equal terms and passed
Indifferent down, until at last
His only kind of grandeur would have been,
50 Apparently, in being seen.

[1] In Babylon. See *Book of Daniel*, 3.

He may have had for evil or for good
No argument; he may have had no care
For what without himself went anywhere
To failure or to glory, and least of all
For such a stale, flamboyant miracle;
He may have been the prophet of an art
Immovable to old idolatries;
He may have been a player without a part,
Annoyed that even the sun should have the skies
For such a flaming way to advertise;
He may have been a painter sick at heart
With Nature's toiling for a new surprise;
He may have been a cynic, who now, for all
Of anything divine that his effete
Negation may have tasted,
Saw truth in his own image, rather small,
Forbore to fever the ephemeral,
Found any barren height a good retreat
From any swarming street,
And in the sun saw power superbly wasted;
And when the primitive old-fashioned stars
Came out again to shine on joys and wars
More primitive, and all arrayed for doom,
He may have proved a world a sorry thing
In his imagining,
And life a lighted highway to the tomb.

Or, mounting with infirm unsearching tread,
His hopes to chaos led,
He may have stumbled up there from the past,
And with an aching strangeness viewed the last
Abysmal conflagration of his dreams,—
A flame where nothing seems
To burn but flame itself, by nothing fed;
And while it all went out,
Not even the faint anodyne of doubt
May then have eased a painful going down
From pictured heights of power and lost renown,
Revealed at length to his outlived endeavor
Remote and unapproachable forever;
And at his heart there may have gnawed
Sick memories of a dead faith foiled and flawed
And long dishonored by the living death
Assigned alike by chance
To brutes and hierophants;
And anguish fallen on those he loved around him

5

10

15

20

25

30

35

40

45

May once have dealt the last blow to confound him,
And so have left him as death leaves a child,
Who sees it all too near;
And he who knows no young way to forget
May struggle to the tomb unreconciled.
Whatever suns may rise or set
There may be nothing kinder for him here
Than shafts and agonies;
And under these
He may cry out and stay on horribly;
Or, seeing in death too small a thing to fear,
He may go forward like a stoic Roman
Where pangs and terrors in his pathway lie—
Or, seizing the swift logic of a woman,
Curse God and die.
Or maybe there, like many another one
Who might have stood aloft and looked ahead,
Black-drawn against wild red,
He may have built unawed by fiery gules
That in him no commotion stirred,
A living reason out of molecules
Why molecules occurred,
And one for smiling when he might have sighed
Had he seen far enough
And in the same inevitable stuff
Discovered an odd reason too for pride
In being what he must have been by laws
Infrangible and for no kind of cause.
Deterred by no confusion or surprise
He may have seen with his mechanic eyes
A world without a meaning, and had room,
Alone amid magnificence and doom,
To build himself an airy monument
That should, or fail him in his vague intent,
Outlast an accidental universe—
To call it nothing worse—
Or, by the burrowing guile
Of Time disintegrated and effaced,
Like once-remembered mighty trees go down
To ruin, of which by man may now be traced
No part sufficient even to be rotten,
And in the book of things that are forgotten
Is entered as a thing not quite worth while.
He may have been so great
That satraps would have shivered at his frown,
And all he prized alive may rule a state
No larger than a grave that holds a clown;
He may have been a master of his fate,
And of his atoms—ready as another
In his emergence to exonerate

50

His father and his mother;
He may have been a captain of a host,
Self-eloquent and ripe for prodigies,
Doomed here to swell by dangerous degrees,
And then give up the ghost.
Nahum's great grasshoppers were such as
these,
Sun-scattered and soon lost.

Whatever the dark road he may have taken,
This man who stood on high
And faced alone the sky,
Whatever drove or lured or guided him,—
A vision answering a faith unshaken,
An easy trust assumed of easy trials,
A sick negation born of weak denials,
A crazed abhorrence of an old condition,
A blind attendance on a brief ambition,—
Whatever stayed him or derided him,
His way was even as ours;
And we, with all our wounds and all our
powers,
Must each await alone at his own height
Another darkness or another light;
And there, of our poor self dominion reft,
If inference and reason shun
Hell, Heaven, and Oblivion,
May thwarted will (perforce precarious,
But for our conservation better thus)
Have no misgiving left
Of doing yet what here we leave undone?
Or if unto the last of these we cleave,
Believing or protesting we believe
In such an idle and ephemeral
Florescence of the diabolical—
If, robbed of two fond old enormities,
Our being had no onward auguries,
What then were this great love of ours to say
For launching other lives to voyage again
A little farther into time and pain,
A little faster in a futile chase
For a kingdom and a power and a Race
That would have still in sight
A manifest end of ashes and eternal night?
Is this the music of the toys we shake
So loud,—as if there might be no mistake
Somewhere in our indomitable will?
Are we no greater than the noise we make
Along one blind atomic pilgrimage
Whereon by crass chance billeted we go
Because our brains and bones and cartilage
Will have it so?

If this we say, then let us all be still
About our share in it, and live and die
More quietly thereby.

5 Where was he going, this man against the sky?
You know not, nor do I.
But this we know, if we know anything:
That we may laugh and fight and sing
And of our transience here make offering
10 To an orient Word that will not be erased,
Or, save in incommunicable gleams
Too permanent for dreams,
Be found or known.
No tonic and ambitious irritant
15 Of increase or of want
Has made an otherwise insensate waste
Of ages overthrown
A ruthless, veiled, implacable foretaste
Of other ages that are still to be
20 Depleted and rewarded variously
Because a few, by fate's economy,
Shall seem to move the world the way it goes;
No soft evangel of equality,
Safe-cradled in a communal repose
25 That huddles into death and may at last
Be covered well with equatorial snows—
And all for what, the devil only knows—
Will aggregate an inkling to confirm
The credit of a sage or of a worm,
30 Or tell us why one man in five
Should have a care to stay alive
While in his heart he feels no violence
Laid on his humor and intelligence
When infant Science makes a pleasant face
35 And waves again that hollow toy, the Race;
No planetary trap where souls are wrought
For nothing but the sake of being caught
And sent again to nothing will attune
Itself to any key of any reason
40 Why man should hunger through another
season
To find out why 'twere better late than soon
To go away and let the sun and moon
And all the silly stars illuminate
45 A place for creeping things,
And those that root and trumpet and have
wings,
And herd and ruminate,
Or dive and flash and poise in rivers and seas,
50 Or by their loyal tails in lofty trees
Hang screeching lewd victorious derision
Of man's immortal vision.

Shall we, because Eternity records
Too vast an answer for the time-born words
We spell, whereof so many are dead that once
In our capricious lexicons
Were so alive and final, hear no more   5
The Word itself, the living word
That none alive has ever heard
Or ever spelt,
And few have ever felt
Without the fears and old surrenderings   10
And terrors that began
When Death let fall a feather from his wings
And humbled the first man?
Because the weight of our humility,
Wherefrom we gain   15
A little wisdom and much pain,
Falls here too sore and there too tedious,
Are we in anguish or complacency,
Not looking far enough ahead
To see by what mad couriers we are led   20
Along the roads of the ridiculous,
To pity ourselves and laugh at faith
And while we curse life bear it?
And if we see the soul's dead end in death,
Are we to fear it?   25
What folly is here that has not yet a name
Unless we say outright that we are liars?
What have we seen beyond our sunset fires
That lights again the way by which we came?
Why pay we such a price, and one we give   30
So clamouringly, for each racked empty day
That leads one more last human hope away,
As quiet fiends would lead past our crazed eyes
Our children to an unseen sacrifice?
If after all that we have lived and thought,   35
All comes to Nought—
If there be nothing after Now,
And we be nothing anyhow,
And we know that—why live?
'Twere sure but weaklings' vain distress   40
To suffer dungeons where so many doors
Will open on the cold eternal shores
That look sheer down
To the dark tideless floods of Nothingness
Where all who know may drown.   45

EDGAR LEE MASTERS

With a Kansas and Illinois background, Masters (1869–   ) was well on his way toward a successful career in law after being clerk, collector, and so on. Two forces intervened: poli-

tics and poetry. The success of the Spoon River Anthology *determined his future. With Sandburg, Lindsay, and others, Masters owed some debt to the magazine* Poetry *for his start. Sturdy and tough, he managed in his cemetery monologues to open up a new approach to the heart and mind of America; his frankness in verse was similar to that of Sherwood Anderson and Dreiser in fiction, and received the same mixed reception at first. Although Masters has many titles to his credit—he wrote novels and plays as well as poetry—Spoon River is still his major accomplishment.*

From *Spoon River Anthology**

PETIT, THE POET

Seeds in a dry pod, tick, tick, tick,
Tick, tick, tick, like mites in a quarrel—   20
Faint iambics that the full breeze wakens—
But the pine tree makes a symphony thereof.
Triolets, villanelles, rondels, rondeaus,
Ballades by the score with the same old
      thought:
The snows and roses of yesterday are van-   25
      ished;
And what is love but a rose that fades?
Life all around me here in the village:
Tragedy, comedy, valor and truth,   30
Courage, constancy, heroism, failure—
All in the loom, and oh what patterns!
Woodlands, meadows, streams and rivers—
Blind to all of it all my life long.
Triolets, villanelles, rondels, rondeaus,   35
Seeds in a dry pod, tick, tick, tick,
Tick, tick, tick, what little iambics,
While Homer and Whitman roared in the
      pines?

SETH COMPTON

When I died, the circulating library
Which I built up for Spoon River,
And managed for the good of inquiring minds,
Was sold at auction on the public square,
As if to destroy the last vestige
Of my memory and influence.
For those of you who could not see the virtue

---

* By special permission of Mr. Edgar Lee Masters.

Of knowing Volney's "Ruins"[1] as well as But-
    ler's "Analogy"[2]
And "Faust"[3] as well as "Evangeline,"[4]
Were really the power in the village,
And often you asked me,
"What is the use of knowing the evil in the
    world?"
I am out of your way now, Spoon River,
Choose your own good and call it good.
For I could never make you see
That no one knows what is good
Who knows not what is evil;
And no one knows what is true
Who knows not what is false.

ANNE RUTLEDGE

Out of me unworthy and unknown
The vibrations of deathless music;
"With malice toward none, with charity for
    all."
Out of me the forgiveness of millions toward
    millions,
And the beneficent face of a nation
Shining with justice and truth.
I am Anne Rutledge who sleep beneath these
    weeds,
Beloved in life of Abraham Lincoln,
Wedded to him, not through union,
But through separation.
Bloom forever, O Republic,
From the dust of my bosom!

LUCINDA MATLOCK

I went to the dances at Chandlerville,
And played snap-out at Winchester.
One time we changed partners,
Driving home in the moonlight of middle
    June,
And then I found Davis.
We were married and lived together for
    seventy years,
Enjoying, working, raising the twelve children,
Eight of whom we lost
Ere I had reached the age of sixty.

---

[1] Constantin François Volney: *Ruins of Empire*
(Paris, 1791).
  [2] Joseph Butler: *Analogy of Religion* (1736).
  [3] subject of dramas by Marlowe and Goethe.
  [4] narrative poem by Longfellow (1847).

I spun, I wove, I kept the house, I nursed the
    sick,
I made the garden, and for holiday
Rambled over the fields where sang the larks,
5 And by Spoon River gathering many a shell,
And many a flower and medicinal weed—
Shouting to the wooded hills, singing to the
    green valleys.
At ninety-six I had lived enough, that is all,
10 And passed to a sweet repose.
What is this I hear of sorrow and weariness,
Anger, discontent and drooping hopes?
Degenerate sons and daughters,
Life is too strong for you—
15 It takes life to love Life.

AMY LOWELL

*Amy Lowell (1874–1925), unlike some of her
contemporaries, did not have to worry about
making a living. Descended from an old New
England family of patricians and educators,
she had opportunity to travel and to write at
leisure. After undistinguished early verse she
developed into a poetic force in her day by
leading the school of imagists, a group who
used the language of common speech to create
hard, clear pictures. Miss Lowell wrote criticism, did translations, and engineered a significant life of Keats. In ill health a good part
of her life, always a stormy figure, she developed free verse and for a few years had great
influence. Today she is remembered for three
or four poems; imagism is a moribund term,
and many critics publicly wonder whether she
was really a poet or not (because she rarely
went deep, and because she dodged issues). As
a historical figure, regardless of the critical decision, Miss Lowell seems assured of a kind of
immortality.*[*]

PATTERNS

I walk down the garden paths,
45 And all the daffodils
Are blowing, and the bright blue squills.
I walk down the patterned garden paths
In my stiff, brocaded gown.
With my powdered hair and jeweled fan,

---

[*] The poems by Miss Lowell are reprinted with
the permission of Houghton Mifflin Company, publishers.

I too am a rare
Pattern. As I wander down
The garden paths.
My dress is richly figured,
And the train
Makes a pink and silver stain
On the gravel, and the thrift
Of the borders.
Just a plate of current fashion,
Tripping by in high-heeled, ribboned shoes. 10
Not a softness anywhere about me,
Only whale-bone and brocade.
And I sink on a seat in the shade
Of a lime tree. For my passion
Wars against the stiff brocade. 15
The daffodils and squills
Flutter in the breeze
As they please.
And I weep;
For the lime tree is in blossom 20
And one small flower has dropped upon my
    bosom.

And the plashing of waterdrops
In the marble fountain
Comes down the garden paths.
The dripping never stops.
Underneath my stiffened gown
Is the softness of a woman bathing in a marble
    basin, 30
A basin in the midst of hedges grown
So thick, she cannot see her lover hiding,
But she guesses he is near,
And the sliding of the water
Seems the stroking of a dear 35
Hand upon her.
What is Summer in a fine brocaded gown!
I should like to see it lying in a heap upon the
    ground.
All the pink and silver crumpled up on the 40
    ground.

I would be the pink and silver as I run along
    the paths,
And he would stumble after,
Bewildered by my laughter. 45
I should see the sun flashing from his sword
    hilt and the buckles on his shoes.
I would choose
To lead him in a maze along the patterned 50
    paths,

A bright and laughing maze for my heavy-
    booted lover,
Till he caught me in the shade,
And the buttons of his waistcoat bruised my 5
    body as he clasped me,
Aching, melting, unafraid.
With the shadows of the leaves and the sun-
    drops,
And the plopping of the waterdrops,
All about us in the open afternoon— 10
I am very like to swoon
With the weight of this brocade,
For the sun shifts through the shade.

Underneath the fallen blossom 15
In my bosom,
Is a letter I have hid.
It was brought to me this morning by a rider
    from the Duke.
"Madam, we regret to inform you that Lord 20
    Hartwell
Died in action Thursday se'nnight."
As I read it in the white, morning sunlight,
The letters squirmed like snakes.
"Any answer, Madam?" said my footman. 25
"No," I told him.
"See that the messenger takes some refresh-
    ment.
No, no answer."

And I walked into the garden,
Up and down the patterned paths,
In my stiff, correct brocade.
The blue and yellow flowers stood up proudly
    in the sun, 35
Each one.
I stood upright, too,
Held rigid to the pattern
By the stiffness of my gown.
Up and down I walked, 40
Up and down.

In a month he would have been my husband.
In a month, here, underneath this lime,
We would have broke the pattern; 45
He for me, and I for him,
He as Colonel, I as Lady,
On this shady seat.
He had a whim
That sunlight carried blessing. 50
And I answered, "It shall be as you have said."
Now he is dead.

In Summer and in Winter I shall walk
Up and down
The patterned garden paths
In my stiff, brocaded gown.
The squills and daffodils
Will give place to pillared roses, and to asters,
   and to snow.
I shall go
Up and down,
In my gown.
Gorgeously arrayed,
Boned and stayed.
And the softness of my body will be guarded
   from embrace
By each button, hook, and lace.
For the man who should loose me is dead,
Fighting with the Duke in Flanders,
In a pattern called a war.
Christ! What are patterns for?

ON READING A LINE UNDER-
SCORED BY KEATS

IN A COPY OF *Palmerin of England* [1]

You marked it with light pencil upon a printed
   page,
And, as though your finger pointed along a
   sunny path for my eyes' better direction,
I see "a knight mounted on a mulberry courser
   and attired in green armour."
I think the sky is faintly blue, but with a
   Spring shining about it,
And the new grass scarcely fetlock high in the
   meads.
He rides, I believe, alongside an overflown
   river,
By a path soft and easy to his charger's feet.
My vision confuses you with the green-ar-
   moured knight:
So dight and caparisoned might you be in a
   land of Faery.
Thus, with denoting finger, you make of your-
   self an escutcheon to guide me to that in
   you which is its essence.
But for the rest,
The part which most persists and is remem-
   bered,
I only know I compass it in loving and neither
   have, nor need, a symbol.

ON LOOKING AT A COPY OF ALICE
MEYNELL'S [1] POEMS, GIVEN ME,
YEARS AGO, BY A FRIEND

5 Upon this greying page you wrote
A whispered greeting, long ago.
Faint pencil-marks run to and fro
Scoring the lines I loved to quote.

10 A sea-shore of white, shoaling sand,
Blue creeks zigzagging through marsh-grasses,
Sand pipers, and a wind which passes
Cloudily silent up the land.

15 Upon the high edge of the sea
A great four-master sleeps; three hours
Her bowsprit has not cleared those flowers.
I read and look alternatively.

20 It all comes back again, but dim
As pictures on a winking wall
Hidden save when the dark clouds fall
Or crack to show the moon's bright rim.

25 I will remember what I was,
And what I wanted. You, unwise
With sore unwisdom, had no eyes
For what was patently the cause.

30 So are we sport of others' blindness,
We who could see right well alone.
What were you made of—wood or stone?
Yet I remember you with kindness.

35 You gave this book to me to ease
The smart in me you could not heal.
Your gift a mirror—woe or weal.
We sat beneath the apple-trees.

40 And I remember how they rang,
These words, like bronze cathedral bells
Down ancient lawns, or citadels
Thundering with gongs where choirs sang.

45 Silent the sea, the earth, the sky,
And in my heart a silent weeping.
Who has not sown can know no reaping!
Bitter conclusion and no lie.

50 O heart that sorrows, heart that bleeds,

---

[1] sixteenth-century chivalric romance.

[1] 1850–1922.

Heart that was never mine, your words
Were like the pecking Autumn birds
Stealing away my garnered seeds.

No future where there is no past!
O cherishing grief which laid me bare,
I wrapped you like a wintry air
About me. Poor enthusiast!

How strange that tumult, looking back.
The ink is pale, the letters fade.
The verses seem to be well made,
But I have lived the almanac.

And you are dead these drifted years,
How many I forget. And she
Who wrote the book, her tragedy
Long since dried up its scalding tears.

I read of her death yesterday,
Frail lady whom I never knew
And knew so well. Would I could strew
Her grave with pansies, blue and grey.

Would I could stand a little space
Under a blowing, brightening sky,
And watch the sad leaves fall and lie
Gently upon that lonely place.

So cried her heart, a feverish thing.
But clay is still, and clay is cold,
And I was young, and I am old
And in December what birds sing!

Go, wistful book, go back again
Upon your shelf and gather dust.
I've seen the glitter through the rust
Of old, long years, I've known the pain.

I've recollected both of you,
But I shall recollect no more.
Between us I must shut the door.
The living have so much to do.

ROBERT FROST*

MENDING WALL

Something there is that doesn't love a wall,
That sends the frozen-ground-swell under it,

And spills the upper boulders in the sun;
And makes gaps even two can pass abreast.
The work of hunters is another thing:
I have come after them and made repair
5 Where they have left not one stone on a stone,
But they would have the rabbit out of hiding,
To please the yelping dogs. The gaps I mean,
No one has seen them made or heard them made,
10 But at spring mending-time we find them there.
I let my neighbor know beyond the hill;
And on a day we meet to walk the line
And set the wall between us once again.
15 We keep the wall between us as we go.
To each the boulders that have fallen to each.
And some are loaves and some so nearly balls
We have to use a spell to make them balance:
"Stay where you are until our backs are
20 turned!"
We wear our fingers rough with handling them.
Oh, just another kind of out-door game,
One on a side. It comes to little more:
25 There where it is we do not need the wall:
He is all pine and I am apple orchard.
My apple trees will never get across
And eat the cones under his pines, I tell him.
He only says, "Good fences make good neigh-
30 bors."
Spring is the mischief in me, and I wonder
If I could put a notion in his head:
"*Why* do they make good neighbors? Isn't it
Where there are cows? But here there are no
35 cows.
Before I built a wall I'd ask to know
What I was walling in or walling out,
And to whom I was like to give offense.
Something there is that doesn't love a wall,
40 That wants it down." I could say "Elves" to him,
But it's not elves exactly, and I'd rather
He said it for himself. I see him there
Bringing a stone grasped firmly by the top
45 In each hand, like an old-stone savage armed.
He moves in darkness as it seems to me,
Not of woods only and the shade of trees.
He will not go behind his father's saying,
And he likes having thought of it so well

* For introductory sketch see I, 186. The selections which follow are from *Collected Poems of*

He says again, "Good fences make good neighbors."

BIRCHES

When I see birches bend to left and right
Across the lines of straighter darker trees,
I like to think some boy's been swinging them.
But swinging doesn't bend them down to stay.
Ice-storms do that. Often you must have seen 10
them
Loaded with ice a sunny winter morning
After a rain. They click upon themselves
As the breeze rises, and turn many-colored
As the stir cracks and crazes their enamel.
Soon the sun's warmth makes them shed crys-
tal shells
Shattering and avalanching on the snow-
crust—
Such heaps of broken glass to sweep away 20
You'd think the inner dome of heaven had
fallen.
They are dragged to the withered bracken by
the load,
And they seem not to break; though once they 25
are bowed
So low for long, they never right themselves:
You may see their trunks arching in the woods
Years afterwards, trailing their leaves on the
ground 30
Like girls on hands and knees that throw their
hair
Before them over their heads to dry in the sun.
But I was going to say when Truth broke in
With all her matter-of-fact about the ice-storm 35
(Now am I free to be poetical?)
I should prefer to have some boy bend them
As he went out and in to fetch the cows—
Some boy too far from town to learn baseball,
Whose only play was what he found himself, 40
Summer or winter, and could play alone.
One by one he subdued his father's trees
By riding them down over and over again
Until he took the stiffness out of them,
And not one but hung limp, not one was left 45
For him to conquer. He learned all there was
To learn about not launching out too soon
And so not carrying the tree away
Clear to the ground. He always kept his poise
To the top branches, climbing carefully 50
With the same pains you use to fill a cup
Up to the brim, and even above the brim.

Then he flung outward, feet first, with a swish,
Kicking his way down through the air to the
ground.
So was I once myself a swinger of birches.
And so I dream of going back to be. 5
It's when I'm weary of considerations,
And life is too much like a pathless wood
Where your face burns and tickles with the
cobwebs
Broken across it, and one eye is weeping
From a twig's having lashed across it open.
I'd like to get away from earth awhile
And then come back to it and begin over.
May no fate willfully misunderstand me
And half grant what I wish and snatch me 15
away
Not to return. Earth's the right place for love:
I don't know where it's likely to go better.
I'd like to go by climbing a birch tree,
And climb black branches up a snow-white 20
trunk
Toward heaven, till the tree could bear no
more,
But dipped its top and set me down again.
That would be good both going and coming 25
back.
One could do worse than be a swinger of
birches.

THE ROAD NOT TAKEN

Two roads diverged in a yellow wood,
And sorry I could not travel both
And be one traveler, long I stood
And looked down one as far as I could
To where it bent in the undergrowth;

Then took the other, as just as fair,
And having perhaps the better claim,
Because it was grassy and wanted wear;
Though as for that the passing there
Had worn them really about the same,

And both that morning equally lay
In leaves no step had trodden black.
Oh, I kept the first for another day!
Yet knowing how way leads on to way,
I doubted if I should ever come back.

I shall be telling this with a sigh
Somewhere ages and ages hence:
Two roads diverged in a wood, and I—

I took the one less traveled by,
And that has made all the difference.

CARL SANDBURG

Sandburg (1878–), the son of Swedish immigrants, is the living embodiment of the familiar American idea that after hard knocks and adventure a good man can reach the top. Before Poetry circulated his poems he had tried various means of making a living, had enlisted for the Spanish-American War, and had then enrolled at Lombard College. In the earthy, vigorous tradition of Whitman, Sandburg continued to sing the songs of the people, introducing topics and scenes unknown among the earlier Americans, who so often concentrated on flowers or birds and avoided unpleasantness or controversy. He has done a monumental study of Lincoln, written tales for children, and collected ballads and songs. His lectures and song programs are familiar to large audiences throughout the land. Literary history will probably mark Sandburg as a trail blazer who made poems to fit the tempo of a machine age in which "The People, Yes" proved that a functional democracy could be made up of many races and creeds.

CHICAGO*

Hog Butcher for the World,
Tool Maker, Stacker of Wheat,
Player with Railroads and the Nation's
   Freight Handler;
Stormy, husky, brawling,
City of the Big Shoulders:

They tell me you are wicked, and I believe
   them; for I have seen your painted
   women under the gas lamps luring the
   farm boys.
And they tell me you are crooked, and I answer: Yes, it is true I have seen the gun-
   man kill and go free to kill again.
And they tell me you are brutal, and my reply
   is: On the faces of women and children I
   have seen the marks of wanton hunger.
And having answered so I turn once more to

those who sneer at this my city, and I give
   them back the sneer and say to them:
Come and show me another city with lifted
   head singing so proud to be alive and
   coarse and strong and cunning.
Flinging magnetic curses amid the toil of piling job on job, here is a tall bold slugger
   set vivid against the little soft cities;
Fierce as a dog with tongue lapping for action,
   cunning as a savage pitted against the wilderness,
      Bareheaded,
      Shovelling,
      Wrecking,
      Planning,
      Building, breaking, rebuilding,
Under the smoke, dust all over his mouth,
   laughing with white teeth,
Under the terrible burden of destiny laughing
   as a young man laughs,
Laughing even as an ignorant fighter laughs
   who has never lost a battle,
Bragging and laughing that under his wrist is
   the pulse, and under his ribs the heart of
   the people,
         Laughing!
Laughing the stormy, husky, brawling laughter of Youth, half-naked, sweating, proud
   to be Hog Butcher, Tool Maker, Stacker
   of Wheat, Player with Railroads and
   Freight Handler to the Nation.

GRASS*

Pile the bodies high at Austerlitz and Water-
   loo.
Shovel them under and let me work—
         I am the grass; I cover all.

And pile them high at Gettysburg
And pile them high at Ypres and Verdun.
Shovel them under and let me work.
Two years, ten years, and passengers ask the
   conductor:
         What place is this?
         Where are we now?

         I am the grass.
         Let me work.

COOL TOMBS

When Abraham Lincoln was shovelled into the
tombs, he forgot the copperheads and the
assassin . . . in the dust, in the cool
tombs.

And Ulysses Grant lost all thought of con men
and Wall Street, cash and collateral
turned ashes . . . in the dust, in the cool
tombs.

Pocahontas' body, lovely as a poplar, sweet as
a red haw in November or a pawpaw in
May, did she wonder? does she remember? . . . in the dust, in the cool tombs?

Take any streetful of people buying clothes
and groceries, cheering a hero or throwing confetti and blowing tin horns . . .
tell me if the lovers are losers . . . tell
me if any get more than the lovers . . .
in the dust . . . in the cool tombs.

SMOKE AND STEEL*

Smoke of the fields in spring is one,
Smoke of the leaves in autumn another.
Smoke of a steel-mill roof or a battleship fun-
nel,
They all go up in a line with a smokestack,
Or they twist . . . in the slow twist . . . of
the wind.

If the north wind comes they run to the south.
If the west wind comes they run to the east.
    By this sign
    all smokes
    know each other.
Smoke of the fields in spring and leaves in
autumn,
Smoke of the finished steel, chilled and blue,
By the oath of work they swear: 'I know
you.'

Hunted and hissed from the centre
Deep down long ago when God made us over,
Deep down are the cinders we came from—
You and I and our heads of smoke.

* From *Smoke and Steel* by Carl Sandburg,
copyright, 1920, by Harcourt, Brace and Company, Inc.

Some of the smokes God dropped on the job
Cross on the sky and count our years
And sing in the secrets of our numbers;
Sing their dawns and sing their evenings,
Sing an old log-fire song:
        You may put the damper up,
        You may put the damper down,
        The smoke goes up the chimney just
        the same.

Smoke of a city sunset skyline,
Smoke of a country dusk horizon—
        They cross on the sky and count our
        years.

Smoke of a brick-red dust
        Winds on a spiral
        Out of the stacks
For a hidden and glimpsing moon.
This, said the bar-iron shed to the blooming
mill,
This is the slang of coal and steel.
The day-gang hands it to the night-gang,
The night-gang hands it back.

Stammer at the slang of this—
Let us understand half of it.
        In the rolling mills and sheet mills,
        In the harr and boom of the blast fires,
        The smoke changes its shadow
        And men change their shadow;
        A nigger, a wop, a bohunk changes.
        A bar of steel—it is only
Smoke at the heart of it, smoke and the blood
        of a man.
A runner of fire ran in it, ran out, ran some-
        where else,
And left—smoke and the blood of a man
And the finished steel, chilled and blue.

So fire runs in, runs out, runs somewhere else
        again,
And the bar of steel is a gun, a wheel, a nail,
        a shovel,
A rudder under the sea, a steering-gear in the
        sky;
And always dark in the heart and through it,
        Smoke and the blood of a man.
Pittsburg, Youngstown, Gary—they make their
        steel with men.
In the blood of men and the ink of chimneys

The smoke nights write their oaths:
Smoke into steel and blood into steel;
Homestead, Braddock, Birmingham, they make
    their steel with men.
Smoke and blood is the mix of steel.   5

    The birdmen drone
    in the blue; it is steel
    a motor sings and zooms.

     10

Steel barb-wire around The Works.
Steel guns in the holsters of the guards at the
    gates of The Works.
Steel ore-boats bring the loads clawed from
    the earth by steel, lifted and lugged by   15
    arms of steel, sung on its way by the
    clanking clam-shells.
The runners now, the handlers now, are steel;
    they dig and clutch and haul; they hoist
    their automatic knuckles from job to job;   20
    they are steel making steel.
Fire and dust and air fight in the furnaces;
    the pour is timed, the billets wriggle; the
    clinkers are dumped:
Liners on the sea, skyscrapers on the land;   25
    diving steel in the sea, climbing steel in
    the sky.

   .   .   .   .   .

Finders in the dark, you Steve with a dinner
    bucket, you Steve clumping in the dusk   30
    on the sidewalks with an evening paper
    for the woman and kids, you Steve with
    your head wondering where we all end
    up—
Finders in the dark, Steve: I hook my arm in   35
    cinder sleeves; we go down the street to-
    gether; it is all the same to us; you Steve
    and the rest of us end on the same stars;
    we all wear a hat in hell together, in hell
    or heaven.   40

    Smoke nights now, Steve.
    Smoke, smoke, lost in the sieves of
      yesterday;
    Dumped again to the scoops and hooks   45
      to-day.
    Smoke like the clocks and whistles, al-
      ways.
      Smoke nights now.
      To-morrow something else.   50

   .   .   .   .   .
Luck moons come and go;

Five men swim in a pot of red steel.
Their bones are kneaded into the bread of
    steel:
Their bones are knocked into coils and anvils
And the sucking plungers of sea-fighting tur-
    bines.
Look for them in the woven frame of a wireless
    station.
So ghosts hide in steel like heavy-armed men
    in mirrors.
Peepers, skulkers—they shadow-dance in
    laughing tombs.
They are always there and they never answer.

One of them said: 'I like my job, the company
    is good to me, America is a wonderful
    country.'
One: 'Jesus, my bones ache; the company is a
    liar; this is a free country, like hell.'
One: 'I got a girl, a peach; we save up and go
    on a farm and raise pigs and be the boss
    ourselves.'
And the others were roughneck singers a long
    ways from home.
Look for them back of a steel vault door.

    They laugh at the cost.
    They lift the birdmen into the blue.
    It is steel a motor sings and zooms.

In the subway plugs and drums,
In the slow hydraulic drills, in gumbo or
    gravel,
Under dynamo shafts in the webs of armature
    spiders,
They shadow-dance and laugh at the cost.

   .   .   .   .   .

The ovens light a red dome.
Spools of fire wind and wind.
Quadrangles of crimson sputter.
The lashes of dying maroon let down.
Fire and wind wash out the slag.
Forever the slag gets washed in fire and wind
The anthem learned by the steel is:
    Do this or go hungry.
Look for our rust on a plough.
Listen to us in a threshing-engine razz.
Look at our job in the running wagon wheat.

   .   .   .   .   .
Fire and wind wash at the slag.
Box-cars, clocks, steam-shovels, churns, pis-

tons, boilers, scissors—
Oh, the sleeping slag from the mountains, the slag-heavy pig-iron will go down many roads.
Men will stab and shoot with it, and make [5] butter and tunnel rivers, and mow hay in swaths, and slit hogs and skin beeves, and steer airplanes across North America, Europe, Asia, round the world.

Hacked from a hard rock country, broken and baked in mills and smelters, the rusty dust waits
Till the clean hard weave of its atoms cripples and blunts the drills chewing a hole in it. [15]
The steel of its plinths and flanges is reckoned, O God, in one-millionth of an inch.

. . . .

Once when I saw the curves of fire, the rough scarf women dancing,
Dancing out of the flues and smokestacks— [20] flying hair of fire, flying feet upside down;
Buckets and baskets of fire exploding and chortling, fire running wild out of the steady and fastened ovens; [25]
Sparks cracking a harr-harr-huff from a solar-plexus of rock-ribs of the earth taking a laugh for themselves;
Ears and noses of fire, gibbering gorilla arms of fire, gold mud-pies, gold bird-wings, red [30] jackets riding purple mules, scarlet autocrats tumbling from the humps of camels, assassinated czars straddling vermilion balloons;
I saw then the fires flash one by one: good- [35] bye: then smoke, smoke;
And in the screens the great sisters of night and cool stars, sitting women arranging their hair,
Waiting in the sky, waiting with slow easy [40] eyes, waiting and half-murmuring:
    'Since you know all
    and I know nothing,
    tell me what I dreamed last night.'

. . . .

Pearl cobwebs in the windy rain, [45]
in only a flicker of wind,
are caught and lost and never known again.

A pool of moonshine comes and waits, [50]
but never waits long: the wind picks up
loose gold like this and is gone.

A bar of steel sleeps and looks slant-eyed
on the pearl cobwebs, the pools of moonshine;
sleeps slant-eyed a million years,
sleeps with a coat of rust, a vest of moths,
a shirt of gathering sod and loam.

The wind never bothers . . . a bar of steel.
The wind picks only . . . pearl cobwebs . . .
    pools of moonshine.

JOHN MASEFIELD

Poet laureate after Bridges, John Masefield (1878–   ) began life in sail (see Salt-Water Ballads) and moved around soaking up experience which included humble odd jobs in New York. He found fame in The Everlasting Mercy *but was criticized for dealing too forthrightly with life in the raw. Masefield wrote with vigor, turning out plays and essays as well as poetry. He could generally be counted on to spin a good yarn. Recent poems, many written for occasions in his capacity as laureate, have not been outstanding.**

CARGOES

Quinquireme[1] of Nineveh from distant Ophir,
Rowing home to haven in sunny Palestine,
With a cargo of ivory,
And apes and peacocks,
Sandalwood, cedarwood, and sweet white wine.

Stately Spanish galleon coming from the Isthmus,
Dipping through the Tropics by the palm-green shores,
With a cargo of diamonds,
Emeralds, amethysts,
Topazes, and cinnamon, and gold moidores.

Dirty British coaster with a salt-caked smoke stack,
Butting through the Channel in the mad March days,
With a cargo of Tyne coal,

---

* The following selections are from John Masefield, *Poems,* copyright, 1935. By permission of The Macmillan Company, publishers.
[1] ancient boat with five banks of oars.

Road-rails, pig-lead,
Firewood, iron-ware, and cheap tin trays.

LONDON TOWN

Oh, London Town's a fine town, and London
    sights are rare,
And London ale is right ale, and brisk's the
    London air,
And busily goes the world there, but crafty 10
    grows the mind,
And London Town of all towns I'm glad to
    leave behind.

Then hey for croft and hop-yard, and hill, and 15
    field, and pond,
With Bredon Hill before me and Malvern Hill
    beyond.
The hawthorn white i' the hedgerow, and all
    the spring's attire 20
In the comely land of Teme and Lugg, and
    Clent, and Clee, and Wyre.

Oh, London girls are brave girls, in silk and
    cloth o' gold,
And London shops are rare shops where gal- 25
    lant things are sold,
And bonnily clinks the gold there, but drowsily
    blinks the eye,
And London Town of all towns I'm glad to 30
    hurry by.

Then hey for covert and woodland, and ash
    and elm and oak,
Tewkesbury inns, and Malvern roofs, and 35
    Worcester chimney smoke,
The apple trees in the orchard, the cattle in
    the byre,
And all the land from Ludlow town to Bredon
    church's spire. 40

Oh, London tunes are new tunes, and London
    books are wise,
And London plays are rare plays, and fine to
    country eyes, 45
But wretchedly fare the most there and merrily
    fare the few,
And London Town of all towns I'm glad to
    hurry through. 50

So hey for the road, the west road, by mill and
    forge and fold,

Scent of the fern and song of the lark by brook,
    and field, and wold,
To the comely folk at the hearth-stone and the
    talk beside the fire,
In the hearty land, where I was bred, my land 5
    of heart's desire.

ON GROWING OLD

Be with me, Beauty, for the fire is dying;
My dog and I are old, too old for roving.
Man, whose young passion sets the spindrift
    flying,
Is soon too lame to march, too cold for loving.

I take the book and gather to the fire,
Turning old yellow leaves; minute by minute
The clock ticks to my heart; a withered wire
Moves a thin ghost of music in the spinet.

I cannot sail your seas, I cannot wander
Your corn-land nor your hill-land nor your val-
    leys
Ever again, nor share the battle yonder
Where the young knight the broken squadron
    rallies;

Only stay quiet, while my mind remembers
The beauty of fire from the beauty of embers.

Beauty, have pity, for the strong have power,
The rich their wealth, the beautiful their grace,
Summer of man its sunlight and its flower,
Springtime of man all April in a face.

Only, as in the jostling in the Strand,[1]
Where the mob thrusts or loiters or is loud,
The beggar with the saucer in his hand
Asks only a penny from the passing crowd,

So, from this glittering world with all its fash-
    ion,
Its fire and play of men, its stir, its march,
Let me have wisdom, Beauty, wisdom and
    passion,
Bread to the soul, rain where the summers
    parch.

Give me but these, and though the darkness
    close
Even the night will blossom as the rose.

[1] in London.

VACHEL LINDSAY

Lindsay (1879–1931), like Sandburg, was born in Illinois and tried odd jobs (after a period as art student). He spent considerable time vaga- bonding up and down the land, lecturing and peddling poems for bread. He developed chant-like verses with refrain effects which al- lowed for audience participation in the man- ner of the old ballads but with more showman- ship and not a little touch of the theater. His best poems, however, show a feeling for satire and a tired, pitying philosophy concerning man's muddling efforts to retain individuality in a genteel society. Although Lindsay eventu- ally found life a wearing experience (he died by his own hand), his poems are always filled with a notable vitality.*

THE GHOSTS OF THE BUFFALOES

Last night at black midnight I woke with a
cry,
The windows were shaking, there was thunder
on high,
The floor was atremble, the door was ajar,
White fires, crimson fires, shone from afar.
I rushed to the dooryard. The city was gone.
My home was a hut without orchard or lawn.
It was mud-smear and logs near a whispering
stream,
Nothing else built by man could I see in my
dream . . .

Then . . .
Ghost-kings came headlong, row upon row,
Gods of the Indians, torches aglow.
They mounted the bear and the elk and the
deer,
And eagles gigantic, agèd and sere,
They rode long-horn cattle, they cried
"A-la-la."
They lifted the knife, the bow, and the spear,
They lifted ghost-torches from dead fires be-
low,
The midnight made grand with the cry
"A-la-la."

* The material which follows is from Lindsay's
Collected Poems, copyright, 1925. By permission of
The Macmillan Company, publishers.

The midnight made grand with a red-god
charge,
A red-god show,
A red-god show,
"A-la-la, a-la-la, a-la-la, a-la-la."

With bodies like bronze, and terrible eyes
Came the rank and the file, with catamount
cries,
Gibbering, yipping, with hollow-skull clacks,
Riding white bronchos with skeleton backs,
Scalp-hunters, beaded and spangled and bad,
Naked and lustful and foaming and mad,
Flashing primeval demoniac scorn,
Blood-thirst and pomp amid darkness reborn,
Power and glory that sleep in the grass
While the winds and the snows and the great
rains pass.
They crossed the gray river, thousands abreast,
They rode out in infinite lines to the west,
Tide upon tide of strange fury and foam,
Spirits and wraiths, the blue was their home,
The sky was their goal where the star-flags are
furled,
And on past those far golden splendors they
whirled.
They burned to dim meteors, lost in the deep,
And I turned in dazed wonder, thinking of
sleep.

And the wind crept by
Alone, unkempt, unsatisfied,
The wind cried and cried—
Muttered of massacres long past,
Buffaloes in shambles vast . . .
An owl said, "Hark, what is a-wing?"
I heard a cricket caroling,
I heard a cricket caroling,
I heard a cricket caroling.

Then . . .
Snuffing the lightning that crashed from on
high
Rose royal old buffaloes, row upon row.
The lords of the prairie came galloping by.
And I cried in my heart "A-la-la, a-la-la.
A red-god show,
A red-god show,
A-la-la, a-la-la, a-la-la."
Buffaloes, buffaloes, thousands abreast,
A scourge and amazement, they swept to the
west.

[359]

With black bobbing noses, with red rolling
    tongues,
Coughing forth steam from their leather-
    wrapped lungs,
Cows with their calves, bulls big and vain,   5
Goring the laggards, shaking the mane,
Stamping flint feet, flashing moon eyes,
Pompous and owlish, shaggy and wise.

Like sea-cliffs and caves resounded their ranks 10
With shoulders like waves, and undulant
    flanks.
Tide upon tide of strange fury and foam,
Spirits and wraiths, the blue was their home,
The sky was their goal where the star-flags are 15
    furled,
And on past those far golden splendors they
    whirled.
They burned to dim meteors, lost in the deep,
And I turned in dazed wonder, thinking of 20
    sleep.

I heard a cricket's cymbals play,
A scarecrow lightly flapped his rags,
And a pan that hung by his shoulder rang, 25
Rattled and thumped in a listless way,
And now the wind in the chimney sang,
The wind in the chimney,
The wind in the chimney,
The wind in the chimney, 30
Seemed to say:—
"Dream, boy, dream,
If you anywise can.
To dream is the work
Of beast or man. 35
Life is the west-going dream-storm's breath,
Life is a dream, the sigh of the skies,
The breath of the stars, that nod on their pil-
    lows
With their golden hair mussed over their eyes." 40
The locust played on his musical wing,
Sang to his mate of love's delight.
I heard the whippoorwill's soft fret.
I heard a cricket caroling,
I heard a cricket caroling, 45
I heard a cricket say: "Good-night, good-night,
Good-night, good-night, . . . good-night."

FACTORY WINDOWS ARE
ALWAYS BROKEN

Factory windows are always broken. 50
Somebody's always throwing bricks,

Somebody's always heaving cinders,
Playing ugly Yahoo[1] tricks.

Factory windows are always broken.
Other windows are let alone.
No one throws through the chapel-window
The bitter, snarling derisive stone.

Factory windows are always broken.
Something or other is going wrong.
Something is rotten—I think, in Denmark.
End of the factory-window song.

ABRAHAM LINCOLN WALKS
AT MIDNIGHT
(IN SPRINGFIELD, ILLINOIS)

It is portentous, and a thing of state
That here at midnight, in our little town
A mourning figure walks, and will not rest,
Near the old court-house pacing up and down.

Or by his homestead, or in shadowed yards
He lingers where his children used to play,
Or through the market, on the well-worn
    stones
He stalks until the dawn-stars burn away.

A bronzed, lank man! His suit of ancient black,
A famous high top-hat and plain worn shawl
Make him the quaint great figure that men
    love,
The prairie-lawyer, master of us all.

He cannot sleep upon his hillside now.
He is among us:—as in times before!
And we who toss and lie awake for long
Breathe deep, and start, to see him pass the
    door.

His head is bowed. He thinks on men and
    kings.
Yes, when the sick world cries, how can he
    sleep?
Too many peasants fight, they know not why,
Too many homesteads in black terror weep.

The sins of all the war-lords burn his heart.
He sees the dreadnaughts scouring every main.

[1] in *Gulliver's Travels* a dirty, degenerate form
of man.

He carries on his shawl-wrapped shoulders now
The bitterness, the folly and the pain.

He cannot rest until a spirit-dawn 5
Shall come;—the shining hope of Europe free:
The league of sober folk, the Workers' Earth,
Bringing long peace to Cornland, Alp and Sea.

It breaks his heart that kings must murder still, 10
That all his hours of travail here for men
Seem yet in vain. And who will bring white peace
That he may sleep upon his hill again?

15

THE LEADEN-EYED

Let not young souls be smothered out before
They do quaint deeds and fully flaunt their 20 pride.
It is the world's one crime its babes grow dull,
Its poor are ox-like, limp and leaden-eyed.

Not that they starve, but starve so dreamlessly, 25
Not that they sow, but that they seldom reap,
Not that they serve, but have no gods to serve,
Not that they die but that they die like sheep.

30

WALLACE STEVENS

A Harvard man, Stevens (1879–   ) is an officer in a well-known insurance company. Influenced by French symbolists, he developed 35 *an original form of poetry which has won him many critics' awards. He was recently mentioned prominently in the press coverages of Poetry's 35th anniversary. Stevens has a restricted appeal because of his concern with* 40 *sound effects, moving words about, creating impressions. A student who knows only traditional verse may have trouble working out his titles and symbols, but with effort may experience the pleasure of recognizing wit, neatness,* 45 *and, subtly hidden, a deep preoccupation with human values on the one hand and polished form on the other.**

THE PALTRY NUDE STARTS ON A SPRING VOYAGE

But not on a shell, she starts,
Archaic, for the sea.
But on the first-found weed
She scuds the glitters,
Noiselessly, like one more wave.

She too is discontent
And would have purple stuff upon her arms,
Tired of the salty harbors,
Eager for the brine and bellowing
Of the high interiors of the sea.

The wind speeds her,
Blowing upon her hands
And watery back.
She touches the clouds, where she goes
In the circle of her traverse of the sea.

Yet this is meagre play
In the scurry and water-shine,
As her heels foam—
Not as when the goldener nude
Of a later day

Will go, like the centre of sea-green pomp,
In an intenser calm,
Scullion of fate,
Across the spick torrent, ceaselessly,
Upon her irretrievable way.

THE EMPEROR OF ICE-CREAM

Call the roller of big cigars,
The muscular one, and bid him whip
In kitchen cups concupiscent curds.
Let the wenches dawdle in such dress
As they are used to wear, and let the boys
Bring flowers in last month's newspapers.
Let be be finale of seem.
The only emperor is the emperor of ice-cream.

Take from the dresser of deal,
Lacking the three glass knobs, that sheet
On which she embroidered fantails once
And spread it so as to cover her face.
If her horny feet protrude, they come
To show how cold she is, and dumb.
Let the lamp affix its beam.
The only emperor is the emperor of ice-cream.

PETER QUINCE AT THE CLAVIER

1

Just as my fingers on these keys
Make music, so the self-same sounds   5
On my spirit make a music too.

Music is feeling then, not sound;
And thus it is that what I feel,
Here in this room, desiring you,   10

Thinking of your blue-shadowed silk,
Is music. It is like the strain
Waked in the elders by Susanna:[1]

Of a green evening, clear and warm,
She bathed in her still garden, while
The red-eyed elders, watching, felt

The basses of their being throb   20
In witching chords, and their thin blood
Pulse pizzicati of Hosanna.

2

In the green evening, clear and warm,   25
Susanna lay.
She searched
The touch of springs,
And found
Concealed imaginings.   30
She sighed,
For so much melody.

Upon the bank, she stood
In the cool
Of spent emotions.   35
She felt, among the leaves,
The dew
Of old devotions.

She walked upon the grass,
Still quavering.
The winds were like her maids
On timid feet,
Fetching her woven scarves,   45
Yet wavering.

A breath upon her hand
Muted the night.

---

[1] See *History of Susanna* in apochryphal books of Old Testament.

She turned—
A cymbal crashed,
And roaring horns.

3

Soon, with a noise like tambourines,
Came her attendant Byzantines.

They wondered why Susanna cried
Against the elders by her side;

And as they whispered, the refrain
Was like a willow swept by rain.

Anon their lamps' uplifted flame
Revealed Susanna and her shame.

And then the simpering Byzantines,
Fled, with a noise like tambourines.

4

Beauty is momentary in the mind—
The fitful tracing of a portal;
But in the flesh it is immortal.

The body dies; the body's beauty lives.
So evenings die, in their green going,
A wave, interminably flowing.

So gardens die, their meek breath scenting
The cowl of Winter, done repenting.
So maidens die to the auroral
Celebration of a maiden's choral.

Susanna's music touched the bawdy strings
Of those white elders; but, escaping,
Left only Death's ironic scraping.
Now in its immortality, it plays
On the clear viol of her memory,
And makes a constant sacrament of praise.

WITTER BYNNER

Bynner (1881–   ) began writing while he was at Harvard. His successive volumes showed a growing lyric talent. Living most of the time in New Mexico, Bynner has had the wisdom to use the Indian background of the region, thus opening up much unfamiliar material which is part of our national heritage. In another field Bynner has shown unusual interest—transla-

tion from the Chinese. Years ago he received much publicity for participating in a successful literary hoax in which the work of two "new" poets (using pseudonyms) appeared and was soberly reviewed.

WHITMAN*

As voices enter earth,
Into your great frame and windy beard
Have entered many voices,
And out of your great frame and windy beard,
As out of earth,
They are shaken free again . . .

With the thunder and the butterfly,
With the sea crossing like runners the tape of
    the beach,
With machinery and tools and the sweat of
    men,
With all lovers and comrades combining,
With the odour of redwoods and the whisper
    of death,
Comes your prophetic presence,
Never to be downed, never to be dissuaded
    from singing
The comfortable counsel of the earth
And from moving—athletic, intimate, sure,
    nonchalant—
Friending whoever is friends with himself,
Accusing only avoiders, tamperers, fabricators,
And yet touching with your finger-tips
All men,
As Michael-Angelo imagined God
Touching with sap the finger-tips of Adam.

A FARMER REMEMBERS
LINCOLN**

"Lincoln?—
Well, I was in the old Second Maine,
The first regiment in Washington from the Pine
    Tree State.

Of course I didn't get the butt of the clip;
We was there for guardin' Washington—
We was all green.

5 "I ain't never ben to but one theatre in my
    life—
I didn't know how to behave.
I ain't never ben since.
I can see as plain as my hat the box where he
10   sat in
When he was shot.
I can tell you, sir, there was a panic
When we found our President was in the shape
    he was in!
15 Never saw a soldier in the world but what
    liked him.

"Yes, sir. His looks was kind o' hard to forget.
He was a spare man,
20 An old farmer.
Everything was all right, you know,
But he wan't a smooth-appearin' man at all—
Not in no ways;
Thin-faced, long-necked,
25 And a swellin' kind of a thick lip like.

"And he was a jolly old fellow—always cheer-
    ful;
He wan't so high but the boys could talk to
30   him their own ways.
While I was servin' at the hospital,
He'd come in and say, "You look nice in here,"
Praise us up, you know.
And he'd bend over and talk to the boys—
35 And he'd talk so good to 'em—so close—
That's why I call him a farmer.
I don't mean that everything about him wan't
    all right, you understand,
It's just—well, I was a farmer—
40 And he was my neighbour, anybody's neigh-
    bour.

"I guess even you young folks would 'a' liked
    him."
45

A DANCE FOR RAIN

(COCHITI)

50 You may never see rain, unless you see
A dance for rain at Cochiti,[1]

    [1] near Santa Fe, N. M.

Never hear thunder in the air
Unless you hear the thunder there,
Nor know the lightning in the sky
If there's no pole to know it by.
They dipped the pole just as I came,   5
And I can never be the same
Since those feathers gave my brow
The touch of wind that's on it now,
Bringing over the arid lands
Butterfly gestures from Hopi hands   10
And holding me, till earth shall fail,
As close to earth as a fox's tail.

    I saw them, naked, dance in line
Before the candles of a leafy shrine: 15
Before a saint in a Christian dress
I saw them dance their holiness,
I saw them reminding him all day long
That death is weak and life is strong
And urging the fertile earth to yield   20
Seed from the loin and seed from the field.
A feather in the hair and a shell at the throat
Were lifting and falling with every note
Of the chorus-voices and the drum,
Calling for the rain to come.   25
A fox on the back, and shaken on the thigh
Rain-cloth woven from the sky,
And under the knee a turtle-rattle
Clacking with the toes of sheep and cattle—
These were the men, their bodies painted   30
Earthen, with a white rain slanted;
These were the men, a windy line,
Their elbows green with a growth of pine.
And in among them, close and slow,
Women moved, the way things grow,   35
With a mesa-tablet on the head
And a little grassy creeping tread
And with sprays of pine moved back and forth,
While the dance of the men blew from the
    north,   40
Blew from the south and east and west
Over the field and over the breast.
And the heart was beating in the drum,
Beating for the rain to come.

    Dead men out of earlier lives,   45
Leaving their graves, leaving their wives,
Were partly flesh and partly clay,
And their heads were corn that was dry and
    gray.   50
They were ghosts of men and once again
They were dancing like a ghost of rain;

For the spirits of men, the more they eat,
Have happier hands and lighter feet,
And the better they dance the better they
    know
How to make corn and children grow.   5

    And so in Cochiti that day,
They slowly put the sun away
And they made a cloud and they made it break
And they made it rain for the children's sake.   10
And they never stopped the song or the drum
Pounding for the rain to come.

    The rain made many suns to shine,
Golden bodies in a line   15
With leaping feather and swaying pine.
And the brighter the bodies, the brighter the
    rain
Where thunder heaped it on the plain.
Arroyos had been empty, dry,   20
But now were running with the sky;
And the dancers' feet were in a lake,
Dancing for the people's sake.
And the hands of a ghost had made a cup
For scooping handfuls of water up;   25
And he poured it into a ghostly throat,
And he leaped and waved with every note
Of the dancers' feet and the songs of the drum
That had called the rain and made it come.

    For this was not a god of wood,
This was a god whose touch was good,
You could lie down in him and roll
And wet your body and wet your soul;
For this was not a god in a book,   35
This was a god that you tasted and took
Into a cup that you made with your hands,
Into your children and into your lands,
This was a god that you could see,
Rain, rain, in Cochiti!   40

SARA TEASDALE

*Sara Teasdale (1884–1933) sometimes reads
like a later Christina Rossetti or an early Millay; she wrote personally in a tradition of female frankness which Emily Dickinson established. Like Emily, Sara lived in obscurity—in*   50
*her case, however, because her marriage had
failed. She, too, was a prolific writer with
much public favor. Her mood poetry shows*

great capability and marked clarity. She kept away from external questions but, while singing her own emotions, reached universal desires and frustrations. Her strange and premature death stopped abruptly a voice which must have had more lovely things to say.

BURIED LOVE*

I have come to bury Love
    Beneath a tree,
In the forest tall and black
    Where none can see.

I shall put no flowers at his head,
    Nor stone at his feet,
For the mouth I loved so much
    Was bittersweet.

I shall go no more to his grave,
    For the woods are cold.
I shall gather as much of joy
    As my hands can hold.

I shall stay all day in the sun
    Where the wide winds blow,—
But oh, I shall cry at night
    When none will know.

I SHALL NOT CARE

When I am dead and over me bright April
    Shakes out her rain-drenched hair,
Though you should lean above me broken-
        hearted,
    I shall not care.

I shall have peace, as leafy trees are peaceful
    When rain bends down the bough,
And I shall be more silent and cold-hearted
    Than you are now.

BARTER

Life has loveliness to sell,
    All beautiful and splendid things,
Blue waves whitened on a cliff,

Soaring fire that sways and sings,
And children's faces looking up,
Holding wonder like a cup.

Life has loveliness to sell,
    Music like a curve of gold,
Scent of pine trees in the rain,
    Eyes that love you, arms that hold,
And for your spirit's still delight,
Holy thoughts that star the night.

Spend all you have for loveliness,
    Buy it and never count the cost;
For one white singing hour of peace
    Count many a year of strife well lost,
And for a breath of ecstasy
Give all you have been, or could be.

WISDOM

It was a night of early spring,
    The winter-sleep was scarcely broken;
Around us shadows and the wind
    Listened for what was never spoken.

Though half a score of years are gone,
    Spring comes as sharply now as then—
But if we had it all to do
    It would be done the same again.

It was a spring that never came;
    But we have lived enough to know
That what we never have, remains;
    It is the things we have that go.

ELINOR WYLIE

Elinor Wylie (1885–1928) came from an old, distinguished family. She was born in Society (Washington, D. C.) and lived in it. After an uneven love life marked by romantic elopement she married the poet, William Rose Benét (her third husband). Well read, educated in private schools, Miss Wylie displayed her erudition in novels and poems wherein the influence of Shelley, Peacock, and Donne is particularly marked. (As Keats was to Amy Lowell, Shelley was to Elinor Wylie.) Her romantic work was first published in England, but she eventually won fame in the land of her birth. (For further biographical details see II, 380.)

---

* "Buried Love" is from Sara Teasdale, *Helen of Troy & Other Poems,* copyright, 1911. The other three poems are from Sara Teasdale, *Collected Poems,* copyright, 1937. All are reprinted by permission of The Macmillan Company, publishers.

Possessing an unusual mind and strong emo-
tions, the poet managed to avoid pure feeling
or dry intellectualism by steering a melodious
*middle course.** 5

THE EAGLE AND THE MOLE

Avoid the reeking herd,
Shun the polluted flock,
Live like that stoic bird, 10
The eagle of the rock.

The huddled warmth of crowds
Begets and fosters hate;
He keeps, above the clouds, 15
His cliff inviolate.

When flocks are folded warm,
And herds to shelter run,
He sails above the storm, 20
He stares into the sun.

If in the eagle's track
Your sinews cannot leap,
Avoid the lathered pack, 25
Turn from the steaming sheep.

If you would keep your soul
From spotted sight or sound,
Live like the velvet mole; 30
Go burrow underground.

And there hold intercourse
With roots of trees and stones,
With rivers at their source, 35
And disembodied bones.

COLD-BLOODED CREATURES

Man, the egregious egoist 40
(In mystery the twig is bent),
Imagines, by some mental twist,
That he alone is sentient

Of the intolerable load 45

Which on all living creatures lies,
Nor stoops to pity in the toad
The speechless sorrow of its eyes.

He asks no questions of the snake,
Nor plumbs the phosphorescent gloom
Where lidless fishes, broad awake,
Swim staring at a night-mare doom.

VELVET SHOES

Let us walk in the white snow
    In a soundless space;
With footsteps quiet and slow,
    At a tranquil pace,
    Under veils of white lace.

I shall go shod in silk,
    And you in wool,
White as a white cow's milk,
    More beautiful
    Than the breast of a gull.

We shall walk through the still town
    In a windless peace;
We shall step upon white down,
    Upon silver fleece,
    Upon softer than these.

We shall walk in velvet shoes:
    Wherever we go
Silence will fall like dews
    On white silence below.
    We shall walk in the snow.

LOVE SONG

Had I concealed my love
And you so loved me longer,
Since all the wise reprove
Confession of that hunger
In any human creature,
It had not been my nature.

I could not so insult
The beauty of that spirit
Who like a thunderbolt
Has broken me, or near it;
To love I have been candid,
Honest, and open-handed.

Although I love you well
And shall for ever love you,
I set that archangel
The depths of heaven above you;
And I shall lose you, keeping   5
His word, and no more weeping.

SIEGFRIED SASSOON

Sassoon (1886–   ), a Cambridge man, be-
came one of the outstanding young poets of
World War I. Although he was decorated for
valiant performance, he rarely found war any-
thing but a nightmare of folly. His attitude of
indignation and bitterness over the horrors of
modern warfare is at the opposite pole from
Rupert Brooke's. With peace Sassoon could
resume a more pleasant life which included
fox hunting, a sport which gives title to his
Memoirs of a Fox-Hunting Man. During
World War II he moderated his earlier stand
and campaigned vigorously to awake Britain to
*the necessity for all-out defense.**

THE REAR-GUARD

Groping along the tunnel, step by step,
He winked his prying torch with patching
     glare
From side to side, and sniffed the unwhole-
     some air.
Tins, boxes, bottles, shapes too vague to know,
A mirror smashed, the mattress from a bed;
And he, exploring fifty feet below
The rosy gloom of battle overhead.
Tripping, he grabbed the wall; saw someone
     lie
Humped at his feet, half-hidden by a rug,
And stooped to give the sleeper's arm a tug.
"I'm looking for headquarters." No reply.
"God blast your neck!" (For days he'd had no
     sleep.)
"Get up and guide me through this stinking
     place."
Savage, he kicked a soft, unanswering heap,
And flashed his beam across the livid face
Terribly glaring up, whose eyes yet wore
Agony dying hard ten days before;
And fists of fingers clutched a blackening

* The poems which follow are from *Counter*
Attack, published by E. P. Dutton & Co., Inc.
Copyright, 1940, by Siegfried Sassoon.

wound.
Alone he staggered on until he found
Dawn's ghost that filtered down a shafted stair
To the dazed, muttering creatures under-
     ground   5
Who hear the boom of shells in muffled sound.
At last, with sweat of horror in his hair,
He climbed through darkness to the twilight
     air,
Unloading hell behind him step by step.   10

COUNTER-ATTACK

We'd gained our first objective hours before
While dawn broke like a face with blinking   15
     eyes,
Pallid, unshaved and thirsty, blind with smoke.
Things seemed all right at first. We held their
     line,
With bombers posted, Lewis guns well placed, 20
And clink of shovels deepening the shallow
     trench.
The place was rotten with dead; green clumsy
     legs
High-booted, sprawled and groveled along the 25
     saps;
And trunks, face downward in the sucking
     mud,
Wallowed like trodden sand-bags, loosely
     filled;   30
And naked, sodden buttocks, mats of hair,
Bulged, clotted heads, slept in the plastering
     slime.
And then the rain began—the jolly old rain!
                                                 35
A yawning soldier knelt against the bank,
Staring across the morning blear with fog;
He wondered when the Allemands would get
     busy;
And then, of course, they started with five-   40
     nines
Traversing, sure as fate, and never a dud.
Mute in the clamor of shells he watched them
     burst
Spouting dark earth and wire with gusts from   45
     hell,
While posturing giants dissolved in drifts of
     smoke.
He crouched and flinched, dizzy with gallop-
     ing fear,   50
Sick for escape,—loathing the strangled horror
And butchered, frantic gestures of the dead.

An officer came blundering down the trench:
"Stand-to and man the fire-step!" On he
went. . . .
Gasping and bawling, "Fire-step . . . counter-
attack!"
Then the haze lifted. Bombing on the right   5
Down the old sap: machine guns on the left;
And stumbling figures looming out in front.
"O Christ, they're coming at us!" Bullets spat,
And he remembered his rifle . . . rapid   10
fire . . .
And started blazing wildly . . . then a bang
Crumpled and spun him sideways, knocked
him out
To grunt and wriggle: none heeded him; he   15
choked
And fought the flapping veils of smothering
gloom,
Lost in a blurred confusion of yells and
groans . . .   20
Down, and down, and down, he sank and
drowned,
Bleeding to death. The counter-attack had
failed.

DOES IT MATTER?

Does it matter?—losing your leg? . . .
For people will always be kind,
And you need not show that you mind   30
When the others come in after hunting
To gobble their muffins and eggs.

Does it matter?—losing your sight? . . .
There's such splendid work for the blind;   35
And people will always be kind,
As you sit on the terrace remembering
And turning your face to the light.

Do they matter?—those dreams from the   40
pit? . . .
You can drink and forget and be glad,
And people won't say that you're mad;
For they'll know that you've fought for your
country,   45
And no one will worry a bit.

RUPERT BROOKE

*Brilliant and promising member of an unusu-
ally gifted group of young British war poets,
Brooke (1887–1915) died of illness on his way
to the Dardanelles. His verses are remarkable
for their spirit of youth, their basic idealism,
patriotism, and sheer singing joy in life; his attitude toward war, perhaps because he did not
live to see much of it, is in sharp contrast to the
tired cynicism, however justifiable, of Sassoon
and Owen.**

THE GREAT LOVER

I have been so great a lover: filled my days
So proudly with the splendor of Love's praise,
The pain, the calm, and the astonishment,
Desire illimitable, and still content,
And all dear names men use, to cheat despair,   5
For the perplexed and viewless streams that
bear
Our hearts at random down the dark of life.
Now, ere the unthinking silence on that strife
Steals down, I would cheat drowsy Death so   20
far,
My night shall be remembered for a star
That outshone all the suns of all men's days.
Shall I not crown them with immortal praise
Whom I have loved, who have given me, dared   25
with me
High secrets, and in darkness knelt to see
The inenarrable[1] godhead of delight?
Love is a flame:—we have beaconed the
world's night.
A city:—and we have built it, these and I.
An emperor:—we have taught the world to
die.
So, for their sakes I loved, ere I go hence,
And the high cause of Love's magnificence,   35
And to keep loyalties young, I'll write those
names
Golden for ever, eagles, crying flames,
And set them as a banner, that men may
know,   40
To dare the generations, burn, and blow
Out on the wind of Time, shining and stream-
ing. . . .

These I have loved: 45
    White plates and cups, clean-gleaming,

[1] indescribable.

Ringed with blue lines; and feathery, faëry
  dust;
Wet roofs, beneath the lamp-light; the strong
  crust
Of friendly bread; and many-tasting food;
Rainbows; and the blue bitter smoke of wood;
And radiant raindrops couching in cool flow-
  ers;
And flowers themselves, that sway through
  sunny hours,
Dreaming of moths that drink them under the
  moon;
Then, the cool kindliness of sheets, that soon
Smooth away trouble; and the rough male kiss
Of blankets; grainy wood; live hair that is
Shining and free; blue-massing clouds; the
  keen
Unpassioned beauty of a great machine;
The benison of hot water; furs to touch;
The good smell of old clothes; and other
  such—
The comfortable smell of friendly fingers,
Hair's fragrance, and the musty reek that
  lingers
About dead leaves and last year's ferns. . . .

                        Dear names,
And thousand others throng to me! Royal
  flames;
Sweet water's dimpling laugh from tap or
  spring;
Holes in the ground; and voices that do sing:
Voices in laughter, too; and body's pain,
Soon turned to peace; and the deep-panting
  train;
Firm sands; the little dulling edge of foam
That browns and dwindles as the wave goes
  home;
And washen stones, gay for an hour; the cold
Graveness of iron; moist black earthen mold;
Sleep; and high places; footprints in the dew;
And oaks; and brown horse-chestnuts, glossy-
  new;
And new-peeled sticks; and shining pools on
  grass;—
All these have been my loves. And these shall
  pass,
Whatever passes not, in the great hour,
Nor all my passion, all my prayers, have
  power
To hold them with me through the gate of
  Death.

They'll play deserter, turn with the traitor
  breath,
Break the high bond we made, and sell Love's
  trust
And sacramental covenant to the dust.
—Oh, never a doubt but, somewhere, I shall
  wake,
And give what's left of love again, and make
New friends now strangers. . . .
                        But the best I've known
Stays here, and changes, breaks, grows old, is
  blown
About the winds of the world, and fades from
  brains
Of living men, and dies.
                        Nothing remains.

O dear my loves, O faithless, once again
This one last gift I give: that after men
Shall know, and later lovers, far-removed
Praise you, "All these were lovely"; say, "He
  loved."

THE DEAD

These hearts were woven of human joys and
  cares,
  Washed marvelously with sorrow, swift to
  mirth.
The years had given them kindness.
    Dawn was theirs,
  And sunset, and the colors of the earth.
These had seen movement, and heard music;
  known
  Slumber and waking; loved; gone proudly
  friended;
Felt the quick stir of wonder; sat alone;
  Touched flowers and furs and cheeks.
    All this is ended.
There are waters blown by changing winds to
  laughter
And lit by the rich skies, all day. And after,
  Frost, with a gesture, stays the waves that
  dance
And wandering loveliness. He leaves a white
  Unbroken glory, a gathered radiance,
  A width, a shining peace, under the night.

THE SOLDIER

If I should die, think only this of me;
  That there's some corner of a foreign field

That is for ever England. There shall be
  In that rich earth a richer dust concealed;
A dust whom England bore, shaped, made
    aware,
    Gave, once, her flowers to love, her ways to 5
      roam,
A body of England's breathing English air,
  Washed by the rivers, blest by suns of home.

And think, this heart, all evil shed away, 10
  A pulse in the eternal mind, no less
    Gives somewhere back the thoughts by
      England given;
Her sights and sounds; dreams happy as her
    day; 15
  And laughter, learnt of friends; and gentle-
    ness,
    In hearts at peace, under an English
      heaven. 20

ROBINSON JEFFERS

Jeffers (1887–   ) was schooled abroad and in America (Occidental College and University of Southern California). He might have been a 25 lawyer or some other type of professional man if interest in poetry and a timely legacy had not combined to woo him away to the shores of the Pacific, where he lives in a tower-house hewn out with his own hands. Roan Stallion 30 made his name known. There have been many other long poems impossible to anthologize for various reasons. Violent drama plays a large part in Jeffers's work. His characters have strong passions and lead unconventional lives. 35 Against the background of Carmel and Monterey trees, rocks, and sea Jeffers poses his men and women. Most of them are doomed; whatever life there is seems to be for those who live in an elemental state of emotion. Naturally 40 there are episodes of considerable power in Tamar, Thurso's Landing, and the rest; but there are also characters who are stupid or spineless instead of being tragic; and the stories tend to repeat ideas, situations, and words, 45 especially place names like Point Lobos, until the cumulative effect is not overwhelming, but monotonous. On the whole, as Untermeyer has said, it is "poetry we may never love but which we cannot forget." The shorter pieces which follow are rather conventional, unsensational (many readers of Jeffers are not interested in

*poetry but in another form of vicarious experience), yet illustrative of the poet's abilities.**

SHINE, PERISHING REPUBLIC

While this America settles in the mould of its
    vulgarity,
  heavily thickening to empire,
And protest, only a bubble in the molten mass,
    pops and
  sighs out, and the mass hardens,

I sadly remember that the flower fades to
    make fruit,
  the fruit rots to make earth.
Out of the mother; and through the spring
    exultances,
  ripeness and decadence; and home to the
    mother.

You making haste haste on decay: not blame-
    worthy; life is
  good, be it stubbornly long or suddenly
A mortal splendor: meteors are not needed
    less than
  mountains: shine, perishing republic.

But for my children, I would rather have them
    keep their distance
  from the thickening center; corruption
Never has been compulsory, when the cities
    lie at the
  monster's feet there are left the mountains.

And boys, be in nothing so moderate as in love
    of man, a
  clever servant, insufferable master.
There is the trap that catches noblest spirits,
    that caught—
  they say—God, when he walked on earth.

NEW MEXICAN MOUNTAIN

I watch the Indians dancing to help the young
    corn at Taos
  pueblo. The old men squat in a ring
And make the song, the young women with fat
    bare arms, and a

        ————

few shame-faced young men, shuffle the dance.

The lean-muscled young men are naked to the narrow loins,
their breasts and backs daubed with white clay,
Two eagle-feathers plume the black heads. They dance with
reluctance, they are growing civilized; the old men persuade them.

Only the drum is confident, it thinks the world has not changed;
the beating heart, the simplest of rhythms,
It thinks the world has not changed at all; it is only a dreamer,
a brainless heart, the drum has no eyes.

These tourists have eyes, the hundred watching the dance, white
Americans, hungrily too, with reverence, not laughter;
Pilgrims from civilization, anxiously seeking beauty, religion,
poetry; pilgrims from the vacuum.

People from cities, anxious to be human again. Poor show how
they suck you empty! The Indians are emptied,
And certainly there was never religion enough, nor beauty nor
poetry here . . . to fill Americans.

Only the drum is confident, it thinks the world has not changed.
Apparently only myself and the strong
Tribal drum, and the rockhead of Taos mountain, remember
that civilization is a transient sickness.

BOATS IN A FOG

Sports and gallantries, the stage, the arts, the antics of dancers,
The exuberant voices of music,
Have charm for children but lack nobility; it is bitter earnestness
That makes beauty; the mind
Knows, grown adult.
　　A sudden fog-drift muffled the ocean,

A throbbing of engines moved in it,
At length, a stone's throw out, between the rocks and the vapor,
One by one moved shadows
5 Out of the mystery, shadows, fishing-boats, trailing each other
Following the cliff for guidance,
Holding a difficult path between the peril of the sea-fog
10 And the foam on the shore granite.
One by one, trailing their leader, six crept by me,
Out of the vapor and into it,
The throb of their engines subdued by the fog,
15 patient and cautious,
Coasting all round the peninsula
Back to the buoys in Monterey harbor. A flight of pelicans
Is nothing lovelier to look at;
20 The flight of the planets is nothing nobler; all the arts lose virtue
Against the essential reality
Of creatures going about their business among the equally
25 Earnest elements of nature.

HOPE IS NOT FOR THE WISE

30 Hope is not for the wise, fear is for fools;
Change and the world, we think, are racing to a fall,
Open-eyed and helpless, in every newscast that is the news:
35 The time's events would seem mere chaos but all
Drift the one deadly direction. But this is only
The August thunder of the age, not the November.
40 Wise men hope nothing, the wise are naturally lonely
And think November as good as April, the wise remember
That Caesar and even final Augustulus had
45 heirs,
And men lived on; rich unplanned life on earth
After the foreign wars and the civil wars, the border wars
And the barbarians: music and religion, honor
50 and mirth
Renewed life's lost enchantments. But if life even

Had perished utterly, Oh perfect loveliness of
    earth and heaven.

T. S. ELIOT

*T. S. Eliot (1888–   ) is among the most dis-
cussed of modern American poets. After being
exposed to Harvard and Oxford, Eliot did lecturing and editing in London, and eventually
became a British subject. He has published
poetry and criticism and has lectured on both
sides of the Atlantic. His poems have been attacked by some for their obscurity, their lack
of music or joy; they have been called "devoid
of beauty," "over-intellectual," etc. Certainly
Eliot is rich in allusion and symbolism.
Whether the pleasure of recognizing his allusions is a poetic experience (or merely an expression of egotistic delight); what the ratio of
beauty to intellectualism is; how many people
have to appreciate a poet to justify his being
taken seriously, and what people—these are
some questions for the student to consider.
Even Eliot seems to be uncertain, to be tortured with the doubts of Donne. The former
prophet of the Waste Land has shown signs of
going back to God; the critic who blasted Milton is now praising his strength. For better or
worse, Eliot has had an effect on other poets
and has shaken off many conventional bonds of
subject matter and technique. Whether one
likes or dislikes his work, it won for the poet
a Nobel Prize in 1948.** *

THE LOVE SONG OF J. ALFRED
PRUFROCK

*S'io credesse che mia risposta fosse
A persona che mai tornasse al mondo,
Questa fiamma staria senza piu scosse.
Ma perciocche giammai di questo fondo
Non torno vivo alcun, s'i'odo il vero,
Senza tema d'infamia ti rispondo.*[1]

---

* The selections which follow are from *Collected
Poems 1909–1935* by T. S. Eliot, copyright, 1934,
1936, by Harcourt, Brace and Company, Inc. Reprinted by permission of Harcourt, Brace, and of
Faber and Faber, Ltd.
[1] See Dante's *Inferno,* XXVII, 61–66. Freely
translated, this speech of Guido da Montefeltro
reads: "If I thought that I were answering some-

Let us go then, you and I,
When the evening is spread out against the sky
Like a patient etherized upon a table;
Let us go, through certain half-deserted
    streets,
5 The muttering retreats
Of restless nights in one-night cheap hotels
And sawdust restaurants with oyster-shells:
Streets that follow like a tedious argument
10 Of insidious intent
To lead you to an overwhelming ques-
    tion. . . .
Oh, do not ask, "What is it?"
Let us go and make our visit.

15 In the room the women come and go
Talking of Michelangelo.

The yellow fog that rubs its back upon the
    window-panes,
20 The yellow smoke that rubs its muzzle on the
    window-panes,
Licked its tongue into the corners of the eve-
    ning,
25 Lingered upon the pools that stand in drains,
Let fall upon its back the soot that falls from
    chimneys,
Slipped by the terrace, made a sudden leap,
And seeing that it was a soft October night,
30 Curled once about the house, and fell asleep.

And indeed there will be time
For the yellow smoke that slides along the
    street,
35 Rubbing its back upon the window panes;
There will be time, there will be time
To prepare a face to meet the faces that you
    meet;
There will be time to murder and create,
40 And time for all the works and days of hands
That lift and drop a question on your plate;
Time for you and time for me,
And time yet for a hundred indecisions,
And for a hundred visions and revisions,
45 Before the taking of a toast and tea.

In the room the women come and go
Talking of Michelangelo.

---

one who could ever go back to the world, this
flame would stand still. But since, if I have been
correctly informed, nobody ever did return, I reply without fear of infamy."

And indeed there will be time
To wonder, "Do I dare?" and, "Do I dare?"
Time to turn back and descend the stair,
With a bald spot in the middle of my hair—
(They will say: "How his hair is growing   5
    thin!")
My morning coat, my collar mounting firmly to
    the chin,
My necktie rich and modest, but asserted by a
    simple pin—
(They will say: "But how his arms and legs   10
are thin!")
Do I dare
Disturb the universe?
In a minute there is time
For decisions and revisions which a minute   15
will reverse.

For I have known them all already, known
    them all:
Have known the evenings, mornings, after-
    noons,
I have measured out my life with coffee
    spoons;
I know the voices dying with a dying fall
Beneath the music from a farther room.
    So how should I presume?

And I have known the eyes already, known
    them all—   30
The eyes that fix you in a formulated phrase,
And when I am formulated, sprawling on a
    pin,
When I am pinned and wriggling on the wall,
Then how should I begin   35
To spit out all the butt-ends of my days and
    ways?
    And how should I presume?

And I have known the arms already, known   40
    them all—
Arms that are braceleted and white and bare
(But in the lamplight, downed with light
    brown hair!)
Is it perfume from a dress
That makes me so digress?   45
Arms that lie along a table, or wrap about a
    shawl,
    And should I then presume?
    And how should I begin?

.   .   .   .

Shall I say, I have gone at dusk through nar-

row streets
And watched the smoke that rises from the
    pipes
Of lonely men in shirt-sleeves, leaning out of
    windows? . . .

I should have been a pair of ragged claws
Scuttling across the floors of silent seas.

.   .   .   .

And the afternoon, the evening, sleeps so   10
    peacefully!
Smoothed by long fingers,
Asleep . . . tired . . . or it malingers,
Stretched on the floor, here beside you and me.
Should I, after tea and cakes and ices,   15
Have the strength to force the moment to its
    crisis?
But though I have wept and fasted, wept and
    prayed,
Though I have seen my head (grown slightly   20
    bald) brought in upon a platter,
I am no prophet—and here's no great matter;
I have seen the moment of my greatness
    flicker,
And I have seen the eternal Footman hold my   25
    coat, and snicker,
And in short, I was afraid.

And would it have been worth it, after all,
After the cups, the marmalade, the tea,   30
Among the porcelain, among some talk of you
    and me,
Would it have been worth while,
To have bitten off the matter with a smile,
To have squeezed the universe into a ball   35
To roll it toward some overwhelming question,
To say: "I am Lazarus, come from the dead,
Come back to tell you all, I shall tell you all"—
If one, settling a pillow by her head,
    Should say: "That is not what I meant at all;   40
    That is not it, at all."

And would it have been worth it, after all,
Would it have been worth while,
After the sunsets and the dooryards and the   45
    sprinkled streets,
After the novels, after the teacups, after the
    skirts that trail along the floor—
And this, and so much more?—
It is impossible to say just what I mean!   50
But as if a magic lantern threw the nerves in
    patterns on a screen:

Would it have been worth while
If one, settling a pillow or throwing off a
   shawl,
And turning toward the window, should say:
  "That is not it at all,
  That is not what I meant, at all."

    .   .   .   .   .   .

No! I am not Prince Hamlet, nor was meant to
   be;
Am an attendant lord, one that will do
To swell a progress, start a scene or two,
Advise the prince; no doubt, an easy tool.
Deferential, glad to be of use,
Politic, cautious, and meticulous;
Full of high sentence, but a bit obtuse;
At times, indeed, almost ridiculous—
Almost, at times, the Fool.

I grow old. . . . I grow old. . . .
I shall wear the bottoms of my trousers rolled. 20

Shall I part my hair behind? Do I dare to eat a
   peach?
I shall wear white flannel trousers, and walk
   upon the beach.
I have heard the mermaids singing, each to
   each.

I do not think that they will sing to me.

I have seen them riding seaward on the waves
Combing the white hair of the waves blown
   back
When the wind blows the water white and
   black.

We have lingered in the chambers of the sea
By sea-girls wreathed with seaweed red and
   brown
Till human voices wake us, and we drown. 40

THE HOLLOW MEN

Mistah Kurtz—he dead[1]

              A penny for the Old Guy[2] 45

1

We are the hollow men
We are the stuffed men

---
[1] a line from Conrad, apparently to set the mood.
[2] phrase used by English children on Guy Fawkes
Day.

Leaning together
Headpiece filled with straw. Alas!
Our dried voices, when
We whisper together
Are quiet and meaningless 5
As wind in dry grass
Or rats' feet over broken glass
In our dry cellar

Shape without form, shade without color, 10
Paralyzed force, gesture without motion;

Those who have crossed
With direct eyes, to death's other Kingdom
Remember us—if at all—not as lost 15
Violent souls, but only
As the hollow men
The stuffed men.

2

Eyes I dare not meet in dreams
In death's dream kingdom
These do not appear:
There, the eyes are
Sunlight on a broken column 25
There, is a tree swinging
And voices are
In the wind's singing
More distant and more solemn
Than a fading star. 30

Let me be no nearer
In death's dream kingdom
Let me also wear
Such deliberate disguises 35
Rat's coat, crowskin, crossed staves
In a field
Behaving as the wind behaves
No nearer—

Not that final meeting
In the twilight kingdom

3

This is the dead land 45
This is cactus land
Here the stony images
Are raised, here they receive
The supplication of a dead man's hand
Under the twinkle of a fading star. 50

Is it like this

In death's other kingdom
Waking alone
At the hour when we are
Trembling with tenderness
Lips that would kiss
From prayers to broken stone.

4

The eyes are not here
There are no eyes here
In this valley of dying stars
In this hollow valley
This broken jaw of our lost kingdoms

In this last of meeting places
We grope together
And avoid speech
Gathered on this beach of the tumid river

Sightless, unless
The eyes reappear
As the perpetual star
Multifoliate rose
Of death's twilight kingdom
The hope only
Of empty men.

5

Here we go round the prickly pear
Prickly pear prickly pear
Here we go round the prickly pear
At five o'clock in the morning.

Between the idea
And the reality
Between the motion
And the act
Falls the Shadow

For Thine is the Kingdom

Between the conception
And the creation
Between the emotion
And the response
Falls the Shadow

Life is very long

Between the desire
And the spasm
Between the potency

And the existence
Between the essence
And the descent
Falls the Shadow 5

For Thine is the Kingdom

For Thine is
Life is
10 For Thine is the

This is the way the world ends
This is the way the world ends
This is the way the world ends
15 *Not with a bang but a whimper.*

JOURNEY OF THE MAGI

20 "A cold coming we had of it,
Just the worst time of the year
For a journey, and such a long journey:
The ways deep and the weather sharp,
The very dead of winter."
25 And the camels galled, sore-footed, refractory,
Lying down in the melting snow.
There were times we regretted
The summer palaces on slopes, the terraces,
And the silken girls bringing sherbet.
30 Then the camel men cursing and grumbling
And running away, and wanting their liquor
and women,
And the night-fires going out, and the lack of
shelters,
35 And the cities hostile and the towns unfriendly
And the villages dirty and charging high
prices:
A hard time we had of it.
At the end we preferred to travel all night,
40 Sleeping in snatches,
With the voices singing in our ears, saying
That this was all folly.

Then at dawn we came down to a temperate
45 valley,
Wet, below the snow line, smelling of vegeta-
tion;
With a running stream and a water-mill beating the darkness,
50 And three trees on the low sky,
And an old white horse galloped away in the
meadow.

Then we came to a tavern with vine-leaves
over the lintel,
Six hands at an open door dicing for pieces of
silver,
And feet kicking the empty wine-skins. 5
But there was no information, and so we continued
And arriving at evening, not a moment too
soon
Finding the place; it was (you may say) satis- 10
factory.

All this was a long time ago, I remember,
And I would do it again, but set down
This set down
This: were we led all that way for 15
Birth or Death? There was a Birth, certainly,
We had evidence and no doubt. I had seen
birth and death,
But had thought they were different; this Birth 20
was
Hard and bitter agony for us, like Death, our
death.
We returned to our places, these Kingdoms,
But no longer at ease here, in the old dispensa- 25
tion,
With an alien people clutching their gods.
I should be glad of another death.

30

JOHN CROWE RANSOM*

SURVEY OF LITERATURE

In all the good Greek of Plato
I lack my roast beef and potato. 35

A better man with Aristotle,
Pulling steady on the bottle.

I dip my hat to Chaucer
Swilling soup from his saucer, 40

And to Master Shakespeare
Who wrote big on small beer. 45

The abstemious Wordsworth
Subsisted on a curd's-worth,

But a slick one was Tennyson,
Putting gravy on his venison.

What these men had to eat and drink
Is what we say and what we think.

The flatulence of Milton
Come out of wry Stilton.

Sing a song for Percy Shelley,
Drowned in pale lemon jelly,

And for precious John Keats,
Dripping blood of pickled beets.

Then there was poor Willie Blake,
He foundered on sweet cake.

God have mercy on the sinner
Who must write with no dinner,

No gravy and no grub,
No pewter and no pub,

No belly and no bowels,
Only consonants and vowels.

HERE LIES A LADY

Here lies a lady of beauty and high degree.
Of chills and fever she died, of fever and chills,
The delight of her husband, her aunts, an in-
fant of three,
And of medicos marvelling sweetly on her ills.

For either she burned, and her confident eyes 40
would blaze,
And her fingers fly in a manner to puzzle their
heads—
What was she making? Why, nothing; she sat
in a maze
Of old scraps of laces, snipped into curious
shreds—

Or this would pass, and the light of her fire de- 50
cline
Till she lay discouraged and cold as a thin stalk
white and blown,

And would not open her eyes, to kisses, to
wine;
The sixth of these states was her last; the cold
settled down.

Sweet ladies, long may ye bloom, and toughly
I hope ye may thole,
But was she not lucky? In flowers and lace and
mourning,
In love and great honour we bade God rest her
soul
After six little spaces of chill, and six of burn-
ing.

THE EQUILIBRISTS

Full of her long white arms and milky skin
He had a thousand times remembered sin.
Alone in the press of people traveled he,
Minding her jacinth, and myrrh, and ivory.

Mouth he remembered: the quaint orifice
From which came heat that flamed upon the
kiss,
Till cold words came down spiral from the
head,
Grey doves from the officious tower illsped.

Body: it was a white field ready for love,
On her body's field, with the gaunt tower
above,
The lilies grew, beseeching him to take,
If he would pluck and wear them, bruise and
break.

Eyes talking: Never mind the cruel words,
Embrace my flowers, but not embrace the
swords.
But what they said, the doves come straight-
way flying
And unsaid: Honor, Honor, they came crying.

Importunate her doves. Too pure, too wise,
Clambering on his shoulder, saying, Arise,
Leave me now, and never let us meet,
Eternal distance now command thy feet.

Predicament indeed, which thus discovers
Honor among thieves, Honor between lovers.
O such a little word is Honor, they feel!
But the grey word is between them cold as
steel.

At length I saw these lovers fully were come
Into their torture of equilibrium;
Dreadfully had forsworn each other, and yet
They were bound each to each, and they did
not forget.

And rigid as two painful stars, and twirled
About the clustered night their prison world,
They burned with fierce love always to come
near,
But Honor beat them back and kept them
clear.

Ah, the strict lovers, they are ruined now!
I cried in anger. But with puddled brow
Devising for those gibbeted and brave
Came I descanting: Man, what would you
have?

For spin your period out, and draw your
breath,
A kinder saeculum begins with Death.
Would you ascend to Heaven and bodiless
dwell?
Or take your bodies honorless to Hell?

In Heaven you have heard no marriage is,
No white flesh tinder to your lecheries,
Your male and female tissue sweetly shaped
Sublimed away, and furious blood escaped.

Great lovers lie in Hell, the stubborn ones
Infatuate of the flesh upon the bones;
Stuprate, they rend each other when they kiss,
The pieces kiss again, no end to this.

But still I watched them spinning, orbited
nice.
Their flames were not more radiant than their
ice.
I dug in the quiet earth and wrought the tomb
And made these lines to memorize their
doom:—

EPITAPH

Equilibrists lie here; stranger, tread light;
Close, but untouching in each other's sight;
Mouldered the lips and ashy the tall skull,
Let them lie perilous and beautiful.[1]

[1] Cf. Browning's "The Statue and the Bust,"
I, 162.

EDNA ST. VINCENT MILLAY

*Edna St. Vincent Millay (1892–   ) is the best-known living woman poet in America. Her reputation is securely based on several volumes (Renascence, Harp Weaver, Fatal Interview, for example), but it must be said that her most recent work has been overloaded with honest preaching rather than good poetry. A product of Vassar, Miss Millay is in the tradition of the emancipated woman singing freely of her joys and passions. Her best-known love sonnets are hardly profound, but they are nicely turned in a way that combines the lyric touch of the Elizabethans with a modern attitude toward an age-old subject. She has had great popular appeal, and has been commercially successful. During World War II the poet showed growth in ideas and sympathies, treating major issues long neglected; as poetry, however, the war pieces seemed more like sermons that merely happened to be in verse form. Miss Millay, along with Sara Teasdale, Elinor Wylie, and a half-dozen other able women whose names are familiar to anthologists, has done much for the cause of feminism in the arts; she has been especially popular with college students, who often find her particular work the stepping stone to enjoyment of poetry in general.**

WHAT LIPS MY LIPS HAVE KISSED

What lips my lips have kissed, and where, and why,
I have forgotten, and what arms have lain
Under my head till morning; but the rain
Is full of ghosts tonight, that tap and sigh
Upon the glass and listen for reply,
And in my heart there stirs a quiet pain
For unremembered lads that not again
Will turn to me at midnight with a cry.

Thus in the winter stands the lonely tree,
Nor knows what birds have vanished one by one,

* The first two poems are from *The Harp Weaver and Other Poems*, published by Harper & Brothers. Copyright, 1920, by Edna St. Vincent Millay. "Not in a Silver Casket Cool with Pearls" is from *Fatal Interview*, published by Harper & Brothers. Copyright, 1930, by Edna St. Vincent Millay.

Yet knows its boughs more silent than before:
I cannot say what loves have come and gone,
I only know that summer sang in me
A little while, that in me sings no more.

EUCLID ALONE HAS LOOKED ON BEAUTY BARE

Euclid alone has looked on Beauty bare.
Let all that prate of Beauty hold their peace,
And lay them prone upon the earth, and cease
To ponder on themselves, the while they stare
At nothing, intricately drawn nowhere
In shapes of shifting lineage. Let geese
Gabble and hiss, but heroes seek release
From dusty bondage into luminous air.

Oh, blinding hour—oh, holy terrible day—
When first the shaft into his vision shone
Of light anatomized! Euclid alone
Has looked on Beauty bare; fortunate they
Who though once only, and then but far away,
Have heard her massive sandal set on stone.

NOT IN A SILVER CASKET COOL WITH PEARLS

Not in a silver casket cool with pearls
Or rich with red corundum or with blue,
Locked, and the key withheld, as other girls
Have given their loves, I give my love to you;
Not in a lovers'-knot, not in a ring
Worked in such fashion, and the legend plain—
Semper fidelis, where a secret spring
Kennels a drop of mischief for the brain:
Love in the open hand, no thing but that,
Ungemmed, unhidden, wishing not to hurt,
As one should bring you cowslips in a hat
Swung from the hand, or apples in her skirt,
I bring you, calling out as children do:
"Look what I have!—And these are all for you."

WILFRED OWEN

Owen (1893–1918), another young British university man like Sassoon and Graves, went off to World War I, was invalided home, returned to action, won a decoration, and was killed in action a week before the Armistice. He may well stand in this collection for many young

British and American poets of both world wars who were tragically taken before they realized their potentialities. An experimental craftsman in words, Owen indicated in his war verse that he might well have become a major figure if he had lived.*

ANTHEM FOR DOOMED YOUTH

What passing-bells for these who die as cattle?
Only the monstrous anger of the guns.
Only the stuttering rifles' rapid rattle
Can patter out their hasty orisons.
No mockeries for them; no prayers nor bells,
Nor any voice of mourning save the choirs,— 15
The shrill, demented choirs of wailing shells;
And bugles calling for them from sad shires.

What candles may be held to speed them all?
Not in the hands of boys, but in their eyes 20
Shall shine the holy glimmers of good-bys.
The pallor of girls' brows shall be their pall;
Their flowers the tenderness of patient minds,
And each slow dusk a drawing-down of blinds.

DULCE ET DECORUM EST

Bent double, like old beggars under sacks,
Knock-kneed, coughing like hags, we cursed 30
  through sludge,
Till on the haunting flares we turned our
  backs,
And towards our distant rest began to trudge.
Men marched asleep. Many had lost their 35
  boots,
But limped on, blood-shod. All went lame, all
  blind;
Drunk with fatigue; deaf even to the hoots
Of gas-shells dropping softly behind.

Gas! Gas! Quick, boys!—An ecstasy of fum- 40
  bling,
Fitting the clumsy helmets just in time,
But someone still was yelling out and stum- 45
  bling
And flound'ring like a man in fire or lime.
Dim through the misty panes and thick green
  light,
As under a green sea, I saw him drowning. 50

In all my dreams before my helpless sight
He plunges at me, guttering, choking, drowning.

If in some smothering dreams, you too could 5
  pace
Behind the wagon that we flung him in,
And watch the white eyes wilting in his face,
His hanging face, like a devil's sick of sin,
If you could hear, at every jolt, the blood 10
Come gargling from the froth-corrupted lungs
Bitten as the cud
Of vile, incurable sores on innocent tongues,—
My friend, you would not tell with such high
  zest
To children ardent for some desperate glory,
The old lie: *Dulce et decorum est*
Pro patria mori.[1]

GREATER LOVE

Red lips are not so red
  As the stained stones kissed by the English
  dead.
Kindness of wooed and wooer
Seems shame to their love pure.
O Love, your eyes lose lure
  When I behold eyes blinded in my stead!

Your slender attitude
  Trembles not exquisite like limbs knife-
  skewed,
Rolling and rolling there
Where God seems not to care;
Till the fierce love they bear
  Cramps them in death's extreme decrepi-
  tude.

Your voice sings not so soft,—
  Though even as wind murmuring through
  raftered loft,—
Your dear voice is not clear,
Gentle, and evening clear,
As theirs whom none now hear
  Now earth has stopped their piteous mouths
  that coughed.

Heart, you were never hot,
  Nor large, nor full like hearts made great
  with shot;

* The poems which follow are reprinted by arrangement with Messrs. Chatto & Windus, London.

[1] It is sweet and fitting to die for one's country.

And though your hand be pale,
Paler are all which trail
Your cross through flame and hail:
    Weep, you may weep, for you may touch
      them not.   5

E. E. CUMMINGS

A Harvard man who saw service in World War 10
*I, Cummings (1894–   ) attracted attention
by his novel,* The Enormous Room, *which was
based on wartime prison experience. In poetry
he has received considerable publicity because
of extreme practices, such as not using capital* 15
*letters, and spraying words and letters hap-
hazardly over the page (he says this latter
method is an aid to correct stress in reading).
Cummings can be, by turns, sentimental or
cynical, pleasantly humorous or bitterly satir-* 20
*ical. He is obviously original and versatile; he
also draws and paints ably. And in spite of
box-office tactics that remind one of a show-
man, he has too many fine qualities to be called
a poseur. A psychiatrist might even find reason* 25
*to call him a frustrated romanticist; let the
reader test Cumming's printed works and decide which seem most sincere, most deeply felt.*

ALL IN GREEN WENT   30
MY LOVE RIDING*

All in green went my love riding
on a great horse of gold
into the silver dawn.   35

four lean hounds crouched low and smiling
the merry deer ran before.

Fleeter be they than dappled dreams   40
the swift sweet deer
the red rare deer.

Four red roebuck at a white water
the cruel bugle sang before.   45

Horn at hip went my love riding
riding the echo down
into the silver dawn.

four lean hounds crouched low and smiling
the level meadows ran before.

Softer be they than slippered sleep
the lean lithe deer
the fleet flown deer.

Four fleet does at a gold valley
the famished arrow sang before.

Bow at belt went my love riding
riding the mountain down
into the silver dawn.

four lean hounds crouched low and smiling
the sheer peaks ran before.

Paler be they than daunting death
the sleek slim deer
the tall tense deer.

Four tall stags at a green mountain
the lucky hunter sang before.

All in green went my love riding
on a great horse of gold
into the silver dawn.

four lean hounds crouched low and smiling
my heart fell dead before.

MY SWEET OLD ETCETERA*

my sweet old etcetera
aunt lucy during the recent

war could and what
is more did tell you just
what everybody was fighting

for,
my sister

isabel created hundreds
(and
hundreds) of socks not to
mention shirts fleaproof earwarmers

etcetera wristers etcetera, my
mother hoped that

i would die etcetera
bravely of course my father used
to become hoarse talking about how it was
a privilege and if only he
could meanwhile my

self etcetera lay quietly
in the deep mud et
cetera
(dreaming,
et
   cetera, of
Your smile
eyes knees and of your Etcetera)

I GO TO THIS WINDOW

i go to this window

just as day dissolves
when it is twilight (and
looking up in fear

i see the new moon
thinner than a hair)

making me feel
how myself has been coarse and dull
compared with you, silently who are
and cling
to my mind always

But now she sharpens and becomes crisper
until i smile with knowing
—and all about
herself

the sprouting largest final air

plunges inward with hurled
downward thousands of enormous dreams

ALLEN TATE

*Tate (1899–   ), like Ransom, is a Southerner
with agrarian-sectionalist philosophy (he has
written on Stonewall Jackson and Jefferson
Davis). His career is likewise linked with colleges: he has been a professor of English at the
University of the South, and editor of the
Sewanee Review. As a free-lance writer Tate
has published his polished verse, his essays,*
*and his criticism in many periodicals and
books. He is a careful poet, sometimes too metaphysical for average tastes, often harsh; but
his most effective work gets under the skin and
is not quickly forgotten. He seems to do in
poetry what Gamaliel Bradford does in biography (see II, 330)—he stalks around his subject, studies it, absorbs the "feel" of it, and then
gives forth a picture of its soul.*

ODE TO THE CONFEDERATE
DEAD

Row after row with strict impunity
15 The headstones yield their names to the ele-
    ment,
The wind whirrs without recollection;
In the riven troughs the splayed leaves
Pile up, of nature the casual sacrament
20 To the seasonal eternity of death,
Then driven by the fierce scrutiny
Of heaven to their business in the vast breath,
They sough the rumor of mortality.

25 Autumn is desolation in the plot
Of a thousand acres, where these memories
    grow
From the inexhaustible bodies that are not
Dead, but feed the grass row after rich row:
30 Remember now the autumns that have gone—
Ambitious November with the humors of the
    year,
With a particular zeal for every slab,
Staining the uncomfortable angels that rot
35 On the slabs, a wing chipped here, an arm
    there:
The brute curiosity of an angel's stare
Turns you like them to stone,
Transforms the heaving air,
40 Till plunged to a heavier world below
You shift your sea-space blindly,
Heaving, turning like the blind crab.

Dazed by the wind, only the wind
45 The leaves flying, plunge

You know who have waited by the wall
The twilit certainty of an animal;

* The selections which follow are reprinted from
Selected Poems by Allen Tate; copyright 1928,
1937 by Charles Scribner's Sons; used by permission of the publishers.

Those midnight restitutions of the blood
You know—the immitigable pines, the smoky frieze
Of the sky, the sudden call; you know the rage—
The cold pool left by the mounting flood—
The rage of Zeno and Parmenides.
You who have waited for the angry resolution
Of those desires that should be yours tomorrow,
You know the unimportant shrift of death
And praise the vision
And praise the arrogant circumstance
Of those who fall
Rank upon rank, hurried beyond decision—
Here by the sagging gate, stopped by the wall.

Seeing, seeing only the leaves
Flying, plunge and expire

Turn your eyes to the immoderate past
Turn to the inscrutable infantry rising
Demons out of the earth—they will not last.
Stonewall, Stonewall—and the sunken fields of hemp
Shiloh, Antietam, Malvern Hill, Bull Run.
Lost in that orient of the thick and fast
You will curse the setting sun.

Cursing only the leaves crying
Like an old man in a storm

You hear the shout—the crazy hemlocks point
With troubled fingers to the silence which
Smothers you, a mummy, in time. The hound bitch
Toothless and dying, in a musty cellar
Hears the wind only.
                    Now that the salt of their blood
Stiffens the saltier oblivion of the sea,
Seals the malignant purity of the flood,
What shall we, who count our days and bow
Our heads with a commemorial woe,
In the ribboned coats of grim felicity,
What shall we say of the bones, unclean—
Their verduous anonymity will grow—
The ragged arms, the ragged heads and eyes
Lost in these acres of the insane green?
The grey lean spiders come; they come and go;
In a tangle of willows without light

The singular screech-owl's bright
Invisible lyric seeds the mind
With the furious murmur of their chivalry.

5   We shall say only, the leaves
     Flying, plunge and expire

We shall say only, the leaves whispering
In the improbable mist of nightfall
10 That flies on multiple wing:
Night is the beginning and the end,
And in between the ends of distraction
Waits mute speculation, the patient curse
That stones the eyes, or like the jaguar leaps
15 For his own image in a jungle pool, his victim.
What shall we say who have knowledge
Carried to the heart? Shall we take the act
To the grave? Shall we, more hopeful, set up the grave
20   In the house? The ravenous grave?

                            Leave now
The turnstile and the old stone wall:
25 The gentle serpent, green in the mulberry bush,
Riots with his tongue through the hush—
Sentinel of the grave who counts us all!

30

IDIOT

The idiot greens the meadows with his eyes,
The meadow creeps implacable and still;
35 A dog barks, the hammock swings, he lies.
One two three the cows bulge on the hill.

Motion that is not time erects snowdrifts
While sister's hand sieves waterfalls of lace.
40 With a palm fan closer than death he lifts
The Ozarks and tilted seas across his face.

In the long sunset where impatient sound
Strips niggers to a multiple of backs
45 Flies yield their heat, magnolias drench the ground
With Appomattox! The shadows lie in stacks.

The julep glass weaves echoes in Jim's kinks
50 While ashy Jim puts murmurs in the day:
Now in the idiot's heart a chamber stinks
Of dead asters, as the potter's field of May.

All evening the marsh is a slick pool
Where dream wild hares, witch hazel, pretty
    girls.
"Up from the important picnic of a fool
Those rotted asters!" Eddy on eddy swirls   5

The innocent mansion of a panther's heart!
It crumbles, tick-tick time drags it in
Till now his arteries lag and now they start
Reverence with the frigid gusts of sin—   10

The stillness pelts the eye, assaults the hair;
A beech sticks out a branch to warm the stars,
A lightning-bug jerks angles in the air,
Diving. "I am the captain of new wars!"   15

The dusk runs down the lane driven like hail;
Far off a precise whistle is escheat
To the dark; and then the towering weak and
    pale   20
Covers his eyes with memory like a sheet.

THE MEDITERRANEAN

Quem das finem, rex magne, dolorum? [1]

Where we went in the boat was a long bay
A sling-shot wide walled in by towering
    stone—
Peaked margin of antiquity's delay,
And we went there out of time's monotone:

Where we went in the black hull no light
    moved
But a gull white-winged along the feckless   35
    wave;
The breeze unseen but fierce as a body loved,
That boat drove onward like a willing slave.

Where we went in the small ship the seaweed 40
Parted and gave to us the murmuring shore
And we made feast and in our secret need
Devoured the very plates Aeneas bore:

Where derelict you see through the low twi- 45
    light
The green coast that you thunder-tossed
    would win,

Drop sail, and hastening to drink all night
Eat dish and bowl—to take that sweet land in!

Where we feasted and caroused on the sand-
    less
Pebbles, affecting our day of piracy,
What prophecy of eaten plates could landless
Wanderers fulfill by the ancient sea?

We for that time might taste the famous age   10
Eternal here yet hidden from our eyes
When lust of power undid its stuffless rage;
They, in a wineskin, bore earth's paradise.

—Let us lie down once more by the breathing 15
    side
Of ocean, where our live forefathers sleep
As if the Known Sea still were a month wide—
Atlantis howls but is no longer steep!

What country shall we conquer, what fair land
Unman our conquest and locate our blood?
We've cracked the hemispheres with careless
    hand!
Now, from the Gates of Hercules we flood 25

Westward, westward till the barbarous brine
Whelms us to the tired world where tasseling
    corn,
Fat beans, grapes sweeter than muscadine 30
Rot on the vine: in that land were we born.

ROBERT PENN WARREN

Warren (1905–   ) follows the familiar pat-
tern of Ransom and Tate: the South; the Fugi-
tive; reviews (Southern and Kenyon); associa-
tion with colleges (Vanderbilt, California, Yale,
Oxford); teaching (Louisiana State and Minne-
sota). Although he is represented here by his
thoughtful verse, Warren has also written a
prose study of John Brown and has edited vari-
ous textbooks. After two or three early novels,
he made quite a stir with All the King's Men,
a novel based on the Huey Long saga, and has
also successfully invaded the short-story field.
As the youngest of the established Southern
group, with a brilliant academic record, War-
*ren has rich possibilities for the future.**

---

[1] What end of griefs, great king, do you give?
The line, ordinarily rendered *Quem das finem, rex magne, laborum?* is from the *Aeneid,* Bk. I, 1. 241.

* The selections which follow are from *Selected Poems 1923–1943* by Robert Penn Warren, copyright, 1944, by Harcourt, Brace and Company, Inc.

LETTER FROM A COWARD
TO A HERO

What did the day bring?
The sharp fragment,   5
The shard,
The promise half-meant,
The impaired thing,
At dusk the hard word,
Good action by good will marred . . .   10
All
In the trampled stall:
    I think you deserved better;
    Therefore I am writing you this letter.
The scenes of childhood were splendid,   15
And the light that there attended,
But is rescinded:
The cedar,
The lichened rocks,
The thicket where I saw the fox,   20
And where I swam, the river.
These things are hard
To reconstruct:
The word
Is memory's gelded usufruct.   25
But piety is simple,
And should be ample.
    Though late at night we have talked,
    I cannot see what ways your feet in child-
        hood walked.   30
    In what purlieus was courage early caulked?
Guns blaze in autumn and
The quail falls and
Empires collide with a bang
That shakes the pictures where they hang   35
And democracy shows signs of dry rot
And Dives[1] has and Lazarus not
And the time is out of joint:
But a good pointer holds the point
And is not gun-shy;   40
But I
Am gun-shy.

Though young, I do not like loud noise:
The sudden backfire,   45
The catcall of boys,
Drums beating for
The big war,
Or clocks that tick all night, and will not stop.
If you should lose your compass and map   50

[1] See Luke 16:19–31.

Or a mouse get into the wall,
For sleep try love or veronal,
Though some prefer, I know, philology.
Does the airman scream in the flaming tra-
    jectory?

You have been strong in love and hate.
Disaster owns less speed than you have got,
But he will cut across the back lot
To lurk and lie in wait.
Admired of children, gathered for their games,
Disaster, like the dandelion, blooms,
And the delicate film is fanned
To seed the shaven lawn.
Rarely, you've been unmanned;
I have not seen your courage put to pawn.

At the blind hour of unaided grief,
Of addition and subtraction,
Of compromise,
Of the smoky lecher, the thief,
Of regretted action,
At the hour to close the eyes,
At the hour when lights go out in the
    houses . . .
Then wind rouses
The kildees from their sodden ground:
Their commentary is part of the wind's sound.
What is that other sound,
Surf or distant cannonade?
You are what you are without our aid.
No doubt, when corridors are dumb
And the bed is made,
It is your custom to recline,
Clutching between the forefinger and thumb
Honor, for death shy valentine.

BEARDED OAKS

The oaks, how subtle and marine,
Bearded, and all the layered light
Above them swims; and thus the scene,
Recessed, awaits the positive night.

So, waiting, we in the grass now lie
Beneath the languorous tread of light:
The grasses, kelp-like, satisfy
The nameless motions of the air.

Upon the floor of light, and time,
Unmurmuring, of polyp made,

We rest; we are, as light withdraws,
Twin atolls on a shelf of shade.

Ages to our construction went,
Dim architecture, hour by hour: 5
And violence, forgot now, lent
The present stillness all its power.

The storm of noon above us rolled,
Of light the fury, furious gold,   10
The long drag troubling us, the depth:
Dark is unrocking, unrippling, still.

Passion and slaughter, ruth, decay
Descend, minutely whispering down,   15
Silted down swaying streams, to lay
Foundation for our voicelessness.

All our debate is voiceless here,
As all our rage, the rage of stone;   20
If hope is hopeless, then fearless fear,
And history is thus undone.

Our feet once wrought the hollow street
With echo when the lamps were dead   25
At windows, once our headlight glare
Disturbed the doe that, leaping, fled.

I do not love you less that now
The caged heart makes iron stroke,   30
Or less that all that light once gave
The graduate dark should now revoke.

We live in time so little time
And we learn all so painfully,   35
That we may spare this hour's term
To practice for eternity.

RESOLUTION

Time's secret pulse
The huddled jockey knows;
Between the bull's
Horns, as the cape flows,
The matador;   45
The pitcher on his mound,
Sun low, tied score;
The plowman when drouth-bit ground
Deflects the plow;
The pickpocket in the press.   50
Your pulse, these know;
But all than lovers less.

Than lovers less?
What word had touched the heart
I cannot guess:
It was a place apart,
Of rock and sea,
Salt grass, and the salt wind,
And wind-crooked tree.
Sun gilded sea and land,
Like golden rime.
I spoke of Time. You said:
There is no Time.
Since then some friends are dead;
Hates cold, once hot;
Ambitions thewless grown;
Old slights forgot:
And the weeper is made stone.
We, too, have lain
Apart, with continents
And seas between.
Your words' most brave contents
Came narrowly.
I tried to frame your face
In the mind's eye;
And could, a little space.
Though pondering it,
The chapters glad or sorry,
I can commit
No moral from our story.

Old winnower!
I praise your pacèd power:
Not truth I fear.
How ripe is turned the hour.

LOUIS MAC NEICE

An Irishman and an Oxford product, MacNeice (1907–) has been called the "ablest and robustest" of the modern English group of poets. This bishop's son became a lecturer in classics at Birmingham and London universities. He has written outstanding reviews and criticism (see Modern Poetry*). Although his poems belong to a period marked by obscurity and symbolism, he manages to steer a middle course, detached but never too far away.**

AND LOVE HUNG STILL

And love hung still as crystal over the bed
And filled the corners of the enormous room;

---

* The selections which follow are copyright, 1940, by Louis MacNeice.

The boom of dawn that left her sleeping, show-
    ing
    The flowers mirrored in the mahogany table.

O my love, if only I were able
    To protract this hour of quiet after passion,
Not ration happiness but keep this door for
    ever
    Closed on the world, its own world closed
    within it.

But dawn's waves trouble with the bubbling
    minute,
    The names of books come clear upon their
    shelves,
The reason delves for duty and you will wake
    With a start and go on living on your own.

The first train passes and the windows groan,
    Voices will hector and your voice become
A drum in tune with theirs, which all last night
    Like sap that fingered through a hungry tree
Asserted our one night's identity.

BIRMINGHAM

Smoke from the train-gulf hid by hoardings
    blunders upward, the brakes of cars
Pipe as the policeman pivoting round raises his
    flat hand, bars
With his figure of a monolith Pharaoh the
    queue of fidgety machines
(Chromium dogs on the bonnet, faces behind
    the triplex screens)
Behind him the streets run away between the
    proud glass of shops
Cubical scent-bottles artificial legs arctic foxes
    and electric mops
But beyond this center the slumward vista
    thins like a diagram:
There, unvisited, are Vulcan's forges who
    doesn't care a tinker's damn.

Splayed outwards through the suburbs houses,
    houses for rest
Seducingly rigged by the builder, half-tim-
    bered houses with lips pressed
So tightly and eyes staring at the traffic
    through bleary haws
And only a six-inch grip of the racing earth
    in their concrete claws;

In these houses men as in a dream pursue the
    Platonic Forms
With wireless and cairn terriers and gadgets
    approximating to the fickle norms
And endeavor to find God and score one over
    the neighbor
By climbing tentatively upward on jerry-built
    beauty and sweated labor.

The lunch hour: the shops empty, shopgirls'
    faces relax
Diaphanous as green glass empty as old alma-
    nacs
As incoherent with ticketed gewgaws tiered
    behind their heads
As the Burne-Jones windows in St. Philip's
    broken by crawling leads
Insipid color, patches of emotion, Saturday
    thrills—
(This theater is sprayed with "June")—the
    gutter take our old playbills,
Next week-end it is likely in the heart's funfair
    we shall pull
Strong enough on the handle to get back our
    money; or at any rate it is possible.

On shining lines the trams like vast sarcophagi
    move
Into the sky, plum after sunset, merging to
    duck's egg, barred with mauve
Zeppelin clouds, and pentecost-like the cars'
    headlights bud
Out from sideroads and the traffic signals,
    crème-de-menthe or bull's blood,
Tell one to stop, the engine gently breathing,
    or to go on
To where like black pipes of organs in the
    frayed and fading zone
Of the West the factory chimneys on sullen
    sentry will all night wait
To call, in the harsh morning, sleep-stupid
    faces through the daily gate.

SUNDAY MORNING

Down the road someone is practising scales,
The notes like little fishes vanish with a wink
    of tails,
Man's heart expands to tinker with his car
For this is Sunday morning, Fate's great ba-
    zaar,

Regard these means as ends, concentrate on
    this Now,
And you may grow to music or drive beyond
    Hindhead anyhow,
Take corners on two wheels until you go so   5
    fast
That you can clutch a fringe or two of the
    windy past,
That you can abstract this day and make it to
    the week of time   10
A small eternity, a sonnet self-contained in
    rhyme.

But listen, up the road, something gulps, the
    church spire   15
Opens its eight bells out, skulls' mouths which
    will not tire
To tell how there is no music or movement
    which secures
Escape from the weekday time. Which deadens   20
    and endures.

STEPHEN SPENDER

*Along with MacNeice, Auden, Lewis, and one
or two others, Spender (1909–   ) is outstanding among modern British poets. An Oxford poet who also wrote short stories, Spender
began by printing his own material, soon succumbed to the machine age as a dominating
force in determining his subjects and treat-
ments. He is a fertile producer with definite
emotional power. His poetry has a marked
socialistic tinge; more than once his appeal to
the world to look out for the common man has
the ring of Shelley's early poetry and political
pamphlets.**

MOVING THROUGH THE SILENT
CROWD

Moving through the silent crowd
Who stand behind dull cigarettes
These men who idle in the road,
I have the sense of falling light.

They lounge at corners of the street
And greet friends with a shrug of shoulder,
And turn their empty pockets out,
The cynical gestures of the poor.

---

* The selections which follow are copyright,
1934, by The Modern Library.

Now they've no work, like better men
Who sit at desks and take much pay
They sleep long nights and rise at ten
To watch the hours that drain away.

I'm jealous of the weeping hours
They stare through with such hungry eyes.
I'm haunted by these images,
I'm haunted by their emptiness.

THE FUNERAL

Death is another milestone on their way.
With laughter on their lips and with winds
    blowing round them
They record simply
How this one excelled all others in making
    driving-belts.

This is festivity, it is the time of statistics
When they record what one unit contributed:
They are glad as they lay him back in the
    earth
And thank him for what he gave them.

They walk home remembering the straining
    red flags,
And with pennons of song still fluttering
    through their blood
They speak of the world-state
With its towns like brain-centers and its puls-
    ing arteries.

They think how one life hums, revolves and
    toils,
One cog in a golden and singing hive:
Like spark from fire, its task happily achieved,
It falls away quietly.

No more are they haunted by the individual
    grief
Nor the crocodile tears of European genius,
The decline of a culture
Mourned by scholars who dream of the ghosts
    of Greek boys.

THE EXPRESS

After the first powerful plain manifesto
The black statement of pistons, without more
    fuss
But gliding like a queen, she leaves the station.

Without bowing and with restrained uncon-
    cern
She passes the houses which humbly crowd
    outside,
The gasworks and at last the heavy page   5
Of death, printed by gravestones in the ceme-
    tery.
Beyond the town there lies the open country
Where, gathering speed, she acquires mystery,
The luminous self-possession of ships on ocean. 10
It is now she begins to sing—at first quite low
Then loud, and at last with a jazzy madness—
The song of her whistle screaming at curves,
Of deafening tunnels, brakes, innumerable
    bolts.   15
And always light, aerial, underneath
Goes the elate meter of her wheels.
Steaming through metal landscape on her lines
She plunges new eras of wild happiness
Where speed throws up strange shapes, broad 20
    curves
And parallels clean like the steel of guns.
At last, further than Edinburgh or Rome,
Beyond the crest of the world, she reaches
    night
Where only a low streamline brightness   25
Of phosphorus on the tossing hills is white.
Ah, like a comet through flames she moves en-
    tranced
Wrapt in her music no bird song, no, nor 30
    bough
Breaking with honey buds, shall ever equal.

KARL SHAPIRO

*Shapiro (1913–   ) stands here as a repre-
sentative of a group of established younger
poets; space does not permit the inclusion of a
handful of others whose followers may well 40
press the cause of their favorites. Shapiro attended Virginia and Johns Hopkins, later studied to be a librarian, but in 1941 found himself
in the Army. Poetry awards helped to develop
him. In 1944 he won the Pulitzer Prize for 45
V-Letter. In 1946 he was adviser on poetry for
the Library of Congress. Recently a contribution to the long history of poetic criticism appeared: Essay on Rime. Shapiro has vigor, and
a facility which has moved critics to note the
influence of recent British verse. But the idiom
and the toughness—occasionally shocking to*
*an older, more genteel generation—are purely
American.**

BUICK

As a sloop with a sweep of immaculate wing
    on her delicate spine
And a keel as steel as a root that holds in the
    sea as she leans,
Leaning and laughing, my warm-hearted 10
    beauty, you ride, you ride,
You tack on the curves with parabola speed
    and a kiss of goodbye,
Like a thoroughbred sloop, my new high-spir-
    ited spirit, my kiss. 15

As my foot suggests that you leap in the air
    with your hips of a girl,
My finger that praises your wheel and an-
    nounces your voices of song,
Flouncing your skirts, you blueness of joy, you 20
    flirt of politeness,
You leap, you intelligence, essence of wheel-
    ness with silvery nose,
And your platinum clocks of excitement stir 25
    like the hairs of a fern.

But how alien you are from the booming belts
    of your birth and the smoke
Where you turned on the stinging lathes of 30
    Detroit and Lansing at night
And shrieked at the torch in your secret parts
    and the amorous tests,
But now with your eyes that enter the future of
    roads you forget; 35
You are all instinct with your phosphorous
    glow and your streaking hair.

And now when we stop it is not as the bird
    from the shell that I leave
Or the leathery pilot who steps from his bird
    with a sneer of delight,
And not as the ignorant beast do you squat and
    watch me depart,
But with exquisite breathing you smile, with 45
    satisfaction of love,
And I touch you again as you tick in the
    silence and settle in sleep.

HOLLYWOOD

Farthest from any war, unique in time
Like Athens or Baghdad, this city lies
Between dry purple mountains and the sea.
The air is clear and famous, every day
Bright as a postcard, bringing bungalows
   And sights. The broad nights advertise
For love and music and astronomy.

Heart of the continent, the hearts converge
On open boulevards where palms are nursed
With flare-pots like a grove, on villa roads
Where castles cultivated like a style
Breed fabulous metaphors in foreign stone,
   And on enormous movie lots
Where history repeats its vivid blunders.

Alice and Cinderella are most real.
Here may the tourist, quite sincere at last,   20
Rest from his dream of travels. All is new,
No ruins claim his awe, and permanence,
Despised like customs, fails at every turn.
   Here where the eccentric thrives,
Laughter and love are leading industries.   25

Luck is another. Here the body-guard,
The parasite, the scholar are well paid,
The quack erects his alabaster office,
The moron and the genius are enshrined,   30
And the mystic makes a fortune quietly;
   Here all superlatives come true
And beauty is marketed like a basic food.

O can we understand it? Is it ours,
A crude whim of a beginning people,
A private orgy in a secluded spot?
Or alien like the word *harem*, or true   5
Like hideous Pittsburgh or depraved Atlanta?
   Is adolescence just as vile
As this its architecture and its talk?

Or are they parvenues, like boys and girls?
Or ours and happy, cleverest of all?   10
Yes. Yes. Though glamorous to the ignorant
This is the simplest city, a new school.
What is more nearly ours? If soul can mean
   The civilization of the brain,
This is a soul, a possibly proud Florence.   15

THE CONTRABAND

I dreamed I held a poem and knew
The capture of a living thing.
Boys in a Grecian circle sang
And women at their harvesting.

Slowly I tried to wake and draw
The vision after, word by word,
But sleep was covetous: the song
The singers and the singing blurred.

The paper flowers of everynight
All die. Day has no counterpart,
Where memory writes its boldface wish
And swiftly punishes the heart.

GLOSSARY

ALEXANDRINE: a six-foot line in iambics—in English the best example is the final line in the *Faerie Queene* stanza. The term may come from its use in early French heroic poetry on Alexander.

ALLEGORY: a device by which people, scenes, and objects may stand for something besides their apparent significance. In the *Faerie Queene*, for example, Una is a girl, and in a moral allegory, virtue, and in a political allegory, Queen Elizabeth.

ALLITERATION: figure of speech in which two or more words begin with same letter or sound ("furrow followed free").

ANAPEST: a metrical foot of two short syllables followed by one long (to the end).

ANTISTROPHE: see ODE, STROPHE.

APOSTROPHE: figure of speech in which the poet formally addresses a person, abstraction, muse, etc.

ASSONANCE: similarity in sound between vowels; differs from rhyme in that final consonants involved are not the same (wine—lime).

BALLAD: originally a song, then a narrative poem with popular and literary traditions (see introduction to ballad on I, 65), and today (a loose use of the term) a melodramatic or amatory song.

BALLAD STANZA: commonly a four-line stanza with second and fourth lines rhyming and the meter running tetrameter, trimeter, tetrameter, trimeter in order. Many variations exist, however.

BALLADE GROUP: a group of technical forms including the ballade and variations, the chant royal, etc. It includes subtypes of verse often called "French forms"; they are tricky and involved, usually poets' playgrounds rather than steady fare for readers. The ballade, for example, has three stanzas, each with the following rhyme scheme: ababbcbC (refrain line); it ends with an envoi: bcbC.

BLANK VERSE: unrhymed iambic pentameter used in dignified and lofty passages of epic poetry, drama, etc. See Surrey, Marlowe, Milton, Shakespeare.

CADENCE: recognizable beat and rhythmic flow of phrase without formal stress pattern, in verse or prose.

CAESURA: a pause within a line of poetry, as in Old English verse, where it comes after the second foot. See *Beowulf*.

CANTO: a section of a long poem; similar to a "book."

CAVALIER LYRICS: term applied to the light verse of the court poets under Charles I (Suckling, Lovelace, *et al.*).

COMMON METER: see BALLAD STANZA.

CONCEIT: term applied to a strained or involved comparison or idea, as in seventeenth-century metaphysical poetry; see John Donne.

COUPLET: a pair of successive lines of verse, especially such as rhyme together and are of identical length. See HEROIC COUPLET.

DACTYL: a metrical foot consisting of an accented syllable followed by two unaccented ones (mur'-mŭring).

DIMETER: a line of poetry made up of two feet.

DIRGE: a subtype of poetry given over to lyrical lamentation—in Scottish ballads, a coronach. See ELEGY.

DRAMATIC MONOLOGUE: a poem in which one character speaks to one or more mute listeners and incidentally reveals his own psychological make-up. See Tennyson's "Ulysses" and Browning's "My Last Duchess."

ELEGY: a formal poem of mourning or brooding on the subject of death. See Gray's "Elegy" and Milton's "Lycidas."

ENJAMBMENT: the use of run-on lines, that is, lines which do not end with a completed phrase, completed sentence, or full stop. For comic effect, a final word in a line may be split into syllables with the conclusion on the following line. See Byron's *Don Juan*.

EPIC: a poetic type marked by its length, seriousness, noble characters, central hero, etc. Minor features may include invoking the muse, beginning in the middle, cataloguing, incorporating catastrophe, formal simile, etc. See *Beowulf*, *Faerie Queene*, *Paradise Lost*.

[390]

EPIC SIMILE: an involved stated comparison marked by length and often the introductory phrase "as when"—peculiar to the epic.

EPIGRAM: a short, pithy saying or poem; Coleridge defined an epigram by writing one:
"What is an epigram? A dwarfish whole;
Its body brevity, and wit its soul."

EPITAPH: a subtype, a short poem suitable for a gravestone or valedictory. Sometimes synonymous with epigram on death. Sometimes wryly humorous like Gay's, written for himself:
"Life is a jest, and all things show it;
I thought so once, but now I know it."

EPITHALAMION: a subtype, a hymn, song, poem written for a wedding.

EPITHET: an adjective or phrase aptly describing or underlining an outstanding quality in a person, object, scene, etc.

EPODE: see STROPHE.

FIGURE OF SPEECH: a word or combination of words used to get a specific stylistic effect; metaphors, similes, hyperbole, etc., are included.

FOOT: the basic rhythmic unit in a recognizable metric pattern. In English the commonest feet are iambic, trochaic, anapestic, and dactylic (which see).

FREE VERSE: verse which has no regular metrical pattern, but which does have cadence, often set up irregularly as to length of line to "look like" poetry; employs imagery and figures of conventional verse and definitely has some organization or over-all unity of effect. Not to be confused with blank verse. Often referred to as *vers libre*.

HEPTAMETER: a line of poetry having seven feet.

HEROIC COUPLET: a pair of rhyming lines in iambic pentameter; may be a "closed" couplet with a unit organization of its own, or one unit with other continuous "open" couplets, with run-on lines. See Pope.

HEXAMETER: a line of poetry having six feet.

HYPERBOLE: figure of speech in which exaggeration is used for dramatic or comic effect.

IAMBIC: common type of foot with an unaccented syllable followed by an accented one (ŏmit′).

INCREMENTAL REPETITION: a form of repetition which adds or changes slight details from stanza to stanza instead of reiterating. See BALLAD.

KENNING: an early form of metaphor (see *Beowulf*) marked my compounds—"whale-road" for ocean, etc.

LIGHT VERSE: term (not to be confused with blank verse or free verse) applied to those forms (limericks, triolets, certain songs) which are light in touch but which require deftness and dexterity nevertheless. Among moderns, consult Ogden Nash, Dorothy Parker, Samuel Hoffenstein (who have serious moods also).

LIMERICK: a light-verse form consisting of one five-line stanza, the first, second, and fifth lines usually having three main stresses, the others two. American limericks generally use the rhyme scheme aabba. English limericks (Edward Lear) often repeat line one as line five.

LYRIC: originally a poem to be sung to lyre accompaniment, hence melodic; today, however, generally a short poem with strong emotional basis and marked individual personality evident.

MADRIGAL: a polyphonic song for a half-dozen voices singing unaccompanied. Singers traditionally sit around a table. Because every voice carries an equal load, the effect is different from that of an "air," which has one tune harmonized upon by several voices. The term is also applied to a short love poem suitable for musical arrangement. See Elizabethan verse.

METAPHOR: a suggested comparison, a figure of speech in which a term usually having one literal meaning is used in a different sense to create a literary effect or to intensify meaning (a "knotty" problem). In a general sense, metaphor may include other figures involving comparison. See SIMILE.

METAPHYSICAL POETRY: loosely, poetry dealing with reasoning processes and philosophical complexities; in the seventeenth century, it is marked by intellectual pyrotechnics, conceits, subtleties, unusual comparisons. See Donne and Herbert.

METER: a term used as a combining form to designate the number of feet to a line (pentameter equals five-foot line, etc.). Not in combination, the word refers to any formal arrangement of rhythm.

METONYMY: a figure of speech in which for rhetorical effect a word is used in place of another which is close in meaning and easily associated with it: "The pen is mightier than the sword" equals "Writing is mightier than fighting." See SYNECDOCHE.

MOCK EPIC: a poem which burlesques the machinery of the conventional epic. See *Don Juan* and *The Rape of the Lock*.

MONOMETER: literally, a line of poetry having only one foot, obviously seldom found.

MUSES: nine goddesses of letters, arts, and science in Greek mythology. The poet customarily addressed the one whose specific help he needed; or figuratively, he might appeal to the muse in a routine way without specifying.

NONAMETER: a line of poetry having nine feet.

OCCASIONAL VERSE: poetry written for a special occasion such as a wedding, death, coronation, etc.

OCTAMETER: a line of poetry having eight feet.

OCTAVE: a group of eight lines of poetry; generally refers to the first eight lines of an Italian sonnet (see Wyatt and Surrey) which was adapted to English; rhyme scheme: abba, abba.

ODE: a subtype of lyric poetry with serious tone, addressed in praise to a person, object, or idea. The Pindaric ode is made up of strophe, antistrophe, and epode, with involved metrical structure. The Cowley ode is irregular, imitation Pindaric. The stanzaic ode is an ode only in a loose sense, that of a poem of address, but is more common in modern poetry than the complicated formal ode.

ONOMATOPOEIA: the use of words whose sound indicates meaning or sense—"gurgle," "plopping," etc.

OTTAVA RIMA: a stanza of eight lines with this rhyme scheme: abababcc. See *Don Juan.*

PASTORAL: a term, adjective or noun, applied to poetry or music or romance dealing with shepherds, flocks, fields, farms, etc. Classically it is an artificial form with lofty language, set themes, conventional names, etc. See "Lycidas."

PENTAMETER: a line of poetry having five feet.

PETRARCHAN (ITALIAN) SONNET: a fourteen-line love poem originally, introduced to England by Wyatt and Surrey. The first eight lines (octave) rhyme abba, abba; the last six (sestet) may take one of several patterns or be irregular, though strictly the last two lines should not rhyme.

PROSODY: the study of metrical structure.

QUATRAIN: a four-line stanza or a unit group of four lines in a long composition.

REFRAIN: the repeated portion of a poem, ballad, song—used for choral effect, audience participation, etc.

RHYME: repetition of sound at the end of poetic lines (or at the middle and end of a line—"internal" rhyme). Stressed vowels and following consonants should be identical (wine—mine); see ASSONANCE.

RIME ROYAL: a stanza of seven iambic pentameter lines with this rhyme scheme: ababbcc.

ROMANCE: a term originally referring to the Old French language, then to stories of knights in O.F. literature—hence "medieval romance." See *Gawain and the Green Knight.* Later, with Sidney (pastoral romance in *Arcadia*) and Scott, the term suggests a novel of love and adventure; in nineteenth-century poetry the word in adjective form (romantic) suggests the opposite of classic. It cannot be defined except in specialized uses.

RONDEAU (RONDEAU GROUP): special "French forms," like the ballade and ballade group, ordinarily but not necessarily gay, and complicated in structure. The roundel, rondel, triolet, etc., belong here. These subtypes are largely showpieces, not common enough to be represented in this text. For examples, see Untermeyer and Cooper in poetry bibliography, below.

SCANSION: the act of dividing a line of poetry into feet, placing accent marks, deciding meter, and perhaps reading aloud. The commonest lines in English are tetrameter, pentameter, and hexameter; the four familiar patterns are iambic, trochaic, anapestic, and dactylic.

SESTET: the last six lines of an Italian or Petrarchan sonnet (*q.v.*).

SESTINA: one of the "French forms" with six stanzas, envoi, repetition of end-words, and complicated artificial pattern.

SHAKESPEAREAN (ENGLISH) SONNET: a form taking its name from the poet who handled it best, although Surrey introduced it. The fourteen lines are divided into three quatrains and a couplet with the inflexible rhyme scheme: abab, cdcd, efef, gg.

SIMILE: a figure of speech which offers an expressed comparison (where the metaphor in its limited sense *suggests* the likeness) for rhetorical effect. It is introduced by "like," "as," or "as when." (He ran like a deer.)

SONNET: a subtype of poetry identified as fourteen lines in iambic pentameter with several possible rhyme schemes (see Petrarchan, Spenserian, and Shakespearean sonnet). In its long history it has been amatory, autobiographical, philosophical, topical.

SPENSERIAN SONNET: a sonnet form with the following rhyme scheme: abab, bcbc, cdcd, ee. Superficially, it resembles the Shakespearean, but uses fewer rhymes, achieves coherence by the linking repetitions.

SPENSERIAN (*Faerie Queene*) STANZA: a nine-line stanza employed in the *Faerie Queene;* its iambic pentameter lines are grouped according to this rhyme scheme: ababbcbcc. The last line is an Alexandrine (*q.v.*).

SPONDEE: a foot consisting of two accented syllables, used to prevent monotony in conjunction with commoner set patterns.

STANZA: the equivalent in a poem to the paragraph in prose; a unit of verse marked by distinct rhyme, meter, or subject pattern. It is recognized by spacing or indentation.

STROPHE: in the Pindaric ode (see Ode), the first stanza and every third stanza thereafter. In the Greek form, the chorus moved up one side of the stage while the strophe was chanted, down with the antistrophe, and remained in place with the epode.

SYNECDOCHE: a figure of speech close to metonymy (*q.v.*) in meaning, except that a part is used for the whole: "ten head" for ten cattle, "a hundred sail" for a hundred ships.

TERZA RIMA: a stanza form marked by a series of tercets or triplets. Each group of three lines after the first takes as its initial and final rhymes the sound of the middle line of the preceding tercet; the middle line in each new group takes a new sound, thus: aba, bcb, cdc, etc.

TETRAMETER: a line of poetry having four feet.

TRIMETER: a line of poetry having three feet.

TRIOLET: a member of the rondeau group (*q.v.*).

TROCHEE: a metrical foot consisting of an accented syllable followed by an unaccented one (trip′ ĭt).

VERS LIBRE: See FREE VERSE.

VERSE: technically, a single line of poetry; also a synonym for poetry; in modern songs another name for stanza.

VILLANELLE: one of the complicated forms in the rondeau group (*q.v.*).

FURTHER READINGS IN POETRY

PRE-RENAISSANCE

Brooke, S. A., *English Literature from the Beginning to the Norman Conquest*, 1926.

Child, F. J., *English and Scottish Popular Ballads*, 1898.

Cook, A. S., and Tinker, C. B., *Select Translations from Old English Prose*, 1908.

Cook, A. S., and Tinker, C. B., *Select Translations from Old English Poetry*, 1926.

Coulton, G. G., *Medieval Panorama*, 1938.

French, R. D., *A Chaucer Handbook*, 1927.

Hustvedt, S. B., *Ballad Books and Ballad Men*, 1930.

Ker, W. P., *English Literature, Medieval*, 1912.

Kittredge, G. L., *Chaucer and His Poetry*, 1915.

Kittredge, G. L., *Gawain and the Green Knight*, 1916.

Klaeber, F., *Beowulf*, 1928.

Lawrence, W. W., *Beowulf and Epic Tradition*, 1928.

Lewis, C. S., *The Allegory of Love*, 1938.

Pound, L., *Poetic Origins and the Ballad*, 1921.

Power, E., *Medieval People*, 1924.

Root, R. K., *The Poetry of Chaucer*, 1922.

Schofield, W. H., *English Literature from the Norman Conquest to Chaucer*, 1925.

Spaeth, J. D., *Old English Poetry*, 1921.

Taylor, H. O., *The Medieval Mind*, 1927.

Voretsch, K., *Introduction to the Study of Old French Literature*, 1931.

Weston, J., *Romance, Vision and Satire*, 1912.

Weston, J., *The Chief Middle English Poets*, 1914.

Wilson, R. M., *Early Middle English Literature*, 1939.

Wimberly, L. C., *Folklore in the English and Scottish Ballads*, 1928.

SIXTEENTH CENTURY

Black, J. B., *The Reign of Elizabeth*, 1936.

Craig, H., *The Enchanted Glass*, 1936.

Dunn, E. C., *The Literature of Shakespeare's England*, 1936.

Harrison, G. B., *Elizabethan England*, 1904.

Harrison, G. B., *The Elizabethan Journals*, 1939.

Hebel, J. W., and Hudson, H., *Poetry of the English Renaissance*, 1929.

Jones, H. S. V., *A Spenser Handbook*, 1930.

Lamson, R., and Smith, H., *The Golden Hind*, 1942.

Pinto, V. de S., *The English Renaissance*, 1938.

Rollins, H. E., ed., *Tottel's Miscellany*, 1928.

Tillyard, E. M. W., *The Elizabethan World Picture*, 1944.

Wright, L. B., *Middle-Class Culture in Elizabethan England*, 1935.

SEVENTEENTH CENTURY

Brinkley, F., *English Poetry of the Seventeenth Century*, 1942.

Bush, D., *English Literature in the Earlier Seventeenth Century*, 1946.

Clark, G. N., *The Seventeenth Century*, 1929.
Coffin, R. P. T., and Witherspoon, A., *Seventeenth Century Prose and Poetry*, 1946.
Grierson, H., *Cross-Currents in English Literature of the 17th Century*, 1929.

Hanford, J. H., *A Milton Handbook*, 1946.
Tillyard, E. M. W., *Milton*, 1930.
Tillyard, E. M. W., *The Miltonic Setting*, 1938.
Wolfe, D., *Milton in the Puritan Revolution*, 1941.

EIGHTEENTH CENTURY

Plowman, M., *An Introduction to the Study of Blake*, 1927.
Railo, E., *The Haunted Castle*, 1927.
Root, R. K., *The Poetical Career of Alexander Pope*, 1938.

Snyder, F. B., *The Life of Robert Burns*, 1932.
Turberville, A. S., *English Men and Manners in the Eighteenth Century*, 1929.
Turberville, A. S., *Johnson's England*, 1933.

NINETEENTH CENTURY

Allen, H., *Israfel*, 1934.
Babbitt, I., *Rousseau and Romanticism*, 1919.
Barzun, J., *Romanticism and the Modern Ego*, 1943.
Brailsford, H. N., *Shelley, Godwin and Their Circle*, 1913.
Brinton, C. C., *Political Ideas of the English Romanticists*, 1926.
Clutton-Brock, A., *William Morris: His Work and Influence*, 1914.
Colvin, J., *John Keats*, 1925.
De Vane, W. C., *A Browning Handbook*, 1936.
Evans, B. J., *English Poetry in the Later Nineteenth Century*, 1933.
Finney, C. L., *The Evolution of Keats's Poetry*, 1936.
Gaunt, W., *The Pre-Raphaelite Tragedy*, 1943.
Gaunt, W., *The Aesthetic Adventure*, 1945.
Godwin, P., *Biography of William Cullen Bryant*, 1883.
Hardy, F. E., *The Early Life and Later Years of Thomas Hardy* (2 vols.), 1928, 1930.
Herford, C. H., *Wordsworth*, 1930.
Longfellow, S., *The Life of Henry Wadsworth Longfellow*, 1891.
Lowell, A., *John Keats*, 1925.

Lowes, J. L., *The Road to Xanadu*, 1927.
Lucas, F. L., *The Decline and Fall of the Romantic Ideal*, 1936.
Mayne, E., *Byron*, 1913.
Nicolson, H. G., *Tennyson*, 1923.
Page, C. H., *The Chief American Poets*, 1905.
Perry, B., *John G. Whittier*, 1907.
Perry, B., *Heart of Emerson's Journals*, 1926.
Perry, B., *Emerson Today*, 1931.
Phelps, W. L., *Robert Browning: How to Know Him*, 1932.
Quennell, P., *Byron*, 1935.
Read, H., *Wordsworth*, 1930.
Selincourt, E. de, *The Early Wordsworth*, 1936.
Shaw, G. B., *William Morris as I Knew Him*, 1936.
Symons, A., *The Romantic Movement in English Poetry*, 1909.
Tinker, C. B., and Lowry, H. F., *The Poetry of Matthew Arnold*, 1940.
Walker, H., *The Literature of the Victorian Era*, 1921.
White, N., *Shelley*, 1940.
Winwar, F., *Poor Splendid Wings*, 1933.
Winwar, F., *The Romantic Rebels*, 1935.
Winwar, F., *Oscar Wilde and the Yellow Nineties*, 1940.

MODERN PERIOD AND GENERAL CRITICISM

Baugh, A. C., ed., *A Literary History of England*, 1948.
Bennett, A., *Literary Taste*, 1939.
Brooks, C., and Warren, R. P., *Understanding Poetry*, 1938.
Cooper, C. W., *Preface to Poetry*, 1946.
Daiches, D., *Poetry and the Modern World*, 1940.

Earnest, E., *A Foreword to Literature*, 1945.
Eastman, M., *The Enjoyment of Poetry*, 1939.
Gregory, H., and Zaturenska, M., *A History of Modern Poetry*, 1946.
Grierson, H., and Smith, J. C., *A Critical History of English Poetry*, 1946.
Hart, J. D., *The Oxford Companion to American*

Literature, 1948.

Harvey, P., *The Oxford Companion to English Literature*, 1937.

Hillyer, R., *First Principles of Verse*, 1938.

Housman, A. E., *The Name and Nature of Poetry*, 1933.

Lewisohn, L., *Expression in America*, 1932.

Lieder, P., and Withington, R., *The Art of Literary Criticism*, 1941.

Lowes, J. L., *Convention and Revolt in Poetry*, 1930.

MacNeice, L., *Modern Poetry*, 1938.

Monroe, H., *Poets and Their Art*, 1932.

Ransom, J. C., *The World's Body*, 1938.

Richards, I. A., *Practical Criticism*, 1939.

Ridley, M. R., *Poetry and the Ordinary Reader*, 1939.

Roberts, M., *Critique of Poetry*, 1934.

Sampson, G., *The Concise Cambridge History of English Literature*, 1941.

Sanders, G., and Nelson, J. H., *The Chief Modern Poets of England and America*, 1943.

Stauffer, D. A., *The Nature of Poetry*, 1946.

Thomas, W., and Brown, S. G., *Reading Poems*, 1941.

Thrall, W. F., and Hibbard, A., *A Handbook to Literature*, 1936.

Untermeyer, L., ed., *Modern American Poetry and Modern British Poetry*, 1942.

Untermeyer, L., and Davidson, C., *Poetry: Its Appreciation and Enjoyment*, 1934.

PART II
THE DRAMA

THE DRAMA

Our lives are surrounded by drama in some form or other—whether it be the drama of the latest movie thriller, a human-interest story in yesterday's tabloid, or a scene in a park witnessed from a nearby apartment. When people meet, talk, and move, new behavior patterns result. And because people the world over are ruled by much the same passions, have much the same frustrations, want alike to be appreciated, and hope for illusory beauties and gains, they are naturally interested in other people's successes and failures.

If these "other people" live far back in history, or if they are great and powerful, or if they take great risks, or if they do murder in a tenement—in short, if they somehow illuminate the universal pattern—they provide alluring vicarious experience for the amusement, horror, or education of their less-publicized fellow human beings. For out of people, dialogue, and action set against a backdrop come many other components of the drama-scheme of life: motives, morals, conflicts, causes, and so on. Place all this in a building called a theater, add lighting effects, music effects, costume, trained actors, and an intelligent version of some little fable of human life, and you have drama in a technical, indeed in a magic, sense.

Plays, of course, should be seen. But a reader with a spectator intelligence can "see" a play by reading it, and although he naturally misses much of the visual detail, he can compensate for his loss by a leisurely opportunity to reread lines or to study stage directions. Now it is undeniable that a literate person can get much enjoyment from reading a good play even if he hasn't much technical background or training. He cannot, however, be said to possess real understanding of the play without knowing the rules, any more than a profes-

sional football player can be said to understand his first tennis exhibition beyond an appreciation of grace, speed, rhythm—basic points common to all sports. Thus in textbooks we inevitably find introductions, notes, and comment designed to help the reader to achieve a richer experience. Frequently such scholarly impedimenta actually impede because of pedantry or erudition—or failure on the reader's part to realize that learning the rules of a new game doesn't come without practice. Students assigned to read the plays which follow must some day read many books and articles, listen to lectures, participate in discussions before they can hope to feel reasonably sure of their critical reactions, especially to older drama. But there is always a beginning, and, for some, this brief introduction may have to suffice.

THE DEVELOPMENT OF DRAMA

"There is always a beginning." The history of drama is long and broad. We can touch here upon only a few outstanding features of that history. (The plays of India, Japan, modern continental Europe, for example, must pass unnoticed in a text which concentrates on British and American literature and has space for only brief mention of outside influence.) For convenience, then, we begin with the Greeks and Romans. We might not have to go back even that far except for the fact that the English theater owes its present form partly to the historical influence of works by men who wrote before the time of Christ.

In most instances drama begins with some form of religious observance—with the Greeks in ceremonies in honor of Dionysus (Bacchus), a god of fertility, drinking, and revelry. The basic features of religious ritual include offering (gesture, posturing) and recitation or chanting of set speeches. The modern responsive reading in church was anticipated by the Greeks in the dialogue between leader and chorus. In time a second and third "leader" (actor) were evolved, and the chorus lost some of its prominence. Repeated ritual naturally grew in complexity under able hands (Thespis —sixth century B.C.—is the first Greek dramatist on record), and a new form was born which quickly lost its original limitations. The fifth century before Christ saw the work of three master tragedians—Aeschylus, Sophocles, and Euripides—and a major figure in comedy, Aristophanes. The writers of tragedy dealt with known stories of gods and heroes, stories showing characters dogged by fate or suffering from a fatal weakness. The starkness of their themes is seen in the familiar story of Oedipus, who, through a combination of circumstances, murdered his father, married his mother, and blinded himself. Comedy at first was coarse and remained racy (Aristophanes' superb piece, *Lysistrata*, still has trouble with modern censors); this is not surprising since it began as an offshoot of the licentious by-play connected with the Dionysian revels. As comedy matured, it veered toward satire and eventually domesticity, undergoing minor transformations as well; by the time of the Romans, for example, the chorus in comedy had disappeared.

The modern student who thinks of a domestic tragedy in terms of a Broadway production would find many surprises if he went back via a Wellsian time-machine to ancient Greece. Early performances did not enjoy the luxury of a raised stage, although that did develop; audiences sat outdoors in a bowl-like structure. There was no scenery, almost nothing in the way of props. The chorus commented on the action. Deaths occurred offstage and were announced by messenger. When matters got hopelessly tangled the *deus ex machina* (see Glossary, I, 629) was used. One or more of the unities of time, place, and action was observed. A well-made tragedy was expected to produce a catharsis (see Glossary) in the audience. Masks were employed (a device revived by Eugene O'Neill). The story was familiar to onlookers. But unlike typical modern theatergoers, the Greeks did not go to a play for enter-

tainment in the modern sense—the whole production was a serious undertaking for serious people who were moved by language and theme to a point of intellectual and spiritual growth. The modern bystander would note many other differences, but these few will serve to create a superficial impression. Many Greek conventions were taken over by the Romans and eventually by Elizabethan playwrights, including Shakespeare. They have a long and honorable history which must be read elsewhere in full by any serious-minded student of the drama.

When the Romans took over Greek civilization they took over the Greek theater in wholesale fashion. Seneca, the outstanding Roman tragedian, is typical of his group in his adaptation (and debasement) of Greek technique; we are not certain whether his plays were intended for regular performance, for recitation, or for reading alone. When Seneca was imitated in England there was no doubt about performance. The Romans loved spectacle (some of their shows included gladiatorial combats, sham naval battles, and the like); it is not surprising, therefore, to find blood-and-thunder, the ghost, and expansive rhetoric in their plays. The Elizabethans were to borrow these, too. In comedy, where Terence and Plautus excelled, the Romans were clever enough to cast an influence on the early school plays in England and (as in *The Comedy of Errors,* based on the *Menaechmi* of Plautus) on Shakespeare himself. Fortunately for a brief introduction—and for the student—with the fall of Rome the curtain descends for roughly a thousand years, and we may now turn directly to England.

English drama, like the Greek, began in religious ceremony (the possibility of independent evolution with wandering singers or folk shows remains, but the evidence is not convincing). As early as the ninth or tenth century on the Continent bits of Latin dialogue had been inserted in divine services to clarify or enliven proceedings; these early units of drama— called tropes—are best illustrated by the famous "Quem quaeritis" dialogue in which the earth-dwellers seeking Jesus are told by the angels that He has risen; here we have only a few lines with no stage business, and yet these tropes were popular, so popular that as they developed in form they were eventually presented out of doors. These new plays soon became unmanageable and were handed over by their parent to the medieval guilds for production. The guilds vied with each other in open competition for the best performance. Although we read of platforms on trestles and an occasional open-space arrangement with fixed stations for various scenes, in England these guild plays were generally acted on pageant-wagons, two-decker affairs with dressing rooms and storage below, and "stage" above. A wagon would draw up to a specified location, its section of a particular cycle of plays would be acted out, and the vehicle would move on, to be followed by another, and so on. Primitive as this system may sound, it worked; relatively speaking, it was enough. Some of the stage effects (Hell-mouth, for example) must have been sufficiently terrifying, and the costumes at least adequate, judging from the surviving account books with their bills for repairs to angels' wings or a new coat for Noah.

Medieval English religious plays, as given by the guilds, were at first deadly serious. They are sometimes divided into *miracles* (saints' lives); *mysteries* (Bible history); and *moralities* (didactic pieces with personified virtues and vices as characters—see *Everyman* for the classic example). Since there are objections to the use of the term "mystery" on grounds of insufficiently clear historical meaning or distinction, such labels must be handled with care. These were all serious plays whether stories of Abraham or of Good Deeds; like the Greeks, Englishmen at first went to a performance for illustration of familiar ideas or themes. The only note of frivolity in the early days was sounded in a burlesque of the Mass which was tolerated in the hands of theological students, but this was not true public theater. However, a public which knew the antics of traveling troupes at fairs was ready for comedy. It remained for the author of *The Second Shepherds' Play* (see I, 407) and others like him to provide it.

Sixteenth-century drama is marked among other things by a progression from religious to secular plays; increasing influence of Latin and Greek materials; a tightening in organization (the five-act formula, unities, etc.); the impact of the Senecan form on tragedy (the ghost, blood, stock characters, declamation); and the growth of the production scene from wagons and platforms through inn yards to an actual theater building. The evolution of a national comedy from the early Mak episode in *Second Shepherd* to the prose comedy of the University Wits and the major works of Shakespeare is first seen in the racy, farcical interludes like Heywood's *Four P's* and the first straight comedies like *Fulgens and Lucrece* and *Ralph Roister Doister*. Crude as these plays are, they still can be read with more than historical interest. The pioneer blank-verse tragedy, *Gorboduc*, seems a poor thing compared to Kyd's *Spanish Tragedy*, and a hardly recognizable competitor beside Marlowe's *Dr. Faustus* or *Jew of Malta*. Marlowe, who first made blank verse a ringing mighty line, is the giant of the days shortly before Shakespeare achieved his top place in the literary hierarchy. If Marlowe (see I, 198) had lived a normal span of years, there is no telling what heights he might have reached. As it is, he made passion convincing on stage, developed the art of characterization, and clearly showed that the English language was a fit vehicle for dramatic art.

Shakespeare (see I, 419) is, of course, in a class by himself. Of his many able contemporaries, Ben Jonson (see I, 212) is perhaps the runner-up. His comedies of the humours (see Glossary) lack the poetry of Shakespeare but are tight in construction and have a satiric touch which is foreign to the master. Jonson excelled as well in the dramatic form known as the masque—a hodgepodge of plot, song, dance, and elaborate stage effects—which he produced in collaboration with the famous designer, Inigo Jones. The period is also marked by the rise of acting companies subsidized by prominent people; there were even groups of capable child actors who gave the professionals a good run for their money.

One or two other developments should be briefly mentioned. A real theater building had finally come into being, but its existence was in jeopardy. A round structure—or an octagon giving a round effect—it was open to the sky except for a thatch roof running around the rim. Performances were by daylight. The common man stood where the modern orchestra seats are, and there were galleries for the affluent. The stage projected into the audience. There were almost no props, but the costumes were elaborate. No general curtain, no spotlights, no real scenery were to be had. (There was a small gallery over the back of the stage, serving for height effects—walls, cliffs, etc.; underneath was a curtained area available for storage or for actual use as an inner stage.) With a constant hubbub from the beholders, a small area in which to work, boys taking women's roles, and numerous other handicaps, it is a wonder that the magic of the lines or the antics of low comedians could ever get across. But plays were popular and often financially successful. There was one ominous note, however, sounded early when the new playhouses had had to be located out of town because of critical pressure. The Puritans, who hated the theater for moral and political reasons, were slowly growing in power. In 1642 they were to close the houses for almost twenty years, an act which was to have direct and indirect influences on theatrical traditions down to the present day.

After Shakespeare died in 1616 there were many able playwrights still attracting attention in addition to some already named; Marston, Dekker, Middleton, Massinger, Ford, Shirley, and Webster are a few of the many names which are to be found in any good anthology of Jacobean drama (see bibliography, I, 631). But no plays were written which were in the same class with *Hamlet* or *Macbeth;* as a matter of fact, Shakespeare himself showed signs of being "written out" as early as 1609, faded badly in his last plays, borrowing from himself and turning out two or three feeble efforts (with a notable exception, a final puff of brilliance, *The Tempest*). In spite of the interest in the War of the Theaters, the popularity of collaborators like Beaumont and Fletcher and Massinger, or the personal charm of Dekker, it can be said that drama began to run downhill after 1609. By the time Webster's *Duchess of Malfi* appeared (1623), the theater looked like the theater of Kyd's day, with revenge the motif, and dead hands, madmen, waxworks, and torture again playing their Senecan roles. The *Duchess* is not a bad play; Webster has refined the revenge story; revival groups and college classes can have fun with the stout central character and the deep-dyed villains—but

it still reads and plays like a period piece, whereas Shakespeare continues in his major plays to defy time.

By 1642 the Puritans, as has been said, were strong enough to close the theaters, and they stayed closed until the Restoration. Heavy penalties were exacted for producing or attending "bootleg" plays. The only exceptions seem to have been provincial shows and private staging of "drolls," short scenes reworked from full-length plays, which apparently got by, but were no more than small beer after the heady brew of the good old days.

After the repressive methods of the Puritans it is not surprising to find Restoration comedy almost deliberately going to extremes. Its dialogue sparkles with wit and apt phrase. Its tone varies from sophisticatedly racy to plain coarse. Its characters are stock types made over from Jonson's humors with a dash of new French sauce. Its plots are commonplace. Its glitter is false. And yet from the point of view of good theater the best work of Wycherley, Congreve, Vanbrugh, Farquhar, and others can stand up today alongside New York's and London's best. (As a matter of fact, a revival of *The Country Wife,* with Ruth Gordon, was a hit on Broadway a few years ago.) These comedies, of course, are not for Puritans; they are ordinarily not included in college anthologies on the theory that mixed classes would suffer embarrassment if they were. This is unfortunate, for the plays also happen at times to be brilliant, vigorous, artful. The victory of the non-Puritans in 1660 was a Pyrrhic victory.

Of Restoration tragedy little need be said. It is as decorous as the comedy is indecorous. It is also dull. (Not that it is safe or true to conclude that virtue is unattractive and vice rewarding.) This late seventeenth-century tragedy is heroic; the topics are love, valor, honor; the speeches are long, the people wooden. Let the student read Dryden's *Conquest of Granada,* Otway's *Venice Preserved,* and one of Rowe's plays at the turn of the century, and he will see this period's tragedy at its best. He need read no more. "Hopelessly heroic," Nicoll calls them, and there can be no rebuttal.

If the Restoration shocks in one field and bores in another, it can lay claim to other laurels, for it is the time when women play women's roles for the first time in England, theaters have roofs and interior furnishings and effects imitative of the Continent's, and a rapport exists between actor and audience which the Puritan, for all of his virtues, could not comprehend.

Relatively speaking, the eighteenth and nineteenth centuries are as unimportant in the history of English drama as they are significant in the development of, say, the novel and poetry. This is not to say that there was no theater; it is to say that the playwrights of first rank in that long period can be counted on the fingers of one hand. After the excesses of the Restoration there was, not unexpectedly, a reaction. An Age of Reason could not cope with an overplay of emotion or a pyrotechnic display of double meanings. It took an opposite course—toward genteelism, sentiment, decorum. Sheridan (see I, 459) and Goldsmith (I, 255 and II, 52) managed to steer a middle course. Although they are capable of innuendo and not devoid of sentiment, they manage to avoid the Scylla of indecency and the Charybdis of sentimentality in the Steele (see II, 38) tradition. Both men attempted (in *The Rivals* and *She Stoops to Conquer*, for example) to keep the authentic sparkle of Restoration situation and dialogue while cleaning things up a bit, and they succeeded. The plays of both men are still revived with good effect. The minor plays of the period, experiments like Lillo's in prose tragedy, the burlesque of Fielding, the new acting methods under Garrick, and the efforts of the elder Colman in straight comedy—these and other subjects can be discussed and must be in any complete history of the stage; but their importance is secondary, and we have, regretfully, no time for them here.

The nineteenth century is a virtual void in English drama until the end of the period. The early and middle portions are marked by dramatic experiments conducted by poets: Shelley (I, 276), Byron (I, 123), Tennyson (I, 150), and Browning (I, 158), for example. Their work is either closet drama or undramatic stage drama and, however interesting to the historian, is not a major contribution. At the end of the century, however, the modern movement in the theater began. In the plays of Robertson (*Caste*), Pinero (*The Second Mrs. Tanqueray*), and Wilde (see I, 502), there was a noticeable progression respectively toward realism in topic and setting, courage in handling forbidden subjects, and outspokenness in a revived comedy which, however, had its roots in Congreve and Sheridan. The greatest influence on the new theater was not English but Scandinavian; it remained for Ibsen to unlock the door to the forbidden room and, for the first time since the Elizabethans, to present serious plays close to life, written in no uncertain terms, presenting problems with understanding and, above all, compassion. The high poetry of the Elizabethans was gone and the captains and kings had departed in favor of tradesmen and politicians, but at long last and in a new idiom the drama was again at grips with universals.

Modern Drama

The student who picks up a modern play will be aware immediately of many superficial differences between the drama of today and that of yesterday: plays do not have to be five acts long, poetry is rarely used (see Anderson, I, 567, for an exception), stage directions are more elaborate, the mechanics of staging are vastly improved. Under the surface there are differences, too: less genteelism, less sentimentalism, more coming to grips with basic problems. Sex is prominent; the new psychology has introduced a long list of clinical studies; many isms—naturalism, expressionism, impressionism—have been introduced into the jargon of the theater; one-act plays and little theaters have their day. This does not mean that the modern theater is therefore automatically great—as a matter of fact, we are too close to the picture to get a true perspective. No Shakespeares have appeared. And for all the technical improvements there have been dozens of bad plays, so trite, so poorly executed that any intelligent audience might well wonder why anyone ever wasted money on their production.

With new developments not unexpectedly came new problems. To get rid of Victorian prudery was one thing. But there was a danger in going to the other extreme, parading sex in a series of cheap, disgusting "plays" of a kind popular during the last war and still to be seen in some burlesque theaters. To introduce real issues was an excellent thing. But the danger was, and is, that some playwrights merely preach, and no drama results; or they reduce life to a study of test tubes, which, however interesting in the laboratory, does not always make for good theater. But honesty of approach, scientific method, and sociological criticism in the new plays were steps ahead.

Among the leaders in the new drama in England were Shaw, Barrie (see I, 529), Galsworthy, and a long list of others including Granville-Barker and Maugham; in the Irish renascence Lord Dunsany, Lady Gregory, Yeats, Synge (see I, 539), and O'Casey were prominent. Shaw, a follower of Ibsen in the early days, is not impressive in recent plays, but in his prime, in dramas like *Arms and the Man, Candida, Major Barbara, Pygmalion,* and *Saint Joan,* he showed the unmistakable touch of a first-rate writer. He needled people, made them angry but made them think, and cleaned away loads of traditional rubbish almost single-handedly. He wrote long prefaces and made plays that seemed more like sermons. Even at his best he also alienated people by his egotism and his prejudices; nevertheless, like Milton (see I, 87 and II, 21), no matter what one thinks of him, Shaw was a force, the first force in the English theater for a long time. Perhaps his greatest service was making the way easier for later playwrights.[1]

Barrie is still worth going back to. He was known before Shaw, went into partial eclipse, but has never quite disappeared. It is unfortunate in a way that the average man thinks of him as the author of *Peter Pan,* despite its charm, for a "typing" impression remains, in the Hollywood sense of the word. Barrie is whimsical, but tough, capable of criticizing mankind. (Some of his most revealing phrases occur in his stage directions.) Galsworthy (see II, 197), on the other hand, wrote with understanding and patrician intelligence, but today he does not get under one's skin. He recognized inequalities, pointed them out (which is enough service), but offered no solutions. He seems detached or unemotional to a modern generation fed on a diet of proletarian plays, problem plays, and satire. Nevertheless, Galsworthy knew his trade.

---

[1] It is to be regretted that Shaw does not allow his plays to be reprinted in anthologies designed for college and university use.

Space or proximity in time does not allow for even passing mention of other names and titles. A good play here, a capable author there —the list is long; the best procedure for the student is to consult reading lists, anthologies of the drama, and the bibliography in this text. Coward, Milne, Masefield (see I, 357), Priestley (II, 277), and others must await the test of time. The Irish school, represented here by Synge in drama and in poetry by Yeats, is a good product of a national literary renascence. The poverty, bellicoseness, faith, superstition, and humor of the Irish have been made familiar to American audiences on stage and screen by a coterie of artists since the early days of the traveling Abbey players. Such plays as *John Ferguson* and *Shadow and Substance* are typical of second-generation offerings which have pleased on both sides of the Atlantic.

THE PLAY IN AMERICA

American drama—that is, first-rate American drama—has a short history. It is possible to make a historical survey of plays from the Revolution to the present, and some authorities are apparently enthusiastic over certain early authors. For practical purposes, however, American drama begins with Eugene O'Neill in the twentieth century. In terms of world-wide reception, again as with Shaw in terms of impact, O'Neill is to our drama what Whitman (see I, 308) was to our poetry. There had been men who knew their craft—Thomas, Moody, Fitch, to name a trio—earnest men who sometimes produced well-made plays. But until O'Neill, with rare exceptions, playwrights had done what the English had done in the dramatic doldrums; they sheered away from the unpleasant, they sentimentalized, or they skimmed the surface of problems.

O'Neill, of course, can be criticized, and has been for such recent offerings as *The Iceman Cometh. Beyond the Horizon,* which brought his first success, now sounds foolish in places. In Greek moods like that of *Mourning Becomes Electra,* overwhelming fate is melodramatically handled so that the result may be absorbing theater, but the audience is more likely to be revolted or upset than to experience a catharsis. But with O'Neill there is generally evidence of intelligence, passion, knowledge, courage in experiment (masks, asides, etc.). The new psychology, which has affected poetry and the novel as well, accounts for some of the power in O'Neill; it also accounts for the occasional feeling that one is reading a textbook rather than witnessing a play. A winner of many prizes, O'Neill can be given the title of first master in the American theater for *Desire Under the Elms, The Emperor Jones, The Hairy Ape* (see I, 545), *Anna Christie*, and others.

Perhaps Maxwell Anderson (see I, 567) comes closest to O'Neill in terms of output, courage in experiment (revival of verse plays), and popular success. He has been successful with historical offerings like *Mary of Scotland, Elizabeth the Queen*, and the relatively recent *Joan of Lorraine. Winterset* (I, 567), like the best of O'Neill, shows interest in conflict, and pity for the trapped human being. An evening in the theater with Anderson is more than surface entertainment.

There is a temptation to mention a fairly long list of other established modern American playwrights. Barry in drawing-room comedy; Behrman in didactic comedy; Sherwood in comedy and history (*Abe Lincoln in Illinois*); Howard in a problem play like *The Silver Cord;* Rice in social satire and expressionism (see *The Adding Machine*, I, 605); Odets in plays of the proletariat—and a host of others deserve consideration. But nothing can be said for or against authors of one or two good plays, or for the dozen writers of recent Broadway hits; again the test of time must be invoked. The brief bibliography (I, 631) should be enough for a start if any reader wants to bring his historical background up to date in detail or to make his own guesses as to who will survive and who will be forgotten.

STUDY AIDS

A student who knows his way in the theater needs no introductory helps. A beginner must look to his instructor for assistance over rough spots and for answers to specific questions. But in the isolation of the study room a few questions may be of help in organizing reading with some purpose. (See also the Glossary, I, 629.)

1. Can you, after preliminary quick reading of an assigned play, state the plot in your own words as if it were simply a story?

2. How many conventions can you recognize (soliloquies, asides, etc.)? Are there any stock or type characters?

3. Is there a marked conflict, or is the play relatively static? Can you trace rising action to a climax? How is falling action handled?

4. Can you detect any use of forecast, any hints to the audience? How is action occurring prior to the opening of the play presented?

5. If the play is a comedy, is the emphasis on making a point clear, sheer entertainment, dialogue, situation, satire, or what combination?

6. If the play is serious, do you experience any feeling of being a wiser person for having read it? In what respects?

7. If the play is a problem play, what do you think of the author's presentation and prejudices? Does the playwright have an ax to grind? How obviously does he do it? Does he take any liberties with facts?

8. Study the stage directions. Compare them with earlier or later play directions. What is their function?

9. Consider the setting. How would the play look on stage? Is the setting important in the action or could the play have occurred almost anywhere?

10. How are the characters presented (by what they say, what others say, what they do, soliloquy—or a combination of these)? Can you label each clearly?

11. Is there anything in the action or characterization which is hard to swallow? Is the main idea sound? How much use is made of coincidence?

12. If the play is not modern, what differences in reaction do you experience if you read it twice, once from today's point of view, and again from yesterday's? If some details or ideas are definitely dated, how much of the total effect is spoiled thereby?

13. Are there any language difficulties? Do allusions and historical references bother you?

14. Are there any moral problems involved which threaten to complicate your literary judgment?

15. Is there any evidence that the author knows box-office appeal as well as his art?

16. Would the play make an acceptable moving picture or radio script? What changes would have to be made?

17. How does the method of the dramatist differ from that of a novelist handling the same theme?

18. Read two or three pages aloud with the help of some friends. What comes out in the oral exercise, amateurish though your acting may be?

19. Would you read the play again with profit and enjoyment if it were not reassigned?

20. Has the play—apart from its value as a theater piece—taught you anything about manners, customs, language, etc.?

THE SECOND SHEPHERDS' PLAY*

AUTHOR UNKNOWN
14th Century

The Second Shepherds' Play *is the work of an unknown artist sometimes called the Wakefield Master because the play belongs to the Towneley cycle, which probably was produced by the guilds of Wakefield. Along with* Abraham and Isaac, *a miracle play, and* Everyman, *a morality,* Second Shepherd, *a "mystery," may serve as a good example of drama in the early stage immediately after the Church handed over its overgrown stepchild to new guardians. It is distinguished from others by its comic episode involving Mak and the theft of a sheep. The blending of the serious and comic themes and the careful working-out of the symbols in Mak's unfortunate affair attest to the art of the unknown author who paved the way for full-length comedy. Recent scholarship has established this artful organization especially in regard to what has hitherto been thought of only as horseplay. (See H. A. Watt, "The Dramatic Unity of the 'Secunda Pastorum,'" in* Essays *and* Studies *in Honor of Carleton Brown,* New York, 1940; *and, especially, C. Chidamian, "Mak and the Tossing in the Blanket," in* Speculum, *April, 1947.)*

The FIRST SHEPHERD (PRIMUS PASTOR) *enters*

PRIMUS PASTOR. Lord, but this weather is 30
cold, and I am ill wrapped!

Nigh dazed, were the truth told, so long have
    I napped;
My legs under me fold; my fingers are
    chapped—
5 With such like I don't hold, for I am all lapt
        In sorrow.
    In storms and tempest,
    Now in the east, now in the west,
    Woe is him has never rest
        Midday nor morrow!

But we seely[1] shepherds that walk on the
    moor,
In faith we're nigh at hand to be put out of
    door.
15 No wonder, as it doth stand, if we be poor,
For the tilth of our land lies fallow as the floor,
        As ye ken.
    We're so burdened and banned,
20 Over-taxed and unmanned,
    We're made tame to the hand
        Of these gentry men.

Thus they rob us of our rest, our Lady them
    harry!
These men bound to their lords' behest, they
    make the plough tarry,
What men say is for the best, we find the
    contrary,—
30 Thus are husbandmen oppressed, in point to
    miscarry,
        In life,

---

* This text of the play, edited by Professor Child, is reproduced by permission of the Houghton Mifflin Company.

[1] poor.

[407]

Thus hold they us under
And from comfort sunder.
It were great wonder,
    If ever we should thrive.

For if a man may get an embroidered sleeve or
    a brooch now-a-days,
Woe is him that may him grieve, or a word
    in answer says!
No blame may he receive, whatever pride he 10
    displays;
And yet may no man believe one word that he
    says,
    Not a letter.
His daily needs are gained 15
By boasts and bragging feigned,
And in all he's maintained
    By men that are greater.

Proud shall come a swain as a peacock may go, 20
He must borrow my wain,[2] my plough also,
Then I am full fain to grant it ere he go.
Thus live we in pain, anger, and woe
    By night and day!
He must have it, if he choose, 25
Though I should it lose,
I were better hanged than refuse,
    Or once say him nay!

It does me good as I walk thus alone 30
Of this world for to talk and to make my
    moan.
To my sheep will I stalk, and hearken anon,
There wait on a balk,[3] or sit on a stone.
    Full soon,
For I trow, perdie,[4] 35
True men if they be,
We shall have company,
    Ere it be noon.

The FIRST SHEPHERD *goes to one side. The* 40
    SECOND SHEPHERD *enters*

SECUNDUS PASTOR. Ben'cite[5] and Dominus!
    What may this mean?
Why fares the world thus! The like often we've 45
    seen!
Lord, but it is spiteful and grievous, this
    weather so keen!
And the frost so hideous—it waters mine een!
    That's no lie! 50

Now in dry, now in wet,
Now in snow, now in sleet,
When my shoes freeze to my feet,
    It's not all easy!

5

But so far as I ken, wherever I go,
We seely weeded[6] men suffer mickle woe,
We have sorrow once and again, it befalls oft
    so.
Seely Capel, our hen, both to and fro
    She cackles,
But if she begins to croak,
To grumble or cluck,
Then woe be to our cock,
    For he is in the shackles!

These men that are wed have not all their
    will;
When they're full hard bestead, they sigh
    mighty still;
God knows the life they are led is full hard
    and full ill,
Nor thereof in bower or bed may they speak
    their will,
    This tide.
My share I have found,
Know my lesson all round,
Woe is him that is bound,
    For he must it abide!

But now late in men's lives (such a marvel
    to me
That I think my heart rives such wonders to
    see,
How that destiny drives that it should so be!)
Some men will have two wives and some men
    three
    In store.
Some are grieved that have any,
But I'll wager my penny
Woe is him that has many,
    For he feels sore!

But young men as to wooing, for God's sake
    that you bought,
Beware well of wedding, and hold well in
    thought,
"Had I known" is a thing that serves you
    nought.
Much silent sorrowing has a wedding home
    brought,

---

[2] wagon.   [3] ridge.
[4] by God.   [5] *Benedicite*, bless you.   [6] married.

And grief gives,
With many a sharp shower—
For thou mayest catch in an hour
What shall taste thee full sour
    As long as one lives!

For—if ever read I epistle!—I have one by my
    fire,
As sharp as a thistle, as rough as a briar,
She has brows like a bristle and a sour face by 10
    her;
If she had once wet her whistle, she might
    sing clearer and higher
      Her pater-noster;
She is as big as a whale,
She has a gallon of gall,—
By him that died for us all,
    I wish I had run till I had lost her!

    PRIMUS PASTOR. "God look over the row!" 20
    like a deaf man ye stand.
    SECUNDUS PASTOR. Yea, sluggard, the devil
    thy maw burn with his brand!
Didst see aught of Daw?
    PRIMUS PASTOR. Yea, on the pasture-land
I heard him blow just before; he comes nigh
    at hand
      Below there.
Stand still.
    SECUNDUS PASTOR. Why?
    PRIMUS PASTOR. For he comes, hope I.
    SECUNDUS PASTOR. He'll catch us both with
    some lie
      Unless we beware.

The THIRD SHEPHERD *enters, at first without*
seeing them

    TERTIUS PASTOR. Christ's cross me speed
    and St. Nicholas!
Thereof in sooth I had need, it is worse than 40
    it was.
Whoso hath knowledge, take heed, and let the
    world pass,
You may never trust it, indeed,—it's as brittle
    as glass,
      As it rangeth.
Never before fared this world so,
With marvels that greater grow,
Now in weal, now in woe,
    And everything changeth.

There was never since Noah's flood such floods

    seen,
Winds and rains so rude and storms so keen;
Some stammered, some stood in doubt, as I
    ween.—
5 Now God turn all to good, I say as I mean!
      For ponder
How these floods all drown
Both in fields and in town,
And bear all down,
      And that is a wonder!

We that walk of nights our cattle to keep,
    [*catches sight of the others*]
We see startling sights when other men sleep.
15 Yet my heart grows more light—I see shrews[7]
    a-peep.
Ye are two tall wights—I will give my sheep
      A turn, below.
But my mood is ill-sent;
As I walk on this bent,
I may lightly repent,
      If I stub my toe.

Ah, sir, God you save and my master sweet!
25 A drink I crave, and somewhat to eat.
    PRIMUS PASTOR. Christ's curse, my knave,
    thou'rt a lazy cheat!
    SECUNDUS PASTOR. Lo, the boy lists to rave!
      Wait till later for meat,
      We have eat it.
Ill thrift on thy pate!
Though the rogue came late,
Yet is he in state
      To eat, could he get it.

35
    TERTIUS PASTOR. That such servants as I,
    that sweat and swink,[8]
Eat our bread full dry gives me reason to
    think.
Wet and weary we sigh while our masters
    wink,[9]
Yet full late we come by our dinner and drink—
      But soon thereto
Our dame and sire,
45 When we've run in the mire,
Take a nip from our hire,
      And pay slow as they care to.

But hear my oath, master, since you find fault
50   this way,

---

[7] rogues.   [8] work.   [9] sleep.

[409]

I shall do this hereafter—work to fit my pay;
I'll do just so much, sir, and now and then
　　play,
For never yet supper in my stomach lay
　　In the fields.
But why dispute so?
Off with staff I can go.
"Easy bargain," men say,
　　"But a poor return yields."

PRIMUS PASTOR. Thou wert an ill lad for
　　work to ride wooing
From a man that had but little for spending.
SECUNDUS PASTOR. Peace, boy, I bade! No
　　more jangling,
Or I'll make thee full sad, by the Heaven's
　　King,
　　With thy gauds![10]
Where are our sheep, boy? Left lorn?
TERTIUS PASTOR. Sir, this same day at morn,
I them left in the corn
　　When they rang Lauds.

They have pasture good, they cannot go
　　wrong.
PRIMUS PASTOR. That is right. By the Rood,
　　these nights are long!
Ere we go now, I would someone gave us a
　　song.
SECUNDUS PASTOR. So I thought as I stood,
　　to beguile us along.
TERTIUS PASTOR. I agree.
PRIMUS PASTOR. The tenor I'll try.
SECUNDUS PASTOR. And I the treble so high.

TERTIUS PASTOR. Then the mean shall be I.
　　How ye chant now, let's see! [They
　　sing (the song is not given)]

Tunc entrat MAK, *in clamide se super togam*
　　vestitus[11]

MAK. Now, Lord, by thy seven names'
　　spell, that made both moon and stars on
　　high,
Full more than I can tell, by the will for me,
　　Lord, lack I.
I am all at odds, nought goes well—that oft
　　doth my temper try.
Now would God I might in heaven dwell, for

there no children cry,
　　So still.
PRIMUS PASTOR. Who is that pipes so poor?
MAK. Would God ye knew what I endure!
[PRIMUS PASTOR.] Lo, a man that walks on
　　the moor,
　　And has not all his will!

SECUNDUS PASTOR. Mak, whither dost speed?
　　What news do you bring?
TERTIUS PASTOR. Is he come? Then take
　　heed each one to his thing. [*Et accipit
　　clamidem ab ipso*][12]
MAK. What! I am a yeoman—since there's
　　need I should tell you—of the King,
That self-same, indeed, messenger from a great
　　lording,
　　And the like thereby.
Fie on you! Go hence
Out of my presence!
I must have reverence,
　　And you ask "who am I"!

PRIMUS PASTOR. Why dress ye it up so
　　quaint? Mak, ye do ill!
SECUNDUS PASTOR. But, Mak, listen, ye saint,
　　I believe what ye will!
TERTIUS PASTOR. I trow the knave can feint,
　　by the neck the devil him kill!
MAK. I shall make complaint, and you'll
　　all get your fill,
　　At a word from me—
And tell your doings, forsooth!
PRIMUS PASTOR. But, Mak, is that truth?
Now take out that southern tooth
　　And stick in a flea!
SECUNDUS PASTOR. Mak, the devil be in your
　　eye, verily! to a blow I'd fain treat you.
TERTIUS PASTOR. Mak, know you not me?
　　By God, I could beat you!

MAK. God keep you all three! Me thought
　　I had seen you—I greet you,
Ye are a fair company!
PRIMUS PASTOR. Oh, now you remember,
　　you cheat, you!
SECUNDUS PASTOR. Shrew, jokes are cheap!
When thus late a man goes,
What will folk suppose?—
You've a bad name, God knows,
　　For stealing of sheep!

---

[10] tricks.
[11] Then enters Mak with a cloak over his smock.

[12] He takes the cloak from him.

THE SECOND SHEPHERDS' PLAY · THE DRAMA

MAK. And true as steel am I, all men know
and say,
But a sickness I feel, verily, that grips me hard,
night and day.
My belly is all awry, it is out of play——
TERTIUS PASTOR. "Seldom doth the Devil lie
dead by the way—"
MAK. Therefore
Full sore am I and ill,
Though I stand stone still;
I've not eat a needle
This month and more.

PRIMUS PASTOR. How fares thy wife, by my
hood, how fares she, ask I?
MAK. Lies asprawl, by the Rood, lo, the fire
close by,
And a house-full of home-brewed she drinks
full nigh—
Ill may speed any good thing that she will try
Else to do!—
Eats as fast as may be,
And each year there'll a day be
She brings forth a baby,
And some years two.

But were I now kinder, d'ye hear, and far
richer in purse,
Still were I eaten clear out of house and home,
sirs.
And she's a foul-favored dear, see her close,
by God's curse!
No one knows or may hear, I trow, of a worse,
Not any!
Now will ye see what I proffer?—
To give all in my coffer,
To-morrow next to offer
Her head-mass[13] penny.

SECUNDUS PASTOR. Faith, so weary and
worn is there none in this shire.
I must sleep, were I shorn of a part of my
hire.
TERTIUS PASTOR. I'm naked, cold, and for-
lorn, and would fain have a fire.
PRIMUS PASTOR. I'm clean spent, for, since
morn, I've run in the mire.
Watch thou, do!
SECUNDUS PASTOR. Nay, I'll lie down hereby,
For I must sleep, truly.
TERTIUS PASTOR. As good a man's son was I,

As any of you! [*They prepare to lie
down*]
But, Mak, come lie here in between, if you
please.
5   MAK. You'll be hindered, I fear, from talk-
ing at ease,
Indeed! [*He yields and lies down*]
From my top to my toe,
Manus tuas commendo,
10 *Poncio Pilato,*
Christ's cross me speed! [*Tunc surgit,
pastoribus dormientibus et dicit:*][14]
Now 'twere time a man knew, that lacks what
he'd fain hold,
15 To steal privily through then into a fold,
And then nimbly his work do—and be not too
bold,
For his bargain he'd rue, if it were told
At the ending
20 Now 'twere time their wrath to tell!—
But he needs good counsel
That fain would fare well,
And has but little for spending.

25 But about you a circle as round as a moon, [*He
draws the circle*]
Till I have done what I will, till that it be noon,
That ye lie stone still, until I have done;
And I shall say thereto still, a few good words
30   soon
Of might:
Over your heads my hand I lift.
Out go your eyes! Blind be your sight!
But I must make still better shift,
35   If it's to be right.

Lord, how hard they sleep—that may ye all
hear!
I never herded sheep, but I'll learn now, that's
40   clear.
Though the flock be scared a heap, yet shall I
slip near. [*He captures a sheep*]
Hey—hitherward creep! Now that betters our
cheer
45   From sorrow.
A fat sheep, I dare say!
A good fleece, swear I may!
When I can, then I'll pay,
But this I will borrow! [MAK *goes to his
50   house, and knocks at the door*]

[14] Then he gets up, the shepherds being asleep,
and speaks.

[13] money for funeral service.

MAK. Ho, Gill, art thou in? Get us a light!
UXOR EIUS.[15] Who makes such a din at this
 time of night?
I am set for to spin, I think not I might
Rise a penny to win! Curses loud on them light 5
  Trouble cause!
A busy house-wife all day
To be called thus away!
No work's done, I say,
  Because of such small chores! 10

  MAK. The door open, good Gill. See'st thou
  not what I bring?
  UXOR. Draw the latch, an thou will. Ah,
  come in, my sweeting!
  MAK. Yea, thou need'st not care didst thou
  kill me with such long standing!
  UXOR. By the naked neck still thou art likely
  to swing.
  MAK. Oh, get away!
I am worthy of my meat,
For at a pinch I can get
More than they that swink and sweat
  All the long day.

Thus it fell to my lot, Gill! Such luck came my
  way! 25
  UXOR. It were a foul blot to be hanged for
  it some day.
  MAK. I have often escaped, Gillot, as risky 30
  a play.
  UXOR. But "though long goes the pot to the
  water," men say,
    "At last
Comes it home broken." 35
  MAK. Well know I the token,
But let it never be spoken—
    But come and help fast!

I would he were slain, I would like well to eat, 40
This twelvemonth was I not so fain to have
  some sheep's meat.
  UXOR. Should they come ere he's slain and
  hear the sheep bleat—
  MAK. Then might I be ta'en. That were a 45
  cold sweat!
    The door—
Go close it!
  UXOR. Yes, Mak,—
For if they come at thy back—— 50

MAK. Then might I suffer from the whole
  pack
    The devil, and more!

  UXOR. A good trick have I spied, since thou
  thinkest of none,
Here shall we him hide until they be gone—
In my cradle he'll bide—just you let me
  alone—
And I shall lie beside in childbed and groan.
  MAK.   Well said!
And I shall say that this night
A boy child saw the light.
  UXOR. Now that day was bright
    That saw me born and bred!

This is a good device and a far cast.
Ever a woman's advice gives help at the last!
I care not who spies! Now go thou back fast!
  MAK. Save I come ere they rise, there'll
  blow a cold blast! [MAK *goes back to the
  moor, and prepares to lie down*]
    I will go sleep.
Still sleeps all this company,
And I shall slip in privily
As it had never been I
    That carried off their sheep.

  PRIMUS PASTOR. *Resurrex a mortruis!* Reach
  me a hand!
Judas carnas dominus![16] I can hardly stand!
My foot's asleep, by Jesus, and my mouth's
  dry as sand.
I thought we had laid us full nigh to England!
  SECUNDUS PASTOR.   Yea, verily!
Lord, but I have slept well.
As fresh as an eel,
As light do I feel,
  As leaf on the tree.

  TERTIUS PASTOR. Ben'cite be herein! So my
  body is quaking,
My heart is out of my skin with the to-do it's
  making.
Who's making all this din, so my head's set to
  aching?
To the doer I'll win! Hark, you fellows, be
  waking!
    Four we were—
See ye aught of Mak now?

---

[15] his wife.   [16] pig Latin.

PRIMUS PASTOR. We were up ere thou.
SECUNDUS PASTOR. Man, to God I vow,
    Not once did he stir.

TERTIUS PASTOR. Methought he was lapt in   5
    a wolf's skin.
PRIMUS PASTOR. So many are wrapped now
    —namely within.
TERTIUS PASTOR. When we had long napped,
    methought with a gin   10
A fat sheep he trapped, but he made no din.
SECUNDUS PASTOR. Be still!
Thy dream makes thee mad,
It's a nightmare you've had.
PRIMUS PASTOR. God bring good out of bad, 15
    If it be his will!

SECUNDUS PASTOR. Rise, Mak, for shame!
    Right long dost thou lie.
MAK. Now Christ's Holy Name be with us 20
    for aye!
What's this? by Saint James, I can't move
    when I try.
I suppose I'm the same. Oo-o, my neck's lain
    awry   25
        Enough, perdie—
Many thanks!—since yester even.
Now, by Saint Stephen,
I was plagued by a sweven,[17]
        Knocked the heart of me.   30

I thought Gill began to croak and travail full
    sad,
Well-nigh at the first cock, with a young lad
To add to our flock. Of that I am never glad, 35
I have "tow on my rock more than ever I had."[18]
        Oh, my head!
A house full of young banes—
The devil knock out their brains!
Woe is him many gains,   40
        And thereto little bread.

I must go home, by your leave, to Gill, as I
    thought.
Prithee look in my sleeve that I steal naught.
I am loath you to grieve, or from you take 45
    aught.
TERTIUS PASTOR. Go forth—ill may'st thou
    thrive! [MAK *goes*] Now I would that we
    sought   50

---
[17] dream.
[18] Freely, "I've more to do than ever."

This morn,
That we had all our store.
PRIMUS PASTOR. But I will go before. Let us
    meet.
SECUNDUS PASTOR. Where, Daw?
TERTIUS PASTOR. At the crooked thorn.
    [*They go out*]

MAK *enters and knocks at his door*

MAK. Undo the door, see who's here! How
    long must I stand?
UXOR EIUS. Who's making such gear? Now
    "walk in the wenyand."[19]
MAK. Ah, Gill, what cheer? It is I, Mak,
    your husband.
UXOR. Then may we "see here the devil in
    a band,"
        Sir Guile!
Lo, he comes with a note
As he were held by the throat.
And I cannot devote
        To my work any while.

MAK. Will ye hear the pother she makes to
    get her a gloze[20]—
Naught but pleasure she takes, and curls up
    her toes.
UXOR. Why, who runs, who wakes, who
    comes, who goes,
Who brews, who bakes, what makes me hoarse,
    d'ye suppose!
        And also,
It is ruth to behold,
Now in hot, now in cold,
Full woeful is the household
        That no woman doth know!

But what end hast thou made with the shep-
    herds, Mak?
MAK. The last word that they said when I
    turned my back
Was they'd see that they had of their sheep
    all the pack.
They'll not be pleased, I'm afraid, when they
    their sheep lack,
        Perdie.
But how so the game go,
They'll suspect me, whether or no,

---
[19] Literally, "Walk in the waning of the moon,"
an unlucky time; actually, the sense is "Go to the
devil."
[20] excuse.

And raise a great bellow,
     And cry out upon me.

But thou must use thy sleight.
     UXOR. Yea, I think it not ill.
I shall swaddle him aright in my cradle with
     skill.
Were it yet a worse plight, yet a way I'd find
     still. [GILL *meanwhile swaddles the sheep
     and places him in the cradle*]
I will lie down forthright. Come tuck me up.
     MAK. That I will.
     UXOR. Behind! [MAK *tucks her in at the
     back*]
If Coll come and his marrow,[21]
They will nip us full narrow.
     MAK. But I may cry out "Haro,"
          The sheep if they find.
     UXOR. Hearken close till they call—they
     will come anon.
Come and make ready all, and sing thou
     alone—
Sing lullaby, thou shalt, for I must groan
And cry out by the wall on Mary and John
          Full sore.
Sing lullaby on fast.
When thou hear'st them at last,
And, save I play a shrewd cast,
          Trust me no more.

The SHEPHERDS *enter on the moor and meet*
     TERTIUS PASTOR. Ah, Coll, good morn! Why
     sleepest thou not?
     PRIMUS PASTOR. Alas, that ever I was born!
     We have a foul blot.
A fat wether have we lorn.
     TERTIUS PASTOR. Marry, God forbid, say it
     not!
     SECUNDUS PASTOR. Who should do us that
     scorn? That were a foul spot.
     PRIMUS PASTOR. Some shrew.
I have sought with my dogs
All Horbury Shrogs,
And of fifteen hogs
          Found I all but one ewe.

     TERTIUS PASTOR. Now trust me, if you will,
     by Saint Thomas of Kent,
Either Mak or Gill their aid thereto lent!
     PRIMUS PASTOR. Peace, man, be still! I saw

when he went.
Thou dost slander him ill. Thou shouldest
     repent
          At once, indeed!
5   SECUNDUS PASTOR. So may I thrive, perdie,
Should I die here where I be,
I would say it was he
          That did that same deed!

10   TERTIUS PASTOR. Go we thither, quick
     sped, and run on our feet,
I shall never eat bread till I know all com-
     plete!
     PRIMUS PASTOR. Nor drink in my head till
15   with him I meet.
     SECUNDUS PASTOR. In no place will I bed
     until I him greet,
          My brother!
One vow I will plight,
20 Till I see him in sight,
I will ne'er sleep one night
          Where I do another! [*They go to* MAK's
          house. MAK, *hearing them coming,
          begins to sing lullaby at the top of his
25   voice, while* GILL *groans in concert*]

     TERTIUS PASTOR. Hark the row they make!
List our sire there croon!
     PRIMUS PASTOR. Never heard I voice break
30   so clear out of tune.
Call to him.
     SECUNDUS PASTOR. Mak, wake there! Undo
     your door soon!
     MAK. Who is that spake as if it were noon?
35   Aloft?
Who is that, I say?
     TERTIUS PASTOR. Good fellows, if it were
     day— [*mocking* MAK]
     MAK. As far as ye may,
          Kindly, speak soft;

O'er a sick woman's head in such grievous
     throes!
I were liefer dead than she should suffer such
     woes.
     UXOR. Go elsewhere, well sped. Oh, how
     my pain grows—
Each footfall ye tread goes straight through
     my nose
          So loud, woe's me!
     PRIMUS PASTOR. Tell us, Mak, if ye may,
How fare ye, I say?

---
[21] companion.

MAK. But are ye in this town to-day—
　　Now how fare ye?

Ye have run in the mire and are wet still a bit,
I will make you a fire, if ye will sit.　　　5
A nurse I would hire—can you help me in it?
Well quit is my hire—my dream the truth
　　hit—
　　　In season.
I have bairns, if ye knew,　　　10
Plenty more than will do,
But we must drink as we brew,
　　And that is but reason.

I would ye would eat ere ye go. Methinks that 15
　　ye sweat.
SECUNDUS PASTOR. Nay, no help could we
　　know in what's drunken or eat.
MAK. Why, sir, ails you aught but good,
　　though?　　　20
TERTIUS PASTOR. Yea, our sheep that we get
Are stolen as they go; our loss is great.
　　MAK.　　Sirs, drink!
Had I been there,
Some one had bought it sore, I swear.　　25
PRIMUS PASTOR. Marry, some men trow that
　　ye were,
　　　And that makes us think!

SECUNDUS PASTOR. Mak, one and another 30
　　trows it should be ye.
TERTIUS PASTOR. Either ye or your spouse,
　　so say we.
MAK. Now if aught suspicion throws on
　　Gill or me,　　　35
Come and search our house, and then may ye
　　see
　　　Who had her—
If I any sheep got,
Or cow or stot;[22]　　　40
And Gill, my wife, rose not,
　　Here since we laid her.

As I am true and leal,[23] to God, here I pray
That this is the first meal that I shall eat this 45
　　day.
PRIMUS PASTOR. Mak, as may I have weal,
　　advise thee, I say—
"He learned timely to steal that could not say
　　nay."　　　50

UXOR. Me, my death you've dealt!
Out, ye thieves, nor come again,
Ye've come just to rob us, that's plain.
　　MAK. Hear ye not how she groans amain—
　　　Your hearts should melt!

UXOR. From my child, thieves, begone. Go
　　nigh him not,—there's the door!
MAK. If ye knew all she's borne, your hearts
　　would be sore.
Ye do wrong, I you warn, thus to come in
　　before
A woman that has borne—but I say no more.
　　UXOR. Oh, my middle—I die!
I vow to God so mild,
If ever I you beguiled,
That I will eat this child
　　That doth in this cradle lie!

MAK. Peace, woman, by God's pain, and
　　cry not so.
Thou dost hurt thy brain and fill me with woe.
　　SECUNDUS PASTOR. I trow our sheep is slain.
　　What find ye two, though?
Our work's all in vain. We may as well go.
　　Save clothes and such matters
I can find no flesh
Hard or nesh,[24]
Salt nor fresh,
　　Except two empty platters.

Of any "cattle" but this, tame or wild, that we
　　see,
None, as may I have bliss, smelled as loud as
　　he.
UXOR. No, so God joy and bliss of my child
　　may give me!
PRIMUS PASTOR. We have aimed amiss; de-
　　ceived, I trow, were we.
SECUNDUS PASTOR. Sir, wholly each one.
Sir, Our Lady him save!
Is your child a knave?
　　MAK. Any lord might him have,
　　　This child, for his son.

When he wakes, so he grips, it's a pleasure
　　to see.
TERTIUS PASTOR. Good luck to his hips, and
　　blessing, say we!
But who were his gossips,[25] now tell who they
　　be?

---

[22] steer.　　　[23] loyal.　　　[24] soft.　　　[25] godparents.

MAK. Blest be their lips—— [*hesitates, at a loss*]

PRIMUS PASTOR. [*aside*] Hark a lie now, trust me!

MAK. So may God them thank,
Parkin and Gibbon Waller, I say,
And gentle John Horn, in good fey—
He made all the fun and play—
    With the great shank.

SECUNDUS PASTOR. Mak, friends will we be, for we are at one.

MAK. We!—nay, count not on me, for amends get I none.
Farewell, all three! Glad 'twill be when ye're 15 gone! [*The* SHEPHERDS *go*]

TERTIUS PASTOR. "Fair words there may be, but love there is none
    This year."

PRIMUS PASTOR. Gave ye the child any- 20 thing?

SECUNDUS PASTOR. I trow, not one farthing.

TERTIUS PASTOR. Fast back I will fling.
    Await ye me here. [DAW *goes back. The other* SHEPHERDS *turn and follow him* 25 *slowly, entering while he is talking with* MAK]

[TERTIUS PASTOR.] Mak, I trust thou'lt not grieve, if I go to thy child.

MAK. Nay, great hurt I receive,—thou hast 30 acted full wild.

TERTIUS PASTOR. Thy bairn 'twill not grieve, little day-star so mild.
Mak, by your leave, let me give your child
    But six-pence. [DAW *goes to cradle, and* 35 *starts to draw away the covering*]

MAK. Nay, stop it—he sleeps!

TERTIUS PASTOR. Methinks he peeps—

MAK. When he wakens, he weeps;
    I pray you go hence! [*The other* SHEP- 40 HERDS *return*]

TERTIUS PASTOR. Give me leave him to kiss, and lift up the clout.
What the devil is this?—he has a long snout! 45

PRIMUS PASTOR. He's birth-marked amiss. We waste time hereabout.

SECUNDUS PASTOR. "A weft[26] that ill-spun is comes ever foul out." [*He sees the sheep*]
    Aye—so!
He is like to our sheep! 50

TERTIUS PASTOR. Ho, Gib, may I peep?

PRIMUS PASTOR. I trow "Nature will creep Where it may not go."[27]

SECUNDUS PASTOR. This was a quaint gaud and a far cast.
It was a high fraud.

TERTIUS PASTOR. Yea, sirs, that was't.
Let's burn this bawd, and bind her fast.
"A false scold," by the Lord, "will hang at the last!"
    So shalt thou!
Will ye see how they swaddle
His four feet in the middle!
Saw I never in the cradle
    A horned lad ere now!

MAK. Peace, I say! Tell ye what, this to-do ye can spare! [*pretending anger*]
It was I him begot and yon woman him bare.

PRIMUS PASTOR. What the devil for name has he got? Mak?—Lo, God, Mak's heir!

SECUNDUS PASTOR. Come, joke with him not. Now, may God give him care, I say!

UXOR. A pretty child is he
As sits on a woman's knee,
A dilly-down, perdie,
    To make a man gay.

TERTIUS PASTOR. I know him by the earmark —that is a good token.

MAK. I tell you, sirs, hark, his nose was broken—
Then there told me a clerk he'd been mis-spoken.[28]

PRIMUS PASTOR. Ye deal falsely and dark; I would fain be wroken.[29]
    Get a weapon,—go!

UXOR. He was taken by an elf,
I saw it myself.
When the clock struck twelve,
    Was he mis-shapen so.

SECUNDUS PASTOR. Ye two are at one, that's plain, in all ye've done and said.

PRIMUS PASTOR. Since their theft they main-tain, let us leave them dead!

MAK. If I trespass again, strike off my head!
At your will I remain.

TERTIUS PASTOR. Sirs, take my counsel in-

---

[26] woof.   [27] walk.   [28] bewitched.   [29] avenged.

stead.
    For this trespass
We'll neither curse nor wrangle in spite,
Chide nor fight,
But have done forthright,
    And toss him in canvas. [*They toss* MAK
in one of GILL's *canvas sheets till they are
tired. He disappears groaning into his
house. The* SHEPHERDS *pass over to the
moor on the other side of the stage*] 10

    PRIMUS PASTOR. Lord, lo! but I am sore, like
        to burst, in back and breast.
In faith, I may no more, therefore will I rest.
    SECUNDUS PASTOR. Like a sheep of seven 15
        score he weighed in my fist.
To sleep anywhere, therefore seemeth now
        best.
    TERTIUS PASTOR. Now I you pray,
On this green let us lie. 20
    PRIMUS PASTOR. O'er those thieves yet
        chafe I.
    TERTIUS PASTOR. Let your anger go by,—
        Come do as I say.

As they are about to lie down THE ANGEL *appears*
[ANGELUS *cantat "Gloria in excelsis." Postea
dicat:*][30]

ANGELUS. Rise, herdsmen gentle, attend ye, 30
    for now is he born
From the fiend that shall rend what Adam had
    lorn,
That warlock to shend,[31] this night is he born,
God is made your friend now on this morn. 35
    Lo! thus doth he command—
Go to Bethlehem, see
Where he lieth so free,[32]
In a manger full lowly
    'Twixt where twain beasts stand. [THE 40
ANGEL *goes*]

    PRIMUS PASTOR. This was a fine voice, even
        as ever I heard.
It is a marvel, by St. Stephen, thus with dread 45
    to be stirred.
    SECUNDUS PASTOR. 'Twas of God's Son from
        heaven he these tidings averred.
All the wood with a levin,[33] methought at his
    50

---

word
    Shone fair.
    TERTIUS PASTOR. Of a Child did he tell,
In Bethlehem, mark ye well.
    PRIMUS PASTOR. That this star yonder doth
        spell—
    Let us seek him there.

    SECUNDUS PASTOR. Say, what was his song—
        how it went, did ye hear?
Three breves[34] to a long—
    TERTIUS PASTOR. Marry, yes, to my ear
There was no crotchet[35] wrong, naught it
    lacked and full clear!
    PRIMUS PASTOR. To sing it here, us among,
        as he nicked it, full near,
    I know how—
    SECUNDUS PASTOR. Let's see how you croon!
Can you bark at the moon?
    TERTIUS PASTOR. Hold your tongues, have
        done!
    Hark after me now! [*They sing*]

    SECUNDUS PASTOR. To Bethlehem he bade
        that we should go.
I am sore adrad that we tarry too slow.
    TERTIUS PASTOR. Be merry, and not sad—
        our song's of mirth not of woe,
To be forever glad as our meed may we know,
    Without noise.
    PRIMUS PASTOR. Hie we thither, then,
        speedily,
Though we be wet and weary,
To that Child and that Lady!—
    We must not lose those joys!

    SECUNDUS PASTOR. We find by the prophecy
        —let be your din!—
David and Isaiah, and more that I mind me
    therein,
They prophesied by clergy, that in a virgin,
Should he alight and lie, to assuage our sin,
    And slake it,
Our nature, from woe,
For it was Isaiah said so,
"*Ecce virgo
    Concipiet*"[36] a child that is naked.

    TERTIUS PASTOR. Full glad may we be and
        await that day
That lovesome one to see, that all mights doth

---

[30] The angel sings "Glory in the highest," next
is to say.
[31] That devil to destroy.   [32] noble.
[33] lightning flash.

[34] short notes.   [35] quarter-note.
[36] Behold, a virgin shall conceive.

sway.
Lord, well it were with me, now and for aye,
Might I kneel on my knee some word for to
say
    To that child. 5
But the angel said
In a crib was he laid,
He was poorly arrayed,
    Both gracious and mild.
                  10

PRIMUS PASTOR. Patriarchs that have been
    and prophets beforne,
They desired to have seen this child that
    is born.
They are gone full clean,—that have they lorn. 15
We shall see him, I ween, ere it be morn,
    For token.
When I see him and feel,
I shall know full well,
It is true as steel, 20
    What prophets have spoken,

To so poor as we are that he would appear,
First find and declare by his messenger.
    SECUNDUS PASTOR. Go we now, let us fare, 25
    the place is us near.
    TERTIUS PASTOR. I am ready and eager to be
there; let us together with cheer
    To that bright one go.
Lord, if thy will it be, 30
Untaught are we all three,
Some kind of joy grant us, that we
    Thy creature, comfort may know!

They enter the stable and adore the infant 35
Savior

    PRIMUS PASTOR. Hail, thou comely and clean
    one! Hail, young Child!
Hail, Maker, as I mean, from a maiden so mild!
Thou hast harried, I ween, the warlock so 40
    wild,—
The false beguiler with his teen[37] now goes be-
guiled.
    Lo, he merries,
Lo, he laughs, my sweeting! 45
A happy meeting!
Here's my promised greeting,—
    Have a bob[38] of cherries!

    SECUNDUS PASTOR. Hail, sovereign Savior, 50
    for thou hast us sought!
Hail, noble nursling and flower, that all things

hast wrought!
Hail, thou, full of gracious power, that made
    all from nought!
Hail, I kneel and I cower! A bird have I
    brought
    To my bairn from far.
Hail, little tiny mop!
Of our creed thou art the crop,
I fair would drink in thy cup,
    Little day-star!

    TERTIUS PASTOR. Hail, darling dear one, full
    of Godhead indeed!
I pray thee be near, when I have need.
Hail, sweet is thy cheer! My heart would bleed
To see thee sit here in so poor a weed,
    With no pennies.
Hail, put forth thy dall,[39]
I bring thee but a ball,
Keep it, and play with it withal,
    And go to the tennis.

    MARIA. The Father of Heaven this night,
    God omnipotent,
That setteth all things aright, his Son hath he
    sent.
My name he named and did light on me ere
    that he went.
I conceived him forthright through his might
    as he meant,
    And now he is born.
May he keep you from woe!
I shall pray him do so.
Tell it, forth as ye go,
    And remember this morn.

    PRIMUS PASTOR. Farewell, Lady, so fair to be-
    hold
With thy child on thy knee!
    SECUNDUS PASTOR. But he lies full cold!
Lord, 'tis well with me! Now we go, behold!
    TERTIUS PASTOR. Forsooth, already it seems
    to be told
    Full oft!
    PRIMUS PASTOR. What grace we have found!
    SECUNDUS PASTOR. Now are we won safe and
    sound.
    TERTIUS PASTOR. Come forth, to sing are we
    bound.
    Make it ring then aloft! [*They depart
singing*]
    Explicit pagina Pastorum.[40]

---

[37] sorrow.   [38] bunch.   [39] hand.   [40] The Shepherds' play ends.

THE FIRST PART OF KING HENRY THE FOURTH*

WILLIAM SHAKESPEARE

Shakespeare (1564–1616) was born in Stratford, where for a number of years his father was a prosperous tradesman and holder of municipal offices. Presumably Shakespeare had a local grammar-school education; we have no evidence of further formal instruction. Late in his teens he went through a sudden marriage ceremony with Anne Hathaway, several years his senior; their union produced three children. There are several unsubstantiated tales about the young Shakespeare—that he was arrested for poaching, and that he taught school, for example. Otherwise we do not know much about him until he went to London, where his rise was to be rapid.

In the London theater, Shakespeare went up the ladder by acting minor roles, helping to arrange texts, collaborating, and branching out on his own. Somehow he won the patronage of Southampton, to whom he dedicated the non-dramatic poems, The Rape of Lucrece and Venus and Adonis, and whom he probably had in mind when he wrote the sonnets, 154 of them, composed in the 1590's and published in 1609 by Thorpe. (See comment on songs and sonnets, I, 201.)

Shakespeare was successful at the box office, prospered, bought real estate, applied for a grant of a coat of arms. As a shareholder in various acting companies the maturing dramatist wrote, produced, and shared in the profits. It is customary to divide his plays into four periods from 1590 to 1610: early experiment in comedy, history, and tragedy; great histories and comedies; great tragedies and dark comedies; romances, weak attempts to recapture the old fire, and one last good comedy. In competition with Jonson, Beaumont, Fletcher, and others Shakespeare revealed an incomparable genius which eventually was to be recognized the world around. Apparently written out, he may have retired to Stratford, where, at any rate, he was buried.

Shakespeare's reputation does not depend on his plots, which were based largely on borrowed material; rather, his development of character and mastery of the poetic line were responsible for his rise to the heights. It is impossible to pick one of his plays for an anthology and satisfy everyone, or do more than hint at his power and universality. Your editors, like others before them, have chosen Henry IV, Part One, because it combines history with comedy and more than a hint of tragedy. (It is fondly to be hoped that a great comedy and a great tragedy—Twelfth Night and Hamlet, say —can be included in outside reading.) Henry IV, based on Holinshed and a few details from an old play, is interesting for its relationship to Richard II, Henry IV, Part Two, and Henry V. For action, fine major and minor characters, comedy, and all-around good theater this play is a fitting place to begin a study of the dramatist's abilities.

* The Kittredge text of this play is here reprinted by permission of Ginn and Company, publishers.

Dramatis Personae

KING HENRY THE FOURTH

HENRY, PRINCE OF WALES, } *sons to the*
PRINCE JOHN OF LANCASTER, } KING   5

EARL OF WESTMORELAND

SIR WALTER BLUNT

THOMAS PERCY, *Earl of Worcester*

HENRY PERCY, *Earl of Northumberland*

HENRY PERCY, surnamed HOTSPUR, *his son*   10

EDMUND MORTIMER, *Earl of March*

RICHARD SCROOP, *Archbishop of York*

ARCHIBALD, *Earl of Douglas*

OWEN GLENDOWER

SIR RICHARD VERNON   15

SIR JOHN FALSTAFF

SIR MICHAEL, *a friend to the* ARCHBISHOP OF YORK

POINS

GADSHILL   20

PETO

BARDOLPH

LADY PERCY, *wife to* HOTSPUR, *and sister to* MORTIMER

LADY MORTIMER, *daughter to* GLENDOWER, *and*   25 *wife to* MORTIMER

MISTRESS QUICKLY *hostess of the Boar's Head in Eastcheap*

Lords, Officers, Sheriff, Vintner, Chamberlain, Drawers, two Carriers, Travellers, and At-   30 *tendants*

SCENE. England and Wales

ACT I

SCENE I.

London. The Palace

Enter the KING, LORD JOHN OF LANCASTER,   40
EARL OF WESTMORELAND, [SIR WALTER BLUNT,] *with others*

KING. So shaken as we are, so wan with care,
Find we a time for frighted peace to pant   45
And breathe short-winded accents of new broils
To be commenc'd in stronds[1] afar remote.
No more the thirsty entrance of this soil
Shall daub her lips with her own children's   50 blood.

No more shall trenching war channel her fields,
Nor bruise her flow'rets with the armed hoofs
Of hostile paces. Those opposed eyes
Which, like the meteors of a troubled heaven,
All of one nature, of one substance bred,   5
Did lately meet in the intestine shock
And furious close of civil butchery,
Shall now in mutual well-beseeming ranks
March all one way and be no more oppos'd
Against acquaintance, kindred, and allies.   10
The edge of war, like an ill-sheathed knife,
No more shall cut his master. Therefore, friends,
As far as to the sepulchre of Christ—
Whose soldier now, under whose blessed **cross**   15
We are impressed and engag'd to fight—
Forthwith a power of English shall we levy,
Whose arms were moulded in their mother's womb
To chase these pagans in those holy fields   20
Over whose acres walk'd those blessed feet
Which fourteen hundred years ago were nail'd
For our advantage on the bitter cross.
But this our purpose now is twelvemonth old,
And bootless 'tis to tell you we will go.   25
Therefore we meet not now. Then let me hear
Of you, my gentle cousin[2] Westmoreland,
What yesternight our Council did decree
In forwarding this dear expedience.

WEST. My liege, this haste was hot in ques-   30 tion
And many limits of the charge set down
But yesternight; when all athwart there came
A post from Wales, loaden with heavy news;
Whose worst was that the noble Mortimer,   35
Leading the men of Herefordshire to fight
Against the irregular and wild Glendower,
Was by the rude hands of that Welshman taken,
A thousand of his people butchered;   40
Upon whose dead corpse there was such misuse,
Such beastly shameless transformation,
By those Welshwomen done as may not be
Without much shame retold or spoken of.   45

KING. It seems then that the tidings of this broil
Brake off our business for the Holy Land.

WEST. This, match'd with other, did, my gracious lord;   50

---

[1] shores.

[2] kinsman.

For more uneven and unwelcome news
Came from the North, and thus it did import:
On Holy-rood Day[3] the gallant Hotspur there,
Young Harry Percy, and brave Archibald,
That ever-valiant and approved Scot,   5
At Holmedon met,
Where they did spend a sad and bloody hour;
As by discharge of their artillery
And shape of likelihood the news was told;
For he that brought them, in the very heat   10
And pride of their contention did take horse,
Uncertain of the issue any way.
   KING. Here is a dear, a true-industrious
    friend,
Sir Walter Blunt, new lighted from his horse, 15
Stain'd with the variation of each soil
Betwixt that Holmedon and this seat of ours,
And he hath brought us smooth and welcome
   news.
The Earl of Douglas is discomfited;   20
Ten thousand bold Scots, two-and-twenty
   knights,
Balk'd[4] in their own blood did Sir Walter see
On Holmedon's plains. Of prisoners, Hotspur
   took   25
Mordake Earl of Fife and eldest son
To beaten Douglas, and the Earl of Athol,
Of Murray, Angus, and Menteith.
And is not this an honourable spoil?
A gallant prize? Ha, cousin, is it not?   30
   WEST. In faith,
It is a conquest for a prince to boast of.
   KING. Yea, there thou mak'st me sad, and
    mak'st me sin
In envy that my Lord Northumberland
Should be the father to so blest a son—
A son who is the theme of honour's tongue,
Amongst a grove the very straightest plant;
Who is sweet Fortune's minion and her pride;
Whilst I, by looking on the praise of him,   40
See riot and dishonour stain the brow
Of my young Harry. O that it could be prov'd
That some night-tripping fairy had exchang'd
In cradle clothes our children where they lay,
And call'd mine Percy, his Plantagenet!   45
Then would I have his Harry, and he mine.
But let him from my thoughts. What think you,
   coz,
Of this young Percy's pride? The prisoners
Which he in this adventure hath surpris'd   50
To his own use he keeps, and sends me word

I shall have none but Mordake Earl of Fife.
   WEST. This is his uncle's teaching, this is
    Worcester,
Malevolent to you in all aspects,
Which makes him prune himself and bristle   5
   up
The crest of youth against your dignity.
   KING. But I have sent for him to answer this;
And for this cause awhile we must neglect
Our holy purpose to Jerusalem.   10
Cousin, on Wednesday next our council we
Will hold at Windsor. So inform the lords;
But come yourself with speed to us again;
For more is to be said and to be done
Than out of anger can be uttered.   15
   WEST. I will, my liege.   [*exeunt.*]

SCENE II.

London. An apartment of the PRINCE'S   20

Enter PRINCE OF WALES *and*
SIR JOHN FALSTAFF

   FAL. Now, Hal, what time of day is it, lad?
   PRINCE. Thou art so fat-witted with drinking   25
of old sack,[5] and unbuttoning thee after supper, and sleeping upon benches after noon,
that thou hast forgotten to demand that truly
which thou wouldest truly know. What a devil
hast thou to do with the time of the day? Un- 30
less hours were cups of sack, and minutes ca-
pons, and clocks the tongues of bawds, and
dials the signs of leaping houses, and the
blessed sun himself a fair hot wench in flame-
coloured taffeta, I see no reason why thou   35
shouldst be so superfluous to demand the time
of the day.
   FAL. Indeed you come near me now, Hal;
for we that take purses go by the moon and
the seven stars, and not by Phœbus,[6] he, that 40
wand'ring knight so fair. And I prithee, sweet
wag, when thou art king, as, God save thy
Grace—Majesty I should say, for grace thou
wilt have none——
   PRINCE. What, none?   45
   FAL. No, by my troth; not so much as will
serve to be prologue to an egg and butter.
   PRINCE. Well, how then? Come, roundly,
roundly.
   FAL. Marry, then, sweet wag, when thou art 50

---

[3] Sept. 14.   [4] piled up in ridges.
[5] sherry, or wine of a sherry type.
[6] the sun.

king, let not us that are squires of the night's body be called thieves of the day's beauty. Let us be Diana's Foresters, Gentlemen of the Shade, Minions of the Moon; and let men say we be men of good government, being gov- 5 erned as the sea is, by our noble and chaste mistress the moon, under whose countenance we steal.

PRINCE. Thou sayest well, and it holds well too; for the fortune of us that are the moon's 10 men doth ebb and flow like the sea, being governed, as the sea is, by the moon. As, for proof now: a purse of gold most resolutely snatch'd on Monday night and most dissolutely spent on Tuesday morning; got with swearing 15 'Lay by,' and spent with crying 'Bring in'; now in as low an ebb as the foot of the ladder,[7] and by-and-by in as high a flow as the ridge of the gallows.

FAL. By the Lord, thou say'st true, lad—and 20 is not my hostess of the tavern a most sweet wench?

PRINCE. As the honey of Hybla,[8] my old lad of the castle—and is not a buff jerkin a most sweet robe of durance? 25

FAL. How now, how now, mad wag? What, in thy quips and thy quiddities? What a plague have I to do with a buff jerkin?

PRINCE. Why, what a pox have I to do with my hostess of the tavern? 30

FAL. Well, thou hast call'd her to a reckoning many a time and oft.

PRINCE. Did I ever call for thee to pay thy part?

FAL. No; I'll give thee thy due, thou hast 35 paid all there.

PRINCE. Yea, and elsewhere, so far as my coin would stretch; and where it would not, I have used my credit.

FAL. Yea, and so us'd it that, were it not here 40 apparent that thou art heir apparent—But I prithee, sweet wag, shall there be gallows standing in England when thou art king? and resolution thus fubb'd[9] as it is with the rusty curb of old father antic the law? Do not thou, 45 when thou art king, hang a thief.

PRINCE. No; thou shalt.

FAL. Shall I? O rare! By the Lord, I'll be a brave judge.

PRINCE. Thou judgest false already. I mean, 50 thou shalt have the hanging of the thieves and

so become a rare hangman.

FAL. Well, Hal, well; and in some sort it jumps with my humour[10] as well as waiting in the court, I can tell you.

PRINCE. For obtaining of suits?

FAL. Yea, for obtaining of suits, whereof the hangman hath no lean wardrobe. 'Sblood,[11] I am as melancholy as a gib cat or a lugg'd bear.[12]

PRINCE. Or an old lion, or a lover's lute.

FAL. Yea, or the drone of a Lincolnshire bagpipe.

PRINCE. What sayest thou to a hare, or the melancholy of Moor Ditch?

FAL. Thou hast the most unsavoury similes, and art indeed the most comparative, rascalliest, sweet young prince. But, Hal, I prithee trouble me no more with vanity. I would to God thou and I knew where a commodity of good names were to be bought. An old lord of 20 the Council rated me the other day in the street about you, sir, but I mark'd him not; and yet he talk'd very wisely, but I regarded him not; and yet he talk'd wisely, and in the street too. 25

PRINCE. Thou didst well; for wisdom cries out in the streets, and no man regards it.

FAL. O, thou hast damnable iteration, and art indeed able to corrupt a saint. Thou hast 30 done much harm upon me, Hal—God forgive thee for it! Before I knew thee, Hal, I knew nothing; and now am I, if a man should speak truly, little better than one of the wicked. I must give over this life, and I will give it over! 35 By the Lord, an I do not, I am a villain! I'll be damn'd for never a king's son in Christendom.

PRINCE. Where shall we take a purse tomorrow, Jack?

FAL. Zounds,[13] where thou wilt, lad! I'll 40 make one. An I do not, call me villain and baffle[14] me.

PRINCE. I see a good amendment of life in thee—from praying to purse-taking.

FAL. Why, Hal, 'tis my vocation, Hal. 'Tis 45 no sin for a man to labour in his vocation.

Enter POINS

Poins! Now shall we know if Gadshill have set a match. O, if men were to be saved by merit,

---

[7] of the gallows.   [8] in Sicily.   [9] thwarted.

[10] disposition.   [11] God's blood.
[12] tom cat or baited bear.
[13] God's wounds.   [14] disgrace.

what hole in hell were hot enough for him? This is the most omnipotent villain that ever cried 'Stand!' to a true man.

PRINCE. Good morrow, Ned.

POINS. Good morrow, sweet Hal. What says Monsieur Remorse? What says Sir John Sack and Sugar? Jack, how agrees the devil and thee about thy soul, that thou soldest him on Good Friday last for a cup of Madeira and a cold capon's leg?

PRINCE. Sir John stands to his word, the devil shall have his bargain; for he was never yet a breaker of proverbs. He will give the devil his due.

POINS. Then art thou damn'd for keeping thy word with the devil.

PRINCE. Else he had been damn'd for cozening the devil.

POINS. But, my lads, my lads, to-morrow morning, by four o'clock early, at Gadshill![15] There are pilgrims going to Canterbury with rich offerings, and traders riding to London with fat purses. I have vizards[16] for you all; you have horses for yourselves. Gadshill lies tonight in Rochester. I have bespoke supper tomorow night in Eastcheap. We may do it as secure as sleep. If you will go, I will stuff your purses full of crowns; if you will not, tarry at home and be hang'd!

FAL. Here ye, Yedward: if I tarry at home and go not, I'll hang you for going.

POINS. You will, chops?

FAL. Hal, wilt thou make one?

PRINCE. Who, I rob? I a thief? Not I, by my faith.

FAL. There's neither honesty, manhood, nor good fellowship in thee, nor thou cam'st not of the blood royal if thou darest not stand for ten shillings.[17]

PRINCE. Well then, once in my days I'll be a madcap.

FAL. Why, that's well said.

PRINCE. Well, come what will, I'll tarry at home.

FAL. By the Lord, I'll be a traitor then, when thou art king.

PRINCE. I care not.

POINS. Sir John, I prithee, leave the Prince and me alone. I will lay him down such reasons for this adventure that he shall go.

FAL. Well, God give thee the spirit of persuasion and him the ears of profiting, that what thou speakest may move and what he hears may be believed, that the true prince may (for recreation sake) prove a false thief; for the poor abuses of the time want countenance. Farewell; you shall find me in Eastcheap.

PRINCE. Farewell, thou latter spring! farewell, All-hallown summer![18] [*exit* FALSTAFF]

POINS. Now, my good sweet honey lord, ride with us to-morrow. I have a jest to execute that I cannot manage alone. Falstaff, Bardolph, Peto, and Gadshill shall rob those men that we have already waylaid; yourself and I will not be there; and when they have the booty, if you and I do not rob them, cut this head off from my shoulders.

PRINCE. How shall we part with them in setting forth?

POINS. Why, we will set forth before or after them and appoint them a place of meeting, wherein it is at our pleasure to fail; and then will they adventure upon the exploit themselves; which they shall have no sooner achieved, but we'll set upon them.

PRINCE. Yea, but 'tis like that they will know us by our horses, by our habits, and by every other appointment, to be ourselves.

POINS. Tut! our horses they shall not see— I'll tie them in the wood; our vizards we will change after we leave them; and, sirrah, I have cases of buckram for the nonce, to immask our noted outward garments.

PRINCE. Yea, but I doubt they will be too hard for us.

POINS. Well, for two of them, I know them to be as true-bred cowards as ever turn'd back; and for the third, if he fight longer than he sees reason, I'll forswear arms. The virtue of this jest will be the incomprehensible lies that this same fat rogue will tell us when we meet at supper: how thirty, at least, he fought with; what wards, what blows, what extremities he endured; and in the reproof of this lies the jest.

PRINCE. Well, I'll go with thee. Provide us

---

[15] a hill near Rochester; also note, the name of a character in the play.
[16] masks.
[17] pun on "royal" (coin worth 10s.) and "stand for."

[18] equivalent to our Indian summer; Falstaff has taken a new lease on life.

all things necessary and meet me to-night in
Eastcheap. There I'll sup. Farewell.

POINS. Farewell, my lord.   [*exit*]

PRINCE. I know you all, and will awhile uphold

5 The unyok'd humour of your idleness.
Yet herein will I imitate the sun,
Who doth permit the base contagious clouds
To smother up his beauty from the world,
That, when he please again to be himself,
10 Being wanted, he may be more wond'red at
By breaking through the foul and ugly mists
Of vapours that did seem to strangle him.
If all the year were playing holidays,
To sport would be as tedious as to work;
15 But when they seldom come, they wish'd-for
come,
And nothing pleaseth but rare accidents.
So, when this loose behaviour I throw off
And pay the debt I never promised,
20 By how much better than my word I am,
By so much shall I falsify men's hopes;
And, like bright metal on a sullen ground,
My reformation, glitt'ring o'er my fault,
Shall show more goodly and attract more eyes
25 Than that which hath no foil to set it off.
I'll so offend to make offence a skill,
Redeeming time when men think least I will.

[*exit*]

SCENE III.

London. The palace

Enter the KING, NORTHUMBERLAND, WORCES-
TER, HOTSPUR, SIR WALTER BLUNT, *with others*

KING. My blood hath been too cold and
temperate,
Unapt to stir at these indignities,
And you have found me, for accordingly
You tread upon my patience; but be sure
I will from henceforth rather be myself,
Mighty and to be fear'd, than my condition,
45 Which hath been smooth as oil, soft as young
down,
And therefore lost that title of respect
Which the proud soul ne'er pays but to the
proud.
WOR. Our house, my sovereign liege, little 50
deserves
The scourge of greatness to be us'd on it—

And that same greatness too which our own
hands
Have holp to make so portly.
NORTH. My lord——
5 KING. Worcester, get thee gone; for I do see
Danger and disobedience in thine eye.
O, sir, your presence is too bold and
peremptory,
And majesty might never yet endure
10 The moody frontier of a servant brow.
You have good leave to leave us. When we
need
Your use and counsel, we shall send for you.

[*exit* WORCESTER]

You were about to speak.
NORTH.   Yea, my good lord.
Those prisoners in your Highness' name de-
manded
20 Which Harry Percy here at Holmedon took,
Were, as he says, not with such strength de-
nied
As is delivered to your Majesty.
Either envy, therefore, or misprision
25 Is guilty of this fault, and not my son.
HOT. My liege, I did deny no prisoners.
But I remember, when the fight was done,
When I was dry with rage and extreme toil,
Breathless and faint, leaning upon my sword,
30 Came there a certain lord, neat and trimly
dress'd,
Fresh as a bridegroom; and his chin new
reap'd
Show'd like a stubble land at harvest home.
35 He was perfumed like a milliner,
And 'twixt his finger and his thumb he held
A pouncet box[19] which ever and anon
He gave his nose, and took't away again;
Who therewith angry, when it next came there,
40 Took it in snuff; and still he smil'd and
talk'd;
And as the soldiers bore dead bodies by,
He call'd them untaught knaves, unmannerly,
To bring a slovenly unhandsome corse
45 Betwixt the wind and his nobility.
With many holiday and lady terms
He questioned me, amongst the rest demanded
My prisoners in your Majesty's behalf.
I then, all smarting with my wounds being
50 cold,

[19] a box containing something aromatic, to ward
off odors.

To be so pest'red with a popingay,
Out of my grief and my impatience
Answer'd neglectingly, I know not what—
He should, or he should not; for he made me
    mad
To see him shine so brisk, and smell so sweet,
And talk so like a waiting gentlewoman
Of guns and drums and wounds—God save the
    mark!—
And telling me the sovereignest thing on earth 10
Was parmacity[20] for an inward bruise;
And that it was great pity, so it was,
This villanous saltpetre should be digg'd
Out of the bowels of the harmless earth,
Which many a good tall fellow had destroy'd 15
So cowardly; and but for these vile guns,
He would himself have been a soldier.
This bald unjointed chat of his, my lord,
I answered indirectly, as I said,
And I beseech you, let not his report 20
Come current for an accusation
Betwixt my love and your high majesty.
    BLUNT. The circumstance considered, good
    my lord,
Whate'er Lord Harry Percy then had said
To such a person, and in such a place, 25
At such a time, with all the rest retold,
May reasonably die, and never rise
To do him wrong, or any way impeach
What then he said, so he unsay it now.
    KING. Why, yet he doth deny his prisoners, 30
But with proviso and exception,
That we at our own charge shall ransom
    straight
His brother-in-law, the foolish Mortimer;[21]
Who, on my soul, hath wilfully betray'd 35
The lives of those that he did lead to fight
Against that great magician, damn'd
    Glendower,
Whose daughter, as we hear, the Earl of
    March
Hath lately married. Shall our coffers, then, 40
Be emptied to redeem a traitor home?
Shall we buy treason? and indent with fears
When they have lost and forfeited themselves? 45
No, on the barren mountains let him starve!
For I shall never hold that man my friend
Whose tongue shall ask me for one penny cost

To ransom home revolted Mortimer.
    HOT. Revolted Mortimer?
He never did fall off, my sovereign liege,
But by the chance of war. To prove that true
Needs no more but one tongue for all those 5
    wounds,
Those mouthed wounds, which valiantly he
    took
When on the gentle Severn's sedgy bank,
In single opposition hand to hand, 10
He did confound[22] the best part of an hour
In changing hardiment[23] with great
    Glendower.
Three times they breath'd, and three times did
    they drink,
Upon agreement, of swift Severn's flood; 15
Who then, affrighted with their bloody looks,
Ran fearfully among the trembling reeds
And hid his crisp head in the hollow bank,
Bloodstained with these valiant combatants. 20
Never did base and rotten policy
Colour her working with such deadly wounds;
Nor never could the noble Mortimer
Receive so many, and all willingly.
Then let not him be slandered with revolt. 25
    KING. Thou dost belie him, Percy, thou dost
    belie him!
He never did encounter with Glendower.
I tell thee
He durst as well have met the devil alone 30
As Owen Glendower for an enemy.
Art thou not asham'd? But, sirrah, henceforth
Let me not hear you speak of Mortimer.
Send me your prisoners with the speediest
    means, 35
Or you shall hear in such a kind from me
As will displease you. My Lord Northumber-
    land,
We license your departure with your son.—
Send us your prisoners, or you will hear of it. 40

        exeunt KING, [BLUNT, *and* TRAIN]

    HOT. An if the devil come and roar for them,
I will not send them. I will after straight
And tell him so; for I will ease my heart, 45
Albeit I make a hazard of my head.
    NORTH. What, drunk with choler? Stay, and
    pause awhile.
Here comes your uncle.

---

[20] spermaceti.
[21] Shakespeare, like Holinshed, his historical source, confuses two Edmund Mortimers, uncle and nephew.

---

[22] use up.
[23] matching valor.

. *Enter* WORCESTER

HOT.   Speak of Mortimer?
Zounds, I will speak of him, and let my soul
Want mercy if I do not join with him!
Yea, on his part I'll empty all these veins,
And shed my dear blood drop by drop in the
       dust,
But I will lift the downtrod Mortimer
As high in the air as this unthankful king,
As this ingrate and cank'red Bolingbroke.
   NORTH. Brother, the King hath made your
       nephew mad.
   WOR. Who struck this heat up after I was
       gone?
   HOT. He will (forsooth) have all my
       prisoners;
And when I urg'd the ransom once again
Of my wife's brother, then his cheek look'd
       pale,
And on my face he turn'd an eye of death,
Trembling even at the name of Mortimer.
   WOR. I cannot blame him. Was not he
       proclaim'd
By Richard that dead is, the next of blood?
   NORTH. He was; I heard the proclamation.
And then it was when the unhappy King
(Whose wrongs in us God pardon!) did set
       forth
Upon his Irish expedition;
From whence he intercepted did return
To be depos'd, and shortly murdered.
   WOR. And for whose death we in the world's
       wide mouth
Live scandaliz'd and foully spoken of.
   HOT. But soft, I pray you. Did King Richard
       then
Proclaim my brother Edmund Mortimer
Heir to the crown?
   NORTH.   He did; myself did hear it.
   HOT. Nay, then I cannot blame his cousin
       king,
That wish'd him on the barren mountains
       starve.
But shall it be that you, that set the crown
Upon the head of this forgetful man,
And for his sake wear the detested blot
Of murtherous subornation—shall it be
That you a world of curses undergo,
Being the agents or base second means,
The cords, the ladder, or the hangman rather?
O, pardon me that I descend so low

To show the line and the predicament
Wherein you range under this subtile king!
Shall it for shame be spoken in these days,
Or fill up chronicles in time to come,
That men of your nobility and power
Did gage them both in an unjust behalf
(As both of you, God pardon it! have done)
To put down Richard, that sweet lovely rose,
And plant this thorn, this canker,[24]
       Bolingbroke?
And shall it in more shame be further spoken
That you are fool'd, discarded, and shook off
By him for whom these shames ye underwent?
No! yet time serves wherein you may redeem
Your banish'd honours and restore yourselves
Into the good thoughts of the world again;
Revenge the jeering and disdain'd contempt
Of this proud king, who studies day and night
To answer all the debt he owes to you
Even with the bloody payment of your deaths.
Therefore I say——
   WOR.   Peace, cousin, say no more;
And now I will unclasp a secret book,
And to your quick-conceiving discontents
I'll read you matter deep and dangerous,
As full of peril and adventurous spirit
As to o'erwalk a current roaring loud
On the unsteadfast footing of a spear.
   HOT. If he fall in, good night, or sink or
       swim!
Send danger from the east unto the west,
So honour cross it from the north to south,
And let them grapple. O, the blood more stirs
To rouse a lion than to start a hare!
   NORTH. Imagination of some great exploit
Drives him beyond the bounds of patience.
   HOT. By heaven, methinks it were an easy
       leap
To pluck bright honour from the pale-fac'd
       moon,
Or dive into the bottom of the deep,
Where fadom line could never touch the
       ground,
And pluck up drowned honour by the locks,
So he that doth redeem her thence might wear
Without corrival all her dignities;
But out upon this half-fac'd fellowship!
   WOR. He apprehends a world of figures here,
But not the form of what he should attend.
Good cousin, give me audience for a while.

——————
[24] dog rose.

HOT. I cry you mercy.

WOR.   Those same noble Scots
That are your prisoners——

HOT.   I'll keep them all.
By God, he shall not have a Scot of them!
No, if a Scot would save his soul, he shall not.
I'll keep them, by this hand!

WOR.   You start away.
And lend no ear unto my purposes.
Those prisoners you shall keep.

HOT.   Nay, I will! That's flat!
He said he would not ransom Mortimer,
Forbade my tongue to speak of Mortimer,
But I will find him when he lies asleep,
And in his ears I'll holloa 'Mortimer.'
Nay;
I'll have a starling shall be taught to speak
Nothing but 'Mortimer,' and give it him
To keep his anger still in motion.

  WOR. Hear you, cousin, a word.

  HOT. All studies here I solemnly defy[25]
Save how to gall and pinch this Bolingbroke;
And that same sword-and-buckler Prince of
      Wales—
But that I think his father loves him not
And would be glad he met with some mis-
      chance,
I would have him poisoned with a pot of ale.

  WOR. Farewell, kinsman. I will talk to you
When you are better temper'd to attend.

  NORTH. Why, what a wasp-stung and im-
      patient fool
Art thou to break into this woman's mood,
Tying thine ear to no tongue but thine own!

  HOT. Why, look you, I am whipp'd and
      scourg'd with rods,
Nettled, and stung with pismires when I hear
Of this vile politician, Bolingbroke.
In Richard's time—what do you call the
      place?—
A plague upon it! it is in Gloucestershire—
'Twas where the madcap Duke his uncle
      kept[26]—
His uncle York—where I first bow'd my knee
Unto this king of smiles, this Bolingbroke—
'Sblood!
When you and he came back from Ravens-
      purgh——

  NORTH. At Berkeley Castle.

  HOT. You say true.

Why, what a candy deal of courtesy
This fawning greyhound then did proffer me!
Look, 'when his infant fortune came to age,'
And 'gentle Harry Percy,' and 'kind cousin'—
O, the devil take such cozeners!—God forgive
  me!
Good uncle, tell your tale, for I have done.

  WOR. Nay, if you have not, to it again.
We will stay your leisure.

  HOT.   I have done, i' faith.

  WOR. Then once more to your Scottish pris-
      oners.
Deliver them up without their ransom straight,
And make the Douglas' son your only mean
For powers in Scotland; which, for divers rea-
      sons
Which I shall send you written, be assur'd
Will easily be granted. [*to* NORTHUMBER-
      LAND] You, my lord,
Your son in Scotland being thus employ'd,
Shall secretly into the bosom creep
Of that same noble prelate well-belov'd,
The Archbishop.

  HOT.   Of York, is it not?

  WOR. True; who bears hard
His brother's death at Bristow, the Lord Scroop.
I speak not this in estimation,
As what I think might be, but what I know
Is ruminated, plotted, and set down,
And only stays but to behold the face
Of that occasion that shall bring it on.

  HOT. I smell it. Upon my life, it will do well.

  NORTH. Before the game is afoot thou still
      let'st slip.[27]

  HOT. Why, it cannot choose but be a noble
      plot.
And then the power of Scotland and of York
To join with Mortimer, ha?

  WOR.   And so they shall.

  HOT. In faith, it is exceedingly well aim'd.

  WOR. And 'tis no little reason bids us speed,
To save our heads by raising of a head;[28]
For, bear ourselves as even as we can,
The King will always think him in our debt,
And think we think ourselves unsatisfied,
Till he hath found a time to pay us home.
And see already how he doth begin
To make us strangers to his looks of love.

  HOT. He does, he does! We'll be reveng'd on
      him.

25 renounce.   26 lived.

27 loose the dogs.
28 an army (pun).

WOR. Cousin, farewell. No further go in this
Than I by letters shall direct your course.
When time is ripe, which will be suddenly,
I'll steal to Glendower and Lord Mortimer,
Where you and Douglas, and our pow'rs at 5
      once,
As I will fashion it, shall happily meet,
To bear our fortunes in our own strong arms,
Which now we hold at much uncertainty.

    NORTH. Farewell, good brother. We shall 10
      thrive, I trust.

    HOT. Uncle, adieu. O, let the hours be short
Till fields and blows and groans applaud our
    sport!   *[exeunt]*
                              15

ACT II

SCENE I.

Rochester. An inn yard   20

Enter a CARRIER *with a lantern in his hand*

    1. CAR. Heigh-ho! an it be not four by the
day, I'll be hang'd. Charles' wain[29] is over the 25
new chimney, and yet our horse not pack'd.—
What, ostler!

    OST. *[within]* Anon, anon.

    1. CAR. I prithee, Tom, beat Cut's saddle,
put a few flocks in the point. Poor jade is 30
wrung in the withers out of all cess.[30]

Enter another CARRIER

    2. CAR. Peas and beans are as dank here as a
dog, and that is the next way to give poor jades 35
the bots. This house is turned upside down
since Robin Ostler died.

    1. CAR. Poor fellow never joyed since the
price of oats rose. It was the death of him.

    2. CAR. I think this be the most villanous 40
house in all London road for fleas. I am stung
like a tench.

    1. CAR. Like a tench? By the mass, there is
ne'er a king christen[31] could be better bit than
I have been since the first cock.   45

    2. CAR. Why, they will allow us ne'er a jor-
dan, and then we leak in your chimney, and
your chamber-lye breeds fleas like a loach.

    1. CAR. What, ostler! come away and be
hang'd! come away!   50

    2. CAR. I have a gammon of bacon and two
razes[32] of ginger, to be delivered as far as
Charing Cross.

    1. CAR. God's body! the turkeys in my pan-
nier are quite starved. What, ostler! A plague
on thee! hast thou never an eye in thy head?
Canst not hear? An 'twere not as good deed
as drink to break the pate on thee, I am a very
villain. Come, and be hang'd! Hast no faith in
thee?

Enter GADSHILL

    GADS. Good morrow, carriers. What's o'clock?

    1. CAR. I think it be two o'clock.

    GADS. I prithee lend me thy lantern to see
my gelding in the stable.

    1. CAR. Nay, by God, soft! I know a trick
worth two of that, i' faith.

    GADS. I pray thee lend me thine.

    2. CAR. Ay, when? canst tell? Lend me thy
lantern, quoth he? Marry, I'll see thee hang'd
first!

    GADS. Sirrah carrier, what time do you mean
to come to London?

    2. CAR. Time enough to go to bed with a
candle, I warrant thee. Come, neighbour
Mugs, we'll call up the gentlemen. They will
along with company, for they have great
charge.   *exeunt* [CARRIERS]

    GADS. What, ho! chamberlain!

Enter CHAMBERLAIN

    CHAM. At hand, quoth pickpurse.

    GADS. That's even as fair as—'at hand, quoth
the chamberlain'; for thou variest no more
from picking of purses than giving direction
doth from labouring: thou layest the plot how.

    CHAM. Good morrow, Master Gadshill. It
holds current that I told you yesternight.
There's a franklin in the Wild of Kent hath
brought three hundred marks with him in gold.
I heard him tell it to one of his company last
night at supper—a kind of auditor; one that
hath abundance of charge too, God knows
what. They are up already and call for eggs
and butter. They will away presently.

    GADS. Sirrah, if they meet not with Saint
Nicholas' clerks,[33] I'll give thee this neck.

    CHAM. No, I'll none of it. I pray thee keep
that for the hangman; for I know thou wor- 50

---

[29] Big Dipper.   [30] measure.   [31] Christian.   [32] roots.   [33] highwaymen.

shippest Saint Nicholas as truly as a man of falsehood may.

GADS. What talkest thou to me of the hang-man? If I hang, I'll make a fat pair of gal-lows; for if I hang, old Sir John hangs with me, and thou knowest he is no starveling. Tut! there are other Troyans that thou dream'st not of, the which for sport sake are content to do the profession some grace; that would (if mat-ters should be look'd into) for their own credit sake make all whole. I am joined with no foot landrakers, no long-staff sixpenny strikers, none of these mad mustachio purple-hued malt-worms;[34] but with nobility and tranquillity, burgomasters and great oneyers, such as can hold in, such as will strike sooner than speak, and speak sooner than drink, and drink sooner than pray; and yet, zounds, I lie; for they pray continually to their saint, the commonwealth, or rather, not pray to her, but prey on her, for they ride up and down on her and make her their boots.

CHAM. What, the commonwealth their boots? Will she hold out water in foul way?

GADS. She will, she will! Justice hath liq-uor'd[35] her. We steal as in a castle, cocksure. We have the receipt of fernseed, we walk in-visible.[36]

CHAM. Nay, by my faith, I think you are more beholding to the night than to fernseed for your walking invisible.

GADS. Give me thy hand. Thou shalt have a share in our purchase, as I am a true man.

CHAM. Nay, rather let me have it, as you are a false thief.

GADS. Go to; 'homo' is a common name to all men. Bid the ostler bring my gelding out of the stable. Farewell, you muddy knave.

[exeunt]

Scene II.

The highway near Gadshill

Enter PRINCE and POINS

POINS. Come, shelter, shelter! I have remov'd Falstaff's horse, and he frets like a gumm'd vel-vet.

PRINCE. Stand close.　　　　[they step aside]

---

[34] no footpads, no thugs, no drunks.
[35] waterproofed by greasing.
[36] Fern seed was supposed to be able to make people invisible.

Enter FALSTAFF

FAL. Poins! Poins, and be hang'd! Poins!

PRINCE. [comes forward] Peace, ye fat-kid-ney'd rascal! What a brawling dost thou keep!

FAL. Where's Poins, Hal?

PRINCE. He is walk'd up to the top of the hill. I'll go seek him.　　　[steps aside]

FAL. I am accurs'd to rob in that thief's com-pany. The rascal hath removed my horse and tied him I know not where. If I travel but four foot by the squire[37] further afoot, I shall break my wind. Well, I doubt not but to die a fair death for all this, if I scape hanging for killing that rogue. I have forsworn his company hourly any time this two-and-twenty years, and yet I am bewitch'd with the rogue's company. If the rascal have not given me medicines to make me love him, I'll be hang'd. It could not be else. I have drunk medicines. Poins! Hal! A plague upon you both! Bardolph! Peto! I'll starve ere I'll rob a foot further. An 'twere not as good a deed as drink to turn true man and to leave these rogues, I am the veriest varlet that ever chewed with a tooth. Eight yards of uneven ground is threescore and ten miles afoot with me, and the stony-hearted villains know it well enough. A plague upon it when thieves cannot be true one to another! [they whistle.] Whew! A plague upon you all! Give me my horse, you rogues! give me my horse and be hang'd!

PRINCE. [comes forward] Peace, ye fat-guts! Lie down, lay thine ear close to the ground, and list if thou canst hear the tread of travel-lers.

FAL. Have you any levers to lift me up again, being down? 'Sblood, I'll not bear mine own flesh so far afoot again for all the coin in thy father's exchequer. What a plague mean ye to colt[38] me thus?

PRINCE. Thou liest; thou art not colted, thou art uncolted.

FAL. I prithee, good Prince Hal, help me to my horse, good king's son.

PRINCE. Out, ye rogue! Shall I be your ostler?

FAL. Go hang thyself in thine own heir-ap-parent garters! If I be ta'en, I'll peach for this. An I have not ballads made on you all, and

---

[37] carpenter's square.　　　[38] trick.

sung to filthy tunes, let a cup of sack be my poison. When a jest is so forward—and afoot too—I hate it.

Enter GADSHILL, [BARDOLPH *and* PETO *with him*]

GADS. Stand!

FAL. So I do, against my will.

POINS. [*comes forward*] O, 'tis our setter.[39] I know his voice. Bardolph, what news?

BAR. Case ye, case ye![40] On with your vizards! There's money of the King's coming down the hill; 'tis going to the King's exchequer.

FAL. You lie, ye rogue! 'Tis going to the King's tavern.

GADS. There's enough to make us all.

FAL. To be hang'd.

PRINCE. Sirs, you four shall front them in the narrow lane; Ned Poins and I will walk lower. If they scape from your encounter, then they light on us.

PETO. How many be there of them?

GADS. Some eight or ten.

FAL. Zounds, will they not rob us?

PRINCE. What, a coward, Sir John Paunch?

FAL. Indeed, I am not John of Gaunt, your grandfather; but yet no coward, Hal.

PRINCE. Well, we leave that to the proof.

POINS. Sirrah Jack, thy horse stands behind the hedge. When thou need'st him, there thou shalt find him. Farewell and stand fast.

FAL. Now cannot I strike him, if I should be hang'd.

PRINCE. [*aside to* POINS] Ned, where are our disguises?

POINS. [*aside to* PRINCE] Here, hard by. Stand close.   [*exeunt* PRINCE *and* POINS]

FAL. Now, my masters, happy man be his dole, say I. Every man to his business.

Enter the TRAVELLERS

TRAVELLER. Come, neighbour. The boy shall lead our horses down the hill; we'll walk afoot awhile and ease our legs.

THIEVES. Stand!

TRAVELLER. Jesus bless us!

FAL. Strike! down with them! cut the villains' throats! Ah, whoreson caterpillars! bacon-fed knaves! they hate us youth. Down with them! fleece them!

TRAVELLER. O, we are undone, both we and ours for ever!

FAL. Hang ye, gorbellied[41] knaves, are ye undone? No, ye fat chuffs;[42] I would your store were here! On, bacons, on! What, ye knaves! young men must live. You are grand-jurors, are ye? We'll jure ye, faith! [*here they rob and bind them; exeunt*]

Enter the PRINCE *and* POINS [*in buckram suits*]

PRINCE. The thieves have bound the true men. Now could thou and I rob the thieves and go merrily to London, it would be argument for a week, laughter for a month, and a good jest for ever.

POINS. Stand close! I hear them coming.

[*they stand aside*]

Enter the THIEVES *again*

FAL. Come, my masters, let us share, and then to horse before day. An the Prince and Poins be not two arrant cowards, there's no equity stirring. There's no more valour in that Poins than in a wild duck.

PRINCE. Your money!
POINS. Villains!

[*as they are sharing, the* PRINCE *and* POINS *set upon them. They all run away, and* FALSTAFF, *after a blow or two, runs away too, leaving the booty behind them.*]

PRINCE. Got with much ease. Now merrily to horse.
The thieves are scattered, and possess'd with fear
So strongly that they dare not meet each other.
Each takes his fellow for an officer.
Away, good Ned. Falstaff sweats to death
And lards the lean earth as he walks along.
Were't not for laughing, I should pity him.

POINS. How the rogue roar'd!   [*exeunt*]

[39] member of a gang who acts as decoy, or who sets the scene by preliminary investigation; in modern slang, he "cases the job."
[40] Put on masks.
[41] fat.   [42] misers.

SCENE III.

Warkworth Castle

Enter HOTSPUR *solus, reading a letter*

HOT. 'But, for mine own part, my lord, I could be well contented to be there, in respect of the love I bear your house.' He could be contented—why is he not then? In respect of the love he bears our house! He shows in this he loves his own barn better than he loves our house. Let me see some more. 'The purpose you undertake is dangerous'—Why, that's certain! 'Tis dangerous to take a cold, to sleep, to drink; but I tell you, my lord fool, out of this nettle, danger, we pluck this flower, safety. 'The purpose you undertake is dangerous, the friends you have named uncertain, the time itself unsorted, and your whole plot too light for the counterpoise of so great an opposition.' Say you so, say you so? I say unto you again, you are a shallow, cowardly hind, and you lie. What a lack-brain is this! By the Lord, our plot is a good plot as ever was laid; our friends true and constant: a good plot, good friends, and full of expectation; an excellent plot, very good friends. What a frosty-spirited rogue is this! Why, my Lord of York commends the plot and the general course of the action. Zounds, an I were now by this rascal, I could brain him with his lady's fan. Is there not my father, my uncle, and myself; Lord Edmund Mortimer, my Lord of York, and Owen Glendower? Is there not, besides, the Douglas? Have I not all their letters to meet me in arms by the ninth of the next month, and are they not some of them set forward already? What a pagan rascal is this! an infidel! Ha! you shall see now, in very sincerity of fear and cold heart will he to the King and lay open all our proceedings. O, I could divide myself and go to buffets for moving such a dish of skim milk with so honourable an action! Hang him, let him tell the King! we are prepared. I will set forward to-night.

Enter his LADY

How now, Kate? I must leave you within these two hours.

LADY. O my good lord, why are you thus alone?
For what offence have I this fortnight been

A banish'd woman from my Harry's bed?
Tell me, sweet lord, what is't that takes from thee
Thy stomach, pleasure, and thy golden sleep?
Why dost thou bend thine eyes upon the earth,
And start so often when thou sit'st alone?
Why hast thou lost the fresh blood in thy cheeks
And given my treasures and my rights of thee
To thick-ey'd musing and curs'd melancholy?
In thy faint slumbers I by thee have watch'd,
And heard thee murmur tales of iron wars,
Speak terms of manage to thy bounding steed,
Cry 'Courage! to the field!' And thou hast talk'd
Of sallies and retires, of trenches, tents,
Of palisadoes, frontiers, parapets,
Of basilisks,[43] of cannon, culverin,[44]
Of prisoners' ransom, and of soldiers slain,
And all the currents of a heady fight.
Thy spirit within thee hath been so at war,
And thus hath so bestirr'd thee in thy sleep,
That beads of sweat have stood upon thy brow
Like bubbles in a late-disturbed stream,
And in thy face strange motions have appear'd,
Such as we see when men restrain their breath
On some great sudden hest.[45] O, what portents are these?
Some heavy business hath my lord in hand,
And I must know it, else he loves me not.

HOT. What, ho!

Enter a SERVANT

      Is Gilliams with the packet gone?
SERV. He is, my lord, an hour ago.
HOT. Hath Butler brought those horses from the sheriff?
SERV. One horse, my lord, he brought even now.
HOT. What horse? A roan, a crop-ear, is it not?
SERV. It is, my lord.
HOT.   That roan shall be my throne.
Well, I will back him straight. O esperance![46]
Bid Butler lead him forth into the park.
                     [exit SERVANT*]*
LADY. But hear you, my lord.
HOT. What say'st thou, my lady?
LADY. What is it carries you away?

_____

43 heavy cannon.   44 light cannon.
45 emergency.   46 hope.

HOT. Why, my horse, my love—my horse!

LADY. Out, you mad-headed ape!
A weasel hath not such a deal of spleen
As you are toss'd with. In faith,
I'll know your business, Harry; that I will!   5
I fear my brother Mortimer doth stir
About his title and hath sent for you
To line his enterprise; but if you go—

HOT. So far afoot, I shall be weary, love.

LADY. Come, come, you paraquito, answer   10
me
Directly unto this question that I ask.
In faith, I'll break thy little finger, Harry,
An if thou wilt not tell me all things true.

HOT. Away,
Away, you trifler! Love? I love thee not;   15
I care not for thee, Kate. This is no world
To play with mammets[47] and to tilt with lips.
We must have bloody noses and crack'd
crowns,
And pass them current too. Gods me,[48] my   20
horse!
What say'st thou, Kate? What wouldst thou
have with me?

LADY. Do you not love me? do you not in-   25
deed?
Well, do not then; for since you love me not,
I will not love myself. Do you not love me?
Nay, tell me if you speak in jest or no.

HOT. Come, wilt thou see me ride?   30
And when I am a-horseback, I will swear
I love thee infinitely. But hark you, Kate:
I must not have you henceforth question me
Whither I go, nor reason whereabout.
Whither I must, I must; and to conclude,   35
This evening must I leave you, gentle Kate.
I know you wise; but yet no farther wise
Than Harry Percy's wife; constant you are,
But yet a woman and for secrecy,
No lady closer, for I well believe   40
Thou wilt not utter what thou dost not know,
And so far will I trust thee, gentle Kate.

LADY. How? so far?

HOT. Not an inch further. But hark you,
Kate: 45
Whither I go, thither shall you go too;
To-day will I set forth, to-morrow you.
Will this content you, Kate?

LADY.   It must of force.
                                     [*exeunt*]   50

---

[47] dolls.   [48] God save me.

Eastcheap. The Boar's Head Tavern

Enter PRINCE *and* POINS

PRINCE. Ned, prithee come out of that fat-
room[49] and lend me thy hand to laugh a little.

POINS. Where hast been, Hal?

PRINCE. With three or four loggerheads
amongst three or fourscore hogsheads. I have
sounded the very bass-string of humility. Sirrah, I am sworn brother to a leash of drawers[50]
and can call them all by their christen names,
as Tom, Dick, and Francis. They take it already upon their salvation that, though I be
but Prince of Wales, yet I am the king of
courtesy; and tell me flatly I am no proud Jack
like Falstaff, but a Corinthian,[51] a lad of mettle, a good boy (by the Lord, so they call me!),
and when I am King of England I shall command all the good lads in Eastcheap. They call
drinking deep, dying scarlet; and when you
breathe in your watering, they cry 'hem!' and
bid you play it off. To conclude, I am so good
a proficient in one quarter of an hour that I
can drink with any tinker in his own language
during my life. I tell thee, Ned, thou hast lost
much honour that thou wert not with me in
this action. But, sweet Ned—to sweeten which
name of Ned, I give thee this pennyworth of
sugar, clapp'd even now into my hand by an
under-skinker,[52] one that never spake other
English in his life than 'Eight shillings and six-
pence,' and 'You are welcome,' with this shrill
addition, 'Anon, anon, sir! Score a pint of
bastard in the Half-moon,'[53] or so—but, Ned,
to drive away the time till Falstaff come, I
prithee do thou stand in some by-room while I
question my puny drawer to what end he gave
me the sugar; and do thou never leave calling
'Francis!' that his tale to me may be nothing
but 'Anon!' Step aside, and I'll show thee a
precedent.

POINS. Francis!

PRINCE. Thou art perfect.

POINS. Francis!   [*exit* POINS]

---

[49] vat room.
[50] a set of tapsters.
[51] a drunk or sport.
[52] assistant tapster.
[53] Charge a pint of sweet Spanish wine (to the
customer) in the Half-moon Room.

Enter [FRANCIS, *a*] *Drawer*

FRAN. Anon, anon, sir.—Look down into the Pomgarnet,[54] Ralph.

PRINCE. Come hither, Francis.

FRAN. My lord?

PRINCE. How long hast thou to serve, Francis?

FRAN. Forsooth, five years, and as much as to——

POINS. [*within*] Francis!

FRAN. Anon, anon, sir.

PRINCE. Five year! by'r Lady, a long lease for the clinking of pewter. But, Francis, darest thou be so valiant as to play the coward with thy indenture and show it a fair pair of heels and run from it?

FRAN. O Lord, sir, I'll be sworn upon all the books in England I could find in my heart——

POINS. [*within*] Francis!

FRAN. Anon, sir.

PRINCE. How old art thou, Francis?

FRAN. Let me see. About Michaelmas[55] next I shall be——

POINS. [*within*] Francis!

FRAN. Anon, sir. Pray stay a little, my lord.

PRINCE. Nay, but hark you, Francis. For the sugar thou gavest me—'twas a pennyworth, was't not?

FRAN. O Lord! I would it had been two!

PRINCE. I will give thee for it a thousand pound. Ask me when thou wilt, and thou shalt have it.

POINS. [*within*] Francis!

FRAN. Anon, anon.

PRINCE. Anon, Francis? No, Francis; but to-morrow, Francis; or, Francis, a Thursday; or indeed, Francis, when thou wilt. But Francis——

FRAN. My lord?

PRINCE. Wilt thou rob this leathern-jerkin, crystal-button, not-pated,[56] agate-ring, puke-stocking,[57] caddis-garter,[58] smooth-tongue, Spanish-pouch——

FRAN. O Lord, sir, who do you mean?

PRINCE. Why then, your brown bastard is your only drink; for look you, Francis, your white canvas doublet will sully. In Barbary, sir, it cannot come to so much.

FRAN. What, sir?

POINS. [*within*] Francis!

PRINCE. Away, you rogue! Dost thou not hear them call? [*here they both call him. The Drawer stands amazed, not knowing which way to go*]

Enter VINTNER

VINT. What, stand'st thou still, and hear'st such a calling? Look to the guests within. [*exit* FRANCIS] My lord, old Sir John, with half-a-dozen more, are at the door. Shall I let them in?

PRINCE. Let them alone awhile, and then open the door. [*exit* VINTNER] Poins!

POINS. [*within*] Anon, anon, sir.

Enter POINS

PRINCE. Sirrah, Falstaff and the rest of the thieves are at the door. Shall we be merry?

POINS. As merry as crickets, my lad. But hark ye; what cunning match have you made with this jest of the drawer? Come, what's the issue?

PRINCE. I am now of all humours that have showed themselves humours since the old days of goodman Adam to the pupil age of this present twelve o'clock at midnight.

[*Enter* FRANCIS]

What's o'clock, Francis?

FRAN. Anon, anon, sir.   [*exit*]

PRINCE. That ever this fellow should have fewer words than a parrot, and yet the son of a woman! His industry is upstairs and down-stairs, his eloquence the parcel of a reckoning. I am not yet of Percy's mind, the Hotspur of the North; he that kills me some six or seven dozen of Scots at a breakfast, washes his hands, and says to his wife, 'Fie upon this quiet life! I want work.' 'O my sweet Harry,' says she, 'how many hast thou kill'd to-day?' 'Give my roan horse a drench,'[59] says he, and an-swers 'Some fourteen,' an hour after, 'a trifle, a trifle.' I prithee call in Falstaff. I'll play Percy, and that damn'd brawn shall play Dame Mortimer his wife. 'Rivo!'[60] says the drunkard. Call in ribs, call in tallow.

Enter FALSTAFF, [GADSHILL, BARDOLPH *and* PETO; FRANCIS *follows with wine*]

---

[54] another room in the inn.
[55] Sept. 29.   [56] short-haired.
[57] dark gray stockinged.   [58] tape garter.

[59] a dose of medicine.   [60] a drinker's cry.

POINS. Welcome, Jack. Where hast thou been?

FAL. A plague of all cowards, I say, and a vengeance too! Marry and amen! Give me a cup of sack, boy. Ere I lead this life long, I'll sew nether-stocks,[61] and mend them and foot them too. A plague of all cowards! Give me a cup of sack, rogue. Is there no virtue extant?

[he drinketh]

PRINCE. Didst thou never see Titan[62] kiss a dish of butter? Pitiful-hearted butter, that melted at the sweet tale of the sun! If thou didst, then behold that compound.[63]

FAL. You rogue, here's lime in this sack too! There is nothing but roguery to be found in villanous man. Yet a coward is worse than a cup of sack with lime in it—a villanous coward! Go thy ways, old Jack, die when thou wilt; if manhood, good manhood, be not forgot upon the face of the earth, then am I a shotten herring.[64] There lives not three good men unhang'd in England; and one of them is fat, and grows old. God help the while! A bad world, I say. I would I were a weaver; I could sing psalms or anything. A plague of all cowards I say still!

PRINCE. How now, woolsack? What mutter you?

FAL. A king's son! If I do not beat thee out of thy kingdom with a dagger of lath and drive all thy subjects afore thee like a flock of wild geese, I'll never wear hair on my face more. You Prince of Wales?

PRINCE. Why, you whoreson round man, what's the matter?

FAL. Are not you a coward? Answer me to that—and Poins there?

POINS. Zounds, ye fat paunch, an ye call me coward, by the Lord, I'll stab thee.

FAL. I call thee coward? I'll see thee damn'd ere I call thee coward, but I would give a thousand pound I could run as fast as thou canst. You are straight enough in the shoulders; you care not who sees your back. Call you that backing of your friends? A plague upon such backing! Give me them that will face me. Give me a cup of sack. I am a rogue if I drunk to-day.

PRINCE. O villain! thy lips are scarce wip'd since thou drunk'st last.

FAL. All is one for that. [he drinketh] A plague of all cowards still say I.

PRINCE. What's the matter?

FAL. What's the matter? There be four of us here have ta'en a thousand pound this day morning.

PRINCE. Where is it, Jack? Where is it?

FAL. Where is it? Taken from us it is. A hundred upon poor four of us!

PRINCE. What, a hundred, man?

FAL. I am a rogue if I were not at half-sword with a dozen of them two hours to-gether. I have scap'd by miracle. I am eight times thrust through the doublet, four through the hose; my buckler cut through and through; my sword hack'd like a hand-saw—ecce signum![65] I never dealt better since I was a man. All would not do. A plague of all cowards! Let them speak. If they speak more or less than truth, they are villains and the sons of darkness.

PRINCE. Speak, sirs. How was it?

GADS. We four set upon some dozen——

FAL. Sixteen at least, my lord.

GADS. And bound them.

PETO. No, no, they were not bound.

FAL. You rogue, they were bound, every man of them, or I am a Jew else—an Ebrew Jew.

GADS. As we were sharing, some six or seven fresh men set upon us——

FAL. And unbound the rest, and then come in the other.

PRINCE. What, fought you with them all?

FAL. All? I know not what you call all, but if I fought not with fifty of them, I am a bunch of radish! If there were not two or three and fifty upon poor old Jack, then am I no two-legg'd creature.

PRINCE. Pray God you have not murd'red some of them.

FAL. Nay, that's past praying for. I have pepper'd two of them. Two I am sure I have paid, two rogues in buckram suits. I tell thee what, Hal—if I tell thee a lie, spit in my face, call me horse. Thou knowest my old ward. Here I lay, and thus I bore my point. Four rogues in buckram let drive at me.

---

61 stockings.   62 the sun.
63 Falstaff.
64 a herring that has cast its roe.

65 behold the evidence.

PRINCE. What, four? Thou saidst but two even now.

FAL. Four, Hal. I told thee four.

POINS. Ay, ay, he said four.

FAL. These four came all afront and mainly thrust at me. I made me no more ado but took all their seven points in my target,[66] thus.

PRINCE. Seven? Why, there were but four even now.

FAL. In buckram?

POINS. Ay, four, in buckram suits.

FAL. Seven, by these hilts, or I am a villain else.

PRINCE. [*aside to* POINS] Prithee let him alone. We shall have more anon.

FAL. Dost thou hear me, Hal?

PRINCE. Ay, and mark thee too, Jack.

FAL. Do so, for it is worth the list'ning to. These nine in buckram that I told thee of——

PRINCE. So, two more already.

FAL. Their points being broken——

POINS. Down fell their hose.

FAL. Began to give me ground; but I followed me close, came in, foot and hand, and with a thought seven of the eleven I paid.

PRINCE. O monstrous! Eleven buckram men grown out of two!

FAL. But, as the devil would have it, three misbegotten knaves in Kendal green came at my back and let drive at me; for it was so dark, Hal, that thou couldst not see thy hand.

PRINCE. These lies are like their father that begets them—gross as a mountain, open, palpable. Why, thou clay-brain'd guts, thou knotty-pated fool, thou whoreson obscene greasy tallow-catch[67]——

FAL. What, art thou mad? art thou mad? Is not the truth the truth?

PRINCE. Why, how couldst thou know these men in Kendal green when it was so dark thou couldst not see thy hand? Come, tell us your reason. What sayest thou to this?

POINS. Come, your reason, Jack, your reason.

FAL. What, upon compulsion? Zounds, an I were at the strappado or all the racks in the world, I would not tell you on compulsion. Give you a reason on compulsion? If reasons were as plentiful as blackberries, I would give no man a reason upon compulsion, I.

PRINCE. I'll be no longer guilty of this sin; this sanguine coward, this bed-presser, this horseback-breaker, this huge hill of flesh—

FAL. 'Sblood, you starveling, you elf-skin, you dried neat's-tongue, you bull's pizzle, you stockfish[68]—O for breath to utter what is like thee!—you tailor's yard, you sheath, you bow-case, you vile standing tuck![69]

PRINCE. Well, breathe awhile, and then to it again; and when thou hast tired thyself in base comparisons, hear me speak but this.

POINS. Mark, Jack.

PRINCE. We two saw you four set on four, and bound them and were masters of their wealth. Mark now how a plain tale shall put you down. Then did we two set on you four and, with a word, outfac'd you from your prize, and have it; yea, and can show it you here in the house. And, Falstaff, you carried your guts away as nimbly, with as quick dexterity, and roar'd for mercy, and still run and roar'd, as ever I heard bullcalf. What a slave art thou to hack thy sword as thou hast done, and then say it was in fight! What trick, what device, what starting hole canst thou now find out to hide thee from this open and apparent shame?

POINS. Come, let's hear, Jack. What trick hast thou now?

FAL. By the Lord, I knew ye as well as he that made ye. Why, hear you, my masters. Was it for me to kill the heir apparent? Should I turn upon the true prince? Why, thou knowest I am as valiant as Hercules; but beware instinct. The lion will not touch the true prince. Instinct is a great matter. I was now a coward on instinct. I shall think the better of myself, and thee, during my life—I for a valiant lion, and thou for a true prince. But, by the Lord, lads, I am glad you have the money. Hostess, clap to the doors. Watch to-night, pray to-morrow. Gallants, lads, boys, hearts of gold, all the titles of good fellowship come to you! What, shall we be merry? Shall we have a play extempore?

PRINCE. Content—and the argument shall be thy running away.

FAL. Ah, no more of that, Hal, an thou lovest me!

---

[66] shield.

[67] either a tub to hold tallow or, simply, a lump of fat.

[68] dried cod.

[69] rapier.

Enter HOSTESS

HOST. O Jesu, my lord the Prince!

PRINCE. How now, my lady the hostess? What say'st thou to me?

HOST. Marry, my lord, there is a nobleman of the court at door would speak with you. He says he comes from your father.

PRINCE. Give him as much as will make him a royal man, and send him back again to my 10 mother.

FAL. What manner of man is he?

HOST. An old man.

FAL. What doth gravity out of his bed at midnight? Shall I give him his answer? 15

PRINCE. Prithee do, Jack.

FAL. Faith, and I'll send him packing. [*exit*]

PRINCE. Now, sirs. By'r lady, you fought fair; so did you, Peto; so did you, Bardolph. You are lions too, you ran away upon instinct, 20 you will not touch the true prince; no—fie!

BARD. Faith, I ran when I saw others run.

PRINCE. Tell me now in earnest, how came Falstaff's sword so hack'd?

PETO. Why, he hack'd it with his dagger, 25 and said he would swear truth out of England but he would make you believe it was done in fight, and persuaded us to do the like.

BARD. Yea, and to tickle our noses with spear-grass to make them bleed, and then to 30 beslubber our garments with it and swear it was the blood of true men. I did that I did not this seven year before—I blush'd to hear his monstrous devices.

PRINCE. O villain! thou stolest a cup of sack 35 eighteen years ago and wert taken with the manner, and ever since thou hast blush'd extempore. Thou hadst fire and sword on thy side, and yet thou ran'st away. What instinct hadst thou for it? 40

BARD. My lord, do you see these meteors? Do you behold these exhalations?

PRINCE. I do.

BARD. What think you they portend?

PRINCE. Hot livers and cold purses. 45

BARD. Choler, my lord, if rightly taken.

PRINCE. No, if rightly taken, halter.

Enter FALSTAFF

Here comes lean Jack; here comes bare-bone. 50
How now, my sweet creature of bombast?
How long is't ago, Jack, since thou sawest

thine own knee?

FAL. My own knee? When I was about thy years, Hal, I was not an eagle's talent[70] in the waist; I could have crept into any alderman's 5 thumb-ring. A plague of sighing and grief! It blows a man up like a bladder. There's villanous news abroad. Here was Sir John Bracy from your father. You must to the court in the morning. That same mad fellow of the North, 10 Percy, and he of Wales that gave Amamon[71] the bastinado, and made Lucifer cuckold, and swore the devil his true liegeman upon the cross of a Welsh hook—what a plague call you him?

POINS. O, Glendower. 15

FAL. Owen, Owen—the same; and his sonin-law Mortimer, and old Northumberland, and that sprightly Scot of Scots, Douglas, that runs a-horseback up a hill perpendicular—

PRINCE. He that rides at high speed and 20 with his pistol kills a sparrow flying.

FAL. You have hit it.

PRINCE. So did he never the sparrow.

FAL. Well, that rascal hath good metal in him; he will not run. 25

PRINCE. Why, what a rascal art thou then, to praise him so for running!

FAL. A-horseback, ye cuckoo! but afoot he will not budge a foot.

PRINCE. Yes, Jack, upon instinct. 30

FAL. I grant ye, upon instinct. Well, he is there too, and one Mordake, and a thousand bluecaps[72] more. Worcester is stol'n away tonight; thy father's beard is turn'd white with the news; you may buy land now as cheap as 35 stinking mack'rel.

PRINCE. Why then, it is like, if there come a hot June, and this civil buffeting hold, we shall buy maidenheads as they buy hobnails, by the hundreds. 40

FAL. By the mass, lad, thou sayest true; it is like we shall have good trading that way. But tell me, Hal, art not thou horrible afeard? Thou being heir apparent, could the world pick thee out three such enemies again as that 45 fiend Douglas, that spirit Percy, and that devil Glendower? Art thou not horribly afraid? Doth not thy blood thrill at it?

PRINCE. Not a whit, i' faith. I lack some of 50 thy instinct.

---

[70] talon. [71] a devil. [72] Scots.

FAL. Well, thou wilt be horribly chid to-morrow when thou comest to thy father. If thou love me, practise an answer.

PRINCE. Do thou stand for my father and examine me upon the particulars of my life.

FAL. Shall I? Content. This chair shall be my state, this dagger my sceptre, and this cushion my crown.

PRINCE. Thy state is taken for a join'd-stool, thy golden sceptre for a leaden dagger, and thy precious rich crown for a pitiful bald crown.

FAL. Well, an the fire of grace be not quite out of thee, now shalt thou be moved. Give me a cup of sack to make my eyes look red, that it may be thought I have wept; for I must speak in passion, and I will do it in King Cambyses' vein.[73]

PRINCE. Well, here is my leg.[74]

FAL. And here is my speech. Stand aside, nobility.

HOST. O Jesu, this is excellent sport, i' faith!

FAL. Weep not, sweet queen, for trickling tears are vain.

HOST. O, the Father, how he holds his countenance!

FAL. For God's sake, lords convey my tristful queen!

For tears do stop the floodgates of her eyes.

HOST. O Jesu, he doth it as like one of these harlotry[75] players as ever I see!

FAL. Peace, good pintpot. Peace, good ticklebrain.[76]—Harry, I do not only marvel where thou spendest thy time, but also how thou art accompanied. For though the camomile, the more it is trodden on, the faster it grows, yet youth, the more it is wasted, the sooner it wears. That thou art my son I have partly thy mother's word, partly my own opinion, but chiefly a villanous trick of thine eye and a foolish hanging of thy nether lip that doth warrant me. If then thou be son to me, here lies the point: why, being son to me, art thou so pointed at? Shall the blessed sun of heaven prove a micher[77] and eat blackberries? A question not to be ask'd. Shall the son of England prove a thief and take purses? A question to be ask'd. There is a thing, Harry, which thou hast often heard of, and it is known to many in our land by the name of pitch. This pitch, as ancient writers do report, doth defile; so doth the company thou keepest. For, Harry, now I do not speak to thee in drink, but in tears; not in pleasure, but in passion; not in words only, but in woes also: and yet there is a virtuous man whom I have often noted in thy company, but I know not his name.

PRINCE. What manner of man, an it like your Majesty?

FAL. A goodly portly man, i' faith, and a corpulent; of a cheerful look, a pleasing eye, and a most noble carriage; and, as I think, his age some fifty, or, by'r Lady, inclining to threescore; and now I remember me, his name is Falstaff. If that man should be lewdly given, he deceiveth me; for, Harry, I see virtue in his looks. If then the tree may be known by the fruit, as the fruit by the tree, then, peremptorily I speak it, there is virtue in that Falstaff. Him keep with, the rest banish. And tell me now, thou naughty varlet, tell me where hast thou been this month?

PRINCE. Dost thou speak like a king? Do thou stand for me, and I'll play my father.

FAL. Depose me? If thou dost it half so gravely, so majestically, both in word and matter, hang me up by the heels for a rabbit-sucker or a poulter's hare.

PRINCE. Well, here I am set.

FAL. And here I stand. Judge, my masters.

PRINCE. Now, Harry, whence come you?

FAL. My noble lord, from Eastcheap.

PRINCE. The complaints I hear of thee are grievous.

FAL. 'Sblood, my lord, they are false! Nay, I'll tickle ye for a young prince, i' faith.

PRINCE. Swearest thou, ungracious boy? Henceforth ne'er look on me. Thou art violently carried away from grace. There is a devil haunts thee in the likeness of an old fat man; a tun of man is thy companion. Why dost thou converse with that trunk of humours, that bolting hutch[78] of beastliness, that swoll'n parcel of dropsies, that huge bombard[79] of sack, that stuff'd cloakbag of guts, that roasted Manningtree ox[80] with the pudding in his belly, that reverend vice, that grey iniquity, that

---

[73] in a ranting manner like that of the character in Preston's play of *Cambises*.
[74] (He bows).   [75] rascally.
[76] strong drink.   [77] truant.

[78] flour bin.
[79] leather drinking vessel.
[80] Manningtree in Essex was famous for oxen.

father ruffian, that vanity in years? Wherein is he good, but to taste sack and drink it? wherein neat and cleanly, but to carve a capon and eat it? wherein cunning, but in craft? wherein crafty, but in villany? wherein villanous, but in all things? wherein worthy, but in nothing?

FAL. I would your Grace would take me with you. Whom means your Grace?

PRINCE. That villanous abominable mis- 10 leader of youth, Falstaff, that old whitebearded Satan.

FAL. My lord, the man I know.

PRINCE. I know thou dost.

FAL. But to say I know more harm in him 15 than in myself were to say more than I know. That he is old (the more the pity) his white hairs do witness it; but that he is (saving your reverence) a whoremaster, that I utterly deny. If sack and sugar be a fault, God help 20 the wicked! If to be old and merry be a sin, then many an old host that I know is damn'd. If to be fat be to be hated, then Pharaoh's lean kine are to be loved. No, my good lord. Banish Peto, banish Bardolph, banish Poins; 25 but for sweet Jack Falstaff, kind Jack Falstaff, true Jack Falstaff, valiant Jack Falstaff, and therefore more valiant being, as he is, old Jack Falstaff, banish not him thy Harry's company, banish not him thy Harry's company. Banish 30 plump Jack, and banish all the world!

PRINCE. I do, I will. [*a knocking heard.*

Exeunt HOSTESS, FRANCIS, *and* BARDOLPH.]

Enter BARDOLPH, *running*

BARD. O, my lord, my lord! the sheriff with 35 a most monstrous watch is at the door.

FAL. Out, ye rogue! Play out the play. I have much to say in the behalf of that Falstaff.

Enter the HOSTESS

HOST. O Jesu, my lord, my lord! 40

PRINCE. Heigh, heigh, the devil rides upon a fiddlestick! What's the matter?

HOST. The sheriff and all the watch are at 45 the door. They are come to search the house. Shall I let them in?

FAL. Dost thou hear, Hal? Never call a true piece of gold a counterfeit. Thou art essentially mad without seeming so.

PRINCE. And thou a natural coward without instinct.

FAL. I deny your major.[81] If you will deny the sheriff, so; if not, let him enter. If I become not a cart as well as another man, a plague on my bringing up! I hope I shall as soon be strangled with a halter as another. 5

PRINCE. Go hide thee behind the arras. The rest walk up above. Now, my masters, for a true face and good conscience.

FAL. Both which I have had; but their date is out, and therefore I'll hide me. [*exit*] 10

PRINCE. Call in the sheriff. [*exeunt; manent the* PRINCE *and* PETO]

Enter SHERIFF *and the* CARRIER

Now, Master Sheriff, what is your will with 15 me?

SHER. First, pardon me, my lord. A hue and cry

Hath followed certain men unto this house.

PRINCE. What men? 20

SHER. One of them is well known, my gracious lord—

A gross fat man.

CARRIER.   As fat as butter.

PRINCE. The man, I do assure you, is not here,

For I myself at this time have employ'd him.

And, sheriff, I will engage my word to thee

That I will by to-morrow dinner time

Send him to answer thee, or any man, 30

For anything he shall be charg'd withal;

And so let me entreat you leave the house.

SHER. I will, my lord. There are two gentlemen

Have in this robbery lost three hundred 35 marks.

PRINCE. It may be so. If he have robb'd these men,

He shall be answerable; and so farewell.

SHER. Good night, my noble lord. 40

PRINCE. I think it is good morrow, is it not?

SHER. Indeed, my lord, I think it be two o'clock. *exit* [*with* CARRIER]

PRINCE. This oily rascal is known as well as 45 Paul's.[82] Go call him forth.

PETO. Falstaff! Fast asleep behind the arras, and snorting like a horse.

PRINCE. Hark how hard he fetches breath. 50 Search his pockets. [*he searcheth his pockets*

---

[81] major premise.   [82] St. Paul's Cathedral.

and findeth certain papers]
What hast thou found?

PETO. Nothing but papers, my lord.

PRINCE. Let's see what they be. Read them.

PETO. [*reads*]

> 'Item, A capon . . . ii s. ii d.
> Item, Sauce . . . . iiii d.
> Item, Sack two gallons v s. viii d.
> Item, Anchovies and
> Sack after supper . ii s. vi d.
> Item, Bread . . . . ob.' [83]

PRINCE. O monstrous! but one halfpenny-worth of bread to this intolerable deal of sack! What there is else, keep close; we'll read it at more advantage. There let him sleep till day. I'll to the court in the morning. We must all to the wars, and thy place shall be honourable. I'll procure this fat rogue a charge of foot; and I know his death will be a march of twelve score. The money shall be paid back again with advantage. Be with me betimes in the morning, and so good morrow, Peto.

PETO. Good morrow, good my lord. [*exeunt*]

ACT III

SCENE I.

Bangor. The Archdeacon's house

Enter HOTSPUR, WORCESTER, LORD MORTIMER,
OWEN GLENDOWER

MORT. These promises are fair, the parties sure,
And our induction full of prosperous hope.

HOT. Lord Mortimer, and cousin Glendower,
Will you sit down?
And uncle Worcester. A plague upon it!
I have forgot the map.

GLEND. No, here it is.
Sit, cousin Percy; sit, good cousin Hotspur,
For by that name as oft as Lancaster
Doth speak of you, his cheek looks pale, and with
A rising sigh he wisheth you in heaven.

HOT. And you in hell, as oft as he hears
Owen Glendower spoke of.

GLEND. I cannot blame him. At my nativity
The front of heaven was full of fiery shapes

Of burning cressets,[84] and at my birth
The frame and huge foundation of the earth
Shak'd like a coward.

HOT. Why, so it would have done at the same season, if your mother's cat had but kitten'd though yourself had never been born.

GLEND. I say the earth did shake when I was born.

HOT. And I say the earth was not of my mind,
If you suppose as fearing you it shook.

GLEND. The heavens were all on fire, the earth did tremble.

HOT. O, then the earth shook to see the heavens on fire,
And not in fear of your nativity.
Diseased nature oftentimes breaks forth
In strange eruptions; oft the teeming earth
Is with a kind of colic pinch'd and vex'd
By the imprisoning of unruly wind
Within her womb, which, for enlargement striving,
Shakes the old beldame earth and topples down
Steeples and mossgrown towers. At your birth
Our grandam earth, having this distemp'rature,
In passion shook.

GLEND. Cousin, of many men
I do not bear these crossings. Give me leave
To tell you once again that at my birth
The front of heaven was full of fiery shapes,
The goats ran from the mountains, and the herds
Were strangely clamorous to the frighted fields.
These signs have mark'd me extraordinary,
And all the courses of my life do show
I am not in the roll of common men.
Where is he living, clipp'd in with the sea
That chides the banks of England, Scotland, Wales,
Which calls me pupil or hath read to me?
And bring him out that is but woman's son
Can trace me in the tedious ways of art
And hold me pace in deep experiments.

HOT. I think there's no man speaks better Welsh. I'll to dinner.

MORT. Peace, cousin Percy; you will make him mad.

GLEND. I can call spirits from the vasty deep.

HOT. Why, so can I, or so can any man;
But will they come when you do call for them?

---

[83] ob. equals *obolus*, halfpenny.

[84] torches.

GLEND. Why, I can teach you, cousin, to
command
The devil.

HOT. And I can teach thee, coz, to shame
the devil— 5
By telling truth. Tell truth and shame the
devil.
If thou have power to raise him, bring him
hither,
And I'll be sworn I have power to shame him 10
hence.
O, while you live, tell truth and shame the
devil!

MORT. Come, come, no more of this unprofitable chat. 15

GLEND. Three times hath Henry Bolingbroke
made head
Against my power; thrice from the banks of
Wye
And sandy-bottom'd Severn have I sent him 20
Bootless home and weather-beaten back.

HOT. Home without boots, and in foul
weather too?
How scapes he agues, in the devil's name?

GLEND. Come, here's the map. Shall we di- 25
vide our right
According to our threefold order ta'en?

MORT. The Archdeacon hath divided it
Into three limits very equally.
England, from Trent and Severn hitherto, 30
By south and east is to my part assign'd;
All westward, Wales beyond the Severn shore,
And all the fertile land within that bound,
To Owen Glendower; and, dear coz, to you
The remnant northward lying off from Trent. 35
And our indentures tripartite are drawn;
Which being sealed interchangeably
(A business that this night may execute),
To-morrow, cousin Percy, you and I
And my good Lord of Worcester will set forth 40
To meet your father and the Scottish power,
As is appointed us, at Shrewsbury.
My father Glendower is not ready yet,
Nor shall we need his help these fourteen
days. 45
[*To* GLEND.] Within that space you may have
drawn together
Your tenants, friends, and neighbouring gen-
tlemen.

GLEND. A shorter time shall send me to you, 50
lords;
And in my conduct shall your ladies come,

From whom you now must steal and take no
leave,
For there will be a world of water shed
Upon the parting of your wives and you.

HOT. Methinks my moiety,[85] north from
Burton here,
In quantity equals not one of yours.
See how this river comes me cranking in
And cuts me from the best of all my land
A huge half-moon, a monstrous cantle[86] out.
I'll have the current in this place damm'd up,
And here the smug and silver Trent shall run
In a new channel fair and evenly.
It shall not wind with such a deep indent
To rob me of so rich a bottom here.

GLEND. Not wind? It shall, it must! You see
it doth.

MORT. Yea, but
Mark how he bears his course, and runs me
up
With like advantage on the other side,
Gelding the opposed continent as much
As on the other side it takes from you.

WOR. Yea, but a little charge will trench him
here
And on this north side win this cape of land;
And then he runs straight and even.

HOT. I'll have it so. A little charge will do it.

GLEND. I will not have it alt'red.

HOT.   Will not you?

GLEND. No, nor you shall not.

HOT.   Who shall say me nay?

GLEND. Why, that will I.

HOT. Let me not understand you then;
speak it in Welsh.

GLEND. I can speak English, lord, as well as
you;
For I was train'd up in the English court,
Where, being but young, I framed to the harp
Many an English ditty lovely well,
And gave the tongue a helpful ornament—
A virtue that was never seen in you.

HOT. Marry,
And I am glad of it with all my heart!
I had rather be a kitten and cry mew
Than one of these same metre ballet-mongers.[87]
I had rather hear a brazen canstick[88] turn'd
Or a dry wheel grate on the axletree,
And that would set my teeth nothing on edge,

---

[85] share.   [86] piece.
[87] ballad writers or singers.   [88] candlestick.

Nothing so much as mincing poetry.
'Tis like the forc'd gait of a shuffling nag.
  GLEND. Come, you shall have Trent turn'd.
  HOT. I do not care. I'll give thrice so much land
To any well-deserving friend;
But in the way of bargain, mark ye me,
I'll cavil on the ninth part of a hair.
Are the indentures drawn? Shall we be gone?
  GLEND. The moon shines fair; you may away by night.
I'll haste the writer, and withal
Break with your wives of your departure hence.
I am afraid my daughter will run mad,
So much she doteth on her Mortimer. [*exit*]
  MORT. Fie, cousin Percy! how you cross my father!
  HOT. I cannot choose. Sometime he angers me
With telling me of the moldwarp[89] and the ant,
Of the dreamer Merlin and his prophecies,
And of a dragon and a finless fish,
A clip-wing'd griffin and a moulten raven,
A couching lion and a ramping cat,
And such a deal of skimble-skamble stuff
As puts me from my faith. I tell you what—
He held me last night at least nine hours
In reckoning up the several devils' names
That were his lackeys. I cried 'hum,' and 'Well,
  go to!'
But mark'd him not a word. O, he is as tedious
As a tired horse, a railing wife;
Worse than a smoky house. I had rather live
With cheese and garlic in a windmill far
Than feed on cates and have him talk to me
In any summer house in Christendom.
  MORT. In faith, he is a worthy gentleman,
Exceedingly well read, and profited
In strange concealments, valiant as a lion,
And wondrous affable, and as bountiful
As mines of India. Shall I tell you, cousin?
He holds your temper in a high respect
And curbs himself even of his natural scope
When you come 'cross his humour. Faith, he
  does.
I warrant you that man is not alive
Might so have tempted him as you have done
Without the taste of danger and reproof.
But do not use it oft, let me entreat you.

  WOR. In faith, my lord, you are too wilful-blame,
And since your coming hither have done enough
5 To put him quite besides his patience.
You must needs learn, lord, to amend this fault.
Though sometimes it show greatness, courage, blood—
And that's the dearest grace it renders you—
10 Yet oftentimes it doth present harsh rage,
Defect of manners, want of government,
Pride, haughtiness, opinion, and disdain;
The least of which haunting a nobleman
15 Loseth men's hearts, and leaves behind a stain
Upon the beauty of all parts besides,
Beguiling them of commendation.
  HOT. Well, I am school'd. Good manners be your speed!
20 Here come our wives, and let us take our leave.

Enter GLENDOWER *with the* LADIES

  MORT. This is the deadly spite that angers me—
My wife can speak no English, I no Welsh.
  GLEND. My daughter weeps; she will not part with you;
She'll be a soldier too, she'll to the wars.
  MORT. Good father, tell her that she and my aunt Percy
Shall follow in your conduct speedily. [GLEN-DOWER *speaks to her in Welsh, and she answers him in the same*]
  GLEND. She is desperate here. A peevish self-will'd harlotry,[90]
One that no persuasion can do good upon. [*the* LADY *speaks in Welsh*]
  MORT. I understand thy looks. That pretty Welsh
40 Which thou pourest down from these swelling heavens
I am too perfect in; and, but for shame,
In such a parley should I answer thee. [*the* LADY *again in Welsh*]
45 I understand thy kisses, and thou mine,
And that's a feeling disputation.
But I will never be a truant, love,
Till I have learnt thy language; for thy tongue
Makes Welsh as sweet as ditties highly penn'd,
50 Sung by a fair queen in a summer's bow'r,

---

[89] mole.

[90] wench.

With ravishing division, to her lute.

GLEND. Nay, if you melt, then will she run mad. [*the* LADY *speaks again in Welsh*]

MORT. O, I am ignorance itself in this!

GLEND. She bids you on the wanton[91] rushes 5
lay you down
And rest your gentle head upon her lap,
And she will sing the song that pleaseth you
And on your eyelids crown the god of sleep,
Charming your blood with pleasing heaviness, 10
Making such difference 'twixt wake and sleep
As is the difference betwixt day and night
The hour before the heavenly-harness'd team
Begins his golden progress in the East.

MORT. With all my heart I'll sit and hear her 15
sing.
By that time will our book, I think, be drawn.

GLEND.   Do so,
And those musicians that shall play to you
Hang in the air a thousand leagues from hence, 20
And straight they shall be here. Sit, and at-
tend.

HOT. Come, Kate, thou art perfect in lying
down. Come, quick, quick, that I may lay my
head in thy lap.

LADY. Go, ye giddy goose. [*the music plays*] 25

HOT. Now I perceive the devil understands
Welsh;
And 'tis no marvel, he is so humorous.[92]
By'r Lady, he is a good musician.

LADY P. Then should you be nothing but 30
musical; for you are altogether govern'd by
humours. Lie till, ye thief, and hear the lady
sing in Welsh.

HOT. I had rather hear Lady, my brach,[93] 35
howl in Irish.

LADY P. Wouldst thou have thy head broken?

HOT. No.

LADY P. Then be still. 40

HOT. Neither! 'Tis a woman's fault.

LADY P. Now God help thee!

HOT. To the Welsh lady's bed.

LADY P. What's that?

HOT. Peace! she sings. [*here the* LADY *sings* 45
a Welsh song]
Come, Kate, I'll have your song too.

LADY P. Not mine, in good sooth.

HOT. Not yours, in good sooth? Heart! you
swear like a comfit-maker's[94] wife. 'Not you, 50

in good sooth!' and 'as true as I live!' and 'as
God shall mend me!' and 'as sure as day!'
And givest such sarcenet[95] surety for thy oaths
As if thou ne'er walk'st further than Finsbury.
Swear me, Kate, like a lady as thou art,
A good mouth-filling oath; and leave 'in sooth'
And such protest of pepper gingerbread
To velvet guards[96] and Sunday citizens.
Come, sing.

LADY P. I will not sing.

HOT. 'Tis the next way to turn tailor or be
redbreast-teacher. An the indentures be drawn,
I'll away within these two hours; and so come
in when ye will.   [*exit*]

GLEND. Come, come, Lord Mortimer. You
are as slow
As hot Lord Percy is on fire to go.
By this our book is drawn; we'll but seal,
And then to horse immediately.

MORT.   With all my heart. [*exeunt*]

SCENE II.

London. The palace

Enter the KING, PRINCE OF WALES, *and others*

KING. Lords, give us leave. The Prince of
Wales and I
Must have some private conference; but be
near at hand, 30
For we shall presently have need of you.
                              [*exeunt Lords*]
I know not whether God will have it so,
For some displeasing service I have done,
That, in his secret doom, out of my blood
He'll breed revengement and a scourge for me;
But thou dost in thy passages of life
Make me believe that thou art only mark'd
For the hot vengeance and the rod of heaven
To punish my mistreadings. Tell me else, 40
Could such inordinate and low desires,
Such poor, such bare, such lewd, such mean
attempts,
Such barren pleasures, rude society,
As thou art match'd withal and grafted to,
Accompany the greatness of thy blood
And hold their level with thy princely heart?

PRINCE. So please your Majesty, I would I
could

---

[91] luxuriant.   [92] moody.
[93] hound.   [94] confectioner's.

[95] flimsy.
[96] women wearing velvet-trimmed dresses.

Quit all offences with as clear excuse
As well as I am doubtless I can purge
Myself of many I am charg'd withal.
Yet such extenuation let me beg
As, in reproof of many tales devis'd,
Which oft the ear of greatness needs must hear
By smiling pickthanks[97] and base news-mon-
    gers,
I may, for some things true wherein my youth
Hath faulty wand'red and irregular,
10 Find pardon on my true submission.
    KING. God pardon thee! Yet let me wonder,
    Harry,
At thy affections, which do hold a wing
Quite from the flight of all thy ancestors.
Thy place in Council thou hast rudely lost,
Which by thy younger brother is supplied,
And art almost an alien to the hearts
Of all the court and princes of my blood.
The hope and expectation of thy time
Is ruin'd and the soul of every man
Prophetically do forethink thy fall.
Had I so lavish of my presence been,
So common-hackney'd in the eyes of men,
So stale and cheap to vulgar company,
Opinion, that did help me to the crown,
Had still kept loyal to possession
And left me in reputeless banishment,
A fellow of no mark nor likelihood.
By being seldom seen, I could not stir
But, like a comet, I was wond'red at;
That men would tell their children, 'This is he!'
Others would say, 'Where? Which is Boling-
    broke?'
And then I stole all courtesy from heaven,
And dress'd myself in such humility
That I did pluck allegiance from men's hearts,
Loud shouts and salutations from their mouths
Even in the presence of the crowned King.
Thus did I keep my person fresh and new,
My presence, like a robe pontifical,
Ne'er seen but wond'red at; and so my state,
Seldom but sumptuous, show'd like a feast
And won by rareness such solemnity.
The skipping King, he ambled up and down
With shallow jesters and rash bavin[98] wits,
Soon kindled and soon burnt; carded[99] his
    state;

Mingled his royalty with cap'ring fools;
Had his great name profaned with their scorns
And gave his countenance, against his name,
To laugh at gibing boys and stand the push
5 Of every beardless vain comparative;
Grew a companion to the common streets,
Enfeoff'd[100] himself to popularity;
That, being daily swallowed by men's eyes,
They surfeited with honey and began
10 To loathe the taste of sweetness, whereof a
    little
More than a little is by much too much.
So, when he had occasion to be seen,
He was but as the cuckoo is in June,
15 Heard, not regarded—seen, but with such eyes
As, sick and blunted with community,
Afford no extraordinary gaze,
Such as is bent on sunlight majesty
When it shines seldom in admiring eyes;
20 But rather drows'd and hung their eyelids
    down,
Slept in his face, and rend'red such aspect
As cloudy men use to their adversaries,
Being with his presence glutted, gorg'd and
25   full.
And in that very line, Harry, standest thou;
For thou hast lost thy princely privilege
With vile participation. Not an eye
But is aweary of thy common sight,
30 Save mine, which hath desir'd to see thee
    more;
Which now doth that I would not have it do—
Make blind itself with foolish tenderness.
    PRINCE. I shall hereafter, my thrice-gracious
35   lord,
Be more myself.
    KING.   For all the world,
As thou art to this hour, was Richard then
When I from France set foot at Ravenspurgh;
40 And even as I was then is Percy now.
Now, by my sceptre, and my soul to boot,
He hath more worthy interest to the state
Than thou, the shadow of succession;
For of no right, nor colour like to right,
45 He doth fill fields with harness[101] in the realm,
Turns head against the lion's armed jaws,
And, being no more in debt to years than
    thou,
Leads ancient lords and reverend bishops on
50 To bloody battles and to bruising arms.

---

[97] parasites.
[98] superficial (literally brushwood which ignites
easily and burns out at once).
[99] debased his rank.

[100] surrendered.   [101] men in armor.

What never-dying honour hath he got
Against renowmed Douglas! whose high deeds,
Whose hot incursions and great name in arms
Holds from all soldiers chief majority
And military title capital
Through all the kingdoms that acknowledge
  Christ.
Thrice hath this Hotspur, Mars in swathling
  clothes,
This infant warrior, in his enterprises
Discomfited great Douglas; ta'en him once, 10
Enlarged him, and made a friend of him,
To fill the mouth of deep defiance up
And shake the peace and safety of our throne.
And what say you to this? Percy, Northumber-
  land,   15
The Archbishop's Grace of York, Douglas,
  Mortimer
Capitulate against us and are up.
But wherefore do I tell these news to thee? 20
Why, Harry, do I tell thee of my foes,
Which art my nearest and dearest enemy?
Thou that art like enough, through vassal fear,
Base inclination, and the start of spleen,
To fight against me under Percy's pay, 25
To dog his heels and curtsy at his frowns,
To show how much thou art degenerate.
  PRINCE. Do not think so. You shall not find
    it so.
And God forgive them that so much have 30
  sway'd
Your Majesty's good thoughts away from me!
I will redeem all this on Percy's head
And, in the closing of some glorious day,
Be bold to tell you that I am your son, 35
When I will wear a garment all of blood,
And stain my favours[102] in a bloody mask,
Which, wash'd away, shall scour my shame
  with it.
And that shall be the day, whene'er it lights, 40
That this same child of honour and renown,
This gallant Hotspur, this all-praised knight,
And your unthought-of Harry chance to meet.
For every honour sitting on his helm,
Would they were multitudes, and on my head 45
My shames redoubled! For the time will come
That I shall make this Northern youth ex-
  change
His glorious deeds for my indignities.
Percy is but my factor, good my lord, 50

To engross up glorious deeds on my behalf;
And I will call him to so strict account
That he shall render every glory up,
Yea, even the slightest worship of his time,
Or I will tear the reckoning from his heart. 5
This in the name of God I promise here;
The which if he be pleas'd I shall perform,
I do beseech your Majesty may salve
The long-grown wounds of my intemperance.
If not, the end of life cancels all bands, 10
And I will die a hundred thousand deaths
Ere break the smallest parcel of this vow.
  KING. A hundred thousand rebels die in this!
Thou shalt have charge and sovereign trust
  herein. 15

Enter BLUNT

How now, good Blunt? Thy looks are full of
  speed.
  BLUNT. So hath the business that I come to 20
    speak of.
Lord Mortimer of Scotland hath sent word
That Douglas and the English rebels met
The eleventh of this month at Shrewsbury.
A mighty and a fearful head they are, 25
If promises be kept on every hand,
As ever off'red foul play in a state.
  KING. The Earl of Westmoreland set forth
    to-day;
With him my son, Lord John of Lancaster; 30
For this advertisement is five days old.
On Wednesday next, Harry, you shall set for-
  ward;
On Thursday we ourselves will march. Our
  meeting 35
Is Bridgenorth; and, Harry, you shall march
Through Gloucestershire; by which account,
Our business valued, some twelve days hence
Our general forces at Bridgenorth shall meet.
Our hands are full of business. Let's away. 40
Advantage feeds him fat while men delay.
                              [*exeunt*]

SCENE III.

Eastcheap. The Boar's Head Tavern

Enter FALSTAFF *and* BARDOLPH

  FAL. Bardolph, am I not fall'n away vilely
since this last action? Do I not bate? Do I not 50
dwindle? Why, my skin hangs about me like an
old lady's loose gown! I am withered like an

---

[102] features.

old apple John.[103] Well, I'll repent, and that suddenly, while I am in some liking. I shall be out of heart shortly, and then I shall have no strength to repent. An I have not forgotten what the inside of a church is made of, I am a [5] peppercorn, a brewer's horse. The inside of a church! Company, villanous company, hath been the spoil of me.

BARD. Sir John, you are so fretful you cannot live long. [10]

FAL. Why, there is it! Come, sing me a bawdy song; make me merry. I was as virtuously given as a gentleman need to be, virtuous enough: swore little, dic'd not above seven times a week, went to a bawdy house not [15] above once in a quarter—of an hour, paid money that I borrowed—three or four times, lived well, and in good compass; and now I live out of all order, out of all compass.

BARD. Why, you are so fat, Sir John, that you [20] must needs be out of all compass—out of all reasonable compass, Sir John.

FAL. Do thou amend thy face, and I'll amend my life. Thou art our admiral, thou bearest the lantern in the poop—but 'tis in the [25] nose of thee. Thou art the Knight of the Burning Lamp.

BARD. Why, Sir John, my face does you no harm.

FAL. No, I'll be sworn. I make as good use [30] of it as many a man doth of a death's-head or a memento mori.[104] I never see thy face but I think upon hellfire and Dives that lived in purple; for there he is in his robes, burning, burning.[105] If thou wert any way given to vir- [35] tue, I would swear by thy face; my oath should be 'By this fire, that's God's angel.' But thou art altogether given over, and wert indeed, but for the light in thy face, the son of utter darkness. When thou ran'st up Gadshill [40] in the night to catch my horse, if I did not think thou hadst been an ignis fatuus[106] or a ball of wildfire, there's no purchase in money. O, thou art a perpetual triumph, an everlasting bonfire-light! Thou hast saved me a thou- [45] sand marks in links[107] and torches, walking with thee in the night betwixt tavern and tavern; but the sack that thou hast drunk me would have bought me lights as good cheap

at the dearest chandler's in Europe. I have maintained that salamander of yours with fire any time this two-and-thirty years. God reward me for it!

BARD. 'Sblood, I would my face were in your [5] belly!

FAL. God-a-mercy! so should I be sure to be heart-burn'd.

Enter HOSTESS

How now, Dame Partlet the hen?[108] Have you enquir'd yet who pick'd my pocket?

HOST. Why, Sir John, what do you think, Sir John? Do you think I keep thieves in my house? I have search'd, I have enquired, so has my husband, man by man, boy by boy, servant by servant. The tithe of a hair was never lost in my house before.

FAL. Ye lie, hostess. Bardolph was shav'd and lost many a hair, and I'll be sworn my pocket was pick'd. Go to, you are a woman, go!

HOST. Who, I? No; I defy thee! God's light, I was never call'd so in mine own house before!

FAL. Go to, I know you well enough.

HOST. No, Sir John; you do not know me, Sir John. I know you, Sir John. You owe me money, Sir John, and now you pick a quarrel to beguile me of it. I bought you a dozen of shirts to your back.

FAL. Dowlas, filthy dowlas![109] I have given them away to bakers' wives; they have made bolters[110] of them.

HOST. Now, as I am a true woman, holland of eight shillings an ell. You owe money here besides, Sir John, for your diet and by-drinkings, and money lent you, four-and-twenty pound.

FAL. He had his part of it; let him pay.

HOST. He? Alas, he is poor; he hath nothing.

FAL. How? Poor? Look upon his face. What call you rich? Let them coin his nose, let them coin his cheeks. I'll not pay a denier. What, will you make a younker[111] of me? Shall I not take mine ease in mine inn but I shall have my pocket pick'd? I have lost a seal-ring of my grandfather's worth forty mark.

HOST. O Jesu, I have heard the Prince tell

---

[103] shriveled apple.   [104] reminder of death.
[105] see Luke 16:19 ff.   [106] will o' the wisp.
[107] small torches.

[108] See Chaucer's *Nun's Priest's Tale.*
[109] coarse linen.   [110] sifting cloths.
[111] greenhorn.

him, I know not how oft, that that ring was copper!

FAL. How? the Prince is a Jack, a sneak-cup. 'Sblood, an he were here, I would cudgel him like a dog if he would say so.

Enter the PRINCE [*and* POINS], *marching; and* FALSTAFF *meets them, playing upon his truncheon like a fife*

How now, lad? Is the wind in that door, i' faith? Must we all march? 10

BARD. Yea, two and two, Newgate fashion.[112]

HOST. My lord, I pray you hear me.

PRINCE. What say'st thou, Mistress Quickly? How doth thy husband? I love him well; he is an honest man. 15

HOST. Good my lord, hear me.

FAL. Prithee let her alone and list to me.

PRINCE. What say'st thou, Jack?

FAL. The other night I fell asleep here behind the arras and had my pocket pick'd. This 20 house is turn'd bawdy house; they pick pockets.

PRINCE. What didst thou lose, Jack?

FAL. Wilt thou believe me, Hal? Three or four bonds of forty pound apiece and a seal-ring of my grandfather's. 25

PRINCE. A trifle, some eightpenny matter.

HOST. So I told him, my lord, and I said I heard your Grace say so; and, my lord, he speaks most vilely of you, like a foul-mouth'd man as he is, and said he would cudgel you. 30

PRINCE. What! he did not?

HOST. There's neither faith, truth, nor womanhood in me else.

FAL. There's no more faith in thee than in a 35 stewed prune, nor no more truth in thee than in a drawn fox; and for womanhood, Maid Marian[113] may be the deputy's wife of the ward to thee. Go, you thing, go!

HOST. Say, what thing? what thing? 40

FAL. What thing? Why, a thing to thank God on.

HOST. I am no thing to thank God on, I would thou shouldst know it! I am an honest man's wife, and, setting thy knighthood aside, 45 thou art a knave to call me so.

---

[112] like prisoners in Newgate Prison.

[113] The gist of this remark is that compared with the hostess, Maid Marian (not too virtuous) would seem a respectable official's wife; Marian appears in morris dances and Robin Hood stories.

FAL. Setting thy womanhood aside, thou art a beast to say otherwise.

HOST. Say, what beast, thou knave, thou?

FAL. What beast? Why, an otter.

PRINCE. An otter, Sir John? Why an otter? 5

FAL. Why, she's neither fish nor flesh; a man knows not where to have her.

HOST. Thou are an unjust man in saying so. Thou or any man knows where to have me, thou knave, thou! 10

PRINCE. Thou say'st true, hostess, and he slanders thee most grossly.

HOST. So he doth you, my lord, and said this other day you ought him a thousand pound. 15

PRINCE. Sirrah, do I owe you a thousand pound?

FAL. A thousand pound, Hal? A million! Thy love is worth a million; thou owest me thy love. 20

HOST. Nay, my lord, he call'd you Jack and said he would cudgel you.

FAL. Did I, Bardolph?

BARD. Indeed, Sir John, you said so.

FAL. Yea, if he said my ring was copper. 25

PRINCE. I say 'tis copper. Darest thou be as good as thy word now?

FAL. Why, Hal, thou knowest, as thou art but man, I dare; but as thou art Prince, I fear thee as I fear the roaring of the lion's whelp. 30

PRINCE. And why not as the lion?

FAL. The King himself is to be feared as the lion. Dost thou think I'll fear thee as I fear thy father? Nay, an I do, I pray God my girdle break. 35

PRINCE. O, if it should, how would thy guts fall about thy knees! But, sirrah, there's no room for faith, truth, nor honesty in this bosom of thine. It is all fill'd up with guts and midriff. Charge an honest woman with picking thy 40 pocket? Why, thou whoreson, impudent, emboss'd[114] rascal, if there were anything in thy pocket but tavern reckonings, memorandums of bawdy houses, and one poor pennyworth of sugar candy to make thee long-winded—if thy 45 pocket were enrich'd with any other injuries but these, I am a villain. And yet you will stand to it; you will not pocket up wrong. Art thou not ashamed?

FAL. Dost thou hear, Hal? Thou knowest in 50

---

[114] blown up.

the state of innocency Adam fell; and what should poor Jack Falstaff do in the days of villany? Thou seest I have more flesh than another man, and therefore more frailty. You confess then, you pick'd my pocket?

PRINCE. It appears so by the story.

FAL. Hostess, I forgive thee. Go make ready breakfast. Love thy husband, look to thy servants, cherish thy guests. Thou shalt find me tractable to any honest reason. Thou seest I 10 am pacified.—Still?—Nay, prithee be gone. [exit HOSTESS] Now, Hal, to the news at court. For the robbery, lad—how is that answered?

PRINCE. O my sweet beef, I must still be good angel to thee. The money is paid back 15 again.

FAL. O, I do not like that paying back! 'Tis a double labour.

PRINCE. I am good friends with my father, and may do anything. 20

FAL. Rob me the exchequer the first thing thou doest, and do it with unwash'd hands[115] too.

BARD. Do, my lord.

PRINCE. I have procured thee, Jack, a charge 25 of foot.

FAL. I would it had been of horse. Where shall I find one that can steal well? O for a fine thief of the age of two-and-twenty or thereabouts! I am heinously unprovided. Well, 30 God be thanked for these rebels. They offend none but the virtuous. I laud them, I praise them.

PRINCE. Bardolph!

BARD. My lord? 35

PRINCE. Go bear this letter to Lord John of Lancaster,
To my brother John; this to my Lord of Westmoreland. [exit BARDOLPH]
Go, Poins, to horse, to horse; for thou and I 40
Have thirty miles to ride yet ere dinner time. [exit POINS]
Jack, meet me to-morrow in the Temple Hall
At two o'clock in the afternoon.
There shalt thou know thy charge, and there 45 receive
Money and order for their furniture.
The land is burning; Percy stands on high;
And either they or we must lower lie. [exit]

FAL. Rare words! brave world! Hostess, my 50

breakfast, come.
O, I could wish this tavern were my drum![116] [exit]

ACT IV

SCENE I.

The rebel camp near Shrewsbury

Enter HARRY HOTSPUR, WORCESTER, and DOUGLAS

HOT. Well said, my noble Scot. If speaking truth
In this fine age were not thought flattery,
Such attribution should the Douglas have
As not a soldier of this season's stamp
Should go so general current through the world.
By God, I cannot flatter, I defy
The tongues of soothers! but a braver place
In my heart's love hath no man than yourself.
Nay, task me to my word; approve me,[117] lord.

DOUG. Thou art the king of honour.
No man so potent breathes upon the ground
But I will beard him.
Enter one with letters
HOT. Do so, and 'tis well.—
What letters hast thou there? I can but thank you.

MESSENGER. These letters come from your father.

HOT. Letters from him? Why comes he not himself?

MESS. He cannot come, my lord; he is grievous sick.

HOT. Zounds! how has he the leisure to be sick
In such a justling time? Who leads his power?
Under whose government come they along?

MESS. His letters bears his mind, not I, my lord.

WOR. I prithee tell me, doth he keep his bed?

MESS. He did, my lord, four days ere I sat forth,
And at the time of my departure thence
He was much fear'd by his physicians.

WOR. I would the state of time had first been whole

---

[115] at once.

[116] to attract recruits.
[117] test me.

Ere he by sickness had been visited.
His health was never better worth than now.
  HOT. Sick now? droop now? This sickness
    doth infect
The very lifeblood of our enterprise.
'Tis catching hither, even to our camp.
He writes me here that inward sickness—
And that his friends by deputation could not
So soon be drawn; nor did he think it meet
To lay so dangerous and dear a trust
On any soul remov'd but on his own.
Yet doth he give us bold advertisement,
That with our small conjunction we should on,
To see how fortune is dispos'd to us;
For, as he writes, there is no quailing now,
Because the King is certainly possess'd
Of all our purposes. What say you to it?
  WOR. Your father's sickness is a maim to us.
  HOT. A perilous gash, a very limb lopp'd off.
And yet, in faith, it is not! His present want
Seems more than we shall find it. Were it good
To set the exact wealth of all our states
All at one cast? to set so rich a main[118]
On the nice[119] hazard of one doubtful hour?
It were not good; for therein should we read
The very bottom and the soul of hope,
The very list,[120] the very utmost bound
Of all our fortunes.
  DOUG.   Faith, and so we should;
Where now remains a sweet reversion.
We may boldly spend upon the hope of what
Is to come in.
A comfort of retirement lives in this.
  HOT. A rendezvous, a home to fly unto,
If that the devil and mischance look big
Upon the maidenhead of our affairs.
  WOR. But yet I would your father had been
    here.
The quality and hair[121] of our attempt
Brooks no division. It will be thought
By some that know not why he is away,
That wisdom, loyalty, and mere dislike
Of our proceedings kept the Earl from hence.
And think how such an apprehension
May turn the tide of fearful faction
And breed a kind of question in our cause.
For well you know we of the off'ring side
Must keep aloof from strict arbitrement,
And stop all sight-holes, every loop from
    whence

The eye of reason may pry in upon us.
This absence of your father's draws a curtain
That shows the ignorant a kind of fear
Before not dreamt of.
  HOT.   You strain too far.
I rather of his absence make this use:
It lends a lustre and more great opinion,
A larger dare to our great enterprise,
Than if the Earl were here; for men must
    think,
If we, without his help, can make a head
To push against a kingdom, with his help
We shall o'erturn it topsy-turvy down.
Yet all goes well; yet all our joints are whole.
  DOUG. As heart can think. There is not such
    a word
Spoke of in Scotland as this term of fear.

Enter SIR RICHARD VERNON

  HOT. My cousin Vernon! welcome, by my
    soul.
  VER. Pray God my news be worth a welcome,
    lord.
The Earl of Westmoreland, seven thousand
    strong,
Is marching hitherwards; with him Prince
    John.
  HOT. No harm. What more?
  VER.   And further, I have learn'd
The King himself in person is set forth,
Or hitherwards intended speedily,
With strong and mighty preparation.
  HOT. He shall be welcome too. Where is his
    son,
The nimble-footed madcap Prince of Wales,
And his comrades, that daff'd[122] the world
    aside
And bid it pass?
  VER.   All furnish'd, all in arms;
All plum'd like estridges[123] that with the wind
Bated[124] like eagles having lately bath'd;
Glittering in golden coats like images;
As full of spirit as the month of May
And gorgeous as the sun at midsummer;
Wanton as youthful goats, wild as young bulls.
I saw young Harry with his beaver[125] on,
His cushes[126] on his thighs, gallantly arm'd,
Rise from the ground like feathered Mercury,
And vaulted with such ease into his seat

---

118 stake.   119 doubtful, delicate.   123 ostriches.
120 limit.   121 synonymous with quality.   125 helmet.
122 pushed.   124 flapped.   126 armor.

As if an angel dropp'd down from the clouds
To turn and wind a fiery Pegasus
And witch the world with noble horsemanship.
  HOT. No more, no more! Worse than the sun in March,
This praise doth nourish agues. Let them come.
They come like sacrifices in their trim,
And to the fire-ey'd maid of smoky war[127]
All hot and bleeding will we offer them.
The mailed Mars shall on his altar sit
Up to the ears in blood. I am on fire
To hear this rich reprisal is so nigh,
And yet not ours. Come, let me taste my horse,
Who is to bear me like a thunderbolt
Against the bosom of the Prince of Wales.
Harry to Harry shall, hot horse to horse,
Meet, and ne'er part till one drop down a corse.
O that Glendower were come!
  VER.   There is more news.
I learn'd in Worcester, as I rode along,
He cannot draw his power this fourteen days.
  DOUG. That's the worst tidings that I hear of yet.
  WOR. Ay, by my faith, that bears a frosty sound.
  HOT. What may the King's whole battle reach unto?
  VER. To thirty thousand.
  HOT.   Forty let it be.
My father and Glendower being both away,
The powers of us may serve so great a day.
Come, let us take a muster speedily.
Doomsday is near. Die all, die merrily.
  DOUG. Talk not of dying. I am out of fear
Of death or death's hand for this one half-year.
                        [exeunt]

SCENE II.

A public road near Coventry

Enter FALSTAFF *and* BARDOLPH

  FAL. Bardolph, get thee before to Coventry; fill me a bottle of sack. Our soldiers shall march through. We'll to Sutton Co'fil'[128] to-night.
  BARD. Will you give me money, Captain?

  FAL. Lay out, lay out.
  BARD. This bottle makes an angel.[129]
  FAL. An if it do, take it for thy labour; an if it make twenty, take them all; I'll answer the coinage. Bid my lieutenant Peto meet me at town's end.
  BARD. I will, Captain. Farewell.   *[exit]*
  FAL. If I be not ashamed of my soldiers, I am a sous'd gurnet.[130] I have misused the King's press damnably. I have got, in exchange of a hundred and fifty soldiers, three hundred and odd pounds. I press me none but good householders, yeomen's sons; inquire me out contracted bachelors, such as had been ask'd twice on the banes[131]—such a commodity of warm slaves as had as lieve hear the devil as a drum; such as fear the report of a caliver worse than a struck fowl or a hurt wild duck. I press'd me none but such toasts-and-butter, with hearts in their bellies no bigger than pins' heads, and they have bought out their services; and now my whole charge consists of ancients, corporals, lieutenants, gentlemen of companies—slaves as ragged as Lazarus in the painted cloth, where the glutton's dogs licked his sores; and such as indeed were never soldiers, but discarded unjust serving-men, younger sons to younger brothers, revolted tapsters, and ostlers trade-fall'n; the cankers of a calm world and a long peace; ten times more dishonourable ragged than an old fac'd ancient; and such have I to fill up the rooms of them that have bought out their services that you would think that I had a hundred and fifty tattered Prodigals lately come from swine-keeping, from eating draff[132] and husks. A mad fellow met me on the way, and told me I had unloaded all the gibbets and press'd the dead bodies. No eye hath seen such scarecrows. I'll not march through Coventry with them, that's flat. Nay, and the villains march wide betwixt the legs, as if they had gyves[133] on; for indeed I had the most of them out of prison. There's but a shirt and a half in all my company; and the half-shirt is two napkins tack'd together and thrown over the shoulders like a herald's coat without sleeves; and the shirt, to say the truth, stol'n from my host at Saint Alban's, or the red-nose innkeeper of Daventry. But that's

---

[127] Bellona, goddess of war.
[128] Sutton Coldfield, near Coventry.
[129] I owe an angel, a coin worth 10 shillings.
[130] pickled fish.   [131] banns.
[132] swill.   [133] fetters.

all one; they'll find linen enough on every
hedge.

Enter the PRINCE *and the* LORD OF WEST-
MORELAND

PRINCE. How now, blown Jack? How now,
quilt?

FAL. What, Hal? How now, mad wag? What
a devil dost thou in Warwickshire? My good
Lord of Westmoreland, I cry you mercy. I 10
thought your honour had already been at
Shrewsbury.

WEST. Faith, Sir John, 'tis more than time
that I were there, and you too; but my powers
are there already. The King, I can tell you, 15
looks for us all. We must away all, to-night.

FAL. Tut, never fear me. I am as vigilant as
a cat to steal cream.

PRINCE. I think, to steal cream indeed, for
thy theft hath already made thee butter. But 20
tell me, Jack, whose fellows are these that
come after?

FAL. Mine, Hal, mine.

PRINCE. I did never see such pitiful rascals.

FAL. Tut, tut! good enough to toss; food 25
for powder, food for powder. They'll fill a pit
as well as better. Tush, man, mortal men, mortal men.

WEST. Ay, but, Sir John, methinks they are
exceeding poor and bare—too beggarly. 30

FAL. Faith, for their poverty, I know not
where they had that; and for their bareness, I
am sure they never learn'd that of me.

PRINCE. No, I'll be sworn, unless you call
three fingers on the ribs bare. But, sirrah, 35
make haste. Percy is already in the field. [*exit*]

FAL. What, is the King encamp'd?

WEST. He is, Sir John. I fear we shall stay
too long.   [*exit*]

FAL. Well,   40
To the latter end of a fray and the beginning
of a feast
Fits a dull fighter and a keen guest.   [*exit*]

SCENE III.   45

The rebel camp near Shrewsbury

Enter HOTSPUR, WORCESTER, DOUGLAS, VERNON

HOT. We'll fight with him to-night.
WOR.   It may not be.   50
DOUG. You give him then advantage.

VER.   Not a whit.
HOT. Why say you so? Looks he not for
supply?
VER. So do we.
HOT.   His is certain, ours is doubtful.
WOR. Good cousin, be advis'd; stir not to-
night.
VER. Do not, my lord.
DOUG.   You do not counsel well.
You speak it out of fear and cold heart.
VER. Do me no slander, Douglas. By my
life—
And I dare well maintain it with my life—
If well-respected honour bid me on,
I hold as little counsel with weak fear
As you, my lord, or any Scot that this day lives.
Let it be seen to-morrow in the battle
Which of us fears.
DOUG.   Yea, or to-night.
VER.   Content.
HOT. To-night, say I.
VER. Come, come, it may not be. I wonder
much,
Being men of such great leading as you are,
That you foresee not what impediments
Drag back our expedition. Certain horse
Of my cousin Vernon's are not yet come up.
Your uncle Worcester's horse came but to-day;
And now their pride and mettle is asleep,
Their courage with hard labour tame and dull,
That not a horse is half the half of himself.
HOT. So are the horses of the enemy,
In general journey-bated and brought low.
The better part of ours are full of rest.
WOR. The number of the King exceedeth
ours.
For God's sake, cousin, stay till all come in.
                    [*the trumpet sounds a parley*]

Enter SIR WALTER BLUNT

BLUNT. I come with gracious offers from the
King,
If you vouchsafe me hearing and respect.
HOT. Welcome, Sir Walter Blunt, and would
to God
You were of our determination!
Some of us love you well; and even those some
Envy your great deservings and good name,
Because you are not of our quality,
But stand against us like an enemy.
BLUNT. And God defend but still I should
stand so,

So long as out of limit and true rule
You stand against anointed majesty!
But to my charge. The King hath sent to know
The nature of your griefs; and whereupon
You conjure from the breast of civil peace 5
Such bold hostility, teaching his duteous land
Audacious cruelty. If that the King
Have any way your good deserts forgot,
Which he confesseth to be manifold,
He bids you name your griefs, and with all 10
 speed
You shall have your desires with interest,
And pardon absolute for yourself and these
Herein misled by your suggestion.
 HOT. The King is kind; and well we know 15
 the King
Knows at what time to promise, when to pay.
My father and my uncle and myself
Did give him that same royalty he wears;
And when he was not six-and-twenty strong, 20
Sick in the world's regard, wretched and low,
A poor unminded outlaw sneaking home,
My father gave him welcome to the shore;
And when he heard him swear and vow to
 God 25
He came but to be Duke of Lancaster,
To sue his livery[134] and beg his peace,
With tears of innocency and terms of zeal,
My father, in kind heart and pity mov'd,
Swore him assistance, and perform'd it too. 30
Now when the lords and barons of the realm
Perceiv'd Northumberland did lean to him,
The more and less came in with cap and knee;
Met him in boroughs, cities, villages,
Attended him on bridges, stood in lanes, 35
Laid gifts before him, proffer'd him their oaths,
Gave him their heirs as pages, followed him
Even at the heels in golden multitudes.
He presently, as greatness knows itself,
Steps me a little higher than his vow 40
Made to my father, while his blood was poor,
Upon the naked shore at Ravenspurgh;
And now, forsooth, takes on him to reform
Some certain edicts and some strait decrees
That lie too heavy on the commonwealth; 45
Cries out upon abuses, seems to weep
Over his country's wrongs; and by this face,
This seeming brow of justice, did he win
The hearts of all that he did angle for;
Proceeded further—cut me off the heads 50

Of all the favourites that the absent King
In deputation left behind him here
When he was personal in the Irish war.
 BLUNT. Tut! I came not to hear this.
 HOT. Then to the point.
In short time after he depos'd the King;
Soon after that depriv'd him of his life;
And in the neck of that task'd[135] the whole
 state;
To make that worse, suff'red his kinsman
 March
(Who is, if every owner were well plac'd,
Indeed his king) to be engag'd in Wales,
There without ransom to lie forfeited;
Disgrac'd me in my happy victories,
Sought to entrap me by intelligence;
Rated mine uncle from the Council board;
In rage dismiss'd my father from the court;
Broke oath on oath, committed wrong on
 wrong;
And in conclusion drove us to seek out
This head of safety, and withal to pry
Into his title, the which we find
Too indirect for long continuance.
 BLUNT. Shall I return this answer to the
 King?
 HOT. Not so, Sir Walter. We'll withdraw
 awhile.
Go to the King; and let there be impawn'd
Some surety for a safe return again,
And in the morning early shall mine uncle
Bring him our purposes; and so farewell.
 BLUNT. I would you would accept of grace
 and love.
 HOT. And may be so we shall.
 BLUNT. Pray God you do.
 [exeunt]

SCENE IV.

York. The Archbishop's palace

Enter the ARCHBISHOP OF YORK *and* SIR
 MICHAEL

 ARCH. Hie, good Sir Michael; bear this
 sealed brief
With winged haste to the Lord Marshal;
This to my cousin Scroop; and all the rest
To whom they are directed. If you knew

---
[134] to make legal claim to his inheritance.   [135] taxed.

[451]

How much they do import, you would make
    haste.
  SIR M. My good lord,
I guess their tenour.
    ARCH.   Like enough you do.   5
To-morrow, good Sir Michael, is a day
Wherein the fortune of ten thousand men
Must bide the touch;[136] for, sir, at Shrewsbury,
As I am truly given to understand,
The King with mighty and quick-raised power 10
Meets with Lord Harry; and I fear, Sir
    Michael,
What with the sickness of Northumberland,
Whose power was in the first proportion,
And what with Owen Glendower's absence 15
    thence,
Who with them was a rated sinew too
And comes not in, overrul'd by prophecies—
I fear the power of Percy is too weak
To wage an instant trial with the King.   20
  SIR M. Why, my good lord, you need not
    fear;
There is Douglas and Lord Mortimer.
  ARCH. No, Mortimer is not there.
  SIR M. But there is Mordake, Vernon, Lord 25
    Harry Percy,
And there is my Lord of Worcester, and a head
Of gallant warriors, noble gentlemen.
  ARCH. And so there is; but yet the King hath
    drawn
The special head of all the land together— 30
The Prince of Wales, Lord John of Lancaster,
The noble Westmoreland and warlike Blunt,
And many moe corrivals and dear men[137]
Of estimation and command in arms.   35
  SIR M. Doubt not, my lord, they shall be well
    oppos'd.
  ARCH. I hope no less, yet needful 'tis to
    fear;
And, to prevent the worst, Sir Michael, speed. 40
For if Lord Percy thrive not, ere the King
Dismiss his power, he means to visit us,
For he hath heard of our confederacy,
And 'tis but wisdom to make strong against
    him.   45
Therefore make haste. I must go write again
To other friends; and so farewell, Sir Michael.
                         [exeunt]

---

[136] must be tested.
[137] And many more companions and valuable
men.

ACT V

SCENE I.

The King's camp near Shrewsbury

Enter the KING, PRINCE OF WALES, LORD JOHN
OF LANCASTER, SIR WALTER BLUNT, FALSTAFF

  KING. How bloodily the sun begins to peer
Above yon busky[138] hill! The day looks pale
At his distemp'rature.[139]
  PRINCE.   The southern wind
Doth play the trumpet to his purposes
And by his hollow whistling in the leaves
Foretells a tempest and a blust'ring day.
  KING. Then with the losers let it sympathize,
For nothing can seem foul to those that win.
                     [the trumpet sounds]

Enter WORCESTER *[and* VERNON]

How now, my Lord of Worcester? 'Tis not well
That you and I should meet upon such terms
As now we meet. You have deceiv'd our trust
And made us doff our easy robes of peace
To crush our old limbs in ungentle steel.
This is not well, my lord; this is not well.
What say you to it? Will you again unknit
This churlish knot of all-abhorred war,
And move in that obedient orb again
Where you did give a fair and natural light,
And be no more an exhal'd meteor,
A prodigy of fear, and a portent
Of broached mischief to the unborn times?
  WOR. Hear me, my liege.
For mine own part, I could be well content
To entertain the lag-end of my life
With quiet hours; for I do protest
I have not sought the day of this dislike.
  KING. You have not sought it! How comes it
    then?
  FAL. Rebellion lay in his way, and he
    found it.
  PRINCE. Peace, chewet,[140] peace!
  WOR. It pleas'd your Majesty to turn your
    looks
Of favour from myself and all our house;
And yet I must remember you, my lord,
We were the first and dearest of your friends.
For you my staff of office did I break

---

[138] bushy.   [139] unusual appearance.
[140] jackdaw.

In Richard's time, and posted day and night
To meet you on the way and kiss your hand
When yet you were in place and in account
Nothing so strong and fortunate as I.
It was myself, my brother, and his son   5
That brought you home and boldly did
    outdare
The dangers of the time. You swore to us,
And you did swear that oath at Doncaster,
That you did nothing purpose 'gainst the state, 10
Nor claim no further than your new-fall'n
    right,
The seat of Gaunt, dukedom of Lancaster.
To this we swore our aid. But in short space
It rain'd down fortune show'ring on your
    head,
And such a flood of greatness fell on you—   15
What with our help, what with the absent
    King,
What with the injuries of a wanton time,
The seeming sufferances that you had borne,
And the contrarious winds that held the King
So long in his unlucky Irish wars
That all in England did repute him dead—
And from this swarm of fair advantages
You took occasion to be quickly woo'd
To gripe the general sway into your hand;
Forgot your oath to us at Doncaster;
And, being fed by us, you us'd us so
As that ungentle gull, the cuckoo's bird,   30
Useth the sparrow—did oppress our nest;
Grew by our feeding to so great a bulk
That even our love durst not come near your
    sight
For fear of swallowing; but with nimble wing   35
We were enforc'd for safety sake to fly
Out of your sight and raise this present head;
Whereby we stand opposed by such means
As you yourself have forg'd against yourself
By unkind usage, dangerous countenance,   40
And violation of all faith and troth
Sworn to us in your younger enterprise.
    KING. These things, indeed, you have articu-
    late,
Proclaim'd at market crosses, read in churches, 45
To face the garment of rebellion
With some fine colour that may please the eye
Of fickle changelings and poor discontents,
Which gape and rub the elbow at the news
Of hurlyburly innovation.   50
And never yet did insurrection want
Such water colours to impaint his cause,

Nor moody beggars, starving for a time
Of pell-mell havoc and confusion.
    PRINCE. In both our armies there is many a
    soul
Shall pay full dearly for this encounter,   5
If once they join in trial. Tell your nephew
The Prince of Wales doth join with all the
    world
In praise of Henry Percy. By my hopes,
This present enterprise set off his head,   10
I do not think a braver gentleman,
More active-valiant or more valiant-young,
More daring or more bold, is now alive
To grace this latter age with noble deeds.
For my part, I may speak it to my shame,   15
I have a truant been to chivalry;
And so I hear he doth account me too.
Yet this before my father's Majesty—
I am content that he shall take the odds
Of his great name and estimation,   20
And will, to save the blood on either side,
Try fortune with him in a single fight.
    KING. And, Prince of Wales, so dare we ven-
    ture thee,
Albeit considerations infinite   25
Do make against it. No, good Worcester, no!
We love our people well; even those we love
That are misled upon your cousin's part;
And, will they take the offer of our grace,
Both he, and they, and you, yea, every man 30
Shall be my friend again, and I'll be his.
So tell your cousin, and bring me word
What he will do. But if he will not yield,
Rebuke and dread correction wait on us,
And they shall do their office. So be gone.   35
We will not now be troubled with reply.
We offer fair; take it advisedly.
                exit WORCESTER [*with* VERNON]
    PRINCE. It will not be accepted, on my life.
The Douglas and the Hotspur both together   40
Are confident against the world in arms.
    KING. Hence, therefore, every leader to his
    charge;
For, on their answer, will we set on them,
And God befriend us as our cause is just!   45
        [*exeunt; manent* PRINCE, FALSTAFF]
    FAL. Hal, if thou see me down in the battle
and bestride me, so! 'Tis a point of friendship.
    PRINCE. Nothing but a Colossus can do thee
that friendship. Say thy prayers, and farewell.   50
    FAL. I would 'twere bedtime, Hal, and all
well.

PRINCE. Why, thou owest God a death.

[*exit*]

FAL. 'Tis not due yet. I would be loath to pay him before his day. What need I be so forward with him that calls not on me? Well, 'tis no matter; honour pricks me on. Yea, but how if honour prick me off when I come on? How then? Can honour set to a leg? No. Or an arm? No. Or take away the grief of a wound? No. Honour hath no skill in surgery then? No. What is honour? A word. What is that word honour? Air. A trim reckoning! Who hath it? He that died a Wednesday. Doth he feel it? No. Doth he hear it? No. 'Tis insensible then? Yea, to the dead. But will it not live with the living? No. Why? Detraction will not suffer it. Therefore I'll none of it. Honour is a mere scutcheon—and so ends my catechism. [*exit*]

SCENE II.

The rebel camp

Enter WORCESTER *and* SIR RICHARD VERNON

WOR. O no, my nephew must not know, Sir Richard,
The liberal and kind offer of the King.
VER. 'Twere best he did.
WOR.   Then are we all undone.
It is not possible, it cannot be,
The King should keep his word in loving us.
He will suspect us still and find a time
To punish this offence in other faults.
Suspicion all our lives shall be stuck full of eyes;
For treason is but trusted like the fox,
Who, ne'er so tame, so cherish'd and lock'd up,
Will have a wild trick of his ancestors.
Look how we can, or sad or merrily,
Interpretation will misquote our looks,
And we shall feed like oxen at a stall,
The better cherish'd, still the nearer death.
My nephew's trespass may be well forgot;
It hath the excuse of youth and heat of blood,
And an adopted name of privilege—
A hare-brain'd Hotspur, govern'd by a spleen.
All his offences live upon my head
And on his father's. We did train him on;
And, his corruption being ta'en from us,
We, as the spring of all, shall pay for all.

Therefore, good cousin, let not Harry know,
In any case, the offer of the King.

Enter HOTSPUR [*and* DOUGLAS]

VER. Deliver what you will, I'll say 'tis so.
Here comes your cousin.
HOT.   My uncle is return'd.
Deliver up my Lord of Westmoreland.
Uncle, what news?
WOR. The King will bid you battle presently.
DOUG. Defy him by the Lord of Westmoreland.
HOT. Lord Douglas, go you and tell him so.
DOUG. Marry, and shall, and very willingly.

[*exit*]

WOR. There is no seeming mercy in the King.
HOT. Did you beg any? God forbid!
WOR. I told him gently of our grievances,
Of his oath-breaking; which he mended thus,
By now forswearing that he is forsworn.
He calls us rebels, traitors, and will scourge
With haughty arms this hateful name in us.

Enter DOUGLAS

DOUG. Arm, gentlemen! to arms! for I have thrown
A brave defiance in King Henry's teeth,
And Westmoreland, that was engag'd,[141] did bear it;
Which cannot choose but bring him quickly on.
WOR. The Prince of Wales stepp'd forth before the King
And, nephew, challeng'd you to single fight.
HOT. O, would the quarrel lay upon our heads,
And that no man might draw short breath today
But I and Harry Monmouth! Tell me, tell me,
How show'd his tasking?[142] Seem'd it in contempt?
VER. No, by my soul. I never in my life
Did hear a challenge urg'd more modestly,
Unless a brother should a brother dare
To gentle exercise and proof of arms.
He gave you all the duties of a man;
Trimm'd up your praises with a princely tongue;
Spoke your deservings like a chronicle;

———

[141] held as hostage.   [142] challenge

Making you ever better than his praise
By still dispraising praise valued with you;
And, which became him like a prince indeed,
He made a blushing cital[143] of himself,
And chid his truant youth with such a grace
As if he mast'red there a double spirit
Of teaching and of learning instantly.
There did he pause; but let me tell the world,
If he outlive the envy of this day,
England did never owe[144] so sweet a hope,
So much misconstrued in his wantonness.
  HOT. Cousin, I think thou art enamoured
Upon his follies. Never did I hear
Of any prince so wild a libertine.
But be he as he will, yet once ere night
I will embrace him with a soldier's arm,
That he shall shrink under my courtesy.
Arm, arm with speed! and, fellows, soldiers, friends,
Better consider what you have to do
Than I, that have not well the gift of tongue,
Can lift your blood up with persuasion.

Enter a MESSENGER

  MESS. My lord, here are letters for you.
  HOT. I cannot read them now.—
O gentlemen, the time of life is short!
To spend that shortness basely were too long
If life did ride upon a dial's point,
Still ending at the arrival of an hour.
An if we live, we live to tread on kings;
If die, brave death, when princes die with us!
Now for our consciences, the arms are fair,
When the intent of bearing them is just.

Enter another MESSENGER

  MESS. My lord, prepare. The King comes on apace.
  HOT. I thank him that he cuts me from my tale,
For I profess not talking. Only this—
Let each man do his best; and here draw I
A sword whose temper I intend to stain
With the best blood that I can meet withal
In the adventure of this perilous day.
Now, Esperance! Percy! and set on.
Sound all the lofty instruments of war,
And by that music let us all embrace;
For, heaven to earth, some of us never shall
A second time do such a courtesy.

---

[143] recital.   [144] own.

Here they embrace. The trumpets sound.
[exeunt]

SCENE III.

Plain between the camps

The KING *enters with his Power. Alarum to the battle. Then enter* DOUGLAS *and* SIR WALTER BLUNT

  BLUNT. What is thy name, that in the battle thus
Thou crossest me? What honour dost thou seek
Upon my head?
  DOUG. Know then my name is Douglas,
And I do haunt thee in the battle thus
Because some tell me that thou art a king.
  BLUNT. They tell thee true.
  DOUG. The Lord of Stafford dear to-day hath bought
Thy likeness; for instead of thee, King Harry,
This sword hath ended him. So shall it thee,
Unless thou yield thee as my prisoner.
  BLUNT. I was not born a yielder, thou proud Scot;
And thou shalt find a king that will revenge
Lord Stafford's death.
  They fight. DOUGLAS *kills* BLUNT

Then enter HOTSPUR

  HOT. O Douglas, hadst thou fought at Holmedon thus,
I never had triumph'd upon a Scot.
  DOUG. All's done, all's won. Here breathless lies the King.
  HOT. Where?
  DOUG. Here.
  HOT. This, Douglas? No. I know this face full well.
A gallant knight he was, his name was Blunt;
Semblably furnish'd like the King himself.
  DOUG. A fool go with thy soul, whither it goes!
A borrowed title hast thou bought too dear:
Why didst thou tell me that thou wert a king?
  HOT. The King hath many marching in his coats.
  DOUG. Now, by my sword, I will kill all his coats;
I'll murder all his wardrop, piece by piece,
Until I meet the King.

HOT.   Up and away!
Our soldiers stand full fairly for the day.

                         [*exeunt*]

Alarum. Enter FALSTAFF *solus*

FAL. Though I could scape shot-free at London, I fear the shot here. Here's no scoring but
upon the pate. Soft! who are you? Sir Walter
Blunt. There's honour for you! Here's no vanity! I am as hot as molten lead, and as heavy 10
too. God keep lead out of me! I need no more
weight than mine own bowels. I have led my
rag-of-muffins where they are pepper'd.
There's not three of my hundred and fifty left
alive; and they are for the town's end, to beg 15
during life. But who comes here?

Enter the PRINCE

PRINCE. What, stand'st thou idle here? Lend
    me thy sword.   20
Many a nobleman lies stark and stiff
Under the hoofs of vaunting enemies,
Whose deaths are yet unreveng'd. I prithee
Lend me thy sword.
    FAL. O Hal, I prithee give me leave to 25
breathe awhile. Turk Gregory[145] never did
such deeds in arms as I have done this day.
I have paid Percy; I have made him sure.
    PRINCE. He is indeed, and living to kill thee.
I prithee lend me thy sword.   30
    FAL. Nay, before God, Hal, if Percy be alive,
thou get'st not my sword; but take my pistol,
if thou wilt.
    PRINCE. Give it me. What, is it in the case?
    FAL. Ay, Hal. 'Tis hot, 'tis hot. There's that 35
will sack a city. [*the* PRINCE *draws it out and
finds it to be a bottle of sack*]
    PRINCE. What, is it a time to jest and dally
now?   [*he throws the bottle at him; exit*]
    FAL. Well, if Percy be alive, I'll pierce him. 40
If he do come in my way, so; if he do not, if
I come in his willingly, let him make a car-
bonado[146] of me. I like not such grinning honour as Sir Walter hath. Give me life; which if I
can save, so; if not, honour comes unlook'd for, 45
and there's an end.   [*exit*]

---

[145] Pope Gregory VII, a former militant friar,
had a reputation among Protestants for being
ferocious.   50
[146] meat pounded and slashed for tenderness in
broiling.

SCENE IV.

Another part of the field

Alarum. Excursions. Enter the KING, *the* 5
PRINCE, LORD JOHN OF LANCASTER, EARL
OF WESTMORELAND

KING. I prithee,
Harry, withdraw thyself; thou bleedest too
    much.
Lord John of Lancaster, go you with him.
    JOHN. Not I, my lord, unless I did bleed too.
    PRINCE. I do beseech your Majesty make up,
Lest your retirement do amaze your friends.
    KING. I will do so.
My Lord of Westmoreland, lead him to his
    tent.
    WEST. Come, my lord, I'll lead you to your
    tent.
    PRINCE. Lead me, my lord? I do not need
    your help;
And God forbid a shallow scratch should drive
The Prince of Wales from such a field as this,
Where stain'd nobility lies trodden on,
And rebels' arms triumph in massacres!
    JOHN. We breathe too long. Come, cousin
    Westmoreland,
Our duty this way lies. For God's sake, come.
    [*exeunt* PRINCE JOHN *and* WESTMORE-
    LAND]
    PRINCE. By God, thou hast deceiv'd me,
    Lancaster!
I did not think thee lord of such a spirit.
Before, I lov'd thee as a brother, John;
But now, I do respect thee as my soul.
    KING. I saw him hold Lord Percy at the
    point
With lustier maintenance than I did look for
Of such an ungrown warrior.
    PRINCE.   O, this boy
Lends mettle to us all!   [*exit*]

Enter DOUGLAS

DOUG. Another king? They grow like Hydra's
    heads.[147]
I am the Douglas, fatal to all those
That wear those colours on them. What art
    thou
That counterfeit'st the person of a king?

---

[147] a nine-headed monster killed by Hercules; if
one head was lopped off, two grew in its place.

KING. The King himself, who, Douglas, grieves at heart
So many of his shadows thou hast met,
And not the very King. I have two boys
Seek Percy and thyself about the field;
But, seeing thou fall'st on me so luckily,
I will assay thee. So defend thyself.

DOUG. I fear thou art another counterfeit;
And yet, in faith, thou bearest thee like a king.
But mine I am sure thou art, whoe'er thou be, 10
And thus I win thee.

They fight. The KING being in danger, enter PRINCE OF WALES

PRINCE. Hold up thy head, vile Scot, or thou 15
art like
Never to hold it up again! The spirits
Of valiant Shirley, Stafford, Blunt are in my
arms.
It is the Prince of Wales that threatens thee, 20
Who never promiseth but he means to pay.
[*they fight; DOUGLAS flieth*]
Cheerly, my lord. How fares your Grace?
Sir Nicholas Gawsey hath for succour sent,
And so hath Clifton. I'll to Clifton straight. 25
KING. Stay and breathe awhile.
Thou hast redeem'd thy lost opinion,
And show'd thou mak'st some tender of my life,
In this fair rescue thou hast brought to me.
PRINCE. O God! they did me too much 30
injury
That ever said I heark'ned for your death.
If it were so, I might have let alone
The insulting hand of Douglas over you,
Which would have been as speedy in your end 35
As all the poisonous potions in the world,
And sav'd the treacherous labour of your son.
KING. Make up to Clifton; I'll to Sir Nicholas
Gawsey. [*exit*]

Enter HOTSPUR

HOT. If I mistake not, thou art Harry Monmouth.
PRINCE. Thou speak'st as if I would deny
my name.
HOT. My name is Harry Percy. 45
PRINCE. Why, then I see
A very valiant rebel of the name.
I am the Prince of Wales; and think not, Percy,
To share with me in glory any more. 50
Two stars keep not their motion in one sphere,
Nor can one England brook a double reign

Of Harry Percy and the Prince of Wales.
HOT. Nor shall it, Harry; for the hour is
come
To end the one of us; and would to God
Thy name in arms were now as great as mine! 5
PRINCE. I'll make it greater ere I part from
thee,
And all the budding honours on thy crest
I'll crop to make a garland for my head.
HOT. I can no longer brook thy vanities.
[*they fight*]

Enter FALSTAFF

FAL. Well said, Hal! to it, Hal! Nay, you
shall find no boy's play here, I can tell you. 15
*Enter DOUGLAS. He fighteth with FAL-
STAFF, who falls down as if he were
dead* [*exit DOUGLAS*]

The PRINCE killeth PERCY

HOT. O Harry, thou hast robb'd me of my
youth! 20
I better brook the loss of brittle life
Than those proud titles thou hast won of me.
They wound my thoughts worse than thy
sword my flesh. 25
But thoughts, the slaves of life, and life, time's
fool,
And time, that takes survey of all the world,
Must have a stop. O, I could prophesy, 30
But that the earthy and cold hand of death
Lies on my tongue. No, Percy, thou art dust,
And food for— [*dies*]
PRINCE. For worms, brave Percy. Fare thee
well, great heart!
Ill-weav'd ambition, how much art thou
shrunk!
When that this body did contain a spirit,
A kingdom for it was too small a bound;
But now two paces of the vilest earth 40
Is room enough. This earth that bears thee
dead
Bears not alive so stout a gentleman.
If thou wert sensible of courtesy,
I should not make so dear a show of zeal. 45
But let my favours hide thy mangled face;
And, even in thy behalf, I'll thank myself
For doing these fair rites of tenderness.
Adieu, and take thy praise with thee to 50
heaven!
Thy ignominy sleep with thee in the grave,
But not rememb'red in thy epitaph! [*he spieth*

FALSTAFF *on the ground*]

What, old acquaintance? Could not all this
flesh
Keep in a little life? Poor Jack, farewell!
I could have better spar'd a better man.
O, I should have a heavy miss of thee   5
If I were much in love with vanity!
Death hath not struck so fat a deer to-day,
Though many dearer, in this bloody fray.
Embowell'd will I see thee by-and-by;
Till then in blood by noble Percy lie.   [*exit*]   10

FALSTAFF *riseth up*

FAL. Embowell'd? If thou embowel me to-
day, I'll give you leave to powder me and   15
eat me too to-morrow. 'Sblood, 'twas time to
counterfeit, or that hot termagant Scot had
paid me scot and lot too. Counterfeit? I lie;
I am no counterfeit. To die is to be a counterfeit; for he is but the counterfeit of a man   20
who hath not the life of a man; but to counterfeit dying when a man thereby liveth, is to
be no counterfeit, but the true and perfect
image of life indeed. The better part of valour
is discretion; in the which better part I have   25
saved my life. Zounds, I am afraid of this
gunpowder Percy, though he be dead. How
if he should counterfeit too, and rise? By my
faith, I am afraid he would prove the better
counterfeit. Therefore I'll make him sure; yea,   30
and I'll swear I kill'd him. Why may not he
rise as well as I? Nothing confutes me but eyes,
and nobody sees me. Therefore, sirrah [*stabs
him*], with a new wound in your thigh, come
you along with me.   35

He takes up HOTSPUR *on his back. Enter*
PRINCE, *and* JOHN OF LANCASTER

PRINCE. Come, brother John; full bravely
    hast thou flesh'd   40
Thy maiden sword.
JOHN.   But, soft! whom have we here?
Did you not tell me this fat man was dead?
PRINCE. I did; I saw him dead,
Breathless and bleeding on the ground. Art   45
    thou alive,
Or is it fantasy that plays upon our eyesight?
I prithee speak. We will not trust our eyes
Without our ears. Thou art not what thou
    seem'st.   50
FAL. No, that's certain! I am not a double
man; but if I be not Jack Falstaff, then am

I a Jack. There is Percy. If your father will do
me any honour, so; if not, let him kill the
next Percy himself. I look to be either earl or
duke, I can assure you.
PRINCE. Why, Percy I kill'd myself, and saw
    thee dead!
FAL. Didst thou? Lord, Lord, how this
world is given to lying! I grant you I was
down, and out of breath, and so was he; but
we rose both at an instant and fought a long
hour by Shrewsbury clock. If I may be be-
liev'd, so; if not, let them that should reward
valour bear the sin upon their own heads. I'll
take it upon my death, I gave him this wound
in the thigh. If the man were alive and would
deny it, zounds! I would make him eat a
piece of my sword.
JOHN. This is the strangest tale that ever I
    heard.
PRINCE. This is the strangest fellow, brother
    John.
Come, bring your luggage nobly on your back.
For my part, if a lie may do thee grace,
I'll gild it with the happiest terms I have.
                    [*a retreat is sounded*]
The trumpet sounds retreat; the day is ours.
Come, brother, let's to the highest of the field,
To see what friends are living, who are dead.
    Exeunt [PRINCE HENRY *and* PRINCE JOHN]
FAL. I'll follow, as they say, for reward. He
that rewards me, God reward him! If I do
grow great, I'll grow less; for I'll purge, and
leave sack, and live cleanly, as a nobleman
should do   *Exit* [*bearing off the body*]

SCENE V.

Another part of the field

The trumpets sound. Enter the KING,
    PRINCE OF WALES, LORD JOHN OF
    LANCASTER, EARL OF WESTMORE-
    LAND, *with* WORCESTER *and* VER-
    NON *prisoners*

KING. Thus ever did rebellion find rebuke.
Ill-spirited Worcester! did not we send grace,
Pardon, and terms of love to all of you?
And wouldst thou turn our offers contrary?
Misuse the tenour of thy kinsman's trust?
Three knights upon our party slain to-day,
A noble earl, and many a creature else
Had been alive this hour,

If like a Christian thou hadst truly borne
Betwixt our armies true intelligence.
  WOR. What I have done my safety urg'd me
    to;
And I embrace this fortune patiently,
Since not to be avoided it falls on me.
  KING. Bear Worcester to the death, and Ver-
    non too;
Other offenders we will pause upon.
    Exeunt WORCESTER *and* VERNON [*guarded*] 10
How goes the field?
  PRINCE. The noble Scot, Lord Douglas, when
    he saw
The fortune of the day quite turn'd from him,
The noble Percy slain, and all his men 15
Upon the foot of fear, fled with the rest;
And falling from a hill, he was so bruis'd
That the pursuers took him. At my tent
The Douglas is, and I beseech your Grace
I may dispose of him. 20
  KING.   With all my heart.
  PRINCE. Then, brother John of Lancaster, to
    you
This honourable bounty shall belong.

Go to the Douglas and deliver him
Up to his pleasure, ransomless and free.
His valour shown upon our crests to-day
Hath taught us how to cherish such high deeds,
Even in the bosom of our adversaries. 5
  JOHN. I thank your Grace for this high cour-
    tesy,
Which I shall give away immediately.
  KING. Then this remains, that we divide our
    power.
You, son John, and my cousin Westmoreland,
Towards York shall bend you with your dearest
    speed
To meet Northumberland and the prelate
    Scroop,
Who, as we hear, are busily in arms.
Myself and you, son Harry, will towards Wales
To fight with Glendower and the Earl of
    March.
Rebellion in this land shall lose his sway, 20
Meeting the check of such another day;
And since this business so fair is done,
Let us not leave till all our own be won.
                          [*exeunt*]

THE SCHOOL
FOR SCANDAL*

RICHARD BRINSLEY SHERIDAN

Sheridan (1751–1816) was born to the theater, his father having been an actor and writer. He met his future wife at Bath, where his father had opened a school of oratory, and, in a romantic courtship marked by duels and a quick trip to France, won her hand. Needing money, he turned to writing plays, of which the two comedies, The Rivals (1775) and The

School for Scandal (1777), are the best known. As writer, theater manager, and man-about-town Sheridan achieved great popularity and was nominated for membership in The Club by Dr. Johnson himself. His place in the theater has been discussed in the introduction to drama, I, 399.

In 1780 Sheridan entered Parliament and remained in public service thereafter. He was prominent in the Warren Hastings case and held a high post as Treasurer of the Navy.

Dogged by debt and disease he finally finished a useful life and was honored by a public funeral and eulogistic testimony from many prominent men who had admired his wit, his liberalism, and his personality.

Dramatis Personæ

SIR PETER TEAZLE	CRABTREE
SIR OLIVER SURFACE	SIR BENJAMIN BACKBITE
JOSEPH SURFACE	ROWLEY
CHARLES	MOSES
TRIP	LADY TEAZLE
SNAKE	MARIA
CARELESS	LADY SNEERWELL
SIR HARRY BUMPER	MRS. CANDOUR

A PORTRAIT

Addressed to Mrs. Crewe,[1] with the Comedy of The School for Scandal

BY R. B. SHERIDAN, ESQ.

Tell me, ye prim adepts in Scandal's school,
Who rail by precept, and detract by rule,
Lives there no character, so tried, so known,
So deck'd with grace, and so unlike your own,
That even you assist her fame to raise,
Approve by envy, and by silence praise?
Attend!—a model shall attract your view—
Daughters of calumny, I summon you!
You shall decide if this a portrait prove,
Or fond creation of the Muse and Love.
Attend, ye virgin critics, shrewd and sage,
Ye matron censors of this childish age,
Whose peering eye and wrinkled front declare
A fixed antipathy to young and fair;
By cunning, cautious; or by nature, cold,
In maiden madness, virulently bold!
Attend! ye skilled to coin the precious tale,
Creating proof, where innuendoes fail!
Whose practised memories, cruelly exact,
Omit no circumstance, except the fact!
Attend, all ye who boast—or old or young
The living libel of a slanderous tongue!
So shall my theme as far contrasted be,
As saints by fiends, or hymns by calumny.

[1] Mrs. John Crewe, beauty and wit, friend of Sheridan, Fox, *et al.*

Come, gentle Amoret[2] (for 'neath that name,
In worthier verse is sung thy beauty's fame);
Come—for but thee who seeks the Muse? and while
5 Celestial blushes check thy conscious smile,
With timid grace and hesitating eye,
The perfect model, which I boast, supply.
Vain Muse! couldst thou the humblest sketch create
Of her, or slightest charm couldst imitate—
10 Could thy blest strain in kindred colors trace
The faintest wonder of her form and face—
Poets would study the immortal line,
And *Reynolds*[3] own *his* art subdued by thine;
15 That art, which well might added lustre give
To Nature's best, and Heaven's superlative:
On *Granby's*[4] cheek might bid new glories rise,
Or point a purer beam from *Devon's*[5] eyes!
Hard is the task to shape that beauty's praise,
20 Whose judgment scorns the homage flattery pays!
But praising Amoret we cannot err,
No tongue o'ervalues Heaven, or flatters her!
Yet she by Fate's perverseness—she alone
25 Would doubt our truth, nor deem such praise her own!
Adorning Fashion, unadorn'd by dress,
Simple from taste, and not from carelessness;
Discreet in gesture, in deportment mild,
30 Not stiff with prudence, nor uncouthly wild:
No state has *Amoret!* no studied mien;
She frowns no *goddess*, and she moves no *queen*.
The softer charm that in her manner lies
35 Is framed to captivate, yet not surprise;
It justly suits th' expression of her face—
'Tis less than dignity, and more than grace!
On her pure cheek the native hue is such,
That form'd by Heav'n to be admired so much,
40 The hand divine, with a less partial care,
Might well have fix'd a fainter crimson there,
And bade the gentle inmate of her breast—
Inshrined Modesty!—supply the rest.
But who the peril of her lips shall paint?
45 Strip them of smiles—still, still all words are faint!

[2] name from *Faerie Queene*, here a pet name for Mrs. Crewe.
[3] Sir Joshua Reynolds.
[4] the Marchioness of Granby.
[5] the Duchess of Devonshire.

But moving Love himself appears to teach
Their action, though denied to rule her speech;
And thou who seest her speak and dost not
    hear,
Mourn not her distant accents 'scape thine ear;
Viewing those lips, thou still may'st make 5
    pretence
To judge of what she says, and swear 'tis
    sense:
Cloth'd with such grace, with such expression 10
    fraught,
They move in meaning, and they pause in
    thought!
But dost thou farther watch, with charm'd
    surprise,
The mild irresolution of her eyes,
Curious to mark how frequent they repose,
In brief eclipse and momentary close—
Ah! seest thou not an ambush'd Cupid there,
Too tim'rous of his charge, with jealous care 20
Veils and unveils those beams of heav'nly
    light,
Too full, too fatal else, for mortal sight?
Nor yet, such pleasing vengeance fond to meet,
In pard'ning dimples hope a safe retreat.
What though her peaceful breast should ne'er 25
    allow
Subduing frowns to arm her alter'd brow,
By Love, I swear, and by his gentle wiles,
More fatal still the mercy of her smiles!
Thus lovely, thus adorn'd, possessing all 30
Of bright or fair that can to woman fall.
The height of vanity might well be thought
Prerogative in her, and Nature's fault.
Yet gentle *Amoret*, in mind supreme 35
As well as charms, rejects the vainer theme;
And half mistrustful of her beauty's store,
She barbs with wit those darts too keen be-
    fore:—
Read in all knowledge that her sex should 40
    reach,
Though *Greville*,[6] or the *Muse*, should deign
    to teach,
Fond to improve, nor tim'rous to discern
How far it is a woman's grace to learn;
In Millar's[7] dialect she would not prove
Apollo's priestess, but Apollo's love,
Graced by those signs, which truth delights

    to own,
The timid blush, and mild submitted tone:
Whate'er she says, though sense appear
    throughout,
Displays the tender hue of female doubt; 5
Deck'd with that charm, how lovely wit ap-
    pears,
How graceful *science*, when that robe she
    wears!
Such too her talents, and her bent of mind,
As speak a sprightly heart by thought refined,
A taste for mirth, by contemplation school'd,
A turn for ridicule, by candour ruled,
A scorn of folly, which she tries to hide;
An awe of talent, which she owns with pride! 15
    Peace! idle Muse, no more thy strain pro-
    long,
But yield a theme, thy warmest praises
    wrong;
Just to her merit, though thou canst not raise 20
Thy feeble voice, behold th' acknowledged
    praise
Has spread conviction through the envious
    train,
And cast a fatal gloom o'er Scandal's reign! 25
And lo! each pallid hag, with blister'd tongue,
Mutters assent to all thy zeal has sung—
Owns all the colors just—the outline true;
Thee my inspirer, and my *model*—CREWE!

PROLOGUE

WRITTEN BY MR. GARRICK[8]

A SCHOOL FOR SCANDAL! tell me, I beseech 35
    you,
Needs there a school this modish art to teach
    you?
No need of lessons now, the knowing think;
We might as well be taught to eat and drink. 40
Caused by a dearth of scandal, should the
    vapors[9]
Distress our fair ones—let them read the
    papers;
Their powerful mixtures such disorders hit; 45
Crave what you will—there's *quantum
    sufficit*.[10]

---

[6] Mrs. Fulke Greville, Mrs. Crewe's mother.
[7] Lady Millar was a famous hostess at literary salons.

[8] David Garrick, actor, dramatist, theater manager.
[9] melancholy, the "blues."
[10] enough to go around.

"Lord!" cries my Lady *Wormwood* (who loves
    tattle,
And puts much salt and pepper in her prattle),
Just ris'n at noon, all night at cards when
    threshing   5
Strong tea and scandal—"Bless me, how re-
    freshing!
"Give me the papers, *Lisp*—how bold and
    free! (*sips*)
"*Last night Lord L. (sips) was caught with* 10
    Lady D.
"For aching heads what charming *sal volatile!*
    (*sips.*)
"*If Mrs. B. will still continue flirting,*
"*We hope she'll* DRAW, *or we'll* UNDRAW *the* 15
    curtain.
"Fine satire, poz[11]—in public all abuse it,
"But, by ourselves (*sips*), our praise we can't
    refuse it.
"Now, *Lisp*, read you—there, at that dash 20
    and star."
"Yes, ma'am—*A certain lord had best beware,*
"*Who lives not twenty miles from Grosvenor*
    Square;
"*For should he Lady W. find willing,* 25
"*Wormwood is bitter*"—"Oh, that's me, the
    villain!
"Throw it behind the fire, and never more
"Let that vile paper come within my door."
Thus at our friends we laugh, who feel the 30
    dart;
To reach our feelings, we ourselves must
    smart.
Is our young bard so young, to think that he
Can stop the full spring-tide of calumny? 35
Knows he the world so little, and its trade?
Alas! the devil's sooner raised than laid.
So strong, so swift, the monster there's no
    gagging:
Cut Scandal's head off, still the tongue is 40
    wagging.
Proud of your smiles once lavishly bestow'd,
Again our young Don Quixote takes the road;
To show his gratitude he draws his pen,
And seeks this hydra, Scandal, in his den. 45
For your applause all perils he would
    through—
He'll fight—that's write—a cavalliero true,
Till every drop of blood—that's ink—is spilt
    for you. 50

—————
[11] positively.

ACT I

SCENE I.

LADY SNEERWELL's house

Discovered LADY SNEERWELL *at the dressing-*
table; SNAKE *drinking chocolate*

LADY SNEER. The paragraphs, you say, Mr.
Snake, were all inserted?

SNAKE. They were, madam; and as I copied
them myself in a feigned hand, there can be
no suspicion whence they came.

LADY SNEER. Did you circulate the report of
Lady Brittle's intrigue with Captain Boastall?

SNAKE. That's in as fine a train as your ladyship could wish. In the common course of
things, I think it must reach Mrs. Clackitt's
ears within four-and-twenty hours; and then,
you know, the business is as good as done.

LADY SNEER. Why, truly, Mrs. Clackitt has
a very pretty talent, and a great deal of industry.

SNAKE. True, madam, and has been toler-
ably successful in her day. To my knowledge
she has been the cause of six matches being
broken off, and three sons disinherited; of four
forced elopements, and as many close con-
finements; nine separate maintenances, and
two divorces. Nay, I have more than once
traced her causing a *tête-à-tête* in the *Town
and Country Magazine*, when the parties, perhaps, had never seen each other's face before
in the course of their lives.

LADY SNEER. She certainly has talents, but
her manner is gross.

SNAKE. 'Tis very true. She generally designs well, has a free tongue, and a bold invention; but her coloring is too dark, and her
outlines often extravagant. She wants that deli-
cacy of tint, and mellowness of sneer, which
distinguish your ladyship's scandal.

LADY SNEER. You are partial, Snake.

SNAKE. Not in the least; everybody allows
that Lady Sneerwell can do more with a word
or a look than many can with the most labored
detail, even when they happen to have a little
truth on their side to support it.

LADY SNEER. Yes, my dear Snake; and I am
no hypocrite to deny the satisfaction I reap
from the success of my efforts. Wounded myself in the early part of my life by the en-

venomed tongue of slander, I confess I have since known no pleasure equal to the reducing others to the level of my own injured reputation.

SNAKE. Nothing can be more natural. But, Lady Sneerwell, there is one affair in which you have lately employed me, wherein, I confess, I am at a loss to guess your motives.

LADY SNEER. I conceive you mean with respect to my neighbor, Sir Peter Teazle, and his family?

SNAKE. I do. Here are two young men, to whom Sir Peter has acted as a kind of guardian since their father's death; the eldest possessing the most amiable character, and universally well spoken of; the youngest, the most dissipated and extravagant young fellow in the kingdom, without friends or character: the former an avowed admirer of your ladyship, and apparently your favorite; the latter attached to Maria, Sir Peter's ward, and confessedly beloved by her. Now, on the face of these circumstances, it is utterly unaccountable to me, why you, the widow of a city knight, with a good jointure, should not close with the passion of a man of such character and expectations as Mr. Surface; and more so why you should be so uncommonly earnest to destroy the mutual attachment subsisting between his brother Charles and Maria.

LADY SNEER. Then at once to unravel this mystery, I must inform you that love has no share whatever in the intercourse between Mr. Surface and me.

SNAKE. No!

LADY SNEER. His real attachment is to Maria, or her fortune; but finding in his brother a favored rival, he has been obliged to mask his pretensions, and profit by my assistance.

SNAKE. Yet still I am more puzzled why you should interest yourself in his success.

LADY SNEER. How dull you are! Cannot you surmise the weakness which I hitherto, through shame, have concealed even from you? Must I confess that Charles, that libertine, that extravagant, that bankrupt in fortune and reputation, that he it is for whom I'm thus anxious and malicious, and to gain whom I would sacrifice everything?

SNAKE. Now, indeed, your conduct appears consistent; but how came you and Mr. Surface so confidential?

LADY SNEER. For our mutual interest. I have found him out a long time since. I know him to be artful, selfish, and malicious; in short, a sentimental knave; while with Sir Peter, and indeed with all his acquaintance, he passes for a youthful miracle of prudence, good sense, and benevolence.

SNAKE. Yes; yet Sir Peter vows he has not his equal in England; and above all, he praises him as a man of sentiment.

LADY SNEER. True; and with the assistance of his sentiment and hypocrisy, he has brought Sir Peter entirely into his interest with regard to Maria; while poor Charles has no friend in the house, though, I fear, he has a powerful one in Maria's heart, against whom we must direct our schemes.

Enter SERVANT

SERV. Mr. Surface.

LADY SNEER. Show him up. [*exit* SERVANT]

Enter JOSEPH SURFACE

JOSEPH S. My dear Lady Sneerwell, how do you do to-day? Mr. Snake, your most obedient.

LADY SNEER. Snake has just been rallying me on our mutual attachment; but I have informed him of our real views. You know how useful he has been to us, and, believe me, the confidence is not ill placed.

JOSEPH S. Madam, it is impossible for me to suspect a man of Mr. Snake's sensibility and discernment.

LADY SNEER. Well, well, no compliments now; but tell me when you saw your mistress, Maria; or, what is more material to me, your brother.

JOSEPH S. I have not seen either since I left you; but I can inform you that they never meet. Some of your stories have taken a good effect on Maria.

LADY SNEER. Ah! my dear Snake! the merit of this belongs to you; but do your brother's distresses increase?

JOSEPH S. Every hour. I am told he has had another execution[12] in the house yesterday. In short, his dissipation and extravagance exceed anything I have ever heard of.

LADY SNEER. Poor Charles!

---

[12] seizure or sale of goods by the authorities.

JOSEPH S. True, madam; notwithstanding his vices, one can't help feeling for him. Poor Charles! I'm sure I wish it were in my power to be of any essential service to him; for the man who does not share in the distresses of a brother, even though merited by his own misconduct, deserves——

LADY SNEER. O Lud! you are going to be moral, and forget that you are among friends.

JOSEPH S. Egad, that's true! I'll keep that sentiment till I see Sir Peter; however, it certainly is a charity to rescue Maria from such a libertine, who, if he is to be reclaimed, can be so only by a person of your ladyship's superior accomplishments and understanding.

SNAKE. I believe, Lady Sneerwell, here's company coming; I'll go and copy the letter I mentioned to you. Mr. Surface, your most obedient. [*exit* SNAKE]

JOSEPH S. Sir, your very devoted. Lady Sneerwell, I am very sorry you have put any further confidence in that fellow.

LADY SNEER. Why so?

JOSEPH S. I have lately detected him in frequent conference with old Rowley, who was formerly my father's steward, and has never, you know, been a friend of mine.

LADY SNEER. And do you think he would betray us?

JOSEPH S. Nothing more likely; take my word for't, Lady Sneerwell, that fellow hasn't virtue enough to be faithful even to his own villainy. Ah! Maria!

Enter MARIA

LADY SNEER. Maria, my dear, how do you do? What's the matter?

MARIA. Oh! there is that disagreeable lover of mine, Sir Benjamin Backbite, has just called at my guardian's, with his odious uncle, Crabtree; so I slipped out, and ran hither to avoid them.

LADY SNEER. Is that all?

JOSEPH S. If my brother Charles had been of the party, madam, perhaps you would not have been so much alarmed.

LADY SNEER. Nay, now you are severe; for I dare swear the truth of the matter is, Maria heard *you* were here. But, my dear, what has Sir Benjamin done, that you would avoid him so?

MARIA. Oh, he has done nothing; but 'tis for what he has said: his conversation is a perpetual libel on all his acquaintance.

JOSEPH S. Ay, and the worst of it is, there is no advantage in not knowing him; for he'll abuse a stranger just as soon as his best friend; and his uncle's as bad.

LADY SNEER. Nay, but we should make allowance; Sir Benjamin is a wit and a poet.

MARIA. For my part, I confess, madam, wit loses its respect with me, when I see it in company with malice. What do you think, Mr. Surface?

JOSEPH S. Certainly, madam; to smile at the jest which plants a thorn in another's breast is to become a principal in the mischief.

LADY SNEER. Pshaw! there's no possibility of being witty without a little ill nature: the malice of a good thing is the barb that makes it stick. What's your opinion, Mr. Surface?

JOSEPH S. To be sure, madam; that conversation, where the spirit of raillery is suppressed, will ever appear tedious and insipid.

MARIA. Well, I'll not debate how far scandal may be allowable; but in a man, I am sure, it is always contemptible. We have pride, envy, rivalship, and a thousand motives to depreciate each other; but the male slanderer must have the cowardice of a woman before he can traduce one.

Enter SERVANT

SERV. Madam, Mrs. Candour is below, and if your ladyship's at leisure, will leave her carriage.

LADY SNEER. Beg her to walk in. [*exit* SERVANT] Now, Maria, here is a character to your taste; for though Mrs. Candour is a little talkative, everbody allows her to be the best natured and best sort of woman.

MARIA. Yes, with a very gross affectation of good nature and benevolence, she does more mischief than the direct malice of old Crabtree.

JOSEPH S. I' faith that's true, Lady Sneerwell: whenever I hear the current running against the characters of my friends, I never think them in such danger as when Candour undertakes their defence.

LADY SNEER. Hush! here she is!

Enter MRS. CANDOUR

MRS. CAN. My dear Lady Sneerwell, how have you been this century? Mr. Surface, what news do you hear? though indeed it is no matter, for I think one hears nothing else but scandal.

JOSEPH S. Just so, indeed, ma'am.

MRS. CAN. Oh, Maria! child, what, is the whole affair off between you and Charles? His extravagance, I presume; the town talks of nothing else.

MARIA. Indeed! I am very sorry, ma'am, the town is not better employed.

MRS. CAN. True, true, child; but there's no stopping people's tongues. I own I was hurt to hear it, as I indeed was to learn, from the same quarter, that your guardian, Sir Peter, and Lady Teazle have not agreed lately as well as could be wished.

MARIA. 'Tis strangely impertinent for people to busy themselves so.

MRS. CAN. Very true, child; but what's to be done? People will talk; there's no preventing it. Why, it was but yesterday I was told Miss Gadabout had eloped with Sir Filigree Flirt. But, Lord! there's no minding what one hears; though, to be sure, I had this from very good authority.

MARIA. Such reports are highly scandalous.

MRS. CAN. So they are, child; shameful! shameful! But the world is so censorious, no character escapes. Lord, now who would have suspected your friend, Miss Prim, of an indiscretion? Yet such is the ill-nature of people, that they say her uncle stopped her last week, just as she was stepping into the York diligence[13] with her dancing-master.

MARIA. I'll answer for't there are no grounds for that report.

MRS. CAN. Ah, no foundation in the world, I dare swear: no more, probably, than for the story circulated last month, of Mrs. Festino's affair with Colonel Cassino; though, to be sure, that matter was never rightly cleared up.

JOSEPH S. The licence of invention some people take is monstrous indeed.

MARIA. 'Tis so; but, in my opinion, those who report such things are equally culpable.

MRS. CAN. To be sure they are; tale-bearers are as bad as the tale-makers; 'tis an old observation, and a very true one. But what's to be done, as I said before? How will you prevent people from talking? To-day, Mrs. Clackitt assured me, Mr. and Mrs. Honeymoon were at last become mere man and wife, like the rest of their acquaintance. She likewise hinted that a certain widow, in the next street, had got rid of her dropsy and recovered her shape in a most surprising manner. And at the same time, Miss Tattle, who was by, affirmed that Lord Buffalo had discovered his lady at a house of no extraordinary fame; and that Sir H. Bouquet and Tom Saunter were to measure swords on a similar provocation. But, Lord, do you think I would report these things? No, no! tale-bearers, as I said before, are just as bad as the tale-makers.

JOSEPH S. Ah Mrs. Candour, if everybody had your forbearance and good-nature!

MRS. CAN. I confess, Mr. Surface, I cannot bear to hear people attacked behind their backs; and when ugly circumstances come out against our acquaintance, I own I always love to think the best. By-the-bye, I hope 'tis not true that your brother is absolutely ruined?

JOSEPH S. I am afraid his circumstances are very bad indeed, ma'am.

MRS. CAN. Ah! I heard so; but you must tell him to keep up his spirits; everybody almost is in the same way—Lord Spindle, Sir Thomas Splint, Captain Quinze, and Mr. Nickit—all up, I hear, within this week; so if Charles is undone, he'll find half his acquaintance ruined too, and that, you know, is a consolation.

JOSEPH S. Doubtless, ma'am; a very great one.

Enter SERVANT

SERV. Mr. Crabtree and Sir Benjamin Backbite. [*exit* SERVANT]

LADY SNEER. So, Maria, you see your lover pursues you; positively you sha'n't escape.

Enter CRABTREE *and* SIR BENJAMIN BACKBITE

CRABT. Lady Sneerwell, I kiss your hand. Mrs. Candour, I don't believe you are acquainted with my nephew, Sir Benjamin Backbite? Egad! ma'am, he has a pretty wit, and is a pretty poet too; isn't he, Lady Sneerwell?

SIR BENJ. B. O fie, uncle!

CRABT. Nay, egad, it's true; I back him at a rebus or a charade against the best rhymer in the kingdom. Has your ladyship heard the epigram he wrote last week on Lady Frizzle's feather catching fire? Do, Benjamin, repeat it,

---

[13] coach.

or the charade you made last night extempore at Mrs. Drowzie's conversazione. Come now; your first is the name of a fish, your second a great naval commander, and—

SIR BENJ. B. Uncle, now—pr'ythee—

CRABT. I' faith, ma'am, 'twould surprise you to hear how ready he is at all these fine sort of things.

LADY SNEER. I wonder, Sir Benjamin, you never publish anything.

SIR BENJ. B. To say truth, ma'am, 'tis very vulgar to print; and as my little productions are mostly satires and lampoons on particular people, I find they circulate more by giving copies in confidence to the friends of the parties. However, I have some love elegies, which, when favored with this lady's smiles, I mean to give the public.

CRABT. 'Fore heaven, ma'am, they'll immortalize you! You will be handed down to posterity, like Petrarch's Laura,[14] or Waller's Sacharissa.[15]

SIR BENJ. B. Yes, madam, I think you will like them, when you shall see them on a beautiful quarto page, where a neat rivulet of text shall meander through a meadow of margin. 'Fore Gad, they will be the most elegant things of their kind!

CRABT. But, ladies, that's true. Have you heard the news?

MRS. CAN. What, sir, do you mean the report of—

CRABT. No, ma'am, that's not it. Miss Nicely is going to be married to her own footman.

MRS. CAN. Impossible!

CRABT. Ask Sir Benjamin.

SIR BENJ. B. 'Tis very true, ma'am; everything is fixed, and the wedding liveries bespoke.

CRABT. Yes; and they do say there were pressing reasons for it.

LADY SNEER. Why, I have heard something of this before.

MRS. CAN. It can't be, and I wonder any one should believe such a story of so prudent a lady as Miss Nicely.

SIR BENJ. B. O Lud! ma'am, that's the very reason 'twas believed at once. She has always been so cautious and so reserved, that everybody was sure there was some reason for it at bottom.

MRS. CAN. Why, to be sure, a tale of scandal is as fatal to the credit of a prudent lady of her stamp, as a fever is generally to those of the strongest constitutions. But there is a sort of puny, sickly reputation, that is always ailing, yet will outlive the robuster characters of a hundred prudes.

SIR BENJ. B. True, madam, there are valetudinarians in reputation as well as constitution; who, being conscious of their weak part, avoid the least breath of air, and supply their want of stamina by care and circumspection.

MRS. CAN. Well, but this may be all a mistake. You know, Sir Benjamin, very trifling circumstances often give rise to the most injurious tales.

CRABT. That they do, I'll be sworn, ma'am. Did you ever hear how Miss Piper came to lose her lover and her character last summer at Tunbridge? Sir Benjamin, you remember it?

SIR BENJ. B. Oh, to be sure! The most whimsical circumstance.

LADY SNEER. How was it, pray?

CRABT. Why, one evening, at Mrs. Ponto's assembly, the conversation happened to turn on the breeding of Nova Scotia sheep in this country. Says a young lady in company, I have known instances of it, for Miss Letitia Piper, a first cousin of mine, had a Nova Scotia sheep that produced her twins. What! cries the Lady Dowager Dundizzy (who, you know, is as deaf as a post), has Miss Piper had twins? This mistake, as you may imagine, threw the whole company into a fit of laughter. However, 'twas the next morning everywhere reported, and in a few days believed by the whole town, that Miss Letitia Piper had actually been brought to bed of a fine boy and a girl; and in less than a week there were some people who could name the father, and the farmhouse where the babies were put to nurse.

LADY SNEER. Strange, indeed!

CRABT. Matter of fact, I assure you. O Lud! Mr. Surface, pray is it true that your uncle, Sir Oliver, is coming home?

JOSEPH S. Not that I know of, indeed, sir.

CRABT. He has been in the East Indies a

---

[14] The fourteenth-century Italian poet Petrarch wrote his sonnets to a lady named Laura.

[15] The seventeenth-century English poet Edmund Waller wrote some of his verse to "Sacharissa," generally identified as Lady Dorothy Sidney.

long time. You can scarcely remember him, I believe? Sad comfort whenever he returns, to hear how your brother has gone on!

JOSEPH S. Charles has been imprudent, sir, to be sure; but I hope no busy people have already prejudiced Sir Oliver against him. He may reform.

SIR BENJ. B. To be sure he may; for my part, I never believed him to be so utterly void of principle as people say; and though he has lost all his friends, I am told nobody is better spoken of by the Jews.

CRABT. That's true, egad, nephew. If the Old Jewry was a ward, I believe Charles would be an alderman. No man more popular there, 'fore Gad! I hear he pays as many annuities as the Irish tontine; and that whenever he is sick, they have prayers for the recovery of his health in all the synagogues.

SIR BENJ. B. Yet no man lives in greater splendor. They tell me, when he entertains his friends he will sit down to dinner with a dozen of his own securities; have a score of tradesmen waiting in the antechamber, and an officer behind every guest's chair.

JOSEPH S. This may be entertainment to you, gentlemen, but you pay very little regard to the feelings of a brother.

MARIA. Their malice is intolerable. Lady Sneerwell, I must wish you a good morning: I'm not very well. [*exit* MARIA]

MRS. CAN. O dear! she changes color very much.

LADY SNEER. Do, Mrs. Candour, follow her: she may want assistance.

MRS. CAN. That I will, with all my soul, ma'am. Poor dear girl, who knows what her situation may be! [*exit*]

LADY SNEER. 'Twas nothing but that she could not bear to hear Charles reflected on, notwithstanding their difference.

SIR BENJ. B. The young lady's *penchant* is obvious.

CRABT. But, Benjamin, you must not give up the pursuit for that: follow her, and put her into good humor. Repeat her some of your own verses. Come, I'll assist you.

SIR BENJ. B. Mr. Surface, I did not mean to hurt you; but, depend on't, your brother is utterly undone.

CRABT. O Lud, ay! undone as ever man was. Can't raise a guinea!

SIR BENJ. B. And everything sold, I'm told, that was movable.

CRABT. I have seen one that was at his house. Not a thing left but some empty bottles that were overlooked, and the family pictures, which I believe are framed in the wainscots.

SIR BENJ. B. And I'm very sorry, also, to hear some bad stories against him. [*going*]

CRABT. Oh! he has done many mean things, that's certain.

SIR BENJ. B. But, however, as he's your brother——[*going*]

CRABT. We'll tell you all another opportunity. [*ex(eunt)* CRABTREE *and* SIR BENJAMIN]

LADY SNEER. Ha! ha! 'tis very hard for them to leave a subject they have not quite run down.

JOSEPH S. And I believe the abuse was no more acceptable to your ladyship than Maria.

LADY SNEER. I doubt her affections are farther engaged than we imagine. But the family are to be here this evening, so you may as well dine where you are, and we shall have an opportunity of observing farther; in the meantime, I'll go and plot mischief, and you shall study sentiment. [*exeunt*]

SCENE II.

SIR PETER's house

Enter SIR PETER

SIR PETER T. When an old bachelor marries a young wife, what is he to expect? 'Tis now six months since Lady Teazle made me the happiest of men; and I have been the most miserable dog ever since! We tifted a little going to church, and fairly quarrelled before the bells had done ringing. I was more than once nearly choked with gall during the honeymoon, and had lost all comfort in life before my friends had done wishing me joy. Yet I chose with caution—a girl bred wholly in the country, who never knew luxury beyond one silk gown, nor dissipation above the annual gala of a race ball. Yet now she plays her part in all the extravagant fopperies of the fashion and the town, with as ready a grace as if she had never seen a bush or a grass-plot out of Grosvenor Square! I am sneered at by all my acquaintance, and paragraphed in the newspapers. She dissipates my fortune, and contradicts all my humors: yet the worst of it is, I doubt I love her, or I should never bear all this. However, I'll never be weak enough to own it.

Enter ROWLEY

ROWLEY. Oh! Sir Peter, your servant; how is it with you, sir?

SIR PETER T. Very bad, Master Rowley, very bad. I meet with nothing but crosses and vexations.

ROWLEY. What can have happened to trouble you since yesterday?

SIR PETER T. A good question to a married man!

ROWLEY. Nay, I'm sure your lady, Sir Peter, can't be the cause of your uneasiness.

SIR PETER T. Why, has anybody told you she was dead?

ROWLEY. Come, come, Sir Peter, you love her, notwithstanding your tempers don't exactly agree.

SIR PETER T. But the fault is entirely hers, Master Rowley. I am, myself, the sweetest tempered man alive, and hate a teasing temper; and so I tell her a hundred times a day.

ROWLEY. Indeed!

SIR PETER T. Ay; and what is very extraordinary, in all our disputes she is always in the wrong! But Lady Sneerwell, and the set she meets at her house, encourage the perverseness of her disposition. Then, to complete my vexation, Maria, my ward, whom I ought to have the power of a father over, is determined to turn rebel too, and absolutely refuses the man whom I have long resolved on for her husband; meaning, I suppose, to bestow herself on his profligate brother.

ROWLEY. You know, Sir Peter, I have always taken the liberty to differ with you on the subject of these two young gentlemen. I only wish you may not be deceived in your opinion of the elder. For Charles, my life on't! he will retrieve his errors yet. Their worthy father, once my honored master, was, at his years, nearly as wild a spark; yet, when he died, he did not leave a more benevolent heart to lament his loss.

SIR PETER T. You are wrong, Master Rowley. On their father's death, you know, I acted as a kind of guardian to them both, till their uncle Sir Oliver's liberality gave them an early independence: of course, no person could have more opportunities of judging of their hearts, and I was never mistaken in my life. Joseph is indeed a model for the young men of the age. He is a man of sentiment, and acts up to the *sentiments* he professes; but for the other, take my word for't, if he had any grain of virtue by descent, he has dissipated it with the rest of his inheritance. Ah! my old friend, Sir Oliver, will be deeply mortified when he finds how part of his bounty has been misapplied.

ROWLEY. I am sorry to find you so violent against the young man, because this may be the most critical period of his fortune. I came hither with news that will surprise you.

SIR PETER T. What! let me hear.

ROWLEY. Sir Oliver *is* arrived, and at this moment in town.

SIR PETER T. How! you astonish me! I thought you did not expect him this month.

ROWLEY. I did not; but his passage has been remarkably quick.

SIR PETER T. Egad, I shall rejoice to see my old friend. 'Tis fifteen years since we met. We have had many a day together; but does he still enjoin us not to inform his nephews of his arrival?

ROWLEY. Most strictly. He means, before it is known, to make some trial of their dispositions.

SIR PETER T. Ah! there needs no art to discover their merits; he shall have his way. But, pray, does he know I am married?

ROWLEY. Yes, and will soon wish you joy.

SIR PETER T. What, as we drink health to a friend in a consumption! Ah! Oliver will laugh at me. We used to rail at matrimony together, and he has been steady to his text. Well, he must be soon at my house, though! I'll instantly give orders for his reception. But, Master Rowley, don't drop a word that Lady Teazle and I ever disagree.

ROWLEY. By no means.

SIR PETER T. For I should never be able to stand Noll's jokes; so I'd have him think, Lord forgive me! that we are a very happy couple.

ROWLEY. I understand you; but then you must be very careful not to differ while he is in the house with you.

SIR PETER T. Egad, and so we must, and that's impossible. Ah! Master Rowley, when an old bachelor marries a young wife, he deserves

—no—the crime carries its punishment along with it. [*exeunt*]

ACT II

Scene I.

[SIR PETER's house]

Enter SIR PETER *and* LADY TEAZLE

SIR PETER T. Lady Teazle, Lady Teazle, I'll not bear it!

LADY T. Sir Peter, Sir Peter, you may bear it or not, as you please; but I ought to have my own way in everything, and what's more, I will, too. What! though I was educated in the country, I know very well that women of fashion in London are accountable to nobody after they are married.

SIR PETER T. Very well, ma'am, very well; so a husband is to have no influence, no authority?

LADY T. Authority! No, to be sure, if you wanted authority over me, you should have adopted me, and not married me: I am sure you were old enough.

SIR PETER T. Old enough! ay, there it is. Well, well, Lady Teazle, though my life may be made unhappy by your temper, I'll not be ruined by your extravagance.

LADY T. My extravagance! I'm sure I'm not more extravagant than a woman of fashion ought to be.

SIR PETER T. No, no, madam, you shall throw away no more sums on such unmeaning luxury. 'Slife! to spend as much to furnish your dressing-room with flowers in winter as would suffice to turn the Pantheon[16] into a green-house, and give a *fête champêtre*[17] at Christmas.

LADY T. And am I to blame, Sir Peter, because flowers are dear in cold weather? You should find fault with the climate, and not with me. For my part, I'm sure, I wish it was spring all the year round, and that roses grew under our feet.

SIR PETER T. Oons! madam; if you had been born to this, I shouldn't wonder at your talking thus; but you forget what your situation was when I married you.

LADY T. No, no, I don't; 'twas a very disagreeable one, or I should never have married you.

SIR PETER T. Yes, yes, madam; you were then in somewhat a humbler style: the daughter of a plain country squire. Recollect, Lady Teazle, when I saw you first sitting at your tambor,[18] in a pretty figured linen gown, with a bunch of keys at your side; your hair combed smooth over a roll, and your apartment hung round with fruits in worsted, of your own working.

LADY T. Oh, yes! I remember it very well, and a curious life I led. My daily occupation to inspect the dairy, superintend the poultry, make extracts from the family receipt book, and comb my aunt Deborah's lap-dog.

SIR PETER T. Yes, yes, ma'am, 'twas so indeed.

LADY T. And then, you know, my evening amusements! To draw patterns for ruffles, which I had not materials to make up; to play Pope Joan[19] with the curate; to read a sermon to my aunt; or to be stuck down to an old spinet to strum my father to sleep after a fox-chase.

SIR PETER T. I am glad you have so good a memory. Yes, madam, these were the recreations I took you from; but now you must have your coach—*vis-à-vis*[20]—and three powdered footmen before your chair; and in the summer, a pair of white cats[21] to draw you to Kensington Gardens. No recollection, I suppose, when you were content to ride double, behind the butler, on a docked coach-horse?

LADY T. No; I swear I never did that. I deny the butler and the coach-horse.

SIR PETER T. This, madam, was your situation; and what have I done for you? I have made you a woman of fashion, of fortune, of rank; in short, I have made you my wife.

LADY T. Well, then, and there is but one thing more you can make me to add to the obligation, and that is——

SIR PETER T. My widow, I suppose?

LADY T. Hem! hem!

SIR PETER T. I thank you, madam; but don't flatter yourself; for though your ill conduct may disturb my peace, it shall never break

---

[16] here, a London concert hall.
[17] garden party.

[18] embroidery frame.   [19] card game.
[20] that is, the occupants sit face to face.
[21] horses.

my heart, I promise you; however, I am equally obliged to you for the hint.

LADY T. Then why will you endeavor to make yourself so disagreeable to me, and thwart me in every little elegant expense?

SIR PETER T. 'Slife, madam, I say, had you any of these little elegant expenses when you married me?

LADY T. Lud, Sir Peter! would you have me be out of the fashion?

SIR PETER T. The fashion, indeed! what had you to do with the fashion before you married me?

LADY T. For my part, I should think you would like to have your wife thought a woman of taste.

SIR PETER T. Ay, there again; taste! Zounds! madam, you had no taste when you married me!

LADY T. That's very true indeed, Sir Peter; and after having married you, I should never pretend to taste again, I allow. But now, Sir Peter, if we have finished our daily jangle, I presume I may go to my engagement at Lady Sneerwell's.

SIR PETER T. Ah, there's another precious circumstance; a charming set of acquaintance you have made there.

LADY T. Nay, Sir Peter, they are all people of rank and fortune, and remarkably tenacious of reputation.

SIR PETER T. Yes, egad, they are tenacious of reputation with a vengeance; for they don't choose anybody should have a character but themselves! Such a crew! Ah! many a wretch has rid on a hurdle[22] who has done less mischief than these utterers of forged tales, coiners of scandal, and clippers of reputation.

LADY T. What! would you restrain the freedom of speech?

SIR PETER T. Ah! they have made you just as bad as any one of the society.

LADY T. Why, I believe I do bear a part with a tolerable grace. But I vow I bear no malice against the people I abuse. When I say an ill-natured thing, 'tis out of pure good humor; and I take it for granted, they deal exactly in the same manner with me. But, Sir Peter, you know you promised to come to Lady Sneerwell's too.

SIR PETER T. Well, well, I'll call in just to look after my own character.

LADY T. Then indeed you must make haste after me, or you'll be too late. So, good-bye to ye. [*exit* LADY TEAZLE]

SIR PETER T. So, I have gained much by my intended expostulation; yet, with what a charming air she contradicts everything I say, and how pleasingly she shows her contempt for my authority! Well, though I can't make her love me, there is great satisfaction in quarreling with her; and I think she never appears to such advantage as when she is doing everything in her power to plague me. [*exit*]

SCENE II.

AT LADY SNEERWELL'S

Enter LADY SNEERWELL, MRS. CANDOUR, CRABTREE, SIR BENJAMIN BACKBITE, *and* JOSEPH SURFACE

LADY SNEER. Nay, positively, we will hear it.

JOSEPH S. Yes, yes, the epigram, by all means.

SIR BENJ. B. O plague on't, uncle! 'tis mere nonsense.

CRABT. No, no; 'fore Gad, very clever for an extempore!

SIR BENJ. B. But, ladies, you should be acquainted with the circumstances. You must know, that one day last week, as Lady Betty Curricle was taking the dust in Hyde Park, in a sort of duodecimo[23] phaeton, she desired me to write some verses on her ponies, upon which I took out my pocket-book, and in one moment produced the following:

Sure never were seen two such beautiful ponies;
Other horses are clowns, but these macaronies:[24]
To give them this title I'm sure can't be wrong,
Their legs are so slim, and their tails are so long.

CRABT. There, ladies, done in the smack of a whip, and on horseback too.

_____

[22] cart for carrying the condemned to execution.

[23] tiny (as a duodecimo volume).
[24] fops, dandies.

JOSEPH S. A very Phœbus mounted, indeed, Sir Benjamin.

SIR BENJ. B. O dear sir! trifles, trifles.

Enter LADY TEAZLE *and* MARIA

MRS. CAN. I must have a copy.

LADY SNEER. Lady Teazle, I hope we shall see Sir Peter?

LADY T. I believe he'll wait on your lady- ship presently.

LADY SNEER. Maria, my love, you look grave. Come, you shall set down to piquet with Mr. Surface.

MARIA. I take very little pleasure in cards; however, I'll do as you please.

LADY T. [*aside*] I am surprised Mr. Surface should sit down with her; I thought he would have embraced this opportunity of speaking to me, before Sir Peter came.

MRS. CAN. Now, I'll die, but you are so scandalous. I'll forswear your society.

LADY T. What's the matter, Mrs. Candour?

MRS. CAN. They'll not allow our friend, Miss Vermilion, to be handsome.

LADY SNEER. Oh, surely she is a pretty woman.

CRABT. I'm very glad you think so, ma'am.

MRS. CAN. She has a charming fresh color.

LADY T. Yes, when it is fresh put on.

MRS. CAN. O fie! I'll swear her color is nat- ural; I have seen it come and go.

LADY T. I dare swear you have, ma'am; it goes off at night, and comes again in the morn- ing.

SIR BENJ. B. True, ma'am, it not only comes and goes, but what's more, egad! her maid can fetch and carry it.

MRS. CAN. Ha! ha! ha! how I hate to hear you talk so! But surely, now, her sister *is*, or *was*, very handsome.

CRABT. Who? Mrs. Evergreen? O Lord! she's six and fifty if she's an hour.

MRS. CAN. Now, positively you wrong her; fifty-two or fifty-three is the utmost; and I don't think she looks more.

SIR BENJ. B. Ah! there's no judging by her looks, unless one could see her face.

LADY SNEER. Well, well, if Mrs. Evergreen *does* take some pains to repair the ravages of time, you must allow she effects it with great ingenuity, and surely that's better than the careless manner in which the widow Ochre caulks her wrinkles.

SIR BENJ. B. Nay, now, Lady Sneerwell, you are severe upon the widow. Come, come, t'is not that she paints so ill, but when she has finished her face, she joins it so badly to her neck, that she looks like a mended statue, in which the connoisseur sees at once that the head's modern though the trunk's antique.

CRABT. Ha! ha! ha! well said, nephew.

MRS. CAN. Ha! ha! ha! well, you make me laugh, but I vow I hate you for it. What do you think of Miss Simper?

SIR BENJ. B. Why, she has very pretty teeth.

LADY T. Yes, and on that account, when she is neither speaking nor laughing (which very seldom happens), she never absolutely shuts her mouth, but leaves it on ajar, as it were—thus——[*shows her teeth*]

MRS. CAN. How can you be so ill-natured?

LADY T. Nay, I allow even that's better than the pains Mrs. Prim takes to conceal her losses in front. She draws her mouth till it positively resembles the aperture of a poor's box, and all her words appear to slide out edgewise, as it were thus, *How do you do, madam? Yes, madam.*

LADY SNEER. Very well, Lady Teazle; I see you can be a little severe.

LADY T. In defence of a friend it is but jus- tice. But here comes Sir Peter to spoil our pleasantry.

Enter SIR PETER TEAZLE

SIR PETER T. Ladies, your most obedient. [*aside*] Mercy on me! here is the whole set! a character dead at every word, I suppose.

MRS. CAN. I am rejoiced you are come, Sir Peter. They have been so censorious; and Lady Teazle as bad as any one.

SIR PETER T. It must be very distressing to *you*, Mrs. Candour, I dare swear.

MRS. CAN. Oh, they will allow good quali- ties to nobody; not even good nature to our friend Mrs. Pursy.

LADY T. What, the fat dowager who was at Mrs. Quadrille's last night?

MRS. CAN. Nay, her bulk is her misfortune; and when she takes such pains to get rid of it, you ought not to reflect on her.

LADY SNEER. That's very true, indeed.

LADY T. Yes, I know she almost lives on acids and small whey; laces herself by pullies; and often in the hottest noon in summer, you may see her on a little squat pony, with her hair plaited up behind like a drummer's, and puffing round the Ring on a full trot.

MRS. CAN. I thank you, Lady Teazle, for defending her.

SIR PETER T. Yes, a good defence, truly!

MRS. CAN. Truly, Lady Teazle is as censorious as Miss Sallow.

CRABT. Yes, and she is a curious being to pretend to be censorious—an awkward gawky, without any one good point under heaven.

MRS. CAN. Positively you shall not be so very severe. Miss Sallow is a near relation of mine by marriage, and as for her person, great allowance is to be made; for, let me tell you, a woman labors under many disadvantages who tries to pass for a girl at six-and-thirty.

LADY SNEER. Though, surely, she is handsome still; and for the weakness in her eyes, considering how much she reads by candlelight, it is not to be wondered at.

MRS. CAN. True, and then as to her manner; upon my word I think it is particularly graceful, considering she had never had the least education; for you know her mother was a Welsh milliner, and her father a sugar-baker at Bristol.

SIR BENJ. B. Ah! you are both of you too good natured!

SIR PETER T. [aside] Yes, damned good natured! This their own relation! mercy on me!

MRS. CAN. For my part, I own I cannot bear to hear a friend ill spoken of.

SIR PETER T. No, to be sure!

SIR BENJ. B. Oh! you are of a moral turn. Mrs. Candour and I can sit for an hour and hear Lady Stucco talk sentiment.

LADY T. Nay, I vow Lady Stucco is very well with the dessert after dinner; for she's just like the French fruits one cracks for mottoes—made up of paint and proverb.

MRS. CAN. Well, I never will join in ridiculing a friend; and so I constantly tell my cousin Ogle, and you all know what pretensions she has to be critical on beauty.

CRABT. Oh, to be sure! she has herself the oddest countenance that ever was seen; 'tis a collection of features from all the different countries of the globe.

SIR BENJ. B. So she has, indeed—an Irish front——

CRABT. Caledonian locks——

SIR BENJ. B. Dutch nose——

CRABT. Austrian lips——

SIR BENJ. B. Complexion of a Spaniard——

CRABT. And teeth *à la Chinois*.[25]

SIR BENJ. B. In short, her face resembles a *table d'hôte* at Spa,[26] where no two guests are of a nation——

CRABT. Or a congress at the close of a general war—wherein all the members, even to her eyes, appear to have a different interest, and her nose and chin are the only parties likely to join issue.

MRS. CAN. Ha! ha! ha!

SIR PETER T. [aside] Mercy on my life!— a person they dine with twice a week.

LADY SNEER. Go, go; you are a couple of provoking toads.

MRS. CAN. Nay, but I vow you shall not carry the laugh off so; for give me leave to say that Mrs. Ogle——

SIR PETER T. Madam, madam, I beg your pardon; there's no stopping these good gentlemen's tongues. But when I tell you, Mrs. Candour, that the lady they are abusing is a particular friend of mine, I hope you'll not take her part.

LADY SNEER. Ha! ha! ha! Well said, Sir Peter! But you are a cruel creature—too phlegmatic yourself for a jest, and too peevish to allow wit in others.

SIR PETER T. Ah! madam, true wit is more nearly allied to good nature than your ladyship is aware of.

LADY T. True, Sir Peter. I believe they are so near akin that they can never be united.

SIR BENJ. B. Or rather, madam, suppose them to be man and wife, because one seldom sees them together.

LADY T. But Sir Peter is such an enemy to scandal, I believe he would have it put down by Parliament.

SIR PETER T. 'Fore heaven, madam, if they were to consider the sporting with reputation of as much importance as poaching on manors, and pass an Act for the preservation of fame,

---

[25] in the Chinese manner.
[26] originally a Belgian resort, now a term for any watering place.

I believe there are many would thank them for the bill.

LADY SNEER. O Lud! Sir Peter; would you deprive us of our privileges?

SIR PETER T. Ay, madam; and then no person should be permitted to kill characters and run down reputations, but qualified old maids and disappointed widows.

LADY SNEER. Go, you monster!

MRS. CAN. But, surely, you would not be quite so severe on those who only report what they hear?

SIR PETER T. Yes, madam, I would have law merchant[27] for them too; and in all cases of slander currency, whenever the drawer of the lie was not to be found, the injured parties should have a right to come on any of the indorsers.

CRABT. Well, for my part, I believe there never was a scandalous tale without some foundation.

SIR PETER T. Oh, nine out of ten of the malicious inventions are founded on some ridiculous misrepresentation.

LADY SNEER. Come, ladies, shall we sit down to cards in the next room?

Enter a SERVANT, *who whispers to* SIR PETER

SIR PETER T. I'll be with them directly. [*apart*] I'll get away unperceived.

LADY SNEER. Sir Peter, you are not going to leave us?

SIR PETER T. Your ladyship must excuse me; I'm called away by particular business. But I leave my character behind me. [*exit* SIR PETER]

SIR BENJ. B. Well; certainly, Lady Teazle, that lord of yours is a strange being; I could tell you some stories of him would make you laugh heartily if he were not your husband.

LADY T. Oh, pray don't mind that; come, do let's hear them. [*joins the rest of the company going into the next room*]

JOSEPH S. Maria, I see you have no satisfaction in this society.

MARIA. How is it possible I should? If to raise malicious smiles at the infirmities or misfortunes of those who have never injured us be the province of wit or humor, Heaven grant me a double portion of dullness!

JOSEPH S. Yet they appear more ill-natured than they are; they have no malice at heart.

MARIA. Then is their conduct still more contemptible; for, in my opinion, nothing could excuse the interference of their tongues, but a natural and uncontrollable bitterness of mind.

JOSEPH S. Undoubtedly, madam; and it has always been a sentiment of mine, that to propagate a malicious truth wantonly is more despicable than to falsify from revenge. But can you, Maria, feel thus for others, and be unkind to me alone? Is hope to be denied the tenderest passion?

MARIA. Why will you distress me by renewing the subject?

JOSEPH S. Ah, Maria! you would not treat me thus, and oppose your guardian, Sir Peter's will, but that I see that profligate Charles is still a favored rival.

MARIA. Ungenerously urged! But whatever my sentiments are for that unfortunate young man, be assured I shall not feel more bound to give him up, because his distresses have lost him the regard even of a brother.

JOSEPH S. Nay, but Maria. do not leave me with a frown; by all that's honest, I swear [*kneels*]——

[Re-enter LADY TEAZLE, *behind]*

[*Aside*] Gad's life, here's Lady Teazle! [*Aloud to* MARIA] You must not; no, you shall not; for, though I have the greatest regard for Lady Teazle——

MARIA. Lady Teazle!

JOSEPH S. Yet were Sir Peter to suspect——

LADY T. [*coming forward*] What is this, pray? Do you take her for me? Child, you are wanted in the next room. [*exit* MARIA] What is all this, pray?

JOSEPH S. O, the most unlucky circumstance in nature! Maria has somehow suspected the tender concern I had for your happiness, and threatened to acquaint Sir Peter with her suspicions, and I was just endeavoring to reason with her when you came in.

LADY T. Indeed! but you seemed to adopt a very tender mode of reasoning; do you usually argue on your knees?

JOSEPH S. Oh, she's a child, and I thought a little bombast—— But, Lady Teazle, when are you to give me your judgment on my library, as you promised?

LADY T. No, no; I begin to think it would be

---

[27] commercial law.

imprudent, and you know I admit you as a lover no farther than fashion sanctions.

JOSEPH S. True, a mere platonic cicisbeo[28]—what every wife is entitled to.

LADY T. Certainly, one must not be out of the fashion. However, I have so much of my country prejudices left, that, though Sir Peter's ill-humor may vex me ever so, it never shall provoke me to——

JOSEPH S. The only revenge in your power. Well; I applaud your moderation.

LADY T. Go; you are an insinuating wretch. But we shall be missed; let us join the company.

JOSEPH S. But we had best not return together.

LADY T. Well, don't stay; for Maria sha'n't come to hear any more of your reasoning, I promise you. [*exit* LADY TEAZLE]

JOSEPH S. A curious dilemma my politics have run me into! I wanted, at first, only to ingratiate myself with Lady Teazle, that she might not be my enemy with Maria; and I have, I don't know how, become her serious lover. Sincerely I begin to wish I had never made such a point of gaining so very good a character, for it has led me into so many cursed rogueries that I doubt I shall be exposed at last. [*exit*]

SCENE III.

SIR PETER TEAZLE'S

Enter ROWLEY *and* SIR OLIVER SURFACE

SIR OLIVER S. Ha! ha! ha! So my old friend is married, hey?—a young wife out of the country. Ha! ha! ha! that he should have stood bluff to old bachelor so long, and sink into a husband at last.

ROWLEY. But you must not rally him on the subject, Sir Oliver; 'tis a tender point, I assure you, though he has been married only seven months.

SIR OLIVER S. Then he has been just half a year on the stool of repentance! Poor Peter! But you say he has entirely given up Charles; never sees him, hey?

ROWLEY. His prejudice against him is aston-ishing, and I am sure greatly increased by a jealousy of him with Lady Teazle, which he has industriously been led into by a scandalous society in the neighborhood, who have contributed not a little to Charles's ill name. Whereas the truth is, I believe, if the lady is partial to either of them, his brother is the favorite.

SIR OLIVER S. Ay, I know there is a set of malicious, prating, prudent gossips, both male and female, who murder characters to kill time; and will rob a young fellow of his good name, before he has years to know the value of it. But I am not to be prejudiced against my nephew by such, I promise you. No, no; if Charles has done nothing false or mean, I shall compound[29] for his extravagance.

ROWLEY. Then, my life on't, you will reclaim him. Ah, sir! it gives me new life to find that *your* heart is not turned against him; and that the son of my good old master has one friend, however, left.

SIR OLIVER S. What, shall I forget, Master Rowley, when I was at his years myself? Egad, my brother and I were neither of us very prudent youths; and yet, I believe, you have not seen many better men than your old master was.

ROWLEY. Sir, 'tis this reflection gives me assurance that Charles may yet be a credit to his family. But here comes Sir Peter.

SIR OLIVER S. Egad, so he does. Mercy on me! he's greatly altered, and seems to have a settled married look! One may read *husband* in his face at this distance!

Enter SIR PETER TEAZLE

SIR PETER T. Ha! Sir Oliver, my old friend! Welcome to England a thousand times!

SIR OLIVER S. Thank you—thank you, Sir Peter! and i' faith I am glad to find you well, believe me.

SIR PETER T. Oh! 'tis a long time since we met—fifteen years, I doubt, Sir Oliver, and many a cross accident in the time.

SIR OLIVER S. Ay, I have had my share. But what! I find you are married, hey? Well, well, it can't be helped; and so—I wish you joy with all my heart.

---

[28] lover or escort of a married woman.

[29] make allowances (in the settlement).

SIR PETER T. Thank you, thank you, Sir Oliver. Yes, I have entered into—the happy state; but we'll not talk of that now.

SIR OLIVER S. True, true, Sir Peter; old friends should not begin on grievances at first meeting; no, no, no.

ROWLEY. Take care, pray, sir.

SIR OLIVER S. Well; so one of my nephews is a wild fellow, hey?

SIR PETER T. Wild! Ah! my old friend, I grieve for your disappointment there; he's a lost young man, indeed. However, his brother will make you amends. Joseph is, indeed, what a youth should be. Everybody in the world speaks well of him.

SIR OLIVER S. I am sorry to hear it; he has too good a character to be an honest fellow. Everybody speaks well of him! Pshaw! then he has bowed as low to knaves and fools as to the honest dignity of genius and virtue.

SIR PETER T. What, Sir Oliver! do you blame him for not making enemies?

SIR OLIVER S. Yes, if he has merit enough to deserve them.

SIR PETER T. Well, well; you'll be convinced when you know him. 'Tis edification to hear him converse; he professes the noblest sentiments.

SIR OLIVER S. Oh! plague of his sentiments! If he salutes me with a scrap of morality in his mouth, I shall be sick directly. But, however, don't mistake me, Sir Peter; I don't mean to defend Charles's errors; but before I form my judgment of either of them, I intend to make a trial of their hearts; and my friend Rowley and I have planned something for the purpose.

ROWLEY. And Sir Peter shall own for once he has been mistaken.

SIR PETER T. Oh! my life on Joseph's honor.

SIR OLIVER S. Well—come, give us a bottle of good wine, and we'll drink the lad's health, and tell you our scheme.

SIR PETER T. *Allons,*[30] then!

SIR OLIVER S. And don't, Sir Peter, be so severe against your old friend's son. Odds my life! I am not sorry that he has run out of the course a little; for my part I hate to see prudence clinging to the green suckers of youth; 'tis like ivy round a sapling, and spoils the growth of the tree. [*exeunt*]

[30] Let's go.

ACT III

SCENE I.

SIR PETER TEAZLE'S

Enter SIR PETER TEAZLE, SIR OLIVER SURFACE, *and* ROWLEY

SIR PETER T. Well, then, we will see this fellow first, and have our wine afterwards; but how is this, Master Rowley? I don't see the jest of your scheme.

ROWLEY. Why, sir, this Mr. Stanley, who I was speaking of, is nearly related to them by their mother. He was a merchant in Dublin, but has been ruined by a series of undeserved misfortunes. He has applied, by letter, to Mr. Surface and Charles; from the former he has received nothing but evasive promises of future service, while Charles has done all that his extravagance has left him power to do, and he is, at this time, endeavoring to raise a sum of money, part of which, in the midst of his own distresses, I know he intends for the service of poor Stanley.

SIR OLIVER S. Ah! he is my brother's son.

SIR PETER T. Well, but how is Sir Oliver personally to——

ROWLEY. Why, sir, I will inform Charles and his brother that Stanley has obtained permission to apply personally to his friends, and as they have neither of them ever seen him, let Sir Oliver assume his character, and he will have a fair opportunity of judging, at least, of the benevolence of their dispositions; and believe me, sir, you will find in the youngest brother one who, in the midst of folly and dissipation, has still, as our immortal bard expresses it, "a heart to pity, and a hand, open as day, for melting charity."[31]

SIR PETER T. Pshaw! What signifies his having an open hand or purse either, when he has nothing left to give? Well, well, make the trial, if you please. But where is the fellow whom you brought for Sir Oliver to examine, relative to Charles's affairs?

ROWLEY. Below, waiting his commands, and no one can give him better intelligence. This, Sir Oliver, is a friendly Jew, who, to do him justice, has done everything in his power to

[31] misquoted from *Henry IV, Part Two.*

bring your nephew to a proper sense of his extravagance.

SIR PETER T. Pray let us have him in.

ROWLEY. [*apart to* SERVANT] Desire Mr. Moses to walk upstairs.

SIR PETER T. But pray, why should you suppose he will speak the truth?

ROWLEY. Oh! I have convinced him that he has no chance of recovering certain sums advanced to Charles, but through the bounty of Sir Oliver, who he knows is arrived, so that you may depend on his fidelity to his own interests. I have also another evidence in my power—one Snake, whom I have detected in a matter little short of forgery, and shall speedily produce him to remove some of your prejudices.

SIR PETER T. I have heard too much on that subject.

ROWLEY. Here comes the honest Israelite.

Enter MOSES

This is Sir Oliver.

SIR OLIVER S. Sir, I understand you have lately had great dealings with my nephew, Charles.

MOSES. Yes, Sir Oliver, I have done all I could for him; but he was ruined before he came to me for assistance.

SIR OLIVER S. That was unlucky, truly; for you have had no opportunity of showing your talents.

MOSES. None at all; I hadn't the pleasure of knowing his distresses till he was some thousands worse than nothing.

SIR OLIVER S. Unfortunate, indeed! But I suppose you have done all in your power for him, honest Moses?

MOSES. Yes, he knows that. This very evening I was to have brought him a gentleman from the city, who does not know him, and will, I believe, advance him some money.

SIR PETER T. What! one Charles has never had money from before?

MOSES. Yes; Mr. Premium, of Crutched Friars, formerly a broker.

SIR PETER T. Egad, Sir Oliver, a thought strikes me! Charles, you say, does not know Mr. Premium?

MOSES. Not at all.

SIR PETER T. Now then, Sir Oliver, you may have a better opportunity of satisfying yourself than by an old romancing tale of a poor relation. Go with my friend Moses, and represent Premium, and then, I'll answer for it, you'll see your nephew in all his glory.

SIR OLIVER S. Egad, I like this idea better than the other, and I may visit Joseph afterwards as Old Stanley.

SIR PETER T. True, so you may.

ROWLEY. Well, this is taking Charles rather at a disadvantage, to be sure. However, Moses, you understand Sir Peter, and will be faithful.

MOSES. You may depend upon me. This is near the time I was to have gone.

SIR OLIVER S. I'll accompany you as soon as you please, Moses. But hold! I have forgot one thing—how the plague shall I be able to pass for a Jew?

MOSES. There's no need—the principal is Christian.

SIR OLIVER S. Is he? I'm very sorry to hear it. But then, again, a'n't I rather too smartly dressed to look like a money lender?

SIR PETER T. Not at all; 'twould not be out of character if you went in your own carriage—would it, Moses?

MOSES. Not in the least.

SIR OLIVER S. Well, but how must I talk? There's certainly some cant of usury and mode of treating that I ought to know.

SIR PETER T. Oh! there's not much to learn. The great point, as I take it, is to be exorbitant enough in your demands—hey, Moses?

MOSES. Yes, that's a very great point.

SIR OLIVER S. I'll answer for't I'll not be wanting in that. I'll ask him eight or ten per cent. on the loan, at least.

MOSES. If you ask him no more than that, you'll be discovered immediately.

SIR OLIVER S. Hey! what the plague! How much, then?

MOSES. That depends upon the circumstances. If he appears not very anxious for the supply, you should require only forty or fifty per cent.; but if you find him in great distress, and want the moneys very bad, you may ask double.

SIR PETER T. A good honest trade you're learning, Sir Oliver!

SIR OLIVER S. Truly, I think so; and not unprofitable.

MOSES. Then, you know, you hav'n't the

moneys yourself, but are forced to borrow them for him of an old friend.

SIR OLIVER S. Oh! I borrow it of a friend, do I?

MOSES. And your friend is an unconscionable dog; but you can't help that.

SIR OLIVER S. My friend an unconscionable dog?

MOSES. Yes, and he himself has not the moneys by him, but is forced to sell stock at a great loss.

SIR OLIVER S. He is forced to sell stock at a great loss, is he? Well, that's very kind of him.

SIR PETER T. I' faith, Sir Oliver—Mr. Premium, I mean—you'll soon be master of the trade. But, Moses! would not you have him run out a little against the Annuity Bill? That would be in character, I should think.

MOSES. Very much.

ROWLEY. And lament that a young man now must be at years of discretion before he is suffered to ruin himself?

MOSES. Ay, great pity!

SIR PETER T. And abuse the public for allowing merit to an Act whose only object is to snatch misfortune and imprudence from the rapacious grip of usury, and give the minor a chance of inheriting his estate without being undone by coming into possession.

SIR OLIVER S. So, so; Moses shall give me further instructions as we go together.

SIR PETER T. You will not have much time, for your nephew lives hard by.

SIR OLIVER S. Oh! never fear; my tutor appears so able, that though Charles lived in the next street, it must be my own fault if I am not a complete rogue before I turn the corner. [*exeunt* SIR OLIVER SURFACE *and* MOSES]

SIR PETER T. So now, I think Sir Oliver will be convinced. You are partial, Rowley, and would have prepared Charles for the other plot.

ROWLEY. No, upon my word, Sir Peter.

SIR PETER T. Well, go bring me this Snake, and I'll hear what he has to say presently. I see Maria, and want to speak with her. [*exit* ROWLEY] I should be glad to be convinced my suspicions of Lady Teazle and Charles were unjust. I have never yet opened my mind on this subject to my friend Joseph. I am determined I will do it; he will give me his opinion sincerely.

Enter MARIA

So, child, has Mr. Surface returned with you?

MARIA. No, sir; he was engaged.

SIR PETER T. Well, Maria, do you not reflect, the more you converse with that amiable young man, what return his partiality for you deserves?

MARIA. Indeed, Sir Peter, your frequent importunity on this subject distresses me extremely; you compel me to declare that I know no man who has ever paid me a particular attention whom I would not prefer to Mr. Surface.

SIR PETER T. So, here's perverseness! No, no, Maria, 'tis Charles only whom you would prefer. 'Tis evident his vices and follies have won your heart.

MARIA. This is unkind, sir. You know I have obeyed you in neither seeing nor corresponding with him. I have heard enough to convince me that he is unworthy my regard. Yet I cannot think it culpable, if, while my understanding severely condemns his vices, my heart suggests some pity for his distresses.

SIR PETER T. Well, well, pity him as much as you please; but give your heart and hand to a worthier object.

MARIA. Never to his brother!

SIR PETER T. Go, perverse and obstinate! But take care, madam; you have never yet known what the authority of a guardian is. Don't compel me to inform you of it.

MARIA. I can only say, you shall not have just reason. 'Tis true, by my father's will, I am for a short period bound to regard you as his substitute; but must cease to think you so, when you would compel me to be miserable. [*exit* MARIA]

SIR PETER T. Was ever man so crossed as I am? Everything conspiring to fret me! I had not been involved in matrimony a fortnight, before her father, a hale and hearty man, died, on purpose, I believe, for the pleasure of plaguing me with the care of his daughter. But here comes my helpmate! She appears in great good humor. How happy I should be if I could tease her into loving me, though but a little!

Enter LADY TEAZLE

LADY T. Lud! Sir Peter, I hope you hav'n't been quarrelling with Maria? It is not using me well to be ill humored when I am not by.

SIR PETER T. Ah! Lady Teazle, you might have the power to make me good humored at all times.

LADY T. I am sure I wish I had; for I want you to be in a charming sweet temper at this moment. Do be good humored now, and let me have two hundred pounds, will you?

SIR PETER T. Two hundred pounds! What, a'n't I to be in a good humor without paying for it? But speak to me thus, and i' faith there's nothing I could refuse you. You shall have it; but seal me a bond for the repayment.

LADY T. Oh, no—there. My note of hand will do as well. [offering her hand]

SIR PETER T. And you shall no longer reproach me with not giving you an independent settlement. I mean shortly to surprise you. But shall we always live thus, hey?

LADY T. If you please. I'm sure I don't care how soon we leave off quarrelling, provided you'll own you were tired first.

SIR PETER T. Well, then let our future contest be, who shall be most obliging.

LADY T. I assure you, Sir Peter, good nature becomes you. You look now as you did before we were married, when you used to walk with me under the elms, and tell me stories of what a gallant you were in your youth, and chuck me under the chin, you would; and ask me if I thought I could love an old fellow who would deny me nothing—didn't you?

SIR PETER T. Yes, yes; and you were as kind and attentive——

LADY T. Ay, so I was, and would always take your part, when my acquaintance used to abuse you, and turn you into ridicule.

SIR PETER T. Indeed!

LADY T. Ay, and when my cousin Sophy has called you a stiff, peevish old bachelor, and laughed at me for thinking of marrying one who might be my father, I have always defended you, and said, I didn't think you so ugly by any means, and I dared say you'd make a very good sort of a husband.

SIR PETER T. And you prophesied right; and we shall now be the happiest couple——

LADY T. And never differ again?

SIR PETER T. No, never! Though at the same time, indeed, my dear Lady Teazle, you must watch your temper very seriously; for in all our little quarrels, my dear, if you recollect, my love, you always began first.

LADY T. I beg your pardon, my dear Sir Peter: indeed, you always gave the provocation.

SIR PETER T. Now see, my angel! take care; contradicting isn't the way to keep friends.

LADY T. Then don't you begin it, my love!

SIR PETER T. There, now! you—you are going on. You don't perceive, my life, that you are just doing the very thing which you know always makes me angry.

LADY T. Nay, you know if you will be angry without any reason, my dear——

SIR PETER T. There! now you want to quarrel again.

LADY T. No, I am sure I don't; but if you will be so peevish——

SIR PETER T. There now! who begins first?

LADY T. Why you, to be sure. I said nothing; but there's no bearing your temper.

SIR PETER T. No, no, madam; the fault's in your own temper.

LADY T. Ay, you are just what my cousin Sophy said you would be.

SIR PETER T. Your cousin Sophy is a forward, impertinent gipsy.

LADY T. You are a great bear, I'm sure, to abuse my relations.

SIR PETER T. Now may all the plagues of marriage be doubled on me, if ever I try to be friends with you any more!

LADY T. So much the better.

SIR PETER T. No, no, madam; 'tis evident you never cared a pin for me, and I was a madman to marry you—a pert, rural coquette, that had refused half the honest squires in the neighborhood.

LADY T. And I am sure I was a fool to marry you; an old dangling bachelor, who was single at fifty, only because he never could meet with any one who would have him.

SIR PETER T. Ay, ay, madam; but you were pleased enough to listen to me; you never had such an offer before.

LADY T. No! didn't I refuse Sir Tivy Terrier, who everybody said would have been a better match? for his estate is just as good as yours, and he has broke his neck since we have been married.

SIR PETER T. I have done with you, madam! You are an unfeeling, ungrateful—but there's an end to everything. I believe you capable of everything that is bad. Yes, madam, I now believe the reports relative to you and Charles, madam. Yes, madam, *you* and Charles are—not without grounds——

LADY T. Take care, Sir Peter; you had better not insinuate any such thing! I'll not be suspected without cause, I promise you.

SIR PETER T. Very well, madam! very well! A separate maintenance as soon as you please. Yes, madam, or a divorce! I'll make an example of myself for the benefit of all old bachelors. Let us separate, madam.

LADY T. Agreed, agreed! And now, my dear Sir Peter, we are of a mind once more, we may be the happiest couple, and never differ again, you know—ha! ha! ha! Well, you are going to be in a passion, I see, and I shall only interrupt you; so, bye—bye. [*exit*]

SIR PETER T. Plagues and tortures! Can't I make her angry either! Oh, I am the most miserable fellow! but I'll not bear her presuming to keep her temper; no! she may break my heart, but she sha'n't keep her temper. [*exit*]

SCENE II.

CHARLES SURFACE'S house

Enter TRIP, MOSES, *and* SIR OLIVER SURFACE

TRIP. Here, Master Moses! if you'll stay a moment, I'll try whether—what's the gentleman's name?

SIR OLIVER S. Mr. Moses, what is my name?

MOSES. Mr. Premium.

TRIP. Premium—very well. [*exit* TRIP, *taking snuff*]

SIR OLIVER S. To judge by the servants, one wouldn't believe the master was ruined. But what!—sure, this was my brother's house?

MOSES. Yes, sir; Mr. Charles bought it of Mr. Joseph, with the furniture, pictures, &c., just as the old gentleman left it. Sir Peter thought it a piece of extravagance in him.

SIR OLIVER S. In my mind, the other's economy in selling it to him was more reprehensible by half.

Enter TRIP

TRIP. My master says you must wait, gentlemen; he has company, and can't speak with you yet.

SIR OLIVER S. If he knew who it was wanted to see him, perhaps he would not send such a message?

TRIP. Yes, yes, sir; he knows you are here. I did not forget little Premium; no, no, no.

SIR OLIVER S. Very well; and I pray, sir, what may be your name?

TRIP. Trip, sir; my name is Trip, at your service.

SIR OLIVER S. Well, then, Mr. Trip, you have a pleasant sort of place here, I guess?

TRIP. Why, yes; here are three or four of us pass our time agreeably enough; but then our wages are sometimes a little in arrear—and not very great either—but fifty pounds a year, and find our own bags and bouquets.

SIR OLIVER S. [*aside*] Bags and bouquets! halters and bastinadoes!

TRIP. And, *à propos*, Moses; have you been able to get me that little bill discounted?

SIR OLIVER S. [*aside*] Wants to raise money too! mercy on me! Has his distresses too, I warrant, like a lord, and affects creditors and duns.

MOSES. 'Twas not to be done, indeed, Mr. Trip.

TRIP. Good lack, you surprise me! My friend Brush has indorsed it, and I thought when he put his name on the back of a bill 'twas the same as cash.

MOSES. No! 'twouldn't do.

TRIP. A small sum; but twenty pounds. Hark'ee, Moses, do you think you couldn't get it me by way of annuity?

SIR OLIVER S. [*aside*] An annuity! ha! ha! a footman raise money by way of annuity! Well done, luxury, egad!

MOSES. Well, but you must insure your place.

TRIP. Oh, with all my heart! I'll insure my place, and my life, too, if you please.

SIR OLIVER S. [*aside*] It is more than I would your neck.

MOSES. But is there nothing you could deposit?

TRIP. Why, nothing capital of my master's wardrobe has dropped lately; but I could give you a mortgage on some of his winter clothes, with equity of redemption before November; or you shall have the reversion of the French velvet, or a post-obit[32] on the blue and silver:

32 *post obitum*, Latin for "after death"; here, a note secured by expected legacy.

these, I should think, Moses, with a few pair of point ruffles, as a collateral security; hey, my little fellow?

MOSES. Well, well.   [*bell rings*]

TRIP. Egad, I heard the bell! I believe, gentlemen, I can now introduce you. Don't forget the annuity, little Moses! This way, gentlemen. I'll insure my place, you know.

SIR OLIVER S. If the man be a shadow of the master, this is the temple of dissipation indeed. 10 [*exeunt*]

SCENE III.

CHARLES SURFACE, [SIR HARRY BUMPER,] CARELESS, &c., &c. [*discovered*] *at a table* 15 *with wine, &c.*

CHARLES S. 'Fore heaven, 'tis true! there's the great degeneracy of the age. Many of our acquaintance have taste, spirit, and politeness; 20 but, plague on't, they won't drink.

CARELESS. It is so indeed, Charles! they give in to all the substantial luxuries of the table, and abstain from nothing but wine and wit. Oh, certainly society suffers by it intolerably; 25 for now, instead of the social spirit of raillery that used to mantle over a glass of bright Burgundy, their conversation is become just like the Spa water they drink, which has all the pertness and flatulence of Champagne, 30 without the spirit or flavor.

1ST GENT. But what are they to do who love play better than wine?

CARELESS. True; there's Sir Harry diets himself for gaming, and is now under a hazard 35 regimen.

CHARLES S. Then he'll have the worst of it. What! you wouldn't train a horse for the course by keeping him from corn? For my part, egad, I am never so successful as when I am a little 40 merry; let me throw on a bottle of Champagne, and I never lose; at least, I never feel my losses, which is exactly the same thing.

2ND GENT. Ay, that I believe.

CHARLES S. And then, what man can pre- 45 tend to be a believer in love, who is an abjurer of wine? 'Tis the test by which the lover knows his own heart. Fill a dozen bumpers to a dozen beauties, and she that floats atop is the maid that has bewitched you.   50

CARELESS. Now then, Charles, be honest, and give us your real favorite.

CHARLES S. Why, I have withheld her only

in compassion to you. If I toast her, you must give a round of her peers, which is impossible —on earth.

CARELESS. Oh! then we'll find some canonized vestals or heathen goddesses that will do, I warrant!

CHARLES S. Here then, bumpers, you rogues! bumpers! Maria! Maria!

SIR HARRY B. Maria who?

CHARLES S. Oh, damn the surname; 'tis too formal to be registered in Love's calendar; but now, Sir Harry, beware, we must have beauty superlative.

CARELESS. Nay, never study, Sir Harry; we'll stand to the toast, though your mistress should want an eye, and you know you have a song will excuse you.

SIR HARRY B. Egad, so I have! and I'll give him the song instead of the lady.

SONG

Here's to the maiden of bashful fifteen;
    Here's to the widow of fifty;
Here's to the flaunting extravagant quean,
    And here's to the housewife that's thrifty.

Chorus.   Let the toast pass,
                 Drink to the lass,
I'll warrant she'll prove an excuse for the glass.

Here's to the charmer whose dimples we prize;
    Now to the maid who has none, sir;
Here's to the girl with a pair of blue eyes,
    And here's to the nymph with but *one*, sir.
Chorus.   Let the toast pass, &c.

Here's to the maid with a bosom of snow;
    Now to her that's as brown as a berry;
Here's to the wife with a face full of woe,
    And now to the girl that is merry.
Chorus.   Let the toast pass, &c.

For let 'em be clumsy, or let 'em be slim,
    Young or ancient, I care not a feather;
So fill a pint bumper quite up to the brim,
    And let us e'en toast them together.
Chorus.   Let the toast pass, &c.

ALL. Bravo! bravo!

Enter TRIP, *and whispers to* CHARLES
SURFACE

CHARLES S. Gentlemen, you must excuse me a little. Careless, take the chair, will you?

CARELESS. Nay, pr'ythee, Charles, what now? This is one of your peerless beauties, I suppose, has dropt in by chance?

CHARLES S. No, faith! To tell you the truth 'tis a Jew and a broker, who are come by appointment.

CARELESS. Oh, damn it! let's have the Jew in.

1ST GENT. Ay, and the broker too, by all means.

2ND GENT. Yes, yes, the Jew and the broker.

CHARLES S. Egad, with all my heart! Trip, bid the gentlemen walk in; though there's one of them a stranger, I can tell you.

CARELESS. Charles, let us give them some generous Burgundy, and perhaps they'll grow conscientious.

CHARLES S. Oh, hang 'em, no! wine does but draw forth a man's natural qualities, and to make them drink would only be to whet their knavery.

Enter TRIP, SIR OLIVER SURFACE, *and*
MOSES

CHARLES S. So, honest Moses, walk in; walk in, pray, Mr. Premium—that's the gentleman's name, isn't it, Moses?

MOSES. Yes, sir.

CHARLES S. Set chairs, Trip—sit down, Mr. Premium—glasses, Trip—sit down, Moses. Come, Mr. Premium, I'll give you a sentiment; here's *Success to usury!* Moses, fill the gentleman a bumper.

MOSES. *Success to usury!*

CARELESS. Right, Moses; usury is prudence and industry, and deserves to succeed.

SIR OLIVER S. Then, *here's all the success it deserves!*

CARELESS. No, no, that won't do! Mr. Premium, you have demurred at the toast, and must drink it in a pint bumper.

1ST GENT. A pint bumper, at least.

MOSES. Oh, pray, sir, consider; Mr. Premium's a gentleman.

CARELESS. And therefore loves good wine.

2ND GENT. Give Moses a quart glass; this is mutiny, and a high contempt for the chair.

CARELESS. Here, now for't! I'll see justice done, to the last drop of my bottle.

SIR OLIVER S. Nay, pray, gentlemen; I did not expect this usage.

CHARLES S. No, hang it, you sha'n't! Mr. Premium's a stranger.

SIR OLIVER S. [*aside*] Odd! I wish I was well out of their company.

CARELESS. Plague on 'em, then! if they don't drink, we'll not sit down with them. Come, Harry, the dice are in the next room. Charles, you'll join us when you have finished your business with the gentlemen!

CHARLES S. I will! I will! [*exeunt*] Careless!

CARELESS. [*returning*] Well!

CHARLES S. Perhaps I may want you.

CARELESS. Oh, you know I am always ready: word, note, or bond, 'tis all the same to me. [*exit*]

MOSES. Sir, this is Mr. Premium, a gentleman of the strictest honor and secrecy and always performs what he undertakes. Mr. Premium, this is—

CHARLES S. Pshaw! have done. Sir, my friend Moses is a very honest fellow, but a little slow at expression: he'll be an hour giving us our titles. Mr. Premium, the plain state of the matter is this: I am an extravagant young fellow who wants to borrow money; you I take to be a prudent old fellow, who have got money to lend. I am blockhead enough to give fifty per cent. sooner than not have it; and you, I presume, are rogue enough to take a hundred if you can get it. Now, sir, you see we are acquainted at once, and may proceed to business without further ceremony.

SIR OLIVER S. Exceeding frank, upon my word. I see, sir, you are not a man of many compliments.

CHARLES S. Oh, no, sir! plain dealing in business I always think best.

SIR OLIVER S. Sir, I like you the better for it; however, you are mistaken in one thing; I have no money to lend, but I believe I could procure some of a friend; but then he's an unconscionable dog, isn't he, Moses?

MOSES. But you can't help that.

SIR OLIVER S. And must sell stock to accommodate you—mustn't he, Moses?

MOSES. Yes, indeed! You know I always speak the truth, and scorn to tell a lie!

CHARLES S. Right. People that speak truth generally do: but these are trifles, Mr. Premium. What! I know money isn't to be bought without paying for't!

SIR OLIVER S. Well; but what security could you give? You have no land, I suppose?

CHARLES S. Not a molehill, nor a twig, but what's in the bough-pots out of the window!

SIR OLIVER S. Nor any stock, I presume?

CHARLES S. Nothing but live stock, and that's

only a few pointers and ponies. But pray, Mr. Premium, are you acquainted at all with any of my connections?

SIR OLIVER S. Why, to say truth, I am.

CHARLES S. Then you must know that I have a dev'lish rich uncle in the East Indies, Sir Oliver Surface, from whom I have the greatest expectations?

SIR OLIVER S. That you have a wealthy uncle I have heard; but how your expectations will turn out is more, I believe, than you can tell.

CHARLES S. Oh, no! there can be no doubt. They tell me I'm a prodigious favorite, and that he talks of leaving me everything.

SIR OLIVER S. Indeed! this is the first I've heard of it.

CHARLES S. Yes, yes, 'tis just so. Moses knows 'tis true; don't you, Moses?

MOSES. Oh, yes! I'll swear to't.

SIR OLIVER S. [aside] Egad, they'll persuade me presently I'm at Bengal.

CHARLES S. Now, I propose, Mr. Premium, if it's agreeable to you, a post-obit on Sir Oliver's life; though at the same time the old fellow has been so liberal to me that I give you my word I should be very sorry to hear that anything had happened to him.

SIR OLIVER S. Not more than I should, I assure you. But the bond you mention happens to be just the worst security you could offer me, for I might live to a hundred, and never see the principal.

CHARLES S. Oh, yes, you would; the moment Sir Oliver dies, you know, you would come on me for the money.

SIR OLIVER S. Then I believe I should be the most unwelcome dun you ever had in your life.

CHARLES S. What! I suppose you're afraid that Sir Oliver is too good a life?

SIR OLIVER S. No, indeed, I am not; though I have heard he is as hale and healthy as any man of his years in Christendom.

CHARLES S. There again now you are misinformed. No, no, the climate has hurt him considerably, poor uncle Oliver! Yes, yes, he breaks apace, I'm told, and is so much altered lately that his nearest relations don't know him.

SIR OLIVER S. No! ha! ha! ha! so much altered lately, that his nearest relations don't know him! ha! ha! ha! egad—ha! ha! ha!

CHARLES S. Ha! ha! you're glad to hear that, little Premium?

SIR OLIVER S. No, no, I'm not.

CHARLES S. Yes, yes, you are—ha! ha! ha! You know that mends your chance.

SIR OLIVER S. But I'm told Sir Oliver is coming over? Nay, some say he is actually arrived?

CHARLES S. Pshaw! Sure I must know better than you whether he's come or not. No, no; rely on't, he's at this moment at Calcutta. Isn't he, Moses?

MOSES. Oh, yes, certainly.

SIR OLIVER S. Very true, as you say, you must know better than I, though I have it from pretty good authority. Haven't I, Moses?

MOSES. Yes, most undoubted!

SIR OLIVER S. But, sir, as I understand you want a few hundreds immediately, is there nothing you could dispose of?

CHARLES S. How do you mean?

SIR OLIVER S. For instance, now, I have heard that your father left behind him a great quantity of massive old plate?

CHARLES S. O Lud! that's gone long ago. Moses can tell you how better than I can.

SIR OLIVER S. [aside] Good lack! all the family race-cups and corporation-bowls!—[aloud] Then it was also supposed that his library was one of the most valuable and compact—

CHARLES S. Yes, yes, so it was—vastly too much so for a private gentleman. For my part, I was always of a communicative disposition, so I thought it a shame to keep so much knowledge to myself.

SIR OLIVER S. [aside] Mercy upon me! Learning that had run in the family like an heirloom!—[aloud] Pray, what are become of the books?

CHARLES S. You must inquire of the auctioneer, Master Premium, for I don't believe even Moses can direct you.

MOSES. I know nothing of books.

SIR OLIVER S. So, so, nothing of the family property left, I suppose?

CHARLES S. Not much, indeed; unless you have a mind to the family pictures. I have got a room full of ancestors above, and if you have a taste for paintings, egad, you shall have 'em a bargain.

SIR OLIVER S. Hey! what the devil! sure, you wouldn't sell your forefathers, would you?

CHARLES S. Every man of them to the best bidder.

SIR OLIVER S. What! your great uncles and aunts?

CHARLES S. Ay, and my great grandfathers and grandmothers too.

SIR OLIVER S. [aside] Now I give him up.— [aloud] What the plague, have you no bowels for your own kindred? Odd's life, do you take me for Shylock in the play, that you would raise money of me on your own flesh and blood?

CHARLES S. Nay, my little broker, don't be angry: what need you care if you have your money's worth?

SIR OLIVER S. Well, I'll be the purchaser: I think I can dispose of the family canvas.— [aside] Oh, I'll never forgive him this! never!

Enter CARELESS

CARELESS. Come, Charles, what keeps you?

CHARLES S. I can't come yet: i'faith, we are going to have a sale above stairs; here's little Premium will buy all my ancestors.

CARELESS. Oh, burn your ancestors!

CHARLES S. No, he may do that afterwards, if he pleases. Stay, Careless, we want you; egad, you shall be auctioneer; so come along with us.

CARELESS. Oh, have with you, if that's the case. [I can] handle a hammer as well as a dice-box!

SIR OLIVER S. [aside] Oh, the profligates!

CHARLES S. Come, Moses, you shall be appraiser, if we want one. Gad's life, little Premium, you don't seem to like the business?

SIR OLIVER S. Oh, yes, I do, vastly. Ha! ha! ha! yes, yes, I think it a rare joke to sell one's family by auction—ha! ha!—[aside] Oh, the prodigal!

CHARLES S. To be sure! when a man wants money, where the plague should he get assistance if he can't make free with his own relations? [exeunt]

ACT IV

Scene I.

Picture room at CHARLES'S

Enter CHARLES SURFACE, SIR OLIVER SURFACE, MOSES, *and* CARELESS

CHARLES S. Walk in, gentlemen; pray walk in. Here they are, the family of the Surfaces, up to the Conquest.

SIR OLIVER S. And, in my opinion, a goodly collection.

CHARLES S. Ay, ay; these are done in the true spirit of portrait painting; no *volontièr* [e] *grace*[33] and expression. Not like the works of your modern Raphaels, who give you the strongest resemblance, yet contrive to make your portrait independent of you; so that you may sink the original and not hurt the picture. No, no; the merit of these is the inveterate likeness—all stiff and awkward as the originals, and like nothing in human nature besides.

SIR OLIVER S. Ah! we shall never see such figures of men again.

CHARLES S. I hope not. Well, you see, Master Premium, what a domestic character I am. Here I sit of an evening surrounded by my family. But come, get to your pulpit, Mr. Auctioneer; here's an old gouty chair of my grandfather's will answer the purpose.

CARELESS. Ay, ay, this will do. But, Charles, I hav'n't a hammer; and what's an auctioneer without his hammer?

CHARLES S. Egad, that's true. What parchment have we here? Oh, our genealogy in full. Here, Careless, you shall have no common bit of mahogany; here's the family tree, for you, you rogue; this shall be your hammer, and now you may knock down my ancestors with their own pedigree.

SIR OLIVER S. [aside] What an unnatural rogue! an *ex post facto*[34] parricide!

CARELESS. Yes, yes, here's a bit of your generation indeed; faith, Charles, this is the most convenient thing you could have found for the business, for 'twill serve not only as a hammer, but a catalogue into the bargain. Come, begin,—A-going, a-going, a-going!

CHARLES S. Bravo, Careless! Well, here's my great uncle, Sir Richard Raveline, a marvellous good general in his day, I assure you. He served in all the Duke of Marlborough's wars, and got that cut over his eye at the battle of Malplaquet. What say you, Mr. Premium? look at him; there's a hero, not cut out of his feathers, as your modern clipp'd captains are, but enveloped in wig and regimentals, as a general should be. What do you bid?

MOSES. Mr. Premium would have *you* speak.

CHARLES S. Why, then, he shall have him for ten pounds, and I'm sure that's not dear for a staff-officer.

[33] freely tossed-off slickness.
[34] retroactive.

SIR OLIVER S. [*aside*] Heaven deliver me! his famous uncle Richard for ten pounds!—[*aloud*] Well, sir, I take him at that.

CHARLES S. Careless, knock down my uncle Richard. Here, now, is a maiden sister of his, my great aunt Deborah, done by Kneller,[35] thought to be in his best manner, and a very formidable likeness. There she is, you see, a shepherdess feeding her flock. You shall have her for five pounds ten; the sheep are worth the money.

SIR OLIVER S. [*aside*] Ah! poor Deborah; a woman who set such a value on herself!—[*aloud*] Five pounds ten; she's mine.

CHARLES S. Knock down my aunt Deborah! Here, now, are two that were a sort of cousins of theirs. You see, Moses, these pictures were done sometime ago, when beaux wore wigs, and the ladies their own hair.

SIR OLIVER S. Yes, truly, headdresses appear to have been a little lower in those days.

CHARLES S. Well, take that couple for the same.

MOSES. 'Tis a good bargain.

CHARLES S. Careless! This, now, is a grandfather of my mother, a learned judge, well known on the Western Circuit. What do you rate him at, Moses?

MOSES. Four guineas.

CHARLES S. Four guineas! Gad's life, you don't bid me the price of his wig. Mr. Premium, you have more respect for the woolsack;[36] do let us knock his lordship down at fifteen.

SIR OLIVER S. By all means.

CARELESS. Gone!

CHARLES S. And there are two brothers of his, William and Walter Blunt, Esquires, both members of Parliament, and noted speakers, and what's very extraordinary, I believe, this is the first time they were ever bought or sold.

SIR OLIVER S. That is very extraordinary, indeed! I'll take them at your own price, for the honor of Parliament.

CARELESS. Well said, little Premium! I'll knock them down at forty.

CHARLES S. Here's a jolly fellow; I don't know what relation, but he was mayor of Man-chester. Take him at eight pounds.

SIR OLIVER S. No, no; six will do for the mayor.

CHARLES S. Come, make it guineas, and I'll throw you the two aldermen there into the bargain.

SIR OLIVER S. They're mine.

CHARLES S. Careless, knock down the mayor and aldermen. But, plague on't, we shall be all day retailing in this manner. Do let us deal wholesale; what say you, little Premium? Give us three hundred pounds for the rest of the family in the lump.

CARELESS. Ay, ay, that will be the best way.

SIR OLIVER S. Well, well, anything to accommodate you—they are mine. But there is one portrait which you have always passed over.

CARELESS. What, that ill-looking little fellow over the settee?

SIR OLIVER S. Yes, sir, I mean that; though I don't think him so ill-looking a little fellow, by any means.

CHARLES S. What, that? Oh! that's my uncle Oliver; 'twas done before he went to India.

CARELESS. Your uncle Oliver! Gad, then, you'll never be friends, Charles. That, now, to me, is as stern a looking rogue as ever I saw—an unforgiving eye, and a damned disinheriting countenance! an inveterate knave, depend on't. Don't you think so, little Premium?

SIR OLIVER S. Upon my soul, sir, I do not. I think it is as honest a looking face as any in the room, dead or alive. But I suppose uncle Oliver goes with the rest of the lumber?

CHARLES S. No, hang it! I'll not part with poor Noll. The old fellow has been very good to me, and, egad, I'll keep his picture while I've a room to put it in.

SIR OLIVER S. [*aside*] The rogue's my nephew after all!—[*aloud*] But, sir, I have somehow taken a fancy to that picture.

CHARLES S. I'm sorry for't, for you certainly will not have it. Oons, haven't you got enough of them?

SIR OLIVER S. [*aside*] I forgive him everything!—[*aloud*] But, sir, when I take a whim in my head I don't value money. I'll give you as much for that as for all the rest.

CHARLES S. Don't tease me, master broker. I tell you I'll not part with it, and there's an end of it.

SIR OLIVER S. [*aside*] How like his father the

---

[35] Sir Godfrey Kneller (1646–1723).
[36] literally, the cushion used by the Lord Chancellor in the House of Lords; actually, the meaning here is respect for the law.

dog is!—[*aloud*] Well, well, I have done.— [*aside*] I did not perceive it before, but I think I never saw such a striking resemblance.—Here is a draft for your sum.

CHARLES S. Why, 'tis for eight hundred pounds.

SIR OLIVER S. You will not let Sir Oliver go?

CHARLES S. Zounds! no! I tell you once more.

SIR OLIVER S. Then never mind the difference, we'll balance that another time. But give me your hand on the bargain; you are an honest fellow, Charles. I beg pardon, sir, for being so free. Come, Moses.

CHARLES S. Egad, this is a whimsical old fellow! But hark'ee, Premium, you'll prepare lodgings for these gentlemen?

SIR OLIVER S. Yes, yes, I'll send for them in a day or two.

CHARLES S. But, hold; do now send a genteel conveyance for them, for, I assure you, they were most of them used to ride in their own carriages.

SIR OLIVER S. I will, I will; for all but Oliver.

CHARLES S. Ay, all but the little nabob.

SIR OLIVER S. You're fixed on that?

CHARLES S. Peremptorily.

SIR OLIVER S. [*aside*] A dear extravagant rogue!—[*aloud*] Good day! Come, Moses. Let me hear now who calls him profligate! [*exeunt* SIR OLIVER SURFACE *and* MOSES]

CARELESS. Why, this is the oddest genius of the sort I ever saw!

CHARLES S. Egad! he's the prince of brokers, I think. I wonder how Moses got acquainted with so honest a fellow. Ha! here's Rowley; do, Careless, say I'll join the company in a few moments.

CARELESS. I will; but don't let that old blockhead persuade you to squander any of that money on old musty debts, or any such nonsense; for tradesmen, Charles, are the most exorbitant fellows.

CHARLES S. Very true, and paying them is only encouraging them.

CARELESS. Nothing else.

CHARLES S. Ay, ay, never fear. [*exit* CARELESS] So! this was an odd old fellow, indeed. Let me see; two-thirds of this is mine by right, five hundred and thirty odd pounds. 'Fore heaven! I find one's ancestors are more valuable relations than I took them for! Ladies and gentlemen, your most obedient and very grateful servant.

Enter ROWLEY

Ha! old Rowley; egad, you are just come in time to take leave of your old acquaintance.

ROWLEY. Yes, I heard they were a-going. But I wonder you can have such spirits under so many distresses.

CHARLES S. Why, there's the point! my distresses are so many, that I can't afford to part with my spirits; but I shall be rich and splenetic, all in good time. However, I suppose you are surprised that I am not more sorrowful at parting with so many near relations; to be sure 'tis very affecting; but you see they never move a muscle, so why should I?

ROWLEY. There's no making you serious a moment.

CHARLES S. Yes, faith, I am so now. Here, my honest Rowley, here, get me this changed directly, and take a hundred pounds of it immediately to old Stanley.

ROWLEY. A hundred pounds! Consider only—

CHARLES S. Gad's life, don't talk about it; poor Stanley's wants are pressing, and if you don't make haste, we shall have some one call that has a better right to the money.

ROWLEY. Ah! there's the point! I never will cease dunning you with the old proverb—

CHARLES S. "Be just before you're generous." Why, so I would if I could; but Justice is an old, lame, hobbling beldame, and I can't get her to keep pace with Generosity for the soul of me.

ROWLEY. Yet, Charles, believe me, one hour's reflection—

CHARLES S. Ay, ay, it's all very true; but, hark'ee, Rowley, while I have, by heaven, I'll give; so damn your economy, and now for hazard. [*exeunt*]

SCENE II.

The parlor

Enter SIR OLIVER SURFACE *and* MOSES

MOSES. Well, sir, I think, as Sir Peter said, you have seen Mr. Charles in high glory; 'tis great pity he's so extravagant.

SIR OLIVER S. True, but he would not sell my picture.

MOSES. And loves wine and women so much.

SIR OLIVER S. But he would not sell my picture.

MOSES. And games so deep.

SIR OLIVER S. But he would not sell my picture. Oh, here's Rowley.

Enter ROWLEY

ROWLEY. So, Sir Oliver, I find you have made a purchase—

SIR OLIVER S. Yes, yes; our young rake has parted with his ancestors like old tapestry.

ROWLEY. And here has he commissioned me to re-deliver you part of the purchase money. I mean, though, in your necessitous character of old Stanley.

MOSES. Ah! there is the pity of it all; he is so damned charitable.

ROWLEY. And I left a hosier and two tailors in the hall, who, I'm sure, won't be paid, and this hundred would satisfy them.

SIR OLIVER S. Well, well, I'll pay his debts, and his benevolence too. But now I am no more a broker, and you shall introduce me to the elder brother as old Stanley.

ROWLEY. Not yet a while; Sir Peter, I know, means to call there about this time.

Enter TRIP

TRIP. Oh, gentlemen, I beg pardon for not showing you out; this way. Moses, a word. [*exeunt* TRIP *and* MOSES]

SIR OLIVER S. There's a fellow for you! Would you believe it, that puppy intercepted the Jew on our coming, and wanted to raise money before he got to his master.

ROWLEY. Indeed!

SIR OLIVER S. Yes, they are now planning an annuity business. Ah! Master Rowley, in my days servants were content with the follies of their masters, when they were worn a little threadbare; but now, they have their vices, like their birthday clothes, with the gloss on. [*exeunt*]

SCENE III.

A library

[*Discovered*] JOSEPH SURFACE *and a* SERVANT

JOSEPH S. No letter from Lady Teazle?

SERV. No, sir.

JOSEPH S. I am surprised she has not sent,

if she is prevented from coming. Sir Peter certainly does not suspect me. Yet, I wish I may not lose the heiress, through the scrape I have drawn myself into with the wife; however, Charles's imprudence and bad character are great points in my favor. [*knocking heard without*]

SERV. Sir, I believe that must be Lady Teazle.

JOSEPH S. Hold! see whether it is or not before you go to the door: I have a particular message for you, if it should be my brother.

SERV. 'Tis her ladyship, sir; she always leaves her chair at the milliner's in the next street.

JOSEPH S. Stay, stay; draw that screen before the window—that will do; my opposite neighbor is a maiden lady of so anxious a temper. [SERVANT *draws the screen, and exit*] I have a difficult hand to play in this affair. Lady Teazle has lately suspected my views on Maria; but she must by no means be let into that secret—at least, till I have her more in my power.

Enter LADY TEAZLE

LADY T. What, sentiment in soliloquy now? Have you been very impatient? O Lud! don't pretend to look grave. I vow I couldn't come before.

JOSEPH S. Oh, madam, punctuality is a species of constancy, a very unfashionable quality in a lady.

LADY T. Upon my word you ought to pity me. Do you know, Sir Peter is grown so ill-natured to me of late, and so jealous of Charles too; that's the best of the story, isn't it?

JOSEPH S. [*aside*] I am glad my scandalous friends keep that up.

LADY T. I am sure I wish he would let Maria marry him, and then perhaps he would be convinced. Don't you, Mr. Surface?

JOSEPH S. [*aside*] Indeed I do not.—Oh, certainly I do! for then my dear Lady Teazle would also be convinced how wrong her suspicions were of my having any design on the silly girl.

LADY T. Well, well, I'm inclined to believe you. But isn't it provoking, to have the most ill-natured things said of one? And there's my friend, Lady Sneerwell, has circulated I don't know how many scandalous tales of me, and all without any foundation too; that's what vexes me.

JOSEPH S. Ay, madam, to be sure, that is the provoking circumstance—without foundation. Yes, yes, there's the mortification, indeed; for when a scandalous story is believed against one, there certainly is no comfort like the consciousness of having deserved it.

LADY T. No, to be sure, then I'd forgive their malice; but to attack me, who am really so innocent, and who never say an ill-natured thing of anybody—that is, of any friend; and then Sir Peter too, to have him so peevish, and so suspicious, when I know the integrity of my own heart! indeed 'tis monstrous!

JOSEPH S. But, my dear Lady Teazle, 'tis your own fault if you suffer it. When a husband entertains a groundless suspicion of his wife, and withdraws his confidence from her, the original compact is broken, and she owes it to the honor of her sex to outwit him.

LADY T. Indeed! so that if he suspects me without cause, it follows, that the best way of curing his jealousy is to give him reason for't.

JOSEPH S. Undoubtedly; for your husband should never be deceived in you; and in that case it becomes you to be frail in compliment to his discernment.

LADY T. To be sure, what you say is very reasonable, and when the consciousness of my innocence—

JOSEPH S. Ah! my dear madam, there is the great mistake: 'tis this very conscious innocence that is of the greatest prejudice to you. What is it makes you negligent of forms and careless of the world's opinion? Why, the consciousness of your own innocence. What makes you thoughtless in your own conduct, and apt to run into a thousand little imprudences? Why, the consciousness of your own innocence. What makes you impatient of Sir Peter's temper, and outrageous of his suspicions? Why, the consciousness of your innocence.

LADY T. 'Tis very true!

JOSEPH S. Now, my dear Lady Teazle, if you would but once make a trifling *faux pas,* you can't conceive how cautious you would grow, and how ready to humor and agree with your husband.

LADY T. Do you think so?

JOSEPH S. Oh! I'm sure on't; and then you would find all scandal would cease at once;

for, in short, your character at present is like a person in a plethora, absolutely dying from too much health.

LADY T. So, so; then I perceive your prescription is, that I must sin in my own defence, and part with my virtue to secure my reputation?

JOSEPH S. Exactly so, upon my credit, ma'am.

LADY T. Well, certainly this is the oddest doctrine and the newest receipt for avoiding calumny!

JOSEPH S. An infallible one, believe me. Prudence, like experience, must be paid for.

LADY T. Why, if my understanding were once convinced—

JOSEPH S. Oh, certainly, madam, your understanding should be convinced. Yes, yes; heaven forbid I should persuade you to do anything you thought wrong. No, no, I have too much honor to desire it.

LADY T. Don't you think we may as well leave *honor* out of the question?

JOSEPH S. Ah! the ill effects of your country education, I see, still remain with you.

LADY T. I doubt they do indeed; and I will fairly own to you, that if I could be persuaded to do wrong, it would be by Sir Peter's ill usage sooner than your *honorable logic,* after all.

JOSEPH S. Then, by this hand, which he is unworthy of—[*taking her hand*]

Enter SERVANT

'Sdeath, you blockhead! What do you want?

SERV. I beg your pardon, sir, but I thought you would not choose Sir Peter to come up without announcing him.

JOSEEPH S. Sir Peter! Oons—the devil!

LADY T. Sir Peter! O Lud, I'm ruined! I'm ruined!

SERV. Sir, 'twasn't I let him in.

LADY T. Oh, I'm quite undone! What will become of me? Now, Mr. Logic. Oh! he's on the stairs. I'll get behind here; and if ever I'm so imprudent again—[*Goes behind the screen*]

JOSEPH S. Give me that book. [*sits down.* SERVANT *pretends to adjust his hair*]

Enter SIR PETER

SIR PETER T. Ay, ever improving himself. Mr. Surface! Mr. Surface!

JOSEPH S. Oh! my dear Sir Peter, I beg your pardon. [*gaping, throws away the book*] I have been dozing over a stupid book. Well, I am much obliged to you for this call. You haven't been here, I believe, since I fitted up this room. Books, you know, are the only things in which I am a coxcomb.

SIR PETER T. 'Tis very neat indeed. Well, well, that's proper; and you can make even your screen a source of knowledge; hung, I perceive, with maps.

JOSEPH S. Oh, yes, I find great use in that screen.

SIR PETER T. I dare say, you must, certainly, when you want to find anything in a hurry.

JOSEPH S. [*aside*] Ay, or to hide anything in a hurry, either.

SIR PETER T. Well, I have a little private business—

JOSEPH S. [*to the* SERVANT] You need not stay.

SERV. No, sir. [*exit*]

JOSEPH S. Here's a chair, Sir Peter, I beg—

SIR PETER T. Well, now we are alone, there is a subject, my dear friend, on which I wish to unburden my mind to you—a point of the greatest moment to my peace; in short, my dear friend, Lady Teazle's conduct of late has made me extremely unhappy.

JOSEPH S. Indeed! I am very sorry to hear it.

SIR PETER T. Ay, 'tis too plain she has not the least regard for me; but, what's worse, I have pretty good authority to suppose she has formed an attachment to another.

JOSEPH S. Indeed! you astonish me!

SIR PETER T. Yes; and, between ourselves, I think I've discovered the person.

JOSEPH S. How! you alarm me exceedingly.

SIR PETER T. Ay, my dear friend, I knew you would sympathize with me!

JOSEPH S. Yes, believe me, Sir Peter, such a discovery would hurt me just as much as it would you.

SIR PETER T. I am convienced of it. Ah! it is a happiness to have a friend whom we can trust even with one's family secrets. But have you no guess who I mean?

JOSEPH S. I haven't the most distant idea. It can't be Sir Benjamin Backbite!

SIR PETER T. Oh, no! What say you to Charles?

JOSEPH S. My brother! impossible!

SIR PETER T. Oh! my dear friend, the goodness of your own heart misleads you. You judge of others by yourself.

JOSEPH S. Certainly, Sir Peter, the heart that is conscious of its own integrity is ever slow to credit another's treachery.

SIR PETER T. True; but your brother has no sentiment; you never hear him talk so.

JOSEPH S. Yet I can't but think Lady Teazle herself has too much principle.

SIR PETER T. Ay; but what is principle against the flattery of a handsome, lively young fellow?

JOSEPH S. That's very true.

SIR PETER T. And then, you know, the difference of our ages makes it very improbable that she should have any very great affection for me; and if she were to be frail, and I were to make it public, why the town would only laugh at me, the foolish old bachelor, who had married a girl.

JOSEPH S. That's true, to be sure; they would laugh.

SIR PETER T. Laugh—ay, and make ballads, and paragraphs, and the devil knows what of me.

JOSEPH S. No; you must never make it public.

SIR PETER T. But then again—that the nephew of my old friend, Sir Oliver, should be the person to attempt such a wrong, hurts me more nearly.

JOSEPH S. Ay, there's the point. When ingratitude barbs the dart of injury, the wound has double danger in it.

SIR PETER T. Ay, I, that was, in a manner, left his guardian; in whose house he had been so often entertained; who never in my life denied him—my advice.

JOSEPH S. Oh, 'tis not to be credited. There may be a man capable of such baseness, to be sure; but, for my part, till you can give me positive proofs, I cannot but doubt it. However, if it should be proved on him, he is no longer a brother of mine. I disclaim kindred with him; for the man who can break the laws of hospitality, and tempt the wife of his friend, deserves to be branded as the pest of society.

SIR PETER T. What a difference there is between you! What noble sentiments!

JOSEPH S. Yet, I cannot suspect Lady Teazle's honor.

SIR PETER T. I am sure I wish to think well of her, and to remove all ground of quarrel between us. She has lately reproached me more than once with having made no settlement on her; and, in our last quarrel, she almost hinted that she should not break her heart if I was dead. Now, as we seem to differ in our ideas of expense, I have resolved she shall have her own way, and be her own mistress in that respect for the future; and if I were to die, she will find I have not been inattentive to her interest while living. Here, my friend, are the drafts of the two deeds, which I wish to have your opinion on. By one, she will enjoy eight hundred a year independent while I live; and, by the other, the bulk of my fortune at my death.

JOSEPH S. This conduct, Sir Peter, is indeed truly generous.—[*aside*] I wish it may not corrupt my pupil.

SIR PETER T. Yes, I am determined she shall have no cause to complain, though I would not have her acquainted with the latter instance of my affection yet awhile.

JOSEPH S. [*aside*] Nor I, if I could help it.

SIR PETER T. And now, my dear friend, if you please, we will talk over the situation of your affairs with Maria.

JOSEPH S. [*softly*] Oh, no, Sir Peter; another time, if you please.

SIR PETER T. I am sensibly chagrined at the little progress you seem to make in her affections.

JOSEPH S. [*softly*] I beg you will not mention it. What are my disappointments when your happiness is in debate!—[*aside*] 'Sdeath, I shall be ruined every way.

SIR PETER T. And though you are so averse to my acquainting Lady Teazle with your passion for Maria, I'm sure she's not your enemy in the affair.

JOSEPH S. Pray, Sir Peter, now, oblige me. I am really too much affected by the subject we have been speaking of to bestow a thought on my own concerns. The man who is intrusted with his friend's distresses can never——

Enter SERVANT

Well, sir?

SERV. Your brother, sir, is speaking to a gentleman in the street, and says he knows you are within.

JOSEPH S. 'Sdeath, blockhead, I'm not within; I'm out for the day.

SIR PETER T. Stay—hold—a thought has struck me: you shall be at home.

JOSEPH S. Well, well, let him up. [*exit* SERVANT]

[*Aside*] He'll interrupt Sir Peter, however.

SIR PETER T. Now, my good friend, oblige me, I entreat you. Before Charles comes, let me conceal myself somewhere; then do you tax him on the point we have been talking, and his answer may satisfy me at once.

JOSEPH S. O fie, Sir Peter! would you have me join in so mean a trick?—to trepan my brother, too?

SIR PETER T. Nay, you tell me you are sure he is innocent; if so, you do him the greatest service by giving him an opportunity to clear himself, and you will set my heart at rest. Come, you shall not refuse me; here, behind this screen will be—Hey! what the devil! there seems to be one listener there already. I'll swear I saw a petticoat!

JOSEPH S. Ha! ha! ha! Well, this is ridiculous enough. I'll tell you, Sir Peter, though I hold a man of intrigue to be a most despicable character, yet, you know it does not follow that one is to be an absolute Joseph[37] either! Hark'ee, 'tis a little French milliner—a silly rogue that plagues me—and having some character to lose, on your coming, sir, she ran behind the screen.

SIR PETER T. Ah! you rogue! But egad, she has overheard all I have been saying of my wife.

JOSEPH S. Oh, 'twill never go any farther, you may depend upon it.

SIR PETER T. No; then, faith, let her hear it out. Here's a closet will do as well.

JOSEPH S. Well, go in there.

SIR PETER T. Sly rogue! sly rogue! [*going into the closet*]

JOSEPH S. A narrow escape, indeed! and a curious situation I'm in, to part man and wife in this manner.

LADY T. [*peeping*] Couldn't I steal off?

JOSEPH S. Keep close, my angel!

SIR PETER T. [*peeping*] Joseph, tax him home.

JOSEPH S. Back, my dear friend!

---

[37] that is, virtuous like the Biblical Joseph.

LADY T. [*peeping*] Couldn't you lock Sir Peter in?

JOSEPH S. Be still, my life!

SIR PETER T. [*peeping*] You're sure the little milliner won't blab?

JOSEPH S. In, in, my good Sir Peter. [*aside*] 'Fore Gad, I wish I had a key to the door.

Enter CHARLES SURFACE

CHARLES S. Holloa! brother, what has been the matter? Your fellow would not let me up at first. What! have you had a Jew or a wench with you?

JOSEPH S. Neither, brother, I assure you.

CHARLES S. But what has made Sir Peter steal off? I thought he had been with you.

JOSEPH S. He *was,* brother; but hearing you were coming, he did not choose to stay.

CHARLES S. What! was the old gentleman afraid I wanted to borrow money of him?

JOSEPH S. No, sir; but I am sorry to find, Charles, you have lately given that worthy man grounds for great uneasiness.

CHARLES S. Yes, they tell me I do that to a great many worthy men. But how so, pray?

JOSEPH S. To be plain with you, brother, he thinks you are endeavoring to gain Lady Teazle's affections from him.

CHARLES S. Who, I? O Lud! not I, upon my word. Ha! ha! ha! ha! so the old fellow has found out that he has got a young wife, has he? Or, what is worse, Lady Teazle has found out she has an old husband?

JOSEPH S. This is no subject to jest on, brother. He who can laugh——

CHARLES S. True, true, as you were going to say—then, seriously, I never had the least idea of what you charge me with, upon my honor.

JOSEPH S. [*raising his voice*] Well, it will give Sir Peter great satisfaction to hear this.

CHARLES S. To be sure, I once thought the lady seemed to have taken a fancy to me; but, upon my soul, I never gave her the least encouragement; besides, you know my attachment to Maria.

JOSEPH S. But sure, brother, even if Lady Teazle had betrayed the fondest partiality for you——

CHARLES S. Why, look'ee, Joseph, I hope I shall never deliberately do a dishonorable action; but if a pretty woman was purposely to throw herself in my way; and that pretty woman married to a man old enough to be her father——

JOSEPH S. Well——

CHARLES S. Why, I believe I should be obliged to borrow a little of your morality, that's all. But, brother, do you know now that you surprise me exceedingly, by naming *me* with Lady Teazle? for, 'faith, I always understood you were her favorite.

JOSEPH S. Oh, for shame, Charles! This retort is foolish.

CHARLES S. Nay, I swear I have seen you exchange such significant glances——

JOSEPH S. Nay, nay, sir, this is no jest.

CHARLES S. Egad, I'm serious. Don't you remember one day when I called here——

JOSEPH S. Nay, prithee, Charles——

CHARLES S. And found you together——

JOSEPH S. Zounds, sir! I insist——

CHARLES S. And another time when your servant——

JOSEPH S. Brother, brother, a word with you!——[*aside*] Gad, I must stop him.

CHARLES S. Informed, I say, that——

JOSEPH S. Hush! I beg your pardon, but Sir Peter has overheard all we have been saying. I knew you would clear yourself, or I should not have consented.

CHARLES S. How, Sir Peter! Where is he?

JOSEPH S. Softly; there! [*points to the closet*]

CHARLES S. Oh, 'fore heaven, I'll have him out. Sir Peter, come forth!

JOSEPH S. No, no——

CHARLES S. I say, Sir Peter, come into court. [*pulls in* SIR PETER] What! my old guardian! What! turn inquisitor, and take evidence incog?

SIR PETER T. Give me your hand, Charles. I believe I have suspected you wrongfully; but you mustn't be angry with Joseph; 'twas my plan!

CHARLES S. Indeed!

SIR PETER T. But I acquit you. I promise you I don't think near so ill of you as I did. What I have heard has given me great satisfaction.

CHARLES S. Egad, then, 'twas lucky you didn't hear any more; [*apart to* JOSEPH] wasn't it, Joseph?

SIR PETER T. Ah! you would have retorted on him.

CHARLES S. Ay, ay, that was a joke.

SIR PETER T. Yes, yes, I know his honor too well.

CHARLES S. But you might as well have suspected *him* as *me* in this matter, for all that; [*apart to* JOSEPH] mightn't he, Joseph?

SIR PETER T. Well, well, I believe you.

JOSEPH S. [*aside*] Would they were both well out of the room!

Enter SERVANT, *and whispers to* JOSEPH
SURFACE

SIR PETER T. And in future perhaps we may not be such strangers.

JOSEPH S. Gentlemen, I beg pardon, I must wait on you downstairs; here is a person come on particular business.

CHARLES S. Well, you can see him in another room. Sir Peter and I have not met a long time, and I have something to say to him.

JOSEPH S. [*aside*] They must not be left together.—I'll send this man away, and return directly. [*apart to* SIR PETER] Sir Peter, not a word of the French milliner.

SIR PETER T. [*apart to* JOSEPH] I! not for the world—[*exit* JOSEPH] Ah! Charles, if you associated more with your brother, one might indeed hope for your reformation. He is a man of sentiment. Well, there is nothing in the world so noble as a man of sentiment.

CHARLES S. Pshaw! he is too moral by half, and so apprehensive of his good name, as he calls it, that I suppose he would as soon let a priest into his house as a girl.

SIR PETER T. No, no; come, come; you wrong him. No, no! Joseph is no rake, but he is no such saint either in that respect.—[*aside*] I have a great mind to tell him; we should have a laugh at Joseph.

CHARLES S. Oh, hang him! He's a very anchorite, a young hermit.

SIR PETER T. Hark'ee; you must not abuse him; he may chance to hear of it again, I promise you.

CHARLES S. Why, you won't tell him?

SIR PETER T. No—but—this way. [*aside*] Egad, I'll tell him.—[*aloud*] Hark'ee; have you a mind to have a good laugh at Joseph?

CHARLES S. I should like it of all things.

SIR PETER T. Then, i'faith, we will; I'll be quit with him for discovering me. He had a girl with him when I called.

CHARLES S. What! Joseph? you jest.

SIR PETER T. Hush! a little French milliner, and the best of the jest is, she's in the room now.

CHARLES S. The devil she is!

SIR PETER T. Hush! I tell you! [*points*]

CHARLES S. Behind the screen! 'Slife, let's unveil her!

SIR PETER T. No, no—he's coming—you sha'n't, indeed!

CHARLES S. Oh, egad, we'll have a peep at the little milliner!

SIR PETER T. Not for the world; Joseph will never forgive me——

CHARLES S. I'll stand by you——

SIR PETER T. Odds, here he is.

JOSEPH SURFACE *enters just as* CHARLES
SURFACE *throws down the screen*

CHARLES S. Lady Teazle, by all that's wonderful!

SIR PETER T. Lady Teazle, by all that's damnable!

CHARLES S. Sir Peter, this is one of the smartest French milliners I ever saw. Egad, you seem all to have been diverting yourselves here at hide and seek, and I don't see who is out of the secret. Shall I beg your ladyship to inform me? Not a word! Brother, will you be pleased to explain this matter? What! is Morality dumb too? Sir Peter, though I found you in the dark, perhaps you are not so now! All mute! Well, though I can make nothing of the affair, I suppose you perfectly understand one another, so I'll leave you to yourselves. [*going*] Brother, I'm sorry to find you have given that worthy man cause for so much uneasiness. Sir Peter! there's nothing in the world so noble as a man of sentiment! [*exit* CHARLES] [*they stand for some time looking at each other*]

JOSEPH S. Sir Peter—notwithstanding—I confess—that appearances are against me—if you will afford me your patience—I make no doubt—but I shall explain everything to your satisfaction.

SIR PETER T. If you please, sir.

JOSEPH S. The fact is, sir, that Lady Teazle, knowing my pretensions to your ward Maria— I say, sir, Lady Teazle, being apprehensive of the jealousy of your temper—and knowing my friendship to the family—She, sir, I say— called here—in order that—I might explain these pretensions—but on your coming—being apprehensive—as I said—of your jealousy—she withdrew—and this, you may depend on it, is the whole truth of the matter.

SIR PETER T. A very clear account, upon my word; and I dare swear the lady will vouch for every article of it.

LADY T. For not one word of it, Sir Peter!

SIR PETER T. How! don't you think it worth while to agree in the lie?

LADY T. There is not one syllable of truth in what that gentleman has told you.

SIR PETER T. I believe you, upon my soul, ma'am!

JOSEPH S. [aside to LADY TEAZLE] 'Sdeath, madam, will you betray me?

LADY T. Good Mr. Hypocrite, by your leave, I'll speak for myself.

SIR PETER T. Ay, let her alone, sir; you'll find she'll make out a better story than you, without prompting.

LADY T. Hear me, Sir Peter! I came hither on no matter relating to your ward, and even ignorant of this gentleman's pretensions to her. But I came seduced by his insidious arguments, at least to listen to his pretended passion, if not to sacrifice your honor to his baseness.

SIR PETER T. Now, I believe, the truth is coming indeed!

JOSEPH S. The woman's mad!

LADY T. No, sir, she has recovered her senses, and your own arts have furnished her with the means. Sir Peter, I do not expect you to credit me, but the tenderness you expressed for me, when I am sure you could not think I was a witness to it, has penetrated so to my heart, that had I left the place without the shame of this discovery, my future life should have spoken the sincerity of my gratitude. As for that smooth-tongued hypocrite, who would have seduced the wife of his too credulous friend, while he affected honorable addresses to his ward, I behold him now in a light so truly despicable that I shall never again respect myself for having listened to him. [exit LADY TEAZLE]

JOSEPH S. Notwithstanding all this, Sir Peter, Heaven knows——

SIR PETER T. That you are a villain! and so I leave you to your conscience.

JOSEPH S. You are too rash, Sir Peter; you shall hear me. The man who shuts out convic-tion by refusing to——[exeunt SIR PETER and SURFACE talking]

ACT V

SCENE I.

The library [in JOSEPH SURFACE's house]

Enter JOSEPH SURFACE *and* SERVANT

JOSEPH S. Mr. Stanley? and why should you think I would see him? you must know he comes to ask something.

SERV. Sir, I should not have let him in, but that Mr. Rowley came to the door with him.

JOSEPH S. Pshaw! blockhead! to suppose that I should now be in a temper to receive visits from poor relations! Well, why don't you show the fellow up?

SERV. I will, sir. Why, sir, it was not my fault that Sir Peter discovered my lady——

JOSEPH S. Go, fool! [exit SERVANT] Sure Fortune never played a man of my policy such a trick before. My character with Sir Peter, my hopes with Maria, destroyed in a moment! I'm in a rare humor to listen to other people's distresses! I sha'n't be able to bestow even a benevolent sentiment on Stanley. So! here he comes, and Rowley with him. I must try to recover myself, and put a little charity into my face, however. [exit]

Enter SIR OLIVER SURFACE *and* ROWLEY

SIR OLIVER S. What! does he avoid us? That was he, was it not?

ROWLEY. It was, sir. But I doubt you are come a little too abruptly. His nerves are so weak that the sight of a poor relation may be too much for him. I should have gone first to break it to him.

SIR OLIVER S. Oh, plague of his nerves! Yet this is he whom Sir Peter extols as a man of the most benevolent way of thinking!

ROWLEY. As to his way of thinking, I cannot pretend to decide; for, to do him justice, he appears to have as much speculative benevolence as any private gentleman in the kingdom, though he is seldom so sensual as to indulge himself in the exercise of it.

SIR OLIVER S. Yet he has a string of charitable sentiments at his fingers' ends.

ROWLEY. Or rather at his tongue's end, Sir Oliver; for I believe there is no sentiment he has such faith in as that "Charity begins at home."

SIR OLIVER S. And his, I presume, is of that domestic sort which never stirs abroad at all?

ROWLEY. I doubt you'll find it so; but he's coming. I mustn't seem to interrupt you; and, you know, immediately as you leave him, I come in to announce your arrival in your real character.

SIR OLIVER S. True; and afterwards you'll meet me at Sir Peter's.

ROWLEY. Without losing a moment. [*exit*]

SIR OLIVER S. I don't like the complaisance of his features.

Enter JOSEPH SURFACE

JOSEPH S. Sir, I beg you ten thousand pardons for keeping you a moment waiting. Mr. Stanley, I presume.

SIR OLIVER S. At your service.

JOSEPH S. Sir, I beg you will do me the honor to sit down. I entreat you, sir!

SIR OLIVER S. Dear sir, there's no occasion. —[*aside*] Too civil by half!

JOSEPH S. I have not the pleasure of knowing you, Mr. Stanley, but I am extremely happy to see you look so well. You were nearly related to my mother, I think, Mr. Stanley?

SIR OLIVER S. I was, sir; so nearly, that my present poverty, I fear, may do discredit to her wealthy children, else I should not have presumed to trouble you.

JOSEPH S. Dear sir, there needs no apology; he that is in distress, though a stranger, has a right to claim kindred with the wealthy. I am sure I wish I was of that class, and had it in my power to offer you even a small relief.

SIR OLIVER S. If your uncle, Sir Oliver, were here, I should have a friend.

JOSEPH S. I wish he was, sir, with all my heart: you should not want an advocate with him, believe me, sir.

SIR OLIVER S. I should not need one—my distresses would recommend me. But I imagined his bounty would enable you to become the agent of his charity.

JOSEPH S. My dear sir, you were strangely misinformed. Sir Oliver is a worthy man, a very worthy man; but avarice, Mr. Stanley, is the vice of age. I will tell you, my good sir, in confidence, what he has done for me has been a mere nothing; though people, I know, have

thought otherwise, and, for my part, I never chose to contradict the report.

SIR OLIVER S. What! has he never transmitted you bullion—rupees—pagodas?[38]

JOSEPH S. Oh, dear sir, nothing of the kind. No, no; a few presents, now and then—china, shawls, congou tea, avadavats,[39] and Indian crackers; little more, believe me.

SIR OLIVER S. [*aside*] Here's gratitude for twelve thousand pounds! Avadavats and Indian crackers!

JOSEPH S. Then, my dear sir, you have heard, I doubt not, of the extravagance of my brother; there are very few would credit what I have done for that unfortunate young man.

SIR OLIVER S. [*aside*] Not I, for one!

JOSEPH S. The sums I have lent him! Indeed I have been exceedingly to blame; it was an amiable weakness; however, I don't pretend to defend it; and now I feel it doubly culpable, since it has deprived me of the pleasure of serving you, Mr. Stanley, as my heart dictates.

SIR OLIVER S. [*aside*] Dissembler!—[*aloud*] Then, sir, you can't assist me?

JOSEPH S. At present, it grieves me to say, I cannot; but, whenever I have the ability, you may depend upon hearing from me.

SIR OLIVER S. I am extremely sorry——

JOSEPH S. Not more than I, believe me; to pity without the power to relieve is still more painful than to ask and be denied.

SIR OLIVER S. Kind sir, your most obedient humble servant.

JOSEPH S. You leave me deeply affected, Mr. Stanley. William, be ready to open the door.

SIR OLIVER S. Oh, dear sir, no ceremony.

JOSEPH S. Your very obedient.

SIR OLIVER S. Sir, your most obsequious.

JOSEPH S. You may depend upon hearing from me, whenever I can be of service.

SIR OLIVER S. Sweet sir, you are too good!

JOSEPH S. In the meantime I wish you health and spirits.

SIR OLIVER S. Your ever grateful and perpetual humble servant.

JOSEPH S. Sir, yours as sincerely.

SIR OLIVER S. [*aside*] Charles, you are my heir! [*exit*]

JOSEPH S. This is one bad effect of a good

---

[38] Indian coins.   [39] Indian songbirds.

character; it invites application from the unfortunate, and there needs no small degree of
address to gain the reputation of benevolence
without incurring the expense. The silver ore
of pure charity is an expensive article in the
catalogue of a man's good qualities; whereas
the sentimental French plate I use instead of
it, makes just as good a show, and pays no tax.

Enter ROWLEY

ROWLEY. Mr. Surface, your servant. I was
apprehensive of interrupting you, though my
business demands immediate attention, as this
note will inform you.

JOSEPH S. Always happy to see Mr. Rowley.
[*reads the letter*] Sir Oliver Surface! My uncle
arrived!

ROWLEY. He is, indeed; we have just parted
—quite well, after a speedy voyage, and impatient to embrace his worthy nephew.

JOSEPH S. I am astonished! William! stop
Mr. Stanley, if he's not gone.

ROWLEY. Oh! he's out of reach, I believe.

JOSEPH S. Why did you not let me know
this when you came in together?

ROWLEY. I thought you had particular business; but I must be gone to inform your
brother, and appoint him here to meet your
uncle. He will be with you in a quarter of an
hour.

JOSEPH S. So he says. Well, I am strangely
overjoyed at his coming.—[*aside*] Never, to
be sure, was anything so damned unlucky.

ROWLEY. You will be delighted to see how
well he looks.

JOSEPH S. Ah! I'm rejoiced to hear it.——
[*aside*] Just at this time!

ROWLEY. I'll tell him how impatiently you
expect him.

JOSEPH S. Do, do; pray give my best duty
and affection. Indeed, I cannot express the
sensations I feel at the thought of seeing him.
[*exit* ROWLEY] Certainly his coming just at this
time is the cruelest piece of ill fortune! [*exit*]

SCENE II.

SIR PETER TEAZLE'S

Enter MRS. CANDOUR *and* MAID

MAID. Indeed, ma'am, my lady will see nobody at present.

MRS. CAN. Did you tell her it was her friend
Mrs. Candour?

MAID. Yes, ma'am; but she begs you will excuse her.

MRS. CAN. Do go again; I shall be glad to
see her, if it be only for a moment, for I am
sure she must be in great distress. [*exit* MAID]
Dear heart, how provoking! I'm not mistress of
half the circumstances! We shall have the
whole affair in the newspapers, with the names
of the parties at length, before I have dropped
the story at a dozen houses.

Enter SIR BENJAMIN BACKBITE

Oh, Sir Benjamin, you have heard, I suppose——

SIR BENJ. B. Of Lady Teazle and Mr. Surface——

MRS. CAN. And Sir Peter's discovery——

SIR BENJ. B. Oh! the strangest piece of business, to be sure!

MRS. CAN. Well, I never was so surprised in
my life. I am so sorry for all parties, indeed.

SIR BENJ. B. Now, I don't pity Sir Peter at
all; he was so extravagantly partial to Mr. Surface.

MRS. CAN. Mr. Surface! Why, 'twas with
Charles Lady Teazle was detected.

SIR BENJ. B. No, no, I tell you; Mr. Surface
is the gallant.

MRS. CAN. No such thing! Charles is the
man. 'Twas Mr. Surface brought Sir Peter on
purpose to discover them.

SIR BENJ. B. I tell you I had it from one——

MRS. CAN. And I have it from one——

SIR BENJ. B. Who had it from one, who had
it——

MRS. CAN. From one immediately—but here
comes Lady Sneerwell; perhaps she knows the
whole affair.

Enter LADY SNEERWELL

LADY SNEER. So, my dear Mrs. Candour,
here's a sad affair of our friend, Lady Teazle.

MRS. CAN. Ay, my dear friend, who would
have thought——

LADY SNEER. Well, there is no trusting appearances; though, indeed, she was always too
lively for me.

MRS. CAN. To be sure, her manners were a
little too free; but then she was young!

LADY SNEER. And had, indeed, some good qualities.

MRS. CAN. So she had, indeed. But have you heard the particulars?

LADY SNEER. No; but everybody says that Mr. Surface——

SIR BENJ. B. Ay, there; I told you Mr. Surface was the man.

MRS. CAN. No, no; indeed the assignation was with Charles.

LADY SNEER. With Charles! You alarm me, Mrs. Candour!

MRS. CAN. Yes, yes, he was the lover. Mr. Surface, to do him justice, was only the informer.

SIR BENJ. B. Well, I'll not dispute with you, Mrs. Candour; but, be it which it may, I hope that Sir Peter's wound will not——

MRS. CAN. Sir Peter's wound! Oh, mercy! I didn't hear a word of their fighting.

LADY SNEER. Nor I, a syllable.

SIR BENJ. B. No! what, no mention of the duel?

MRS. CAN. Not a word.

SIR BENJ. B. Oh, yes; they fought before they left the room.

LADY SNEER. Pray, let us hear.

MRS. CAN. Ay, do oblige us with the duel.

SIR BENJ. B. "Sir," says Sir Peter, immediately after the discovery, "you are a most ungrateful fellow."

MRS. CAN. Ay, to Charles.

SIR BENJ. B. No, no, to Mr. Surface—"a most ungrateful fellow; and, old as I am, sir," says he, "I insist on immediate satisfaction."

MRS. CAN. Ay, that must have been to Charles; for 'tis very unlikely Mr. Surface should fight in his own house.

SIR BENJ. B. Gad's life, ma'am, not at all. "Giving me satisfaction." On this, ma'am, Lady Teazle, seeing Sir Peter in such danger, ran out of the room in strong hysterics, and Charles after her, calling out for hartshorn and water; then, madam, they began to fight with swords.

Enter CRABTREE

CRABT. With pistols, nephew—pistols. I have it from undoubted authority.

MRS. CAN. Oh, Mr. Crabtree, then it is all true!

CRABT. Too true, indeed, madam, and Sir Peter is dangerously wounded—

SIR BENJ. B. By a thrust in second[40] quite through his left side——

CRABT. By a bullet lodged in the thorax.

MRS. CAN. Mercy on me! Poor Sir Peter!

CRABT. Yes, madam; though Charles would have avoided the matter, if he could.

MRS. CAN. I knew Charles was the person.

SIR BENJ. B. My uncle, I see, knows nothing of the matter.

CRABT. But Sir Peter taxed him with the basest ingratitude.

SIR BENJ. B. That I told you, you know—

CRABT. Do, nephew, let me speak! and insisted on immediate——

SIR BENJ. B. Just as I said——

CRABT. Odds life, nephew, allow others to know something too. A pair of pistols lay on the bureau (for Mr. Surface, it seems, had come home the night before late from Salthill, where he had been to see the Montem with a friend, who has a son at Eton), so, unluckily, the pistols were left charged.

SIR BENJ. B. I heard nothing of this.

CRABT. Sir Peter forced Charles to take one, and they fired, it seems, pretty nearly together. Charles's shot took effect as I tell you, and Sir Peter's missed; but what is very extraordinary, the ball struck against a little bronze Shakespeare that stood over the fireplace, grazed out of the window, at a right angle, and wounded the postman, who was just coming to the door with a double letter from Northamptonshire.

SIR BENJ. B. My uncle's account is more circumstantial, I confess; but I believe mine is the true one, for all that.

LADY SNEER. [*aside*] I am more interested in this affair than they imagine, and must have better information. [*exit* LADY SNEERWELL]

SIR BENJ. B. Ah! Lady Sneerwell's alarm is very easily accounted for.

CRABT. Yes, yes, they certainly do say; but that's neither here nor there.

MRS. CAN. But, pray, where is Sir Peter at present?

CRABT. Oh! they brought him home, and he is now in the house, though the servants are ordered to deny him.

MRS. CAN. I believe so, and Lady Teazle, I suppose, attending him.

[40] a parry.

CRABT. Yes, yes; and I saw one of the faculty enter just before me.

SIR BENJ. B. Hey, who comes here?

CRABT. Oh, this is he: the physician, depend on't.

MRS. CAN. Oh, certainly: it must be the physician; and now we shall know.

Enter SIR OLIVER SURFACE

CRABT. Well, doctor, what hopes?

MRS. CAN. Ah, doctor, how's your patient?

SIR BENJ. B. Now, doctor, isn't it a wound with a small sword?

CRABT. A bullet lodged in the thorax, for a hundred!

SIR OLIVER S. Doctor! a wound with a small sword! and a bullet in the thorax! Oons! are you mad, good people?

SIR BENJ. B. Perhaps, sir, you are not a doctor?

SIR OLIVER S. Truly, I am to thank you for my degree if I am.

CRABT. Only a friend of Sir Peter's, then, I presume. But, sir, you must have heard of his accident?

SIR OLIVER S. Not a word!

CRABT. Not of his being dangerously wounded?

SIR OLIVER S. The devil he is!

SIR BENJ. B. Run through the body——

CRABT. Shot in the breast——

SIR BENJ. B. By one Mr. Surface——

CRABT. Ay, the younger.

SIR OLIVER S. Hey! what the plague! you seem to differ strangely in your accounts: however, you agree that Sir Peter is dangerously wounded.

SIR BENJ. B. Oh, yes, we agree there.

CRABT. Yes, yes, I believe there can be no doubt of that.

SIR OLIVER S. Then, upon my word, for a person in that situation, he is the most imprudent man alive; for here he comes, walking as if nothing at all was the matter.

Enter SIR PETER TEAZLE

Odds heart, Sir Peter, you are come in good time, I promise you; for we had just given you over.

SIR BENJ. B. Egad, uncle, this is the most sudden recovery!

SIR OLIVER S. Why, man, what do you out of

bed with a small sword through your body, and a bullet lodged in your thorax?

SIR PETER T. A small sword, and a bullet!

SIR OLIVER S. Ay, these gentlemen would have killed you without law or physic, and wanted to dub me a doctor, to make me an accomplice.

SIR PETER T. Why, what is all this?

SIR BENJ. B. We rejoice, Sir Peter, that the story of the duel is not true, and are sincerely sorry for your other misfortune.

SIR PETER T. [*aside*] So, so; all over the town already.

CRABT. Though, Sir Peter, you were certainly vastly to blame to marry at your years.

SIR PETER T. Sir, what business is that of yours?

MRS. CAN. Though, indeed, as Sir Peter made so good a husband, he's very much to be pitied.

SIR PETER T. Plague on your pity, ma'am! I desire none of it.

SIR BENJ. B. However, Sir Peter, you must not mind the laughing and jests you will meet with on the occasion.

SIR PETER T. Sir, sir, I desire to be master in my own house.

CRABT. 'Tis no uncommon case, that's one comfort.

SIR PETER T. I insist on being left to myself; without ceremony. I insist on your leaving my house directly.

MRS. CAN. Well, well, we are going, and depend on't we'll make the best report of it we can. [*exit*]

SIR PETER T. Leave my house!

CRABT. And tell how hardly you've been treated. [*exit*]

SIR PETER T. Leave my house!

SIR BENJ. B. And how patiently you bear it. [*exit*]

SIR PETER T. Fiends! vipers! furies! Oh! that their own venom would choke them!

SIR OLIVER S. They are very provoking, indeed, Sir Peter.

Enter ROWLEY

ROWLEY. I heard high words; what has ruffled you, sir?

SIR PETER T. Pshaw! what signifies asking? Do I ever pass a day without my vexations?

ROWLEY. Well, I'm not inquisitive.

SIR OLIVER S. Well, Sir Peter, I have seen both my nephews in the manner we proposed.

SIR PETER T. A precious couple they are!

ROWLEY. Yes, and Sir Oliver is convinced that your judgment was right, Sir Peter.

SIR OLIVER S. Yes, I find Joseph is indeed the man, after all.

ROWLEY. Ay, as Sir Peter says, he is a man of sentiment.

SIR OLIVER S. And acts up to the sentiments he professes.

ROWLEY. It certainly is edification to hear him talk.

SIR OLIVER S. Oh, he's a model for the young men of the age! But how's this, Sir Peter? you don't join us in your friend Joseph's praise, as I expected.

SIR PETER T. Sir Oliver, we live in a damned wicked world, and the fewer we praise the better.

ROWLEY. What! do you say so, Sir Peter, who were never mistaken in your life?

SIR PETER T. Pshaw! Plague on you both! I see by your sneering you have heard the whole affair. I shall go mad among you!

ROWLEY. Then, to fret you no longer, Sir Peter, we are indeed acquainted with it all. I met Lady Teazle coming from Mr. Surface's so humbled that she deigned to request me to be her advocate with you.

SIR PETER T. And does Sir Oliver know all this?

SIR OLIVER S. Every circumstance.

SIR PETER T. What, of the closet and the screen, hey?

SIR OLIVER S. Yes, yes, and the little French milliner. Oh, I have been vastly diverted with the story! Ha! ha! ha!

SIR PETER T. 'Twas very pleasant.

SIR OLIVER S. I never laughed more in my life, I assure you. Ha! ha! ha!

SIR PETER T. Oh, vastly diverting! Ha! ha! ha!

ROWLEY. To be sure, Joseph with his sentiments; ha! ha! ha!

SIR PETER T. Yes, yes, his sentiments! Ha! ha! ha! Hypocritical villain!

SIR OLIVER S. Ay, and that rogue Charles to pull Sir Peter out of the closet: ha! ha! ha!

SIR PETER T. Ha! ha! 'twas devilish entertaining, to be sure!

SIR OLIVER S. Ha! ha! ha! Egad, Sir Peter, I should like to have seen your face when the screen was thrown down: ha! ha!

SIR PETER T. Yes, yes, my face when the screen was thrown down: ha! ha! ha! Oh, I must never show my head again!

SIR OLIVER S. But come, come, it isn't fair to laugh at you neither, my old friend; though, upon my soul, I can't help it.

SIR PETER T. Oh, pray don't restrain your mirth on my account; it does not hurt me at all! I laugh at the whole affair myself. Yes, yes, I think being a standing jest for all one's acquaintance a very happy situation. Oh, yes, and then of a morning to read the paragraphs about Mr. S—, Lady T—, and Sir P—, will be so entertaining!

ROWLEY. Without affection, Sir Peter, you may despise the ridicule of fools; but I see Lady Teazle going towards the next room. I am sure you must desire a reconciliation as earnestly as she does.

SIR OLIVER S. Perhaps my being here prevents her coming to you. Well, I'll leave honest Rowley to mediate between you; but he must bring you all presently to Mr. Surface's, where I am now returning, if not to reclaim a libertine, at least to expose hypocrisy.

SIR PETER T. Ah, I'll be present at your discovering yourself there with all my heart; though 'tis a vile unlucky place for discoveries.

ROWLEY. We'll follow. [*exit* SIR OLIVER]

SIR PETER T. She is not coming here, you see, Rowley.

ROWLEY. No, but she has left the door of that room open, you perceive. See, she is in tears.

SIR PETER T. Certainly a little mortification appears very becoming in a wife. Don't you think it will do her good to let her pine a little?

ROWLEY. Oh, this is ungenerous in you!

SIR PETER T. Well, I know not what to think. You remember the letter I found of hers, evidently intended for Charles?

ROWLEY. A mere forgery, Sir Peter, laid in your way on purpose. This is one of the points which I intend Snake shall give you conviction of.

SIR PETER T. I wish I were once satisfied of that. She looks this way. What a remarkably elegant turn of the head she has! Rowley, I'll go to her.

ROWLEY. Certainly.

SIR PETER T. Though when it is known that we are reconciled, people will laugh at me ten times more.

ROWLEY. Let them laugh, and retort their malice only by showing them you are happy in spite of it.

SIR PETER T. I'faith, so I will! And if I'm not mistaken, we may yet be the happiest couple in the country.

ROWLEY. Nay, Sir Peter, he who once lays aside suspicion——

SIR PETER T. Hold, Master Rowley! if you have any regard for me, let me never hear you utter anything like a sentiment. I have had enough of them to serve me the rest of my life. [*exeunt*]

SCENE III.

The library [in JOSEPH SURFACE'S house]

Enter JOSEPH SURFACE *and* LADY
SNEERWELL

LADY SNEER. Impossible! Will not Sir Peter immediately be reconciled to Charles, and, of course, no longer oppose his union with Maria? The thought is distraction to me.

JOSEPH S. Can passion furnish a remedy?

LADY SNEER. No, nor cunning neither. O! I was a fool, an idiot, to league with such a blunderer!

JOSEPH S. Lady Sneerwell, I am the greatest sufferer; yet you see I bear the accident with calmness.

LADY SNEER. Because the disappointment doesn't reach your heart; your interest only attached you to Maria. Had you felt for her what I have for that ungrateful libertine, neither your temper nor hypocrisy could prevent your showing the sharpness of your vexation.

JOSEPH S. But why should your reproaches fall on me for this disappointment?

LADY SNEER. Are you not the cause of it? Had you not a sufficient field for your roguery in imposing upon Sir Peter, and supplanting your brother, but you must endeavor to seduce his wife? I hate such an avarice of crimes; 'tis an unfair monopoly, and never prospers.

JOSEPH S. Well, I admit I have been to blame. I confess I deviated from the direct road of wrong, but I don't think we're so totally defeated neither.

LADY SNEER. No!

JOSEPH S. You tell me you have made a trial of Snake since we met, and that you still believe him faithful to us.

LADY SNEER. I do believe so.

JOSEPH S. And that he has undertaken, should it be necessary, to swear and prove, that Charles is at this time contracted by vows and honor to your ladyship, which some of his former letters to you will serve to support?

LADY SNEER. This, indeed, might have assisted.

JOSEPH S. Come, come; it is not too late yet. [*knocking at the door*] But hark! this is probably my uncle, Sir Oliver; retire to that room, we'll consult farther when he is gone.

LADY SNEER. Well, but *if he* should find you out too?

JOSEPH S. Oh, I have no fear of that. Sir Peter will hold his tongue for his own credit's sake; and you may depend on it I shall soon discover Sir Oliver's weak side!

LADY SNEER. I have no diffidence of your abilities! only be constant to one roguery at a time. [*exit* LADY SNEERWELL]

JOSEPH S. I will, I will. So! 'tis confounded hard, after such bad fortune, to be baited by one's confederate in evil. Well, at all events my character is so much better than Charles's that I certainly—hey!—what!—this is not Sir Oliver, but old Stanley again. Plague on't that he should return to tease me just now. I shall have Sir Oliver come and find him here—and——

Enter SIR OLIVER SURFACE

Gad's life, Mr. Stanley, why have you come back to plague me at this time? You must not stay now, upon my word.

SIR OLIVER S. Sir, I hear your uncle Oliver is expected here, and though he has been so penurious to you, I'll try what he'll do for me.

JOSEPH S. Sir, 'tis impossible for you to stay now, so I must beg—come any other time, and I promise you, you shall be assisted.

SIR OLIVER S. No; Sir Oliver and I must be acquainted.

JOSEPH S. Zounds, sir! then I insist on your quitting the room directly.

SIR OLIVER S. Nay, sir——

JOSEPH S. Sir, I insist on't; here, William! show this gentleman out. Since you compel me, sir, not one moment; this is such insolence! [*going to push him out*]

Enter CHARLES SURFACE

CHARLES S. Hey day! what's the matter now! What the devil, have you got hold of my little broker here? Zounds, brother! don't hurt little Premium. What's the matter, my little fellow?

JOSEPH S. So! he has been with you too, has he?

CHARLES S. To be sure he has. Why he's as honest a little—— But sure, Joseph, you have not been borrowing money too, have you?

JOSEPH S. Borrowing! no! But, brother, you know we expect Sir Oliver here every——

CHARLES S. Oh, Gad, that's true! Noll mustn't find the little broker here, to be sure.

JOSEPH S. Yet Mr. Stanley insists——

CHARLES S. Stanley! why his name's Premium.

JOSEPH S. No, sir, Stanley.

CHARLES S. No, no, Premium.

JOSEPH S. Well, no matter which—but——

CHARLES S. Ay, ay, Stanley or Premium, 'tis the same thing, as you say; for I suppose he goes by half a hundred names, besides A. B. at the coffee-house. [*knocking*]

JOSEPH S. 'Sdeath, here's Sir Oliver at the door. Now I beg, Mr. Stanley——

CHARLES S. Ay, ay, and I beg, Mr. Premium——

SIR OLIVER S. Gentlemen——

JOSEPH S. Sir, by heaven you shall go!

CHARLES S. Ay, out with him, certainly!

SIR OLIVER. This violence——

JOSEPH S. Sir, 'tis your own fault.

CHARLES S. Out with him, to be sure. [*both forcing* SIR OLIVER *out*]

Enter SIR PETER *and* LADY TEAZLE, MARIA, *and* ROWLEY

SIR PETER T. My old friend, Sir Oliver; hey! What in the name of wonder; here are dutiful nephews; assault their uncle at a first visit!

LADY T. Indeed, Sir Oliver, 'twas well we came in to rescue you.

ROWLEY. Truly, it was; for I perceive, Sir Oliver, the character of old Stanley was no protection to you.

SIR OLIVER S. Nor of Premium either: the necessities of the former could not extort a shilling from that benevolent gentleman; and

now, egad, I stood a chance of faring worse than my ancestors, and being knocked down without being bid for.

JOSEPH S. Charles!

CHARLES S. Joseph!

JOSEPH S. 'Tis now complete!

CHARLES S. Very!

SIR OLIVER S. Sir Peter, my friend, and Rowley too—look on that elder nephew of mine. You know what he has already received from my bounty; and you also know how gladly I would have regarded half my fortune as held in trust for him; judge then my disappointment in discovering him to be destitute of faith, charity, and gratitude.

SIR PETER T. Sir Oliver, I should be more surprised at this declaration, if I had not myself found him to be mean, treacherous, and hypocritical.

LADY T. And if the gentleman pleads not guilty to these, pray let him call *me* to his character.

SIR PETER T. Then, I believe, we need add no more: if he knows himself, he will consider it as the most perfect punishment that he is known to the world.

CHARLES S. [*aside*] If they talk this way to Honesty, what will they say to me, by and by?

SIR OLIVER S. As for that prodigal, his brother, there——

CHARLES S. [*aside*] Ay, now comes my turn; the damned family pictures will ruin me.

JOSEPH S. Sir Oliver—uncle, will you honor me with a hearing?

CHARLES S. [*aside*] Now if Joseph would make one of his long speeches, I might recollect myself a little.

SIR OLIVER S. [*to* JOSEPH] I suppose you would undertake to justify yourself entirely.

JOSEPH S. I trust I could.

SIR OLIVER S. [*to* CHARLES] Well, sir! and you could justify yourself too, I suppose?

CHARLES S. Not that I know of, Sir Oliver.

SIR OLIVER S. What! Little Premium has been let too much into the secret, I suppose?

CHARLES S. True, sir; but they were *family* secrets, and should not be mentioned again, you know.

ROWLEY. Come, Sir Oliver, I know you cannot speak of Charles's follies with anger.

SIR OLIVER S. Odd's heart, no more can I; nor with gravity either. Sir Peter, do you know the rogue bargained with me for all his ancestors; sold me judges and generals by the foot, and maiden aunts as cheap as broken china.

CHARLES S. To be sure, Sir Oliver, I did make a little free with the family canvas, that's the truth on't. My ancestors may rise in judgment against me, there's no denying it; but believe me sincere when I tell you—and upon my soul I would not say so if I was not—that if I do not appear mortified at the exposure of my follies, it is because I feel at this moment the warmest satisfaction in seeing you, my liberal benefactor.

SIR OLIVER S. Charles, I believe you; give me your hand again; the ill-looking little fellow over the settee has made your peace.

CHARLES S. Then, sir, my gratitude to the original is still increased.

LADY T. Yet, I believe, Sir Oliver, here is one whom Charles is still more anxious to be reconciled to.

SIR OLIVER S. Oh, I have heard of his attachment there; and, with the young lady's pardon, if I construe right—that blush——

SIR PETER T. Well, child, speak your sentiments!

MARIA. Sir, I have little to say, but that I shall rejoice to hear that he is happy; for me—whatever claim I had to his affection, I willingly resign to one who has a better title.

CHARLES S. How, Maria!

SIR PETER T. Hey day! what's the mystery now? While he appeared an incorrigible rake, you would give your hand to no one else; and now that he is likely to reform, I'll warrant you won't have him.

MARIA. His own heart and Lady Sneerwell know the cause.

CHARLES S. Lady Sneerwell!

JOSEPH S. Brother, it is with great concern I am obliged to speak on this point, but my regard to justice compels me, and Lady Sneerwell's injuries can no longer be concealed. [*opens the door*]

Enter LADY SNEERWELL

SIR PETER T. So! another French milliner! Egad, he has one in every room of the house, I suppose.

LADY SNEER. Ungrateful Charles! Well may you be surprised, and feel for the indelicate situation your perfidy has forced me into.

CHARLES S. Pray, uncle, is this another plot of yours? For, as I have life, I don't understand it.

JOSEPH S. I believe, sir, there is but the evidence of one person more necessary to make it extremely clear.

SIR PETER T. And that person, I imagine, is Mr. Snake. Rowley, you were perfectly right to bring him with us, and pray let him appear.

ROWLEY. Walk in, Mr. Snake.

Enter SNAKE

I thought his testimony might be wanted; however, it happens unluckily that he comes to confront Lady Sneerwell, not to support her.

LADY SNEER. A villain! Treacherous to me at last! Speak, fellow; have you too conspired against me?

SNAKE. I beg your ladyship ten thousand pardons; you paid me extremely liberally for the lie in question; but I unfortunately have been offered double to speak the truth.

SIR PETER T. Plot and counter-plot, egad!

LADY SNEER. The torments of shame and disappointment on you all. [*going*]

LADY T. Hold, Lady Sneerwell; before you go, let me thank you for the trouble you and that gentleman have taken, in writing letters from me to Charles, and answering them yourself; and let me also request you to make my respects to the scandalous college, of which you are president, and inform them that Lady Teazle, licentiate, begs leave to return the diploma they gave her, as she leaves off practice, and kills characters no longer.

LADY SNEER. You too, madam—provoking—insolent. May your husband live these fifty years. [*exit*]

SIR PETER T. Oons! what a fury!

LADY T. A malicious creature, indeed!

SIR PETER T. Hey! Not for her last wish?

LADY T. Oh, no!

SIR OLIVER S. Well, sir, and what have you to say now?

JOSEPH S. Sir, I am so confounded, to find that Lady Sneerwell could be guilty of suborning Mr. Snake in this manner, to impose on us all, that I know not what to say; however, lest her revengeful spirit should prompt her to injure my brother, I had certainly better follow her directly. [*exit*]

SIR PETER T. Moral to the last drop!

SIR OLIVER S. Ay, and marry her, Joseph, if you can. Oil and vinegar, egad! you'll do very well together.

ROWLEY. I believe we have no more occasion for Mr. Snake at present?

SNAKE. Before I go, I beg pardon once for all, for whatever uneasiness I have been the humble instrument of causing to the parties present.

SIR PETER T. Well, well, you have made atonement by a good deed at last.

SNAKE. But I must request of the company that it shall never be known.

SIR PETER T. Hey! What the plague! Are you ashamed of having done a right thing once in your life?

SNAKE. Ah, sir! consider; I live by the badness of my character. I have nothing but my infamy to depend on! and if it were once known that I had been betrayed into an honest action, I should lose every friend I have in the world.

SIR OLIVER S. Well, well; we'll not traduce you by saying anything in your praise, never fear. [*exit* SNAKE]

SIR PETER T. There's a precious rogue!

LADY T. See, Sir Oliver, there needs no persuasion now to reconcile your nephew and Maria.

SIR OLIVER S. Ay, ay, that's as it should be, and, egad, we'll have the wedding tomorrow morning.

CHARLES S. Thank you, dear uncle!

SIR PETER T. What, you rogue! don't you ask the girl's consent first?

CHARLES S. Oh, I have done that a long time—a minute ago—and she has looked *yes*.

MARIA. For shame, Charles! I protest, Sir Peter, there has not been a word.

SIR OLIVER S. Well, then, the fewer the better. May your love for each other never know abatement!

SIR PETER T. And may you live as happily together as Lady Teazle and I intend to do!

CHARLES S. Rowley, my old friend, I am sure you congratulate me; and I suspect that I owe you much.

SIR OLIVER S. You do indeed, Charles.

ROWLEY. If my efforts to serve you had not succeeded, you would have been in my debt for the attempt: but deserve to be happy, and you overpay me.

SIR PETER T. Ay, honest Rowley always said you would reform.

CHARLES S. Why, as to reforming, Sir Peter, I'll make no promises, and that I take to be a proof that I intend to set about it; but here shall be my monitor—my gentle guide. Ah! can I leave the virtuous path those eyes illumine?

Though thou, dear maid, shouldst waive thy
    beauty's sway,
Thou still must rule, because I will obey:
An humble fugitive from Folly view,
No sanctuary near but Love and you.
                                  [*to the audience*]
You can, indeed, each anxious fear remove,
For even Scandal dies if you approve.

EPILOGUE

BY MR. COLMAN[41]

Spoken by Lady Teazle

I, who was late so volatile and gay,
Like a trade wind must now blow all one
    way,
Bend all my cares, my studies, and my vows,
To one dull rusty weathercock—my spouse!
So wills our virtuous bard—the motley Bayes[42]
Of crying epilogues and laughing plays!
Old bachelors, who marry smart young wives,
Learn from our play to regulate your lives:
Each bring his dear to town, all faults upon
    her,
London will prove the very source of honor.
Plunged fairly in, like a cold bath it serves,
When principles relax, to brace the nerves.
Such is my case; and yet I must deplore
That the gay dream of dissipation's o'er.
And say, ye fair, was ever lively wife,
Born with a genius for the highest life,
Like me untimely blasted in her bloom,
Like me condemn'd to such a dismal doom?
Save money—when I just knew how to waste
    it!
Leave London—just as I began to taste it!
    Must I then watch the early crowing cock,
The melancholy ticking of a clock;

_____

[41] George Colman, the elder, theater manager and playwright.
[42] In *The Rehearsal* by Buckingham, Bayes was a burlesque of Dryden; by extension, the name means simply dramatist.

In a lone rustic hall for ever pounded,[43]
With dogs, cats, rats, and squalling brats sur-
   rounded?
With humble curate can I now retire
(While good Sir Peter boozes with the squire), 5
And at backgammon mortify my soul,
That pants for loo[44] or flutters at a vole?[45]
Seven's the main![46] Dear sound that must ex-
   pire,
Lost at hot cockles[47] round a Christmas fire! 10
The transient hour of fashion too soon spent,
Farewell the tranquil mind, farewell content!
Farewell the plumèd head, the cushioned tête,
That takes the cushion from its proper seat!
The spirit-stirring drum! card drums[48] I mean, 15

Spadille—odd trick—pam—basto—king and
   queen![49]
And you, ye knockers, that, with brazen throat,
The welcome visitors' approach denote;
Farewell all quality of high renown,
Pride, pomp, and circumstance of glorious
   town!
Farewell! your revels I partake no more,
And Lady Teazle's occupation's o'er!
All this I told our bard; he smiled, and said 10
   'twas clear
I ought to play deep tragedy next year;
Meanwhile he drew wise morals from his play,
And in these solemn periods stalk'd away:—
"Blest were the fair like you! her faults who 15
   stopp'd,
And closed her follies when the curtain
   dropp'd!
No more in vice or error to engage,
Or play the fool at large on life's great stage." 20

---

[43] impounded.
[44] a card game.
[45] a slam in cards.
[46] the "point" in dice.
[47] blindman's buff.
[48] parties.

---

[49] names of cards in the game of ombre.

LADY WINDERMERE'S FAN

OSCAR WILDE

Wilde (1856–1900) was educated in Dublin and at Oxford, where he won a poetry prize and dabbled in the aesthetic life under the influence of Pater. He wrote undistinguished early poetry, fiction (The Picture of Dorian Gray), four comedies of manners, other plays, and the popular Ballad of Reading Gaol, a work based on his imprisonment on charges of homosexuality. At one time Wilde toured America, giving lectures and impressing audiences with his strange mannerisms and his wit. Broken and disillusioned, he died in Paris. His place in the theater is relatively secure (see I, 403). Criticism of his way of life varies from stern moral disapproval to understanding sympathy.

Dramatis Personæ

LORD WINDERMERE
LORD DARLINGTON
LORD AUGUSTUS LORTON
MR. CECIL GRAHAM
MR. DUMBY

MR. HOPPER
PARKER, *butler*
LADY WINDERMERE
THE DUCHESS OF BERWICK
LADY AGATHA CARLISLE
LADY PLYMDALE
LADY JEDBURGH
LADY STUTFIELD
MRS. COWPER-COWPER
MRS. ERLYNNE
ROSALIE, *maid*

THE SCENES OF THE PLAY

ACT I. Morning-Room in Lord Winder-mere's House
ACT II. Drawing-Room in Lord Winder-mere's House
ACT III. Lord Darlington's Rooms
ACT IV. Same as Act I

TIME—The Present

PLACE—London

The action of the play takes place within twenty-four hours, beginning on a Tuesday afternoon at five o'clock, and ending the next day at 1:30 P.M.

ACT I

SCENE—*morning-room of* LORD WINDER-MERE'S *house in Carlton House Terrace. Doors* C. *and* R. *Bureau with books and papers* R. *Sofa with small tea-table* L. *Window opening on to terrace* L. *Table* R.

LADY WINDERMERE *is at table* R. *arranging roses in a blue bowl.*

Enter PARKER

PARKER. Is your ladyship at home this afternoon?
LADY W. Yes—who has called?
PARKER. Lord Darlington, my lady.
LADY W. [*hesitates for a moment*] Show him up—and I'm at home to anyone who calls.
PARKER. Yes, my lady. [*exit* C.]
LADY W. It's best for me to see him before to-night. I'm glad he's come.

Enter PARKER (C.)

PARKER. Lord Darlington.

Enter LORD D. (C.) *Exit* PARKER

LORD D. How do you do, Lady Windermere?
LADY W. How do you do, Lord Darlington? No, I can't shake hands with you. My hands are all wet with these roses. Aren't they lovely? They came up from Selby this morning.
LORD D. They are quite perfect. [*sees a fan lying on the table*] And what a wonderful fan! May I look at it?
LADY W. Do. Pretty, isn't it! It's got my name on it, and everything. I have only just seen it myself. It's my husband's birthday present to me. You know to-day is my birthday?
LORD D. No? Is it really?
LADY W. Yes; I'm of age to-day. Quite an important day in my life, isn't it? That is why I am giving this party to-night. Do sit down. [*still arranging flowers*]
LORD D. [*sitting down*] I wish I had known it was your birthday, Lady Windermere. I would have covered the whole street in front of your house with flowers to walk on. They are made for you. [*a short pause*]
LADY W. Lord Darlington, you annoyed me last night at the Foreign Office. I am afraid you are going to annoy me again.
LORD D. I, Lady Windermere?

Enter PARKER *and* FOOTMAN (C.) *with tray and tea-things*

LADY W. Put it there, Parker. That will do. [*wipes her hands with her pocket-handkerchief, goes to tea-table* L. *and sits down*] Won't you come over, Lord Darlington? [*exit* PARKER C.]
LORD D. [*takes chair and goes across* L. C.] I am quite miserable, Lady Windermere. You must tell me what I did. [*sits down at table* L.]
LADY W. Well, you kept paying me elaborate compliments the whole evening.
LORD D. [*smiling*] Ah, nowadays we are all of us so hard up, that the only pleasant things to pay *are* compliments. They're the only things we *can* pay.
LADY W. [*shaking her head*] No, I am talking very seriously. You mustn't laugh, I am quite serious. I don't like compliments, and I don't see why a man should think he is pleasing a woman enormously when he says to her a whole heap of things that he doesn't mean.

LORD D. Ah, but I did mean them. [*takes tea which she offers him*]

LADY W. [*gravely*] I hope not. I should be sorry to have to quarrel with you, Lord Darlington. I like you very much, you know that. But I shouldn't like you at all if I thought you were what most other men are. Believe me, you are better than most other men, and I sometimes think you pretend to be worse.

LORD D. We all have our little vanities, Lady Windermere.

LADY W. Why do you make that your special one? [*still seated at table* L.]

LORD D. [*still seated* L. C.] Oh, nowadays so many conceited people go about Society pretending to be good, that I think it shows rather a sweet and modest disposition to pretend to be bad. Besides, there is this to be said. If you pretend to be good, the world takes you very seriously. If you pretend to be bad, it doesn't. Such is the astounding stupidity of optimism.

LADY W. Don't you *want* the world to take you seriously, then, Lord Darlington?

LORD D. No, not the world. Who are the people the world takes seriously? All the dull people one can think of, from the bishops down to the bores. I should like *you* to take me very seriously, Lady Windermere, *you* more than anyone else in life.

LADY W. Why—why me?

LORD D. [*after a slight hesitation*] Because I think we might be great friends. Let us be great friends. You may want a friend some day.

LADY W. Why do you say that?

LORD D. Oh!—we all want friends at times.

LADY W. I think we're very good friends already, Lord Darlington. We can always remain so as long as you don't—

LORD D. Don't what?

LADY W. Don't spoil it by saying extravagant, silly things to me. You think I am a Puritan, I suppose? Well, I have something of the Puritan in me. I was brought up like that. I am glad of it. My mother died when I was a mere child. I lived always with Lady Julia, my father's eldest sister, you know. She was stern to me, but she taught me what the world is forgetting, the difference that there is between what is right and what is wrong. *She* allowed of no compromise. *I* allow of none.

LORD D. My dear Lady Windermere!

LADY W. [*leaning back on the sofa*] You look on me as being behind the age.—Well, I am! I should be sorry to be on the same level as an age like this.

LORD D. You think the age very bad?

LADY W. Yes. Nowadays people seem to look on life as a speculation. It is not a speculation. It is a sacrament. Its ideal is Love. Its purification is sacrifice.

LORD D. [*smiling*] Oh, anything is better than being sacrificed!

LADY W. [*leaning forward*] Don't say that.

LORD D. I do say it. I feel it—I know it.

Enter PARKER (C.)

PARKER. The men want to know if they are to put the carpets on the terrace for to-night, my lady?

LADY W. You don't think it will rain, Lord Darlington, do you?

LORD D. I won't hear of its raining on your birthday!

LADY W. Tell them to do it at once, Parker. [*exit* PARKER C.]

LORD D. [*still seated*] Do you think, then—of course I am only putting an imaginary instance—do you think, that in the case of a young married couple, say about two years married, if the husband suddenly becomes the intimate friend of a woman of—well, more than doubtful character, is always calling upon her, lunching with her, and probably paying her bills—do you think that the wife should not console herself?

LADY W. [*frowning*] Console herself?

LORD D. Yes, I think she should—I think she has the right.

LADY W. Because the husband is vile should the wife be vile also?

LORD D. Vileness is a terrible word, Lady Windermere.

LADY W. It is a terrible thing, Lord Darlington.

LORD D. Do you know I am afraid that good people do a great deal of harm in this world. Certainly the greatest harm they do is that they make badness of such extraordinary importance. It is absurd to divide people into good and bad. People are either charming or tedious. I take the side of the charming, and you, Lady Windermere, can't help belonging to them.

LADY W. Now, Lord Darlington. [*rising and crossing* R., *front of him*] Don't stir, I am merely going to finish my flowers. [*goes to table* R. C.]

LORD D. [*rising and moving chair*] And I must say I think you are very hard on modern life, Lady Windermere. Of course there is much against it, I admit. Most women, for instance, nowadays, are rather mercenary.

LADY W. Don't talk about such people.

LORD D. Well, then, setting mercenary people aside, who, of course, are dreadful, do you think seriously that women who have committed what the world calls a fault should never be forgiven?

LADY W. [*standing at table*] I think they should never be forgiven.

Lord D. And me? Do you think that there should be the same laws for men as there are for women?

LADY W. Certainly!

LORD D. I think life too complex a thing to be settled by these hard-and-fast rules.

LADY W. If we had "these hard-and-fast rules," we should find life much more simple.

LORD D. You allow of no exceptions?

LADY W. None!

LORD D. Ah, what a fascinating Puritan you are, Lady Windermere!

LADY W. The adjective was unnecessary, Lord Darlington.

LORD D. I couldn't help it. I can resist everything except temptation.

LADY W. You have the modern affectation of weakness.

LORD D. [*looking at her*] It's only an affectation, Lady Windermere.

Enter PARKER (C.)

PARKER. The Duchess of Berwick and Lady Agatha Carlisle. [*exit* PARKER (C.)]

Enter the DUCHESS OF B. *and* LADY A. C. (C.)

DUCHESS OF B. [*coming down* C. *and shaking hands*] Dear Margaret, I am so pleased to see you. You remember Agatha, don't you? [*crossing* L. C.] How do you do, Lord Darlington? I won't let you know my daughter, you are far too wicked.

LORD D. Don't say that, Duchess. As a wicked man I am a complete failure. Why, there are lots of people who say I have never really done anything wrong in the whole course of my life. Of course they only say it behind my back.

DUCHESS OF B. Isn't he dreadful? Agatha, this is Lord Darlington. Mind you don't believe a word he says. [LORD DARLINGTON *crosses* R. C.] No, no tea, thank you, dear. [*crosses and sits on sofa*] We have just had tea at Lady Markby's. Such bad tea, too. It was quite undrinkable. I wasn't at all surprised. Her own son-in-law supplies it. Agatha is looking forward so much to your ball to-night, dear Margaret.

LADY W. [*seated* L. C.] Oh, you mustn't think it is going to be a ball, Duchess. It is only a dance in honor of my birthday. A small and early.

LORD D. [*standing* L. C.] Very small, very early, and very select, Duchess.

DUCHESS OF B. [*on sofa* L.] Of course it's going to be select. But we know *that*, dear Margaret, about *your* house. It is really one of the few houses in London where I can take Agatha, and where I feel perfectly secure about poor Berwick. I don't know what Society is coming to. The most dreadful people seem to go everywhere. They certainly come to my parties—the men get quite furious if one doesn't ask them. Really, someone should make a stand against it.

LADY W. *I* will, Duchess, I will have no one in my house about whom there is any scandal.

LORD D. (R. C.) Oh, don't say that, Lady Windermere. I should never be admitted! [*sitting*]

DUCHESS OF B. Oh, men don't matter. With women it is different. We're good. Some of us are, at least. But we are positively getting elbowed into the corner. Our husbands would really forget our existence if we didn't nag at them from time to time, just to remind them that we have a perfect legal right to do so.

LORD D. It's a curious thing, Duchess, about the game of marriage—a game, by the way, that is going out of fashion—the wives hold all the honors, and invariably lose the odd trick.

DUCHESS OF B. The odd trick? Is that the

husband, Lord Darlington?

LORD D. It would be rather a good name for the modern husband.

DUCHESS OF B. Dear Lord Darlington, how thoroughly depraved you are!

LADY W. Lord Darlington is trivial.

LORD D. Ah, don't say that, Lady Windermere.

LADY W. Why do you *talk* so trivially about life, then?

LORD D. Because I think that life is far too important a thing ever to talk seriously about it. [*moves up* C.]

DUCHESS OF B. What does he mean? Do, as a concession to my poor wits, Lord Darlington, just explain to me what you really mean?

LORD D. [*coming down back of table*] I think I had better not, Duchess. Nowadays to be intelligible is to be found out. Good-bye! [*shakes hands with* DUCHESS] And now [*goes up stage*] Lady Windermere, good-bye. I may come to-night, mayn't I? Do let me come.

LADY W. [*standing up stage with* LORD D.] Yes, certainly. But you are not to say foolish, insincere things to people.

LORD D. [*smiling*] Ah, you are beginning to reform me. It is a dangerous thing to reform anyone, Lady Windermere. [*bows, and exit* C.]

DUCHESS OF B. [*who has risen, goes* C.] What a charming, wicked creature! I like him so much. I'm quite delighted he's gone! How sweet you're looking! Where *do* you get your gowns? And now I must tell you how sorry I am for you, dear Margaret. [*crosses to sofa and sits with* LADY W.] Agatha, darling!

LADY A. Yes, mamma. [*rises*]

DUCHESS OF B. Will you go and look over the photograph album that I see there?

LADY A. Yes, mamma. [*goes to table* L.]

DUCHESS OF B. Dear girl! She is so fond of photographs of Switzerland. Such a pure taste, I think. But I really am so sorry for you, Margaret.

LADY W. [*smiling*] Why, Duchess?

DUCHESS OF B. Oh, on account of that horrid woman. She dresses so well, too, which makes it much worse, sets such a dreadful example. Augustus—you know my disreputable brother —such a trial to us all—well, Augustus is completely infatuated about her. It is quite scandalous, for she is absolutely inadmissible into society. Many a woman has a past, but I am told that she has at least a dozen, and that they all fit.

LADY W. Whom are you talking about, Duchess?

DUCHESS OF B. About Mrs. Erlynne.

LADY W. Mrs. Erlynne? I never heard of her, Duchess. And what *has* she to do with me?

DUCHESS OF B. My poor child! Agatha, darling!

LADY A. Yes, mamma.

DUCHESS OF B. Will you go out on the terrace and look at the sunset?

LADY A. Yes, mamma. [*exit through window* L.]

DUCHESS OF B. Sweet girl! So devoted to sunsets! Shows such refinement of feeling, does it not? After all, there is nothing like nature, is there?

LADY W. But what is it, Duchess? Why do you talk to me about this person?

DUCHESS OF B. Don't you really know? I assure you we're all so distressed about it. Only last night at dear Lady Jansen's everyone was saying how extraordinary it was that, of all men in London, Windermere should behave in such a way.

LADY W. My husband—what has *he* to do with any woman of that kind?

DUCHESS OF B. Ah, what indeed, dear? That is the point. He goes to see her continually, and stops for hours at a time, and while he is there she is not at home to anyone. Not that many ladies call on her, dear, but she has a great many disreputable men friends—my own brother in particular, as I told you—and that is what makes it so dreadful about Windermere. We looked upon *him* as being such a model husband, but I am afraid there is no doubt about it. My dear nieces—you know the Saville girls, don't you?—such nice domestic creatures—plain, dreadfully plain, but so good —well, they're always at the window doing fancy work, and making ugly things for the poor, which I think so useful of them in these dreadful socialistic days, and this terrible woman has taken a house in Curzon Street, right opposite them—such a respectable street, too. I don't know what we're coming to! And they tell me that Windermere goes there four and five times a week—they *see* him. They can't help it—and although they never talk scandal, they—well, of course—they remark on it to everyone. And the worst of it all is that I have been told that this woman has got a great deal of money out of somebody, for it seems that she came to London six months ago without anything at all to speak of, and now she has this charming house in Mayfair, drives her pony in the Park every afternoon, and all— well, all—since she has known poor dear Windermere.

LADY W. Oh, I can't believe it!

DUCHESS OF B. But it's quite true, my dear. The whole of London knows it. That is why I felt it was better to come and talk to you, and advise you to take Windermere away at once to Homburg or to Aix[1] where he'll have something to amuse him, and where you can watch him all day long. I assure you, my dear, that on several occasions after I was first married I had to pretend to be very ill, and was obliged to drink the most unpleasant mineral waters, merely to get Berwick out of town. He was so extremely susceptible. Though I am bound to say he never gave away any large sums of money to anybody. He is far too high-principled for that.

LADY W. [interrupting] Duchess, Duchess, it's impossible! [rising and crossing stage C.] We are only married two years. Our child is but six months old. [sits in chair R. of L. table]

DUCHESS OF B. Ah, the dear, pretty baby! How is the little darling? Is it a boy or a girl? I hope a girl—— Ah, no, I remember it's a boy! I'm so sorry. Boys are so wicked. My boy is excessively immoral. You wouldn't believe at what hours he comes home. And he's only left Oxford a few months—I really don't know what they teach them there.

LADY W. Are all men bad?

DUCHESS OF B. Oh, all of them, my dear, all of them, without any exception. And they never grow any better. Men become old, but they never become good.

LADY W. Windermere and I married for love.

DUCHESS OF B. Yes, we begin like that. It was only Berwick's brutal and incessant threats of suicide that made me accept him at all, and before the year was out he was running after all kinds of petticoats, every color, every shape, every material. In fact, before the honeymoon

was over, I caught him winking at my maid, a most pretty, respectable girl. I dismissed her at once without a character.—No, I remember I passed her on to my sister; poor dear Sir George is so short-sighted, I thought it wouldn't matter. But it did, though—it was most unfortunate. [rises] And now, my dear child, I must go, as we are dining out. And mind you don't take this little aberration of Windermere's too much to heart. Just take him abroad, and he'll come back to you all right.

LADY W. Come back to me? [C.]

DUCHESS OF B. (L. C.) Yes, dear, these wicked women get our husbands away from us, but they always come back, slightly damaged, of course. And don't make scenes, men hate them!

LADY W. It is very kind of you, Duchess, to come and tell me all this. But I can't believe that my husband is untrue to me.

DUCHESS OF B. Pretty child! I was like that once. Now I know that all men are monsters. [LADY W. rings bell] The only thing to do is to feed the wretches well. A good cook does wonders, and that I know you have. My dear Margaret, you are not going to cry?

LADY W. You needn't be afraid, Duchess, I never cry.

DUCHESS OF B. That's quite right, dear. Crying is the refuge of plain women, but the ruin of pretty ones. Agatha, darling.

LADY A. [entering L.] Yes, mamma. [stands back of table L. C.)

DUCHESS OF B. Come and bid good-bye to Lady Windermere, and thank her for your charming visit. [coming down again] And by the way, I must thank you for sending a card to Mr. Hopper—he's that rich young Australian people are taking such notice of just at present. His father made a great fortune by selling some kind of food in circular tins— most palatable, I believe—I fancy it is the thing the servants always refuse to eat. But the son is quite interesting. I think he's attracted by dear Agatha's clever talk. Of course, we should be very sorry to lose her, but I think that a mother who doesn't part with a daughter every season has no real affection. We're coming to-night, dear. [PARKER opens C. doors] And remember my advice, take the poor fellow out of town at once, it is the only thing to do. Good-bye, once more; come, Agatha. [exeunt

[1] Continental watering places.

DUCHESS *and* LADY A. (C.)]

LADY W. How horrible! I understand now what Lord Darlington meant by the imaginary instance of the couple not two years married. Oh! it can't be true—she spoke of enormous sums of money paid to this woman. I know where Arthur keeps his bank book—in one of the drawers of that desk. I might find out by that. I *will* find out. [*opens drawer*] No, it is some hideous mistake. [*rises and goes* C.] Some silly scandal! He loves *me!* He loves *me!* But why should I not look? I am his wife, I have a right to look! [*returns to bureau, takes out book and examines it, page by page, smiles and gives a sigh of relief*] I knew it, there is not a word of truth in this stupid story. [*puts book back in drawer. As she does so, starts and takes out another book*] A second book—private—locked! [*tries to open it, but fails. Sees paper knife on bureau, and with it cuts cover from book. Begins to start at the first page*] Mrs. Erlynne—£600—Mrs. Erlynne—£700 —Mrs. Erlynne—£400. Oh! it is true! it is true! How horrible! [*throws book on floor*]

Enter LORD W. (C.)

LORD W. Well, dear, has the fan been sent home yet? [*going* R. C. *sees book*] Margaret, you have cut open my bank book. You have no right to do such a thing!

LADY W. You think it wrong that you are found out, don't you?

LORD W. I think it wrong that a wife should spy on her husband.

LADY W. I did not spy on you. I never knew of this woman's existence till half an hour ago. Someone who pitied me was kind enough to tell me what everyone in London knows already—your daily visits to Curzon Street, your mad infatuation, the monstrous sums of money you squander on this infamous woman! [*crossing* L.]

LORD W. Margaret, don't talk like that of Mrs. Erlynne, you don't know how unjust it is!

LADY W. [*turning to him*] You are very jealous of Mrs. Erlynne's honor. I wish you had been jealous of mine.

LORD W. Your honor is untouched, Margaret. You don't think for a moment that—— [*puts book back into desk*]

LADY W. I think that you spend your money strangely. That is all. Oh, don't imagine I mind about the money. As far as I am concerned, you may squander everything we have. But what I *do* mind is that you who have loved me, you who have taught me to love you, should pass from the love that is given to the love that is bought. Oh, it's horrible! [*sits on sofa*] And it is I who feel degraded. *You* don't feel anything. I feel stained, utterly stained. You can't realize how hideous the last six months seem to me now—every kiss you have given me is tainted in my memory.

LORD W. [*crossing to her*] Don't say that, Margaret, I never loved anyone in the whole world but you.

LADY W. [*rises*] Who is this woman, then? Why do you take a house for her?

LORD W. I did not take a house for her.

LADY W. You gave her the money to do it, which is the same thing.

LORD W. Margaret, as far as I have known Mrs. Erlynne——

LADY W. Is there a Mr. Erlynne—or is he a myth?

LORD W. Her husband died many years ago. She is alone in the world.

LADY W. No relations? [*a pause*]

LORD W. None.

LADY W. Rather curious, isn't it? [L.]

LORD W. (L. C.). Margaret, I was saying to you—and I beg you to listen to me—that as far as I have known Mrs. Erlynne, she has conducted herself well. If years ago——

LADY W. Oh! [*crossing* R. C.] I don't want details about her life.

LORD W. I am not going to give you any details about her life. I tell you simply this— Mrs. Erlynne was once honored, loved, respected. She was well born, she had a position —she lost everything—threw it away, if you like. That makes it all the more bitter. Misfortunes one can endure—they come from outside, they are accidents. But to suffer for one's own faults—ah! there is the sting of life. It was twenty years ago, too. She was little more than a girl then. She had been a wife for even less time than you have.

LADY W. I am not interested in her—and— you should not mention this woman and me in the same breath. It is an error of taste. [*sitting* R. *at desk*]

LORD W. Margaret, you could save this woman. She wants to get back into society, and she wants you to help her. [crossing to her]

LADY W. Me!

LORD W. Yes, you.

LADY W. How impertinent of her! [a pause]

LORD W. Margaret, I came to ask you a great favor, and I still ask it of you, though you have discovered what I had intended you should never have known, that I have given Mrs. Erlynne a large sum of money. I want you to send her an invitation for our party to-night. [standing L. of her]

LADY W. You are mad. [rises]

LORD W. I entreat you. People may chatter about her, do chatter about her, of course, but they don't know anything definite against her. She has been to several houses—not to houses where you would go, I admit, but still to houses where women who are in what is called Society nowadays do go. That does not content her. She wants you to receive her once.

LADY W. As a triumph for her, I suppose.

LORD W. No; but because she knows that you are a good woman—and that if she comes here once she will have a chance of a happier, a surer life, than she has had. She will make no further effort to know you. Won't you help a woman who is trying to get back?

LADY W. No! If a woman really repents, she never wishes to return to the society that has made or seen her ruin.

LORD W. I beg of you.

LADY W. [crossing to door R.] I am going to dress for dinner, and don't mention the subject again this evening. Arthur [going to him C.], you fancy because I have no father or mother that I am alone in the world and you can treat me as you choose. You are wrong, I have friends, many friends.

LORD W. (L. C.) Margaret, you are talking foolishly, recklessly. I won't argue with you, but I insist upon your asking Mrs. Erlynne to-night.

LADY W. (R. C.) I shall do nothing of the kind. [crossing L. C.]

LORD W. (C.) You refuse?

LADY W. Absolutely!

LORD W. Ah, Margaret, do this for my sake; it is her last chance.

LADY W. What has that to do with me?

LORD W. How hard good women are!

LADY W. How weak bad men are!

LORD W. Margaret, none of us men may be good enough for the women we marry—that is quite true—but you don't imagine I would ever—oh, the suggestion is monstrous!

LADY W. Why should you be different from other men? I am told that there is hardly a husband in London who does not waste his life over some shameful passion.

LORD W. I am not one of them.

LADY W. I am not sure of that.

LORD W. You are sure in your heart. But don't make chasm after chasm between us. God knows the last few minutes have thrust us wide enough apart. Sit down and write the card.

LADY W. Nothing in the whole world would induce me.

LORD W. [crossing to the bureau] Then I will. [rings electric bell, sits down and writes card]

LADY W. You are going to invite this woman? [crossing to him]

LORD W. Yes. [pause]

Enter PARKER

LORD W. Parker!

PARKER. Yes, my lord. [comes down L. C.]

LORD W. Have this note sent to Mrs. Erlynne at No. 84A Curzon Street. [crossing to L. C. and giving note to PARKER] There is no answer. [exit PARKER (C.)]

LADY W. Arthur, if that woman comes here I shall insult her.

LORD W. Margaret, don't say that.

LADY W. I mean it.

LORD W. Child, if you did such a thing, there's not a woman in London who wouldn't pity you.

LADY W. There is not a good woman in London who would not applaud me. We have been too lax. We must make an example. I propose to begin to-night. [picking up fan] Yes, you gave me this fan today; it was your birthday present. If that woman crosses my threshold, I shall strike her across the face with it.

LORD W. Margaret, you couldn't do such a thing.

LADY W. You don't know me! [moves R.]

Enter PARKER

LADY W. Parker!

PARKER. Yes, my lady.

LADY W. I shall dine in my own room. I 5
don't want dinner, in fact. See that everything
is ready by half-past ten. And, Parker, be sure
you pronounce the names of the guests very
distinctly to-night. Sometimes you speak so fast
that I miss them. I am particularly anxious to 10
hear the names quite clearly, so as to make no
mistake. You understand, Parker?

PARKER. Yes, my lady.

LADY W. That will do! [*exit* PARKER (C.)]
[*speaking to* LORD W.] Arthur, if that woman 15
comes here—I warn you——

LORD W. Margaret, you'll ruin us!

LADY W. Us! From this moment my life is
separate from yours. But if you wish to avoid
a public scandal, write at once to this woman, 20
and tell her that I forbid her to come here!

LORD W. I will not!—I cannot—she must
come!

LADY W. Then I shall do exactly as I have
said. [*goes* R.] You leave me no choice. 25
[*exit* R.]

LORD W. [*calling after her*] Margaret! Margaret! [*a pause*] My God! What shall I do! I
dare not tell her who this woman really is. The
shame would kill her. [*sinks down into a chair* 30
and buries his face in his hands.]

ACT II

SCENE—*Drawing-room in* LORD W.'s *house.
Door* R. U. *opening into ballroom, where band
is playing. Door* L. *through which guests are* 35
entering. Door L. U. *opens on an illuminated
terrace. Palms, flowers, and brilliant lights.
Room crowded with guests.* LADY W. *is receiving them.*

DUCHESS OF B. [*up* C.] So strange Lord 40
Windermere isn't here. Mr. Hopper is very
late, too. You have kept those five dances for
him, Agatha? [*comes down*]

LADY A. Yes, mamma.

DUCHESS OF B. [*sitting on sofa*] Just let me 45
see your card. I'm so glad Lady Windermere
has revived cards.—They're a mother's only
safeguard. You dear simple little thing! 50
[*scratches out two names*] No nice girl should
ever waltz with such particularly younger sons!

It looks so fast! The last two dances you must
pass on the terrace with Mr. Hopper.

Enter MR. DUMBY *and* LADY PLYMDALE *from
the ballroom*

LADY A. Yes, mamma.

DUCHESS OF B. [*fanning herself*] The air is
so pleasant there.

PARKER. Mrs. Cowper-Cowper. Lady Stutfield. Sir James Royston. Mr. Guy Berkeley.

These people enter as announced

DUMBY. Good evening, Lady Stutfield. I
suppose this will be the last ball of the season?

LADY S. I suppose so, Mr. Dumby. It's been
a delightful season, hasn't it?

DUMBY. Quite delightful! Good evening,
Duchess. I suppose this will be the last ball of
the season?

DUCHESS OF B. I suppose so, Mr. Dumby.
It has been a very dull season, hasn't it?

DUMBY. Dreadfully dull! Dreadfully dull!

MRS. C.-C. Good evening, Mr. Dumby. I
suppose this will be the last ball of the season?

DUMBY. Oh, I think not. There'll probably
be two more. [*wanders back to* LADY P.]

PARKER. Mr. Rufford. Lady Jedburgh and
Miss Graham. Mr. Hopper.

These people enter as announced

HOPPER. How do you do, Lady Windermere? How do you do, Duchess? [*bows to*
LADY A.]

DUCHESS OF B. Dear Mr. Hopper, how nice
of you to come so early. We all know how you
are run after in London.

HOPPER. Capital place, London! They are
not nearly so exclusive in London as they are
in Sydney.

DUCHESS OF B. Ah! we know your value, Mr.
Hopper. We wish there were more like you. It
would make life so much easier. Do you know,
Mr. Hopper, dear Agatha and I are so much
interested in Australia. It must be so pretty
with all the dear little kangaroos flying about.
Agatha has found it on the map. What a curious shape it is! Just like a large packing-case.
However, it is a very young country, isn't it?

HOPPER. Wasn't it made at the same time as
the others, Duchess?

DUCHESS OF B. How clever you are, Mr.
Hopper. You have a cleverness quite of your

own. Now I mustn't keep you.

HOPPER. But I should like to dance with Lady Agatha, Duchess.

DUCHESS OF B. Well, I *hope* she has a dance left. Have you got a dance left, Agatha?

LADY A. Yes, mamma.

DUCHESS OF B. The next one?

LADY A. Yes, mamma.

HOPPER. May I have the pleasure? [LADY AGATHA *bows*]

DUCHESS OF B. Mind you take great care of my little chatter-box, Mr. Hopper. [LADY A. *and* MR. H. *pass into ballroom*]

Enter LORD W. (C.)

LORD W. Margaret, I want to speak to you.

LADY W. In a moment. [*the music stops*]

PARKER. Lord Augustus Lorton.

Enter LORD A.

LORD A. Good evening, Lady Windermere.

DUCHESS OF B. Sir James, will you take me into the ballroom? Augustus has been dining with us to-night. I really have had quite enough of dear Augustus for the moment. [SIR JAMES R. *gives the* DUCHESS *his arm and escorts her into the ballroom*]

PARKER. Mr. and Mrs. Arthur Bowden. Lord and Lady Paisley. Lord Darlington.

These people enter as announced

LORD A. [*coming up to* LORD W.] Want to speak to you particularly, dear boy. I'm worn to a shadow. Know I don't look it. None of us men do look what we really are. Demmed good thing, too. What I want to know is this. Who is she? Where does she come from? Why hasn't she got any demmed relations? Demmed nuisance, relations! But they make one so demmed respectable.

LORD W. You are talking of Mrs. Erlynne, I suppose? I only met her six months ago. Till then I never knew of her existence.

LORD A. You have seen a good deal of her since then.

LORD W. [*coldly*] Yes, I have seen a good deal of her since then. I have just seen her.

LORD A. Egad! the women are very down on her. I have been dining with Arabella this evening! By Jove! you should have heard what she said about Mrs. Erlynne. She didn't leave a rag on her. . . . [*aside*] Berwick and I told her that didn't matter much, as the lady in question must have an extremely fine figure. You should have seen Arabella's expression! . . . But, look here, dear boy. I don't know what to do about Mrs. Erlynne. Egad! I might be married to her; she treats me with such demmed indifference. She's deuced clever, too! She explains everything. Egad! She explains you. She has got any amount of explanations for you—and all of them different.

LORD W. No explanations are necessary about my friendship with Mrs. Erlynne.

LORD A. Hem! Well, look here, dear old fellow. Do you think she will ever get into this demmed thing called Society? Would you introduce her to your wife? No use beating about the confounded bush. Would you do that?

LORD W. Mrs. Erlynne is coming here to-night.

LORD A. Your wife has sent her a card?

LORD W. Mrs. Erlynne has received a card.

LORD A. Then she's all right, dear boy. But why didn't you tell me that before? It would have saved me a heap of worry and demmed misunderstandings! [LADY A. *and* MR. H. *cross and exit on terrace* L. U. E.]

PARKER. Mr. Cecil Graham!

Enter MR. CECIL G.

CECIL G. [*bows to* LADY W., *passes over and shakes hands with* LORD W.] Good evening, Arthur. Why don't you ask me how I am? I like people to ask me how I am. It shows a widespread interest in my health. Now tonight I am not at all well. Been dining with my people. Wonder why it is one's people are always so tedious? My father would talk morality after dinner. I told him he was old enough to know better. But my experience is that as soon as people are old enough to know better, they don't know anything at all. Hullo, Tuppy! Hear you're going to be married again; thought you were tired of that game.

LORD A. You're excessively trivial, my dear boy, excessively trivial!

CECIL G. By the way, Tuppy, which is it? Have you been twice married and once divorced, or twice divorced and once married? I say, you've been twice divorced and once married. It seems so much more probable.

LORD A. I have a very bad memory. I really don't remember which. [*moves away* R.]

LADY P. Lord Windermere, I've something most particular to ask you.

LORD W. I am afraid—if you will excuse me —I must join my wife.

LADY P. Oh, you mustn't dream of such a thing. It's most dangerous nowadays for a husband to pay any attention to his wife in public. It always makes people think that he beats her when they're alone. The world has grown so suspicious of anything that looks like a happy married life. But I'll tell you what it is at supper. [*moves towards door of ballroom*]

LORD W. (C.) Margaret, I *must* speak to you.

LADY W. Will you hold my fan for me, Lord Darlington? Thanks. [*comes down to him*]

LORD W. [*crossing to her*] Margaret, what you said before dinner was, of course, impossible?

LADY W. That woman is not coming here to-night!

LORD W. (R. C.) Mrs. Erlynne is coming here, and if you in any way annoy or wound her, you will bring shame and sorrow on us both. Remember that! Ah, Margaret! only trust me! A wife should trust her husband!

LADY W. (C.) London is full of women who trust their husbands. One can always recognize them. They look so thoroughly unhappy. I am not going to be one of them. [*moves up*] Lord Darlington, will you give me back my fan, please? Thanks. . . . A useful thing, a fan, isn't it? . . . I want a friend to-night, Lord Darlington. I didn't know I would want one so soon.

LORD D. Lady Windermere! I knew the time would come some day; but why to-night!

LORD W. I *will* tell her. I must. It would be terrible if there were any scene. Margaret——

PARKER. Mrs. Erlynne.

[LORD W. *starts.* MRS. E. *enters, very beautifully dressed and very dignified.* LADY w. *clutches at her fan, then lets it drop on the floor. She bows coldly to* MRS. E., *who bows to her sweetly in turn, and sails into the room*]

LORD D. You have dropped your fan, Lady Windermere. [*picks it up and hands it to her*]

MRS. E. [C.] How do you do again, Lord Windermere? How charming your sweet wife looks! Quite a picture!

LORD W. [*in a low voice*] It was terribly rash of you to come!

MRS. E. [*smiling*] The wisest thing I ever did in my life. And, by the way, you must pay me a good deal of attention this evening. I am afraid of the women. You must introduce me to some of them. The men I can always manage. How do you do, Lord Augustus? You have quite neglected me lately. I have not seen you since yesterday. I am afraid you're faithless. Everyone told me so.

LORD A. (R.) Now really, Mrs. Erlynne, allow me to explain.

MRS. E. (R. C.) No, dear Lord Augustus, you can't explain anything. It is your chief charm.

LORD A. Ah! if you find charms in me, Mrs. Erlynne——[*they converse together.* LORD W. *moves uneasily about the room watching* MRS E.]

LORD D. [*to* LADY W.] How pale you are!

LADY W. Cowards are always pale.

LORD D. You look faint. Come out on the terrace.

LADY W. Yes. [*to* PARKER] Parker, send my cloak out.

MRS. E. [*crossing to her*] Lady Windermere, how beautifully your terrace is illuminated. Reminds me of Prince Doria's at Rome. [LADY w. *bows coldly, and goes off with* LORD D.] Oh, how do you do, Mr. Graham? Isn't that your aunt, Lady Jedburgh? I should so much like to know her.

CECIL G. [*after a moment's hesitation and embarrassment*] Oh, certainly, if you wish it. Aunt Caroline, allow me to introduce Mrs. Erlynne.

MRS. E. So pleased to meet you, Lady Jedburgh. [*sits beside her on the sofa*] Your nephew and I are great friends. I am so much interested in his political career. I think he's sure to be a wonderful success. He thinks like a Tory, and talks like a Radical, and that's so important nowadays. He's such a brilliant talker, too. But we all know from whom he inherits that. Lord Allendale was saying to me only yesterday, in the Park, that Mr. Graham talks almost as well as his aunt.

LADY J. (R.) Most kind of you to say these charming things to me! [MRS. E. *smiles and continues conversation*]

DUMBY [*to* CECIL G.] Did you introduce Mrs. Erlynne to Lady Jedburgh?

CECIL G. Had to, my dear fellow. Couldn't help it. That woman can make one do anything she wants. How, I don't know.

DUMBY. Hope to goodness she won't speak to me! [*saunters towards* LADY P.]

MRS. E. [C. *to* LADY J.] On Thursday? With great pleasure. [*rises and speaks to* LORD W. *laughing*] What a bore it is to have to be civil to these old dowagers. But they always insist on it.

LADY P. [*to* MR. D.] Who is that well-dressed woman talking to Windermere?

DUMBY. Haven't got the slightest idea. Looks like an *édition de luxe* of a wicked French novel, meant specially for the English market.

MRS. E. So that is poor Dumby with Lady Plymdale? I hear she is frightfully jealous of him. He doesn't seem anxious to speak to me to-night. I suppose he is afraid of her. Those straw-colored women have dreadful tempers. Do you know, I think I'll dance with you first, Windermere. [LORD W. *bites his lip and frowns*] It will make Lord Augustus so jealous! Lord Augustus! [LORD A. *comes down*] Lord Windermere insists on my dancing with him first, and, as it's his own house, I can't well refuse. You know I would much sooner dance with you.

LORD A. [*with a low bow*] I wish I could think so, Mrs. Erlynne.

MRS. E. You know it far too well. I can fancy a person dancing through life with you and finding it charming.

LORD A. [*placing his hand on his white waist-coat*] Oh, thank you, thank you. You are the most adorable of all ladies!

MRS. E. What a nice speech! So simple and so sincere! Just the sort of speech I like. Well, you shall hold my bouquet. [*goes towards ball-room on* LORD W.*'s arm*] Ah, Mr. Dumby, how are you? I am so sorry I have been out the last three times you have called. Come and lunch on Friday.

DUMBY [*with perfect nonchalance*] Delighted. [LADY P. *glares with indignation at* MR. D. LORD A. *follows* MRS. E. *and* LORD W. *into the ballroom holding bouquet*]

LADY P. [*to* MR. D.] What an absolute brute you are! I never can believe a word you say! Why did you tell me you didn't know her? What do you mean by calling on her three times running? You are not to go to lunch there; of course you understand that?

DUMBY. My dear Laura, I wouldn't dream of going!

LADY P. You haven't told me her name yet. Who is she?

DUMBY. [*coughs slightly and smoothes his hair*] She's a Mrs. Erlynne.

LADY P. *That* woman!

DUMBY. Yes, that is what everyone calls her.

LADY P. How very interesting! How intensely interesting! I really must have a good stare at her. [*goes to door of ballroom and looks in*] I have heard the most shocking things about her. They say she is ruining poor Windermere. And Lady Windermere, who goes in for being so proper, invites her! How extremely amusing! It takes a thoroughly good woman to do a thoroughly stupid thing. You are to lunch there on Friday.

DUMBY. Why?

LADY P. Because I want you to take my husband with you. He has been so attentive lately that he has become a perfect nuisance. Now, this woman is just the thing for him. He'll dance attendance upon her as long as she lets him, and won't bother me. I assure you, women of that kind are most useful. They form the basis of other people's marriages.

DUMBY. What a mystery you are!

LADY P. [*looking at him*] I wish *you* were!

DUMBY. I am—to myself. I am the only person in the world I should like to know thoroughly; but I don't see any chance of it just at present. [*they pass into the ballroom, and* LADY W. *and* LORD D. *enter from the terrace*]

LADY W. Yes. Her coming here is monstrous, unbearable. I know now what you meant to-day at tea-time. Why didn't you tell me right out? You should have!

LORD D. I couldn't! A man can't tell these things about another man! But if I had known he was going to make you ask her here to-night, I think I would have told you. That insult, at any rate, you would have been spared.

LADY W. I did not ask her. He insisted on her coming—against my entreaties—against my commands. Oh! the house is tainted for me! I feel that every woman here sneers at me as she dances by with my husband. What have I done to deserve this? I gave him all my life. He took it—used it—spoiled it! I am degraded in my own eyes; and I lack courage—I am a coward! [*sits down on sofa*]

LORD D. If I know you at all, I know that you can't live with a man who treats you like this! What sort of life would you have with him? You would feel that he was lying to you every moment of the day. You would feel that the look in his eyes was false, his voice false, his touch false, his passion false. He would come to you when he was weary of others; you would have to comfort him. He would come to you when he was devoted to others; you would have to charm him. You would have to be to him the mask of his real life, the cloak to hide his secret.

LADY W. You are right—you are terribly right. But where am I to turn? You said you would be my friend, Lord Darlington.—Tell me, what am I to do? Be my friend now.

LORD D. Between men and women there is no friendship possible. There is passion, enmity, worship, love, but no friendship. I love you——

LADY W. No, no! [*rises*]

LORD D. Yes, I love you! You are more to me than anything in the whole world. What does your husband give you? Nothing. Whatever is in him he gives to this wretched woman, whom he has thrust into your society, into your home, to shame you before every one. I offer you my life——

LADY W. Lord Darlington!

LORD D. My life—my whole life. Take it, and do with it what you will. . . . I love you—love you as I have never loved any living thing. From the moment I met you I loved you, loved you blindly, adoringly, madly! You did not know it then—you know it now! Leave this house to-night. I won't tell you that the world matters nothing, or the world's voice, or the voice of Society. They matter a good deal. They matter far too much. But there are moments when one has to choose between living one's own life, fully, entirely, completely—or dragging out some false, shallow, degrading existence that the world in its hypocrisy demands. You have that moment now. Choose! Oh, my love, choose!

LADY W. [*moving slowly away from him, and looking at him with startled eyes*] I have not the courage.

LORD D. [*following her*] Yes; you have the courage. There may be six months of pain, of disgrace even, but when you no longer bear his name, when you bear mine, all will be well. Margaret, my love, my wife that shall be some day—yes, my wife! You know it! What are you now? This woman has the place that belongs by right to you. Oh! go—go out of this house, with head erect, with a smile upon your lips, with courage in your eyes. All London will know why you did it; and who will blame you? No one. If they do, what matter? Wrong? What is wrong? It's wrong for a man to abandon his wife for a shameless woman. It is wrong for a wife to remain with a man who so dishonors her. You said once you would make no compromise with things. Make none now. Be brave! Be yourself!

LADY W. I am afraid of being myself. Let me think! Let me wait! My husband may return to me. [*sits down on sofa*]

LORD D. And you would take him back! You are not what I thought you were. You are just the same as every other woman. You would stand anything rather than face the censure of a world whose praise you would despise. In a week you will be driving with this woman in the Park. She will be your constant guest—your dearest friend. You would endure anything rather than break with one blow this monstrous tie. You are right. You have no courage; none.

LADY W. Ah, give me time to think. I cannot answer you now. [*passes her hand nervously over her brow*]

LORD D. It must be now or not at all.

LADY W. [*rising from the sofa*] Then not at all! [*a pause*]

LORD D. You break my heart!

LADY W. Mine is already broken. [*a pause*]

LORD D. To-morrow I leave England. This is the last time I shall ever look on you. You will never see me again. For one moment our lives met—our souls touched. They must never meet or touch again. Good-bye, Margaret. [*exit*]

LADY W. How alone I am in life! How terribly alone! [*the music stops*]

Enter the DUCHESS OF B. *and* LORD P. *laughing and talking. Other guests come in from ballroom*

DUCHESS OF B. Dear Margaret, I've just been

having such a delightful chat with Mrs. Erlynne. I am so sorry for what I said to you this afternoon about her. Of course, she must be all right if *you* invite her. A most attractive woman, and has such sensible views on life. Told me she entirely disapproved of people marrying more than once, so I feel quite safe about poor Augustus. Can't imagine why people speak against her. It's those horrid nieces of mine—the Saville girls—they're always talking scandal. Still, I should go to Homburg, dear, I really should. She is just a little too attractive. But where is Agatha? Oh, there she is. [LADY A. *and* MR. H. *enter from the terrace* L. U. E.] Mr. Hopper, I am very angry with you. You have taken Agatha out on the terrace, and she is so delicate.

HOPPER (L. C.) Awfully sorry, Duchess. We went out for a moment and then got chatting together.

DUCHESS OF B. (C.) Ah, about dear Australia, I suppose?

HOPPER. Yes.

DUCHESS OF B. Agatha, darling! [*beckons her over*]

LADY A. Yes, mamma!

DUCHESS OF B. [*aside*] Did Mr. Hopper definitely——

LADY A. Yes, mamma.

DUCHESS OF B. And what answer did you give him, dear child?

LADY A. Yes, mamma.

DUCHESS OF B. [*affectionately*] My dear one! You always say the right thing. Mr. Hopper! James! Agatha has told me everything. How cleverly you have both kept your secret.

HOPPER. You don't mind my taking Agatha off to Australia, then, Duchess?

DUCHESS OF B. [*indignantly*] To Australia? Oh, don't mention that dreadful vulgar place.

HOPPER. But she said she'd like to come with me.

DUCHESS OF B. [*severely*] Did you say that, Agatha?

LADY A. Yes, mamma.

DUCHESS OF B. Agatha, you say the most silly things possible. I think on the whole that Grosvenor Square would be a more healthy place to reside in. There are lots of vulgar people live in Grosvenor Square, but at any rate there are no horrid kangaroos crawling about. But we'll talk about that to-morrow. James, you

can take Agatha down. You'll come to lunch, of course, James. At half-past one instead of two. The Duke will wish to say a few words to you, I am sure.

HOPPER. I should like to have a chat with the Duke, Duchess. He has not said a single word to me yet.

DUCHESS OF B. I think you'll find he will have a great deal to say to you to-morrow. [*exit* LADY A. *with* MR. H.] And now good night, Margaret. I'm afraid it's the old, old story, dear. Love—well, not love at first sight, but love at the end of the season, which is so much more satisfactory.

LADY W. Good night, Duchess. [*exit the* DUCHESS OF B. *on* LORD P.'s *arm*]

LADY P. My dear Margaret, what a handsome woman your husband has been dancing with! I should be quite jealous if I were you! Is she a great friend of yours?

LADY W. No!

LADY P. Really? Good night, dear. [*looks at* MR. D. *and exit*]

DUMBY. Awful manners young Hopper has!

CECIL G. Ah! Hopper is one of Nature's gentlemen, the worst type of gentleman I know.

DUMBY. Sensible woman, Lady Windermere. Lots of wives would have objected to Mrs. Erlynne coming. But Lady Windermere has that uncommon thing called common sense.

CECIL G. And Windermere knows that nothing looks so like innocence as an indiscretion.

DUMBY. Yes; dear Windermere is becoming almost modern. Never thought he would. [*bows to* LADY W. *and exit*]

LADY J. Good night, Lady Windermere. What a fascinating woman Mrs. Erlynne is! She is coming to lunch on Thursday; won't you come too? I expect the Bishop and dear Lady Merton.

LADY W. I am afraid I am engaged, Lady Jedburgh.

LADY J. So sorry. Come, dear. [*exeunt* LADY J. *and* MISS G.]

Enter MRS. E. *and* LORD W.

MRS. E. Charming ball it has been! Quite reminds me of old days. [*sits on the sofa*] And I see that there are just as many fools in society as there used to be. So pleased to find that nothing has altered! Except Margaret. She's grown quite pretty. The last time I saw her— twenty years ago—she was a fright in flannel. Positive fright, I assure you. The dear Duchess! and that sweet Lady Agatha! Just the type of girl I like. Well, really, Windermere, if I am to be the Duchess's sister-in-law——

LORD W. [*sitting* L. *of her*] But are you—? [*exit* MR. CECIL G. *with rest of guests.* LADY W. *watches with a look of scorn and pain* MRS. E. *and her husband. They are unconscious of her presence*]

MRS. E. Oh, yes! He's to call to-morrow at twelve o'clock. He wanted to propose to-night. In fact he did. He kept on proposing. Poor Augustus, you know how he repeats himself. Such a bad habit! But I told him I wouldn't give him an answer till to-morrow. Of course I am going to take him. And I dare say I'll make him an admirable wife, as wives go. And there is a great deal of good in Lord Augustus. Fortunately it is all on the surface. Just where good qualities should be. Of course you must help me in this matter.

LORD W. I am not called on to encourage Lord Augustus, I suppose?

MRS. E. Oh, no! I do the encouraging. But you will make me a handsome settlement, Windermere, won't you?

LORD W. [*frowning*] Is that what you want to talk to me about to-night?

MRS. E. Yes.

LORD W. [*with a gesture of impatience*] I will not talk of it here.

MRS. E. [*laughing*] Then we will talk of it on the terrace. Even business should have a picturesque background. Should it not, Windermere? With a proper background women can do anything.

LORD W. Won't to-morrow do as well?

MRS. E. No; you see, to-morrow I am going to accept him. And I think it would be a good thing if I was able to tell him that—well, what shall I say—£2000 a year left me by a third cousin—or a second husband—or some distant relative of that kind. It would be an additional attraction, wouldn't it? You have a delightful opportunity now of paying me a compliment, Windermere. But you are not very clever at paying compliments. I am afraid Margaret doesn't encourage you in that excellent habit. It's a great mistake on her part. When men give

up saying what is charming, they give up thinking what is charming. But seriously, what do you say to £2000? £2500, I think. In modern life margin is everything. Windermere, don't you think the world an intensely amusing place? I do! [*exit on terrace with* LORD W. *Music strikes up in ballroom*]

LADY W. To stay in this house any longer is impossible. To-night a man who loves me offered me his whole life. I refused it. It was foolish of me. I will offer him mine now. I will give him mine. I will go to him! [*puts on cloak and goes to door, then turns back. Sits down at table and writes a letter, puts it into an envelope and leaves it on table*] Arthur has never understood me. When he reads this, he will. He may do as he chooses now with his life. I have done with mine as I think best, as I think right. It is he who has broken the bond of marriage—not I. I only break its bondage. [*exit*]

PARKER *enters* L. *and crosses towards the ballroom* R. *Enter* MRS. E.

MRS. E. Is Lady Windermere in the ballroom?

PARKER. Her ladyship has just gone out.

MRS. E. Gone out? She's not on the terrace?

PARKER. No, madam. Her ladyship has just gone out of the house.

MRS. E. [*starts and looks at the servant with a puzzled expression on her face*] Out of the house?

PARKER. Yes, madam—her ladyship told me she had left a letter for his lordship on the table.

MRS. E. A letter for Lord Windermere?

PARKER. Yes, madam.

MRS. E. Thank you. [*exit* PARKER. *The music in the ballroom stops*] Gone out of her house! A letter addressed to her husband! [*goes over to table and looks at letter. Takes it up and lays it down again with a shudder of fear*] No, no! It would be impossible! Life doesn't repeat its tragedies like that! Oh, why does this horrible fancy come across me? Why do I remember now the one moment of my life I most wish to forget? Does life repeat its tragedies? [*tears letter open and reads it, then sinks down into a chair with a gesture of anguish*] Oh, how terrible! the same words that twenty years ago I wrote to her father!

and how bitterly I have been punished for it! No; my punishment, my real punishment is to-night, is now! [*still seated* R.]

Enter LORD W. (L. U. E.)

LORD W. Have you said good night to my wife?

MRS. E. [*crushing letter in her hand*] Yes.

LORD W. Where is she?

MRS. E. She is very tired. She has gone to bed. She said she had a headache.

LORD W. I must go to her. You'll excuse me?

MRS. E. [*rising hurriedly*] Oh, no! It's nothing serious. She's only very tired, that is all. Besides, there are people still in the supper-room. She wants you to make her apologies to them. She said she didn't wish to be disturbed. [*drops letter*] She asked me to tell you.

LORD W. [*picks up letter*] You have dropped something.

MRS. E. Oh, yes, thank you, that is mine. [*puts out her hand to take it*]

LORD W. [*still looking at letter*] But it's my wife's handwriting, isn't it?

MRS. E. [*takes the letter quickly*] Yes, it's— an address. Will you ask them to call my carriage, please?

LORD W. Certainly. [*goes* L. *and exit*]

MRS. E. Thanks.—What can I do? What can I do? I feel a passion awakening within me that I never felt before. What can it mean? The daughter must not be like the mother—that would be terrible. How can I save her? How can I save my child? A moment may ruin a life. Who knows that better than I? Windermere must be got out of the house; that is absolutely necessary. [*goes* L.] But how shall I do it? It must be done somehow. Ah!

Enter LORD A. (R. U. E.) *carrying bouquet*

LORD A. Dear lady, I am in such suspense! May I not have an answer to my request?

MRS. E. Lord Augustus, listen to me. You are to take Lord Windermere down to your club at once and keep him there as long as possible. You understand?

LORD A. But you said you wished me to keep early hours!

MRS. E. [*nervously*] Do what I tell you. Do what I tell you.

LORD A. And my reward?

MRS. E. Your reward? Your reward? Oh!

ask me that to-morrow. But don't let Windermere out of your sight to-night. If you do I will never forgive you. I will never speak to you again. I'll have nothing to do with you. Remember you are to keep Windermere at your club, and don't let him come back to-night. [*exit*]

LORD A. Well, really, I might be her husband already. Positively I might. [*follows her in a bewildered manner.*]

ACT III

SCENE—LORD DARLINGTON'S *rooms. A large sofa is in front of fireplace* R. *At the back of the stage a curtain is drawn across the window. Doors* L. *and* R. *Table* R. *with writing materials. Table* C. *with syphons, glasses, and Tantalus frame.*[2] *Table* L. *with cigars and cigarette box. Lamps lit.*

LADY W. [*standing by the fireplace*] Why doesn't he come? This waiting is horrible. He should be here. Why is he not here, to wake by passionate words some fire within me? I am cold—cold as a loveless thing. Arthur must have read my letter by this time. If he cared for me, he would have come after me, would have taken me back by force. But he doesn't care. He's entrammeled by this woman—fascinated by her—dominated by her. If a woman wants to hold a man, she has merely to appeal to what is worst in him. We make gods of men, and they leave us. Others make brutes of them, and they fawn and are faithful. How hideous life is! . . . Oh! it was mad of me to come here, horribly mad. And yet which is the worst, I wonder, to be at the mercy of a man who loves one, or the wife of a man who in one's own house dishonors one? What woman knows? What woman in the whole world? But will he love me always, this man to whom I am giving my life? What do I bring him? Lips that have lost the note of joy, eyes that are blighted by tears, chill hands and icy heart. I bring him nothing. I must go back—no; I can't go back,

---

[2] a contrivance for holding two or three decanters of liquor, which, however, cannot be poured from until a metal bar over the stoppers is unlocked or removed (a tantalizing arrangement for anyone but the owner); see Tantalus in *The American College Dictionary* and compounds of the term in *OED.*

my letter has put me in their power—Arthur would not take me back! That fatal letter! No! Lord Darlington leaves England to-morrow. I will go with him—I have no choice. [*sits down for a few moments. Then starts up and puts on her cloak*] No, no! I will go back, let Arthur do with me what he pleases. I can't wait here. It has been madness my coming. I must go at once. As for Lord Darlington—Oh! here he is! What shall I do? What can I say to him? Will he let me go away at all? I have heard that men are brutal, horrible. . . . Oh! [*hides her face in her hands*]

Enter MRS. E. (L.)

MRS. E. Lady Windermere! [LADY W. *starts and looks up. Then recoils in contempt*] Thank Heaven I am in time. You must go back to your husband's house immediately.

LADY W. Must?

MRS. E. [*authoritatively*] Yes, you must! There is not a second to be lost. Lord Darlington may return at any moment.

LADY W. Don't come near me!

MRS. E. Oh! you are on the brink of ruin; you are on the brink of a hideous precipice. You must leave this place at once, my carriage is waiting at the corner of the street. You must come with me and drive straight home. [LADY W. *throws off her cloak and flings it on the sofa*] What are you doing?

LADY W. Mrs. Erlynne—if you had not come here, I would have gone back. But now that I see you, I feel that nothing in the whole world would induce me to live under the same roof as Lord Windermere. You fill me with horror. There is something about you that stirs the wildest rage within me. And I know why you are here. My husband sent you to lure me back that I might serve as a blind to whatever relations exist between you and him.

MRS. E. Oh! You don't think that—you can't.

LADY W. Go back to my husband, Mrs. Erlynne. He belongs to you and not to me. I suppose he is afraid of a scandal. Men are such cowards. They outrage every law of the world, and are afraid of the world's tongue. But he had better prepare himself. He shall have a scandal. He shall have the worst scandal there has been in London for years. He shall see his name in every vile paper, mine on every hideous placard.

MRS. E. No—no—

LADY W. Yes! he shall. Had he come himself, I admit I would have gone back to the life of degradation you and he had prepared for me—I was going back—but to stay himself at home, and send you as his messenger—oh! it was infamous—infamous.

MRS. E. [C.] Lady Windermere, you wrong me horribly—you wrong your husband horribly. He doesn't know you are here—he thinks you are safe in your own house. He thinks you are asleep in your own room. He never read the mad letter you wrote to him!

LADY W. [R.] Never read it!

MRS. E. No—he knows nothing about it.

LADY W. How simple you think me! [*going to her*] You are lying to me!

MRS. E. [*restraining herself*] I am not. I am telling you the truth.

LADY W. If my husband didn't read my letter, how is it that you are here? Who told you I had left the house you were shameless enough to enter? Who told you where I had gone to? My husband told you, and sent you to decoy me back. [*crosses* L.]

MRS. E. (R. C.) Your husband has never seen the letter. I—saw it, I opened it. I—read it.

LADY W. [*turning to her*] You opened a letter of mine to my husband? You wouldn't dare!

MRS. E. Dare! Oh! to save you from the abyss into which you are falling, there is nothing in the world I would not dare, nothing in the whole world. Here is the letter. Your husband has never read it. He never shall read it. [*going to fireplace*] It should never have been written. [*tears it and throws it into the fire*]

LADY W. [*with infinite contempt in her voice and look*] How do I know that was my letter after all? You seem to think the commonest device can take me in!

MRS. E. Oh! Why do you disbelieve everything I tell you! What object do you think I have in coming here, except to save you from utter ruin, to save you from the consequence of a hideous mistake? That letter that is burning now *was* your letter. I swear it to you!

LADY W. [*slowly*] You took good care to burn it before I had examined it. I cannot trust you. You, whose whole life is a lie, how could you speak the truth about anything? [*sits down*]

MRS. E. [*hurriedly*] Think as you like about me—say what you choose against me, but go back, go back to the husband you love.

LADY W. [*sullenly*] I do *not* love him!

MRS. E. You do, and you know that he loves you.

LADY W. He does not understand what love is. He understands it as little as you do—but I see what you want. It would be a great advantage for you to get me back. Dear Heaven! what a life I would have then! Living at the mercy of a woman who has neither mercy nor pity in her, a woman whom it is an infamy to meet, a degradation to know, a vile woman, a woman who comes between husband and wife!

MRS. E. [*with a gesture of despair*] Lady Windermere, Lady Windermere, don't say such terrible things. You don't know how terrible they are, how terrible and how unjust. Listen, you must listen! Only go back to your husband, and I promise you never to communicate with him again on any pretext—never to see him—never to have anything to do with his life or yours. The money that he gave me, he gave me not through love, but through hatred, not in worship, but in contempt. The hold I have over him—

LADY W. [*rising*] Ah! you admit you have a hold!

MRS. E. Yes, and I will tell you what it is. It is his love for you, Lady Windermere.

LADY W. You expect me to believe that?

MRS. E. You must believe it! It is true. It is his love for you that has made him submit to—oh! call it what you like, tyranny, threats, anything you choose. But it is his love for you. His desire to spare you—shame, yes, shame and disgrace.

LADY W. What do you mean? You are insolent! What have I to do with you?

MRS. E. [*humbly*] Nothing. I know it—but I tell you that your husband loves you—that you may never meet with such love again in your whole life—that such love you will never meet—and that if you throw it away, the day may come when you will starve for love and it will not be given to you, beg for love and it will be denied you—Oh! Arthur loves you!

LADY W. Arthur? And you tell me there is nothing between you?

MRS. E. Lady Windermere, before Heaven your husband is guiltless of all offense towards you! And I—I tell you that had it ever occurred to me that such a monstrous suspicion would have entered your mind, I would have died rather than have crossed your life or his —oh! died, gladly died! [*moves away to sofa* R.]

LADY W. You talk as if you had a heart. Women like you have no hearts. Heart is not in you. You are bought and sold. [*sits* L. C.]

MRS. E. [*starts, with a gesture of pain. Then restrains herself, and comes over to where* LADY w. *is sitting. As she speaks, she stretches out her hands towards her, but does not dare to touch her*] Believe what you choose about me, I am not worth a moment's sorrow. But don't spoil your beautiful young life on my account! You don't know what may be in store for you, unless you leave this house at once. You don't know what it is to fall into the pit, to be despised, mocked, abandoned, sneered at—to be an outcast! to find the door shut against one, to have to creep in by hideous byways, afraid every moment lest the mask should be stripped from one's face, and all the while to hear the laughter, the horrible laughter of the world, a thing more tragic than all the tears the world has ever shed. You don't know what it is. One pays for one's sin, and then one pays again, and all one's life one pays. You must never know that.—As for me, if suffering be an expiation, then at this moment I have expiated all my faults, whatever they have been; for tonight you have made a heart in one who had it not, made it and broken it.—But let that pass. I may have wrecked my own life, but I will not let you wreck yours. You—why, you are a mere girl, you would be lost. You haven't got the kind of brains that enables a woman to get back. You have neither the wit nor the courage. You couldn't stand dishonor. No! Go back, Lady Windermere, to the husband who loves you, whom you love. You have a child, Lady Windermere. Go back to that child who even now, in pain or in joy, may be calling to you. [LADY w. *rises*] God gave you that child. He will require from you that you make his life fine, that you watch over him. What answer will you make to God if his life is ruined through you? Back to your house, Lady Windermere—your husband loves you. He has never swerved for a moment from the love he bears you. But even if he had a thousand loves, you must stay with your child. If he was harsh to you, you must stay with your child. If he ill-treated you, you must stay with your child. If he abandoned you, your place is with your child. [LADY W. *bursts into tears and buries her face in her hands*] [*rushing to her*] Lady Windermere!

LADY W. [*holding out her hands to her, helplessly, as a child might do*] Take me home. Take me home.

MRS. E. [*is about to embrace her. Then restrains herself. There is a look of wonderful joy in her face*] Come! Where is your cloak? [*getting it from sofa*] Here. Put it on. Come at once! [*they go to the door*]

LADY W. Stop! Don't you hear voices?

MRS. E. No, no! There is no one!

LADY W. Yes, there is! Listen! Oh! that is my husband's voice! He is coming in! Save me! Oh, it's some plot! You have sent for him! [*voices outside*]

MRS. E. Silence! I am here to save you if I can. But I fear it is too late! There! [*points to the curtain across the window*] The first chance you have, slip out, if you ever get a chance!

LADY W. But you!

MRS. E. Oh! never mind me. I'll face them. [LADY W. *hides herself behind the curtain*]

LORD A. [*outside*] Nonsense, dear Windermere, you must not leave me!

MRS. E. Lord Augustus! Then it is I who am lost! [*hesitates for a moment, then looks round and sees door* R., *and exit through it*]

Enter LORD D., MR. D., LORD W., LORD A. L., *and* CECIL G.

DUMBY. What a nuisance their turning us out of the club at this hour! It's only two o'clock. [*sinks into a chair*] The lively part of the evening is only just beginning. [*yawns and closes his eyes*]

LORD W. It is very good of you, Lord Darlington, allowing Augustus to force our company on you, but I'm afraid I can't stay long.

LORD D. Really! I am so sorry! You'll take a cigar, won't you?

LORD W. Thanks! [*sits down*]

LORD A. [*to* LORD W.] My dear boy, you must not dream of going. I have a great deal to talk to you about, of demmed importance, too. [*sits down with him at* L. *table*]

CECIL G. Oh! we all know what that is! Tuppy can't talk about anything but Mrs. Erlynne!

LORD W. Well, that is no business of yours is it, Cecil?

CECIL G. None! That is why it interests me. My own business always bores me to death. I prefer other people's.

LORD D. Have something to drink, you fellows. Cecil, you'll have a whiskey and soda?

CECIL G. Thanks. [*goes to the table with* LORD D.] Mrs. Erlynne looked very handsome to-night, didn't she?

LORD D. I am not one of her admirers.

CECIL G. I usen't to be, but I am now. Why! she actually made me introduce her to poor dear Aunt Caroline. I believe she is going to lunch there.

LORD D. [*in surprise*] No?

CECIL G. She is, really.

LORD D. Excuse me, you fellows. I'm going away to-morrow. And I have to write a few letters. [*goes to writing-table and sits down*]

DUMBY. Clever woman, Mrs. Erlynne.

CECIL G. Hallo, Dumby! I thought you were asleep.

DUMBY. I am, I usually am!

LORD A. A very clever woman. Knows perfectly well what a demmed fool I am—knows it as well as I do myself. [CECIL G. *comes towards him laughing*] Ah! you may laugh, my boy, but it is a great thing to come across a woman who thoroughly understands one.

DUMBY. It is an awfully dangerous thing. They always end by marrying one.

CECIL G. But I thought, Tuppy, you were never going to see her again. Yes! you told me so yesterday evening at the club. You said you'd heard—[*whispering to him*]

LORD A. Oh, she's explained that.

CECIL G. And the Wiesbaden affair?

LORD A. She's explained that, too.

DUMBY. And her income, Tuppy? Has she explained that?

LORD A. [*in a very serious voice*] She's going to explain that to-morrow. [CECIL G. *goes back to* C. *table*]

DUMBY. Awfully commercial, women nowadays. Our grandmothers threw their caps over the mills, of course, but by Jove, their granddaughters only throw their caps over mills that can raise the wind for them.

LORD A. You want to make her out a wicked woman. She is not!

CECIL G. Oh! Wicked women bother one. Good women bore one. That is the only difference between them.

LORD A. [*puffing a cigar*] Mrs. Erlynne has a future before her.

DUMBY. Mrs. Erlynne has a past before her.

LORD A. I prefer women with a past. They're always so demmed amusing to talk to.

CECIL G. Well, you'll have lots of topics of conversation with *her,* Tuppy. [*rising and going to him*]

LORD A. You're getting annoying, dear boy; you're getting demmed annoying.

CECIL G. [*puts his hands on his shoulders*] Now, Tuppy, you've lost your figure and you've lost your character. Don't lose your temper; you have only got one.

LORD A. My dear boy, if I wasn't the most good-natured man in London—

CECIL G. We'd treat you with more respect, wouldn't we, Tuppy? [*strolls away*]

DUMBY. The youth of the present day are quite monstrous. They have absolutely no respect for dyed hair. [LORD A. *looks round angrily*]

CECIL G. Mrs. Erlynne has a very great respect for dear Tuppy.

DUMBY. Then Mrs. Erlynne sets an admirable example to the rest of her sex. It is perfectly brutal the way most women nowadays behave to men who are not their husbands.

LORD W. Dumby, you are ridiculous, and Cecil, you let your tongue run away with you. You must leave Mrs. Erlynne alone. You don't really know anything about her, and you're always talking scandal against her.

CECIL G. [*coming towards him* L. C.] My dear Arthur, *I* never talk scandal. *I* only talk gossip.

LORD W. What is the difference between scandal and gossip?

CECIL G. Oh! gossip is charming! History is merely gossip. But scandal is gossip made tedious by morality. Now I never moralize. A man who moralizes is usually a hypocrite, and a woman who moralizes is invariably plain. There is nothing in the whole world so unbecoming to a woman as a Nonconformist con-

science. And most women know it, I'm glad to say.

LORD A. Just my sentiments, dear boy, just my sentiments.

CECIL G. Sorry to hear it, Tuppy; whenever people agree with me, I always feel I must be wrong.

LORD A. My dear boy, when I was your age—

CECIL G. But you never were, Tuppy, and you never will be. [*goes up* C.] I say, Darlington, let us have some cards. You'll play, Arthur, won't you?

LORD W. No, thanks, Cecil.

DUMBY. [*with a sigh*] Good Heavens! how marriage ruins a man! It's as demoralizing as cigarettes, and far more expensive.

CECIL G. You'll play, of course, Tuppy?

LORD A. [*pouring himself out a brandy and soda at table*] Can't, dear boy. Promised Mrs. Erlynne never to play or drink again.

CECIL G. Now, my dear Tuppy, don't be led astray into the paths of virtue. Reformed, you would be perfectly tedious. That is the worst of women. They always want one to be good. And if we are good, when they meet us, they don't love us at all. They like to find us quite irretrievably bad, and to leave us quite unattractively good.

LORD D. [*rising from* R. *table, where he has been writing letters*] They always do find us bad!

DUMBY. I don't think we are bad. I think we are all good except Tuppy.

LORD D. No, we are all in the gutter, but some of us are looking at the stars. [*sits down at* C. *table*]

DUMBY. We are all in the gutter, but some of us are looking at the stars? Upon my word, you are very romantic to-night, Darlington.

CECIL G. Too romantic! You must be in love. Who is the girl?

LORD D. The woman I love is not free, or thinks she isn't. [*glances instinctively at* LORD W. *while he speaks*]

CECIL G. A married woman, then! Well, there's nothing in the world like the devotion of a married woman. It's a thing no married man knows anything about.

LORD D. Oh! she doesn't love me. She is a good woman. She is the only good woman I have ever met in my life.

CECIL G. The only good woman you have ever met in your life?

LORD D. Yes!

CECIL G. [*lighting a cigarette*] Well, you are a lucky fellow! Why, I have met hundreds of good women. I never seem to meet any but good women. The world is perfectly packed with good women. To know them is a middle-class education.

LORD D. This woman has purity and innocence. She has everything we men have lost.

CECIL G. My dear fellow, what on earth should we men do going about with purity and innocence? A carefully thought-out buttonhole is much more effective.

DUMBY. She doesn't really love you then?

LORD D. No, she does not!

DUMBY. I congratulate you, my dear fellow. In this world there are only two tragedies. One is not getting what one wants, and the other is getting it. The last is much the worst, the last is a real tragedy! But I am interested to hear she does not love you. How long could you love a woman who didn't love you, Cecil?

CECIL G. A woman who didn't love me? Oh, all my life!

DUMBY. So could I. But it's so difficult to meet one.

LORD D. How can you be so conceited, Dumby?

DUMBY. I didn't say it as a matter of conceit. I said it as a matter of regret. I have been wildly, madly adored. I am sorry I have. It has been an immense nuisance. I should like to be allowed a little time to myself, now and then.

LORD A. [*looking round*] Time to educate yourself, I suppose.

DUMBY. No, time to forget all I have learned. That is much more important, dear Tuppy. [LORD A. *moves uneasily in his chair*]

LORD D. What cynics you fellows are!

CECIL G. What is a cynic? [*sitting on the back of the sofa*]

LORD D. A man who knows the price of everything and the value of nothing.

CECIL G. And a sentimentalist, my dear Darlington, is a man who sees an absurd value in everything, and doesn't know the market price of any single thing.

LORD D. You always amuse me, Cecil. You talk as if you were a man of experience.

CECIL G. I am. [*moves up to front of fireplace*]

LORD D. You are far too young!

CECIL G. That is a great error. Experience is a question of instinct about life. I have got it. Tuppy hasn't. Experience is the name Tuppy gives to his mistakes. That is all. [LORD A. *looks round indignantly*]

DUMBY. Experience is the name everyone gives to their mistakes.

CECIL G. [*standing with his back to fireplace*] One shouldn't commit any. [*sees* LADY W.'s *fan on sofa*]

DUMBY. Life would be very dull without them.

CECIL G. Of course you are quite faithful to this woman you are in love with, Darlington, to this good woman?

LORD D. Cecil, if one really loves a woman, all other women in the world become absolutely meaningless to one. Love changes one— I am changed.

CECIL G. Dear me! How very interesting. Tuppy, I want to talk to you. [LORD A. *takes no notice*]

DUMBY. It's no use talking to Tuppy. You might as well talk to a brick wall.

CECIL G. But I like talking to a brick wall— it's the only thing in the world that never contradicts me! Tuppy!

LORD A. Well, what is it? What is it? [*rising and going over to* CECIL G.]

CECIL G. Come over here. I want you particularly. [*aside*] Darlington has been moralizing and talking about the purity of love, and that sort of thing, and he has got some woman in his rooms all the time.

LORD A. No, really! really!

CECIL G. [*in a low voice*] Yes, here is her fan. [*points to the fan*]

LORD A. [*chuckling*] By Jove! By Jove!

LORD W. [*up by door*] I am really off now, Lord Darlington. I am sorry you are leaving England so soon. Pray call on us when you come back! My wife and I will be charmed to see you!

LORD D. [*up stage with* LORD W.] I am afraid I shall be away for many years. Good night!

CECIL G. Arthur!

LORD W. What?

CECIL G. I want to speak to you for a moment. No, do come!

LORD W. [*putting on his coat*] I can't—I'm off!

CECIL G. It is something very particular. It will interest you enormously.

LORD W. [*smiling*] It is some of your nonsense, Cecil.

CECIL G. It isn't. It isn't really!

LORD A. [*going to him*] My dear fellow, you mustn't go yet. I have a lot to talk to you about. And Cecil has something to show you.

LORD W. [*walking over*] Well, what is it?

CECIL G. Darlington has got a woman here in his rooms. Here is her fan. Amusing, isn't it? [*a pause*]

LORD W. Good God! [*seizes the fan—* DUMBY *rises*]

CECIL G. What is the matter?

LORD W. Lord Darlington!

LORD D. [*turning round*] Yes!

LORD W. What is my wife's fan doing here in your rooms? Hands off, Cecil. Don't touch me.

LORD D. Your wife's fan?

LORD W. Yes, here it is!

LORD D. [*walking towards him*] I don't know!

LORD W. You must know. I demand an explanation. [*to* CECIL G.] Don't hold me, you fool.

LORD D. [*aside*] She is here after all!

LORD W. Speak, sir! Why is my wife's fan here? Answer me, by God! I'll search your rooms, and if my wife's here, I'll— [*moves*]

LORD D. You shall not search my rooms. You have no right to do so. I forbid you.

LORD W. You scoundrel! I'll not leave your room till I have searched every corner of it! What moves behind that curtain? [*rushes towards the curtain* C.]

MRS. E. [*enters behind* R.] Lord Windermere!

LORD W. Mrs. Erlynne! [*everyone starts and turns round.* LADY W. *slips out from behind the curtain and glides from the room* L.]

MRS. E. I am afraid I took your wife's fan in mistake for my own, when I was leaving your house to-night. I am so sorry. [*takes fan from him.* LORD W. *looks at her in contempt,* LORD D. *in mingled astonishment and anger.* LORD A. *turns away. The other men smile at each other*]

ACT IV

SCENE—*Same as in Act I.*

LADY W. [*lying on sofa*] How can I tell him? I can't tell him. It would kill me. I wonder what happened after I escaped from that horrible room. Perhaps she told them the true reason of her being there, and the real meaning of that—fatal fan of mine. Oh, if he knows—how can I look him in the face again? He would never forgive me. [*touches bell*] How securely one thinks one lives—out of reach of temptation, sin, folly. And then suddenly—Oh! Life is terrible. It rules us, we do not rule it.

Enter ROSALIE (R.)

ROSALIE. Did your ladyship ring for me?

LADY W. Yes. Have you found out at what time Lord Windermere came in last night?

ROSALIE. His lordship did not come in till five o'clock.

LADY W. Five o'clock! He knocked at my door this morning, didn't he?

ROSALIE. Yes, my lady—at half-past nine. I told him your ladyship was not awake yet.

LADY W. Did he say anything?

ROSALIE. Something about your ladyship's fan. I didn't quite catch what his lordship said. Has the fan been lost, my lady? I can't find it, and Parker says it was not left in any of the rooms. He has looked in all of them and on the terrace as well.

LADY W. It doesn't matter. Tell Parker not to trouble. That will do. [*exit* ROSALIE] [*rising*] She is sure to tell him. I can fancy a person doing a wonderful act of self-sacrifice, doing it spontaneously, recklessly, nobly—and afterwards finding out that it costs too much. Why should she hesitate between her ruin and mine? . . . How strange! I would have publicly disgraced her in my own house. She accepts public disgrace in the house of another to save me. . . . There is a bitter irony in things, a bitter irony in the way we talk of good and bad women. . . . Oh, what a lesson! and what a pity that in life we only get our lessons when they are of no use to us! For even if she doesn't tell, I must. Oh! the shame of it, the shame of it! To tell it is to live through it all again. Actions are the first tragedy in life, words are the second. Words are perhaps the worst. Words are merciless. . . . Oh! [*starts as* LORD W. *enters*]

LORD W. [*kisses her*] Margaret—how pale you look!

LADY W. I slept very badly.

LORD W. [*sitting on sofa with her*] I am so sorry. I came in dreadfully late, and I didn't like to wake you. You are crying, dear.

LADY W. Yes, I am crying, for I have some-10 thing to tell you, Arthur.

LORD W. My dear child, you are not well. You've been doing too much. Let us go away to the country. You'll be all right at Selby. The season is almost over. There is no use staying 15 on. Poor darling! We'll go away to-day, if you like. [*Rises*] We can easily catch the 4:30. I'll send a wire to Fannen. [*crosses and sits down at table to write a telegram*]

LADY W. Yes; let us go away to-day. No; I 20 can't go away to-day, Arthur. There is someone I must see before I leave town—someone who has been kind to me.

LORD W. [*rising and leaning over sofa*] Kind to you? 25

LADY W. Far more than that. [*rises and goes to him*] I will tell you, Arthur, but only love me, love me as you used to love me.

LORD W. Used to? You are not thinking of that wretched woman who came here last 30 night? [*coming round and sitting* R. *of her*] You don't still imagine—no, you couldn't.

LADY W. I don't. I know now I was wrong and foolish.

LORD W. It was very good of you to receive 35 her last night—but you are never to see her again.

LADY W. Why do you say that? [*a pause*]

LORD W. [*holding her hand*] Margaret, I thought Mrs. Erlynne was a woman more 40 sinned against than sinning, as the phrase goes. I thought she wanted to be good, to get back into a place that she had lost by a moment's folly, to lead again a decent life. I believed what she told me—I was mistaken in her. She 45 is bad—as bad as a woman can be.

LADY W. Arthur, Arthur, don't talk so bitterly about any woman. I don't think now that people can be divided into the good and the bad, as though they were two separate races or 50 creations. What are called good women may have terrible things in them, mad moods of recklessness, assertion, jealousy, sin. Bad women, as they are termed, may have in them sorrow, repentance, pity, sacrifice. And I don't think Mrs. Erlynne a bad woman—I know 5 she's not.

LORD W. My dear child, the woman's impossible. No matter what harm she tries to do us, you must never see her again. She is inadmissible anywhere.

LADY W. But I want to see her. I want her to come here.

LORD W. Never!

LADY W. She came here once as *your* guest. She must come now as *mine*. That is but fair.

LORD W. She should never have come here.

LADY W. [*rising*] It is too late, Arthur, to say that now. [*moves away*]

LORD W. [*rising*] Margaret, if you knew where Mrs. Erlynne went last night, after she 20 left this house, you would not sit in the same room with her. It was absolutely shameless, the whole thing.

LADY W. Arthur, I can't bear it any longer. I must tell you. Last night——

Enter PARKER *with a tray on which lie*
LADY W.'s *fan and a card*

PARKER. Mrs. Erlynne has called to return your ladyship's fan which she took away by mistake last night. Mrs. Erlynne has written a message on the card.

LADY W. Oh, ask Mrs. Erlynne to be kind enough to come up. [*reads card*] Say I shall be very glad to see her. [*exit* PARKER] She wants to see me, Arthur.

LORD W. [*takes card and looks at it*] Margaret, I *beg* you not to. Let me see her first, at any rate. She's a very dangerous woman. She is the most dangerous woman I know. You don't realize what you're doing.

LADY W. It is right that I should see her.

LORD W. My child, you may be on the brink of a great sorrow. Don't go to meet it. It is absolutely necessary that I should see her before you do.

LADY W. Why should it be necessary?

Enter PARKER

PARKER. Mrs. Erlynne.

Enter MRS. E. *Exit* PARKER

MRS. E. How do you do, Lady Windermere? [*to* LORD W.] How do you do? Do you know, Lady Windermere, I am so sorry about your fan. I can't imagine how I made such a silly mistake. Most stupid of me. And as I was driving in your direction, I thought I would take the opportunity of returning your property in person, with many apologies for my carelessness, and of bidding you good-bye.

LADY W. Good-bye? [*moves towards sofa with* MRS. E. *and sits down beside her*] Are you going away, then, Mrs. Erlynne?

MRS. E. Yes; I am going to live abroad again. The English climate doesn't suit me. My —heart is affected here, and that I don't like. I prefer living in the south. London is too full of fogs and—serious people, Lord Windermere. Whether the fogs produce the serious people or whether the serious people produce the fogs, I don't know, but the whole thing rather gets on my nerves, and so I'm leaving this afternoon by the Club Train.

LADY W. This afternoon? But I wanted so much to come and see you.

MRS. E. How kind of you! But I am afraid I have to go.

LADY W. Shall I never see you again, Mrs. Erlynne?

MRS. E. I am afraid not. Our lives lie too far apart. But there is a little thing I would like you to do for me. I want a photograph of you, Lady Windermere—would you give me one? You don't know how gratified I should be.

LADY W. Oh, with pleasure. There is one on that table. I'll show it to you. [*goes across to the table*]

LORD W. [*coming up to* MRS. E. *and speaking in a low voice*] It is monstrous your intruding yourself here after your conduct last night.

MRS. E. [*with an amused smile*] My dear Windermere, manners before morals!

LADY W. [*returning*] I'm afraid it is very flattering—I am not so pretty as that. [*showing photograph*]

MRS. E. You are much prettier. But haven't you got one of yourself with your little boy?

LADY W. *I have.* Would you prefer one of those?

MRS. E. Yes.

LADY W. I'll go and get it for you, if you'll excuse me for a moment. I have one upstairs.

MRS. E. So sorry, Lady Windermere, to give you so much trouble.

LADY W. [*moves to door* R.] No trouble at all, Mrs. Erlynne.

MRS. E. Thanks so much. [*exit* LADY W. (R.)] You seem rather out of temper this morning, Windermere. Why should you be? Margaret and I get on charmingly together.

LORD W. I can't bear to see you with her. Besides, you have not told me the truth, Mrs. Erlynne.

MRS. E. I have not told *her* the truth, you mean.

LORD W. [*standing* C.] I sometimes wish you had. I should have been spared then the misery, the anxiety, the annoyance of the last six months. But rather than my wife should know—that the mother whom she was taught to consider as dead, the mother whom she has mourned as dead, is living—a divorced woman going about under an assumed name, a bad woman preying upon life, as I know you now to be—rather than that, I was ready to supply you with money to pay bill after bill, extravagance after extravagance, to risk what occurred yesterday, the first quarrel I have ever had with my wife. You don't understand what that means to me. How could you? But I tell you that the only bitter words that ever came from those sweet lips of hers were on your account, and I hate to see you next her. You sully the innocence that is in her. [*moves* L. C.] And then I used to think that with all your faults you were frank and honest. You are not.

MRS. E. Why do you say that?

LORD W. You made me get you an invitation to my wife's ball.

MRS. E. For my daughter's ball—yes.

LORD W. You came, and within an hour of your leaving the house, you are found in a man's rooms—you are disgraced before everyone. [*goes up stage* C.]

MRS. E. Yes.

LORD W. [*turning round on her*] Therefore I have a right to look upon you as what you are—a worthless, vicious woman. I have the right to tell you never to enter this house, never to attempt to come near my wife——

MRS. E. [*coldly*] My daughter, you mean.

LORD W. You have no right to claim her as your daughter. You left her, abandoned her, when she was but a child in the cradle, abandoned her for your lover, who abandoned you in turn.

MRS. E. [*rising*] Do you count that to his credit, Lord Windermere—or to mine?

LORD W. To his, now that I know you.

MRS. E. Take care—you had better be careful.

LORD W. Oh, I am not going to mince words for you. I know you thoroughly.

MRS. E. [*looking steadily at him*] I question that.

LORD W. I *do* know you. For twenty years of your life you lived without your child, without a thought of your child. One day you read in the papers that she had married a rich man. You saw your hideous chance. You knew that to spare her the ignominy of learning that a woman like you was her mother, I would endure anything. You began your blackmailing.

MRS. E. [*shrugging her shoulders*] Don't use ugly words, Windermere. They are vulgar. I saw my chance, it is true, and took it.

LORD W. Yes, you took it—and spoiled it all last night by being found out.

MRS. E. [*with a strange smile*] You are quite right, I spoiled it all last night.

LORD W. And as for your blunder in taking my wife's fan from here, and then leaving it about in Darlington's rooms, it is unpardonable. I can't bear the sight of it now. I shall never let my wife use it again. The thing is soiled for me. You should have kept it and not brought it back.

MRS. E. I think I *shall* keep it. [*goes up*] It's extremely pretty. [*takes up fan*] I shall ask Margaret to give it to me.

LORD W. I hope my wife will give it you.

MRS. E. Oh, I'm sure she will have no objection.

LORD W. I wish that at the same time she would give you a miniature she kisses every night before she prays—— It's the miniature of a young, innocent-looking girl with beautiful dark hair.

MRS. E. Ah, yes, I remember. How long ago that seems! [*goes to sofa and sits down*] It was done before I was married. Dark hair and an innocent expression were the fashion then, Windermere! [*a pause*]

LORD W. What do you mean by coming here this morning? What is your object? [*crossing L. C. and sitting*]

MRS. E. [*with a note of irony in her voice*] To bid good-bye to my dear daughter, of course. [LORD W. *bites his under lip in anger.* MRS. E. *looks at him, and her voice and manner become serious. In her accents as she talks there is a note of deep tragedy. For a moment she reveals herself*] Oh, don't imagine I am going to have a pathetic scene with her, weep on her neck and tell her who I am, and all that kind of thing. I have no ambition to play the part of a mother. Only once in my life have I known a mother's feelings. That was last night. They were terrible—they made me suffer—they made me suffer too much. For twenty years, as you say, I have lived childless—I want to live childless still. [*hiding her feelings with a trivial laugh*] Besides, my dear Windermere, how on earth could I pose as a mother with a grown-up daughter? Margaret is twenty-one, and I have never admitted that I am more than twenty-nine, or thirty at the most. Twenty-nine when there are pink shades, thirty when there are not. So you see what difficulties it would involve. No, as far as I am concerned, let your wife cherish the memory of this dead, stainless mother. Why should I interfere with her illusions? I find it hard enough to keep my own. I lost one illusion last night. I thought I had no heart. I find I have, and a heart doesn't suit me, Windermere. Somehow it doesn't go with modern dress. It makes one look old. [*takes up hand-mirror from table and looks into it*] And it spoils one's career at critical moments.

LORD W. You fill me with horror—with absolute horror.

MRS. E. [*rising*] I suppose, Windermere, you would like me to retire into a convent or become a hospital nurse or something of that kind, as people do in silly modern novels. That is stupid of you, Arthur; in real life we don't do such things—not as long as we have any good looks left, at any rate. No—what consoles one nowadays is not repentance, but pleasure. Repentance is quite out of date. And, besides, if a woman really repents, she has to go to a bad dressmaker, otherwise no one believes in her. And nothing in the world would induce me to do that. No; I am going to pass entirely out of your two lives. My coming into them has been a mistake—I discovered that last night.

LORD W. A fatal mistake.

MRS. E. [*smiling*] Almost fatal.

LORD W. I am sorry now I did not tell my wife the whole thing at once.

MRS. E. I regret my bad actions. You regret your good ones—that is the difference between us.

LORD W. I don't trust you. I *will* tell my wife. It's better for her to know, and from me. It will cause her infinite pain—it will humiliate her terribly, but it's right that she should know.

MRS. E. You propose to tell her?

LORD W. I am going to tell her.

MRS. E. [*going up to him*] If you do, I will make my name so infamous that it will mar every moment of her life. It will ruin her and make her wretched. If you dare to tell her, there is no depth of degradation I will not sink to, no pit of shame I will not enter. You shall not tell her—I forbid you.

LORD W. Why?

MRS. E. [*after a pause*] If I said to you that I cared for her, perhaps loved her even—you would sneer at me, wouldn't you?

LORD W. I should feel it was not true. A mother's love means devotion, unselfishness, sacrifice. What could you know of such things?

MRS. E. You are right. What could I know of such things? Don't let us talk any more about it; as for telling my daughter who I am, that I do not allow. It is my secret, it is not yours. If I make up my mind to tell her, and I think I will, I shall tell her before I leave this house—if not, I shall never tell her.

LORD W. [*angrily*] Then let me beg of you to leave our house at once. I will make your excuses to Margaret.

Enter LADY W. (R.) *She goes over to* MRS. E. *with the photograph in her hand.* LORD W. *moves to back of sofa, and anxiously watches* MRS. E. *as the scene progresses*

LADY W. I am so sorry, Mrs. Erlynne, to have kept you waiting. I couldn't find the photograph anywhere. At last I discovered it in my husband's dressing-room—he had stolen it.

MRS. E. [*takes the photograph from her and looks at it*] I am not surprised—it is charming. [*goes over to sofa with* LADY W. *and sits down beside her. Looks again at the photograph*] And so that is your little boy! What is he called?

LADY W. Gerard, after my dear father.

MRS. E. [*laying the photograph down*] Really?

LADY W. Yes. If it had been a girl, I would have called it after my mother. My mother had the same name as myself, Margaret.

MRS. E. My name is Margaret, too.

LADY W. Indeed!

MRS. E. Yes. [*pause*] You are devoted to your mother's memory, Lady Windermere, your husband tells me.

LADY W. We all have ideals in life. At least we all should have. Mine is my mother.

MRS. E. Ideals are dangerous things. Realities are better. They wound, but they are better.

LADY W. [*shaking her head*] If I lost my ideals, I should lose everything.

MRS. E. Everything?

LADY W. Yes. [*pause*]

MRS. E. Did your father often speak to you of your mother?

LADY W. No, it gave him too much pain. He told me how my mother had died a few months after I was born. His eyes filled with tears as he spoke. Then he begged me never to mention her name to him again. It made him suffer even to hear it. My father—my father really died of a broken heart. His was the most ruined life I know.

MRS. E. [*rising*] I am afraid I must go now, Lady Windermere.

LADY W. [*rising*] Oh, no, don't.

MRS. E. I think I had better. My carriage must have come back by this time. I sent it to Lady Jedburgh's with a note.

LADY W. Arthur, would you mind seeing if Mrs. Erlynne's carriage has come back?

MRS. E. Pray don't trouble Lord Windermere, Lady Windermere.

LADY W. Yes, Arthur, do go, please. [LORD W. *hesitates for a moment and looks at* MRS. E. *She remains quite impassive. He leaves the room*] [*To* MRS. E.] Oh, what am I to say to you? You saved me last night! [*goes toward her*]

MRS. E. Hush—don't speak of it.

LADY W. I must speak of it. I can't let you think that I am going to accept this sacrifice. I am not. It is too great. I am going to tell my husband everything. It is my duty.

MRS. E. It is not your duty—at least you

have duties to others besides him. You say you owe me something?

LADY W. I owe you everything.

MRS. E. Then pay your debt by silence. That is the only way in which it can be paid. Don't spoil the one good thing I have done in my life by telling it to anyone. Promise me that what passed last night will remain a secret between us. You must not bring misery into your husband's life. Why spoil his love? You must not spoil it. Love is easily killed. Oh, how easily love is killed! Pledge me your word, Lady Windermere, that you will *never* tell him. I insist upon it.

LADY W. [*with bowed head*] It is your will, not mine.

MRS. E. Yes, it is my will. And never forget your child—I like to think of you as a mother. I like you to think of yourself as one.

LADY W. [*looking up*] I always will now. Only once in my life I have forgotten my own mother—that was last night. Oh, if I had remembered her, I should not have been so foolish, so wicked.

MRS. E. [*with a slight shudder*] Hush, last night is quite over.

Enter LORD W.

LORD W. Your carriage has not come back yet, Mrs. Erlynne.

MRS. E. It makes no matter. I'll take a hansom. There is nothing in the world so respectable as a good Shrewsbury and Talbot. And now, dear Lady Windermere, I am afraid it is really good-bye. [*moves up* C.] Oh, I remember. You'll think me absurd, but do you know, I've taken a great fancy to this fan that I was silly enough to run away with last night from your ball. Now, I wonder would you give it to me? Lord Windermere says you may. I know it is his present.

LADY W. Oh, certainly, if it will give you any pleasure. But it has my name on it. It has "Margaret" on it.

MRS. E. But we have the same Christian name.

LADY W. Oh, I forgot. Of course, do have it. What a wonderful chance our names being the same!

MRS. E. Quite wonderful. Thanks—it will always remind me of you. [*shakes hands with her*]

Enter PARKER

PARKER. Lord Augustus Lorton. Mrs. Erlynne's carriage has come.

Enter LORD A.

LORD A. Good morning, dear boy. Good morning, Lady Windermere. [*sees* MRS. E.] Mrs. Erlynne!

MRS. E. How do you do, Lord Augustus? Are you quite well this morning?

LORD A. [*coldly*] Quite well, thank you, Mrs. Erlynne.

MRS. E. You don't look at all well, Lord Augustus. You stop up too late—it is so bad for you. You really should take more care of yourself. Good-bye, Lord Windermere. [*goes towards door with a bow to* LORD A. *Suddenly smiles, and looks back at him*] Lord Augustus! Won't you see me to my carriage? You might carry the fan.

LORD W. Allow me!

MRS. E. No, I want Lord Augustus. I have a special message for the dear Duchess. Won't you carry the fan, Lord Augustus?

LORD A. If you really desire it, Mrs. Erlynne.

MRS. E. [*laughing*] Of course I do. You'll carry it so gracefully. You would carry off anything gracefully, dear Lord Augustus. [*when she reaches the door she looks back for a moment at* LADY W. *Their eyes meet. Then she turns, and exit* C., *followed by* LORD A.]

LADY W. You will never speak against Mrs. Erlynne again, Arthur, will you?

LORD W. [*gravely*] She is better than one thought her.

LADY W. She is better than I am.

LORD W. [*smiling as he strokes her hair*] Child, you and she belong to different worlds. Into your world evil has never entered.

LADY W. Don't say that, Arthur. There is the same world for all of us, and good and evil, sin and innocence, go through it hand in hand. To shut one's eyes to half of life that one may live securely is as though one blinded oneself that one might walk with more safety in a land of pit and precipice.

LORD W. [*moves down with her*] Darling, why do you say that?

LADY W. [*sits on sofa*] Because I, who had shut my eyes to life, came to the brink. And one who had separated us——

LORD W. We were never parted.

LADY W. We never must be again. Oh, Arthur, don't love me less, and I will trust you more. I will trust you absolutely. Let us go to Selby. In the Rose Garden at Selby, the roses are white and red.

Enter LORD A.

LORD A. Arthur, she has explained everything! [LADY W. *looks horribly frightened.* LORD W. *starts.* LORD A. *takes* LORD W. *by the arm, and brings him to front of stage*] My dear fellow, she has explained every demmed thing. We all wronged her immensely. It was entirely for my sake she went to Darlington's rooms— called first at the club. Fact is, wanted to put me out of suspense, and being told I had gone on—followed—naturally frightened when she heard a lot of men coming in—retired to another room—I assure you, most gratifying to me, the whole thing. We all behaved brutally to her. She is just the woman for me. Suits me down to the ground. All the condition she makes is that we live out of England—a very good thing, too!—Demmed clubs, demmed climate, demmed cooks, demmed everything! Sick of it all.

LADY W. [*frightened*] Has Mrs. Erlynne——?

LORD A. [*advancing towards her with a bow*] Yes, Lady Windermere, Mrs. Erlynne has done me the honor of accepting my hand.

LORD W. Well, you are certainly marrying a very clever woman.

LADY W. [*taking her husband's hand*] Ah! you're marrying a very good woman.

THE TWELVE-POUND LOOK *

JAMES M. BARRIE

Sir James M. Barrie (1860–1937) was born in Scotland and studied at Edinburgh University. As journalist and novelist in the nineties, he slowly made his way up the literary ladder. The dramatized version of his novel, The Little Minister, "made" him in a commercial sense. Although Barrie (see I, 404) has been called egotist, sentimentalist, children's writer, canny Scot, the "Great Comforter," and other names, he remains a capable and successful playwright; from an early burlesque of Ibsen, Barrie progressed to a high place in early twenti-eth-century British drama with The Admirable Crichton, Quality Street, and What Every Woman Knows. One critic has written that the dramatist's charm lay in his being "inoffensive." This is negative and misleading; Barrie could show up the human race as well as comfort it. In a positive way, outside the theater, the Great Comforter became a baronet in 1913, received the Order of Merit, and assumed the posts of Rector (1922) and Chancellor (1930) of Edinburgh University.

If quite convenient (as they say about cheques) you are to conceive that the scene is laid in your own house, and that HARRY SIMS is you. Perhaps the ornamentation of the house is a trifle ostentatious, but if you cavil at that we are willing to re-decorate: you don't get out of being HARRY SIMS on a mere matter of plush and dados. It pleases us to make him a city man, but (rather than lose you) he can be turned with a scrape of the pen into a K. C.,[1] fashionable doctor, Secretary of State, or what you will. We conceive him of a pleasant rotundity with a thick red neck, but we shall waive that point if you know him to be thin.

It is that day in your career when everything went wrong just when everything seemed to be superlatively right.

In HARRY's case it was a woman who did the mischief. She came to him in his great hour and told him she did not admire him. Of course he turned her out of the house and was soon himself again, but it spoilt the morning for him. This is the subject of the play, and quite enough too.

HARRY is to receive the honour of knighthood in a few days, and we discover him in the sumptuous "snuggery" of his home in Kensington (or is it Westminster?), rehearsing the ceremony with his wife. They have been at it all the morning, a pleasing occupation. MRS. SIMS (as we may call her for the last time, as it were, and strictly as a good-natured joke) is wearing her presentation gown, and personates the august one who is about to dub her HARRY knight. She is seated regally. Her jewelled shoulders proclaim aloud her husband's generosity. She must be an extraordinarily proud and happy woman, yet she has a drawn face and shrinking ways as if there were some one near her of whom she is afraid. She claps her hands, as the signal to HARRY. He enters bowing, and with a graceful swerve of the leg. He is only partly in costume, the sword and the real stockings not having arrived yet. With a gliding motion that is only delayed while one leg makes up to the other, he reaches his wife, and, going on one knee, raises her hand superbly to his lips. She taps him on the shoulder with a paper-knife and says huskily, "Rise, Sir Harry." He rises, bows, and glides about the room, going on his knees to various articles of furniture, and rises from each a knight. It is a

[1] King's Counsel (or possibly a colloquial shortening of K. C. B., Knight Commander of the Bath).

radiant domestic scene, and HARRY is as dignified as if he knew that royalty was rehearsing it at the other end.

SIR HARRY. [complacently] Did that seem all right, eh?

LADY SIMS. [much relieved] I think perfect.

SIR HARRY. But was it dignified?

LADY SIMS. Oh, very. And it will be still more so when you have the sword.

SIR HARRY. The sword will lend it an air. There are really the five moments—[suiting the action to the word]—the glide—the dip—the kiss—the tap—and you back out a knight. It's short, but it's a very beautiful ceremony. [kindly] Anything you can suggest?

LADY SIMS. No—oh no. [nervously, seeing him pause to kiss the tassel of a cushion] You don't think you have practised till you know what to do almost too well? [He has been in a blissful temper, but such niggling criticism would try any man]

SIR HARRY. I do not. Don't talk nonsense. Wait till your opinion is asked for.

LADY SIMS. [abashed] I'm sorry, Harry. [a perfect butler appears and presents a card] "The Flora Typewriting Agency."

SIR HARRY. Ah, yes. I telephoned them to send some one. A woman, I suppose, Tombes?

TOMBES. Yes, Sir Harry.

SIR HARRY. Show her in here. [He has very lately become a stickler for etiquette] And, Tombes, strictly speaking, you know, I am not Sir Harry till Thursday.

TOMBES. Beg pardon, sir, but it is such a satisfaction to us.

SIR HARRY. [good-naturedly] Ah, they like it downstairs, do they?

TOMBES. [unbending] Especially the females, Sir Harry.

SIR HARRY. Exactly. You can show her in, Tombes. [the butler departs on his mighty task] You can tell the woman what she is wanted for, Emmy, while I change. [He is too modest to boast about himself, and prefers to keep a wife in the house for that purpose] You can tell her the sort of things about me that will come better from you. [smiling happily] You heard what Tombes said, "Especially the females." And he is right. Success! The women like it even better than the men. And rightly. For they share. You share, Lady Sims. Not a woman will see that gown without being sick with envy of it. I know them. Have all our lady friends in to see it. It will make them ill for a week. [*These sentiments carry him off lightheartedly, and presently the disturbing element is shown in. She is a mere typist, dressed in uncommonly good taste, but at contemptibly small expense, and she is carrying her typewriter in a friendly way rather than as a badge of slavery, as of course it is. Her eye is clear; and in odd contrast to* LADY SIMS, *she is self-reliant and serene*]

KATE. [*respectfully, but she should have waited to be spoken to*] Good morning, madam.

LADY SIMS. [*in her nervous way, and scarcely noticing that the typist is a little too ready with her tongue*] Good morning. [*As a first impression she rather likes the woman, and the woman, though it is scarcely worth mentioning, rather likes her.* LADY SIMS *has a maid for buttoning and unbuttoning her, and probably another for waiting on the maid, and she gazes with a little envy perhaps at a woman who does things for herself*] Is that the type-writing machine?

KATE. [*who is getting it ready for use*] Yes. [*not "Yes, madam," as it ought to be*] I suppose if I am to work here I may take this off. I get on better without it. [*She is referring to her hat*]

LADY SIMS. Certainly. [*But the hat is already off*] I ought to apologise for my gown. I am to be presented this week, and I was trying it on. [*Her tone is not really apologetic. She is rather clinging to the glory of her gown, wistfully, as if not absolutely certain, you know, that it is a glory*]

KATE. It is beautiful, if I may presume to say so. [*She frankly admires it. She probably has a best, and a second best of her own: that sort of thing*]

LADY SIMS. [*with a flush of pride in the gown*] Yes, it is very beautiful. [*The beauty of it gives her courage*] Sit down, please.

KATE. [*the sort of woman who would have sat down in any case*] I suppose it is some copying you want done? I got no particulars. I was told to come to this address, but that was all.

LADY SIMS. [*almost with the humility of a servant*] Oh, it is not work for me, it is for my husband, and what he needs is not exactly copying. [*swelling, for she is proud of* HARRY] He wants a number of letters answered—hundreds of them—letters and telegrams of congratulation.

KATE. [*as if it were all in the day's work*] Yes?

LADY SIMS. [*remembering that* HARRY *expects every wife to do her duty*] My husband is a remarkable man. He is about to be knighted. [*pause, but* KATE *does not fall to the floor*] He is to be knighted for his services to— [*on reflection*]—for his services. [*She is conscious that she is not doing* HARRY *justice*] He can explain it so much better than I can.

KATE. [*in her business-like way*] And I am to answer the congratulations?

LADY SIMS. [*afraid that it will be a hard task*] Yes.

KATE. [*blithely*] It is work I have had some experience of. [*she proceeds to type*]

LADY SIMS. But you can't begin till you know what he wants to say.

KATE. Only a specimen letter. Won't it be the usual thing?

LADY SIMS [*to whom this is a new idea*] Is there a usual thing?

KATE. Oh, yes. [*she continues to type, and* LADY SIMS, *half-mesmerised, gazes at her nimble fingers. The useless woman watches the useful one, and she sighs, she could not tell why*]

LADY SIMS. How quickly you do it! It must be delightful to be able to do something, and to do it well.

KATE. [*thankfully*] Yes, it is delightful.

LADY SIMS. [*again remembering the source of all her greatness*] But, excuse me, I don't think that will be any use. My husband wants me to explain to you that his is an exceptional case. He did not try to get this honour in any way. It was a complete surprise to him——

KATE. [*who is a practical* KATE *and no dealer in sarcasm*] That is what I have written.

LADY SIMS. [*in whom sarcasm would meet a dead wall*] But how could you know?

KATE. I only guessed.

LADY SIMS. Is that the usual thing?

KATE. Oh, yes.

LADY SIMS. They don't try to get it?

KATE. I don't know. That is what we are told to say in the letters. [*To her at present the only important thing about the letters is that they are ten shillings the hundred*]

LADY SIMS. [*returning to surer ground*] I should explain that my husband is not a man who cares for honours. So long as he does his duty——

KATE. Yes, I have been putting that in.

LADY SIMS. Have you? But he particularly wants it to be known that he would have declined a title were it not——

KATE. I have got it here.

LADY SIMS. What have you got?

KATE. [*reading*] "Indeed, I would have asked to be allowed to decline had it not been that I want to please my wife."

LADY SIMS. [*heavily*] But how could you know it was that?

KATE. Is it?

LADY SIMS. [*who after all is the one with the right to ask questions*] Do they all accept it for that reason?

KATE. That is what we are told to say in the letters.

LADY SIMS. [*thoughtlessly*] It is quite as if you knew my husband.

KATE. I assure you, I don't even know his name.

LADY SIMS. [*suddenly showing that she knows him*] Oh, he wouldn't like that! [*And it is here that* HARRY *re-enters in his city garments, looking so gay, feeling so jolly that we bleed for him. However, the annoying* KATHERINE *is to get a shock also*]

LADY SIMS. This is the lady, Harry.

SIR HARRY. [*shooting his cuffs*] Yes, yes. Good morning, my dear. [*Then they see each other, and their mouths open, but not for words. After the first surprise* KATE *seems to find some humour in the situation, but* HARRY *lowers like a thundercloud*]

LADY SIMS. [*who has seen nothing*] I have been trying to explain to her——

SIR HARRY. Eh—what? [*he controls himself*] Leave it to me, Emmy; I'll attend to her. [LADY SIMS *goes, with a dread fear that somehow she has vexed her lord, and then* HARRY *attends to the intruder*]

SIR HARRY. [*with concentrated scorn*] You!

KATE. [*as if agreeing with him*] Yes, it's funny.

SIR HARRY. The shamelessness of your daring to come here.

KATE. Believe me, it is not less a surprise to me than it is to you. I was sent here in the ordinary way of business. I was given only the number of the house. I was not told the name.

SIR HARRY. [*withering her*] The ordinary way of business! This is what you have fallen to—a typist!

KATE. [*unwithered*] Think of it!

SIR HARRY. After going through worse straits, I'll be bound.

KATE. [*with some grim memories*] Much worse straits.

SIR HARRY. [*alas, laughing coarsely*] My congratulations!

KATE. Thank you, Harry.

SIR HARRY. [*who is annoyed, as any man would be, not to find her abject*] Eh? What was that you called me, madam?

KATE. Isn't it Harry? On my soul, I almost forget.

SIR HARRY. It isn't Harry to you. My name is Sims, if you please.

KATE. Yes, I had not forgotten that. It was my name, too, you see.

SIR HARRY. [*in his best manner*] It was your name till you forfeited the right to bear it.

KATE. Exactly.

SIR HARRY. [*gloating*] I was furious to find you here, but on second thoughts it pleases me. [*from the depths of his moral nature*] There is a grim justice in this.

KATE. [*sympathetically*] Tell me?

SIR HARRY. Do you know what you were brought here to do?

KATE. I have just been learning. You have been made a knight, and I was summoned to answer the messages of congratulation.

SIR HARRY. That's it, that's it. You come on this day as my servant!

KATE. I, who might have been Lady Sims.

SIR HARRY. And you are her typist instead. And she has four men-servants. Oh, I am glad you saw her in her presentation gown.

KATE. I wonder if she would let me do her washing, Sir Harry? [*Her want of taste disgusts him*]

SIR HARRY. [*with dignity*] You can go. The mere thought that only a few flights of stairs separates such as you from my innocent children——[*He will never know why a new light has come into her face*]

KATE. [*slowly*] You have children?

SIR HARRY. [*inflated*] Two. [*He wonders why she is so long in answering*]

KATE. [*resorting to impertinence*] Such a nice number.

SIR HARRY. [*with an extra turn of the screw*] Both boys.

KATE. Successful in everything. Are they like you, Sir Harry?

SIR HARRY. [*expanding*] They are very like me.

KATE. That's nice. [*even on such a subject as this she can be ribald*]

SIR HARRY. Will you please to go.

KATE. Heigho! What shall I say to my employer?

SIR HARRY. That is no affair of mine.

KATE. What will you say to Lady Sims?

SIR HARRY. I flatter myself that whatever I say, Lady Sims will accept without comment. [*She smiles, heaven knows why, unless her next remark explains it*]

KATE. Still the same Harry.

SIR HARRY. What do you mean?

KATE. Only that you have the old confidence in your profound knowledge of the sex.

SIR HARRY. [*beginning to think as little of her intellect as of her morals*] I suppose I know my wife.

KATE. [*hopelessly dense*] I suppose so. I was only remembering that you used to think you knew her in the days when I was the lady. [*He is merely wasting his time on her, and he indicates the door. She is not sufficiently the lady to retire worsted*] Well, good-bye, Sir Harry. Won't you ring, and the four men-servants will show me out? [*But he hesitates*]

SIR HARRY. [*in spite of himself*] As you are here, there is something I want to get out of you. [*wishing he could ask it less eagerly*] Tell me, who was the man? [*The strange woman— it is evident now that she has always been strange to him—smiles tolerantly*]

KATE. You never found out?

SIR HARRY. I could never be sure.

KATE. [*reflectively*] I thought that would worry you.

SIR HARRY. [*sneering*] It's plain that he soon left you.

KATE. Very soon.

SIR HARRY. As I could have told you. [*But still she surveys him with the smile of Mona Lisa. The badgered man has to entreat*] Who was he? It was fourteen years ago, and cannot matter to any of us now. Kate, tell me who he was? [*It is his first youthful moment, and perhaps because of that she does not wish to hurt him*]

KATE. [*shaking a motherly head*] Better not ask.

SIR HARRY. I do ask. Tell me.

KATE. It is kinder not to tell you.

SIR HARRY. [*violently*] Then, by James, it was one of my own pals. Was it Bernard Roche? [*she shakes her head*] It may have been some one who comes to my house still.

KATE. I think not. [*reflecting*] Fourteen years! You found my letter that night when you went home?

SIR HARRY. [*impatient*] Yes.

KATE. I propped it against the decanters. I thought you would be sure to see it there. It was a room not unlike this, and the furniture was arranged in the same attractive way. How it all comes back to me. Don't you see me, Harry, in hat and cloak, putting the letter there, taking a last look round, and then stealing out into the night to meet——

SIR HARRY. Whom?

KATE. Him. Hours pass, no sound in the room but the tick-tack of the clock, and then about midnight you return alone. You take——

SIR HARRY. [*gruffly*] I wasn't alone.

KATE. [*the picture spoilt*] No? oh. [*plaintively*] Here have I all these years been conceiving it wrongly. [*she studies his face*] I believe something interesting happened?

SIR HARRY. [*growling*] Something confoundedly annoying.

KATE. [*coaxing*] Do tell me.

SIR HARRY. We won't go into that. Who was the man? Surely a husband has a right to know with whom his wife bolted.

KATE. [*who is detestably ready with her tongue*] Surely the wife has a right to know how he took it. [*The woman's love of bargaining comes to her aid*] A fair exchange. You tell me what happened, and I will tell you who he was.

SIR HARRY. You will? Very well. [*It is the first point on which they have agreed, and, forgetting himself, he takes a place beside her on the fire-seat. He is thinking only of what he is to tell her, but she, woman-like, is conscious of their proximity*]

KATE. [*tastelessly*] Quite like old times. [*he moves away from her indignantly*] Go on, Harry.

SIR HARRY. [*who has a manful shrinking from saying anything that is to his disadvantage*] Well, as you know, I was dining at the club that night.

KATE. Yes.

SIR HARRY. Jack Lamb drove me home. Mabbett Green was with us, and I asked them to come in for a few minutes.

KATE. Jack Lamb, Mabbett Green? I think I remember them. Jack was in Parliament.

SIR HARRY. No, that was Mabbett. They came into the house with me and—[*with sudden horror*]—was it him?

KATE. [*bewildered*] Who?

SIR HARRY. Mabbett?

KATE. What?

SIR HARRY. The man?

KATE. What man? [*understanding*] Oh, no. I thought you said he came into the house with you.

SIR HARRY. It might have been a blind.

KATE. Well, it wasn't. Go on.

SIR HARRY. They came in to finish a talk we had been having at the club.

KATE. An interesting talk, evidently.

SIR HARRY. The papers had been full that evening of the elopement of some countess woman with a fiddler. What was her name?

KATE. Does it matter?

SIR HARRY. No. [*Thus ends the countess*] We had been discussing the thing and—[*he pulls a wry face*]—and I had been rather warm——

KATE. [*with horrid relish*] I begin to see. You had been saying it served the husband right, that the man who could not look after his wife deserved to lose her. It was one of your favorite subjects. Oh, Harry, say it was that!

SIR HARRY. [*sourly*] It may have been something like that.

KATE. And all the time the letter was there, waiting; and none of you knew except the clock. Harry, it is sweet of you to tell me. [*His face is not sweet. The illiterate woman has used the wrong adjective*] I forget what I said precisely in the letter.

SIR HARRY. [*pulverising her*] So do I. But I have it still.

KATE. [*not pulverised*] Do let me see it again. [*She has observed his eye wandering to the desk*]

SIR HARRY. You are welcome to it as a gift. [*The fateful letter, a poor little dead thing, is brought to light from a locked drawer*]

KATE. [*taking it*] Yes, this is it. Harry, how you did crumple it! [*she reads, not without curiosity*] "Dear husband—I call you that for the last time—I am off. I am what you call making a bolt of it. I won't try to excuse myself nor to explain, for you would not accept the excuses nor understand the explanation. It will be a little shock to you, but only to your pride; what will astound you is that any woman could be such a fool as to leave such a man as you. I am taking nothing with me that belongs to you. May you be very happy.—Your ungrateful Kate. P.S.—You need not try to find out who he is. You will try, but you won't succeed." [*she folds the nasty little thing up*] I may really have it for my very own?

SIR HARRY. You really may.

KATE. [*impudently*] If you would care for a typed copy—?

SIR HARRY. [*in a voice with which he used to frighten his grandmother*] None of your sauce! [*wincing*] I had to let them see it in the end.

KATE. I can picture Jack Lamb eating it.

SIR HARRY. A penniless parson's daughter.

KATE. That is all I was.

SIR HARRY. We searched for the two of you high and low.

KATE. Private detectives?

SIR HARRY. They couldn't get on the track of you.

KATE. [*smiling*] No?

SIR HARRY. But at last the courts let me serve the papers by advertisement on a man unknown, and I got my freedom.

KATE. So I saw. It was the last I heard of you.

SIR HARRY. [*each word a blow for her*] And I married again just as soon as ever I could.

KATE. They say that is always a compliment to the first wife.

SIR HARRY. [*violently*] I showed them.

KATE. You soon let them see that if one woman was a fool, you still had the pick of the basket to choose from.

SIR HARRY. By James, I did.

KATE. [*bringing him to earth again*] But still, you wondered who he was.

SIR HARRY. I suspected everybody—even my pals. I felt like jumping at their throats and crying, "It's you!"

KATE. You had been so admirable to me, an instinct told you that I was sure to choose another of the same.

SIR HARRY. I thought, it can't be money, so it must be looks. Some dolly face. [*he stares at her in perplexity*] He must have had something wonderful about him to make you willing to give up all that you had with me.

KATE. [*as if he was the stupid one*] Poor Harry.

SIR HARRY. And it couldn't have been going on for long, for I would have noticed the change in you.

KATE. Would you?

SIR HARRY. I knew you so well.

KATE. You amazing man.

SIR HARRY. So who was he? Out with it.

KATE. You are determined to know?

SIR HARRY. Your promise. You gave your word.

KATE. If I must—[*She is the villain of the piece, but it must be conceded that in this matter she is reluctant to pain him*] I am sorry I promised. [*looking at him steadily*] There was no one, Harry; no one at all.

SIR HARRY. [*rising*] If you think you can play with me—

KATE. I told you that you wouldn't like it.

SIR HARRY. [*rasping*] It is unbelievable.

KATE. I suppose it is; but it is true.

SIR HARRY. Your letter itself gives you the lie.

KATE. That was intentional. I saw that if the truth were known you might have a difficulty in getting your freedom; and as I was getting mine it seemed fair that you should have yours also. So I wrote my good-bye in words that would be taken to mean what you thought they meant, and I knew the law would back you in your opinion. For the law, like you, Harry, has a profound understanding of women.

SIR HARRY. [*trying to straighten himself*] I don't believe you yet.

KATE. [*looking not unkindly into the soul of this man*] Perhaps that is the best way to take

it. It is less unflattering than the truth. But you were the only one. [*summing up her life*] You sufficed.

SIR HARRY. Then what mad impulse—

KATE. It was no impulse, Harry. I had thought it out for a year.

SIR HARRY. A year? [*dazed*] One would think to hear you that I hadn't been a good husband to you.

KATE. [*with a sad smile*] You were a good husband according to your lights.

SIR HARRY. [*stoutly*] I think so.

KATE. And a moral man, and chatty, and quite the philanthropist.

SIR HARRY. [*on sure ground*] All women envied you.

KATE. How you loved me to be envied.

SIR HARRY. I swaddled you in luxury.

KATE. [*making her great revelation*] That was it.

SIR HARRY. [*blankly*] What?

KATE. [*who can be serene because it is all over*] How you beamed at me when I sat at the head of your fat dinners in my fat jewellery, surrounded by our fat friends.

SIR HARRY. [*aggrieved*] They weren't so fat.

KATE. [*a side issue*] All except those who were so thin. Have you ever noticed, Harry, that many jewels make women either incredibly fat or incredibly thin?

SIR HARRY. [*shouting*] I have not. [*Is it worth while to argue with her any longer?*] We had all the most interesting society of the day. It wasn't only business men. There were politicians, painters, writers——

KATE. Only the glorious, dazzling successes. Oh, the fat talk while we ate too much—about who had made a hit and who was slipping back, and what the noo house cost and the noo motor and the gold soup-plates, and who was to be the noo knight.

SIR HARRY. [*who it· will be observed is unanswerable from first to last*] Was anybody getting on better than me, and consequently you?

KATE. Consequently me! Oh, Harry, you and your sublime religion.

SIR HARRY. [*honest heart*] My religion? I never was one to talk about religion, but——

KATE. Pooh, Harry, you don't even know what your religion was and is and will be till the day of your expensive funeral. [*And here is the lesson that life has taught her*] One's religion is whatever he is most interested in, and yours is Success.

SIR HARRY. [*quoting from his morning paper*] Ambition—it is the last infirmity of noble minds.

KATE. Noble minds!

SIR HARRY. [*at last grasping what she is talking about*] You are not saying that you left me because of my success?

KATE. Yes, that was it. [*And now she stands revealed to him*] I couldn't endure it. If a failure had come now and then—but your success was suffocating me. [*She is rigid with emotion*] The passionate craving I had to be done with it, to find myself among people who had not got on.

SIR HARRY. [*with proper spirit*] There are plenty of them.

KATE. There were none in our set. When they began to go down-hill they rolled out of our sight.

SIR HARRY. [*clenching it*] I tell you I am worth a quarter of a million.

KATE. [*unabashed*] That is what you are worth to yourself. I'll tell you what you are worth to me: exactly twelve pounds. For I made up my mind that I could launch myself on the world alone if I first proved my mettle by earning twelve pounds; and as soon as I had earned it I left you.

SIR HARRY. [*in the scales*] Twelve pounds!

KATE. That is your value to a woman. If she can't make it she has to stick to you.

SIR HARRY. [*remembering perhaps a rectory garden*] You valued me at more than that when you married me.

KATE. [*seeing it also*] Ah, I didn't know you then. If only you had been a man, Harry.

SIR HARRY. A man? What do you mean by a man?

KATE. [*leaving the garden*] Haven't you heard of them? They are something fine; and every woman is loath to admit to herself that her husband is not one. When she marries, even though she has been a very trivial person, there is in her some vague stirring toward a worthy life, as well as a fear of her capacity for evil. She knows her chance lies in him. If there is something good in him, what is good in her finds it, and they join forces against the baser parts. So I didn't give you up willingly,

Harry. I invented all sorts of theories to explain you. Your hardness—I said it was a fine want[2] of mawkishness. Your coarseness—I said it goes with strength. Your contempt for the weak—I called it virility. Your want of ideals was clear-sightedness. Your ignoble views of women—I tried to think them funny. Oh, I clung to you to save myself. But I had to let go; you had only the one quality, Harry, success; you had it so strong that it swallowed all the others.

SIR HARRY. [*not to be diverted from the main issue*] How did you earn that twelve pounds?

KATE. It took me nearly six months; but I earned it fairly. [*She presses her hand on the typewriter as lovingly as many a woman has pressed a rose*] I learned this. I hired it and taught myself. I got some work through a friend, and with my first twelve pounds I paid for my machine. Then I considered that I was free to go, and I went.

SIR HARRY. All this going on in my house while you were living in the lap of luxury! [*she nods*] By God, you were determined.

KATE. [*briefly*] By God, I was.

SIR HARRY. [*staring*] How you must have hated me.

KATE. [*smiling at the childish word*] Not a bit—after I saw that there was a way out. From that hour you amused me, Harry; I was even sorry for you, for I saw that you couldn't help yourself. Success is just a fatal gift.

SIR HARRY. Oh, thank you.

KATE. [*thinking, dear friends in front, of you and me perhaps*] Yes, and some of your most successful friends knew it. One or two of them used to look very sad at times, as if they thought they might have come to something if they hadn't got on.

SIR HARRY. [*who has a horror of sacrilege*] The battered crew you live among now— what are they but folk who have tried to succeed and failed?

KATE. That's it; they try, but they fail.

SIR HARRY. And always will fail.

KATE. Always. Poor souls—I say of them. Poor soul—they say of me. It keeps us human. That is why I never tire of them.

SIR HARRY. [*comprehensively*] Bah! Kate, I tell you I'll be worth half a million yet.

KATE. I'm sure you will. You're getting stout, Harry.

---

[2] lack.

SIR HARRY. No, I'm not.

KATE. What was the name of that fat old fellow who used to fall asleep at our dinner-parties?

SIR HARRY. If you mean Sir William Crackley——

KATE. That was the man. Sir William was to me a perfect picture of the grand success. He had got on so well that he was very, very stout, and when he sat on a chair it was thus [*her hands meeting in front of her*]—as if he were holding his success together. That is what you are working for, Harry. You will have that and the half million about the same time.

SIR HARRY. [*who has surely been very patient*] Will you please to leave my house?

KATE. [*putting on her gloves, soiled things*] But don't let us part in anger. How do you think I am looking, Harry, compared to the dull, inert thing that used to roll round in your padded carriages?

SIR HARRY. [*in masterly fashion*] I forget what you were like. I'm very sure you never could have held a candle to the present Lady Sims.

KATE. That is a picture of her, is it not?

SIR HARRY. [*seizing his chance again*] In her wedding-gown. Painted by an R.A.[3]

KATE. [*wickedly*] A knight?

SIR HARRY. [*deceived*] Yes.

KATE. [*who likes* LADY SIMS: *a piece of presumption on her part*] It is a very pretty face.

SIR HARRY. [*with the pride of possession*] Acknowledged to be a beauty everywhere.

KATE. There is a merry look in the eyes, and character in the chin.

SIR HARRY. [*like an auctioneer*] Noted for her wit.

KATE. All her life before her when that was painted. It is a *spirituelle*[4] face too. [*Suddenly she turns on him with anger, for the first and only time in the play*] Oh, Harry, you brute!

SIR HARRY. [*staggered*] Eh, What?

KATE. That dear creature capable of becoming a noble wife and mother—she is the spiritless woman of no account that I saw here a few minutes ago. I forgive you for myself, for I escaped, but that poor lost soul, oh, Harry, Harry.

_____

[3] a member of the Royal Academy.
[4] intelligent, alive.

SIR HARRY. [*waving her to the door*] I'll thank you—— If ever there was a woman proud of her husband and happy in her married life, that woman is Lady Sims.

KATE. I wonder.

SIR HARRY. Then you needn't wonder.

KATE. [*slowly*] If I was a husband—it is my advice to all of them—I would often watch my wife quietly to see whether the twelve-pound look was not coming into her eyes. Two boys, did you say, and both like you?

SIR HARRY. What is that to you?

KATE. [*with glistening eyes*] I was only thinking that somewhere there are two little girls who, when they grow up—the dear, pretty girls who are all meant for the men that don't get on! Well, good-bye, Sir Harry.

SIR HARRY. [*showing a little human weakness, it is to be feared*] Say first that you're sorry.

KATE. For what?

SIR HARRY. That you left me. Say you regret it bitterly. You know you do. [*She smiles and shakes her head. He is pettish. He makes a terrible announcement*] You have spoilt the day for me.

KATE. [*to hearten him*] I am sorry for that; but it is only a pin-prick, Harry. I suppose it is a little jarring in the moment of your triumph to find that there is—one old friend—who does not think you a success; but you will soon forget it. Who cares what a typist thinks?

SIR HARRY. [*heartened*] Nobody. A typist at eighteen shillings a week!

KATE. [*proudly*] Not a bit of it, Harry. I double that.

SIR HARRY. [*neatly*] Magnificent! [*There is a timid knock at the door*]

LADY SIMS. May I come in?

SIR HARRY. [*rather appealingly*] It is Lady Sims.

KATE. I won't tell. She is afraid to come into her husband's room without knocking!

SIR HARRY. She is not. [*uxoriously*] Come in, dearest. [*Dearest enters carrying the sword. She might have had the sense not to bring it in while this annoying person is here*]

LADY SIMS. [*thinking she has brought her welcome with her*] Harry, the sword has come.

SIR HARRY. [*who will dote on it presently*] Oh, all right.

LADY SIMS. But I thought you were so eager

to practice with it. [*The person smiles at this. He wishes he had not looked to see if she was smiling*]

SIR HARRY. [*sharply*] Put it down. [LADY SIMS *flushes a little as she lays the sword aside*]

KATE. [*with her confounded courtesy*] It is a beautiful sword, if I may say so.

LADY SIMS. [*helped*] Yes. [*The person thinks she can put him in the wrong, does she? He'll show her*]

SIR HARRY. [*with one eye on* KATE] Emmy, the one thing your neck needs is more jewels.

LADY SIMS. [*faltering*] More!

SIR HARRY. Some ropes of pearls. I'll see to it. It's a bagatelle to me. [KATE *conceals her chagrin, so she had better be shown the door. He rings*] I won't detain you any longer, miss.

KATE. Thank you.

LADY SIMS. Going already? You have been very quick.

SIR HARRY. The person doesn't suit, Emmy.

LADY SIMS. I'm sorry.

KATE. So am I, madam, but it can't be helped. Good-bye, your ladyship—good-bye, Sir Harry. [*There is a suspicion of an impertinent curtsy, and she is escorted off the premises by* TOMBES. *The air of the room is purified by her going.* SIR HARRY *notices it at once*]

LADY SIMS. [*whose tendency is to say the wrong thing*] She seemed such a capable woman.

SIR HARRY. [*on his hearth*] I don't like her style at all.

LADY SIMS. [*meekly*] Of course you know best. [*This is the right kind of woman*]

SIR HARRY. [*rather anxious for corroboration*]

Lord, how she winced when I said I was to give you those ropes of pearls.

LADY SIMS. Did she? I didn't notice. I suppose so.

SIR HARRY. [*frowning*] Suppose? Surely I know enough about women to know that.

LADY SIMS. Yes, oh yes.

SIR HARRY. [*odd that so confident a man should ask this*] Emmy, I know you well, don't I? I can read you like a book, eh?

LADY SIMS. [*nervously*] Yes, Harry.

SIR HARRY. [*jovially, but with an inquiring eye*] What a different existence yours is from that poor lonely wretch's.

LADY SIMS. Yes, but she has a very contented face.

SIR HARRY. [*with a stamp of his foot*] All put on. What?

LADY SIMS. [*timidly*] I didn't say anything.

SIR HARRY. [*snapping*] One would think you envied her.

LADY SIMS. Envied? Oh no—but I thought she looked so alive. It was while she was working the machine.

SIR HARRY. Alive! That's no life. It is you that are alive. [*curtly*] I'm busy, Emmy. [*he sits at his writing table*]

LADY SIMS. [*dutifully*] I'm sorry; I'll go, Harry. [*inconsequentially*] Are they very expensive?

SIR HARRY. What?

LADY SIMS. Those machines? [*When she has gone the possible meaning of her question startles him. The curtain hides him from us, but we may be sure that he will soon be bland again. We have a comfortable feeling, you and I, that there is nothing of* HARRY SIMS *in us.*]

RIDERS TO THE SEA*

JOHN M. SYNGE

Synge (1871–1909) left Trinity College, Dublin, to travel, and eventually settled down in Paris, where he lived a bohemian existence. He was luckily set on a new track by Yeats, who suggested that he write of the primitive existence on the Aran Isles; Riders to the Sea (1904), a modern classic, was the result. It has been called the greatest of one-act plays and has been compared with Greek tragedy in its impact on an audience. Synge later became a prominent director of the Abbey Theatre and, with six plays to his credit, seemed destined for the heights; cancer cut off his career at the age of thirty-eight. His Playboy of the Western World (1907), a comedy which offended Irish audiences at first, is a notable effort. Along with other prominent dramatists Synge belongs to the Irish literary renaissance as one of its most revered prophets (see I, 404).

Persons

MAURYA, AN OLD WOMAN
BARTLEY, HER SON
CATHLEEN, HER DAUGHTER
NORA, A YOUNGER DAUGHTER
MEN AND WOMEN

SCENE—An Island off the West of Ireland. Cottage kitchen, with nets, oilskins, spinning wheel, some new boards standing by the wall, etc. CATHLEEN, a girl of about twenty, finishes kneading cake, and puts it down in the pot-oven by the fire; then wipes her hands, and begins to spin at the wheel. NORA, a young girl, puts her head in at the door.

* Reprinted by permission of Random House, Inc.

NORA. [in a low voice] Where is she?

CATHLEEN. She's lying down, God help her, and may be sleeping, if she's able. [NORA comes in softly, and takes a bundle from under her shawl]

CATHLEEN. [spinning the wheel rapidly] What is it you have?

NORA. The young priest is after bringing them. It's a shirt and a plain stocking were got off a drowned man in Donegal. [CATHLEEN stops her wheel with a sudden movement and leans out to listen]

NORA. We're to find out if it's Michael's they are; some time herself will be down looking by the sea.

CATHLEEN. How would they be Michael's, Nora? How would he go the length of that way to the far north?

NORA. The young priest says he's known the like of it. "If it's Michael's they are," says he, "you can tell herself he's got a clean burial by the grace of God, and if they're not his, let no one say a word about them, for she'll be getting her death," says he, "with crying and lamenting." [the door which NORA half closed is blown open by a gust of wind]

CATHLEEN. [looking out anxiously] Did you ask him would he stop Bartley going this day with the horses to the Galway fair?

NORA. "I won't stop him," says he, "but let you not be afraid. Herself does be saying prayers half through the night, and the Almighty God won't leave her destitute," says he, "with no son living."

CATHLEEN. Is the sea bad by the white rocks, Nora?

NORA. Middling bad, God help us. There's a great roaring in the west, and it's worse it'll be getting when the tide's turned to the wind.

[*she goes over to the table with the bundle*] Shall I open it now?

CATHLEEN. Maybe she'd wake up on us, and come in before we'd done. [*coming to the table*] It's a long time we'll be, and the two of us crying.

NORA. [*goes to the inner door and listens*] She's moving about on the bed. She'll be coming in a minute.

CATHLEEN. Give me the ladder, and I'll put them up in the turf-loft, the way she won't know of them at all, and maybe when the tide turns, she'll be going down to see would he be floating from the east. [*they put the ladder against the gable of the chimney;* CATHLEEN *goes up a few steps and hides the bundle in the turf-loft.* MAURYA *comes from the inner room*]

MAURYA. [*looking up at* CATHLEEN *and speaking querulously*] Isn't it turf enough you have for this day and evening?

CATHLEEN. There's a cake baking at the fire for a short space [*throwing down the turf*] and Bartley will want it when the tide turns if he goes to Connemara. [NORA *picks up the turf and puts it round the pot-oven*]

MAURYA. [*sitting down on a stool at the fire*] He won't go this day with the wind rising from the south and west. He won't go this day, for the young priest will stop him surely.

NORA. He'll not stop him, mother, and I heard Eamon Simon and Stephen Pheety and Colum Shawn saying he would go.

MAURYA. Where is he itself?

NORA. He went down to see would there be another boat sailing in the week, and I'm thinking it won't be long till he's here now, for the tide's turning at the green head, and the hooker's tacking from the east.

CATHLEEN. I hear some one passing the big stones.

NORA. [*looking out*] He's coming now, and he in a hurry.

BARTLEY. [*comes in and looks round the room; speaking sadly and quietly*] Where is the bit of new rope, Cathleen, was bought in Connemara?

CATHLEEN. [*coming down*] Give it to him, Nora; it's on a nail by the white boards. I hung it up this morning, for the pig with the black feet was eating it.

NORA. [*giving him a rope*] Is that it, Bartley?

MAURYA. You'd do right to leave that rope, Bartley, hanging by the boards. [BARTLEY *takes the rope*] It will be wanting in this place, I'm telling you, if Michael is washed up tomorrow morning, or the next morning, or any morning in the week, for it's a deep grave we'll make him by the grace of God.

BARTLEY. [*beginning to work with the rope*] I've no halter the way I can ride down on the mare, and I must go now quickly. This is the one boat going for two weeks or beyond it, and the fair will be a good fair for horses I heard them saying below.

MAURYA. It's a hard thing they'll be saying below if the body is washed up and there's no man in it to make the coffin, and I after giving a big price for the finest white boards you'd find in Connemara. [*she looks round at the boards*]

BARTLEY. How would it be washed up, and we after looking each day for nine days, and a strong wind blowing a while back from the west and south?

MAURYA. If it wasn't found itself, that wind is raising the sea, and there was a star up against the moon, and it rising in the night. If it was a hundred horses, or a thousand horses you had itself, what is the price of a thousand horses against a son where there is one son only?

BARTLEY. [*working at the halter, to* CATHLEEN] Let you go down each day, and see the sheep aren't jumping in on the rye, and if the jobber comes, you can sell the pig with the black feet if there is a good price going.

MAURYA. How would the like of her get a good price for a pig?

BARTLEY. [*to* CATHLEEN] If the west wind holds with the last bit of the moon, let you and Nora get up weed enough for another cock for the kelp. It's hard set we'll be from this day with no one in it but one man to work.

MAURYA. It's hard set we'll be surely the day you're drownd'd with the rest. What way will I live and the girls with me, and I an old woman looking for the grave? [BARTLEY *lays down the halter, takes off his old coat, and puts on a newer one of the same flannel*]

BARTLEY. [*to* NORA] Is she coming to the pier?

NORA. [*looking out*] She's passing the green head and letting fall her sails.

BARTLEY. [*getting his purse and tobacco*]

I'll have half an hour to go down, and you'll see me coming again in two days, or in three days, or maybe in four days if the wind is bad.

MAURYA. [*turning round to the fire, and putting her shawl over her head*] Isn't it a hard and cruel man won't hear a word from an old woman, and she holding him from the sea?

CATHLEEN. It's the life of a young man to be going on the sea, and who would listen to an old woman with one thing and she saying it over?

BARTLEY. [*taking the halter*] I must go now quickly. I'll ride down on the red mare, and the gray pony'll run behind me. . . . The blessing of God on you. [*he goes out*]

MAURYA. [*crying out as he is in the door*] He's gone now, God spare us, and we'll not see him again. He's gone now, and when the black night is falling, I'll have no son left me in the world.

CATHLEEN. Why wouldn't you give him your blessing and he looking round in the door? Isn't it sorrow enough is on every one in this house without your sending him out with an unlucky word behind him, and a hard word in his ear? [MAURYA *takes up the tongs and begins raking the fire aimlessly without looking round*]

NORA. [*turning toward her*] You're taking away the turf from the cake.

CATHLEEN. [*crying out*] The Son of God forgive us, Nora, we're after forgetting his bit of bread. [*she comes over to the fire*]

NORA. And it's destroyed he'll be going till dark night, and he after eating nothing since the sun went up.

CATHLEEN. [*turning the cake out of the oven*] It's destroyed he'll be, surely. There's no sense left on any person in a house where an old woman will be talking forever. [MAURYA *sways herself on her stool*]

CATHLEEN. [*cutting off some of the bread and rolling it in a cloth; to* MAURYA] Let you go down now to the spring well and give him this and he passing. You'll see him then and the dark word will be broken, and you can say "God speed you," the way he'll be easy in his mind.

MAURYA. [*taking the bread*] Will I be in it as soon as himself?

CATHLEEN. If you go now quickly.

MAURYA. [*standing up unsteadily*] It's hard set I am to walk.

CATHLEEN. [*looking at her anxiously*] Give her the stick, Nora, or maybe she'll slip on the big stones.

NORA. What stick?

CATHLEEN. The stick Michael brought from Connemara.

MAURYA. [*taking a stick* NORA *gives her*] In the big world the old people do be leaving things after them for their sons and children, but in this place it is the young men do be leaving things behind for them that do be old. [*she goes out slowly.* NORA *goes over to the ladder*]

CATHLEEN. Wait, Nora, maybe she'd turn back quickly. She's that sorry, God help her, you wouldn't know the thing she'd do.

NORA. Is she gone round by the bush?

CATHLEEN. [*looking out*] She's gone now. Throw it down quickly, for the Lord knows when she'll be out of it again.

NORA. [*getting the bundle from the loft*] The young priest said he'd be passing tomorrow, and we might go down and speak to him below if it's Michael's they are surely.

CATHLEEN. [*taking the bundle*] Did he say what way they were found?

NORA. [*coming down*] "There were two men," says he, "and they rowing round with poteen[1] before the cocks crowed, and the oar of one of them caught the body, and they passing the black cliffs of the north."

CATHLEEN. [*trying to open the bundle*] Give me a knife, Nora; the string's perished with the salt water, and there's a black knot on it you wouldn't loosen in a week.

NORA. [*giving her a knife*] I've heard tell it was a long way to Donegal.

CATHLEEN. [*cutting the string*] It is surely. There was a man in here a while ago— the man sold us that knife—and he said if you set off walking from the rocks beyond, it would be seven days you'd be in Donegal.

NORA. And what time would a man take, and he floating? [CATHLEEN *opens the bundle and takes out a bit of a stocking. They look at them eagerly*]

CATHLEEN. [*in a low voice*] The Lord spare us, Nora! isn't it a queer hard thing to say if it's his they are surely?

---

[1] moonshine, bootleg whisky.

NORA. I'll get his shirt off the hook the way we can put the one flannel on the other. [*she looks through some clothes hanging in the corner*] It's not with them, Cathleen, and where will it be?

CATHLEEN. I'm thinking Bartley put it on him in the morning, for his own shirt was heavy with the salt in it. [*pointing to the corner*] There's a bit of a sleeve was of the same stuff. Give me that, and it will do. [NORA *brings it to her, and they compare the flannel*] It's the same stuff, Nora; but if it is itself, aren't there great rolls of it in the shops of Galway, and isn't it many another man may have a shirt of it as well as Michael himself?

NORA. [*who has taken up the stocking and counted the stitches, crying out*] It's Michael, Cathleen, it's Michael; God spare his soul, and what will herself say when she hears this story, and Bartley on the sea?

CATHLEEN. [*taking the stocking*] It's a plain stocking.

NORA. It's the second one of the third pair I knitted, and I put up three score stitches, and I dropped four of them.

CATHLEEN. [*counts the stitches*] It's that number is in it. [*crying out*] Ah, Nora, isn't it a bitter thing to think of him floating that way to the far north, and no one to keen[2] him but the black hags[3] that do be flying on the sea?

NORA. [*swinging herself round, and throwing out her arms on the clothes*] And isn't it a pitiful thing when there is nothing left of a man who was a great rower and fisher but a bit of an old shirt and a plain stocking?

CATHLEEN. [*after an instant*] Tell me is herself coming, Nora? I hear a little sound on the path.

NORA. [*looking out*] She is, Cathleen. She's coming up to the door.

CATHLEEN. Put these things away before she'll come in. Maybe it's easier she'll be after giving her blessing to Bartley, and we won't let on we've heard anything the time he's on the sea.

NORA. [*helping* CATHLEEN *to close the bundle*] We'll put them here in the corner. [*they put them into a hole in the chimney corner.* CATHLEEN *goes back to the spinning wheel*] Will she see it was crying I was?

CATHLEEN. Keep your back to the door the way the light'll not be on you. [NORA *sits down at the chimney corner, with her back to the door.* MAURYA *comes in very slowly, without looking at the girls, and goes over to her stool at the other side of the fire. The cloth with the bread is still in her hand. The girls look at each other, and* NORA *points to the bundle of bread*]

CATHLEEN. [*after spinning for a moment*] You didn't give him his bit of bread? [MAURYA *begins to keen softly, without turning round*]

CATHLEEN. Did you see him riding down? [MAURYA *goes on keening*]

CATHLEEN. [*a little impatiently*] God forgive you; isn't it a better thing to raise your voice and tell what you seen, than to be making lamentation for a thing that's done? Did you see Bartley, I'm saying to you?

MAURYA. [*with a weak voice*] My heart's broken from this day.

CATHLEEN. [*as before*] Did you see Bartley?

MAURYA. I seen the fearfulest thing.

CATHLEEN. [*leaves her wheel and looks out*] God forgive you; he's riding the mare now over the green head, and the gray pony behind him.

MAURYA. [*starts, so that her shawl falls back from her head and shows her white tossed hair. With a frightened voice*] The gray pony behind him.

CATHLEEN. [*coming to the fire*] What is it ails you, at all?

MAURYA. [*speaking very slowly*] I've seen the fearfulest thing any person has seen, since the day Bride Dara seen the dead man with a child in his arms.

CATHLEEN AND NORA. Uah! [*they crouch down in front of the old woman at the fire*]

NORA. Tell us what it is you seen.

MAURYA. I went down to the spring well, and I stood there saying a prayer to myself. Then Bartley came along, and he riding on the red mare with the gray pony behind him. [*she puts up her hands, as if to hide something from her eyes*] The Son of God spare us, Nora!

CATHLEEN. What is it you seen?

MAURYA. I seen Michael himself.

CATHLEEN. [*speaking softly*] You did not, mother; it wasn't Michael you seen, for his body is after being found in the far north, and he's got a clean burial by the grace of God.

MAURYA. [*a little defiantly*] I'm after seeing

---

[2] to lament by wailing.   [3] sea witches.

him this day, and he riding and galloping. Bartley came first on the red mare; and I tried to say, "God speed you!" but something choked the words in my throat. He went by quickly; and "the blessing of God on you," says he, and I could say nothing. I looked up then, and I crying, at the gray pony, and there was Michael upon it—with fine clothes on him, and new shoes on his feet.

CATHLEEN. [*begins to keen*] It's destroyed we are from this day. It's destroyed, surely.

NORA. Didn't the young priest say the Almighty God wouldn't leave her destitute with no son living?

MAURYA. [*in a low voice, but clearly*] It's little the like of him knows of the sea. . . . Bartley will be lost now, and let you call in Eamon and make me a good coffin out of the white boards, for I won't live after them. I've had a husband, and a husband's father, and six sons in this house—six fine men, though it was a hard birth I had with every one of them and they coming into the world—and some of them were found and some of them were not found, but they're gone now with the lot of them . . . There were Stephen, and Shawn, were lost in the great wind, and found after in the Bay of Gregory of the Golden Mouth, and carried up the two of them on the one plank, and in by that door. [*she pauses for a moment; the girls start as if they heard something through the door that is half open behind them*]

NORA. [*in a whisper*] Did you hear that, Cathleen? Did you hear a noise in the northeast?

CATHLEEN. [*in a whisper*] There's some one after crying out by the seashore.

MAURYA. [*continues without hearing anything*] There was Sheamus and his father, and his own father again, were lost in a dark night, and not a stick or sign was seen of them when the sun went up. There was Patch after was drowned out of a curagh[4] that turned over. I was sitting here with Bartley, and he a baby, lying on my two knees, and I seen two women, and three women, and four women coming in, and they crossing themselves, and not saying a word. I looked out then, and there were men coming after them, and they holding a thing in

the half of a red sail, and water dripping out of it—it was a dry day, Nora—and leaving a track to the door. [*she pauses again with her hand stretched out toward the door. It opens softly and old women begin to come in, crossing themselves on the threshold, and kneeling down in front of the stage with red petticoats over their heads*]

MAURYA. [*half in a dream, to* CATHLEEN] Is it Patch, or Michael, or what is it at all?

CATHLEEN. Michael is after being found in the far north, and when he is found there, how could he be here in this place?

MAURYA. There does be a power of young men floating round in the sea, and what way would they know if it was Michael they had, or another man like him, for when a man is nine days in the sea, and the wind blowing, it's hard set his own mother would be to say what man was it.

CATHLEEN. It's Michael, God spare him, for they're after sending us a bit of his clothes from the far north. [*she reaches out and hands* MAURYA *the clothes that belong to* MICHAEL. MAURYA *stands up slowly, and takes them in her hands.* NORA *looks out*]

NORA. They're carrying a thing among them and there's water dripping out of it and leaving a track by the big stones.

CATHLEEN. [*in a whisper to the women who have come in*] Is it Bartley it is?

ONE OF THE WOMEN. It is surely, God rest his soul. [*two younger women come in and pull out the table. Then men carry in the body of* BARTLEY, *laid on a plank, with a bit of sail over it, and lay it on the table*]

CATHLEEN. [*to the women, as they are doing so*] What way was he drowned?

ONE OF THE WOMEN. The gray pony knocked him into the sea, and he was washed out where there is a great surf on the white rocks. [MAURYA *has gone over and knelt down at the head of the table. The women are keening softly and swaying themselves with a slow movement.* CATHLEEN *and* NORA *kneel at the other end of the table. The men kneel near the door*]

MAURYA. [*raising her head and speaking as if she did not see the people around her*] They're all gone now, and there isn't anything more the sea can do to me. . . . I'll have no call now to be up crying and praying when

---

[4] a small, frail boat.

the wind breaks from the south, and you can hear the surf is in the east, and the surf is in the west, making a great stir with the two noises, and they hitting one on the other. I'll have no call now to be going down and getting Holy Water in the dark nights after Samhain,[5] and I won't care what way the sea is when the other women will be keening. [*to* NORA] Give me the Holy Water, Nora; there's a small sup still on the dresser. [NORA *gives it to her.* MAURYA *drops* MICHAEL's *clothes across* BART-LEY's *feet, and sprinkles the Holy Water over him*] It isn't that I haven't prayed for you, Bartley, to the Almighty God. It isn't that I haven't said prayers in the dark night till you wouldn't know what I'd be saying; but it's a great rest I'll have now, and it's time surely. It's a great rest I'll have now, and great sleeping in the long nights after Samhain, if it's only a bit of wet flour we do have to eat, and maybe a fish that would be stinking. [*she kneels down again, crossing herself, and saying prayers under her breath*]

CATHLEEN. [*to an old man*] Maybe yourself and Eamon would make a coffin when the sun rises. We have fine white boards herself bought, God help her, thinking Michael would be found, and I have a new cake you can eat while you'll be working.

THE OLD MAN. [*looking at the boards*] Are there nails with them?

CATHLEEN. There are not, Colum; we didn't think of the nails.

ANOTHER MAN. It's a great wonder she

─────────
[5] All Souls' Day (November 2).

wouldn't think of the nails, and all the coffins she's seen made already.

CATHLEEN. It's getting old she is, and broken. [MAURYA *stands up again very slowly and spreads out the pieces of* MICHAEL's *clothes beside the body, sprinkling them with the last of the Holy Water*]

NORA. [*in a whisper to* CATHLEEN] She's quiet now and easy; but the day Michael was drowned you could hear her crying out from this to the spring well. It's fonder she was of Michael, and would anyone have thought that?

CATHLEEN. [*slowly and clearly*] An old woman will be soon tired with anything she will do, and isn't it nine days herself is after crying and keening, and making great sorrow in the house?

MAURYA. [*puts the empty cup mouth downwards on the table, and lays her hands together on* BARTLEY's *feet*] They're all together this time, and the end is come. May the Almighty God have mercy on Bartley's soul, and on Michael's soul, and on the souls of Sheamus and Patch, and Stephen and Shawn [*bending her head*]; and may He have mercy on my soul, Nora, and on the soul of every one is left living in the world. [*she pauses, and the keen rises a little more loudly from the women, then sinks away*]

MAURYA. [*continuing*] Michael has a clean burial in the far north by the grace of the Almighty God. Bartley will have a fine coffin out of the white boards, and a deep grave surely. What more can we want than that? No man at all can be living forever, and we must be satisfied. [*she kneels down again and the curtain falls slowly*]

THE HAIRY APE*

A COMEDY OF ANCIENT AND MODERN LIFE IN EIGHT SCENES

EUGENE O'NEILL

O'Neill (1888–   ) was born into the theater; his father was an actor, and the boy spent years on tour with him. Finding college not to his liking, O'Neill went to sea, was frequently "on the beach" (unengaged), had a spell at reporting, tried odd jobs all over the world, and eventually found himself back behind academic walls, this time at Harvard in the famous dramatic workshop of Professor Baker. Early experimental plays produced by the Provincetown Players and the notable full-length Beyond the Horizon started him on the way to the top position in the American theater (see I, 404). The golden period of The Emperor Jones, The Hairy Ape (q.v.), and Anna Christie was followed by a half-dozen interesting but uneven plays, and then came Strange Interlude and Mourning Becomes Electra. (It is significant that with one notable exception O'Neill deals exclusively with tragedy.) After the last war the playwright emerged from a long retirement, from which had come stories of a massive chain of plays, illness, mental trouble, and destruction of manuscripts. Two of the new plays have appeared without causing much stir; a third is to appear long after his death.

O'Neill has won Pulitzer and Nobel prizes along with other honors. He has made money in the theater, though he is far from being a millionaire. He has been translated and produced all over the globe. Almost single-handedly he made the American theater grow up. Few have doubted his power and courage, although he has been attacked for concentrating on muddled people, for never quite mastering the poetic impulses which often produce equally muddled lines. Nevertheless, O'Neill stands today as the first American dramatist to clear away the lumber of tradition; without too much preaching he has probed deep into the heart of man and, like Marlowe, once more made human passion real on stage.

Characters

ROBERT SMITH, "YANK"
PADDY
LONG
MILDRED DOUGLAS
HER AUNT
SECOND ENGINEER
A GUARD
A SECRETARY OF AN ORGANIZATION
STOKERS, LADIES, GENTLEMEN, ETC.

SCENE I. The firemen's forecastle of an ocean liner—an hour after sailing from New York
SCENE II. Section of promenade deck, two days out—morning
SCENE III. The stokehole. A few minutes later
SCENE IV. Same as Scene I. Half an hour later
SCENE V. Fifth Avenue, New York. Three weeks later
SCENE VI. An island near the city. The next night
SCENE VII. In the city. About a month later
SCENE VIII. In the city. Twilight of the next day

SCENE I.

SCENE—The firemen's forecastle of a transatlantic liner an hour after sailing from New

*York for the voyage across. Tiers of narrow,
steel bunks, three deep, on all sides. An entrance in rear. Benches on the floor before the
bunks. The room is crowded with men, shouting, cursing, laughing, singing—a confused, in-* 5
*choate uproar swelling into a sort of unity, a
meaning—the bewildered, furious, baffled defiance of a beast in a cage. Nearly all the men
are drunk. Many bottles are passed from hand
to hand. All are dressed in dungaree pants,* 10
*heavy ugly shoes. Some wear singlets, but the
majority are stripped to the waist.*

*The treatment of this scene, or of any other
scene in the play, should by no means be nat-
uralistic. The effect sought after is a cramped* 15
*space in the bowels of a ship, imprisoned by
white steel. The lines of bunks, the uprights
supporting them, cross each other like the steel
framework of a cage. The ceiling crushes down
upon the men's heads. They cannot stand up-* 20
*right. This accentuates the natural stooping
posture which shoveling coal and the resultant
over-development of back and shoulder muscles have given them. The men themselves
should resemble those pictures in which the ap-* 25
*pearance of Neanderthal Man is guessed at. All
are hairy-chested, with long arms of tremendous power, and low, receding brows above
their small, fierce, resentful eyes. All the civilized white races are represented, but except* 30
*for the slight differentiation in color of hair,
skin, eyes, all these men are alike.*

The curtain rises on a tumult of sound. YANK
*is seated in the foreground. He seems broader,
fiercer, more truculent, more powerful, more* 35
*sure of himself than the rest. They respect his
superior strength—the grudging respect of
fear. Then, too, he represents to them a self-
expression, the very last word in what they are,
their most highly developed individual.* 40

VOICES. Gif me trink dere, you!
    'Ave a wet!
    Salute!
    Gesundheit!
    Skoal![1] 45
    Drunk as a lord, God stiffen you!
    Here's how!
    Luck!
    Pass back that bottle, damn you! 50

_____
[1] Here's how, your health (in three languages).

Pourin' it down his neck!
Ho, Froggy! Where the devil have
    you been?
La Touraine.
I hit him smash in yaw, py Gott!
Jenkins—the First—he's a rotten
    swine——
And the coppers nabbed him—and
    I run——
I like peer better. It don't pig head
    gif you.
A slut, I'm sayin'! She robbed me
    aslape——
To hell with 'em all!
You're a bloody liar!
Say dot again! [*commotion. Two
    men about to fight are pulled
    apart*]
No scrappin' now!
Tonight——
See who's the best man!
Bloody Dutchman!
Tonight on the for'ard square.
I'll bet on Dutchy.
He packa da wallop, I tella you!
Shut up, Wop!
No fightin', maties. We're all
    chums, ain't we?
[*a voice starts bawling a song*]
"Beer, beer, glorious beer!
Fill yourself right up to here."

YANK. [*for the first time seeming to take notice of the uproar about him, turns around
threateningly—in a tone of contemptuous authority*] Choke off dat noise! Where d'yuh get
dat beer stuff? Beer, hell! Beer's for goils—
and Dutchmen. Me for somep'n wit a kick to
it! Gimme a drink, one of youse guys. [*several
bottles are eagerly offered. He takes a tremendous gulp at one of them; then, keeping
the bottle in his hand, glares belligerently at
the owner, who hastens to acquiesce in this
robbery by saying*] All righto, Yank. Keep it
and have another. [YANK *contemptuously turns
his back on the crowd again. For a second
there is an embarrassed silence. Then—*]
VOICES. We must be passing the Hook.
    She's beginning to roll to it.
    Six days in hell—and then South-
        ampton.
    Py Yesus, I vish somepody take my
        first vatch for me!

Gittin' seasick, Square-head?
Drink up and forget it!
What's in your bottle?
Gin.
Dot's nigger trink.
Absinthe? It's doped. You'll go off
    your chump, Froggy!
Cochon![2]
Whisky, that's the ticket!
Where's Paddy?
Going asleep.
Sing us that whisky song, Paddy.
[*They all turn to an old, wizened Irishman
who is dozing, very drunk, on the benches for-
ward. His face is extremely monkey-like with
all the sad, patient pathos of that animal in his
small eyes*]

    Singa da song, Caruso Pat!
    He's gettin' old. The drink is too
        much for him.
    He's too drunk.

PADDY. [*blinking about him, starts to his feet
resentfully, swaying, holding on to the edge
of a bunk*] I'm never too drunk to sing. 'Tis
only when I'm dead to the world I'd be wishful
to sing at all. [*with a sort of sad contempt*]
"Whisky Johnny," ye want? A chanty, ye
want? Now that's a queer wish from the ugly
like of you, God help you. But no mather. [*he
starts to sing in a thin, nasal, doleful tone*]
Oh, whisky is the life of man!
    Whisky! O Johnny! [*they all join in on
    this*]
Oh, whisky is the life of man!
    Whisky for my Johnny [*again chorus*]
Oh, whisky drove my old man mad!
    Whisky! O Johnny!
Oh, whisky drove my old man mad!
    Whisky for my Johnny!

YANK. [*again turning around scornfully*] Aw
hell! Nix on dat old sailing ship stuff! All dat
bull's dead, see? And you're dead, too, yuh
damned old Harp, on'y yuh don't know it.
Take it easy, see. Give us a rest. Nix on de
loud noise. [*with a cynical grin*] Can't youse
see I'm tryin' to t'ink?

ALL. [*repeating the word after him, as one,
with the same cynical amused mockery*] Think!
[*the chorused word has a brazen metallic
quality as if their throats were phonograph
horns. It is followed by a general uproar of
hard, barking laughter*]

    VOICES. Don't be cracking your head wid ut,
        Yank.
    You gat headache, py yingo!
    One thing about it—it rhymes with
        drink!
    Ha, ha, ha!
    Drink, don't think!
    Drink, don't think!
    Drink, don't think! [*a whole chorus
of voices has taken up this refrain, stamping
on the floor, pounding on the benches with
fists*]

YANK. [*taking a gulp from his bottle—good-
naturedly*] Aw right. Can de noise. I got yuh
de foist time. [*the uproar subsides. A very
drunken sentimental tenor begins to sing*]
    Far away in Canada,
    Far across the sea,
    There's a lass who fondly waits
    Making a home for me——

YANK. [*fiercely contemptuous*] Shut up, yuh
lousy boob! Where d'yuh get dat tripe? Home?
Home, hell! I'll make a home for yuh! I'll
knock yuh dead. Home! T'hell wit home!
Where d'yuh get dat tripe? Dis is home, see?
What d'yuh want wit home? [*proudly*] I
runned away from mine when I was a kid.
On'y too glad to beat it, dat was me. Home
was lickings for me, dat's all. But yuh can bet
your shoit no one ain't never licked me since!
Wanter try it, any of youse? Huh! I guess not.
[*in a more placated but still contemptuous
tone*] Goils waitin' for yuh, huh? Aw, hell!
Dat's all tripe. Dey don't wait for no one.
Dey'd double-cross yuh for a nickel. Dey're all
tarts, get me? Treat 'em rough, dat's me. To
hell wit 'em. Tarts, dat's what, de whole bunch
of 'em.

LONG. [*very drunk, jumps on a bench excitedly, gesticulating with a bottle in his hand*]
Listen 'ere, Comrades! Yank 'ere is right. 'E
says this 'ere stinkin' ship is our 'ome. And 'e
says as 'ome is 'ell. And 'e's right. This is 'ell.
We lives in 'ell, Comrades—and right enough
we'll die in it. [*raging*] And who's ter blame,
I arsks yer. We ain't. We wasn't born this rotten way. All men is born free and ekal. That's
in the bleedin' Bible, maties. But what d'they
care for the Bible—them lazy, bloated swine
what travels first cabin? Them's the ones. They

---

[2] Pig.

dragged us down 'til we're on'y wage slaves in the bowels of a bloody ship, sweatin', burnin' up, eatin' coal dust! Hit's them's ter blame—the damned Capitalist clarss! [*there had been a gradual murmur of contemptuous resentment rising among the men until now he is interrupted by a storm of catcalls, hisses, boos, hard laughter*]

VOICES. Turn it off!
Shut up!
Sit down!
Closa da face!
Tamn fool! [*etc.*]

YANK. [*standing up and glaring at* LONG] Sit down before I knock yuh down! [LONG *makes haste to efface himself.* YANK *goes on contemptuously*] De Bible, huh? De Cap'tlist class, huh? Aw, nix on dat Salvation Army-Socialist bull. Git a soapbox! Hire a hall! Come and be saved, huh? Jerk us to Jesus, huh? Aw g'wan! I've listened to lots of guys like you, see? Yuh're all wrong. Wanter know what I t'ink? Yuh ain't no good for no one. Yuh're de bunk. Yuh ain't got no noive, get me? Yuh're yellow, dat's what. Yellow, dat's you. Say! What's dem slobs in de foist cabin got to do wit us? We're better men dan dey are, ain't we? Sure! One of us guys could clean up de whole mob wit one mit. Put one of 'em down here for one watch in de stokehole, what'd happen? Dey'd carry him off on a stretcher. Dem boids don't amount to nothin'. Dey're just baggage. Who makes dis old tub run? Ain't it us guys? Well den, we belong, don't we? We belong and dey don't. Dat's all. [*a loud chorus of approval.* YANK *goes on*] As for dis bein' hell—aw, nuts! Yuh lost your noive, dat's what. Dis is a man's job, get me? It belongs. It runs dis tub. No stiffs need apply. But yuh're a stiff, see? Yuh're yellow, dat's you.

VOICES. [*with a great hard pride in them*]
Righto!
A man's job!
Talk is cheap, Long.
He never could hold up his end.
Divil take him!
Yank's right. We make it go.
Py Gott, Yank say right ting!
We don't need no one cryin' over us.
Makin' speeches.
Throw him' out!
Yellow!

Chuck him overboard!
I'll break his jaw for him!
[*They crowd around* LONG *threateningly.*]

YANK. [*half good-natured again—contemptuously*] Aw, take it easy. Leave him alone. He ain't woith a punch. Drink up. Here's how, whoever owns dis. [*he takes a long swallow from his bottle. All drink with him. In a flash all is hilarious amiability again, back-slapping, loud talk, etc.*]

PADDY. [*who has been sitting in a blinking, melancholy daze—suddenly cries out in a voice full of old sorrow*] We belong to this, you're saying? We make the ship to go, you're saying? Yerra then, that Almighty God have pity on us! [*his voice runs into the wail of a keen; he rocks back and forth on his bench. The men stare at him, startled and impressed in spite of themselves*] Oh, to be back in the fine days of my youth, ochone! Oh, there was fine beautiful ships them days—clippers wid tall masts touching the sky—fine strong men in them—men that was sons of the sea as if 'twas the mother that bore them. Oh, the clean skins of them, and the clear eyes, the straight backs and full chests of them! Brave men they was, and bold men surely! We'd be sailing out, bound down round the Horn maybe. We'd be making sail in the dawn, with a fair breeze, singing a chanty song wid no care to it. And astern the land would be sinking low and dying out, but we'd give it no heed but a laugh, and never a look behind. For the day that was, was enough, for we was free men—and I'm thinking 'tis only slaves do be giving heed to the day that's gone or the day to come—until they're old like me. [*with a sort of religious exaltation*] Oh, to be scudding south again wid the power of the Trade Wind driving her on steady through the nights and the days! Full sail on her! Nights and days! Nights when the foam of the wake would be flaming wid fire, when the sky'd be blazing and winking wid stars. Or the full of the moon maybe. Then you'd see her driving through the gray night, her sails stretching aloft all silver and white, not a sound on the deck, the lot of us dreaming dreams, till you'd believe 'twas no real ship at all you was on but a ghost ship like the Flying Dutchman they say does be roaming the seas forevermore widout touching a port. And there was the days, too. A warm sun on the clean decks. Sun warming the blood of you, and wind over the miles of shiny green ocean like strong drink to your lungs. Work—aye, hard work—but who'd mind that at all? Sure, you worked under the sky and 'twas work wid skill and daring to it. And wid the day done, in the dog watch, smoking me pipe at ease, the lookout would be raising land maybe, and we'd see the mountains of South Americy wid the red fire of the setting sun painting their white tops and the clouds floating by them! [*his tone of exaltation ceases. He goes on mournfully*] Yerra, what's the use of talking? 'Tis a dead man's whisper. [*to* YANK *resentfully*] 'Twas them days men belonged to ships, not now. 'Twas them days a ship was part of the sea, and a man was part of a ship, and the sea joined all together and made it one. [*scornfully*] Is it one wid this you'd be, Yank—black smoke from the funnels smudging the sea, smudging the decks—the bloody engines pounding and throbbing and shaking—wid divil a sight of sun or a breath of clean air—choking our lungs wid coal dust—breaking our backs and hearts in the hell of the stokehole—feeding the bloody furnace—feeding our lives along wid the coal, I'm thinking—caged in by steel from a sight of the sky like bloody apes in the Zoo! [*with a harsh laugh*] Ho-ho, divil mend you! Is it to belong to that you're wishing? Is it a flesh and blood wheel of the engines you'd be?

YANK. [*who has been listening with a contemptuous sneer, barks out the answer*] Sure ting! Dat's me. What about it?

PADDY. [*as if to himself—with great sorrow*] Me time is past due. That a great wave wid sun in the heart of it may sweep me over the side sometime I'd be dreaming of the days that's gone!

YANK. Aw, yuh crazy Mick! [*he springs to his feet and advances on Paddy threateningly —then stops, fighting some queer struggle within himself—lets his hands fall to his sides —contemptuously*] Aw, take it easy. Yuh're aw right, at dat. Yuh're bugs, dat's all—nutty as a cuckoo. All dat tripe yuh been pullin'— Aw, dat's all right. On'y it's dead, get me? Yuh don't belong no more, see. Yuh don't get de stuff. Yuh're too old. [*disgustedly*] But aw say, come up for air onct in a while, can't yuh? See what's happened since yuh croaked. [*he sud-*denly bursts forth vehemently, growing more and more excited*] Say! Sure! Sure I meant it! What de hell— Say, lemme talk! Hey! Hey, you old Harp! Hey, youse guys! Say, listen to me—wait a moment—I gotta talk, see. I belong and he don't. He's dead but I'm livin'. Listen to me! Sure I'm part of de engines! Why de hell not? Dey move, don't dey? Dey're speed, ain't dey? Dey smash trou, don't dey? Twenty-five knots a hour! Dat's goin' some! Dat's new stuff! Dat belongs! But him, he's too old. He gets dizzy. Say listen. All dat crazy tripe about nights and days; all dat crazy tripe about stars and moons; all dat crazy tripe about suns and winds, fresh air and de rest of it—Aw hell, dat's all a dope dream! Hittin' de pipe of de past, dat's what he's doin'. He's old and don't belong no more. But me, I'm young! I'm in de pink! I move wit it! It, get me! I mean de ting dat's de guts of all dis. It ploughs trou all de tripe he's been sayin'. It blows dat up! It knocks dat dead! It slams dat offen de face of de oith! It, get me! De engines and de coal and de smoke and all de rest of it! He can't breathe and swallow coal dust, but I kin, see? Dat's fresh air for me! Dat's food for me! I'm new, get me? Hell in de stokehole? Sure! It takes a man to work in hell. Hell, sure, dat's my fav'rite climate. I eat it up! I git fat on it! It's me makes it hot! It's me makes it roar! It's me makes it move! Sure, on'y for me everyting stops. It all goes dead, get me? De noise and smoke and all de engines movin' de woild, dey stop. Dere ain't nothin' no more! Dat's what I'm sayin'. Everyting else dat makes de woild move, somep'n makes it move. It can't move without somep'n else, see? Den yuh get down to me. I'm at de bottom, get me! Dere ain't nothin' foither. I'm de end! I'm de start! I start somep'n and de woild moves! It—dat's me!—de new dat's moiderin' de old! I'm de ting in coal dat makes it boin; I'm steam and oil for de engines; I'm de ting in noise dat makes yuh hear it; I'm smoke and express trains and steamers and factory whistles; I'm de ting in gold dat makes money! And I'm what makes iron into steel! Steel, dat stands for de whole ting! And I'm steel—steel—steel! I'm de muscles in steel, de punch behind it! [*as he says this he pounds with his fist against the steel bunks. All the men roused to a pitch of frenzied self-glorification by his speech, do like-*

wise. There is a deafening metallic roar, through which YANK's *voice can be heard bellowing*] Slaves, hell! We run de whole woiks. All de rich guys dat tink dey're somep'n, dey ain't nothin'! Dey don't belong. But us guys, we're in de move, we're at de bottom, de whole ting is us! [PADDY *from the start of* YANK's *speech has been taking one gulp after another from his bottle, at first frightenedly, as if he were afraid to listen, then desperately, as if to drown his senses, but finally has achieved complete indifferent, even amused, drunkenness.* YANK *sees his lips moving. He quells the uproar with a shout*] Hey, youse guys, take it easy! Wait a moment! De nutty Harp is sayin' somep'n.

PADDY. [*is heard now—throws his head back with a mocking burst of laughter*] Ho-ho-ho-ho-ho—

YANK. [*drawing back his fist, with a snarl*] Aw! Look out who yuh're givin' the bark!

PADDY. [*begins to sing the "Miller of Dee" with enormous good nature*]

> I care for nobody, no, not I,
> And nobody cares for me.

YANK. [*good-natured himself in a flash, interrupts* PADDY *with a slap on the bare back like a report*] Dat's de stuff! Now yuh're gettin' wise to somep'n. Care for nobody, dat's de dope! To hell wit 'em all! And nix on nobody else carin'. I kin care for myself, get me! [*eight bells sound, muffled, vibrating through the steel walls as if some enormous brazen gong were imbedded in the heart of the ship. All the men jump up mechanically, file through the door silently close upon each other's heels in what is very like a prisoners' lockstep.* YANK *slaps* PADDY *on the back*] Our watch, yuh old Harp! [*mockingly*] Come on down in hell. Eat up de coal dust. Drink in de heat. It's it, see! Act like yuh liked it, yuh better—or croak yuhself.

PADDY. [*with jovial defiance*] To the divil wid it! I'll not report this watch. Let thim log me and be damned. I'm no slave the like of you. I'll be sittin' here at me ease, and drinking, and thinking, and dreaming dreams.

YANK. [*contemptuously*] Tinkin' and dreamin', what'll that get yuh? What's tinkin' got to do wit it? We move, don't we? Speed, ain't it? Fog, dat's all you stand for. But we drive trou dat, don't we? We split dat up and

smash trou—twenty-five knots a hour! [*turns his back on* PADDY *scornfully*] Aw, yuh make me sick! Yuh don't belong! [*he strides out the door in rear.* PADDY *hums to himself, blinking drowsily*]

[*Curtain*]

SCENE II.

SCENE—*Two days out. A section of the promenade deck.* MILDRED DOUGLAS *and her aunt are discovered reclining in deck chairs. The former is a girl of twenty, slender, delicate, with a pale, pretty face marred by a self-conscious expression of disdainful superiority. She looks fretful, nervous and discontented, bored by her own anemia. Her aunt is a pompous and proud—and fat—old lady. She is a type even to the point of a double chin and lorgnette. She is dressed pretentiously, as if afraid her face alone would never indicate her position in life.* MILDRED *is dressed all in white.*

The impression to be conveyed by this scene is one of the beautiful, vivid life of the sea all about—sunshine on the deck in a great flood, the fresh sea wind blowing across it. In the midst of this, these two incongruous, artificial figures, inert and disharmonious, the elder like a gray lump of dough touched up with rouge, the younger looking as if the vitality of her stock had been sapped before she was conceived, so that she is the expression not of its life energy but merely of the artificialities that energy had won for itself in the spending.

MILDRED. [*looking up with affected dreaminess*] How the black smoke swirls back against the sky! Is it not beautiful?

AUNT. [*without looking up*] I dislike smoke of any kind.

MILDRED. My great-grandmother smoked a pipe—a clay pipe.

AUNT. [*ruffling*] Vulgar!

MILDRED. She was too distant a relative to be vulgar. Time mellows pipes.

AUNT. [*pretending boredom but irritated*] Did the sociology you took up at college teach you that—to play the ghoul on every possible occasion, excavating old bones? Why not let your great-grandmother rest in her grave?

MILDRED. [*dreamily*] With her pipe beside her—puffing in Paradise.

AUNT. [*with spite*] Yes, you are a natural born ghoul. You are even getting to look like one, my dear.

MILDRED. [*in a passionless tone*] I detest you, Aunt. [*looking at her critically*] Do you know what you remind me of? Of a cold pork pudding against a background of linoleum tablecloth in the kitchen of a—but the possibilities are wearisome. [*she closes her eyes*]

AUNT. [*with a bitter laugh*] Merci for your candor. But since I am and must be your chaperon—in appearance, at least—let us patch up some sort of armed truce. For my part you are quite free to indulge any pose of eccentricity that beguiles you—as long as you observe the amenities——

MILDRED. [*drawling*] The inanities?

AUNT. [*going on as if she hadn't heard*] After exhausting the morbid thrills of social service work on New York's East Side—how they must have hated you, by the way, the poor that you made so much poorer in their own eyes!—you are now bent on making your slumming international. Well, I hope Whitechapel will provide the needed nerve tonic. Do not ask me to chaperon you there, however. I told your father I would not. I loathe deformity. We will hire an army of detectives and you may investigate everything—they allow you to see.

MILDRED. [*protesting with a trace of genuine earnestness*] Please do not mock at my attempts to discover how the other half lives. Give me credit for some sort of groping sincerity in that at least. I would like to help them. I would like to be some use in the world. Is it my fault I don't know how? I would like to be sincere, to touch life somewhere. [*with weary bitterness*] But I'm afraid I have neither the vitality nor integrity. All that was burnt out in our stock before I was born. Grandfather's blast furnaces, flaming to the sky, melting steel, making millions—then father keeping those home fires burning, making more millions—and little me at the tail-end of it all. I'm a waste product in the Bessemer process—like the millions. Or rather, I inherit the acquired trait of the by-product, wealth, but none of the energy, none of the strength of the steel that made it. I am sired by gold and dammed by it, as they say at the race track—damned in more ways than one. [*she laughs mirthlessly*]

AUNT. [*unimpressed—superciliously*] You seem to be going in for sincerity today. It isn't becoming to you, really—except as an obvious pose. Be as artificial as you are, I advise. There's a sort of sincerity in that, you know. And, after all, you must confess you like that better.

MILDRED. [*again affected and bored*] Yes, I suppose I do. Pardon me for my outburst. When a leopard complains of its spots, it must sound rather grotesque. [*in a mocking tone*] Purr, little leopard. Purr, scratch, tear, kill, gorge yourself and be happy—only stay in the jungle where your spots are camouflage. In a cage they make you conspicuous.

AUNT. I don't know what you are talking about.

MILDRED. It would be rude to talk about anything to you. Let's just talk. [*she looks at her wrist watch*] Well, thank goodness, it's about time for them to come for me. That ought to give me a new thrill, Aunt.

AUNT. [*affectedly troubled*] You don't mean to say you're really going? The dirt—the heat must be frightful——

MILDRED. Grandfather started as a puddler. I should have inherited an immunity to heat that would make a salamander shiver. It will be fun to put it to the test.

AUNT. But don't you have to have the captain's—or someone's—permission to visit the stokehole?

MILDRED. [*with a triumphant smile*] I have it—both his and the chief engineer's. Oh, they didn't want to at first, in spite of my social service credentials. They didn't seem a bit anxious that I should investigate how the other half lives and works on a ship. So I had to tell them that my father, the president of Nazareth Steel, chairman of the board of directors of this line, had told me it would be all right.

AUNT. He didn't.

MILDRED. How naïve age makes one! But I said he did, Aunt. I even said he had given me a letter to them—which I had lost. And they were afraid to take the chance that I might be lying. [*excitedly*] So it's ho! for the stokehole. The second engineer is to escort me. [*looking at her watch again*] It's time. And here he comes, I think. [*the SECOND ENGINEER enters. He is a husky, fine-looking man of thirty-five or so. He stops before the two and tips his cap, visibly embarrassed and ill-at-ease*]

SECOND ENGINEER. Miss Douglas?

MILDRED. Yes. [*throwing off her rugs and getting to her feet*] Are we all ready to start?

SECOND ENGINEER. In just a second, ma'am. I'm waiting for the Fourth. He's coming along.

MILDRED. [*with a scornful smile*] You don't care to shoulder this responsibility alone, is that it?

SECOND ENGINEER. [*forcing a smile*] Two are better than one. [*disturbed by her eyes, glances out to sea—blurts out*] A fine day we're having.

MILDRED. Is it?

SECOND ENGINEER. A nice warm breeze——

MILDRED. It feels cold to me.

SECOND ENGINEER. But it's hot enough in the sun——

MILDRED. Not hot enough for me. I don't like Nature. I was never athletic.

SECOND ENGINEER. [*forcing a smile*] Well, you'll find it hot enough where you're going.

MILDRED. Do you mean hell?

SECOND ENGINEER. [*flabbergasted, decides to laugh*] Ho-ho! No, I mean the stokehole.

MILDRED. My grandfather was a puddler. He played with boiling steel.

SECOND ENGINEER. [*all at sea—uneasily*] Is that so? Hum, you'll excuse me, ma'am, but are you intending to wear that dress?

MILDRED. Why not?

SECOND ENGINEER. You'll likely rub against oil and dirt. It can't be helped.

MILDRED. It doesn't matter. I have lots of white dresses.

SECOND ENGINEER. I have an old coat you might throw over——

MILDRED. I have fifty dresses like this. I will throw this one into the sea when I come back. That ought to wash it clean, don't you think?

SECOND ENGINEER. [*doggedly*] There's ladders to climb down that are none too clean—and dark alleyways——

MILDRED. I will wear this very dress and none other.

SECOND ENGINEER. No offense meant. It's none of my business. I was only warning you——

MILDRED. Warning? That sounds thrilling.

SECOND ENGINEER. [*looking down the deck —with a sigh of relief*] There's the Fourth now. He's waiting for us. If you'll come——

MILDRED. Go on. I'll follow you. [*he goes. MILDRED turns a mocking smile on her* AUNT] An oaf—but a handsome, virile oaf.

AUNT. [*scornfully*] Poser!

MILDRED. Take care. He said there were dark alleyways——

AUNT. [*in the same tone*] Poser!

MILDRED. [*biting her lips angrily*] You are right. But would that my millions were not so anemically chaste!

AUNT. Yes, for a fresh pose I have no doubt you would drag the name of Douglas in the gutter!

MILDRED. From which it sprang. Good-by, Aunt. Don't pray too hard that I may fall into the fiery furnace.

AUNT. Poser!

MILDRED. [*viciously*] Old hag! [*she slaps her aunt insultingly across the face and walks off, laughing gaily*]

AUNT. [*screams after her*] I said poser!

[*Curtain*]

SCENE III.

SCENE—*The stokehole. In the rear, the dimly outlined bulks of the furnaces and boilers. High overhead one hanging electric bulb sheds just enough light through the murky air laden with coal dust to pile up masses of shadows everywhere. A line of men, stripped to the waist, is before the furnace doors. They bend over, looking neither to right nor left, handling their shovels as if they were part of their bodies, with a strange, awkward, swinging rhythm. They use the shovels to throw open the furnace doors. Then from these fiery round holes in the black a flood of terrific light and heat pours full upon the men who are outlined in silhouette in the crouching, inhuman attitudes of chained gorillas. The men shovel with a rhythmic motion, swinging as on a pivot from the coal which lies in heaps on the floor behind to hurl it into the flaming mouths before them. There is a tumult of noise—the brazen clang of the furnace doors as they are flung open or slammed shut, the grating, teeth-gritting grind of steel against steel, of crunching coal. This clash of sound stuns one's ears with its rending dissonance. But there is order in it, rhythm, a mechanical regulated recurrence, a tempo. And rising above all, making the air hum with the quiver of liberated energy, the roar of leaping flames in the furnaces, the monotonous throbbing beat of the engines.*

As the curtain rises, the furnace doors are shut. The men are taking a breathing spell. One or two are arranging the coal behind them, pulling it into more accessible heaps. The others can be dimly made out leaning on their shovels in relaxed attitudes of exhaustion.

PADDY. [*from somewhere in the line—plaintively*] Yerra, will this divil's own watch nivir end? Me back is broke. I'm destroyed entirely.

YANK. [*from the center of the line—with exuberant scorn*] Aw, yuh make me sick! Lie down and croak, why don't yuh? Always beefin', dat's you! Say, dis is a cinch! Dis was made for me! It's my meat, get me! [*a whistle is blown—a thin, shrill note from somewhere overhead in the darkness.* YANK *curses without resentment*] Dere's dat damn engineer crackin' de whip. He tinks we're loafin'.

PADDY. [*vindictively*] God stiffen him!

YANK. [*in an exultant tone of command*] Come on, youse guys! Git into de game! She's gittin' hungry! Pile some grub in her. Trow it into her belly! Come on now, all of youse! Open her up! [*at this last all the men, who have followed his movements of getting into position, throw open their furnace doors with a deafening clang. The fiery light floods over their shoulders as they bend round for the coal. Rivulets of sooty sweat have traced maps on their backs. The enlarged muscles form bunches of high light and shadow*]

YANK. [*chanting a count as he shovels without seeming effort*] One—two—tree—[*his voice rising exultantly in the joy of battle*] Dat's de stuff! Let her have it! All togedder now! Sling it into her! Let her ride! Shoot de piece now! Call de toin on her! Drive her into it! Feel her move! Watch her smoke! Speed, dat's her middle name! Give her coal, youse guys! Coal, dat's her booze! Drink it up, baby! Let's see yuh sprint! Dig in and gain a lap! Dere she go-o-es. [*this last in the chanting formula of the gallery gods at the six-day bike race. He slams his furnace door shut. The others do likewise with as much unison as their wearied bodies will permit. The effect is of*

one fiery eye after another being blotted out with a series of accompanying bangs]

PADDY. [*groaning*] Me back is broke. I'm bate out—bate—[*there is a pause. Then the inexorable whistle sounds again from the dim regions above the electric light. There is a growl of cursing rage from all sides*]

YANK. [*shaking his fist upward—contemptuously*] Take it easy dere, you! Who d'yuh tinks runnin' dis game, me or you? When I git ready, we move. Not before! When I git ready, get me!

VOICES. [*approvingly*] That's the stuff!
Yank tal him, py golly!
Yank ain't afeerd.
Goot poy, Yank!
Give him hell!
Tell 'im 'e's a bloody swine!
Bloody slave-driver!

YANK. [*contemptuously*] He ain't got no noive. He's yellow, get me? All de engineers is yellow. Dey got streaks a mile wide. Aw, to hell with him! Let's move, youse guys. We had a rest. Come on, she needs it! Give her pep! It ain't for him. Him and his whistle, dey don't belong. But we belong, see! We gotter feed de baby! Come on! [*he turns and flings his furnace door open. They all follow his lead. At this instant the* SECOND *and* FOURTH ENGINEERS *enter from the darkness on the left with* MILDRED *between them. She starts, turns paler, her pose is crumbling, she shivers with fright in spite of the blazing heat, but forces herself to leave the* ENGINEERS *and take a few steps near the men. She is right behind* YANK. *All this happens quickly while the men have their backs turned*]

YANK. Come on, youse guys! [*he is turning to get coal when the whistle sounds again in a peremptory, irritating note. This drives* YANK *into a sudden fury. While the other men have turned full around and stopped dumbfounded by the spectacle of* MILDRED *standing there in her white dress,* YANK *does not turn far enough to see her. Besides, his head is thrown back, he blinks upward through the murk trying to find the owner of the whistle, he brandishes his shovel murderously over his head in one hand, pounding on his chest, gorilla-like, with the other, shouting*] Toin off dat whistle! Come down outa dere, yuh yellow, brass-buttoned, Belfast bum, yuh! Come down and I'll knock yer brains out! Yuh lousy, stinkin', yellow mut of a Catholic-moiderin' bastard! Come down and I'll moider yuh! Pullin' dat whistle on me, huh? I'll show yuh! I'll crash yer skull in! I'll drive yer teet' down yer throat! I'll slam yer nose trou de back of yer head! I'll cut yer guts out for a nickel, yuh lousy boob, yuh dirty, crummy, muck-eatin' son of a——[*suddenly he becomes conscious of all the other men staring at something directly behind his back. He whirls defensively with a snarling, murderous growl, crouching to spring, his lips drawn back over his teeth, his small eyes gleaming ferociously. He sees* MILDRED, *like a white apparition in the full light from the open furnace doors. He glares into her eyes, turned to stone. As for her, during his speech she has listened, paralyzed with horror, terror, her whole personality crushed, beaten in, collapsed, by the terrific impact of this unknown, abysmal brutality, naked and shameless. As she looks at his gorilla face, as his eyes bore into hers, she utters a low, choking cry and shrinks away from him, putting both hands up before her eyes to shut out the sight of his face, to protect her own. This startles* YANK *to a reaction. His mouth falls open, his eyes grow bewildered*]

MILDRED. [*about to faint—to the* ENGINEERS, *who now have her one by each arm—whimperingly*] Take me away! Oh, the filthy beast! [*she faints. They carry her quickly back, disappearing in the darkness at the left, rear. An iron door clangs shut. Rage and bewildered fury rush back on* YANK. *He feels himself insulted in some unknown fashion in the very heart of his pride. He roars*] God damn yuh! [*and hurls his shovel after them at the door which has just closed. It hits the steel bulkhead with a clang and falls clattering on the steel floor. From overhead the whistle sounds again in a long, angry, insistent command.*]

[*Curtain*]

SCENE IV.

SCENE—*The firemen's forecastle.* YANK's *watch has just come off duty and had dinner. Their faces and bodies shine from a soap and water scrubbing but around their eyes, where a hasty dousing does not touch, the coal dust sticks like black make-up, giving them a queer, sinister expression.* YANK *has not washed either* face or body. *He stands out in contrast to them, a blackened, brooding figure. He is seated forward on a bench in the exact attitude of Rodin's "The Thinker." The others, most of them smoking pipes, are staring at* YANK *half-apprehensively, as if fearing an outburst; half-amusedly, as if they saw a joke somewhere that tickled them.*

VOICES. He ain't ate nothin'.
        Py golly, a fallar gat to gat grub in
            him.
        Divil a lie.
        Yank feeda da fire, no feeda da
            face.
        Ha-ha.
        He ain't even washed hisself.
        He's forgot.
        Hey, Yank, you forgot to wash.
YANK. [*sullenly*] Forgot nothin'! To hell wit washin'.
VOICES. It'll stick to you.
        It'll get under your skin.
        Give yer the bleedin' itch, that's
            wot.
        It makes spots on you—like a
            leopard.
        Like a piebald nigger, you mean.
        Better wash up, Yank.
        You sleep better.
        Wash up, Yank.
        Wash up! Wash up!
YANK. [*resentfully*] Aw say, youse guys. Lemme alone. Can't youse see I'm tryin' to tink?
ALL. [*repeating the word after him, as one, with cynical mockery*] Think! [*the word has a brazen, metallic quality as if their throats were phonograph horns. It is followed by a chorus of hard, barking laughter*]
YANK. [*springing to his feet and glaring at them belligerently*] Yes, tink! Tink, dat's what I said! What about it? [*they are silent, puzzled by his sudden resentment at what used to be one of his jokes.* YANK *sits down again in the same attitude of "The Thinker"*]
VOICES. Leave him alone.
        He's got a grouch on.
        Why wouldn't he?
PADDY. [*with a wink at the others*] Sure I know what's the matther. 'Tis aisy to see. He's fallen in love, I'm telling you.

ALL. [*repeating the word after him, as one, with cynical mockery*] Love! [*the word has a brazen, metallic quality as if their throats were phonograph horns. It is followed by a chorus of hard, barking laughter*]

YANK. [*with a contemptuous snort*] Love, hell! Hate, dat's what. I've fallen in hate, get me?

PADDY. [*philosophically*] 'Twould take a wise man to tell one from the other. [*with a bitter, ironical scorn, increasing as he goes on*] But I'm telling you it's love that's in it. Sure what else but love for us poor bastes in the stokehole would be bringing a fine lady, dressed like a white quane, down a mile of ladders and steps to be havin' a look at us? [*a growl of anger goes up from all sides*]

LONG. [*jumping on a bench—hectically*] Hinsultin' us! Hinsultin' us, the bloody cow! And them bloody engineers! What right 'as they got to be exhibitin' us 's if we was bleedin' monkeys in a menagerie? Did we sign for hinsults to our dignity as 'onest workers? Is that in the ship's articles? You kin bloody well bet it ain't! But I knows why they done it. I arsked a deck steward 'oo she was and 'e told me. 'Er old man's a bleedin' millionaire, a bloody Capitalist! 'E's got enuf bloody gold to sink this bleedin' ship! 'E makes arf the bloody steel in the world! 'E owns this bloody boat! And you and me, Comrades, we're 'is slaves! And the skipper and mates and engineers, they're 'is slaves! And she's 'is bloody daughter and we're all 'er slaves, too! And she gives 'er orders as 'ow she wants to see the bloody animals below decks and down they takes 'er! [*there is a roar of rage from all sides*]

YANK. [*blinking at him bewilderedly*] Say! Wait a moment! Is all dat straight goods?

LONG. Straight as string! The bleedin' steward as waits on 'em, 'e told me about 'er. And what're we goin' ter do, I arsks yer? 'Ave we got ter swaller 'er hinsults like dogs? It ain't in the ship's articles. I tell yer we got a case. We kin go ter law——

YANK. [*with abysmal contempt*] Hell! Law!

ALL. [*repeating the word after him, as one, with cynical mockery*] Law! [*the word has a brazen metallic quality as if their throats were phonograph horns. It is followed by a chorus of hard, barking laughter*]

LONG. [*feeling the ground slipping from un-der his feet—desperately*] As voters and citizens we kin force the bloody governments——

YANK. [*with abysmal contempt*] Hell! Governments!

ALL. [*repeating the word after him, as one, with cynical mockery*] Governments! [*the word has a brazen metallic quality as if their throats were phonograph horns. It is followed by a chorus of hard, barking laughter*]

LONG. [*hysterically*] We're free and equal in the sight of God——

YANK. [*with abysmal contempt*] Hell! God!

ALL. [*repeating the word after him, as one, with cynical mockery*] God! [*the word has a brazen metallic quality as if their throats were phonograph horns. It is followed by a chorus of hard, barking laughter*]

YANK. [*witheringly*] Aw, join de Salvation Army!

ALL. Sit down! Shut up! Damn fool! Sea-lawyer! [LONG *slinks back out of sight*]

PADDY. [*continuing the trend of his thoughts as if he had never been interrupted—bitterly*] And there she was standing behind us, and the Second pointing at us like a man you'd hear in a circus would be saying: In this cage is a queerer kind of baboon than ever you'd find in darkest Africy. We roast them in their own sweat—and be damned if you won't hear some of thim saying they like it! [*he glances scornfully at* YANK]

YANK. [*with a bewildered uncertain growl*] Aw!

PADDY. And there was Yank roarin' curses and turning round wid his shovel to brain her —and she looked at him, and him at her——

YANK. [*slowly*] She was all white. I tought she was a ghost. Sure.

PADDY. [*with heavy, biting sarcasm*] 'Twas love at first sight, divil a doubt of it! If you'd seen the endearin' look on her pale mug when she shriveled away with her hands over her eyes to shut out the sight of him! Sure, 'twas as if she'd seen a great hairy ape escaped from the Zoo!

YANK. [*stung—with a growl of rage*] Aw!

PADDY. And the loving way Yank heaved his shovel at the skull of her, only she was out the door! [*a grin breaking over his face*] 'Twas touching, I'm telling you! It put the touch of home, swate home in the stokehole. [*there is a roar of laughter from all*]

YANK. [*glaring at* PADDY *menacingly*] Aw, choke dat off, see!

PADDY. [*not heeding him—to the others*] And her grabbin' at the Second's arm for protection. [*with a grotesque imitation of a woman's voice*] Kiss me, Engineer dear, for it's dark down here and me old man's in Wall Street making money. Hug me tight, darlin', for I'm afeerd in the dark and me mother's on deck makin' eyes at the skipper! [*another roar of laughter*]

YANK. [*threateningly*] Say! What yuh tryin' to do, kid me, yuh old Harp?

PADDY. Divil a bit! Ain't I wishin' myself you'd brained her?

YANK. [*fiercely*] I'll brain her! I'll brain her yet, wait 'n' see! [*coming over to* PADDY—*slowly*] Say, is dat what she called me—a hairy ape?

PADDY. She looked it at you if she didn't say the word itself.

YANK. [*grinning horribly*] Hairy ape, huh? Sure! Dat's de way she looked at me, aw right. Hairy ape! So dat's me, huh? [*bursting into rage—as if she were still in front of him*] Yuh skinny tart! Yuh white-faced bum, yuh! I'll show yuh who's a ape! [*turning to the others, bewilderment seizing him again*] Say, youse guys. I was bawlin' him out for pullin' de whistle on us. You heard me. And den I seen youse lookin' at somep'n and I tought he'd sneaked down to come up in back of me, and I hopped round to knock him dead wit de shovel. And dere she was wit de light on her! Christ, yuh coulda pushed me over wit a finger! I was scared, get me? Sure! I tought she was a ghost, see? She was all in white like dey wrap around stiffs. You seen her. Kin yuh blame me? She didn't belong, dat's what. And den when I come to and seen it was a real skoit and seen de way she was lookin' at me—like Paddy said —Christ, I was sore, get me? I don't stand for dat stuff from nobody. And I flung de shovel— on'y she'd beat it. [*furiously*] I wished it'd banged her! I wished it'd knocked her block off!

LONG. And be 'anged for murder or 'lectrocuted? She ain't bleedin' well worth it.

YANK. I don't give a damn what! I'd be square wit her, wouldn't I? Tink I wanter let her put somep'n over on me? Tink I'm goin' to let her git away wit dat stuff? Yuh don't know me! No one ain't never put nothin' over on me and got away wit it, see!—not dat kind of stuff—no guy and no skoit neither! I'll fix her! Maybe she'll come down again——

VOICE. No chance, Yank. You scared her out of a year's growth.

YANK. I scared her? Why de hell should I scare her? Who de hell is she? Ain't she de same as me? Hairy ape, huh? [*with his old confident bravado*] I'll show her I'm better'n her, if she on'y knew it. I belong and she don't, see! I move and she's dead! Twenty-five knots a hour, dat's me! Dat carries her but I make dat. She's on'y baggage. Sure! [*again bewilderedly*] But, Christ, she was funny lookin'! Did yuh pipe her hands? White and skinny. Yuh could see de bones through 'em. And her mush, dat was dead white, too. And her eyes, dey was like dey'd seen a ghost. Me, dat was! Sure! Hairy ape! Ghost, huh? Look at dat arm! [*he extends his right arm, swelling out the great muscles*] I coulda took her wit dat, wit just my little finger even, and broke her in two. [*again bewilderedly*] Say, who is dat skoit, huh? What is she? What's she come from? Who made her? Who give her de noive to look at me like dat? Dis ting's got my goat right. I don't get her. She's new to me. What does a skoit like her mean, huh? She don't belong, get me! I can't see her. [*with growing anger*] But one ting I'm wise to, aw right, aw right! Youse all kin bet your shoits I'll git even wit her. I'll show her if she tinks she— She grinds de organ and I'm on de string, huh? I'll fix her! Let her come down again and I'll fling her in de furnace! She'll move den! She won't shiver at nothin', den! Speed, dat'll be her! She'll belong den! [*he grins horribly*]

PADDY. She'll never come. She's had her belly-full, I'm telling you. She'll be in bed now, I'm thinking, wid ten doctors and nurses feedin' her salts to clean the fear out of her.

YANK. [*enraged*] Yuh tink I made her sick, too, do yuh? Just lookin' at me, huh? Hairy ape, huh? [*in a frenzy of rage*] I'll fix her! I'll tell her where to git off! She'll git down on her knees and take it back or I'll bust de face offen her! [*shaking one fist upward and beating on his chest with the other*] I'll find yuh! I'm comin', d'yuh hear? I'll fix yuh, God damn yuh! [*he makes a rush for the door*]

VOICES. Stop him!

He'll get shot!
He'll murder her!
Trip him up!
Hold him!
He's gone crazy!
Gott, he's strong!
Hold him down!
Look out for a kick!
Pin his arms!

[*They have all piled on him and, after a fierce struggle, by sheer weight of numbers have borne him to the floor just inside the door*]

PADDY. [*who has remained detached*] Kape him down till he's cooled off. [*scornfully*] Yerra, Yank, you're a great fool. Is it payin' attention at all you are to the like of that skinny sow widout one drop of rale blood in her?

YANK. [*frenziedly, from the bottom of the heap*] She done me doit! She done me doit, didn't she? I'll git square wit her! I'll get her some way! Git offen me, youse guys! Lemme up! I'll show her who's a ape!

[*Curtain*]

SCENE V.

SCENE—*Three weeks later. A corner of Fifth Avenue in the Fifties on a fine Sunday morning. A general atmosphere of clean, well-tidied, wide street; a flood of mellow, tempered sunshine; gentle, genteel breezes. In the rear, the show windows of two shops, a jewelry establishment on the corner, a furrier's next to it. Here the adornments of extreme wealth are tantalizingly displayed. The jeweler's window is gaudy with glittering diamonds, emeralds, rubies, pearls, etc., fashioned in ornate tiaras, crowns, necklaces, collars, etc. From each piece hangs an enormous tag from which a dollar sign and numerals in intermittent electric lights wink out the incredible prices. The same in the furrier's. Rich furs of all varieties hang there bathed in a downpour of artificial light. The general effect is of a background of magnificence cheapened and made grotesque by commercialism, a background in tawdry disharmony with the clear light and sunshine on the street itself.*

Up the side street YANK *and* LONG *come swaggering.* LONG *is dressed in shore clothes, wears a black Windsor tie, cloth cap.* YANK *is in his dirty dungarees. A fireman's cap with black peak is cocked defiantly on the side of his head. He has not shaved for days and around his fierce, resentful eyes—as around those of* LONG *to a lesser degree—the black smudge of coal dust still sticks like make-up. They hesitate and stand together at the corner, swaggering, looking about them with a forced, defiant contempt.*

LONG. [*indicating it all with an oratorical gesture*] Well, 'ere we are. Fif' Avenoo. This 'ere's their bleedin' private lane, as yer might say. [*bitterly*] We're trespassers 'ere. Proletarians keep orf the grass!

YANK. [*dully*] I don't see no grass, yuh boob. [*staring at the sidewalk*] Clean, ain't it? Yuh could eat a fried egg offen it. The white wings got some job sweepin' dis up. [*looking up and down the avenue—surlily*] Where's all de white-collar stiffs yuh said was here—and de skoits—*her* kind?

LONG. In church, blarst 'em! Arskin' Jesus to give 'em more money.

YANK. Choich, huh? I useter go to choich onct—sure—when I was a kid. Me old man and woman, dey made me. Dey never went demselves, dough. Always got too big a head on Sunday mornin', dat was dem. [*with a grin*] Dey was scrappers for fair, bot' of dem. On Satiday nights when dey bot' got a skinful dey could put up a bout oughter been staged at de Garden. When dey got trough dere wasn't a chair or table wit a leg under it. Or else dey bot' jumped on me for somep'n. Dat was where I loined to take punishment. [*with a grin and a swagger*] I'm a chip offen de old block, get me?

LONG. Did yer old man follow the sea?

YANK. Naw. Worked along shore. I runned away when me old lady croaked wit de tremens. I helped at truckin' and in de market. Den I shipped in de stokehole. Sure. Dat belongs. De rest was nothin'. [*looking around him*] I ain't never seen dis before. De Brooklyn waterfront, dat was where I was dragged up. [*taking a deep breath*] Dis ain't so bad at dat, huh?

LONG. Not bad? Well, we pays for it wiv our bloody sweat, if yer wants to know!

YANK. [*with sudden angry disgust*] Aw, hell! I don't see no one, see—like her. All dis gives me a pain. It don't belong. Say, ain't dere a back room around dis dump? Let's go shoot a ball. All dis is too clean and quiet and dolled-up, get me? It gives me a pain.

LONG. Wait and yer'll bloody well see——

YANK. I don't wait for no one. I keep on de move. Say, what yuh drag me up here for, anyway? Tryin' to kid me, yuh simp, yuh?

LONG. Yer wants to get back at 'er, don't yer? That's what yer been sayin' every bloomin' hour since she hinsulted yer.

YANK. [*vehemently*] Sure ting I do! Didn't I try to get even wit her in Southampton? Didn't I sneak on de deck and wait for her by de gangplank? I was goin' to spit in her pale mug, see! Sure, right in her pop-eyes! Dat woulda made me even, see? But no chanct. Dere was a whole army of plainclothes bulls around. Dey spotted me and gimme de bum's rush. I never seen her. But I'll git square wit her yet, you watch! [*furiously*] De lousy tart! She tinks she kin get away wit moider—but not wit me! I'll fix her! I'll tink of a way!

LONG. [*as disgusted as he dares to be*] Ain't that why I brought yer up 'ere—to show yer? Yer been lookin' at this 'ere 'ole affair wrong. Yer been actin' an' talkin' 's if it was all a bleedin' personal matter between yer and that bloody cow. I wants to convince yer she was on'y a representative of 'er clarss. I wants to awaken yer bloody clarss consciousness. Then yer'll see it's 'er clarss ye've got to fight, not 'er alone. There's a 'ole mob of 'em like 'er, Gawd blind 'em!

YANK. [*spitting on his hands—belligerently*] De more de merrier when I gits started. Bring on de gang!

LONG. Yer'll see 'em in arf a mo', when that church lets out. [*he turns and sees the window display in the two stores for the first time*] Blimey! Look at that, will yer? [*they both walk back and stand looking in the jeweler's. LONG flies into a fury*] Just look at this 'ere bloomin' mess! Just look at it! Look at the bleedin' prices on 'em—more'n our 'ole bloody stokehole makes in ten voyages sweatin' in 'ell! And they—'er and 'er bloody clarss—buys 'em for toys to dangle on 'em! One of these 'ere would buy scoff for a starvin' family for a year!

YANK. Aw, cut de sob stuff! T' hell wit de starvin' family! Yuh'll be passin' de hat to me next. [*with naïve admiration*] Say, dem tings is pretty, huh? Bet yuh dey'd hock for a piece of change aw right. [*then turning away, bored*] But, aw hell, what good are dey? Let her have 'em. Dey don't belong no more'n she does. [*with a gesture of sweeping the jeweler's into oblivion*] All dat don't count, get me?

LONG. [*who has moved to the furrier's—indignantly*] And I s'pose this 'ere don't count neither—skins of poor, 'armless animals slaughtered so as 'er and 'ers can keep their bleedin' noses warm!

YANK. [*who has been staring at something inside—with queer excitement*] Take a slant at dat! Give it de once-over! Monkey fur—two t'ousand bucks! [*bewilderedly*] Is dat straight goods—monkey fur? What de hell——?

LONG. [*bitterly*] It's straight enuf. [*with grim humor*] They wouldn't bloody well pay that for a 'airy ape's skin—no, nor for the 'ole livin' ape with all 'is 'ead, and body, and soul thrown in!

YANK. [*clenching his fists, his face growing pale with rage as if the skin in the window were a personal insult*] Trowin' it up in my face! Christ! I'll fix her!

LONG. [*excitedly*] Church is out. 'Ere they come, the bleedin' swine. [*after a glance at YANK's lowering face—uneasily*] Easy goes, Comrade. Keep yer bloomin' temper. Remember force defeats itself. It ain't our weapon. We must impress our demands through peaceful means—the votes of the on-marching proletarians of the bloody world!

YANK. [*with abysmal contempt*] Votes, hell! Votes is a joke, see. Votes for women! Let dem do it!

LONG. [*still more uneasily*] Calm, now. Treat 'em wiv the proper contempt. Observe the bleedin' parasites but 'old yer 'orses.

YANK. [*angrily*] Git away from me! Yuh're yellow, dat's what. Force, dat's me! De punch, dat's me every time, see! [*the crowd from church enter from the right, sauntering slowly and affectedly, their heads held stiffly up, looking neither to right nor left, talking in toneless, simpering voices. The women are rouged, calcimined, dyed, overdressed to the nth degree. The men are in Prince Alberts, high hats, spats, canes, etc. A procession of gaudy marionettes, yet with something of the relentless horror of Frankenstein monsters in their detached, mechanical unawareness*]

VOICES. Dear Doctor Caiaphas! He is so
sincere!

What was the sermon? I dozed off.

About the radicals, my dear—and
the false doctrines that are being
preached.

We must organize a hundred per
cent American bazaar.

And let everyone contribute one
one-hundredth per cent of their
income tax.

What an original idea!

We can devote the proceeds to re-
habilitating the veil of the temple.

But that has been done so many
times.

YANK. [*glaring from one to the other of them
—with an insulting snort of scorn*] Huh! Huh!
[*without seeming to see him, they make wide
detours to avoid the spot where he stands in
the middle of the sidewalk*]

LONG. [*frightenedly*] Keep yer bloomin'
mouth shut, I tells yer.

YANK. [*viciously*] G'wan! Tell it to Sweeney!
[*he swaggers away and deliberately lurches
into a top-hatted gentleman, then glares at him
pugnaciously*] Say, who d'yuh tink yuh're
bumpin'? Tink yuh own de oith?

GENTLEMAN. [*coldly and affectedly*] I beg
your pardon. [*he has not looked at* YANK *and
passes on without a glance, leaving him bewildered*]

LONG. [*rushing up and grabbing* YANK's *arm*]
'Ere! Come away! This wasn't what I meant.
Yer'll 'ave the bloody coppers down on us.

YANK. [*savagely—giving him a push that
sends him sprawling*] G'wan!

LONG. [*picks himself up—hysterically*] I'll
pop orf then. This ain't what I meant. And
whatever 'appens, yer can't blame me. [*he
slinks off left*]

YANK. T'hell wit youse! [*he approaches a
lady—with a vicious grin and a smirking wink*]
Hello, Kiddo. How's every little ting? Got any-
ting on for tonight? I know an old boiler down
to de docks we kin crawl into. [*the lady stalks
by without a look, without a change of pace.*
YANK *turns to others—insultingly*] Holy
smokes, what a mug! Go hide yuhself before de
horses shy at yuh. Gee, pipe de heine on dat
one! Say, youse, yuh look like de stoin of a

ferry-boat. Paint and powder! All dolled up to
kill! Yuh look like stiffs laid out for de bone-
yard! Aw, g'wan, de lot of youse! Yuh give me
de eyeache. Yuh don't belong, get me! Look
at me, why don't youse dare? I belong, dat's
me! [*pointing to a skyscraper across the street
which is in process of construction—with bravado*] See dat building goin' up dere? See de
steel work? Steel, dat's me! Youse guys live on
it and tink yuh're somep'n. But I'm *in* it, see!
I'm de hoistin' engine dat makes it go up! I'm
it—de inside and bottom of it! Sure! I'm steel
and steam and smoke and de rest of it! It moves
—speed—twenty-five stories up—and me at de
top and bottom—movin'! Youse simps don't
move. Yuh're on'y dolls I winds up to see'm
spin. Yuh're de garbage, get me—de leavins—
de ashes we dump over de side! Now, whata
yuh gotto say? [*but as they seem neither to see
nor hear him, he flies into a fury*] Bums! Pigs!
Tarts! Bitches! [*he turns in a rage on the men,
bumping viciously into them but not jarring
them the least bit. Rather it is he who recoils
after each collision. He keeps growling*] Git off
de oith! G'wan, yuh bum! Look where yuh're
goin', can't yuh? Git outa here! Fight, why
don't yuh? Put up yer mits! Don't be a dog!
Fight or I'll knock yuh dead! [*but, without
seeming to see him, they all answer with mechanical affected politeness*] I beg your pardon.
[*then at a cry from one of the women, they all
scurry to the furrier's window*]

THE WOMAN. [*ecstatically, with a gasp of delight*] Monkey fur! [*the whole crowd of men
and women chorus after her in the same tone of
affected delight*] Monkey fur!

YANK. [*with a jerk of his head back on his
shoulders, as if he had received a punch full in
the face—raging*] I see yuh, all in white! I see
yuh, yuh white-faced tart, yuh! Hairy ape, huh?
I'll hairy ape yuh! [*he bends down and grips
at the street curbing as if to pluck it out and
hurl it. Foiled in this, snarling with passion, he
leaps to the lamp-post on the corner and tries
to pull it up for a club. Just at that moment a
bus is heard rumbling up. A fat, high-hatted,
spatted gentleman runs out from the side street.
He calls out plaintively: "Bus! Bus! Stop there!"
and runs full tilt into the bending, straining*
YANK, *who is bowled off his balance*]

YANK. [*seeing a fight—with a roar of joy as
he springs to his feet*] At last! Bus, huh? I'll

bust yuh! [*he lets drive a terrific swing, his fist landing full on the fat gentleman's face. But the gentleman stands unmoved as if nothing had happened*]

GENTLEMAN. I beg your pardon. [*then ir-* 5 *ritably*] You have made me lose my bus. [*he claps his hands and begins to scream*] Officer! Officer! [*many police whistles shrill out on the instant and a whole platoon of policemen rush in on* YANK *from all sides. He tries to fight but* 10 *is clubbed to the pavement and fallen upon. The crowd at the window have not moved or noticed this disturbance. The clanging gong of the patrol wagon approaches with a clamoring din.*] 15

[*Curtain*]

SCENE VI.

SCENE—*Night of the following day. A row* 20 *of cells in the prison on Blackwells Island. The cells extend back diagonally from right front to left rear. They do not stop, but disappear in the dark background as if they ran on, numberless, into infinity. One electric bulb from the low* 25 *ceiling of the narrow corridor sheds its light through the heavy steel bars of the cell at the extreme front and reveals part of the interior.* YANK *can be seen within, crouched on the edge of his cot in the attitude of Rodin's "The* 30 *Thinker." His face is spotted with black and blue bruises. A blood-stained bandage is wrapped around his head.*

YANK. [*suddenly starting as if awakening* 35 *from a dream, reaches out and shakes the bars —aloud to himself, wonderingly*] Steel. Dis is de Zoo, huh? [*a burst of hard, barking laughter comes from the unseen occupants of the cells, runs back down the tier, and abruptly ceases*] 40
VOICES. [*mockingly*] The Zoo? That's a new name for this coop—a damn good name!
    Steel, eh? You said a mouthful. This is the old iron house. 45
    Who is that boob talkin'?
    He's the bloke they brung in out of his head. The bulls had beat him up fierce.
YANK. [*dully*] I musta been dreamin'. I 50 tought I was in a cage at de Zoo—but de apes don't talk, do dey?

VOICES. [*with mocking laughter*] You're in a cage aw right.
    A coop!
    A pen!
    A sty!
    A kennel! [*hard laughter—a pause*]
    Say, guy! Who are you? No, never mind lying. What are you?
    Yes, tell us your sad story. What's your game?
    What did they jug yuh for?
YANK. [*dully*] I was a fireman—stokin' on de liners. [*then with sudden rage, rattling his cell bars*] I'm a hairy ape, get me? And I'll bust youse all in de jaw if yuh don't lay off kiddin' me.
VOICES. Huh! You're a hard boiled duck, ain't you!
    When you spit, it bounces! [*laughter*]
    Aw, can it. He's a regular guy. Ain't you?
    What did he say he was—a ape?
YANK. [*defiantly*] Sure ting! Ain't dat what youse all are—apes? [*a silence. Then a furious rattling of bars from down the corridor*]
A VOICE. [*thick with rage*] I'll show yuh who's a ape, yuh bum!
VOICES. Ssshh! Nix!
    Can de noise!
    Piano!
    You'll have the guard down on us!
YANK. [*scornfully*] De guard? Yuh mean de keeper, don't yuh? [*angry exclamations from all the cells*]
VOICE. [*placatingly*] Aw, don't pay no attention to him. He's off his nut from the beatin'-up he got. Say, you guy! We're waitin' to hear what they landed you for—or ain't yuh tellin'?
YANK. Sure, I'll tell youse. Sure! Why de hell not? On'y—youse won't get me. Nobody gets me but me, see? I started to tell de Judge and all he says was: "Toity days to tink it over." Tink it over! Christ, dat's all I been doin' for weeks! [*after a pause*] I was tryin' to git even wit someone, see?—someone dat done me doit.
VOICES. [*cynically*] De old stuff, I bet.
    Your goil, huh?
    Give yuh the double-cross, huh?
    That's them every time!
    Did yuh beat up de odder guy?
YANK. [*disgustedly*] Aw, yuh're all wrong!

Sure dere was a skoit in it—but not what youse mean, not dat old tripe. Dis was a new kind of skoit. She was dolled up all in white—in de stokehole. I tought she was a ghost. Sure.

[*a pause*]

VOICES. [*whispering*] Gee, he's still nutty.

Let him rave. It's fun listenin'.

YANK. [*unheeding—groping in his thoughts*] Her hands—dey was skinny and white like dey wasn't real but painted on somep'n. Dere was a million miles from me to her—twenty-five knots a hour. She was like some dead ting de cat brung in. Sure, dat's what. She didn't belong. She belonged in de window of a toy store, or on de top of a garbage can, see! Sure! [*he breaks out angrily*] But would yuh believe it, she had de noive to do me doit. She lamped me like she was seein' somep'n broke loose from de menagerie. Christ, yuh'd oughter seen her eyes! [*he rattles the bars of his cell furiously*] But I'll get back at her yet, you watch! And if I can't find her I'll take it out on de gang she runs wit. I'm wise to where dey hangs out now. I'll show her who belongs! I'll show her who's in de move and who ain't. You watch my smoke!

VOICES. [*serious and joking*] Dat's de talkin'!

Take her for all she's got!

What was this dame, anyway?

Who was she, eh?

YANK. I dunno. First cabin stiff. Her old man's a millionaire, dey says—name of Douglas.

VOICES. Douglas? That's the president of the Steel Trust, I bet.

Sure. I seen his mug in de papers. He's filthy with dough.

VOICE. Hey, feller, take a tip from me. If you want to get back at that dame, you better join the Wobblies. You'll get some action then.

YANK. Wobblies? What de hell's dat?

VOICE. Ain't you ever heard of the I.W.W.?

YANK. Naw. What is it?

VOICE. A gang of blokes—a tough gang. I been readin' about 'em today in the paper. The guard give me the *Sunday Times*. There's a long spiel about 'em. It's from a speech made in the Senate by a guy named Senator Queen. [*he is in the cell next to* YANK's. *There is a rustling of paper*] Wait'll I see if I got light enough and I'll read you. Listen. [*he reads*] "There is a menace existing in this country to-

day which threatens the vitals of our fair Republic—as foul a menace against the very life-blood of the American Eagle as was the foul conspiracy of Catiline against the eagles of ancient Rome!"

VOICE. [*disgustedly*] Aw, hell! Tell him to salt de tail of dat eagle!

VOICE. [*reading*] "I refer to that devil's brew of rascals, jailbirds, murderers, and cutthroats who libel all honest working men by calling themselves the Industrial Workers of the World; but in the light of their nefarious plots, I call them the Industrious *Wreckers* of the World!"

YANK. [*with vengeful satisfaction*] Wreckers, dat's de right dope! Dat belongs! Me for dem!

VOICE. Ssshh! [*reading*] "This fiendish organization is a foul ulcer on the fair body of our Democracy——"

VOICE. Democracy, hell! Give him the boid, fellers—the raspberry! [*they do*]

VOICE. Ssshh! [*reading*] "Like Cato I say to this Senate, the I.W.W. must be destroyed! For they represent an ever-present dagger pointed at the heart of the greatest nation the world has ever known, where all men are born free and equal, with equal opportunities to all, where the Founding Fathers have guaranteed to each one happiness, where Truth, Honor, Liberty, Justice, and the Brotherhood of Man are a religion absorbed with one's mother's milk, taught at our father's knee, sealed, signed, and stamped in the glorious Constitution of these United States!" [*a perfect storm of hisses, cat-calls, boos, and hard laughter*]

VOICES. [*scornfully*] Hurrah for de Fort' of July!

Pass de hat!

Liberty!

Justice!

Honor!

Opportunity!

Brotherhood!

ALL. [*with abysmal scorn*] Aw, hell!

VOICE. Give the Queen Senator guy the bark! All togedder now—one—two—three——[*a terrific chorus of barking and yapping*]

GUARD. [*from a distance*] Quiet there, youse—or I'll git the hose. [*the noise subsides*]

YANK. [*with growling rage*] I'd like to catch dat senator guy alone for a second. I'd loin him some trute!

VOICE. Ssshh! Here's where he gits down to cases on the Wobblies. [*reads*] "They plot with fire in one hand and dynamite in the other. They stop not before murder to gain their ends, nor at the outraging of defenseless womanhood. They would tear down society, put the lowest scum in the seats of the mighty, turn Almighty God's revealed plan for the world topsy-turvy, and make of our sweet and lovely civilization a shambles, a desolation where man, God's masterpiece, would soon degenerate back to the ape!"

VOICE. [*to* YANK] Hey, you guy. There's your ape stuff again.

YANK. [*with a growl of fury*] I got him. So dey blow up tings, do they? Dey turn tings round, do dey? Hey, lend me dat paper, will yuh?

VOICE. Sure. Give it to him. On'y keep it to yourself, see? We don't wanter listen to no more of that slop.

VOICE. Here you are. Hide it under your mattress.

YANK. [*reaching out*] Tanks. I can't read much but I kin manage. [*he sits, the paper in the hand at his side, in the attitude of Rodin's "The Thinker." A pause. Several snores from down the corridor. Suddenly* YANK *jumps to his feet with a furious groan as if some appalling thought had crashed on him—bewilderedly*] Sure—her old man—president of de Steel Trust—makes half de steel in de world—steel —where I thought I belonged—drivin' trou— movin'—in dat—to make* her—*and cage me in for her to spit on! Christ! [*he shakes the bars of his cell door till the whole tier trembles. Irritated, protesting exclamations from those awakened or trying to get to sleep*] He made dis—dis cage! Steel! *It* don't belong, dat's what! Cages, cells, locks, bolts, bars—dat's what it means!—holdin' me down with him at de top! But I'll drive trou! Fire, dat melts it! I'll be fire—under de heap—fire dat never goes out—hot as hell—breakin' out in de night—— [*while he has been saying this last he has shaken his cell door to a clanging accompaniment. As he comes to the "breakin' out" he seizes one bar with both hands and, putting his two feet up against the others so that his position is parallel to the floor like a monkey's, he gives a great wrench backwards. The bar bends like a licorice stick under his tremendous*

strength. *Just at this moment the* PRISON GUARD *rushes in, dragging a hose behind him*]

GUARD. [*angrily*] I'll loin youse bums to wake me up! [*sees* YANK] Hello, it's you, huh? Got the D.Ts., hey? Well, I'll cure 'em. I'll drown your snakes for yuh! [*noticing the bar*] Hell, look at dat bar bended! On'y a bug is strong enough for dat!

YANK. [*glaring at him*] Or a hairy ape, yuh big yellow bum! Look out! Here I come! [*he grabs another bar*]

GUARD. [*scared now—yelling off left*] Toin de hose on, Ben!—full pressure! And call de others—and a straitjacket [*the curtain is falling. As it hides* YANK *from view, there is a splattering smash as the stream of water hits the steel of* YANK's *cell.*]

[*Curtain*]

SCENE VII.

SCENE—*Nearly a month later. An I.W.W. local near the waterfront, showing the interior of a front room on the ground floor, and the street outside. Moonlight on the narrow street, buildings massed in black shadow. The interior of the room, which is general assembly room, office, and reading room, resembles some dingy settlement boys' club. A desk and high stool are in one corner. A table with paper, stacks of pamphlets, chairs about it, is at center. The whole is decidedly cheap, banal, commonplace, and unmysterious as a room could well be. The* SECRETARY *is perched on the stool making entries in a large ledger. An eye shade casts his face into shadows. Eight or ten* MEN, LONG-SHOREMEN, IRON WORKERS, *and the like, are grouped about the table. Two are playing checkers. One is writing a letter. Most of them are smoking pipes. A big signboard is on the wall at the rear, "Industrial Workers of the World—Local No. 57."* YANK *comes down the street outside. He is dressed as in Scene V. He moves cautiously, mysteriously. He comes to a point opposite the door; tiptoes softly up to it, listens, is impressed by the silence within, knocks carefully, as if he were guessing at the password to some secret rite. Listens. No answer. Knocks again a bit louder. No answer. Knocks impatiently, much louder.*

SECRETARY. [*turning around on his stool*] What the devil is that—someone knocking?

[*shouts*] Come in, why don't you? [*all the men in the room look up.* YANK *opens the door slowly, gingerly, as if afraid of an ambush. He looks around for secret doors, mystery, is taken aback by the commonplaceness of the room and the men in it, thinks he may have gotten in the wrong place, then sees the signboard on the wall and is reassured*]

YANK. [*blurts out*] Hello.

MEN. [*reservedly*] Hello.

YANK. [*more easily*] I tought I'd bumped into de wrong dump.

SECRETARY. [*scrutinizing him carefully*] Maybe you have. Are you a member?

YANK. Naw, not yet. Dat's what I come for —to join.

SECRETARY. That's easy. What's your job— longshore?

YANK. Naw. Fireman—stoker on de liners.

SECRETARY. [*with satisfaction*] Welcome to our city. Glad to know you people are waking up at last. We haven't got many members in your line.

YANK. Naw. Dey're all dead to de woild.

SECRETARY. Well, you can help to wake 'em. What's your name? I'll make out your card.

YANK. [*confused*] Name? Lemme tink.

SECRETARY. [*sharply*] Don't you know your own name?

YANK. Sure; but I been just Yank for so long —Bob, dat's it—Bob Smith.

SECRETARY. [*writing*] Robert Smith. [*fills out the rest of card*] Here you are. Cost you half a dollar.

YANK. Is dat all—four bits? Dat's easy. [*gives the* SECRETARY *the money*]

SECRETARY. [*throwing it in drawer*] Thanks. Well, make yourself at home. No introductions needed. There's literature on the table. Take some of those pamphlets with you to distribute aboard ship. They may bring results. Sow the seeds, only go about it right. Don't get caught and fired. We got plenty out of work. What we need is men who can hold their jobs —and work for us at the same time.

YANK. Sure. [*but he still stands, embarrassed and uneasy*]

SECRETARY. [*looking at him—curiously*] What did you knock for? Think we had a coon in uniform to open doors?

YANK. Naw. I tought it was locked—and dat yuh'd wanter give me the once-over trou a peephole or somep'n to see if I was right.

SECRETARY. [*alert and suspicious but with an easy laugh*] Think we were running a crap game? That door is never locked. What put that in your nut?

YANK. [*with a knowing grin, convinced that this is all camouflage, a part of the secrecy*] Dis burg is full of bulls, ain't it?

SECRETARY. [*sharply*] What have the cops got to do with us? We're breaking no laws.

YANK. [*with a knowing wink*] Sure. Youse wouldn't for woilds. Sure. I'm wise to dat.

SECRETARY. You seem to be wise to a lot of stuff none of us knows about.

YANK. [*with another wink*] Aw, dat's aw right, see. [*then made a bit resentful by the suspicious glances from all sides*] Aw, can it! Youse needn't put me trou de toid degree. Can't youse see I belong? Sure! I'm reg'lar. I'll stick, get me? I'll shoot de woiks for youse. Dat's why I wanted to join in.

SECRETARY. [*breezily, feeling him out*] That's the right spirit. Only are you sure you understand what you've joined? It's all plain and aboveboard; still, some guys get a wrong slant on us. [*sharply*] What's your notion of the purpose of the I.W.W.?

YANK. Aw, I know all about it.

SECRETARY. [*sarcastically*] Well, give us some of your valuable information.

YANK. [*cunningly*] I know enough not to speak outa my toin. [*then resentfully again*] Aw, say! I'm reg'lar. I'm wise to de game. I know yuh got to watch your step wit a stranger. For all youse know, I might be a plain-clothes dick, or somep'n, dat's what yuh're tinkin', huh? Aw, forget it! I belong, see? Ask any guy down to de docks if I don't.

SECRETARY. Who said you didn't?

YANK. After I'm 'nitiated, I'll show yuh.

SECRETARY. [*astounded*] Initiated? There's no initiation.

YANK. [*disappointed*] Ain't there no pass-word—no grip nor nothin'?

SECRETARY. What'd you think this is—the Elks—or the Black Hand?

YANK. De Elks, hell! De Black Hand, dey're a lot of yellow backstickin' Ginees.[3] Naw. Dis is a man's gang, ain't it?

SECRETARY. You said it! That's why we stand

---

[3] Italians.

on our two feet in the open. We got no secrets.

YANK. [*surprised but admiringly*] Yuh mean to say yuh always run wide open—like dis?

SECRETARY. Exactly.

YANK. Den yuh sure got your noive wit youse!

SECRETARY. [*sharply*] Just what was it made you want to join us? Come out with that straight.

YANK. Yuh call me? Well, I got noive, too! Here's my hand. Yuh wanter blow tings up, dont' yuh? Well, dat's me! I belong!

SECRETARY. [*with pretended carelessness*] You mean change the unequal conditions of society by legitimate direct action—or with dynamite?

YANK. Dynamite! Blow it offen de oith—steel—all de cages—all de factories, steamers, buildings, jails—de Steel Trust and all dat makes it go.

SECRETARY. So—that's your idea, eh? And did you have any special job in that line you wanted to propose to us? [*he makes a sign to the men, who get up cautiously one by one and group behind YANK*]

YANK. [*boldly*] Sure, I'll come out wit it. I'll show youse I'm one of de gang. Dere's dat millionaire guy, Douglas—

SECRETARY. President of the Steel Trust, you mean? Do you want to assassinate him?

YANK. Naw, dat don't get yuh nothin'. I mean blow up de factory, de woiks, where he makes de steel. Dat's what I'm after—to blow up de steel, knock all de steel in de woild up to de moon. Dat'll fix tings! [*eagerly, with a touch of bravado*] I'll do it by me lonesome! I'll show yuh! Tell me where his woiks is, how to git there, all de dope. Gimme de stuff, de old butter—and watch me do de rest! Watch de smoke and see it move! I don't give a damn if dey nab me—long as it's done! I'll soive life for it—and give 'em de laugh! [*half to himself*] And I'll write her a letter and tell her de hairy ape done it. Dat'll square tings.

SECRETARY. [*stepping away from YANK*] Very interesting. [*he gives a signal. The men, huskies all, throw themselves on YANK and before he knows it they have his legs and arms pinioned. But he is too flabbergasted to make a struggle, anyway. They feel him over for weapons*]

MAN. No gat, no knife. Shall we give him

what's what and put the boots to him?

SECRETARY. No. He isn't worth the trouble we'd get into. He's too stupid. [*he comes closer and laughs mockingly in* YANK's *face*] Ho-ho! By God, this is the biggest joke they've put up on us yet. Hey, you Joke! Who sent you—Burns or Pinkerton?[4] No, by God, you're such a bonehead I'll bet you're in the Secret Service! Well, you dirty spy, you rotten agent provocator, you can go back and tell whatever skunk is paying you blood-money for betraying your brothers that he's wasting his coin. You couldn't catch a cold. And tell him that all he'll ever get on us, or ever has got, is just his own sneaking plots that he's framed up to put us in jail. We are what our manifesto says we are, neither more nor less—and we'll give him a copy of that any time he calls. And as for you ——[*he glares scornfully at* YANK, *who is sunk in an oblivious stupor*] Oh, hell, what's the use of talking? You're a brainless ape.

YANK. [*aroused by the word to fierce but futile struggles*] What's dat, yuh Sheeny bum, yuh!

SECRETARY. Throw him out, boys. [*in spite of his struggles, this is done with gusto and éclat. Propelled by several parting kicks,* YANK *lands sprawling in the middle of the narrow cobbled street. With a growl he starts to get up and storm the closed door, but stops bewildered by the confusion of his brain, pathetically impotent. He sits there, brooding, in as near to the attitude of Rodin's "Thinker" as he can get in his position*]

YANK. [*bitterly*] So dem boids don't tink I belong, neider. Aw, to hell with 'em! Dey're in de wrong pew—de same old bull—soapboxes and Salvation Army—no guts! Cut out an hour offen de job a day and make me happy! Gimme a dollar more a day and make me happy! Tree square a day, and cauliflowers in de front yard—ekal rights—a woman and kids—a lousy vote—and I'm all fixed for Jesus, huh? Aw, hell! What does dat get yuh? Dis ting's in your inside, but it ain't your belly. Feedin' your face—sinkers and coffee—dat don't touch it. It's way down—at de bottom. Yuh can't grab it, and yuh can't stop it. It moves, and everyting moves. It stops and de whole woild stops. Dat's me now—I don't tick, see?—I'm a busted In-

---

[4] detective agencies.

gersoll,[5] dat's what. Steel was me, and I owned de woild. Now I ain't steel, and de woild owns me. Aw, hell! I can't see—it's all dark, get me? It's all wrong! [*he turns a bitter mocking face up like an ape gibbering at the moon*] Say, youse up dere, Man in de Moon, yuh look so wise, gimme de answer, huh? Slip me de inside dope, de information right from de stable —where do I get off at, huh?

A POLICEMAN. [*who has come up the street in time to hear this last—with grim humor*] You'll get off at the station, you boob, if you don't get up out of that and keep movin'.

YANK. [*looking up at him—with a hard, bitter laugh*] Sure! Lock me up! Put me in a cage! Dat's de on'y answer yuh know. G'wan, lock me up!

POLICEMAN. What you been doin'?

YANK. Enuf to gimme life for! I was born, see? Sure, dat's de charge. Write it in de blotter. I was born, get me?

POLICEMAN. [*jocosely*] God pity your old woman! [*then matter-of-fact*] But I've no time for kidding. You're soused. I'd run you in but it's too long a walk to the station. Come on now, get up, or I'll fan your ears with this club. Beat it now! [*he hauls* YANK *to his feet*]

YANK. [*in a vague mocking tone*] Say, where do I go from here?

POLICEMAN. [*giving him a push—with a grin, indifferently*] Go to hell.

[*Curtain*]

SCENE VIII.

SCENE—*Twilight of the next day. The monkey house at the Zoo. One spot of clear gray light falls on the front of one cage so that the interior can be seen. The other cages are vague, shrouded in shadow from which chatterings pitched in a conversational tone can be heard. On the one cage a sign from which the word "gorilla" stands out. The gigantic* ANIMAL *himself is seen squatting on his haunches on a bench in much the same attitude as Rodin's "Thinker."*

YANK *enters from the left. Immediately a chorus of angry chattering and screeching breaks out. The* GORILLA *turns his eyes but makes no sound or move.*

----

[5] a low-priced watch.

YANK. [*with a hard, bitter laugh*] Welcome to your city, huh? Hail, hail, de gang's all here! [*at the sound of his voice the chattering dies away into an attentive silence.* YANK *walks up to the* GORILLA's *cage and, leaning over the railing, stares in at its occupant, who stares back at him, silent and motionless. There is a pause of dead stillness. Then* YANK *begins to talk in a friendly confidential tone, half-mockingly, but with a deep undercurrent of sympathy*] Say, yuh're some hard-lookin' guy, ain't yuh? I seen lots of tough nuts dat de gang called gorillas, but yuh're de foist real one I ever seen. Some chest yuh got, and shoulders, and dem arms and mits! I bet yuh got a punch in eider fist dat'd knock 'em all silly! [*this with genuine admiration. The* GORILLA, *as if he understood, stands upright, swelling out his chest and pounding on it with his fist.* YANK *grins sympathetically.*] Sure, I get yuh. Yuh challenge de whole woild, huh? Yuh got what I was sayin' even if yuh muffed de woids. [*then bitterness creeping in*] And why wouldn't yuh get me? Ain't we both members of de same club— de Hairy Apes? [*they stare at each other—a pause—then* YANK *goes on slowly and bitterly*] So yuh're what she seen when she looked at me, de white-faced tart! I was you to her, get me? On'y outa de cage—broke out—free to moider her, see? Sure! Dat's what she tought. She wasn't wise dat I was in a cage, too— worser'n yours—sure—a damn sight—'cause you got some chanct to bust loose—but me—— [*he grows confused*] Aw, hell! It's wrong, ain't it? [*a pause*] I s'pose yuh wanter know what I'm doin' here, huh? I been warmin' a bench down to de Battery—ever since last night. Sure. I seen de sun come up. Dat was pretty, too— all red and pink and green. I was lookin' at de skyscrapers—steel—and all de ships comin' in, sailin' out, all over de oith—and dey was steel, too. De sun was warm, dey wasn't no clouds, and dere was a breeze blowin'. Sure, it was great stuff. I got it aw right—what Paddy said about dat bein' de right dope—on'y I couldn't get *in* it, see? I couldn't belong in dat. It was over my head. And I kept tinkin'—and den I beat it up here to see what youse was like. And I waited till dey was all gone to git yuh alone. Say, how d'yuh feel sittin' in dat pen all de time, havin' to stand for 'em comin' and starin' at yuh—de white-faced, skinny tarts and de boobs what marry 'em—makin' fun of yuh, laughin' at yuh, gittin' scared of yuh—damn 'em! [*he pounds on the rail with his fist. The* GORILLA *rattles the bars of his cage and snarls. All the other monkeys set up an angry chattering in the darkness.* YANK *goes on excitedly*] Sure! Dat's de way it hits me, too. On'y yuh're lucky, see? Yuh don't belong wit 'em and yuh know it. But me, I belong wit 'em—but I don't, see? Dey don't belong wit me, dat's what. Get me? Tinkin' is hard——[*he passes one hand across his forehead with a painful gesture. The* GORILLA *growls impatiently.* YANK *goes on gropingly*] It's dis way, what I'm drivin' at. Youse can sit and dope dream in de past, green woods, de jungle, and de rest of it. Den yuh belong and dey don't. Den yuh kin laugh at 'em, see? Yuh're de champ of de woild. But me —I ain't got no past to tink in, nor nothin' dat's comin', on'y what's now—and dat don't belong. Sure, you're de best off! Yuh can't tink, can yuh? Yuh can't talk neider. But I kin make a bluff at talkin' and tinkin'—a'most git away wit it—a'most!—and dat's where de joker comes in. [*he laughs*] I ain't on oith and I ain't in heaven, get me? I'm in de middle tryin' to separate 'em, takin' all de woist punches from bot' of 'em. Maybe dat's what dey call hell, huh? But you, yuh're at de bottom. You belong! Sure! Yuh're de on'y one in de woild dat does, yuh lucky stiff! [*the* GORILLA *growls proudly*] And dat's why dey gotter put yuh in a cage, see? [*the* GORILLA *roars angrily*] Sure! Yuh get me. It beats it when you try to tink it or talk it—it's way down—deep—behind—you 'n' me we feel it. Sure! Bot' members of dis club! [*he laughs—then in a savage tone*] What de hell! T' hell wit it! A little action, dat's our meat! Dat belongs! Knock 'em down and keep bustin' 'em till dey croaks yuh wit a gat—wit steel! Sure! Are yuh game? Dey've looked at youse, ain't dey—in a cage? Wanter git even? Wanter wind up like a sport 'stead of croakin' slow in dere? [*the* GORILLA *roars an emphatic affirmative.* YANK *goes on with a sort of furious exaltation*] Sure! Yuh're reg'lar! Yuh'll stick to de finish! Me 'n' you, huh?—bot' members of this club! We'll put up one last star bout dat'll knock 'em

offen deir seats! Dey'll have to make de cages stronger after we're trou! [*the* GORILLA *is straining at his bars, growling, hopping from one foot to the other.* YANK *takes a jimmy from under his coat and forces the lock on the cage door. He throws this open*] Pardon from de governor! Step out and shake hands! I'll take yuh for a walk down Fif' Avenoo. We'll knock 'em offen de oith and croak wit de band playin'. Come on, Brother. [*the* GORILLA *scrambles gingerly out of his cage. Goes to* YANK *and stands looking at him.* YANK *keeps his mocking tone—holds out his hand*] Shake—de secret grip of our order. [*something, the tone of mockery, perhaps, suddenly enrages the* AN-IMAL. *With a spring he wraps his huge arms around* YANK *in a murderous hug. There is a crackling snap of crushed ribs—a gasping cry, still mocking, from* YANK] Hey, I didn't say kiss me! [*the* GORILLA *lets the crushed body slip to the floor; stands over it uncertainly, considering; then picks it up, throws it in the cage, shuts the door, and shuffles off menacingly into the darkness at left. A great uproar of frightened chattering and whimpering comes from the other cages. Then* YANK *moves, groaning, opening his eyes, and there is silence. He mutters painfully*] Say—dey oughter match him wit Zybszko.[6] He got me, aw right. I'm trou. Even him didn't tink I belonged. [*then, with sudden passionate despair*] Christ, where do I get off at? Where do I fit in? [*checking himself as suddenly*] Aw, what de hell! No squawkin', see! No quittin', get me! Croak wit your boots on! [*he grabs hold of the bars of the cage and hauls himself painfully to his feet—looks around him bewilderedly—forces a mocking laugh*] In de cage, huh? [*in the strident tones of a circus barker*] Ladies and gents, step forward and take a slant at de one and only—[*his voice weakening*]—one and original—Hairy Ape from de wilds of——[*he slips in a heap on the floor and dies. The monkeys set up a chattering, whimpering wail. And, perhaps, the Hairy Ape at last belongs.*]

[*Curtain*]

---

[6] a contemporary champion wrestler.

*WINTERSET**

MAXWELL ANDERSON

Anderson (1888–   ) attended North Dakota
and Stanford universities, earned an M.A. degree, and taught English for a while. After a period of editorial writing for San Francisco and
New York papers, he tried the drama, and with
his second effort, What Price Glory? (with Lau-
rence Stallings), won a reputation which has
been growing ever since. He is a prolific author. Saturday's Children was a commercial
success, and his historical studies (see I, 405)
have won the approval of critics and public
alike. Anderson is a careful and thoughtful
writer who has definite ideas about the theater,
especially on the nature of tragedy. The Winterset story (he had done an earlier sketch of
Sacco) is a fitting example of its author's ideas
and style. Anderson's revival of verse (which
must be accepted as a device to make manifest
the inherent dignity in normally inarticulate
people) is an interesting departure. Like O'Neill,
Anderson wrestles with grand themes and, unlike him, often succeeds in showing man capable of great moments, even comic moments, in
a confused existence. He has been condemned
for writing too much too fast, but his best
works insure his position at present as the second most significant name in the contemporary
American theater.

Characters

TROCK	HERMAN
SHADOW	LUCIA
GARTH	PINY
MIRIAMNE	A SAILOR

* This play is reprinted by arrangement with
Anderson House, publishers.

ESDRAS	STREET URCHIN
THE HOBO	POLICEMAN
1ST GIRL	RADICAL
2ND GIRL	SERGEANT
JUDGE GAUNT	*Non-speaking*
MIO	URCHINS
CARR	TWO MEN IN BLUE SERGE

ACT I

SCENE I.

SCENE—*The scene is the bank of a river under a bridgehead. A gigantic span starts from
the rear of the stage and appears to lift over
the heads of the audience and out to the left.
At the right rear is a wall of solid supporting
masonry. To the left an apartment building
abuts against the bridge and forms the left wall
of the stage with a dark basement window and
a door in the brick wall. To the right, and in the
foreground, an outcropping of original rock
makes a barricade behind which one may enter
through a cleft. To the rear, against the masonry, two sheds have been built by waifs and
strays for shelter. The river bank, in the foreground, is black rock worn smooth by years of
trampling. There is room for exit and entrance
to the left around the apartment house, also
around the rock to the right. A single street
lamp is seen at the left—and a glimmer of
apartment lights in the background beyond. It
is an early, dark December morning.*

TWO YOUNG MEN IN SERGE *lean against the
masonry, matching bills.* TROCK *and* SHADOW
come in from the left.

TROCK. Go back and watch the car. [*The*
TWO YOUNG MEN *go out.* TROCK *walks to the
corner and looks toward the city*]

You roost of punks and gulls! Sleep, sleep it off,
whatever you had last night, get down in warm,
one big ham-fat against another—sleep,
cling, sleep and rot! Rot out your pasty guts
with diddling, you had no brain to begin. If
  you had
there'd be no need for us to sleep on iron
who had too much brains for you.
  SHADOW. Now look, Trock, look,
what would the warden say to talk like that?
  TROCK. May they die as I die!
By God, what life they've left me
they shall keep me well! I'll have that out of
  them—
these pismires that walk like men!
  SHADOW. Because, look, chief,
it's all against science and penology
for you to get out and begin to cuss that way
before your prison vittles are out of you. Hell,
you're supposed to leave the pen full of high
  thought,
kind of noble-like, loving toward all mankind,
ready to kiss their feet—or whatever parts
they stick out toward you. Look at me!
  TROCK. I see you.
And even you may not live as long as you
  think.
You think too many things are funny. Well,
  laugh.
But it's not so funny.
  SHADOW. Come on, Trock, you know me.
Anything you say goes, but give me leave
to kid a little.
  TROCK. Then laugh at somebody else!
It's a lot safer! They've soaked me once too
  often
in that vat of poisoned hell they keep up-state
to soak men in, and I'm rotten inside, I'm all
one liquid puke inside where I had lungs
once, like yourself! And now they want to get
  me
and stir me in again—and that'd kill me—
and that's fine for them. But before that happens to me
a lot of these healthy boys'll know what it's like
when you try to breathe and have no place to
  put air—
they'll learn it from me!
  SHADOW. They've got nothing on you, chief.
  TROCK. I don't know yet. That's what I'm
  here to find out.
If they've got what they might have

it's not a year this time—
no, nor ten. It's screwed down under a lid.—
I can die quick enough, without help.
  SHADOW. You're the skinny kind
that lives forever.
  TROCK. He gave me a half a year,
the doc at the gate.
  SHADOW. Jesus.
  TROCK. Six months I get,
and the rest's dirt, six feet. [LUCIA, *the street-
piano man, comes in right from behind the
rock and goes to the shed where he keeps his
piano.* PINY, *the apple-woman, follows and
stands in the entrance.* LUCIA *speaks to ES-
TRELLA, who still stands facing* SHADOW]
  LUCIA. Morning. [TROCK *and* SHADOW *go out
round the apartment house without speaking*]
  PINY. Now what would you call them?
  LUCIA. Maybe someting da river washed up.
  PINY. Nothing ever washed him—that black
  one.
  LUCIA. Maybe not, maybe so. More like his
pa and ma raise-a heem in da cella. [*He wheels
out the piano*]
  PINY. He certainly gave me a turn. [*She lays
a hand on the rock*]
  LUCIA. You don' live-a right, o' gal. Take
heem easy. Look on da bright-a side. Never
say-a die. Me, every day in every way I getta
be da regular heller. [*He starts out*]
    [*Curtain*]

SCENE II.

SCENE—*A cellar apartment under the apartment building, floored with cement and roofed
with huge boa constrictor pipes that run slant-
wise from left to right, dwarfing the room. An
outside door opens to the left and a door at the
right rear leads to the interior of the place. A
low squat window to the left. A table at the
rear and a few chairs and books make up the
furniture.* GARTH, *son of* ESDRAS, *sits alone,
holding a violin upside down to inspect a crack
at its base. He lays the bow on the floor and
runs his fingers over the joint.* MIRIAMNE *enters from the rear, a girl of fifteen.* GARTH
looks up, then down again.

  MIRIAMNE. Garth—
  GARTH. The glue lets go. It's the steam,
  I guess.

It splits the hair on your head.

MIRIAMNE. It can't be mended?

GARTH. I can't mend it.
No doubt there are fellows somewhere
who'd mend it for a dollar—and glad to do it. 5
That is if I had a dollar.—Got a dollar?
No, I thought not.

MIRIAMNE. Garth, you've sat at home here
three days now. You haven't gone out at all.
Something frightens you. 10

GARTH. Yes?

MIRIAMNE. And father's frightened.
He reads without knowing where. When a
    shadow falls
across the page he waits for a blow to follow 15
after the shadow. Then in a little while
he puts his book down softly and goes out
to see who passed.

GARTH. A bill collector, maybe.
We haven't paid the rent. 20

MIRIAMNE. No.

GARTH. You're a bright girl, sis.—
You see too much. You run along and cook.
Why don't you go to school?

MIRIAMNE. I don't like school.
They whisper behind my back. 25

GARTH. Yes? about what?

MIRIAMNE. What did the lawyer mean that
wrote to you?

GARTH. [rising] What lawyer? 30

MIRIAMNE. I found a letter
on the floor of your room. He said, "Don't get
    me wrong,
but stay in out of the rain the next few days,
just for instance." 35

GARTH. I thought I burned that letter.

MIRIAMNE. Afterward you did. And then
    what was printed
about the Estrella gang—you hid it from me,
you and father. What is it—about this 40
    murder—?

GARTH. Will you shut up, you fool!

MIRIAMNE. But if you know
why don't you tell them, Garth?
If it's true—what they say— 45
you knew all the time Romagna wasn't guilty,
and could have said so——

GARTH. Everybody knew
Romagna wasn't guilty! But they weren't
    listening 50
to evidence in his favor. They didn't want it.
They don't want it now.

MIRIAMNE. But was that why
they never called on you?—

GARTH. So far as I know
they never'd heard of me—and I can assure
    you
I knew nothing about it—

MIRIAMNE. But something's wrong—
and it worries father——

GARTH. What could be wrong?

MIRIAMNE. I don't know.

[A pause]

GARTH. And I don't know. You're a good
    kid, Miriamne,
but you see too many movies. I wasn't mixed
    up
in any murder, and I don't mean to be.
If I had a dollar to get my fiddle fixed
and another to hire a hall, by God I'd fiddle
some of the prodigies back into Sunday School
where they belong, but I won't get either, and
    so
I sit here and bite my nails—but if you hoped
I had some criminal romantic past
you'll have to look again!

MIRIAMNE. Oh, Garth, forgive me—
But I want you to be so far above such things
nothing could frighten you. When you seem
    to shrink
and be afraid, and you're the brother I love,
I want to run there and cry, if there's any
    question
they care to ask, you'll be quick and glad to
    answer,
for there's nothing to conceal!

GARTH. And that's all true——

MIRIAMNE. But then I remember—
how you dim the lights—
and we go early to bed—and speak in
    whispers—
and I could think there's a death somewhere
    behind us—
an evil death——

GARTH. [hearing a step] Now for God's sake,
    be quiet!

ESDRAS, an old rabbi with a kindly face,
enters from the outside. He is hurried and
troubled

ESDRAS. I wish to speak alone with someone
    here
if I may have this room. Miriamne—

MIRIAMNE. [turning to go] Yes, father. [The

outer door is suddenly thrown open. TROCK
appears]

TROCK. [*after a pause*] You'll excuse me for
not knocking. [SHADOW *follows* TROCK *in*]
Sometimes it's best to come in quiet. Sometimes
it's a good way to go out. Garth's home, I see.
He might not have been here if I made a point
of knocking at doors.

GARTH. How are you, Trock?

TROCK. I guess
you can see how I am. [*To* MIRIAMNE] Stay
here. Stay where you are.
We'd like to make your acquaintance.
—If you want the facts
I'm no better than usual, thanks. Not enough
sun,
my physician tells me. Too much close con-
finement.
A lack of exercise and an overplus
of beans in the diet. You've done well, no
doubt?

GARTH. I don't know what makes you think
so.

TROCK. Who's the family?

GARTH. My father and my sister.

TROCK. Happy to meet you.
Step inside a minute. The boy and I
have something to talk about.

ESDRAS. No, no—he's said nothing—
nothing, sir, nothing!

TROCK. When I say go out, you go——

ESDRAS. [*pointing to the door*] Miriamne——

GARTH. Go on out, both of you!

ESDRAS. Oh, sir—I'm old—
old and unhappy——

GARTH. Go on! [MIRIAMNE *and* ESDRAS *go
inside*]

TROCK. And if you listen
I'll riddle that door! [SHADOW *shuts the door
behind them and stands against it*]
I just got out, you see,
and I pay my first call on you.

GARTH. Maybe you think
I'm not in the same jam you are.

TROCK. That's what I do think.
Who started looking this up?

GARTH. I wish I knew,
and I wish he was in hell! Some damned professor
with nothing else to do. If you saw his stuff
you know as much as I do.

TROCK. It wasn't you

turning state's evidence?

GARTH. Hell, Trock, use your brain!
The case was closed. They burned Romagna
for it
and that finished it. Why should I look for
trouble
and maybe get burned myself?

TROCK. Boy, I don't know,
but I just thought I'd find out.

GARTH. I'm going straight, Trock.
I can play this thing, and I'm trying to make
a living.
I haven't talked and nobody's talked to me.
Christ—it's the last thing I'd want!

TROCK. Your old man knows.

GARTH. That's where I got the money that
last time
when you needed it. He had a little saved up,
but I had to tell him to get it. He's as safe
as Shadow there.

TROCK. [*looking at* SHADOW] There could be
people safer
than that son-of-a-bitch.

SHADOW. Who?

TROCK. You'd be safer dead
along with some other gorillas.

SHADOW. It's beginning to look
as if you'd feel safer with everybody dead,
the whole god-damn world.

TROCK. I would. These Jesus-bitten
professors! Looking up their half-ass cases!
We've got enough without that.

GARTH. There's no evidence
to reopen the thing.

TROCK. And suppose they called on you
and asked you to testify?

GARTH. Why then I'd tell 'em
that all I know is what I read in the papers.
And I'd stick to that.

TROCK. How much does your sister know?

GARTH. I'm honest with you, Trock. She
read my name
in the professor's pamphlet, and she was scared
the way anybody would be. She got nothing
from me, and anyway she'd go to the chair
herself before she'd send me there.

TROCK. Like hell.

GARTH. Besides, who wants to go to trial
again
except the radicals?—You and I won't spill
and unless we did there's nothing to take to
court

as far as I know. Let the radicals go on howling
about getting a dirty deal. They always howl
and nobody gives a damn. This professor's
red—

everybody knows it.

TROCK. You're forgetting the judge.
Where's the damn judge?

GARTH. What judge?

TROCK. Read the morning papers.
It says Judge Gaunt's gone off his nut. He's got
that damn trial on his mind, and been going
round
proving to everybody he was right all the time
and the radicals were guilty—stopping people
in the street to prove it—and now he's nuts
entirely
and nobody knows where he is.

GARTH. Why don't they know?

TROCK. Because he's on the loose somewhere!
They've got
the police of three cities looking for him.

GARTH. Judge Gaunt?

TROCK. Yes, Judge Gaunt.

SHADOW. Why should that worry you?
He's crazy, ain't he? And even if he wasn't
he's arguing on your side. You're jittery, chief.
God, all the judges are looney. You've got the
jitters,
and you'll damn well give yourself away some
time
peeing yourself in public. [TROCK *half turns toward* SHADOW *in anger*] Don't jump the
gun now,
I've got pockets in my clothes, too. [*His hand
is in his coat pocket*]

TROCK. All right. Take it easy. [*He takes his
hand from his pocket, and* SHADOW *does
the same. To* GARTH]
Maybe you're lying to me and maybe you're
not.
Stay at home a few days.

GARTH. Sure thing. Why not?

TROCK. And when I say stay home I mean
stay home.
If I have to go looking for you you'll stay a
long time
wherever I find you.
[*To* SHADOW] Come on. We'll get out of here.
[*To* GARTH] Be seeing you. [SHADOW *and*
TROCK *go out. After a pause* GARTH *walks over
to his chair and picks up the violin. Then he
puts it down and goes to the inside door, which*

he opens]
GARTH. He's gone.

MIRIAMNE *enters*, ESDRAS *behind her*

MIRIAMNE. [*going up to* GARTH] Let's not
stay here. [*She puts her hands on his
arms*]
I thought he'd come for something—horrible.
Is he coming back?

GARTH. I don't know.

MIRIAMNE. Who is he, Garth?

GARTH. He'd kill me if I told you who he is,
that is, if he knew.

MIRIAMNE. Then don't say it——

GARTH. Yes, and I'll say it! I was with a gang
one time
that robbed a pay roll. I saw a murder done,
and Trock Estrella did it. If that got out
I'd go to the chair and so would he—that's
why
he was here today——

MIRIAMNE. But that's not true——

ESDRAS. He says it
to frighten you, child.

GARTH. Oh, no I don't! I say it
because I've held it in too long! I'm damned
if I sit here forever and look at the door,
waiting for Trock with his sub-machine gun,
waiting
for police with a warrant!—I say I'm damned,
and I am,
no matter what I do! These piddling scales
on a violin—first position, third, fifth,
arpeggios in E—and what I'm thinking
is Romagna dead for the murder—dead while
I sat here
dying inside—dead for the thing Trock did
while I looked on—and I could have saved
him, yes—
but I sat here and let him die instead of me
because I wanted to live! Well, it's no life,
and it doesn't matter who I tell, because
I mean to get it over!

MIRIAMNE. Garth, it's not true!

GARTH. I'd take some scum down with me if
I died—
that'd be one good deed——

ESDRAS. Son, son, you're mad—
someone will hear——

GARTH. Then let them hear! I've lived
with ghosts too long, and lied too long. God
damn you if you keep me

from the truth!— [*He turns away*]
Oh, God damn the world!
I don't want to die! [*He throws himself down*]
    ESDRAS. I should have known.
I thought you hard and sullen,
Garth, my son. And you were a child, and hurt
with a wound that might be healed.
—All men have crimes,
and most of them are hidden, and many are
    heavy
as yours must be to you. [GARTH *sobs*] They
    walk the streets
to buy and sell, but a spreading crimson stain
tinges the inner vestments, touches flesh,
and burns the quick. You're not alone.
    GARTH. I'm alone
in this.
    ESDRAS. Yes, if you hold with the world that
    only
those who die suddenly should be revenged.
But those whose hearts are cancered, drop by
    drop
in small ways, little by little, till they've borne
all they can bear, and die—these deaths will go
unpunished now as always. When we're young
we have faith in what is seen, but when we're
    old
we know that what is seen is traced in air
and built on water. There's no guilt under
    heaven,
just as there's no heaven, till men believe it—
no earth, till men have seen it, and have a word
to say this is the earth.
    GARTH. Well, I say there's an earth,
and I say I'm guilty on it, guilty as hell.
    ESDRAS. Yet till it's known you bear no guilt
    at all—
unless you wish. The days go by like film,
like a long written scroll, a figured veil
unrolling out of darkness into fire
and utterly consumed. And on this veil,
running in sounds and symbols of men's minds
reflected back, life flickers and is shadow
going toward flame. Only what men can see
exists in that shadow. Why must you rise and
    cry out:
That was I, there in the ravelled tapestry,
there, in that pistol flash, when the man was
    killed.
I was there, and was one, and am bloodstained!
Let the wind
and fire take that hour to ashes out of time

and out of mind! This thing that men call
    justice,
this blind snake that strikes men down in the
    dark,
mindless with fury, keep your hand back from
    it,
pass by in silence—let it be forgotten, for-
    gotten!—
Oh, my son, my son—have pity!
    MIRIAMNE. But if it was true
and someone died—then it was more than
    shadow—
and it doesn't blow away——
    GARTH. Well, it was true.
    ESDRAS. Say it if you must. If you have heart
    to die,
say it, and let them take what's left—there was
    little
to keep, even before——
    GARTH. Oh, I'm a coward—
I always was. I'll be quiet and live. I'll live
even if I have to crawl. I know. [*He gets up
    and goes into the inner room*]
    MIRIAMNE. Is it better
to tell a lie and live?
    ESDRAS. Yes, child. It's better.
    MIRIAMNE. But if I had to do it—
I think I'd die.
    ESDRAS. Yes, child. Because you're young.
    MIRIAMNE. Is that the only reason?
    ESDRAS. The only reason.

       [*Curtain*]

SCENE III.

    SCENE—*Under the bridge, evening of the
same day. When the curtain rises* MIRIAMNE *is
sitting alone on the ledge at the rear of the
apartment house. A spray of light falls on her
from a street lamp above. She shivers a little
in her thin coat, but sits still as if heedless of
the weather. Through the rocks on the other
side a* TRAMP *comes down to the river bank,
hunting a place to sleep. He goes softly to the
apple-woman's hut and looks in, then turns
away, evidently not daring to preëmpt it. He
looks at* MIRIAMNE *doubtfully. The door of the
street-piano man is shut. The vagabond passes
it and picks carefully among some rags and
shavings to the right.* MIRIAMNE *looks up and
sees him but makes no sign. She looks down*

[572]

again, and the man curls himself up in a make-shift bed in the corner, pulling a piece of sacking over his shoulders. TWO GIRLS *come in round the apartment house.*

1ST GIRL. Honest, I never heard of anything so romantic. Because you never liked him.

2ND GIRL. I certainly never did.

1ST GIRL. You've got to tell me how it happened. You've got to.

2ND GIRL. I couldn't. As long as I live I couldn't. Honest, it was terrible. It was terrible.

1ST GIRL. What was so terrible?

2ND GIRL. The way it happened.

1ST GIRL. Oh, please—not to a soul, never.

2ND GIRL. Well, you know how I hated him because he had such a big mouth. So he reached over and grabbed me, and I began all falling to pieces inside, the way you do—and I said, "Oh no you don't mister," and started screaming and kicked a hole through the windshield and lost a shoe, and he let go and was cursing and growling because he borrowed the car and didn't have money to pay for the windshield, and he started to cry, and I got so sorry for him I let him, and now he wants to marry me.

1ST GIRL. Honest, I never heard of anything so romantic! [*She sees the sleeping* TRAMP] My God, what you won't see! [*They give the* TRAMP *a wide berth, and go out right. The* TRAMP *sits up looking about him.* JUDGE GAUNT, *an elderly, quiet man, well dressed but in clothes that have seen some weather, comes in uncertainly from the left. He holds a small clipping in his hand and goes up to the* HOBO]

GAUNT. [*tentatively*] Your pardon, sir. Your pardon, but perhaps you can tell me the name of this street.

HOBO. Huh?

GAUNT. The name of this street?

HOBO. This ain't no street.

GAUNT. There, where the street lamps are.

HOBO. That's the alley.

GAUNT. Thank you. It has a name, no doubt?

HOBO. That's the alley.

GAUNT. I see. I won't trouble you. You wonder why I ask, I daresay.—I'm a stranger.—Why do you look at me? [*He steps back*] I—I'm not the man you think. You've mistaken me, sir.

HOBO. Huh?

JUDGE. Perhaps misled by a resemblance. But you're mistaken—I had an errand in this city. It's only by accident that I'm here——

HOBO. [*muttering*] You go to hell.

JUDGE. [*going nearer to him, bending over him*] Yet why should I deceive you? Before God, I held the proofs in my hands. I hold them still. I tell you the defense was cunning beyond belief, and unscrupulous in its use of propaganda—they gagged at nothing—not even— [*He rises*] No, no—I'm sorry—this will hardly interest you. I'm sorry. I have an errand. [*He looks toward the street.* ESDRAS *enters from the basement and goes to* MIRIAMNE. *The* JUDGE *steps back into the shadows*]

ESDRAS. Come in, my daughter. You'll be cold here.

MIRIAMNE. After a while.

ESDRAS. You'll be cold. There's a storm coming.

MIRIAMNE. I didn't want him to see me crying. That was all.

ESDRAS. I know.

MIRIAMNE. I'll come soon. [ESDRAS *turns reluctantly and goes out the way he came.* MIRIAMNE *rises to go in, pausing to dry her eyes.* MIO *and* CARR, *road boys of seventeen or so, come round the apartment house. The* JUDGE *has disappeared*]

CARR. Thought you said you were never coming east again.

MIO. Yeah, but—I heard something changed my mind.

CARR. Same old business?

MIO. Yes, just as soon not talk about it.

CARR. Where did you go from Portland?

MIO. Fishing—I went fishing. God's truth.

CARR. Right after I left?

MIO. Fell in with a fisherman's family on the coast and went after the beautiful mackerel fish that swim in the beautiful sea. Family of Greeks—Aristides Marinos was his lovely name. He sang while he fished. Made the pea-green Pacific ring with his bastard Greek chanties. Then I went to Hollywood High School for a while.

CARR. I'll bet that's a seat of learning.

MIO. It's the hind end of all wisdom. They kicked me out after a time.

CARR. For cause?

MIO. Because I had no permanent address, you see. That means nobody's paying school taxes for you, so out you go. [*To* MIRIAMNE] What's the matter, Kid?

MIRIAMNE. Nothing. [*she looks up at him, and they pause for a moment*] Nothing.

MIO. I'm sorry.

MIRIAMNE. It's all right. [*She withdraws her eyes from his and goes out past him. He turns and looks after her*]

CARR. Control your chivalry.

MIO. A pretty kid.

CARR. A baby.

MIO. Wait for me.

CARR. Be a long wait? [MIO *steps swiftly out after* MIRIAMNE, *then returns*] Yeah?

MIO. She's gone.

CARR. Think of that.

MIO. No, but I mean—vanished. Presto—into nothing—prodigioso.

CARR. Damn good thing, if you ask me. The homely ones are bad enough, but the lookers are fatal.

MIO. You exaggerate, Carr.

CARR. I doubt it.

MIO. Well, let her go. This river bank's loaded with typhus rats, too. Might as well die one death as another.

CARR. They say chronic alcoholism is nice but expensive. You can always starve to death.

MIO. Not always. I tried it. After the second day I walked thirty miles to Niagara Falls and made a tour of the plant to get the sample of shredded wheat biscuit on the way out.

CARR. Last time I saw you you couldn't think of anything you wanted to do except curse God and pass out. Still feeling low?

MIO. Not much different. [*He turns away, then comes back*] Talk about the lost generation, I'm the only one fits that title. When the State executes your father, and your mother dies of grief, and you know damn well he was innocent, and the authorities of your home town politely inform you they'd consider it a favor if you lived somewhere else—that cuts you off from the world—with a meat-axe.

CARR. They asked you to move?

MIO. It came to that.

CARR. God, that was white of them.

MIO. It probably gave them a headache just to see me after all that agitation. They knew as well as I did my father never staged a holdup. Anyway, I've got a new interest in life now.

CARR. Yes—I saw her.

MIO. I don't mean the skirt.—No, I got wind of something, out west, some college professor investigating the trial and turning up new evidence. Couldn't find anything he'd written out there, so I beat it east and arrived on this blessed island just in time to find the bums holing up in the public library for the winter. I know now what the unemployed have been doing since the depression started. They've been catching up on their reading in the main reference room. Man, what a stench! Maybe I stank, too, but a hobo has the stench of ten because his shoes are poor.[1]

CARR. Tennyson.

MIO. Right. Jeez, I'm glad we met up again! Never knew anybody else that could track me through the driven snow of Victorian literature.

CARR. Now you're cribbing from some half-forgotten criticism of Ben Jonson's Roman plagiarisms.

MIO. Where did you get your education, sap?

CARR. Not in the public library, sap. My father kept a news-stand.

MIO. Well, you're right again. [*There is a faint rumble of thunder*] What's that? Winter thunder?

CARR. Or Mister God, beating on His little tocsin. Maybe announcing the advent of a new social order.

MIO. Or maybe it's going to rain coffee and doughnuts.

CARR. Or maybe it's going to rain.

MIO. Seems more likely. [*Lowering his voice*] Anyhow, I found Professor Hobhouse's discussion of the Romagna case. I think he has something. It occurred to me I might follow it up by doing a little sleuthing on my own account.

CARR. Yes?

MIO. I have done a little. And it leads me to somewhere in that tenement house that backs up against the bridge. That's how I happen to be here.

CARR. They'll never let you get anywhere with it, Mio. I told you that before.

MIO. I know you did.

CARR. The State can't afford to admit it was

---

[1] a parody of Tennyson's "Sir Galahad":
"My strength is as the strength of ten,
Because my heart is pure."

wrong, you see. Not when there's been that
much of a row kicked up over it. So for all
practical purposes the State was right and your
father robbed the payroll.

MIO. There's still such a thing as evidence.

CARR. It's something you can buy. In fact,
at the moment I don't think of anything you
can't buy, including life, honor, virtue, glory,
public office, conjugal affection and all kinds of
justice, from the traffic court to the immortal
nine. Go out and make yourself a pot of money
and you can buy all the justice you want.
Convictions obtained, convictions averted.
Lowest rates in years.

MIO. I know all that.

CARR. Sure.

MIO. This thing didn't happen to you.
They've left you your name
and whatever place you can take. For my heritage
they've left me one thing only, and that's to be
my father's voice crying up out of the earth
and quicklime where they stuck him. Electro-
cution
doesn't kill, you know. They eviscerate them
with a turn of the knife in the dissecting room.
The blood spurts out. The man was alive. Then
into
the lime pit, leave no trace. Make it short shrift
and chemical dissolution. That's what they
thought
of the man that was my father. Then my
mother—
I tell you these county burials are swift
and cheap and run for profit! Out of the house
and into the ground, you wife of a dead dog.
Wait,
here's some Romagna spawn left.
Something crawls here—
something they called a son. Why couldn't he
die
along with his mother? Well, ease him out of
town,
ease him out, boys, and see you're not too
gentle.
He might come back. And, by their own living
Jesus,
I will go back, and hang the carrion
around their necks that made it!
Maybe I can sleep then.
Or even live.

CARR. You have to try it?

MIO. Yes.
Yes. It won't let me alone. I've tried to live
and forget it—but I was birthmarked with hot
iron
into the entrails. I've got to find out who did it
and make them see it till it scalds their eyes
and make them admit it till their tongues are
blistered
with saying how black they lied!

HERMAN, *a gawky shoe salesman, enters
from the left*

HERMAN. Hello. Did you see a couple of
girls go this way?

CARR. Couple of girls? Did we see a couple
of girls?

MIO. No.

CARR. No. No girls. [HERMAN *hesitates, then
goes out right.* LUCIA *comes in from the left,
trundling his piano.* PINY *follows him, weeping*]

PINY. They've got no right to do it——

LUCIA. All right, hell what, no matter, I got
to put him away, I got to put him away, that's
what the hell! [TWO STREET URCHINS *follow him
in*]

PINY. They want everybody on the relief
rolls and nobody making a living?

LUCIA. The cops, they do what the big boss
say. The big boss, that's the mayor, he says he
heard it once too often, the sextette——

PINY. They want graft, that's all. It's a new
way to get graft——

LUCIA. Oh, no, no, no! He's a good man, the
mayor. He's just don't care for music, that's all.

PINY. Why shouldn't you make a living on
the street? The National Biscuit Company ropes
off Eighth Avenue—and does the mayor do
anything? No, the police hit you over the head
if you try to go through!

LUCIA. You got the big dough, you get the
pull, fine. No big dough, no pull, what the hell,
get off the city property! Tomorrow I start
cooking chestnuts . . . [*He strokes the piano
fondly.* The TWO GIRLS *and* HERMAN *come back
from the right*] She's a good little machine, this
baby. Cost plenty—and two new records I only
played twice. See this one. [*He starts turning
the crank, talking while he plays*] Two weeks
since they play this one in a picture house. [*A
SAILOR wanders in from the left. One of the
STREET URCHINS begins suddenly to dance a*

wild rumba, the others watch] Good boy—see, it's a lulu—it itches in the feet! [HERMAN, *standing with his girl, tosses the boy a penny. He bows and goes on dancing; the other* URCHIN *joins him. The* SAILOR *tosses a coin*]

SAILOR. Go it, Cuba! Go it! [LUCIA *turns the crank, beaming*]

2ND GIRL. Oh, Herman! [*She throws her arms round* HERMAN *and they dance*]

1ST URCHIN. Hey, pipe the professionals!

1ST GIRL. Do your glide, Shirley! Do your glide!

LUCIA. Maybe we can't play in front, maybe we can play behind! [*The* HOBO *gets up from his nest and comes over to watch.* A YOUNG RADICAL *wanders in*] Maybe you don't know, folks! Tonight we play good-bye to the piano! Good-bye forever! No more piano on the streets! No more music! No more money for the music-man! Last time, folks! Good-bye to the piano—good-bye forever! [MIRIAMNE *comes out the rear door of the apartment and stands watching.* THE SAILOR *goes over to the* 1ST GIRL *and they dance together*] Maybe you don't know, folks! Tomorrow will be sad as hell, tonight we dance! Tomorrow no more Verdi, no more rumba, no more good time! Tonight we play good-bye to the piano, good-bye forever! [*The* RADICAL *edges up to* MIRIAMNE, *and asks her to dance. She shakes her head and he goes to* PINY, *who dances with him. The* HOBO *begins to do a few lonely curvets on the side above*] Hoy! Hoy! Pick 'em up and take 'em around! Use the head, use the feet! Last time forever! [*He begins to sing to the air*]

MIO. Wait for me, will you?

CARR. Now's your chance. [MIO *goes over to* MIRIAMNE *and holds out a hand, smiling. She stands for a moment uncertain, then dances with him.* ESDRAS *comes out to watch.* JUDGE GAUNT *comes in from the left. There is a rumble of thunder*]

LUCIA. Hoy! Hoy! Maybe it rains tonight, maybe it snows tomorrow! Tonight we dance good-bye. [*He sings the air lustily.* A POLICEMAN *comes in from the left and looks on.* TWO OR THREE PEDESTRIANS *follow him*]

POLICEMAN. Hey you! [LUCIA *goes on singing*] Hey, you!

LUCIA. [*still playing*] What you want?

POLICEMAN. Sign off!

LUCIA. What you mean? I get off the street!

POLICEMAN. Sign off!

LUCIA. [*still playing*] What you mean? [*The* POLICEMAN *walks over to him.* LUCIA *stops playing and the* DANCERS *pause*]

POLICEMAN. Cut it.

LUCIA. Is this a street?

POLICEMAN. I say cut it out. [*The* HOBO *goes back to his nest and sits in it, watching*]

LUCIA. It's the last time. We dance good-bye to the piano.

POLICEMAN. You'll dance good-bye to something else if I catch you cranking that thing again.

LUCIA. All right.

PINY. I'll bet you don't say that to the National Biscuit Company!

POLICEMAN. Lady, you've been selling apples on my beat for some time now, and I said nothing about it—

PINY. Selling apples is allowed—

POLICEMAN. You watch yourself—[*He takes a short walk around the place and comes upon the* HOBO] What are you doing here? [*The* HOBO *opens his mouth, points to it, and shakes his head*] Oh, you are, are you? [*He comes back to* LUCIA] So you trundle your so-called musical instrument to wherever you keep it, and don't let me hear it again. [*The* RADICAL *leaps on the base of the rock at right. The* 1ST GIRL *turns away from the* SAILOR *toward the* 2ND GIRL *and* HERMAN]

SAILOR. Hey, captain, what's the matter with the music?

POLICEMAN. Not a thing, admiral.

SAILOR. Well, we had a little party going here—

POLICEMAN. I'll say you did.

2ND GIRL. Please, officer, we want to dance.

POLICEMAN. Go ahead. Dance.

2ND GIRL. But we want music!

POLICEMAN. [*turning to go*] Sorry. Can't help you.

RADICAL. And there you see it, the perfect example of capitalistic oppression! In a land where music should be free as air and the arts should be encouraged, a uniformed minion of the rich, a guardian myrmidon of the Park Avenue pleasure hunters, steps in and puts a limit on the innocent enjoyments of the poor! We don't go to theatres! Why not? We can't afford it! We don't go to night clubs, where women dance naked and the music drips from saxo-

phones and leaks out of Rudy Vallee—we can't
afford that either!—But we might at least dance
on the river bank to the strains of a barrel organ—! [GARTH *comes out of the apartment and
listens*]

POLICEMAN. It's against the law!

RADICAL. What law? I challenge you to tell
me what law of God or man—what ordinance
—is violated by this spontaneous diversion?
None! I say none! An official whim of the masters who should be our servants!—

POLICEMAN. Get down! Get down and shut
up!

RADICAL. By what law, by what ordinance
do you order me to be quiet?

POLICEMAN. Speaking without a flag. You
know it.

RADICAL. [*pulling out a small American flag*]
There's my flag! There's the flag of this United
States which used to guarantee the rights of
man—the rights of man now violated by every
third statute of the commonweal—

POLICEMAN. Don't try to pull tricks on me!
I've seen you before! You're not making any
speech, and you're climbing down—

JUDGE GAUNT [*who has come quietly forward*]. One moment, officer. There is some difference of opinion even on the bench as to the
elasticity of police power when applied in minor emergencies to preserve civil order. But the
weight of authority would certainly favor the
defendant in any equable court, and he would
be upheld in his demand to be heard.

POLICEMAN. Who are you?

JUDGE GAUNT. Sir, I am not accustomed to
answer that question.

POLICEMAN. I don't know you.

GAUNT. I am a judge of some standing, not
in your city but in another with similar statutes.
You are aware, of course, that the bill of rights
is not to be set aside lightly by the officers of
any municipality——

POLICEMAN. [*looking over GAUNT's somewhat
bedraggled costume*] Maybe they understand
you better in the town you come from, but I
don't get your drift.—[*To the RADICAL*] I don't
want any trouble, but if you ask for it you'll get
plenty. Get down!

RADICAL. I'm not asking for trouble, but I'm
staying right here. [*The POLICEMAN moves towards him*]

GAUNT. [*taking the POLICEMAN's arm, but

shaken off roughly] I ask this for yourself,
truly, not for the dignity of the law nor the
maintenance of precedent. Be gentle with them
when their threats are childish—be tolerant
while you can—for your least harsh word will
return on you in the night—return in a storm
of cries!—[*He takes the POLICEMAN's arm
again*] Whatever they may have said or done,
let them disperse in peace! It is better that they
go softly, lest when they are dead you see their
eyes pleading, and their outstretched hands
touch you, fingering cold on your heart!—I
have been harsher than you. I have sent men
down that long corridor into blinding light and
blind darkness! [*He suddenly draws himself
erect and speaks defiantly*] And it was well that
I did so! I have been an upright judge! They
are all liars! Liars!

POLICEMAN. [*shaking GAUNT off so that he
falls*] Why, you fool, you're crazy!

GAUNT. Yes, and there are liars on the force!
They came to me with their shifty lies! [*He
catches at the POLICEMAN, who pushes him
away with his foot*]

POLICEMAN. You think I've got nothing better to do than listen to a crazy fool?

1ST GIRL. Shame, shame!

POLICEMAN. What have I got to be ashamed
of? And what's going on here, anyway? Where
in hell did you all come from?

RADICAL. Tread on him! That's right! Tread
down the poor and the innocent! [*There is a
protesting murmur in the crowd*]

SAILOR. [*moving in a little*] Say, big boy,
you don't have to step on the guy.

POLICEMAN. [*facing them, stepping back*]
What's the matter with you! I haven't stepped
on anybody!

MIO. [*at the right, across from the POLICE-
MAN*]
Listen now, fellows, give the badge a chance.
He's doing his job, what he gets paid to do,
the same as any of you. They're all picked men,
these metropolitan police, hand picked
for loyalty and a fine up-standing pair
of shoulders on their legs—it's not so easy
to represent the law. Think what he does
for all of us, stamping out crime!
Do you want to be robbed and murdered in
    your beds?

SAILOR. What's eating you?

RADICAL. He must be a capitalist.

MIO. They pluck them fresh,
from Ireland, and a paucity of headpiece
is a prime prerequisite. You from Ireland,
   buddy?
   POLICEMAN. [*surly*] Where are you from?
   MIO. Buddy, I tell you flat
I wish I was from Ireland, and could boast
some Tammany connections. There's only one
   drawback
about working on the force. It infects the brain,
it eats the cerebrum. There've been cases
   known,
fine specimens of manhood, too, where autop-
   sies,
conducted in approved scientific fashion,
revealed conditions quite incredible
in policemen's upper layers. In some, a trace,
in others, when they've swung a stick too long,
there was nothing there!—but nothing! Oh, my
   friends,
this fine athletic figure of a man
that stands so grim before us, what will they
   find
when they saw his skull for the last inspec-
   tion?
I fear me a little puffball dust will blow away
rejoining earth, our mother—and this same
   dust,
this smoke, this ash on the wind, will represent
all he had left to think with!
   THE HOBO. Hooray! [*The* POLICEMAN *turns
on his heel and looks hard at the* HOBO, *who
slinks away*]
   POLICEMAN. Oh, yeah?
   MIO. My theme
gives ears to the deaf and voice to the dumb!
   But now
forgive me if I say you were most unkind
in troubling the officer. He's a simple man
of simple tastes, and easily confused
when faced with complex issues. He may reflect
on returning home, that is, so far as he
is capable of reflection, and conclude
that he was kidded out of his uniform pants,
and in his fury when this dawns on him
may smack his wife down!
   POLICEMAN. That'll be about enough from
you, too, professor!
   MIO. May I say that I think you have managed this whole situation rather badly, from the
beginning?——
   POLICEMAN. You may not!

TROCK *slips in from the background. The*
TWO YOUNG MEN IN SERGE *come with
him*

5   MIO. Oh, but your pardon, sir! It's apparent
to the least competent among us that you
should have gone about your task more subtly
—the glove of velvet, the hand of iron, and all
that sort of thing——

10   POLICEMAN. Shut that hole in your face!
   MIO. Sir, for that remark I shall be satisfied
with nothing less than an unconditional apology! I have an old score to settle with policemen, brother, because they're fools and fat-

15   heads, and you're one of the most fatuous fat-
heads that ever walked his feet flat collecting
graft! Tell that to your sergeant back in the
booby-hatch.
   POLICEMAN. Oh, you want an apology, do

20   you? You'll get an apology out of the other side
of your mouth! [*He steps toward* MIO. CARR
suddenly stands in his path] Get out of my
way! [*He pauses and looks round him; the
crowd looks less and less friendly. He lays a

25   hand on his gun and backs to a position where
there is nobody behind him*] Get out of here,
all of you! Get out! What are you trying to do
—start a riot?
   MIO. There now, that's better! That's in the

30   best police tradition. Incite a riot yourself and
then accuse the crowd.
   POLICEMAN. It won't be pleasant if I decide
to let somebody have it! Get out! [*The onlookers begin to melt away. The* SAILOR *goes out

35   left with the* GIRLS *and* HERMAN. CARR *and* MIO
go out right, CARR *whistling "The Star Spangled
Banner." The* HOBO *follows them. The* RADICAL
walks past with his head in the air. PINY *and*
LUCIA *leave the piano where it stands and slip

40   away to the left. At the end the* POLICEMAN *is
left standing in the center, the* JUDGE *near him.*
ESDRAS *stands in the doorway.* MIRIAMNE *is left
sitting half in shadow and unseen by* ESDRAS]
   JUDGE GAUNT. [*to the* POLICEMAN] Yes, but

45   should a man die, should it be necessary that
one man die for the good of many, make not
yourself the instrument of death, lest you sleep
to wake sobbing! Nay, it avails nothing that
you are the law—this delicate ganglion that is

50   the brain, it will not bear these things—! [*The*
POLICEMAN *gives the* JUDGE *the once-over,
shrugs, decides to leave him there and starts*

out left. GARTH *goes to his father—a fine sleet begins to fall through the street lights.* TROCK *is still visible*]

GARTH. Get him in here, quick.

ESDRAS. Who, son?

GARTH. The Judge, damn him!

ESDRAS. Is it Judge Gaunt?

GARTH. Who did you think it was? He's crazy as a bedbug and telling the world. Get him inside! [*He looks round*]

ESDRAS. [*going up to* GAUNT] Will you come in, sir?

GAUNT. You will understand, sir. We old men know how softly we must proceed with these things.

ESDRAS. Yes, surely, sir.

GAUNT. It was always my practice—always. They will tell you that of me where I am known. Yet even I am not free of regret—even I. Would you believe it?

ESDRAS. I believe we are none of us free of regret.

GAUNT. None of us? I would it were true. I would I thought it were true.

ESDRAS. Shall we go in, sir? This is sleet that's falling.

GAUNT. Yes. Let us go in. [ESDRAS, GAUNT *and* GARTH *enter the basement and shut the door.* TROCK *goes out with his men. After a pause* MIO *comes back from the right, alone. He stands at a little distance from* MIRIAMNE]

MIO. Looks like rain. [*She is silent*] You live around here? [*She nods gravely*] I guess you thought I meant it—about waiting here to meet me. [*She nods again*] I'd forgotten about it till I got that winter across the face. You'd better go inside. I'm not your kind. I'm nobody's kind but my own. I'm waiting for this to blow over. [*She rises*] I lied. I meant it— I meant it when I said it—but there's too much black whirling inside me—for any girl to know. So go on in. You're somebody's angel child and they're waiting for you.

MIRIAMNE. Yes. I'll go. [*She turns*]

MIO. And tell them when you get inside where it's warm, And you love each other, and mother comes to kiss her darling, tell them

to hang on to it while they can, believe while they can
it's a warm safe world, and Jesus finds his lambs
and carries them in his bosom.—I've seen some lambs
that Jesus missed. If they ever want the truth
tell them that nothing's guaranteed in this climate
except it gets cold in winter, nor on this earth
except you die sometime. [*He turns away*]

MIRIAMNE. I have no mother.
And my people are Jews.

MIO. Then you know something about it.

MIRIAMNE. Yes.

MIO. Do you have enough to eat?

MIRIAMNE. Not always.

MIO. What do you believe in?

MIRIAMNE. Nothing.

MIO. Why?

MIRIAMNE. How can one?

MIO. It's easy if you're a fool. You see the words
in books. Honor, it says there, chivalry, freedom,
heroism, enduring love—and these
are words on paper. It's something to have them there.
You'll get them nowhere else.

MIRIAMNE. What hurts you?

MIO. Just that.
You'll get them nowhere else.

MIRIAMNE. Why should you want them?

MIO. I'm alone, that's why. You see those lights,
along the river, cutting across the rain—?
those are the hearths of Brooklyn, and up this way
the love-nests of Manhattan—they turn their points
like knives against me—outcast of the world,
snake in the streets.—I don't want a hand-out.
I sleep and eat.

MIRIAMNE. Do you want me to go with you?

MIO. Where?

MIRIAMNE. Where you go.
[*A pause. He goes nearer to her*]

MIO. Why, you god-damned little fool—
what made you say that?

MIRIAMNE. I don't know.

MIO. If you have a home
stay in it. I ask for nothing. I've schooled myself

[579]

to ask for nothing, and take what I can get,
and get along. If I fell for you, that's my lookout,
and I'll starve it down.
    MIRIAMNE. Wherever you go, I'd go.
    MIO. What do you know about loving?
How could you know?
Have you ever had a man?
    MIRIAMNE. [*after a slight pause*] No. But I
    know.
Tell me your name.
    MIO. Mio. What's yours?
    MIRIAMNE. Miriamne.
    MIO. There's no such name.
    MIRIAMNE. But there's no such name as Mio!
M.I.O. It's no name.
    MIO. It's for Bartolomeo.
    MIRIAMNE. My mother's name was Miriam,
so they called me Miriamne.
    MIO. Meaning little Miriam?
    MIRIAMNE. Yes.
    MIO. So now little Miriamne will go in
and take up quietly where she dropped them
    all
her small housewifely cares.—When I first saw
    you,
not a half-hour ago, I heard myself saying,
this is the face that launches ships for me—
and if I owned a dream—yes, half a dream—
we'd share it. But I have no dream. This earth
came tumbling down from chaos, fire and rock,
and bred up worms, blind worms that sting
    each other
here in the dark. These blind worms of the
    earth
took out my father—and killed him, and set a
    sign
on me—the heir of the serpent—and he was a
    man
such as men might be if the gods were men—
but they killed him—
as they'll kill all others like him
till the sun cools down to the stabler molecules,
yes, till men spin their tent-worm webs to the
    stars
and what they think is done, even in the think-
    ing,
and they are the gods, and immortal, and con-
    stellations
turn for them all like mill wheels—still as they
    are
they will be, worms and blind. Enduring love,

oh gods and worms, what mockery!—And yet
I have blood enough in my veins. It goes like
    music,
singing, because you're here. My body turns
as if you were the sun, and warm. This men
    called love
in happier times, before the Freudians taught
    us
to blame it on the glands. Only go in
before you breathe too much of my atmosphere
and catch death from me.
    MIRIAMNE. I will take my hands
and weave them to a little house, and there
you shall keep a dream—
    MIO. God knows I could use a dream
and even a house.
    MIRIAMNE. You're laughing at me, Mio!
    MIO. The worms are laughing.
I tell you there's death about me
and you're a child! And I'm alone and half mad
with hate and longing. I shall let you love me
and love you in return, and then, why then
God knows what happens!
    MIRIAMNE. Something most unpleasant?
    MIO. Love in a box car—love among the
    children.
I've seen too much of it. Are we to live
in this same house you make with your two
    hands
mystically, out of air?
    MIRIAMNE. No roof, no mortgage!
Well, I shall marry a baker out in Flatbush,
it gives hot bread in the morning! Oh, Mio,
    Mio,
in all the unwanted places and waste lands
that roll up into the darkness out of sun
and into sun out of dark, there should be one
    empty
for you and me.
    MIO. No.
    MIRIAMNE. Then go now and leave me.
I'm only a girl you saw in the tenements,
and there's been nothing said.
    MIO. Miriamne. [*She takes a step toward
    him*]
    MIRIAMNE. Yes. [*He kisses her lips lightly*]
    MIO. Why, girl, the transfiguration on the
    mount
was nothing to your face. It lights from
    within—
a white chalice holding fire, a flower in flame,
this is your face.

MIRIAMNE. And you shall drink the flame
and never lessen it. And round your head
the aureole shall burn that burns there now,
forever. This I can give you. And so forever
the Freudians are wrong.

MIO. They're well-forgotten
at any rate.

MIRIAMNE. Why did you speak to me
when you first saw me?

MIO. I knew then.

MIRIAMNE. And I came back
because I must see you again. And we danced
together
and my heart hurt me. Never, never, never,
though they should bind me down and tear out
my eyes,
would I ever hurt you now. Take me with you,
Mio,
let them look for us, whoever there is to look,
but we'll be away. [MIO *turns away toward the
tenement*]

MIO. When I was four years old
we climbed through an iron gate, my mother
and I,
to see my father in prison. He stood in the
death-cell
and put his hand through the bars and said,
My Mio,
I have only this to leave you, that I love you,
and will love you after I die. Love me then,
Mio,
when this hard thing comes on you, that you
must live
a man despised for your father. That night the
guards,
walking in flood-lights brighter than high noon,
led him between them with his trousers slit
and a shaven head for the cathodes. This sleet
and rain
that I feel cold here on my face and hands
will find him under thirteen years of clay
in prison ground. Lie still and rest, my father,
for I have not forgotten. When I forget
may I lie blind as you. No other love,
time passing, nor the spaced light-years of
suns
shall blur your voice, or tempt me from the path
that clears your name—
till I have these rats in my grip
or sleep deep where you sleep. [*To* MIRIAMNE]
I have no house,
nor home, nor love of life, nor fear of death,

nor care for what I eat, or who I sleep with,
or what color of calcimine the Government
will wash itself this year or next to lure
the sheep and feed the wolves. Love somewhere else,
and get your children in some other image
more acceptable to the State! This face of mine
is stamped for sewage! [*She steps back, sur-
mising*]

MIRIAMNE. Mio——

MIO. My road is cut
in rock, and leads to one end. If I hurt you, I'm
sorry.
One gets over hurts.

MIRIAMNE. What was his name—
your father's name?

MIO. Bartolomeo Romagna.
I'm not ashamed of it.

MIRIAMNE. Why are you here?

MIO. For the reason
I've never had a home. Because I'm a cry
out of a shallow grave, and all roads are mine
that might revenge him!

MIRIAMNE. But Mio—why here—why here?

MIO. I can't tell you that.

MIRIAMNE. No—but—there's someone
lives here—lives not far—and you mean to see
him—
you mean to ask him—— [*She pauses*]

MIO. Who told you that?

MIRIAMNE. His name
is Garth—Garth Esdras——

MIO. [*after a pause, coming nearer*]
Who are you, then? You seem
to know a good deal about me.—Were you sent
to say this?

MIRIAMNE. You said there was death about
you! Yes,
but nearer than you think! Let it be as it is—
let it all be as it is, never see this place
nor think of it—forget the streets you came
when you're away and safe! Go before you're
seen
or spoken to!

MIO. Will you tell me why?

MIRIAMNE. As I love you
I can't tell you—and I can never see you——

MIO. I walk where I please——

MIRIAMNE. Do you think it's easy for me
to send you away? [*She steps back as if to go*]

MIO. Where will I find you then
if I should want to see you?

MIRIAMNE. Never—I tell you
I'd bring you death! Even now. Listen!

SHADOW *and* TROCK *enter between the
bridge and the tenement house.* MIRI-
AMNE *pulls* MIO *back into the shadow
of the rock to avoid being seen*

TROCK. Why, fine.
SHADOW. You watch it now—just for the
record, Trock—
you're going to thank me for staying away from
it
and keeping you out. I've seen men get that
way,
thinking they had to plug a couple of guys
and then a few more to cover it up, and then
maybe a dozen more. You can't own all
and territory adjacent, and you can't
slough all the witnesses, because every man
you put away has friends——
TROCK. I said all right.
I said fine.
SHADOW. They're going to find this judge,
and if they find him dead it's just too bad,
and I don't want to know anything about it—
and you don't either.
TROCK. You all through?
SHADOW. Why sure.
TROCK. All right.
We're through, too, you know.
SHADOW. Yeah? [*He becomes wary*]
TROCK. Yeah, we're through.
SHADOW. I've heard that said before, and
afterwards
somebody died.
[TROCK *is silent*] Is that what you mean?
TROCK. You can go.
I don't want to see you.
SHADOW. Sure, I'll go.
Maybe you won't mind if I just find out
what you've got on you. Before I turn my back.
I'd like to know. [*Silently and expertly he
touches* TROCK's *pockets, extracting a gun*]
Not that I'd distrust you,
but you know how it is. [*He pockets the gun*]
So long, Trock.
TROCK. So long.
SHADOW. I won't talk.
You can be sure of that.
TROCK. I know you won't. [SHADOW *turns
and goes out right, past the rock and along the
bank. As he goes the* TWO YOUNG MEN IN BLUE

SERGE *enter from the left and walk slowly after*
SHADOW. *They look toward* TROCK *as they enter
and he motions with his thumb in the direction
taken by* SHADOW. *They follow* SHADOW *out
without haste.* TROCK *watches them disappear,
then slips out the way he came.* MIO *comes a
step forward, looking after the two men. Two
or three shots are heard, then silence.* MIO
starts to run after SHADOW]
MIRIAMNE. Mio!
MIO. What do you know about this?
MIRIAMNE. The other way,
Mio—quick! [CARR *slips in from the right, in
haste*]
CARR. Look, somebody's just been shot.
He fell in the river. The guys that did the
shooting
ran up the bank.
MIO. Come on. [MIO *and* CARR *run out right.*
MIRIAMNE *watches uncertainly, then slowly
turns and walks to the rear door of the tene-
ment. She stands there a moment, looking after*
MIO, *then goes in, closing the door.* CARR *and*
MIO *return*]
CARR. There's a rip tide past the point.
You'd never find him.
MIO. No.
CARR. You know a man really ought to carry
insurance living around here.—God, it's easy,
putting a fellow away. I never saw it done be-
fore.
MIO. [*looking at the place where* MIRIAMNE
stood] They have it all worked out.
CARR. What are you doing now?
MIO. I have a little business to transact in
this neighborhood.
CARR. You'd better forget it.
MIO. No.
CARR. Need any help?
MIO. Well, if I did I'd ask you first. But I
don't see how it would do any good. So you
keep out of it and take care of yourself.
CARR. So long, then.
MIO. So long, Carr.
CARR. [*looking down-stream*] He was drifting face up. Must be halfway to the island the
way the tide runs. [*He shivers*] God, it's cold
here. Well——[*He goes out to the left.* MIO
sits on the edge of the rock. LUCIA *comes
stealthily back from between the bridge and the
tenement, goes to the street-piano and wheels it
away.* PINY *comes in. They take a look at* MIO,

but say nothing. LUCIA *goes into his shelter and* PINY *into hers.* MIO *rises, looks up at the tenement, and goes out to the left*]

[*Curtain*]

ACT II

SCENE—*The basement as in Scene II of Act I. The same evening.* ESDRAS *sits at the table reading,* MIRIAMNE *is seated at the left, listening and intent. The door of the inner room is half open and* GARTH's *violin is heard. He is playing the theme from the third movement of Beethoven's Archduke Trio.* ESDRAS *looks up.*

ESDRAS. I remember when I came to the end
of all the Talmud said, and the commentaries,
then I was fifty years old—and it was time
to ask what I had learned. I asked this question
and gave myself the answer. In all the Talmud
there was nothing to find but the names of
        things,
set down that we might call them by those
        names
and walk without fear among things known.
        Since then
I have had twenty years to read on and on
and end with Ecclesiastes. Names of names,
evanid days, evanid nights and days
and words that shift their meaning. Space is
        time,
that which was is now—the men of tomorrow
live, and this is their yesterday. All things
that were and are and will be, have their being
then and now and to come. If this means little
when you are young, remember it. It will return
to mean more when you are old.
MIRIAMNE. I'm sorry—I
was listening for something.
ESDRAS. It doesn't matter.
It's a useless wisdom. It's all I have,
but useless. It may be there is no time,
but we grow old. Do you know his name?
MIRIAMNE. Whose name?
ESDRAS. Why, when we're young and listen
        for a step
the step should have a name——[MIRIAMNE, *not hearing, rises and goes to the window.* GARTH *enters from within, carrying his violin and carefully closing the door*]
GARTH. [*as* ESDRAS *looks at him*] Asleep.

ESDRAS. He may
sleep on through the whole night—then in the
        morning
we can let them know.
5   GARTH. We'd be wiser to say nothing—
let him find his own way back.
ESDRAS. How did he come here?
GARTH. He's not too crazy for that. If he
        wakes again
10 we'll keep him quiet and shift him off tomorrow.
Somebody'd pick him up.
ESDRAS. How have I come
to this sunken end of a street, at a life's end—?
15 GARTH. It was cheaper here—not to be transcendental—
So—we say nothing——?
ESDRAS. Nothing.
MIRIAMNE. Garth, there's no place
in this whole city—not one—
where you wouldn't be safer
than here—tonight—or tomorrow.
GARTH. [*bitterly*] Well, that may be.
What of it?
25 MIRIAMNE. If you slipped away and took
a place somewhere where Trock couldn't find
        you—
GARTH. Yes—
using what for money? and why do you think
30 I've sat here so far—because I love my home
so much? No, but if I stepped around the
        corner
it'd be my last corner and my last step.
MIRIAMNE. And yet—
35 if you're here—they'll find you here—
Trock will come again—
and there's worse to follow——
GARTH. Do you want to get me killed?
MIRIAMNE. No.
40 GARTH. There's no way out of it. We'll wait
and take what they send us.
ESDRAS. Hush! You'll wake him.
GARTH. I've done it.
I hear him stirring now. [*They wait quietly.*
45 JUDGE GAUNT *opens the door and enters*]
GAUNT. [*in the doorway*] I beg your pardon—
no, no, be seated—keep your place—I've made
your evening difficult enough, I fear;
and I must thank you doubly for your kindness,
for I've been ill—I know it.
ESDRAS. You're better, sir?

[583]

GAUNT. Quite recovered, thank you. Able, I
   hope,
to manage nicely now. You'll be rewarded
for your hospitality—though at this moment
   [*he smiles*]
I'm low in funds. [*He inspects his billfold*]
Sir, my embarrassment
is great indeed—and more than monetary,
for I must own my recollection's vague
of how I came here—how we came together—
and what we may have said. My name is Gaunt,
Judge Gaunt, a name long known in the criminal courts,
and not unhonored there.
   ESDRAS. My name is Esdras—
and this is Garth, my son. And Miriamne,
the daughter of my old age.
   GAUNT. I'm glad to meet you.
Esdras. Garth Esdras. [*He passes a hand over
   his eyes*]
It's not a usual name.
Of late it's been connected with a case—
a case I knew. But this is hardly the man.
Though it's not a usual name. [*They are silent*]
Sir, how I came here,
as I have said, I don't well know. Such things
are sometimes not quite accident.
   ESDRAS. We found you
outside our door and brought you in.
   GAUNT. The brain
can be overworked, and weary, even when the
   man
would swear to his good health. Sir, on my
   word
I don't know why I came here, nor how, nor
   when,
nor what would explain it. Shall we say the machine
begins to wear? I felt no twinge of it.—
You will imagine how much more than gall-
   ing
I feel it, to ask my way home—and where I
   am—
but I do ask you that.
   ESDRAS. This is New York City—
or part of it.
   GAUNT. Not the best part, I presume? [*He
   smiles grimly*] No, not the best.
   ESDRAS. Not typical, no.
   GAUNT. And you—[*To* GARTH]
you are Garth Esdras?
   GARTH. That's my name.

GAUNT. Well, sir, [*To* ESDRAS]
I shall lie under the deepest obligation
if you will set an old man on his path,
for I lack the homing instinct, if the truth
were known. North, east and south mean nothing to me
here in this room.
   ESDRAS. I can put you in your way.
   GARTH. Only you'd be wiser to wait a
   while—
if I'm any judge.——
   GAUNT. It happens I'm the judge—[*With
   stiff humor*]
in more ways than one. You'll forgive me if I
   say
I find this place and my predicament
somewhat distasteful. [*He looks round him*]
   GARTH. I don't doubt you do;
but you're better off here.
   GAUNT. Nor will you find it wise
to cross my word as lightly as you seem
inclined to do. You've seen me ill and shaken—
and you presume on that.
   GARTH. Have it your way.
   GAUNT. Doubtless what information is required
we'll find nearby.
   ESDRAS. Yes, sir—the terminal,——
if you could walk so far.
   GAUNT. I've done some walking—
to look at my shoes. [*He looks down, then puts
   out a hand to steady himself*]
   That—that was why I came—
never mind—it was there—and it's gone.
[*To* GARTH] Professor Hobhouse—
that's the name—he wrote some trash about
   you
and printed it in a broadside.
   —Since I'm here I can tell you
it's a pure fabrication—lacking facts
and legal import. Senseless and impudent,
written with bias—with malicious intent
to undermine the public confidence
in justice and the courts. I knew it then—
all he brings out about this testimony
you might have given. It's true I could have
   called you,
but the case was clear—Romagna was known
   guilty,
and there was nothing to add. If I've endured
some hours of torture over their attacks
upon my probity—and in this torture

have wandered from my place, wandered perhaps
in mind and body—and found my way to face
you—
why, yes, it is so—I know it—I beg of you
say nothing. It's not easy to give up
a fair name after a full half century
of service to a state. It may well rock
the surest reason. Therefore I ask of you
say nothing of this visit.

GARTH. I'll say nothing.
ESDRAS. Nor any of us.
GAUNT. Why, no—for you'd lose, too.
You'd have nothing to gain.
ESDRAS. Indeed we know it.
GAUNT. I'll remember you kindly. When I've
returned,
there may be some mystery made of where I
was—
we'll leave it a mystery?
GARTH. Anything you say.
GAUNT. Why, now I go with much more
peace of mind—if I can call you friends.
ESDRAS. We shall be grateful
for silence on your part, Your Honor.
GAUNT. Sir—
if there were any just end to be served
by speaking out, I'd speak! There is none. No—
bear that in mind!
ESDRAS. We will, Your Honor.
GAUNT. Then—
I'm in some haste. If you can be my guide,
we'll set out now.
ESDRAS. Yes, surely. [*There is a knock at the
door. The four look at each other with some apprehension.* MIRIAMNE *rises*]
I'll answer it.
MIRIAMNE. Yes. [*She goes into the inner
room and closes the door.* ESDRAS *goes to the
outer door. The knock is repeated. He opens
the door.* MIO *is there*]
ESDRAS. Yes, sir.
MIO. May I come in?
ESDRAS. Will you state your business, sir?
It's late—and I'm not at liberty——
MIO. Why, I might say
that I was trying to earn my tuition fees
by peddling magazines. I could say that,
or collecting old newspapers—paying cash—
highest rates—no questions asked——[*He
looks round sharply*]
GARTH. We've nothing to sell.

What do you want?
MIO. Your pardon, gentlemen.
My business is not of an ordinary kind,
and I felt the need of this slight introduction
while I might get my bearings. Your name is
Esdras,
or they told me so outside.
GARTH. What do you want?
MIO. Is that the name?
GARTH. Yes.
MIO. I'll be quick and brief.
I'm the son of a man who died many years ago
for a pay roll robbery in New England. You
should be Garth Esdras, by what I've heard.
You have
some knowledge of the crime, if one can believe
what he reads in the public prints, and it might
be
that your testimony, if given, would clear my
father
of any share in the murder. You may not care
whether he was guilty or not. You may not
know.
But I do care—and care deeply, and I've come
to ask you face to face.
GARTH. To ask me what?
MIO. What do you know of it?
ESDRAS. This man Romagna,
did he have a son?
MIO. Yes, sir, this man Romagna,
as you choose to call him, had a son, and I
am that son, and proud.
ESDRAS. Forgive me.
MIO. Had you known him,
and heard him speak, you'd know why I'm
proud, and why
he was no malefactor.
ESDRAS. I quite believe you.
If my son can help he will. But at this moment,
as I told you—could you, I wonder, come to-
morrow,
at your own hour?
MIO. Yes.
ESDRAS. By coincidence
we too of late have had this thing in mind—
there have been comments printed, and much
discussion
which we could hardly avoid.
MIO. Could you tell me then
in a word?—What you know—
is it for him or against him?—

that's all I need.

ESDRAS. My son knows nothing.

GARTH. No.
The picture-papers lash themselves to a fury
over any rumor—make them up when they're 5
short
of bedroom slops.—This is what happened. I
had known a few members of a gang one time
up there—and after the murder they picked
me up 10
because I looked like someone that was seen
in what they called the murder car. They held
me
a little while, but they couldn't identify me
for the most excellent reason I wasn't there 15
when the thing occurred. A dozen years later
now
a professor comes across this, and sees red
and asks why I wasn't called on as a witness
and yips so loud they syndicate his picture 20
in all the rotos. That's all I know about it.
I wish I could tell you more.

ESDRAS. Let me say too
that I have read some words your father said,
and you were a son fortunate in your father, 25
whatever the verdict of the world.

MIO. There are few
who think so, but it's true, and I thank you.
Then—
that's the whole story?

GARTH. All I know of it.

MIO. They cover their tracks well, the inner
ring
that distributes murder. I came three thousand
miles to this dead end. 35

ESDRAS. If he was innocent
and you know him so, believe it, and let the
others
believe as they like.

MIO. Will you tell me how a man's 40
to live, and face his life, if he can't believe
that truth's like a fire,
and will burn through and be seen
though it takes all the years there are?
While I stand up and have breath in my lungs 45
I shall be one flame of that fire;
it's all the life I have.

ESDRAS. Then you must live so.
One must live as he can.

MIO. It's the only way 50
of life my father left me.

ESDRAS. Yes? Yet it's true

the ground we walk on is impacted down
and hard with blood and bones of those who
died
unjustly. There's not one title to land or life,
even your own, but was built on rape and 5
murder,
back a few years. It would take a fire indeed
to burn out all this error.

MIO. Then let it burn down,
all of it! 10

ESDRAS. We ask a great deal of the world
at first—then less—and then less.
We ask for truth
and justice. But this truth's a thing unknown
in the lightest, smallest matter—and as for jus- 15
tice,
who has once seen it done? You loved your
father,
and I could have loved him, for every word he
spoke 20
in his trial was sweet and tolerant, but the
weight
of what men are and have, rests heavy on
the graves of those who lost. They'll not rise
again, 25
and their causes lie there with them.

GAUNT. If you mean to say
that Bartolomeo Romagna was innocent,
you are wrong. He was guilty.
There may have been injustice 30
from time to time, by regrettable chance, in
our courts,
but not in that case, I assure you.

MIO. Oh, you assure me!
You lie in your scrag teeth, whoever you are! 35
My father was murdered!

GAUNT. Romagna was found guilty
by all due process of law, and given his chance
to prove his innocence.

MIO. What chance? When a court 40
panders to mob hysterics, and the jury
comes in loaded to soak an anarchist
and a foreigner, it may be due process of law
but it's also murder!

GAUNT. He should have thought of that 45
before he spilled blood.

MIO. He?

GAUNT. Sir, I know too well
that he was guilty.

MIO. Who are you? How do you know? 50
I've searched the records through, the trial and
what

came after, and in all that million words
I found not one unbiased argument
to fix the crime on him.
    GAUNT. And you yourself,
were you unprejudiced?
    MIO. Who are you?
    ESDRAS. Sir,
this gentleman is here, as you are here,
to ask my son, as you have asked, what ground
there might be for this talk of new evidence   10
in your father's case. We gave him the same
    answer
we've given you.
    MIO. I'm sorry. I'd supposed
his cause forgotten except by myself. There's   15
    still
a defense committee then?
    GAUNT. There may be. I
am not connected with it.
    ESDRAS. He is my guest,
and asks to remain unknown.   20
    MIO. [*after a pause, looking at* GAUNT] The
    judge at the trial
was younger, but he had your face. Can it be
that you're the man?—Yes—Yes.—The jury   25
    charge—
I sat there as a child and heard your voice,
and watched that Brahminical mouth. I knew
    even then
you meant no good to him. And now you're   30
    here
to winnow out truth and justice—the fountain-
    head
of the lies that slew him! Are you Judge Gaunt?
    GAUNT. I am.   35
    MIO. Then tell me what damnation to what
    inferno
would fit the toad that sat in robes and lied
when he gave the charge, and knew he lied!
    Judge that,   40
and then go to your place in that hell!
    GAUNT. I know and have known
what bitterness can rise against a court
when it must say, putting aside all weakness,
that a man's to die. I can forgive you that,   45
for you are your father's son, and you think of
    him
as a son thinks of his father. Certain laws
seem cruel in their operation; it's necessary
that we be cruel to uphold them. This cruelty   50
is kindness to those I serve.
    MIO. I don't doubt that.

I know who it is you serve.
    GAUNT. Would I have chosen
to rack myself with other men's despairs,
stop my ears, harden my heart, and listen only
to the voice of law and light, if I had hoped   5
some private gain for serving? In all my years
on the bench of a long-established common-
    wealth
not once has my decision been in question
save in this case. Not once before or since.
For hope of heaven or place on earth, or power
or gold, no man has had my voice, nor will
while I still keep the trust that's laid on me
to sentence and define.
    MIO. Then why are you here?
    GAUNT. My record's clean. I've kept it so.
    But suppose
with the best intent, among the myriad tongues
that come to testify, I had missed my way
and followed a perjured tale to a lethal end   20
till a man was forsworn to death? Could I rest
    or sleep
while there was doubt of this,
even while there was question in a layman's
    mind?
For always, night and day,
there lies on my brain like a weight, the ad-
    monition:
see truly, let nothing sway you; among all
    functions
there's but one godlike, to judge. Then see
    to it
you judge as a god would judge, with clarity,
with truth, with what mercy is found consonant
with order and law. Without law men are   35
    beasts,
and it's a judge's task to lift and hold them
above themselves. Let a judge be once mis-
    taken
or step aside for a friend, and a gap is made   40
in the dykes that hold back anarchy and chaos,
and leave men bound but free.
    MIO. Then the gap's been made,
and you made it.
    GAUNT. I feared that too. May you be a   45
    judge
sometime, and know in what fear,
through what nights long
in fear, I scanned and verified and compared
the transcripts of the trial.
    MIO. Without prejudice,
no doubt. It was never in your mind to prove

that you'd been right.

GAUNT. And conscious of that, too—
that that might be my purpose—watchful of
that,
and jealous as his own lawyer of the rights
that should hedge the defendant!
And still I found no error,
shook not one staple of the bolts that linked
the doer to the deed! Still following on from
step to step, I watched all modern comment,
and saw it centered finally on one fact—
Garth Esdras was not called. This is Garth
Esdras,
and you have heard him. Would his deposition
have justified a new trial?

MIO. No. It would not.

GAUNT. And there I come, myself. If the
man were still
in his cell, and waiting, I'd have no faint excuse
for another hearing.

MIO. I've told you that I read
the trial from beginning to end. Every word
you spoke
was balanced carefully to keep the letter
of the law and still convict—convict, by Christ,
if it tore the seven veils! You stand here now
running cascades of casuistry, to prove
to yourself and me that no judge of rank and
breeding
could burn a man out of hate! But that's what
you did
under all your varnish!

GAUNT. I've sought for evidence,
and you have sought. Have you found it? Can
you cite
one fresh word in defence?

MIO. The trial itself
was shot full of legerdemain, prearranged to
lead
the jury astray——

GAUNT. Could you prove that?

MIO. Yes!

GAUNT. And if
the jury were led astray, remember it's
the jury, by our Anglo-Saxon custom,
that finds for guilt or innocence. The judge
is powerless in that matter.

MIO. Not you! Your charge
misled the jury more than the evidence,
accepted every biased meaning, distilled
the poison for them!

GAUNT. But if that were so
I'd be the first, I swear it, to step down
among all men, and hold out both my hands
for manacles—yes, publish it in the streets,
that all I've held most sacred was defiled
by my own act. A judge's brain becomes
a delicate instrument to weigh men's lives
for good and ill—too delicate to bear
much tampering. If he should push aside
the weights and throw the beam, and say, this
once
the man is guilty, and I will have it so
though his mouth cry out from the ground,
and all the world
revoke my word, he'd have a short way to go
to madness. I think you'd find him in the
squares,
stopping the passers-by with arguments,—
see, I was right, the man was guilty there—
this was brought in against him, this—and
this—
and I was left no choice! It's no light thing
when a long life's been dedicate to one end
to wrench the mind awry!

MIO. By your own thesis
you should be mad, and no doubt you are.

GAUNT. But my madness
is only this—that I would fain look back
on a life well spent—without one stain—one
breath
of stain to flaw the glass—not in men's minds
nor in my own. I take my God as witness
I meant to earn that clearness, and believe
that I have earned it. Yet my name is clouded
with the blackest, fiercest scandal of our age
that's touched a judge. What I can do to wipe
that smutch from my fame I will. I think you
know
how deeply I've been hated, for no cause
that I can find there. Can it not be—and I
ask this
quite honestly—that the great injustice lies
on your side and not mine? Time and time
again
men have come before me perfect in their
lives,
loved by all who knew them, loved at home,
gentle, not vicious, yet caught so ripe red-
handed
in some dark violence there was no denying
where the onus lay.

MIO. That was not so with my father!

GAUNT. And yet it seemed so to me. To other men

who sat in judgment on him. Can you be sure—
I ask this in humility—that you,

who were touched closest by the tragedy,

may not have lost perspective—may have brooded

day and night on one theme—till your eyes are tranced

and show you one side only?

MIO. I see well enough.

GAUNT. And would that not be part of the malady—

to look quite steadily at the drift of things

but see there what you wish—not what is there—

not what another man to whom the story

was fresh would say is there?

MIO. You think I'm crazy.

Is that what you meant to say?

GAUNT. I've seen it happen

with the best and wisest men. I but ask the question.

I can't speak for you. Is it not true wherever

you walk, through the little town where you knew him well,

or flying from it, inland or by the sea,

still walking at your side, and sleeping only

when you too sleep, a shadow not your own

follows, pleading and holding out its hands

to be delivered from shame?

MIO. How you know that

by God I don't know.

GAUNT. Because one spectre haunted you and me—

and haunts you still, but for me it's laid to rest

now that my mind is satisfied. He died

justly and not by error.

[A pause]

MIO. [stepping forward]

Do you care to know

you've come so near to death it's miracle

that pulse still beats in your splotchy throat?

Do you know

there's murder in me?

GAUNT. There was murder in your sire,

and it's to be expected! I say he died

justly, and he deserved it!

MIO. Yes, you'd like too well

to have me kill you! That would prove your case

and clear your name, and dip my father's name

in stench forever! You'll not get that from me!
Go home and die in bed, get it under cover,
your lux-et-lex[2] putrefaction of the right thing,
you man that walks like a god!

GAUNT. Have I made you angry
by coming too near the truth?

MIO. This sets him up,
this venomous slug, this sets him up in a gown,
deciding who's to walk above the earth
and who's to lie beneath! And giving reasons!
The cobra giving reasons; I'm a god,
by Buddha, holy and worshipful my fang,
and can I sink it in! [He pauses, turns as if to go, then sits] This is no good.
This won't help much. [The JUDGE and ESDRAS look at each other]

GAUNT. We should be going.

ESDRAS. Yes. [They prepare to go] I'll lend you my coat.

GAUNT. [looking at it with distaste]
No, keep it. A little rain
shouldn't matter to me.

ESDRAS. It freezes as it falls,
and you've a long way to go.

GAUNT. I'll manage, thank you. [GAUNT and ESDRAS go out, ESDRAS obsequious, closing the door.]

GARTH. [looking at MIO's back] Well?

MIO. [not moving] Let me sit here a moment. [GARTH shrugs his shoulders and goes toward the inner door. MIRIAMNE opens it and comes out. GARTH looks at her, then at MIO, then lays his fingers on his lips. She nods. GARTH goes out. MIRIAMNE sits and watches MIO. After a little he turns and sees her]

MIO. How did you come here?

MIRIAMNE. I live here.

MIO. Here?

MIRIAMNE. My name is Esdras. Garth
is my brother. The walls are thin.
I heard what was said.

MIO. [stirring wearily] I'm going. This is no place for me.

MIRIAMNE. What place would be better?

MIO. None. Only it's better to go.
Just to go. [She comes over to him, puts her arm around him and kisses his forehead]

MIRIAMNE. Mio.

MIO. What do you want?
Your kisses burn me—and your arms. Don't offer

_____
[2] light and law.

what I'm never to have! I can have nothing.
   They say
they'll cross the void sometime to the other
   planets
and men will breathe in that air.
Well, I could breathe there,
but not here now. Not on this ball of mud.
I don't want it.

  MIRIAMNE. They can take away so little
with all their words. For you're a king among 10
   them.
I heard you, and loved your voice.

  MIO. I thought I'd fallen
so low there was no further, and now a pit
opens beneath. It was bad enough that he 15
should have died innocent, but if he were
   guilty—
then what's my life—what have I left to do—?
The son of a felon—and what they spat on me
was earned—and I'm drenched with the stuff. 20
Here on my hands
and cheeks, their spittle hanging! I liked my
   hands
because they were like his. I tell you I've lived
by his innocence, lived to see it flash 25
and blind them all—

  MIRIAMNE. Never believe them, Mio,
never. [*She looks toward the inner door*]

  MIO. But it was truth I wanted, truth—
not the lies you'd tell yourself, or tell a woman, 30
or a woman tells you! The judge with his cobra
   mouth
may have spat truth—and I may be mad! For
   me—
your hands are too clean to touch me. I'm to 35
   have
the scraps from hotel kitchens—and instead of
   love
those mottled bodies that hitch themselves
   through alleys 40
to sell for dimes or nickles. Go, keep yourself
   chaste
for the baker bridegroom—baker and son of a
   baker,
let him get his baker's dozen on you! 45

  MIRIAMNE. No—
say once you love me—say it once; I'll never
ask to hear it twice, nor for any kindness,
and you shall take all I have! 50

   GARTH *opens the inner door and comes out*

   GARTH. I interrupt

a love scene, I believe. We can do without
your adolescent mawkishness.
[*To* MIRIAMNE] You're a child.
You'll both remember that.

  MIRIAMNE. I've said nothing to harm you—
and will say nothing.

  GARTH. You're my sister, though,
and I take a certain interest in you. Where
have you two met?

  MIRIAMNE. We danced together.

  GARTH. Then
the dance is over, I think.

  MIRIAMNE. I've always loved you
and tried to help you, Garth. And you've been
   kind.
Don't spoil it now.

  GARTH. Spoil it how?

  MIRIAMNE. Because I love him.
I didn't know it would happen. We danced together.
And the world's all changed. I see you through
   a mist,
and our father, too. If you brought this to
   nothing
I'd want to die.

  GARTH. [*to* MIO] You'd better go.

  MIO. Yes, I know. [*He rises. There is a
trembling knock at the door.* MIRIAMNE *goes
to it. The* HOBO *is there shivering*]

  HOBO. Miss, could I sleep under the pipes
   tonight, miss?
Could I, please?

  MIRIAMNE. I think—not tonight.

  HOBO. There won't be any more nights—
if I don't get warm, miss.

  MIRIAMNE. Come in. [*The* HOBO *comes in,
looks round deprecatingly, then goes to a corner
beneath a huge heating pipe, which he crawls
under as if he'd been there before*]

  HOBO. Yes, miss, thank you.

  GARTH. Must we put up with that?

  MIRIAMNE. Father let him sleep there—
last winter.

  GARTH. Yes, God, yes.

  MIO. Well, good night.

  MIRIAMNE. Where will you go?

  MIO. Yes, where? As if it mattered.

  GARTH. Oh, sleep here, too.
We'll have a row of you under the pipes.

  MIO. No, thanks.

  MIRIAMNE. Mio, I've saved a little money.
   It's only

some pennies, but you must take it. [*She shakes some coins out of a box into her hand*]

MIO. No, thanks.

MIRIAMNE. And I love you.
You've never said you love me.

MIO. Why wouldn't I love you
when you're clean and sweet,
and I've seen nothing sweet or clean
this last ten years? I love you. I leave you that
for what good it may do you. It's none to me. 10

MIRIAMNE. Then kiss me.

MIO. [*looking at* GARTH] With that scowling
over us? No.
When it rains, some spring
on the planet Mercury, where the spring comes 15
often,
I'll meet you there, let's say. We'll wait for that.
It may be some time till then. [*The outside door
opens and* ESDRAS *enters with* JUDGE GAUNT,
then, after a slight interval,* TROCK *follows.* 20
TROCK *surveys the interior and its occupants
one by one, carefully*]

TROCK. I wouldn't want to cause you in-
convenience,
any of you, and especially the Judge. 25
I think you know that. You've all got things
to do—
trains to catch, and so on. But trains can wait.
Hell, nearly anything can wait, you'll find,
only I can't. I'm the only one that can't 30
because I've got no time. Who's all this here?
Who's that? [*He points to the* HOBO]

ESDRAS. He's a poor half-wit, sir,
that sometimes sleeps there.

TROCK. Come out. I say come out, 35
whoever you are. [*The* HOBO *stirs and looks up*]
Yes, I mean you. Come out. [*The* HOBO
emerges]
What's your name?

HOBO. They mostly call me Oke.

TROCK. What do you know? 40

HOBO. No, sir.

TROCK. Where are you from?

HOBO. I got a piece of bread. [*He brings it
out, trembling*]

TROCK. Get back in there! [*The* HOBO *crawls 45
back into his corner*]
Maybe you want to know why I'm doing this.
Well, I've been robbed, that's why—
robbed five or six times; 50
the police can't find a thing—so I'm out for
myself—

if you want to know.
[*To* MIO] Who are you?

MIO. Oh, I'm a half-wit,
came in here by mistake. The difference is 5
I've got no piece of bread.

TROCK. What's your name?

MIO. My name?
Theophrastus Such.[3] That's respectable.
You'll find it all the way from here to the coast
on the best police blotters. 10
Only the truth is we're a little touched in the
head,
Oke and me. You'd better ask somebody else.

TROCK. Who is he?

ESDRAS. His name's Romagna. He's the son. 15

TROCK. Then what's he doing here? You
said you were on the level.

GARTH. He just walked in. On account of the
stuff in the papers. We didn't ask him.

TROCK. God, we are a gathering. Now if we
had Shadow we'd be all here, huh? Only I
guess we won't see Shadow. No, that's too
much to ask.

MIO. Who's Shadow?

TROCK. Now you're putting questions. 25
Shadow was just nobody, you see. He blew
away. It might happen to anyone. [*He looks at*
GARTH] Yes, anyone at all.

MIO. Why do you keep your hand in your
pocket, friend? 30

TROCK. Because I'm cold, punk. Because I've
been outside and it's cold as the tomb of Christ.
[*To* GARTH] Listen, there's a car waiting up at
the street to take the Judge home. We'll take
him to the car. 35

GARTH. That's not necessary.

ESDRAS. No.

TROCK. I say it is, see? You wouldn't want to
let the Judge walk, would you? The Judge is
going to ride where he's going, with a couple 40
of chauffeurs, and everything done in style.
Don't you worry about the Judge. He'll be
taken care of. For good.

GARTH. I want no hand in it.

TROCK. Anything happens to me happens to 45
you too, musician.

GARTH. I know that.

TROCK. Keep your mouth out of it then. And
you'd better keep the punk here tonight, just
for luck. [*He turns toward the door. There is a* 50

[3] See *Impressions of Theophrastus Such,* satirical essays by George Eliot (1879).

brilliant lightning flash through the windows, followed slowly by dying thunder. TROCK *opens the door. The rain begins to pour in sheets*] Jesus, somebody tipped it over again! [*A cough racks him*] Wait till it's over. It takes ten days 5 off me every time I step into it. [*He closes the door*] Sit down and wait. [*Lightning flashes again. The thunder is fainter.* ESDRAS, GARTH *and the* JUDGE *sit down*]

GAUNT. We were born too early. Even you 10
who are young
are not of the elect. In a hundred years
man will put his finger on life itself, and then
he will live as long as he likes. For you and me
we shall die soon—one day, one year more or 15
less,
when or where, it's no matter. It's what we call
an indeterminate sentence. I'm hungry. [GARTH
   looks at MIRIAMNE]

MIRIAMNE. There was nothing left 20
tonight.

HOBO. I've got a piece of bread. [*He breaks his bread in two and hands half to the JUDGE*]

GAUNT. I thank you, sir. [*He eats*] 25
This is not good bread. [*He rises*]
Sir, I am used
to other company. Not better, perhaps, but
   their clothes
were different. These are what it's the fashion 30
   to call
the underprivileged.

TROCK. Oh, hell! [*He turns toward the door*]

MIO. [*to* TROCK] It would seem that you and
   the Judge know each other.
[TROCK *faces him*] 35

TROCK. I've been around.

MIO. Maybe you've met before.

TROCK. Maybe we have.

MIO. Will you tell me where?

TROCK. How long do you want to live? 40

MIO. How long? Oh, I've got big ideas about
   that.

TROCK. I thought so. Well, so far I've got
nothing against you but your name, see? You 45
keep it that way. [*He opens the door. The rain still falls in torrents. He closes the door. As he turns from it, it opens again, and* SHADOW, *white, bloodstained and dripping, stands in the doorway.* GARTH *rises.* TROCK *turns*] 50

GAUNT. [*to the* HOBO] Yet if one were careful of his health, ate sparingly, drank not at all,

used himself wisely, it might be that even an old man could live to touch immortality. They may come on the secret sooner than we dare hope. You see? It does no harm to try.

TROCK. [*backing away from* SHADOW] By 5
God, he's out of his grave!

SHADOW. [*leaning against the doorway, holding a gun in his hands*] Keep your hands where they belong, Trock.
You know me. 10

TROCK. Don't! Don't! I had nothing to do
   with it! [*He backs to the opposite wall*]

SHADOW. You said the doctor gave you six
months to live—well, I don't give you that 15
much. That's what you had, six months, and so
you start bumping off your friends to make sure
of your damn six months. I got it from you. I
know where I got it.
Because I wouldn't give it to the Judge. 20
So he wouldn't talk.

TROCK. Honest to God—

SHADOW. What God?
The one that let you put three holes in me
when I was your friend? Well, He let me get 25
up again and walk till I could find you. That's
as far as I get, but I got there, by God! And I
can hear you
even if I can't see! [*He takes a staggering step forward*] A man needs blood
to keep going. I got this far.—And now I can't 30
see!
It runs out too fast—too fast—
when you've got three slugs
clean through you.
Show me where he is, you fools? He's here! 35
I got here! [*He drops the gun*]
Help me! Help me! Oh, God! Oh, God!
I'm going to die! Where does a man lie down?
I want to lie down! [MIRIAMNE *starts toward*
SHADOW. GARTH *and* ESDRAS *help him into the* 40
next room, MIRIAMNE *following.* TROCK *squats in his corner, breathing hard, looking at the door.* MIO *stands, watching* TROCK. GARTH *returns, wiping his hand with a handkerchief.*
MIO *picks up and pockets the gun.* MIRIAMNE 45
comes back and leans against the door jamb]

GAUNT. You will hear it said that an old man
makes a good judge, being calm, clear-eyed,
without passion. But this is not true. Only the 50
young love truth and justice. The old are savage, wary, violent, swayed by maniac desires,
cynical of friendship or love, open to bribery

and the temptations of lust, corrupt and dastardly to the heart. I know these old men. What have they left to believe, what have they left to lose? Whorers of daughters, lickers of girls' shoes, contrivers of nastiness in the night, purveyors of perversion, worshippers of possession! Death is the only radical. He comes late, but he comes at last to put away the old men and give the young their places. It was time. [*He leers*]

Here's one I heard yesterday:

> Marmaduke behind the barn
> got his sister in a fix;
> he says damn instead of darn;
> ain't he cute? He's only six!

THE HOBO. He, he, he!

GAUNT.

> And the hoot-owl hoots all night,
> and the cuckoo cooks all day,
> and what with a minimum grace of God
> we pass the time away.

THE HOBO. He, he, he—I got ya! [*He makes a sign with his thumb*]

GAUNT. [*sings*]

> And he led her all around
> and laid her on the ground
> and he ruffled up the feathers of her
> cuckoo's nest!

HOBO. Ho, ho, ho!

GAUNT. I am not taken with the way you laugh. You should cultivate restraint.

ESDRAS *reënters*

TROCK. Shut the door.

ESDRAS. He won't come back again.

TROCK. I want the door shut! He was dead, I tell you! [ESDRAS *closes the door*] And Romagna was dead, too, once! Can't they keep a man under ground?

MIO. No. No more! They don't stay under ground any more, and they don't stay under water! Why did you have him killed?

TROCK. Stay away from me! I know you!

MIO. Who am I, then?

TROCK. I know you, damn you! Your name's Romagna!

MIO. Yes! And Romagna was dead, too, and Shadow was dead, but the time's come when you can't keep them down, these dead men! They won't stay down! They come in with their heads shot off and their entrails dragging! Hundreds of them! One by one—all you ever killed!

Watch the door! See!—It moves!

TROCK. [*looking, fascinated, at the door*] Let me out of here! [*He tries to rise*]

MIO. [*the gun in his hand*] Oh, no! You'll sit there and wait for them! One by one they'll come through that door, pulling their heads out of the gunny-sacks where you tied them—glauming over you with their rotten hands! They'll see without eyes and crawl over you—Shadow and the paymaster and all the rest of them—putrescent bones without eyes! Now! Look! Look! For I'm first among them!

TROCK. I've done for better men than you! And I'll do for you!

GAUNT. [*rapping on the table*] Order, gentlemen, order! The witness will remember that a certain decorum is essential in the court-room!

MIO. By God, he'll answer me!

GAUNT. [*thundering*] Silence! Silence! Let me remind you of courtesy toward the witness! What case is this you try?

MIO. The case of the state against Bartolomeo Romagna for the murder of the paymaster!

GAUNT. Sir, that was disposed of long ago!

MIO. Never disposed of, never, not while I live!

GAUNT. Then we'll have done with it now! I deny the appeal! I have denied the appeal before and I do so again!

HOBO. He, he!—He think's he's in the moving pictures! [*A flash of lightning*]

GAUNT. Who set that flash! Bailiff, clear the court! This it not Flemington,[4] gentlemen! We are not conducting this case to make a journalistic holiday! [*The thunder rumbles faintly.* GARTH *opens the outside door and faces a solid wall of rain*] Stop that man! He's one of the defendants! [GARTH *closes the door*]

MIO. Then put him on the stand!

GARTH. What do you think you're doing?

MIO. Have you any objection?

GAUNT. The objection is not sustained. We will hear the new evidence. Call your witness.

MIO. Garth Esdras!

GAUNT. He will take the stand!

GARTH. If you want me to say what I said before I'll say it!

---

[4] town in New Jersey where the Lindbergh kidnapping case was tried; feature writers, cameramen, and publicity seekers turned the trial into a sideshow.

MIO. Call Trock Estrella then!

GAUNT. Trock Estrella to the stand!

TROCK. No, by God!

MIO. Call Shadow, then! He'll talk! You thought he was dead, but he'll get up again and talk!

TROCK. [*screaming*] What do you want of me?

MIO. You killed the paymaster! You!

TROCK. You lie! It was Shadow killed him!

MIO. And now I know! Now I know!

GAUNT. Again I remind you of courtesy toward the witness!

MIO. I know them now!
Let me remind you of courtesy toward the dead!
He says that Shadow killed him! If Shadow were here
he'd say it was Trock! There were three men involved
in the new version of the crime for which
my father died! Shadow and Trock Estrella
as principals in the murder—Garth as witness!—
Why are they here together?—and you—the Judge—
why are you here? Why, because you were all afraid
and you drew together out of that fear to arrange
a story you could tell! And Trock killed Shadow
and meant to kill the Judge out of that same fear—
to keep them quiet! This is the thing I've hunted
over the earth to find out, and I'd be blind
indeed if I missed it now!
[*To* GAUNT.] You heard what he said:
It was Shadow killed him! Now let the night conspire
with the sperm of hell! It's plain beyond denial
even to this fox of justice—and all his words
are curses on the wind! You lied! You lied!
You knew this too!

GAUNT. [*low*] Let me go. Let me go!

MIO. Then why
did you let my father die?

GAUNT. Suppose it known,
but there are things a judge must not believe
though they should head and fester underneath
and press in on his brain. Justice once rendered
in a clear burst of anger, righteously,

upon a very common laborer,
confessed an anarchist, the verdict found
and the precise machinery of law
invoked to know him guilty—think what furor
would rock the state if the court then flatly said:
all this was lies—must be reversed? It's better,
as any judge can tell you, in such cases,
holding the common good to be worth more
than small injustice, to let the record stand,
let one man die. For justice, in the main,
is governed by opinion. Communities
will have what they will have, and it's quite as well,
after all, to be rid of anarchists. Our rights
as citizens can be maintained as rights
only while we are held to be the peers
of those who live about us. A vendor of fish
is not protected as a man might be
who kept a market. I own I've sometimes wished
this was not so, but it is. The man you defend
was unfortunate—and his misfortune bore
almost as heavily on me.—I'm broken—
broken across. You're much too young to know
how bitter it is when a worn connection chars
and you can't remember—can't remember.
[*He steps forward*] You
will not repeat this? It will go no further?

MIO. No.
No further than the moon takes the tides—no further
than the news went when he died—
when you found him guilty
and they flashed that round the earth. Wherever men
still breathe and think, and know what's done to them
by the powers above, they'll know. That's all I ask.
That'll be enough. [TROCK *has risen and looks darkly at* MIO]

GAUNT. Thank you. For I've said some things
a judge should never say.

TROCK. Go right on talking.
Both of you. It won't get far, I guess.

MIO. Oh, you'll see to that?

TROCK. I'll see to it. Me and some others.
Maybe I lost my grip there just for a minute.
That's all right.

MIO. Then see to it! Let it rain!

What can you do to me now when the night's
  on fire
with this thing I know? Now I could almost
  wish
there was a god somewhere—I could almost 5
  think
there was a god—and he somehow brought me
  here
and set you down before me here in the rain
where I could wring this out of you! For it's 10
  said,
and I've heard it, and I'm free! He was as I
  thought him,
true and noble and upright, even when he went
to a death contrived because he was as he was 15
and not your kind! Let it rain! Let the night
  speak fire
and the city go out with the tide, for he was
  a man
and I know you now, and I have my day! 20
  [*There is a heavy knock at the outside
  door.* MIRIAMNE *opens it, at a glance from*
  GARTH. *The* POLICEMAN *is there in oilskins*]
  POLICEMAN. Evening. [*He steps in, followed* 25
  by a SERGEANT, *similarly dressed*]
We're looking for someone
might be here. Seen an old man around
acting a little off?
[*To* ESDRAS] You know the one
I mean. You saw him out there. Jeez! You've got 30
a funny crowd here! [*He looks round. The* HOBO
  shrinks into his corner]
That's the one I saw.
What do you think? 35
  SERGEANT. That's him. You mean to say
you didn't know him by his pictures? [*He goes
  to* GAUNT] Come on, old man.
You're going home.
  GAUNT. Yes, sir. I've lost my way. 40
I think I've lost my way.
  SERGEANT. I'll say you have.
About three hundred miles. Now don't you
  worry.
We'll get you back. 45
  GAUNT. I'm a person of some rank
in my own city.
  SERGEANT. We know that. One look at you
and we'd know that.
  GAUNT. Yes, sir. 50
  POLICEMAN. If it isn't Trock!
Trock Estrella. How are you, Trock?

  TROCK. Pretty good,
Thanks.
  POLICEMAN. Got out yesterday again, I
  hear?
  TROCK. That's right.
  SERGEANT. Hi'ye, Trock?
  TROCK. O.K.
  SERGEANT. You know we got orders
to watch you pretty close. Be good now, baby,
or back you go. Don't try to pull anything,
not in my district.
  TROCK. No, sir.
  SERGEANT. No bumping off.
If you want my advice quit carrying a gun.
Try earning your living for once.
  TROCK. Yeah.
  SERGEANT. That's an idea.
Because if we find any stiffs on the river bank
we'll know who to look for.
  MIO. Then look in the other room!
I accuse that man of murder! Trock Estrella!
He's a murderer!
  POLICEMAN. Hello. I remember you.
  SERGEANT. Well, what murder?
  MIO. It was Trock Estrella
that robbed the pay roll thirteen years ago
and did the killing my father died for! You
  know
the Romagna case! Romagna was innocent,
and Trock Estrella guilty!
  SERGEANT. [*disgusted*] Oh, what the hell!
That's old stuff—the Romagna case.
  POLICEMAN. Hey, Sarge! [*The* SERGEANT *and*
  POLICEMAN *come closer together*]
The boy's a professional kidder. He took me
  over
about half an hour ago. He kids the police
and then ducks out!
  SERGEANT. Oh, yeah?
  MIO. I'm not kidding now.
You'll find a dead man there in the next room
and Estrella killed him!
  SERGEANT. Thirteen years ago?
And nobody smelled him yet?
  MIO. [*pointing*] I accuse this man
of two murders! He killed the paymaster long
  ago
and had Shadow killed tonight. Look, look for
  yourself!
He's there all right!
  POLICEMAN. Look boy. You stood out there
and put the booby sign on the dumb police

because they're fresh out of Ireland. Don't try
it twice.

SERGEANT. [*to* GARTH] Any corpses here?

GARTH. Not that I know of.

SERGEANT. I thought so. [MIO *looks at* MIRI-
AMNE]

[*To* MIO] Think up a better one.

MIO. Have I got to drag him
out here where you can see him?
[*He goes toward the inner door*] Can't you
scent a murder
when it's under your nose? Look in!

MIRIAMNE. No, no—there's no one—there's
no one there!

SERGEANT. [*looking at* MIRIAMNE] Take a
look inside.

POLICEMAN. Yes, sir. [*He goes into the inside room. The* SERGEANT *goes up to the
door. The* POLICEMAN *returns*]
He's kidding, Sarge. If there's a cadaver
in here I don't see it.

MIO. You're blind then! [*He goes into the
room, the* SERGEANT *following him*]

SERGEANT. What do you mean? [*He comes
out,* MIO *following him*]
When you make a charge of murder it's better
to have
the *corpus delicti,* son. You're the kind puts in
fire alarms to see the engine!

MIO. By God, he was there.
He went in there to die.

SERGEANT. I'll bet he did.
And I'm Haile Selassie's[5] aunt! What's your
name?

MIO. Romagna. [*To* GARTH] What have you
done with him?

GARTH. I don't know what you mean.

SERGEANT. [*to* GARTH] What's he talking
about?

GARTH. I wish I could tell you.
I don't know.

SERGEANT. He must have seen something.

POLICEMAN. He's got
the Romagna case on the brain. You watch
yourself,
chump, or you'll get run in.

MIO. Then they're in it together!
All of them! [*To* MIRIAMNE] Yes, and you!

GARTH. He's nuts, I say.

MIRIAMNE. [*gently*] You have dreamed

---

[5] ruler of Ethiopia prominent in conflict with
Italy under Mussolini.

something—isn't it true?
You've dreamed—
But truly, there was no one——[MIO *looks at
her comprehendingly*]

MIO. You want me to say it. [*He pauses*]
Yes, by God, I was dreaming.

SERGEANT. [*to* POLICEMAN] I guess you're
right.
We'd better be going. Haven't you got a coat?

GAUNT. No, sir.

SERGEANT. I guess I'll have to lend you mine.
[*He puts his oilskins on* GAUNT]
Come on, now. It's getting late. [GAUNT, *the*
POLICEMAN *and the* SERGEANT *go out*]

TROCK. They're welcome to him.
His fuse is damp. Where is that walking fool
with the three slugs in him?

ESDRAS. He fell in the hall beyond
and we left him there.

TROCK. That's lucky for some of us. Is he out
this time
or is he still butting around?

ESDRAS. He's dead.

TROCK. That's perfect. [*To* MIO] Don't try
using your firearms, *amigo* baby,
the Sarge is outside. [*He turns to go*]
Better ship that carrion
back in the river! The one that walks when he's
dead;
maybe he'll walk the distance for you.

GARTH. Coming back?

TROCK. Well, if I come back,
you'll see me. If I don't, you won't. Let the
punk
go as far as he likes. Turn him loose and let him
go.
And may you all rot in hell. [*He pulls his coat
around him and goes to the left.* MIRIAMNE
climbs up to look out a window]

MIRIAMNE. He's climbing up to the street,
along the bridgehead. [*She turns*]
Quick, Mio! It's safe now! Quick!

GARTH. Let him do as he likes.

MIRIAMNE. What do you mean? Garth! He
means to kill him!
You know that!

GARTH. I've no doubt Master Romagna
can run his own campaign.

MIRIAMNE. But he'll be killed!

MIO. Why did you lie about Shadow? [*There
is a pause.* GARTH *shrugs, walks across the
room, and sits*]

You were one of the gang!

GARTH. I can take a death if I have to! Go
    tell your story,
only watch your step, for I warn you, Trock's
    out gunning   5
and you may not walk very far. Oh, I could de-
    fend it
but it's hardly worth while.
If they get Trock they get me too.
Go tell them. You owe me nothing.   10

ESDRAS. This Trock you saw,
no one defends him. He's earned his death so
    often
there's nobody to regret it. But his crime,
his same crime that has dogged you, dogged us 15
    down
from what little we had, to live here among the
    drains,
where the waterbugs break out like a scrofula
on what we eat—and if there's lower to go   20
we'll go there when you've told your story. And
    more
that I haven't heart to speak——

MIO. [to GARTH] My father died
in your place. And you could have saved him! 25
You were one of the gang!

GARTH. Why, there you are.
You certainly owe me nothing.

MIRIAMNE. [moaning] I want to die.
I want to go away.   30

MIO. Yes, and you lied!
And trapped me into it!

MIRIAMNE. But Mio, he's my brother.
I couldn't give them my brother.

MIO. No. You couldn't.   35
You were quite right. The gods were damned
    ironic
tonight, and they've worked it out.

ESDRAS. What will be changed
if it comes to trial again? More blood poured 40
    out
to a mythical justice, but your father lying still
where he lies now.

MIO. The bright, ironical gods!
What fun they have in heaven! When a man 45
    prays hard
for any gift, they give it, and then one more
to boot that makes it useless.
[To MIRIAMNE] You might have picked
some other stranger to dance with!   50

MIRIAMNE. I know.

MIO. Or chosen

some other evening to sit outside in the rain.
But no, it had to be this. All my life long
I've wanted only one thing, to say to the world
and prove it: the man you killed was clean and
    true
and full of love as the twelve-year-old that
    stood
and taught in the temple. I can say that now
and give my proofs—and now you stick a girl's
    face
between me and the rites I've sworn the dead
shall have of me! You ask too much! Your
    brother
can take his chance! He was ready enough to
    let
an innocent man take certainty for him
to pay for the years he's had. That parts us,
    then,
but we're parted anyway, by the same dark
    wind
that blew us together. I shall say what I have
    to say.
[He steps back] And I'm not welcome here.

MIRIAMNE. But don't go now! You've stayed
too long! He'll be waiting!

MIO. Well, is this any safer?
Let the winds blow, the four winds of the
    world,
and take us to the four winds.
[The three are silent before him. He turns and
    goes out.]

[Curtain]

ACT III

SCENE—*The river bank outside the tenement, a little before the close of the previous
act. The rain still falls through the street lamps.
The* TWO NATTY YOUNG MEN IN SERGE AND
GRAY *are leaning against the masonry in a ray
of light, concentrating on a game of chance.
Each holds in his hand a packet of ten or fifteen
crisp bills. They compare the numbers on the
top notes and immediately a bill changes hands.
This goes on with varying fortune until the tide
begins to run toward the* 1ST GUNMAN, *who has
accumulated nearly the whole supply. They
play on in complete silence, evidently not wishing to make any noise. Occasionally they raise
their heads slightly to look carefully about.
Luck begins to favor the* 2ND GUNMAN, *and the
notes come his way. Neither evinces the slight-*

est interest in how the game goes. They merely play on, bored, half-absorbed. There is a slight noise at the tenement door. They put the bills away and watch. TROCK *comes out, pulls the door shut and comes over to them. He says a few words too low to be heard, and without changing expression the* YOUNG MEN *saunter toward the right.* TROCK *goes out to the left, and the* 2ND PLAYER, *watching that out of the corner of his eye, lingers in a glimmer of light to go on with the game. The* 1ST, *with an eye on the tenement door, begins to play without ado, and the bills again shift back and forth, then concentrate in the hands of the* 1ST GUN-MAN. *The* 2ND *shrugs his shoulders, searches his pockets, finds one bill, and playing with it begins to win heavily. They hear the door opening, and putting the notes away, slip out in front of the rock.* MIO *emerges, closes the door, looks round him and walks to left. Near the corner of the tenement he pauses, reaches out his hand to try the rain, looks up toward the street, and stands uncertainly a moment. He returns and leans against the tenement wall.* MIRIAMNE *comes out.* MIO *continues to look off into space as if unaware of her. She looks away.*

MIO. This rather takes one off his high horse. —What I mean, tough weather for a hegira. You see, this is my sleeping suit, and if I get it wet—*basta!*

MIRIAMNE. If you could only hide here.

MIO. Hide?

MIRIAMNE. Lucia would take you in. The street-piano man.

MIO. At the moment I'm afflicted with claustrophobia. I prefer to die in the open, seeking air.

MIRIAMNE. But you could stay there till daylight.

MIO. You're concerned about me.

MIRIAMNE. Shall I ask him?

MIO. No. On the other hand there's a certain reason in your concern. I looked up the street and our old friend Trock hunches patiently under the warehouse eaves.

MIRIAMNE. I was sure of that.

MIO. And here I am, a young man on a cold night, waiting the end of the rain. Being read my lesson by a boy, a blind boy—you know the one I mean. Knee-deep in the salt-marsh, Miriamne, bitten from within, fought.

MIRIAMNE. Wouldn't it be better if you came back in the house?

MIO. You forget my claustrophobia.

MIRIAMNE. Let me walk with you, then. Please. If I stay beside you he wouldn't dare.

MIO. And then again he might.—We don't speak the same language, Miriamne.

MIRIAMNE. I betrayed you. Forgive me.

MIO. I wish I knew this region. There's probably a path along the bank.

MIRIAMNE. Yes. Shadow went that way.

MIO. That's true, too. So here I am, a young man on a wet night, and blind in my weather eye. Stay and talk to me.

MIRIAMNE. If it happens—it's my fault.

MIO. Not at all, sweet. You warned me to keep away. But I would have it. Now I have to find a way out. It's like a chess game. If you think long enough there's always a way out.— For one or the other.—I wonder why white always wins and black always loses in the problems. White to move and mate in three moves. But what if white were to lose—ah, what then? Why, in that case, obviously black would be white and white would be black.—As it often is.—As we often are.—Might makes white. Losers turn black. Do you think I'd have time to draw a gun?

MIRIAMNE. No.

MIO. I'm a fair shot. Also I'm fair game. [*The door of the tenement opens and* GARTH *comes out to look about quickly. Seeing only* MIO *and* MIRIAMNE *he goes in and comes out again almost immediately carrying one end of a door on which a body lies covered with a cloth. The* HOBO *carries the other end. They go to the right with their burden*]
This is the burial of Shadow, then;
feet first he dips, and leaves the haunts of
    men.
Let us make mourn for Shadow, wetly lying,
in elegiac stanzas and sweet crying.
Be gentle with him, little cold waves and fishes;
nibble him not, respect his skin and tissues——

MIRIAMNE. Must you say such things?

MIO. My dear, some requiem is fitting over
    the dead, even
for Shadow. But the last rhyme was bad.

Whittle him not, respect his dying wishes.

That's better. And then to conclude:

His aromatic virtues, slowly rising
will circumnamb the isle, beyond disguising.
He clung to life beyond the wont of men.
Time and his silence drink us all. Amen.

How I hate these identicals. The French allow them, but the French have no principles
anyway. You know, Miriamne, there's really
nothing mysterious about human life. It's
purely mechanical, like an electric appliance.
Stop the engine that runs the generator and
the current's broken. When we think the brain
gives off a small electrical discharge—quite
measurable, and constant within limits. But
that's not what makes your hair stand up when
frightened.

MIRIAMNE. I think it's a mystery.

MIO. Human life? We'll have to wear veils
if we're to keep it a mystery much longer. Now
if Shadow and I were made up into sausages
we'd probably make very good sausages.

MIRIAMNE. Don't——

MIO. I'm sorry. I speak from a high place,
far off, long ago, looking down. The cortège returns. [GARTH *and the* HOBO *return, carrying
the door, the cloth lying loosely over it*] I hope
you placed an obol in his mouth to pay the fer-
ryman? Even among the Greeks a little money
was prerequisite to Elysium. [GARTH *and the*
HOBO *go inside, silent*] No? It's grim to think of
Shadow lingering among lesser shades on the
hither side. For lack of a small gratuity. [ES-
DRAS *comes out the open door and closes it behind him*]

ESDRAS. You must wait here, Mio, or go inside. I know
you don't trust me, and I haven't earned your
trust.
You're young enough to seek truth—
and there is no truth;
and I know that—
but I shall call the police and see that you
get safely off.

MIO. It's a little late for that.

ESDRAS. I shall try.

MIO. And your terms? For I daresay you
make terms?

ESDRAS. No.

MIO. Then let me remind you what will happen.
The police will ask some questions.

When they're answered
they'll ask more, and before they're done with
it
your son will be implicated.

ESDRAS. Must he be?

MIO. I shall not keep quiet.

[*A pause*]

ESDRAS. Still, I'll go.

MIO. I don't ask help, remember. I made no
truce.
He's not on my conscience, and I'm not on
yours.

ESDRAS. But you
could make it easier, so easily.
He's my only son. Let him live.

MIO. His chance of survival's
better than mine, I'd say.

ESDRAS. I'll go.

MIO. I don't urge it.

ESDRAS. No. I put my son's life in your
hands.
When you're gone,
that may come to your mind.

MIO. Don't count on it.

ESDRAS. Oh,
I count on nothing. [*He turns to go.* MIRIAMNE
*runs over to him and silently kisses his
hands*]
Not mine, not mine, my daughter!
They're guilty hands. [*He goes out left.*
GARTH'S *violin is heard within*]

MIO. There was a war in heaven
once, all the angels on one side, and all
the devils on the other, and since that time
disputes have raged among the learned, concerning
whether the demons won, or the angels. Maybe
the angels won, after all.

MIRIAMNE. And again, perhaps
there are no demons or angels.

MIO. Oh, there are none.
But I could love your father.

MIRIAMNE. I love him. You see,
he's afraid because he's old. The less one has
to lose the more he's afraid.

MIO. Suppose one had
only a short stub end of life, or held
a flashlight with the batteries run down
till the bulb was dim, and knew that he could
live
while the glow lasted. Or suppose one knew
that while he stood in a little shelter of time

[599]

under a bridgehead, say, he could live, and
    then,
from then on, nothing. Then to lie and turn
with the earth and sun, and regard them not in
    the least
when the bulb was extinguished or he stepped
    beyond
his circle into the cold? How would he live
that last dim quarter-hour, before he went,
minus all recollection, to grow in grass
between cobblestones?

    MIRIAMNE. Let me put my arms round you,
    Mio.
Then if anything comes, it's for me, too. [*She
    puts both arms round him*]

    MIO. Only suppose
this circle's charmed! To be safe until he steps
from this lighted space into dark! Time pauses
    here
and high eternity grows in one quarter-hour
in which to live.

    MIRIAMNE. Let me see if anyone's there—
there in the shadows. [*She looks toward the
    right*]

    MIO. It might blast our eternity—
blow it to bits. No, don't go. This is forever,
here where we stand. And I ask you, Miriamne,
how does one spend a forever?

    MIRIAMNE. You're frightened?

    MIO. Yes.
So much that time stands still.

    MIRIAMNE. Why didn't I speak—
tell them—when the officers were here? I failed
    you
in that one moment.

    MIO. His life for mine? Oh, no.
I wouldn't want it, and you couldn't give it.
And if I should go on living we're cut apart
by that brother of yours.

    MIRIAMNE. Are we?

    MIO. Well, think about it.
A body lies between us, buried in quicklime.
Your allegiance is on the other side of that
    grave and not to me.

    MIRIAMNE. No, Mio! Mio, I love you!

    MIO. I love you, too, but in case my life
    went on
beyond that barrier of dark—then Garth
would run his risk of dying.

    MIRIAMNE. He's punished, Mio.
His life's been torment to him. Let him go,
for my sake, Mio.

    MIO. I wish I could. I wish
I'd never seen him—or you. I've steeped too
    long
in this thing. It's in my teeth and bones. I can't
let go or forget. And I'll not add my lie
to the lies that cumber his ground. We live our
    days
in a storm of lies that drifts the truth too deep
for path or shovel; but I've set my foot on a
    truth
for once, and I'll trail it down!

    [*A silence.* MIRIAMNE *looks out to the right*]

    MIRIAMNE. There's someone there—
I heard——

CARR *comes in from the right*

    MIO. It's Carr.

    CARR. That's right. No doubt about it.
Excuse me.

    MIO. Glad to see you. This is Miriamne.
Carr's a friend of mine.

    CARR. You're better employed
than when I saw you last.

    MIO. Bow to the gentleman,
Miriamne. That's meant for you.

    MIRIAMNE. Thank you, I'm sure.
Should I leave you, Mio? You want to talk?

    MIO. Oh, no,
we've done our talking.

    MIRIAMNE. But——

    CARR. I'm the one's out of place—
I wandered back because I got worried about
    you,
that's the truth.—Oh—those two fellows with
    the hats
down this way, you know, the ones that ran
after we heard the shooting—they're back
    again,
lingering or malingering down the bank,
revisiting the crime, I guess. They may
mean well.

    MIO. I'll try to avoid them.

    CARR. I didn't care
for the way they looked at me.—No luck, I
    suppose,
with that case history? The investigation
you had on hand?

    MIO. I can't say. By the way,
the stiff that fell in the water and we saw swirl-
    ing
down the eddy, he came trudging up, later on,

long enough to tell his name. His name was
   Shadow
but he's back in the water now. It's all in an
   evening.
These things happen here.
   CARR. Good God!
   MIO. I know.
I wouldn't believe it if you told it.
   CARR. But—
the man was alive?
   MIO. Oh, not for long! He's dunked
for good this time. That's all that's happened.
   CARR. Well,
if you don't need me——
   MIRIAMNE. You had a message to send—
have you forgotten——?
   MIO. I?—Yes, I had a message—
but I won't send it—not now.
   MIRIAMNE. Then I will——!
   MIO. No.
Let it go the way it is! It's all arranged
another way. You've been a good scout, Carr,
the best I ever knew on the road.
   CARR. That sounds
like making your will.
   MIO. Not yet, but when I do
I've thought of something to leave you. It's the
   view
of Mt. Rainier from the Seattle jail,
snow over cloud. And the rusty chain in my
   pocket from a pair of handcuffs my father
   wore. That's all the worldly goods I'm
   seized of.
   CARR. Look, Mio—hell—
if you're in trouble——
   MIO. I'm not. Not at all. I have
a genius that attends me where I go,
and guards me now. I'm fine.
   CARR. Well, that's good news.
He'll have his work cut out.
   MIO. Oh, he's a genius.
   CARR. I'll see you then.
I'll be at the Grand Street place. I'm lucky to-
   night,
and I can pay. I could even pay for two.
   MIO. Thanks, I may take you up.
   CARR. Good night.
   MIO. Right, Carr.
   CARR. [to MIRIAMNE] Good night.
   MIRIAMNE. [after a pause] Good night.
   [CARR goes out to the left]
Why did you do that? He's your genius, Mio,

and you let him go.
   MIO. I couldn't help it.
   MIRIAMNE. Call him.
Run after him and call him!
   MIO. I tried to say it
and it strangled in my throat. I might have
   known
you'd win in the end.
   MIRIAMNE. Is it for me?
   MIO. For you?
It stuck in my throat, that's all I know.
   MIRIAMNE. Oh, Mio,
I never asked for that! I only hoped
Garth could go clear.
   MIO. Well, now he will.
   MIRIAMNE. But you—
It was your chance!
   MIO. I've lost
my taste for revenge if it falls on you. Oh, God,
deliver me from the body of this death
I've dragged behind me all these years! Miri-
   amne!
Miriamne!
   MIRIAMNE. Yes!
   MIO. Miriamne, if you love me
teach me a treason to what I am, and have
   been,
till I learn to live like a man! I think I'm wak-
   ing
from a long trauma of hate and fear and death
that's hemmed me from my birth—and glimpse
   a life
to be lived in hope—but it's young in me yet,
   I can't
get free, or forgive! But teach me how to live
and forget to hate!
   MIRIAMNE. He would have forgiven.
   MIO. He?
   MIRIAMNE. Your father. [A pause]
   MIO. Yes. [Another pause]
You'll think it strange, but I've never
   remembered that.
   MIRIAMNE. How can I help you?
   MIO. You have.
   MIRIAMNE. If I were a little older—if I knew
the things to say! I can only put out my hands
and give you back the faith you bring to me
by being what you are. Because to me
you are all hope and beauty and brightness
   drawn
across what's black and mean!
   MIO. He'd have forgiven—

[601]

Then there's no more to say—I've groped long
    enough
through this everglades of old revenges—here
the road ends.—Miriamne, Miriamne,
the iron I wore so long—it's eaten through
and fallen from me. Let me have your arms.
They'll say we're children—Well—the world's
    made up of children.
    MIRIAMNE. Yes.
    MIO. But it's too late for me.
    MIRIAMNE. No. [*She goes into his arms, and*
they kiss for the first time]
Then we'll meet again?
    MIO. Yes.
    MIRIAMNE. Where?
    MIO. I'll write—
or send Carr to you.
    MIRIAMNE. You won't forget?
    MIO. Forget?
Whatever streets I walk, you'll walk them, too,
from now on, and whatever roof or stars
I have to house me, you shall share my roof
and stars and morning. I shall not forget.
    MIRIAMNE. God keep you!
    MIO. And keep you. And this to remember!
if I should die, Miriamne, this half-hour
is our eternity. I came here seeking
light in darkness, running from the dawn,
and stumbled on a morning. [*One of the* YOUNG
MEN IN SERGE *strolls in casually from the right,*
looks up and down without expression, then,
seemingly having forgotten something, retraces
his steps and goes out. ESDRAS *comes in slowly*
from the left. He has lost his hat, and his face is
bleeding from a slight cut on the temple. He
stands abjectly near the tenement]
    MIRIAMNE. Father—what is it? [*She goes*
toward ESDRAS]
    ESDRAS. Let me alone. [*He goes nearer to*
    MIO] He wouldn't let me pass.
The street's so icy up along the bridge
I had to crawl on my knees—he kicked me
    back
three times—and then he held me there—I
    swear
what I could do I did! I swear to you
I'd save you if I could.
    MIO. What makes you think
that I need saving?
    ESDRAS. Child, save yourself if you can!
He's waiting for you.
    MIO. Well, we knew that before.

    ESDRAS. He won't wait much longer. He'll
    come here—
he told me so. Those damned six months of
    his—
he wants them all—and you're to die—you'd
    spread
his guilt—I had to listen to it—
    MIO. Wait—[*He walks forward and looks*
    casually to the right, then returns]
There must be some way up through the house
    and out
across the roof——
    ESDRAS. He's watching that. But come in—
and let me look.—
    MIO. I'll stay here, thanks. Once in
and I'm a rat in a deadfall—I'll stay here—
look for me if you don't mind.
    ESDRAS. Then watch for me—
I'll be on the roof——[*He goes in hurriedly*]
    MIO. [*looking up*] Now all you silent powers
that make the sleet and dark, and never yet
have spoken, give us a sign, let the throw be
    ours
this once, on this longest night, when the winter
    sets
his foot on the threshold leading up to spring
and enters with remembered cold—let fall
some mercy with the rain. We are two lovers
here in your night, and we wish to live.
    MIRIAMNE. Oh, Mio—
if you pray that way, nothing good will come!
You're bitter, Mio.
    MIO. How many floors has this building?
    MIRIAMNE. Five or six. It's not as high as the
    bridge.
    MIO. No, I thought not. How many pome-
    granate seeds
did you eat, Persephone?[6]
    MIRIAMNE. Oh, darling, darling,
if you die, don't die alone.
    MIO. I'm afraid I'm damned
to hell, and you're not damned at all. Good
    God,
how long he takes to climb!
    MIRIAMNE. The stairs are steep.
                        [*A slight pause*]

---

[6] daughter of Zeus and Demeter who had been
carried off by Hades, or Pluto, and made queen
of the lower world. Her mother moved Zeus to
allow the girl to return, but since she had eaten
pomegranate seeds in the lower world, she was
allowed to spend only half of each year on earth.

MIO. I'll follow him.

MIRIAMNE. He's there—at the window—now.

He waves you to go back, not to go in.
Mio, see, that path between the rocks—
they're not watching that—they're out at the river—
I can see them there—they can't watch both—
it leads to a street above.

MIO. I'll try it, then.
Kiss me. You'll hear. But if you never hear—
then I'm the king of hell, Persephone,
and I'll expect you.

MIRIAMNE. Oh, lover, keep safe.

MIO. Good-bye. [*He slips out quickly between the rocks. There is a quick machine gun rat-tat. The violin stops.* MIRIAMNE *runs toward the path.* MIO *comes back slowly, a hand pressed under his heart*]
It seems you were mistaken.

MIRIAMNE. Oh, God, forgive me! [*She puts an arm round him. He sinks to his knees*]
Where is it, Mio? Let me help you in! Quick, quick,
let me help you!

MIO. I hadn't thought to choose—this—ground—
but it will do. [*He slips down*]

MIRIAMNE. Oh, God, forgive me!

MIO. Yes?
The king of hell was not forgiven then,
Dis is his name, and Hades is his home—
and he goes alone—

MIRIAMNE. Why does he bleed so? Mio, if you go
I shall go with you.

MIO. It's better to stay alive.
I wanted to stay alive—because of you—
I leave you that—and what he said to me dying:
I love you, and will love you after I die.
Tomorrow, I shall still love you, as I've loved
the stars I'll never see, and all the mornings
that might have been yours and mine. Oh, Miriamne,
you taught me this.

MIRIAMNE. If only I'd never seen you
then you could live—

MIO. That's blasphemy—Oh, God,
there might have been some easier way of it.
You didn't want me to die, did you,
Miriamne—?

You didn't send me away——?

MIRIAMNE. Oh, never, never——

MIO. Forgive me—kiss me—I've got blood on your lips—
I'm sorry—it doesn't matter—I'm sorry——

ESDRAS *and* GARTH *come out*

MIRIAMNE. Mio—
I'd have gone to die myself—you must hear this, Mio,
I'd have died to help you—you must listen, sweet,
you must hear it—[*She rises*]
I can die, too, see! You! There!
You in the shadows!—You killed him to silence him! [*She walks toward the path*]
But I'm not silenced! All that he knew I know,
and I'll tell it tonight! Tonight—
tell it and scream it
through all the streets—that Trock's a murderer
and he hired you for this murder!
Your work's not done—
and you won't live long! Do you hear?
You're murderers, and I know who you are!
   [*The machine gun speaks again. She sinks to her knees.* GARTH *runs to her.*]

GARTH. You little fool! [*He tries to lift her*]

MIRIAMNE. Don't touch me! [*She crawls toward* MIO]
Look, Mio! They killed me, too. Oh, you can believe me
now, Mio. You can believe I wouldn't hurt you,
because I'm dying! Why doesn't he answer me?
Oh, now he'll never know! [*She sinks down, her hand over her mouth, choking.* GARTH *kneels beside her, then rises, shuddering. The* HOBO *comes out.* LUCIA *and* PINY *look out.*]

ESDRAS. It lacked only this.

GARTH. Yes. [ESDRAS *bends over* MIRIAMNE, *then rises slowly*]
Why was the bastard born? Why did he come here?

ESDRAS. Miriamne—Miriamne—yes, and Mio,
one breath shall call you now—forgive us both—
forgive the ancient evil of the earth
that brought you here——

GARTH. Why must she be a fool?

ESDRAS. Well, they were wiser than you and I. To die

when you are young and untouched, that's beg-
    gary
to a miser of years, but the devils locked in
    synod
shake and are daunted when men set their   5
    lives
at hazard for the heart's love, and lose. And
    these,
who were yet children, will weigh more than
    all
a city's elders when the experiment   10
is reckoned up in the end. Oh, Miriamne,
and Mio—Mio, my son—know this where you
    lie,
this is the glory of earth-born men and women,   15
not to cringe, never to yield, but standing,
take defeat implacable and defiant,
die unsubmitting. I wish that I'd died so,
long ago; before you're old you'll wish
that you had died as they have. On this star,   20

in this hard star-adventure, knowing not
what the fires mean to right and left, nor
    whether
a meaning was intended or presumed,
man can stand up, and look out blind, and say:
in all these turning lights I find no clue,
only a masterless night, and in my blood
no certain answer, yet is my mind my own,
yet is my heart a cry toward something dim
in distance, which is higher than I am
and makes me emporor of the endless dark
even in seeking! What odds and ends of life
men may live otherwise, let them live, and then
go out, as I shall go, and you. Our part
is only to bury them. Come, take her up.
They must not lie here.
[LUCIA *and* PINY *come near to help.* ESDRAS *and*
    GARTH *stoop to carry* MIRIAMNE.]
      [*Curtain*]

THE ADDING
*MACHINE**

ELMER RICE

Rice (1892–   ), *whose plays appear at regular intervals on Broadway, has been chosen
for last position in the drama section of this anthology. He thus represents a group of recognized playwrights (see I, 405), any one of whom*
might equally well stand here. After taking a
law degree, Rice tried playwriting, and his
first play, On Trial, *was successful. From early
work with little theater groups he progressed*

---

to a point at which he attracted wide attention (1923) with The Adding Machine, *a truly original American play and an early experiment in expressionism.* Street Scene *and other social plays followed.* Cousellor-at-Law *was a hit on stage and screen, and Rice has since continued popular. His 1930 novel,* Voyage to Purilia, *was a satire on the movies. From 1935 to 1937 he was a regional director for the Federal Theatre Project. With two dozen plays to his credit (some in collaboration) and a sheaf of articles on the theater, Rice is a typical first-rank playwright of the older modern generation.*

Characters

MR. ZERO

MRS. ZERO

DAISY DIANA DOROTHEA DEVORE

THE BOSS

MR. ONE

MRS. ONE

MR. TWO

MRS. TWO

MR. THREE

MRS. THREE

MR. FOUR

MRS. FOUR

MR. FIVE

MRS. FIVE

MR. SIX

MRS. SIX

POLICEMAN

JUDY O'GRADY

YOUNG MAN

SHRDLU

A HEAD

LIEUTENANT CHARLES

JOE

SCENE I. A bedroom

SCENE II. An office

SCENE III. A living room

SCENE IV. A place of justice

SCENE V. A graveyard

SCENE VI. A pleasant place

SCENE VII. Another office

SCENE I.

SCENE—*A bedroom. A small room containing an "instalment-plan" bed, dresser, and chairs. An ugly electric-light fixture over the* bed with a single glaring naked lamp. One small window with the shade drawn. The walls are papered with sheets of foolscap covered with columns of figures.

MR. ZERO *is lying in the bed, facing the audience, his head and shoulders visible. He is thin, sallow, under-sized, and partially bald.* MRS. ZERO *is standing before the dresser arranging her hair for the night. She is forty-five, sharp-featured, gray streaks in her hair. She is shapeless in her long-sleeved cotton nightgown. She is wearing her shoes, over which sag her ungartered stockings.*

MRS. ZERO. [*as she takes down her hair*] I'm gettin' sick o' them Westerns. All them cowboys ridin' around an' foolin' with them ropes. I don't care nothin' about that. I'm sick of 'em. 5 I don't see why they don't have more of them stories like "For Love's Sweet Sake." I like them sweet little love stories. They're nice an' wholesome. Mrs. Twelve was sayin' to me only yesterday, "Mrs. Zero," says she, "what I like 10 is one of them wholesome stories, with just a sweet, simple little love story." "You're right, Mrs. Twelve," I says. "That's what I like, too." They're showin' too many Westerns at the Rosebud. I'm gettin' sick of them. I think we'll 15 start goin' to the Peter Stuyvesant. They got a good bill there Wednesday night. There's a Chubby Delano comedy called "Sea-Sick." Mrs. Twelve was tellin' me about it. She says it's a scream. They're havin' a picnic in the country 20 and they sit Chubby next to an old maid with a great big mouth. So he gets sore an' when she ain't lookin' he goes and catches a frog and drops it in her clam chowder. An' when she goes to eat the chowder the frog jumps out of it 25 an' right into her mouth. Talk about laugh! Mrs. Twelve was tellin' me she laughed so she nearly passed out. He sure can pull some funny ones. An' they got that big Grace Darling feature, "A Mother's Tears." She's sweet. But I don't like 30 her clothes. There's no style to them. Mrs. Nine was tellin' me she read in *Pictureland* that she ain't livin' with her husband. He's her second, too. I don't know whether they're divorced or just separated. You wouldn't think it to see her 35 on the screen. She looks so sweet and innocent. Maybe it ain't true. You can't believe all you read. They say some Pittsburgh millionaire is crazy about her and that's why she ain't livin' with her husband. Mrs. Seven was tellin' me her brother-in-law has a friend that used to go to school with Grace Darling. He says her name ain't Grace Darling at all. Her right name is Elizabeth Dugan, he says, an' all them stories about her gettin' five thousand a week is the bunk, he says. She's sweet, though. Mrs. Eight was tellin' me that "A Mother's Tears" is the best picture she ever made. "Don't miss it, Mrs. Zero," she says. "It's sweet," she says. "Just sweet and wholesome. Cry!" she says, "I nearly cried my eyes out." There's one part in it where this big bum of an Englishman—he's a married man, too—an' she's this little simple country girl. An' she nearly falls for him, too. But she's sittin' out in the garden one day, and she looks up and there's her mother lookin' at her, right out of the clouds. So that night she locks the door of her room. An' sure enough, when everybody's in bed, along comes this big bum of an Englishman an' when she won't let him in what does he do but go an' kick open the door. "Don't miss it, Mrs. Zero," Mrs. Eight was tellin' me. It's at the Peter Stuyvesant Wednesday night, so don't be tellin' me you want to go to the Rosebud. The Eights seen it downtown at the Strand. They go downtown all the time. Just like us—nit! I guess by the time it gets to the Peter Stuyvesant all that part about kickin' in the door will be cut out. Just like they cut out that big cabaret scene in "The Price of Virtue." They sure are pullin' some rough stuff in the pictures nowadays. "It's no place for a young girl," I was tellin' Mrs. Eleven, only the other day. An' by the time they get uptown half of it is cut out. But you wouldn't go downtown —not if wild horses was to drag you. You can wait till they come uptown! Well, I don't want to wait, see? I want to see 'em when everybody else is seein' them an' not a month later. Now don't go tellin' me you ain't got the price. You could dig up the price all right, all right, if you wanted to. I notice you always got the price to go to the ball game. But when it comes to me havin' a good time then it's always: "I ain't got the price, I gotta start savin'." A fat lot you'll ever save! I got all I can do now makin' both ends meet an' you talkin' about savin'. [*She seats herself on a chair and begins removing her shoes and stockings*] An' don't go pullin' that stuff about bein' tired. "I been workin' hard all day. Twice a day in the subway's enough for me." Tired! Where do you get that tired stuff, anyhow? What about me? Where do I come in? Scrubbin' floors an' cookin' your meals an' washin' your dirty clothes. An' you sittin' on a chair all day, just addin' figgers an' waitin' for five-thirty. There's no five-thirty for me. I don't wait for no whistle. I don't get no vacations neither. And what's more I don't get no pay envelope every Saturday night neither. I'd like to know where you'd be without me. An' what have I got to show for it?—slavin' my life away to give you a home. What's in it for me, I'd like to know? But it's my own fault, I guess. I was a fool for marryin' you. If I'd 'a' had any sense, I'd 'a' known what you were from the start. I wish I had it to do over again, I hope to tell you. You was goin' to do wonders, you was! You wasn't goin' to be a bookkeeper long—oh, no, not you. Wait till you got started—you was goin' to show 'em. There wasn't no job in the store that was too big for you. Well, I've been waitin'—waitin' for you to get started—see? It's been a good long wait, too. Twenty-five years! An' I ain't seen nothin' happen. Twenty-five years in the same job. Twenty-five years tomorrow! You're proud of it, ain't you? Twenty-five years in the same job an' never missed a day! That's somethin' to be proud of, ain't it? Sittin' for twenty-five years on the same chair, addin' up figures. What about bein' store-manager? I guess you forgot about that, didn't you? An' me at home here lookin' at the same four walls an' workin' my fingers to the bone to make both ends meet. Seven years since you got a raise! An' if you don't get one tomorrow, I'll bet a nickel you won't have the guts to go an' ask for one. I didn't pick much when I picked you, I'll tell the world. You ain't much to be proud of. [*She rises, goes to the window, and raises the shade. A few lighted windows are visible on the other side of the closed court. Looking out for a moment*] She ain't walkin' around tonight, you can bet your sweet life on that. An' she won't be walkin' around any more nights, neither. Not in this house, anyhow. [*She turns away from the window*] The dirty bum! The idea of her comin' to live in a house with respectable people. They should 'a' gave her six years, not six months. If I was the judge I'd of gave her life. A bum like that. [*She approaches the bed and stands there a moment*] I guess you're sorry she's gone. I guess you'd like to sit home every night an' watch her goin's-on. You're somethin' to be proud of, you are! [*She stands on the bed and turns out the light. . . . A thin stream of moonlight filters in from the court. The two figures are dimly visible.* MRS. ZERO *gets into bed*] You'd better not start nothin' with women, if you know what's good for you. I've put up with a lot, but I won't put up with that. I've been slavin' away for twenty-five years, makin' a home for you an' nothin' to show for it. If you was any kind of a man you'd have a decent job by now an' I'd be gettin' some comfort out of life—instead of bein' just a slave, washin' pots an' standin' over the hot stove. I've stood it for twenty-five years an' I guess I'll have to stand it twenty-five more. But don't you go startin' nothin' with women——[*She goes on talking as the curtain falls.*]

SCENE II.

SCENE—*An office in a department store. Wood and glass partitions. In the middle of the room, two tall desks back to back. At one desk on a high stool is* ZERO. *Opposite him at the other desk, also on a high stool, is* DAISY DIANA DOROTHEA DEVORE, *a plain, middle-aged woman. Both wear green eye shades and paper sleeve protectors. A pendent electric lamp throws light upon both desks.* DAISY *reads aloud figures from a pile of slips which lie before her. As she reads the figures,* ZERO *enters them upon a large square sheet of ruled paper which lies before him.*

DAISY. [*reading aloud*] Three ninety-eight. Forty-two cents. A dollar fifty. A dollar fifty. A dollar twenty-five. Two dollars. Thirty-nine cents. Twenty-seven fifty.

ZERO. [*petulantly*] Speed it up a little, cancha?

DAISY. What's the rush? Tomorrer's another day.

ZERO. Aw, you make me sick.

DAISY. An' you make me sicker.

ZERO. Go on. Go on. We're losin' time.

DAISY. Then quit bein' so bossy. [*She reads*] Three dollars. Two sixty-nine. Eighty-one fifty. Forty dollars. Eight seventy-five. Who do you think you are, anyhow?

ZERO. Never mind who I think I am. You tend to your work.

DAISY. Aw, don't be givin' me so many orders. Sixty cents. Twenty-four cents. Seventy-five cents. A dollar fifty. Two fifty. One fifty. One fifty. Two fifty. I don't have to take it from you and what's more I won't.

ZERO. Aw, quit talkin'.

DAISY. I'll talk all I want. Three dollars. Fifty cents. Fifty cents. Seven dollars. Fifty cents. Two fifty. Three fifty. Fifty cents. One fifty. Fifty cents. [*She goes on, bending over the slips and transferring them from one pile to another.* ZERO *bends over his desk, busily entering the figures*]

ZERO. [*without looking up*] You make me sick. Always shootin' off your face about somethin'. Talk, talk, talk. Just like all the other women. Women make me sick.

DAISY. [*busily fingering the slips*] Who do you think you are, anyhow? Bossin' me around. I don't have to take it from you, and what's more I won't. [*They both attend closely to their work, neither looking up*]

ZERO. Women make me sick. They're all alike. The judge gave her six months. I wonder what they do in the workhouse. Peel potatoes. I'll bet she's sore at me. Maybe she'll try to kill me when she gets out. I better be careful. Hello. Girl Slays Betrayer. Jealous Wife Slays Rival. You can't tell what a woman's liable to do. I better be careful.

DAISY. I'm gettin' sick of it. Always pickin' on me about somethin'. Never a decent word out of you. Not even the time o' day.

ZERO. I guess she wouldn't have the nerve at that. Maybe she don't even know it's me. They didn't even put my name in the paper, the big bums. Maybe she's been in the workhouse before. A bum like that. She didn't have nothin' on that one time—nothin' but a shirt. [*He glances up quickly, then bends over again*] You make me sick. I'm sick of lookin' at your face.

DAISY. Gee, ain't that whistle ever goin' to blow? You didn't used to be like that. Not even good mornin' or good evenin'. I ain't done nothin' to you. It's the young girls. Goin' around without corsets.

ZERO. Your face is gettin' all yeller. Why don't you put some paint on it? She was puttin' on paint that time. On her cheeks and on her lips. And that blue stuff on her eyes. Just sittin' there in a shimmy puttin' on the paint. An' walkin' around the room with her legs all bare.

DAISY. I wish I was dead.

ZERO. I was a goddam fool to let the wife get on to me. She oughta get six months at that. The dirty bum. Livin' in a house with respectable people. She'd be livin' there yet, if the wife hadn't o' got on to me. Damn her!

DAISY. I wish I was dead.

ZERO. Maybe another one'll move in. Gee, that would be great. But the wife's got her eye on me now.

DAISY. I'm scared to do it, though.

ZERO. You oughta move into that room. It's cheaper than where you're livin' now. I better tell you about it. I don't mean to be always pickin' on you.

DAISY. Gas. The smell of it makes me sick. [ZERO *looks up and clears his throat*] [*Looking up, startled*] Whadja say?

ZERO. I didn't say nothin'.

DAISY. I thought you did.

ZERO. You thought wrong.

[*They bend over their work again*]

DAISY. A dollar sixty. A dollar fifty. Two ninety. One sixty-two.

ZERO. Why the hell should I tell you? Fat chance of you forgettin' to pull down the shade!

DAISY. If I asked for carbolic they might get on to me.

ZERO. Your hair's gettin' gray. You don't wear them shirt waists any more with the low collars. When you'd bend down to pick somethin' up——

DAISY. I wish I knew what to ask for. Girl Takes Mercury After All-Night Party. Woman In Ten-Story Death Leap.

ZERO. I wonder where'll she go when she gets out. Gee, I'd like to make a date with her. Why didn't I go over there the night my wife went to Brooklyn? She never woulda found out.

DAISY. I seen Pauline Frederick[1] do it once. Where could I get a pistol though?

ZERO. I guess I didn't have the nerve.

DAISY. I'll bet you'd be sorry then that you been so mean to me. How do I know, though? Maybe you wouldn't.

ZERO. Nerve! I got as much nerve as anybody. I'm on the level, that's all. I'm a married man and I'm on the level.

DAISY. Anyhow, why ain't I got a right to

---

[1] an early movie queen.

live? I'm as good as anybody else. I'm too refined, I guess. That's the whole trouble.

ZERO. The time the wife had pneumonia I thought she was goin' to pass out. But she didn't. The doctor's bill was eighty-seven dollars. [*Looking up*] Hey, wait a minute! Didn't you say eighty-seven dollars?

DAISY. [*looking up*] What?

ZERO. Was the last you said eighty-seven dollars?

DAISY. [*consulting the slip*] Forty-two fifty.

ZERO. Well, I made a mistake. Wait a minute. [*He busies himself with an eraser*] All right. Shoot.

DAISY. Six dollars. Three fifteen. Two twenty-five. Sixty-five cents. A dollar twenty. You talk to me as if I was dirt.

ZERO. I wonder if I could kill the wife without anybody findin' out. In bed some night. With a pillow.

DAISY. I used to think you was stuck on me.

ZERO. I'd get found out, though. They always have ways.

DAISY. We used to be so nice and friendly together when I first came here. You used to talk to me then.

ZERO. Maybe she'll die soon. I noticed she was coughin' this mornin'.

DAISY. You used to tell me all kinds o' things. You were goin' to show them all. Just the same, you're still sittin' here.

ZERO. Then I could do what I damn please. Oh, boy!

DAISY. Maybe it ain't all your fault neither. Maybe if you'd had the right kind of wife—somebody with a lot of common-sense, somebody refined—me!

ZERO. At that, I guess I'd get tired of bummin' around. A feller wants some place to hang his hat.

DAISY. I wish she would die.

ZERO. And when you start goin' with women you're liable to get into trouble. And lose your job maybe.

DAISY. Maybe you'd marry me.

ZERO. Gee, I wish I'd gone over there that night.

DAISY. Then I could quit workin'.

ZERO. Lots o' women would be glad to get me.

DAISY. You could look a long time before you'd find a sensible, refined girl like me.

ZERO. Yes, sir, they could look a long time before they'd find a steady meal-ticket like me.

DAISY. I guess I'd be too old to have any kids. They say it ain't safe after thirty-five.

ZERO. Maybe I'd marry you. You might be all right, at that.

DAISY. I wonder—if you don't want kids—whether—if there's any way——

ZERO. [looking up] Hey! Hey! Can't you slow up? What do you think I am—a machine?

DAISY. [looking up] Say, what do you want, anyhow? First it's too slow an' then it's too fast. I guess you don't know what you want.

ZERO. Well, never mind about that. Just you slow up.

DAISY. I'm gettin' sick o' this. I'm goin' to ask to be transferred.

ZERO. Go ahead. You can't make me mad.

DAISY. Aw, keep quiet. [She reads] Two forty-five. A dollar twenty. A dollar fifty. Ninety cents. Sixty-three cents.

ZERO. Marry you! I guess not! You'd be as bad as the one I got.

DAISY. You wouldn't care if I did ask. I got a good mind to ask.

ZERO. I was a fool to get married.

DAISY. Then I'd never see you at all.

ZERO. What chance has a guy got with a woman tied around his neck?

DAISY. That time at the store picnic—the year your wife couldn't come—you were nice to me then.

ZERO. Twenty-five years holdin' down the same job!

DAISY. We were together all day—just sittin' around under the trees.

ZERO. I wonder if the boss remembers about it bein' twenty-five years.

DAISY. And comin' home that night—you sat next to me in the big delivery wagon.

ZERO. I got a hunch there's a big raise comin' to me.

DAISY. I wonder what it feels like to be really kissed. Men—dirty pigs! They want the bold ones.

ZERO. If he don't come across I'm goin' right up to the front office and tell him where he gets off.

DAISY. I wish I was dead.

ZERO. "Boss," I'll say, "I want to have a talk with you." "Sure," he'll say, "sit down. Have a Corona Corona." "No," I'll say, "I don't smoke."

"How's that?" he'll say. "Well, boss," I'll say, "it's this way. Every time I feel like smokin' I just take a nickel and put it in the old sock. A penny saved is a penny earned, that's the way I look at it." "Damn sensible," he'll say. "You got a wise head on you, Zero."

DAISY. I can't stand the smell of gas. It makes me sick. You coulda kissed me if you wanted to.

ZERO. "Boss," I'll say, "I ain't quite satisfied. I been on the job twenty-five years now and if I'm gonna stay I gotta see a future ahead of me." "Zero," he'll say, "I'm glad you came in. I've had my eye on you, Zero! Nothin' gets by me." "Oh, I know that, boss," I'll say. That'll hand him a good laugh, that will. "You're a valuable man, Zero," he'll say, "and I want you right up here with me in the front office. You're done addin' figgers. Monday mornin' you move up here."

DAISY. Them kisses in the movies—them long ones—right on the mouth——

ZERO. I'll keep a-goin' right on up after that. I'll show some of them birds where they get off.

DAISY. That one the other night—"The Devil's Alibi"—he put his arms around her—and her head fell back and her eyes closed—like she was in a daze.

ZERO. Just give me about two years and I'll show them birds where they get off.

DAISY. I guess that's what it's like—a kinda daze—when I see them like that, I just seem to forget everything.

ZERO. Then me for a place in Jersey. And maybe a little Buick. No tin Lizzie for mine. Wait till I get started—I'll show 'em.

DAISY. I can see it now when I kinda half-close my eyes. The way her head fell back. And his mouth pressed right up against hers. Oh, Gawd! it must be grand! [There is a sudden shrill blast from a steam whistle]

DAISY AND ZERO. [together] The whistle! [With great agility they get off their stools, remove their eye shades and sleeve protectors and put them on the desks. Then each produces from behind the desk a hat—ZERO, a dusty derby, DAISY, a frowsy straw. . . . DAISY puts on her hat and turns towards ZERO as though she were about to speak to him. But he is busy cleaning his pen and pays no attention to her. She sighs and goes towards the door at the left]

ZERO. [looking up] G'night, Miss Devore. [But she does not hear him and exits. ZERO takes up his hat and goes left. The door at the right opens and the BOSS enters—middle-aged, stoutish, bald, well dressed]

THE BOSS. [calling] Oh—er—Mister—er—— [ZERO turns in surprise, sees who it is and trembles nervously]

ZERO. [obsequiously] Yes, sir. Do you want me, sir?

BOSS. Yes. Just come here a moment, will you?

ZERO. Yes, sir. Right away, sir. [He fumbles his hat, picks it up, stumbles, recovers himself, and approaches the BOSS, every fiber quivering]

BOSS. Mister—er—er——

ZERO. Zero.

BOSS. Yes, Mr. Zero. I wanted to have a little talk with you.

ZERO. [with a nervous grin] Yes sir, I been kinda expectin' it.

BOSS. [staring at him] Oh, have you?

ZERO. Yes, sir.

BOSS. How long have you been with us, Mister—er—Mister——

ZERO. Zero.

BOSS. Yes, Mister Zero.

ZERO. Twenty-five years today.

BOSS. Twenty-five years! That's a long time.

ZERO. Never missed a day.

BOSS. And you've been doing the same work all the time?

ZERO. Yes, sir. Right here at this desk.

BOSS. Then, in that case, a change probably won't be unwelcome to you.

ZERO. No, sir, it won't. And that's the truth.

BOSS. We've been planning a change in this department for some time.

ZERO. I kinda thought you had your eye on me.

BOSS. You were right. The fact is that my efficiency experts have recommended the installation of adding machines.

ZERO. [staring at him] Addin' machines?

BOSS. Yes, you've probably seen them. A mechanical device that adds automatically.

ZERO. Sure. I've seen them. Keys—and a handle that you pull. [He goes through the motions in the air]

BOSS. That's it. They do the work in half the time and a high-school girl can operate them.

Now, of course, I'm sorry to lose an old and faithful employee——

ZERO. Excuse me, but would you mind sayin' that again?

BOSS. I say I'm sorry to lose an employee who's been with me for so many years—— [Soft music is heard—the sound of the mechanical player of a distant merry-go-round. The part of the floor upon which the desk and stools are standing begins to revolve very slowly] But, of course, in an organization like this, efficiency must be the first consideration— [The music becomes gradually louder and the revolutions more rapid] You will draw your salary for the full month. And I'll direct my secretary to give you a letter of recommendation——

ZERO. Wait a minute, boss. Let me get this right. You mean I'm canned?

BOSS. [barely making himself heard above the increasing volume of sound] I'm sorry—no other alternative—greatly regret—old employee — efficiency — economy — business — business—BUSINESS——[His voice is drowned by the music. The platform is revolving rapidly now. ZERO and the BOSS face each other. They are entirely motionless save for the BOSS's jaws, which open and close incessantly. But the words are inaudible. The music swells and swells. To it is added every off-stage effect of the theatre: the wind, the waves, the galloping horses, the locomotive whistle, the sleigh bells, the automobile siren, the glass-crash. New Year's Eve, Election Night, Armistice Day, and the Mardi-Gras. The noise is deafening, maddening, unendurable. Suddenly it culminates in a terrific peal of thunder. For an instant there is a flash of red and then everything is plunged into blackness.]

[Curtain]

SCENE III.

SCENE—The ZERO dining room. Entrance door at right. Doors to kitchen and bedroom at left. The walls, as in the first scene, are paper with foolscap sheets covered with columns of figures. In the middle of the room, upstage, a table set for two. Along each side wall seven chairs are ranged in symmetrical rows.

At the rise of the curtain MRS. ZERO is seen seated at the table looking alternately at the en-

trance door and a clock on the wall. She wears a bungalow apron over her best dress.

After a few moments, the entrance door opens and ZERO *enters. He hangs his hat on a rack behind the door and coming over to the table seats himself at the vacant place. His movements throughout are quiet and abstracted.*

MRS. ZERO. [*breaking the silence*] Well, it was nice of you to come home. You're only an hour late and that ain't very much. The supper don't get very cold in an hour. An' of course the part about our havin' a lot of company tonight don't matter. [*They begin to eat*] Ain't you even got sense enough to come home on time? Didn't I tell you we're goin' to have a lot o' company tonight? Didn't you know the Ones are comin'? An' the Twos? An' the Threes? An' the Fours? An' the Fives? And the Sixes? Didn't I tell you to be home on time? I might as well talk to a stone wall. [*They eat for a few moments in silence*] I guess you musta had some important business to attend to. Like watchin' the score-board. Or was two kids havin' a fight an' you was the referee? You sure do have a lot of business to attend to. It's a wonder you have time to come home at all. You gotta tough life, you have. Walk in, hang up your hat, an' put on the nose-bag. An' me in the hot kitchen all day, cookin' your supper an' waitin' for you to get good an' ready to come home! [*Again they eat in silence*] Maybe the boss kept you late tonight. Tellin' you what a big noise you are and how the store couldn't 'a' got along if you hadn't been pushin' a pen for twenty-five years. Where's the gold medal he pinned on you? Did some blind old lady take it away from you or did you leave it on the seat of the boss's limousine when he brought you home? [*Again a few moments of silence*] I'll bet he gave you a big raise, didn't he? Promoted you from the third floor to the fourth, maybe. Raise? A fat chance you got o' gettin' a raise. All they gotta do is put an ad in the paper. There's ten thousand like you layin' around the streets. You'll be holdin' down the same job at the end of another twenty-five years —if you ain't forgot how to add by that time. [*A noise is heard off-stage, a sharp clicking such as is made by the operation of the keys and levers of an adding machine.* ZERO *raises his*

head for a moment, but lowers it almost instantly] There's the door-bell. The company's here already. And we ain't hardly finished supper. [*She rises*] But I'm goin' to clear off the table whether you're finished or not. If you want your supper, you got a right to be home on time. Not standin' around lookin' at score-boards. [*As she piles up the dishes,* ZERO *rises and goes towards the entrance door*] Wait a minute! Don't open the door yet. Do you want the company to see all the mess? An' go an' put on a clean collar. You got red ink all over it. [ZERO *goes towards bedroom door*] I should think after pushin' a pen for twenty-five years, you'd learn how to do it without gettin' ink on your collar. [ZERO *exits to bedroom.* MRS. ZERO *takes dishes to kitchen, talking as she goes*] I guess I can stay up all night now washin' dishes. You should worry! That's what a man's got a wife for, ain't it? Don't he buy her her clothes an' let her eat with him at the same table? An' all she's gotta do is cook the meals an' do the washin' an' scrub the floor, an' wash the dishes, when the company goes. But, believe me, you're goin' to sling a mean dish-towel when the company goes tonight! [*While she is talking* ZERO *enters from bedroom. He wears a clean collar and is cramming the soiled one furtively into his pocket.* MRS. ZERO *enters from kitchen. She has removed her apron and carries a table cover which she spreads hastily over the table. The clicking noise is heard again*] There's the bell again. Open the door, cancha? [ZERO *goes to the entrance door and opens it. Six men and six women file into the room in a double column. The men are all shapes and sizes, but their dress is identical with that of* ZERO *in every detail. Each, however, wears a wig of a different color. The women are all dressed alike, too, except that the dress of each is of a different color*] [*Taking the first woman's hand*] How de do, Mrs. One.

MRS. ONE. How de do, Mrs. Zero. [MRS. ZERO *repeats this formula with each woman in turn.* ZERO *does the same with the men except that he is silent throughout. The files now separate, each man taking a chair from the right wall and each woman one from the left wall. Each sex forms a circle with the chairs very close together. The men—all except* ZERO—*smoke cigars. The women munch chocolates*]

SIX. Some rain we're havin'.

FIVE. Never saw the like of it.

FOUR. Worst in fourteen years, paper says.

THREE. Y' can't always go by the papers.

TWO. No, that's right, too.

ONE. We're liable to forget from year to year.

SIX. Yeh, come t' think, last year was pretty bad, too.

FIVE. An' how about two years ago?

FOUR. Still this year's pretty bad.

THREE. Yeh, no gettin' away from that.

TWO. Might be a whole lot worse.

ONE. Yeh, it's all the way you look at it. Some rain, though.

MRS. SIX. I like them little organdie dresses.

MRS. FIVE. Yeh, with a little lace trimmin' on the sleeves.

MRS. FOUR. Well, I like 'em plain myself.

MRS. THREE. Yeh, what I always say is the plainer the more refined.

MRS. TWO. Well, I don't think a little lace does any harm.

MRS. ONE. No, it kinda dresses it up.

MRS. ZERO. Well, I always say it's all a matter of taste.

MRS. SIX. I saw you at the Rosebud Movie Thursday night, Mr. One.

ONE. Pretty punk show, I'll say.

TWO. They're gettin' worse all the time.

MRS. SIX. But who was the charming lady, Mr. One?

ONE. Now don't you go makin' trouble for me. That was my sister.

MRS. FIVE. Oho! That's what they all say.

MRS. FOUR. Never mind! I'll bet Mrs. One knows what's what, all right.

MRS. ONE. Oh, well, he can do what he likes —'slong as he behaves himself.

THREE. You're in luck at that, One. Fat chance I got of gettin' away from the frau even with my sister.

MRS. THREE. You oughta be glad you got a good wife to look after you.

THE OTHER WOMEN. [*in unison*] That's right, Mrs. Three.

FIVE. I guess I know who wears the pants in your house, Three.

MRS. ZERO. Never mind. I saw them holdin' hands at the movie the other night.

THREE. She musta been tryin' to get some money away from me.

MRS. THREE. Swell chance anybody'd have

of gettin' any money away from you. [*General laughter*]

FOUR. They sure are a loving couple.

MRS. TWO. Well, I think we oughta change the subject.

MRS. ONE. Yes, let's change the subject.

SIX. [*sotto voce*] Did you hear the one about the travellin' salesman?

FIVE. It seems this guy was in a sleeper.

FOUR. Goin' from Albany to San Diego.

THREE. And in the next berth was an old maid.

TWO. With a wooden leg.

ONE. Well, along about midnight——[*They all put their heads together and whisper*]

MRS. SIX. [*sotto voce*] Did you hear about the Sevens?

MRS. FIVE. They're gettin' a divorce.

MRS. FOUR. It's the second time for him.

MRS. THREE. They're two of a kind, if you ask me.

MRS. TWO. One's as bad as the other.

MRS. ONE. Worse.

MRS. ZERO. They say that she——

[*They all put their heads together and whisper*]

SIX. I think this woman suffrage is the bunk.

FIVE. It sure is! Politics is a man's business.

FOUR. Woman's place is in the home.

THREE. That's it! Lookin' after the kids, 'stead of hangin' around the streets.

TWO. You hit the nail on the head that time.

ONE. The trouble is they don't know what they want.

MRS. SIX. Men sure get me tired.

MRS. FIVE. They sure are a lazy lot.

MRS. FOUR. And dirty.

MRS. THREE. Always grumblin' about somethin'.

MRS. TWO. When they're not lyin'!

MRS. ONE. Or messin' up the house.

MRS. ZERO. Well, believe me, I tell mine where he gets off.

SIX. Business conditions are sure bad.

FIVE. Never been worse.

FOUR. I don't know what we're comin' to.

THREE. I look for a big smash-up in about three months.

TWO. Wouldn't surprise me a bit.

ONE. We're sure headin' for trouble.

MRS. SIX. My aunt has gall-stones.

MRS. FIVE. My husband has bunions.

MRS. FOUR. My sister expects next month.

MRS. THREE. My cousin's husband has erysipelas.

MRS. TWO. My niece has St. Vitus's dance.

MRS. ONE. My boy has fits.

MRS. ZERO. I never felt better in my life. Knock wood!

SIX. Too damn much agitation, that's at the bottom of it.

FIVE. That's it! Too damn many strikes.

FOUR. Foreign agitators, that's what it is.

THREE. They ought to be run outa the country.

TWO. What the hell do they want, anyhow?

ONE. They don't know what they want, if you ask me.

SIX. America for the Americans is what I say!

ALL. [in unison] That's it! Damn foreigners! Damn dagoes! Damn Catholics! Damn sheenies! Damn niggers! Jail 'em! shoot 'em! hang 'em! lynch 'em! burn 'em! [They all rise] [Sing in unison]

> My country 'tis of thee,
> Sweet land of liberty!

MRS. FOUR. Why so pensive, Mr. Zero?

ZERO. [speaking for the first time] I'm thinkin'.

MRS. FOUR. Well, be careful not to sprain your mind. [Laughter]

MRS. ZERO. Look at the poor men all by themselves. We ain't very sociable.

ONE. Looks like we're neglectin' the ladies. [The women cross the room and join the men, all chattering loudly. The door-bell rings]

MRS. FOUR. Sh! The door-bell! [The volume of sound slowly diminishes. Again the door-bell]

ZERO. [quietly] I'll go. It's for me. [They watch curiously as ZERO goes to the door and opens it, admitting a policeman. There is a murmur of surprise and excitement]

POLICEMAN. I'm lookin' for Mr. Zero. [They all point to ZERO]

ZERO. I've been expectin' you.

POLICEMAN. Come along!

ZERO. Just a minute. [He puts his hand in his pocket]

POLICEMAN. What's he tryin' to pull? [He draws a revolver] I got you covered.

ZERO. Sure, that's all right. I just want to give you somethin'. [He takes the collar from his pocket and gives it to the policeman]

POLICEMAN. [suspiciously] What's that?

ZERO. The collar I wore.

POLICEMAN. What do I want it for?

ZERO. It's got blood-stains on it.

POLICEMAN. [pocketing it] All right, come along!

ZERO. [turning to MRS. ZERO] I gotta go with him. You'll have to dry the dishes yourself.

MRS. ZERO. [rushing forward] What are they takin' you for?

ZERO. [calmly] I killed the boss this afternoon.

[Quick curtain as the POLICEMAN takes him off.]

SCENE IV.

SCENE—A court of justice. Three bare white walls without door or windows except for a single door in the right wall. At the right is a jury-box in which are seated MESSRS. ONE, TWO, THREE, FOUR, FIVE, and SIX, and their respective wives. On either side of the jury-box stands a uniformed OFFICER. Opposite the jury-box is a long, bare oak table piled high with law books. Behind the books ZERO is seated, his face buried in his hands. There is no other furniture in the room. A moment after the rise of the curtain, one of the officers rises and, going around the table, taps ZERO on the shoulder. ZERO rises and accompanies the OFFICER. The OFFICER escorts him to the great empty space in the middle of the courtroom, facing the jury. He motions to ZERO to stop, then points to the jury and resumes his place beside the jury-box. ZERO stands there looking at the jury, bewildered and half afraid. The JURORS give no sign of having seen him. Throughout they sit with folded arms, staring stolidly before them.

ZERO. [beginning to speak; haltingly] Sure I killed him. I ain't sayin' I didn't, am I? Sure I killed him. Them lawyers! They give me a good stiff pain, that's what they give me. Half the time I don't know what the hell they're talkin' about. Objection sustained. Objection overruled. What's the big idea, anyhow? You ain't heard me do any objectin', have you? Sure not! What's the idea of objectin'? You got a right to know. What I say is if one bird kills another bird, why you got a right to call him for it. That's what I say. I know all about that. I been on the jury, too. Them lawyers! Don't let 'em fill you full of bunk. All that bull about it bein' red ink on the bill-file. Red ink nothin'! It was blood, see? I want you to get that right. I killed him, see? Right through the heart with the bill-file, see? I want you to get that right—all of you. One, two, three, four, five, six, seven, eight, nine, ten, eleven, twelve. Twelve of you. Six and six. That makes twelve. I figgered it up often enough. Six and six makes twelve. And five is seventeen. And eight is twenty-five. And three is twenty-eight. Eight and carry two. Aw, cut it out! Them damn figgers! I can't forget 'em. Twenty-five years, see? Eight hours a day, exceptin' Sundays. And July and August half-day Saturday. One week's vacation with pay. And another week without pay if you want it. Who the hell wants it? Layin' around the house listenin' to the wife tellin' you where you get off. Nix! An' legal holidays. I nearly forgot them. New Year's, Washington's Birthday, Decoration Day, Fourth o' July, Labor Day, Election Day, Thanksgivin', Christmas. Good Friday if you want it. An' if you're a Jew, Young Kipper an' the other one—I forget what they call it. The dirty sheenies—always gettin' two to the other bird's one. An' when a holiday comes on Sunday, you get Monday off. So that's fair enough. But when the Fourth o' July comes on Saturday, why you're out of luck on account of Saturday bein' a half-day anyhow. Get me? Twenty-five years—I'll tell you somethin' funny. Decoration Day an' the Fourth o' July are always on the same day o' the week. Twenty-five years. Never missed a day, and never more'n five minutes late. Look at my time card if you don't believe me. Eight twenty-seven, eight thirty, eight twenty-nine, eight twenty-seven, eight thirty-two. Eight an' thirty-two's forty an'—Goddam them figgers! I can't forget 'em. They're funny things, them figgers. They look like people sometimes. The eights, see? Two dots for the eyes and a dot for the nose. An' a line. That's the mouth, see? An' there's others remind you of other things—but I can't talk about them, on account of there bein' ladies here. Sure I killed him. Why didn't he shut up? If he'd only shut up! Instead o' talkin' an' talkin' about how sorry he was an' what a good guy I was an' this an' that. I felt like sayin' to him: "For Christ's sake, shut up!" But I didn't have the nerve, see? I didn't have

the nerve to say that to the boss. An' he went on talkin', sayin' how sorry he was, see? He was standin' right close to me. An' his coat only had two buttons on it. Two an' two makes four an' —aw, can it! An' there was the bill-file on the desk. Right where I could touch it. It ain't right to kill a guy. I know that. When I read all about him in the paper an' about his three kids I felt like a cheap skate, I tell you. They had the kids' pictures in the paper, right next to mine. An' his wife, too. Gee, it must be swell to have a wife like that. Some guys sure is lucky. An' he left fifty thousand dollars just for a rest-room for the girls in the store. He was a good guy, at that. Fifty thousand. That's more'n twice as much as I'd have if I saved every nickel I ever made. Let's see. Twenty-five an' twenty-five an' twenty-five an'—aw, cut it out! An' the ads had a big, black border around 'em; an' all it said was that the store would be closed for three days on account of the boss bein' dead. That nearly handed me a laugh, that did. All them floor-walkers an' buyers an' high-muck-a-mucks havin' me to thank for gettin' three days off. I hadn't oughta killed him. I ain't sayin' nothin' about that. But I thought he was goin' to give me a raise, see? On account of bein' there twenty-five years. He never talked to me before, see? Except one mornin' we happened to come in the store together and I held the door open for him and he said "Thanks." Just like that, see? "Thanks!" That was the only time he ever talked to me. An' when I see him comin' up to my desk, I didn't know where I got off. A big guy like that comin' up to my desk. I felt like I was chokin' like and all of a sudden I got a kind o' bad taste in my mouth like when you get up in the mornin'. I didn't have no right to kill him. The district attorney is right about that. He read the law to you right out o' the book. Killin' a bird—that's wrong. But there was that girl, see? Six months they gave her. It was a dirty trick tellin' the cops on her like that. I shouldn't 'a' done that. But what was I gonna do? The wife wouldn't let up on me. I hadda do it. She used to walk around the room, just in her undershirt, see? Nothin' else on. Just her undershirt. An' they gave her six months. That's the last I'll ever see of her. Them birds—how do they get away with it? Just grabbin' women, the way you see 'em do in the pictures. I've seen lots I'd like to grab like that, but I ain't got the nerve—in the subway an' on the street an' in the store buyin' things. Pretty soft for them shoe-salesmen, I'll say, lookin' at women's legs all day. Them lawyers! They give me a pain, I tell you—a pain! Sayin' the same thing over an' over again. I never said I didn't kill him. But that ain't the same as bein' a regular murderer. What good did it do me to kill him? I didn't make nothin' out of it. Answer yes or no! Yes or no, me elbow! There's some things you can't answer yes or no. Give me the once-over, you guys. Do I look like a murderer? Do I? I never did no harm to nobody. Ask the wife. She'll tell you. Ask anybody. I never got into trouble. You wouldn't count that one time at the Polo Grounds. That was just fun like. Everybody was yellin', "Kill the umpire! Kill the umpire!" An' before I knew what I was doin' I fired the pop bottle. It was on account of everybody yellin' like that. Just in fun like, see? The yeller dog! Callin' that one a strike—a mile away from the plate. Anyhow, the bottle didn't hit him. An' when I seen the cop comin' up the aisle, I beat it. That didn't hurt nobody. It was just in fun like, see? An' that time in the subway. I was readin' about a lynchin', see? Down in Georgia. They took the nigger an' they tied him to a tree. An' they poured kerosene on him and lit a big fire under him. The dirty nigger! Boy, I'd of liked to been there, with a gat in each hand, pumpin' him full of lead. I was readin' about it in the subway, see? Right at Times Square where the big crowd gets on. An' all of a sudden this big nigger steps right on my foot. It was lucky for him I didn't have a gun on me. I'd of killed him sure, I guess. I guess he couldn't help it all right on account of the crowd, but a nigger's got no right to step on a white man's foot. I told him where he got off all right. The dirty nigger. But that didn't hurt nobody, either. I'm a pretty steady guy, you gotta admit that. Twenty-five years in one job an' I never missed a day. Fifty-two weeks in a year. Fifty-two an' fifty-two an' fifty-two an'— They didn't have t' look for me, did they? I didn't try to run away, did I? Where was I goin' to run to! I wasn't thinkin' about it at all, see? I'll tell you what I was thinkin' about— how I was goin' to break it to the wife about bein' canned. He canned me after twenty-five years, see? Did the lawyers tell you about that? I forget. All that talk gives me a headache. Ob-

jection sustained. Objection overruled. Answer yes or no. It gives me a headache. And I can't get the figgers outta my head. But that's what I was thinkin' about—how I was goin' t' break it to the wife about bein' canned. An' what Miss Devore would think when she heard about me killin' him. I bet she never thought I had the nerve to do it. I'd of married her if the wife had passed out. I'd be holdin' down my job yet, if he hadn't o' canned me. But he kept talkin' an' talkin'. An' there was the bill-file right where I could reach it. Do you get me? I'm just a regular guy like anybody else. Like you birds, now. [*For the first time the* JURORS *relax, looking indignantly at each other and whispering*] Suppose you was me, now. Maybe you'd 'a' done the same thing. That's the way you oughta look at it, see? Suppose you was me——

THE JURORS. [*rising as one and shouting in unison*] GUILTY! [ZERO *falls back, stunned for a moment by their vociferousness. The* JURORS *right-face in their places and file quickly out of the jury-box and towards the door in a double column*]

ZERO. [*recovering speech as the* JURORS *pass out at the door*] Wait a minute. Jest a minute. You don't get me right. Jest give me a chance an' I'll tell you how it was. I'm all mixed up, see? On account of them lawyers. And the figgers in my head. But I'm goin' to tell you how it was. I was there twenty-five years, see? An' they gave her six months, see?
[*He goes on haranguing the empty jury-box as the curtain falls.*]

SCENE V.

SCENE—*A grave-yard in full moonlight. It is a second-rate grave-yard—no elaborate tombstones or monuments—just simple headstones and here and there a cross. At the back is an iron fence with a gate in the middle. At first no one is visible, but there are occasional sounds throughout: the hooting of an owl, the whistle of a distant whippoorwill, the croaking of a bull-frog, and the yowling of a serenading cat. After a few moments two figures appear outside the gate—a man and a woman. She pushes the gate and it opens with a rusty creak. The couple enter. They are now fully visible in the moonlight—*JUDY O'GRADY *and a* YOUNG MAN.

JUDY. [*advancing*] Come on, this is the place.

YOUNG MAN. [*hanging back*] This! Why this here is a cemetery.

JUDY. Aw, quit yer kiddin'!

YOUNG MAN. You don't mean to say——

JUDY. What's the matter with this place?

YOUNG MAN. A cemetery!

JUDY. Sure. What of it?

YOUNG MAN. You must be crazy.

JUDY. This place is all right, I tell you. I been here lots o' times.

YOUNG MAN. Nix on this place for me!

JUDY. Ain't this place as good as another? Whaddya afraid of? They're all dead ones here! They don't bother you. [*With sudden interest*] Oh, look, here's a new one.

YOUNG MAN. Come on out of here.

JUDY. Wait a minute. Let's see what it says. [*She kneels on a grave in the foreground and putting her face close to headstone spells out the inscription*] Z-E-R-O. Z-e-r-o. Zero! Say, that's the guy——

YOUNG MAN. Zero? He's the guy killed his boss, ain't he?

JUDY. Yeh, that's him, all right. But what I'm thinkin' of is that I went to the hoosegow on account of him.

YOUNG MAN. What for?

JUDY. You know, same old stuff. Tenement House Law. [*Mincingly*] Section blaa-blaa of the Penal Code. Third Offence. Six months.

YOUNG MAN. And this bird——

JUDY. [*contemptuously*] Him? He was mamma's white-haired boy. We lived in the same house. Across the airshaft, see? I used to see him lookin' in my window. I guess his wife musta seen him, too. Anyhow, they went and turned the bulls on me. And now I'm out and he's in. [*Suddenly*] Say—say—[*She bursts into a peal of laughter*]

YOUNG MAN. [*nervously*] What's so funny?

JUDY. [*rocking with laughter*] Say, wouldn't it be funny—if—if—[*She explodes again*] That would be a good joke on him, all right. He can't do nothin' about it now, can he?

YOUNG MAN. Come on out of here. I don't like this place.

JUDY. Aw, you're a bum sport. What do you want to spoil my joke for? [*A cat yammers mellifluously*]

YOUNG MAN. [*half hysterically*] What's that?

JUDY. It's only the cats. They seem to like it here all right. But come on if you're afraid. [*They go towards the gate. As they go out*] You nervous men sure are the limit. [*They go out through the gate. As they disappear* ZERO's *grave opens suddenly and his head appears*]

ZERO. [*looking about*] That's funny! I thought I heard her talkin' and laughin'. But I don't see nobody. Anyhow, what would she be doin' here? I guess I must 'a' been dreamin'. But how could I be dreamin' when I ain't been asleep? [*He looks about again*] Well, no use goin' back. I can't sleep, anyhow. I might as well walk around a little. [*He rises out of the ground, very rigidly. He wears a full-dress suit of very antiquated cut and his hands are folded stiffly across his breast*] [*Walking woodenly*] Gee! I'm stiff! [*He slowly walks a few steps, then stops*] Gee, it's lonesome here! [*He shivers and walks on aimlessly*] I should 'a' stayed where I was. But I thought I heard her laughin'. [*A loud sneeze is heard.* ZERO *stands motionless, quaking with terror. The sneeze is repeated*] [*Hoarsely*] What's that?

A MILD VOICE. It's all right. Nothing to be afraid of. [*From behind a headstone* SHRDLU *appears. He is dressed in a shabby and ill-fitting cutaway. He wears silver-rimmed spectacles and is smoking a cigarette*]

SHRDLU.[2] I hope I didn't frighten you.

ZERO. [*still badly shaken*] No-o. It's all right. You see, I wasn't expectin' to see anybody.

SHRDLU. You're a newcomer, aren't you?

ZERO. Yeh, this is my first night. I couldn't seem to get to sleep.

SHRDLU. I can't sleep either. Suppose we keep each other company, shall we?

ZERO. [*eagerly*] Yeh, that would be great. I been feelin' awful lonesome.

SHRDLU. [*nodding*] I know. Let's make ourselves comfortable. [*He seats himself easily on a grave.* ZERO *tries to follow his example but he is stiff in every joint and groans with pain*]

ZERO. I'm kinda stiff.

SHRDLU. You mustn't mind the stiffness. It wears off in a few days. [*He seats himself on the grave beside* ZERO *and produces a package of cigarettes*] Will you have a Camel?

[2] The name, formed from the letters on one bank of keys on a linotype machine, preserves the wooden anonymity of most of the play's characters.

ZERO. No, I don't smoke.

SHRDLU. I find it helps keep the mosquitoes away. [*He lights a cigarette. Suddenly taking the cigarette out of his mouth*] Do you mind if I smoke, Mr.—Mr.——?

ZERO. No, go right ahead.

SHRDLU. [*replacing the cigarette*] Thank you. I didn't catch your name. [ZERO *does not reply*] [*Mildly*] I say I didn't catch your name.

ZERO. I heard you the first time. [*Hesitantly*] I'm scared if I tell you who I am and what I done, you'll be off me.

SHRDLU. [*sadly*] No matter what your sins may be, they are as snow compared to mine.

ZERO. You got another guess comin'. [*He pauses dramatically*] My name's Zero. I'm a murderer.

SHRDLU. [*nodding calmly*] Oh, yes, I remember reading about you, Mr. Zero.

ZERO. [*a little piqued*] And you still think you're worse than me?

SHRDLU. [*throwing away his cigarette*] Oh, a thousand times worse, Mr. Zero—a million times worse.

ZERO. What did you do?

SHRDLU. I, too, am a murderer.

ZERO. [*looking at him in amazement*] Go on! You're kiddin' me!

SHRDLU. Every word I speak is the truth, Mr. Zero. I am the foulest, the most sinful of murderers! You only murdered your employer, Mr. Zero. But I—I murdered my mother. [*He covers his face with his hands and sobs*]

ZERO. [*horrified*] The hell yer say!

SHRDLU. [*sobbing*] Yes, my mother!—my beloved mother!

ZERO. [*suddenly*] Say, you don't mean to say you're Mr.——

SHRDLU. [*nodding*] Yes. [*He wipes his eyes, still quivering with emotion*]

ZERO. I remember readin' about you in the papers.

SHRDLU. Yes, my guilt has been proclaimed to all the world. But that would be a trifle if only I could wash the stain of sin from my soul.

ZERO. I never heard of a guy killin' his mother before. What did you do it for?

SHRDLU. Because I have a sinful heart—there is no other reason.

ZERO. Did she always treat you square and all like that?

SHRDLU. She was a saint—a saint, I tell you.

She cared for me and watched over me as only a mother can.

ZERO. You mean to say you didn't have a scrap or nothin'?

SHRDLU. Never a harsh or an unkind word. Nothing except loving care and good advice. From my infancy she devoted herself to guiding me on the right path. She taught me to be thrifty, to be devout, to be unselfish, to shun evil companions and to shut my ears to all the temptations of the flesh—in short, to become a virtuous, respectable, and God-fearing man. [*He groans*] But it was a hopeless task. At fourteen I began to show evidence of my sinful nature.

ZERO. [*breathlessly*] You didn't kill anybody else, did you?

SHRDLU. No, thank God, there is only one murder on my soul. But I ran away from home.

ZERO. You did!

SHRDLU. Yes. A companion lent me a profane book—the only profane book I have ever read, I'm thankful to say. It was called *Treasure Island.*[3] Have you ever read it?

ZERO. No, I never was much on readin' books.

SHRDLU. It is a wicked book—a lurid tale of adventure. But it kindled in my sinful heart a desire to go to sea. And so I ran away from home.

ZERO. What did you do—get a job as a sailor?

SHRDLU. I never saw the sea—not to the day of my death. Luckily, my mother's loving intuition warned her of my intention and I was sent back home. She welcomed me with open arms. Not an angry word, not a look of reproach. But I could read the mute suffering in her eyes as we prayed together all through the night.

ZERO. [*sympathetically*] Gee, that must 'a' been tough. Gee, the mosquitoes are bad, ain't they? [*He tries awkwardly to slap at them with his stiff hands*]

SHRDLU. [*absorbed in his narrative*] I thought that experience had cured me of evil and I began to think about a career. I wanted to go in foreign missions at first, but we couldn't bear the thought of the separation. So we finally decided that I should become a proofreader.

[3] R. L. Stevenson's anything-but-profane novel of one boy's adventures.

ZERO. Say, slip me one o' them Camels, will you? I'm gettin' all bit up.

SHRDLU. Certainly. [*He hands* ZERO *cigarettes and matches*]

ZERO. [*lighting up*] Go ahead. I'm listenin'.

SHRDLU. By the time I was twenty I had a good job reading proof for a firm that printed catalogues. After a year they promoted me and let me specialize in shoe catalogues.

ZERO. Yeh? That must 'a' been a good job.

SHRDLU. It was a very good job. I was on the shoe catalogues for thirteen years. I'd been on them yet, if I hadn't——[*He chokes back a sob*]

ZERO. They oughta put a shot o' citronella in that embalmin'-fluid.

SHRDLU. [*he sighs*] We were so happy together. I had my steady job. And Sundays we would go to morning, afternoon, and evening service. It was an honest and moral mode of life.

ZERO. It sure was.

SHRDLU. Then came that fatal Sunday. Dr. Amaranth, our minister, was having dinner with us—one of the few pure spirits on earth. When he had finished saying grace, we had our soup. Everything was going along as usual—we were eating our soup and discussing the sermon, just like every other Sunday I could remember. Then came the leg of lamb—[*He breaks off, then resumes in a choking voice*] I see the whole scene before me so plainly—it never leaves me—Dr. Amaranth at my right, my mother at my left, the leg of lamb on the table in front of me and the cuckoo clock on the little shelf between the windows. [*He stops and wipes his eyes*]

ZERO. Yeh, but what happened?

SHRDLU. Well, as I started to carve the lamb ——Did you ever carve a leg of lamb?

ZERO. No, corned beef was our speed.

SHRDLU. It's very difficult on account of the bone. And when there's gravy in the dish there's danger of spilling it. So Mother always used to hold the dish for me. She leaned forward, just as she always did, and I could see the gold locket around her neck. It had my picture in it and one of my baby curls. Well, I raised my knife to carve the leg of lamb—and instead I cut my mother's throat! [*He sobs*]

ZERO. You must 'a' been crazy!

SHRDLU. [*raising his head, vehemently*] No! Don't try to justify me. I wasn't crazy. They tried to prove at the trial that I was crazy. But Dr. Amaranth saw the truth! He saw it from the first! He knew that it was my sinful nature —and he told me what was in store for me.

ZERO. [*trying to be comforting*] Well, your troubles are over now.

SHRDLU. [*his voice rising*] Over! Do you think this is the end?

ZERO. Sure. What more can they do to us?

SHRDLU. [*his tones growing shriller and shriller*] Do you think there can ever be any peace for such as we are—murderers, sinners? Don't you know what awaits us—flames, eternal flames!

ZERO. [*nervously*] Keep your shirt on, Buddy —they wouldn't do that to us.

SHRDLU. There's no escape—no escape for us, I tell you. We're doomed! We're doomed to suffer unspeakable torments through all eternity. [*His voice rises higher and higher*] [*A grave opens suddenly and a head appears*]

THE HEAD. Hey, you birds! Can't you shut up and let a guy sleep? [ZERO *scrambles painfully to his feet*]

ZERO. [*to* SHRDLU] Hey, put on the soft pedal.

SHRDLU. [*too wrought up to attend*] It won't be long now! We'll receive our summons soon.

THE HEAD. Are you goin' to beat it or not? [*He calls into the grave*] Hey, Bill, lend me your head a minute. [*A moment later his arm appears holding a skull*]

ZERO. [*warningly*] Look out! [*He seizes* SHRDLU *and drags him away just as* THE HEAD *throws the skull*]

THE HEAD. [*disgustedly*] Missed 'em. Damn old tabby cats! I'll get 'em next time. [*A prodigious yawn*] Ho-hum! Me for the worms!

[THE HEAD *disappears as the curtain falls.*]

SCENE VI.

SCENE—*A pleasant place. A scene of pastoral loveliness. A meadow dotted with fine old trees and carpeted with rich grass and field flowers. In the background are seen a number of tents fashioned of gay-striped silks and beyond gleams a meandering river. Clear air and a fleckless sky. Sweet distant music throughout. At the rise of the curtain,* SHRDLU *is seen seated under a tree in the foreground in an attitude of deep dejection. His knees are drawn up* and his head is buried in his arms. He is dressed as in the preceding scene.

A few minutes later, ZERO enters at right. He walks slowly and looks about him with an air of half-suspicious curiosity. He, too, is dressed as in the preceding scene. Suddenly he sees SHRDLU seated under the tree. He stands still and looks at him half fearfully. Then, seeing something familiar in him, goes closer. SHRDLU is unaware of his presence. At last ZERO recognizes him and grins in pleased surprise.

ZERO. Well, if it ain't——! [He claps SHRDLU on the shoulder] Hello, Buddy! [SHRDLU looks up slowly, then recognizing ZERO, he rises gravely and extends his hand courteously]

SHRDLU. How do you do, Mr. Zero? I'm very glad to see you again.

ZERO. Same here. I wasn't expectin' to see you, either. [Looking about] This is a kinda nice place. I wouldn't mind restin' here a while.

SHRDLU. You may if you wish.

ZERO. I'm kinda tired. I ain't used to bein' outdoors. I ain't walked so much in years.

SHRDLU. Sit down here, under the tree.

ZERO. Do they let you sit on the grass?

SHRDLU. Oh, yes.

ZERO. [seating himself] Boy, this feels good. I'll tell the world my feet are sore. I ain't used to so much walkin'. Say, I wonder would it be all right if I took my shoes off; my feet are tired.

SHRDLU. Yes. Some of the people here go barefoot.

ZERO. Yeh? They sure must be nuts. But I'm goin' t' leave 'em off for a while. So long as it's all right. The grass feels nice and cool. [He stretches out comfortably] Say, this is the life of Riley all right, all right. This sure is a nice place. What do they call this place, anyhow?

SHRDLU. The Elysian Fields.[4]

ZERO. The which?

SHRDLU. The Elysian Fields.

ZERO. [dubiously] Oh! Well, it's a nice place, all right.

SHRDLU. They say that this is the most desirable of all places. Only the most favored remain here.

ZERO. Yeh? Well, that let's me out, I guess. [Suddenly] But what are you doin' here? I thought you'd be burned by now.

_____
[4] the mythological paradise.

SHRDLU. [sadly] Mr. Zero, I am the most unhappy of men.

ZERO. [in mild astonishment] Why, because you ain't bein' roasted alive?

SHRDLU. [nodding] Nothing is turning out as I expected. I saw everything so clearly—the flames, the tortures, an eternity of suffering as the just punishment for my unspeakable crime. And it has all turned out so differently.

ZERO. Well, that's pretty soft for you, ain't it?

SHRDLU. [wailingly] No, no, no! It's right and just that I should be punished. I could have endured it stoically. All through those endless ages of indescribable torment I should have exulted in the magnificence of divine justice. But this—this is maddening! What becomes of justice? What becomes of morality? What becomes of right and wrong? It's maddening—simply maddening! Oh, if Dr. Amaranth were only here to advise me! [He buries his face and groans]

ZERO. [trying to puzzle it out] You mean to say they ain't called you for cuttin' your mother's throat?

SHRDLU. No! It's terrible—terrible! I was prepared for anything—anything but this.

ZERO. Well, what did they say to you?

SHRDLU. [looking up] Only that I was to come here and remain until I understood.

ZERO. I don't get it. What do they want you to understand?

SHRDLU. [despairingly] I don't know—I don't know! If I only had an inkling of what they meant——[Interrupting him] Just listen quietly for a moment; do you hear anything? [They are both silent, straining their ears]

ZERO. [at length] Nope.

SHRDLU. You don't hear any music? Do you?

ZERO. Music? No, I don't hear nothin'.

SHRDLU. The people here say that the music never stops.

ZERO. They're kiddin' you.

SHRDLU. Do you think so?

ZERO. Sure thing. There ain't a sound.

SHRDLU. Perhaps. They're capable of anything. But I haven't told you of the bitterest of my disappointments.

ZERO. Well, spill it. I'm gettin' used to hearin' bad news.

SHRDLU. When I came to this place, my first thought was to find my dear mother. I wanted to ask her forgiveness. And I wanted her to help me to understand.

ZERO. An' she couldn't do it?

SHRDLU. [*with a deep groan*] She's not here! Mr. Zero! Here where only the most favored dwell, that wisest and purest of spirits is nowhere to be found. I don't understand it.

A WOMAN'S VOICE. [*in the distance*] Mr. Zero! Oh, Mr. Zero! [ZERO *raises his head and listens attentively*]

SHRDLU. [*going on, unheedingly*] If you were to see some of the people here—the things they do——

ZERO. [*interrupting*] Wait a minute, will you? I think somebody's callin' me.

THE VOICE. [*somewhat nearer*] Mr. Ze-ro! Oh! Mr. Ze-ro!

ZERO. Who the hell's that now? I wonder if the wife's on my trail already. That would be swell, wouldn't it? An' I figured on her bein' good for another twenty years, anyhow.

THE VOICE. [*nearer*] Mr. Ze-ro! Yoo-hoo!

ZERO. No. That ain't her voice. [*Calling, savagely*] Yoo-hoo. [*To* SHRDLU] Ain't that always the way? Just when a guy is takin' life easy an' havin' a good time! [*He rises and looks off left*] Here she comes, whoever she is. [*In sudden amazement*] Well, I'll be——! Well, what do you know about that! [*He stands looking in wonderment, as* DAISY DIANA DOROTHEA DEVORE *enters. She wears a much-beruffled white muslin dress which is a size too small and fifteen years too youthful for her. She is red-faced and breathless*]

DAISY. [*panting*] Oh! I thought I'd never catch up to you. I've been followin' you for days—callin' an' callin'. Didn't you hear me?

ZERO. Not till just now. You look kinda winded.

DAISY. I sure am. I can't hardly catch my breath.

ZERO. Well, sit down an' take a load off your feet. [*He leads her to the tree*] [DAISY *sees* SHRDLU *for the first time and shrinks back a little*] It's all right, he's a friend of mine. [*To* SHRDLU] Buddy, I want you to meet my friend, Miss Devore.

SHRDLU. [*rising and extending his hand courteously*] How do you do, Miss Devore?

DAISY. [*self-consciously*] How do!

ZERO. [*to* DAISY] He's a friend of mine. [*To* SHRDLU] I guess you don't mind if she sits here

a while an' cools off, do you?

SHRDLU. No, no, certainly not. [*They all seat themselves under the tree.* ZERO *and* DAISY *are a little self-conscious.* SHRDLU *gradually becomes absorbed in his own thoughts*]

ZERO. I was just takin' a rest myself. I took my shoes off on account of my feet bein' so sore.

DAISY. Yeh, I'm kinda tired, too. [*Looking about*] Say, ain't it pretty here, though?

ZERO. Yeh, it is at that.

DAISY. What do they call this place?

ZERO. Why—er—let's see. He was tellin' me just a minute ago. The—er—I don't know. Some kind o' fields. I forget now. [*To* SHRDLU] Say, Buddy, what do they call this place again? [SHRDLU, *absorbed in his thoughts, does not hear him. To* DAISY] He don't hear me. He's thinkin' again.

DAISY. [*sotto voce*] What's the matter with him?

ZERO. Why, he's the guy that murdered his mother—remember?

DAISY. [*interested*] Oh, yeh! Is that him?

ZERO. Yeh. An' he had it all figgered out how they was goin' t' roast him or somethin'. And now they ain't goin' to do nothin' to him an' it's kinda got his goat.

DAISY. [*sympathetically*] Poor feller!

ZERO. Yeh. He takes it kinda hard.

DAISY. He looks like a nice young feller.

ZERO. Well, you sure are good for sore eyes. I never expected to see you here.

DAISY. I thought maybe you'd be kinda surprised.

ZERO. Surprised is right. I thought you was alive an' kickin'. When did you pass out?

DAISY. Oh, right after you did—a coupla days.

ZERO. [*interested*] Yeh? What happened? Get hit by a truck or somethin'?

DAISY. No. [*Hesitantly*] You see—it's this way. I blew out the gas.

ZERO. [*astonished*] Go on! What was the big idea?

DAISY. [*falteringly*] Oh, I don't know. You see, I lost my job.

ZERO. I'll bet you're sorry you did it now, ain't you?

DAISY. [*with conviction*] No, I ain't sorry. Not a bit. [*Then hesitantly*] Say, Mr. Zero, I been thinkin'—— [*She stops*]

ZERO. What?

DAISY. [*plucking up courage*] I been thinkin' it would be kinda nice—if you an' me—if we could kinda talk things over.

ZERO. Yeh. Sure. What do you want to talk about?

DAISY. Well—I don't know—but you and me—we ain't really ever talked things over, have we?

ZERO. No, that's right, we ain't. Well, let's go to it.

DAISY. I was thinkin' if we could be alone— just the two of us, see?

ZERO. Oh, yeh! Yeh, I get you. [*He turns to* SHRDLU *and coughs loudly.* SHRDLU *does not stir. To* DAISY] He's dead to the world. [*He turns to* SHRDLU] Say, Buddy! [*No answer*] Say, Buddy!

SHRDLU. [*looking up with a start*] Were you speaking to me?

ZERO. Yeh. How'd you guess it? I was thinkin' that maybe you'd like to walk around a little and look for your mother.

SHRDLU. [*shaking his head*] It's no use. I've looked everywhere. [*He relapses into thought again*]

ZERO. Maybe over there they might know.

SHRDLU. No, no! I've searched everywhere. She's not here. [ZERO *and* DAISY *look at each other in despair*]

ZERO. Listen, old shirt, my friend here and me—see?—we used to work in the same store. An' we got some things to talk over—business, see?—kinda confidential. So if it ain't askin' too much——

SHRDLU. [*springing to his feet*] Why, certainly! Excuse me! [*He bows politely to* DAISY *and walks off.* DAISY *and* ZERO *watch him until he has disappeared*]

ZERO. [*with a forced laugh*] He's a good guy at that. [*Now that they are alone, both are very self-conscious, and for a time they sit in silence*]

DAISY. [*breaking the silence*] It sure is pretty here, ain't it?

ZERO. Sure is.

DAISY. Look at the flowers! Ain't they just perfect! Why, you'd think they was artificial, wouldn't you?

ZERO. Yeh, you would.

DAISY. And the smell of them. Like perfume.

ZERO. Yeh.

DAISY. I'm crazy about the country, ain't you?

ZERO. Yeh. It's nice for a change.

DAISY. Them store picnics—remember?

ZERO. You bet. They sure was fun.

DAISY. One time—I guess you don't remember—the two of us—me and you—we sat down on the grass together under a tree—just like we're doin' now.

ZERO. Sure I remember.

DAISY. Go on! I'll bet you don't.

ZERO. I'll bet I do. It was the year the wife didn't go.

DAISY. [*her face brightening*] That's right! I didn't think you'd remember.

ZERO. An' comin' home we sat together in the truck.

DAISY. [*eagerly, rather shamefacedly*] Yeh! There's somethin' I've always wanted to ask you.

ZERO. Well, why didn't you?

DAISY. I don't know. It didn't seem refined. But I'm goin' to ask you now, anyhow.

ZERO. Go ahead. Shoot.

DAISY. [*falteringly*] Well—while we was comin' home—you put your arm up on the bench behind me—and I could feel your knee kinda pressin' against mine. [*She stops*]

ZERO. [*becoming more and more interested*] Yeh—well—what about it?

DAISY. What I wanted to ask you was—was it just kinda accidental?

ZERO. [*with a laugh*] Sure it was accidental. Accidental on purpose.

DAISY. [*eagerly*] Do you mean it?

ZERO. Sure I mean it. You mean to say you didn't know it?

DAISY. No. I've been wantin' to ask you——

ZERO. Then why did you get sore at me?

DAISY. Sore? I wasn't sore! When was I sore?

ZERO. That night. Sure you was sore. If you wasn't sore why did you move away?

DAISY. Just to see if you meant it. I thought if you meant it you'd move up closer. An' then when you took your arm away I was sure you didn't mean it.

ZERO. An' I thought all the time you was sore. That's why I took my arm away. I thought if I moved up you'd holler and then I'd be in a jam, like you read in the paper all the time about guys gettin' pulled in for annoyin' women.

DAISY. An' I was wishin' you'd put your arm

around me—just sittin' there wishin' all the way home.

ZERO. What do you know about that? That sure is hard luck, that is. If I'd 'a' only knew! You know what I felt like doin'—only I didn't have the nerve? 5

DAISY. What?

ZERO. I felt like kissin' you.

DAISY. [*fervently*] I wanted you to.

ZERO. [*astonished*] You would 'a' let me? 10

DAISY. I wanted you to! I wanted you to! Oh, why didn't you—why didn't you?

ZERO. I didn't have the nerve. I sure was a dumbbell.

DAISY. I would 'a' let you all you wanted to. 15 I wouldn't 'a' cared. I know it would 'a' been wrong but I wouldn't 'a' cared. I wasn't thinkin' about right an' wrong at all. I didn't care—see? I just wanted you to kiss me.

ZERO. [*feelingly*] If I'd only knew. I wanted 20 to do it, I swear I did. But I didn't think you cared nothin' about me.

DAISY. [*passionately*] I never cared nothin' about nobody else.

ZERO. Do you mean it—on the level? You 25 ain't kiddin' me, are you?

DAISY. No, I ain't kiddin'. I mean it. I'm tellin' you the truth. I ain't never had the nerve to tell you before—but now I don't care. It don't make no difference now. I mean it—every 30 word of it.

ZERO. [*dejectedly*] If I'd only knew it.

DAISY. Listen to me. There's somethin' else I want to tell you. I may as well tell you everything now. It don't make no difference now. 35 About my blowin' out the gas—see? Do you know why I done it?

ZERO. Yeh, you told me—on account o' bein' canned.

DAISY. I just told you that. That ain't the real 40 reason. The real reason is on account o' you.

ZERO. You mean to say on account o' me passin' out——?

DAISY. Yeh. That's it. I didn't want to go on livin'. What for? What did I want to go on livin' 45 for? I didn't have nothin' to live for with you gone. I often thought of doin' it before. But I never had the nerve. An' anyhow I didn't want to leave you.

ZERO. An' me bawlin' you out, about readin' 50 too fast an' readin' too slow.

DAISY. [*reproachfully*] Why did you do it?

ZERO. I don't know, I swear I don't. I was always stuck on you. An' while I'd be addin' them figgers, I'd be thinkin' how if the wife died, you an' me could get married.

DAISY. I used to think o' that, too.

ZERO. An' then before I knew it, I was bawlin' you out.

DAISY. Them was the times I'd think o' blowin' out the gas. But I never did till you was gone. There wasn't nothin' to live for then. But it wasn't so easy to do, anyhow. I never could stand the smell o' gas. An' all the while I was gettin' ready, you know, stuffin' up all the cracks, the way you read about in the paper —I was thinkin' of you and hopin' that maybe I'd meet you again. An' I made up my mind if I ever did see you, I'd tell you.

ZERO. [*taking her hand*] I'm sure glad you did. I'm sure glad. [*ruefully*] But it don't do much good now, does it?

DAISY. No, I guess it don't. [*summoning courage*] But there's one thing I'm goin' to ask you.

ZERO. What's that?

DAISY. [*in a low voice*] I want you to kiss me.

ZERO. You bet I will! [*He leans over and kisses her cheek*]

DAISY. Not like that. I don't mean like that. I mean really kiss me. On the mouth. I ain't never been kissed like that. [ZERO *puts his arms about her and presses his lips to hers. A long embrace. At last they separate and sit side by side in silence*] [*Putting her hands to her cheeks*] So that's what it's like. I didn't know it could be like that. I didn't know anythin' could be like that.

ZERO. [*fondling her hand*] Your cheeks are red. They're all red. And your eyes are shinin'. I never seen your eyes shinin' like that before.

DAISY. [*holding up her hand*] Listen—do you hear it? Do you hear the music?

ZERO. No, I don't hear nothin'!

DAISY. Yeh—music. Listen an' you'll hear it. [*They are both silent for a moment*]

ZERO. [*excitedly*] Yeh! I hear it! He said there was music, but I didn't hear it till just now.

DAISY. Ain't it grand?

ZERO. Swell! Say, do you know what?

DAISY. What?

ZERO. It makes me feel like dancin'.

DAISY. Yeh? Me, too.

ZERO. [*springing to his feet*] Come on! Let's dance! [*He seizes her hands and tries to pull her up*]

DAISY. [*resisting laughingly*] I can't dance. I ain't danced in twenty years.

ZERO. That's nothin'. I ain't, neither. Come on! I feel just like a kid! [*He pulls her to her feet and seizes her about the waist*]

DAISY. Wait a minute! Wait till I fix my skirt. [*She turns back her skirts and pins them above the ankles*] [ZERO *seizes her about the waist. They dance clumsily but with gay abandon.* DAISY's *hair becomes loosened and tumbles over her shoulders. She lends herself more and more to the spirit of the dance. But* ZERO *soon begins to tire and dances with less and less zest*]

ZERO. [*stopping at last, panting for breath*] Wait a minute! I'm all winded. [*He releases* DAISY, *but before he can turn away, she throws her arms about him and presses her lips to his*] Wait a minute! Let me get my wind! [*He limps to the tree and seats himself under it, gasping for breath.* DAISY *looks after him, her spirits rather dampened*] Whew! I sure am winded! I ain't used to dancin'. [*He takes off his collar and tie and opens the neckband of his shirt.* DAISY *sits under the tree near him, looking at him longingly. But he is busy catching his breath*] Gee, my heart's goin' a mile a minute.

DAISY. Why don't you lay down an' rest? You could put your head on my lap.

ZERO. That ain't a bad idea. [*He stretches out, his head in* DAISY's *lap*]

DAISY. [*fondling his hair*] It was swell, wasn't it?

ZERO. Yeh. But you gotta be used to it.

DAISY. Just imagine if we could stay here all the time—you an' me together—wouldn't it be swell?

ZERO. Yeh. But there ain't a chance.

DAISY. Won't they let us stay?

ZERO. No. This place is only for the good ones.

DAISY. Well, we ain't so bad, are we?

ZERO. Go on! Me a murderer an' you committin' suicide. Anyway, they wouldn't stand for this—the way we been goin' on.

DAISY. I don't see why.

ZERO. You don't! You know it ain't right. Ain't I got a wife?

DAISY. Not any more you ain't. When you're dead that ends it. Don't they always say "until death do us part"?

ZERO. Well, maybe you're right about that, but they wouldn't stand for us here.

DAISY. It would be swell—the two of us together—we could make up for all them years.

ZERO. Yeh, I wish we could.

DAISY. We sure were fools. But I don't care. I've got you now. [*She kisses his forehead and cheeks and mouth*]

ZERO. I'm sure crazy about you. I never saw you lookin' so pretty before, with your cheeks all red. An' your hair hangin' down. You got swell hair. [*He fondles and kisses her hair*]

DAISY. [*ecstatically*] We got each other now, ain't we?

ZERO. Yeh. I'm crazy about you. Daisy! That's a pretty name. It's a flower, ain't it? Well—that's what you are—just a flower.

DAISY. [*happily*] We can always be together now, can't we?

ZERO. As long as they'll let us. I sure am crazy about you. [*Suddenly he sits upright*] Watch your step!

DAISY. [*alarmed*] What's the matter?

ZERO. [*nervously*] He's comin' back.

DAISY. Oh, is that all? Well, what about it?

ZERO. You don't want him to see us layin' around like this, do you?

DAISY. I don't care if he does.

ZERO. Well, you oughta care. You don't want him to think you ain't a refined girl, do you? He's an awful moral bird, he is.

DAISY. I don't care nothin' about him. I don't care nothin' about anybody but you.

ZERO. Sure, I know. But we don't want people talkin' about us. You better fix your hair an' pull down your skirts. [DAISY *complies rather sadly. They are both silent as* SHRDLU *enters*] [*With feigned nonchalance*] Well, you got back all right, didn't you?

SHRDLU. I hope I haven't returned too soon.

ZERO. No, that's all right. We were just havin' a little talk. You know—about business an' things.

DAISY. [*boldly*] We were wishin' we could stay here all the time.

SHRDLU. You may if you like.

ZERO AND DAISY. [*in astonishment*] What!

SHRDLU. Yes. Any one who likes may remain——

ZERO. But I thought you were tellin' me——

SHRDLU. Just as I told you, only the most favored do remain. But any one may.

ZERO. I don't get it. There's a catch in it somewheres.

DAISY. It doesn't matter as long as we can stay.

ZERO. [*to* SHRDLU] We were thinkin' about gettin' married, see?

SHRDLU. You may or not, just as you like.

ZERO. You don't mean to say we could stay if we didn't, do you?

SHRDLU. Yes. They don't care.

ZERO. An' there's some here that ain't married?

SHRDLU. Yes.

ZERO. [*to* DAISY] I don't know about this place, at that. They must be kind of a mixed crowd.

DAISY. It don't matter, so long as we got each other.

ZERO. Yeh, I know, but you don't want to mix with people that ain't respectable.

DAISY. [*to* SHRDLU] Can we get married right away? I guess there must be a lot of ministers here, ain't there?

SHRDLU. Not as many as I had hoped to find. The two who seem most beloved are Dean Swift and the Abbé Rabelais.[5] They are both much admired for some indecent tales which they have written.

ZERO. [*shocked*] What! Ministers writin' smutty stories! Say, what kind of a dump is this, anyway?

SHRDLU. [*despairingly*] I don't know, Mr. Zero. All these people here are so strange, so unlike the good people I've known. They seem to think of nothing but enjoyment or of wasting their time in profitless occupations. Some paint pictures from morning until night, or carve blocks of stone. Others write songs or put

---

[5] Jonathan Swift (1667–1745), author of *Gulliver's Travels*, and François Rabelais (1494?–1553), author of *Gargantua and Pantagruel*. Both works contain vulgar passages and satirize mankind; the managers of the Elysian Fields, however, prefer to overlook the vulgarity in favor of the fact that both authors may have written as they did to "needle" man into improving himself, and thus both really loved man in the best humanistic manner. Or, again, Swift and Rabelais may have been admitted simply because they created laughter and enjoyment.

words together, day in and day out. Still others do nothing but lie under the trees and look at the sky. There are men who spend all their time reading books and women who think only of adorning themselves. And for ever they are telling stories and laughing and singing and drinking and dancing. There are drunkards, thieves, vagabonds, blasphemers, adulterers. There is one——

ZERO. That's enough. I heard enough. [*He seats himself and begins putting on his shoes*]

DAISY. [*anxiously*] What are you goin' to do?

ZERO. I'm goin' to beat it, that's what I'm goin' to do.

DAISY. You said you liked it here.

ZERO. [*looking at her in amazement*] Liked it! Say, you don't mean to say you want to stay here, do you, with a lot of rummies an' loafers an' bums?

DAISY. We don't have to bother with them. We can just sit here together an' look at the flowers an' listen to the music.

SHRDLU. [*eagerly*] Music! Did you hear music?

DAISY. Sure. Don't you hear it?

SHRDLU. No, they say it never stops. But I've never heard it.

ZERO. [*listening*] I thought I heard it before but I don't hear nothin' now. I guess I must 'a' been dreamin'. [*Looking about*] What's the quickest way out of this place?

DAISY. [*pleadingly*] Won't you stay just a little longer?

ZERO. Didn't yer hear me say I'm goin'? Good-bye, Miss Devore. I'm goin' to beat it. [*He limps off at the right.* DAISY *follows him slowly*]

DAISY. [*to* SHRDLU] I won't ever see him again.

SHRDLU. Are you goin' to stay here?

DAISY. It don't make no difference now. Without him I might as well be alive. [*She goes off right.* SHRDLU *watches her a moment, then sighs and, seating himself under the tree, buries his head on his arm. Curtain falls.*]

SCENE VII.

SCENE—*Before the curtain rises the clicking of an adding machine is heard. The curtain rises upon an office similar in appearance to that in Scene II except that there is a door in the back wall through which can be seen a glimpse of the corridor outside. In the middle of the room* ZERO *is seated completely absorbed in the operation of an adding machine. He presses the keys and pulls the lever with mechanical precision. He still wears his full-dress suit but he has added to it sleeve protectors and a green eye shade. A strip of white paper-tape flows steadily from the machine as* ZERO *operates. The room is filled with this tape—streamers,* 10 *festoons, billows of it everywhere. It covers the floor and the furniture, it climbs the walls and chokes the doorways. A few moments later,* LIEUTENANT CHARLES *and* JOE *enter at the left.* LIEUTENANT CHARLES *is middle-aged and in-* 15 *clined to corpulence. He has an air of world-weariness. He is bare-footed, wears a Panama hat, and is dressed in bright red tights which are a very bad fit—too tight in some places, badly wrinkled in others.* JOE *is a youth with a* 20 *smutty face dressed in dirty blue overalls.*

CHARLES. [*after contemplating* ZERO *for a few moments*] All right, Zero, cease firing.

ZERO. [*looking up, surprised*] Whaddja say? 25

CHARLES. I said stop punching that machine.

ZERO. [*bewildered*] Stop? [*He goes on working mechanically*]

CHARLES. [*impatiently*] Yes. Can't you stop? Here, Joe, give me a hand. He can't stop. [JOE 30 *and* CHARLES *each take one of* ZERO's *arms and with enormous effort detach him from the machine. He resists passively—mere inertia. Finally they succeed and swing him around on his stool.* CHARLES *and* JOE *mop their fore-* 35 *heads*]

ZERO. [*querulously*] What's the idea?. Can't you lemme alone?

CHARLES. [*ignoring the question*] How long have you been here? 40

ZERO. Jes' twenty-five years. Three hundred months, ninety-one hundred thirty-one days, one hundred thirty-six thousand——

CHARLES. [*impatiently*] That'll do! That'll do! 45

ZERO. [*proudly*] I ain't missed a day, not an hour, not a minute. Look at all I got done. [*He points to the maze of paper*]

CHARLES. It's time to quit.

ZERO. Quit? Whaddye mean quit? I ain't 50 goin' to quit!

CHARLES. You've got to.

ZERO. What for? What do I have to quit for?

CHARLES. It's time for you to go back.

ZERO. Go back where? Whaddya talkin' about?

CHARLES. Back to earth, you dub. Where do 5 you think?

ZERO. Aw, go on, Cap, who are you kiddin'?

CHARLES. I'm not kidding anybody. And don't call me Cap. I'm a lieutenant.

ZERO. All right, Lieutenant, all right. But what's this you're tryin' to tell me about goin' back?

CHARLES. Your time's up. I'm telling you. You must be pretty thick. How many times do 15 you want to be told a thing?

ZERO. This is the first time I heard about goin' back. Nobody ever said nothin' to me about it before.

CHARLES. You didn't think you were going to stay here for ever, did you?

ZERO. Sure. Why not? I did my bit, didn't I? Forty-five years of it. Twenty-five years in the store. Then the boss canned me and I knocked him cold. I guess you ain't heard about that——

CHARLES. [*interrupting*] I know all about that. But what's that got to do with it?

ZERO. Well, I done my bit, didn't I? That oughta let me out.

CHARLES. [*jeeringly*] So you think you're all through, do you?

ZERO. Sure, I do. I did the best I could while I was there and then I passed out. And now I'm sittin' pretty here.

CHARLES. You've got a fine idea of the way 35 they run things, you have. Do you think they're going to all the trouble of making a soul just to use it once?

ZERO. Once is often enough, it seems to me.

CHARLES. It seems to you, does it? Well, who 40 are you? And what do you know about it? Why, man, they use a soul over and over again—over and over until it's worn out.

ZERO. Nobody ever told me.

CHARLES. So you thought you were all 45 through, did you? Well, that's a hot one, that is.

ZERO. [*sullenly*] How was I to know?

CHARLES. Use your brains! Where would we put them all! We're crowded enough as it is. Why, this place is nothing but a kind of repair 50 and service station—a sort of cosmic laundry, you might say. We get the souls in here by the bushelful. Then we get busy and clean them up. And you ought to see some of them. The muck and slime. Phoo! And as full of holes as a flour-sifter. But we fix them up. We disinfect them and give them a kerosene rub and mend the holes and back they go—practically as good as new.

ZERO. You mean to say I've been here before—before the last time, I mean?

CHARLES. Been here before! Why, you poor boob—you've been here thousands of times—fifty thousand, at least.

ZERO. [*suspiciously*] How is it I don't remember nothin' about it?

CHARLES. Well—that's partly because you're stupid. But it's mostly because that's the way they fix it. [*Musingly*] They're funny that way —every now and then they'll do something white like that—when you'd least expect it. I guess economy's at the bottom of it, though. They figure that the souls would get worn out quicker if they remembered.

ZERO. And don't any of 'em remember?

CHARLES. Oh, some do. You see there's different types: there's the type that gets a little better each time it goes back—we just give them a wash and send them right through. Then there's another type—the type that gets a little worse each time. That's where you belong!

ZERO. [*offended*] Me? You mean to say I'm gettin' worse all the time?

CHARLES. [*nodding*] Yes. A little worse each time.

ZERO. Well—what was I when I started? Somethin' big?—A king or somethin'?

CHARLES. [*laughing derisively*] A king! That's a good one! I'll tell you what you were the first time—if you want to know so much— a monkey.

ZERO. [*shocked and offended*] A monkey!

CHARLES. Yes, sir—just a hairy, chattering, long-tailed monkey.

ZERO. That musta been a long time ago.

CHARLES. Oh, not so long. A million years or so. Seems like yesterday to me.

ZERO. Then look here, whaddya mean by sayin' I'm gettin' worse all the time?

CHARLES. Just what I said. You weren't so bad as a monkey. Of course, you did just what all the other monkeys did, but still it kept you out in the open air. And you weren't women

shy—there was one little red-headed monkey—— Well, never mind. Yes, sir, you weren't so bad then. But even in those days there must have been some bigger and brainier monkey that you kowtowed to. The mark of the slave was on you from the start.

ZERO. [*sullenly*] You ain't very particular about what you call people, are you?

CHARLES. You wanted the truth, didn't you? If there ever was a soul in the world that was labelled slave it's yours. Why, all the bosses and kings that there ever were have left their trademarks on your backside.

ZERO. It ain't fair, if you ask me.

CHARLES. [*shrugging his shoulders*] Don't tell me about it. I don't make the rules. All I know is you've been getting worse—worse each time. Why, even six thousand years ago you weren't so bad. That was the time you were hauling stones for one of those big pyramids in a place they call Africa. Ever hear of the pyramids?

ZERO. Them big pointy things?

CHARLES. [*nodding*] That's it.

ZERO. I seen a picture of them in the movies.

CHARLES. Well, you helped build them. It was a long step down from the happy days in the jungle, but it was a good job—even though you didn't know what you were doing and your back was striped by the foreman's whip. But you've been going down, down. Two thousand years ago you were a Roman galley-slave. You were on one of the triremes that knocked the Carthaginian fleet for a goal. Again the whip. But you had muscles then—chest muscles, back muscles, biceps. [*He feels* ZERO's *arm gingerly and turns away in disgust*] Phoo! a bunch of mush! [*He notices that* JOE *has fallen asleep. Walking over, he kicks him in the shin*] Wake up, you mutt! Where do you think you are! [*He turns to* ZERO *again*] And then another thousand years and you were a serf—a lump of clay digging up other lumps of clay. You wore an iron collar then—white ones hadn't been invented yet. Another long step down. But where you dug, potatoes grew and that helped fatten the pigs. Which was something. And now—well, I don't want to rub it in——

ZERO. Rub it in is right! Seems to me I got a pretty healthy kick comin'. I ain't had a square deal! Hard work! That's all I've ever had!

CHARLES. [*callously*] What else were you ever good for?

ZERO. Well, that ain't the point. The point is I'm through! I had enough! Let 'em find somebody else to do the dirty work. I'm sick of bein' the goat! I quit right here and now! [*He glares about defiantly. There is a thunderclap and a bright flash of lightning. Screaming*] Ooh! What's that? [*He clings to* CHARLES]

CHARLES. It's all right. Nobody's going to hurt you. It's just their way of telling you that they don't like you to talk that way. Pull yourself together and calm down. You can't change the rules—nobody can—they've got it all fixed. It's a rotten system—but what are you going to do about it?

ZERO. Why can't they stop pickin' on me? I'm satisfied here—doin' my day's work. I don't want to go back.

CHARLES. You've got to, I tell you. There's no way out of it.

ZERO. What chance have I got—at my age? Who'll give me a job?

CHARLES. You big boob, you don't think you're going back the way you are, do you?

ZERO. Sure, how then?

CHARLES. Why, you've got to start all over.

ZERO. All over?

CHARLES. [*nodding*] You'll be a baby again —a bald, red-faced little animal, and then you'll go through it all again. There'll be millions of others like you—all with their mouths open, squawking for food. And then when you get a little older you'll begin to learn things— and you'll learn all the wrong things and learn them all in the wrong way. You'll eat the wrong food and wear the wrong clothes and you'll live in swarming dens where there's no light and no air! You'll learn to be a liar and a bully and a braggart and a coward and a sneak. You'll learn to fear the sunlight and to hate beauty. By that time you'll be ready for school. There they'll tell you the truth about a great many things that you don't give a damn about and they'll tell you lies about all the things you ought to know—and about all the things you want to know they'll tell you nothing at all. When you get through you'll be equipped for your life-work. You'll be ready to take a job.

ZERO. [*eagerly*] What'll my job be? Another adding machine?

CHARLES. Yes. But not one of these anti-quated adding machines. It will be a superb, super-hyper-adding machine, as far from this old piece of junk as you are from God. It will be something to make you sit up and take notice, that adding machine. It will be an adding machine which will be installed in a coal mine and which will record the individual output of each miner. As each miner down in the lower galleries takes up a shovelful of coal, the impact of his shovel will automatically set in motion a graphite pencil in your gallery. The pencil will make a mark in white upon a blackened, sensitised drum. Then your work comes in. With the great toe of your right foot you release a lever which focuses a violet ray on the drum. The ray playing upon and through the white mark, falls upon a selenium cell which in turn sets the keys of the adding apparatus in motion. In this way the individual output of each miner is recorded without any human effort except the slight pressure of the great toe of your right foot.

ZERO. [*in breathless, round-eyed wonder*] Say, that'll be some machine, won't it?

CHARLES. Some machine is right. It will be the culmination of human effort—the final triumph of the evolutionary process. For millions of years the nebulous gases swirled in space. For more millions of years the gases cooled and then through inconceivable ages they hardened into rocks. And then came life. Floating green things on the waters that covered the earth. More millions of years and a step upward—an animate organism in the ancient slime. And so on—step by step, down through the ages—a gain here, a gain there—the mollusc, the fish, the reptile, then mammal, man! And all so that you might sit in the gallery of a coal mine and operate the super-hyper-adding machine with the great toe of your right foot!

ZERO. Well, then—I ain't so bad, after all.

CHARLES. You're a failure, Zero, a failure. A waste product. A slave to a contraption of steel and iron. The animal's instincts, but not his strength and skill. The animal's appetites, but not his unashamed indulgence of them. True, you move and eat and digest and excrete and reproduce. But any microscopic organism can do as much. Well—time's up! Back you go—back to your sunless groove—the raw material of slums and wars—the ready prey of the first jingo or demagogue or political adventurer who takes the trouble to play upon your ignorance and credulity and provincialism. You poor, spineless, brainless boob—I'm sorry for you!

ZERO. [*falling to his knees*] Then keep me here! Don't send me back! Let me stay!

CHARLES. Get up. Didn't I tell you I can't do anything for you? Come on, time's up!

ZERO. I can't! I can't! I'm afraid to go through it all again.

CHARLES. You've got to, I tell you. Come on, now!

ZERO. What did you tell me so much for? Couldn't you just let me go, thinkin' everythin' was goin' to be all right?

CHARLES. You wanted to know, didn't you?

ZERO. How did I know what you were goin' to tell me? Now I can't stop thinkin' about it! I can't stop thinkin'! I'll be thinkin' about it all the time.

CHARLES. All right! I'll do the best I can for you. I'll send a girl with you to keep you company.

ZERO. A girl? What for? What good will a girl do me?

CHARLES. She'll help make you forget.

ZERO. [*eagerly*] She will? Where is she?

CHARLES. Wait a minute, I'll call her. [*He calls in a loud voice*] Oh! Hope! Yoo-hoo! [*He turns his head aside and says in the manner of a ventriloquist imitating a distant feminine voice*] Ye-es. [*Then in his own voice*] Come here, will you? There's a fellow who wants you to take him back. [*Ventriloquously again*] All right. I'll be right over, Charlie dear. [*He turns to* ZERO] Kind of familiar, isn't she? Charlie dear!

ZERO. What did you say her name is?

CHARLES. Hope. H-o-p-e.

ZERO. Is she good-lookin'?

CHARLES. Is she good-looking! Oh, boy, wait until you see her! She's a blonde with big blue eyes, red lips, little white teeth and——

ZERO. Say, that listens good to me. Will she be long?

CHARLES. She'll be here right away. There she is now! Do you see her?

ZERO. No. Where?

CHARLES. Out in the corridor. No, not there. Over farther. To the right. Don't you see her blue dress? And the sunlight on her hair?

ZERO. Oh, sure! Now I see her! What's the matter with me, anyhow? Say, she's some jane! Oh, you baby vamp!

CHARLES. She'll make you forget your troubles.

ZERO. What troubles are you talkin' about?

CHARLES. Nothing. Go on. Don't keep her waiting.

ZERO. You bet I won't! Oh, Hope! Wait for me! I'll be right with you! I'm on my way! [*He stumbles out eagerly*] [JOE *bursts into uproarious laughter*]

CHARLES. [*eyeing him in surprise and anger*] What in hell's the matter with you?

JOE. [*shaking with laughter*] Did you get that? He thinks he saw somebody and he's following her! [*He rocks with laughter*]

CHARLES. [*punching him in the jaw*] Shut your face!

JOE. [*nursing his jaw*] What's the idea? Can't I even laugh when I see something funny?

CHARLES. Funny! You keep your mouth shut or I'll show you something funny. Go on, hustle out of here and get something to clean up this mess with. There's another fellow moving in. Hurry now. [*He makes a threatening gesture.* JOE *exits hastily.* CHARLES *goes to chair and seats himself. He looks weary and dispirited. Shaking his head*] Hell, I'll tell the world this is a lousy job! [*He takes a flask from his pocket, uncorks it, and slowly drains it.*]

[*Curtain*]

GLOSSARY

ACADEMIC DRAMA: a term applied to plays imitating the ancient classics and to original plays produced in Renaissance England by schools and universities. These plays were instrumental in transmitting classical influence to the professional theater.

ALLEGORY: in drama, a story in which the characters and action present a moral, political, or religious meaning beyond the obvious narrative.

ANTAGONIST: a character who opposes the protagonist (q.v.) in a play.

ASIDE: term applied to an old convention which allowed an actor to speak directly to the audience supposedly without being heard by other actors on stage.

CATASTROPHE: usually the death or destruction of the major figures in a tragedy, near the end, but after the climax.

CATHARSIS: the purging of audience emotions by vicarious experience. The term is generally applied to classic drama, the witnessing of which gave the beholder a cleansing of fear and pity, leaving him as spent as if he had actually suffered real-life tragedy.

CHRONICLE PLAY: a history play (Renaissance England) with emphasis on royal careers and spectacle.

CLIMAX: the point in a play where the knot of plot is untied, where action falls off because major issues are settled; loose ends remain, perhaps, and catastrophe may yet occur, but the high point has been reached.

CLOSET DRAMA: drama to be read in private, not intended for performance.

COINCIDENCE: chance meetings, the arrival of a check just before eviction, and so on. An overuse or implausible use of coincidence weakens or wrecks a play, even if life occasionally offers similar happenings.

COMEDY OF HUMORS: a term applied to Jonsonian comedy which had characters distinguished by a dominating trait or "humor" in the old sense. Their names usually indicated their personalities (Volpone equals fox, and so on). Restoration comedy and later writers like Sheridan adapted the technique.

COMEDY OF MANNERS: in one sense, comedy of wit set in high social circles.

CONFLICT: the tangle of opposing forces producing the central interest in a play; it may concern one character against another, against his inner self, against society, and so on.

CONVENTIONS: devices used in presenting a play which the audience, as the traditional thing to do, must accept—the use of asides, soliloquies, scenery, masks, etc.; the term also applies to set styles of writing in period pieces.

DENOUEMENT: the untying of the knot of plot, sometimes the climax, generally the explanation of unsettled details; occasionally referred to as "falling action."

DEUS EX MACHINA (dē′əs ĕks măk′ənə): literally "god out of the machine" from a classical device of having a god or gods descend to earth to settle the outcome of a difficult dramatic situation; hence today an arbitrary or unmotivated way of resolving the plot—the long-lost uncle, affluent, returns at the crucial moment to save the family from the poorhouse.

DOMESTIC TRAGEDY: a play which concerns the private lives of ordinary people, as contrasted with classical tragedy, which dealt with nobility and great issues.

DRAMATIC IRONY: a term used to fit a situation in which matters turn out contrary to normal expectations of cause and effect; the phrase is used particularly when the audience, knowing facts unknown to a stage character, reads a meaning into his lines which he cannot intend.

EXCITING FORCE: the force which begins to establish a conflict in a play, following a certain amount of scene-setting and preliminary information.

FALLING ACTION: that part of a play which follows the climax, gives minor conclusions, tapers off to the actual termination.

FARCE: in modern times, exaggerated comedy aiming to produce laughter without too much concern for probability, taste, depth of characterization, etc.

FIVE-ACT FORMULA: a term applied to the custom of writing plays always in five acts, in imitation of the Roman method; in England, five acts were the rule, almost without exception, down to the end of the nineteenth century.

FORESHADOWING: preparing an audience in advance to expect certain subsequent action—by establishing patterns, hints, etc.

HEROIC DRAMA: a form popular in late seventeenth-century England in which characters debated the themes of love and honor at great length.

HIGH COMEDY: comedy that has enough wit and substance to appeal primarily to the intelligence.

INTERLUDE: a short comic skit which could in sixteenth-century England be played in intermissions of serious presentations or between courses at a state dinner.

LITURGICAL DRAMA: a term applied to the medieval "plays" which were performed in or by the church.

LOW COMEDY: comedy which appeals not primarily to the intelligence (see HIGH COMEDY) but to the comic sense which reacts to noise, slapstick, vulgarity, obvious broad allusions, etc. —producing "belly-laughs."

MASQUE: a dramatic form reaching a climax in Jonson's day; a loosely organized structure of spoken lines, singing, dancing, elaborate stage machinery (relatively speaking)—all intended to delight the eye and ear. Masques were performed privately for special occasions, such as weddings, birthdays, holidays.

MELODRAMA: exaggerated tragedy or serious drama, the counterpart of farce. Emphasis falls on thrills, sensationalism, surface emotion, with little regard for depth, consistency, or subtlety.

MIRACLE PLAY: in a restricted sense, a medieval play based on saints' lives.

MISE EN SCÈNE (mē zän sĕn'): the stage setting.

MORALITY PLAY: a medieval form (with occasional modern adaptations) in which the characters are personified virtues and vices.

MOTIVATION: paving the way for action so that it seems logical and right—usually through careful build-up of character.

MYSTERY PLAY: a medieval form based on Bible stories.

ONE-ACT PLAY: a modern form developing from curtain-raisers and skits into a full-fledged genre possessing unity and concentration like that of the short story.

PANTOMIME: acting without speaking; a story told by gesture, movement, music.

PLOT: the "story" of a play in which actions, characters, and other forces become tangled, work to a climax, and fall off to a conclusion.

PROBLEM PLAY: a form in which the author is primarily concerned with presenting or solving a major issue, such as labor relations, war, disease, etc.

PROTAGONIST: the central character in a play.

RISING ACTION: that part of a play covering the introduction of a complicating force, the growth of conflict, and the last steps in the advance toward climax.

SENECAN TRAGEDY: a play by Seneca or imitating his style; employing ghosts, blood-and-thunder, exaggerated rhetoric.

SENTIMENTAL COMEDY: a term applied particularly to eighteenth-century English comedy which revolted against the excesses of the Restoration theater. It was "moral," gushy, and didactic.

SETTING: the background of a play—scene, architecture, furniture, and other details which help establish correct atmosphere and authentic tone.

SOCK AND BUSKIN: a phrase referring to the low-heeled shoe and high boot worn respectively by Greek comic and tragic actors; by extension, comedy and tragedy.

SOLILOQUY: a convention by which a character is allowed to think out loud (Hamlet's "To be, or not to be").

STOCK CHARACTER, RESPONSE, SITUATION: a role, remark, or event recognizable at once as having been often used in "just that way" before; "stock" is opposed to original or fresh.

STRUCTURE: the manner of arranging, organizing, and welding the parts of a play.

SUBPLOT: a secondary or minor thread of story running parallel to the main plot, either directly related or almost independent; the Gloucester story in *Lear* is remarkably similar in detail and character to the main plot, has much independent development, but is significantly intertwined with the major theme and action.

THEME: in satire, didactic plays, and the like, the theme is the underlying subject—mother love, for example.

TRAGICOMEDY: a play which mixes tragedy and comedy, or a play which begins seriously, seems headed for disaster, but ends happily.

TROPE: a composition of words and music inserted in the medieval liturgy to add interest; its dialogue led to the early development of English church drama.

UNITIES: a term applied to the Renaissance "rules" of drama which called for unity of *time* (action should cover only one day); *place* (only one scene); *action* (concentration on one tight plot). Though credited to Aristotle, the three unities developed from his remarks on the unity of action alone.

FURTHER READINGS
IN DRAMA

EARLY PERIOD

Chambers, E. K., *The Medieval Stage*, 1903.
Pollard, A. W., *English Miracle Plays, Moralities, and Interludes*, 1923.

Young, K., *The Drama of the Medieval Church*, 1933.

RENAISSANCE PERIOD

Adams, J. Q., *Shakespearean Playhouses*, 1917.
Alden, R. M., *A Shakespeare Handbook*, 1935.
Boas, F. S., *Tudor Drama*, 1933.
Brooke, C. F. T., *The Tudor Drama*, 1911.
Brooke, C. F. T., and Paradise, N., eds., *English Drama: 1580–1642*, 1933.

Chambers, E. K., *The Elizabethan Stage*, 1923.
Harrison, G. B., *Introducing Shakespeare*, 1939.
Spencer, H., *The Art and Life of William Shakespeare*, 1940.
Wilson, J. D., *The Essential Shakespeare*, 1932.

RESTORATION—MODERN

Dobrée, B., *Restoration Comedy*, 1924.
Dobrée, B., *Restoration Tragedy*, 1929.
Hampden, J., ed., *Eighteenth Century Plays*, 1936.
McMillan, D., and Jones, H. M., eds., *Plays of the Restoration and Eighteenth Century*, 1931.
Moses, M. J., ed., *Representative British Dramas, Victorian and Modern*, 1931.

Nettleton, G. H., *English Drama of the Restoration and 18th Century*, 1932.
Nicoll, A., *Restoration Drama*, 1923.
Nicoll, A., *History of Late 18th Century Drama*, 1927.
Schelling, F. E., and Black, M. W. (eds.), *Typical Elizabethan Plays*, rev. ed., 1948.
Summers, M., *The Restoration Theatre*, 1934.

MODERN AND GENERAL

Baker, G. P., *Dramatic Technique*, 1919.
Baugh, A. C., ed., *A Literary History of England*, 1948.
Brooks, C., and Heilman, R. B., *Understanding Drama*, 1945.
Buck, P., et al., eds., *A Treasury of the Theatre*, 1940.
Cheney, S., *The Theatre*, 1929.
Clark, B. H., *A Study of the Modern Drama*, 1928.
Clark, B. H., and Freedley, G., *A History of Modern Drama*, 1947.
Drew, E., *Discovering Drama*, 1937.
Gassner, J., *Masters of the Drama*, 1945.
Hart, J. D., *Oxford Companion to American Literature*, 1948.

Harvey, P., *Oxford Companion to English Literature*, 1937.
Morgan, A. E., *Tendencies of Modern English Drama*, 1924.
Nicoll, A., *The Development of the Theatre*, 1927.
Quinn, A. H., *A History of the American Drama from the Civil War to the Present Day*, 1936.
Sampson, G., *Concise Cambridge History of English Literature*, 1941.
Tucker, S. M., and Downer, A. S. (eds.), *Twenty-five Modern Plays*, rev. ed., 1949.
Yeats, W. B., *Synge and the Ireland of His Time*, 1911.

FURTHER READINGS IN DRAMA

EARLY PERIOD

Chambers, E. K. The Mediæval Stage, 1903.
Pollard, A. W. English Miracle Plays, Moralities and Interludes, 1928.

Young, K. The Drama of the Mediæval Church, 1933.

RENAISSANCE PERIOD

Adams, J. Q. Shakespearean Playhouses, 1917.
Alden, R. M. A Shakespeare Handbook, 1925.
Boas, F. S. Tudor Drama, 1933.
Brooke, C. F. T. The Tudor Drama, 1911.
Brooke, C. F. T. and Paradise, N., eds. English Drama 1580-1642, 1933.

Chambers, E. K. The Elizabethan Stage, 1923.
Harrison, G. B. Introducing Shakespeare, 1939.
Spencer, H. The Art and Life of William Shakespeare, 1940.
Wilson, J. D. The Essential Shakespeare, 1932.

RESTORATION—MODERN

Dobrée, B. Restoration comedy, 1924.
Dobrée, B. Restoration Tragedy, 1929.
Hampden, J., ed. Eighteenth Century Plays, 1930.
MacMillan, D. and Jones, H. M., eds. Plays of the Restoration and Eighteenth Century, 1931.
Moses, M. J., ed. Representative British Dramas, Victorian and Modern, 1931.

Nettleton, G. H. English Drama of the Restoration and 18th Century, 1932.
Nicoll, A. Restoration Drama, 1923.
Nicoll, A. History of Late 18th Century Drama, 1927.
Schelling, F. E. and Black, M. W., eds. Typical Elizabethan Plays, rev. ed., 1949.
Summers, M. The Restoration Theatre, 1934.

MODERN AND GENERAL

Baker, G. P. Dramatic Technique, 1919.
Bouyn, A. C., ed. A Literary History of England, 1948.
Brooks, C. and Heilman, R. B. Understanding Drama, 1945.
Brock, P. et al., eds. A Treasury of the Theatre, 1940.
Cheney, S. The Theatre, 1929.
Clark, B. H. A Study of the Modern Drama, 1925.
Clark, B. H. and Freedley, G. A History of Modern Drama, 1947.
Drew, E. Discovering Drama, 1937.
Gassner, J. Masters of the Drama, 1940.
Hart, J. D. Oxford Companion to American Literature, 1948.

Harvey, P. Oxford Companion to English Literature, 1937.
Morgan, A. E. Tendencies of Modern English Drama, 1924.
Nicoll, A. The Development of the Theatre, 1927.
Quinn, A. H. A History of the American Drama from the Civil War to the Present Day, 1936.
Sampson, G. Concise Cambridge History of English Literature, 1941.
Tucker, S. M. and Downer, A. S. (eds.), Twenty-five Modern Plays, rev. ed., 1949.
Yeats, W. B. Synge and the Ireland of His Time, 1911.

PROMINENT SUBTYPES
OF POETRY

The following list contains titles of only those poems in this volume which fit into the more prominent subtypes of poetry. All such grouping is necessarily somewhat inexact; actually, some poems have such distinct narrative and lyric qualities in combination that they cannot be rigidly classified in these major divisions. Furthermore, poems may be grouped according to meter-and-rhyme schemes, subject matter, purpose, or tone. The following table, however, may prove useful in focusing attention upon specific forms, ideas, and moods.

THE EPIC AND MOCK-EPIC

THE ROMANCE

THE TALE

THE BALLAD

THE DRAMATIC MONOLOGUE

THE SONG

THE PASTORAL

THE ODE

THE ELEGY AND ELEGIAC VERSE

THE DIRGE AND EPITAPH

THE SONNET

INDEXES

INDEX
OF FIRST LINES

INDEX

(Bold face figures after a writer's name indicate selections)

[647]

"Mean to Attain Happy Life, The," 196–197
Measure for Measure, song from, 203
"Mediocrity in Love Rejected," 220
"Mediterranean, The," 383
Medley-poem, Italianate, 123
Melodrama defined, 630
Menaechmi, 400
"Mending Wall," 352–353
Merchant of Venice, The, song from, 202
Metaphor, compared with simile, 392; defined, 381
    See also Kenning
Meter, common, 390; defined, 391; in ballads, 390
Metonymy defined, 391
"Metropolitan Nightmare," 191–193
"Michael," 109–114
MIDDLETON, THOMAS, 402
MILLAY, EDNA ST. VINCENT, 378
MILNE, A. A., 404
MILTON, JOHN, introductory note, 87–88; lyric poetry, 222–228; narrative poetry, 87–100
"Miniver Cheevy," 181–182
Miracle play, 401; defined, 630
Mise en scène defined, 630
Monologue, dramatic, defined, 390
Monometer defined, 391
MOODY, WILLIAM VAUGHAN, 404
Morality play, 401; defined, 630
MORLEY, THOMAS, 208–209
MORRIS, WILLIAM, 174–180
"Morte d'Arthur," 153–156
Motivation in drama defined, 630
Mourning Becomes Electra, 404
"Moving Through the Silent Crowd," 387
Much Ado About Nothing, song from, 202
Muses, 391
Musical Humors, song from, 209
"Musketaquid," 291–292
"My Heart Leaps Up," 271
"My Last Duchess," 159
"My Lost Youth," 293–294
"my sweet old etcetera," 380–381
Mystery play, 401; defined, 630
"Myth of the Sheaf-Child, The" (from "Beowulf"), 11–24

Narrative poetry, 11–194; Anglo-Saxon, 11–28; Elizabethan, 79–87; Middle English, 28–76; Renaissance, 76–87; 17th century, 87–100; 18th century, 101–108; 19th century, 108–180; 20th century, 181–194
"New Mexican Mountain," 370–371
"Nightmare Number Three," 193–194
Nonameter defined, 391
"Not in a Silver Casket Cool with Pearls," 378
"Nymph's Reply to the Shepherd, The," 198–199

O'CASEY, SEAN, 404
Octameter defined, 391
Octave, defined, 391–392; rhyme in, 392
Ode, defined, 392; forms of, 392
"Ode" (Collins), 255
"Ode: Intimations of Immortality," 272–274
"Ode on a Grecian Urn," 283–284

"Ode on Melancholy," 283
"Ode to a Nightingale," 284–285
"Ode to Evening," 254–255
"Ode to the Confederate Dead," 381–382
"Ode to the Virginian Voyage," 200–201
"Ode to the West Wind," 279–280
ODETS, CLIFFORD, 405
OEDIPUS, 400
"Oh, When I Was in Love with You," 340
"On a Girdle," 221–222
"On First Looking into Chapman's Homer," 282
"On Growing Old," 358
"On His Blindness," 228
"On His Having Arrived to the Age of Twenty-Three," 225
"On Looking at a Copy of Alice Meynell's Poems," 351–352
"On My First Son," 213
"On Reading a Line Underscored by Keats," 351
O'NEILL, EUGENE, 404, 545–566; introductory note, 545; use of masks, 400
Onomatopoeia defined, 392
Ottava rima, 123; defined, 392
OTWAY, THOMAS, 402
OWEN, WILFRED, 378–380
"Ozymandias," 278

Pageant-wagons, 401
"Paltry Nude Starts on a Spring Voyage, The," 361
Pantisocracy, 114
Pantomime defined, 630
"Paradise Lost," 88–100
"Pardoner's Tale, The" (from "The Canterbury Tales"), 58–65
Passionate Pilgrim, The, song from, 206–207
"Passionate Shepherd to His Love, The," 198
Pastoral defined, 392
Patient Grissill, song from, 206
"Patterns," 349–351
"Peace," 238
Pentameter defined, 392
"Persuasions to Enjoy," 221
Peter Pan, 404
"Peter Quince at the Clavier," 362
"Petit, the Poet," 348
Petrarchan sonnet, *see* Sonnet
"Phillida Flouts Me," 207–208
Pindaric ode, 392
PINERO, ARTHUR WING, 403
Place, unity of, 630
PLAUTUS, 400
Play, one-act, defined, 630; problem, defined, 630; school, in England, 400
    See also Drama
Plot defined, 630
POE, EDGAR ALLAN, 287–290
Poetic experience, 3, 4
Poetry, a language phenomenon, 7; allusion in, 7; and civilization, 3; and custom, 4; and inspiration, 4; and moral codes, 4; and prose, 4; appeal of, 4; appreciation of, 3, 4–5; as entertainment, 4; bibliography, 394–396; characteristics of, 7;